The
INTERNATIONAL CRITICAL COMMENTARY
on the Holy Scriptures of the Old and New Testaments

GENERAL EDITORS:

J. A. EMERTON, F.B.A.
Fellow of St. John's College
Regius Professor of Hebrew in the University of Cambridge
Honorary Canon of St. George's Cathedral, Jerusalem

C. E. B. CRANFIELD, F.B.A.
Emeritus Professor of Theology in the University of Durham

AND

G. N. STANTON
Professor of New Testament Studies,
King's College, University of London

FORMERLY UNDER THE EDITORSHIP OF

S. R. DRIVER
A. PLUMMER
C. A. BRIGGS

THE GOSPEL ACCORDING TO SAINT MATTHEW

VOLUME II

A CRITICAL AND EXEGETICAL COMMENTARY

ON

THE GOSPEL ACCORDING TO SAINT MATTHEW

BY

W. D. DAVIES, F.B.A.

Fellow of the American Academy of Arts and Sciences
Emeritus Professor of Christian Origins, Duke University

AND

DALE C. ALLISON, Jr., Ph.D.

Research Fellow, New College, Friends University, Wichita

IN THREE VOLUMES

VOLUME II

Commentary on Matthew VIII–XVIII

EDINBURGH
T&T CLARK, 59 GEORGE STREET

T&T CLARK
59 GEORGE STREET
EDINBURGH EH2 2LQ
SCOTLAND

First published 1991

British Library Cataloguing in Publication Data
Davies, W. D. (William David) 1911–
A critical and exegetical commentary on the Gospel
according to Saint Matthew.
Vol. 2, Matthew 8–18
1. Bible. N. T. Matthew – Commentaries
I. Title   II. Allison, Dale C.   III. Series
226.206

ISBN 0–567–09545–2

TYPESET BY C. R. BARBER & PARTNERS (HIGHLANDS) LTD, FORT WILLIAM
PRINTED IN GREAT BRITAIN BY
MARTIN'S OF BERWICK LTD

Dedicated
to
Eurwen and Kristine
οὐκ ἔχομεν ἀνταποδοῦναι ὑμῖν

PREFACE

The increasing attention now being paid to the Gospel according to Matthew is in marked contrast to the comparative neglect of it when we began our study. Particularly noteworthy is the recent appearance of commentaries by J. Gnilka, U. Luz, D. Patte, and A. Sand. We have much benefited from these and other recent studies. The warm reception given to our own volume I by reviewers and readers alike we here gratefully acknowledge. We welcome any constructive comments or corrections of errors in the printing.

As will be clear from our exegesis, the division of the text at the end of chapter 7 is highly artificial and arbitrary. This we emphasize. The Sermon on the Mount is retrospective: it is inseparable from what precedes it in chapters 1–4. But it is also prospective, equally inseparable from what follows it in chapters 8–28. The division of our volumes between chapters 7 and 8 has been required solely by the exigencies of printing. It does not indicate a caesura.

Permission to print materials from publications by Harvard University Press and Sheffield Academic Press is gratefully acknowledged.

There remains only to recognize Mrs. Jean Bradford-Armstrong of Midland, Texas. Like that of her family, her generosity in establishing the Bradford Distinguished Chair in Religious Studies at Texas Christian University made possible the continuation of our work.

W. D. Davies
Dale C. Allison, Jr.

December, 1989

CONTENTS OF VOLUME II

ABBREVIATIONS AND BIBLIOGRAPHY SUPPLEMENT

Journals and Series: Supplement
AJT: *American Journal of Theology* (Chicago)
AUSS: *Andrews University Seminary Studies* (Berrien Springs)
BibRev: *Bible Review* (Washington, D.C.)
BibTerreS: *Bible et terre sainte* (Paris)
BibTod: *The Bible Today* (Collegeville)
BLE: *Bulletin de Littérature Ecclésiastique* (Toulouse)
CR: *Clergy Review* (London)
CurrTM: *Currents in Theology and Mission* (St. Louis, Chicago)
EAJET: *East African Journal of Evangelical Theology* (Machakos)
EpRev: *Epworth Review* (London)
EspVie: *Esprit et Vie* (Langres)
FZBT: *Freiburger Zeitschrift für Philosophie und Theologie* (Fribourg)
GkOTRev: *Greek Orthodox Theological Review* (Brookline)
LuthQ: *Lutheran Quarterly* (Gettysburg)
McQ: *McCormick Quarterly* (Chicago)
RevAfThéol: *Revue Africaine de Théologie* (Kinshasa-Limete)
SNTU: *Studien zum Neuen Testament und seiner Umwelt* (Aufsätze)
 (Linz, Wien, München)
SWJT: *Southwestern Journal of Theology* (Fort Worth)
ThViat: *Theologia Viatorum* (Berlin)
TPQ: *Theologisch-Praktische Quartalschrift* (Linz)
TSFB: *TSF Bulletin* (Madison)
TToday: *Theology Today* (Princeton)
VD: *Verbum Domini* (Rome)
ZRG: *Zeitschrift für Religions- und Geistesgeschichte* (Erlangen)

Commentaries and Other Literature: Supplement[1]
Aland and Aland: K. Aland and B. Aland, *The Text of the New Testament* (trans. of *Der Text des Neuen Testaments*, 1981), Grand Rapids, 1987.
Baarlink: H. Baarlink, *Die Eschatologie der synoptischen Evangelien*, Stuttgart, 1986.
Bauckham: R. J. Bauckham, *Jude, 2 Peter*, Word Biblical Commentary, Waco, 1983.
Bayer: H. F. Bayer, *Jesus' Predictions of Vindication and Resurrection*, WUNT 2/20, Tübingen, 1986.
Betz, *Messias*: O. Betz, *Jesus. Der Messias Israels*, WUNT 42, Tübingen, 1987.

[1] A double asterisk (**) indicates a commentary on Matthew.

xiii

Borg, *Jesus*: M. J. Borg, *Jesus: A New Vision*, New York, 1988.

Brandon: S. G. F. Brandon, *The Fall of Jerusalem and the Christian Church*, 2nd ed., London, 1957.

Brooks: S. H. Brooks, *Matthew's Community: The Evidence of His Special Sayings Material*, JSNTSS 16, Sheffield, 1987.

Brunner, *Christbook*: F. D. Brunner, *The Christbook. An Historical/Theological Commentary. Matthew 1–12*, Waco, 1987.

Camponovo: O. Camponovo, *Königtum, Königsherrschaft und Reich Gottes in den frühjüdischen Schriften*, OBO 58, Göttingen, 1984.

Carson, 'Matthew': D. A. Carson, 'Matthew', in F. E. Gaebelein, ed., *The Expositor's Bible Commentary* 8, Grand Rapids, 1985, pp. 1–599.

Chilton and McDonald: B. D. Chilton and J. I. .H. McDonald, *Jesus and the Ethics of the Kingdom*, London, 1987.

Chordat: J.-L. Chordat, *Jésus devant sa mort dans l'évangile de Marc*, Paris, 1970.

Crossan, *Cliffs*: J. D. Crossan, *Cliffs of Fall*, New York, 1980.

idem, *Parables*: J. .D. Crossan, *In Parables*, New York, 1973.

Cullmann, *Peter*: O. Cullmann, *Peter: Disciple, Apostle, Martyr* (trans. of *Petrus*, 1960), 2nd ed., London, 1962.

Daniélou, *Bible*: J. Daniélou, *The Bible and Liturgy* (trans. *Bible et Liturgie*, 1951), Ann Arbor, 1979.

Descamps, *Jésus*: A. Descamps, *Jésus et l'Eglise*, BETL 77, Leuven, 1987.

de Vaux: R. de Vaux, *Ancient Israel* (trans. of *Les Institutions de l'Ancien Testament*, 1958, 1960), 2 vols., London, 1961.

De Kruijf: Th. De Kruijf, *Der Sohn des Lebendigen Gottes*, AnBib 14, Rome, 1962.

Dix: G. Dix, *The Shape of the Liturgy*, 2nd ed., London, 1945.

Donahue, *Parable*: J. R. Donahue, *The Gospel in Parable*, Philadelphia, 1988.

Drury: J. Drury, *The Parables in the Gospels*, New York, 1985.

Ehrman: B. D. Ehrman, *Didymus the Blind and the Text of the Gospels*, Atlanta, 1986.

**Erasmus: Erasmus, *In Evangelium Matthaei Paraphrasis*, in *Opera omnia VII*, Hildesheim, 1962, pp. 1–146.

Ernst, *Lukas*: J. Ernst, *Das Evangelium nach Lukas*, RNT, Regensburg, 1977.

idem, *Markus*: J. Ernst, *Das Evangelium nach Markus*, RNT, Regensburg, 1981.

Fiedler: P. Fiedler, *Jesus und die Sünder*, Beiträge zur biblischen Exegese und Theologie 3, Frankfurt am Main, 1976.

Flusser, *Gleichnisse*: D. Flusser, *Die rabbinischen Gleichnisse und der Gleichniserzähler Jesus I*, Bern, 1981.

**France, *Matthew*: R. T. France, *Matthew*, Leicester, 1985.

Freyne, *Jesus*: S. Freyne, *Galilee, Jesus and the Gospels*, Philadelphia, 1988.

Geist: H. Geist, *Menschensohn und Gemeinde*, FB 57, Würzburg, 1986.

Gils: F. Gils, *Jésus prophète d'après les évangiles synoptiques*, Leuven, 1957.

**Gnilka, *Matthäusevangelium* 1, 2: J. Gnilka, *Das Matthäusevangelium*, HTKNT I/1, 2, Freiburg, 1986, 1988.

J. B. Green: J. B. Green, *The Death of Jesus*, WUNT 2/33, Tübingen, 1988.

Guelich, *Mark*: R. A. Guelich, *Mark 1–8.26*, Waco, 1989.

Havener: I. Havener, *Q: The Sayings of Jesus*, Wilmington, 1987.

Hawthorne and Betz: G. F. Hawthorne and O. Betz, *Tradition and Interpretation in the New Testament*, Grand Rapids, 1987.

Hendrickx, *Miracle Stories*: H. Hendrickx, *The Miracle Stories*, London, 1987.

idem, *Parables*: H. Hendrickx, *The Parables of Jesus*, London, 1986.

Horstmann: M. Horstmann, *Studien zur markinischen Christologie*, Münster, 1969.

Houlden, *Light*: J. L. Houlden, *Backward into Light: The Passion and Resurrection of Jesus according to Matthew and Mark*, London, 1987.

Howard: G. Howard, *The Gospel of Matthew according to a Primitive Hebrew Text*, Macon, 1987.

Juel, *Exegesis*: D. Juel, *Messianic Exegesis*, Philadelphia, 1987.

Kingsbury, *Story*: J. D. Kingsbury, *Matthew as Story*, Philadelphia, 1986.

Kloppenborg: J. S. Kloppenborg, *The Formation of Q*, Philadephia, 1987.

Köhler: W.-D. Köhler, *Die Rezeption des Matthäusevangeliums in der Zeit vor Irenäus*, WUNT 2/24, Tübingen, 1987.

Landry: B. Landry, *L'évangile selon Matthieu commenté par les Pères*, Paris, 1985.

Leivestad: R. Leivestad, *Jesus in his own Perspective* (trans. of *Hvem ville Jesus voere?*, 1982), Minneapolis, 1987.

Léon-Dufour, *Life*: X. Léon-Dufour, *Life and Death in the New Testament* (trans of *Face à la mort*, 1979), San Francisco, 1986.

**Levertoff: P. Levertoff, 'Matthew', in *A New Commentary on Holy Scripture including the Apocrypha*, ed. C. Gore et al., London, 1928.

**Limbeck: M. Limbeck, *Matthäus-Evangelium*, Stuttgart, 1986.

Lohfink, *Community*: G. Lohfink, *Jesus and Community* (trans. of *Wie hat Jesus Gemeinde gewollt?*, 1982), Philadelphia, 1984.

Matera: J. Matera, *Passion Narratives and Gospel Theologies*, New York, 1986.

Mann, *Mark*: C. S. Mann, *Mark*, AB 27, Garden City, 1986.

**Minear: P. Minear, *Matthew: The Teacher's Gospel*, New York, 1982.

Neuhäusler: E. Neuhäusler, *Anspruch und Antwort Gottes*, Düsseldorf, 1962.

Nielsen: H. K. Nielsen, *Heilung und Verkündigung*, Leiden, 1987.

Oakman: D. E. Oakman, *Jesus and the Economic Questions of His Day*, Lewiston/Queenston, 1986.

Orchard and Riley: B. Orchard and H. Riley, *The Order of the Synoptic Gospels*, Macon, 1987.

Patsch: H. Patsch, *Abendmahl und historischer Jesus*, Stuttgart, 1972.

**Patte: D. Patte, *The Gospel According to Matthew*, Philadelphia, 1987.

Piper: R. A. Piper, *Wisdom in the Q Tradition*, Cambridge, 1988.
Popkes: W. Popkes, *Christus Traditus*, ATANT 49, Zürich, 1967.
Pregeant: R. Pregeant, *Christology beyond Dogma: Matthew's Christ in Process Hermeneutic*, Philadelphia, 1978.
Reicke: B. Reicke, *The Roots of the Synoptic Gospels*, Philadelphia, 1986.
J. A. Robinson: J. A. Robinson, *St Paul's Epistle to the Ephesians*, 2nd ed., London, n.d.
SacPag.: Sacra Pagina, ed. J. Coppens et al., Leuven, 1959.
**Sand, *Matthäus*: A. Sand, *Das Evangelium nach Matthäus*, Regensburger Neues Testament, 1986.
Sanders, *Gospels*: E. P. Sanders, ed., *Jesus, the Gospels and the Church*, Macon, 1987.
Sato: M. Sato, *Q und Prophetie*, WUNT 2/29, Tübingen, 1988.
Schenk, *Sprache*: W. Schenk, *Die Sprache des Matthäus*, Göttingen, 1987.
Schenke, *Matthäusevangelium*: L. Schenke, ed., *Studien zum Matthäusevangelium*, Stuttgart, 1988.
Schlosser, *Dieu*: J. Schlosser, *Le Dieu de Jésus*, LD 129, Paris, 1987.
T. E. Schmidt: T. E. Schmidt, *Hostility to Wealth in the Synoptic Tradition*, JSNTSS 15, Sheffield, 1987.
Schmithals, *Wunder*: W. Schmithals, *Wunder und Glaube*, Neukirchen-Vluyn, 1970.
**Schnackenburg, *Matthäusevangelium*: R. Schnackenburg, *Matthäusevangelium*, 2 vols., Würzburg, 1985, 1987.
Sigal: P. Sigal, *The Halakah of Jesus of Nazareth according to the Gospel of Matthew*, Lanham and London, 1986.
**R. H. Smith: R. H. Smith, *Matthew*, Minneapolis, 1988.
Tagawa: P. K. Tagawa, *Miracles et Évangile*, Paris, 1966.
Thysman: R. Thysman, *Communauté et directives éthiques*, Gembloux, 1974.
Trautmann: M. Trautmann, *Zeichenhafte Handlungen Jesu*, FB 37, Würzburg, 1980.
Trilling, *Hausordnung*: W. Trilling, *Hausordnung Gottes*, Düsseldorf, 1960.
idem, *Studien*: W. Trilling, *Studien zur Jesusüberlieferung*, Stuttgart, 1988.
Tuckett, *Nag Hammadi*: C. M. Tuckett, *Nag Hammadi and the Gospel Tradition*, Edinburgh, 1986.
Verseput: D. Verseput, *The Rejection of the Humble Messianic King*, Frankfurt am Main, 1986.
**Viviano, 'Matthew': B. T. Viviano, 'The gospel according to Matthew', in *The Jerome Biblical Commentary*, rev. ed., forthcoming.
Wailes: S. L. Wailes, *Medieval Allegories of Jesus' Parables*, Berkeley, 1987.
**Wansbrough: H. Wansbrough, 'St. Matthew', in *A New Catholic Commentary on Holy Scripture*, ed. R. C. Fuller et al., London, 1975, pp. 709–43.
**Weiss, *Matthäus-Evangelium*: J. Weiss, *Das Matthäus-Evangelium*, 2nd ed., Göttingen, 1907.

Wenham and Blomberg: D. Wenham and C. Blomberg, *The Miracles of Jesus*, Gospel Perspectives 6, Sheffield, 1986.

**J. Wilkens: J. Wilkens, *Der König Israels*, 2 vols., Berlin, 1934.

Witherington: B. Witherington, *Women in the Ministry of Jesus*, SNTSMS 51, Cambridge, 1984.

Wrede: W. Wrede, *The Messianic Secret* (trans. of *Das Messiasgeheimnis in den Evangelien*, 1901), London, 1971.

A. F. Zimmermann, *Die urchristlichen Lehrer*, WUNT 2/12, Tübingen, 1984.

Classical Sources

Quotations from classical sources are usually from the translations in The Loeb Classical Library and are used by permission.

Note

Throughout this volume and the next an asterisk (*) after a Greek word or phrase signifies that that word or phrase is listed in vol. 1 on pp. 75–9 and so is characteristic of the First Evangelist.

EXCURSUS V

MATTHEW 8–9

Scholars generally agree that Mt 8–9 is the second half of a two-panel presentation which typifies Jesus' ministry. In 5–7 Jesus speaks. In 8–9 he (for the most part) acts. It is thereby shown that God in Christ heals both by words and by mighty deeds (cf. Clement of Alexandria, *Paed.* 1.2.6). There are also some other points upon which there is a measure of scholarly agreement. For example, the people healed in Mt 8–9 are generally recognized to be either from the margins of Jewish society or to be without public status or power: a leper, a Roman's servant, Peter's mother-in-law, two demoniacs, a paralytic, an unnamed, unclean woman, an unnamed little girl, two blind men, and a dumb demoniac. Usually observed too is the way in which the miracles in 8–9 have been selected with an eye towards the scripture quoted in 11.4–6 (see pp. 139, 242). But the leading themes of Mt 8–9 are in dispute, as are the structure of the section and the leading christological conception.[1]

A. *Structure.* (1) E. Klostermann, p. 72, and Schoeps, *Theologie*, p. 93, have discovered the key to Mt 8–9 in the number ten. In their judgement, Jesus performs ten miracles, a fact which should recall the ten miracles Moses worked in Egypt (Exod 7–12). In Mt 8–9 Jesus is, therefore, a new Moses (cf. Grundmann, pp. 245–6). The proposition is attractive. Elsewhere in the First Gospel the shadow that Jesus casts definitely bears distinctly Mosaic features (see e.g. on 2.20; 5.1–2; 8.1; 11.27–30; 17.1–8). Yet one hesitates. There may be ten *miracles* in Mt 8–9. But there are only nine *miracle stories*. (9.18–26, the healing of a ruler's daughter and of the woman with an issue of blood, is a unit—just as 8.28–34, which is about two demoniacs, and 9.27–31, which is about two blind men, are units.) Even more problematic is the observation that the miracle stories of 8–9 are parcelled out into three different groups—8.2–15; 8.23–9.8; and 9.18–34. Why? There is nothing

---

[1] Lit.: C. Burger, 'Jesu Taten nach Matthäus 8 und 9', *ZTK* 70 (1973), pp. 272–87; Davies, *SSM*, pp. 86–93; P. F. Ellis, pp. 40–6; Gerhardsson, *Acts*, pp. 39–40; K. Gatzweiler, 'Les récits de miracles dans l'Évangile selon saint Matthieu', in Didier, pp. 209–20: J. P. Heil, 'Significant Aspects of the Healing Miracles in Matthew', *CBQ* 41 (1979), pp. 274–87; Held, in *TIM*, pp. 165–299; J. D. Kingsbury, 'Observations on the "Miracle Chapters" of Matthew 8–9', *CBQ* 40 (1978), pp. 559–73; U. Luz, 'Die Wundergeschichten von Mt 8–9', in Hawthorne and Betz, pp. 149–65; J. Moiser, 'The Structure of Matthew 8–9: A Suggestion', *ZNW* 76 (1985), pp. 117–18; Rigaux, *Testimony*, pp. 41–8; Theissen, *Stories*, pp. 209–11; W. G. Thompson, 'Reflections on the Composition of Mt 8.1–9.34', *CBQ* 33 (1971), pp. 365–88.

1

corresponding to this in Exodus. Finally, Jesus' mighty deeds are anything but plagues: they are deeds of compassion done for the benefit of others. For additional criticism see Davies, *SSM*, pp. 86–93.

(2) G. Theissen has tentatively discerned a geographical arrangement in Mt 8–9, one based on Mt 4.15, which refers first to 'the sea', then to the region 'across the sea', then to 'Galilee of the Gentiles' (*Stories*, p. 210). Supposedly the movement of Jesus in 8–9 literally fulfils the prophecy of 4.15–16. The problems with this are several. First, Capernaum, while prominent in 8–9, is not mentioned in 4.15–16 (although note 4.13). Secondly, even if Theissen were correct, 4.15–16 could only point forward to chapter 8, where Jesus is by the sea (8.5–22), then crosses to the other side (8.23–7), and finally lands in what may be Gentile territory (8.28; cf. the healing of a Gentile in 8.5–13). Theissen's conjecture does nothing to help us understand the structure of chapter 9. Next, there are no geographical catchword connexions between 4.15 and 8.1–9.34. Why, if Matthew were intent upon correlating chapters 8–9 with 4.15–16, is Capernaum not said to be by the sea? And why is the Jordan not named? And why is the Gentile character of the Gadarenes not explicit? Lastly, where else in Matthew does a formula quotation not find its fulfilment in its immediate context? There are three whole chapters between 4.16 and 8.1.

(3) Cope, pp. 65–73, has proposed that the citation of Hos 6.6 in 9.13 is a 'mid-point' text which states the theme of 9.10–34. Thus the issue of 'mercy not sacrifice', which Cope interprets as the issue of Jesus' mercy versus Torah-piety, is the key to each pericope. 9.10–13 concerns fellowship with sinners, 9.14–17 treats the problem of fasting, and 9.18–26 has to do with Jesus touching a dead—and therefore unclean—person. Similarly, in 9.20–2 Jesus is touched by an unclean woman, in 9.27–31 he heals two blind men (which Cope supposes were also unclean), and in 9.32–4 Jesus heals a dumb demoniac, an act which involves him in contact with demons.

There are several problems with Cope's proposals (which do not in any event help one to understand the structure of 8.1–9.9). First, the common theme of mercy is not so significant as one might imagine: it is part of every story in which Jesus heals a sick individual. Secondly, the problem of Torah-piety is nowhere explicit in the last three paragraphs, 9.18–26, 27–31, and 32–4. Thirdly, Matthew fails to call attention to the fact that the dead child and the bleeding woman are unclean.

(4) Fenton, pp. 119–21, states that perhaps our two chapters should be divided in the following manner—

a leper, 8.1–4	woman with the hemorrhage, 9.20–2
Peter's mother-in-law, 8.14–15	the ruler's daughter, 9.23–6
two demoniacs, 8.28–34	two blind men, 9.27–31
a paralytic, 9.1–8	a dumb demoniac, 9.32–4

Fenton draws correlations in the following manner—leprosy and hemorrhage are both causes of uncleanness in Lev 14–15; Peter's mother-in-law and the ruler's daughter rise to Jesus' touch; the two demoniacs and the two blind men are both pairs of individuals; and in both the accounts of the healing of the paralytic and the healing of the dumb demoniac the reaction of the crowd is mentioned. In our estimation Fenton has let his imagination get the better of him. Correlations of some sort could be drawn between almost any two synoptic paragraphs.[2] And why does the Gentile character of the centurion mean that the healing of his son or servant must be excluded from the series?

(5) H. J. Held, in *TIM*, pp. 246–53, has divided 8.1–9.31 into three sections: 8.2–17, the subject being Christology; 8.18–9.17, the subject being discipleship; 9.18–31, the subject being faith. W. G. Thompson (as in n. 1) and Sabourin, p. 455, concur. This analysis probably points us in the right direction. It recognizes that the miracles of 8–9 fall into three separate sections. Yet the attempt to discern a thematic unity in 8.2–17 or 8.18–9.17 or 9.18–31 does not seem credible. 8.16f. does make Jesus' healing ministry the fulfilment of Isa 53.4, which concerns the servant, a christological title; but this circumstance does not suffice to make Christology the dominant theme of all of 8.2–17. As for 8.18–9.17, the theme of discipleship is prominent in 8.18–27 and 9.9–13, but what of 8.28–9.8 and 9.14–17? These cannot really be said to treat of discipleship in any obvious or special fashion. With regard to 9.18–22, while faith is a central idea (see 9.22, 28f.), πίστις and πιστεύω are also present in 8.1–9.17 (see 8.10, 13, 26; 9.2). If the mention of faith in two miracle stories in the third section makes faith the dominant theme, why does not the mention of faith in 8.26 and 9.2 make faith the major theme of the second section?

(6) C. Burger (as in n. 1) and J. D. Kingsbury (as in n. 1) have put forward a modified version of Held's thesis. They both find a four-fold division: 8.1–15(17) (Christology and 'outcasts'), 18–34 (discipleship); 9.1–17 (Jesus and Israel), 9.18–34 (faith). The drawback to this is that it fails to take into account what is the most obvious structural clue, namely, Matthew's grouping of miracle stories into three separate sections—8.2–15; 8.23–9.8; 9.18–34. Moreover, for the reasons cited when discussing Held's scheme, the thematic unity of the proposed units hangs in doubt.

(7) J. Moiser (as in n. 1) has suggested that 8–9 might be the structural twin of 5–7, and he has tried to correlate sequentially sections in the latter with sections in the former. The hypothesis is very speculative. Where else has a major Matthean discourse supplied the structural foundation for subsequent narrative material? Furthermore, the order of Mt 9 is largely a reproduction of a Markan sequence (see below), so how can it be correlated with portions of the sermon on the mount?

(8) Our own proposal, which we have already introduced (1, pp. 67 and 102), takes as its point of departure Matthew's love of the triad, the number of miracle stories in 8–9 (nine), and the fact that the miracle stories appear in three different groups.[3] All this leads us to the arrangement set out in 1, p. 67. The point to stress is that the key to unlocking the structure cannot be found in topical interests

---

[2] See Allison, 'Structure', pp. 424–9.
[3] Cf. Gaechter, *Kommentar*, p. 259; Moiser (v).

(Christology, discipleship, faith). Not that there are no thematic threads. 8.14f. (the formula quotation) follows nicely after three healing stories, and 8.18–22 (on discipleship) is neatly placed into a context where Jesus' disciples literally follow him around. Further, in 9.9–17, the very first verse (the call of Levi, 9.9) appropriately picks up once again the theme of discipleship, and 9.10–13 (on toll collectors and sinners) gains meaning from the low social status of most of those healed in Mt 8–9. But the arrangement of the entire section is dictated by a formal consideration, the triad.

B. *Christology.* In the view of Kingsbury (as in n. 1), chapters 8–9 present Jesus Messiah basically as the Son of God. This seems to us misleading. The title, 'Son of God', occurs only once in these chapters, in 8.29.[4] Moreover, Kingsbury underplays the importance of the quotation in 8.17, which makes Jesus the servant of Deutero-Isaiah (see on 8.17), and he never justifies the assumption that one christological title must be dominant. In our judgement, the concatenation of various christological appellations in our two chapters should not be muted, as they are when each is subsumed under 'Son of God'. Jesus is Lord (8.2, 6, 21, 25; 9.28), Son of man (8.20; 9.6), Son of David (9.27), Son of God (8.29), and the servant of Isaiah (8.17). This variety is itself expressive of one of the evangelist's major concerns. Just as the fullness of Jesus cannot be captured by any one pericope, so it can not be captured by any one christological title. In Matthew's mind, Jesus is many things: the object of messianic hopes, fulfiller of the Torah, Lord of the church, healer of the infirm, servant of the Lord, saviour of Israel, eschatological judge, exorcist without peer—and on and on it goes. This explains why throughout the First Gospel, including chapters 8–9, no one christological title crowds out the others. On the contrary: the more appellations that can be piled up, the greater the glory that is given to the gospel's subject.

C. *The function of Mt 8–9.* According to Klostermann, Schoeps, and Grundmann, the leading theme of the narrative history in chapters 8–9 is Christology: Jesus is the Mosaic eschatological prophet, the new Moses (see above). But according to Schlatter, pp. 266–8, the central concern of Matthew's miracle cycle is faith; and because (in his judgement) the dominant note of the sermon on the mount is love, Mt 5–9 as a whole gives expression to the themes of love and faith. Different again is the approach of C. Burger (as in n. 1). He discerns in Mt 8–9 an ecclesiological dimension. Indeed, he finds recounted the beginnings of the church (cf. Luz, as in n. 1).

Given the variety of opinions, one might wish to argue that just as it is a mistake to latch on to any one title and make it the key to the Christology of 8–9, so too is it dubious to perceive one theological idea at the heart of these chapters. The material placed after the sermon on the mount addresses and raises a host of different issues and questions, so does not undue concentration on any one inevitably prevent justice

---

[4] Kingsbury, however, has an explanation for this: apart from supernatural beings (God, Satan, demons), it is only by revelation that one can confess Jesus to be the Son of God (16.16–7); thus, when Jesus is in public, as in chapters 8–9, we learn only what the crowds called him.

being done to the others (cf. Gnilka, *Matthäusevangelium* 1, p. 350)?
One should not overlook the variety of interests enshrined in our
narrative—faith, discipleship, Christology, the response of Israel, etc.
The text moves in several directions at once.

Having said this, however, we nevertheless contend that Mt 8–9, *in
relation to Matthew's structure and plot*, is a unit whose primary
functions can be specified. In other words, while 8.1ff. touches a variety
of subjects and themes, within the total context of Matthew the section
is a unified whole which serves in specific ways to forward Matthew's
story. After the title (1.1) and the genealogy (1.2–17) there are three
narrative pieces (1.18–2.23; 3.1–17; 4.1–22; see 1, pp. 66–70). Their
primary purpose is introductory: Jesus' 'pre-history', his early history,
his preparation for the ministry, and his saving purpose are all set
forth with clarity. Next follows the sermon on the mount (4.23–7.28),
which gives us Jesus' words, primarily about three topics: the law, cult,
and social issues. And then comes the cycle of miracle stories. Clearly
it is the complement of the great sermon. In chapters 5–7 we have the
challenge of Jesus' words, in 8–9 the challenge of his activities. More is
involved than making the Messiah the incarnation of his speech,
although that is an important consideration. In the first place, chapters
5–7 and 8–9 prepare for chapter 10, in which Jesus instructs his
missionaries on what they should preach and how they should act. The
many parallels between what Jesus has already said and done and what
the disciples will say and do demand that one function of the miracle
chapters is to set up an example: like master, like disciple (cf. 10.24f.).
The Jesus of Mt 8–9 is a model. One must not only learn his words (5–
7) but copy his acts, that is, imitate his behaviour (cf. p. 197). As
pupil with rabbi, the disciple of Jesus learns by normative precept (5–7)
and by normative example (8–9). In the second place, one must not
lose sight of the focus upon Israel throughout the first half of
Matthew's gospel. The sermon on the mount is addressed to Jewish
disciples and to a Jewish crowd (cf. 7.27f.). The events of chapters 8–9
involve Jews (exceptions in 8.5–13 and perhaps 8.28–34). And the
disciples go only to the lost sheep of the house of Israel (10.5–6; cf.
15.24). What we have in Mt 5–10 is not the founding of the church—
that does not come until the fourth narrative section, 13.53–17.27—but
Jesus' challenge to Israel, the people of God. He speaks. He acts. And
he sends out others to speak and act as his representatives. In sum,
therefore, Mt 5–10 depicts the mission to the lost sheep of the house of
Israel, that is, the demands made on and benefits offered to the chosen
people by God in Christ. It is therefore no surprise that chapters 11–12
are largely occupied with the theme of the corporate response of Israel
to her Messiah, and that the section begins with a comprehensive
reference to 'the deeds of Christ' (11.2) and poses in a straightforward
manner the question of Jesus' identity (11.3). It is true that the issue of
response is already prominent in chapters 8–9 (cf. especially the
conclusion in 9.33f.). But the failure of corporate Israel does not
become manifest until chapters 11–12 (where the theme is almost
systematically treated). Which is to say: Mt 5–7 (the words of Jesus),
8–9 (the deeds of Jesus), and 10 (the words and deeds of the disciples)
largely record an overture, chapters 11 and 12 a response.

XVII

A TRIAD OF MIRACLE STORIES
(8.1–22)

(i) Structure

The section consists of two basic units. The first is comprised of the three miracle stories in vv. 1–4, 5–13, and 14–15, the second of vv. 16–22 (a summary statement and teaching on discipleship). In all this there is resemblance with both 8.23– 9.17 and 9.18–38, which also consist of three miracle stories plus added material (see below).

The healing narratives in 8.1–15 exhibit certain formal similarities. Each begins with a participial clause describing movement of Jesus (v. 1: καταβάντος; v. 5: εἰσελθόντος; v. 14: ἐλθών) and follows this with a preposition (v. 1: ἀπό; v. 5: εἰς; v. 14: εἰς). Moreover, vv. 1–4 and vv. 5–13 have additional similarities. The former opens with καταβάντος δὲ αὐτοῦ, the latter with εἰσελθόντος δὲ αὐτοῦ. In each instance the individual making request is introduced with a form of προσέρχομαι, λέγων is used, and Jesus is addressed as κύριε. Finally, Jesus' concluding command begins in both cases with ὕπαγε. Clearly some assimilation has taken place.

As for 8.16–22, it is a unit designed to separate 8.1–15 from 8.23–9.8. Like 9.9–17, it functions as the boundary marker between two larger blocks of material, each of which contains three miracle stories. Pictorially:

1 – 2 – 3		1 – 2 – 3		1 – 2 – 3
miracles	8.16–22	miracles	9.9–17	miracles
8.1–15		8.23–9.8		9.18–34

See further Excursus V.

8.16–22 itself contains two subunits, 8.16f. and 8.18–22. The first looks back on 8.1–15 and offers interpretation: Jesus' merciful acts of healing fulfil the ancient oracle in Isa 53.4. Vv. 18–22, in contrast, look forward. They reveal that the following pericope, about peril at sea (8.23–7), is to be understood as a parable about discipleship.

6

(ii) Sources

(1) 8.1–4 is a passage to which both the followers of Griesbach and the proponents of the two-source theory have appealed for support. The several minor agreements between Matthew and Luke against Mark[1] are taken by some to be more than the fruit of coincidence (cf. Farmer, *Problem*, pp. 144–5). But those who favour Markan priority—ourselves included—ask whether one can satisfactorily explain what the Griesbach hypothesis must regard as Markan additions (e.g. ὀργισθείς in Mk 1.41, ἐμβριμησάμενος in Mk 1.43, the notice in 1.45 that the leper disobeyed Jesus' command). For our part we find it easier to tackle the minor agreements than what would have to be considered from the Griesbach perspective Markan additions (see pp. 109–14 of the Introduction). It must be conceded, however, that the implications of Mk 1.40–5 par. for the synoptic problem may be perceived as ambiguous. The signs can be said to point in two different directions. Thus the passage, instead of contributing to the solution of the riddle of synoptic relationships, simply typifies the problem.

(2) Although 8.5–13 = Lk 7.1–10, the healing of a Gentile παῖς, does not much bear on the question of Markan priority (there is no parallel in Mark), the pericope is of importance for the Q hypothesis (see Wegner (v), pp. 277–334). The words of Jesus in Matthew and Luke tend to be very close; but the narrative framework in the two gospels is very different indeed (see the commentary). We shall argue that the differences are explicable in terms of editorial licence: both Matthew and Luke have, for literary and theological reasons, modified certain narrative elements. In this connexion one must remember that Q was primarily a collection of sayings, and its narrative portions were minimal. So in Mt 8.5–13 par. as elsewhere the First and Third Evangelists were all but invited to go their own ways: the sparse narrative framework left room for clarification and expansion. (Wegner (v), pp. 239ff., however, reminds us that Matthew and Luke may have known slightly different versions of the same story (cf. our comments on Q^mt and Q^lk: vol. 1, 121), and perhaps we have to some extent overestimated the contributions of *both* evangelists.)

(3) Concerning 8.14f. = Mk 1.29–31, the healing of Peter's mother-in-law, we believe that it supplies a good argument for Markan priority. Matthew's version is perfectly explicable as arising from two motives— the desire to abbreviate and the desire to assign all the initiative to Jesus. When one takes the other view and interprets Mk 1.29–31 as a revision of Mt 8.14.f, obvious motives no longer appear. One must think long and hard to come up with an explanation for Mark's hypothetical treatment of Matthew. Why increase the verbiage—Mark's account is longer—without adding substance? Why shift the initiative away from Jesus towards others?

(4) 8.16 is, on the two-source theory, a redactional creation based upon Mk 1.32–4 (cf. Lk 4.40f.) whereas 8.17 is Matthean redaction

---

[1] Including the addition of ἰδού and κύριε and the omission of αὐτῷ ὅτι, σπλαγχνισθείς, αὐτῷ, and μηδέν.

without parallel in Mark or Luke. Any theory of synoptic relationships which, against this, postulates Matthean priority, requires that Mark and/or Luke omitted 8.17. One should also note that, on the Griesbach hypothesis, Mark must have altered Matthew's 'they brought to him *many* who were possessed with demons, and he cast out the spirits with a word and healed *all* who were sick' (8.16) to the potentially problematic 'they brought to him *all* who were sick or possessed with demons . . . and he healed *many* who were sick with various diseases, and cast out *many* demons . . .' (Mk 1.32–4). Only Mark's text leaves open the possibility that not everyone brought to Jesus was healed.[2]

(5) 8.18–22 is, with the exception of v. 18 (based on Mk 4.35), Q material. As is so often the case, Matthew and Luke come closer in relating Jesus' words than in depicting the setting.

(iii) *Exegesis*

Two themes are highlighted by 8.1–22. First, the three healing stories and the summary in vv. 16–17 show forth Jesus' rôle as compassionate healer and extraordinary miracle worker. Secondly, those healed all belong to the fringes of Jewish society: a leper, a Gentile youth, a woman, demoniacs. This fact reflects the universalism of Matthew's Jesus: the salvation he offers is for all. It is not for any privileged group.

A LEPER CLEANSED (8.1–4)

Leaving behind the formidable eschatological warnings of chapter 7, Jesus (at the foot of the mountain?) becomes once again a healer (cf. 4.23–5). The narrative—a healing story with apophthegmatic character—would appear to have this fundamental structure:

8.1 transition/introduction
8.2a action
8.2b speech
8.3a action
8.3b speech
8.3c action
8.4 speech

Following the transition/introduction, there are three actions, three speeches, and no narrative conclusion. (8.5a in effect serves as this last.)

Matthew has, on the whole, abbreviated the narrative proper

---

[2] On the alleged conflation of Matthew and Luke in Mk 1.32 see on 8.16.

as over against Mark. This makes for greater concentration on Jesus' words. Our evangelist has also emptied the Markan story of all its emotional features. Jesus is not moved with pity or anger, and we do not hear that he was stern (contrast Mk 1.40–5).

According to Bultmann, *History*, p. 240, the miracle story in Mk 1.40–5 par. goes back to Jewish Christian circles. This is a judgement shared by most modern interpreters. But there has been disagreement over whether the episode records an event in the life of Jesus. Pesch (v) thinks not. For him the narrative is too stylized, it reflects Christian discussion over the status of the Mosaic law, and it presents Jesus as the eschatological prophet like Elijah (the latter healed a leper). Gnilka, *Markus* 1, p. 94, agrees. But Marshall, pp. 207–8, finds the case against authenticity to be indecisive and affirms probable historicity (cf. Taylor, *Mark*, p. 186). Sabourin, p. 457, even goes so far as to assert (without clear reason) that 'the historical authenticity of the cleansing of the leper can hardly be doubted'. While this evaluation is scarcely called for, the arguments against an historical kernel are not in fact compelling. Further, Jesus did, according to his own words, heal lepers (see on 11.5), and we believe he lived his life within the confines of the Torah. We therefore consider it not unlikely that Mk 1.40–5 par. records the memory of an actual occurrence, one on which Jesus healed a man of a skin disorder and directed him to go to a priest.

1. In this redactional verse (without synoptic parallel), Jesus descends the mountain he ascended in 5.1, and he is followed by the crowds already mentioned in 4.25–5.1 and 7.28f.

καταβάντος δὲ αὐτοῦ ἀπὸ τοῦ ὄρους.[3] This is almost identical with Exod 34.29 LXX A, which recounts Moses' descent from Sinai: καταβαίνοντος δὲ αὐτοῦ ἀπὸ τοῦ ὄρους . . . (cf. also 19.14; 32.1, 15). Moreover, a participial form of καταβαίνω + δέ + αὐτοῦ + ἀπό + τοῦ ὄρους appears only once in the OT, in the passage quoted (LXX B has ἐκ for ἀπό). So Mt 8.1, just like 5.1–2, sends the reader's thoughts back to Moses and Sinai. The redactor is drawing a parallel between Jesus and Moses and between Sinai and the mount of Jesus' sermon (cf. Allison (v)). The supposition is supported by 17.9 = Mk 9.9, which has this: καταβαινόντων αὐτῶν ἐκ[4] τοῦ ὄρους. The Mosaic colouring of the narrative to which this belongs is clear (cf. pp. 685–87).

ἠκολούθησαν αὐτῷ ὄχλοι πολλοί. This phrase also appeared immediately before the sermon, in 4.25. See our comments there. It serves to make an *inclusio* and also provides the audience for 8.10–12.

---

[3] καταβαντι δε αυτω appears in ℵ* K M (Δ) 565 1010 1241 1424 Maj k? See BDF § 423.1, 3.

[4] There is an interesting interchange between ἐκ and ἀπό in Matthew; compare 6.27 with 27.21; 7.20 with 12.33; 14.2 with 17.9. In the LXX both translate *min*.

2. Matthew now turns to Mk 1.40–5 (= Lk 5.12–16). The story is placed here primarily because of the reference to what Moses commanded. Jesus' injunction to follow the Pentateuchal legislation happily illustrates one of the central themes of the sermon on the mount: Jesus did not come to do away with Moses (cf. 5.17–19).[5] **καὶ ἰδού.** So also Lk 5.12. The expression (see on 1.20 and 3.16) is not in Mark. Compare Num 12.10: 'behold, Miriam was leprous'. Note the typical absence of introductory details (something also characteristic of rabbinic miracle stories): 'And behold, a leper coming . . .'. The leper's name, his motivation, and the place and time of his encounter with Jesus are passed over in silence. For other units which open with καὶ ἰδού see 9.2; 19.16; and 27.51; also Schrenk, *Sprache*, pp. 297–98. **λεπρὸς προσελθὼν προσεκύνει αὐτῷ λέγων.** Compare Mk 1.40: καὶ ἔρχεται πρὸς αὐτὸν λεπρὸς παρακαλῶν αὐτὸν καὶ γονυπετῶν καὶ λέγων αὐτῷ ὅτι. Matthew has revised Mark so as to obtain (i) a shorter sentence, (ii) a line with favourite expressions (προσελθών[6], προσκυνέω* + αὐτῷ[7]), and (iii) an introduction for direct speech.[8]

Should the movement of the leper (προσελθών) be taken as symbolic? The leper comes forward and seeks Jesus out of the crowd. This might illustrate the asking, seeking, and knocking of 7.7–11. Certainly faith in the First Gospel is praying faith.[9] Grundmann, p. 248, goes even further in detecting symbolism. For him, Jesus is in 8.1–4 the new cultic centre: a leper comes to him, worships him, and makes petition. This interpretation, which makes Jesus the functional equivalent of the temple or its altar, could well be correct in view of the cultic connotations of προσέρχομαι and προσέρχομαι + προσκυνέω.[10]

λεπρός[11]—note the *inclusio* the word makes with v. 4—is traditionally rendered 'leper', λέπρα by 'leprosy'. The translations are misleading. The ṣāraʿat or negaʿ-ṣāraʿat of the OT or the λέπρα of the

---

[5] Cf. Gnilka, *Matthäusevangelium* 1, p. 297. Pace Sabourin, p. 457, who thinks that Mt 8.1–4 illustrates Jesus' freedom from the purity laws.

[6] Cf. 9.18; 20.20; 28.9.

[7] Mt: 9; Mk: 1; Lk: 0.

[8] Luke has also omitted αὐτῷ ὅτι.

[9] See Held, in *TIM*, pp. 284–8.

[10] See 1, pp. 236f. 360, and J. R. Edwards, 'The Use of Προσέρχεσθαι in the Gospel of Matthew', *JBL* 106 (1987), pp. 65–74.

[11] See 1, pp. SB 4, pp. 745–63; L. Goldman et al., 'White Spots in Biblical Times', *Archives of Dermatology* 93 (1966), pp. 744–53; J. J. Pilch, 'Biblical Leprosy and Body Symbolism', *BTB* 11 (1981), pp. 108–13; E. V. Hulse, 'The Nature of Biblical Leprosy and the Use of Alternative Medical Terms in Modern Translations of the Bible', *PEQ* 107 (1975), pp. 87–105; Paul (v); de Vaux 2, pp. 462–4; J. Wilkinson, 'Leprosy and Leviticus', *SJT* 31 (1978), pp. 153–66.

NT is almost certainly not to be identified with, or at least not exclusively with, what we know and refer to as 'leprosy', that is, Hansen's disease or Elephantiasis Graecorum. In the Bible, 'leprosy' is apparently used to cover a variety of skin diseases, including the different forms of psoriasis and vitiligo (cf. Philo, *Spec. leg.* 1.80; *Som.* 1.202; *Poster C.* 47). These diseases were associated with uncleanness and entailed exclusion from Jerusalem and other walled cities, and great social stigma was inevitable.[12] There are even texts which attribute leprosy to demons (e.g. *b. Ḥor.* 10a). The instructions for dealing with leprosy are given in the post-exilic passage, Lev 13–14 (cf. CD 15.7–8). For rabbinic legislation see the mishnaic tractate, *Negaim*, which is based on Lev 13–4. Popular imagination tends to think of lepers living together in colonies (like the Lazaries or leper houses of the Middle Ages), and in this it could be correct. Although Lev 13.46 is not proof, the idea is attested in the targum on 2 Chr 26.21 and may be presupposed by 11QTemple 46.16–18. Yet *m. Neg.* indicates that lepers could sit (by themselves) in synagogue[13], and the NT and rabbinic literature show that lepers were not completely isolated from the rest of society (cf. SB 4, p. 752). So if there were leper colonies or 'hospitals' they were not prisons; that is, their inhabitants were evidently free to come and go as they pleased.

The notion that lepers were the living dead is reflected in several texts, including Num 12.12; 2 Kgs 5.7; Job 18.13; *b. Sanh.* 47a; and *b. Ned.* 64b. For leprosy as the visitation of divine judgement see Lev 14.34; Deut 24.8–9; 2 Chr 26.20.

There are, in the OT, two stories about lepers being healed. The first is found in Num 12, the tale of Miriam's seven-day leprosy. The other appears in 2 Kgs 5.1–14, Elisha's healing of Naaman (cf. L. Proph. Elijah 12). The second is of particular interest for Mk 1.40–5 and its Matthean and Lukan parallels. This is because the OT narrative makes the ability to heal a leper the sign of a prophet (2 Kgs 5.8); and, given the early church's belief that Jesus was an eschatological prophet (Mt 21.11; Jn 4.19; etc.), it could well be that Mk 1.40–5 was once interpreted as evidence for Jesus' status as such. Compare 11.5: the cleansing of lepers is listed as one of the signs of messianic fulfilment. (That Moses too healed a leper—Num 12—might also be taken to hint at this, for some early Christians held Jesus to be the prophet like Moses; see, e.g., Acts 3.22f.)

The evidence for Jesus' association with lepers is surprisingly scanty. In fact it consists of only five items: the healing story in Mt 8.2–4 par., the saying in Mt 11.5 = Lk 7.22 (Q), the healing story in Lk 17.11–19, the saying in Mt 10.8 (redactional), and the notice that Jesus ate in the

---

[12] See Num 5.2; 2 Kgs 7.3–10; 15.5; 2 Chron 26.16–21; 11QTemple 45.17–18; 46.16–18; 49.4; 1QSa 2.3–4; Josephus, *Ant.* 3.261, 264; *C. Ap.* 1.281; *m. Kel.* 1.7; *b. Pesaḥ.* 85b. Note should be taken of the polemical tradition according to which the Egyptians exiled the Jews because they were lepers; see Josephus, *C. Ap.* 1.229, 289, 305, and J. G. Gager, *Moses in Greco-Roman Paganism*, SBLMS 16, Nashville, 1972, p. 129.

[13] In mediaeval churches 'lepers' could view the Mass through a small opening (hagioscope) in the chancel wall.

house of 'Simon the leper'. Pesch, *Taten*, has argued that the first three of these texts will not stand up to critical scrutiny: Mk 1.40–5 is a product of Hellenistic Jewish Christianity which shows Jesus to be faithful to Moses; Mt 11.4–6 is not authentic but a community product which makes Jesus out to be an end-time prophet like Elijah; and Lk 17.11–19 is a secondary creation based on Mk 1.40–5. We, however, shall contend that Mt 11.5 = Lk 7.22 probably goes back to Jesus; and the possibility that Mk 1.40–5 preserves an historical memory can hardly be excluded (see above). In our judgement, then, Jesus was accurately remembered as a man whose healing ministry encompassed even lepers. In accordance with his tendency to emphasize mercy over holiness (see on 5.48), Jesus reached out to people on society's fringes, including lepers. (Pesch himself, *Markusevangelium* 2, p. 335, admits that at least Mk 14.3 preserves historical reminiscence: Jesus supped in the house of a leper. But in *Taten*, pp. 49–51, he argues that Simon may have been a leper only at one time (and not when Jesus ate with him), or that others were living in his house, or that he used to own the house in which Jesus stayed; and in any case there is no remark on Simon having been healed by Jesus.)

What is the significance of the theme of leprosy in the First Gospel? First, the saying of Jesus in 11.5 makes the cleansing of lepers an item of eschatological expectation. So 8.1–4 stands to 11.5 as fulfilment to prophecy. Secondly, Matthew alone adds to Jesus' instructions to missionaries the command to heal lepers (10.8). This helps extend the idea of the *imitatio Christi*: the disciples should do what their Lord did.

κύριε, ἐὰν θέλῃς δύνασαί με καθαρίσαι. So Mark, without 'Lord' (also added by Luke).[14] Compare 9.21 = Mk 5.28. The leper, instead of crying, 'Unclean, unclean' (Lev 13.45–6), asks for help. On the title 'Lord' see on 8.6.

καθαρίζω is a late word, rare outside the LXX (where it occurs most often for a form of *ṭāhēr*) and the NT. It here refers to the healing and to its effect (cf. 2 Kgs 5.10, 14; 5ApocSyrPs 3.13), not to the declaration of cultic cleanness (Lev 13.6, 7, etc.).

The sovereign authority and divine power of Jesus are presupposed by the leper, a man obviously full of faith. When he remarks that what Jesus wills he is able to do (cf. Job 42.2; Isa 55.11), the outcast knows that everything depends solely upon Jesus' gracious will. This is why, instead of asking, 'If you are able, will you?', he says, 'If you will you are able'. Compare the formula, ἐὰν θεὸς θέλῃ[15] and Wisd 12.18 ('Thou (God) hast power to act (δύνασαι) whenever you will' (θέλῃς)). Even though

---

[14] One cannot make much of this, in view of the fact that Matthew and Luke, on the two-source theory, insert κύριε (Mt: 30; Mk: 2; Lk: 25) on a number of occasions.

[15] See G. Schrenk, *TWNT* 3, p. 46.

Jesus has not yet 'received all authority in heaven and on earth' (28.18), his ἐξουσία (cf. 7.29) is remarkable: his will is done. Note Chrysostom, *Hom. on Mt.* 25.2: 'For neither did he (the leper) say, "If thou request it of God", nor "If thou pray", but "If thou wilt, thou canst make me clean". Nor did he say, "Lord, cleanse me", but (he) leaves all to him, and makes his recovery depend on him, and testifies that all authority is his'. Contrast *b. Ber.* 34b, where Hanina ben Dosa heals others *by praying to God.* Contrast also 2 Kgs 5.11, where Elijah is expected to heal a leper *by calling on the name of the Lord.*

3. The evangelist has constructed this verse so that it resembles v. 2. Both have this structure: participle + finite verb + 'saying' + direct speech (cf. Thompson, p. 89). The heightened parallelism is typical.

καὶ ἐκτείνας τὴν χεῖρα ἥψατο αὐτοῦ λέγων. Compare LXX Judg 6.21; 4 Βασ 5.11; Jer 1.9. Luke has this with εἰπών at the end. Both Matthew and Luke probably found ὀργισθείς (directed against whom or what?) in their copies of Mark, not σπλαγχνισθείς. This would readily explain the common omission. One would certainly be hard pressed to urge that both evangelists omitted σπλαγχνισθείς (cf. Mt 9.36; 14.14; 15.32; 18.27; 20.34).

Assuming that Mark originally had αὐτοῦ ἥψατο (but see Streeter, pp. 309–10), Matthew and Luke have, naturally enough, independently moved αὐτοῦ so that it no longer qualifies 'hand' but instead becomes the object of 'touch'. (The verb cries out for an object; cf. 8.15; 9.20; 17.7; Lk 6.19; 18.15; Jn 20.17). Matthew also alters Mark's 'touched and says' because, as Allen, p. 75, observed, our author prefers subordinate to co-ordinate clauses (contrast 8.25; 9.14; 14.27; 20.30; 21.1–2; 26.67–8; and 21.23 with their Markan counterparts). On the element of touch in miracle stories see on 9.28 and Theissen, *Stories*, pp. 62–3, to which add *b. Ber.* 5b. The idea that benefit and power or energy flow through the extremities of a healer or holy man is found in all religions.

If Jesus did in fact touch a leper, that would not, strictly speaking, have been a transgression of Jewish law (contrast Chrysostom, *Hom. on Mt.* 25.2).[16] But would it have brought ceremonial uncleanness (cf. Josephus, *C. Ap.* 1.281)? Whether rightly or wrongly, Matthew would not have thought so. When Jesus touches the man, leprosy does not spread to the healer; rather, healing power goes forth to conquer the disease. The leprosy is rendered impotent.

θέλω, καθαρίσθητι. So also Mark and Luke. Compare 4 Βασ 5.13: καθαρίσθητι. The combination of a word of power with a healing touch is common in the synoptics as elsewhere in the ancient world (e.g. Mt 9.29; Mk 7.33–4; Acts 9.40; 28.8).

[16] Neither Moses (Num 12.9–15) nor Elisha (2 Kgs 5.1–14) touched the leper he healed.

καὶ εὐθέως ἐκαθαρίσθη αὐτοῦ ἡ λέπρα. Compare 2 Kgs 5.14. Luke, like Matthew, substitutes εὐθέως* for εὐθύς.[17] For the rest he is much closer to Mark than is Matthew. The First Gospel is a condensation of the Second. 'With him speaking, immediately the leprosy went from him and he became cleansed' has become 'and immediately his leprosy was cleansed.' Jesus does not here use any magical word or formula. 'Be clean' is simply an unqualified imperative. Power and mystery reside in the speaker, not in what is spoken.[18] Further, Jesus says simply, 'I will'. He does not say, 'God wills'. Jesus himself is in control, and he is the source of healing power.

4. Jesus tells the healed leper to show himself to the priest. Eusebius' words are apt: 'Nor could our Lord have said to the leper, "Going show thyself to the priest and offer the gift which Moses commanded" . . . if he did not consider it right for the legal observances to be carried out there as in a holy place worthy of God' (*Dem. ev.* 8.2 (401c)). Thus it is that Mt 8.4 'plays the role in the miracles that Mt 5.17–20 played in the teachings' (Brunner, p. 302).

καὶ λέγει αὐτῷ ὁ 'Ιησοῦς. Matthew has added the subject, as often (cf. 1, p. 78).

ὅρα μηδενὶ εἴπῃς. Compare 9.30; 12.16. Mark has μηδέν after μηδενί, which Matthew and Luke have dropped as redundant (it is also missing in many Markan mss.). ὅρα here has the sense 'see to it' (cf. 18.10; 1 Thess 5.15; Did. 6.1). Why is the man to say nothing? The answer to this difficult question is bound up with the problem of the so-called 'messianic secret'.[19] For our purposes the significant fact is that the difficulty modern scholars have had in sorting out Mark's commands to secrecy (1.25, 34, 44 etc.) was evidently shared by our evangelist. That he too was not a little nonplussed appears from this, that he dropped no less than six of the relevant Markan texts and passed on the others without significant alteration. Seemingly 'the idea of the messianic secret no longer has the importance for Matthew that it has for Mark' (Wrede, p. 154). The one pattern that does exist in Matthew, as compared with Mark, is that in the former Jesus never silences demons. This is probably because the practice was associated with magical notions about the power of names (cf. Mk 1.24), and Matthew wanted Jesus

---

[17] On the motif of immediacy in healings (more common in Mark than Matthew) see Theissen, *Stories*, p. 66. Compare 14.31; 20.34; Jn 5.9; Acts 9.34; Tacitus, *Hist.* 4.81.

[18] Contrast Mk 5.41; 7.34; *PGM* 4.1609–11; 8.20–1. See Theissen, *ibid.*, pp. 63–5.

[19] See esp. the collection of essays in C. M. Tuckett, ed., *The Messianic Secret*, London, 1984; and for Matthew Wrede, pp. 152–64.

divorced as much as possible from the accusation of magic.[20]
Beyond this, we can say no more than that Matthew, following
his tradition, connected the commands to silence with Jesus'
healing ministry (see 12.15-21).

What was the original function of the command to silence in Mk
1.44? Perhaps it served to confirm Jesus as upholder of the Torah.
Jesus is apprehensive lest the leper begin to mingle with others (to tell
of the mighty deed) before officially being declared clean by a priest.
Such a result would give offence because, according to Lev 13-14, it is
the priest, and no one else, who is to pronounce a person clean. Thus
Jesus must request the priestly judgement. If all this is correct, our
pericope would seem to have its *Sitz im Leben* either in a Jewish
Christian community which felt the need to emphasize its faithfulness
to Moses or in the ministry of Jesus (he presumably had to defend
himself against charges of antinomianism).

ἀλλὰ ὕπαγε σεαυτὸν δεῖξον τῷ ἱερεῖ. Compare 8.13; Lk 17.14;
and *Pap. Eg.* 2 fol. 1r 10 (πορε[υθεὶς ἐπίδειξον σεαυτὸ]ν
τοῖ[ς ἱερεῦσι). The dismissal formula is taken over without
change from Mark. δεῖξον τῷ ἱερεῖ is from LXX Lev 13.49.
Luke, by placing the pronoun immediately before τῷ, weakens
the scriptural allusion. Jesus tells the leper to go to the priest for
three reasons, one implicit, the other two explicit. (i) Implicit is
the need to be pronounced clean by a priest: without a priest's
word of approval, reintegration into Jewish society would not be
possible. (Does the injunction envisage first the seeking out of a
local priest (cf. *t. Ned.* 8.2) and then a journey to Jerusalem,
where the sacrifice can be offered?) (ii) Explicit is the need to
fulfil a cultic requirement. The law must be obeyed. Note *m.
Neg.* 3.1: 'Only a priest may declare them [lepers] unclean or
clean' (cf. LAB 13.3). (iii) Also explicit is the desire to provide a
'witness' or 'testimony' (on this see below).

καὶ προσένεγκον τὸ δῶρον. καὶ προσένεγκε περὶ τοῦ καθαρισμοῦ
σου appears in Mark. Matthew has altered Mark in order to
get a construction he is fond of, one with a biblical ring:
προσφέρω* + δῶρον* (see 1, pp. 248).[21]

In Lev 14.4 the offering for leprosy is two clean birds, cedarwood,
scarlet stuff, hyssop, in Lev 14.10 two male lambs without blemish, one
ewe lamb, a cereal offering, and one log of oil (cf. 11QTemple 48.17–49.4).

ὃ προσέταξεν Μωϋσῆς.[22] So Mark, with ἅ for ὅ. The reference
is to Lev 13.49 (cf. 14.2–32; LAB 13.3).

[20] Is this because Matthew's Jewish opponents accused Jesus of being a
magician? Cf. Justin, *Dial.* 69; *b. Šabb.* 104b; *b. Sanh.* 43a. See further Smith,
Magician, pp. 21–67.
[21] Cf. *qārab* + *qorbān* and see LXX Gen 43.26; Lev 1.2; 2.1; 4.23; 9.15; etc.
[22] The Diatessaron apparently referred to the law in its version of Mt 8.4 par.
See W. L. Petersen, 'Romanos and the Diatessaron', *NTS* 29 (1983), pp. 493–4.

εἰς μαρτύριον αὐτοῖς. So also Mark and Luke. Compare Mk 6.11 = Mt 10.18; Mk 13.9 = Mt 24.14.

εἰς μαρτύριον (= *lĕ'ēd*) was a fixed expression.[23] Here the RSV translates, 'For a proof to the people'. There is, however, no clear antecedent, and 'people' must be read in. 'Them' could just as easily refer to the priests.[24] In this case, and if the phrase be taken in a negative sense, it would harmonize with Matthew's penchant for criticizing the Jewish leaders in particular. The point would be that if the priests do recognize the leper's recovery, then they cannot persist in unbelief without incriminating themselves.[25] On the other hand, εἰς κ.τ.λ. has been taken positively. (i) Jesus could be showing the Jewish leaders or the people in general that he keeps the law ('a testimony to them that I uphold the Torah'). (ii) Or he could be making it possible for the leper to re-enter society ('a testimony to them that the outcast has been made whole'). (iii) Or the witness could concern the miracle itself ('a testimony to them that I have done this great work'). There is also the possibility that εἰς κ.τ.λ. simply means 'as a statute for Israel'. See further Cranfield, *Mark*, p. 95.

Matthew and Luke have omitted Mk 1.45, a verse which can be taken to imply that the leper disobeys Jesus' order to keep silent.[26] The motive for the omission is plain. The evangelists do not want Jesus' authority to be violated, especially by one who has just shown faith and been cured.

Egerton Papyrus 2 fol. lr° 8–10 reads: 'And behold, a leper coming to him says, "Teacher Jesus, journeying with lepers and eating with them in the inn I myself also became a leper. If therefore thou wilt, I am made clean." The Lord then said to him, "I will; be clean." And straightway the leprosy departed from him. (And the Lord said to him,) "Go(ing, show yourself) to th(e priests . . .)"'. A knowledge of Matthew appears probable,[27] this because λεπρὸς προσελθὼν . . . αὐτῷ λέγων is redactional in Matthew and also appears in the papyrus.

[23] See LXX Gen 31.44; Deut 31.26; Josh 24.27; Job 16.9; Prov 29.14; Hos 2.12; Amos 1.11; Mic 1.2; 7.18; Zeph 3.8; Jas 5.3; Ignatius, *Trall.* 12.3; Barn. 9.3.
[24] *Pap. Eg.* 2 h sy^pal turn the 'priest' of 8.4 into 'priests', thus making the connexion with 'them' firm. See further Zahn, p. 336.
[25] Cf. E. Lohmeyer, *Lord of the Temple* (trans. of *Kultus und Evangelium*, 1942), London, 1962, pp. 25–6.
[26] Nineham, p. 86, however, observes that the Greek could equally mean: 'And he (Jesus) went out and preached (the gospel) constantly and spread abroad the word . . .'.
[27] So also Pesch, *Taten*, pp. 107–13; Neirynck (v); and D. F. Wright, 'Apocryphal Gospels and the "Unknown Gospel"', in Wenham, *Tradition*, pp. 216–17; against Mayeda and Koester (see 1, p. 713, n. 31). Crossan, *Four*, p. 75, entertains the possibility of Matthew's dependence upon *Egerton Papyrus* 2.

THE CENTURION'S SERVANT (8.5–13)

In Mark, the healing of the leper (1.40–5) is followed by the
healing of a paralytic in Capernaum (2.1–12). But Matthew,
wishing to stress at this juncture the great authority of Jesus,
puts this last story off for a time (see 9.2–8) and now turns to a
pericope which, in Q, immediately followed the sermon on the
mount/plain (cf. Lk 7.1–10; there is nothing corresponding to
this in Mark). Matthew was no doubt encouraged in his choice
or substitution by the fact that both Mk 2.1–12 and the Q story
are set in Capernaum.

The structure of 8.5–13, which is more a pronouncement story *M*
than a miracle story,[28] may be set forth in more than one way. */*
The following analysis highlights the fact that 8.5–13 consists
primarily not of description but dialogue.

8.5   introduction/setting
8.6   speech of centurion (brief)
8.7   speech of Jesus (brief)
8.8–9   speech of centurion (protracted)
8.10–13a   speech of Jesus (protracted)
8.13b   conclusion

Despite some minor differences, no one would claim that Mt 8.5–13
and Lk 7.1–10 recount different incidents (although some earlier
commentators did; see Strauss, pp. 463–64). Matters are otherwise with
Jn 4.46–54. Although Irenaeus, *Adv. haer.* 2.22.3, identified John's story
with that in the synoptics, others have held a different opinion (cf.
Chrysostom, *Hom. on Mt.* 26.4) or been unsure (cf. Dodd, *Tradition*,
pp. 193–4). This is because John's account departs from Matthew and
Luke in several important particulars. In the Fourth Gospel (i) Jesus is
in Cana of Galilee, not Capernaum, (ii) the man of rank is not called a
centurion but a βασιλικός, and (iii) instead of commending the officer's
faith, Jesus seems to display disillusionment; in addition (iv) while in
Matthew the boy or servant is a paralytic, in John he has a fever. These
differences are, however, far outweighed by the similarities. Following
Brown, *John* 1, pp. 192f., the common elements are these: (i) an official
lives in or is temporarily residing in Capernaum; (ii) he asks a favour of
Jesus; (iii) the favour concerns a boy (so Luke) or servant (so John) in
the man's household; (iv) the boy or servant is ill; (v) Jesus determines
to heal him; (vi) the healing is accomplished at a distance; (vii) John and
Matthew both write that the healing took place 'at that very hour'. In
our judgement, these parallels indicate that the same incident or story
lies behind Mt 8.5–13 par. and Jn 4.46–54 (although it is just possible
that we have to do with two different incidents or stories which were

---

[28] Compare the story in *b. Ber.* 34b. Here, as in Mt 8.5–13, we have a healing
at a distance (see also 15.21–8; 2 Kgs 5.1–14; Lk 17.11–19; Acts 19.11–12;
Philostratus, *V.A.* 3.38; *b. Bab. Qam.* 50a; discussion in Wegner (v), pp. 344–61)
in which the dialogue element is large and in which the motif of 'that hour' is
important.

assimilated to each other in the tradition). We are also strongly inclined to believe that Jn 4.46–54 does not directly depend upon either Matthew or Luke. It is, admittedly, theoretically possible to explain John's version as a radical rewriting of the synoptic tale; but the common vocabulary is very slight, the synoptic dialogue has no counterpart in John, and certain details in John (e.g. βασιλικός and the diagnosis of fever) are almost impossible to account for as redactional alterations of Matthew or Luke (cf. Wegner (v), pp. 32–7). There is, accordingly, every reason to suppose that Jn 4.46–54 and its synoptic relatives are independent formulations which go back to a common oral tradition.

The genesis of Mt 8.5–13 par. has been discussed at length by Wegner (v), pp. 403–28. Opposing Bultmann's conclusion (the story is a variant of Mk 7.24–31 and an imaginary product of the church: *History*, pp. 38f.), he makes several points, including these: (i) the story has multiple attestation (Q and John); (ii) stylistic criteria make a primitive Aramaic source possible;[29] (iii) nothing fails to fit the situation in pre-70 Palestine; (iv) the rôle of faith and Jesus' remarks about it seem characteristic of him; and (v) the pericope hardly answers any of the burning questions which the Gentile mission produced (e.g.circumcision or the place of the law). In view of all this, Wegner, along with Hahn, *Mission*, p. 32, and Gnilka, *Matthäusevangelium* 1, p. 304, are probably correct: Mt 8.5–13 par. preserves a concrete memory from the ministry of Jesus.

5. The scene is an odd one. A Roman[30] is asking for help from a Jew, a commander is playing the part of a supplicant.

εἰσελθόντος δὲ αὐτοῦ εἰς Καφαρναούμ. Compare 17.22. The form, participle + δέ + αὐτοῦ/αὐτῶν + preposition is a redactional feature.[31] Note the lack of any chronological specifics. This is typical of our evangelist. Also typical is the naming of the subject (αὐτοῦ): Jesus is always named first in the Matthean healing narratives. Lk 7.1 has this: 'After he had ended all his words in the hearing of the people, εἰσῆλθεν εἰς Καφαρναούμ'. Matthew and Luke have both rewritten Q, which had a form of εἰσέρχομαι + εἰς Καφαρναούμ.[32] On Capernaum and Matthew's interest in it see on 4.13 and 8.14.

προσῆλθεν αὐτῷ ἑκατόνταρχος παρακαλῶν αὐτόν.[33] Except for the one word, 'centurion',[34] Luke has something completely

---

[29] Possible Semitisms include: verb before noun, parataxis, ἄνθρωπος = τις, synonymous parallelism. See Wegner (v), pp. 409–18; also Schulz, *Q*, p. 242, n. 440.

[30] He is reminiscent of the pious Gentiles who occasionally cross the pages of the OT—Abimelech (Gen 20–1), Rahab (Josh 2), Ruth (Ruth 1–4), and esp. Naaman (2 Kgs 5).

[31] Cf. 8.1; 17.22, 24; 24.3; 27.19.

[32] Luke's hand is revealed by word statistics. ἐπειδή: Mt: 0; Mk: 0; Lk: 2; Acts: 3. πληρόω with profane sense: Mt: 0; Mk: 1; Lk: 1; Acts: 8. πάντα τὰ ῥήματα: Mt: 0; Mk: 0; Lk: 4. εἰς + τὰς ἀκοάς: Mt: 0; Mk: 0; Lk: 1; Acts: 1. λαός: Mt: 14; Mk: 2; Lk: 36; Acts: 48.

[33] χιλίαρχης, found in sy[s] Cl[hom] Eus here and in vv. 8 and 13, is favoured by Zuntz; but see Wegner (v), pp. 78–9.

different: 'A certain centurion had a slave who was dear to him, who was sick and about to die . . .'. προσῆλθεν* is Matthean, as is the sentence structure.[35] Luke, with the exception perhaps of adjectival τις, probably comes closer to Q.[36]

The ἑκατόνταρχος[37] (= κεντυρίων, lat. *centurio*) was the officer in charge of a Roman 'century', that is, one hundred foot soldiers. He was often an ordinary soldier of a legion who had been promoted, although the post was also held by magistrates or lower members of the equestrian order. His responsibilities were vast and included field command and the supervision of capital penalties.[38]

In the NT the prominence of the centurion in the Roman world is manifest. One is said to have built a synagogue (Lk 7.5). Another conducts Paul safely to Rome (Acts 27.1) while yet another stands near Jesus at the crucifixion and confesses him to the Son of God (Mk 15.39). And when the centurion Cornelius is converted in Acts, Luke devotes an entire chapter (10) to the event. Whatever the reason, the favourable picture of the centurion painted in Mt 8.5–13 = Lk 7.1–10 is typical of the NT. Roman centurions not only merit respect but are also pious. This is somewhat surprising given the hostility many first-century Jews felt towards the invincible Roman army.[39]

What is the significance of the centurion in Mt 8.5–13? He is first of all a Gentile. The man thus foreshadows (as did the magi) the successful evangelization of the nations (28.16–20). In the second place, the centurion is a paradigm for the believer in so far as he exhibits true faith: the ear of his soul is open. The man trusts implicitly in Jesus' power and authority. This is why his faith is mentioned not once but twice (8.10, 13).

6. **καὶ λέγων.** Compare Josephus, *Ant.* 8.213 (προσελθόντες . . . παρεκάλουν λέγοντες). *Pace* Schulz, *Q*, p. 237, Matthew has probably turned indirect speech (so Luke and Jn 4.47) into direct speech, as in 26.1–2 diff. Mk 14.1. This puts the Jewish elders in Luke = Q out of the picture and requires certain other changes, such as the omission of Lk 7.4–5 (see below). The upshot is that the First Gospel is shorter and comes more quickly to the point.

κύριε, ὁ παῖς μου βέβληται ἐν τῇ οἰκίᾳ παραλυτικός, δεινῶς

---

[34] On the form of the word see BDF § 50.

[35] προσέρχμαι* + αὐτῷ + subject + participle: Mt: 12–13; Mk: 0; Lk: 0.

[36] See Jeremias, *Lukasevangelium*, pp. 151–2; Wegner (v), pp. 127–33.

[37] Mt: 4 (redactional in 27.54); Mk: 0; Lk: 3; LXX: ca. 20, for *śar hammeʾôt* or *śar meʾôt*.

[38] For lit. see BAGD, s.v., and B. Dobson, 'The Significance of the Centurion and "Primipilaris" in the Roman Army and Administration', *ANRW* II/1 (1974), pp. 395–433.

[39] Is it possible to identify Q's 'centurion' with John's βασιλικός? See A. H. Mead, 'The βασιλικός in John 4.46–53', *JSNT* 23 (1985), pp. 69–72; also Wegner (v), pp. 57–72.

βασανιζόμενος.[40] Lk 7.2–5 is much longer. Matthew has, presumably, severely abbreviated Q, just as he has elsewhere shortened many Markan miracle stories.[41]

As in 8.2, Matthew has added 'Lord'. Q itself had the word in 8.8 = Lk 7.6. Our evangelist very much likes to use 'Lord' in healing stories. When a supplicant addresses Jesus, more often than not the title appears.[42] For discussion of 'Lord' in the NT and its Jewish background see esp. Fitzmyer, *Aramean*, pp. 115–42, and *Advance*, pp. 218–35. It now seems certain that the application of 'Lord' to Jesus originated either (a) out of the religious title *'ādôn* or *mārê'* used by Palestinian Jews of Yahweh[43] or (b) out of secular usage, 'Lord' being used of Jesus already during the ministry, with the sense of something like 'sir'.[44]

How is 'Lord' employed in Matthew? It is not, *pace* Trilling and Frankemölle, the primary christological title. For one thing, it is not distinctive of Jesus. It is as often as not an appellation for God himself (1.20, 22; etc.). And in other places it bears a totally secular sense (e.g. 13.27 and 21.30). 'Lord' is also never part of a confession. There is no 'Thou art the Lord' (contrast the confession of 'Son (of God)' and 'Christ' in 3.17; 16.16; and 17.5). Despite the varying senses of 'Lord', the title is always positive in Matthew. This is why Jesus' opponents never address him as such. But what is the specific content of 'Lord' as applied precisely to Jesus? Its use by supplicants in the healing narratives and by the disciples in 8.25 and 14.28–30 connects it with Jesus' majestic ἐξουσία. It would be hazardous, however, to venture much more than this. The significance of the title is nowhere delimited, and only in a few places do we seem to have the full Christian meaning of the term (e.g. 7.21f.; 24.42; 25.37). Gerhardsson is probably right in affirming that 'Lord' was 'open to humbler or more elevated interpretation', and that in the therapeutic narratives the supplicants are 'on the right track without realizing anything like the whole truth about Jesus' (*Acts*, p. 86).

Concerning ὁ παῖς μου: throughout the present pericope Matthew has only παῖς, Luke παῖς and δοῦλος. Is Luke's 'servant' redactional? Gundry, *Commentary*, p. 142, thinks not, arguing that Matthew changed 'servant' (so Q) in order to gain a parallel with 8.8, where ὁ παῖς μου appears. But (i) Matthew shows no avoidance of δοῦλος;[45] (ii) John has υἱός (4.46), and granted his independence from the synoptics in the present instance, this would argue for the

---

[40] κυριε is omitted by ℵ* k sy[s.c] Or Hil. See Wegner (v), pp. 79–80.

[41] On the traditional and redactional elements in Lk 7.2–5 see Wegner (v), pp. 142–9, 161–88. A pre-Lukan basis for Lk 7.2–5 is indicated by several facts, including some expressions not typical of Luke (e.g. κακῶς ἔχων and ἤμελλεν τελευτᾶν) and Jn 4.47, which agrees with Luke that the servant or son was at the point of death.

[42] 8.2, 6, 8; 9.28; 15.22, 25, 27; 17.15; 20.30, 31.

[43] So Fitzmyer, citing Ps 114.7; 151.4; Ecclus 10.7; 11QtgJob 24.6–7; 1QapGen 20.12–13; 4QEn[b] 1.4.5.

[44] This is the position of Hahn, *Titles*, pp. 73–89. Cf. Fuller, *Mission*, p. 112.

[45] δοῦλος: Mt: 30; Mk: 5; Lk: 26.

originality of Matthew's ambiguous παῖς, which like the Hebrew *na'ar* or the Aramaic *ṭalyā'* can mean either 'son' (cf. John) or 'servant' (cf. Luke); (iii) παῖς appears in Jn 4.49; (iv) παῖς did undoubtedly appear in Q (cf. Lk 7.7), at least at one point; (v) Luke may have been interested in the parallelism between Lk 7 and the story of Cornelius in Acts 10,[46] and Cornelius had servants (Acts 10.7); (vi) Luke shows a tendency to substitute synonymous terms for one another.[47] With all this in mind, the παῖς in Mt 8.5 and 13 may very well be original.[48]

How should the word be translated? It can mean either 'son' or 'servant'. Although the equation with 'servant' increases the distance between our story and the healings in 9.23–6 (the daughter of the synagogue ruler) and 15.21–8 (the daughter of the Canaanite woman), yet only once in the NT does παῖς clearly mean 'son' (Jn 4.51). For the rest it seems to mean 'servant' (cf. Mt 14.2; 12.18) or 'youngster' (cf. 17.18). And in the LXX παῖς rarely translates *bēn*: it is most commonly the equivalent of *'ebed*. So we prefer to translate 'servant'. One should think of a house slave.

With βέβληται[49] ἐν τῇ οἰκίᾳ παραλυτικός compare 8.14 diff. Mk 1.30 and 9.2 diff. Mk 2.3. Lk 7.2 has: κακῶς ἔχων ἤμελλεν τελευτᾶν (not an expected description of a paralytic), Jn 4.46f.: ἠσθένει ... ἤμελλεν ... ἀποθνήσκειν. Matthew shows a tendency to specify sicknesses, and perhaps his formulation has been affected by Mk 2.1–12, a story which in Mark follows the healing of the leper (Mk 1.40–5 = Mt 8.2–4): 'paralytic' occurs there. 'In the house' has been added (cf. Wegner (v), p. 139) because, given the changes vis-à-vis Q, we would not otherwise know that Jesus was not near the sick servant and that healing occurred at a distance.

Concerning δεινῶς βασανιζόμενος, the adverb (= 'terribly') is a Matthean *hapax*. It here serves to underline the severity of the affliction and so magnify the act of healing. For βασανίζω (= 'torment'; cf. 8.29; 14.24; also the use of βάσανος in 4.24) see Horsley 4, p. 142, and BAGD, s.v., documenting its application to physical illness.

7. καὶ λέγει αὐτῷ· ἐγὼ ἐλθὼν θεραπεύσω αὐτόν; The formulation may be editorial.[50] The main issue concerning 8.7 is whether Jesus' words show compliance or resistance. Is the proper translation: 'I coming will heal him' or 'Should I coming

---

[46] See Talbert, pp. 16, 19.

[47] H. J. Cadbury, 'Four Features of Lukan Style', in *Studies in Luke-Acts*, ed. L. E. Keck and J. Louis Martyn, Philadelphia, 1980, pp. 88–97.

[48] So also Schulz, *Q*, p. 236.

[49] βάλλω*. Cf. *mûṭṭāl*, as in *b*. Qidd. 82b (other texts in SB 1, p. 475 and Schlatter, p. 274; *mûṭṭāl* means both 'to be thrown' and 'to lie').

[50] *Pace* Wegner (v), p. 157. λέγω in the historical present: Mt: 71; Mk: 73; Mk: 4. ἐλθών/-όντες and other genders used circumstantially: Mt: 28; Mk: 16; Lk: 12. θεραπεύω: Mt: 16; Mk: 5; Lk: 14; with αὐτόν/αὐτούς as direct object: Mt: 8; Mk: 1; Lk: 1.

heal him"? The versions and commentators are divided.[51] While eschewing certainty, we concur with those who have taken 8.7 to be a question. (i) In the story of the Syro-Phoenician woman (15.21–8), which in so many ways is so similar to 8.5–13, a Gentile's request for her daughter's healing is initially met with a negative response. (ii) Hesitation to help a Gentile would accord with the view that Jesus came only for the lost sheep of the house of Israel (10.6; 15.24). (iii) In Jn 4.46–54 Jesus responds to the official's plea with this: 'Unless you see signs and wonders you will not believe'. This shows that, in at least one stream of the tradition, Jesus' reaction was not unambiguously positive; so Mt 8.7, understood as a question or an attempt to assay the centurion's faith, could have a pre-Matthean basis. (iv) ἐγώ, placed at the beginning of the sentence, seems emphatic: 'Should *I* . . .?'.[52] (v) If Matthew were a Jew, he might have thought that his law-abiding Lord, in the days of his earthly ministry and before the directive in 28.16–20, would have avoided entrance into a Gentile residence.[53]

8. The centurion ὁ responds to Jesus in words which largely agree with Luke's version. If 8.7 be understood as a question and test, then the soldier now proves himself and clarifies his request: You need not even come into my house but need only say the word. If, however, 8.7 records Jesus' readiness to offer aid, 8.8 becomes a declaration either of surprise or gratitude: Even though you are willing to enter my house, do not trouble yourself; just say the word. In either case, faith is the victor on the battlefield of the centurion's heart.

In Lk 7.6 the centurion himself does not directly address Jesus: 'When he was not far from the house, the centurion sent friends to him, saying to him: "Lord, do not trouble yourself, for I am not worthy to have you come under my roof; and for this reason I did not presume to come to you myself"'. Because the words that follow (cf. 8.8–9) are more fitting coming from the centurion himself, it may be that Luke is responsible for artificially attributing the second speech of supplication to messengers, thus bringing it into line with the first speech (cf. Strauss, p. 466).[54]

καὶ ἀποκριθεὶς ὁ ἑκατόνταρχος ἔφη. Although Q named the subject (see Lk 7.6), ἀποκριθείς* and ἔφη[55] may well be

[51] Schlatter, pp. 274–5; Lagrange, p. 165; Gundry, *Commentary*, pp. 142–3; and the RSV, JB, and NEB opt for the first alternative, Zahn, pp. 338–9; Allen, p. 77; Lohmeyer, p. 157; Wegner (v), pp. 375–80; and Gnilka, *Matthäusevangelium* 1, p. 301, for the second.
[52] Unemphatic pronouns are not placed first in NT Greek; see BDF § 473.1.
[53] Cf. Jn 18.28; Acts 10.28; 11.12; *m. Ohol.* 18.7.
[54] In Luke the messengers have replaced the centurion in the second encounter, in order to illustrate the latter's 'authority' and to sound the theme of believing without seeing.
[55] φημι* is often redactional.

Matthean—although καὶ ἀποκριθείς . . . ἔφη is found nowhere else in the First Gospel (or the NT). **κύριε, οὐκ εἰμὶ ἱκανὸς ἵνα μου ὑπὸ τὴν στέγην εἰσέλθῃς.** οὐκ εἰμὶ ἱκανός was a fixed expression.⁵⁶ Luke has μὴ σκύλλου (= 'do not trouble yourself') after 'Lord' (cf. Lk 8.49), οὐ γάρ instead of οὐκ, and 'I am' after, not before, 'worthy'. The only other difference is the placement of 'my'. In Luke it comes after 'roof'. Has Matthew moved the pronoun forward to highlight the contrast with Jesus' ἐγώ? Or do we have here an instance of the rule that unemphatic pronouns are usually placed near (but not at) the beginning of a clause (BDF § 473.1)? **ἀλλὰ μόνον εἰπὲ λόγῳ καὶ ἰαθήσεται.**⁵⁷ Compare Ps 107.20 ('He sent forth his word and healed them') and Mt 8.16 (Jesus 'cast out the spirits λόγῳ'). Luke does not have μόνον*, an adverb which Matthew inserts⁵⁸ to emphasize the ease with which Jesus exercises his power. Compare Lactantius, *Div. inst.* 4.15: 'He did all these things not by his hands or the application of any charm but by word and command'. Luke employs the aorist imperative passive of 'heal' instead of the future indicative passive. Has Matthew turned a petition into a prediction?

9. This verse, which agrees exactly with Lk 7.8 save for one word, supplies the reason for the confidence conveyed in 8.8. The implicit logic is from the lesser to the greater: if the centurion, a man under authority, can command power with a word, how much more Jesus, who is under no earthly authority at all.⁵⁹

καὶ γὰρ ἐγὼ ἄνθρωπός εἰμι ὑπὸ ἐξουσίαν.⁶⁰ Luke has τασσόμενος⁶¹ at the end (it is added in some Matthean texts). ἄνθρωπος is unnecessary and may be a Semitism (1, p. 81).

'For also I am a man under authority' proved problematic for some later Christians. Jesus, the text may be thought to imply, is, like the centurion, under some authority. This explains the reading of syˢ·ᶜ: 'I am a man *having* authority'.⁶² But it is not clear that καὶ γάρ requires

⁵⁶ Cf. LXX Exod 4.10; Mt 3.11; 1 Cor 15.9. Comparable is the rabbinic *'ênî kĕda'y*, as in *b. B. Bat.* 165b; *b. Giṭ.* 90b.
⁵⁷ HG and NA²⁶ have ο παις μου at the end. It is omitted by f¹ k sa mae boᵐˢˢ Or, and this may well be original. The subject is named in the Lukan parallel, and so could have come into Matthew through harmonization. Metzger's explanation (p. 20) we do not understand: 'the eyes of copyists passed from ἰαθήσεται to the following και, omitting the intervening words'. But then why does the omission not include και?
⁵⁸ Cf. Wegner (v), pp. 206–7.
⁵⁹ Should we, following Ps.-Clem. Hom. 9.21; Rec. 4.33, draw out the analogy so as to make Jesus the commander of demons? Cf. Chrysostom, *Hom. on Mt* 26.4.
⁶⁰ ℵ B pc it vgᶜˡ add τασσομενος (from Lk 7.8).
⁶¹ Redactional: so Wegner (v), p. 208.
⁶² Cf. Hooke (v). Jeremias, *Promise*, p. 30, n. 4, supposes that the Syriac

that Jesus be under authority,[63] and it is quite hazardous to find any christological point in 8.9a.

ἔχων ὑπ' ἐμαυτὸν στρατιώτας. So Luke. Should the verb receive the emphasis, thus making the previous clause concessive: '*Although* I am a man under authority . . .'?

καὶ λέγω τούτῳ· πορεύθητι, καὶ πορεύεται, καὶ ἄλλῳ· ἔρχου, καὶ ἔρχεται, καὶ τῷ δούλῳ μου· ποίησον τοῦτο, καὶ ποιεῖ. So Luke, which entails that this perfectly balanced triad comes from Q. The words illustrate the previous clause. A similar construction appears in Epictetus, *Diss.* 1.25.10: 'Agamemnon says to me, "Go . . .". I go. "Come". I come'.

10. Jesus now marvels—only here in Matthew—at the noble simplicity of the centurion's faith (cf. 15.28).

ἀκούσας δὲ ὁ 'Ιησοῦς ἐθαύμασεν. Compare Mk 6.6 (where Jesus marvels at unbelief). It is rare for Matthew to record Jesus' emotional state (cf. 1, pp. 104–5).

Luke has ταῦτα after δέ and αὐτόν after the second verb. In line with his tendency to abbreviate miracle stories, Matthew has probably omitted 'him' as unnecessary. ταῦτα, on the other hand, could be Lukan, since the Third Evangelist has sometimes added it to Mark.[64]

καὶ εἶπεν τοῖς ἀκολουθοῦσιν. Compare 8.1. Luke has: 'And turning, he said to the crowd following him'. στρέφω may or may not be Lukan; and although Luke likes to set participles between articles and substantives,[65] 'the crowd following him' is a construction he uses only here. Gundry, *Commentary*, p. 144, suggests that Matthew has abbreviated in order to focus completely on Jesus' words. But Wegner (v), pp. 211–12, thinks Matthew closer to Q.

ἀμὴν λέγω ὑμῖν. Matthew has probably added 'amen'*. It makes for solemnity. See on 5.18.

When Jesus speaks not to the centurion but to the crowd, he is no longer addressing a Gentile but Jews.[66] The switch in addressees adds poignancy. Jesus is speaking directly to those who have not lived up to their calling as the people of God.

παρ' οὐδενὶ τοσαύτην πίστιν ἐν τῷ 'Ισραὴλ εὖρον. Compare Lk

---

accurately represents the Aramaic ('in authority') which the Greek mistakenly rendered 'under authority'. Cf. the similar proposals of Zuntz (v), pp. 184–5, and Black, pp. 158–9. Criticism in Wegner (v), pp. 82–5.

[63] καὶ γάρ may mean either 'yes, even' or simply 'for'; cf. T. Abr. A 18.7 and see BDF § 452.

[64] E.g. 5.27; 8.8; 9.34; 18.23; 21.9.

[65] See 1.1; 21.1 (diff. Mk 12.41); 23.48.

[66] Chrysostom, *Hom. on Mt* 26.5, must be mistaken in thinking that Jesus is addressing Gentiles from Galilee.

18.8: 'Nonetheless, when the Son of man comes, will he find faith on the earth?' Lk 7.9 opens with οὐδέ (= 'not even') and immediately follows with 'in Israel' (so also some Matthean mss., under Lukan influence). Otherwise there is agreement.

ἐν τῷ Ἰσραήλ may refer either to an ethnic unit (the Jewish people) or, in view of our discussion below, to a geographical entity (the land of Israel).

When Jesus speaks of the faith of the centurion, this is typical. Elsewhere in the gospels, miracles of healing and faith are intimately connected.[67] The association (cf. Jas 5.15f.) probably goes back to Jesus himself; for despite the undoubted tendency of the tradition to introduce sayings about faith (cf. 15.28 and Lk 8.12f.), the logion in 17.20 par. is dominical (see the commentary), and it makes faith the door to miraculous powers. Further, in the synoptic sayings about faith, Jesus is rarely the explicit object, in contrast with early kerygmatic usage.[68]

In the First Gospel, πίστις and πιστεύω are used, roughly, in three ways.[69] There is first the secular sense, intellectual assent (24.23, 26). This is of no theological significance. Secondly, 'faith' is, as in Paul, a comprehensive term meaning acceptance of, loyalty to, and trust in Jesus and his message: it characterizes the essence of Christian existence (18.6; 21.25; 27.42; cf. 23.23). Thirdly, there is the use of 'faith' in the miracle stories. This is belief in Jesus and his power as miracle worker. It is the faith which moves mountains (8.13; 9.22, 28f; 15.28; cf. 17.20; 21.21). Without it there are no miracles (13.58). Matthew's favourite ὀλιγόπιστος is to be explained in terms of this third category. Paradoxically, even a believer may not fully believe, and one with faith may be deficient in faith (cf. 6.30; 8.26; 14.31; 16.8).

The fundamental importance of faith for Matthew is revealed by this, that in the only two places where Jesus grants a Gentile's request, it is because of his or her faith (8.5–13; 15.21–8). Although Jesus has come only for the lost sheep of Israel, the restriction is overcome when he meets genuine belief. Faith conquers the separation between Jew and Gentile; it cannot but gain Jesus' kindly help. 'As you have believed, be it done to you' (8.13). 'Your faith has saved you' (9.22). 'According to your faith be it done to you' (9.29). These remarks are applicable to all. Regardless of social status or ethnic origin, faith is salvation.

11. In this verse and the next Matthew interpolates a saying which had a different context in Q; see Lk 13.28f.[70] His purpose is to highlight the contrast between the faith of a Gentile and the unbelief of 'the sons of the kingdom'.

[67] E.g. Mk 2.5; 5.34, 36; 9.19, 23–4; 10.52.
[68] Cf. Jeremias, *Theology*, pp. 159–62.
[69] In addition to what follows see Barth, in *TIM*, pp. 112–16; Held, in *TIM*, pp. 178–81, 193–200, 275–96; and U. Luz, 'The Disciples in the Gospel of Matthew', in Stanton, pp. 103–4, 107.
[70] See Wegner (v), pp. 3–5.

There are four clauses in Mt 8.11f. Their order is this:
1. many will come . . . (11a)
2. they will recline with Abraham . . . (11b)
3. the sons of the kingdom will be cast out . . . (12a)
4. there will be weeping . . . (12b)

In Luke the order is 4, 3, 1, 2, and the patriarchs are named not in 2 but in a clause which has no Matthean parallel:
4. there will be weeping . . . (28a)
   whenever you see Abraham . . . (28b)
3. but you will be cast out (28c)
1. they will come . . . (29a)
2. they will recline . . . (29b)

Although some have despaired of making sense of these different orders, a conjectural explanation in terms of Matthean redaction commends itself.[71] (i) Lk 13.23–30 consists entirely of Q material, it makes fair sense as it stands, and as Luke is much more apt than Matthew to preserve Q material intact, presumption favours taking Lk 13.23–30 as a block from the sayings source.[72] (ii) Because it is Matthew who has displaced Lk 13.28–9 from its Q context into another, we may expect *a priori* that he might need to make alterations for the new fitting.[73] (iii) Matthew cannot open with Lk 13.28a because as of yet there is no antecedent for ἐκεῖ (in Luke the reference is to those outside the door: 13.24–7). So he goes instead to 13.29a. (iv) Having begun with 13.29a he naturally goes on to 13.29b: the two belong together. (v) Having used 13.29, this leaves 13.28. But there is still no antecedent for ἐκεῖ. He therefore moves it to the end where it will have one—a change which accords with his tendency to put the phrase, 'the weeping and gnashing of teeth', at the end of sections (13.50; 24.51; 25.30). (vi) This leaves 13.28b-c, and because Matthew has already mentioned the patriarchs (8.11), he begins with the saying about 'the sons of the kingdom' (28c).

λέγω δὲ ὑμῖν ὅτι. The phrase, without Lukan parallel, is redactional.[74]

πολλοὶ ἀπὸ ἀνατολῶν καὶ δυσμῶν ἥξουσιν. Compare 24.27 and Ps 107.1–3. Luke lacks 'many',[75] has the verb at the front (more Semitic), and adds καὶ ἀπὸ βορρᾶ καὶ νότου.[76] See further Allison, 'East and West' (v).

---

[71] Cf. Trilling, pp. 88–9; Schlosser 2, pp. 608–14. For a different conclusion see Chilton, *Strength*, pp. 184–8; Kloppenborg, pp. 226–7.—Our judgement on this matter requires that the version of the saying in Justin, *Dial.* 76, 120, and 140 has been influenced by Matthew's text.

[72] Cf. Gundry, *Commentary*, p. 146; and (cautiously) Schweizer, *Luke*, pp. 225–6; contrast F. Mussner, 'Das "Gleichnis" vom gestrengen Mahlherrn (Lk 13.22–30)', in *Praesentia Salutis*, Düsseldorf, 1967, pp. 113–24; Chilton, *Strength*, pp. 184–6.

[73] We have already seen the extent to which Matthew was moved to revise other sayings from Lk 13.23–30; see on 7.13–14 and 7.22–3.

[74] λέγω + ὑμῖν/σοι: Mt: 58; Mk: 16; Lk: 45.

[75] πολύς may be redactional, for Matthew has elsewhere added it to Mark (cf. Schulz, *Q*, pp. 323–4). .

[76] Cf. Irenaeus, *Adv. haer.* 4.8.1. The phrase is missing from *Adv. haer.* 4.36.8 and Justin (see n. 71).

Who are the many who come from east and west? Almost all ancient and modern exegetes assume that Gentiles are meant. This is, we think, very far from self-evident, whether one is thinking of Jesus or even of Matthew.

(i) Gentiles are not explicitly named.

(ii) The clear allusion to Ps 107.3 sends thoughts back to a passage about the return of Jewish exiles to the land. In the OT text the Gentiles are out of the picture.

(iii) The phrase, 'east and west', is, in Jewish texts, frequently associated with the return of diaspora Jews to their land.[77] In this connexion the directions refer to Babylon and Egypt respectively, the two centres of the diaspora.[78] At the same time, we have failed to find any instances in which the phrase is used of the eschatological pilgrimage of the Gentiles.

(iv) In the OT the coming of the Gentiles is never conceived of as a judgement upon Israel or those in the land. On the contrary, the Gentile pilgrimage serves to exalt Zion (Zeller (v)). Thus the usual interpretation requires that Mt 8.11f. turns a traditional motif on its head in order to deny Jewish hopes. But did not Jesus and Matthew look forward to the fulfilment of God's promises to Israel? It suffices to recall Mt 19.28, which looks forward to the twelve disciples sitting upon twelve thrones judging the twelve tribes of Israel. This text presupposes that the scattered tribes have returned to the land; see our commentary.

(v) If 'the sons of the kingdom' are simply identified with the Jews as a whole in contrast to Gentiles (those from east and west), then our saying, at least hyperbolically, consigns all of Israel to perdition. Is this credible? Leaving aside the fact that Jesus and his disciples were, like the First Evangelist, themselves Jews, we are confronted by all the promises of the OT (cf. 1, pp. 23–4). These make it incredible that either Jesus or Matthew could have seriously entertained the possibility that Israel as a whole was doomed for hell. On this subject they could not have differed from Paul (cf. 1, Rom 11).

(vi) 'There are . . . many passages in the Old Testament that speak of the nations making their way to Zion at the end of the age to pay homage to Yahweh and to Israel (e.g., Isa. 2.1ff.), but in none of these is mention made of the nations sharing in the feast of the kingdom of God. On the other hand, Isaiah 25.6ff., which provides the classic description of the feast for the nations given by God, makes no mention of the peoples streaming from all parts of the world to Zion . . .' (Beasley-Murray, p. 170). But in Ps 107; Isa 25–7; 49; and Ezek 37–9, the theme of the pilgrimage of the diaspora Jews *is* brought into connexion with the messianic feast, so once more the usual interpretation is not what comes to mind to one steeped in the OT.

[77] Isa 43.5; Zech 8.7; Bar 4.37; 5.5; Ps. Sol. 11.2; 1 En. 57.1. Cf. LXX Deut 30.4.
[78] See Isa 27.13; Hos 11.10–11; Zech 10.10; Sib. Orac. 5.113.

In the light of these points, we suggest that, as spoken by Jesus, Mt 8.11f. par. was intended to draw a stark contrast not between unbelieving Jews and believing Gentiles but between privileged and unprivileged Jews. Jesus seems to have believed that those who rejected him and his message would suffer judgement on the last day (cf. 10.32f.; 11.21–4). In particular, he seems to have delivered dire warnings especially to some of the Jewish leaders, including the Pharisees. When to this one adds that he thought of such people as being good and pious in their own eyes (cf. Mt 23), might he not have ironically labelled them 'sons of the kingdom'[79] and foretold their condemnation? Recall the use of 'the righteous' in 9.13 par. and the use of 'the wise' in 11.25 par. If Mt 8.11f. par. was originally addressed to the Pharisees or to the Jerusalem establishment or to some other group of powerful religious Jews which Jesus perceived to be opposed to him, the text can be understood as yet one more example of the conviction that the first will be last, the last first. The 'sons of the kingdom' will have a tragic end because of their response to Jesus and his preaching while others, less privileged because they have not lived in the land or heard Jesus, will find eschatological salvation. The privileged will have their places taken by the underprivileged. The poor will enter the kingdom. The meek will inherit the earth.

But what of Matthew? One could argue that as the saying in Q was isolated he may not have known its original meaning and so came to misinterpret it. Confirmation of this could be found in the Matthean context, where the faith of a Gentile serves to condemn Israel's unbelief. Yet the inference is not inevitable. How can one square it with 19.28, which looks forward to the restoration of Israel? Given Matthew's intimate acquaintance with the OT, would he not have recognized that those from 'east and west' must be Jews of the diaspora? If so, he must have understood 'in Israel' (v. 10) not in an ethnic fashion but—and this certainly accords with his story line, for Jesus does not go beyond the borders of Israel—in a geographical sense: 'in (the land of) Israel'. The point of 8.11f. would then lie not in the salvation of the Gentiles as opposed to the damnation of all Jews but in the salvation of the seemingly unfortunate as opposed to 'the sons of the kingdom', the wise and privileged who have lived in Eretz Israel and beheld the Messiah, and yet do not believe. On this reading, the many from east and west would serve primarily as a foil. All the emphasis would lie upon the miserable lot of those who fail to welcome the Messiah.

Taken at face value, Mt 8.11–2 possesses a geographical dimension.

---

[79] But this also may be redactional. Luke's 'you' could be original. For Jewish texts which idealize exiles at the expense of those in the land see T. A. Bergren, 'The "People coming from the East" in 5 Ezra 1.38', *JBL* 108 (1989), pp. 675–83. Note esp. Jer 24; Ezek 11; Davies, *GL*, pp. 38–45.

People come from east and west. As the speaker is standing within Israel, the saying presupposes that the Jewish land will be the geographical centre of the eschatological events. This lines up with a large number of Jewish texts which anticipate that Israel and its capital, Jerusalem, will be the hub of God's end-time activity. One recalls, for instance, passages which announce that the Lord will set David's throne in Jerusalem (e.g. Jer 17.25), or that the resurrection of the dead will take place in the land (e.g. *b. Ketub.* 111a), or that a new temple will appear in the holy city (e.g. Tob 14.5; Jub. 1.27f.). So should we not think that Mt 8.11 envisages the celebration of the messianic banquet as taking place inside the borders of Israel? We are unsure. Certainly it will not do to argue (assuming that the many are Gentiles: but they may not be) that, as both the Gentile mission and the kingdom of God are present realities (see on 4.17), Mt 8.11 must be fulfilled in the evangelization of the Gentiles.[80] Should one then think of a literal pilgrimage by Jews or Gentiles to Palestine? While this cannot be excluded, one must always reckon with a good measure of symbolism in Jewish and Christian eschatological texts. This is especially true in the present case in view of the tendency of early Christianity to move away from Judaism's focus on the land (Davies, *GL* pp. 161–376). So we have the same problem as in the third beatitude: has the land been transcendentalized (cf. T. Job 33)? Although Matthew does not directly address the issue, it is telling that the First Gospel, unlike 4 Ezra and some rabbinic texts, fails to draw a distinction between a millennial kingdom or messianic age and the age to come: the book looks forward to only one fulfilment, inaugurated with the return of Jesus the Son of man and the general resurrection. When this fact is coupled with the lack of a territorial dimension to such passages as 24.29–31 and 25.31–46, one is inclined to think that for Matthew, as for others,[81] the eschatological promises are to find their realization not in this world as it is but in a re-created world, an old world made new, in which the boundaries between heaven and earth will begin to disappear. If so, any mundane or literal interpretation of Matthew's eschatological expectations would seem to be excluded.

καὶ ἀνακλιθήσονται μετὰ 'Αβραὰμ καὶ 'Ισαὰκ καὶ 'Ιακὼβ ἐν τῇ βασιλείᾳ τῶν οὐρανῶν. Compare 22.32. The mention of the patriarchs makes for a 'sharper sting' (Chrysostom, *Hom. on Mt* 22.32).

'And will recline in the kingdom of God' appears in Lk 13.29b, 'whenever you will see Abraham and Isaac and Jacob and all the prophets in the kingdom of God' in Lk 13.28b. 'Of the heavens' is Matthean redaction. 'All the prophets', which is awkwardly tacked on to a fixed OT expression (Exod 3.6; Acts 7.32; etc.), is Lukan.[82]

---

[80] This is the interpretation of Ps.-Clem. Hom. 8.4; but the text also retained its eschatological sense for many Christian writers; see e.g. Justin, *Dial.* 140; Ambrose, *De bono mort.* 12.53–4; Patrick, *Ep.* 18.

[81] E.g. 1 En 6–36; Sib. Orac. 3; Ps. Sol. 17; 1 En. 37–71.

[82] Cf. 11.50; 24.27; Acts 3.18, 24; 10.43; elsewhere in the NT only in Mt 11.13. (Narrative of Joseph 3 adds 'Moses' after 'Jacob'.)

ἀνακλίνω⁸³ appears in the LXX only once, in 3 Macc 5.16. For reclining at meals—'the *kline* was pre-eminently a Greek style of banqueting' and in the gospels is 'evidence from Palestine for the ubiquitous spread of Hellenism' (Horsley 1, p. 9)—see Jdt 12.15; Mt 20.28 D; Mk 6.39; *b. Ber.* 42a. On formal occasions, tables were, as in the Graeco-Roman world, arranged to form a U, and the guests reclined on pillows or couches around the outside, propping themselves up on their elbows. The space in the centre was left for the servants.

Although there are texts in which the faithful meet one or more of the patriarchs immediately after death,⁸⁴ in Mt 8.11 par. the resurrection (cf. T. Jud. 25.1) and the messianic banquet are in view.⁸⁵ The redeemed will mingle with the fathers of Israel at the great heavenly banquet. Are we to think of Abraham, Isaac, and Jacob as the hosts or the guests of honour?

12. **οἱ δὲ υἱοὶ τῆς βασιλείας ἐκβληθήσονται εἰς τὸ σκότος τὸ ἐξώτερον.**⁸⁶ Compare Apoc. Pet. 78.23f. ('the workers who will be cast into the farthest darkness'). Lk 13.28c reads: 'But you yourselves will be cast out'. The 'farthest darkness' (cf. T. Jacob 5.9) is Matthean redaction (cf. 22.13; 25.30). Our author, like most of his Jewish and Christian contemporaries, imagined the place of perdition to be, despite its fire, dark.⁸⁷ He also thought of it as being removed as far as possible from God and his light.

'Sons of the kingdom' (= natural or rightful heirs of the kingdom) appears also in 13.38 (q.v.), where the reference is to Christians who 'shine like the sun in the kingdom of their father'. Compare Hist. Rechab. 10.2: 'obedient sons of our kingdom'. The expression is a Semitism.⁸⁸ Similar are 'sons of his covenant' (1QM 17.8), 'sons of this age' (Lk 16.8), and 'son(s) of the world to come' (a fixed rabbinic phrase). Because Matthew is fond of υἱός constructions,⁸⁹ 'sons of the

⁸³ Mt: 2; Mk: 1; Lk: 3. LXX: 1 (3 Macc 5.16). Cf. the Aramaic *'ashar*. (In *y. Ta'an.* 68a the patriarchs are, even in their graves, lying as though they were at a meal or banquet.)
⁸⁴ E.g. 4 Macc 13.17; Lk 16.22; T. Abr. A 20.14.
⁸⁵ To the texts cited in vol. 1, p. 453, add: Ezek 39.17–20; Mk 14.25; Rev 19.9; 2 Bar. 29.4; 2 En 42.5; 3 En 48 A 10; Clement of Alexandria, *Paed.* 1.9, quoting the lost Apocryphon of Ezekiel; *b. Pesah.* 119b; also SB 4, pp. 1154–65.
⁸⁶ Chilton, *Strength*, pp. 181–3, argues for the originality of εξελευσονται (so ℵ* 0250 k syˢ·ᶜ·ᵖ) over against εκβληθησονται. It is not easy to see how the variant might have arisen, yet we prefer the reading which agrees with Matthew's usage elsewhere (cf. 22.13; 25.30).
⁸⁷ Cf. Wisd 17.21; Tob 14.10; 1 En 63.6; 108.14; Ps. Sol. 14.9; 15.10; 2 Pet 2.17; Jude 13. For darkness and fire together see 1QS 4.13; Sib. Orac. 4.43; 1 En 103.7; 2 En 10.2.
⁸⁸ Deissmann, *Studies*, pp. 161–6; SB 1, pp. 476–8.
⁸⁹ 5.9, 45; 9.15; 12.27; 13.38; 23.31; etc.

kingdom' could be redactional.[90] For the unqualified 'kingdom' see also 4.23; 9.35; 13.19, 38; 24.14.
According to Trilling (v), Mt 8.12 entails no future conversion of Israel. We must demur. Even if one rejects our proposal that the many from east and west are not Gentiles but diaspora Jews, several points must be considered. (i) There is no πάντες before the 'sons of the kingdom'. (ii) The definite article may indicate no more than many of the named class will be cast out (cf. Zahn, p. 341). (iii) While the centurion is a Gentile, the leper of 9.1–4 and Peter's mother-in-law are Jews, and all of the others who are healed in Mt 8–9 are Jews who have faith in Jesus' healing power. Thus the context of 8.11f. encourages one to think that there is faith in Israel: not all are lost. (iv) Hyperboles abound in the synoptic tradition, and the searing antithesis in Mt 8.11f., with its seemingly sweeping condemnation of a whole class, is the kind of black and white declaration one hesitates to take at face value. Poetic licence must be given its due. (v) Leaving aside 8.11–12, there are good reasons for thinking that the First Evangelist looked for the salvation of Israel (cf. p. 27; also 1, pp. 23–4, and our commentary on 19.28). (vi) Perhaps 8.11f. should be understood as a prophetic threat, a word which speaks of damnation not as a certainty but as a prospect demanding repentance. See Beasley-Murray, p. 173.

ἐκεῖ ἔσται ὁ κλαυθμὸς καὶ ὁ βρυγμὸς τῶν ὀδόντων. So Lk 13.28a. Matthew has made this expression his own.[91] κλαυθμός* (cf. 2.18) = 'weeping' (cf. Acts 20.37). If, after the judgement, the saints neither mourn nor weep any longer (5.4; Rev 21.4), it is just the opposite with sinners (Lk 6.25; 1 En. 108.3; 2 En. 40.12). βρυγμός* here means 'gnashing' or 'chattering' and connotes anger. For βρύχω with ὀδούς see LXX Job 16.9; Ps 34.16; 36.12; 111.10; Lam 2.16; Acts 7.54. The entire line may be Q redaction, added to link Lk 13.28 to 13.27.

13. In this, the conclusion to 8.5–13, Jesus turns away from the crowd, back to the Gentile full of faith. The emphasis is clear: faith has brought healing.

If Q had a conclusion to the story about the centurion it cannot now be reconstructed. Lk 7.10 has this: 'and returning to the house those who had been sent found the sick servant healed'. This appears redactional.[92] But Matthew's final verse equally seems to contain redactional traits (see below).

καὶ εἶπεν ὁ Ἰησοῦς τῷ ἑκατοντάρχῃ. 'Centurion' harks back to 8.5 and forms an inclusio. εἶπεν ὁ Ἰησοῦς + dative appears only here in Matthew.

ὕπαγε. Compare 8.4, 32; 9.6 (all addressed by Jesus to people he has healed).

[90] Cf. Schlosser 2, p. 607; Chilton, Strength, pp. 191–2.
[91] 13.42, 50; 22.13; 24.51; 25.30.
[92] See Jeremias, Lukasevangelium, p. 156.

ὡς ἐπίστευσας γενηθήτω σοι.⁹³ Compare 9.29; 15.28. Whether we are to think of Jesus' assurance as involving some sort of 'clairvoyance' or as stemming from absolute faith in God or his own powers is left unsaid. γίνομαι + dative: Mt: 5; Mk: 2; Lk: 1.

καὶ ἰάθη ὁ παῖς ἐν τῇ ὥρᾳ ἐκείνῃ.⁹⁴ Despite the parallels in 9.22; 15.28 diff. Mk 7.29–30; and 17.18 diff. Mk 9.25–6, the redactional use of ἰάομαι (cf. 8.8 = Lk 7.7) in 15.28, and Matthew's fondness for ὥρα + ἐκείνη* (vol. 1, pp. 78, 82), our line could have some basis in the tradition, for Jn 4.53 ('The father knew that was the hour when Jesus had said to him, "Your son will live"') is similar.

THE HEALING OF PETER'S MOTHER-IN-LAW (8.14–15)

With 8.14–15 Matthew reverts to Mk 1.29–31 (cf. Lk 4.38f.). This gives him a third healing for 8.1–22 and exhausts the material he wants to borrow from Mk 1.

There are three or four keys to understanding the Matthean redaction of Mark 1.29–31, whose simple and sparse character, combined with unusually concrete details (Peter's house, his mother-in-law), have led most to postulate historical tradition. First, the evangelist, as is usual in healing stories, abbreviates. Next, he focuses all the attention on Jesus, who takes all the initiatives. Thus, in contrast with Mark's account, Jesus alone is named as entering the house; and Jesus, without prompting from others, sees the condition of Peter's relative; and Jesus alone is served by the woman—she does not serve 'them' (so Mark). Thirdly, Matthew's love of the triad has moved him to restructure the Markan narrative. Mt 8.14–15 falls into two halves. The first part recounts the actions of Jesus, the second part recounts the results of his actions:

8.14–5a	Jesus' actions
8.14a	He comes into the house
8.14b	He sees Peter's mother-in-law
8.15a	He touches her hand
8.15b–d	The result
8.15b	The fever leaves
8.15c	The woman rises
8.15d	The woman serves Jesus

Clearly Matthew has rewritten Mark so that there are three main verbs associated with Jesus and three main verbs associated with the woman and her healing.⁹⁵

---

⁹³ C L Θ 0233 f¹·¹³ Maj lat syʰ boᵐˢ and HG add και before ως.

⁹⁴ NA²⁶ (against NA²⁵) adds αυτου (in brackets) after παις; so C L W Θ 0233 f¹³ Maj sy. HG omits (cf. 17.18). See Wegner (v), p. 86.

⁹⁵ For a chiastic outline see B. Olsson's scheme, as reported by Gerhardsson, *Acts*, p. 40.

14. This verse introduces as succinctly as possible the setting for a healing miracle. Still in Capernaum, Jesus enters the house of Peter and sees Peter's mother-in-law lying with fever. Not one word in Matthew's record is superfluous.

καὶ ἐλθὼν ὁ Ἰησοῦς εἰς τὴν οἰκίαν Πέτρου. Compare 9.23. Matthew, like Luke, has abbreviated Mk 1.29 ('And immediately going out of the synagogue he (or: they) went into the house of Simon and Andrew with James and John'). εὐθύς is, as frequently, dropped. 'Going out of the synagogue' falls away because, in the new Matthean context, 8.14f. does not follow upon a synagogue scene. 'And Andrew with James and John' is omitted (so also Luke) for the sake of brevity, and we are left with the possible impression that Jesus alone entered Peter's house. 'Jesus' is added because the subject of the previous sentence (8.13c) was someone else. Why does 'Simon' become 'Peter'? Matthew never lets 'Simon' stand alone. It is always followed by 'the one called Peter' (4.18; 10.2), or combined with another name (Simon Peter, Simon Bar-Jona, 16.16, 17), or directly preceded by the use of 'Peter' (17.25).[96] Perhaps a second Simon was known to Matthew's community and it was therefore necessary or customary to distinguish Simon Peter from his namesake. Certainly 'Simon' was a popular name. There are at least ten of them in the NT. For the name 'Peter' see on 4.18.

Chrysostom, *Hom. on Mt* 27.1, speculates about Peter's 'mean hut' and declares that Jesus displayed humility entering it. However that may be, it should be observed that archaeologists may have located Peter's house in Capernaum. Less than one hundred feet from what is left of Capernaum's magnificent ancient synagogue lie the remains of a fifth century church with three concentric octagonal walls. This church in turn incorporates a fourth century house church whose central hall was originally part of a house built ca. 63 B.C. This original house, which appears to have been quite ordinary, seems to have become a public meeting place during the last half of the first century A.D.: the floor, walls, and ceiling of the central room were plastered at that time, and to judge from the pottery, the place was no longer the site of domestic activities. When to this one adds that the graffiti on the walls refer to Jesus as Christ and Lord, one suspects that archaeologists may have unearthed a first century house church. Moreover, the octagonal shape of the fifth century structure would seem to indicate a venerated place (cf. the octagonal church at the cave in Bethlehem), and we know that Christian pilgrims of the fourth and sixth centuries recorded having seen in Capernaum a house church made out of Peter's house. There is a good chance, then, that sometime during the first century A.D. Peter's residence in Capernaum was

[96] Contrast Mk 1.16, 29, 30, 36; Lk 4.38; 5.3; 24.34.

turned into a Christian centre and that this church was eventually converted into the octagonal structure whose ruins now lie midway between the Jewish synagogue and the Sea of Galilee.[97] The scene of Jesus in a house with his disciples is very common in the synoptic tradition (e.g. Mk 1.29; 2.15; etc.). If more than historical reminiscence is to be discerned in this fact, perhaps we should recall the OT texts in which the prophets Elisha (2 Kgs 5.9; 6.1–2, 32) and Ezekiel (3.24) stay in houses.[98] Also important might be the setting of early Christian gatherings. According to the NT, believers in Jesus gathered in homes (cf. Rom 16.5; Col 4.15; 2 Jn 10; etc.). One accordingly wonders whether the stories of Jesus ministering and teaching in houses helped to legitimate the new location, the new ritual centre. Temple and synagogue no longer had a monopoly on holy space. The presence of Jesus made space sacred, and during his earthly ministry he chose to bless houses with his presence.

εἶδεν τὴν πενθερὰν αὐτοῦ βεβλημένην καὶ πυρέσσουσαν. This is based upon Mk 1.30a: 'The mother-in-law of Peter lay (κατ-έκειτο) sick with a fever'. Matthew's 'he saw' makes Jesus the initiator (cf. 4.18, 21). He knows the trouble and does not need to be told. Contrast Mk 1.30 (omitted by Matthew): 'and immediately they speak to him concerning her'. 'Of Peter' becomes 'of him' (cf. 4.18 diff. Mk 1.16). κατέκειτο, a word Matthew never uses, becomes βεβλημένην (cf. 8.6 diff. Lk 7.2; 9.2 diff. Mk 2.3). The meaning is 'lie on a sick bed'. πυρέσσω (only here in Matthew; LXX: 0) = 'suffer with a fever'. Obviously more than an innocuous symptom is meant (cf. SB 1, pp. 479–80). Perhaps we should think of malaria (*IDB* 2, p. 266). πενθερά (cf. 10.35) is 'mother-in-law'. We know independently from Paul that Peter was married (1 Cor 9.5).

15. καὶ ἥψατο τῆς χειρὸς αὐτῆς. Compare Acts 28.8, where Publius' father, sick with fever, is cured by Paul's touch. Mk 1.31a has: 'And coming he raised her, taking her by the hand'. ἅπτω + body part + possessive pronoun (cf. LXX Job 2.5; Isa 6.7; Jer 1.9) is also redactional in 9.29. For touching in miracle stories see Theissen, *Stories*, pp. 62–3.

καὶ ἀφῆκεν αὐτὴν ὁ πυρετός. So Mark. Compare Jn 4.52 (ἀφῆκεν αὐτὸν ὁ πυρετός) and *b. Šabb.* 137a (ḥǎlāṣattô ḥammâ). πυρετός appears once in the LXX, in Deut 28.22, for qaddaḥat. For other NT healings of fever see Jn 4.52 and Acts 28.8. It is unclear whether we should think of the fever as caused

---

[97] See further J. F. Strange and H. Shanks, 'Has the House where Jesus stayed in Capernaum been found?', *BAR* 8 (1982), pp. 26–37. But Robertson, *Priority*, pp. 50–1, considers it probable that the house was that of Jesus himself.

[98] See further H. M. I. Gevaryahu, 'Privathäuser als Versammlungsstätten von Meister und Jüngern', *ASTI* 12 (1983), pp. 5–12.

by a demon and thus of the cure as an exorcism. Luke certainly seems to have been so disposed (4.39: 'he rebuked the fever'), and the connexion between demons and fever was perhaps common (cf. T. Sol. 7.5–7). For a record of the (mostly magical) methods purportedly endorsed by some rabbis for the healing of fevers see *b. Sabb.* 66b–7a.

καὶ ἠγέρθη καὶ διηκόνει αὐτῷ. This is a demonstration which confirms the miracle: the woman can do what she could not do before. Compare Mk 1.31: 'And he raised her up and the fever left her; and she served them'. 'Served him' means 'served him (at table)'. The motive is gratitude. Observe that nothing is said of any time needed for recovery. Not only is the fever gone, but full health and vigour have evidently been restored instantly. Note also that Mark's 'she served them' has become 'she served him' (see p. 32). Without exception, Jesus is, in the First Gospel, either the subject or object of διακονέω.

For other instances of women waiting on Jesus see Mk 15.41; Lk 8.3; Jn 12.2. It is doubtful that these texts present Jesus as flouting custom. Although *b. Qidd.* 70a advises against letting oneself be served by a woman, there is no solid evidence that such a sentiment was universally embraced by the learned at the time of Jesus; and this is confirmed by the failure of the gospels to record any objection to Jesus' association with women.[99] An uncritical transfer of later rabbinic ideas to first-century realities has made Jesus' attitude towards women appear more radical than it probably was. See W. Horbury in *CHJ*, 3 (forthcoming).

THE SICK HEALED AT EVENING (8.16–17)

8.16–17, a brief summary between the more comprehensive summaries in 4.23–5 and 9.35, concludes the day that began with the sermon on the mount. One is reminded of Mk 1.21–34. Mark too opens his account of Jesus' ministry by recounting the several events of a single day. But despite the similarities and the dependence of one gospel upon the other, the records of the two evangelists display significant differences. For instance, although both Matthew and Mark bring the day to a close with Mt 8.14f. = Mk 1.29–31 and 8.16f. = Mk 1.32–4, the First Gospel places the healing of the leper on the same day as the events of 8.14–17 whereas in the Second that healing occurs on the next day (Mk 1.35–45). Again, while in Mark the day in Capernaum is a Sabbath (cf. Mk 1.21, 29), it apparently is not in Matthew. Clearly Matthew did not feel bound to follow his predecessor's chronology.

Mt 4.23–5 and 9.35–8 frame 5.1–9.34 and alert the reader

[99] Cf. Montefiore, *Rabbinic Literature*, p. 218.

that the five chapters concern τὰ λεχθέντα καὶ τὰ πραχθέντα by Jesus. But the summary which occurs in 8.16f. mentions only Jesus' deeds. This implies that whereas the emphasis in 5–7 is upon the things said, in 8–9 it is upon the things done. **16.** This is the introduction to the formula quotation. Matthew is less vivid and abbreviated than Mark. ὀψίας δὲ γενομένης. So Mk 1.32a. The same phrase (LXX: 0) occurs in Mt 14.15, 23; 16.2; 20.8; 27.57 (cf. Josephus, *Ant.* 5.7).

Matthew has dropped Mark's 'when the sun set'. Because Luke retains this but lacks 'when it became evening', it has been urged that Mark is explicable as a conflation of Matthew and Luke (Farmer, *Problem*, pp. 81–4). This is not, however, the only satisfactory solution. The theory of Markan priority can explain things just as easily. Matthew has omitted 'when the sun set' in accordance with his tendency to abbreviate.[100] As for Luke, he has failed to reproduce all six of Mark's ὀψία phrases.[101] So the absence from his Gospel of 'when it became evening' is scarcely cause for surprise.

προσήνεγκαν αὐτῷ δαιμονιζομένους πολλούς. Jesus the mighty healer draws the sick and the suffering like a magnet. Compare Mk 1.32: 'they brought to him (ἔφερον πρὸς αὐτόν) all those sick and possessed by demons'. προσφέρω* and προσήνεγκαν + αὐτῷ + δαιμονιζομένους/ον (Mt: 4; Mk: 0; Lk: 0) are Matthean favourites; φέρω + πρός (Mt: 0; Mk: 6; Lk: 0), a Semitic vulgarism, he avoids. 'Many' comes forward from Mk 1.34 ('he cast out many demons'). In Mark people bring 'all' and Jesus heals 'many'. In Matthew they bring 'many' and Jesus heals 'all'. This avoids the implication that Jesus did not heal everybody (cf. 1, p. 105). Matthew, like Luke, has omitted Mk 1.33 ('and all the city was gathered at the door').[102]

καὶ ἐξέβαλεν τὰ πνεύματα λόγῳ. This is editorial. For demons as spirits see 1 βασ 16.23; CD 12.2; 1 En. 15.4–16.1; 99.7; LAB 60; Mk 3.11; Acts 5.16. λόγος is editorial in 8.8 and 22.46. As elsewhere Matthew emphasizes the ease with which Jesus works wonders.

The mention of 'word' helps bind together Jesus' teaching and his healing ministry. Both are to be traced to the same *logos*. It should be recalled that even though Mt 8–9 consists firstly of miracle stories, these are interspersed with teaching material. Thus the two are inseparable. Word and deed are one. Compare Philo, *Vit. Mos.* 1. 29: Moses 'exemplified his philosophical creed by his daily actions. His words expressed his feelings, and his actions accorded with his words, so that speech and life were in harmony, and thus through their mutual agreement were found to make melody together as on a musical instrument'.

[100] Also, because in Matthew, unlike Mark, it is not the Sabbath, there is no need to postpone the carrying of the sick until dark.
[101] Cf. the Lukan parallels to Mk 1.32; 4.35; 6.47; 11.11; 14.17; 15.42.
[102] For other omissions of Markan references to a house see 9.2; 15.12–15, 21; 17.19; 18.1; 19.9.

καὶ πάντας τοὺς κακῶς ἔχοντας ἐθεράπευσεν. This combines a phrase from Mk 1.32 ('all who were sick') with Mk 1.34 ('he healed many who were sick with various diseases'). Matthew prefers 'all' to 'many' for obvious reasons (cf. 4.23; 9.35; 10.1). θεραπεύω + πᾶς* is editorial. The verb occurs also in the summaries of 4.23f.; 9.35; 12.15; 19.2; 21.14. πάντας τοὺς κακῶς ἔχοντας reappears in 4.24 and 14.35 (Mt: 3; Mk: 1; Lk: 0). Note the chiastic arrangement of 8.16c–d: verb/object/object/verb.

17. In this verse, which contains the only explicit citation of Isa 53 in the synoptics, 'the spotlight is not giving a broad and general sweep over what is now happening in Israel but is directed right at *Jesus' person and ministry*; thus the primary function of the quotation is a Christological one. The prophetic words seem to be usable because Jesus is considered as "the Servant of the Lord"'.[103]

ὅπως πληρωθῇ τὸ ῥηθὲν διὰ Ἠσαΐου τοῦ προφήτου λέγοντος. On the introductions to the Matthean formula quotations see on 1.22. ὅπως* likewise introduces the OT citations in 2.23 and 13.35, and Isaiah is mentioned in the formula quotations in 4.14 and 12.17 (cf. 3.3). Matthew associates the prophet and his book with Jesus as the bringer of salvation; see on 4.14.

αὐτὸς τὰς ἀσθενείας ἡμῶν ἔλαβεν καὶ τὰς νόσους ἐβάστασεν. Compare Ignatius, *Polyc.* 1.3 ('Bear the infirmities of all'). The Scripture prophesied that Jesus the Servant would heal others. His miracles are, therefore, not simply the sensational workings of an extraordinary man but rather the fulfilment of the Scriptures and the exhibition of God's almighty will (cf. 11.2–6). Isa 53.4 MT reads: 'ākēn ḥŏlāyēnû hûʾ nāśāʾ ûmakʾōbênû sĕbālām. The LXX has: οὗτος τὰς ἁμαρτίας ἡμῶν φέρει καὶ περὶ ἡμῶν ὀδυνᾶται (cf. 1 Pet 2.24). Matthew has obviously not followed the LXX (which is here a very loose translation). His agreements with it are minimal. He has instead translated the text from the Hebrew and worded it to serve the purposes of his narrative (cf. Schlatter, pp. 282–3).

(i) Nothing corresponds to 'ākēn (cf. the LXX). (ii) ḥŏlāyēnû is properly translated by 'our sicknesses'.[104] (iii) hûʾ is the equivalent of Matthew's αὐτός (cf. Aq.). The placement at the beginning accords with Matthew's usual custom (cf. 1.21; 3.4, 11; etc.). (iv) nāśāʾ = ἔλαβεν as in LXX Gen 21.18; Exod 20.7; etc. (Matthew's ἔλαβεν[105] instead of the LXX's φέρει eliminates the possibility that Jesus himself was sick. Removal, not contraction, is the picture.) (v) καί = wĕ. (vi) τὰς

[103] Gerhardsson, *Acts*, p. 25. For other NT texts which presuppose Jesus' identity as the servant of Isaiah see 12.15–21; Lk 4.17–21; Jn 12.38; Acts 8.30–5; 1 Pet 2.22–5.

[104] Even though the LXX never renders ḥŏlî by ἀσθένεια, the verb ἀσθενεῖν does represent ḥālâ in Judg 16.7, 11, 17; Ezek 34.4; Dan 8.27. ἀσθεν- in Matthew: 8.17; 10.8; 25.36, 39, 43–4; 26.41.

[105] Cf. the ἀνέλαβεν of Aq., Symm.

νόσους (cf. 4.23–4; 9.35; 10.1) is a correct rendering of *mak'ōbênû*. Although the LXX does not use νόσος* for *mak'ōb*, the latter refers to physical and/or mental pain, and the former means 'illness' or 'anguish' (see the dictionaries). The Greek word selected by Matthew puts the emphasis upon physical difficulties. (vii) Concerning βαστάζω, its meanings according to BAGD, s.v., are 'take up', 'carry, bear', and 'carry away, remove', while according to BDB, s.v., *sābal* means 'bear a heavy load'; and the one is used for the other in Aq. Isa 53.11. To sum up, then, Mt 8.17 qualifies as a literal translation of the Hebrew (cf. Zahn, p. 344).

Even though Mt 8.17 is a possible rendering of Isa 53.4, it cannot be rightly said that the NT verse captures the true sense of the OT text. In Isaiah the servant suffers vicariously, carrying infirmities in himself; in the Gospel he heals the sick by *taking away* their diseases.[106] In the OT the distress seems to be mental or spiritual;[107] in Matthew physical illnesses are the subject. So a text about vicarious suffering has become a text about healing, and two different pictures are involved. Can Matthew be delivered from the charge of eisegesis? Perhaps he understood the healing ministry to be a type of Jesus' redemptive suffering; or maybe the association between sin and the distasteful reality of disease was so intimate (cf. Jn 9.2) that the healing of sickness could be conceived of as a taking away of sins. There is also the possibility that there was precedent in Jewish circles for a literal interpretation of Isa 53.4. Certainly the tradition in *b. Sanh.* 98a–b, although rather different in sense from Mt 8.17, seems to take the OT prophecy literally: 'Surely he hath borne our griefs and carried our sins, yet we did esteem him stricken with leprosy, and smitten of God and afflicted.'[108]

Although rabbinic texts know a messianic interpretation of Isa 53 (SB 1, pp. 481–3), would Isa 53.4 have been a messianic text to Jews of the first century? The lengthy debate on this issue has been inconclusive.[109]

By associating the servant motif with the ministry of miracles, Matthew shows us that Jesus' healings are 'to be understood as a work of his obedience and his humiliation' (Barth, in *TIM*, p. 128). The miracles flow from Jesus' meekness and mercy; his task is not grand or glorious or in any way self-serving. Rather, his portion is with lepers and demoniacs, and he identifies himself with humanity in its suffering.

---

[106] Both λαμβάνω and βαστάζω can imply removal; see the dictionaries.

[107] This is the justification for the targum and LXX interpreting 'sickness' as 'sin'.

[108] Cf. perhaps T. Jos. 17.7: 'All their suffering was my suffering, and all their sickness was my infirmity' (ἀσθένειά μου): so Joseph, speaking of his brothers.

[109] For discussion and lit. see S. H. T. Page, 'The Suffering Servant Between the Testaments', *NTS* 31 (1985), pp. 481–97.

THE COST OF DISCIPLESHIP (8.18–22)

Before Matthew moves on to recount the next three miracles
there is a section on the hardship of following Jesus. The
teaching is from Q (cf. Lk 9.57–60) but has been inserted into a
narrative framework from Mark. Mt 8.18 draws upon Mk 4.35
while Mt 8.23–7 is the equivalent of Mk 4.36–41. So our
evangelist, displaying freedom *vis-à-vis* the Markan chronology,
has inserted his Q material between Mk 4.35 and 36. The result
is that between the time Jesus decides to go to the other side of
the Sea of Galilee and the moment he boards a boat, he has
conversations with two people on the high cost of discipleship.

Why has Matthew placed 8.18–22 precisely where it is?
Probably because for him the tale of the stilling of the storm is
a parable, a symbolic illustration of what it means to 'follow'
Jesus. In other words, a story about discipleship is prefaced by
teaching on discipleship. Perhaps there is also a subsidiary
motive. 8.1–17 has demonstrated the great authority of Jesus,
and the proper response to this authority is 'following', which
therefore now becomes the main theme.[110]

The parallelism between 8.19f. and 8.21f. should not cause
one to overlook the differences between the two scenes. The
parallelism is really antithetical, not synthetic. This has been
convincingly argued by Kingsbury, 'Following' (v). He has made
these points. (i) While it is a scribe who addresses Jesus in 8.19,
a disciple comes forward in 8.21. (ii) While Jesus is addressed as
a teacher in 8.19, in 8.21 he is called 'Lord'. (iii) While the
scribe in 8.19 asks to follow Jesus, in 8.21 Jesus asks the disciple
to follow him. These contrasts are striking. The man in 8.19–20
bears a title ('scribe') which often in Matthew belongs to Jesus'
opponents. The man calls Jesus 'teacher'—an appellation which
does not in itself connote faith and which is used by unbelieving
scribes in 12.38. And in 8.19–20 the would-be follower asks to
come with Jesus—which is how Jewish students picked rabbis
but not how Jesus selected his disciples (cf. 4.18–22; 9.9). In
contrast to all this, 8.21f. involves a disciple who calls Jesus
'Lord', and this man is beckoned to discipleship by Jesus
himself: 'Follow me'. The conclusion is inescapable. 8.18–22
first offers a negative example and follows with a positive
presentation of genuine discipleship.

In Luke alone there is a third encounter between Jesus and a would-

---

[110] Lk 9.57–62 immediately precedes the missionary discourse in Lk 10, and
in Matthew there is no Q material between 8.22 and its missionary discourse.
From this we surmise that, in Q, Lk 9.57–62 introduced Jesus' instructions to
his disciples.

be follower: 'Another said: "I will follow you, Lord; but let me first say farewell to those at my home" '. Jesus said to him, "No one who puts his hand to the plough and looks back is fit for the kingdom of God" ' (9.61f.; cf. 1 Kgs 19.19–21). While this contains some Lukan vocabulary, the unit is not readily attributed to Luke's imagination.[111] Perhaps it belonged only to Q^{1k}, or perhaps it is L material which Luke revised and tacked on, or perhaps Matthew deliberately omitted the two verses.[112]

According to Gnilka, *Matthäusevangelium* 1, pp. 314f., one should not doubt the historicity of the story in 8.21f. Most scholars would rightly agree and as justification refer to Hengel's monograph on the subject. What of 8.19f.? Gnilka thinks them a community creation. His main point is that the text presupposes the equation, Jesus = Wisdom, and that this must come from the Q community. But it is not at all clear that 8.20 identifies Jesus with Wisdom. Beyond this, the saying can be translated into Aramaic without difficulty (Casey (v)), it harmonizes with the itinerant nature of Jesus' ministry, and (*pace* Bultmann, *History*, pp. 28 and 98) there is no solid evidence that the words preserve a traditional proverb. It would not be unreasonable to affirm a dominical origin, even if the setting may be secondary (cf. M. H. Smith (v)).

18. Jesus must move on. Are we to imagine that the great crowds around Peter's house have become troublesome and that Jesus is seeking repose? Or is Jesus' movement a challenge to the crowds to follow him?[113]

ἰδὼν δὲ ὁ Ἰησοῦς πολλοὺς ὄχλους περὶ αὐτὸν ἐκέλευσεν ἀπελθεῖν εἰς τὸ πέραν.[114] Mk 4.35 ('And he says to them in that day, when evening had come: "Let us go across to the other side" ') and Mk 4.36a ('And leaving the crowd') have been combined and modified. (i) 'In that day' has been omitted (it is unnecessary). (ii) 'When evening had come' drops out to avoid a clash with 8.16. (iii) The swelling of the crowds comes in, probably to supply Jesus' motivation (see n. 113). (iv) Direct speech has become indirect speech. Both ἰδών + 'crowds' as direct object* and κελεύω* are redactional. Although εἰς τὸ

[111] For non-Lukan features see Jeremias, *Lukasevangelium*, pp. 182–3.
[112] Hengel, *Leader*, p. 4, n. 5, favours the last possibility. Cf. Crossan (v). Matthew's propensity to abbreviate might well have moved him to drop the lines, which would ruin the antithetical parallelism now apparent (p. 39). (Lk 9.61–2 is closer to 9.59–60 than to 9.57–8: the first two concern doing something before following Jesus, and in both instances family ties are the subject. In view of this, we can understand why, if Matthew were to drop anything, it would be either 9.59–60 or 61–2.)
[113] Discussion in Kingsbury, 'Following' (v), pp. 46–7. He urges, probably rightly, that 'he commanded' does not involve a general command to discipleship and that it is the disciples alone who are directed to cross.
[114] οχλους is read by א* f¹ pc bo, οχλον by B sa^{mss} and NA^{26}. The external evidence favours πολλους οχλους, the reading of א² C L Θ 0233 f¹³ Maj lat sy; so HG.

πέραν[115] is editorial in 16.5, it is here from Mk 4.35. Observe that it is Jesus who makes the decision to take a boat. He is in command of the situation. No one advises him or has to bring circumstances to his attention.

19. καὶ προσελθὼν εἷς γραμματεὺς εἶπεν αὐτῷ. Compare Lk 9.57: 'And with him going in the way someone said to him'. Matthew and Luke agree exactly only in having καί + εἶπεν. προσέρχομαι* and εἷς* are Matthean, as is the sentence structure: προσέρχομαι + subject + verb of speech + αὐτῷ/αὐτοῖς (Mt: 6; Mk: 0; Lk: 1). Is Luke closer to Q?[116] Pace Gundry, Commentary, pp. 151–2, and others, εἷς is not to be paired with the ἕτερος of 8.21, as though Matthew first introduces 'a scribe, one (of the disciples)' and then later 'another disciple'. εἷς may here function, as in 21.19 and 26.69, as an indefinite article.[117] Or, because Matthew tends to place εἷς = τις after substantives, it could be independent: 'one, a scribe' (so Zahn, p. 347).[118] Whether or not γραμματεύς (see on 2.4) is redactional, we do not, against many, consider the scribe a disciple.[119] The man is not a friendly inquirer who is (implicitly) bidden to follow Jesus. On the contrary, the scribe, we are to think, is turned away.[120]

διδάσκαλε. This vocative (Mt: 6; Mk: 10; Lk: 12), which means more coming from a scribe, is perhaps a redactional addition. It is missing from Lk 9.57. Although Jesus is, for Matthew, the teacher par excellence, 'teacher' remains only a minor christological title. The disciples, in fact, never employ it.[121] By contrast, outsiders, in particular the Jewish leaders, often do.[122] It seems to be the equivalent of 'rabbi'[123] and is usually addressed to Jesus out of respect. It seems a good guess that Matthew, despite his strong emphasis on Jesus' teaching, did not turn 'teacher' into a major christological title in part because it, like 'rabbi', was, in common parlance, a title claimed by many, including Jewish scholars known to the evangelist.[124]

ἀκολουθήσω σοι ὅπου ἐὰν ἀπέρχῃ. So Lk 9.57. Compare

[115] Cf. LXX Num 21.13; Deut 30.13; Josh 1.15; 1 Macc 9.48; Liv.Proph. Ezek 10.
[116] For the Lukan and non-Lukan features of Lk 9.57 see Jeremias, Lukasevangelium, pp. 180–1.
[117] So BDF § 247.2 and Kingsbury, 'Following' (v), p. 48.
[118] Schlatter, p. 284, cites instances of ḥad in first position, and this too may be relevant.
[119] Pace Lagrange, p. 171; Hummel, p. 27; Gundry, Commentary, p. 151.
[120] Cf. Gnilka, Matthäusevangelium 1, pp. 310–1; Kingsbury, 'Following' (v).
[121] Contrast Mk 4.38; 9.38; 10.35; 13.1.
[122] 8.19; 9.11; 12.38; 17.24; 19.16; 22.16, 24, 36.
[123] Cf. 23.8; Jn 1.38.
[124] Cf. LXX Est 6.1; 2 Macc 1.10; Lk 2.46; 3.12; Jn 3.10; Josephus, Ant. 17.334. See further on 23.8.

Josephus, *Ant.* 6.77 (ἀκολουθήσουσιν αὐτῷ). The scribe states that he will literally follow Jesus around and (this is implicit) learn from him. This reflects the custom of the day. The student picked' his teacher or rabbi (Davies, *SSM*, pp. 455–7). Jesus, however, has another idea of discipleship, so the next verse holds correction. On 'following' see further 1, pp. 399–400.

20. Jesus answers the scribe with a hard saying which presupposes that Jesus is an itinerant and that therefore those who follow him will have to live on the road, uncertain whether the night will bring a friendly haven or not.[125] Matthew will have understood 8.20 in terms of the incredible contrast between the Son of man on earth and the Son of man in his kingdom. Before coming in glory with his angels to judge the quick and the dead, the Son of man must first suffer humiliation and rejection.

καὶ λέγει αὐτῷ ὁ Ἰησοῦς. See on 9.28. Luke has εἶπεν. Except for this minor disagreement, Lk 9.58 = Mt 8.20. (In Mt 8.19–22, λέγει is used of Jesus, εἶπεν of the other parties. It is otherwise in Lk 9.57–60. Evidently Matthew has used the verbs to add to the parallelism between 8.19 and 21 and between 8.20 and 22.)

αἱ ἀλώπεκες φωλεοὺς ἔχουσιν. ἀλώπηξ (cf. the Aramaic *taʿălāʾ*) bears its literal sense ('fox'), as everywhere in the LXX (for *šûʿāl*); contrast Lk 13.32, where it is used figuratively of Herod. φωλεός (LXX: 0) = 'den', 'hole' (cf. Josephus, *Bell.* 4.507). Plutarch, *T.G.* 9.5, supplies an interesting parallel: 'The wild beasts grazing in Italy have dens (φωλεόν), and there is for each of them a lair and a hiding place; but those fighting and dying for Italy have no share in such things, only air and light, and they are forced to wander unsettled with their wives and children'.

καὶ τὰ πετεινὰ τοῦ οὐρανοῦ κατασκηνώσεις. On 'the birds of heaven' see 1, p. 648. κατασκήνωσις (Mt: 1) translates *bānâ* in 1 Chron 28.2 and *miškān* in Ezek 37.27 (cf. Symm. Ps 45.5; 48.12). It means 'a place to live' (BAGD, s.v.) and may translate the Aramaic *miškan*.

ὁ δὲ υἱὸς τοῦ ἀνθρώπου οὐκ ἔχει ποῦ τὴν κεφαλὴν κλίνῃ. Compare *m. Qidd.* 4.14: 'R. Simeon b. Eleazar says, Have you ever seen a wild animal or bird practising a craft, yet they are sustained without care, and were they not created for no other purpose than to serve me? But I was created to serve my maker. How much more then ought I to be sustained without care? But I have done evil, and forfeited my sustenance' (cf. *b. Qidd.* 82b). οὐκ ἔχει ποῦ = 'has no place'. Compare LXX Josh 8.20 (καὶ

---

[125] Cf. the interpretation in Bonaventure, *Legenda maior* 7.2. For the parallel with Paul see C. Wolff, 'Niedrigkeit und Verzicht in Wort und Weg Jesu und in der apostolischen Existenz des Paulus', *NTS* 34 (1988), pp. 183–5.

οὐκέτι εἶχον ποῦ φύγωσιν ὧδε ἢ ὧδε) and Lk 12.17. Despite his spending much time at Capernaum, Jesus' mission and the hostility of Israel keep him moving.[126]

Some scholars[127] find an allusion to Wisdom in 8.20: the Son of man (=Wisdom) can find no dwelling place on earth. Although the themes of rejection and homelessness are at home in the Wisdom tradition,[128] and although there are possible connexions between the Son of man and wisdom in Jewish literature,[129] we consider the proposed interpretation rather remote. 'While it is true that the sages portray the power by which God created the world as seeking a resting place, they assert in the next breath that she in fact found one, either in Israel (Sir 24.7f.) or among the angels in heaven (1 Enoch 42.1f.). In the gospel logion ... there is no claim that 'the son of man' has been looking for a permanent abode, much less any hint that he will ever have one' (M. H. Smith (v), pp. 96f.).

EXCURSUS VI

THE SON OF MAN

Study of the mysterious synoptic title, 'the Son of man', has become a specialized field of its own wherein scholarly discord reigns supreme. Everyone concurs that the awkward ὁ υἱὸς τοῦ ἀνθρώπου is not a native Greek expression[130] and that the explanation for it must rather lie in the Hebrew or Aramaic background of the gospels. Scholars have also tended to agree that it is pedagogically profitable to divide the synoptic Son of man sayings into three categories:
1. Those which concern the earthly activity of the Son of man
2. Those which concern the sufferings of the Son of man
3. Those which concern the future coming of the Son of man in glory
Beyond these two items of agreement, however, the ever-mushrooming literature on the Son of man offers a host of conflicting and sometimes confusing claims and counter claims.

Contemporary solutions to the problem of the Son of man can, for convenience, be placed in four categories. First, it is possible, with reference especially to 1 En. 37–71 (the parables) and 4 Ezra 13, to argue that 'Son of man' was, in first-century Judaism, an established title of messianic significance, denoting a supernatural, eschatological figure of judgement. Some who think this deny that Jesus himself ever

[126] Cf. Kingsbury, 'Following' (v), p. 50, citing 2.13–14; 12.14–15; 14.1–3; 15.12–14, 21; 16.1–5.

[127] E.g. Hamerton-Kelly, p. 29, and Gnilka, *Matthäusevangelium* 1, pp. 311–12.

[128] Note Prov 1.20–33; Bar 4.19; 1 En 42.1–2; 94.5.

[129] J. Muilenberg, 'The Son of Man in Daniel and the Ethiopic Apocalypse of Enoch', *JBL* 79 (1960), pp. 197–209.

[130] 'The Son of man' is only one of many Semitisms in Matthew: cf. 1, pp. 80–5.

used the phrase.[131] Those who are prepared to trace the title back to Jesus of Nazareth disagree as to whether he used it of himself[132] or of another still to come.[133] Secondly, it is possible to find the background of the title in the Scriptures. In this connexion Dan 7 has been most frequently cited, some arguing that Jesus saw himself and his ministry in the light of the destiny of the 'one like a son of man',[134] others that the church made Jesus the object of Daniel's prophecy.[135] But Ezekiel has also been made the point of departure for interpreting the term. Eduard Schweizer, for example, has proposed that Jesus called himself 'son of man' in the way Ezekiel did—Ezekiel is called 'son of man' (*ben 'ādām*) over eighty-five times—in order to describe the commission he had received from God to serve in lowliness and suffering.[136]

Thirdly, there are those who have undertaken to resolve matters by recourse to Aramaic idiom. According to Geza Vermes, *bar nāšā'* was, in Galilean Aramaic, sometimes employed as a circumlocution, that is, it could serve as a substitute for the personal pronoun, 'I', and was used especially in contexts alluding to danger or death, or where humility or modesty was appropriate.[137] Only those sayings of Jesus that can be explained in terms of this idiom are authentic (e.g. Mk 2.10; 2.28; Mt 12.40 = Lk 11.30; Lk 19.10); the others have been added by the church, largely under the influence of Dan 7. According to P. M. Casey, Jesus, in accordance with first-century Aramaic idiom, uttered general statements, in which the expression 'man' was *bar 'ĕnāšā'/'ĕnāš*, in order to say things about himself. Thus those sayings that can be fitted into this usage are genuine (e.g. Mt 8.20 = Lk 9.58; Mt 11.19 = Lk 7.34; Mt 12.32 = Lk 12.10; Lk 22.48). All the others, including every reference to Dan 7, are creations of the church.[138] B. Lindars has made a similar case. He claims, however, to have found examples of the idiomatic use of the generic article in which the speaker refers to a class of persons with whom he identifies himself ('a man in

[131] E.g. P. Vielhauer, 'Jesus und der Menschensohn: zur Diskussion mit Heinz Eduard Tödt und Eduard Schweizer', *ZTK* 60 (1963), pp. 133–77.

[132] E.g. Kümmel, *Theology*, pp. 76–95; Jeremias, *Theology*, pp. 257–76.

[133] E.g. Bultmann, *Theology* 1, pp. 26–31; Tödt, *Son of Man*; Hahn, *Titles*, pp. 15–53; A. Y. Collins, 'The Origin of the Designation of Jesus as "Son of Man"', *HTR* 80 (1987), pp. 391–407.

[134] T. W. Manson, 'The Son of Man in Daniel, Enoch, and the Gospels', in *Studies in the Gospel and Epistles*, ed. M. Black, Manchester, 1962, pp. 123–45; Moule, *Christology*, pp. 11–22; M. D. Hooker, 'Is the Son of Man Problem really insoluble?', in *Text and Interpretation*, ed. E. Best and R. McL. Wilson, Cambridge, 1979, pp. 155–68; Kim, pp. 32–7.

[135] Perrin, *Rediscovering*, pp. 164–99; W. O. Walker, 'The Son of Man: Some Recent Developments', *CBQ* 45 (1983), pp. 584–607.

[136] Schweizer, *Mark*, pp. 166–71.

[137] See Vermes in Black, pp. 310–28; idem, *Jesus the Jew*, pp. 160–91; idem, 'The Present State of the Son of Man Debate', *JJS* 29 (1978), pp. 123–34; idem, '"The Son of Man" Debate', *JSNT* 1 (1978), pp. 19–32; idem, *World*, pp. 89–99.

[138] Casey, *Son of Man*; also idem (v); idem, 'Aramaic Idiom and Son of Man Sayings', *ExpT* 96 (1985), pp. 233–6; idem, 'General, Generic and Indefinite: The Use of the Term "Son of Man" in Aramaic Sources and in the Teaching of Jesus', *JSNT* 29 (1987), pp. 21–56.

my position'). In other words, 'man' did not necessarily include each and every man but could denote a particular class of men.[139]

Fourthly, F. H. Borsch has attempted to set the Son of man sayings within the context of speculation about the First Man and his son. The king was often thought of as the son of the Primal Man, and when Jesus spoke of the Son of man he was picking up a widespread idea that had deep roots in Near Eastern mythology.[140]

This all-too-brief and condensed sketch of the different resolutions to the issue of the Son of man must pass over possible points of overlap. It also leaves several options altogether out of account. But any attempt to set forth adequately the course of the discussion would take us too far afield. For this we must refer to the surveys that others have made.[141] What we wish to do herein is make some observations and offer our own very tentative conclusions concerning the on-going Son of man debate.

(1) Was 'Son of man' a well-established title in first-century Judaism? Was the central figure of the eschatological judgement already known in Jesus' time as 'the Son of man'? The Similitudes of Enoch (1 En. 37–71), which in the past have been the principal source for this supposition, cannot bear the burden of proof. Many are persuaded that the Similitudes are not pre-Christian.[142] Much more importantly, even if they are, probably Perrin and others are correct in concluding that the Son of man in 1 En. 37–71 is no independent conception with a title which is itself a sufficient designation of that conception. Rather, the Similitudes depend upon an exegesis of Dan 7, as the definite article attests: the Son of man is always *that* Son of man, that is, the one in Dan 7.[143] It is the same with 4 Ezra 13: 'that man' refers back to 'the figure of a man' and thus supplies Danielic imagery which helps

[139] Lindars, *Son of Man*; see also idem, 'The New Look on the Son of Man', *BJRL* 63 (1981), pp. 437–62.

[140] F. H. Borsch, *The Son of Man in Myth and History*, London, 1967.

[141] A. J. B. Higgins, 'Son of Man-*Forschung* since "The Teaching of Jesus"', in *New Testament Essays*, ed. A. J. B. Higgins, Manchester, 1959, pp. 119–35; idem, 'Is the Son of Man Problem insoluble?', in *Neotestamentica et Semitica*, ed. E. E. Ellis and M. Wilcox, Edinburgh, 1969, pp. 70–87; J. R. Donahue, 'Recent Studies on the Origin of "Son of Man" in the Gospels', *CBQ* 48 (1986), pp. 484–98.

[142] For discussion see M. Black, 'The Composition, Character and Date of the "Second Vision of Enoch"', in *Text-Wort-Glaube*, ed. M. Brecht, Berlin, 1980, pp. 19–30; J. C. Greenfield and M. E. Stone, 'The Enochic Pentateuch and the Date of the Similitudes', *HTR* 70 (1977), pp. 51–65; M. Knibb, 'The Date of the Parables of Enoch: A Critical Review', *NTS* 25 (1979), pp. 345–59; G. W. E. Nickelsburg, *Jewish Literature Between the Bible and the Mishnah*, Philadelphia, 1981, pp. 221–3. J. T. Milik, *The Books of Enoch*, ed. with the collaboration of M. Black, Oxford, 1976, pp. 91–2, has argued that the Parables of Enoch are a Christian composition. On this point he has not persuaded others.

[143] See Perrin, *Rediscovering*, pp. 167–70. Cf. Moule, *Christology*, pp. 15–16; M. Casey, 'The Use of the Term "son of man" in the Similitudes of Enoch', *JSJ* 7 (1976), pp. 11–29.

to paint a vision of the Messiah.[144] Therefore, until further evidence is forthcoming, it appears methodologically unsound to approach the synoptic data with the assumption that most first-century Jews, upon hearing the phrase, 'Son of man', would immediately have thought of a transcendent redeemer figure, the judge of the last day. The most one can say is that the phrase, within the appropriate context or with the appropriate markers, could cause one to recall the theophany of Dan 7.

(2) Vermes, Casey, and Lindars agree that the son of man idiom could include the speaker. But whereas Vermes prefers to speak of a circumlocution for 'I', Casey stresses that there are no known examples of the indefinite application of the idiom to the speaker alone; and Lindars for his part clarifies all by referring to the 'generic article'. It is not clear how these three different approaches are to be evaluated and related to one another. Vermes seems to regard his differences with Casey as minimal (*World*, p. 92: 'it would be ungracious to quibble over inessentials'). And Casey has in one place accepted Lindars' evaluation of the Aramaic evidence in terms of generic usage as 'satisfactory'. Lindars, however, faults both Vermes and Casey, the latter for taking the general statement in which the speaker includes himself as the key to the synoptic sayings, the former for implying the possibility of exclusive self-reference. All this is quite confusing. Are there really significant differences between the positions of the three scholars or is the impression left by Lindars somewhat misleading? Both Vermes and Casey complain that they have been misunderstood. Vermes says that his critics have failed to appreciate 'that a circumlocution is not just a synonym, but by definition roundabout and evasive speech. It is expected to entail ambiguity' (*World*, p. 91). This would seem to imply that, according to Vermes, '(the) son of man' was not used to mean simply 'I and no one else'. In a similar vein, Casey states that his reviewers have mistakenly imagined that general statements with the son of man idiom must be true of everyone. It would appear, then, that even the well-informed Lindars may have slightly misrepresented his discussion partners. Vermes, Casey, and Lindars are at one in concluding that '(the) son of man' was not just the equivalent of 'I' but involved or at least could involve a more general reference; and Casey and Lindars concur that whether one uses the label 'general' or 'generic' or not, statements with the son of man idiom need not apply to every human being.

(3) The one fact that asserts itself above all the others is that the precise significance of '(the) son of man' in first-century Palestinian Aramaic has not yet been fully clarified. Two problems in particular remain to be resolved to the satisfaction of all. Were the definite and indefinite states interchangeable or not?[145] And, if Jesus used '(the) son of man' as an oblique self-reference, are we compelled to think that he always spoke of himself as the member of a particular group or class of men (so Casey and Lindars) or could he have been talking

---

[144] See Perrin, *Rediscovering*, pp. 170–1; Casey, *Son of Man*, pp. 122–9. One should note further the possibility that *'ādām* or *'ĕnāš* originally stood in 4 Ezra 13, not *ben 'ādām* or *bar 'ĕnāš* (cf. Casey, ibid., pp. 124–45).

[145] Casey thinks they were. M. Black, 'Aramaic Barnāshā and the "Son of Man"', *ExpT* 95 (1984), pp. 200–6, thinks they were not.

about one particular 'someone' ('I' being implicit)?[146] Perhaps answers to these disputed questions will come with the future discovery of more Aramaic evidence. In the meanwhile, we should like to propose that there may be another way forward. Attention should be called to an observation of C. M. Tuckett: 'Every culture has its accepted shorthand ways of speaking and writing: e.g. in England, "the war" means the 1939–45 war, even though the word "war" is quite general'.[147] Even if '(the) son of man' simply meant 'man', and even if the absolute and emphatic states were interchangeable, could Jesus not have used the expression in such a way as to give it special content? One might compare the Johannine use of 'I am'. Certainly the simple Greek phrase ἐγώ εἰμί is common enough and not necessarily overloaded with significance; yet because of its associations in the Fourth Gospel, ἐγώ εἰμί becomes pregnant with meaning, gaining the status of a title. Jesus, in like manner, might have used '(the) son of man', a common expression, in an uncommon manner, making it—at least on occasion—take on for himself and for his audience extraordinary associations, associations not present in everyday speech. We recall here an observation made by W. Bousset, pp. 43f.: even if '(the) son of man' was 'in general usage first . . . taken as nothing but an expression for the individual (definite) man, then it is utterly beyond comprehension why a quite general term such as "the man" could not also, under certain conditions, have become a messianic term. Jewish apocalypticism loved to coin such mysterious and enigmatic terms. In it we find such expressions for the Messiah as hbʾ = ὁ ἐρχόμενος, the "shoot" (zemach, ἀνατολή), or even (in later tradition) the leper!' We must, however, inquire whether there is in fact sufficient evidence that Jesus used '(the) son of man' in an unusual or distinctive manner.

(4) In our judgement, the inquiry may best proceed by examining whether the synoptics are credible in making Jesus associate '(the) son of man' with the 'one like a son of man' of Dan 7. The following considerations persuade us that they are.

a. Jesus' apparently novel use of both 'abba' and 'amen' demonstrates that he was deliberately innovative in the linguistic sphere. He was not, that is, bound by conventional usage. The possibility that he employed '(the) son of man' in an uncommon manner is perhaps first suggested by the frequency of the term in the synoptics. If the gospels are reliable, Jesus spoke of '(the) son of man' on many occasions. Our extant sources do not indicate that this was true of anyone else. We concede that the point lacks great force because the literary remains relevant for comparison are fragmentary. Still, one has to wonder whether Jesus' habit of referring to '(the) son of man' was atypically frequent and therefore a hint of some deeper or unconventional meaning. It may also bear remarking that while ὁ υἱὸς τοῦ ἀνθρώπου points to a definite form in the underlying Hebrew or

[146] For this last see R. Bauckham, 'The Son of Man: "A Man in my Position" or "Someone"?', JSNT 23 (1985), pp. 23–33, arguing that Jesus used bar ʾĕnāš with indefinite sense ('a man', 'someone'). For Lindars' response to this article see ibid., pp. 35–41.

[147] C. M. Tuckett, 'The Present Son of Man', JSNT 14 (1982), p. 73, n. 14.

Aramaic, the definite form, 'the son of man', is found less frequently in Aramaic sources than is the indefinite form, 'a son of man', and this is especially true of the earlier materials.

b. In 1 En. 37–71, there is an initial reference to Dan 7 which does not use a definite article (46.1: 'another being whose countenance had the appearance of a man'). Thereafter we read only of '*that* Son of Man' or '*the* Son of Man'. In other words, subsequent references to the Son of Man hark back to 46.1 and to the imagery of Dan 7 there used. C. F. D. Moule has postulated something similar for the Jesus tradition. The definite state or article was a way of alluding back to Daniel's human figure. Jesus used the definite article or a demonstrative pronoun to direct his hearers back to the well-known scene of Dan 7 with its 'one like a son of man'. Moule musters support from this observation: 'there is . . . only one instance in Hebrew literature before the New Testament of the definite article used with the singular, "*the* Son of Man" (though the plural, "the sons of men", is, of course, found); and that, which occurs in the Qumran Manual of Discipline, IQS 11.20, appears to be an afterthought, for the *he* (*h*) of the definite article is placed above the first letter of "Man" (that is, over the *a* (') of '*ādām*). By contrast, in the New Testament, there is only one instance, among all the sayings attributed to Jesus (and the one attributed to Stephen), of the phrase *without* the definite article'.[148]

c. Both Mk 13.26 and 14.62 clearly draw upon Dan 7; and the combination of 'Son of man' with ἔρχομαι in Mk 8.38c (contrast Lk 12.8); in Mt 24.44 = Lk 12.40; in Mt 10.23; 16.28 (contrast Mk 9.1); 25.31; and Lk 18.8 probably also depends upon Dan 7 (7.13: 'there *came* one like a son of man, and he *came* to the Ancient of Days'). Admittedly several of these sayings are not usually traced back to Jesus (e.g. Mk 8.38c; 13.26; Mt 25.31). But opinion is divided over Mk 14.62; Mt 24.44 = Lk 12.40; Mt 10.23; and Lk 18.8. Many would be willing to affirm that these logia go back to Jesus.

d. Dan 7 has left few traces in the New Testament outside the gospels; and apart from the Apocalypse, there are few if any references to the Danielic Son of man. To be sure, scholars have made up the lack by telling us that, despite all appearances, the primitive community of Palestine had as its life-blood a Son of man Christology. But notwithstanding the long-running popularity of this affirmation, it is woefully ill-founded. It forces one to suppose that 'from this Christology not a single formula of the community, neither a kerygma, nor a confession, nor a prayer, outside (or for that matter within) the Gospels would have survived' (Goppelt, *Theology* 1, p. 180). The implausibility of this is enormous. By way of contrast, references to Dan 7 and to the Son of man do certainly occur in materials attributed to Jesus. Moreover, there are synoptic passages in which the Son of man is not mentioned but allusion to Dan 7 is made. For instance, the absolute use of 'kingdom' with 'give' in Lk 12.32 ('Fear not, little flock, for it is your Father's good pleasure to give you the kingdom'), a saying we should probably assign to

---

[148] *Christology*, p. 16.

Jesus,[149] recalls Dan 7.18 and 27, where the saints of the Most High are given the kingdom. And the original form of Lk 22.28–30 = Mt 19.28, which perhaps did not mention the Son of man (contrast the present text of Matthew) and which may go back to Jesus, also depends upon Dan 7. Luke speaks of thrones (cf. Dan 7.9), of the kingdom (cf. Dan 7.18, 27), and of the judgement (cf. Dan 7.10), and the Matthean parallel adds a reference to glory (Dan 7.14). Given the lack of reflection upon Dan 7 outside the gospels, the repeated use of the Son of man in the synoptics, and the likelihood, established even apart from the Son of man sayings, that Jesus was influenced by Dan 7, those who believe that Jesus himself spoke of the Son of man with reference to Dan 7 have grounds for their conviction.

e. As we shall argue in the commentary on Mt 10.32f., Lk 12.8 probably goes back to Jesus, and although scholars have usually missed the saying's dependence upon Dan 7, it is unmistakable.

f. Those who question whether Jesus spoke of the Son of man with reference to Dan 7 or to an established figure of Jewish expectation must suppose that the church formulated a good number of new Son of man sayings. This is true even of those who explain the Son of man sayings in terms of Aramaic idiom; for the postulated idiomatic usage accounts for only a handful of the total number of logia. But what evidence is there that christological terms were readily put into the mouth of Jesus? We know that although 'Lord' and 'Christ' were all-important titles in the early church, they have left scarcely a trace in the tradition of the sayings of Jesus. This is in direct contrast with the Son of man phenomenon. 'The Son of man' occurs again and again in the gospels, and the references to Dan 7 are several. But the title is found in Acts only once and never in the epistles, and allusions to Dan 7 are few and far between. Should this not spell caution for those who would solve the Son of man problem by continual recourse to the creative activities of the early church?

g. If Jesus did sometimes use '(the) son of man' in a 'messianic' sense with reference to Dan 7, it is perhaps worth observing that the basic meaning of 'son of man' is simply 'man', and that 'man' has messianic associations in the Jewish tradition; see, for example, Num 24.7 LXX; Isa 66.7; Zech 6.12; T. Jud. 24.1; Acts 17.31; Sib. Or. 5.414; Tg. on Ps 80.16–18. Discussion in W. Horbury, 'The Messianic Associations of "The Son of man"', *JTS* 36 (1985), pp. 34–55.

h. Casey has urged that '(the) Son of man' could not in and of itself have been a pointer to Dan 7: the phrase was too common. We have reservations. Jesus was no ordinary speaker. He was a prophet, indeed more than a prophet. He and others probably thought of himself as the destined king of Israel, the Messiah. See Excursus XII. If so, then the context of his speech was such that *from the beginning* people would have associated him with the eschatological expectations of the OT, including those in Daniel. Instead of rejecting Son of man sayings because they do not easily fit idiomatic usage (cf. p. 46), why not take them as indication that Jesus was using '(the) Son of man' in a

---

[149] Cf. W. Pesch, 'Zur Formgeschichte und Exegese von Lk. 12.32', *Bib* 41 (1960), pp. 25–40.

special fashion? Why not apply the criterion of dissimilarity and argue for authenticity? Why not suppose that the *Sitz im Leben Jesu* was such that a novel use of '(the) Son of man' might have been enough to provoke reflections about Jesus and Dan 7?

i. The book of Daniel closely associates the 'one like a son of man' with the saints of the Most High (7.17f., 21f., 26f.), and many have supposed that the figure of 7.13f. either represents the saints or is a corporate entity. If the supposition is correct, Daniel shares something important with the gospels. In the Markan passion predictions Jesus is always 'linked in the context with his followers, who are expected to share both his suffering and his glory' (Hooker, *Son of Man*, pp. 181f.). T. W. Manson (n. 134) argued that there is often a corporate dimension to the synoptic sayings about the Son of man. The explanation for this he found in Dan 7, where the one like a son of man and the saints of the Most High are brought together: the fluctuation between individual and community in Dan 7 has its close parallel in the gospels. While it is perhaps more accurate to view the synoptic Son of man as a representative rather than corporate figure, Manson was right to call attention to the similarities between Son of man usage in Daniel and the synoptics: in both the Son of man is more than an isolated individual.[150]

j. Daniel's one like a son of man is a suffering figure—because the saints of the Most High suffer. 'As I looked, this horn made war with the saints, and prevailed over them' (7.21; cf. 7.25). Pious Jews, hearing Dan 7 read, and finding themselves persecuted or in a situation of suffering would no doubt have viewed the events involving the one like a son of man as a promise of passage through affliction to victory: if Daniel's figure had suffered difficulty only to be given the triumph, so too, the listeners might hope, might they be delivered from a painful predicament into the state of salvation.[151] Further, the supposition that Jesus interpreted the Son of man in these terms is credible. Many of the Son of man sayings have to do either with suffering (e.g. Mk 14.21, 41) or with vindication (e.g. Mk 13.26; 14.62) or with both (e.g. Mt 10.23 and the passion predictions). In both Dan 7 and the synoptics, the Son of man first suffers and then finds vindication.

In view of all we have said, we are inclined to think that Jesus used the son of man idiom on more than one occasion in a novel or quasi-titular manner with the intent of directing his hearers to Dan 7, and that he saw in Daniel's eschatological figure a prophecy of his own person and fate. But what of the First Evangelist? What did he make of 'the Son of man'?[152] The phrase appears thirty times, thirteen with

---

[150] See further D. Wenham, 'The Kingdom of God and Daniel', *ExpT* 98 (1987), pp. 132–4, arguing that the primary OT background for Jesus' preaching of the kingdom of God lies in Dan 2 and 7.

[151] Against Casey, for whom the one like a son of man 'is a pure symbol with no experience at all, other than the symbolic ones in vss. 13–14', and for whom Daniel's figure is 'separate . . . dissociated from the suffering of the saints', see F. J. Moloney, 'The End of the Son of Man?', *Downside Review* 98 (1980), p. 284.

[152] Lit.: Kingsbury, *Structure*, pp. 113–22; idem, 'The Figure of Jesus in Matthew's Story: A Literary-Critical Probe', *JSNT* 21 (1984), pp. 22–32; idem,

reference to the future coming of the Son of man, ten with reference to his death and resurrection, seven with reference to his earthly activity. These numbers, along with the fact that most of the redactional instances of the title[153] belong to the first category (cf. 13.41; 16.28; 19.28; 24.30; 25.31), demonstrate Matthew's great interest in Jesus as the coming Son of man. But what is the precise content of his interest? The title seems to be used primarily of Jesus not in his relationship to God (cf. 'Son of God') or to believers alone (cf. 'Lord') or to unbelievers alone (cf. 'rabbi') but to the world at large.[154] This is why in the First Gospel the Son of man is the eschatological judge (13.41; 19.28; 24.30, 39; 25.31); why he will come publicly and be seen by all (10.23; 24.27, 30; 25.31; 26.64); why Jesus answers enemies and outsiders by referring to himself as the Son of man (11.19; 12.32, 40; 26.24, 64); why it is as the Son of man that Jesus suffers at the hands of others (the passion predictions); and why the ransom for *many* is paid by Jesus as the Son of man (20.28).

Decisive for Matthew's understanding of the Son of man is the apocalyptic vision of Dan 7. The dependence of 24.30 and 26.64 upon Daniel's version of the eschatological judgement would have been manifest to our knowledgeable evangelist, and he would not have missed the allusion to Dan 7.13 created by the linking of the Son of man with ἔρχομαι in 10.23; 16.28; 24.44; and 25.31. There are several additional verses which may well allude to Dan 7: 9.6 (cf. Dan 7.14); 19.28 (see above); 28.3 (cf. Dan 7.9); 28.18 (cf. Dan 7.14).

One cannot eliminate the probability that the First Evangelist knew Aramaic and so was aware of the idiomatic usage of '(the) Son of man' (cf. 16.13?). But if so, he must also have believed that Jesus often used the words to allude to Dan 7 (and therefore that his words were sometimes susceptible of being interpreted on two different levels). For this reason, we question Kingsbury, who argues that 'the Son of man' (he translates 'this man' or 'this human being') does not specify 'who Jesus is'. He argues this in part because' he thinks that only Jesus employs the phrase and that the title is not used confessionally. We believe that 9.6 ('But that you may know that the Son of man has authority on earth to forgive sins, he then said to the paralytic') is evidence to the contrary, for on pp. 93–94 we have urged that the verse should be understood by the reader as editorial comment; that is, here 'the Son of man' is used by someone other than Jesus. See also

'The Figure of Jesus in Matthew's Gospel: A Rejoinder to David Hill', *JSNT* 25 (1985), pp. 68–74; D. Hill, 'The Figure of Jesus in Matthew's Story: A Response to Professor Kingsbury's Literary-Critical Probe', *JSNT* 21 (1984), pp. 48–51; M. Pamment, 'The Son of Man in the First Gospel', *NTS* 29 (1983), pp. 116–29; Lindars, *Son of Man*, pp. 115–31; Geist; Schenk, *Sprache*, pp. 305–7

[153] 'Title' is the right word. (i) Our interpretation of 9.6 and 12.8 requires a titular usage (see the commentary). (ii) There is a consistency in how the term is used. (iii) We think that 'the Son of man' was already quasi-titular on the lips of Jesus. (iv) The very similar 'the Son of God' is clearly a title. (Meier, *Vision*, pp. 82–3, wonders whether the absolute 'the Son' is always the simple equivalent of 'the Son of God', and whether 'the Son' should not sometimes be linked with 'the Son of man'. In view of 28.16–20, he may be correct. There 'the Son' appears in a text which alludes to Dan 7.)

[154] This has been rightly stressed by Kingsbury's contributions (n. 152).

pp. 315–16. But even if one thinks otherwise, this does not imply that Matthew must have thought it odd or unfitting for someone to say, 'Jesus is the Son of man'. After all, in Luke only Jesus refers to himself as 'the Son of man', but in Acts this is not the case (see 7.56). The failure of 'the Son of man' to be used confessionally is probably just due to Matthew's faithfulness to his sources. We thus consider it fair to assert that in Matthew 'the Son of man' is a title whose first function is to tell the reader that Jesus is the figure seen in the vision of Dan 7.[155]

How does 'the Son of man' function in 8.20? Matthew probably understood the words in a titular sense. This means the saying contains much irony. The one without a home is the majestic judge of mankind. Hence we have the ultimate illustration of the last being first.

For understanding the logion on Jesus' lips there are two good possibilities. One is the view of Casey (v): 'At the general level, the provision of resting places for foxes/jackals and birds is contrasted with the lack of such provisions for people, who have to build houses to have anywhere to stay'; at the particular level, Jesus was declaring that 'he, in the course of his migratory ministry, had nowhere to go'— and that his followers must expect the same (pp. 8, 13). The other plausible interpretation comes from M. H. Smith (v). He detects an allusion to Ps 8, where 'the son of man' and 'the birds of heaven' both appear. The saying is ironic and proclaims a reversal of everyday values. There is an implicit paradox which is intentionally ambiguous. 'By being called emphatically "the son of man", he who is declared to have "no place to lay his head" is simultaneously seen as one who is usually believed to have "all things under his feet"' (p. 103).[156]

---

[155] Pamment (as in n. 152) claims that in Matthew 'the Son of man' is a representative and exemplary figure. There is substance to this, and it favours seeing a connexion with Dan 7, where the one like a son of man is so closely linked to the saints. —According to Lindars (n. 152), Matthew betrays no awareness that 'the Son of man' was an established messianic title. We wonder. There are quite a few intriguing parallels between Mt 25.31–46 and 1 En 70–1; see D. R. Catchpole, 'The Poor on Earth and the Son of Man in Heaven', *BJRL* 61 (1979), pp. 379–83. These do not suffice to *prove* Matthew's knowledge of 1 Enoch. Nonetheless, the possibility that our evangelist knew some version of 1 Enoch (including the Parables) is real; cf. D. W. Suter, *Tradition and Composition in the Parables of Enoch*, SBLDS 47, Missoula, 1979, pp. 25–9. And a knowledge of 1 Enoch would certainly have encouraged him to think of 'the Son of man' as more than a simple circumlocution and as containing eschatological content. Moreover, although we have stated that it would be methodologically unsound to assume that 'the Son of man' was a title in the days of Jesus or Matthew, we must admit that the titular status of the expression has not been disproved. For the possibility that the targum on Ps 8 and Ps 80 presupposes the equation, 'Son of man' = 'Messiah', see B. McNeil, 'The Son of Man and the Messiah', *NTS* 26 (1980), pp. 419–22, and F. J. Maloney, 'The Reinterpretation of Psalm VIII and the Son of Man Debate', *NTS* 27 (1981), pp. 656–72.

[156] There is no reason to postulate an original 'I' or 'Wisdom' in place of 'the Son of man'.

Gos. Thom. 86 ('Jesus says: [the foxes ha]ve the[ir holes] and birds have their dwellings, but the Son of·man does not have any place to lay his head and rest') differs from Mt 8.20 and Lk 9.58 in several respects: possessive pronouns after 'holes', 'dwellings', and 'head'; no 'of the heavens' after 'birds'; and 'rest' at the end. There is nothing in Thomas to indicate dependence upon the synoptics (although nothing to disprove it either); and it is just possible that 'to rest' is not a late addition but part of the original saying.

21. A second man appears. He too (having just heard the interchange in 8.19–20?) wants to follow Jesus. He feels bound, however, to fulfil a familial obligation—burial of his father. The request ('Let me first go and bury my father') if taken at face value is quite reasonable and in accord with the filial piety enjoined by the decalogue. Moreover, burial of the dead was in Judaism considered an act of lovingkindness and imitation of the deity (God buried Moses!).[157] Its importance is reflected by *m. Ber.* 3.1: 'He whose dead lies unburied before him is exempt from reciting the *Shemaʿ*, from saying the *Tefillah*, and from wearing phylacteries'.[158]

ἕτερος δὲ τῶν μαθητῶν εἶπεν αὐτῷ.[159] Compare Lk 9.59: 'He (Jesus) said to another: "Follow me". But he said . . .'. This makes the Lukan scene a call story.

Against Hengel, *Leader*, pp. 3–4, the arrangement in Matthew is probably secondary—as is shown by the appearance of 'first' in the

---

[157] Cf. *b. Soṭa* 14a. See S. E. Loewenstamm, 'The Death of Moses', in *Studies on the Testament of Moses*, ed. G. W. E. Nickelsburg, Missoula, 1976, pp. 185–217, and K. Haacker and P. Schäfer, 'Nachbiblische Traditionen vom Tod des Mose', in *Josephus-Studien*, ed. O. Betz et al., Göttingen, 1974, pp. 147–74. The key text is Deut 34.6: 'he buried him' (cf. LAB 19.16; *m. Soṭa* 1.9). But in the Slavonic Life of Moses 16 and elsewhere, the angels bury Moses (cf. already (?) the LXX and the Samaritan version: 'they buried'). — For pertinent texts on burial see Gen 47.29–31; 49.29–32; 50.5, 25; 2 Sam 21.10–4; Tob 1.17–18; 4.3–4; 6.14–15; 12.12–13; 14.10; Jub. 23.7; 26.18; 36.1–2; Liv. Proph. Nathan 2–4; the conclusions to the twelve books making up the Testaments of the Twelve Patriarchs; Mt 27.57–61 par.; Josephus, *Bell.* 5.545; T. Abr. A 20.11; T. Job 39; 40.12–13; 52.11–12; and the passages in SB 1, pp. 487–9. Many of these texts refer to burial of father by son. From the Graeco-Roman world note Homer, *Il.* 23.65–92, and for the honouring of parents Diogenes Laertius 8.2; Epictetus, *Diss.* 2.17; Marcus Aurelius Antoninus 5.31. For the denial of burial as a harsh punishment and horror see Deut 28.26; Jer 7.33; 8.1–2; 16.4; 25.33; Ezek 6.5; 29.5; 2 Macc 5.10; 1 En 98.13; Ps Sol. 4.19–20; Josephus, *Bell.* 2.465; 4.317; Suetonius, *Vesp.* 2.3. Recall esp. Sophocles, *Antigone*.

[158] Some texts add: 'and from all duties enjoined in the law' (cf. *b. Ber.* 14b). The importance of mourning should also be remembered; see on 9.23.

[159] NA[26] prints αυτου after μαθητων; so C L W Θ 0250 *f*[1.13] Maj lat sy mae bo. It is omitted by HG on the authority of ℵ B 33 *pc* it sa. Other places where the ms. tradition has qualified the absolute 'the disciples' include 14.15, 22; 15.12, 33, 36; 16.5, 20; 19.25; 26.8, 56.

next line. The adverb makes sense in Luke because the man is answering Jesus' call: 'I will follow you as you command; but *first* ...'. In Matthew, however, 'first' hangs in the air. Matthew, desirous of increasing the parallelism between 8.19–20 and 21–2, has moved Jesus' 'Follow me' so that it is no longer an independent sentence. Schematically, then, Q's arrangement—

Assertion of first man
Jesus' response
Jesus' call of another
Response of second man
Jesus' response

—has become, in the First Gospel, a perfectly balanced dyad:

Assertion of first man
Jesus' response
Request of second man
Jesus' response

ἕτερος can indicate a difference in kind.[160] Perhaps we should translate: 'another man, one of his disciples' (so NEB). The man is not identified (but in Clement of Alexandria, *Strom.* 3.4, he is Philip).

μαθητῶν* is probably redactional. It adds to the (antithetical) parallelism between vv. 19 and 21 (scribe–disciple). The word 'loosely qualifies ἕτερος without implying that the γραμματεύς was a disciple' (Allen, p. 82). It is perhaps odd that a 'disciple' is being called to follow Jesus. One has the impression from 4.18–22 and 9.9 that discipleship is defined precisely as following Jesus, so would a disciple not already be following Jesus? Perhaps by 'disciple' is meant 'one who became a disciple'. Or maybe 8.21–2 has to do with continuing on in a discipleship already entered into: the decision for Jesus must be made again and again.[161]

κύριε. There is no title in the best mss. of Luke. Its insertion here by Matthew adds to the antithetical parallelism with 8.19 (where 'teacher' is the address). See further on 8.6.

ἐπίτρεψόν μοι πρῶτον ἀπελθεῖν καὶ θάψαι τὸν πατέρα μου. Compare 1 Kgs 19.20 ('Let me kiss my father and my mother, and then I will follow you'—so Elisha to Elijah). After 'me' and before 'to bury' Luke has ἀπελθόντι πρῶτον; otherwise there is agreement. The participle + infinitive is probably Lukan.[162] 'To go' is pleonastic and a Semitism. 'First' has temporal sense. (If

---

[160] BAGD, s.v., citing Lk 23.32 and Tebtunis Papyrus 41.9.
[161] Cf. Grundmann, p. 259, who observes the pertinence of this for Matthew's Christian readers; also Gnilka, *Matthäusevangelium* 1, p. 312, supposing this evidence that in Matthew's community Christians were called 'disciples' (cf. Acts).
[162] Jeremias, *Lukasevangelium*, p. 181.

the father is already dead, the disciple is not asking for an
indefinite period of time but perhaps for only a few hours.[163])

22. Jesus' response ('Leave the dead to bury their own dead')
has been called 'both cruel and senseless'.[164] Certainly 'the
sayings of the wise are like goads' (Eccles 12.11), but this remark
seemingly discourages a deed of lovingkindness and leaves one
truly nonplussed.

ὁ δὲ Ἰησοῦς λέγει αὐτῷ. On the difference from Lk 9.60 (εἶπεν
δὲ αὐτῷ) see on 8.20. Against Donn (v), Jesus is addressing not a
third party but the disciple of 8.21.[165]

ἀκολούθει μοι. Compare 8.19; also 9.9. Matthew has moved
this demand from its place in Q (*supra*).[166]

For Matthew and his Christian readers, faith in Jesus and following
Jesus were probably conterminous ideas: to have faith in Jesus was to
follow him. But with regard to the historical Jesus, the two must be
distinguished (cf. Hengel, *Leader*, pp. 61–3). Jesus proclaimed the
kingdom to all Israel. He called only a few, however, to follow him.
Discipleship in that sense was a special 'office', the result of a personal,
concrete encounter. For the purpose of furthering his mission, Jesus
chose a select group to be with him and to engage in missionary work.
These alone 'followed' him.

καὶ ἄφες τοὺς νεκροὺς θάψαι τοὺς ἑαυτῶν νεκρούς. So Luke,
without introductory 'and'. θάπτω (cf. 14.12) = 'bury', 'entomb'.

'In terms of its outward form, Jesus' answer amounts to a
paradoxically formulated single-membered aphorism; by the word-play
contained in it, Jesus shows himself to be someone who formulates *ad
hoc* maxims, and this is something we find also in a great number of
his other logia, and something which is also true of the previous and
subsequent maxims on following him (Lk 9.58 and 9.62)' (so Hengel,
Leader, p. 7).

In the story of Elijah calling Elisha, which should no doubt
here be recalled, the latter asks the former for permission to say
farewell to his parents (1 Kgs 19.19–21). The LXX and Josephus
take the text to imply that such permission was granted (1, p. 393).
This makes for a striking contrast with our passage. Jesus
demands that discipleship take absolute precedence over
everything else. His command brooks no delay, even if the result
is the slighting of one's parents. Who are the dead who should

---

[163] Contrast Diogenes, *Ep.* 38.3: '*From the next day* after he distributed his
property to his relatives, he took up the wallet, doubled his coarse cloak, and
followed me'.

[164] K. Kohler, *The Origins of the Synagogue and the Church*, New York,
1929, p. 212.

[165] According to Donn (v), the disciple is to be equated with the dead.

[166] We note that the synoptic command, 'Follow me', may well be the source
of John's 'I am the way' (14.6).

bury the dead? If they are the physically dead, then, since dead men can do nothing, the meaning must be paradoxical and ironic: let the business of burial take care of itself.[167] It is better, however, to think of the spiritually dead. The figurative use of 'dead' is well-attested in the NT and texts from its world.[168] So the buriers of the dead are those who have rejected Jesus and his proclamation.[169] They love father and mother more than Jesus (10.37) and have chosen death instead of the life of the kingdom. 'Let the living dead who are in the world bury those dead in the body' (John Climacus, *Scal.* 2).

Because Jesus' words about leaving burial for the dead are so scandalous, many scholars have refused to take them at face value. Four different approaches have been adopted. (i) Mistranslation of the Aramaic or textual corruption. According to McNeile, p. 110, the Greek may obscure an Aramaic proverb meaning 'Let the dead past bury its dead'. Perles (v), who was followed by Abrahams, *Studies* 2, pp. 183–4, proposed this original: 'Leave the dead to their undertaker' (cf. Ezek 39.15; criticism in SB 1, p. 489). K. Kohler (n. 164) suggested this: 'Leave it to the men of the town (*mĕtê hāʿîr*) that is, the burial society to bury the dead, and follow me'. Black, p. 208, claimed it 'very probable' that Jesus said: 'Follow me and let the undecided bury their dead'. G. Schwarz (v) has reconstructed this original: 'Leave the dead to the grave diggers'. In the opinion of L. Herrmann (v), Mt 8.22 was once about 'young men' burying the dead. Instead of νεκρούς we should read νεαρούς (cf. Acts 5.6, 10). (ii) Misunderstood idiom. H. G. Howard (v) and W. J. Davies and C. S. S. Ellison (v) have called attention to the fact that in some places today in the middle east 'I must stay and bury my father' would be understood as expressing the duty of caring for one's aged parents until they are dead. (iii) Extenuating circumstances. According to Bengel, *ad loc.*, the man had brothers who could take care of the job. According to Plummer, pp. 129–30, the father had not yet died and the son was asking to stay on until he did[170]—which could have been an indefinite period of time. According to Jeremias, *Theology*, p. 132, the disciple was asking to complete his father's burial by mourning for the customary seven days.[171] According to F. Hauck, Jesus was probably calling the man away from arguments over the inheritance.[172] Finally, according to E. M. Meyers, Jesus' harsh statement may 'refer to second burial which could have seemed a rather excessive display of piety.'[173] (iv) Banks,

---

[167] Cf. Manson, *Sayings*, p. 73; Beare, p. 214; Klemm (v).

[168] Cf. Philo, *Fug.* 56; Lk 15.24, 32; Jn 3.14; Eph 2.1; 1 Tim 5.6; Rev 3.1; Jos. Asen. 20.7; Ignatius, *Phil.* 6.1; Sextus, *Sent.* 175; Gos. Phil. 52.6–15; *b. Ber.* 18b ('the wicked who in their lifetime are called dead'), 63b; *b. Ned.* 64b.

[169] Cf. already Irenaeus, *Adv. haer.* 5.9.1; Clement of Alexandria, *Paed.* 3.11.

[170] Cf. the formulation in Jerome, *Ep.* 14.2: 'wait a little for us to die, and then bury us'.

[171] Cf. Gen 50.10; 2 Sam 31.13; Ecclus 22.12; Jos. Asen. 10.17.

[172] Hauck, *Das Evangelium des Lukas*, Leipzig, 1934, p. 137.

[173] Meyers, *Jewish Ossuaries: Reburial and Rebirth*, Rome, 1971, p. 54, n. 31.

p. 97, considers the words 'purely proverbial' and thus without literal application.

It is common to affirm that all of the preceding conjectures are attempts to avoid the obvious, that they inevitably convert a dramatic and memorable imperative into a palatable, pedestrian utterance, and that it is prudent rather to accept the text as it stands, without in any way weakening it. We concur, and do not endorse any of the proposals just listed. The saying as uttered by Jesus was no doubt shocking and scandalous. There is no way around that. At the same time, we add that 8.21f. is a very brief, stylized narrative. Thus we have no real knowledge of the *immediate* circumstances in which Jesus spoke. One would, for example, very much like to know why the disciple is out in public and listening to Jesus if his father has just died and is about to be interred. (Presumably, the burial took place the day of death; cf. Deut 21.23; Acts 5.5–6, 10.) But this and other questions remain unanswered—which is one reason why it would be unwise to base generalizations about Jesus' attitude towards burial or his respect for the dead (or lack thereof) on an interpretation of 8.22.[174] Certainly it seems improbable that Jesus' attitude was that expressed by Heraclitus, frag. 85: 'Corpses are more worthless than excrement'. Such denigration of the physical body is not likely to have coexisted with hope for the resurrection of the dead (cf. 22.23–33 par.)

Hengel, *Leader*, p. 8, labels 8.22 an attack on the respect for parents demanded by the decalogue. We think this probably goes too far. The verse is not solid evidence of indifference towards the Mosaic law. In Jer 16 the word of the Lord comes to the prophet and tells him not to take a wife, not to enter the house of mourning or lament, and not to go into the house of feasting (16.1–9). And in Ezekiel 24 the word of the Lord instructs Ezekiel, the day before his wife dies, not to mourn for the dead or to eat the bread of mourners. In both cases the prophets transgress custom in order to proclaim through unusual actions the coming judgement of God. When the hour of crisis comes, God communicates through a dramatic and unforgettable flouting of custom, a symbolic action which, because it is outrageous, cannot be ignored (cf. Mk 11.13–14). We do not think of Jeremiah or Ezekiel as setting themselves against Moses. Why then Jesus? Mt 8.22 tells us much more about Jesus' prophetic consciousness than about his understanding of the Mosaic law. And this we think Matthew understood (see below). Compare *Sipre* on Deut 18.15: 'Even though he bid thee transgresses one of the commandments ordained in the Torah, as did Elijah on Mount Carmel, yet according to the need of the hour listen to him' (cf. *b. Yeb.* 90b; *b. Menaḥ.* 99b). Even if Jesus was perceived as asking a man not to honour his father, those who

---

[174] The canonical gospels notably continue to view burial as an act of lovingkindness (27.57–61). So also the early church; cf. 4 Ezra 2.23; Aristides, *Apol.* 15; Jerome, *Ep.* 22.3 (although note Acts Pet 40, citing Mt 8.22). Because Mt 8.22 reflects only a concrete moment and does not contain general or normative teaching on Christian burial, Augustine, in his treatise on the subject, *De cura pro mortuis gerenda*, was justified in not discussing the verse (he nowhere even alludes to it).

accepted Jesus' status as a true prophet would never have concluded from this alone that he was an antinomian.

Several additional points may be made in this regard. (i) One can detect in the synoptic tradition a tendency to tone down sayings that might be seen as undermining the authority of the Torah. Thus Luke or an editor of Q found Lk 16.16 ('The law and the prophets were until John') potentially problematic and so added v. 17: 'But it is easier for heaven and earth to pass away than for one dot of the law to become void'. Similarly, Matthew was moved to drop Mk 7.19c ('He declared all foods clean'). Yet neither Matthew nor Luke was sufficiently troubled by Mt 8.22 = Lk 9.60 so as to leave it out or to modify it in any significant way. (ii) Jesus does not prohibit the burial of the dead father. He simply asserts that the disciple should leave it to others.[175] (iii) Lev 21.11 forbids the high priest to bury his parents, and Num 6.6 issues the same prohibition for Nazirites. These OT injunctions may not have been strictly observed in the time of Jesus,[176] and one certainly hesitates to urge that Jesus spoke Mt 8.22 with Lev 21 or Num 6 in mind. Still the OT does supply precedent for exempting, for religious reasons, certain important people from the duty of burying one's parents. Jesus and Matthew will have known this (cf. Tertullian, *Adv. Marc.* 4.23.10–11).

(iv) *Concluding Observations*

On 8.1–15—

(1) Jesus heals a leper, a Gentile, a woman with fever. He does not heal a priest, a Pharisee, or a Sadducee. Why not? It cannot be because there is no love for the enemy. 5.38–48 excludes that. The answer is instead this. Jesus consciously sides with those without status and power in traditional Jewish society. He aids not those at the top but those on the bottom. Implicit in our gospel, yet still unmistakable, is a dissatisfaction with the world as it is. The Christian Lord is not at home in a place where God's will is not done as it is in heaven. Things have gone awry and need to be righted (cf. 1, p. 283). By showering his compassion on the unfortunate and downtrodden, Jesus rejects the status quo. His eschatological orientation is accordingly understandable. The evils of the present move one to look to God's future.

(2) In 8.1–15, as throughout Matthew, Jesus 'heals' (8.8, 13; 15.28) and 'saves' (8.25; 9.21f.; 14.30) the sick. But both words (σῴζω, ἰάομαι) can bear figurative or more comprehensive sense (cf. 1.21; 13.15 v. 1.; Jn 12.40; etc.). This broader usage

---

[175] Cf. Chrysostom, *Hom. on Mt* 27.6; Zahn, pp. 348–9.

[176] See Hengel, *Leader*, pp. 10–11, citing *Sipra* on Lev 21.11; *b. Zeb.* 100a; and SB 1, pp. 488–9.

encourages one to interpret Matthew's healing stories, as parables, symbols of Christian behaviour and hope.[177] On the one hand, the narratives supply models for imitation. The believer should, like the centurion and the others, approach Jesus, ask for help, and have faith. On the other hand, the promise of reward is there too: faith will grasp what it gropes for, for Jesus the merciful Lord will respond to those who come to him—just as he raised up Peter's mother-in-law. In short, the healing narratives illustrate 7.7: ask and it will be given to you.

On 8.16–22—

(1) Jesus 'cast out spirits with a word'. Even though Matthew distinguishes between word and deed, and even though this distinction accounts for the different sorts of material gathered in chapters 5–7 and 8–9, the text strives to hold together word and deed. In Mt 8–9 Jesus 'does the word' (Philo, *Migr. Abr.* 23.130). Hence throughout the Gospel the correlation between Jesus' actions and God's will is no less perfect than that between God's will and Jesus' words. This is why, in Gerhardsson's words, 'the teaching is healing and the healing is teaching' (*Acts*, p. 46).

(2) The quotation in 8.17 (from Isa 53.4) serves notice that Jesus' ministry fulfils the oracles of Deutero-Isaiah. This was already hinted at in 3.17 and in 5.3–12, and it will become even clearer in 11.2–6 and 12.18–21. By drawing so much attention to Jesus' rôle as the Servant, Matthew lends balance to his christological portrait. One could come away from the First Gospel with an image of Jesus as the fearful, majestic, transcendent Son of man who will return to judge the world (cf. 16.27; 24.30; etc.). But the allusions to and quotations from Isaiah show Jesus as a more sympathetic, understanding figure. He knows sorrow and is acquainted with grief. He is the Servant who preaches to the poor and does not break a bruised reed.

(3) The compassion present in 8.17 ('he bore our diseases') is strikingly juxtaposed with 8.18–22, where Jesus is a harsh master. The scribe is not welcomed by the Son of man, and the disciple is told to let the dead bury their own dead. In this way Matthew informs us that Jesus' compassion is not sentimental. The merciful servant issues excruciating orders. The kindly saviour is the Lord who asks much. Jesus freely dispenses grace, but he is not to be presumed upon. Love gives and demands in equal measure.

[177] Cf. J. P. Heil, 'Significant Aspects of the Healing Miracles in Matthew', *CBQ* 41 (1979), pp. 274–87.

(v) *Bibliography*

D. C. Allison, 'Jesus and Moses (Mt 5:1–2)', *ExpT* 98 (1987), pp. 203–5.

idem, 'Who will come from East and West? Observations on Matt 8.11–12/Luke 13.28–29', *IBS* 11 (1989), pp. 158–70.

Beasley-Murray, pp. 169–74.

M. Black, 'Let the Dead Bury their Dead', *ExpT* 61 (1950), pp. 219–20.

M.-E. Boismard, 'La guérison du lépreux (Mc 1.40–5 et par.)', *Salmanticensis* 28 (1981), pp. 283–91.

M. Casey, 'The Jackals and the Son of Man', *JSNT* 23 (1985), pp. 3–22.

C. H. Cave, 'The Leper: Mark 1.40–5', *NTS* 25 (1979), pp. 245–50.

Chilton, *Strength*, pp. 179–201.

Crossan, *Aphorisms*, pp. 237–44.

W. J. Davies and C. S. S. Ellison, 'Was his Father lying Dead at Home?', *ExpT* 62 (1950–1), p. 92.

J. D. M. Derrett, 'Law in the New Testament: The Syro-Phoenician Woman and the Centurion of Capernaum', *NovT* 15 (1973), pp. 161–86.

idem, 'Two "Harsh" Sayings of Christ Explained', *DR* 103 (1985), pp. 218–29.

T. M. Donn, 'Let the dead bury their dead,' *ExpT* 61 (1950), p. 384.

J. Dupont, '"Beaucoup viendront du levant et du couchant . . ." (Matthieu 8.11–12; Luc 13.28–9)', *Sciences ecclesiastiques* 19 (1967), pp. 153–67.

J. K. Elliott, 'The Healing of the Leper in the Synoptic Parallels', *TZ* 34 (1978), pp. 175–6.

A. Fossion, 'From the Bible Text to the Homily. Cure of a Leper (Mk 1.40–5)', *LumVie* 35 (1980), pp. 279–90.

R. T. France, 'Exegesis in Practice: Two Samples', in *New Testament Interpretation*, ed. I. H. Marshall, Grand Rapids, 1977, pp. 253–64.

M. Frost, 'I also am a man under authority', *ExpT* 45 (1934), pp. 477–78.

A. Fuchs, 'Entwicklungsgeschichtliche Studie zu Mk 1.29–31 par Mt 8.14–15 par Lk 4.38–9', *SNTU* 6 (1981), pp. 21–76.

A. George, 'Guérison de l'esclave d'un centurion: Lc 7.1–10', *AsSeign* 40 (1972), pp. 66–77.

O. Glombitza, 'Die christologische Aussage des Lukas in seiner Gestaltung der drei Nachfolgeworte Lukas IX 57–62', *NovT* 13 (1971), pp. 14–23.

W. Grimm, 'Zum Hintergrund von Mt 8.11f./Lk 13.28f.', *BZ* 16 (1972), pp. 255–6.

E. Haenchen, 'Johanneische Probleme', *ZTK* 56 (1959), pp. 23–31.

Held, in *TIM*, pp. 193–7, 213–5.

F. Helmer, 'Die Heilung eines Aussätzigen (Mk 1.40–5)', *Erbe und Auftrag* 55 (1982), pp. 310–3.

Hendrickx, *Miracle Stories*, pp. 63–103.

Hengel, *Leader*.

L. Herrmann, 'Correction du *k* en *a* dans une phrase de Jésus', *Revue des Études Anciennes* 83 (1981), p. 283.

Hoffmann, *Logienquelle*, pp. 182–7.

S. H. Hooke, 'Jesus and the Centurion: Matthew viii. 5–10', *ExpT* 69 (1957), pp. 79–80.

H. G. Howard, 'Was his Father lying Dead at Home?', *ExpT* 61 (1950), pp. 350–1.

Jeremias, *Promise*, pp. 28–35, 55–73.

Kertelge, *Wunder*, pp. 60–75.

J. D. Kingsbury, 'On Following Jesus: the "Eager" Scribe and "Reluctant" Disciple (Matthew 8.18–22)', *NTS* 34 (1988), pp. 45–59.

H. G. Klemm, 'Das Wort von der Selbstbestattung der Toten', *NTS* 16 (1969), pp. 60–75.

P. Lamarche, 'La guérison de la belle-mère de Pierre et le genre littéraire des évangiles', *NRT* 87 (1965), pp. 515–26.

X. Léon-Dufour, 'La guérison de la belle-mère de Simon-Pierre', *EstB* 24 (1965), pp. 193–216; reprinted in *Études*, pp. 123–48.

van der Loos, pp. 530–5.

S. Luria, 'Zur Quelle von Mt 8.19', *ZNW* 25 (1926), pp. 282–6.

R. A. Martin, 'The Pericope of the Healing of the "Centurion's" Servant/Son', in *Unity and Diversity in New Testament Theology*, ed. R. A. Guelich, Grand Rapids, Michigan, 1978, pp. 14–22.

C. Masson, 'La guérison du lépreux (Marc 1,40–5)', in *Vers les sources d'eau vive*, Lausanne, 1961, pp. 11–19.

J. Mouson, 'Die sanatione pueri centurionis (Mt viii,5–13)', *Collectanea mechliniensia* 29 (1959), pp. 633–6.

F. Neirynck, 'Papyrus Egerton 2 and the Healing of the Leper', *ETL* 61 (1985), pp. 153–60.

A. Paul, 'La guérison d'un lépreux. Approche d'un récit de Marc (1.40–5)', *NRT* 92 (1970), pp. 692–704.

F. Perles, 'Zwei Übersetzungsfehler im Text der Evangelien', *ZNW* 19 (1919), p. 96.

idem, 'Noch einmal Mt 8.22', *ZNW* 25 (1926), pp. 286–7.

R. Pesch, 'Die Heilung der Schwiegermutter des Simon-Petrus', in *Neuere Exegesis—Verlust oder Gewinn?*, Freiburg, 1968, pp. 143–75.

J. J. Pilch, 'Biblical Leprosy and Body Symbolism', *BTB* 11 (1981), pp. 108–13.

Sanders, *Jesus*, pp. 252–55.

Schenke, *Wundererzählungen*, pp. 109–45.

Schlosser 2, pp. 603–69.

R. Schnackenburg, 'Zur Traditionsgeschichte von Joh 4.46–54', *BZ* 8 (1964), pp. 58–88.

Schnider and Stenger, pp. 54–88.

Schulz, *Q*, pp. 236–46, 323–30.

B. Schwank, 'Dort wird Heulen und Zähneknirschen sein', *BZ* 16, (1972), pp. 121–2.

G. Schwarz, "Αφες τοὺς νεκροὺς θάψαι τοὺς ἑαυτῶν νεκρούς', *ZNW* 72 (1981), pp. 272–6.

M. H. Smith, 'No Place for a Son of Man', *Forum* 4/4 (1988), pp. 83–107.

H. F. D. Sparks, 'The Centurion's παῖς', *JTS* 42 (1941), pp. 179–80.

Strauss, pp. 462–71.

A. Strobel, 'Textgeschichtliches zum Thomas-Logion 86 (Mt 8.20/Luk 9.58)', *VC* 17 (1963), pp. 211–24.

G. B. Telford, 'Mark 1.40–5', *Int.* 36 (1982), pp. 54–8.

Wanke, *Bezugs*, pp. 40–4.

U. Wegner, *Der Hauptmann von Kafarnaum*, WUNT 2/14, Tübingen, 1985.

E. Wendling, 'Synoptische Studien: II. Der Hauptmann von Kapernaum', *ZNW* 9 (1908), pp. 96–109.

D. Zeller, 'Die Heilung der Aussätzigen (Mk 1.40–5)', *TTZ* 93 (1984), pp. 138–46.

idem, 'Das Logion Mt 8.11f./Lk 13.28f. und das Motiv der "Völkerwallfahrt"', *BZ* 15 (1971), pp. 222–37; 16 (1972), pp. 84–93.

Zumstein, pp. 220–5.

G. Zuntz, 'The "Centurion" of Capernaum and his Authority (Matth. viii.5–13)', *HTS* 46 (1945), pp. 183–90.

EXCURSUS VII

MIRACLES AND THE HISTORICAL JESUS

There are at least four different ways one might explain or account for the miracle stories of the synoptic gospels. First, one could accept the claim of traditional Christian theology and simply take many or most of them at face value: Jesus did extraordinary things because he was the supernatural figure the church has made him out to be. Secondly, one could argue that, as miracles (defined as the impossible) just do not happen, the stories in the gospels must be the product of religious imagination or theological fancy, and that the history in them is of homeopathic proportions (cf. the work of D. F. Strauss). Thirdly, one might contend that although Jesus carried on a healing ministry, its success need not be put down to supernatural powers at work in him. The ability of the human mind to heal bodily infirmities is extraordinary,[1] so perhaps it was the power of suggestion which worked the wonders.[2] Finally, if one believed that people do sometimes exhibit such controversial powers as telepathy, clairvoyance, or telekinesis, it would be quite possible to explain many of Jesus' miracles as due to his command of certain 'psychic' or 'paranormal' abilities.

It is outside the scope of this commentary to undertake the difficult task of evaluating the arguments which could be mustered for or against the four positions just introduced. There is, however, one issue upon which we do wish to render a verdict, to wit: the presence of a miraculous element in a synoptic pericope is no good reason for considering that pericope late and unhistorical. Or, to put it

---

[1] Lit.: B. O'Regan, *Healing, Remission and Miracle Cures*, Washington, D.C., 1987; E. Rossi, *The Psychobiology of Mind Body Healing*, New York, 1986; L. White, B. Tursky, and G. Schwartz, eds., *Placebo*, New York, 1985.

[2] Such an approach, however, will not explain the so-called nature miracles, those in which Jesus multiplies food, walks on the water, etc.

differently, if a synoptic text recounts an extraordinary occurrence, that in itself has little bearing on whether that text might not rest upon some historical event. Whether or not one thinks that strange things happen, it cannot be denied that many people have thought they do. Moreover, individuals have again and again purported to be eye-witnesses of seemingly supernatural phenomena.[3] To illustrate: the apostle Paul claimed to speak in tongues (1 Cor 14.8), to have out-of-body experiences (2 Cor 12.1–10), and to have done among the Corinthians 'signs and wonders and mighty works' (2 Cor 12.12). Again, Josephus could write: 'I have seen a certain Eleazar, a countryman of mine, in the presence of Vespasian, his sons, tribunes and a number of other soldiers, free men possessed by demons' (*Ant.* 8.46). In like manner, Sulpicius Severus was a personal friend of Bishop Martin of Tours, about whom he composed a famous life which is filled with remarkable miracle stories; and in *De civ. dei* 22.8, Augustine recounts a whole list of miracles performed during his lifetime, some of which he witnessed personally, many of which he learned of from eye-witnesses. One also recalls the miracles which Gregory of Nyssa, in his *Vita Sanctae Macrinae*, spoke of with reference to his sister and other family members, as well as the *Historia religiosa* of Theodoret of Cyrrhus, a book filled with miracle-working monks known to the author. It is important to recognize that it is not just the ancients who purport to have seen miracles. In the December 24–31, 1983 issue of the *British Medical Journal* (vol. 287, pp. 1927–33), Dr. Rex Gardner has gathered together the stories of several modern physicians concerning the inexplicable healings of patients who had been prayed for by others. Also of great interest are the numerous tales about the Brazilian priest Padre Pio[4] as well as the experiences of numerous educated Westerners who have visited the Indian guru Sai Baba, whose countless miracles are so like those recorded in the NT: many have come back believers.[5] One could go on in this vein indefinitely. Faith healers and miracles are still with us. They cannot be dismissed as the product of antique naïveté.

For our immediate purposes, which are strictly historical, it does not matter at all what explanation(s) one might offer for apparent miracles—God, coincidence, conscious deception, the placebo effect, or little recognized human powers. It also does not matter precisely how one defines a miracle, whether as a statistical rarity (so already Augustine and, in our own time, C. S. Lewis) or rather in terms of the violation of natural law (so Hume).[6] All that counts is the undeniable fact that many people have thought themselves to be witnesses to

[3] Helpful source books include H. Thurston, *The Physical Phenomena of Mysticism*, London, 1952; idem, *Surprising Mystics*, London, 1955; and D. S. Rogo, *Miracles*, Chicago, 1983.

[4] See the Duchess of St. Albans, *Magic of a Mystic: Stories of Padre Pio*, New York, 1983.

[5] See E. Haraldsson, *Modern Miracles; An Investigative Report on Psychic Phenomena associated with Sathya Sai Baba*, New York, 1987.

[6] For an historic overview see C. Brown, *Miracles and the Critical mind*, London 1984.

events resembling those recorded in the NT gospels (including the so-called nature miracles). It follows that if a synoptic pericope recounts a miraculous deed, that *by itself* is not sufficient cause for supposing that pericope to have no foundation in the earliest tradition or even in the life of Jesus. Put simply, there is no reason, whatever one's philosophical or religious disposition, to deny that people could have perceived Jesus doing seemingly miraculous things.

Having, however, reached this conclusion, the historian is still faced by very difficult problems. (i) If miracle stories are not necessarily the product of late, legendary development, that is certainly no reason to accept them as historical. (ii) Even if a particular miracle story is deemed to rest upon some historical event, the question of what really happened is still not answered. There is an area the historian cannot penetrate. (iii) A number of the gospel stories are, on formal grounds, largely constructed of motifs common to Graeco-Roman miracle tales, and many of them in many ways resemble each other as well as stories told about OT heroes,[7] Jewish rabbis,[8] and Hellenistic wonder-workers and magicians.[9] They are, therefore, occasionally insufficiently singular or unique to enable us to evaluate with much confidence the issue of historicity—which is why now and then we have come to no conclusion about the origin of a particular miracle story. Certainly Jesus was, among other things, a successful exorcist and healer (cf. Pesch, *Taten*, pp. 15–28); and, in our estimation, those who knew him believed that they had witnessed truly extraordinary events, miracles which fulfilled OT prophecy and revealed the triumph of the kingdom of God. Moreover, the stories in the canonical gospels in all likelihood give us a fairly good feeling for the kind of things Jesus often did. He did direct demons to leave people. He did stress the need for faith. He did on occasion use healing aids (such as spittle and touch). We even consider it highly probable that he was extraordinarily successful in his extraordinary activities, for (i) his opponents did not deny his powers but rather attributed them to Beelzebul (Mt 12.22–30 par.); (ii) Jesus spoke with unbridled confidence about his abilities (e.g. Mt 12.22–30

---

[7] The OT parallels to NT miracle stories have yet—despite the work of D. F. Strauss—to receive their fair share of attention; see, however, B. L. Blackburn, "'Miracle Working ΘΕΙΟΙ ΑΝΔΡΕΣ" in Hellenism (and Hellenistic Judaism)', in Wenham and Blomberg, pp. 185–218.

[8] Relevant lit. includes: P. Fiebig, *Jüdische Wundergeschichten des neutestamentlichen Zeitalters*, Tübingen, 1911; idem, *Rabbinische Wundergeschichten des neutestamentlichen Zeitalters*, Bonn, 1911; W. S. Green, 'Palestinian Holy Men', *ANRW* II.19.2 (1979), pp. 619–47; Vermes, *Jesus the Jew*, pp. 58–82, 202–13. —A critical sifting of the rabbinic materials leaves very few miracles stories from the pre-70 period; see Neusner 3, p. 86. Cf. also Smith, *Tannaitic Parallels*, pp. 81–3.

[9] See Bultmann, *History*, pp. 209–44; Theissen, *Stories*; Smith, *Magician*.— We cannot here enter into the controverted topic of whether there was an established 'divine man' type which Hellenistic Judaism used to interpret its heroes and which early Christianity used to interpret Jesus—although the tendency of recent research is to doubt this; see esp. C. H. Holladay, *Theios Aner in Hellenistic Judaism*, SBLDS 40, Missoula, 1977, and D. L. Tiede, *The Charismatic Figure as Miracle Worker*, SBLDS 1, Missoula, 1972.

par.; 17.20 par.); and (iii) 'through all antiquity no other man is credited with so many' miracles as Jesus (Smith, *Magician*, p. 109). Still, all this does not help us with individual pericopae, especially when one recalls that great men quickly and, it seems, inevitably stimulate the development of legends. We have no reason to think it was otherwise with Jesus.

So what is the conclusion? It is our considered opinion that one should approach any given synoptic miracle story without prejudging the issue of its genesis. In other words, a miracle story should be evaluated in the same way and with the same methods as other items in the tradition. Does the text harmonize with what we otherwise know of Jesus? Can one detect peculiarly Christian concerns? Is a *Sitz im Leben Jesu* credible? What does a form-critical analysis have to contribute? Is there independent attestation in the Gospel of John or another non-synoptic source? Are there reasons to suspect formulation in a Semitic-speaking environment? These are the sorts of questions scholars ask about the sayings attributed to Jesus as well as about other parts of the tradition. The miracle stories should receive precisely the same treatment.[10]

---

[10] One is naturally inclined to suppose that the so-called nature miracles (e.g. walking on the water, multiplying loaves of bread) should invite more doubt than, let us say, an exorcism story, this because they are not so easily related to the psychological arena. Cf. n. 3. Even here, however, caution is prescribed. The NT itself does not distinguish between nature miracles and miracles worked on human beings. More importantly, as we have observed in the appropriate portions of the commentary, even the nature miracles often have parallels in allegedly first-hand accounts. However this fact be explained, it remains a fact.

XVIII

A SECOND TRIAD OF MIRACLE STORIES
(8.23–9.17)

(i) *Structure*

The first miracle triad (8.1–22) contains three healing stories. This second triad is different. Three diverse types of miracles are represented: a sea rescue (8.23–7), an exorcism (8.28–34), a healing (9.1–8). Following the three miracle stories are two episodes which involve no miracles: the call of Levi and its sequel (9.9–13) and the pericope about fasting (9.14–7). The pattern, three miracle stories + added material, also occurs in 8.1ff. and 9.18ff. See further 1, pp. 67, 102, and Excursus V.

The three miracle stories in 8.23–9.8 are closely related in that each lays emphasis upon the reaction of the onlookers. In 8.23–7 the result of Jesus' miracle is wonder and questioning: who is this? The answer is left open. In the next episode, 8.28–34, the response is negative: the people beg Jesus to leave their region; they cannot abide his presence. Lastly, in 9.1–8, the response is positive: the crowds glorify God. The effect of such disparate reactions to the same man and his work is to suggest that the meaning of a miracle lies in the eye of the beholder. Or, put otherwise, one must have eyes to see and ears to hear. Miracles will not compel unbelief to relinquish its doubt.

(ii) *Sources*

These are the parallels to the material in Mt 8.23–9.17:

	Mark	Luke
8.23–7 (the tempest)	4.35–41	8.22–5
8.28–34 (the demoniacs)	5.1–20	8.26–39
9.1–8 (a healing)	2.1–12	5.17–26
9.9–13 (Levi)	2.13–7	5.27–32
9.14–7 (fasting)	2.18–22	5.33–9

Earlier (1, pp. 101–3) we attempted to explain Matthew's procedure according to the theory of Markan priority. Here we should like to list some of the reasons for supposing that in 8.23–9.17 par. it is Mark, not Matthew, which is the more primitive document.

(1) Matthew's text is consistently shorter than Mark's, so if the author of the Second Gospel used the First Gospel he must be viewed as a very creative writer who enjoyed expanding the tradition. There is no insuperable difficulty in this—until, that is, one considers the types of additions with which one would have to credit Mark. Assuming the Griesbach hypothesis, Mark has added, among other things, these items: 'and other boats were with him' (4.36); 'in the stern, on the cushion' (4.38); 'and no one could bind him any more, even with a chain; for he had often been bound with fetters and chains, but the chains he wrenched apart, and the fetters he broke in pieces; and no one had the strength to subdue him. Night and day among the tombs and on the mountains he was always crying out, and bruising himself with stones. And when he saw Jesus from afar, he ran and worshipped him' (5.3–6; parts of this are paralleled in Lk 8.29); 'numbering about two thousand' (5.13); 'And many were gathered together, so that there was no longer room for them, not even about the door' (2.2); 'were sitting there' (2.6); 'in his spirit' (2.8); 'take up your pallet' (2.9); 'He went out again beside the sea; and all the crowd gathered around him, and he taught them' (2.13); 'for there were many who followed him' (2.15); 'Now John's disciples and the Pharisees were fasting' (2.18). If all these lines and phrases are to be regarded as Markan additions, the Second Evangelist must be guilty of adding 'novelistic' elements at every turn. Such uncontrolled expansion of the tradition is hard to imagine. This is especially true when the alleged expansions do not appear to reflect any consistent christological or ecclesiastical interests.

(2) On the Griesbach hypothesis Mark has omitted an extremely high percentage of the words which, on the basis of statistics, one naturally thinks of as Matthean, words such as μαθητής* (8.23, 25), σεισμός* (8.24), προσέρχομαι* (8.25; 9.14), ἐγείρω* (8.25), ὀλιγό-πιστος* (8.26), δύο* (8.28), ἰδού (8.32; 9.2, 3, 10), ὅπως* (8.34), μεταβαίνω* (8.34), πονηρός* (9.4), δίδωμι + ἐξουσία (9.8), ἀνάκειμαι (9.10), μανθάνω (9.13), τότε* (9.14), βάλλω* (9.17). How is this to be explained?

(3) The Christology of Mt 8.23–9.17 is consistently more circumspect than that of Mk 2.1–22; 4.35–5.20. In Mark the disciples take Jesus with them (4.36). In Matthew the disciples follow Jesus (8.23). In Mark the disciples ask a question that can be understood as a reproach: 'Teacher, do you not care if we perish?' (4.38). In Matthew the disciples say, 'Lord, save, we perish' (8.25). In Mark Jesus' command to a demon to come out is not immediately obeyed but leads to a dialogue between exorcist and demoniac (5.7–13). In Matthew the dialogue comes before the command, and once Jesus says 'Go', the demoniacs go (5.29–32).

(4) If one presupposes Markan priority, then almost all of Matthew's alterations of Mark can be attributed to three factors—christological interests, a desire to abbreviate, and stylistic improvements.

(5) There are three inconcinnities in Matthew's text which are readily explained as due to over-zealous abbreviation of Mark. (a) In 8.26 Jesus rebukes the wind, but the wind has not previously been mentioned (contrast Mk 4.37). (b) In Mt 9.2 Jesus sees the faith of those who have brought the paralytic, but only in Mk 2.2 (omitted by Matthew)

do we learn about the men's act of faith (uncovering the roof and lowering the paralytic). (c) In Mt 9.8 the crowd marvels, but the crowd has not heretofore been introduced (contrast Mk 2.2).

Against the five points just made, the Griesbach hypothesis can call upon the minor agreements of Matthew and Luke against Mark, especially those in Mt 9.1–8 par. (see Neirynck (v) and Fitzmyer, *Luke* 1, pp. 578, 586, 595). We have, however, discussed most of these in the commentary proper and found them to be of doubtful significance; see for example on 8.27; 9.2 and 17.

(iii) *Exegesis*

JESUS STILLS THE STORM (8.23–7)

Mt 8.23–7(28), which is Matthew's version of Mk 4.35–41 = Lk 8.22–5, should perhaps be analysed as exhibiting a chiastic structure:

8.23a	Jesus boards
8.23b	the disciples follow
8.24a-b	a storm arises
8.24c	Jesus is sleeping
8.25	the disciples address Jesus
8.26a	Jesus addresses the disciples
8.26b	Jesus arises and rebukes the storm
8.26c	the storm calms
8.27	the disciples are amazed
(8.28	Jesus disembarks)

Acceptance of this scheme would put the conversation between Jesus and his disciples at the centre of the tale (cf. Grundmann, p. 259)

G. Bornkamm, in a very influential article, argued that in Matthew the stilling of the storm is 'a kerygmatic paradigm of the danger and glory of discipleship' ((v), p. 57; cf. the exegesis of Held, in *TIM*, pp. 200–4). There is much to support such a view. (i) The verb, ἀκολουθεῖν, links 8.23–7 with 8.19–22: in both pericopae disciples follow or are called to follow their master. One suspects that the figurative use of the verb in the former paragraph has coloured the usage in the second. (ii) Already in the OT the subduing of the raging flood by Yahweh illustrates the experience of Israel: Ps 29.3; 65.7; 89.9; 93.4; 107.25–32; 124.4–5 (cf. 1QH 3.6; 7.4–5; T. Naph. 6); and the sea and its storms can symbolize chaos or the world and its difficulties (Ps 65.5; 69.1–2; Isa 43.2; 57.20; Dan 7.2–3; cf. Rev 13.1). Note also Philo, *Migr. Abr.* 148: 'Some men are irresolute ... inclining to either side like a boat tossed by winds from opposite quarters'. (iii) In 6.30; 14.31; and 16.8, ὀλιγόπιστος (which also occurs in 8.26) is used to describe the imperfect faith of one who truly believes in Jesus. It is, therefore, a word associated with discipleship; see further on 6.30 and 8.10. (iv) 'And behold, there was a great σεισμός in the sea' is a bit unusual. The Greek word means 'earthquake', and it does not appear in either Mark's or Luke's version of the stilling of the storm. σεισμός does, however, appear in passages depicting the trials of the end times (e.g. 24.7; Mk 13.8; Lk 21.11; Rev 6.12; etc.); and in the Qumran *Hôdāyôt* the image of the storm-tossed ship metaphorically describes the eschatological oppression of the righteous (1QH 3.6, 12–18; 6.22–25; 7.4–5). Thus σεισμός is particularly appropriate for a description of the trials suffered by believers (cf. 7.24–7). (v) The disciples address Jesus as 'Lord' (8.25; contrast Mk 4.38; Lk 8.24). This would encourage the Christian reader to identify with those in the boat. (vi) The identification of the boat with the little ship of the church is found in patristic exegesis (e.g. Tertullian, *De bapt.* 12: 'that little ship presented a figure of the church, in that she is disquieted in the sea, that is in the world, by the waves, that is, by persecutions and temptations . . .').[1]

Despite the previous points, J. P. Heil (v) has disputed Bornkamm's interpretation. In Heil's judgement, Mt 8.23–7 is not simply a story of discipleship, or of the disciples' relationship to Jesus. It is rather a 'sea-rescue epiphany' whose main purpose is to reveal to the disciples that Jesus has divine power to save them from distress (cf. Feiler (v)). 8.23–7 raises a christological question: What sort of man is this, that even the winds and sea obey him? The answer will come in 14.22–32, the sea-walking epiphany: 'Truly you are the Son of God'.

There can be no doubt that Heil has a contribution to make. Bornkamm has almost entirely overlooked the christological elements in 8.23–7. This makes for a one-sided approach. At the same time, Heil has probably gone too far in the other direction. While he concedes that 'the storm-stilling story concerns the disciples' and that 'the readers of Matthew can identify with this unique experience of the disciples' ((v), p. 97), he makes too little of these facts. He also reads too much into 8.27, where the disciples wonder about the identity of Jesus. Heil affirms that the question of 8.27 is not answered until several chapters later, so 'we are left hanging in suspense for an answer to the question of 8.27' (ibid., p. 91). This, however, confuses the knowledge of the

[1] For the church as a boat see Hippolytus, *Antichr.* 59; Apost. Const. 2.57. Lit.: F. J. Dölger, *Sol Salutis*, 2nd ed., Münster, 1925, pp. 272–87; K. Goldammer, 'Navis Ecclesiae', *ZNW* 40 (1941), pp. 76–86; E. Peterson, 'Das Schiff als Symbol der Kirche', *TZ* 6 (1950), pp. 77–9; K. Goldammer, 'Das Schiff der Kirche', *TZ* 6 (1950), pp. 232–7; J. Daniélou, *Primitive Christian Symbols* (trans. of *Les Symbols chrétiens primitifs*, 1961), Baltimore, 1964, pp. 58–70. For the world as a ship see Philostratus, *VA* 3.35. Related is the common likening of the church to Noah's ark, a simile with roots in 1 Pet 3.20–2 and which came in time to illustrate the maxim, *extra ecclesiam nulla salus*.

reader with the knowledge of the disciples. The reader, having already read chapters 1–4, knows that Jesus is God's Son (1.18–25; 2.15; 3.17; 4.1–11). It is the disciples, not the readers, who do not yet understand who Jesus really is. So while there remains a christological question—and therefore suspense—for the disciples, the readers are no longer asking the christological question. So for the implied readers the meaning of 8.23–7 cannot be the disciples' query. Rather, knowing full well all about Jesus' identity, they must ask themselves how they will fare when their ship is tossed about (cf. Chrysostom, *Hom. on Mt.* 28.1). Do they trust their Lord in the storms of life, or are they, despite the revelation made known to them, of little faith?

Mt 8.23–7, it would appear, draws upon the story of Jonah. Cope (v) has listed these parallels. Both stories involve

1. Departure by boat
2. A violent storm at sea
3. A sleeping main character
4. Badly frightened sailors
5. A miraculous stilling related to the main character
6. A marvelling response by the sailors

The verbal parallels between Jonah and the gospel accounts indicate that the synoptic evangelists were probably aware of the close relationship (cf. Mt 8.24 with MT Jon 1.4; Mk 4.41 with LXX Jon 1.16; Lk 8.22–23 with LXX Jon 1.3–4). Moreover, it seems likely that, when our story was first told, its intent was to show that 'a greater than Jonah is here' (Mt 12.41): Jesus is more than a prophet (cf. 8.27) because in rebuking the roaring waves he exercises the power of Yahweh himself (cf. Ps 65.7; 89.8–9; 93.3–4; 106.8–9; 107.23–32; Isa 51.9–10; 2 Macc 9.8; 4Q381; it is striking that, unlike Jonah, Jesus does not pray to God but directly addresses the storm). For his part the First Evangelist has not really developed the parallels between Jesus and Jonah (cf. Cope (v)). That is, in this connexion he has not much added to the tradition.[2]

In addition to the story of Jonah, other parallels to the nature miracle in Mt 8.23–27 par. exist. See for instance *y. Ber.* 13b; Herodotus 7.191; Virgil, *Aeneid* 4.553–83 (where Aeneas sleeps); Pliny, *N. H.* 37.142, 155; Acts 27; Plutarch, *Caesar 38*; Aelius Aristides, *Or.* 42.10; 45.29, 33; Philostratus, *VA* 4.13 (people wished to travel by boat with Apollonius because he had the power to calm storms); Clement of Alexandria, *Strom.* 6.3; Iamblichus, *Vit. Pyth.* 135 (Pythagoras 'calmed rivers and seas so that his companions might cross over easily . . .'); *ARN* 3; *b. B. Meṣ.* 59b.[3]

---

[2] Contrast Gundry, *Commentary*, p. 155: 'The similarity of Matthew's peculiar description of the storm with the phraseology of Jonah 1.4 . . . combines with his distinctive comparison between Jonah's experience and Jesus' rising from the dead (12.40) to confirm the symbolism of the great shaking as a preview of the risen Jesus' authority' (cf. 28.2).

[3] For additional parallels see Bultmann, *History*, pp. 237–8 (who favours a Palestinian origin, p. 240); Deissmann, *Light*, pp. 179–80; and Theissen, *Stories*, pp. 99–103 (he classifies Mt 8.23–7 as a 'rescue miracle').

23. καὶ ἐμβάντι αὐτῷ εἰς πλοῖον.⁴ Compare Mk 4.36a: 'And leaving the crowd, they took him with them as he was in the boat'. Matthew has shortened Mark and made the scene less picturesque. He has also made two other changes. First, whereas in Mark Jesus is already in the boat (cf. 4.1), in Matthew he has to embark (cf. Lk 8.22). Secondly, whereas in Mark the disciples 'take' Jesus with them, in Matthew the disciples, as the next verse will inform us, 'follow' the master (the essence of true discipleship). All the initiative lies with Jesus.

Bengel, *Gnomon, ad loc.*, wrote: 'Jesus had an itinerant school: and in that school his disciples were much more solidly instructed than if they had dwelt under the roof of a single college, without any anxiety or trial'.

ἠκολούθησαν αὐτῷ οἱ μαθηταὶ αὐτοῦ. This replaces the enigmatic Mk 4.36b: 'and other boats were with him'—something Luke also omits.⁵ The Matthean addition stresses two themes, following Jesus (ἠκολούθησαν) and discipleship (μαθηταί), both subjects of the previous pericope (8.19–22). This is one indication of our evangelist's desire to make 8.23–7 bear on the issue of Christian discipleship.

24. καὶ ἰδοὺ σεισμὸς μέγας ἐγένετο ἐν τῇ θαλάσσῃ. Compare 28.2. Mk 4.37 reads: 'and there arose a great storm of wind, and the waves beat against the boat'. Matthew has (i) shortened Mark, (ii) used language more readily transferred to human existence (see p. 69), (iii) perhaps assimilated the line to Jon 1.4⁶ and (iv) substituted favourite vocabulary: καὶ ἰδού (see on 1.20 and 3.16) and σεισμός*⁷.

ὥστε τὸ πλοῖον καλύπτεσθαι ὑπὸ τῶν κυμάτων. Compare Exod 15.10; Ps 78.53; Jer 51.42; T. Naph. 6.5. Mk 4.37 has: 'And the waves beat into the boat, so that the boat was already filling'. Matthew's clause has the same structure as 8.24a: subject + verb + prepositional phrase. For figurative uses of 'wave(s)' see MT Isa 57.20; Wisd 14.1; 1QH 2.12–3, 27–8; 6.23; Jude 13. We are to imagine the boat sunk⁸ in a great trough.

---

⁴ το is added before πλοιον in ℵ*·² LW Θ Maj, followed by NA²⁶. It is omitted by HG on the authority of ℵ¹ B C f¹·¹³ 33 565 892 *pc*. The article may mark assimilation either to Mk 4.36 or 5.18.

⁵ Did the pre-Markan tradition record the sinking of the other boats? For suggestions as to the meaning of 'and other boats were with him' see Pesch 1, p. 270.

⁶ MT: *wayĕhî sa'ar – gādôl bayyām.* LXX: καὶ ἐγένετο κλύδων μέγας ἐν τῇ θαλάσσῃ.

⁷ With μέγας: LXX Jer 10.22; Ezek 3.12; 38.19; Mt 28.2. For σεισμός as a storm in the sea see BAGD, s.v.

⁸ Lit. 'hidden'. καλύπτω: Mt: 2; Mk: 0; Lk: 3. Cf. Exod 15.10. Tertullian, *De bapt.* 12, records the opinion (which he rejects) that Jesus' twelve disciples discharged the duty of Christian baptism when their little boat was immersed by the waves.

αὐτὸς δὲ ἐκάθευδεν. Compare Jon 1.5. Mk 4.38 reads: 'And he was in the stern, sleeping on the pillow'. Matthew abbreviates and omits an irrelevant detail[9] while retaining the allusion to the story of Jonah. Nineham, *Mark*, p. 146, observes that the ability to sleep untroubled is, in the OT, a sign of faith in the protective power of God (Lev 26.6; Job 11.18–9; Ps 3.5; 4.8; Prov 3.23–4). Furthermore, there were moments of disaster or peril when it seemed as though God were asleep, and his people sought to 'wake him up' (Ps 35.23; 44.23–4; 59.4; Isa 51.9).

Is it possible that the ancient motif of the sleeping deity[10] lies behind our story. There are many Ancient Near Eastern texts in which sleep is a symbol of supreme and unchallenged ability: only the one completely in charge can truly sleep in peace (see n. 10). One wonders, therefore, whether B. Batto is not correct: 'The image of the sleeping Jesus is modeled after the sleeping divine king, the sleeping God taking his divine rest. His sleeping indicates not powerlessness but the fullness of absolute rule [cf. Gnilka, *Matthäusevangelium* 1, p. 317]. The power of the demonic kingdom is only apparent, not real, as is evident when Jesus awakes and stills the raging sea, just as ancient tradition required of one possessing divine authority.'[11], [12]

25. This verse records the disciples' plea for help. Are we to recall that at least four of the disciples were fishermen and that they would not have been greatly troubled unless the storm was really out of the ordinary?

καὶ προσελθόντες οἱ μαθηταὶ ἤγειραν αὐτὸν λέγοντες.[13] Compare Mk 4.38: 'And they rouse (διεγείρουσιν) him and say to him'. Matthew's changes are purely stylistic. He likes προσέρχομαι* (see on 4.3), μαθητής*, and ἐγείρω*; and he often prefers to substitute the construction, finite verb + participle, where Mark has finite verb + finite verb (see on 8.3). Note

---

[9] Which might be thought to be at odds with 8.20: the Son of man has nowhere to lay his head.

[10] See on this B. Batto, 'The Sleeping God: An Ancient Near Eastern Motif of Divine Sovereignty', *Bib* 68 (1987), pp. 153–77.

[11] Idem, 'When God sleeps', *BibRev* 3 (1987), p. 23.

[12] Augustine, *Serm.* 31(81).8 well illustrates the typical patristic approach to our story. See also Ambrose, *Hexameron* 4.5(24).

[13] οι μαθηται is printed in HG but not NA[26]. It appears in C²L*f*[13] Maj h arm Eus. It is missing in אB 33[vid] 892 lat sa bo Or. οι μ. αυτου appears in C* W Θ *f*[1] 1424 *al* b g[1] (q) vg[cl] sy mae. Because οι μ. does not appear in the Markan or Lukan parallels its omission may be due to assimilation of the First Gospel to the other gospels.

also the change from Mark's historical present to the aorist tense (cf. Allen, p. xx).[14]

κύριε, σῶσον ἀπολλύμεθα.[15] Compare Jon 1.14: κύριε, μὴ ἀπολώμεθα. In Jonah these words are addressed to God. In Matthew Jesus receives the cry for help. Bonnard, p. 120, suggests that Matthew's words might have a liturgical ring (cf. Beare, p. 215, and recall the κύριε ἐλέησον of the Greek prayer books). Mk 4.38 has this: 'Teacher, do you not care that we perish?' (cf. Jon 1.6). In Matthew 'Lord' (see on 8.6) replaces 'teacher' (see on 8.19), and 'save'[16] (cf. 14.30) replaces 'do you not care that we perish?', an exclamation which might suggest that Jesus is indifferent to the disciples' plight. So the question in Mark has become, in Matthew, a prayer or request for a miracle.

26. Jesus now acts to save. After speaking to the disciples he commands the winds and sea, which dutifully obey him. This reverses the narrative sequence of Mark, where Jesus first rebukes the sea (cf. Luke). The Matthean order is less natural. What is its explanation? In the First Gospel the emphasis is no longer, as in Mark, on the stilling of the storm but rather on the faith of the disciples in a difficult situation.

καὶ λέγει αὐτοῖς. This is from Mk 4.40, with λέγει (historical present for emphasis) for εἶπεν (aorist).

τί δειλοί ἐστε, ὀλιγόπιστοι;[17] Compare 14.31. The disciples came to Jesus and asked for help; they appealed to him as to a guardian angel. Why then are they of 'little faith'? We are probably to see in the exclamation, 'We perish', evidence of anxiety.[18] And anxiety was rebuked in 6.24–34 as evidence of ὀλιγοπιστία. Mk 4.40 has this: τί δειλοί ἐστε οὕτως; οὔπω ἔχετε πίστιν; Matthew has exchanged ὀλιγόπιστος for οὕτως and dropped Mark's second question, Do you not yet have faith? As an explanation for the changes it is sometimes held that Matthew wished to portray the disciples in a better light (cf. Beare, p. 215). This is to put the matter too simply. There is no consistent whitewashing of the disciples in our gospel (see Barth, in *TIM*, pp. 118–21). Furthermore, in the present text the changes *vis-à-vis* Mark have as their explanation this: Matthew cannot conceive of discipleship without faith. He is therefore unable to reproduce

[14] Two of Matthew's changes bring him, whether intentionally or not, closer to the text of Jonah. προσέρχομαι is used in LXX Jon 1.4, and ἤγειραν recalls MT Jon 1.6: 'Rise (*qûm*) and call upon your God'.

[15] ημας appears after σωσον in L W Θ 0242ᵛⁱᵈ Maj latt sy Chr Eus Or eth. It is missing in ℵ B C *f*¹·¹³ 33 892 *pc* boᵐˢˢ. The addition (cf. 14.30) seems easier to explain than omission. Cf. also LXX Jon 1.6 (next note).

[16] Note LXX Jon 1.6: ὅπως διασώσῃ ὁ Θεὸς ἡμᾶς.

[17] One could conceivably put a question mark after τί and begin a new question with δειλοί. Cf. LSJ, s.v., τίς, 8.a.

[18] Captured so well in Rembrandt's 'The Storm in the Sea of Galilee' (1633).

Mark's 'Do you not yet have faith?' In Matthew's mind, the story of the stilling of the tempest is instruction for the faithful. It is a call not to come to faith but rather to exercise the faith one already has.

τότε ἐγερθεὶς ἐπετίμησεν τοῖς ἀνέμοις καὶ τῇ θαλάσσῃ. Compare Ps 65.7; 89.9; 105.9 LXX (ἐπετίμησεν . . . θαλάσσῃ); 107.25–32; Isa 50.2; Nah 1.4. Having calmed the souls of the disciples, Jesus now rises and calms the winds and sea, speaking to them as though they were conscious beings. Mk 4.39 reads: 'And having been awakened (διεγερθείς) he rebuked the wind and said to the sea, "Peace! Be still!"' Matthew has turned 'wind' into 'winds', perhaps because he has already used the plural in 7.25 and 27 to symbolize the trials that come upon all. For other instances of singulars being turned into plurals see Allen, p. 83. Why does our evangelist omit the words, 'Peace! Be still!'? Probably because, with the exception of the simple 'Go' in 8.32, Matthew never records Jesus' direct commands to demons. This fact is likely due to his desire to separate Jesus from any taint of magical method, or from a desire to prevent Christian exorcists from using Jesus' words as though they were magical formulae.

Although the degree to which Matthew thought of the winds and sea as being subject to supernatural or demonic powers is unclear, he may not have conceived of them as we do, that is, as lifeless elements. The primitive 'science' preserved in 1 En. 72–82 reveals plainly enough that the sun, the moon, the stars, the winds, the seasons and other natural phenomena were commonly anthropomorphized by Jews and thought of as ruled by heavenly or supernatural creatures. See further Ps 77.18; 104.7; 1 En. 60.11–25; Rev 14.18; 2 En. 19 (where we read of 'the angels who are over rivers and sea'); and 3 En. 14 (where we are given the names of the princes in charge of the wind, hurricanes, whirlwinds, and other facets of nature). For the wind spirit see Jub. 2.2. For the sea spirit see 1 En. 60.16 and 69.22 (cf. 2 Bar. 10.8; *PGM* 3.226–28). For ἐπιτιμάω in stories of exorcism see 17.18; Mk 1.25; and 9.25.

καὶ ἐγένετο γαλήνη μεγάλη. So Mk 4.39. Compare Jon 1.15. As God once overcame the powers of chaos and limited the sea (cf. Job 38.8–11; Ps 33.7; Prov 8.22–31; Jer 5.22; 31.35), so Jesus overcomes the swirling tempest in the Sea of Galilee. Matthew has omitted as unnecessary Mark's preceding 'and the wind ceased' (cf. Mk 6.51). Note that the 'great calm'[19] is established instantaneously. There is no period in which things get progressively calmer. As in the healing stories so here too Jesus' power works its complete effect immediately.[20]

[19] Taylor, *Mark*, p. 276: 'With unconscious artistry the long vowels of γαλή-νη μεγάλη suggest an atmosphere of complete peace'.

[20] Plummer, p. 131: 'A sudden drop in the wind is possible, but that would not at once calm the sea'.

In the OT the coming of the eschaton is depicted in terms of
Yahweh's victory over the cosmic sea. For example, victory
over the nations in the last days is compared with victory over
the sea (Ps 46; Isa 17.12–4); and the future final conflict between
Yahweh and 'the adversary' is expressed in similar terms (Isa
50.2–3; note also Rev 13.1 and 21.1). It is probably over against
this tradition that we are to understand the description of the
sea, the terror of the disciples, and the action of Jesus in 8.23–7.
The implicit Christology is this. The cosmic forces of evil that
threaten the order of creation are brought under the control of
one who has authority over them, and who, in the latter days,
exercises the sovereign power of God.[21] In his sovereign word
the elements have found their master.

27. οἱ δὲ ἄνθρωποι ἐθαύμασαν λέγοντες. Compare 9.33; 21.20;
Jn 7.15; Acts 2.7. The men marvel because the stilling of the
storm has revealed a previously unknown power of Jesus. Until
now, Jesus has only healed the sick and cast out demons. In
8.23–7 a new ability has manifested itself (cf. Heil, pp. 86–7).

Mk 4.41 reads: 'And they feared greatly, and were saying to
one another' (cf. Jon 1.10, 16). Lk 8.28 has: 'Fearing they
marvelled, saying to one another'. Again Matthew prefers the
construction, finite verb + participle, to Mark's finite verb +
finite verb (cf. on 8.25). 'To one another' is dropped, perhaps to
make it easier for readers to see themselves in the story (cf.
Gundry, *Commentary*, p. 156). Gundry, *ibid.*, pp. 156–7, urges
that Matthew has described the disciples as 'men' in order to
suggest that Jesus the Lord might be more than just a man (cf.
Plummer, p. 131). This is more plausible than the other
proposals heretofore made—that 'men' underlines the disciples'
imperfect faith, or that the word alludes to Jon 1.16 ('the men
feared the Lord'), or that the crew of the boat is in view, or that
a crowd on shore is intended, or that the subject is the occupants
of other boats, or that we are to think of men, after the fact,
marvelling upon hearing of the miracle.

The suggestion that the 'men' are not the disciples or others in the
story but a chorus whose members are made up of the Christian readers
of Matthew[22] raises too many questions. Where else in the gospel do
we find such a choral ending? Are the disciples not 'men'? Cannot the
reader identify with the 'men' even if they are the historical disciples?
Is Matthew not following Mark, in which the disciples ask the question
about Jesus' identity? Why is ἐθαύμασαν in the aorist tense instead of
the present?

[21] See further P. Reymond, *L'eau, sa vie, et sa signification dans l'Ancien
Testament*, Leiden, 1958, pp. 183–96.
[22] E.g. Theissen, *Stories*, p. 165; Grundmann, p. 262.

ἐθαύμασαν occurs not only in Matthew but also in Luke, making
for a minor agreement against Mark. This fact, however, should not be
taken to be obvious support for the followers of Griesbach. On the
contrary, it raises a question mark over one of the arguments they
sometimes make for their position. For example, proponents of the
Griesbach hypothesis have claimed that Mk 1.32 (ὀψίας δὲ γενομένης
ὅτε ἔδυσεν ὁ ἥλιος) is a conflation of Mt 8.16 (ὀψίας δὲ γενομένης) and Lk 4.40 (δύνοντος δὲ τοῦ ἡλίου). Yet in Mt 8.23 par. the
Lukan text (φοβηθέντες δὲ ἐθαύμασαν) could just as easily be regarded
as a conflation of Mt 8.27 (οἱ δὲ ἄνθρωποι ἐθαύμασαν) and Mk 4.41
(ἐφοβήθησαν φόβον μέγαν). And there are other instances of the same
thing, which means that the alleged argument for Markan conflation
needs to be worked out much more carefully than it has been. What is
required is a list containing not only the possible instances of Mark's
conflation of Matthew and Luke but also lists containing what would
theoretically be Matthew's conflations of Mark and Luke and Luke's
conflations of Matthew and Mark. Only then could the supposed
evidence for Mark's conflation of Matthew and Luke be properly
evaluated.[23]

ποταπός ἐστιν οὗτος. Mk 4.41 has: 'Who then is this?' (so
also Lk 8.28). The meaning of ποταπός[24] is not, *pace* Fenton,
p. 131, and Gundry, *Commentary*, p. 157, 'how wonderful' but
'what kind of' (cf. BAGD, s.v.).

ὅτι καὶ οἱ ἄνεμοι καὶ ἡ θάλασσα αὐτῷ ὑπακούουσιν; Mark has
the singular, 'wind', the singular of the verb, and αὐτῷ at the
end; otherwise Matthew and Mark concur. ὅτι = kî (cf. BDF §
456.2), and καί means not 'both' but 'even': the disciples are
amazed because they have witnessed a previously hidden ability.
Jesus can command *even* the winds and sea (cf. BDF § 444.3;
Heil, p. 89). Clearly one greater than Jonah is here (cf. 12.41).

JESUS HEALS TWO DEMONIACS (8.28–34)

Mt 8.28–34, like its fuller and more dramatic parallels in Mk
5.1–20 and Lk 8.26–39, follows the stilling of the sea episode. It
continues the theme of Jesus' ἐξουσία, and its elements are all
typical of tales of exorcism (cf. Theissen, *Stories*, pp. 47–72).

Matthew's episode differs from Mk 5.1–20 in several significant ways.
(i) There are seven verses in Matthew, twenty in Mark, so our evangelist
has greatly compressed his source. At least two ends are thereby
achieved. First, there is more focus upon purely christological themes.

---

[23] For additional reflections on the problem see F. Neirynck, 'Les expressions
doubles chez Marc et le problème synoptique', *ETL* 59 (1983), pp. 303–30.
[24] Mt: 1; Mk: 1; Lk: 2. Cf. ποδαπός. This is a clear instance of a *hapax
legomenon* being redactional, a fact which should serve to warn against an uncritical
use of word statistics.

(Gnilka, *Matthäusevangelium* 1, p. 320, speaks here of 'christologische Konzentration'). Secondly, there is a falling away of motifs associated with ritual exorcism (thus e.g. Jesus no longer asks for a name and there is no formula of exorcism; contrast Mk 5.8–9). (ii) Γερασηνῶν has become Γαδαρηνῶν (see on v. 28). (iii) In Mark there is one demoniac. In Matthew there are two (see on v. 28). (iv) The demons no longer refer to 'Jesus, Son of the Most High God'; rather, they speak simply of God's Son (8.29 diff. Mk 5.7). (v) The addition of 'before the time' in 9.29 diff. Mk 5.7 calls to remembrance the theme of eschatological perdition. (vi) 'And he gave them leave' (Mk 5.13) has become 'And he said to them: Go' (Mt 9.32). (vii) Matthew's version terminates with the negative response of the populace (v. 34); there is no conversation between the healed man and Jesus (contrast Mk 5.18–20, which has strong missionary themes). (viii) καὶ ἰδού (absent from Mark's story) appears in Mt 9.29, 32, and 34. The words mark the dramatic high points (cf. Gnilka, *Matthäusevangelium* 1, p. 320).

As it stands in Mark, our colourful tale is difficult to unravel. It contains both doublets and inconcinnities (Guelich, *Mark* 1, p. 273); and one scholar (Pesch, *Der Besessene*(v)) has even managed to unearth four hypothetical pre-Markan stages through which it has allegedly passed. Even if a complex tradition-history seems called for, one hesitates to think we can now accurately reconstruct it. Is Mk 5.1–20 really a literary onion whose skin can be peeled off layer by layer? We content ourselves with two observations. (i) Nothing proves or disproves the remark of Hill, *Commentary*, p. 167: 'behind the embroidered version and the theological superstructure there may be a kernel of truth about the cure of a deranged person whose final paroxysm frightened a herd of swine and provoked a stampede' (see further Taylor, *Mark*, pp. 277–8). (ii) Isa 65.1–4[25] may have played some rôle in the formation of our story or at least have been recalled by those who passed it on.[26]

The story of the Gadarene demoniacs raises difficult questions for many today. The existence of evil spirits was taken for granted by Jesus and his contemporaries; and exorcism (a world-wide practice) was a recognized means of delivering souls from wicked bondage. Today, however, many no longer believe in the existence of disembodied spirits, good or evil; and individuals who would once have been thought possessed would now be diagnosed in other terms. A psychologist or psychiatrist, for instance, if he could somehow transport himself back in time and meet a so-called demoniac, might want to treat the individual for a severe psychotic disorder. Or perhaps he would find a genuine case of multiple personality. And the sociologist or anthropologist might explain everything in terms of rôle-playing for power: in many societies a person may become possessed, that is, act in a wild and bizarre fashion, in order to gain attention, status, and influence.[27] Torture by evil spirits

[25] The text concerns salvation coming to 'a nation that did not call on my name' and includes the phrases 'sit in tombs' and 'eat swine's flesh'.

[26] Against Derrett, 'Legend' (v), we can find no trace of the influence of either Ps 68.6 or of Nah 1.4, 11–5.

[27] See I. M. Lewis, *Ecstatic Religion*, Baltimore, 1971.

would in any event rank rather low on the list of possible explanations.

Given the nature of this commentary we cannot here address the complex theological or religious issues involved in interpreting the synoptic stories of exorcism; nor shall we discuss whether exorcism might in fact not be an appropriate if dramatic means for dealing with certain 'dissociation disorders which are interpreted by their victims in preternatural categories.[28] But as historians we cannot avoid the issue of historicity, and in this connexion several observations may be registered. Jesus was, without doubt, known in his own lifetime as an exorcist (cf. Pesch, *Taten*, pp. 15–28); and he himself, to judge by Mt 12.28 par., believed he had the power to drive out demons. This is an important fact which has great bearing on the problem of whether the several synoptic stories of Jesus performing exorcisms can go back to concrete events. Only uninformed prejudice would infer the non-historicity of a particular narrative on the grounds that it recorded an allegedly miraculous occurrence. The interpretation of exorcism is one thing, its actual occurrence another. Anthropologists in the field have time and again witnessed the Shammanistic healing of possessed individuals. Exorcism is even occasionally practised in contemporary Christian circles in North America and Europe. And one American qualified as a doctor with the M.D. degree has recently gone on record as confessing that, as a first-hand witness to an exorcism, he saw things which, in his judgement, are not explicable in conventional medical terms.[29] However that may be, the point to be stressed is this: exorcism, even if foreign, and perhaps even distasteful, to many, does take place, no matter what explanation one may give to it. So the simple fact that a synoptic pericope recounts a successful exorcism is hardly reason to doubt the truth of the events recounted. The judgement of the historian will have to rest on other factors.

28. καὶ ἐλθόντος αὐτοῦ εἰς τὸ πέραν. So also Mk 5.1, with ἦλθεν, without αὐτοῦ, and with τῆς θαλάσσης at the end. This last was dropped as strictly unnecessary (cf. 8.18; 1 Macc 9.48). On the genitive absolute with reference to a following dative (an unclassical construction) see BDF § 423.1.

εἰς τὴν χώραν τῶν Γαδαρηνῶν. So Mk 5.1 A C *f*¹³ Maj sy^{p.h}. Γεργυστήνων appears in W sy^{hmg}, Γεργεσηνῶν in א² L Δ Θ *f*¹ 28 33 700 892 *al* sy^s bo, Γερασηνῶν in א* B D latt sa. The mss. for Lk 8.26 are similarly divided: Γαδαρηνῶν (A R W 0135 *f*¹³ Maj sy), Γερασηνῶν (P⁷⁵ B D 0267 latt sy^{hmg}), Γεργεσηνῶν (א L Θ *f*¹ 33

---

[28] Cf. A. Crabtree, *Multiple Man*, New York, 1985; also C. A. León, 'El Duende and other Incubi', *Archives of General Psychiatry* 32 (1975), pp. 155–62; and C. Ward, 'Spirit Possession and Mental Health', *Human Relations* 33 (1980), pp. 149–63. Lewis, as in n. 27, has plausibly argued that shammanistic treatments of possession are really a type of psychotherapy. However that may be, perhaps future generations will find some of our modern therapeutic techniques to be no less strange than exorcistic practices.

[29] M. S. Peck, *People of the Lie*, New York, pp. 182–4. Pertinent also in this connexion is R. Allison, with I. Schwarz, *Mind in Many Pieces*, New York, 1980.

1241 *pc* Epiph). Here is the data for Matthew: Γερασηνῶν (892ᶜlatt syʰᵐᵍ sa mae), Γεργεσηνῶν (ℵ² L W *f*¹·¹³ (syʰᵐᵍ) bo), Γαζαρηνῶν (ℵ*), Γαδαρηνῶν (B C (Δ) Θ 1010 *al* syˢ·ᵖ·ʰ). The problem created by the various readings is notorious. Most modern scholars have concluded that Mark and Luke originally wrote Γερασηνῶν, Matthew Γαδαρηνῶν (see Metzger, pp. 23–4, 84, 145). If in this they are correct, then we are dealing with two regions—that of the Gadarenes (Matthew) and that of the Gerasenes (Mark, Luke). Gadara³⁰ (= Umm Qeis), the capital of a toparchy, was about six miles south-east of the Sea of Galilee, Gerasa³¹ (= Jerash, a city of Peraea) about thirty-three miles. Both cities, which were members of the Decapolis, are troublesome because the texts very strongly imply a location near water.³² It is, therefore, possible that the story originally concerned not the Gadarenes or the Gerasenes but rather the Gergesenes, that is, the people of Gergesa.³³ Gergesa was on the eastern coast of the Sea of Galilee, and the pre-Markan tradition could have confused it with Gerasa (a city much better known). How then explain Matthew's reading? If the First Evangelist knew that Gerasa was too far inland for the requirements of the story, he might have substituted a place closer to the lake and have come up with Gadara.³⁴ But one is still left with the problem of accounting for the reading, Γεργεσηνῶν. McNeile, p. 111, ascribed it to Origen, who observed that 'Gadarenes' and 'Gerasenes' did not harmonize with the sea-side setting (cf. Baarda (v)). Whether or not Origen be responsible for the reading, it does seem reasonable that Γεργεσηνῶν entered the textual tradition because Gergesa was on the coast and not far from a very steep cliff.³⁵ And despite its secondary character, it could well restore a reading lost in the pre-Markan tradition (see above).

ὑπήντησαν αὐτῷ δύο δαιμονιζόμενοι ἐκ τῶν μνημείων ἐξερχόμενοι. Matthew has shortened Mk 5.2, turned one

---

³⁰ See Schürer 2, pp. 132–6.

³¹ See Schürer 2, pp. 149–55.

³² But Gnilka, *Markus* 1, pp. 200–2, has raised the (unlikely) possibility that Mark is responsible for setting the story beside a lake.

³³ Sometimes identified with Chorsia (see Cyrillus Scythopolitanus, *Vit. Sabae* 24) and the modern ruins known as Kursi or Kersa. Schlatter, however, denied the existence of a city named Gergesa (pp. 290–1). Josephus does not mention it.

³⁴ Schürer 2, p. 136, argues that the territory of Gadara reached Lake Gennesaret, in which case Matthew's choice would be even more fitting. But Avi-Yonah, p. 174, gives good reasons for doubting this.

³⁵ For further discussion see Zahn (v); G. A. Smith, p. 286, n. 7; Baarda (v); and E. M. Yamauchi, 'A Decade and a Half of Archaeology in Israel and in Jordan', *JAAR* 42 (1974), p. 722.

man into two, and added δαιμονιζόμενοι (see on 8.16 and cf. Mk 5.15, 16, 18; Lk 8.36).

The truly puzzling change is the second. Why *two* demoniacs? Suggestions abound.[36] (i) Our evangelist had access to independent tradition (cf. Grundmann, pp. 262–3).[37] (ii) In Mark the demoniac's name is 'legion', the explanation for which is, 'for we are many'. Might Matthew not have inferred plurality from this (cf. Wellhausen, *Matthaei*, p. 38)? (iii) Matthew is compensating for the omission of the demoniac in Mk 1.21–8 (cf. McNeile, p. 112; Haenchen, *Weg*, p. 197). (iv) He had a slip of memory (cf. Allen, p. 84). (v) In accordance with the forensic need for more than one witness (Deut 17.6; cf. Mt 18.15–16), Matthew wanted two men to be able to testify to Jesus' mighty work (so Lamarche (v); Loader (v), pp. 580–2).(vi) The evangelist wanted the number of people healed in chapters 8–9 to add up to twelve (cf. Green, p. 102). (vii) According to Bultmann, *History*, p. 316, Matthew simply shows a fondness for doubling, something that is found in other ancient narratives. (viii) Theissen, *Stories*, p. 54, conjectures that Matthew doubles the suppliants because two shout louder than one (cf. 9.27; 20.30). (ix) According to Sand, *Matthäus*, p. 190, the doubling of the difficulty magnifies the power of the healer, Jesus. In our judgement, while none of the nine proposals listed can be declared impossible, none of them is obviously probable. And as we cannot add to the catalogue, we remain unenlightened. All we can do is call attention to the other places where our author multiplies by two (1, p. 87).

χαλεποὶ λίαν. According to this redactional note the demoniacs were exceedingly violent, vicious, dangerous (cf. Ep. Arist. 289; Josephus, *Ant.* 15.98; T. Sol. 1.10). Compare Chrysostom, *Hom. on Mt.* 28.2: 'the sea was not in such a storm as they'. χαλεπός, which translates the niphal of *yārē'* in Isa 18.2, appears only one other time in the NT: 2 Tim 3.1. λίαν appears four times in Matthew (Mk: 4; Lk:1), never with a synoptic parallel.

This clause and the next substitute a broad characterization for the many details offered by Mk 5.2c–6. The effect of Matthew's abbreviation is at least twofold. First, there is greater concentration on the figure of Jesus. Matthew has little interest in the demoniac as such. Secondly, a possible difficulty in the Markan narrative is removed: if the demons fear Jesus, why do they eagerly go out to meet him?

ὥστε μὴ ἰσχύειν τινὰ παρελθεῖν διὰ τῆς ὁδοῦ ἐκείνης. This

[36] See the review of G. Braumann, 'Die Zweizahl und Verdoppelungen im Matthäusevangelium', *TZ* 24 (1968), pp. 255–66.

[37] The Church Fathers tended to argue that while there were in fact two demoniacs, Mark and Luke singled out the fiercest; cf. Chrysostom, *Hom. on Mt.* 28.2.

redactional sentence[38] shifts the accent found in Mark. Whereas in the Second Gospel the emphasis is upon the pitiful state of the demoniac, in Matthew we are told of the effect upon others: they could not pass that way.[39]

29. καὶ ἰδοὺ ἔκραξαν λέγοντες. Compare Mk 5.7. Matthew has added 'and behold' (see on 1.20 and 3.16), dropped Mark's 'with a great voice' (an extraneous detail), and substituted a finite verb + participle for Mark's participle + finite verb, this because he likes participial forms of λέγω meaning 'saying' (Mt: 118; Mk: 36; Lk: 94).

τί ἡμῖν καὶ σοί. So Mark, with ἐμοί. Compare Judg 11.12; 3 Βασ 17.18; 4 Βασ 3.13; 2 Chr 35.21 (the Hebrew—which BDB, s.v. *mâ*, calls 'a formula of repudiation'— always being *mah-lî wālāk*); also 2 Sam 16.10; 19.22; Mk 1.24 (τί ἡμῖν καὶ σοί); Jn 2.4; Acts Thom. 45 (τί ἡμῖν καὶ σοί). The meaning of the idiom is, 'What do we have in common?' See further A. H. Maynard, 'ΤΙ ΕΜΟΙ ΚΑΙ ΣΟΙ', *NTS* 31 (1985), pp. 582–6. He observes that '*every synoptic use* of this idiom involves the recognition of the divine nature of Jesus by demons or by persons possessed by demons'. For classical parallels see LSJ, s.v. εἰμί, C, III.2.

υἱὲ τοῦ θεοῦ; The demons, like the devil (4.3, 6), have supernatural knowledge: they know Jesus' true identity without being told (cf. Mk 3.11; 5.7; Lk 4.41; Acts 16.17). Contrast 9.27, where the disciples still wonder who Jesus is. Mk 5.7 has: 'Jesus, Son of God the Most High'. Matthew is again abbreviating, and he never uses ὕψιστος with θεός (a good LXX locution; cf. Mk 5.7; 8.28; Acts 16.17; Heb 7.1; it is usually found on the lips of non-Jews).

ἦλθες ὧδε πρὸ καιροῦ βασανίσαι ἡμᾶς; Compare Ecclus 51.30; Mk 1.24; 1 Cor 4.5; Acts Thom. 45.[40] Matthew has replaced Mark's 'I adjure you by God, do not torment me' with this question. For Matthew, one may ask Jesus questions, but one should never dream of telling him what to do. The evangelist has in addition given a new dimension to the subject matter: 'the time' refers to the great assize, when evil spirits, along with wicked human beings, will receive recompense from Jesus, the Son of Man (cf. 25.41; also 1 En. 15–6; Jub. 10.8–9; T. Levi

---

[38] ὥστε*, διά + genitive*, and ἐκεῖνος* are all characteristic. ὁδός after διά: Mt: 2; Mk: 0; Lk:0.

[39] ἐκεῖνος is odd: no road has yet been mentioned. This does not, however, justify the speculation of Gundry, who urges that 'by the road' is perhaps a symbolic reference to the way of discipleship: Jesus clears away demonic opposition so that his disciples may pass (*Commentary*, p. 158).

[40] '"What have we to do with thee, apostle of the Most High? . . . Why dost thou wish to destroy us, when our time is not yet come? Why dost thou wish to take our authority? For until the present hour we had hope and time remaining."' This depends upon Matthew.

18.12). So here is an element of 'realized eschatology': the eschatological judge has already appeared, and evil is already being punished (cf. 12.28). For καιρός meaning 'end time' (as in 13.30) see BAGD, s.v., 4; and the commentary on 16.3. For βασανίζω see Rev 9.5; 11.10; 12.2; 14.10; 20.10; Philostratus, VA 4.25. For ὧδε as redactional see on 14.8.

30. Matthew now passes over Mk 5.8–9 because it implies that Jesus' exorcistic command was not immediately obeyed, that it was necessary for Jesus to learn the demons' identity. (Or do we once again have here evidence for Matthew's desire to isolate Jesus from common exorcistic and magical practices? It was usual for the exorcist to learn first the name of the demon.) Our author in addition omits 5.10, it being redundant (see Mk 5.12). In short, Matthew abbreviates and makes Jesus the easy victor.

ἦν δὲ μακρὰν ἀπ' αὐτῶν ἀγέλη χοίρων πολλῶν βοσκομένη. Compare Josephus, *Ant.* 8.294. Mk 5.11 has: ἦν δὲ ἐκεῖ πρὸς τῷ ὄρει ἀγέλη χοίρων μεγάλη βοσκομένη. For Mark's 'there on the mountain' Matthew has the less specific 'some distance from them'. This change puts space between the law-abiding Jesus and the unclean swine and keeps ὄρος free of negative associations (cf. on 5.1).[41]

The word χοῖρος ('young pig', 'swine') is absent from the LXX, which instead uses σῦς and ὗς to translate *ḥăzîr*. For the prohibition against eating swine see Lev 11.7 and Deut 14.8 (cf. Isa 65.4; 66.17). Non-Jews were struck by the Jewish refusal to eat pork (cf. Philo, *Ad Gaium* 361; Plutarch, *Quaest Con.* 4.5; Tacitus, *Hist.* 5.4; Juvenal, *Sat.* 14.98; Epictetus, *Diss.* 1.22.4). When Antiochus Epiphanes sacrificed swine upon the altar of the temple in Jerusalem and tried to compel the priests to eat the remains, Josephus says the nation was incited to war (*Ant.* 13.243; cf. 1 Macc 1.47; 2 Macc 6.18–23).See E. P. Sanders, *Jewish Law from Jesus to the Mishnah*, 1990, pp. 272–3.

Several considerations encourage one to think of the demoniacs as Gentiles. (i) Jesus has crossed over to Gentile territory, to a place east of the Sea of Galilee. (ii) According to *m. B. Qam.* 7.7, 'None [that is, no Jews][42] may rear swine anywhere' (cf. *b. B. Qam.* 82b; *b. Menaḥ.* 64b; *b. Ned.* 49b). (iii) The 'here' of 8.29 might be taken to imply Gentile territory: 'Have you come here [that is, into a pagan country] . . .' (cf. Hill, *Matthew*, p. 168).[43] (iv) If Matthew took the demoniacs to be Gentiles this would account for his omission of Mark's conclusion, with its missionary themes; for our evangelist confines the

---

[41] Hill, *Matthew*, p. 169, tentatively suggests that 'at some distance' 'may be an attempt to reconcile the position of the swine with the location of the incident at Gadara, six miles from the sea'. If so, Matthew must have known Palestinian geography fairly well.

[42] Some texts read, 'No Israelites'.

[43] But this is not the only possibility. 'Here' could refer to the earth: the Messiah has come to the earth to destroy demons.

Gentile mission to the post-Easter period. Nevertheless, it is just possible that for Matthew the demoniacs were Jews, and we wish to leave the issue open. The following points should be noted. (a) Josephus informs us that the population along the east coast of the Sea of Galilee was mixed (*Bell.* 3.51–8). (b) In the parable of the prodigal son, a Jew takes care of swine (Lk 15.15). (c) If the demoniacs are not Jews, how can they converse with Jesus? Or are we to suppose that Jesus could speak Greek? Or were there Gentiles who spoke Aramaic? Or would Matthew just not have thought of the question? Or did he assume that demons could speak foreign languages (cf. Lucian, *Philops.*16)? (d) In the other cases where Jesus bends his rule of confining his mission to the lost sheep of the house of Israel, this becomes plain from the context (cf. Mt 8.5–13; 15.21–8).

31. οἱ δὲ δαίμονες παρεκάλουν αὐτὸν λέγοντες. Matthew has made the subject explicit and the verb a third person plural imperfect (cf. Mk 5.10). δαίμων is a NT *hapax legomenon*. It appears once in the LXX, in Isa 65.11, for *gad* (cf. Josephus, *Bell.* 1.628; T. Jud. 23.1; *PGM* 4.1227). See further E. C. E. Owen, 'Δαίμων and Cognate Words', *JTS* 32 (1931), pp. 133–53. Should we perhaps think not of fallen angels but of spirits of the dead?[44] On demons in the Graeco-Roman world see Hull, pp. 38–41, and the literature cited there.

εἰ ἐκβάλλεις ἡμᾶς. This redactional addition turns an imperative in Mark into a conditional sentence. The effect is heightened respect. The demons do not tell Jesus what to do; they instead display diffidence. Compare Gundry, *Commentary*, p. 160: the demons' words now sound 'less like a command to a Jesus struggling for supremacy and more like a plea to a dominant Jesus'.

ἀπόστειλον ἡμᾶς εἰς τὴν ἀγέλην τῶν χοίρων.[45] Mk 5.12 has this: 'Send us into the swine, that we may go into them'. Our author has shortened Mark ('that we may go into them' is tautologous), substituted ἀποστέλλω[46] for πέμπω[47], and conformed to 5.30, where ἀγέλη χοίρων appeared. In accordance with the belief that evil spirits can leave one body and enter another, the demons now think about a new home (cf. 12.43–5; Mk 9.25).

32. Jesus speaks for the first time. He utters one little word:

[44] Cf. Josephus, *Bell.* 7.185 (defining demons as spirits of the dead); Justin, *1 Apol.* 18; Augustine, *De civ. dei* 9.11; and see E. R. Dodds, *The Ancient Concept of Progress*, Oxford, 1973, pp. 206–9. The idea was rejected by Chrysostom, *Hom. on Mt.* 28.3.

[45] So ℵ B Θ 0242ᵛⁱᵈ *f*¹ 33 892* *pc* lat syˢ co eth Cyr Epiph. επιτρεψον ημιν απελθειν appears in C L W *f*¹³ Maj f h syᵖ·ʰ. Cf. Mk 5.13; Lk 8.32.

[46] Mt: 22; Mk: 20; Lk: 15; with εἰς: Mt: 4; Mk:1; Lk: 2. In Matthew Jesus is usually the subject of this verb.

[47] Mt: 4; Mk: 1; Lk: 10. In Matthew Jesus is never the subject of this verb.

'Go!' The result is dramatic. The herd thunders over a cliff and perishes in the water. The sovereign power of Jesus could not be more effectively presented. His word is compulsion.

καὶ εἶπεν αὐτοῖς· ὑπάγετε. Mk 5.13 has: 'And he permitted them'. Mark's ἐπέτρεψεν is not strong enough for Matthew. He prefers the more forceful ὑπάγετε. In every way the First evangelist is bent upon stressing Jesus' authority.

οἱ δὲ ἐξελθόντες ἀπῆλθον εἰς τοὺς χοίρους. As against Mk 5.13, Matthew has made the subject οἱ, changed the participle accordingly from neuter to masculine, and avoided εἰσῆλθον εἰς.

καὶ ἰδοὺ ὥρμησεν πᾶσα ἡ ἀγέλη κατὰ τοῦ κρημνοῦ εἰς τὴν θάλασσαν. Compared with Mark, Matthew has made only two minor changes. He has added 'behold' (cf. 8.29) and 'all' (often added to Markan material; here it substitutes for Mark's 'about 2,000'). For ὁρμάω of pigs see P. Oxy. 901.6. Whether the swine destroyed themselves or were impelled by the demons is left unsaid.

καὶ ἀπέθανον ἐν τοῖς ὕδασιν. Mk 5.13 has this: 'and ἐπνίγοντο in the sea'. In Matthew ἀποθνήσκω replaces the rarer πνίγω (LXX: 2), and ὕδωρ displaces θάλασσα, avoiding undue repetition. In T. Sol. 5.11 the demon Asmodeus begs not to be sent into water (cf. T. Sol. 11.1–6). Evidently some spirits preferred dry localities (cf. Mt 12.43: unclean spirits pass through waterless places). This may explain why Jesus sends the demons into water: he is tormenting them. (Cf. the Jewish texts in which water is clean and so purifies: Davies, JPS, pp. 74–6.) On the other hand, there are other texts in which demons or spirits are associated with water (see SB 4, pp. 517–8; Böcher, pp. 20–32; Tertullian, De bapt. 5; and note Rev 13.1); so one could conceivably argue that Jesus is sending the demons back to whence they came, back to the watery chaos (cf. 8.23–7). He is restoring order on the land.

33. Following the demonstration (8.32), the witnesses now spread the news of Jesus' mighty conquest.

οἱ δὲ βόσκοντες ἔφυγον. Mark has καί instead of δέ and a superfluous αὐτούς[48] after 'herdsmen'.

καὶ ἀπελθόντες εἰς τὴν πόλιν ἀπήγγειλαν πάντα καὶ τὰ τῶν δαιμονιζομένων. As against Mk 5.14, the following changes have been made. (i) The participle of ἀπέρχομαι* (cf. 8.32) has been added; (ii) 'to the city' has been moved forward so that it no longer goes with 'announced'; (iii) Mark's 'and to the country' drops out; (iv) 'announced' is given two objects—'all' and 'and the things concerning the demoniacs' (cf. 21.21, redactional).

---

[48] Luke also omits this, which makes for a minor agreement, but one which is explicable in terms of independent editing.

34. In response to the report of the herdsmen (8.33), 'all the city' comes out to meet Jesus. Seeing him the people implore him to depart. The reason for their inhospitable attitude is not given in our gospel.[49] In any case, Jesus moves on.

καὶ ἰδοὺ πᾶσα ἡ πόλις ἐξῆλθεν εἰς ὑπάντησιν τῷ Ἰησοῦ.[50] Given what is said next, the crowd is not curious but disturbed. Is it because the swine have stampeded and perished? Mk 5.15a reads: 'And they come to (πρός) Jesus'. Matthew has added both 'behold' (cf. 8.29, 32) and 'all' (cf. 8.32, 33). He has also made the subject explicit ('the city'[51]; cf. 21.10) and, in order to recall 8.28, used ἐξέρχομαι and ὑπάντησις (cf. 25.1). The meeting at the beginning (Jesus and the demoniacs) parallels the meeting at the end (Jesus and the citizens of that region), and hostility is the keynote of both.

καὶ ἰδόντες αὐτόν. Contrast Mk 5.15, where the people see (θεωροῦσιν) the demoniac. Matthew has shifted the focus to Jesus. He is the centre of the picture. (Matthew does not even expressly tell us that the demoniacs were healed; contrast Mk 5.15). What is important is that the people act the way they do because they have a certain feeling about Jesus. In this way, Matthew makes a christological point: one has to respond to Jesus.

παρεκάλεσαν ὅπως μεταβῇ ἀπὸ τῶν ὁρίων αὐτῶν. The last four words are from Mk 5.17. So is the first word, which has become finite in order to fit its Matthean context. Both ὅπως and μεταβῇ (μεταβαίνω*) are redactional. For the motif of the rejection of the miracle worker—characteristic of the synoptics but not non-Christian sources—see Theissen, *Stories*, p. 72. It is the antithesis of acclamation.

JESUS HEALS A MAN SICK WITH PALSY (9.1–8)

In order to complete the second major triad of chapters 8–9 the evangelist returns to Mk 2.1 and gives us his much shortened and less picturesque version of Mk 2.1–12 = Lk 5.17–26. The result is radical disturbance of the Markan sequence (cf. 1, pp. 101–3).

[49] In Mark and Luke the people are afraid.
[50] συναντησιν is read by C L W 0242[vid] f[13] Maj. υπαντησιν appears in ℵ B Θ f[1] 33 399 pc. The latter is original (so also NA[26], against HG). (i) Nowhere else does Matthew use συναντησις (or συνανταω). (ii) υπανταω occurs in 28.9 and could there be redactional (it has no parallel). (iii) εξηλθον εις υπαντησιν has strong attestation in 25.1. (iv) The υπαντησιν of 8.34 forms an *inclusio* with the υπηντησεν of 28.9.
[51] Left unnamed, but one naturally thinks of Gadara (cf. 8.28).

The structure of 9.2–8 may be set forth in this fashion:

9.2a   The paralytic is brought to Jesus (καὶ ἰδού . . .)
9.2b   Jesus forgives the man's sins (καὶ ἰδὼν ὁ Ἰησοῦς . . .)

9.3   The scribes accuse Jesus of blasphemy (καὶ ἰδού . . .)
9.4–6   Jesus responds and instructs the paralytic (καὶ ἰδὼν ὁ Ἰησοῦς . . .)

9.7   The man rises and goes home in obedience (καί . . .)
9.8   The crowd sees and glorifies God (ἰδόντες δὲ οἱ ὄχλοι . . .)

The first couplet (9.2a, 2b) sets the stage. The second (9.3, 4–6) introduces the element of conflict and recounts Jesus' response. The third couplet (9.7, 8) records the outcome. For a similar analysis see Gerhardsson, *Acts*, p. 75; also Gnilka, *Matthäusevangelium* 1, pp. 324–5. For other stories in which a healing is interrupted by offended opponents see Mk 3.1–6 = Mt 12.9–14 and Lk 14.1–6.

Mt 9.2–8 is based upon Mk 2.1–12.[52] Many have believed the Markan passage to be composite, the product of combining a healing miracle with a controversy dialogue.[53] This could well be so. Mk 2.1–5a(5b) + 11–2 is by itself a coherent miracle story which reads smoothly[54] while Mk 2.5b(6)–10, a conflict story, introduces a new theme, scribal opposition. Moreover, Mk 2.12[55] follows better if 2.5b (6)–10 be omitted, this because the 'all' who are amazed and glorify God can scarcely include the scribes of 2.6 and because 2.12 omits any reference to the forgiveness of sins. The objection that Mk 2.5b(6)–10 could not stand by itself does not suffice to overturn the judgement about its secondary character; for Hultgren, p. 107, could be correct: 'whoever composed Mark 2:1–12 in its present form had a miracle story (2:1–5a, 11–2) which he expanded by *composing* 2:5b–10'. On the other hand, some doubt remains. In Theissen's words, if v. 5b ('My son, your sins are forgiven') was part of the traditional miracle story, 'there are difficulties about deleting 6–10 on grounds of both form and content: for formal reasons because an assurance is an anticipated healing but almost never immediately introduces the healing, and for reasons of content because it is scarcely conceivable that the provocative reference to the forgiveness of sins could have remained without an effect on the narrative' (*Stories*, p. 164). We refrain from rendering a final verdict on the issue.[56]

Over against Mark, Matthew has made several characteristic alterations (cf. Greeven (v)).He has (i) retold the story in his own

[52] Against Schramm, pp. 99–103, the few minor agreements between Matthew and Luke do not require use of a non-Markan source.

[53] Cf. Pesch 1, pp. 151–2; Klauck, 'Frage' (v). Contrast Mead (v).

[54] And it could well have its basis in an event in the life of Jesus; cf. Pesch 1, pp. 157–8. For Klauck, 'Vollmacht' (v), the original lies in vv. 3, 4c–f, 5, 11–12.

[55] 'And he rose, and immediately took up the pallet and went out before them all; so that they were all amazed and glorified·God . . .'.

[56] Mk 2.1–12, Matthew's source for 9.1–8, has often been regarded as part of

words; (ii) abbreviated it and made it less vivid; and (iii) placed more emphasis upon the ἐξουσία of the Son of man (cf. 9.8)—which in the context means the power of Jesus to forgive sins.

1. καὶ ἐμβὰς εἰς πλοῖον διεπέρασεν. Compare 14.34; Mk 5.18 and 21 (this last immediately following Mark's equivalent of Mt 8.28–34). See 8.23 and the comments there. διαπεράω (Mt: 2; Mk: 2; Lk:1) appears eight times in the LXX, twice for ʿābar (Deut 30.13; Isa 23.2).

καὶ ἦλθεν εἰς τὴν ἰδίαν πόλιν. 'His own city' is Capernaum, not Nazareth, for according to 4.13 Jesus 'dwelt' at Capernaum. See further on 4.13 and 8.14. Chrysostom, *Hom. on Mt.* 29.1, accurately represents Matthew's conviction: 'That which gave him birth was Bethlehem; that which brought him up, Nazareth; that which had him continually inhabiting it, Capernaum'.

Matthew has eliminated most of Mk 2.1–2, including the reference to Jesus being εἰς οἶκον. For additional omissions of vague references to a house see, with their Markan counterparts, 12.22; 15.15, 21; 17.19; and 19.8.

2. καὶ ἰδού. See on 1.20 and 3.16. Both Matthew and Luke, against Mark, have 'and behold'. Given that both evangelists often insert ἰδού (Mt: 62; Mk: 7; Lk: 57) into Markan material, this minor agreement is insignificant.

προσέφερον αὐτῷ παραλυτικὸν ἐπὶ κλίνης βεβλημένον. Mk 2.3 reads: 'And they come, bringing to him a paralytic, borne of four'. Lk 5.18 reads: 'men bringing on a bed (φέροντες ἐπὶ κλίνης) a man who was paralysed'. προσφέρω* is typically Matthean, as is the elimination of the historic present (Allen, p. xx). Mark's mention of 'four men' has been dropped as an unnecessary detail and because it detracts from the focus upon Jesus. This leaves an indefinite plural ('they brought').

Matthew has added ἐπὶ κλίνης to Mk 2.3, as has Luke. This makes for a minor agreement which has caused some discussion (cf. Farmer, *Problem*, pp. 133–4). What is the explanation? (i) Whether or not κράβαττος (which occurs in Mk 2.4) be considered vulgar, both Matthew and Luke consistently avoid using the word (Mt: 0; Mk: 5; Lk: 0).[57] (ii) ἐπὶ κλίνης, which appears over ten times in the LXX, is hardly an uncommon expression, and its use with προσφέρω is natural.[58] (iii) If ἐπὶ κλίνης is redactional in Lk 17.34 (it has no

---

a pre-Markan collection of controversy stories. For discussion see Kuhn, pp. 18–24, 53–98; Pesch, 1, pp. 149–51; Hultgren, pp. 151–66; J. D. G. Dunn, 'Mark 2.1–3.6: a Bridge between Jesus and Paul on the Question of the Law', *NTS* 30 (1984), pp. 395–415.

[57] Note, however, Acts 5.15.

[58] Cf. Andocides 1.61 (ἐπὶ κλίνης φερόμενος); *SIG* 1169.31; Josephus, *Ant.* 8.326; 17.161, 197 (ἐφέρετο δὲ ἐπὶ κλίνης).

parallel), it can be no surprise to find Luke using the phrase elsewhere, especially with his preference for κλίνη over κράβαττος. (iv) Mark himself has βεβλημένον ἐπὶ τὴν κλίνην in Mk 7.30, and this could have influenced the Matthean formulation (cf. also Rev 2.22). (v) This is especially true since the verb associated with κράβαττος in Mk 2.4 is κατάκειμαι. Matthew never takes this over from Mark (Mt: 0; Mk: 4; Lk: 3), and in 8.14 = Mk 1.30 Mark's κατέκειτο becomes βεβλημένον. So we might have expected the κατέκειτο of Mk 2.4 to become βεβλημένον, which would naturally link up with κλίνη (cf. Mk 7.30; Rev 2.22).[59] (vi) ἐπὶ κλίνης, it should be underlined, is attached to φέροντες in Luke, to βεβλημένον in Matthew, so the agreement is far from perfect.[60]

καὶ ἰδὼν ὁ Ἰησοῦς τὴν πίστιν αὐτῶν εἶπεν τῷ παραλυτικῷ. Compare 9.4a; Acts 14.9. Mk 2.5 agrees, with δέ for καί and λέγει for εἶπεν. (Luke too has εἶπεν). For faith in Matthew and in the healing stories see on 8.10. In Mark the faith Jesus sees has been demonstrated by the digging through the roof: the sick men's friends have overcome difficulty. In Matthew all we read about is the bringing of the paralytic to Jesus: details are not given.[61] This is a bit odd. Everywhere else in Matthew that a person's faith is commented upon it is in view of what he or she has said or because of his or her persistence (8.10; 9.22, 29; 15.28). Does Matthew not presuppose in 9.1–8 the reader's knowledge of the fuller account in Mark? As in 8.5–13, the story of the centurion, it is not the sick person himself who has faith. Just as the centurion's faith can gain healing for his servant, so can the faith of the paralytic's friends save the paralytic (cf. 15.28; Jas 5.15). Yet perhaps too much should not be made of this. For it is not implied that the lame man was being carried to Jesus against his will. Presumably he was a consenting party and also had faith (cf. Chrysostom, *Hom. on Mt.* 29.1).

θάρσει, τέκνον. τέκνον, a term of endearment, is the equivalent of *běnî* (cf. Gen 27.20, 26; Ecclus 2.1; *b. Meg* 24b). Matthew has added a form of θαρσέω (Mt: 3; Mk: 2; Lk: 0). Compare 9.22: θάρσει, θύγατερ (also redactional). The imperative—which means 'Take heart', 'Do not fear'—occurs in the LXX for '*al* + a form of *yārē*' (Gen 35.17; Exod 14.13; 20.20; 3 Βασ 17.13). See also Mk 6.50; 10.49; Jn 16.33; Acts

---

[59] Cf. also the *nāpal lěmiškab* of Exod 21.18 and the rabbinic idiom, *mûṭāl běmiṭṭâ* (on which see Schlatter, p. 274).

[60] For further discussion see C. M. Tuckett, 'On the Relationship between Matthew and Luke', *NTS* 30 (1984), pp. 132–3.

[61] J. Weiss, *Das älteste Evangelium*, Göttingen, 1903, p. 156, as quoted by Held, in *TIM*, p. 175: it belongs 'to the greatest riddles of Gospel criticism how Matthew could deny himself the use of these living details'.

23.11; Josephus, *Ant.* 8.322, 326. For the theme of assurance in miracle stories see Theissen, *Stories*, pp. 58–9.[62] In the synoptics Jesus' words of assurance are often a stimulus for faith.

ἀφίενταί σου αἱ ἁμαρτίαι.[63] So Mk 2.5. ἀφίενται is an 'aoristic present' (BDF § 320). Taylor, *Mark*, p. 195, translates: 'are this moment forgiven'. The passive might be considered a divine passive: God has forgiven the man's sins. In this case, Jesus would not have been forgiving sins but only declaring God's forgiveness. 9.6, however, disallows this interpretation, for it clearly states that the Son of man has authority to forgive sins.[64]

Only one other time in the canonical gospels does Jesus explicitly forgive someone's sins (Lk 7.48). For the connexion between sin and sickness (see on 8.17) see Exod 20.5; Lev 26.14–33; Deut 28.15–68; 2 Chr 21.15, 18–9; Ps 103.3 ('who forgives all your iniquities, who heals all your diseases'); 4Q510; 1QapGen. 20.16–29; 1QS 3.20–4 (both sin and sickness are caused by the angel of darkness); 4QPrNab. (quoted below); Philo, *De praem.* 119, 143–6; Lk 13.2; Jn 5.14; 9.2; 1 Cor 11.29–30; Jas 5.14–5; T Gad 5; T. Sol. passim; *b. Ned.* 41a; *b. Šabb.* 55a. Are we to imagine that a miraculous healing could not take place without the forgiveness of sins, and that forgiveness necessarily entails healing? If so, when Jesus forgives the man's sins, he is not treating a symptom but rooting out the symptom's cause; and the paralytic's ability to walk proves that he has been forgiven (cf. Ps 147.3). Compare Marshall, p. 213: 'The thought of the time certainly associated sin with physical punishment (SB 1, pp. 495–96), and nothing is done here to correct that impression; on the contrary, Jesus' action would suggest that the sin which caused the illness needed to be dealt with before the cure could proceed'.

The forgiveness of sins is a prominent theme in the First Gospel. In 1.21 Jesus' ministry is summed up as a saving of his people from their sins. And in 26.28 (diff. Mark and Luke) Jesus' death is plainly stated to be 'for the forgiveness of sins' (cf. 20.28). Perhaps Matthew's interest in the theme was intensified by the situation after A.D. 70. We know that, with the temple—the centre of the sacrificial system designed to reconcile Israel with God and to assure forgiveness— in ruins, religious Jews had to think anew about atonement, and at such a time it might have been opportune to preach that God, in Jesus, had dealt with sin once and for all. However that may be, Matthew's most characteristic

---

[62] He cites the following: Philostratus, *VA* 3.38; 4.10, 45; 7.38; Lucian, *Philops.* 11; Hymn of Isyllus (*IG* 4.128).

[63] αφεωνται σοι αι αμαρτιαι σου ('your sins *have been* forgiven you') is the reading of Maj. αφιενται is found in ℵ B (D) *pc* lat Ir Aug Cyp Hil eth, σου αι αμαρτιαι in ℵ B C* W *f*¹ 33 892 *pc*.

[64] Although it will not do to interpret the ἀφίενται of Mk 2.5 par. as a divine passive, this is true only for the gospels in their canonical shape. If one were to subtract Mk 2.5b(6)–10 from 2.1–12 (see p. 86) or conclude that Jesus did not utter the saying about the Son of man's authority (see on v. 6), then one could indeed see God as the implicit agent of forgiveness.

contribution to the theological idea of forgiveness is his emphasis upon its pre-conditions. Divine forgiveness cannot be appropriated unless one forgives others (5.21–6; 6.12, 14–5; 18.15–35). For the evangelist, God's forgiveness demands man's forgiveness. Perhaps again we may think of the situation at the end of the first century. The rabbis at Jamnia, aware of the dangers of Jewish disunity, were much concerned with unifying the factions that survived the war.[65] Similarly Matthew, in the face of an increasingly diverse and expanding Christian movement, in which Jewish Christians and Gentile Christians continued to grow apart, may have given much reflection to the need for tolerance and forgiveness.

Mt 9.2 is probably not to be explained in terms of Jesus' office as Messiah. While the messianic age was naturally expected to bring forgiveness (cf. CD 14.19; 11QMelch. 4–9), there is very little evidence that the Messiah himself was expected to intercede or atone for sins. The Messiah does, to be sure, intercede for, although he does not himself forgive, sins in the targum on Isa 53.6–7; but the date of this source is uncertain. Beyond that, the idea is unparalleled in ancient Jewish literature.

Would the idea of a man's forgiving sins have been extraordinary in first-century Judaism? Certainly the scribes in Mk 2.7 must speak for many when they affirm that God alone can forgive sins. But two texts make us wonder whether the action of Jesus in Mt 9.2 par. was absolutely without precedent. 4QPrNab. contains these words: 'The words of the prayer which Nabonidus prayed, the king of [the] la[nd of Bab]ylon, the [great] king, [when he was smitten] with the evil disease by the decree of the [Most High] Go[d] in Teima: ["With the evil disease] was I smitten (for) seven years, and unlike [man] was I made; [and I prayed to the Most High God,] and an exorcist remitted my sins for Him; he (was) a Jew fr[om (among) the deportees. He said to me,] 'Make (it) known and write (it) down, to give glory and gr[eat hono]ur to the name of Go[d Most High'"'.[66] If this Aramaic text has been restored and translated properly, its importance is obvious. Perhaps attention should also be directed to LXX 2 Chron 30.18–9, where Hezekiah prays, 'Let the good Lord pardon every heart that prepareth itself to seek God ... though it not be according to the purification of the sanctuary'.

3. καὶ ἰδού τινες τῶν γραμματέων εἶπαν ἐν ἑαυτοῖς. Compare Mk 2.6: 'there were some of the scribes sitting there and questioning in their hearts'. Matthew has prefaced his line with 'and behold' (cf. 9.2), dropped 'sitting there' (an irrelevant detail), and substituted 'said to themselves' (cf. *'āmar bĕlibbô*, as in Est 6.6; Tob 4.2; 11QTemple 61.2) for the longer and less

---

[65] Cf. S. J. D. Cohen, 'Yavneh Revisited', in *Society of Biblical Literature 1982 Seminar Papers*, ed. K. H. Richards, Chico, 1982, pp. 45–61.

[66] Trans. of J. A. Fitzmyer and D. J. Harrington, *A Manual of Palestinian Aramaic Texts*, Rome, 1978, p. 3. The text is unfortunately damaged and the reading has been disputed; see P. Grelot, 'La prière de Nabonide (4 Q Or. Nab.)', *RevQ* 9 (1978), pp. 483–95, and Tuckett (v), p. 74, n. 29.

decisive 'questioning in their hearts'. On the Jewish scribes in
Matthew see on 2.4. Only in Luke's account do the scribes
speak aloud.

οὗτος βλασφημεῖ. What more horrible thing could one Jew
say about another Jew? Mk 2.7 reads: 'Why does he speak thus?
He blasphemes. Who is able to forgive sins but God alone?'
Matthew has severely abbreviated and given us only the main
point.[67] Matthew does not explain why the outraged scribes
believe Jesus has blasphemed, that is, spoken evil.[68] But it
cannot be because they have misunderstood Jesus, missing the
divine passive in ἀφίενται and therefore erroneously supposing
that Jesus himself forgives sin. 9.6 states clearly enough that the
Son of man does indeed have authority on earth to forgive sins.
So Jesus does more than announce God's forgiveness (contrast
2 Sam 12.13). Are we then to imagine that the difficulty is
forgiveness outside the cult? This is only a very remote
possibility. It seems best to take our clue from Mark's text:
'Who is able to forgive sins but God alone?' (cf. Isa 43.25; Dan
9.9). In Mark and, we may think, in Matthew, Jesus has taken
to himself a divine prerogative. He has made himself out to be
more than an intermediary. He has acted not as a channel of
forgiveness but as its source (cf. Jn 10.33).

4. καὶ ἰδὼν ὁ Ἰησοῦς τὰς ἐνθυμήσεις αὐτῶν εἶπεν.[69] This is
based upon Mk 2.8. Our editor has let Mark's εὐθύς fall away
(cf. Allen, p. xx), changed ἐπιγνοὺς ὅτι to ἰδών (in order to
increase the parallelism with 9.2), dropped τῷ πνεύματι αὐτοῦ as
unnecessary (cf. 16.2 diff. Mk 8.12), substituted the more
compact and determinate τὰς ἐνθυμήσεις αὐτῶν[70] for δια-
λογίζονται ἐν ἑαυτοῖς, and replaced λέγει (the historical
present) with εἶπεν (the same change was just made in 9.2 = Mk
7.5).

[67] The omission of 'Who can forgive sins but God alone' would seem to go
against Gundry's claim (Commentary, p. 163) that in 9.1–8 Matthew simply
equates Jesus with God.
[68] According to m. Sanh. 7.5, 'blasphemy' involved use of the divine name,
and according to 7.4 it was a capital crime (cf. Lev 24.10–23; Num 15.30–1).
This technical understanding of 'blasphemy' was not established by the first
century and should not be connected with our text. In Mk 2.7 par. 'blasphemy'
is simply a word for dishonouring God or his people (cf. 2 Kgs 19.4, 6, 22; 2
Macc 15.24; Rom 14.16; Josephus, C. Ap. 1.59, 223, 279). See further SB 1,
pp. 1008–19, and H. W. Beyer, TWNT 1, pp. 620–4.
[69] ειδως appears in B (Θ) f¹ 565 700 1424 al syᵖ·ʰ sa mae arm Chr, ιδων in ℵ C
D L (N) W 0233 f¹³ Maj latt syˢ bo eth. HG follows B, NA²⁶ does not; see Metzger,
p. 24. ιδων is to be preferred because it fits the scheme outlined on p. 86 and
because 'seeing their thoughts' would have invited the correction, 'knowing
their thoughts'.
[70] ἐνθύμησις (Mt: 2; Mk: 0; Lk: 0) is absent from the LXX, from Philo, and
from Josephus. They instead use ἐνθύμημα.

When we read that Jesus knew 'their thoughts', we are probably to think of paranormal or telepathic knowledge. Jesus did not have to hear speech in order to know people's thoughts: he could read minds (cf. Ambrose, *De Cain et Abel* 1.9(37), assuming Jesus' divinity). Of course the idea that a spiritual master can communicate in ways that do not involve ordinary sensory means is common in world literature (cf. Tacitus, *Ann.* 2.54; Plutarch, *De garr.* 20). Later on in Matthew Jesus will again display supernatural prescience (12.25 and 21.2–3; cf. Jn 1.47–51; 2.24–5; 4.16–26). So just as Jesus is like God in that he has the power to forgive sins (9.6), so is he like God in that he knows what people think in their hearts (cf. 1 Sam 16.7; Jer 11.20; Ps. Sol. 14.8; etc.).

ἱνατί ἐνθυμεῖσθε πονηρὰ ἐν ταῖς καρδίαις ὑμῶν; Compare MT Zech 8.17 and LXX Dan 1.8 (ἐνεθυμήθη Δανιὴλ ἐν τῇ καρδίᾳ). Mk 2.8 has: 'Why (τί) do you question these things in your hearts?' Mark's διαλογίζομαι again drops out, being replaced by ἐνθυμέομαι (which matches the ἐνθυμήσεις of v. 4a). πονηρός* comes in to blacken the scribes' character. As in 27.46 = Mk 15.34, interrogative τίς becomes the stronger ἱνατί. On the meaning of 'heart' see 1, pp. 456 and 632.

5. In response to the scribes' criticism (9.3) Jesus now asks a second rhetorical counter-question. Compare 12.26–9; 21.25; 22.45; Mk 3.4.

τί γάρ ἐστιν εὐκοπώτερον, εἰπεῖν. Compare Ecclus 22.15. So Mk 2.9, without γάρ and with 'to the paralytic' at the end.

ἀφίενταί σου αἱ ἁμαρτίαι. So also Mark. The reference is back to 9.2c = Mk 2.5b, where the same words occurred. Compare also v. 6, where ἀφίημι and ἁμαρτία are joined for the third time.

ἢ εἰπεῖν· ἔγειρε καὶ περιπάτει; Mark has exactly this with 'and take up your κράβαττον' after 'rise'. Luke has independently made the same omission as has Matthew (which does not surprise, given that both Matthew and Luke want a more general statement and given that both consistently avoid κράβαττος). The logic of 9.5 would seem to be this. Although it is certainly not easier to forgive sins than it is to heal disease, it is easier to pronounce the forgiveness of sins than to command someone to walk, this because only the latter can be objectively verified (cf. Chrysostom, *Hom. on Mt.* 29.2). But Jesus, as the following verses show, can in fact heal the paralytic. So he can do the harder thing, and this should cause his critics to wonder whether he cannot also forgive sins (cf. Swete, pp. 36–7).[71] The

---

[71] There is also another possible interpretation: the question about what is easier could be rhetorical because both alternatives are equally difficult. In this case the point would be that since Jesus can do one, he can do the other; cf. Bultmann, *History*, p. 15, n. 2.

point is the more forceful, given the close connection between sin and sickness in ancient Judaism (see on 9.2). Does not Jesus' healing power suggest his authority to forgive transgressions?

6. ἵνα δὲ εἰδῆτε ὅτι ἐξουσίαν ἔχει ὁ υἱὸς τοῦ ἀνθρώπου ἐπὶ τῆς γῆς ἀφιέναι ἁμαρτίας. So Mk 2.10a, but with the order ἀφιέναι ἁμαρτίας ἐπὶ τῆς γῆς. On ἵνα δὲ εἰδῆτε see C. J. Cadoux, 'The imperatival use of ἵνα in the New Testament', JTS 42 (1941), pp. 166–73, and Duplacy (v). The latter cites other examples of a ἵνα-clause introducing independent propositions and he translates the expression as an imperative: 'Know'. On the Son of man see Excursus VI. On Jesus' authority see on 7.29. In the present verse Jesus' ἐξουσία involves both right and power. Matthew will probably have thought of Dan 7.13– 14, where the Son of man is given authority by the Ancient of Days (cf. Tertullian, *Adv. Marc.* 4.10).

'On the earth' can be taken in several different ways. It can, as just suggested, stress the fact that the Son of man has already appeared. But it might also indicate the period of the earthly ministry: even before the resurrection Jesus forgives sins. Or there could be a contrast between heaven and earth: God forgives in heaven, Jesus on the earth. Yet another possibility, one we are attracted to, finds a claim to exclusivity. Jesus is *the only one* on the earth with the power and right to forgive sins. On this interpretation Jesus has replaced the temple in Jerusalem and its priests. 'A greater than the temple is here'.

There is no agreement as to whether 9.6 is an aside to the reader or a continuation of Jesus' speech (in which case the 'you' would be either the scribes or those who brought the paralytic).

Favouring the former option are these facts. (i) The synoptic tradition contains other editorial asides (e.g. Mk 7.3–4, 19c; 13.14 = Mt 24.15). (ii) At least as far as Mark is concerned, 'Son of man' occurs only twice before the confession of Jesus as Messiah in 8.29 (see 2.10 and 28). After this it appears frequently. So if both 2.10 and 28 are, as they can be, interpreted as editorial asides, Mark's narrative would be consistent and give expression to the notion that Jesus spoke of himself as the Son of man only after the revelation at Caesarea Philippi. But what of Matthew? He does not follow the Markan scheme, for in 8.20 Jesus unequivocally, and in public, calls himself the Son of man. Still, this does not exclude the possibility that Matthew understood Mark's apparent intention and that he read and reproduced Mk 2.10 and 28 as editorial remarks. (iii) When Mt 9.6a = Mk 2.10a is removed it does not disrupt the narrative. Indeed, the text reads more easily. This is consistent with 9.6a par being a secondary, editorial insertion, perhaps from Mark's own hand. (iv) Nowhere else in the synoptic tradition is it said that the Son of man has the authority to forgive sins, and the idea has been thought by many to come from the post-Easter period (cf. Gnilka, *Markus* 1, p. 101). (v) If ἵνα κ.τ.λ. addresses the scribes, then Jesus could be accused of healing the paralytic for the benefit of the critical onlookers. Yet nowhere else in the synoptics does Jesus perform signs for his opponents. (vi) Contrary to the influential conclusions of Tödt, C. M. Tuckett (v) has persuasively argued that the concept of authority is, in the Markan Son of man sayings, central only in Mk 2.10 and 28. These two verses therefore distinguish themselves from the other Son of man utterances and may be suspected of coming from Mark himself.

The points just made add up to a powerful argument. What can be said on the other side? (i) There is no decisive grammatical objection to taking ἵνα κ.τ.λ. as addressed to the scribes (BDF § 470.3). (ii) 'The Son of man has authority on the earth to forgive sins' is intelligible as a genuine saying of Jesus. See especially Hooker, *Son of Man*, pp. 81–93, and Kim, pp. 89–91 (both finding an allusion to Dan 7.13–4), also Lindars, *Son of Man*, pp. 44–7 (explaining the words by way of conjectures about the Aramaic original).[72] (iii) While editorial asides can be found in the synoptics, they are rather rare. These three points, however, do not in our judgement overturn the weighty arguments in favour of understanding Mk 2.10a par. as an editorial comment. Mt 9.6a should not be read as a word of Jesus,[73] and Matthew probably did not think it such.

τότε λέγει τῷ παραλυτικῷ. Matthew has added τότε,* which makes the transition from editorial comment to narrative even more abrupt. For the rest there is agreement with Mark.

ἐγερθεὶς ἆρόν σου τὴν κλίνην καὶ ὕπαγε εἰς τὸν οἶκόν σου. Compare Jn 5.8[74] and Lucian, *Philops.* 11.[75] Our evangelist has omitted Mark's σοὶ λέγω (it is unnecessary) and changed the imperative, 'Rise'[76], into a participle (creating a circumstantial participle). He has also exchanged κλίνην for κράβαττον (cf. on 9.2) and moved 'your' before the noun it qualifies (which makes for a less Semitic construction; cf. the position of σου in 9.2 and 5). 'Go to your house' has a biblical ring (2 Sam 14.8; 1 Kgs 1.53; cf. T. Job 12.5; *b. Moʿed Qat.* 21b). On the dismissal (cf. 8.4, 13; Mk 5.19; 10.52) as a formal element in miracle stories see Theissen, *Stories*, pp. 67–8, who cites from outside the NT Lucian, *Philops.* 16, and Diogenes Laertius 8.67.

[72] One wonders, however, whether 'on the earth' is not redundant if 'Son of man' simply translates an Aramaic idiom meaning 'a man'.

[73] So also Dibelius, p. 67; Tuckett (v); Cranfield, *Mark*, pp. 100–1; Fitzmyer, *Luke* 1, pp. 578–9.

[74] 'Jesus said to him: "Rise, take up your pallet, and walk"'.

[75] 'Midas himself picked up the stretcher on which he had been carried and marched off to the fields, so powerful was the spell and the piece from the tombstone'.

[76] Which is awkward in Mark as it is immediately followed by another imperative. Matthew's Greek is an improvement.

7. The paralytic, in immediate response to Jesus' wonder-working command, now obediently rises and goes to his own home (which must be in Capernaum). The power of Jesus is thereby demonstrated.

καὶ ἐγερθεὶς ἀπῆλθεν εἰς τὸν οἶκον αὐτοῦ. Compare Mk 2.12a: 'And he rose and immediately taking the pallet went out before all'. Matthew prefers the circumstantial participle (cf. 9.6), drops 'and immediately taking the pallet' (cf. 9.5 diff. Mk 2.9), and replaces 'went out before all' with 'went away to his home'. The last change (shared by Luke; cf. Lk 1.23) allows use of a biblical phrase[77] and makes the paralytic's actions correspond exactly to the command of 9.6 (cf. 1.20–1 with 24–5; Jn 5.8–9). This is the only place in Matthew where we read that a healed individual went 'to his home'.[78]

8. ἰδόντες δὲ οἱ ὄχλοι ἐφοβήθησαν.[79] See on 14.30. Although this is based upon Mk 2.12b ('so that all were amazed'), no words are shared. Oddly enough, the crowd has not heretofore been mentioned. They were, however, introduced in Mk 2.2, a verse entirely passed over by our evangelist in his desire to abbreviate. It appears, then, that the unprepared and sudden introduction of the crowd in Mt 9.8 is due to imperfect editing (cf. p. 68). ἰδόντες makes for a parallel with 9.2b and 4 (see p. 86). ὄχλοι (see on 4.25) replaces Mark's 'all'. Matthew does not want to leave open the possibility that the scribes might have responded positively. (Such would be as odd as a positive response from the Pharisees.) Mark's ἐξίστημι drops out as it does the other three times Matthew finds it in the Second Gospel. On wonder and fear in the conclusions of miracle stories see Theissen, *Stories*, pp. 69–71. He observes that Matthew typically specifies exactly the object of fear or wonder (contrast Luke) and exactly who the subject is (contrast Mark). See 8.27; 9.8, 33; 12.23; 15.31; 21.20.

καὶ ἐδόξασαν τὸν θεὸν τὸν δόντα ἐξουσίαν τοιαύτην τοῖς ἀνθρώποις. Compare LAB 26.6 ('Blessed be God who has done so many mighty deeds for the sons of men') and T. Sol. prologue ('Blessed are you, Lord God, who have given this authority to

---

[77] Cf. *lĕhālak lĕbêtô* and see Josh 22.4; 1 Βασ 10.26; 23.18; 2 Βασ 12.15; 17.23; Theod. Dan 6.19; 11QTemple 62.3–4 (*yšwb 'l bytw*); Jn 7.53.

[78] Cf. Philostratus, *VA* 4.45: 'and the girl spoke out loud and returned to her father's house'.

[79] εφοβηθησαν is found in א B D W *f*[1] 33 892 1424 *al* lat sy[s.p] co Aug Hil and accepted by HG and NA[26]. But εθαυμασαν just might be pristine. It is read by C L Θ 0233 *f*[13] Maj (f) sy[h] arm. εφοβηθησαν could be due to the influence of Lk 5.26. Moreover, while nowhere else in Matthew do the crowds fear, and while nowhere else does a healing cause anyone to fear, the crowds do marvel (θαυμάζω) after the healings in 9.33 (redactional) and 15.31 (redactional; here too the crowds give glory to God).

Solomon'). Mk 2.10 has: 'and to glorify God [only here in Mark] saying that, "We never did see such as this!"'. Whereas the ending in Mark stresses the miracle, in our gospel the emphasis comes down upon the authority given to Jesus and (implicitly) to his followers (τοῖς ἀνθπώποις is plural, and the dative is not one of advantage, as though we should translate, 'on behalf of men').[80] We are probably to see in Matthew's conclusion an assertion of the right of Christian authorities to pronounce absolution (cf. Jn 20.20–3 and Gnilka, *Matthäusevangelium* 1, p. 327). The practice is legitimated—against the protest of the spiritual descendants of the scribes?—by appeal to the words and deeds of Jesus, who wished his disciples to do what he did (cf. 10.1)

JESUS CALLS LEVI (9.9–13)

Mt 9.10–13, like the story that follows it, may be classified on form-critical grounds as an objection story. In such a story (cf. Bultmann's 'controversy dialogue') opponents object to a word or deed of Jesus. Other examples include Mk 2.18–22, 23–8; 3.1–6, 22–30; 7.1–15; 8.31–3; 9.9–13; 10.23–27 and their synoptic parallels; also Mt 3.13–15; Lk 2.41–51; 11.37–52; 13.10–17; 14.1–6; and 15.1–32. For discussion see R. C. Tannehill, 'Varieties of Synoptic Pronouncement Stories', *Semeia* 20 (1981), pp. 107–11. Also pertinent is Daube, pp. 171–5, who discusses objection stories with a tripartite structure—action of Jesus, protest of opponents, pronouncement of Jesus that silences the critics (cf. Mt 9.10–13).

Mt 9.9 = Mk 2.14, which is an extraordinarily brief story[81], exhibits the same structure as 4.18–22 = Mk 1.16–20. Jesus is (i) walking along; (ii) he sees an individual (whose name is given); (iii) this individual is going about his daily tasks; (iv) Jesus calls the individual to discipleship; and (v) he immediately follows. The dependence of this arrangement upon 1 Kgs 19.19–21 (Elijah's call of Elisha) is obvious. See 1, pp. 392–3.

The similarities between 4.18–22 = Mk 1.16–20 and 9.9 = Mk 2.14 are cause for inferring that one narrative has been modelled upon the other.[82] Given, therefore, the primitive character of 4.18–22 par. and

---

[80] Or, *pace* Schenk (v), 'for the sake of men'.—The 'men' of 9.8 is not to be explained as a correct interpretation of the generic meaning of 'Son of man' in 9.6. Matthew's text is based upon the Greek Mark, and 9.8's ἀνθρώποις has for its explanation theology, not grammar. See further Held, in *TIM*, pp. 273–4.

[81] Cf. Schweizer, *Mark*, p. 63: 'the conciseness of a woodcut in which everything is reduced to the essentials'.

[82] Less probable is independent use of 1 Kgs 19.19–21, this because the synoptic accounts are closer to each other than either is to the OT.

its firm basis in history (see 1, pp. 393–5), 9.9 = Mk 2.14 would appear to be the less original story. How then did it come into being? Pesch, 'Zöllnergastmahl' (v), has made a case for ascribing it to Markan redaction. The story of Jesus at supper (Mk 2.15–17) contained the saying about Jesus eating with toll collectors (2.16); and if the story also identified the house of 2.15 as belonging to Levi (cf. the identification in 14.3), it would have been easy enough to preface 2.15–17 with a concrete example of Jesus calling a toll collector, Levi.

Although Pesch's tradition-history is attractive, it cannot be proven, and there is another possibility that should be considered. According to Crossan, *Aphorisms*, pp. 213–20, Mk 2.15 is to be assigned to Mark's hand (cf. van Iersel (v), pp. 217–18). He created it in order to connect the call of Levi (2.14) with the story of Jesus eating with sinners (2.16f.). In favour of this, 2.15 could have been developed out of the vocabulary of 2.16f. Moreover, *P. Oxy.* 1224 could preserve an independent version of Mk 2.16f: 'And the scribes and [Pharisees] and priests, when they sa[w] him, were angry [that with sin]ners in the midst he [reclined] at table. But Jesus heard [it and said:] the h[ealthy need not the physician]'.

If either Crossan or Pesch be correct, what are we to conclude about the history of Mk 2.15–17? According to Hultgren, pp. 109–11, the story was constructed out of the sayings in Mk 2.17a and 17b, both unauthentic. The reasons put forward for this view are these: first, v. 17a ('Those who are well have no need of a physician, but those who are sick') has parallels in contemporary literature; secondly, v. 17b employs a form (ἤλθον + infinitive) which is attested in post-Easter constructions (e.g. Lk 9.56 Maj.; 1 Tim 1.15; Clement of Alexandria, *Strom.* 3.9.63); and thirdly, can we imagine (scribes and) Pharisees mingling among 'toll collectors and sinners'? In our judgement, however, as we shall argue when discussing 9.12 and 13c, the authenticity of both Mk 2.17a and 17b is more probable than not. And Crossan is right: we 'cannot imagine that the piece of proverbial obviousness . . . in 2.17a, whether stemming from Jesus or the tradition, could ever have been transmitted as an aphorism in search of a setting, as an aphoristic saying on its way to becoming an aphoristic story' (*Aphorisms*, p. 217). Further, the core of Mk 2.15–17 would seem to be at least 2.16–17a. 2.17b (and perhaps 15) could have been added later. So what we seem to have preserved in the story of Jesus eating with toll collectors and sinners is dominical utterances and a context for them which, if not strictly historical, at least faithfully represents a typical problem in the life of Jesus (cf. Braun, *Jesus*, p. 114).[83]

Matthew's redactional contributions include the following: (i) Mark's introduction (2.13) has been discarded, probably in the interests of brevity; (ii) 'Levi the Son of Alphaeus' (Mk 2.14) is now 'Matthew' (see on 9.9); (iii) 'his house' (Mk 2.15) has become 'the house' (9.10, q.v.); (iv) 'For there were many who followed him' (Mk 2.15) has been rejected as unimportant; (v) 'the scribes of the Pharisees' (Mk 2.16) has

[83] For the suggestion that our story was preserved because of its pertinence to the question of table-fellowship in the primitive community see Taylor, *Mark*, p. 204, and Pesch, 'Zöllnergastmahl' (v), pp. 82–4.

been replaced by the simpler 'the Pharisees' (9.11); (vi) only in Matthew is Jesus addressed by his opponents as 'teacher' (9.11); (vii) the citation from Hos 6.6, so important for Matthew's interpretation of the story, has been interpolated.

9. καὶ παράγων ὁ 'Ιησοῦς ἐκεῖθεν εἶδεν ἄνθρωπον καθήμενον ἐπὶ τὸ τελώνιον, Ματθαῖον λεγόμενον. Compare Mk 2.14: 'And passing along he saw Levi the (son) of Alphaeus sitting at the toll booth'.[84] Matthew has named Jesus, added ἐκεῖθεν*, substituted 'a man' for 'Levi the (son) of Alphaeus', and added at the end 'Matthew by name.' The change from 'Levi' (so also Luke) to 'Matthew' has been explained in several different ways (cf. Gnilka, *Matthäusevangelium* 1, pp. 330–1). (i) Our author knew that Levi was also called Matthew.[85] He knew this either through tradition (cf. Allen, p. 89) or because he himself was the man in question (cf. the traditional ascription of our gospel to Matthew).[86] (ii) Our evangelist observed that Levi was not named as one of the twelve (cf. 10.2–5 par.). If, however, Matthew believed that one specially called by Jesus had to be one of the twelve (cf. 4.16–20), then he would have been compelled to identify Mark's Levi with one of the twelve—in which case 'Matthew' may have been as good a name as any.[87,88] (iii) In 10.3 Matthew is called a 'toll collector' (contrast Mark and Luke). If the author of the First Gospel had this information from his tradition, it might have encouraged him to identify Levi the toll collector with Matthew the toll collector (cf. Nineham, *Mark* p. 99).[89] (iv) According to Kiley (v), 'Matthew' was chosen because, through assonance, the name helps stress the theme of discipleship (μαθητής occurs three times in 9.10–13). (v) If, as Kilpatrick has argued (pp. 138–9), the First Gospel was originally a pseudepigraphon with the title 'According to Matthew' placed above it, then 9.9 could be an attempt to inform the readers about the fictitious author (cf. Fenton, p. 136). (vi) Sand, *Matthäus*, p. 196, claims that while

---

[84] Matthew has omitted the redactional Mk 2.13: 'And he went out again by the sea. And all the multitude was coming to him, and he taught them'. Jesus is not teaching the crowds in Mt 8–9.

[85] Some Jews bore two Semitic names. See Acts 4.36; Josephus, *Ant.* 12.285; 18.35, 95; 20.196; and Horsley 1, pp. 89–96. And some have supposed that Jesus gave Levi the name 'Matthew', just as he called Simon 'Peter'.

[86] Bengel, *ad loc.*: 'It is possible that Matthew did not like the name which he had borne as a publican'.

[87] So Beare, p. 225, and Meier, *Commentary*, p. 93.

[88] A parallel to this type of thinking can be seen in Mk 2.14 D Θ *f*[13] *pc* it. Apparently noting that the lists of the twelve mention a certain 'James, son of Alphaeus', D and the other witnesses cited substitute 'James' for 'Levi' in Mk 2.14.

[89] Patristic opinion was not unanimous in identifying Levi and Matthew; see e.g. Clement of Alexandria, *Strom.* 4.9, and Origen, *C. Cels.* 1.62.

Levi was of no interest to the author of the First Gospel and his readers they did know of a Matthew connected with their community and its tradition; thus the substitution.

Of the six options listed, (v) is the least probable. (i) and (iii) cannot be disproved but are unnecessary. (ii) and (vi) are the most satisfactory, although there could also be truth in (iv). One must remain quite uncertain.

Μαθθαῖος (v. 1. Ματθαῖος) occurs five times in the NT, everywhere but here in a list of the twelve (Mt 10.3; Mk 3.18; Lk 6.15; Acts 1.13). The name, which does not appear in the LXX, represents a shortened from of *mattatyâ* or *mattatyâhû* (= 'gift of Yahweh'). It occurs in rabbinic texts (SB 1, p. 536), and in *b. Sanh.* 43a one of Jesus' disciples is 'Matthai'. Some have suggested that Mt 9.9 was one of the factors leading to the ascription of the First Gospel to Matthew. τελώνιον (absent from the LXX) means 'toll office' (cf. *bêt hammekem*, as in *b. Sukka* 30a). Perhaps we are to envisage simply a booth or table. Given the location in Capernaum, maybe one should think of the taxes levied on fishermen (cf. Schlatter, p. 302). On the office of 'toll collector' see on 5.46.

καὶ λέγει αὐτῷ· ἀκολούθει μοι. So Mk 2.14b. On the motif of 'following' see on 4.20; 8.19, and 22. Jesus, it should be underlined, is the one in command. Matthew does not choose Jesus. Jesus chooses Matthew. Compare 1, p. 394.

καὶ ἀναστὰς ἠκολούθει αὐτῷ.[90] So Mk 2.14c. Compare Num 22.20; Judg 13.11; 1 Kgs 19.21; Mt 9.19; Josephus, *Ant.* 9.108. No motive is given for Levi's obedience. So the reader comes away feeling that Jesus' word is truly powerful and effective.

10. καὶ ἐγένετο αὐτοῦ ἀνακειμένου ἐν τῇ οἰκίᾳ. Mk 2.15 begins with καὶ γίνεται κατακεῖσθαι αὐτόν and has 'his' after 'house'. For καὶ ἐγένετο, which here replaces an historic present, see on 7.28. The genitive absolute typifies Matthew's style. ἀνάκειμαι[91] (Mt: 5; Mk: 2; Lk: 2; cf. 1 Esdras 4.10; Tob 9.1 א) means 'be at table'. αὐτοῦ ἀνακειμένου is also redactional in 26.7 diff. Mk 14.3 (cf. Mk 14.18; 16.14). According to Jeremias, *Eucharistic Words*, pp. 48–9, it was custom for Jews to sit for meals; reclining was usually reserved for feasts or parties. If so, then ἀνακειμένου indicates the festive nature of the gathering in 9.9–13 par. See further Horsley 1, p. 9.

Whose house is it? There are three possibilities[92]—Jesus' house (so

[90] The reading is very uncertain. ηκολουθει (so HG) appears in א C^vid D f¹ 892 1010 *pc* geo. NA²⁶ prints ηκολουθησεν (following B Maj Eus Or). It may be due to assimilation to 4.20, 22; Lk 5.11; and/or Jn 1.37.

[91] Matthew never uses κατάκειμαι (Mt: 0; Mk: 4; Lk: 3).

[92] And just perchance a fourth. Perhaps the evangelist himself was uncertain as to which house the tradition indicated and therefore thought it best to leave the matter ambiguous. Note that the house in 2.11 is unqualified also.

apparently Mk 2.15[93]), Matthew's house (so Lk 5.29), or Peter's house (see 8.14). Although commentators have traditionally thought of Matthew's house (cf. Chrysostom, *Hom. on Mt.* 30.2; Zahn, pp. 374–5), the first and third options seem most likely. That Jesus' house is in view would seem to follow from these facts: (i) Matthew has already told us that Jesus dwelt in Capernaum (4.13; cf. 9.1). (ii) In 9.9 Jesus called Matthew to follow him, so Jesus, not the toll collector, has led the way to the house. (iii) While we might imagine Pharisees in Jesus' house, can we imagine them in the house of a toll collector?[94] (iv) συνανέκειντο τῷ 'Ιησοῦ may imply that Jesus is the host. (v) In 9.13 Jesus says, 'I came to call not the righteous but sinners'. This also may imply that Jesus is the host. On the other hand, we must wonder why, if the evangelist had Jesus' house in mind, he has omitted Mark's αὐτοῦ (after οἰκίᾳ: this probably refers to Jesus[95]). Moreover, given Peter's prominence in the First Gospel and the mention of his house in 8.14, maybe we should think of that place. This is especially true in view of 17.25, where the unqualified τὴν οἰκίαν is almost certainly Peter's residence. Perhaps, in fact, the simplest solution is to regard the unqualified ἡ οἰκία of 9.10, 28; 13.1, 36; and 17.25 as in each instance referring back to the house of Peter mentioned in 8.14.

καὶ ἰδοὺ πολλοὶ τελῶναι καὶ ἁμαρτωλοὶ ἐλθόντες συνανέκειντο τῷ 'Ιησοῦ καὶ τοῖς μαθηταῖς αὐτοῦ. So also Mk 2.15b, minus 'behold' (see on 1.20; 3.16) and the participle. On toll collectors (cf. 9.10) see on 5.46. The 'sinners' (cf. 9.11, 13; 11.19; 26.45) are not (*pace* most modern scholars) to be identified with the 'amme hā-'āreṣ, the 'people of the land'. They are rather the 'wicked', the reša'îm, those Jews who, in the eyes of others, have abandoned the law and denied God's covenant with Israel.[96] This explains why 'sinner' is almost the functional equivalent of 'Gentile' (cf. 5.47 diff. Lk 6.33; also Ps 9.17; 1 Macc 2.48; Tob 13.6; Jub. 23. 23–24; Ps. Sol. 2.1–2). In the present context, 'sinners' recalls the previous paragraph, in which Jesus forgives sins. This makes for a thematic link. Jesus eats with sinners after he has forgiven sins.

The phrase, 'toll collectors and sinners', occurs in the gospels in Mk 2.15–16 par., in Mt 11.19 = Lk 7.34 (Q), and in Lk 15.1 (L). It was no doubt first formulated by Jesus' opponents.[97] On its significance see below.

The table fellowship of Jesus—which shows us that his words about

---

[93] See E. S. Malbon, 'τῇ οἰκίᾳ αὐτοῦ: Mark 2.15 in Context', *NTS* 31 (1985), pp. 282–92. Cf. Sand, *Matthäus*, p. 195.

[94] But perhaps the Pharisees are not in the house.

[95] The omission of αὐτοῦ is consistent with the possibility raised in n. 92.

[96] See E. P. Sanders, 'Jesus and the Sinners', *JSNT* 19 (1983), pp. 5–36.

[97] Schweizer, *Mark*, p. 64, and Pesch, 'Zöllnergastmahl' (v), pp. 73–4, propose that the original story referred only to 'toll collectors': 'sinners' was added later in a non-Jewish environment. The suggestion falls short of proof; cf. Gnilka, *Markus* 1, p. 104.

forgiveness were more than mere words—has rightly played a large rôle in recent discussions of the pre-Easter ministry.[98] Two points should be stressed. The first concerns eschatology. Jesus, following established custom, often spoke of the kingdom of God as though it would be a great banquet (cf. 8.11; 22.1–14; 25.1–13; 26.29). But given his 'realized eschatology' (see 1, p. 389), the festive meals in which he participated were in all likelihood interpreted by himself and others as proleptic experiences of the kingdom (cf. 9.15). Secondly, by eating with people who were outcasts Jesus was offering a prophetic symbol.[99] He was announcing that the opportunity to receive God's mercy was being opened to *all* in Israel, including—perhaps especially?—those who had forsaken the covenant and were despised by most pious Jews. In Jesus' view the soteriological scheme of law and covenant had been relativized by his own person: 'Every one who acknowledges me before men, the Son of man also will acknowledge before the angels of God. But he who denies me before men will be denied before the angels of God' (Lk 12.8–9). This meant that all Jews, pious and impious, were faced with the same decision and therefore that all were really in the same situation. So the presence of God's eschatological envoy and the demand for respond to him and his cause gave a new opportunity to the outcasts and at the same time cut the old religious moorings of the 'righteous'.

11. καὶ ἰδόντες οἱ Φαρισαῖοι. These words are all from Mk 2.16, which Matthew has much abbreviated. *P. Oxy* 1224 mentions the scribes, the Pharisees, and the priests. On the Pharisees see on 3.7 and 5.20.

ἔλεγον τοῖς μαθηταῖς αὐτοῦ. So Mk 2.16. The Pharisees' objection is directed towards the disciples and not Jesus himself (cf. Mk 3.22).

διὰ τί μετὰ τῶν τελωνῶν καὶ ἁμαρτωλῶν ἐσθίει ὁ διδάσκαλος ὑμῶν; This largely reproduces Mk 2.16, save that this last begins with ὅτι (cf. 17.9 diff. Mk 9.28 and see BDF § 300.2) and ends with 'and drink' (an unnecessary detail). Matthew has also put 'your teacher' on the lips of the Pharisees. This is typical. Throughout the First Gospel Jesus' opponents do him the honour of calling him 'teacher' (see on 8.19). In Luke 'he eats' becomes 'you eat'. The objection is thus not only addressed to the disciples but against them.

Even if Mk 2.15–7 be thought unhistorical, few would deny that it accurately represents the actual dynamics between the historical Jesus and the Pharisees (cf. Haenchen, *Weg*, p. 111). Jesus made enough of an impact upon the populace in Galilee that the Pharisees took notice. And for the most part they raised objections.[100] But what exactly was

---

[98] For a dissenting (but unpersuasive) voice see D. E. Smith, 'The Historical Jesus at Table', in *SBL 1989 Seminar Papers*, ed. D. Lull, Atlanta, 1989, pp. 466–86.

[99] For prophetic actions see the commentary on 21.18–22.

[100] For the possibility that relations between Jesus and the Pharisees were for a period friendly see Davies, *COJ*, pp. 47–9.

it about Jesus that upset them? And, in particular, what was the substance in the charge that Jesus ate with 'toll collectors and sinners'? The issue has been sharply raised by E. P. Sanders: 'If Jesus, by eating with tax collectors, led them to repent, repay those whom they had robbed, and leave off practising their profession, he would have been a national hero' (*Jesus*, p. 203). Here are possible explanations—

(1) Sanders' own solution is this: Jesus offended people because he offered sinners—those who had neglected the law and put themselves outside the covenant—inclusion in the kingdom without requiring repentance as normally understood. That is, he promised them salvation even though they failed to make restitution, offer sacrifice, and submit to the law. One hesitates to follow Sanders for several reasons, one being that while the synoptics cite several reasons why Jesus' contemporaries took offence at him, the issue of restitution is not among them.[101] Also, Sanders is forced to dismiss as unhistorical not only Lk 19.1–10 (the story of Zacchaeus) but also Mk 1.40–5 (where Jesus sends a leper to the priest).

(2) In the judgement of many, Jesus created a tumult because he pronounced forgiveness to sinners *before* requiring repentance of them. This is a real possibility, although it has been dismissed by Sanders as involving a distinction without a difference.[102]

(3) Klausner, p. 274, supposed that Jesus was regarded by many as a Pharisee, and that the stricter Pharisees did not approve of his mingling with the 'dregs' of Jewish society.[103]

(4) Perhaps the accusation against Jesus should be seen as part of a wider issue. If there were people (e.g. Pharisees) who, on other grounds, were not particularly fond of Jesus, might they not have been moved to malign him and the toll collectors—even if the toll collectors (such as Zachaeus) had tried to make restitution? Many must have been troubled by Jesus' claims and actions. In particular, if he did, as the gospels have it, avow that the fate of Jews at the final judgement hinged upon their response to him and his work, and if he was perceived as detracting from the authority of the Torah or the oral tradition, then he could easily have raised strong opposition. And we can readily imagine that, as soon as Jesus began to be taken seriously by a significant number of people, others would have begun hurling verbal attacks; and if it became known that Jesus had even once spent time with a group of toll collectors we can be sure that, no matter what he had asked of them, contemptuous accusations would have been made. It also seems abundantly clear that Jesus, in order to illustrate the radical nature of his soteriological stance, went out of his way to mingle with outcasts. He

---

[101] See further D. C. Allison, Jr., 'Jesus and the Covenant: A Response to E. P. Sanders', *JSNT* 29 (1987), pp. 57–78.

[102] But see N. H. Young, '"Jesus and the Sinners": Some Queries', *JSNT* 24 (1985), pp. 73–5.

[103] While we do not follow Klausner, it is highly significant that the accusation against Jesus assumes that he himself is not a 'sinner'. The Pharisees did not complain that sinners were eating with a sinner.

appears to have been intentionally provocative and outrageous—
like a prophet acting out a parable or setting forth a prophetic
symbol.

12. ὁ δὲ ἀκούσας εἶπεν. Compared with Mk 9.17 Matthew has
replaced καί with δέ, omitted 'Jesus', exchanged the historical
present (λέγει) for an aorist (cf. 9.2 diff. Mk 2.5; 9.4 diff. Mk
2.8), and dropped αὐτοῖς ὅτι (which is unnecessary;
ὅτι *recitativum* is much more common in Mark than in Matthew;
cf. BDF § 470.1). *P. Oxy.* 1224 has this: ὁ] δὲ ᾽Ιη(σοῦς) ἀκούσας
[εἶπεν.

οὐ χρείαν ἔχουσιν οἱ ἰσχύοντες ἰατροῦ ἀλλ᾽ οἱ κακῶς ἔχοντες.
So both Mk 7.12 and Lk 5.31 (the last with ὑγιαίνοντες). The
words reproduce a well-known secular proverb. Compare
Menander, frag. 591K ('For the one whose body is ill needs a
physician'); Plutarch, *Apophth. Lacon.* 230F ('Physicians are not
among the healthy but spend their time among the sick'); Dio
Chrysostom 8.5; Diogenes Laertius 6.1.1 ('Physicians are
commonly with the sick but they do not catch the fever'); *Mek.*
on Exod. 15.26 ('If they are not sick, why do they need a
physician?'). There is also an abbreviated version in *P. Oxy.*
1224: [οὐ χρείαν ἔχ]ουσιν οἱ ὑ[γιαίνοντες ἰατροῦ]. In its
canonical context, the saying presupposes that sin is a disease
(cf. Isa 1.4–5; 53.5).

It is usually very difficult to judge the authenticity of a synoptic
saying which has proverbial parallels. In the present case, however, the
proverb has a natural setting in the pre-Easter period. We have no
trouble imagining that Jesus might have responded to his critics by
recalling to them a known proverb. This is the more true as Jesus
himself is not the subject of the saying: emphasis lies upon the needs of
the sick. Furthermore, the contrast in 9.12 = Mk 2.17 is between οἱ
ἰσχύοντες and οἱ κακῶς ἔχοντες, not (as expected) οἱ ὑγιαίνοντες
and οἱ νοσοῦντες. This points to a Semitic environment, for 'the
strong' is best explained by the Aramaic *bĕrî*, which means either
'strong' or 'healthy' (cf. Jeremias, *Parables*, p. 125, n. 42; Black, p. 196).
For further discussion see Pesch, 'Zöllnergastmahl' (v), pp. 81–2 and
Klauck (v), pp. 154–7. Both accept authenticity.

In its Matthean context, 'It is not the strong that have need
of a physician but the sick' is a parable whose meaning is
transparent: the sick are the toll collectors and sinners, the
strong are those who oppose Jesus, and the physician is Jesus.
If the words are dominical the equations must also have been
implicit for Jesus. Whether this makes the utterance an 'allegory'
could be debated; but the facts are obvious enough.[104]

---

[104] See further C. E. Carlston, 'Parable and Allegory Revisited', *CBQ* 43
(1981), pp. 235–6.

13. πορευθέντες δὲ μάθετε τί ἐστιν. This is redactional. There is no parallel in Mark or Luke. 'Go and learn'[105] (= *śē ûlmōd*) is a rabbinic expression which is particularly appropriate when its audience is considered. In its present context it conveys irony. The Pharisees never go and learn (from the OT) in Matthew. They always misunderstand and raise objections. They receive no education.

'Go and learn' introduces a precept the Pharisees know only too well, so their failing scarcely lies in scriptural ignorance. The problem, rather, is a lack of imagination (cf. the disciples' ὀλιγοπιστία). They cannot see how Hos 6.6 is applicable to the situation that has made them indignant. They cannot see how the words, 'I desire mercy, and not sacrifice', justify Jesus' outreach to sinners. And so is it throughout our narrative. Jesus never informs the Jewish leaders of ideas or principles they do not already know. On the contrary, he typically responds to criticism by recalling the OT or by appealing to common wisdom or common sense (cf. 9.12–3, 15–7; 12.3–8, 11–3, 25–37; 15.3–9; 19.4–9; 22.29–33, 43–5). Persuaded that all is not what it seems to be, Jesus invites his opponents to use their imaginations, to ponder a creative reinterpretation of their tradition (which is also his own). He is, in other words, trying to push their thoughts beyond conventional interpretations, trying to encourage their minds to construe the old in an inventive fashion. Thus what we appear to have implicit in the First Gospel is an anticipation of the profound notion so memorably taught by Blake, and later by the English writer Charles Williams: sin is a consequence of not exercising the imagination.[106]

ἔλεος θέλω καὶ οὐ θυσίαν. Compare 5.7 (without parallel) and 12.7 (redactional). The words are found in Hos 6.6 LXX A Q. LXX B has ἤ for καὶ οὐ. If the reading in A Q (which agrees perfectly with Matthew) is due to assimilation to the Gospel (so Soares Prabhu, p. 78), our author may have consulted the Hebrew. The MT has: *kî ḥesed ḥāpaṣtî wĕlōʾ zābaḥ*. Compare also 1 Sam 15.22; Ps 40.6; Prov 16.7 LXX; Heb 10.5. For rabbinic interpretations of Hos 6.6 see SB 1, p. 500. It is particularly appropriate that the Pharisees should be answered by a citation from the OT (contrast Mark and Luke), for they prided themselves on their knowledge of and faithfulness to God's revelation in the Torah.

In the Introduction, p. 135, we have urged that Mt 9.13a is to be explained not as a word of the historical Jesus but as a redactional interpolation which has its setting in post-Jamnian Judaism. See the discussion there. On mercy in Matthew see on 5.7.

---

[105] μανθάνω: Mt: 3; Mk: 1; Lk: 0. πορεύομαι as nominative participle: Mt: 13; Mk: 0; Lk: 12. Cf. Mt 2.8; 17.27; 18.12; 28.29. For the rabbinic parallels to 'Go and learn' see Schlatter, p. 307, and SB 1, 499.

[106] Matthew would not have had much sympathy for the post-Enlightenment notion that there is no sin but ignorance.

How did Matthew understand 'I desire mercy, not sacrifice'? Against J. P. Meier, who has written that the evangelist 'probably understands the verse as a complete rejection of temple sacrifices' (*Matthew*, p. 94; cf. Ps.-Clem. Rec. 1.37), the issue would be axiomatic after A.D. 70, that is, solved by the destruction of the temple and the cessation of the sacrificial system. Even if that were not so, there is nothing about the temple cult in the Matthean context. Perhaps most contemporary commentators have seen Jesus as here exalting compassion over strict adherence to the law (e.g. Cope, pp. 67–8). But this seemingly fails to explain the use of Hos 6.6 again in Mt 12.7, where the disciples are said to be guiltless of any transgression of the law (12.3–8). Moreover, given Matthew's view of the Torah (see on 5.17f.), we hesitate to discern in 9.13 criticism of the law as such. According to G. Barth, in *TIM*, p. 83, 'I desire mercy, not sacrifice' means, in 12.7, that 'God himself is the merciful one, the gracious one, and that the Sabbath commandment should therefore be looked upon from the point of view of his kindness. Only in this way is there a real connexion with the use of the same quotation in 9.13: if Jesus does not shrink from a defiling association with sinners, it is because God himself is gracious and merciful, and therefore desires that we show mercy'. This interpretation unfortunately fails to explain what 'sacrifice' means in either 9.13 or 12.7. Perhaps, then, we should consider the possibility that ἔλεος still carries for Matthew the connotations of *ḥesed* and that he understands Hos 6.6 as did the prophet: cultic observance without inner faith and heart-felt covenant loyalty is vain. On this interpretation, the Pharisees are castigated because their objections show that despite their concern with external ritual their hearts are far from the God they think they honour (cf. 23.25–6). That is, their religious concerns are not properly animated, with the result that they are hindering God's work in Jesus. Unless informed by a spirit of mercy, observance of the Torah can become uninformed slavery to the traditions of men (cf. 15.5–6).[107]

οὐ γὰρ ἦλθον καλέσαι δικαίους ἀλλὰ ἁμαρτωλούς.[108] So Mk 2.17, minus γάρ.* What precisely the sinners are called to is left unsaid. Is it 'to repentance' (so the Maj. text and the parallel in Lk 5.32)? Is it to the kingdom of heaven? Is it to discipleship?

Variants of the saying appear in several early Christian texts. See, for example, Lk 9.55 v. 1. ('The Son of man did not come to destroy

---

[107] Cf. J. D. Moo, 'Jesus and the Mosaic Law', *JSNT* 20 (1984), p. 10.

[108] εἰς μετανοιαν is found at the end in Maj and many other witnesses, but it is clearly due to assimilation to Lk 5.32.

the souls of men but to save'); Lk 19.10 ('The Son of man came to seek and save the lost'); 1 Tim 1.15 ('Christ Jesus came into the world to save sinners'; this is introduced by 'the saying is sure and worthy of acceptance'); Barn. 5.9 ('he came not to call the righteous but sinners'); 2 Clem. 2 ('another Scripture says: "I came to call not the righteous but sinners"'); Justin, *1 Apol.* 15.8 ('I have not come to call the righteous but sinners to repentance'; cf. Lk 5.32). Because the text of *P. Oxy.* 1224 breaks off after the saying about the physician, we do not know whether 'I came, etc.' belonged originally to that text.

The variants just cited fall into two categories. One contains the righteous/sinner contrast (Mk 2.17; Barn. 5.9; 2 Clem. 2; Justin, *1 Apol.* 15.8), the other does not (Lk 9.55 v. 1.; 19:10; 1 Tim 1.15). The second is probably a development of the first. Note that Lk 9.55 v. 1. and 19.10 and 1 Tim 1.15 have christological titles ('Son of man', 'Christ Jesus'), and that all three have the word, σώζειν.

While Mt 9.13c may have been isolated at one time and only later tacked on to clarify the proverb in 9.12,[109] its authenticity is far from unlikely. (i) Jesus' fellowship with outcasts, with those who were regarded by many Jews as 'sinners', belongs to the bedrock of the tradition. (ii) The use of 'I came' + infinitive (cf. *'ătā̆ + lĕ*) does not disqualify the saying's authenticity (see on 5.17). In addition, the form of 9.13c has a very close parallel in Lk 12.51, a saying whose authenticity should be accepted (cf. Allison, pp. 118–20). 'Think not that I came to cast peace on earth; I came not to cast peace but a sword' is formally very similar to 'I came not to call the righteous, but sinners'. (iii) The antithesis, δίκαιος/ἁμαρτωλός, is common in Semitic sources (cf. *ṣaddîq/rāšā'* and G. Schrenk, *TWNT* 2, p. 191); and it occurs in dominical parables (Lk 15.7; 18.9–14). Furthermore, early Christians called themselves 'the righteous', so are they likely to have formulated a saying in which the righteous are excluded from Jesus' mission? See Mt 10.41; 13.43, 49; Lk 14.14; Rom 1.17; Jas 5.16; 1 Jn 3.7. (iv) 'I came not to call the righteous but sinners' would have been an appropriate response to objections directed at the company Jesus kept (cf. Mt 11.19 = Lk 7.34). (v) Our saying has no christological title (contrast Lk 19.10; 1 Tim 1.15). Also, one might have expected a community formulation to specify the object of Jesus' call (cf. the addition of 'to repentance' in Mt 9.13 v. 1. and Lk 5.32).

The crux of 9.13 is this: what is the status of the 'righteous'?[110] There would seem to be four different possibilities. (i) Jesus did not call the righteous because they were presumed to be saved already (cf. Pry. Man. 8). (ii) Jesus did not call the righteous because he knew it would do no good: they were too stubborn to heed his proclamation (cf. 13.14–15). (iii) All the emphasis lies on the 'sinners' and one should not

---

[109] Cf. Bultmann, *History*, pp. 91–2; Dodd, *Parables*, pp. 90–1.

[110] In its present context, 'the righteous' must be the Pharisees. Patristic opinion, oddly enough, occasionally equated the righteous with angels (e.g. Macarius Magnes, *Apocritus* 4.18).

draw any inferences at all about the status of the righteous.[111]
(iv) Jesus could have been saying that he came to call sinners
only, it being presupposed that everyone is a sinner (cf. 7.11;
Rom 3.9–18). The 'righteous' would then simply be those who
failed to see that they were no better off than everyone else (cf.
Lk 18.9–14). In other words, 'righteous' refers to subjective
opinion, not objective fact (cf. Chrysostom, *Hom. on Mt.* 30.5).
The saying would contain irony. Which interpretation is correct?
With regard to the historical Jesus all four opinions have been
argued, although (iii) or (iv) is the best guess. With regard to
Matthew, only (ii), (iii), and (iv) are possibilities, and we
regrettably fail to see any way to judge between them.

THE QUESTION ABOUT FASTING (9.14–17)

Verses 14–15 constitute a 'paradigm' (Dibelius' term), more
specifically an 'objection story' (p. 96), which preserves an
authentic saying of Jesus (9.15a = Mk 2.19b). In the pre-Markan
tradition the story attracted vv. 16–17 (= Mk 2.21–22), two
dominical parables which were perhaps paired from the
beginning. In both Matthew and Mark the unit follows the
scene where Jesus feasts with toll collectors and sinners. The
sequence is appropriate. After feasting in a manner offensive to
some, Jesus defends his behaviour as regards fasting and
characterizes the present as a time of celebration.

Matthew's version of Mk 2.18–22 distinguishes itself in the following
ways. (i) It is shorter than its source (105 words in Matthew, 132 in Mark).
(ii) The disciples of John alone address Jesus (v. 14; in Mark it is not clear
who is speaking, although it may just be 'people'; cf. Cranfield, *Mark*,
p. 108). (iii) The phrase, 'the disciples of the Pharisees' (Mk 2.18), has been
eliminated. (iv) The fasting of the questioners is now qualified by πολλά,
'much', 'often'. See v. 14. (v) Mk 2.19c ('as long as they have the
bridegroom with them they cannot fast') finds no place in the First Gospel.
(vi) The superfluous 'in that day' of Mk 2.20 has not been reproduced. (vii)
The parables of the patches and wineskins have been revised in such
a way as to lay more stress on the preservation of the old. Note
especially Matthew's redactional conclusion: 'and so both are
preserved' (v. 17).

14. The disciples of John now appear on the stage. They want
to know why Jesus' followers do not fast. Where is their religious
zeal and moral rigour? Why do the disciples of one who preaches
repentance (4.17) not display acts of repentance?[112]

---

[111] In Hebrew and Aramaic sentences with the form, 'not a, but b', the
emphasis is typically on the affirmation about b; see H. Kruse, 'Die "dialektische
Negation" als semitisches Idiom', *VT* 4 (1954), pp. 385–400.

[112] If we are to imagine Jesus sitting in the house (9.10) until he gets up in

τότε προσέρχονται αὐτῷ οἱ μαθηταὶ ᾽Ιωάννου λέγοντες. Matthew has abbreviated Mk 2.18, eliminating the mention of the Pharisees (see below), adding his beloved τότε*, changing ἔρχονται to προσέρχομαι* + αὐτῷ (Mt: 17; Mk: 2; Lk: 0), and preferring the construction, finite verb + participle, to finite verb + finite verb (cf. 2.7, 17; 9.29; 12.38; 15.1; 20.20; 21.1–2; 23.1–2; 26.65; 27.9).

By referring only to 'the disciples of John'[113] Matthew makes 9.14–17 the third story in a row in which a different religious group has shown itself to be at cross purposes with Jesus—the scribes in 9.1–8, the Pharisees in 9.9–13, the disciples of John the Baptist in 9.14–17. A not too dissimilar scheme occurs in Mk 11–12, where Jesus is confronted first by the chief priests (11.27), then by the Pharisees and Herodians (12.13), next by the Sadducees (12.18), and finally by one of the scribes (12.28).

διὰ τί ἡμεῖς καὶ οἱ Φαρισαῖοι νηστεύομεν πολλά.[114] Mk 2.18 has 'the disciples of John' instead of 'we', 'the disciples of the Pharisees' instead of 'the Pharisees', 'they fast' instead of 'we fast', and no qualifying πολλά.[115] Matthew's text is a decided improvement upon Mark's. It is shorter. It flows more smoothly. And there is no doubt as to who is speaking. Moreover, the novel expression, 'the disciples of the Pharisees' (cf. 22.16), is missing—why we cannot guess, unless it be just a desire for brevity.[116]

It has sometimes been proposed that the disciples of John were fasting because of their master's death (cf. Mk 1.13; 6.14–29; cf. Cranfield, *Mark*, pp. 108–9). Whatever be the merit of this as historical speculation (see Kee, 'Fasting' (v), p. 164), it has no foothold in Matthew's text. And if πολλά be retained in 9.14b, our redactor could not have been thinking of a mourning fast. Rather he probably had in mind the voluntary, self-imposed fasts that many pious Jews observed every week.[117] Matthew must have believed that Jesus kept the fast for the day of atonement: it was commanded by Scripture (Lev

9.19, then the disciples of John must be in the house too. Cf. Edwards, *Story*, p. 30: 'the dinner conversation continues'.

[113] 'The disciples of John' (cf. 11.2 = Lk 7.18–9; 14.12 = Mk 6.29; Lk 11.1; Jn 1.35; 3.25; 4.1) are not defined by our text. Whether they are to be thought of on analogy with the disciples of Jesus or whether we should think more broadly of people influenced by the Baptist's preaching is unclear. On the issue of a continuing Baptist movement see on 11.2–3.

[114] πολλα is omitted by ℵ* B *pc* sa^ms geo^B. See Metzger, p. 25.

[115] πολύς as adverb: Mt: 3; Mk: 12; Lk:2.

[116] On the possibly related 'sons of the Pharisees' (cf. 12.27 = Lk 11.19) see the comments of Marshall, p. 224: they are the Pharisees' followers, those who accept the Pharisees' teaching.

[117] Note that, according to 11.18 = Lk 7.33, John the Baptist was known for his fasts.

16.1–34; Num 29.7–11; cf. 11QTemple 25.10–12); and the temptation story in Q tells about a lengthy fast of Jesus (cf. Mk 14.25). So the failure to fast as did the disciples of John and the Pharisees was not, in Matthew's eyes, a failure to fast altogether. What Jesus and his disciples probably did not do, and what Matthew and his community probably did not do, was fast regularly on Mondays and Thursdays (cf. Kee, 'Fasting' (v), p. 162). The custom (whose origins are unknown) of non-obligatory fasting on these two days had already established itself among the first-century Pharisees. See further on 6.16–8.[118]

οἱ δὲ μαθηταί σου οὐ νηστεύουσιν; Compare 11.19, where John's asceticism is contrasted with Jesus' freedom in eating and drinking. John's response to the eschatological crisis was not that of Jesus. John was an ascetic who called people to sombre repentance. Jesus, as Matthew well knew, announced and joyously celebrated the presence of the kingdom.

15. Jesus now answers the question raised by John's disciples. Defending his own followers, he justifies their practice by drawing an analogy. On the responsibility of a rabbi for his pupils see D. Daube, 'Responsibilities of Master and Disciples in the Gospels', *NTS* 19 (1972), pp. 1–15.

καὶ εἶπεν αὐτοῖς ὁ Ἰησοῦς. So also Mk 2.19a.

μὴ δύνανται οἱ υἱοὶ τοῦ νυμφῶνος πενθεῖν ἐφ᾿ ὅσον μετ᾿ αὐτῶν ἐστιν ὁ νυμφίος; Compare Isa 62.4–5. Was the sentiment proverbial (cf. Bultmann, *History*, p. 102, n. 2)? Mk 2.19 has: 'The sons of the bridal chamber are unable, while (ἐν ᾧ) the bridegroom is with them, to fast'. Matthew has moved 'the bridegroom' to the end of the sentence (enhancing the parallelism with the next clause), substituted ἐφ᾿ ὅσον[119] for ἐν ᾧ[120], used πενθεῖν (cf. 5.4) instead of νηστεύειν,[121] and moved the main verb from the second clause to the first (thus again increasing the parallelism with v. 15e). οἱ υἱοὶ τοῦ νυμφῶνος is a Semitism (cf. *běnê haḥûppâ*, as in *t. Ber.* 2.10; *b. Sukka* 25b) meaning either the bridegroom's attendants or, more generally, the wedding guests (see SB 1, pp. 500–4; Feuillet, 'Jeûne' (v), pp. 129–30; Gos. Philip 82.17). νυμφών (cf. 22.10) appears only

[118] Lane, p. 109, suggests that those who questioned Jesus may have been fasting for the coming of the Messiah. This would give added impact to Jesus' answer, which stresses the eschatological dimensions of the present. Cf. Klausner, p. 248. The suggestion is possible for stage I of the tradition (the historical Jesus) but highly unlikely for stage III (the redactional level).

[119] Mt: 3; Mk: 0; Lk: 0. LXX: 0. Cf. 2 Pet 1.13. Schlatter, p. 312, calls attention to Josephus, *Ant.* 10.105, and 13.359 and compares the rabbinic *kol-zěman*.

[120] Matthew never uses this of time (contrast Lk 19.13).

[121] By substituting 'mourn' for 'fast' in 9.15, the First Evangelist strengthens the allusion to Jesus' death. In addition, perhaps we should recall 6.16–8, where fasting is assumed but the outward signs of mourning are prohibited.

twice in the LXX, in Tob 6.13 and 16. The article before υἱοί is generic.

The answer to Jesus' rhetorical question is obvious: wedding guests do not fast during the bridal celebrations.[122] In like manner, Jesus' disciples cannot fast because they are in a time of celebration. The analogy, which centres on the theme of joy, is unmistakable. But what justifies the comparison in the first place? That is, why is the present a time of joy? For Matthew the answer was probably christological. Messiah Jesus is the bridegroom, and while he is with his disciples they cannot mourn. See especially 25.1–12 (cf. 2 Cor 11.2; Rev 19.7).

Matthew's christological interpretation probably marks a slight shift from the original meaning. What would Jesus' hearers have made of his words? Even though the messianic age was sometimes depicted as a wedding feast (Isa 62.5; Rev 19.7; SB 1, pp. 517–18), only in the relatively late *Pesiq. R.* 149a is the Messiah indisputably compared with a bridegroom.[123] In all probability, when Jesus first uttered Mk 2.19 par. (see below), he was probably thinking about the kingdom of God, which was present in his ministry (cf. J. Jeremias, *TWNT* 4, pp. 1095–6). For Jesus the kingdom was like a feast, and it was already present; so the time to feast had come.

The authenticity of v. 15a par. is today usually taken for granted.[124] Further, it is possible that the canonical context for the saying is correct, that Jesus' utterance was occasioned by a question asked by or about the followers of John the Baptist.[125] Compare Perrin, pp. 79–80; Hultgren, pp. 80–1;[126] contrast Carlston, pp. 121–5.[127]

ἐλεύσονται δὲ ἡμέραι ὅταν ἀπαρθῇ ἀπ' αὐτῶν ὁ νυμφίος, καὶ

---

[122] Cf. 1 Macc 9.37–9. According to *b. Sukka* 25b, wedding guests were free from certain religious obligations (cf. *t. Ber.* 2.10).

[123] See Jeremias, *TWNT* 4, pp. 1094–95; Gnilka, 'Bräutigam' (v). For a different assessment see Feuillet, 'Controverse' (v), p. 133, and J. C. O'Neill (v).

[124] But see Kee, 'Question' (v), for the proposal that the disciples of Jesus fasted only in secret (cf. 6.16–8), and that outsiders therefore thought they did not fast at all. This circumstance then led to the accusation against the church recorded in Mk 2.18, which was answered by Mk 2.19–20.

[125] The reference to the Pharisees could be a later addition; so Taylor, *Mark*, pp. 209–10.

[126] Although Hultgren acknowledges a rôle for historical reminiscence, he urges also that the composition of the story was occasioned by an issue in the early church: Christians had been accused of not keeping the same fast days as the Pharisees (viz. Mondays and Thursdays).

[127] The most forceful of Carlston's objections is this: Mark's ἐν ᾧ implies a temporary situation whereas Jesus nowhere else anticipates an end to the joy experienced because of the kingdom. But the Greek can mean 'because' (cf. BDF§ 220.2). More importantly, if we take seriously the possibility that the saying goes back to Jesus, what we have preserved is presumably a translation, which may or may not adequately render the exact force of the Semitic original. One also wonders whether it would be natural to press the temporal dimension of ἐν ᾧ if 9.15b–c stood alone; cf. Gnilka, *Markus* 1, p. 112; Pesch 1, p. 174.

τότε νηστεύσουσιν. Compare Joel 2.16 (which Muddiman (v) unsuccessfully attempts to connect with our verse). Matthew has reproduced Mk 2.20, without Mark's concluding 'in that day'.[128] Matthew has also omitted the last part of Mk 2.19. Did he think this redundant?[129] Luke also dropped it. Concerning καὶ τότε, it is precisely because the bridegroom has been taken away that his friends mourn (cf. 1 Macc 9.37–41; 4 Ezra 10.1–4). From Matthew's point of view this means that the community stands under the cross. Concerning 'the days will come', because these words elsewhere have eschatological import (cf. Isa 39.6; Jer 7.32; 23.5; Amos 4.2; 9.13; Lk 17.22; 21.6), and because the early church tended to see its own time as part of the messianic woes, an eschatological interpretation may be called for: the disciples will fast in the days of eschatological affliction (cf. Ebeling (v)).

Our clause is usually regarded as a secondary addition. After Easter, when fasting was standard Christian practice, Jesus' words required qualification. This was accomplished by making a distinction between the time of Jesus' earthly presence with his disciples and the time of his bodily absence: regular fasting was only inappropriate during the former period. Although less certain than often assumed (cf. Taylor, Mark, pp. 211–12; Hill, Matthew, p. 177), this analysis is probably correct.

Gos. Thom. 104 reads: 'Come, let us pray today and let us fast. Jesus said: What sin have I committed, or by what have I been defeated? But whenever the bridegroom goes out of the bridal chamber, then let them fast and pray'. Although not necessarily dependent upon the synoptics, this can hardly bring us closer to the historical Jesus than they do. Of more interest is Jn 3.29: 'He who has the bride is the bridegroom. But the friend of the bridegroom, who stands and hears him, rejoices with joy at the bridegroom's voice'. This utterance is attributed to the Baptist. Yet given that sometimes sayings of Jesus were assigned to John and vice versa (cf. Mt 3.2; 7.19), the parable may originally have been attributed to Jesus. In any event the parallels with Mt 9.14–15 par. are striking. Both 9.14–15 par. and Jn 3.29 are responses to a question raised by the disciples of John. Both texts implicitly refer to Jesus as the bridegroom. And both texts have joy as their central motif. Furthermore, while Jn 3.29 concerns the 'friend of the bridegroom', 9.14–15 par. is about 'the sons of the bridegroom'. In view of these similarities, one wonders whether Jn 3.29 and its context might not depend ultimately upon the tradition preserved in the synoptics.[130]

[128] Was our evangelist bothered by the singular 'day'? Contrast the 'days' just previously mentioned.
[129] The clause was probably composed by the pre-Markan tradition in order to provide a transition to what follows.
[130] For further discussion see Dodd, Tradition, pp. 282–5, 385–6; and Lindars, John, pp. 167–8.

16. This verse and the next reproduce Mk 2.21–2 (cf. Lk 5.36–9). Matthew has introduced stylistic changes and underlined the continuity between old and new (see below). Like Mark before him,[131] he was content to pass on the parables about the patch and the wineskins as the conclusion to the controversy about fasting. Crossan (v), p. 121, rightly notes the thematic connexion: 9.14f., 16, and 17 'all involve *impossible combinations*: wedding and fasting, unshrunk with shrunk cloth, new wine in old wineskins'. But this is not all. The parables in vv. 16–17 have to do with the old and the new, and their implicit subject is, like the implicit subject of the preceding two verses, the new time that has come with Jesus and its significance for Judaism. The emphasis is upon discontinuity. But the importance of continuity is also voiced. Thus, on the one hand, Jesus makes traditional fasting impossible. Surely for Matthew this circumstance is just one example of a general truth: new wine should not be put into old wineskins. The new is truly new, and it cannot be embodied in old, established norms. The kingdom impels a new kind of behaviour and a new set of rituals. On the other hand, if new wine is put into fresh wineskins, the old wineskins will not be destroyed: 'so both are preserved'. The past is not to be forsaken but adopted and transformed. Compare 5.17–48 and our comments on pp. 564–5. For Matthew Judaism is Christianity's inheritance, and it would be unthinkable to abandon the legacy. Judaism is for him not a past phenomenon external to Christianity but a continuing presence carried on within it.[132]

οὐδεὶς δὲ ἐπιβάλλει ἐπίβλημα ῥάκους ἀγνάφου ἐπὶ ἱματίῳ παλαιῷ. Matthew has, over against Mark, added δέ (making the connexion with 9.15 firmer), turned the accusative after ἐπί into a dative, moved the verb forward from its place before ἐπί (a change which increases the parallelism with 9.17), and substituted for the very rare ἐπιράπτω (= 'sew on'; only here in the Greek Bible) the less vivid ἐπιβάλλω (cf. MHT 4, p. 40). The last change strengthens the link with 9.17 (where βάλλω occurs twice) and gains a cognate for ἐπίβλημα.[133] ἐπίβλημα (cf. LXX Isa 3.22) is a 'patch'. ῥάκος can mean 'rag' or 'tattered garment' (LXX Isa 64.5) but here means 'piece of

[131] Mk 2.21–2 was probably joined to 2.18–20 in the pre-Markan tradition; so Pesch 1, p. 170, and Gnilka 1, pp. 111–12. Crossan (v), p. 121, appears unsure. Muddiman (v) goes so far as to think the link original with Jesus: the subject of a wedding led to thoughts of garments and wine.
[132] Here Matthew and Paul are similar; see Davies, *JPS*, pp. 123–71.
[133] Lk also has ἐπίβαλλει. But one can hardly make much of this, for as Streeter, p. 130, observed, 'the noun ἐπίβλημα almost shouts out to an editor to alter the verb to ἐπίβαλλει'.

cloth' (cf. Jer 45.11; Josephus, *Ant.* 6.289). ἄγναφος (LXX: 0) means 'new' or 'unshrunken' (BAGD, s.v.; for the related γναφεύς see LXX Isa 7.3; 36.2).

αἴρει γὰρ τὸ πλήρωμα αὐτοῦ ἀπὸ τοῦ ἱματίου. This clause and the next explain why people do not put an unshrunk patch on an old garment. Upon washing, there will be a tear. Compare Mk 2.21: εἰ δὲ μή, αἴρει τὸ πλήρωμα ἀπ᾽ αὐτοῦ τὸ καινὸν τοῦ παλαιοῦ. Matthew's construction is smoother and more concise, although it is hardly free of difficulties (see below). εἰ δὲ μή has been eliminated, γάρ* and αὐτοῦ added, and ἀπ᾽ αὐτοῦ κ.τ.λ. shortened to ἀπὸ τοῦ ἱματίου.

τὸ πλήρωμα could mean 'the patch' (so BAGD, s.v.), even though no parallels to such usage are known.[134] Also difficult is αὐτοῦ. It could conceivably refer to the patch, to the unshrunk cloth, or to the old garment. Matters are even more complicated because our sentence does not seem to have a subject. τὸ πλήρωμα could be nominated (so Schlatter, p. 313), but αἴρει would then have no object (see further Zahn, pp. 380–1). Perhaps Steinhauser, 'Patch' (v), has put forward the best solution. He takes τὸ πλήρωμα to refer to the 'fill' of the unshrunk cloth, 'that is the material and the thread with which the unshrunk cloth is sewn to the old cloak'. The subject is supplied from the previous clause: ἐπίβλημα ῥάκους ἀγνάφου (cf. Zahn, p. 381). The meaning then is: 'because the patch of unshrunk cloth draws the fill (that is, the overlapping section of the unshrunk cloth) from the cloak and the tear becomes worse'.

καὶ χεῖρον σχίσμα γίνεται. So also Mark. The deficiency of the old is made manifest when it puts on the new.

17. A second vivid and homely illustration, another lesson from experience, now follows the first. For other examples of paired parables and discussion see Jeremias, *Parables*, pp. 90–6.

οὐδὲ βάλλουσιν οἶνον νέον εἰς ἀσκοὺς παλαιούς. For 'new wine' see LXX Isa 49.26; Ecclus 9.10; 11QTemple 19.14; 21.10; *m.* 'Aboth 4.20; *t.* Pesaḥ. 10.1. For other NT contrasts between old and new see Rom 7.6; Eph 4.22; Col 3.9–10; Heb 8.13. Mark begins with 'no one puts' and continues as does Matthew. Matthew's impersonal plural (cf. 1.23; 5.15; 7.16) is Semitic. οὐδέ* increases the parallelism with 9.16 (δέ). ἀσκός (in the LXX for both ḥēmet and nōʾd) is a wineskin (see SB 1, pp. 518–19). Wineskins were typically made of goat hides.

εἰ δὲ μή γε, ῥήγνυνται οἱ ἀσκοί. Fermentation will swell the

---

[134] It might be an obscure Semitism. According to Black, p. 133, n. 3, 'One use of the Syriac verb mᵉla is "to patch"'. (This verb, like the Greek πληρόω, the cognate of πλήρωμα, means 'fill'.)

wine and burst the old wineskin. The old cannot contain the new. Mark lacks γε[135] and has wine as the subject: 'the wine will burst the skins'. Matthew's present tense harmonizes with the present tense of 9.16 (αἴρει). By making the wineskins the subject Matthew prepares for his editorial comment on preservation; also, one wonders whether Matthew's version is intended to soften the contrast of old and new in the sense that the new wine itself does not burst Judaism but that the effect of it is to reveal the weakness of the skins. Perhaps Mt 9.17 par. was based on a proverbial sentiment. Compare Josh 9.13; Job 32.19 *m*. ᾿*Abot* 4.20.

καὶ ὁ οἶνος ἐκχεῖται καὶ οἱ ἀσκοὶ ἀπόλλυνται. Mk 2.22 according to NA[26] has καὶ ὁ οἶνος ἀπόλλυται καὶ οἱ ἀσκοί but according to HG καὶ ὁ οἶνος ἐκχεῖται καὶ οἱ ἀσκοι ἀπολοῦνται. If the text in HG is correct Matthew has simply changed one verb from a future middle to a present indicative passive. If NA[26] is right Matthew has given the wineskins their own verb and made two clauses out of one.

ἀλλὰ βάλλουσιν οἶνον νέον εἰς ἀσκοὺς καινούς. The only change from Mark is the addition of the verb (βάλλω*). This makes for perfect parallelism with 17a:

17a: nor do they put old wine into old wineskins
17d: but they put new wine into new wineskins

καινός and νέος both mean 'new'. The former is used to describe the wineskins, the latter the wine, because the NT tends to use καινός of quality, νέος of time. The wine is newly made, the wineskins unused.[136]

καὶ ἀμφότεροι συντηροῦνται. This is a redactional addition without parallel in Mark or Luke. συντηρέω (often in the apocrypha) appears only here in the First Gospel (Mk: 1; Lk: 1). ἀμφότεροι (usually for *šĕnayīm* in the LXX) occurs two other times in Matthew, in 13.30 (without parallel) and in 15.14 (from Q; cf. Lk 6.39).

What exactly Jesus meant when he composed the parables of the patched garment and the wineskins is debated.[137] This is largely because we do not know the context(s) in which they

---

[135] Luke also has γε, which makes for a minor agreement. Coincidence is the obvious explanation. εἰ δὲ μή invited γε for εἰ δὲ μή γε was a standard expression; see e.g. LXX Dan 3.15; Bel 8; Mt 6.1; Lk 5.36, 37; 10.6; 13.9; 14.32; 2 Cor 11.16; Josephus, *Bell*. 6.120; *Ant*. 17.113; *P. Oxy*. 1159.6.

[136] Still worth reading on the point is R. C. Trench, *Synonyms of the New Testament*, 9th ed., London 1880, pp. 219–25. Additional lit.: J. Behm, *TWNT* 3, pp. 450–6; 4, pp. 899–903; R. A. Harrisville, 'The Concept of Newness in the New Testament', *JBL* 74 (1955), pp. 69–79.

[137] The parables are generally accepted as dominical; cf. Hahn (v); and Gnilka 1, p. 116. Contrast Carlston, pp. 127–9.

were first spoken (cf. Taylor, *Mark*, p. 212). According to Jeremias, Jesus was taking up traditional metaphors for the new age. 'Tent, sheet, and garment are common symbols of the cosmos. To this context Mark 2.21 belongs: the old world's age has run out; it is compared to the old garment which is no longer worth patching with new cloth; the New Age has arrived' (*Parables*, p. 118; he cites in support Acts 10.9–16; 11.1–18; and Heb 1.10–12). Similarly, wine was a stock symbol for the time of salvation (Jeremias cites Gen 9.20; 49.11–12; Num 13.23–4; Jn 2.1–11). So from Mk 2.21–2 par. we are to infer that the old is past, for the eschatological age has come.

It is difficult to know whether Jeremias has read too much into the garment and the wine. Mk 2.21 and 22 make sense without taking into account the background Jeremias proposes.[138] More importantly, one wonders whether our two parables do not show some concern for the old. Are not the old wineskins and the old garment worth saving (see Kee, 'Coat' (v))? Whatever be the answer to this question with regard to the historical Jesus,[139] Matthew would have returned an affirmative response. Our evangelist has added: 'and both will be preserved'. In its broader context, which concerns fasting, this clause makes for a positive relation between an old practice (fasting) and the newness brought by Jesus. That is, even though the immediate subject of 'and both will be preserved' is the new wine and the new wineskins, the redactor was probably thinking of wineskins as symbols for something from the past, and of the need to preserve them. After all, Jesus has explicitly endorsed fasting in the post-Easter period, so the old has hardly been cancelled. The concern expressed by Mt 9.17 would seem to be the same as that expressed in 5.17–20: Jesus does not destroy the old but fulfils it (cf. 13.52).

Gos. Thom. 47 contains this: 'No one drinks old wine and immediately desires to drink new wine; and they do not put new wine into old wineskins, lest they burst, and they do not put old wine into a new wineskin, lest it spoil it. They do not sew an old patch on a new garment, because there would be a rent'. Crossan (v) argues that this, which against all three synoptics puts the parable about the wineskins before the parable about the patch, is independent of the canonical

[138] He has at least avoided the crime of extreme allegorizing. Contrast Bengel, *ad loc.*: the old bottles are the Pharisees, the new bottles the disciples, and the wine is the gospel.

[139] We cannot assume, in any case, that Mk 2.21 and 22 had to do with Judaism as a whole rather than with some particular aspect of it. The context does not demand such an assumption. Furthermore, Jesus, like Paul after him, hoped for the salvation of 'all Israel'. Judaism was to be renewed, not destroyed or cast away.

gospels; and this contention is crucial for his involved four stage history of the tradition. One strongly suspects, however, that the apocryphal gospel has here been influenced directly or indirectly by Lk 5.36–9, for it too contains the proverb about drinking old wine (cf. Schrage, pp. 112–6). (That Luke, with the exception of 5.39, contains tradition independent of Mark is possible but hardly probable; cf. Fitzmyer, *Luke* 1, pp. 594–5; contrast Crossan (v). Certainly the minor agreements with Matthew do not amount to much.)

(iv) *Concluding Observations*

Two themes dominate 8.23–9.17. The first and most obvious is Jesus' ἐξουσία (cf. 9.6, 8). The sermon on the mount has already demonstrated the authority of Jesus' teaching (cf. 7.28–9). Mt 8–9 next demonstrates the authority of his actions. In 8.23–7 Jesus can command the storm to cease. In 8.28–34 he can cast out demons with the simple word 'Go'. In 9.1–8 Jesus the Son of man can both heal a paralytic and forgive his sins. And in 9.9 Jesus can, with two words, compel a stranger to follow him. In sum, Jesus' authority is such that his word is deed (cf. 8.9). His command is 'compulsion' and is immediately obeyed by nature (8.23–7), by demons (8.28–34), and by people (9.9). The power of Jesus' divine ἐξουσία is seemingly unbounded, as is its sphere (cf. 28.18 and our comments on 7.29).

The second major theme of 8.13–9.17 is mercy (cf. 9.13). In 8.28–34 Jesus reaches out to two men—demoniacs dwelling in a graveyard—who were clearly forsaken by society. In 9.1–8 he compassionately heals a paralytic by saying to him, 'Take heart, my son; your sins are forgiven'. In 9.9–10 Jesus calls a social outcast—Matthew the toll-collector—and then reclines at table with 'sinners'. And in 9.13–14 Jesus the merciful physician explicitly proclaims that he came for the sick, and in order to call sinners.

In presenting so vividly for his readers Jesus' mercy and authority, the evangelist is implicitly offering both paraenesis and encouragement. Certainly the Christian reader must follow in the footsteps of Jesus in that he too must show mercy. Which is to say: one must be the good Samaritan and extend a hand even to those ignored by others. Mercy involves the crossing of boundaries erected by society at large. This is what makes the demand to be merciful so difficult. The hard imperatives of Matthew's Jesus are, however, never made outside the context of grace, and so is it here. Jesus' ἐξουσία is the ground of Christian confidence and boldness, the basis of Christian courage. When Matthew writes of Jesus' authority he always assumes that this is an authority Jesus shares with others. In the First Gospel Christology is · inextricably bound up with ecclesiology. To speak of Christ is to speak of the church. Jesus' divine power and authority are not, after Easter, confined to some far-away heavenly sphere. Rather are they manifested concretely through, to use a Pauline metaphor, the members of his body, the church. While the numerous illustrations throughout Matthew of Jesus' ἐξουσία may indeed show Jesus to be the Messiah and Son of God, they also invite the faithful reader to share in that ἐξουσία. The idea is not far from Phil 4.13: 'I can do all things through him who strengthens me'.

There is also one more way in which the Jesus of 8.23–9.17 must be seen as example and precedent. In 9.1–8 Jesus faces opposition from the Jewish leaders. His response is as far from concession as it could be. Jesus does not apologize or retract his words. He does not keep quiet or appeal to mitigating circumstances. The cold, unyielding eye of the critics does not cause him to wither away. Jesus instead enters into a debate. This is the response he will continue to exhibit throughout our gospel. So far from opposition intimidating Jesus, it serves him as an opportunity to set forth his views and upbraid error. Now Matthew, writing in a time when Jewish Christians were no doubt experiencing considerable harassment from rabbis and synagogue leaders, must have thought of Jesus' outspoken responses as a charge for Christians to speak the truth with discriminating boldness (cf. Jn 9.1–41). One does not put a light under a bushel but on a stand.

The points made thus far all assume that Matthew's Christian readers—who shared Jesus' ἐξουσία, knew themselves commanded to show mercy, and felt in need of inspiration for boldness—would, in reading or hearing the First Gospel, have identified themselves with the hero. This, however, is not necessarily the case. Surely some readers identified themselves firstly not with Jesus but with those he encountered. 8.23–7 (the stilling of the storm) in particular would have encouraged such an approach (see pp. 68–69). The Christian, after all, not only continues his Lord's ministry (cf. 10.40) but is also an object of his Lord's continuing ministry. So people may well have come away from 8.23–9.17 strengthened with the thought that Jesus would rescue them in times of distress (8.23–7), deliver them from demonic influences (8.28–34), and forgive them of all their sins (9.1–8). Certainly Matthew's text does nothing to discourage such a reading.

(v) *Bibliography*

P. J. Achtemeier, 'Person and Deed', *Int* 16 (1962), pp. 169–76.

F. Annen, *Heil für die Heiden: Zur Bedeutung und Geschichte der Tradition vom besessenen Gerasener (Mk 5, 1–20 parr.)*, FTS 20, Frankfurt am Main, 1976.

Arens, pp. 28–63, 212–21.

T. Baarda, 'Gadarenes, Gerasenes, Gergesenes and the "Diatessaron" Traditions', in Ellis, *Neotestamentica*, pp. 181–97.

U. Becker and S. Wibbing, *Wundergeschichten*, Gütersloh, 1965, pp. 12–55.

R. T. Beckwith, 'The Feast of New Wine and the Question of Fasting', *ExpT* 95 (1984), pp. 334–5.

J. Bligh, 'The Gerasene Demoniac and the Resurrection of Jesus', *CBQ* 31 (1969), pp. 383–90.

G. H. Boobyer, 'Mark 2.10a and the Interpretation of the Healing of the Paralytic', *HTR* 47 (1954), pp. 115–20.

G. Bornkamm, 'The Stilling of the Storm in Matthew', in *TIM*, pp. 52–7.

H. Branscomb, 'Mk 2.5: "Son thy sins are forgiven"', *JBL* 53 (1934), pp. 53–60.

G. Braumann, '"Am jenem Tag" Mk 2.20', *NovT* 6 (1963), pp. 264–7.

H. Braun, 'Gott, die Eröffnung des Lebens für die Nonkonformisten. Erwägungen zu Markus 2.15–17', in *Festschrift für Ernst Fuchs*, Tübingen, 1973, pp. 97–101.

G. Brooke, 'The Feast of New Wine and the Question of Fasting', *ExpT* 95 (1984) pp. 175–6.

T. A. Burkill, 'Concerning Mk 5.7 and 5.18–20', *ST* 11 (1957), pp. 159–66.

idem, 'Should Wedding Guests fast? A Consideration of Mk 2.18–20', in *New Light on the Earliest Gospel*, Ithaca and London, 1972, pp. 39–47.

F. C. Burkitt, 'Levi, Son of Alphaeus', *JTS* 28 (1927), pp. 273–4.

A. Cabaniss, 'A fresh Exegesis of Mk 2.1–12', *Int* 11 (1957), pp. 324–7.

Carlston, pp. 10–5, 110–29.

C. H. Cave, 'The Obedience of Unclean Spirits', *NTS* 11 (1964), pp. 93–7.

C. P. Ceroke, 'Is Mk 2.10 a Saying of Jesus?', *CBQ* 22 (1960), pp. 369–90.

H. Conzelmann, 'Auslegung von Markus 4.35–41 par.; Markus 8.31–37 par.; Römer 1.3f.', *Evangelische Erzieher* (Frankfurt) 20 (1968), pp. 249–60.

Cope, pp. 65–73, 96–8.

J. Craghan, 'The Gerasene Demoniac', *CBQ* 30 (1968), pp. 522–36.

W. J. Cratchley, 'Demoniac of Gadara', *ExpT* 63 (1952), pp. 193–4.

F. G. Cremer, 'Christian von Stablo als Exeget. Beobachtungen zur Auslegung von Mt 9.14–17', *RBén* 77 (1967), pp. 328–41.

idem, *Die Fastenansage Jesu Mk 2.20 und Parallelen in der Sicht der patristischen und scholastischen Exegese*, BBB 23, Bonn, 1965.

Crossan, *Aphorisms*, pp. 121–7, 213–20.

J. D. M. Derrett, 'Legend and Event: The Gerasene Demoniac', in Livingstone, pp. 63–73.

idem, 'Contributions to the Study of the Gerasene Demoniac', *JSNT* 3 (1979), pp. 2–17.

R. Dunkerley, 'The Bridegroom Passage', *ExpT* 64 (1953), pp. 303–4.

J. Duplacy, 'Et il y eut un grand calme. . . . La tempête apaisée (Matthieu 8.23–27)', *BVC* 74 (1967), pp. 15–28.

idem, 'Marc II, 10, note de syntax', in *Mélanges A. Robert*, Paris, 1957, pp. 424–6.

J. Dupont, 'Le paralytique pardonné (Mt 9.1–8)', *NRT* 82 (1960), pp. 940–58.

idem, 'Vin vieux, vin nouveau (Luc 5.39)', *CBQ* 25 (1963), pp. 286–304.

P. F. Feiler, 'The Stilling of the Storm in Matthew: A Response to Günther Bornkamm', *JETS* 26 (1983), pp. 399–406.

J. Feliers, 'L'exégèse de la péricope des porcs de Gérasa dans la patristique latine', in *Studia Patristica*, vol. 10, TU 107, ed. F. L. Cross, Berlin, 1970, pp. 225–9.

A. Feuillet, 'Le controverse sur le jeûne', *NRT* 90 (1968), pp. 113–36, 252–77.

idem, 'L'ἐξουσία du fils de l'homme (d'après Mc. II. 10–28 parr.)', *RSR* 42 (1954), pp. 161–92.

Fiedler, pp. 107–12, 119–29.

J. Gnilka, '"Bräutigam"—spätjüdisches Messiasprädikat?', *TTZ* 69 (1960), pp. 298–301.

idem, 'Das Elend vor dem Menschensohn (Mk 2.1–12)', in Pesch, *Menschensohn*, pp. 196–209.

H. Greeven, 'Die Heilung des Gelähmten nach Matthäus', in Lange, *Matthäus*, pp. 205–22.

F. Hahn, 'Die Bildworte vom neuen Flicken und vom jungen Wein', *EvT* 31 (1971), pp. 357–75.

L. S. Hay, 'The Son of Man in Mark 2.10 and 2.28', *JBL* 89 (1970), pp. 69–75.

Heil, pp. 84–103.

H. J. Held, in *TIM*, pp. 172–8, 200–4, 248–9.

Hendrickx, *Miracle Stories*, pp. 104–48, 168–204.

E. Hilgert, 'Symbolismus und Heilsgeschichte in den Evangelien. Ein Beitrag zu den Seesturm – und Gerasenererzählungen', in *Oikonomia. Festschrift für Oscar Cullmann*, ed. F. Christ, Hamburg, 1967, pp. 51–6.

D. Hill, 'On the Use and Meaning of Hosea 6.6 in Matthew's Gospel', *NTS* 24 (1977), pp. 107–19.

Hultgren, pp. 106–11.

H. Jahnow, 'Das Abdecken des Daches, Mk 2.4; Lk 5.19', *ZNW* 24 (1925), pp. 155–8.

Jülicher 2, pp. 174–202.

J. Kahlmeyer, *Seesturm und Schiffbruch als Bild im antiken Schriftum*, Hildesheim, 1934.

A. Kee, 'The Old Coat and the New Wine', *NovT* 12 (1970), pp. 13–21

idem, 'The Question about Fasting', *NovT* 11 (1969), pp. 161–73.

Kertelge, *Wunder*, pp. 75–82, 91–110.

idem, 'Die Vollmacht des Menschensohnes zur Sündenvergebung (Mk 2.10)', in Hoffmann, *Orientierung*, pp. 205–13.

M. Kiley, 'Why "Matthew" in Matt 9.9–13?', *Bib* 65 (1984), pp. 347–51.

Klauck, pp. 148–74, 340–8.

idem, 'Die Frage der Sündenvergebung in der Perikope von der Heilung des Gelähmten (Mk 2.1–12 parr)', *BZ* 25 (1981), pp. 223–48.

J. A. Kleist, 'The Gadarene Demoniacs', *CBQ* 9 (1947), pp. 101–5.

S. Krauss, 'Das Abdecken des Daches', *ZNW* 25 (1926), pp. 307–10.

J. Kreyenbühl, 'Der älteste Auferstehungsbericht und seine Varianten', *ZNW* 9 (1908), pp. 257–96.

Kuhn, pp. 53–98.

P. Lamarche, 'Le Possédé de Gérasa', *NRT* 90 (1968), pp. 581–97.

G. M. Lee, 'They that are whole need not a physician', *ExpT* 76 (1965), p. 254.

F. J. Leenhardt, 'Essai exégétique: Marc 5.1–20', in R. Barthes et al., *Analyse structurale et exégèse biblique*, Neuchâtel, 1971, pp. 95–121.

X. Leon-Dufour, 'La tempête apaisée', in *Études*, pp. 149–82.

W. R. G. Loader, 'Son of David, Blindness, Possession, and Duality in Matthew', *CBQ* 44 (1982), pp. 570–85.

van der Loos, pp. 382–97, 440–49, 638–49.

I. Maisch, *Die Heilung des Gelähmten: Eine exegetisch-traditionsgeschichtliche Untersuchung zu Mk 2.1–12*, SBS 52, Stuttgart, 1971.

R. T. Mead, 'The Healing of the Paralytic—a Unit?', *JBL* 80 (1961), pp. 348–54.

P. Mourlon Beernaert, 'Jésus controversé. Structure et théologie de Marc 2.1–3.6', *NRT* 95 (1973), pp. 129–49.

J. Mouson, '"Non veni vocare iustos, sed peccatores" (Mt 9.13 = Mk 2.17 = Lk 5.32)', *Collectanea Mechliniensia* (Malines) 43 (1958), pp. 134–9.

J. B. Muddiman, 'Jesus and Fasting', in Dupont, *Jésus*, pp. 283–301.

W. Nagel, 'Neuer Wein in alten Schläuchen', *VC* 14 (1960), pp. 1–8.

F. Neirynck, 'Les accords mineurs et la rédaction des Évangiles. L'épisode du paralytique', in *Evangelica*, pp. 781–96.

J. O'Hara, 'Christian Fasting Mk 2.18–22', *Scr* 19 (1967), pp. 82–95.

J. C. O'Neil, 'The Source of the Parables of the Bridegroom and the wicked Husbandmen', *JTS* 39 (1988), pp. 485–9.

R. Pesch, *Der Besessene von Gerasa*, SBS 56, Stuttgart, 1972.

idem, 'Levi-Matthäus (Mc 2.14/Mt 9.9; 10.3)', *ZNW* 59 (1968), pp. 40–56.

idem, 'The Markan Version of the Healing of the Gerasene Demoniac', *ER* 23 (1971), pp. 349–76.

idem, 'Das Zöllnergastmahl (Mk 2.15–17)', in Descampes, *Mélanges*, pp. 63–87.

B. Reicke, 'Die Fastenfrage nach Luk 5.33–39', *TZ* 30 (1974), pp. 321–8.

idem, 'The Synoptic Reports of the Healing of the Paralytic', in *Studies in New Testament Language and Text*, ed. J. K. Elliot, Leiden, 1976, pp. 319–29.

P. Rolland, 'Les prédécesseurs de Marc. Les sources presynoptiques de Mc. II. 18–22 et parallèles', *RB* 89 (1982), pp. 370–405.

Roloff, pp. 164–6, 223–37.

H. Sahlin, 'Die Perikope vom gerasenischen Besessenen und der Plan des Markusevangeliums', *ST* 18 (1964), pp. 159–74.

K. T. Schäfer, '"... und dann werden sie fasten, an jenem Tage" (Mk 2.20 und Parallelen'), in *Synoptische Studien*, ed. J. Schmid and A. Vögtle, Munich, 1953, pp. 124–47.

W. Schenk, '"Den Menschen" Mt 9.8', *ZNW* 54 (1963), pp. 272–5.

Schenke, *Wundererzählungen*, pp. 1–93, 146–60, 173–95, 205–13.

Schille, 'Die Seesturmerzählung Markus 4.35–41 als Beispiel neutestamentlicher Aktualisierung', *ZNW* 56 (1965), pp. 30–40.

W. Schmithals, *Wunder*, pp. 31–68.

Schramm, pp. 93–103, 105–11, 124–6.

A. Schulz, *Nachfolgen und Nachahmen*, SANT 6, Munich, 1962, pp. 97–116.

G. Schwarz, '"Aus der Gegend" (Mk 5.10b)', *NTS* 22 (1976), pp. 215–6.

J. Starobinski, 'An Essay in Literary Analysis—Mk 5.1–20', *ER* 23 (1971), pp. 377–97.

M. G. Steinhauser, 'Neuer Wein braucht neue Schläuche', in *Biblische Randbemerkungen*, ed. H. Merklein and J. Lange, Würzburg, 1974, pp. 113–23.

idem, 'The Patch of Unshrunk Cloth (Mt 9.16)', *ExpT* 87 (1976), pp. 312–3.

Strauss, pp. 319–23, 415–37, 452–7, 496–507.

F. C. Synge, 'Mark 2.21 = Matthew 9.16 = Luke 5.36: The Parable of the Patch', *ExpT* 56 (1944), pp. 26–7.

M. Theobald, 'Der Primat der Synchronie vor der Diachronie als Grundaxiom der Literarkritik. Methodische Erwägungen an Hand von Mk 2.13–17/Mt 9.9–13', *BZ* 22 (1978), pp. 161–86.

W. Thissen, *Erzählung der Befreiung. Eine exegetische Untersuchung zu Mk 2.1–3.6*, FB 21, Würzburg, 1974.

C. M. Tuckett, 'The Present Son of Man', *JSNT* 14 (1982), pp. 58–81.

Trautmann, pp. 132–66, 234–57.

G. B. Twelftree, 'ΕΙ ΔΕ ... ΕΓΩ ΕΚΒΑΛΛΩ ΤΑ ΔΑΙΜΟΝΙΑ', in Wenham and Bloomberg, pp. 361–400.

B. M. F. van Iersel, 'La vocation de Lévi (Mc 2.13–17; Mt 9.9–13; Lc 5.27–32): Traditions et rédactions', in de la Potterie, pp. 212–32.

idem and A. J. M. Linmans, 'The Storm on the Lake, Mk 4.35–41 and Mt 8.18–27 in the Light of Form Criticism', in *Neotestamentica*, NovTSup 48, ed. T. Baarda et al., Leiden, 1978, pp. 17–48.

J. Vencovský, 'Der gadarenische Exorzismus', *CV* 14 (1971), pp. 13–29.

M. Waibel, 'Die Auseinandersetzung mit der Fasten- und Sabbatpraxis Jesu in urchristlichen Gemeinden', in *Zur Geschichte des Urchristentums*, ed. G. Dautzenberg et al., Freiburg, 1979, pp. 63–80.

Wanke, pp. 82–8.

Westerholm, pp. 70–1, 96–110.

S. Wibbing, 'Das Zöllnergastmahl (Mk 2.13–17; vgl. Mt 9.9–13; Lk 5.27–32)', in H. Stock, K. Wegenast, and S. Wibbing, *Streitgespräche*, Gütersloh, 1968, 84–107.

T. Zahn, 'Das Land der Gadarener, Gerasener oder Gergesener', *NKZ* 13 (1902), pp. 923–45.

J. A. Ziesler, 'The Removal of the Bridegroom: A Note on Mark 2.18–22 and Parallels', *NTS* 19 (1973), pp. 190–4.

XIX

A THIRD TRIAD OF MIRACLE STORIES
(9.18–34)

(i) *Structure*

Mt 9.18–34 consists of three progressively shorter miracle stories (9.18–26, 27–31, 32–4) in which Jesus heals five people: the woman with a hemorrhage, the ruler's daughter, two blind men, and a demoniac. Note the numerical advance over the two preceding sections. Three people are healed in 8.1–15, three in 8.23–9.8, five in 9.18–34.

Structurally, the first two paragraphs are very similar. In both Jesus heals two people. In both he speaks about faith (9.22, 28). In both the healing takes place in a house and there is a note of secrecy (9.25, 28, 30). And in both the conclusion tells of Jesus' fame being spread abroad (9.26, 31). If, as we shall urge, 9.27–31 is indeed a redactional construction, it has obviously been much influenced by the pericope it follows.

The basic structure of 9.18–34 as a whole—three successive miracle stories—is the same as that of 8.1–15 and 8.23–9.8. See Excursus V and the diagrams in 1, pp. 67 and 102.

(ii) *Sources*

On the theory of Markan priority, Mt 9.18–26 is a severely abbreviated version of Mk 5.21–43 (cf. Lk 8.40–56), and all seems in order. Matthew's tendency to concentrate on the bare essentials of a miracle story (cf. Augustine, *De con. ev.* 2.28.66) adequately explains 9.18–26. As for the Griesbach theory, it has the merit of being able to explain without difficulty the few minor agreements between Matthew and Luke (for these see Fitzmyer, *Luke* 1, p. 743, to which add the ἰδού in 9.18 = Lk 8.41). Yet if Matthew is in this section thought to be the earliest of our sources, there are a few problems. (i) 'The interpolation of the healing of the woman with a hemorrhage makes sense only in Mark [and Luke], because the child dies while this is taking place; this probably represents the earlier form' (Schweizer, *Matthew*, p. 228). (ii) The woman comes up behind Jesus in order to touch him (9.20). Jesus then turns and sees her. Unless one presupposes the presence of a crowd (so Mk 5.24, 30), it is hard to see how the woman can attempt to touch Jesus without being noticed (cf. Held, in *TIM*, p. 179). There is, however, no crowd in Matthew. Does this not mean that Matthew's account assumes Mark's? (iii) Mk 5.21–43 is free of Matthean redactional matter—ἄρτι* (9.18); ἰδού* (9.18, 20); εἰς* (9.18); προσκυνέω* + dative (9.18); μαθηταί* (9.19); μόνον* (9.21); ἀπὸ τῆς ὥρας ἐκείνης* (9.22); ἀναχωρέω* (9.24); ἐγείρω* (9.25); ὅτε δέ (9.25); γῆ* (9.26).

The two stories in 9.27–34, which are in all probability redactional products, hardly bear on the synoptic problem. They are doublets that, if the Griesbach hypothesis be assumed, both Mark and Luke might have omitted. On the other hand, nothing in 9.27–31 or 32–4 counts against the supposition of Markan priority.

(iii) *Exegesis*

JESUS HEALS A RULER'S DAUGHTER AND A WOMAN WITH A HEMORRHAGE (9.18–26)

Mt 9.18–26, like its Markan source, Mk 5.21–43, is a single miracle story which recounts two healings. Between the request for the daughter's healing and its accomplishment, the story of the cure of a woman with a hemorrhage is inserted. Whether the intercalation is due to Mark[1] or to pre-Markan tradition[2] is disputed. Mt 9.16–26 as it stands contains in any case three scenes, and using Theissen's catalogue of motifs (*Stories*, pp. 48–72) we may diagram the narrative thus:

18b The appearance of the representative ('a ruler came')
18c Description of the distress ('my daughter has just died')
18d Plea and expression of trust ('lay your hands on her', 'she will live')

20a–b The appearance of the distressed person ('behold, a woman')
20a Description of the distress ('a hemorrhage for twelve years')
20c Touch ('she touched the hem of his garment')
22 The miracle-working word ('your faith has made you well')

23 The coming of the miracle-worker ('Jesus came to the ruler's house')
24 Opposition ('they laughed at him')
25b Touch ('he took her by the hand')
25c Demonstration ('the girl arose')
26 The spread of the news ('the report went out')

Note should be taken of the several corresponding formulations (cf. Gnilka, *Matthäusevangelium* 1, p. 340). The ruler asks Jesus to lay his

---

[1] So e.g. Schürmann, *Lukasevangelium* 1, p. 492; Gnilka, *Markus* 1, p. 210.
[2] So e.g. Dibelius, *Tradition*, p. 72; and Pesch 1, p. 295. For the similarities that might have brought the two narratives together see Kertelge, *Wunder*, pp. 110–14. Mk 14.53–72 par. supplies another example of intercalation.

hand on his daughter, that she might live (9.18). In 9.26 Jesus raises
the girl up by taking her by the hand. Similarly, the woman with an
issue says to herself, 'If I only touch his garment, I shall be made well'
(σωθήσομαι, 9.21). When Jesus then speaks he declares: 'Your faith
has made you well' (σέσωκεν, 9.22). So in both stories Jesus' response
matches the expectation of faith. Furthermore, in both stories the
supplicants are introduced with ἰδού (vv. 18, 20; contrast Mark) and
in both καὶ ἰδών is used of Jesus (vv. 22, 23; contrast Mark).

Matthew's narrative distinguishes itself from Mk 5.21–43 in several
respects. (i) It is much briefer (containing a third of the vocabulary) and
less picturesque (Matthew offers little more than an outline of what is in
Mark). (ii) The setting is different. In Mark the healing story begins by
the sea, and Jesus has just disembarked from a boat. In Matthew Jesus
seems to be in a house (in Capernaum; see on 9.10). (iii) In Matthew the
little girl is dead from the beginning of the account, not on the point of
death as in Mark—so the ruler's faith is all the greater. (iv) The magical
elements in Mark are toned down (see on 9.22 and 25). (v) By twice
omitting the disciples (see Mk 5.31 and 37), by deleting the crowd (Mk
5.24), by neglecting to give us the thoughts of the healed woman (Mk
5.33), by omitting the messengers who in Mark announce that the girl
has died (Mk 5.35), and by failing to mention the ruler's family (Mk
5.40), Matthew prevents Jesus from ever leaving centre stage.

Concerning the historicity of our narrative, one has little trouble with
9.20–22: the story of the woman with an issue could easily be understood
in psycho-somatic terms. The capacity of the mind to heal many bodily
infirmities is an established fact. 9.18–19, 23–26 is another matter. The
bringing of a truly dead person back to life goes beyond the bounds of
scientific probability. One could, of course, argue that the ruler's
daughter had not really expired, that she was in a coma or some other
state of suspended animation. Just such an explanation was, in fact,
quite popular among nineteenth-century rationalists (Strauss, pp. 476–
9). And, one must concede, a few of the resurrection tales from
antiquity[3] may well have had their basis in someone's sudden recovery
from a serious unconscious condition (cf. Acts 20.7–12; Pliny, *H.N.*
7.124; 26.14–15; Apuleius, *Florida* 19). But, to state the obvious, those
who recounted the episode of the ruler's daughter—and this includes
Matthew—would hardly have been happy with a rational, medical
explanation. In their view, Jesus possessed a power and ability that
went far beyond the reach of ordinary mortals. So whatever one
makes of the historical issue,[4] the text itself pictures Jesus doing the

[3] Resurrection or resuscitation stories may be found in 1 Kgs 17.17–24; 2 Kgs
4.18–37; Lk 7.11–17; Jn 11; Apuleius, *Metam.* 2.21–30; Lucian, *Philops.* 26;
Diogenes Laertius 8.67; Philostratus, *VA* 4.45; Heliodorus, *Aeth.* 6.14–15;
Augustine, *De civ. dei.* 22.8; b. *'Abod. Zar.* 10b; b. *Meg.* 7b; Gregory the Great,
Dial. 2.11, 32. For a modern, purportedly first-hand account of a modern-day
resurrection in Hawaii see M. F. Lang, *The Secret Science behind Miracles*, 2nd
ed., Vista, 1954, pp. 203–4. For an uncritical collection of Christian resurrection
stories see A. J. Hebert, *Raised from the Dead*, Rockford, 1986.

[4] For a positive estimate of at least an historical core see the authorities cited
in the discussion on 9.24. For a negative assessment see Gnilka, *Markus* 1,
p. 219.—According to Rochais (v), pp. 100–12, the original narrative (in Aramaic)
consisted of Mk 5.22–4a, 38a, 40b, 41, 42a, c.

impossible. Indeed, the impossibility of raising the dead is precisely the point.[5]

18. Jesus is apparently still at table in 'the house' (cf. 9.10) when an unnamed ruler[6] comes and, with complete confidence, asks him to restore his dead daughter to the land of the living.

ταῦτα αὐτοῦ λαλοῦντος αὐτοῖς. This is a redactional introduction which replaces Mk 5.21, a verse which would be inappropriate for the new, Matthean context. Compare 1.20 (ταῦτα δὲ αὐτοῦ + participle + ἰδού); 12.46 diff. Mk 3.31 (αὐτοῦ λαλοῦντος + dative); 17.5 diff. Mk 9.7 (αὐτοῦ λαλοῦντος + ἰδού); and 26.47 = Mk 14.43; also 1 Βασ 17.23 and Mk 5.35. For the genitive absolute followed by a dative (an unclassical construction) see BDF § 423.1.

ἰδοὺ ἄρχων εἷς ἐλθὼν προσεκύνει αὐτῷ λέγων.[7] Compare 8.2; 15.25. As with the magi and the centurion, so too does this notable authority prostrate himself before Jesus. Matthew has shortened Mk 5.22, substituting his own vocabulary,[8] and avoiding the historic present. For other cases in which Jesus is asked for a healing not by the sufferer himself but by another see on 8.6 and compare 1QapGen. 20.21–2 and Philostratus, *VA* 3.38.

While Mark refers to an ἀρχισυνάγωγος (= rōʼš hakkĕneset), Matthew writes of an ἄρχων (cf. the rabbinic 'arkôn).[9] The former was the leader of meetings for worship (cf. Acts 13.15), the latter one of those responsible for the general direction of the synagogue (Schürer 2, pp. 433–6).[10] Sometimes one man held both offices. Abbreviation

---

[5] There is an interesting question concerning the placement of 9.18–26. Why did Matthew fail to make the double healing the third miracle in his third miracle triad? That is, why is 9.18–26 not the climax of chapters 8–9? 9.27–31 and 32–4 are both redactional and so could have been placed anywhere; and 9.18–26 is certainly not where it is because of any respect for the Markan order. Had Matthew moved 9.18–26 to the end, this would not only have been appropriate in view of the difficulty of raising the dead, but also in view of the fact that in 11.5 raising the dead is the last miracle mentioned. The best explanation of Matthew's order is that he needed an exorcism in order to conclude with the Pharisees' charge about Beelzebul, for this charge is part of the introduction to chapter 10.

[6] Both Mark and Luke give him a name: Jairus.

[7] εις ελθων is the reading of Maj d f. The rest of the mss. show a great deal of diversity. See J. O'Callaghan, 'La variante εἷς/ἐλθών en Mt 9.18', *Bib 62* (1981), pp. 104–6.

[8] ἰδού *; προσκυνέω* + dative. Luke has independently added 'and behold' (although it is missing in some mss.). For the possibility that ἰδού stood in Mark see Taylor, *Mark*, p. 287.

[9] Cf. Lk 8.41: ἄρχων τῆς συναγωγῆς. Without a knowledge of Mark or Luke, one would not know whether Matthew's ἄρχων should be identified with a civil or a religious official.

[10] Their leader was the γερουσιάρχης. See further W. Schrage, *TWNT* 7, pp. 842–45; also Horsley 4, pp. 218–20.

probably explains Matthew's substitution, not a desire to disconnect faith from the synagogue.

ἡ θυγάτηρ μου ἄρτι ἐτελεύτησεν.[11] Mk 5.23 has introductory ὅτι, the diminutive τὸ θυγάτριον,[12] and ἐσχάτως ἔχει after μου. ἄρτι* is Matthean. It here denotes immediacy: 'she has just died' (cf. Rev 12.10). The vulgar Markan ἐσχάτως ἔχει, by way of contrast, means 'be at the point of death' (cf. Josephus, Ant. 9.179). Why the change? Matthew's omission of Mk 5.35–7, in which a messenger meets the ruler, tells him that his daughter has died, and then asks, 'Why trouble the teacher any further?', has forced him to place the notice of death at the story's beginning.[13] This has the effect of magnifying the ruler's faith. The man believes not that Jesus can heal his sick daughter but that Jesus can raise her from the dead.

ʿ ἀλλὰ ἐλθὼν ἐπίθες τὴν χεῖρά σου ἐπ' αὐτήν. Matthew's line is more in accord with LXX usage than is Mk 5.23. ἐπιτίθημι + hand(s) + ἐπί is common in the Greek OT; see Exod 29.10, 15, 19; Lev 1.4, 11; Num 27.18 (ἐπιθήσεις τὰς χεῖράς σου ἐπ' αὐτόν); 27.23; etc. (cf. sāmak + yād/yādayim + ʿal). For other instances of ἀλλά before a request or command see Mk 9.22; Acts 10.20; 26.16.

Matthew prefers to write of Jesus' 'hand' (cf. 8.3; 9.18; 12.49; 14.31). The plural is reserved for 19.13–15, where the subject is not healing but the blessing of children. Contrast Mk 5.23; 6.2, 5; 8.23, 25; Lk 4.40; 13.13. Perhaps our author thought of Jesus' right hand as his more powerful and therefore as the hand he used in healing (cf. 3.12?; 5.30; 25.33f.). Or perhaps the switch from two hands to one serves to accentuate Jesus' power: he needs to use only one hand. It is, however, more likely that Matthew was influenced by OT usage. In the OT, the mighty and creative 'hand of God'[14] is almost always singular (exceptions in Exod 15.17; Ps 8.6). So what we may have in the First Gospel is assimilation to an OT image, with the result that the hand (singular) of Jesus is like the hand (singular) of God.[15]

καὶ ζήσεται replaces the final ἵνα-clause of Mk 5.23. In the

[11] So HG. NA[26] prints οτι before η; but it is missing in ℵ D f[1.13] 33 892 pc and could easily have been added (cf. Mk 5.23; Lk 8.42).
[12] This has also been replaced by θυγάτηρ (cf. 9.22) in 15.22 = Mk 7.25: Neither Matthew nor Luke ever uses the word.
[13] Cf. his treatment of Mark in Mt 21.18–22.
[14] On this see E. Lohse, TWNT 9, pp. 413–27; and J. J. M. Roberts, 'The Hand of Yahweh', VT 21 (1971), pp. 244–51.
[15] On the laying on of hands for healing—which is a motif absent from the OT and rabbinic literature, and which is different from the laying on of hands for a blessing—see J. Behm, Die Handauslegung im Urchristentum, Leipzig, 1911, and E. Lohse, TWNT 9, pp. 417–23; also of interest is F. T. Elworthy, The Evil Eye, reprint ed., New York, 1986, pp. 233–76. Note esp. for comparison 1QapGen. 20.28–9; Philostratus, VA 4.45.

future indicative faith is obviously speaking: the man's words are an expression of trust (cf. Theissen, *Stories*, pp. 54f.). Matthew drops as redundant one of Mark's verbs (cf. the Matthean parallels to Mk 1.15, 32; 8.17; 14.45, 61, 68; 15.32).

19. Jesus, evidently arising from the reclining position assumed at banquets, immediately follows the ruler, as do the disciples. Jesus says nothing. His response is action.[16]

καὶ ἐγερθεὶς ὁ Ἰησοῦς ἠκολούθει αὐτῷ καὶ οἱ μαθηταὶ αὐτοῦ.[17] This is largely redactional. Compare 4 Βασ 4.30 ('and Elijah rose and went after her'—the context is a resurrection story) and Acts 9.39. As against Mk 5.24, Matthew has omitted the reference to the crowd[18] and added a reference to the disciples.[19]

20. While Jesus is on his way to the ruler's house his progress is momentarily delayed by a woman who believes that she has only to touch the hem of Jesus' garment in order to be healed. 'Of the details of Mark's presentation of the story only the behaviour of the woman towards Jesus remains, what she did and what she thought (Mt 9.20b and 21)—the things by which her faith becomes known' (so Held, in *TIM*, p. 179).[20]

According to Held's insightful interpretation of 9.20–2, the text, which has a dialogue of sorts at its centre (see n. 27), sets forth faith as the (necessary but not sufficient) condition of miracles, indicates that confidence in the helpful kindness of Jesus—and not special merit or achievement—is what counts, and teaches a lesson about prayer, for faith is praying faith in the Matthean miracle stories. Theissen's analysis, which builds upon that of Held, stresses Jesus' seeming supernatural knowledge (9.22) and rightly argues that petitionary faith in Jesus is like the faith in God one exercises in prayer: one approaches

---

[16] This is the only place in the First Gospel where Jesus follows another. Everywhere else Matthew's emphasis on discipleship requires that the mind's eye see Jesus out in front.

[17] HG and NA[26] print ηκολουθησεν on the authority of B L W Θ *f*[1.13] Maj. But ℵ C D 33 *pc* Hil have − θει, and as Gundry, *Commentary*, p. 173 observes: 'everywhere else in this passage Matthew retains Mark's imperfect whenever he has a corresponding verb'.

[18] Cf. the parallels to Mk 1.33, 45; 2.2, 4; 3.9–10, 20; 6.31.

[19] The vocabulary—ἐγείρω*, Ἰησοῦς*, μαθητής*—is typical of the redactor.

[20] According to Eusebius, *H.E.* 7.18, the unnamed woman was from Caesarea Philippi; and in that city, in front of the gates to her house, was shown in Eusebius' day a statue allegedly depicting her healing by Jesus. At the base of the statue grew a herb that possessed healing powers. In Acts of Pilate 7 the woman of the gospel story is named Bernice (Lat., Veronica); and in a late interpolation she is identified as the woman who wiped sweat from Jesus' brow as he stumbled while carrying the cross (an incident now depicted in the Stations of the Cross). According to the legend, Veronica later discovered that Jesus' image had imprinted itself on the cloth she had used; cf. The Avenging of the Saviour, in ANF 8, pp. 474–6, and Macarius of Magnesia, *Apocritus*, ed. C. Blondel, p. 1.

Jesus as one approaches God (*Stories*, pp. 134f., 138). Also useful is the rhetorical interpretation of Robbins (v). When the woman thinks to herself, 'If only I touch the tassel of his garment I shall be made well,' the reader might wonder about her motivation. Is it simplemindedness, boldness, faith, hope, courage, or despair? Jesus, by naming faith as her impulse, and by affirming that her faith has saved her, not only clarifies the woman's actions but also reveals the tacit reasoning imbedded in the narrative:

Major premise: an act of faith is able to make a person well.
Minor premise: touching Jesus' garment is an act of faith.
Conclusion: therefore the woman is made well.

καὶ ἰδοὺ γυνὴ αἱμορροοῦσα δώδεκα ἔτη. Compare Mk 5.25. Matthew has added ἰδού (cf. 9.18), dropped τις and replaced Mark's οὖσα ἐν ῥύσει αἵματος (cf. Lev 15.19, 25; 20.18) by the rare compound verb αἱμορρέω, a NT *hapax legomenon* found in Hippocrates and occurring also in Lev 15.33 (for *dāweh*). A uterine hemorrhage is undoubtedly meant. For other miracle stories in which the duration of the sickness is given—something that indicates both the difficulty of the cure and the despair of the sufferer—see Mk 9.21; Lk 13.11; Jn 5.5; 9.1; Acts 3.2; 4.22; 9.33; 14.8; and Philostratus, *VA* 6.43. Is 'twelve' just a good, round number?

According to Lev 15.25 a woman who has a discharge of blood for many days and not at the time of her impurity is unclean. And according to 15.19–24 her infectious state can be transmitted through touch (cf. *m. Zabim* 5.1, 6). Other Jewish texts which involve restriction of and repugnance for menstruous women include Ezek 36.17; CD 4.12–5.17; 11QTemple 48.15–17; Josephus, *Bell.* 5.227; *C. Ap.* 2.103–4; *m. Nidda*, passim; and *m. Zabim* 4.1. Mt 9.18–26 seems to offer a contrast. The woman with an issue is presented in a wholly positive light. The subject of her uncleanness is not mentioned or alluded to. Her touch does not effect indignation. Onlookers do not whisper that Jesus has come into contact with an unclean woman. All of this is surprising. But whatever the explanation for the text's silence, it is possible that the woman comes up 'from behind' precisely because she is unclean and must accordingly try to touch Jesus without anyone observing.[21]

προσελθοῦσα ὄπισθεν ἥψατο τοῦ κρασπέδου τοῦ ἱματίου αὐτοῦ. Compare Ahikar 77 (Lindenberger)[22] and *b. Ta'an.* 23b.[23] Mk 5.27 has: 'coming up behind him in the crowd she touched his

---

[21] For rabbinic suggestions as to what should be done for an extended feminine discharge see *b. Šabb.* 110a–b, which includes such remedies as fetching barley grain from the dung of a white mule and holding it for three days and smearing oneself with sixty pieces of sealing clay.

[22] 'If a wicked man grasps the fringe of your garment' (*ršyᵒ bknpy lbšk*).

[23] When the world needed rain school children would go to Ḥanan ha-Neḥba and 'they would take hold of the hem of his garment' (*bšypwly glymyh*).

garment'. Matthew has added προσ- to the verb (cf. Lk 8.44
and Mt 9.14 diff. Mk 2.18), omitted the crowd, and added 'the
tassel'.[24]

The notion that healing power can be transmitted through touch is
common (see on 8.3 and 9.28). It does not seem to matter whether the
healer is laying on hands or whether (as in 9.20–2) the patient is
touching the healer (cf. Hull, pp. 109–10). Moreover, the spread of
divine power from a healer to clothing or cloth is well attested (cf. Acts
19.12; Koran 12.93–6). This last idea seems to presuppose that there is
some sort of energy[25] which can be stored in physical objects and
subsequently drained.[26]

Luke, like Matthew, has the woman with an issue touch τοῦ
κρασπέδου τοῦ ἱματίου αὐτοῦ. This makes for a striking minor
agreement against Mark. Streeter, p. 313, observing that 'the tassel' is
absent from Lk 8.44 D a ff² r l, suggested that the majority reading in
Luke is secondary. This is possible; but the omission could also be
explained as due to *homoioteleuton*: a scribal eye passed from the τοῦ
before 'tassel' to the τοῦ before 'garment'. Probably the best explanation
of the agreement is independent use of Mk 6.56. 'The tassel of his
garment' occurs twice in Matthew (9.20; 14.36), once in· Mark (6.56),
and once in Luke (8.44). The Markan text appears to function as a⁻
climax. In Mk 3.7–12 people touch Jesus. In Mk 5.21–34 a woman
touches his garment. In Mk 6.53–6 people touch only the tassel of his
garment. Because both Matthew and Luke have 'the tassel of his
garment' in their parallels to Mk 5.21–34, neither has followed the
Markan scheme. Perhaps they did not notice the clever arrangement. It
would in any case seem that ἥψατο τοῦ ἱματίου reminded both
Matthew and Luke of the similar and more memorable phrase in Mk
6.56 (τοῦ κρασπέδου τοῦ ἱματίου αὐτοῦ ἅψωνται). They therefore
reproduced it in 9.20 = Lk 8.44 (cf. also Testim. Truth 41.10).

21. ἔλεγεν γὰρ ἐν ἑαυτῇ. Matthew has added 'in herself' (see
on 9.3) and dropped ὅτι.

ἐὰν μόνον ἅψωμαι τοῦ ἱματίου αὐτοῦ σωθήσομαι. Matthew
has added μόνον* and dropped Mark's κἄν (cf. 14.36 diff.
Mk 6.56). μόνον (cf. 14.36) serves to underline Jesus' power:
'*only*' a touch will suffice. Compare 8.8, where the centurion
says to Jesus: 'Only speak the word'. The change from garment*s*
(so Mk 5.28) to garment brings v. 21 into line with v. 20, where
the singular was used.

22. ὁ δὲ Ἰησοῦς στραφεὶς καὶ ἰδὼν αὐτὴν εἶπεν. This is a

---

[24] 'Hem' is also a possible translation; but in 23.5 the meaning of κράσπεδον is
clearly 'tassel' (= ṣîṣît).

[25] Cf. Dibelius, *Tradition*, p. 86: 'An electric contact [is] set up by the fingers
which touch Jesus' garment. Jesus does not feel the contact but rather the
outflow of the dynamic current'.

[26] According to Hutter (v), the grabbing of the garment is a gesture of
supplication, as in 1 Sam 15.24–7 and *b. Taʻan.* 23b. This does not explain
14.36.

radically compressed version of Mk 5.30–4a. In Matthew, as opposed to Mark, Jesus does not feel power go out from him (as though he were surprised or it had happened without his consent), he asks no question, and he commends the woman's faith without being told by her what has occurred. So Matthew's version underlines Jesus' supernatural knowledge. Just as the Father knows his children's requests before they ask him (6.8), so too, apparently, does Jesus know what believers need before they ask. See further on 9.4.[27]

θάρσει, θύγατερ· ἡ πίστις σου σέσωκέν σε. Instead of uncleanness passing from the woman to Jesus, healing power flows from Jesus to the woman. Mk 5.34 lacks 'take heart' (see on 9.2); otherwise there is agreement. For 'daughter' as a term of endearment see Ruth 2.8; 3.10; Ps 45.10; and Schlatter, p. 318. On faith in the Matthean miracle stories see on 8.10. Lest his readers misunderstand what has transpired, the evangelist plainly indicates that it was not the woman's grasp which effected her cure but faith: 'your faith has saved you'. The point is driven home by the next clause, in which 'from that hour' refers not to the woman's action but to Jesus' words (cf. BDF § 291.3). In short, 'everything is at the conscious, personal level. Jesus perceives what the woman wants and what she believes, and he heals her consciously' (so Gerhardsson, Acts, p. 47; cf. Chrysostom, Hom. on Mt. 31.2). (One should recall that those who lay hands on Jesus to arrest him and to strike him are not healed: for a touch to heal it must be accompanied by faith.)

καὶ ἐσώθη ἡ γυνὴ ἀπὸ τῆς ὥρας ἐκείνης. This is redactional. Contrast Mk 5.34c–d: 'Go in peace, and be healed of your disease'. Matthew prefers to close the episode with a stereotypical conclusion. See 8.13 (and the comments there); 15.28; and 17.18. For 'from that hour' (a Septuagintism) see 1, p. 81.

23. καὶ ἐλθὼν ὁ Ἰησοῦς εἰς τὴν οἰκίαν τοῦ ἄρχοντος. Compare Mk 5.38. Mark's historical present has become an aorist (cf. Allen, p. xx). 'Jesus'* has been added. οἶκος (Mt: 10; Mk: 12; Lk: 33) has become οἰκία (Mt: 25; Mk: 18; Lk: 25). 'Synagogue president' has become 'ruler', in accordance with the change already made in 9.18 diff. Mk 5.22.

καὶ ἰδὼν τοὺς αὐλητὰς καὶ τὸν ὄχλον θορυβούμενον. Compare Mk 5.38: 'And he sees (θεωρεῖ) a tumult (θόρυβον) and weeping and much wailing'. αὐλητής (LXX: 0) occurs only twice in the NT, here and in Rev 18.22. The word means 'clarinet-player'. For its connexion with mourning see Josephus, Bell. 3.437 ('for

---

[27] Held, in TIM, p. 216, observes that, since Jesus can read the woman's thoughts, 9.20–2 really constitutes a 'conversation' of sorts.

thirty days the lamentations never ceased in the city, and many of the mourners hired clarinet-players (αὐλητάς) to accompany their funeral dirges'); *m. Ketub.* 4.4 ('R. Judah says: Even the poorest in Israel should hire not less than two clarinets (*ḥalîlîn*) and one wailing woman'); *m. Šabb.* 23.4 ('If a Gentile brought the clarinets (*ḥalîlîn*) on the Sabbath an Israelite may not play dirges on them unless they had been brought from near by'); *m. B. Meṣ.* 6.1 ('pipers (*ḥalîlîn*) for a bride or for a corpse').[28] Whether or not Matthew's αὐλητάς exhibits knowledge of specifically Jewish funeral customs,[29] certainly the insertion of 'clarinet-players' is most appropriate.

The 'crowd making a tumult' should be envisaged as consisting of both professional mourners and friends offering food and consolation (cf. Jer 16.7; Ezek 24.17, 22; Hos 9.4). For rabbinic texts pertaining to professional mourners see SB 1, pp. 521–3. From the OT we learn that the custom of hiring such people[30] for money had long been established (2 Chr 35.25; Eccles 12.5; Jer 9.17–22; Amos 5.16). They apparently were available at a moment's notice. Their function was primarily two-fold. First, they were to wail and make lamentation (cf. *m. Moʿed Qat.* 3.9; *m. Kelim* 16.7 refers to the 'clappers' of wailing women). Secondly, they composed poems that served as funeral dirges,[31] examples of which can be found in *b. Moʿed Qat.* 28b.

24. ἔλεγεν· ἀναχωρεῖτε. Matthew passes over Jesus' rhetorical question recorded in Mk 5.39 because it does little more than reproduce the information of 9.23. The evangelist also shows a tendency to keep Jesus from asking questions (Allen, p. xxxii).

οὐ γὰρ ἀπέθανεν τὸ κοράσιον ἀλλὰ καθεύδει. Compare Par. Jer. 9.11, where a voice from heaven instructs people concerning Jeremiah: 'Do not bury one who still lives, for his soul is returning to his body'. Matthew follows Mark except in these particulars: οὐκ has become οὐ γάρ, and παιδίον has been replaced by κοράσιον (which makes for greater consistency; cf. 9.25 = Mk 5.42) and then moved from the head of the sentence to its middle.

The words, 'she is not dead but sleeping', have occasioned much discussion. At first reading one supposes that Jesus is saying only that bodily death is not necessarily final, and that if he resolves to restore the girl to life, she must in truth be only 'sleeping'. Yet many have inferred

---

[28] See further J. Mann, 'Rabbinic Studies in the Synoptic Gospels', *HUCA* 1 (1924), p. 351, and E. Werner, in *IDB* 3, col. 472a, s.v., 'Musical Instruments'. For death, burial, and mourning customs in general see S. Safrai, in *CRINT* 1/2, pp. 773–87.

[29] Jews were not the only ones to have flute- or clarinet-players at funerals; see G. Stählin, *TWNT* 3, p. 844, n. 96.

[30] They were usually women, but Matthew's αὐλητάς is masculine.

[31] See E. Jacob, in *IDB* 3, coll. 453b–454a, s.v., 'Mourning'. Note Apoc. Zeph. 1.1–2.

that, as a matter of historical fact, the girl was not dead but in a deep trance. See Strauss, pp. 478–9, citing Paulus, Schleiermacher, and Olshausen. This possibility is also urged by Taylor, *Mark*, pp. 285–6, 295. And Pesch 1, pp. 312–14, has even postulated an earlier form of the story in which Jesus only healed Jairus' daughter of a serious illness. Such speculation can never be dismissed out of hand. The tendency of the tradition to magnify the power of Jesus is admitted by all. Nonetheless, 'she is not dead but sleeping' is in itself scarcely strong reason for supposing that the maiden was not really dead. How did Jesus know the child's real state before seeing her? Furthermore, in Jn 11.11–14 Jesus can both affirm that 'Lazarus is dead' and that he 'sleepeth'.[32] This offers a perfect parallel for our passage, in which the girl is dead but, in view of what is about to happen, can be said to be merely 'sleeping'. In any event, one can hardly miss Matthew's intention. According to 11.5 Jesus raised the dead, and 9.18–26 is the only possible illustration of this in the First Gospel.

καὶ κατεγέλων αὐτοῦ. So Mk 5.40a. Compare 2 Chr 30.10; Josephus, *Ant.* 5.144. On the theme of scepticism and mocking in miracle stories see Theissen, *Stories*, p. 56. Here one wonders whether the response is 'triggered by Jesus' statement "she is not dead but sleeping" which the bystanders had interpreted literally' (so Harris (v), p. 307).

25. ὅτε δὲ ἐξεβλήθη ὁ ὄχλος. Despite its laughter, the crowd is subject to Jesus' command. Mk 5.40b has this: 'Driving out all he takes the father of the child and the mother and those with him'. Matthew retains the dismissal of the crowd (cf. 9.23) and then abbreviates. ὅτε δέ (Mt: 3; Mk: 0; Lk: 1) is Matthean. For parallels to excluding the public from a miracle Theissen, *Stories*, p. 61, cites these texts: 1 Kgs 17.19 (a resurrection); 2 Kgs 4.4, 33 (a resurrection); Mk 7.33; 8.23; Acts 9.40 (a resurrection); Ovid, *Met.* 7.255ff.; Heliodorus 6.15; Apuleius, *Apol.* 42; Lucian, *Philops.* 16; *PGM* 3.616–17; 12.36–37; *SIG*³ 3.1173. The idea underlying many of these passages is not too far from Mt 7.6: pearls are not to be thrown before swine. That is, certain doctrines and practices need to be kept private.

εἰσελθὼν ἐκράτησεν τῆς χειρὸς αὐτῆς. Compare 8.15. Mk 5.40f. reads: 'And they go into where the girl was lying. And taking the hand of the child he says to her: *talitha koum*, which is, being interpreted, Girl, I say to you, arise'. Because the preservation of the Aramaic in Mark might be put down to the belief that mysterious foreign words are greater vessels of power

---

[32] For other texts in which the dead 'sleep' see Gen 47.30; Dan 12.2; 2 Macc 12.45; 1 En. 49.3; Mt 27.52; 1 Cor 15.6; Eph 5.14; 2 Pet 3.4; 1 Clem. 44.2. The rabbinic *děmak* means both 'to sleep' and 'to lie in the grave'; cf. Jastrow, s.v.

than ordinary words,[33] and because Matthew wants to dissociate Jesus from magical activity, the omission is understandable.

καὶ ἠγέρθη τὸ κοράσιον. So Mk 5.42, with εὐθὺς ἀνέστη after καί. Matthew often omits Mark's εὐθύς, and he much prefers ἐγείρω* to ἀνίστημι (Mt: 4; Mk: 17; Lk: 17). ἐγείρω can mean either 'rise (from the dead)' or 'rise (up)'. Here both meanings are simultaneously present. In rising up the girl rises from the dead.[34]

26. The report of Jesus' mighty deed sounds forth over 'all that land'. With this Matthew concludes, neglecting to answer the questions of curious readers. What did the girl say? How did her family respond? Did Jesus say anything at all?

καὶ ἐξῆλθεν ἡ φήμη αὕτη εἰς ὅλην τὴν γῆν ἐκείνην.[35] This is readactional. Compare 9.31; 14.35; Mk 1.28, 45. 'All that land' must be the region around Capernaum. McNeile, p. 126, points out that this narrow use of γῆ (=χώρα), which reappears in 2.6; 4.15; 9.31; 10.15; and 11.24, is unattested in Mark or Luke. We may add that εἰς ὅλην τὴν γῆν ἐκείνην is not a LXX locution.

JESUS HEALS TWO BLIND MEN (9.27–31)

The colourless story of Jesus healing two blind men has no true parallel in Mark or Luke and is almost certainly a redactional creation.[36] It most resembles the healing of blind Bartimaeus, Mk 10.46–52 = Mt 20.29–34[37] (cf. also Mk 1.43–5; 8.22–6). It seems probable that the Markan episode has served Matthew as the inspiration for 9.27–31 (cf. Fuchs (v) and Gnilka, *Matthäusevangelium* 1, p. 344).

Two circumstances led to the story's creation. First, Matthew

---

[33] So Pesch 1, p. 310; cf. Mk 7.34; T. Sol. 18; and texts cited by Theissen, *Stories*, p. 64.

[34] The few rabbinic texts which make the resurrection of the dead a work of the Messiah (see SB 1, p. 524; cf. Jn 5.28) are too few and too late to be of any consequence for the interpretation of Mt 9.18–26. But in so far as Matthew thought of Isa 35.5–6 (cf. Mt. 11.5) as fulfilled by Messiah Jesus, he will have thought of resurrection as a messianic task.

[35] αυτη, which is the more difficult reading, is read by NA[26] on the authority of f[13] Maj lat sy. αυτης (sc. το κοπασιον) appears in ℵ C N[vid] Θ f[1] 33 pc mae bo and in HG. αυτου (sc. Jesus) is the reading of D 1424 pc sa bo[ms]. Cf. 4.24.

[36] So perhaps most modern commentators; cf. Bultmann, *History*, p. 214; Held, in *TIM*, pp. 219–20; Fenton, p. 144; Burger, pp. 74–7; Gundry, *Commentary*, p. 176.

[37] Augustine, *De con. ev.* 2.29: 'There is such similarity in the occurrences, that if Matthew himself had not recorded the latter incident (9.27–31) as well as the former (20.29–34), it might have been thought that the one which he relates at present has also been given by these other two evangelists'.

needed a third triad of miracle stories with which to conclude
Mt 8–9. Secondly, in view of the prophecy quoted in 11.5 ('the
blind receive their sight and the lame walk'), he wanted a story
about Jesus healing the blind.[38]

As befits a Matthean creation, there is a high degree of parallelism
between 9.27 and 28 on the one hand and between 9.29 and 30 on the
other (cf. Gundry, *Commentary*, pp. 176–7):

Movement of Jesus ('And with Jesus passing on from there')
  Movement of the blind men ('Two blind men followed him')
    Introduction to speech ('Crying and saying')
      Speech ('Have mercy on us, Son of David')

Movement of Jesus ('And with him entering the house')
  Movement of the blind men ('The blind men came to him')
    Introduction to speech ('Jesus said to him')
      Speech ('Do you believe that . . .')

Action of Jesus ('Then he touched their eyes')
  Speech ('According to your faith . . .')
    Result ('And their eyes opened')

Action of Jesus ('And Jesus sternly charged them')
  Speech ('See that no one knows it')
    Result ('But they went out and spread his fame . . .')

27. καὶ παράγοντι ἐκεῖθεν τῷ Ἰησοῦ. Compare 9.9 diff. Mk
2.14; 20.30 diff. Mk 10.47. With the exception of 5.26, ἐκεῖθεν*
is, in the First Gospel, always used of Jesus leaving a place
(contrast Mk 6.10, 11; Lk 9.4; 12.59; 16.26). Here the precise
referent is ambiguous. Are we to think of the ruler's house? or
of Capernaum? or of the territory around Capernaum (cf.
9.26)?

ἠκολούθησαν αὐτῷ δύο τυφλοὶ κράζοντες καὶ λέγοντες.[39]
κράζω + λέγω (Mt: 9; Mk: 5; Lk: 1) is taken from Mk 10.47 (cf.
Mt 20.30–1). The construction is Septuagintal (e.g. Exod 5.8;
32.17; 2 Βασ 19.5). Our evangelist likes ἀκολουθέω (Mt: 25;
Mk: 18; Lk: 17), δύο* and τυφλός*. On why there are two
blind men instead of one see on 8.28. In 20.29–34 blind
Bartimaeus becomes two blind men.

Given the close connexion between sin and sickness in Jewish
tradition, it is no surprise to learn that blindness was often

---

[38] One must ask whether our evangelist thought himself to be making up
facts. But Matthew believed that Jesus healed the blind (cf. 11.5) and also that
the stories in the tradition only began to cover what Jesus did (cf. 4.24, etc.); so
a non-descript account of Jesus healing two blind men, an account composed
almost solely of traditional motifs, could hardly, in Matthew's mind, have been
fictional.

[39] B D 892 *pc* omit αυτω, and NA[26] puts the word in brackets. But it is part of
the parallelism between v. 27 and v. 28.

regarded as a punishment for wrong-doing (Gen 19.11; Exod 4.11; Deut 28.28–9; 2 Kgs 6.18; Ep. Arist. 316; Mt 12.22; Jn 9.2; Acts 13.11; *b. Ḥag.* 16a; *b. Šabb.* 108b–9a).[40] Moreover, Lev 21.20 prohibits a man with defective sight from joining the priesthood; and in 11QTemple 45.12–14 we read, concerning Jerusalem: 'No blind people may enter it all their days lest they defile the city in whose midst I dwell' (cf. 2 Sam 5.8; 1QSa 2.3– 11; 1QM 7.4–5). Clearly blindness for an ancient Jew could involve not simply poverty and hardship (cf. Judg 16.21; Mk 10.46; *b. Ta'an.* 21a) but also religious alienation.[41] Thus for those who composed the Dead Sea Scrolls, physical disabilities had serious spiritual consequences (Davies, *SSM*, p. 227, n. 2). Some humanitarian provisions for the blind were, however, made by the Torah. Lev 19.14 prohibits putting a stumbling block before the blind, and Deut 27.18 curses those who mislead a blind man 'on the road' (cf. Job 29.15; Ps.-Phoc. 24; *b. Meg.* 24b). Jesus' ministry to the blind is to be interpreted in part as an extension of such humanitarian concern. At the same time, Matthew, as probably Jesus before him, will have seen in cures of the blind the fulfilment of the eschatological expectation of Isa 35.5: 'the blind shall receive their sight' (cf. Isa 29.18; 42.7, 16; *Mek.* on Exod 20.18; *Gen. Rab.* on 46.28; *Midr. Ps.* on 146.8).

There are only a few instances of blind individuals being healed in Jewish sources.[42] See Tob 2.10; 3.16–17; Ep. Arist. 316; LAB 25.12; *b. B. Meṣ.* 85b; *Num. Rab.* on 16.35. None of these Jewish texts tells of a blind man being directly healed by another person. For this one has to go to Graeco-Roman literature. Recall, for instance, the story told of Vespasian in Tacitus, *Hist.* 4.81, and elsewhere: the emperor healed a blind man by putting spittle on his eyes.[43]

ἐλέησον ἡμᾶς, υἱὲ Δαυίδ.[44] Compare 15.22; 17.15; 20.30–1; Mk 10.47–8; and T. Sol. 20.1 ('King Solomon, son of David, have mercy on me'). Matthew, we cannot doubt, thought of 'Son of David' as a messianic title (see on 1.1). But there is very definitely another side to the term in the First Gospel. Jesus several times heals as David's υἱός (9.27; 12.23; 15.22; 20.30–1). This intrigues because, with one exception, *ben Dāwid/* υἱὸς Δαυίδ is always, in the OT, used of Solomon, who was later

[40] But it was also plainly understood that blindness could also be the natural result of becoming old; cf. Gen 27.1 and 1 Kgs 14.4.
[41] One should keep in mind that blind animals were also unacceptable to Yahweh; cf. Lev 22.22; Deut 15.21; Mal 1.8.
[42] For folk remedies for eye problems see *b. Giṭ.* 69a and *b. B. Meṣ.* 85b.
[43] For other healing stories see W. Schrage, *TWNT* 8, pp. 273–5.
[44] So HG. NA²⁶ on the authority of B W 565 (700) *pm* prints υιος. For the tendency to change υιε to υιος see the variants at Mk 10.47–8 and Lk 18.39.

renowned as a mighty healer, exorcist, and magician.[45] Especially significant in this regard is the Testament of Solomon (second century A.D.?). Its use of υἱὸς Δαυίδ in connexion with Solomon the healer does not appear to be under Christian influence (cf. the title; 1.7; 5.10; 20.1; 26.9). Matthew, it seems reasonable to suppose, both knew the Jewish legends about Solomon's powers and probably intended to present Jesus in their light (cf. further on 2.11, where there may be a Solomon typology).

In line with this, one suspects that the pre-Matthean tradition already linked Jesus' healing ministry with his status as David's son. Reference to David's son occurs in a healing in Mark only in 10.47–8. Interestingly enough, in these verses Jesus is directly addressed as υἱὲ Δαυίδ. The titular ὁ υἱὸς Δαυίδ is not used. In fact, the articular ὁ υἱὸς Δαυίδ, with its messianic associations, is confined in the synoptics to Matthew. This raises the possibility that 'David's son' at one time functioned not as a messianic title but to clarify Jesus' ability to heal. Four facts support this proposal. First, its acceptance would help explain Matthew's tendency to use υἱὸς/υἱὲ Δαυίδ in therapeutic contexts. Secondly, with the exception of Mk 12.35–7 par., in Mark and Luke Jesus is called David's υἱός only when a healing is in view; and throughout the synoptics υἱὲ Δαυίδ appears only in healing stories. Thirdly, David himself was remembered as an exorcist and healer (1 Sam 16.14–23; Josephus, *Ant.* 6.166–8; cf. 11QPsᵃ, which refers to psalms David composed for the stricken). This would have encouraged an application of 'David's son' to Jesus, for he was both a healer and a Davidid. Fourthly, as B. D. Chilton has written, 'the connection between Jesus and David in respect of Jesus' descent and in respect of his resurrection are established in the New Testament, but not in the context of healing and without the address of Jesus as David's son. Precisely the last two points, among the most prominent features of New Testament *ben David* usage, are accounted for on the supposition that "David's son" was the address applied to Jesus at the level of tradition when he was to heal or exorcize in a manner reminiscent of Solomon'.[46] That is, Jesus was addressed as David's son because he was known to be descended from David and because he, like Solomon, was a skilled healer.

28. ἐλθόντι δὲ εἰς τὴν οἰκίαν. Compare 2.11; 8.14 diff. Mk 1.29; 9.23 diff. Mk 5.38; 10.12 diff. Lk 10.5–6; and 17.25. τήν could be the generic article ('a house'). If not, the house is probably the same as that in 9.10 (q.v.). For excluding the public from performance of a miracle see on 9.25.

---

[45] See on 1.1 and note K. Berger, 'Die königlichen Messiastraditionen des Neuen Testaments', *NTS* 20 (1973), pp. 1–44; idem, 'Zur Problem der Messianität Jesu', *ZTK* 71 (1974), pp. 1–30; and D. C. Duling, 'Solomon, Exorcism, and the Son of David', *HTR* 68 (1975), pp. 235–52.

[46] B. D. Chilton, 'Jesus *ben David*: reflections on the *Davidssohnfrage*', *JSNT* 14 (1982), p. 97.

προσῆλθον αὐτῷ οἱ τυφλοί.[47] Compare 9.27.

καὶ λέγει αὐτοῖς ὁ 'Ιησοῦς. Compare 8.4, 20; 15.34; Mk 14.27, 30.

πιστεύετε ὅτι δύναμαι τοῦτο ποιῆσαι; In accordance with a tendency to be observed elsewhere, Matthew makes the heart of the story a conversation (see Held, in *TIM*, pp. 233–7). The subject is faith, and the lesson is that of 21.22: 'whatever you ask in prayer you will receive—if you have faith'. On faith in the miracle stories see further on 8.10. πιστεύω + ὅτι appears only here in the First Gospel. The construction is typical of early Christian credal statements (e.g. Rom 10.9; 1 Thess 4.14).[48]

λέγουσιν αὐτῷ· ναί, κύριε. The blind men profess faith and even call Jesus 'Lord' (see on 8.6). It is, therefore, rather odd that the two turn around and disobey Jesus' command (9.30–1). On the asyndetic 'he says'/'they say' see MHT 4, p. 31, where Aramaic influence is detected.

29. τότε ἥψατο τῶν ὀφθαλμῶν αὐτῶν λέγων. Compare 20.34. Jesus, as we have already indicated, may well have been addressed as David's son because he was both a Davidid and, like Solomon, a great healer. If so, one must wonder about the relationship between Jesus the Solomonic healer and Jesus the messianic Son of David. Did the idea that Jesus the wonder-worker was 'David's son' encourage speculation about Jesus being '*the* Son of David'? However one resolves that involved issue, note should be taken of the belief, widespread in antiquity, in 'the king's touch', that is, in the ability of kings to heal their subjects.[49] Did some early Christians, persuaded that Jesus was the Jewish Messiah or king, think that Jesus had the royal touch? Did Matthew think such a thing?

κατὰ τὴν πίστιν ὑμῶν γενηθήτω ὑμῖν. This very much resembles 8.13 and 15.28. According to BDF § 189.1, γίνομαι + dative (Mt: 5; Mk: 2; Lk: 1) stresses the object possessed.

30. This verse and the next have clearly been influenced by Mk 1.43–5. ὅρα(τε) + μή, ἐμβριμάομαι, and διαφημίζω occur in both passages.

καὶ ἠνεῴχθησαν αὐτῶν οἱ ὀφθαλμοί. Compare 20.33; Jn 9.10; Acts 9.8. Jesus' words have power and bring about what they say. ἀνοίγω in the passive + ὀφθαλμοί occurs twice in Matthew, nowhere else in the synoptics. One recalls LXX Isa 35.5: ἀνοιχθήσονται ὀφθαλμοὶ τυφλῶν.

καὶ ἐνεβριμήθη αὐτοῖς ὁ 'Ιησοῦς λέγων· ὁρᾶτε μηδεὶς γινωσκέτω. Compare 8.4; Mk 1.43–4; 14.5. ἐμβριμάομαι appears

---

[47] HG prints προσηλθαν without apparatus.
[48] Schlatter, p. 320, cites for comparison *he'ĕmîn* + *šĕ*, as in *y. Ketub.* 26d.
[49] The idea lived on in the British monarchy.

only here in Matthew (LXX: 1). When used of persons the word means either 'be deeply moved' (cf. Jn 11.38) or (as here) 'strongly rebuke, sternly admonish' (see further Taylor, *Mark*, pp. 188–9, and Lampe, s.v.). Its effect in 9.30 is to make the men's disobedience more pronounced. On the 'messianic secret' see on 8.4.

31. The blind men who have hailed Jesus as David's son and who have had their request granted now openly disobey Jesus' word. Instead of keeping quiet (9.30), they spread the word of Jesus' act. Their disobedience, like the frequent failure of the twelve, shows that first-hand observation or experience of the supernatural scarcely guarantees faithful discipleship. Miracles of themselves eliminate neither little faith nor unbelief.[50]

οἱ δὲ ἐξελθόντες διεφήμισαν αὐτὸν ἐν ὅλῃ τῇ γῇ ἐκείνῃ. Compare 9.26; Mk 1.45. ἐν + ὅλη + geographical term + ἐκείνη is used again in 14.35 (cf. Tob 14.6 א; Mk 6.55).

JESUS HEALS A DEMONIAC (9.32–4)

This exceedingly concise and comparatively unremarkable pronouncement story, in which Jesus' opponents make the pronouncement, is a redactional doublet of 12.22–3.[51] It serves several functions. (i) It completes Matthew's third triad in chapters 8–9. (ii) It prepares for 11.5, which quotes Isa 11.5 as a summary of Jesus' work (κωφοὶ ἀκούουσιν). (iii) The crowds' declaration, 'Never has there appeared anything like this in Israel', appropriately brings chapters 8–9 to a climax. While our author must know that people other than Jesus have worked miracles, he is anxious for us to understand that the success of Jesus' ministry of miracles was in certain respects unprecedented. (iv) 9.34 records the negative reaction of the Pharisees. This helps prepare for the missionary discourse, where the theme of opposition is prominent (note in particular 10.25).

32. αὐτῶν δὲ ἐξερχομένων, ἰδοὺ προσήνεγκαν αὐτῷ ἄνθρωπον κωφὸν δαιμονιζόμενον. The first three words link 9.32–4 to the previous story: 'As they (the two blind men)[52] were going away...'

---

[50] The understandable tendency of interpreters to mute the disobedience of the blind men can be seen as early as Chrysostom, *Hom. on Mt.* 32.1. Roman Catholic commentators have traditionally emphasized the joy of becoming evangelists, which did not permit the men to endure silence, even though enjoined by Jesus himself.

[51] Cf. Bultmann, *History*, p. 212; Fenton, p. 145; Hill, *Matthew*, p. 181; Gundry, *Commentary*, p. 179; Gnilka, *Matthäusevangelium* 1, p. 346.

[52] It is also grammatically possible to equate αὐτῶν with Jesus and the disciples.

(cf. 9.31). ἰδού*, προσφέρω*, and δαιμονίζομαι (see 1, p. 418)
are often redactional. κωφός can mean deaf (as in 11.5) or dumb (as
in 12.22) or—like the rabbinic noun, *hērēš*[53]—both deaf and
dumb (BAGD, s.v.). Because the demoniac, when he is healed,
speaks, 'dumb' would seem to be the appropriate translation. But
because our story looks forward to 11.5, where 'the deaf hear', it is
probably better to translate the κωφόν of 9.32 as 'deaf and dumb'
(cf. Philo, *Spec. leg.* 4.197; in Mt 12.22 b sy[s.c] the man described as
τυφλός and κωφός is said to speak and see and hear).

33. καὶ ἐκβληθέντος τοῦ δαιμονίου ἐλάλησεν ὁ κωφός. Instead
of writing that the man was healed (cf. 12.22b), Matthew writes
that the demon was cast out. The phraseology, along with the
notice that the man was a 'demoniac' (9.32), sets the stage for
9.34, where the Pharisees accuse Jesus of being in league with
the prince of demons.

καὶ ἐθαύμασαν οἱ ὄχλοι λέγοντες. Compare 15.31 and see on
8.27. On the crowds in Matthew see on 4.25.

οὐδέποτε ἐφάνη οὕτως ἐν τῷ Ἰσραήλ. Compare LXX A Judg
19.30 and Mk 2.12. Coming as they do at the end of chapters
8–9, the words probably refer not to the miracle just worked but
to the whole series of miracles Matthew has recounted. οὐδέποτε (Mt: 5; Mk: 2; Lk: 2), φαίνομαι*, and οὕτως* are
redactional favourites. Bengel, *ad loc.*, commenting on 'in
Israel', wrote: 'the nation in which so many things had been
seen'.

**34. οἱ δὲ Φαρισαῖοι ἔλεγον· ἐν τῷ ἄρχοντι τῶν δαιμονίων
ἐκβάλλει τὰ δαιμόνια.**[54] The words anticipate 12.24 and
27. They supply an antecedent for 10.25: 'If they called the
master of the house Beelzebul, how much more those of his
household'. On Beelzebul, the prince or ruler of demons (cf. T.
Sol. 3.1–6), see on 10.25. The Pharisees' statement is to be
closely associated with the utterance of the crowds. The crowds
speak, then the Pharisees speak. The latter are responding not
so much to Jesus himself but to the assertion that 'never has
there appeared anything like this in Israel'. That is, the
Pharisees, the leaders, are addressing the crowds and trying to
convince them that their assertion is wrong (cf. 12.23–4). As
throughout the First Gospel, the Jewish leaders, transparent
symbols of the rabbis and synagogue leaders of Matthew's day,
are the major obstacle between the Jewish masses and faith in
Jesus.

[53] Cf. *m. Ter.* 1.2. The Hebrew verb *ḥārēš* can mean either 'be silent' or 'be
deaf' (BDB, s.v.).
[54] D a k sy[s] Hil omit the entire verse, and Zahn, p. 388, and many others
have rejected the line as an interpolation. But it fits its context perfectly.

(iv) *Concluding Observations*

(1) Like the first and second triads, the third triad of miracle stories in Mt 8–9 underlines the theme of faith; see 8.10, 26; 9.22, 28. But 9.28 introduces an idea not previously explicit. For Matthew, faith is faith in Jesus. Jesus asks the two blind men: 'Do you believe that I am able to do this?' Jewish faith in God presupposed God's omnipotence and anticipated God's saving acts. Matthew's Christian faith is a bit different. It sees Jesus as the concrete manifestation of the divine omnipotence and therefore expects God's saving acts to come through him. In other words, faith is not general faith in God but involves looking to Jesus as the embodiment and channel of God's power and grace (cf. 11.27; 28.18). Jesus himself thus becomes an object of faith (cf. 18.6).[55]

(2) 9.27–31 and 32–4 are, when considered with 11.5, reminiscent of the infancy narrative. This is because the two stories serve to correlate events in the near past with events prophesied long ago in the Scriptures. If Isa 35.5–6 (quoted in 11.5) foretells that the blind will see and that the deaf and dumb will regain their senses, then Jesus, through his healing ministry, has brought these promises to fulfilment. Matthew's notion of promise and fulfilment is anything but vague. Particular events in the life of Jesus precisely match particular events prophesied by the OT. The effect of this is to put into Matthew's hands not only an apologetical weapon (see the next paragraph) but also a hermeneutical key. If ancient prophecies have been plainly fulfilled they can no longer be understood without reference to what has fulfilled them. So while the OT gives meaning to Matthew's story of Jesus, it is not less true that Matthew's story of Jesus gives meaning to the OT. The Matthean perspective can be illustrated and put this way: when reading 9.27–34 one should think of Isa 35.5–6, and when reading Isa 35.5–6 one should think of Mt 9.27–34.

(3) The Pharisees do not deny Jesus' mighty works. The biting assertion which closes 8.1–9.34—'He casts out demons by the prince of demons'—assumes the successful expulsion of evil influences. So the burning issue in 9.34 is not what Jesus did but what his deeds mean. One gets the same impression

---

[55] We cannot here enter into discussion with the important work of W. Cantwell Smith but must mention him. He has urged that the distinctions between faith and belief have been seriously confused by modern Christian thinkers; see *Faith and Belief*, Princeton, 1979, and *Belief and History*, Charlottesville, 1977. His work merits careful attention.

elsewhere in the First Gospel.[56] The author is nowhere concerned to uphold the historical veracity of his narrative by calling upon eye-witnesses or by otherwise gaining the reader's confidence (contrast Lk 1.1–4). What is controversial is not the essentials of Jesus' story but whether one should side with the Christian *interpretation* of that story. How then does Matthew persuade the reader to embrace the Christian interpretation?[57] He has at least three different strategies. First he appeals to the OT as an instrument of persuasion. By constantly citing and alluding to the Scriptures, the evangelist attempts to show that Jesus is the Messiah, the true fulfilment, in letter and spirit, of the oracles of God. Secondly, Matthew claims that Jesus' deeds were in some respects without parallel and that people recognized this: 'Never has there appeared anything like this in Israel' (9.33; cf. 8.27; 9.8; 15.31). Thirdly, our author lets Jesus speak for himself, trusting that his inspired words, by virtue of their undeniable authority, their clarity of religious insight, and their profound moral vision, will have the power. to implant conviction in hearts that are not hardened (cf. 13.1–23).

(4) 9.27–31 and 32–4 help us appreciate the artistic unity of the First Gospel. The two pericopae, in several ways, prepare for the following two chapters. 9.27–31 (the healing of two blind men) looks forward to 11.5 ('the blind receive their sight'). 9.32–4 (the healing of a deaf and dumb demoniac) similarly anticipates 11.5 ('the deaf hear'). 9.33 ('Never has there appeared anything like this in Israel') sets the stage for 9.35ff., where Jesus sends out his messengers to the lost sheep of the house of Israel (10.6). And 9.34 ('He casts out demons by the prince of demons') anticipates 10.25 ('If they have called the master of the house Beelzebul ...'). All this demonstrates that, while composing chapter 9, the evangelist was already thinking about chapters 10 and 11.[58] Nothing could make plainer the folly of interpreting the individual pericopae of the gospel in isolation from each other. The many pieces of Matthew hang together and were intended to shed light upon one another. Meaning resides not just in the parts but in the whole.

[56] E.g. in 28.11–15 the assertion that Jesus' tomb was empty is not rejected. The question is rather *how* it became so.

[57] Although Matthew addressed his gospel first of all to the faithful, this scarcely excludes an apologetical interest. The evangelist may have hoped that his work would come into some non-Christian hands. More importantly, religious apologies tend to be read more by believers than by the unconverted, so their primary function is not to convert the sceptic but to still the doubts in believers' hearts. And Matthew, living in a polemical environment, would certainly have given careful thought to how his book would buttress the faith of people who already believed in Jesus.

[58] Cf. 1, pp. 93–4 of the Introduction, on 'Foreshadowing'.

(v) Bibliography

L. Dambrine, 'Guérison de la femme hémorroisse et résurrection de la fille de Jaire', in *Mélanges S. de Dietrich*, Paris, 1971, pp. 75–81.

J. D. M. Derrett, 'Mark's Technique: The Haemorrhaging Woman and Jairus' Daughter', *Bib* 63 (1982), pp. 474–505.

M. Gourgues, 'Deux miracles, deux démarches de foi (Marc 5.21–43 par)', in *A Cause de l'Évangile*, LD 123, Paris, 1985, pp. 229–49.

A. Fuchs, *Sprachliche Untersuchungen zu Matthäus und Lukas*, AnBib 49, Rome, 1971, pp. 18–170.

M. J. Harris, '"The Dead are restored to life": Miracles of Revivification in the Gospels', in Wenham and Blomberg, pp. 295–326.

Held, in *TIM*, pp. 178–81, 215–19.

M. Hutter, 'Ein altorientalischer Bittgestus in Mt 9.20–2', *ZNW* 75 (1984), pp. 133–5.

Kertelge, *Wunder*, pp. 110–20.

J. Kreyenbühl, 'Ursprung und Stammbaum eines biblischen Wunders', *ZNW* 10 (1909), pp. 265–76.

W. R. G. Loader, 'Son of David, Blindness, Possession and Duality in Matthew', *CBQ* 44 (1982), pp. 570–85.

van der Loos, pp. 509–19, 567–73.

W. Marxsen, 'Bibelarbeit über Mk 5.21–43/Mt 9.18–26', in *Der Exeget als Theologe*, Gütersloh, 1968, pp. 171–82.

V. K. Robbins, 'The Woman who touched Jesus' Garment', *NTS* 33 (1987), pp. 502–15.

G. Rochais, *Les récits de résurrection des morts dans le Nouveau Testament*, SNTSMS 40, Cambridge, 1981, pp. 39–112.

Schenke, *Wundererzählungen*, pp. 196–216.

Schmithals, *Wunder*, pp. 69–91.

M. J. Selvidge, 'Mark 5.25–34 and Leviticus 15.19–20', *JBL* 103 (1984), pp. 619–23.

Strauss, pp. 444–5, 457–62, 476–95.

H. Verweyen, 'Einheit und Vielfalt der Evangelien am Beispiel der Redaktion von Wundergeschichten (inbesondere Mk 5.25–34 parr.)', *Didaskalia* 11 (1981), pp. 3–24.

XX

THE MISSIONARY TASK AND ITS MESSENGERS
(9.35–10.4)

(i) *Structure*

The text resembles two previous units, the first being 4.23–5.2, which introduces the sermon on the mount, the first major discourse (cf. 1, pp. 410–11). Both 4.24–5.2 and 9.35–10.4 consist of two major parts, the first having to do with Jesus and the Jewish multitudes (4.23–5; 9.35–8), the second with Jesus and his disciples (5.1–2; 10.1–4). Especially noteworthy is the fact that 4.23 and 9.35 are nearly identical and form an important *inclusio* (see p. 158). The other passage 9.35–10.4 resembles is 8.16–22. This last follows the miracle stories in 8.1–15. Both paragraphs conclude a miracle triad, contain summary statements about Jesus' healing ministry, and allude to or cite Scripture (8.17; 9.36). See further 1, pp. 67, 102 and Excursus V. The explanation for the obvious resemblances with both 4.24–5.2 and 8.16–22 is this. 9.35–10.4 is a door that closes off one room and opens another. Structurally the pericope belongs equally to what comes before and to what comes after (just as one door belongs to two rooms). So it is no surprise that while 9.35–10.4 resembles another introduction to a major discourse it also recalls the conclusion of another miracle triad.[1]

(ii) *Sources*

On the theory of synoptic relationships adopted in this commentary, Mt 9.35–7 is a redactional piece forged out of three pre-Matthean sources—Mk 6.6b ('And he went among the villages teaching'[2]), Mk

---

[1] Morosco (v) has proposed that Mt 9.35–11.1 is influenced by an OT *Gattung*, that of the commissioning story. The form had these elements: (1) introduction; (2) confrontation; (3) commissioning; (4) objection; (5) reassurance; and (6) conclusion. According to Morosco, 9.35–8 is the introduction, 10.1–4 the confrontation, 10.5–23 the commissioning, 10.24–42 the reassurance, and 11.1 the conclusion. But there is no objection in Matthew's discourse; and the proposal fails to take into account the major triads of the chapter; see Excursus VIII.

[2] This occurs immediately before the missionary charge in Mk 6.7–13.

6.34 ('he saw a great throng, and he had compassion on them, because they were like sheep without a shepherd'[3]), and Q's saying about the eschatological harvest, which introduced the missionary discourse in that document (see Lk 10.2; cf. Jn 4.35). That Matthew's narrative is secondary is perhaps indicated by the transition from v. 36 (sheep without a shepherd) to vv. 37–8 (the harvest lacks reapers). The switch in images is a bit abrupt (cf. Schweizer, *Matthew*, p. 233).[4]

The ἐν τοῖς συναγωγαῖς αὐτῶν of 9.35 holds an important lesson for students of the synoptic problem. M. D. Goulder has observed that there are three words or phrases in Matthew that are strikingly characteristic of Matthew but which occur only once in Luke: ὀλιγό-πιστος, 'and it came to pass, when Jesus had completed all these words', and 'there shall be weeping and gnashing of teeth'. Goulder then proceeds to argue that since it is dubious to maintain that what is characteristic of Matthew was also found in Q, the unbiased critic should infer Luke's knowledge of Matthew.[5] One problem with the argument is this. Why can we not imagine that the First Evangelist repeated words or phrases found only once in his sources? Why must characteristically Matthean vocabulary be unparalleled in the other gospels? The point gains force from the circumstance that συναγωγή + αὐτῶν/ὑμῶν appears six times in Matthew (including 9.35) but only once in Mark (1.39). Here we have an example of a Mattheanism that even Goulder would admit comes from Mark. And there are other examples, such as πατήρ + ὑμῶν/σου/αὐτῶν/ἡμῶν + ὁ ἐν (τοῖς) οὐρανοῖς (Mt: 13; Mk: 1; Lk: 0), πληρόω used of the Scriptures (Mt: 12; Mk: 1; Lk: 2), and ὑποκριτής (Mt: 13; Mk: 1; Lk: 3).

Turning to 10.1–4, v. 1 has parallels in Mk 3.15; 6.7; and Lk 9.1 and appears to be based upon the passages in Mark. 10.2–4 has parallels in Mk 3.16–19; Lk 6.13–16; and Acts 1.13, and again it is Mark who seems to be Matthew's source. Yet there are some minor differences between Mt 10.2–4 and Mk 3.16–19, as the following chart shows:

Matthew	Mark
Simon the one called Peter	Simon Peter
and Andrew his brother	and James the son of Zebedee
James the son of Zebedee	and John the brother of James
	(whom he surnamed Boanerges,
	that is, sons of thunder)
and John his brother	and Andrew
Philip	and Philip
and Bartholomew	and Bartholomew
Thomas	and Matthew
and Matthew the toll collector	and Thomas
James the son of Alphaeus	and James the son of Alphaeus

[3] This appears in Mark's version of the feeding of the five thousand.

[4] There is also some tension between 9.35–8 and 10.1ff.: in the former Jesus lacks missionaries; in the latter they are standing around him.

[5] M. D. Goulder, 'A House built on Sand', in Harvey, *Approaches*, pp. 7–11.

Matthew	*Mark*
Simon the Cananaean	and Simon the Cananaean
and Judas Iscariot who betrayed	and Judas Iscariot who betrayed
him	him[6]

How has Matthew redacted Mark's list? First, he has ordered the first four names so as to make them appear in the sequence in which they appear in 4.18–22 (cf. also Lk 6.14) and to create parallelism not present in Mark: Simon and Andrew his brother/James and John his brother. Secondly, the desire for increased parallelism also explains why Matthew has arranged the list in six pairs: Peter and Andrew, James and John, Philip and Bartholomew, etc.[7] Thirdly, Matthew, like Luke, has omitted the comment on the sons of Zebedee ('whom he surnamed Boanerges . . .'). See on 10.2. Fourthly, our evangelist has, in accordance with the story in 9.9, tacked on 'the toll collector' after 'Matthew'. Finally, Thomas has been placed before rather than after Matthew (contrast Mark and Luke). This is the only change *vis-à-vis* Mark which does not have any obvious explanation. *By itself* it can scarcely be taken to hint at Matthew's use of a source other than Mark.

Is there, nonetheless, reason to suppose some influence from Q?[8] There are several minor agreements between Lk 6.13–16 and Mt 10.2–4: μαθηταί (10.1; Lk 6.13); ἀπόστολοι (10.1; Lk 6.13); the order, Peter, Andrew, James, John; material between 'Simon' and 'Peter' (ὁ λεγόμενος/ὃν καὶ ὠνόμασεν); the designation of Andrew as 'his (sc. Peter's) brother'; the omission of 'whom he surnamed Boanerges . . .'. Most of these agreements can readily be explained as due to the confluence of Matthean and Lukan redactional tendencies.[9] Still, in view of their number and the fact that certain features of Mt 4.24–5.2 are best explained on the supposition that Q prefaced the sermon on the mount/plain with a paragraph recounting Jesus' calling of the twelve (cf. the Lukan sequence and see on 5.1), the possibility that Mt 10.2–4 owes something to Q cannot be excluded.[10]

---

[6] Cf. Lk 6.14–16 and Acts 1.13. Amid all the differences there are some constants. Peter always occupies the first place, Philip the fifth, and James of Alphaeus the ninth. Further, with one exception, the three names after each of these are the same although they may occur in a different order. See further Villegas (v).

[7] Cf. Acts 1.13. Was Matthew influenced by the δύο δύο of Mk 6.7?

[8] So Schürmann, *Lukasevangelium* 1, pp. 316–19, and Donaldson, pp. 109–11. Contrast F. Neirynck, 'The Argument from Order and St. Luke's Transpositions', *ETL* 49 (1973), pp. 784–815. Gundry, *Commentary*, p. 183, takes the minor agreements between the lists of the twelve in Luke and Matthew to be evidence for Luke's knowledge of the First Gospel.

[9] E.g. the omission of the intrusive and difficult, 'whom he surnamed Boanerges . . .', and the coupling of Peter with Andrew and James with John could be due to independent editing.

[10] However one explains the agreements between Matthew and Luke and the differences from Mark, the variation from one list to the other recalls the variants in the OT lists of the twelve tribes of Israel; see e.g. Gen 49; Deut 33; and Ezek 48. It should also be noted that lists of the twelve outside the NT do

(iii) *Exegesis*

THE MISSIONARY TASK (9.35–8)

This passage offers the reader three images of Jesus. The first is of him wandering about cities and villages, carrying out his ministry of teaching, preaching, and healing (v. 35). The second is of him seeking the crowds and feeling compassion for them (v. 36). The third is of him speaking to his disciples, explaining to them the situation and what they must do (vv. 37–8). Notice that the three images become increasingly contracted. We go from Jesus wandering about cities and villages, to Jesus seeing the crowds, to Jesus speaking to his disciples. In this way the narrative naturally gives rise to 10.1–42. The task that the twelve are to perform (vv. 37–8 + 10.1–42) is rooted in Jesus' compassion for the multitude (v. 36) and results from the need for the ministry of teaching, preaching, and healing to be carried out by more than one individual (v. 35).

35. The missionary work of the disciples is introduced by describing the missionary work of Jesus. This is because the two tasks are of a piece. The disciples of Jesus are to do what Jesus did.

καὶ περιῆγεν ὁ Ἰησοῦς τὰς πόλεις πάσας καὶ τὰς κώμας διδάσκων ἐν ταῖς συναγωγαῖς αὐτῶν καὶ κηρύσσων τὸ εὐαγγέλιον τῆς βασιλείας καὶ θεραπεύων πᾶσαν νόσον καὶ πᾶσαν μαλακίαν.[11] This, with minor variations, reproduces 4.23 (to which Matthew's mind turned because of Mk 6.6b: 'and he went among the villages[12] teaching'). On the *inclusio* created by the two verses see on 4.23 and 1, p. 224. On the meaning of 'teaching' and 'preaching' in Matthew see pp. 414–15. Observe that after the main verb and its clause (καὶ περιῆγεν κ.τ.λ.) the evangelist gives us three participles followed (in the Greek) by four or five words:

teaching—in their synagogues
preaching—the gospel of the kingdom
healing—every disease and every infirmity

not always agree with the canonical registers; see W. Bauer, in Hennecke 2, pp. 35–8. There are even a few minor differences between the list in Lk 6 and the list in Acts 1.13.

[11] C³ K Γ Θ 28 700 *pm* c vg^mss add εν τω λαω (from 4.23). The phrase is likewise found in ℵ* L *f*¹³ 1010 1424 *al* g¹, which also add καὶ πολλοι (− ℵ*) ηκολουθησαν αυτω (cf. 4.25; 8.1).

[12] On the relation between 'villages' and 'cities' and the difficulty of distinguishing between them in first-century Palestine see vol. 1, p. 274, and E. Gabba, 'Social and Economic and Political Conditions in Palestine from 63 B.C.E. to 70 C.E.', in *CHJ* 3, forthcoming.

The balance gives the verse a nice rhythm.

36. Having travelled through cities and villages (v. 35), Jesus knows the condition of the multitudes: they are lost. His response to this sad fact is neither anger nor resignation. Rather is it compassion and action. He sees the people as though they were sheep without a shepherd. He sees them as victims, as harassed and cast down. And, in accordance with his messianic mission, he seeks to help.[13]

ἰδὼν δὲ τοὺς ὄχλους. So also 5.1 (q.v.). Compare Mk 6.34.

ἐσπλαγχνίσθη περὶ αὐτῶν. Mk 6.34 has ἐπ' αὐτούς. On περί + the genitive after verbs of emotion see BDF § 229.2; contrast 14.14 and 15.32. The verb[14] is from the noun, σπλάγχνα, which means 'entrails', 'compassion'. Its usage in the gospels[15] is to be explained by the Hebrew *riḥam*.[16] Because σπλαγχνίζομαι is used positively in several dominical parables (18.27; Lk 10.33; 15.20), one suspects that the tradition applied to Jesus a word which had been given special meaning by his speech.

ὅτι ἦσαν ἐσκυλμένοι καὶ ἐρριμμένοι. The last three words are a redactional addition without parallel in Mk 6.34. ἐσκυλμένοι means 'harassed' (see Allen, p. 99). ἐρριμμένοι means, literally, 'lying on the ground' (see BAGD, s.v., ῥίπτω 2); but here it must mean something like 'helpless'. Perhaps 'cast down' is the best equivalent. Do the passives imply a subject (the political and religious leaders)?

ὡσεὶ πρόβατα μὴ ἔχοντα ποιμένα. So Mk 6.34 (omitted in Mt 14.14). ὡς(ει) πρόβατα οἷς οὐκ ἔστιν ποιμήν appears three times in the LXX: Num 27.17; 2 Chr 18.16; and Jth 11.19.[17] Compare also 3 Βασ 22.17; Ezek 34.5–6; Josephus, *Ant.* 8.404; and 2 Bar. 77.13 ('the shepherds of Israel have perished'). Matthew has moved the words from their place in Mark (6.34) because they link up so well with the imperative in 10.6: 'Go rather to the lost sheep of the house of Israel' (cf. also 9.33 and 15.24).

ποιμήν is used three times in Matthew, in 9.36, in 25.32, and in

---

[13] Undoubtedly in this, as in so much else, Jesus is implicitly being presented as a model for Christian behaviour. The community is to perceive outsiders with love and compassion and should be moved to act on their behalf; cf. Chrysostom, *Hom. on Mt.* 32.3.

[14] Cf. Prov 17.5; T. Zeb. 6.4; 7.1–2; 8.3; T. Job 26.5; Par. Jer. 6.21; Hermas, *Sim.* 8.11.1; *Mand.* 4.3.5.

[15] The verb appears in the NT only in the synoptics.

[16] See further H. Koester, *TWNT* 7, pp. 548–59.

[17] The Hebrew for Num 27.17 and 2 Chr 18.16 is: *kaṣṣō'n 'ăšer 'ên-lāhem(n) rō'eh.*

26.31. In 25.32 Jesus, as the eschatological judge, acts like a shepherd who separates the sheep from the goats. In 26.31 Jesus is the shepherd of Zech 13.7; and, being struck, his sheep (= the disiples) are scattered. Probably implicit in 9.36 is the notion that Israel is waiting for her true shepherd, Messiah Jesus. The evangelist has already asserted, on the basis of OT texts, that the Messiah will 'shepherd' Israel (2.6), and there is some evidence that 'shepherd' carried messianic connotations in Judaism (Jer 3.15; 23.4; Ezek 34.23–4; 37.24; Ps. Sol. 17.40; *Midr. Ps.* on 29.1).[18] Is not Jesus the messianic shepherd, whose responsibility it is to gather eschatological Israel?

Is there also a Mosaic typology in the background of 9.36? Moses was a shepherd (Exod 3.1; Philo, *Vit. Mos.* 1.60–6; Josephus, *Ant.* 2.263–4; LAB 19.3, 9); and in Num 27.17 it is the departure of Moses which occasions the concern that Israel might become 'like sheep which have no shepherd'. When one also recalls that there are certainly places in Matthew where Jesus is one like Moses[19] and that some Jews no doubt expected the last redeemer (Messiah) to be like the first redeemer (Moses), the reader should perhaps think that Jesus the shepherd is taking up a Mosaic office when he seeks out the lost sheep of the house of Israel.

The notice that Israel appeared to Jesus as shepherdless sheep harmonizes well with our author's estimate of the Jewish leadership. The scribes and the Pharisees and the others in positions of power and responsibility have, for Matthew, not performed properly, and they are one of the major causes of the people's downfall. Compare Chrysostom, *Hom. on Mt.* 32.4: Jesus' words are a 'charge against the rulers of the Jews, that being shepherds they acted the part of wolves. For so far from amending the multitude, they even marred their progress'.[20]

37. τότε λέγει τοῖς μαθηταῖς αὐτοῦ. τότε + λέγει is distinctively Matthean (Mt: 12; Mk: 0; Lk: 0). Lk 10.2 has: ἔλεγεν δὲ πρὸς αὐτούς. According to Gundry, *Commentary*, p. 181, Matthew's historical present 'makes Jesus' following words an address to the church'. Compare Sand, *Matthäus*, p. 207: the tense adds emphasis.

ὁ μὲν θερισμὸς πολύς, οἱ δὲ ἐργάται ὀλίγοι. So Lk 10.2. Compare Gos. Thom. 73. The agreement with Luke in this clause and the next indicates a common written source. For other ὀλίγος/πολύς contrasts see 7.13–14; 22.14; Lk 7.47; 12.48; 2 Cor 8.15.

Everywhere else in the synoptic tradition, as in the prophets and Jewish apocalyptic literature, the harvest is typically a metaphor for

---

[18] For God himself as the eschatological shepherd see Clement of Alexandria, *Paed.* 1.9, quoting the lost *Apocryphon of Ezekiel*. Cf. Jer 31.10; Ezek 34.7–24.

[19] D. C. Allison, 'Gnilka on Matthew', *Bib.*, 70 (1989), pp. 527–32.

[20] In the OT, shepherd imagery is frequently used of political and military leaders; see J. Jeremias, *TWNT* 6, pp. 484–501.

the divine judgement, and the harvesters, those that gather, are God and the angels (Isa 18.4; 27.12; Jer 51.53; Hos 6.11; Joel 3.13; Mt 3.12; 13.30, 39; Mk 4.26–9; 13.27; Rev 14.14–20; 4 Ezra 4.26–37; 9.17; 2 Bar. 70.1–2; b. B. Meṣ. 83b; Midr. Ps. on 8.1). Here, however, the harvest is a metaphor for mission, and the disciples of Jesus, with their preaching of the kingdom, are the harvesters. So the eschatological harvest has been moved from the future to the present (cf. Dodd, Parables, pp. 143–4). This is some reason for urging that 9.37f. contains an authentic saying of Jesus.[21] On its connexion with Jn 4.35 see Dodd (v).

m. 'Abot 2.15 reads: 'R. Tarfon said: The day is short and the task is great and the labourers are idle and the wage is abundant and the master of the house is urgent'. This saying probably shows us that the application of harvest imagery to a pressing task was traditional. At the same time, the application in the gospels appears to be new. Time is short not because life is short but because the kingdom is at hand.

Because the harvest is, in the OT and other Jewish sources, so frequently associated with eschatological themes, and because the connexion is maintained in the NT, including Matthew, 9.37f. puts what follows in an eschatological context. The mission of the twelve and of the post-Easter church belongs to the latter days. It is not simply a prelude to the end but itself part of the complex of events that make up the end. This means that the evangelist and his community perceived their own time as eschatological time. See further on 10.17–24.

38. Having observed the tragic situation—the harvest is great, the labourers few—, Jesus does not weep and grieve but asks for prayer. Faith responds to the situation of crisis by turning towards God (cf. 24.20; 26.41). This is because 'man cannot create the new situation that is necessary; God alone will choose his messengers' (Schweizer, Matthew, p. 234).

δεήθητε οὖν τοῦ κυρίου τοῦ θερισμοῦ ὅπως ἐκβάλῃ ἐργάτας εἰς τὸν θερισμὸν αὐτοῦ. So Lk 10.2.[22] Compare Gos. Thom. 73 and m. Ma'as. 3.2 (hammôṣîʾ pôʿălîm laśśādeh). The Lord of the harvest is clearly God, not Jesus.[23]

Because the disciples of 9.37 are most naturally identified with the twelve (see 10.1–4), the 'workers' (ἐργάτας; cf. 10.10) are probably, in Matthew's mind, to be identified with the

---

[21] Cf. Hahn (v). Although ἐργάτης was an ecclesiastical term (cf. 2 Cor 11.13; 1 Tim 5.18; 2 Tim 2.15), that is hardly sufficient reason to deny a pre-Easter Sitz im Leben. Perhaps Jesus did in fact utter 9.37–8 par. at a time when he needed more helpers for the task he envisioned.

[22] Although some Lukan mss. (including P⁷⁵ ℵ B) have the less Semitic εργατας εκβαλη (which is the reading adopted by HG and NA²⁶).

[23] ἐκβάλλω need not always connote force (as it does in the exorcism stories). For its weakened sense see BAGD, s.v. 2. Here ἐκβάλῃ is rightly translated by 'send out'.

missionaries of the post-Easter period. If so, their existence is clearly an answer to prayer. Which is to say: not only is the post-Easter mission grounded in the activities of Jesus and the twelve, it is also grounded in the prayer request of Christ the Lord.

THE TWELVE APOSTLES (10.1–4)

This pericope consists of two parts. The first is a general summary of Jesus' charge to his 'twelve disciples' (v. 1). It anticipates 10.8 and stands as a heading for the discourse that follows. The second part is a list, given in six parts, of the names of the twelve (vv. 2–4). This list introduces the original audience for 10.5–42.

The list of the students of a teacher was conventional in both the Jewish and Graeco-Roman worlds. Compare, for example, m. 'Abot 2.8 ('Five disciples had Rabban Johanan b. Zakkai, and these are they: R. Eliezer b. Hyrcanus, and R. Joshua b. Hananiah, and R. Jose the Priest, and R. Simeon b. Nathaniel, and R. Eleazar b. Arak') and Diogenes Laertius 8.46 (the pupils of Philolaus and Eurytus). Unlike a genealogy, in which the names outline a pre-history, a list of students indicates a post-history. In our gospel the genealogy in 1.2–17 shows Jesus' pre-history to lie in Israel, in Abraham's descendants, while the list of disciples in chapter 10 shows his post-history to be in the church which has Peter at its head (cf. pp. 623–24, on the parallels between Peter and Abraham).[24]

1. Jesus summons twelve men and gives them authority for tasks which he himself has already performed. The *imitatio Christi* is implicit. Note that the initiative lies with Jesus. He makes the decisions and issues the call. Note also that Jesus is the sole source of authority for his followers. What they have comes from him. It is consistent with this that no reason is given why the twelve men named were in fact chosen. Their prior accomplishments evidently do not matter. At least they are not recounted. What counts is Jesus' will.

καὶ προσκαλεσάμενος τοὺς δώδεκα μαθητὰς αὐτοῦ. Compare Mk 6.7. Of the four canonical evangelists, only Matthew uses the

---

[24] One should also compare 10.1–4 with the lists of succession in rabbinic literature (e.g. m. 'Abot 1.1) and Graeco-Roman philosophy (see E. Bickermann, 'La chaîne de la tradition pharisienne', *RB* 59 (1952), pp. 44–54, and Davies, *JPS*, pp. 27–48). Does Matthew's gospel imply that Jesus' halakah was passed on through authorities from the pre-Easter period (e.g. Peter)? —There is a list of Jesus' disciples in b. Sanh. 43a: 'Jesus had five disciples: Mathai, Naqai, Nezer, Buni, and Todah'. Only Mathai has any obvious connexion with the disciple lists in the NT, but Todah could be Thaddaeus.

phrase, 'the twelve disciples'. He takes their existence and status for granted (cf. Gnilka, *Matthäusevangelium* 1, p. 355). Mt 10.1–4 combines into one paragraph material that, in Mark, belongs to two very different scenes (Mk 3.13–9; 6.7). The difference is worthy of remark. The evangelist knows that, according to Mark, Jesus called the twelve some time before he sent them out (Mk 3.13–16; 6.7–13; so also Luke). But it would not serve Matthew's literary and theological ends to follow his predecessor in this regard. From 4.23 on the evangelist wants Jesus alone to be in the spotlight. Only after reciting Jesus' words and deeds (chapters 5–9) do the disciples really come into the picture. This is because Jesus and the disciples are two different subjects, and Matthew, with his proclivity for thematic as opposed to historical and chronological thinking, wants to handle one theme at a time. So Jesus, the model, comes first. The disciples, the followers, come second.

The twelve—so abruptly introduced in 10.1—are, for Matthew, the human links between the pre- and post-Easter periods (cf. 28.16–20). They belong both to the period of Jesus and to the period of the church. They thus bridge the times, establishing continuity between Jesus and his church. The twelve are also, in our gospel, eschatological figures. They, like the twelve patriarchs and twelve phylarchs,[25] represent the twelve tribes of Israel (cf. 19.28). This is why, at least initially, their mission is, like that of Jesus (15.24), confined to Israel (10.5–6). Moreover, the Messiah's eschatological task of shepherding Israel (cf. 2.6 and see on 9.36) ultimately involves, among other things, gathering together into one flock those that have been scattered. This is an expectation Matthew seems to have taken very seriously. It is one of the reasons why, despite the Jewish opposition to Jesus and the community, Matthew does not think of the Jews as abandoned by salvation-history. Not only may the unrepentant come to repentance, but eschatological Israel will (in some other-worldly setting) be largely composed of Jews from the diaspora, that is, by Jews who, according to Matthew's eschatological hope, will recognize Jesus as their Messiah.[26]

A few scholars have denied that Jesus ever gathered a select group of twelve disciples. Admittedly, the δώδεκα, according to many reconstructions, were mentioned only once in Q (19.28 par.). However, already in the tradition preserved in 1 Cor 15.5 'the twelve' is a fixed expression.[27] Furthermore, Judas, who was, according to the gospels, chosen by Jesus himself, was known as 'one of the twelve' (26.14, 17, etc.). The community probably would not have invented something so potentially offensive and for which it had to create explanations (see

---

[25] On the phylarchs, the twelve princes of Israel, see the suggestive article of Horbury (v). It is worth remembering that they are closely associated in the Pentateuch with Moses.

[26] See further on 8.11.

[27] The ενδεκα of 1 Cor 15.5 D* D F latt sy[hmg] is almost certainly secondary.

26.25; Jn 6.64, 70–1; 13.11, 27; 17.12). It is also not irrelevant to observe, as Nineham has done (*Mark*, p. 115) that 'the very fact the twelve did not, as a body, have a very important role in the life of the early Church makes it the less likely that the early Church invented ... [the] story of their appointment'.[28] The assertion has added force because 'the general impression we receive is that, while the existence of the Twelve and the nature of their original appointment were firmly rooted in the tradition, apart from Peter, James, and John, most of them had become a somewhat distant memory' (Taylor, *Mark*, pp. 619–20). So Jesus, there is good reason to believe, did in fact single out from among his followers a special group of twelve.[29] His intent in so doing was probably the creation of a prophetic symbol. The eschatological ingathering of scattered Israel was to hand and indeed beginning in Jesus' own ministry. In addition, the twelve were almost certainly involved in a pre-Easter mission. They had all, in effect, been called to be 'fishers of men'.[30]

ἔδωκεν αὐτοῖς ἐξουσίαν πνευμάτων ἀκαθάρτων. So Mk 6.7, with καὶ ἐδίδου and with τῶν both before and after πνευμάτων (cf. Lk 9.1, with ἔδωκεν). Compare Lk 10.19–20. Note also T. Levi 18.12: καὶ δώσει ἐξουσίαν τοῖς τέκνοις αὐτοῦ τοῦ πατεῖν ἐπὶ τὰ πονηρὰ πνεύματα. For the genitive after ἐξουσία see LXX Dan 5.4. 'Unclean spirits' reappears in Mt only in 12.43 (cf. Judg 9.23; 1 Sam 16.14–23; 1 Kgs 22.22–3; Zech 13.2; Rev 16.13; 18.2; LAB 53.3; T. Iss. 7.7; b. Sanh. 65b).

ὥστε ἐκβάλλειν αὐτά. This redactional phrase makes explicit what remains only implicit in Mark: the purpose of having authority over unclean spirits is to cast them out. Perhaps the point needed to be made unambiguous because authority over unclean spirits could theoretically have been used to make those spirits do one's bidding—something Matthew would have found abhorrent.[31]

καὶ θεραπεύειν πᾶσαν νόσον καὶ πᾶσαν μαλακίαν. Compare

---

[28] Pertinent here is É. Trocmé, 'Le christianisme primitif, un mythe historique?', *ETR* 49 (1974), pp. 15–29.

[29] *Pace* Bultmann, *Theology* 1, p. 37; Klein (v). See further R. P. Meye, *Jesus and the Twelve*, Grand Rapids, 1968, pp. 192–209; C. K. Barrett, *The Signs of an Apostle*, Philadelphia, 1972, pp. 23–4; Trilling (v); Trautmann, pp. 179–85; T. Holtz, *EWNT* 1, pp. 878–9; and Sanders, *Jesus*, pp. 98–106.

[30] Cf. Hahn, *Mission*, pp. 40–6; Hengel, *Jesus and Paul*, pp. 60–3; and R. Pesch, 'Voraussetzungen und Anfänge der urchristlichen Mission', in Kertelge, *Mission*, pp. 26–8. —For other groups of twelve in Jewish documents see 1QS 8 (the twelve in the council of the community); 1QM 2.1–3 (twelve priests, twelve Levites, twelve princes); 4QOrdinances 2–4.3–4 (a court of twelve); 11QTemple 57.11–3 (twelve leaders, twelve priests, twelve Levites); Josephus, *Bell.* 2.292 (the twelve leading men of Caesarea). See further J. M. Baumgarten, 'The Duodecimal Courts of Qumran, Revelation, and the Sanhedrin', *JBL* 95 (1976), pp. 59–78.

[31] In T. Sol. 2 Solomon forces a demon to help in the construction of the Jerusalem temple. Cf. Testim. Truth 70.5–9.

Lk 9.1–2. Matthew now repeats a phrase used of Jesus in both 4.23 (q.v.) and 9.35 and thereby drives home once again the correlation between Jesus' deeds and those of his followers: the disciples do what their master did.

2. τῶν δὲ δώδεκα ἀποστόλων τὰ ὀνόματά ἐστιν ταῦτα. Compare Josephus, *Ant.* 3.105. The word 'apostle' appears only here in the First Gospel. According to most scholars, our author identified 'the twelve' with 'the apostles'.[32] No stress, however, is laid on the equation. Perhaps it is just taken for granted. Why does 'apostle' appear only once in Matthew? We can only speculate. U. Luz's suggestion is, however, the most plausible: 'The members of the community could identify with the *mathētai* but not with the *apostoloi* who had already become by that time figures of the past. Conversely, the word *mathētēs* is very well suited for teaching people to understand the essence of being a Christian as a relationship to the historical Jesus'.[33] To be a Christian is, for Matthew, both an act and a process of learning (cf. 11.25–30; 28.16–20).

ἀπόστολος, from the verb ἀποστέλλω (= 'send away'; cf. 10.5, 16), appears only once in the LXX, translating the *šālûaḥ* of 1 Kgs 14.6 (note also Isa 18.2 Sym.). In classical Greek texts the primary meaning of the word is naval expedition or the sending out of a fleet, although Herodotus (1.21; 5.38) already attests to the meaning, 'one who is sent' (LSJ, s.v.). The word occurs once in Josephus, where it means 'sending out' (*Ant.* 17.300; cf. *Ant.* 1.146 v. 1); and in the papyri it mostly means 'bill of lading' (e.g. *P. Oxy.* 9.1197.13). In the NT it, like ἄγγελος, is used of messengers both human and divine (Jn 13.16; 2 Cor 8.3; Phil 2.25; Heb 3.1), especially of '*the* apostles', a special group of men. In this last sense it is a technical term (even though usage appears to differ somewhat from writer to writer). The background of the term and the office it represents have been disputed.[34] But it is clear that secular Greek does not provide the background, and that the LXX and Hellenistic Jewish texts are also barren in this regard. Most twentieth-century scholars have probably been correct in finding the key in the *šālîaḥ* (= 'sent man') of rabbinic Judaism.[35] The *šālîaḥ* was a commissioned agent sent forth in another's name. Acting for an

---

[32] Many have, despite Acts 14.4, 14, made the same claim for Luke.

[33] U. Luz, 'The Disciples in the Gospel according to Matthew', in Stanton, p. 109.

[34] Surveys include E. M. Kredel, 'Der Apostelbegriff in der neueren Exegese', *ZKT* 78 (1956), pp. 169–93, 257–305, and F. H. Agnew, 'The Origin of the New Testament Apostle-Concept: A Review of Research', *JBL* 105 (1986), pp. 75–96.

[35] E.g. J. B. Lightfoot, *St. Paul's Epistle to the Galatians*, 10th ed., London, 1890, pp. 92–100; K. H. Rengstorf, *TWNT* 1, pp. 406–46; and C. K. Barrett, 'Shaliah and Apostle', in *Donum Gentilicium*, ed. E. Bammel, C. K. Barrett, and W. D. Davies, Oxford, 1978, pp. 88–102. The Syriac church translated 'apostle' by *šĕlîḥâ*, and the equation is made by Jerome in his commentary on Galatians (on 1.1).

individual (as in *m. Qidd.* 2.1) or an institution (as in *m. Giṭ.* 3.6), he was an authoritative representative: 'the one sent (*šālîaḥ*) is like the man himself (that is, the sender)' (*m. Ber.* 5.5; *Mek.* on Exod 12.41; etc.). His power to act was determined wholly by his subordinate relationship to the one who charged him (cf. Jn 13.16). The parallels to the NT apostolate are obvious. Yet, because the *šālîaḥ* convention is clearly attested only in texts of the second century A.D. and later, some scholars have affirmed that the apostle was a new figure called forth by the new experience of Christians.[36] Another suggestion has come from W. Schmithals: the apostle was modelled on the earthly redeemer figure found in the Gnostic tradition.[37] Nonetheless, the rabbinic idea of the *šālîaḥ* may very well go back to the first century (our sources remain scanty). In addition, 2 Cor 8.23[38] and Phil 2.25[39] show that in the NT 'apostle' could be used in a semi-technical sense with a meaning very close to the meaning of *šālîaḥ*. Finally, even though *šālîaḥ* and ἀπόστολος are not offices in the OT, already in 2 Chr 17.7–9 and elsewhere the conception represented by the two words in Christian and rabbinic texts is approximated. In view of these facts it seems best to follow those who have traced the NT's 'apostle' to the rabbinic *šālîaḥ*.[40]

πρῶτος Σίμων ὁ λεγόμενος Πέτρος. Mk 3.16 has: καὶ ἐπέθηκεν ὄνομα τῷ Σίμωνι Πέτρον. On 'Simon the one called Peter' see on 4.18. The redactional πρῶτος (cf. 20.27) is of great interest. The word refers not to Peter's having been the first called nor to his being the first to see the risen Lord nor to his being the first on the list. Rather does it indicate his privileged status. He is, as one might expect in a Jewish gospel, the first among equals, the chief of the apostles.[41] Just as Judas, the last on the list, is the most dishonoured apostle, so is Peter, the first, the most honoured. See further Excursus XIII.

καὶ Ἀνδρέας ὁ ἀδελφὸς αὐτοῦ. Compare Lk 6.14 and see on 4.18.

---

[36] But the sages who travelled to various Jewish communities, a fact well attested, were in a sense *šĕlûḥîm*, and the necessity to keep the Diaspora informed of Palestinian affairs made their work necessary before the second century A.D. See Davies *SSM*, p. 295.

[37] W. Schmithals, *The Office of Apostle in the Early Church* (trans. of *Das kirchliche Apostelamt*, 1961), Nashville and New York, 1969.

[38] 'And as for our brethren, they are messengers (ἀπόστολοι) of the churches, the glory of Christ'.

[39] 'I have thought it necessary to send to you Epaphroditus my brother and fellow worker and fellow soldier, and your messenger (ἀπόστολον) and minister to my need'.

[40] The best alternative, in our judgement, is to trace the concept back to Jesus' adoption of a prophetic *topos*: just as God sent forth (*šālaḥ*) OT prophets so does Jesus send forth his 'apostles'. Cf. Isa 6.8; Jer 1.7; Ezek 2.4; Zech 2.12; also Exod 3.12–15. See further B. Gerhardsson, 'Die Boten Gottes und die Apostel Christi', *SEÅ* 27 (1962), pp. 89–131; Hengel, *Leader*, pp. 82–3.

[41] Cf. BAGD, s.v., πρῶτος 1. C.B, and Clement of Alexandria, *Quis div. salv.* 21.

Ἰάκωβος ὁ τοῦ Ζεβεδαίου καὶ Ἰωάννης ὁ ἀδελφὸς αὐτοῦ.[42]
Compare Mk 3.17 and see on 4.21. Matthew, like Luke, has
omitted the enigmatic 'whom he surnamed Boanerges, that is,
sons of thunder'.[43] It adds nothing and would break the rhythm
of Matthew's list.

3. Φίλιππος καὶ Βαρθολομαῖος. In the synoptics Philip[44] is
nothing more than a name. In John he is a major character. See
1.43–51; 6.5; 12.20–2; 14.8. Whatever be the sources of the
Johannine traditions, it is clear that in some Christian circles
the apostle Philip was remembered as a significant figure (cf.
Papias, in Eusebius, *H.E.* 3.31, 39).[45]

Bartholomew[46] is, like Philip, only a name in the synoptics. Unlike
Philip, he is never mentioned by John. Some (e.g. Leidig (v)) have
identified him with the Nathanael of the Fourth Gospel, but the reasons
for this equation are not compelling.[47] According to Eusebius, *H.E.*
5.10, Pantaenus, upon arriving in India, found that the Gospel of
Matthew (in Hebrew letters) had preceded him there, having been left
by Bartholomew.

Θωμᾶς καὶ Μαθθαῖος ὁ τελώνης. On Matthew see 9.9. He is
labelled 'the tax collector' because of the story in chapter 9. The
vocation of no other apostle is given. Our evangelist probably
did not know what the other apostles did, with the exceptions
of Peter, Andrew, James and John; but it would not have been
appropriate to call one or more of them 'the fisherman'.

In the synoptics, Thomas, who is traditionally credited with taking
Christianity to India, is named only in the lists of the twelve. In John
he appears on several occasions, in 11.16; 14.5; 20.24–9; and 21.2. In
three of these places he is called Δίδυμος (= 'twin'), and this is in
fact the meaning of the Aramaic *tẹ̄ōmāʾ*.[48] We do not learn, however,
whose twin he was. If we discount the tradition that he was Jesus' twin

[42] An initial και appears in ℵ[c] B Γ *pc* d sy[hmg]. But it is probably not original.
It disrupts the pattern, name/καί/name, and it is missing in ℵ[*vid.c] C D L W Θ *f*[1.13]
Maj lat sy[h]co. NA[26] retains, HG omits.
[43] On this see J. T. Rook, '"Boanerges, Sons of Thunder" (Mark 3.17)', *JBL*
100 (1981), pp. 94–5.
[44] For the Hebraized forms of this name in the Talmud see Jastrow, s.v.,
pĕlîpāʾ, and SB 1, p. 535.
[45] Despite the Martyrdom of Andrew and Polycrates (cf. Eusebius, *H.E.*
3.31), modern scholars do not usually identify the Philip of Mt 10.3 par. with
the deacon/evangelist who is so prominent in Acts; see 6.5; 8.4–13, 26–40; 21.8–
9. Hengel, however, regards this as a possibility: *Jesus and Paul*, p. 14. Cf.
Villegas (v).
[46] From Aramaic *bar talmay* = 'son of Talmai'. For 'Talmai' see Num 13.22;
Josh 15.14; Judg 1.10; 2 Sam 3.3; 13.37; 1 Chr 3.2; *b. Yoma* 13a.
[47] See U. Holzmeister, 'Nathanael fuitne idem ac S. Bartholomaeus
apostolus?', *Bib* 21 (1940), pp. 28–39.
[48] Cf. Tg. Onq. on Gen 25.24. Incidentally, the word was never simply a
surname.

(so e.g. the Acts of Thomas⁴⁹), we necessarily remain in the dark.⁵⁰ It is not impossible that his personal name was Judas (cf. Jn 14.22 sy⁸·ᶜ; Gos. Thom. title; Acts of Thomas 1.1; Eusebius, *H.E.* 1.13).

Ἰάκωβος ὁ τοῦ Ἀλφαίου καὶ Θαδδαῖος. About James the son of Alphaeus we know next to nothing, although he could be identified with James the son of Mary (Mt 27.56; Mk 15.40; 16.1; Lk 24.10) or with Levi's brother (according to Mk 2.14 Levi was also a son of Alphaeus⁵¹). He is not James 'the just', the brother of the Lord (1 Cor 15.7; Gal 1.19). As for Thaddaeus (= *tadday, tadda'y*), who becomes Λεββαῖος in many mss.,⁵² he too is a faceless figure. Perhaps, as Jeremias, *Theology*, pp. 232f., has maintained, he is the same as Ἰούδας Ἰακώβου (cf. Mt 10.3 sy⁸; Lk 6.16; Acts 1.13; also (?) Jn 14.22). Note that *b. Sanh.* 43a names, as one of Jesus' five disciples, a certain *tôdâ'*. The Agbar legend (Eusebius, *H.E.* 1.13) makes Thaddaeus one of the seventy (cf. Lk 10.1).

4. Σίμων ὁ Καναναῖος καὶ Ἰούδας ὁ Ἰσκαριώτης ὁ καὶ παραδοὺς αὐτόν. Compare Mk 3.18–19. On the name, 'Simon', see on 4.18. 'Simon the Cananaean' is the same as 'Simon the Zealot' (Lk 6.15; Acts 1.13). 'Cananaean' does not derive from 'Canaanite'⁵³ or 'Cana'⁵⁴ but from the Aramaic word for 'zealot' or 'enthusiast': *qan'ān*. Although it is widely held that Simon at one time belonged to the party of the Zealots, it is, notwithstanding Hengel, *Zeloten*, very doubtful whether 'zealot' came to refer distinctively to revolutionaries before the Jewish war in the sixties (cf. Gal 1.14);⁵⁵ and ζηλωτήν may simply be adjectival in Lk 6.15 and Acts 1.13: 'the zealous one' (cf. 4 Macc. 18.12). Also, some might wonder how likely it is that Jesus would have made an (ex-) Zealot part of his inner circle.

The enigmatic Judas Iscariot, who naturally comes last in the apostolic catalogue and who is the only apostle to have his future rôle noted, appears five times in the First Gospel: in 10.4; 26.14–16 (where Judas strikes the deal to deliver up Jesus); 26.20–5 (where Judas is

---

⁴⁹ This makes Thomas, like Jesus, a carpenter.

⁵⁰ Ps.-Clem. Hom. 2.1 makes Thomas the twin of Eliezer.

⁵¹ The identification of Alphaeus with the Cleopas of Lk 24.18 has sometimes been made; see Swete, p. 61.

⁵² So, with differences, D W L Δ Θ Π *f¹* Maj d f k eth arm Or Aug Hes. For a defence of this reading see Zahn, pp. 392–3. But the reading could be due to a desire to get Levi the publican on the list; or it might have arisen as a gloss on Θαδδαῖος: Λεββαῖος probably comes from the Hebrew for heart (*lēb, lēbāb*), and Θαδδαῖος may have been thought of as deriving from *taddā'* = 'breast'.

⁵³ Mt 15.22 has Χαναναία for 'Canaanite'.

⁵⁴ Although the reading of ℵ Maj—Κανανιτης—assumes derivation from the place name 'Cana'.

⁵⁵ See M. Smith, 'Zealots and Sicarii: Their Origins and Relation', *HTR* 64 (1971), pp. 1–19; R. A. Horsley, 'The Zealots', *NovT* 28 (1986), pp. 159–92.

signalled out by Jesus as the one who would deliver him up); 26.47–56 (where Judas leads the crowd to arrest Jesus); and 27.3–10 (Judas' suicide).[56] Except for 27.3–10, Matthew's material comes from Mark, and most of the major motifs associated with Judas in Mark also appear in Matthew: Judas is the one who delivered Jesus up (10.4; 26.25; 27.3) and 'one of the twelve' (10.4; 26.14, 47), and what he did was somehow ordained by or in accordance with the Scriptures (26.53–6; 27.9–10). Matthew has, however, made at least four contributions of his own. He has emphasized Judas' repentance (27.3),[57] underlined his greed (26.14–16), told us of his bleak end (27.3–10), and added to the parallels between Judas and Ahithophel, the trusted friend who betrayed David and then went out and hanged himself.[58] Notably absent from Matthew is any stress on Judas' association with the dark forces of Satan (contrast Lk 22.3–4; Jn 12.1–8; 13.2, 21–30).

By following Mark in labelling Judas as the one who delivered Jesus up (cf. 26.25; 27.3; Jn 12.4; 18.5), Matthew once again anticipates the passion narrative. Long before Jesus goes up to Jerusalem the narrative hints at the coming end. The crucifixion casts its long shadow over the whole gospel.

There has been much discussion concerning the meaning of 'Iscariot', which Mark leaves unexplained. Does it, as most commentators have supposed (cf. SB 1, pp. 537–8), derive from *'îš qěrîyôt* (= 'man of Kerioth')?[59] Or does it derive from the Greek σικάριος, which means 'assassin', 'bandit' (cf. the Latin *sicarius*)?[60] Or does Iscariot equal the Aramaic *'îšqaryā* (= 'the false one'), in which case the name would be *ex eventu*?[61] Still other possibilities include 'man of Jericho', 'man of Issachar', 'man of Coreae' (cf. Josephus, *Bell.* 1.134; 4.449), 'man from Sychar' (= Samaria), 'purse-bearer' (so Lightfoot 2, p. 179), and 'red-head'.[62] There is also the explanation of A. Ehrman: Iscariot derives from the Aramaic *sāqor*, which means 'to dye or paint red' (cf. *m. Bek.* 9.7).[63] This would mean that Judas was a 'dyer'.

[56] 'Judas Iscariot' is the name in the synoptics and Jn 12.4. In Jn 6.71 and 13.2, 26 he is 'Judas, son of Simon Iscariot'. There are also different forms for the Greek: Ἰσκαριώθ (Mk 14.10; Lk 6.16) and Ἰσκαριώτης (Jn 6.71; 12.4; 13.2, 26; 14.22). Σκαριώθ appears in D in Mk 3.19; Jn 6.71. But in Mt 10.4; 26.14; and Mk 14.10 D has Σκαριώτης.

[57] But not because he wishes to exonerate him. The motive is christological: even the betrayer knows Jesus is innocent.

[58] See further B. Gärtner, *Iscariot* (trans. of pp. 37–68 of *Die rätselhaften Termini Nazoräer und Iskariot*, 1957), FBBS, Philadelphia, 1971, pp. 30–9.

[59] For criticism see C. C. Torrey, 'The Name "Iscariot"', *HTR* 36 (1943), pp. 51–62. If Judas was from Kerioth he would be the only disciple not from Galilee. Further, the appearance in Greek of the untranslated 'man' (= Hebrew *'îš*) is unexpected; cf. Schlatter, p. 327. On the other hand, J. B. Lightfoot, *Biblical Essays*, London, 1893, pp. 143–4, observed that the *'îš tôb* (= the men of Tob) of 2 Sam 10.6, 8 becomes Ἴστοβος in Josephus, *Ant.* 7.121.

[60] So Cullmann (v). But the long ι in the initial syllable of σικάριος/*sicarius* is not represented in 'Iscariot'.

[61] So Gärtner (as in n. 58), pp. 6–7, and Torrey (as in n. 59).

[62] For this last see H. Ingholt, 'The Surname of Judas Iscariot', in *Studia Orientalia*, Copenhagen, 1953, pp. 152–62. Judas, as Ingholt observes, is usually a red-head in Christian iconography. Yet the antiquity of this tradition has not been established.

[63] A. Ehrman, 'Judas Iscariot and Abba Saqqara', *JBL* 97 (1978), pp. 572–3;

(iv) *Concluding Observations*

9.35–10.4, which serves both to conclude chapters 8–9 and to introduce the missionary discourse, accomplishes several significant ends. (1) By harking back to 4.23 and forming an *inclusio*, the passage makes Jesus' words (5–7) and deeds (8–9) the fundamental context for understanding 10.1–42. The twelve are to preach and to heal (10.7–8). In this they are clearly following in the footsteps of Jesus. More particularly, since 5.1–7.27 gives content to the command to preach the gospel of the kingdom (10.7), and since 8.1–9.34 gives content to the command to 'heal the sick, raise the dead, cleanse lepers, cast out demons' (10.8), 5.1–9.34 is for the missionary example and precedent. In other words, Matthew's Jesus is in some sense the first Christian missionary, and he is the standard to be followed. The bearers of the gospel are, in their own situations, to proclaim what Jesus proclaimed and to do what Jesus did. It is no surprise that chapter 10 is full of parallels between Jesus and his followers (cf. 10.6, 7, 8, 17, 18, 24–5). The church is the continuation of the life of Jesus.[64]

(2) The polemical dimension of 9.35–10.4 must not be missed. 9.37–8 is prompted by the failure of the Jewish leaders (see on 9.36). This means that in sending out the twelve, Jesus is seeking to right the wrongs done by some of the Pharisees and other Jewish leaders. And in a sense the twelve are taking the place of the Jewish leaders, for if they perform their missionary task, it is implied that Israel will not be shepherdless.

(3) 9.35–8 should alert the careful reader that the following discourse is bound up with eschatological expectation. Not only is the gospel that Jesus (9.35) and others (10.7) preach concerned with the eschatological kingdom of God, but the missionary endeavour is interpreted by a standard eschatological *topos*, the harvest (see on 9.37). Further, the reference to 'sheep without a shepherd' should, within the broader Matthean context, probably be given eschatological content: Israel is waiting for her messianic leader (see on 9.36). The introduction to 10.5–42 is, accordingly, permeated from first to last by eschatological themes. This leads one to anticipate a discourse about the latter days. This expectation, as we shall see, is fully met.

(4) The twelve, as we have observed, are both a symbol of Matthew's eschatological hope (cf. 19.28) and the guarantors of

---

also Y. Arbeitman, 'The Suffix of Iscariot', *JBL* 99 (1980), pp. 122–4. Red was, as Ehrman notes, the dominate colour of the dyer's trade.

[64] Every significant term that has historically come to be used of church leaders—such as deacon, apostle, shepherd, high Priest, bishop—is applied in the NT to Christ himself.

the Christian *halakah* (cf. Hummel). They are also transparent figures whose relationship to their Lord mirrors and informs the experiences of Christians in Matthew's community. It would be an error, we think, to set the evangelist's 'historicizing' of the twelve (Strecker) over against the tendency—manifest in chapter 10—to make them 'transparent' (Luz; see 1, pp. 406–7). The group, as 10.1–4 and other passages make plain, belongs to the unrepeatable past. But just as Jesus is not for Matthew a dead man but a living Lord, so too are the twelve more than just memory. Not only will they one day rise to govern eschatological Israel, but through the Jesus tradition their authority continues to make itself felt while the stories about them remain to instruct. So the twelve disciples belong to the past, to the present, and to the future.

(v) *Bibliography*

O. Cullmann, 'Le douzième apôtre', *RHPR* 42 (1962), pp. 133–40; translated into German in *Vorträge und Aufsätze 1925–62*, Tübingen, 1966, pp. 214–22.

Dodd, *Tradition*, pp. 391–405.

Hahn, *Mission*, pp. 40–3.

W. Horbury, 'The Twelve and the Phylarchs', *NTS* 32 (1986), pp. 503–27.

G. Klein, *Die zwölf Apostel*, FRLANT 77, Göttingen, 1961.

L. Legrand, 'The Harvest is Plentiful (Mt 9.37)', *Scripture* 17 (1965), pp. 1–9.

E. Leidig, 'Natanael, ein Sohn des Tholomäus', *TZ* 36 (1980), pp. 374–5.

B. Lindars, 'Matthew, Levi, Lebbaeus and the Value of the Western Text', *NTS* 4 (1958), pp. 220–2.

U. Luz, 'Die Jünger im Matthäusevangelium', *ZNW* 62 (1971), pp. 141–71; translated into English in Stanton, pp. 98–128 ('The Disciples in the Gospel according to Matthew').

R. E. Morosco, 'Matthew's Formation of a Commissioning Type-Scene', *JBL* 103 (1984), pp. 539–56.

R. Pesch, 'Levi-Matthäus (Mc 2.14/Mt 9.9; 10.3). Ein Beitrag zum Lösung eines alten Problems', *ZNW* 59 (1968), pp. 40–56.

B. Rigaux, 'Die "Zwölf" in Geschichte und Kergyma', in Ristow, pp. 468–86.

Trautmann, pp. 167–233.

W. Trilling, 'Zur Entstehung des Zwölferkreises', in Schnackenburg, *Kirche*, pp. 201–22.

H.-J. Venetz, 'Bittet den Herrn der Ernte. Überlegungen zu Lk 10.2/Mt 9.37', *Diakonia* 11 (1980), pp. 148–61.

B. Villegas, 'Peter, Philip and James of Alphaeus', *NTS* 33 (1987), pp. 292–4.

EXCURSUS VIII

THE STRUCTURE OF THE MISSIONARY DISCOURSE[1]

There is near unanimity that 10.5–15 is the first major subsection of Matthew's missionary discourse, this because the break between vv. 15 and 16 is impossible to miss (cf. Gnilka, *Matthäusevangelium* 1, p. 358). Vv. 5–15, which are united by the theme of movement from place to place (ἀπέρχομαι, v. 5, εἰσέρχομαι, vv. 5, 11, 12, πορεύομαι, vv. 6, 7, ἐξέρχομαι, vv. 11, 14), offer detailed instructions to missionaries: go here, do not go there; do this, do not do that; take this, do not take that. These instructions are combined with words about the reception of missionaries, as is altogether natural. The commands on what to do when one is accepted or when one is rejected inevitably raise the issue of what will happen to those who do not welcome Jesus' representatives (see vv. 11–15). With v. 16 the theme changes. 'Behold, I send you forth as sheep in the midst of wolves' introduces the reader to a list of hardships the missionary can expect to encounter—flogging in synagogues, arrest, rejection by families, death. The list, which thrice uses the key word, παραδίδωμι, concludes, like 10.5–15, with an eschatological declaration introduced by 'amen': οὐ μὴ τελέσητε. . . .

Following the very specific prophecies delivered in vv. 16–23, the next subsection, 10.24–5, contains a more general forecast: the disciple will be treated in the same manner as the master. The short paragraph makes explicit a motif implicit in both of the preceding units, vv. 5–15 and 16–23, namely, the imitation of Christ. In vv. 7 and 8 the twelve apostles are instructed to say what Jesus has said and to do what Jesus has done (see pp. 169–70); and in 10.16–23 the treatment of the disciples recalls for the informed reader the passion narrative and the fate of Jesus (see pp. 180–92).

The centre of chapter 10 would seem to be 10.26–31, which offers

[1] Lit.: H. J. B. Combrinck, 'Structural Analysis of Mt 9.35–11.1',*Neotestamentica* 11 (1977, second edition, 1980), pp. 98–114; Gaechter, *Kunst*, pp. 36–44 (a chiastic analysis which differs from our own only in seeing 10.5b–10 as the introduction); J. A. Grassi, 'The Last Testament-Succession Literary Background of Matthew 9.35–11.1 and its Significance', *BTB* 7 (1977), pp. 172–6 (Mt 10 is a last testament; see esp. Gen 49.1–33); G. Mangatt, 'Reflections on the Apostolic Discourse (Mt 10)', *Biblebhashyam* 6 (1980), pp. 196–206 (he accepts Radermachers' analysis, see below); R. E. Morosco, 'Matthew's Formation of a Commissioning Type-Scene', *JBL* 103 (1984), pp. 539–56 (Matthew has shaped his discourse so that it resembles Moses' call and commission in Exodus); J. Radermachers, 'La Mission, engagement radical: Une lecture de Mt 10', *NRT* 93 (1971), pp. 1072–85 (a chiastic scheme, with vv. 5–15 paired with vv. 34–42, vv. 16–23 with 26–33, and with 10.24–5 at the centre); Rigaux, *Testimony*, pp. 78–81 (these are the units: vv. 5–16, 17–25, 26–33, 34–6, 37–9, 40–2).

consolation and encouragement. The passage is surrounded on all sides by difficult commands and ominous prophecies. It is the contrast between these and 10.26–31 which brings to light the function of the latter. 10.26–31 does not foretell persecution, betrayal, or difficulty. Rather, as Chrysostom, *Hom. on Mt.* 34, rightly stressed, it puts suffering in perspective by turning the mind's eye towards certain spiritual truths. 'Do not fear' means, in effect, 'there is no need to fear.' Note that the section is triadic. There are three 'fear not' imperatives. These mark the three triadic subunits (vv. 26f., 28, 29–31). Further, the μὴ οὖν in both 26a and 31a creates an *inclusio* which shows the boundary of the subsection.

The next paragraph is clearly 10.31f., on confessing and denying Jesus.[2] It reminds one of the earlier 10.24f. Both texts involve Jesus and the disciples doing the same thing (here Jesus and his followers confess one another, there the disciples act like their Lord and are called Beelzebul, as was Jesus). Both feature main sayings which exhibit antithetical parallelism. And both are of the same length (both having about forty words).

After 10.32f. Jesus returns to the theme of persecution and familial division: vv. 34–9.[3] Here πατήρ (vv. 35, 37), μήτηρ (vv. 35, 37), and θυγάτηρ (vv. 35, 37) appear to be the key words, along with the phrase, οὐκ ἔστιν μου ἄξιος (vv. 37 (*bis*), 38).

The missionary discourse winds up with 10.40–2. The theme of this is the reception of missionaries (cf. vv. 11–15). δέχομαι (vv. 40 (four times), 41 (*bis*)) and μισθός (vv. 41 (*bis*), 42) are the chief terms, and the paragraph, just like 10.5–15 and 16–23, ends with an utterance prefaced by 'amen'.

Our conclusions thus far lead to several additional observations. First, 10.26–31, the structural centre of chapter 10, serves a function very reminiscent of 6.25–34 and 7.7–11. The latter two passages—which stand outside the triadic structures of the sermon on the mount (see 1, pp. 63–4)—operate to ease the burden of Mt 5–7 by informing the faithful disciple about the care of the Father in heaven. They give encouraging expression to God's love for his children, to his watching over and hearkening to them. Similarly, 10.26–31, whose threefold μὴ φοβηθῆτε/φοβεῖσθε so strongly recalls the threefold μὴ μεριμνᾶτε/μεριμνήσητε of 6.25–34, employs, like both 6.25–34 and 7.7–11, an argument *a minori ad maius* (10.31; cf. 6.26, 30; 7.11). Perhaps it also merits remarking that the sparrow of 10.26–31 reminds one of the birds of 6.25–34. In any case, 10.26–31, in both its arrangement and manner of argumentation, mirrors 6.25–34 and 7.7–11.

---

[2] Most commentators—P. F. Ellis, pp. 51–2 is an exception—associate vv. 32f. with 26–31. This ignores the closure made by v. 31 and the change of theme (consolation gives way to exhortation). One suspects that scholars have been led astray by the source-critical fact that vv. 26–31 were joined to vv. 32f. in Q (see Lk 12.4–9). But the juxtaposition of units in Q can hardly be decisive for a literary analysis of Matthew. Cf. Sand, *Matthäus*, p. 229.

[3] The unit of this subsection is recognized by many; cf. Gnilka, *Matthäusevangelium* 1, p. 392.

Secondly, it is natural to outline the missionary discourse in such a way that it consists of two triads, vv. 5–15, 16–23, and 24f. on the one hand, 32f., 34–9, and 40–2 on the other—between which has been inserted the section on consolation, 10.26–31. Strong support for this analysis comes not only from the evangelist's proclivity for the triad, but also from the fact that the entire chapter may well be arranged in a chiastic fashion. The first paragraph, like the last, deals with the theme of the reception of missionaries (vv. 5–15, 40–2). The second paragraph, like the sixth, concerns eschatological tribulation and refers to the division of families (vv. 16–23, 34–9). And if the third paragraph, 10.24f., tells of Jesus and his followers being treated in the same fashion (the disciple is like his teacher, the slave like his lord), the fifth paragraph has Jesus confessing those who confess him and denying those who deny him. In both instances the underlying motif is the same: like master, like servant. In conclusion, then, this is our outline of Matthew's second major discourse:

Narrative introduction, 9.35–10.4
    Discourse proper, 10.5–42

> a Instructions to missionaries and their reception, 5–15
>   b Tribulation and familial division, 16–23
>   c Jesus and his disciples are called Beelzebul, 24f.

    d Consolation and encouragement, 26–31

>   c Jesus and his disciples confess/deny each other, 32f.
>   b Tribulation and familial division, 34–9
> a Reception of missionaries and its reward, 40–2

Narrative conclusion, 11.1

XXI

INSTRUCTIONS AND PROSPECTS FOR MISSIONARIES
(10.5–25)

(i) *Structure*

As urged in Excursus VIII, 10.5–25 consists of three progressively shorter subsections: vv. 5–15, 16–23, 24f. The first, which is dominated by the theme of movement from place to place (cf. p. 160), issues instructions to missionaries and tells them about their reception and rejection by others. The second, a list of hardships headed by v. 16, prophesies tribulation. It is built around three key imperatives (προσέχετε, v. 17; μὴ μεριμνήσητε, v. 19; φεύγετε, v. 23). The third subsection, with its three double-membered sentences (vv. 24, 25a–b, 25c–d), forewarns the missionary that he will be treated as Jesus was treated. It makes explicit the theme of the imitation of Christ, a theme implicit in the two previous sections (cf. p. 160). Altogether, 10.5–25 paints a bleak picture: the future holds hard work and fierce persecution. In this way the whole unit prepares for vv. 26–31, where consolation is the theme.

(ii) *Sources*

Mt 10.5–25 is one of the many reasons the synoptic problem is in fact a problem. Mk 6.8–11 as well as Lk 9.2–5 and 10.3–16 could, without too much difficulty, be explained as abbreviations of Matthew's text; for a desire to abbreviate, to eliminate narrow Jewish concerns, and to omit irrelevant instructions could have led to what we now have in the Second and Third Gospels. Furthermore, Luke, followed by Mark (as on the Griesbach hypothesis), might have found most of 10.17–25 to be more appropriate for an eschatological discourse (thus elucidating why the parallels to Mt 10.17–25 appear mostly in Mk 13 and Lk 21). In our estimation, Mt 10 and its synoptic counterparts do not count against Griesbach. At the same time, and we shall argue throughout section (iii), 10.5–25 is also satisfactorily accounted for if one assumes the priority of Mark and Q. The piece is primarily a conflation of Q and Markan materials.

Once the priority of Mark and Q is accepted, the non-Markan parallels between Mt 10 and Lk 10 demand that Q had a mission discourse of its own. Unfortunately, it cannot now be reconstructed exactly. We have little doubt that its core was very close to what is now Lk 10.3–12, and also that the discourse at some point contained Mt 9.37f. = Lk 10.2 and Mt 10.40 = Lk 10.16. Beyond that, uncertainty reigns. Still, one cannot refrain from speculating about the contours of Q, and our tentative suggestion is that in Q the words on mission were arranged like this:

Mt 9.37–8	Lk 10.2
10.5–6	—
10.16, 9–10a, 11–13, 10b, 7f., 14f.	10.3–12
10.23	—
10.40	10.16

Our reasoning is as follows. (i) Mt 10.1–4 is clearly an insertion inspired by Mk 3.13–19. (ii) 10.5f., which confines the missionaries to Israel, has its natural home in a mission discourse. Its omission by Q^{lk} or Luke would be perfectly understandable. And the ὑπάγετε of Lk 10.3a may well be the remnant of the omitted Mt 10.5f.: the specific directions on where to go and not go have been reduced to the simple 'Go'. (iii) The rearrangement of the material in Lk 10.3–12 is accounted for readily. For example Lk 10.3b ('Behold, I send you out as lambs in the midst of wolves') is moved because it fittingly opens Matthew's table of persecution (10.16–23); and Lk 10.9 ('Heal the sick', 'say to them, "The kingdom of God has come near to you"') is expanded (cf. Mk 6.8–11) and moved forward because it summarizes at the beginning—a Matthean tendency—what the disciples should say and do. (iv) Mt 10.23 contains several indications that its pre-Matthean context was a missionary discourse (see on 10.23). Omission by Luke or Q^{lk} would only be expected. An apparently unfulfilled prophecy which limits the disciples to Israel would not have been treasured by everyone. We observe further that 10.23 is naturally thought of together with 10.5–6 (cf. Streeter, p. 255), and that there are reasons for assigning this last to Q's mission discourse. Finally, 10.23 follows nicely upon Lk 10.12, as we shall argue below. (v) Following T. W. Manson, *Sayings*, pp. 76f., Lk 10.13–15 probably owes its placement to Luke or perhaps to a pre-Lukan redactor of Q^{lk}. The paragraph interrupts the link between 10.12 and 16; see Marshall, p. 424. (This overturns the objection (raised by Schürmann, 'Mt 10.23' (v), p. 152) that putting Mt 10.23 after Lk 10.12 wrecks the connexion between Lk 10.12 and 13. That connexion is secondary). (vi) Lk 10.16 = Mt 10.40 concludes the discourses of both Luke and Matthew, so its placement in Q is manifest. (vii) Four Pauline texts remind one of sayings in the synoptic discourses on mission. See 1 Cor 9.4, 14; 10.27; and 1 Thess 4.8. Interestingly enough, the closest parallels belong to material found in Q's mission discourse as we have reconstructed it (Lk 10.7a, 7b, 8, 16). This is some reason for inferring Paul's knowledge of a collection of logia not far from what we have contended belonged to Q (cf. Allison (v)).

(iii) *Exegesis*

THE MISSIONARY TASK (10.5–15)

5. Jesus opens with a prohibition: Do not go to the Gentiles or to the Samaritans. The words are given special prominence by virtue of their initial position in the discourse. And they anticipate 15.24, where Jesus makes it plain that his mission too is only to Israel.

τούτους τοὺς δώδεκα ἀπέστειλεν ὁ Ἰησοῦς παραγγείλας αὐτοῖς λέγων is a redactional link which has been influenced by Mk 6.7f. τούτους refers to the list just given. Matthew probably uses 'the twelve' instead of 'the disciples' or 'the apostles' because Jesus' words confine the mission to Israel: the number of men corresponds to the number of tribes (cf. 19.28). παρα΄γγέλλω is used in the synoptics exclusively of Jesus, and it 'denotes his word of command in his authority as the Christ' (O Schmitz, *TWNT* 5, p. 760).

εἰς ὁδὸν ἐθνῶν μὴ ἀπέλθητε. εἰς ὁδόν, which appears also in Mk 6.8, is a *hapax* for Matthew. Here, followed by ἐθνῶν, it probably refers to a road leading to a Gentile city.[1] For ἔθνος/ἐθνικός* see on 5.47. Perhaps the combination of εἰς with ἀπέρχομαι* (Mt: 12; Mk: 8; Lk: 4) should be considered redactional.

For obvious reasons, 'Do not go among the Gentiles' created problems for the church Fathers. Many of them allegorized the words and applied them to pagan doctrine or behaviour.[2] Exceptions include Tertullian, *De fuga*, and Chrysostom, *Hom. on Mt.* 32.5. See further the texts cited by Manson (v), p. 2.

καὶ εἰς πόλιν Σαμαριτῶν μὴ εἰσέλθητε.[3] This line, which stands in near or perfect parallelism with the preceding clause, is the only one in Matthew to mention the Samaritans or Samaria. The impression left by the First Gospel is that Jesus never entered Samaritan territory (contrast Luke and John).[4]

[1] Cf. *m. ʿAbod. Zar.* 1.4. There were many Hellenistic cities in first-century Palestine; see Schürer 2, pp. 85–183. According to Jeremias, *Promise*, p. 19, n. 4, behind εἰς ὁδόν lies the Aramaic *lᵉʾôraḥ*: 'in the direction of', 'towards'. He cites the targum on 1 Kgs 18.43 and Ezek 8.5; 40.44.
[2] The interpretation was made possible by the use of ὁδός as a moral term, as in 7.13–14; 21.32; Acts 2.28; 16.17; 1 Clem 16.6; etc.
[3] Albright and Mann, p. 119, read πάλιν instead of πόλιν. In support they appeal to Jn 4, where Jesus speaks with a Samaritan woman; and they affirm that Samaritans would surely have been among the lost sheep of the house of Israel. Their conjecture, however, has no support in the mss.
[4] Cf. Trilling, p. 137. Jeremias, *Promise*, p. 19, n. 5, speculates that εἰς πόλιν Σαμαριτῶν mistranslates the Aramaic *mĕdînāʾ*, which here should mean 'province'. This seems an unnecessary hypothesis.

The Samaritans[5] were the inhabitants of Samaria, the territory between Judea and Galilee. Traditionally their roots have been traced back primarily to the Israelites who were not exiled when the northern kingdom fell in 722 B.C. or to the aliens who were settled in Israel by the Assyrian conquerors. Recent scholarship, however, has questioned the traditional view and made it possible to think of the split between Jews and Samaritans as taking place relatively late—in the period from the third century B.C. to the first century B.C. One fact remains undisputed. Before the time of Jesus and Matthew hostility between Jews and Samaritans was commonplace (cf. Ecclus 50.25f.; Lk 10.29–37; Jn 4.9; Josephus, *Ant.* 11; T. Levi 5–7).[6] The causes of enmity were several and included regional prejudices, the erection of a temple on Mount Gerizim, its destruction by a Hasmonaean, John Hyrcanus, in 128 B.C., and Samaritan acceptance of the Pentateuch alone as the authoritative word of God.

Why does Mt 10.5 mention the Samaritans? More is involved than Matthew's rabbinic point of view.[7] The status of the Samaritans was uncertain (cf. *m. Qidd.* 4.3). On the one hand, their forefathers were Jewish (cf. Par. Jer. 8). On the other hand, they were regarded as racially mixed (Josephus, *Ant.* 9.277–91; *b. Qidd.* 75a– 6a). For this reason, a command to go to Jews but not Gentiles might be thought unclear. What about the Samaritans? Are they Jews or Gentiles? Mt 10.5 dispels any doubt. The Samaritans are not Jews; treat them like Gentiles.

But there may be more than this in the verse before us. In Acts the Christian mission proceeds in three stages. The followers of Jesus first preach in Jerusalem and Judea; they then move on to Samaria; finally they reach out to the Gentiles (cf. Acts 1.8). While the scheme is undoubtedly Lukan, it has every chance of being historically correct, which means that others besides Luke probably thought of the gospel as going first to the Jew, then to the Samaritan, then to the Gentile. If so, Mt 10.5f. might have been formulated under the impact of the historical sequence. That is, if the historical pattern was Jew—Samaritan—Gentile, then a post-Easter command about mission might have referred, as does Mt 10.5, to Gentiles, Samaritans, and Jews.[8] (Note that the order in Matthew—Gentiles, Samaritans, Jews—is exactly the opposite of Luke's order: to the Jews, to the Samaritans, to the Gentiles.)

[5] See Schürer 2, pp. 15–20, and the lit. cited there, to which add SB 1, pp. 538–60; also S. Isser, 'The Samaritans and their Sects', in *CHJ* 3, forthcoming.

[6] But for caution in this connextion see R. Pummer, 'Antisamaritanische Polemik in jüdischen Schriften aus der intertestamentarischen Zeit', *BZ* 26 (1982), pp. 224–42.

[7] Kilpatrick, p. 121: Matthew's one reference to the Samaritans 'shows the point of view of Rabbinic Judaism'. He refers to *t. Ḥull.* 2.20–1 and *b. Ḥull.* 13a–b.

[8] Gundry, *Commentary*, p. 185, has raised yet another possibility. Galilee was surrounded by Samaria and Gentile territories, so 10.5–6 restricts the disciples' initial work to Galilee. In this they would be imitating Jesus (cf. 4.14–16).

6. The negative injunction (10.5) is now followed by a positive imperative: Go to the lost sheep of the house of Israel. Clearly the reason for disregarding the Samaritans and Gentiles stems not from prejudice but from the immediate needs of God's people, Israel.

πορεύεσθε δὲ μᾶλλον πρὸς τὰ πρόβατα τὰ ἀπολωλότα οἴκου Ἰσραήλ. Compare 25.9: πορεύεσθε μᾶλλον πρὸς τοὺς πωλοῦντας (without parallel). The verb anticipates 28.19. The phrase, '(the) lost sheep of the house of Israel',[9] appears again in 15.24, where it is redactional. On Israel as sheep see on 9.36. Although not made explicit, it seems reasonable to suppose that, in the evangelist's eyes, the sheep are lost largely because their leaders have gone astray. οἴκου Ἰσραήλ[10] may be either a partitive genitive or an explicative genitive. If the former, then the disciples' mission is limited to a portion of Israel (presumably the sinners and outcasts; cf. 9.13 and Schlatter, p. 329). If the latter, then the disciples are being sent to all Israel, and the people as a whole are characterized as lost sheep. The case for an explicative genitive seems stronger. Not only does 'the lost sheep of the house of Israel' stand over against 'the Gentiles' (all of them) and 'the Samaritans' (all of them), but in Isa 53.6; Jer 50.6; and Ezek 34 all the people of Israel are lost sheep.

Most modern commentators have been puzzled by the presence of 10.5–6 in a gospel which ends with a command to go preach in all the world. It has generally been inferred that 10.5f. was in Matthew's tradition and was reproduced by him even though it did not reflect his own convictions.[11] We, however, hesitate to follow the consensus in this matter. Matthew seems too thoughtful and too thorough in his editing to let obvious contradictions stand in his text.[12] What then of 10.5f.? Our evangelist manifestly believed that the situation after Easter was rather different from the situation before Easter. Thus he reproduces Mk 9.9, where Jesus tells his followers that a certain story should be made public only after the Son of man rises from the dead. And in 9.14f. Matthew's Lord declares that the practice of fasting will be different when the bridegroom is taken away. Is it not plausible that Matthew similarly reconciled the tension between 10.5f. and 28.16–20

[9] Cf. the ṣộ'n 'ōbdôt of Jer 50.6. The LXX (27.6) translates: πρόβατα ἀπολωλότα.

[10] Cf. bêt-yiśrā'ēl. The striking absence of the article with οἴκου is a Semitism (cf. 3 Βασ 12.21; LXX Ps 117.2).

[11] Some earlier critics assigned 10.5–6 and 28.16–20 to different recensions; see Moffatt, p. 255. According to J. S. Kennard, 'The Reconciliation Tendenz in Matthew', *ATR* 28 (1946), pp. 159–63, Matthew's desire to please two different Christian factions accounts for the inclusion of 10.5–6 and 28.19.

[12] For examples of Matthew dropping texts in order to avoid tension see on 7.2 and 10.10.

by thinking of one as appropriate for the pre-Easter period, the other as appropriate for the post-Easter period? 'To the Jew first and also to the Greek' would then be the idea, with Easter marking the point at which the mission goes beyond the borders of Israel.[13],[14]

If this is the correct understanding then it remains to assess just why Matthew adopted such a point of view and what it meant for him theologically. At least three observations are pertinent. First, there was a stubborn historical fact: the Gentile mission did not in truth begin until after the resurrection. There was no getting around the knowledge that Jesus was a minister to the circumcision. Secondly, the focus of Jesus upon his own people is, as H. Frankemölle in particular has argued at length, a sign of God's covenantal faithfulness. Before offering salvation to Gentiles God in Christ offered salvation to Israel. The sending of the Messiah to the Jews, in fulfilment of the OT, is, then, a demonstration of God's love for his chosen people and proof that he is trustworthy: he fulfils his promises. Lastly, Matthew appears to have interpreted the crucifixion and resurrection of Jesus as eschatological events which mark a decisive turning point in salvation-history, the dawn of a new era, the era in which God's OT promises concerning the Gentiles are realized; see especially Meier, *Law*, pp. 30–5. The scheme requires that the Gentiles come into the church *after* the saving events.

There has been much debate concerning the origin of Mt 10.5f. Does the saying go back to Jesus, who was 'a servant to the circumcised' (Rom 15.8)?[15] Or was it manufactured in the post-Easter period by a Jewish Christian community opposed to the Gentile mission?[16] Or did Matthew himself create it in order to advance his own understanding of salvation-history, according to which the gospel was confined to Israel before Easter?[17] Of the three options, the last seems to us the

---

[13] Cf. Tertullian, *Praescr. haer.* 8 and Peter of Laodicea, p. 105 (ed. Heinrici). See further Meier, *Law*, pp. 27–30, and Levine, passim. On the problem of whether the post-Easter mission excludes Israel see on 10.23 and 28.19.

[14] An alternative view is that of N. Walker: for Matthew the Jewish mission continued until 70; after that the mission to the Gentiles began. This does not do justice to 28.16–20, which puts the command to go to the Gentiles immediately after Easter. More plausible is the view of A. E. Harvey, in Harvey, *Approaches*, pp. 90–4. In his opinion, the Jewish-Christians in Matthew's community would have taken 10.5–6 to apply to themselves, 28.16–20 to apply to Gentile missionaries. So what is envisaged is a division of labour. Cf. W. R. Farmer, 'The Post-Sectarian Character of Matthew and Its Post-War Setting in Antioch of Syria', *PRS* 3 (1976), pp. 240–1: while the twelve are to go to Israel, Paul and others are to go to the Gentiles (cf. Gal 2.9). Yet against both Harvey and Farmer, the commands in 10.5–6 and 28.16–20 are delivered to precisely the same group. This also speaks against the thesis of Goulder, pp. 342–3. He claims that 10.5–6 should be understood as addressed to apostles who remained in Palestine, 28.16–20 as addressed to a much wider circle.

[15] So e.g. Kümmel, *Promise*, pp. 84–5; Bartnicki, 'Bereich' (v).

[16] So e.g. Wellhausen, *Matthaei*, p. 44; Hahn, *Mission*, p. 29. Those adopting this position frequently state that 10.5–6 contradicts Lk 9.51–6; 10.29–37; and 17.11–19. This is uncertain. The texts from Luke involve only incidental contact with Samaritans. They have nothing to do with a missionary enterprise.

[17] So e.g. Frankemölle, pp. 123–43, and G. N. Stanton, 'Matthew as Creative Interpreter of the Sayings of Jesus', in Stuhlmacher, pp. 276–7.

least likely; one can scarcely decide between the first two.[18] Against a
redactional origin the following points may be urged. (i) If, as we have
argued, 10.5f. belonged to Q, Luke would have omitted it for obvious
reasons.[19] (ii) εἰς ὁδόν is not characteristic of the redactor. (iii) Only
in the phrase, τὰ πρόβατα τὰ ἀπολωλότα οἴκου Ἰσραήλ (10.6; 15.24),
does Matthew have an attributive between a noun and its genitive
qualifier. (iv) Nowhere else in the First Gospel is there any reference
to Samaria or Samaritans. (v) Although the tension between 10.5f.
and 28.16–20 has been much exaggerated, nowhere has the evangelist
explicitly addressed the issue of how the two texts are to be
harmonized. It is up to the reader to seek for the theological idea
that brings harmony. It seems to us that, if Matthew had been in
the business of creating sayings that would interpret salvation-history,
he would have been a bit more careful and more explicit, and we
should expect to find more than just the uneasy juxtaposition of
10.5f. and 28.16–20. Why not, for instance, a statement such as
'Before the Son of man suffers do not go among the Gentiles'? If
Matthew did in fact create 10.5f. precisely in order to reveal his
notions about salvation-history, his intent has been lost on the vast
majority of modern scholars.

Bound up with the question of the authenticity of 10.5–6 is the issue
of its relationship to 15.24: 'I was sent only to the lost sheep of the
house of Israel' (no Markan or Lukan parallels). The possibilities
include the following: (i) 10.5f. could be a redactional version of the
traditional logion preserved in 15.24 (cf. Strecker, *Weg*, pp. 107, 194–
5); (ii) 15.24 could be a redactional version of the traditional logion
preserved in 10.5f.; (iii) both texts could be redactional (cf. Gundry,
Commentary, pp. 183–5, 312–3); (iv) both texts could be pre-Matthean
variants of the same saying. We must eliminate (i) and (iii) because we
have urged that 10.5f. is not editorial but rather belonged to Q's
missionary discourse. This leaves (ii) and (iv) as possible solutions. See
further on 15.24.

7. Having been instructed on the location of their actions,
the disciples now receive the message they are to deliver: the
kingdom of heaven has drawn near. The words are those Jesus
himself has used (4.17; cf. 9.35). In carrying on the missionary
task, the disciple must be like the master (cf. 10.24f.).

πορευόμενοι δὲ κηρύσσετε λέγοντες ὅτι. The first word (which

[18] Whoever first formulated Mt 10.5–6 would surely have acknowledged the
truth of H. Wheeler Robinson's words: 'Israel's service was unique and
indispensable. Its particularity was the condition of its intensity. The true
universality is not reached by thinning out our convictions so as to make them
spread over as wide a surface as possible. It is reached by so intense a devotion
to them that we penetrate nearer to the centre of things and so draw nearer to
each other. That is the characteristic of Israel's religion at the best and in the
best of her representatives' (*Redemption and Revelation*, New York and London,
1942, p. 91).

[19] Cf. Trautmann, pp. 202–8; Hengel, *Jesus and Paul*, pp. 111–12. Brooks,
pp. 49–50, however, assigns 10.5–6 to M. Cf. Laufen, p. 243.

presupposes itinerant preachers) recalls the πορεύεσθε of 10.6 while the other two verbs recall 4.17, where Jesus 'began *to preach* and *to say* . . .'.

ἤγγικεν ἡ βασιλεία τῶν οὐρανῶν. For discussion see on 4.17. The parallel in Lk 10.9 shows that Q's missionary discourse contained the command to preach the nearness of the kingdom (cf. Lk 9.2).

The proclamation of 10.7 is not only the proclamation of Jesus' twelve but also the proclamation of Matthew's church. This follows from the obvious transparency of chapter 10: while it is addressed to the historical twelve, it is simultaneously addressed to later missionaries. Also telling is the existence of several key terms common to 28.16–20 (which concerns post-Easter proclamation) and chapter 10—μαθηταί, πορεύομαι, δίδωμι, ἐξουσία. Thus there is only one gospel. The proclamation of the pre-Easter epoch and the proclamation of the post-Easter epoch differ mainly—apart, of course, from the all-important fact that it is only in the latter that the crucifixion and resurrection can be proclaimed as already accomplished—in the audience addressed. It is only after the resurrection that Gentiles are sought out. The content of the preaching is in a real sense the same.[20] So the Christian missionary repeats the words of the Lord and the message of the twelve apostles.

8. ἀσθενοῦντας θεραπεύετε. Compare 8.17. Lk 10.9 reads: καὶ θεραπεύετε τοὺς ἐν αὐτῇ ἀσθενεῖς. This or something very like it stood in Q. Matthew, perhaps influenced by Mk 6.13,[21] has chosen to expand the thought. The result is four imperatival phrases in perfect parallelism, each one instructing the disciples to do something Jesus has done. The good news of the kingdom is spread by believers following the example of the Messiah.

νεκροὺς ἐγείρετε.[22] Compare 9.18–26 and 11.5. There is no good reason for taking the language metaphorically (*pace* Fenton (v); cf. 9.18–26; Acts 9.36–43).

λεπροὺς καθαρίζετε. Compare 8.1–4 and 11.5. Nowhere in the NT does anyone but Jesus heal a leper.

δαιμόνια ἐκβάλλετε. Compare 8.28–34 and 9.32–4; also Mk 6.7, 13.

δωρεὰν ἐλάβετε δωρεὰν δότε. These four words, which are presumably redactional and which continue the rhythm of the

---

[20] One is reminded of the analogous situation in Gal 2: the one gospel is to be preached to different audiences by different people (cf. Davies, *JPS*, pp. 185–6).

[21] 'And they cast out many demons, and anointed with oil many that were sick and healed them'.

[22] P W Δ *pc* syʰ place this after λεπροὺς καθαρίζετε and δαιμόνια ἐκβάλλετε. C³ K L Γ Θ 700* Maj f (syᵖ) sa mae omit. See Zahn, p. 397, n. 19.

preceding couplets, presuppose that believers should act towards
others just as God has acted towards them. Because the power
to heal is a gift from God, it in turn must be made a gift for
others. For similar texts see 2 Kgs 5.15f. and the rabbinic
materials in SB 1, pp. 561–4. The imperative has no parallel in
Mark or Luke and may or may not reproduce a word from the
tradition. It has perhaps its closest parallel in Sextus, *Sent.* 242:
'What you freely receive from God also give freely'. Note also
b. Ned. 37a: 'Just as I (taught you) gratuitously, so you must
teach gratuitously'.

9–10. These two verses—which played a decisive rôle in the life
of St Francis (Bonaventure, *Legenda maior* 3.1)—contain a list of
prohibitions (vv. 9–10a) followed by an explanation (10b). The
disciples can and should leave behind gold and silver and copper.
They are not even to take along a travel bag or an extra tunic or
sandals or a staff—the normal and necessary accoutrements of the
traveller (cf. Exod 12.11; Josh 9.3–6; *b. Yeb.* 16.7). Preaching a
kingdom 'not of this world', they have unloosed their ties to the
present age. They are to be 'like slaves that minister to the master
not for the sake of receiving a bounty' (*m. 'Abot* 1.3).

By going about without possessions the disciples not only put
themselves beyond suspicion but also become examples of trust
in God's providential care (cf. 6.24–34). They are, further, signs
that God is working not through the rich or powerful but
through the poor and powerless (cf. 5.3–12).

The relationship between Mt 10.9f and its synoptic parallels is not
easily unravelled. These are the things prohibited:

Mt 10.9f.	Mk 6.8	Lk 9.3	Lk 10.4
gold (1)			
silver (2)		silver (4)	
copper (3)	copper (4)		
wallet (4)	wallet (3)	wallet (2)	wallet (2)
two shirts (5)	two shirts (6)	two shirts (5)	
sandals (6)			sandals (3)
staff (7)		staff (1)	
	bread (2)	bread (3)	
			purse (1)

These are the things allowed:
staff (1)
sandals (5)
(The numerals refer to order of occurrence.)

No synoptic theory can readily explain the similarities and differences
exhibited by Mt 10.9f. par. In the end one may do well to allow some
rôle for the fluidity of oral tradition or the frailty of human memory.
The following observations may, nonetheless, be made. (i) The
permission to take sandals and staff (so Mark) is probably a secondary

development required by the needs of Christian missionaries.[23] (ii) If Lk 10.4 reproduces Q, then Matthew has altered Q's arrangement to: money (gold, silver, copper), wallet (the πήρα was for bread), clothing (tunics, sandals, staff). (iii) The Matthean order, gold, silver, copper, is according to value (cf. Josephus, *Ant.* 8.76).[24] (iv) Matthew's arrangement seems to contain two small triads: gold, silver, copper, and tunics, sandals, staff. (v) Attempts to harmonize Matthew and Mark by urging mistranslations from Aramaic do not persuade; see Black, pp. 216f. (vi) The Lukan prohibitions against taking silver and staff (9.3) may be from Q since they have parallels in Mt 10.9f. (vii) Because the 'wallet' (πήρα) typically contained bread, Matthew probably thought Mark's mention of bread redundant and therefore omitted it. (viii) Mt 10.9f. is almost certainly based on a dominical word. The logion harmonizes with Jesus' other sayings about apostolic hardship and is consistent with his radical attitude towards wealth and property (cf. Hahn (v), p. 46).

μὴ κτήσησθε χρυσὸν μηδὲ ἄργυρον μηδὲ χαλκὸν εἰς τὰς ζώνας ὑμῶν. Coins are meant. On ζώνη (= belt) see on 3.4 and SB 1, pp. 564–5. It was common custom to keep money in one's belt or girdle (cf. LSJ, s.v., ζώνη, I.3; BAGD, s.v.). Matthew is the only gospel to refer to gold (Mt: 4). The First Gospel also mentions silver more than the others (see 1, p. 405). μὴ κτήσησθε could mean 'do not procure', that is, as a provision before starting.[25] But 'do not acquire' seems a better translation.[26] (i) Matthew has not used a form of αἴρω (contrast Mk 6.8; Lk 9.3). (ii) The immediately preceding command to receive freely (10.8) concerns the issue of reward. This colours what follows.

μὴ πήραν εἰς ὁδόν. Compare Acts Pet 12 Apost 3.23, where Jesus has 'no pouch on his back'. The repetition of εἰς ὁδόν (cf. 10.5) underlines the itinerant character of the Christian missionary. The prohibition of a traveller's bag[27] is the one point on which Mt 10.9f. and its parallels agree. Perhaps it is significant that the Hellenistic wandering philosophers carried such bags.[28] Early Christian preachers may have felt a need to distinguish themselves from the Cynics.[29]

[23] It could also reflect Exod 12.11, where the Israelites are, on the eve of the exodus, told to eat with 'your sandals on your feet and your staff in your hand'.

[24] With the exception of Chronicles and Daniel, the OT usually gives silver the priority over gold. The NT, by contrast, places gold first.

[25] So Zahn, pp. 398–9, and McNeile, p. 135.

[26] Cf. Schlatter, pp. 331–2; Bonnard, p. 145.

[27] Cf. Jth 10.5; 13.10, 15, where it carries bread. πήρα has also been thought to be a beggar's bag. See BAGD, s.v., and Deissmann, *Light*, pp. 108–10. Yet see W. Michaelis, *TWNT* 6, pp. 120–1. On the rabbinic *tarmē(î)l* see SB 1, p. 565.

[28] Cf. Epictetus, *Diss.* 1.24.11; Crates, *Ep.* 16; 23; 28; Diogenes, *Ep.* 7; 13; 46; Diogenes Laertius 6.13; Tatian, *Or. Graec.* 25.1.

[29] Because in so many ways they were so close; cf. Justin, *2 Apol.* 3; Acts of Philip, in ANF 9, p. 503; and F. G. Downing, 'Cynics and Christians', *NTS* 30 (1984), pp. 584–92.

μηδὲ δύο χιτῶνας μηδὲ ὑποδήματα μηδὲ ῥάβδον. On the χιτών
see on 5.40.[30] To carry an extra tunic would be a luxury (cf.
Lk 3.11). ὑποδήματα are sandals (on which see SB 1, pp. 566–
9). To be without them was a sign of poverty (cf. Deut 25.10;
Lk 15.22; b. Yoma 77a). That there is any connexion with Isa
52.7 ('How beautiful ... are the feet of him who brings good
tidings') seems remote (although note Ambrose, De fuga saec.
5.25). ῥάβδον is 'staff'. It was not only a walking aid (cf. Gen 32.10;
Exod 21.19) but also used to ward off animals and human
attackers.[31] Perhaps then the lack of a staff is a sign of
pacifism. For the Cynic's staff see Epictetus, Diss. 3.22.50;
Diogenes, Ep. 7. For the travelling staff of the rabbi see the
texts in SB 1, p. 569. If the absence of a traveller's bag serves
to distinguish Christian missionaries from Cynics, is absence
of a staff intended to make for a difference from the
rabbis?

According to m. Ber. 9.5 'one may not enter the holy mount (of the
temple) with his staff or with his shoes or with his money belt ...' (cf.
SB 1, p. 565). T. W. Manson, Sayings, p. 181, commented: 'This is on
account of the holiness of the place. It is possible that the mission of
the disciples is meant to be regarded as a specially sacred undertaking,
and that they are to set out upon it as if they were setting out to
worship in the Temple'. Although it is hard to assess the probability of
this conjecture, it is consistent with Jesus' fondness for parabolic actions
(on which see Jeremias, Parables, pp. 227–9).[32]

In Lk 10.4 Jesus follows up the injunctions about travelling light
with this: 'and greet no one on the road' (cf. 2 Kgs 4.29). Whatever the
original meaning of this very strange prohibition,[33] Matthew has
omitted it. Why? Probably because it seemed to him to contradict his
Jewish sensibilities (see 1, p. 559) as well as 5.47: 'And if you greet
only your brethren, what more are you doing than others? Do not even
the Gentiles do the same?' The implication is that Jesus' followers
should greet all. How then could Matthew have Jesus turn around and
forbid the giving of greetings?

[30] See C. Schneider, TWNT 6, pp. 966–72.
[31] This makes the disciples of Jesus more radical than the Essenes, for
according to Josephus, Bell.2.125, 'they carry nothing whatever with them on
their journeys except arms as a protection against brigands'. Perhaps it is
worth noting that Origen thought Mt 10.9–10 so radical that he could use it
to make his case for not taking Scripture literally (De prin. 4.3.3).
[32] According to J. Neusner, 'The Pharisees', CHJ 3 (forthcoming), at
Jamnia laws applicable to the priests in the temple came to be applied by the
rabbis to those outside the temple. Do we see the same mentality in the gospel
text?
[33] The closest parallel seems to be in 2 Kgs 4.29: 'Gird up your loins, and
take my staff in your hand and go. If you meet any one, do not salute him;
and if any one salutes you, do not reply ...'. Here the explanation for
prohibition of a greeting is haste.

ἄξιος γὰρ ὁ ἐργάτης τῆς τροφῆς αὐτοῦ. Compare Ps Phoc. 19. Lk 10.7 has τοῦ μισθοῦ; otherwise there is agreement. τροφῆς is Matthean (τροφή*). It replaces the μισθοῦ of Q, thereby lessening the tension with 10.8e. For Matthew, the missionary may receive food and accept free lodging, but he should not ask for anything more. Compare Did. 11.6: 'when he departs let the apostle receive nothing except bread, until he finds shelter; but if he asks for money, he is a false prophet'. (Montanus, at the end of the second century, was evidently the first to put missionaries under salary.)

The disciples, who are here identified with the 'workers' of 9.37f., are to live off what is given to them by those who favourably receive them and their message. One is reminded of 6.25–34. If one takes care of God's business, one will be taken care of by God. There is no need to be anxious about food or drink or clothing.

Paul clearly knew the saying about the workman and his reward (in its Lukan form); see 1 Cor 9.14, 17f. and Allison (v). The saying is also echoed in 1 Tim 5.18, again in agreement with Luke. The version presupposed by Did. 13.1–2 (ἄξιός ἐστιν τῆς τροφῆς αὐτοῦ . . . ἐστιν ἄξιος . . . ὁ ἐργάτης τῆς τροφῆς αὐτοῦ) shows knowledge of Matthew (τροφῆς). Note also Dial. Sav. 3.139.9–10: 'The labourer being worthy of his food'.[34]

In Q 'the workman is worthy of his reward' was introduced by this: 'And remain in the same house, eating and drinking what they provide' (Lk 10.7; cf. 1 Cor 10.27; T. Abr. A 4.7). Perhaps Matthew omitted this because he did not want to leave the impression that Jewish Christians, finding themselves among Gentiles, were required to eat food forbidden by the Torah. When Jesus first uttered the words, it was assumed that his hearers would be in Jewish households, so the point was probably the freedom of the disciples over against the ritual concerns of the Pharisees and those like them (and not, as many have supposed, freedom from the OT kosher laws).

11. This and the following four verses are a conflation of Mk 6.10f. and Q (cf. Lk 10.5–8, 10f.). The theme is the reception and rejection of the missionaries and their response to such. The disciples are not to stay just anywhere. They are to be careful in choosing lodging.

εἰς ἣν δ' ἂν πόλιν ἢ κώμην εἰσέλθητε.[35] Mk 6.10 has: ὅπου ἐὰν εἰσέλθητε εἰς οἰκίαν (cf. Lk 9.4). Under the influence of Q (cf. Lk 10.8, 10, both with πόλιν) Matthew has changed 'house' to 'city or village'. He has thus forged a link with 9.35 (q.v.), where Jesus goes about 'all the cities and villages'.

[34] This depends on Matthew; see Tuckett, *Nag Hammadi*, pp. 129–30.
[35] f^1 700 it sy^s omit η κωμην (cf. Lk 10.8). L f^{13} pc co place it at the end. D has the very Semitic: η πολις εις ην αν εισελθητε εις αυτην—which Zahn, p. 400, n. 25 thought original.

ἐξετάσατε τίς ἐν αὐτῇ ἄξιός ἐστιν. This imperative appears to
be editorial. It has no parallel in Mark or Luke. ἄξιος recalls
10.10 ('the workman is *worthy* . . .'). The word, which in its
present context means not so much moral goodness but
willingness to receive Jesus' messengers, occurs nine times in the
First Gospel (Mk: 0; Lk: 8), seven times in chapter 10, all but
one of these (10.10) being redactional (see 10.11, 13 (*bis*), 37
(*bis*), 38). It thus signals a major theme of the Matthean
discourse on mission. This is because the missionary endeavour,
with its terrible hardships, naturally raises for Matthew the
subject of rewards and punishments.

κἀκεῖ μείνατε ἕως ἂν ἐξέλθητε. This is an adaptation of
Mk 6.10c (cf. Lk 9.4; 10.7), which in Mark refers to a house
that will give the apostles food and shelter. In Matthew the
subject has shifted slightly: one is to stay in the house of the
worthy individual. Gundry, *Commentary*, p. 188, is probably
right: 'instead of staying wherever they can find hospitality, the
disciples are to stay where the proclamation of the kingdom has
already found a favorable reception. In Matthew we are reading
about itinerant ministry in evangelized communities rather than
about itinerant ministry in unevangelized communities'. To stay
in one place would accomplish at least three ends. It would cut
the time spent looking for lodging (which would increase every
time one moved); and it would cancel the suspicion that the
disciples want to take as much as possible from as many as
possible. Further, to be content with the place one has stayed in
and to refrain from moving to a better place prevents the making
of invidious comparisons between households, which can only
result in dissensions.

12. εἰσερχόμενοι δὲ εἰς τὴν οἰκίαν ἀσπάσασθε αὐτήν.[36] This
seems to be Matthew's version of Lk 10.5: εἰς ἣν δ' ἂν εἰσέλθητε οἰκίαν, πρῶτον λέγετε· εἰρήνη τῷ οἴκῳ τούτῳ.
The command to 'greet' (ἀσπάσασθε; cf. Lk 10.4) a house is the
idiomatic equivalent of the command to say, 'Peace to this
house' (cf. *b. Ta'an.* 20b and see on 5.47)—although one
unacquainted with the OT or Jewish tradition might have missed
this.[37]

13. καὶ ἐὰν μὲν ᾖ ἡ οἰκία ἀξία. After καὶ ἐάν
Lk 10.6a his this: ἐκεῖ ᾖ υἱὸς εἰρήνης. 'Son of peace' (a
Semitism[38]) appears only here in the NT. It is from Q. Perhaps
Matthew's wording has been influenced by the thought that

---

[36] ℵ*·2 D L W Θ *f*¹ 1010 (1424) *al* it vg^el arm add: λεγοντες· ειρηνην τω οικω
τουτω. This is from Lk 10.5.
[37] ἀσπάζομαι translates *šā'al lěšālôm* in LXX Exod 18.7 and Judg 18.15.
[38] Cf. Ps 41.9; Jer 20.10; 38.22; Obad 7; SB 2, p. 166.

house churches are the bases for Christian mission (cf. Gundry, *Commentary*, p. 189).

ἐλθάτω ἡ εἰρήνη ὑμῶν ἐπ᾽ αὐτήν. The disciples do not make a wish but instead offer a gift, one that can be accepted or rejected. Compare Lk 10.6b: ἐπαναπαήσεται ἐπ᾽ αὐτὸν ἡ εἰρήνη ὑμῶν. Matthew may have replaced the relatively scarce ἐπαναπαύομαι[39] with the common ἔρχομαι.

One must wonder whether the offer of peace reflects more than social convention—first, because our passage rides roughshod over other social conventions, secondly, because the concept of *šālôm* had such strong eschatological associations in ancient Judaism. The messianic or eschatological age was often represented as a time of unprecedented peace: 'there will be deep peace and understanding' (Sib. Or. 2.29); 'all peace will come upon the land of the good' (Sib. Or. 5.780; cf. Isa 9.6; Zech 9.10; 1 En 10.17). Already in the OT the coming day of the Lord is anticipated as a day of universal peace (Mic 5.5; Nah 1.15). Particularly noteworthy is Isa 52.7, a passage which 11QMelch links to an eschatological figure and which the targum associates with the revelation of the kingdom of God: 'How beautiful upon the mountains are the feet of him who brings good tidings' (cf. Acts 10.36; Rom 10.15; Eph 6.15; all three of these texts significantly enough are about preaching the gospel). For Matthew and his tradition the apostolic greeting of peace was probably a sign of the inbreaking of the kingdom, a symbol of God's eschatological work of establishing reconcilation and *šālôm* (cf. Gnilka, *Matthäusevangelium* 1, p. 368).

ἐὰν δὲ μὴ ᾖ ἀξία. Luke has simply εἰ δὲ μή γε. Matthew has presumably sought to increase the parallelism with 10.13a. For the worthy/unworthy contrast in rabbinic texts see Schlatter, p. 333.

ἡ εἰρήνη ὑμῶν πρὸς ὑμᾶς ἐπιστραφήτω. Peace is here spoken of as though it had an objective existence and as though it were subject to the disciples' commands (cf. Isa 45.23; 55.10–11). If Lk 10.6d (ἐφ᾽ ὑμᾶς ἀνακάμψει) reproduces Q (an uncertain issue), Matthew has once again enhanced the parallelism—
13b: verb + 'your peace' + preposition + personal pronoun
13d: 'your peace' + preposition + personal pronoun + verb
The replacement of ἀνακάμψει by a form of ἐπιστρέφω—a word often linked with εἰρήνη in the LXX[40]—does not surprise.

The disciples do not lose their peace if they give it to an unworthy house. When the message of the kingdom is rejected, it is not the proclaimers that suffer loss but those who do not believe.

---

[39] Never with εἰρήνη in the LXX.
[40] E.g. Judg 8.9; 11.13, 31; 2 Βασ 15.27; 2 Chr 18.26, 27; 19.1; 1 Macc 7.35.

Matthew offers examples of antithetical or near-antithetical parallelism in these places:[41] 5.19f.; 6.14f., 19–21, 22f. 24; 7.13f., 17f., 24–7; 10.13, 32f.; 12.33, 35, 37; 16.19; 18.18; 23.12. One text has a parallel in Mark (Mt 6.14–15; cf. Mk 11.25–6). Most have counterparts in Luke and derive from Q: 6.19–21, 22f., 24; 7.13f., 17f., 24–7; 10.13, 32f.; 12.33, 35; 23.12. Four are either editorial or from special tradition, M: 5.19–20; 12.37; 16.19; 18.18. Because the one Markan and the several Lukan texts consistently exhibit less parallelism than those in Matthew and because Matthew's work in such places as 5.19f.; 6.14f.; and 12.33–7 is clear, antithetical parallelism must be reckoned a feature of his style.[42] One might simply attribute this fact to his love of parallelism in general (see 1, pp. 94–5). It is intriguing, however, that rigid antithetical parallelism (in which the same words are used in both lines, only negated in one) is rare in ancient Jewish and Christian sources. The exception is *m. 'Abot* which, although shorter than the First Gospel, contains at least twelve instances of strict antithetical parallelism (e.g. 3.5, 10; 4.6, 9). As in Matthew, the form is used in sayings which distinguish the righteous from the unrighteous. This is support for those who would connect Matthew with scribal rabbinism. In addition, one understands why both emergent rabbinič Judaism and Matthew were fond of the form: it lent itself to the defining of group boundaries, a necessary task for both.

14. 10.14 has a parallel not only in Mk 6.11 = Lk 9.5 but also in Lk 10.10b–1. Here, then, we have an example of a Markan/Q overlap. Matthew has been more influenced by Mark than Q. As to authenticity, the saying has multiple attestation, presupposes a Jewish milieu, and fits the urgency of Jesus' eschatological situation.

καὶ ὃς ἂν μὴ δέξηται ὑμᾶς μηδὲ ἀκούσῃ τοὺς λόγους ὑμῶν. So Mk 6.11, with τόπος after ἂν and ἀκούσωσιν for ἀκούσῃ, and without τοὺς λόγους. Lk 10.10a is rather different, although it does have δέχωνται. Matthew has followed Mark. He has also added 'your words', which shows us that for him the unwelcome missionaries are above all teachers.[43] On δέχομαι as a term for the acceptance of the gospel or its emissaries see W. Grundmann, *TWNT* 2, pp. 52–3; also the commentary on 10.40–1.

ἐξερχόμενοι ἔξω τῆς οἰκίας ἢ τῆς πόλεως ἐκείνης ἐκτινάξατε τὸν κονιορτὸν τῶν ποδῶν ὑμῶν.[44] Mk 6.11b reads:

[41] For what follows we draw upon a letter from Prof. L. M. Wills and his unpublished paper, 'Scribal Methods in Matthew and '*Abot*'.

[42] Bultmann, *History*, p. 112, argued on the contrary that Matthew retained Q's parallelism and that Luke did not.

[43] Matthew is fond of ἀκούω + λόγον/λόγους: Mt: 9; Mk: 3; Lk: 5. As the combination elsewhere always refers to hearing Jesus' words, perhaps it here adds to the Jesus/disciple parallelism.

[44] ℵ C 33 892 1010 *al* lat add εκ before των. HG, following Maj, omits εξω, which appears in ℵ B D 33 Θ *pc* lat co eth.

'Leaving (ἐκπορευόμενοι) there shake off the dust (χοῦν) that is under your feet for a testimony against them'. Lk 10.10b–11 has this: 'Going (ἐξελθόντες) into its streets say: Even the dust (κονιορτόν) of your town that clings to our feet we wipe off against you; nevertheless know this, that the kingdom of God has come near'. This last is probably much closesr to Q than is Mt 10.14b, although Luke may have added 'clings'[45] as well as the reference to 'streets'. Matthew has made several changes. (i) He has taken the opening verb from Q but changed the tense so that it matches Mark's tense. (ii) He has added ἔξω. Thus the εἰς . . . εἰσέλθητε of 10.11 has its antithesis in the ἐξερχόμενοι ἔξω of 10.14. (iii) He has added a reference to 'the house' (cf. 10.12–13). This helps adapt the saying to its Matthean context. (iv) He has preferred Mark's ἐκτινάξατε to Q's ἀπομασσόμεθα. (v) He has taken over Q's κονιορτόν instead of Mark's χοῦν. (Neither word appears elsewhere in the First Gospel. Are they translation variants?) (vi) He has omitted Mark's τὸν ὑποκάτω (cf. Nah 1.3; Acts Barn. 20). And (vii) 'for a testimony against them' has been dropped. It would be redundant for Jewish readers, especially in view of 10.15.

What is the meaning of shaking off dust? According to Schlatter, p. 334, and Jeremias, *Theology*, p. 238, the disciples are to shake off from their cloaks the dust their feet have stirred up (cf. Gundry, *Commentary*, p. 190). According to most commentators, however, the disciples are to wipe their feet or shake off the dust that cleaves to their feet.[46] In favour of the first alternative, both Neh 5.13 and Acts 18.6 involve the shaking of garments as a sign of renunciation. In favour of the second alternative, the Greek of Matthew, Mark, and Luke most naturally brings to mind the image of dust on the feet, and this must be the decisive consideration. It may nevertheless be observed that the shaking of clothing and the cleaning of feet essentially mean the same thing. Both are public demonstrations of the breaking off of communion and the forfeiting of responsibility (cf. the hand-washing of 27.24). So the main point is clear. The disciples will no longer have anything to do with the place that rejects the messengers of God's kingdom. They will without guilt leave it to its fate.[47]

---

[45] κολλάομαι: Mt: 1; Mk: 0; Lk: 2; Acts: 5; never with κονιορτος in the LXX.

[46] Shoes or sandals are not mentioned because the disciples—at least in Matthew and Luke—are barefoot.

[47] In the light of such texts as *m. Ohol.* 2.3 (cf. SB 1, p. 571), T. W. Manson was perhaps correct in adding: 'The significance of the ritual of wiping the feet before leaving the city is that the city is reckoned as heathen, and its inhabitants as no part of the true Israel, even though it is a city of Israel and its people Jews by birth' (*Sayings*, p. 76). For further discussion see H. J. Cadbury, 'Dust and Garments', in *Beginnings* 5, pp. 269–77.

15. ἀμὴν λέγω ὑμῖν. Matthew has added 'amen', which appropriately introduces the concluding sentence of a subsection (as it does also in 10.23 and 42). See further on 5.18.

ἀνεκτότερον ἔσται γῇ Σοδόμων καὶ Γομόρρων ἐν ἡμέρᾳ κρίσεως ἢ τῇ πόλει ἐκείνῃ. Compare 11.22, 24; Lk 10.14. Lk 10.12 has: 'For Sodom in that day it will be easier than for that city'. Matthew has moved ἀνεκτότερον ἔσται to the front, affixed a reference to 'the land' of Sodom (cf. 11.24), added 'Gomorrah' (which makes for a biblical phrase[48]), and changed 'in that day'[49] to 'in the day of judgement'.[50]

Sodom and Gomorrah are, in the biblical tradition, remembered as the cities whose wickedness was so great that God determined to destroy them and make them a 'burned-out waste' (Gen 13.13; 18.20; 19; Deut 29.23). Their overthrow became proverbial and stood as a warning of God's wrath towards sinners (cf. Isa 1.9; 13.19; Jer 23.14; 50.40; Amos 4.11; Jub 16.5; 20.6; Asc. Isa. 3.10; 2 Pet 2.6). In the present text, Jesus' prophecy assumes that greater privileges require greater responsibility. It is an unprecedented honour to hear the disciples' proclamation, and incomparable failure to reject it. To whom much is given, from them will much be required (cf. Amos 3.2). On Sodom in the rabbis see SB 1, pp. 571–4. They tended to refer to Sodom rather than to Sodom and Gomorrah. (And Josephus, who refers often to the former, never mentions the latter.) For '*land of* Sodom' (not in the OT) see *b. Šabb.* 67a.[51]

THE MISSIONARIES' AFFLICTIONS (10.16–23)

There are, as we shall see, a number of items in 10.16–23 which show us that Matthew's text here goes beyond the historical situation of the twelve to include the situation of missionaries in Matthew's own day. The evangelist has accordingly passed from the past to the present without explicitly noting the fact.[52] This has struck many modern commentators as strange. The phenomenon, however, occurs elsewhere in early Christian

[48] 'Sodom and Gomorrah': Gen 18.20; 19.24, 28; Isa 13.19; Jer 49.18; Amos 4.11; Jub 16.5; Jude 7; Sepher Ha-Razim, first firmament, line 75; Gk. Apoc. Ezra 2.19; 7.12.

[49] So Q; cf. Jeremias, *Lukasevangelium*, pp. 139, 186.

[50] ἡμέρα κρίσεως*. Cf. Isa 34.8; Jub 4.19; Ps Sol. 15.12; 2 Pet 2.9; 3.7; 1 Jn 4.17; 4 Ezra 12.34; 2 En 39.1; *y. Ḥag.* 77a. On the omission of the articles see BDF § 259.

[51] If Jesus did, as Mk 6.7 has it, send out his disciples in couples, then originally the situation foreseen by Mt 10.14–15 par. would have been similar to the situation that led to Sodom's destruction: in both Gen 19 and the gospels a city wrongly treats two divinely sent visitors.

[52] Although the future tenses (indicating Matthew's own time) do tend to come thick and fast.

literature.[53] Moreover, the unheralded transition from past to present results naturally from Matthew's typification of the twelve: they stand for the Christian readers—especially missionaries—of Matthew's time. All that Jesus says to the twelve he says to the church;[54] and the mission of the church is a continuation of the mission carried out in Jesus' lifetime.

16. This verse, which incorporates two proverbial expressions, stands as the heading of 10.17ff. (cf. Chrysostom, *Hom. on Mt.* 33.1). That is, 10.17ff. prophesies the fate of those who are like sheep in the midst of wolves.

ἰδοὺ ἐγὼ ἀποστέλλω ὑμᾶς ὡς πρόβατα ἐν μέσῳ λύκων. So Lk 10.3, without ἐγώ and with ἄρνας.[55] Compare Mt 11.10 (where ἰδοὺ ἐγὼ ἀποστέλλω is spoken by God) and 23.34 (diff. Lk 11.49); also Jer 16.16; Hab 1.6; Mal 4.5. In the redactional 7.15, the false prophets have sheep's clothing but are inwardly ravenous wolves. 10.16, by contrast, pictures a few sheep scattered among wolves.

2 Clem 5.2 ('For the Lord says: You will be as ἀρνία ἐν μέσῳ λύκων') could depend upon Luke.[56] The image in any case was common in Jewish and Christian texts (see on 7.15).[57] Gundry, *Commentary*, p. 191, appropriately writes: 'The figure of sheep, which has recently represented the lost and shepherdless people of Israel (9.36; 10.6), now represents Jesus' missionaries, who are threatened by the wolflike leaders of the people. Thus a certain solidarity exists between the persecuted missionaries and the harried people; both suffer from the same source'. We would add only that the leaders are the scribes and Pharisees (cf. Bonnard, p. 146).

γίνεσθε οὖν φρόνιμοι ὡς οἱ ὄφεις καὶ ἀκέραιοι ὡς αἱ περιστεραί. Compare Gen 3.1, where the serpent is φρονιμώτατος of all beasts.[58] The articles are generic. The imperative means, 'show yourselves to be' (cf. 5.45).

Although without synoptic parallel, Mt 10.16b is reproduced (with ὑμεῖς δέ and without οὖν) in *P. Oxy.* 665 IIb = Gos. Thom. 39 (the former is fragmentary). Since the imperative in Matthew is editorial, there is cause to suppose that the author of Thomas or a contributor to

---

[53] Recall for instance the problems of Jn 3.

[54] 10.5–6 does not apply because Jesus clearly abrogates it in 28.16–20.

[55] A NT *hapax legomenon*, probably from Q. Matthew prefers πρόβατον*. ἐγώ is also probably redactional.

[56] Discussion in Donfried, pp. 68–71 (arguing for independence).

[57] See further G. W. H. Lampe, '"Grievous Wolves" (Acts 20.29)', in *Christ and Spirit in the New Testament*, ed. B. Lindars and S. S. Smalley, Cambridge, 1973, pp. 253–68.

[58] By changing οι οφεις to ο οφις, ℵ* Or^pt Epiph create a reference to Gen 3.1. Note Teachings of Silvanus 95.7–11, which contrasts the intelligence of the snake with the innocence of the dove.

his tradition had been influenced[59] by the First Gospel.[60] On the other hand, Rom 16.19[61] is not evidence for Paul's knowledge of the Jesus tradition but for the proverbial character of Mt 10.16b. Note *Midr. Cant.* on 2.4: 'God saith of the Israelites: Towards me they are as sincere as doves, but towards the Gentiles they are as serpents'.[62]

What exactly is meant by ἀκέραιος? The observation that the dove is 'innocent' because it is not a bird of prey does not take us very far. The word literally means 'unmixed' (LSJ, s.v.), and in its figurative usages in early Christianity it comes close to meaning 'child-like simplicity' (cf. Rom 16.19; Phil 2.15). D, interestingly enough, substitutes ἁπλούστατοι (cf. Mt 6.22) here. This is good interpretation. The disciple, with a single-minded devotion to duty—a devotion made manifest by a lack of equipment—has no guile. Like a child his intent is obvious to all. Such 'simplicity' is not inconsistent with the call for practical prudence or shrewdness ('be wise as serpents'), whose object is simple survival (cf. 10.23).

The rabbis applied the proverbial adage about being wise as serpents and innocent as doves to Israel's situation amidst the Gentiles. This matters because the image of sheep in the midst of wolves was similarly applied (see on 7.15). Thus one strongly suspects that the two parts of 10.16 implicitly reinterpret traditional images. The sheep are no longer the Jews but the disciples of Jesus, the wolves no longer the Gentiles but Jews hostile to the Christian mission; and those who are wise and innocent are not Jews surrounded by Gentiles but rather Jesus' followers in a situation of persecution. As elsewhere in the First Gospel, imagery and privileges traditionally associated with Israel are now associated with the church (cf. 5.13–6; 21.43).

17. Following the general warning and admonition in 10.16, the evangelist next offers paraenesis and a detailed description of missionary tribulation. Despite prudence (10.16b), the disciple cannot avoid persecution. Against unjust suffering there is no inbred immunity. It can even be said that suffering as much as anything will characterize the missionary (cf. 5.10–12). As with the master, so with his disciple. Those who follow the Lord will suffer his fate.

The material in 10.17–22 is taken primarily from Mk 13.9–13 (cf. Lk 21.12–19).[63] This fact is a key for the interpreter. Mk 13

---

[59] Directly or indirectly remains unclear.

[60] Cf. also Ignatius, *Polyc.* 2.2: 'Be wise as the serpent in all things and innocent always as the dove'. This too must draw upon Matthew. On the singular 'serpent' see n. 58.

[61] 'I would have you σοφούς as to what is good and ἀκεραίους as to what is evil'.

[62] Cf. also Cant. 5.2; 6.9 Sym.; T. Naph. 8.9–10; SB 1, pp. 574–5; and H. Greeven, *TWNT* 6, p. 65, n. 29.

[63] On the possible authenticity of the material see on 24.9–14.

is above all a description of the woes preceding the second advent of Jesus, and Matthew's treatment of the chapter in Mt 24 reveals that he understood and accepted its eschatological orientation. Further, nothing in chapter 10 tones down the eschatological nature of the Markan material. On the contrary, 10.22 explicitly mentions 'the end' and 10.23 refers to the *parousia*. It follows that Mt 10 views the pre- and post-Easter missions as belonging to the eschatological affliction, the period of trial and tribulation which heralds the coming of God's new world. In other words, Matthew, like many others in the early church, used the idea of the messianic tribulation to interpret the time between the first and second advents (cf. Allison, pp. 40–50).

Matthew's displacement of Mk 13.9–13 is important not only because it informs us about his eschatological perspective but also because it probably tells us something about his church. The missionary discourses in Mark and Q already contained references to persecution. But Matthew has much more on the theme than either one of his sources. Does this not reflect the concrete hardships of the Matthean community (and in turn explain in part Matthew's polemical tendencies)? When our author thinks of the missionary enterprise he thinks of persecution. Indeed, one can argue that Mt 10 is not about mission as such but about mission as tribulation. The chapter is full of references to suffering and persecution (vv. 14–23, 25, 26, 28, 31, 35f.).

προσέχετε δὲ ἀπὸ τῶν ἀνθρώπων.[64] This is based upon Mk 13.9: 'But take heed to yourselves'. Matthew's words turn the reader's mind towards outsiders: 'Beware of men'. The reference is to all men, both Jews and Gentiles (cf. 10.32–3). προσέχω + ἀπό* (cf. *hiššāmēr/hizzāhēr + min*) is a Matthean favourite. For another instance of προσέχετε replacing βλέπετε see 16.6 = Mk 8.15.

παραδώσουσιν γὰρ ὑμᾶς εἰς συνέδρια. So Mk 13.9, without γάρ*. 'Sanhedrins' are probably local (Jewish) councils, not the lesser sanhedrins known from rabbinic sources; see Hare, pp. 101–4. The verb (cf. 4.12) links the disciples' fate with Jesus' fate (cf. 10.4): both are 'handed over'. See further on 17.22. Note that the persecution suffered by the disciples is both public and official.

καὶ ἐν ταῖς συναγωγαῖς αὐτῶν μαστιγώσουσιν ὑμᾶς. Compare Mk 13.9: καὶ εἰς συναγωγὰς δαρήσεσθε. By turning the verb into the third person plural (cf. LXX Deut 25.2–3) and by adding 'you', Matthew has increased the parallelism between vv. 17b

---

[64] δε is omitted by Zahn, p. 402, n. 31, on the authority of D 28 *pc* it sy^s sa^mss mae arm Or. If it is retained (so HG and NA^26) it is best understood as a transitional particle which can be omitted in translation (cf. RSV).

and 17c. On 'their synagogues' see on 4.23. On the change from
εἰς to ἐν see Allen, p. xxvii. μαστιγόω (Mt: 3; Mk: 1; Lk: 1),
which replaces Mark's δέρω (='beat'), means 'whip', 'flog',
'scourge'. The verb is used of Jesus in 20.19. Here it refers
specifically to the punishment of flogging as decreed in Deut
25.1–3 (where the LXX uses μαστιγόω three times). For the
rabbinic rules on scourging see *m. Makkot*. Matthew's text
would seem to imply knowledge of Jewish Christians who have
been flogged in the synagogues (cf. 23.34; also Acts 22.19;
Eusebius, *H.E.* 5.16). (Although rabbinic literature never refers
to flogging inside the synagogues, it does refer to synagogue
officials in connexion with scourging, as in *m. Makk.* 3.12. It is
just possible that Matthew's ἐν is instrumental, meaning not 'in'
but 'by' or 'through' (cf. 5.13; 7.6): 'through their synagogues
they will flog you'.)

Matthew does not, unfortunately, tell us why Christians will be
flogged by the Jewish authorities,[65] and that punishment was meted
out for more than one offence. We can only guess at the crime. But two
possibilities in particular should be considered.[66] (i) Certain Christians,
in their harsh criticism of the Jewish leaders (cf. 23.1ff.), may have
created resentment and been perceived as a threat to the public order
(cf. Hare, pp. 43–6). Compare Josephus, *Bell.* 6.302, where Jesus ben
Ananias is flogged because of 'his evil speaking'. (ii) Maybe some of
the Christian claims about Jesus were taken to be blasphemous (see on
9.3) and therefore deserving of punishment (cf. Mt 26.65–6; Acts 7.54–
8).[67] On either reading, Matthew is familiar with Jewish Christians
who still submit themselves to the authority of the synagogue. (One is
reminded of the situation of Paul.)

18. The mention of sanhedrins and synagogues (v. 17) leads
to the mention of governors and kings. This probably reflects
the story of Jesus: he was first delivered to a Jewish council and
then taken to the governor.

καὶ ἐπὶ ἡγεμόνας δὲ καὶ βασιλεῖς ἀχθήσεσθε ἕνεκεν ἐμοῦ.
Compare Ep. Pet. Phil. 138.25–6. Mark has genitives after ἐπί,
no δέ, and σταθήσεσθε instead of ἀχθήσεσθε. The last change
stresses the activity of the persecutors: the passive disciples (cf.

[65] Being flogged by the synagogue authorities was not simply a theoretical
possibility for Jewish Christians. (i) Paul tells us that he was flogged more than
once (2 Cor 11.25). (ii) Matthew's gospel reflects a hostile environment. (iii) If,
as it seems, Jewish missionaries of Matthew's time were still trying to reach
Jews in the synagogues, it is altogether likely that there were Christians who
continued to place themselves under the synagogal authority. (iv) The charge
about flogging is repeated in 23.34.

[66] Cf. A. E. Harvey, 'Forty Stripes Save One', in Harvey, *Approaches*, pp. 90–
5.

[67] Blasphemy was, according to the Mishnah, subject to extirpation (*m. Ker.*
1.1), and scourging could replace extirpation according to *m. Makk.* 3.15.

5.38–42) will be taken into custody (cf. Mk 13.11). For ἄγω with ἐπί + accusative see Lk 23.1; Acts 18.12; Josephus, *Ant.* 20.4. βασιλεῖς refers to kings or rulers in general. ἡγεμών (cf. the rabbinic *hegmôn*) means here an imperial governor or Roman procurator (cf. Lk 2.2; 1 Pet 2.14). Matthew uses it often of Pontius Pilate (27.1, 11, etc.).

εἰς μαρτύριον αὐτοῖς καὶ τοῖς ἔθνεσιν. Compare Mk 13.9. Matthew, perhaps under the influence of Mk 13.10, has added 'and to the Gentiles'. εἰς μαρτύριον (cf. 8.4) here apparently means not 'for a testimony against them' but 'for a witness to them'; see Hare, pp. 106–7. αὐτοῖς probably refers to the previous clause: 'for a witness to governors and kings' (cf. Hare, p. 108). But it is just possible that αὐτοῖς harks back to v. 17, 'the Gentiles' to v. 18a. μαρτύριον has nothing to do with death or 'martyrdom' (as in later Christian usage). Rather the disciples, through what they say, do, and suffer, become witnesses to the truth. In other words, they spread the gospel about Jesus even after they are handed over (cf. the position of Paul in Philippians). In addition, our text assumes that to speak to governors and kings is to speak to the people they represent, that is, to 'the Gentiles' in general. A 'witness' before the former is simultaneously a 'witness' before the latter.[68] (This is why v. 18 does not necessarily envisage activity outside Palestine. The Gentiles had many representatives in the land of Israel.)

19. 10.19–20 has a parallel not only in Mk 13.11 and Lk 21.14–15 but also in Lk 12.11–12. This last occurs in a Q context, and because it also has some agreements with Matthew against Mark,[69] we evidently have another Markan/Q overlap.[70]

ὅταν δὲ παραδῶσιν ὑμᾶς.[71] This abbreviates Mk 13.11.

μὴ μεριμνήσητε πῶς ἢ τί λαλήσητε. Mk 13.11 has a different verb (προμεριμνᾶτε, a biblical *hapax legomenon*) and lacks πῶς ἤ. Matthew's version agrees with Lk 12.11 on these two points. Note that 'Do not be anxiously worried' recalls 6.25–34 and the reasons there given for not fretting overmuch.

Throughout chapter 10 it is presupposed that Christian missionaries suffer passively. When delivered up and arrested they

---

[68] Cf. 20.19 and 2 Tim 4.16–18, on which see Munck, pp. 332–4.

[69] E.g. μὴ μεριμνήσητε, πῶς ἤ (assuming this is original in Luke), ἐν ... τῇ ὥρᾳ τί λαλήσητε/α δεῖ εἰπεῖν.

[70] Cf. Schulz, *Q*, p. 442. For the suggestion that Mt 10.19–20 = Lk 12.11f. was linked in *Q* to Mt 10.23 see Schürmann, *Untersuchungen*, pp. 150–5. For possible minor agreements between Mt 10.19 and Lk 21.12–15 see Wenham, *Rediscovery*, p. 222.

[71] So ℵ B 0171^vid *f*¹ *pc.* C Θ *f*¹³ Maj have παραδιδωσιν; D L N W 33 1010 1424 *al* have παραδωσουσιν.

do not resist. Their only action is speaking—and then not in their own defence but in order to proclaim the gospel. Mt 10 thus illustrates the humility enjoined by the beatitudes and the meekness demanded by 5.38–48.[72] Compare Chrysostom, *Hom. on Mt.* 33.4.

δοθήσεται γὰρ ὑμῖν ἐν ἐκείνῃ τῇ ὥρᾳ τί λαλήσητε.[73] Mk 13.11 is a bit different: 'But whatever is given to you in that hour, this speak'. Matthew's version of the saying could be under the influence of Q (cf. Lk 12.12). Or, what is no less likely, he may have wanted to strike a more pastoral note. 'For what you are to say will be given to you in that hour' is not a command (contrast Mark) but reassurance. Perhaps Matthew wanted his readers to recall the encouraging words of the Lord to Moses: 'I will be with your mouth and teach you what you shall speak' (Exod 4.12). For other texts in which people are given words to speak see Ps 119.41–6; Jer 1.6–10; and Eph 6.19. Compare also Ahiqar 32 (Lindenberger): 'If he [a young man] is beloved of the gods they will give him something worthwhile to say'. For ἐν ἐκείνῃ τῇ ὥρᾳ (= bĕhahî' ša'ătā') see 18.1; 26.55; Lk 7.21; Rev 11.13; *b. Ta'an.* 22a. The expression does not appear in the LXX.

20. When standing before courts and synagogues, governors and kings, the missionaries are not alone. The πνεῦμα of their Father is with them, as it was with the prophets; and they become trumpets of the Spirit.[74] The connexion between confession before authorities and the inspiration of the Spirit is, one should observe, found often in early Christian texts.[75] See, for example, Acts 4.8; 5.32; 1 Pet 4.12–14; Rev 19.10; Eusebius, *H.E.* 5.1.10. For Jewish parallels see Isa 42.1 (with 43.10); Asc. Isa. 5.14. The Spirit was naturally thought to be most manifest in times of crisis or great difficulty.

οὐ γὰρ ὑμεῖς ἐστε οἱ λαλοῦντες. So Mk 13.11, with the order 1, 2, 4, 3, 5. 6. Was there an early Christian tendency to use λαλέω rather than λέγω of inspired or ecstatic utterance (cf. 1 Cor 12.3; 13.1; 14.2)?

ἀλλὰ τὸ πνεῦμα τοῦ πατρὸς ὑμῶν τὸ λαλοῦν ἐν ὑμῖν. Compare Jn 14.26; 1 Cor 2.4. Perhaps one should recall the baptismal story, where the Spirit comes down and a divine voice speaks.

---

[72] Unlike some of the cruder legends about Christian martyrs (e.g. those about St Kyriaki and St Catherine of Alexandria), there is no interest in seeing revenge meted out against tormentors.

[73] D L 1010 *pc* g[1] k vg[mss] Epiph omit the entire line. No doubt a scribe's eye passed from the τί λαλήσητε of v. 19b to the τί λαλήσητε of v. 19c.

[74] With the possible exception of 3.11, only here do the disciples have God's Spirit.

[75] See G. W. H. Lampe, 'Martyrdom and Inspiration', in Horbury, pp. 118–35.

Mark has simply, 'but the Holy Spirit'. Matthew prefers the unprecedented 'Spirit of your Father' (cf. Jn 14.26). This prepares for 10.21. If the disciples are to be betrayed by their own families, the terrible circumstance can be endured because they know that their real family is another (cf. 12.49–50). Matthew has also added 'speaking through[76] you', which perhaps gains an allusion to 3 Βασ 22.24: ποῖον πνεῦμα κυρίου τὸ λαλῆσαν ἐν σοί.

Two observations are in order. First, elsewhere in Matthew Jesus is the possessor of or vehicle for God's Spirit: 3.16; 12.18, 28. Once again therefore we have a parallel between Jesus and his apostles: both are vessels of the Spirit. Secondly, perhaps for Matthew and/or his tradition the promise of the Spirit was construed in eschatological terms. Judaism looked forward to a special outpouring of God's Spirit in the latter days (see 1, p. 335, with lit.); and Mt 10.20 is from Mk 13.11, where the eschatological context is patent. So given the eschatological dimensions of Mt 10.5–25 (cf. p. 196), maybe the promise of Spirit-inspired utterance is an eschatological motif (cf. Acts 2.17–21, quoting Joel 2.28–32).

21. The subject now becomes familial strife (cf. 10.34–6). Two observations in particular must be registered. First, the narrative's scope here clearly includes the post-Easter situation. Secondly, in the words of Chrysostom, 'here again the consolation is at the doors' (*Hom. on Mt.* 33.4). If vv. 21–2a and 23a–b speak of tribulation, vv. 22b and 23c–d speak of salvation.

παραδώσει δὲ ἀδελφὸς ἀδελφὸν εἰς θάνατον καὶ πατὴρ τέκνον, καὶ ἐπαναστήσονται τέκνα ἐπὶ γονεῖς καὶ θανατώσουσιν αὐτούς, Compare 1 En 100.1–3 and *m. Soṭa* 9.15. The line reproduces Mk 13.12 (with δέ for καί) and recalls LXX Mic 7.6. The theme belongs to eschatological expectation. See further on 10.35f. One should reckon with possible influence from Isa 19.2, which is alluded to in 24.7 = Mk 13.8: 'they will fight, every man against his brother and every man against his neighbour, city against city, kingdom against kingdom'. For παραδίδωμι (cf. 4.12; 10.4, 17, 19) see on 17.22 and compare 2 Bar. 24.19 and Did. 16.4. ἐπανίστημι in connexion with the act of murder is common in the LXX (for *qûm*; cf. Deut 19.11; Judg 9.18; 1 Βασ 17.35). θανατόω here means not 'kill' but 'hand over to be killed'.

The reference to being delivered over to death is striking. The language is very strong indeed. One is initially inclined to dismiss it as

---

[76] ἐν is instrumental, not local; cf. 12.24, 27, 28 and see Zahn, p. 404, n. 39.

hyperbole. One should remember, however, that late first-century Christian communities did have stories about those who gave their lives for the gospel—Stephen, Paul, and Peter, for instance, not to mention John the Baptist and Jesus himself. Even if death for the Christian cause was an unlikely prospect for Matthew and his first readers (cf. Hare, passim), they had sufficient examples to make the possibility seem real to them.

22. καὶ ἔσεσθε μισούμενοι ὑπὸ πάντων διὰ τὸ ὄνομά μου. So Mk 13.13. Compare 5.10–12; Jn 15.19, 21; 16.2; Tg. Ps.-J, on Mic 7.6[77] The same words occur again in 24.9, with τῶν ἐθνῶν added. But the meaning is no different here. The disciples of Jesus will encounter opposition from every quarter. There is no safe haven, in or out of Palestine. In this respect the Holy Land is no better and no worse than other lands (contrast 2 Bar. 29.2; 71.1; *b. Ketub.* 111a).

διὰ τὸ ὄνομά μου (cf. Isa 66.5) explains the persecution as arising from the disciples' identification with Jesus and their confession of him (cf. 1 Pet 4.14; Polycarp, *Ep.* 8.2; Justin, *1 Apol.* 4). What the world hates is not the disciples but their behaviour as followers of Jesus. That is, it is precisely in so far as believers speak and act as did their Lord that they will encounter opposition. On hatred as an eschatological motif see 24.9–10 and Did. 16.3–5. It is here not an emotion but a concrete act of rejection.

ὁ δὲ ὑπομείνας εἰς τέλος οὗτος σωθήσεται. So Mk 13.13 = Mt 24.13. ὁ ὑπομείνας[78] means 'he who endures (in affliction)' (cf. 4 Macc 1.11; 2 Tim 2.12; Heb 10.32–3; Jas 5.11; Did 16.5). It goes with εἰς τέλος,[79] which does not mean 'unto death' (cf. Rev 2.10) or 'finally' (cf. 2 Macc 8.29) or 'continually' (cf. Lk 18.5) but 'until the end (the *parousia*)' (cf. 1 Cor 1.8; Josephus, *Ant.* 19.96; Ignatius, *Eph.* 14.2). For the thought compare Hab 2.3; Mic 7.7; Dan 12.12–13 Theod.; 4 Ezra 6.25. Despite all appearances, the tested and afflicted disciples are really the ones who will be saved and delivered from death to life. All is not what it seems to be.

23. This verse raises five very difficult questions. Is 10.23 redactional? If not, should we assign the saying to Q? Were vv. 23a–b and c–d originally independent of each other? Does 10.23 go back to Jesus? What does it mean?[80] We take up the queries in turn.

---

[77] In this 'a man's enemies' becomes 'those who hate a man'.

[78] For the present participle as future see BDF § 339.2. For ὑπομένω/ὑπομονή in connexion with martyrdom see 4 Macc 1.11; 9.6, 8, 22, 30, etc. In connexion with eschatology see Rev 2.2, 3, 19.

[79] *Pace* McNeile, p. 141, ὑπομείνας is not absolute, i.e. independent of εἰς τέλος.

[80] Künzi (v) provides a good history of the interpretation of 10.23.

(i) There is no parallel to 10.23 in Mark or Luke. Moreover, 10.23a–b has a close parallel in 23.34c, which in its present form is redactional; and the vocabulary of 10.23 as a whole is characteristic of the First Evangelist,[81] while the structure of the saying could be modelled on 10.19–20 (ὅταν δὲ ... ὑμᾶς ... γάρ) and 16.28. Some scholars, not surprisingly, have assigned 10.23 to Matthean redaction.[82] Against this, however, 10.23 is a bit anticlimactic or redundant after 10.22, and a pre-Matthean genesis is not hard to envisage (see below). Beyond this, ταύτῃ has no immediate antecedent, and the article before ἑτέραν is awkward. So the theory of a redactional origin for 10.23 is not free of difficulties. With Geist (v), we prefer to see the verse as the Matthean version of a pre-Matthean logion (cf. McKnight, 'Matthew 10.23', (v)).

(ii) If 10.23 is pre-Matthean there would seem to be two candidates for its provenance. Either Matthew found it in his Q source (either in Q's mission discourse or elsewhere) or it came to him as isolated tradition (M).[83] Schürmann has made the case for Q.[84] He argues that 10.23 followed 10.19–20 = Lk 12.11–12. The form of the two sayings is similar, as is the content. Elimination of 10.23 by Luke would, furthermore, be understandable: it does not correspond to the missionary situation as he knew it. Perhaps in all this Schürmann is correct. Certainly if 10.23 was known by Luke we can fathom his reason for dropping it. But it seems to us that if Matthew found 10.23 in Q, he probably found it in the discourse on mission. This is because the verse links up so well with other material that can be assigned to that discourse. (a) ὅταν δὲ διώκωσιν would fall in nicely with the prophecies of rejection (cf. Lk 10.10–12). (b) Lk 10.5–12 contains a string of (ἐ)άν's which would fittingly be culminated by ὅταν κ.τ.λ. (c) 'This city' could have referred back in Q to the hostile city spoken of in Lk 10.10–12 (which ends with πόλει ἐκείνῃ). (d) The phrase, 'the cities of Israel', is naturally thought of together with 10.5–6, and there are reasons for assigning 10.5–6 to Q's mission discourse. If so, that discourse would have referred to Israel near its beginning and then again near its end. (e) The eschatological urgency of 10.23 has its parallel in Lk 10.2 (about the ripe harvest) and is presupposed in the instructions on equipment. The theme is also sounded by the warning of judgement (Lk 10.12).

If there is good reason to surmise that 10.23 belonged to Q's mission discourse, we must hasten to add that the argument falls short of proof. There is nothing impossible about Schürmann's conjecture, and we cannot altogether exclude the bare possibility that 10.23 came to Matthew as an isolated saying.

---

[81] διώκω, ἀμὴν (γὰρ) λέγω ὑμῖν, τελέω, ἕως ἄν, υἱὸς τοῦ ἀνθρώπου. See 1, pp. 75–9.

[82] E.g. Frankemölle, pp. 130–3; Gundry, *Commentary*, p. 194. For McDermott (v), 23a is pre-Matthean, 23b editorial.

[83] McKnight, 'Matthew 10.23' (v), however, argues that 10.23 belonged to an eschatological discourse related to Mk 13.

[84] 'Mt 10.5–6' (v). For a similar argument see Wenham, *Rediscovery*, pp. 231–43. He tries to link the διώκω of Lk 21.12 with Mt 10.23. Criticism in McKnight, 'Matthew 10.23' (v), p. 510, n. 32.

(iii) According to several authorities, the connexion between 10.23a–b and c–d is probably secondary.[85] In favour of this hypothesis, v. 23c–d could stand on its own, and one can interpret the τελέσητε of v. 23c–d as having nothing to do with persecution. But neither of these observations is decisive, and on the other side v. 23a–b would hardly have had an independent existence. When one adds that both vv. 23a–b and c–d concern eschatological events, that both envision movement from place to place, and that there is a catchword connexion (πόλει/πόλεις), the unity of the verse would seem a reasonable hypothesis.

(iv) Does 10.23 go back to Jesus?[86] Several considerations encourage an affirmative response—although one can speak only of probabilities. The form of the logion has parallels in other dominical utterances (see on 5.18). There are possible Semitisms.[87] The eschatological perspective is consistent with what we otherwise know of Jesus. Lastly, and with reference to the criterion of multiple attestation, 10.23 could conceivably be a variant of the logion preserved independently in Mk 9.1.[88] The two sayings have precisely the same structure: ἀμὴν + λέγω ὑμῖν + statement about what will not happen to the disciples (with οὐ μή) + ἕως ἄν + statement about the coming of the Son of man or the kingdom of God. Further, if we suppose, in the light of Mt 16.28 diff. Mk 9.1 (where Mark's 'kingdom of God' has become in Matthew 'Son of man') and Matthew's fondness for the Son of man title, that the pre-Matthean version of 10.23 referred not to the Son of Man but the kingdom of God,[89] and if we further suppose that the formulation of Mk 9.1 has been influenced by its function as an introduction to the transfiguration narrative,[90] the differences between Mt 10.23 and Mk 9.1 become slight. Both texts promise that the kingdom of God will come before death or persecution overtakes the apostles utterly.

On the lips of Jesus, a saying such as Mt 10.23 would have been a word of encouragement to disciples or missionaries whose

---

[85] E.g. Dupont (v); and Hare, pp. 110–11.

[86] For an affirmative answer see Lindars, *Son of Man*, pp. 122–3; and Hempel (v). For a negative answer see Streeter, pp. 255–6; Merklein, pp. 53–6.

[87] Jeremias, *Promise*, p. 20, calls attention to the superfluous demonstrative in ἐν τῇ πόλει ταύτῃ and the definite article in εἰς τὴν ἑτέραν (cf. BDF § 306.2).

[88] Mk 13.30 also supplies a close parallel, but this last is probably a secondary creation based upon Mk 9.1. Cf. Pesch 2, p. 308; Chilton, *Strength*, pp. 256–7.

[89] See Lindars, *Son of Man*, pp. 122–3, and Hempel (v).

[90] τινες could be Markan and is in any case not original; ὧδε is also secondary, whether added by scribes or by Mark himself. See Chilton, *Strength*, pp. 260–1, and J. C. O'Neil, 'Did Jesus teach that his death would be vicarious?', in Horbury, pp. 17–18. So the saying at one time, and before being brought into connexion with the transfiguration, referred simply to οἱ ἑστηκότες. The meaning would then presumably be: those who 'stand fast' or 'endure' will not taste death until the kingdom comes; cf. Mk 13.13b and 20. For ἵστημι as 'withstand' or 'stand fast' see BAGD, s.v., II.1.d. Cf. Cyril of Jerusalem, *Cat.* 15.16 (citing Dan 12.12) and the use of ὑπομένω in Mt 10.22. In the MT both *qûm* and *ʿāmad* sometimes mean 'endure' or 'stand fast'.

future included suffering in the eschatological tribulation: take heart, for salvation is near to hand. But what of Matthew's understanding? The attempts to interpret 10.23 as a fulfilled prophecy have been numerous. According to Feuillet (v) and others, Matthew saw in the destruction of Jerusalem the realization of the prophecy in 10.23. According to J. P. Meier, the word found its fulfilment for Matthew in the resurrection of Jesus.[91] Chrysostom thought of the pre-Easter reunion of Jesus with his disciples after they returned from their missionary assignment (*Hom. on Mt.* 34.1). Calvin, *ad loc.*, seemingly thought of Pentecost. Against all these interpretations, there is every reason to urge that Matthew identified the coming of the Son of man with the coming of the kingdom of God in its fulness (see on 16.28). According to the First Gospel, when the Son of man comes, the angels will be sent forth, every man will be requited according to his deeds, and Jesus will sit on his throne (cf. 13.41; 16.27; 24.27–44; 25.31). In other words, the coming of the Son of man will mean the final judgement. As there can be no doubt that the final judgement remains outstanding, it follows that 10.23 most likely refers to the *parousia*.

The major objection to this interpretation is that it seemingly makes Matthew's Jesus a false prophet. Obviously the Son of man did not come in glory before the apostles completed their mission to Israel. In our opinion, however, the supposed contradiction rests upon a questionable assumption, namely, that Matthew believed the mission to Israel to be completed. But our evangelist nowhere informs us that the apostles finished their work in Israel. Indeed, while the missionaries are commanded to go out (10.5–6), they are never said to return (contrast Mk 6.30; Lk 10.17). This striking circumstance is a clue to the reader. The mission to Israel, which began in the pre-Easter period, has never concluded (cf. Gnilka, *Matthäusevangelium* 1, p. 379). It continues—which is why the command to go to 'all nations' (28.19) includes Israel. Hence the application of 10.23 to the *parousia* could not, from the Matthean perspective, result in an unfulfilled prophecy.

ὅταν δὲ διώκωσιν ὑμᾶς ἐν τῇ πόλει ταύτῃ, φεύγετε εἰς τὴν ἑτέραν.[92] Compare 23.34; Jn 15.20; Did 16.4; *m. Soṭa* 9.15 (before the Son of David comes 'the people of the frontier shall go about from city to city'). For the motif of eschatological flight see on 3.7 and Bammel (v). There is in our verse no eagerness for martyrdom. In contrast to the attitude of Ignatius and some Christian martyrs, the message of the kingdom is evidently to be

---

[91] Meier, *Matthew*, p. 111. Cf. K. Barth, *CD* 3/2, pp. 499–500; Sabourin, p. 534, finds a reference to the resurrection and the *parousia*.

[92] For ετεραν C D L Θ 0171[vid] Maj have αλλην.

preached even if it means that the missionaries are to flee as though they were cowards.[93] διώκωσιν (cf. on 5.10) has no clear subject. Who are 'they'? In 23.34 those who persecute God's messengers from city to city and physically abuse them (cf. 23.34) are the scribes and Pharisees. So interpreting one verse by another, 'they' should be identified with the spiritual descendants of the scribes and Pharisees, the Jewish leaders of Matthew's own day.[94]

ἀμὴν γὰρ λέγω ὑμῖν. See on 5.18 and 10.15. γάρ* makes 10.23c–d the reason for 23a–b. One should flee because the coming of the Son of man is near. Compare 24.22: God will shorten the days of eschatological tribulation for the sake of the elect. In other words, he who endures to the end will be saved (10.22).

οὐ μὴ τελέσητε τὰς πόλεις τοῦ Ἰσραὴλ ἕως ἂν ἔλθῃ ὁ υἱὸς τοῦ ἀνθρώπου. On the Son of man in Matthew see Excursus VI. Whether 'the cities of Israel' includes for Matthew the diaspora is not clear. With ἕως ἂν κ.τ.λ. compare the fixed rabbinic phrase, 'ad šeyyābô' ben-Dāwid, as in y. Ḥag. 77d. τελέσητε, which makes for a catchword connexion with the previous verse (τέλος), is a problem. τελέω can, with reference to the job of evangelism, mean either 'accomplish' (that is, fulfil the assigned task) or simply 'finish' (that is, finish preaching in all the cities of Israel). But the verb might also refer to flight: you will not have finished fleeing or going through the cities of Israel.[95] Certainly if 10.23 was at one time isolated the verb must have referred to persecution, for that is the subject of the first part of the verse. But given the Matthean context (a missionary discourse), both options are open; that is, τελέσητε could refer to flight or to missionizing. In favour of the former option, τελέσητε and πόλεις link v. 23c–d to vv. 22–3b, where the theme is persecution and fleeing. In favour of the other option, Ἰσραήλ takes the reader's mind back to 10.5–6 and thus conjures up the charge to go to the lost sheep of the house of Israel.[96] Given the conflicting indicators one can hardly render a verdict.

One final point needs to be made regarding 10.23. It has sometimes been suggested that the verse does not reflect Matthew's own perspective: it is nothing more than tradition he

---

[93] Cf. Mart. Polyc. 4: 'We do not commend those who give themselves up (to suffer), seeing the Gospel does not teach so to do'. The idea caused problems. See Tertullian, De fuga, passim, and Origen, C. Cels. 1.65.

[94] Although the First Gospel was composed after A.D. 70, it is unlikely that its author associated our saying with the flight of Christians to Pella (Eusebius, H.E. 3.5.3; Epiphanius, Haer. 29.7; 30.2).

[95] So BAGD, s.v. τελέω; also Jeremias, Theology, p. 136.

[96] Cf. Hill, Matthew, p. 190; also Gnilka, Matthäusevangelium 1, pp. 378–9.

felt compelled to hand on.[97] We dissent. Our author's compositional habits were not like those of a sea-bottom scavenger which picks up everything without discrimination. Matthew, as his treatment of Mark demonstrates, felt quite free to drop what did not impress him as valuable. So it is very hazardous to dismiss any verse in Matthew as without meaning because traditional.[98] But why then the inclusion of 10.23? Matthew was a member of a mixed community at the end of the first century, and he lived at a time when the success of the Gentile mission had come to overshadow the relative failure of the Jewish mission. It must have been a temptation for some missionaries to conclude that it was time to forget about preaching the gospel in the Jewish synagogues. 10.23, however, requires that the Jewish mission continue until the *parousia*. Indeed, it implicitly encourages Jewish missionaries to stick to the task of evangelizing their people no matter how difficult the situation. In other words, 10.23 reflects Matthew's concern that the mission to God's people Israel not be abandoned.[99]

DISCIPLE AND TEACHER, SERVANT AND MASTER (10.24–5)

Between 10.16–23, which deals with persecution, and 10.26–31, which offers consolation, Matthew has inserted 10.24–5. The passage, which probably came to the evangelist as isolated tradition,[100] can be read in two different ways. Taken with what comes before it, the text declares the necessity of suffering: they persecuted the master, surely they will persecute his servants. If, on the other hand, 10.24–5 be taken with what follows, the emphasis would be upon consolation: take heart, for when they persecute you, they are doing no more than they

[97] Hare, e.g., mutes the force of v. 23b by arguing that Matthew wished to use v. 23a, and that v. 23b is where it is because it was already attached to 10.23a (pp. 111–12). See the criticism in Allison, p. 49, n. 11.

[98] Contrast Luz 1, p. 382, commenting on 7.6: the logion has no meaning in its present context; Matthew was a conservative author and took up the saying out of faithfulness to the tradition; it stood in his Q source.

[99] Again one should note the similarity with Paul. The apostle to the Gentiles in Gal 2 indicates that the mission to the Gentiles should not cancel the mission to the Jews; further, Paul did not exclude Jews from his missionary activity; see Davies, *JPS*, pp. 185–6.

[100] The closest Lukan parallel is 6.40. This differs from 10.24–5 in that it has a different context, a different application, a different structure, and abbreviated content. Perhaps Lk 6.40 = Q is an excerpt from the unit preserved independently in M. It is less likely that 10.24–5 comes from Q and that Luke abbreviated the text. We also deem unlikely the suggestion that Mt 10.24–5 is Matthew's expansion of Lk 6.40 = Q, although this is the judgement of Gnilka, *Matthäusevangelium* 1, p. 374; cf. Gundry, *Commentary*, p. 195.

did to your Lord. Three considerations move us to think that the emphasis is upon the necessity of suffering. First, in both Lk 6.40 and Jn 13.16 the saying about disciple and teacher or servant and Lord has nothing to do with consolation but is used in a hortatory context. A paraenetic application may have been traditional. Secondly, in both *b. Ber.* 55b and *Sipre* on Lev 25.23, 'It is enough, etc.' is used to express not consolation but resignation (see further Gruenewald (v)). Thirdly, according to our structural analysis of chapter 10, the passage belongs to the triad 5–15 + 16–23 + 24–5 while 10.26–31 stands by itself. See Excursus VIII. This encourages us to link vv. 24–5 with what precedes, not with what follows.

Mt 10.24–5 has its closest parallel in Jn 13.16 (cf. 15.20). As Dodd's careful investigation of this passage has shown, it is not easily reckoned as an adaptation of Mt 10.24–5 (*Tradition*, pp. 335–8). His conclusion that Jn 13.16 preserves an oral variant of the quatrain in Mt 10.24–5 is well grounded.[101]

Concerning authenticity, one could consider 10.24a a secular proverb which entered the Jesus tradition and then attracted to itself additions (cf. Bultmann, *History*, pp. 86, 99, 103). Yet Jesus himself mined traditional wisdom materials,[102] and if our tradition-history (see below) is correct, 10.24–5 should be treated as a unit independently attested in John's gospel. We are inclined to receive 10.24–5 as dominical. Certainly Jesus during his own ministry was rebuked in the strongest terms (see on 19.12). He was even accused of being in league with Beelzebul (Mk 3.22). If he then had followers who were extensions of his ministry, we can readily imagine that they too sometimes encountered less than a favourable reception. In such a situation Mt 10.24–5 is readily comprehended as a word of Jesus.

24. οὐκ ἔστιν μαθητὴς ὑπὲρ τὸν διδάσκαλον.[103] So Lk 6.40a. The sentiment may well have been proverbial (note the present tense). On Jesus as 'teacher' in Matthew see on 8.19.

οὐδὲ δοῦλος ὑπὲρ τὸν κύριον αὐτοῦ. Compare Jn 13.16. There is for our author no negative connotation to the idea of being a servant or slave. Jesus himself was a servant (cf. 20.28). Christian service is perfect freedom. Compare Philo, *De cherub.* 107: 'To be the slave of God is the highest boast of man, a treasure more precious not only than freedom, but than wealth and power and all that mortals most cherish'.

---

[101] Cf. Brown, *John* 2, pp. 569–72. If Mt 10.24–5 be considered, against our judgement, as mostly redactional, then one would almost be forced to conclude that Matthew's gospel has influenced John: the parallels between Mt 10.24–5 and Jn 13.16 and 15.20 are too close to be accidental.

[102] See Davies, *SSM*, pp. 457–60.

[103] αυτου appears at the end in ℵ W *f*¹³ 1424 *al* sy. It could be original. It increases the parallelism with v. 24b as well as the corresponding clauses in v. 25.

25. Although never the teacher's equal, the disciple can aspire to be like the teacher, and the servant can aspire to be like the Lord. The theme is the imitation of Christ: Christians must follow Christ's example. It should be stressed, however, that in Matthew the idea is neither simplistic nor literal. Our author would hardly have commended the Cerinthians and Ebionites for using Mt 10.25 to urge that, because Jesus was circumcised, Christians should be also (see Epiphanius, *Haer.* 30.26.2). Matthew's text moves much more in the direction of the words attributed to Isaac the Syrian: 'If anyone should ask how to acquire humility, he would answer: "It is enough for the disciple that he be as his master, and the servant as his lord." See how much humility was shown by Him who has given us this commandment and who gives us this gift; imitate Him and you will acquire it' (Theophan, *Philokalia*, Isaac the Syrian 133).

ἀρκετὸν τῷ μαθητῇ ἵνα γένηται ὡς ὁ διδάσκαλος αὐτοῦ. Before ὡς Lk 6.40 has this: κατηρτισμένος δὲ πᾶς ἔσται. Matthew may be responsible for enhancing the parallelism between this clause and v. 24a. ἀρκετός—which here means 'sufficient in the eyes of God' (cf. Bonnard, p. 149)—appears only three times in the NT: Mt 6.34; 10.25; 1 Pet 4.3. For γίνομαι + ὡς[104] see also 6.16; 18.3; 28.4 (all without parallel). ἵνα γένηται also appears in 23.26 (diff. Lk 11.41).

If 10.24 *may* reformulate a secular proverb, 10.25 certainly does. See SB 1, pp. 577–8; Gruenewald (v). Note especially *Sipra* on Lev 25.23: *dayyô lĕʿebed šeyyihyeh kĕrabbô*. Matthew's formulation is closer to the rabbinic parallels than is Luke's; see Schlatter, p. 342.

καὶ ὁ δοῦλος ὡς ὁ κύριος αὐτοῦ. This clause is required in order to maintain the parallelism with v. 24.

εἰ τὸν οἰκοδεσπότην Βεελζεβοὺλ ἐπεκάλεσαν πόσῳ μᾶλλον τοὺς οἰκιακοὺς αὐτοῦ. Compare 1 Pet 4.1. It is precisely because the disciples are members of the Christian household that they are persecuted.

10.25c has no synoptic parallel and might therefore be regarded as redactional. But the word statistics offer little support.[105] In addition, because 10.24–5b has secular parallels and would, standing by itself, be subject to various interpretations, v. 25c probably preserves the original (that is, Jesus') application to the proverbial material. In other words,

---

[104] Often in the LXX for *hāyâ + kaʾăšer*.

[105] Βεελζεβούλ appears only three times, twice with parallels (12.24, 27). πόσῳ μᾶλλον is used only one other time (7.11) and in that instance comes from Q (cf. Lk 11.13). οἰκιακός: Mt: 2 (once in an OT quotation: 10.35); Mk: 0; Lk: 0. The only word possibly characteristic of Matthew is οἰκοδεσπότης (Mt: 7; Mk: 1; Lk: 4). Although Brooks, pp. 51–2 assigns the line to redaction, he admits that 'the study of vocabulary is inconclusive'.

v. 25c is the *raison d'être* for vv. 24–5b, so the two were presumably handed on together. In support of this conclusion, Jn 15.20 takes up Jn 13.16 (see above) and follows it with this: 'If they persecuted me, they will persecute you'. This is evidence that the slave/master saying was associated in the tradition with mistreatment of the disciples. Finally, the juxtaposition of οἰκοδεσπότην and Βεελζεβούλ is telling. The former could be rendered *bĕʿēl-zĕbūl*,[106] which is obviously very close to 'Beelzebul' (cf. Jeremias, *Theology*, p. 7). If not coincidence, either we have before us the translation of a Semitic sentence, or Matthew, although writing in Greek, was thinking in another language.

Who is the subject of ἐπεκάλεσαν? In 9.34 the Pharisees say that Jesus casts out demons by the prince of demons, and 10.25 refers back to this. Further, in 12.24 it is again the Pharisees who level the same charge. So ἐπεκάλεσαν is probably not an impersonal plural. The implicit subject of 10.25c would appear to be the Jewish leaders. It is they who accuse Jesus and his followers of Satanic inspiration.

Βεελζεβούλ[107] (cf. 4 Βασ 1.2 Sym) has been thought by many to derive from the OT god of Ekron, *baʿal zĕbûb* ('Lord of the flies'; cf. the LXX translation—Βααλ μυῖαν θεόν—and Josephus, *Ant.* 9.19); see 2 Kgs 1.2–3, 6, 16. But the best NT mss. have 'Beelzebul' (that is, λ at the end, not β). Also problematic is derivation from *bĕʿēl dĕbāb* (= 'adversary', that is, 'master of complaint'; criticism in SB 1, p. 631) or from *bĕʿel zibbûl* (= 'Lord of dung'; cf. the Βελχειρά = *baʿal ḥārê* in some copies of Asc. Isa 2–3 and 5; but he is neither Satan nor a spirit). The best guess is that Βεελζεβούλ is an ancient name for the Canaanite god Baal, the Lord of the heavens (cf. Albright and Mann, p. 126; supportive is the possible wordplay with οἰκοδεσπότην = 'lord of the dwelling'; see above). In Ugaritic texts he is known as 'Exalted one, Lord of the earth' (= *zbl bʿl arṣ*; see Fitzmyer, *Luke* 2, p. 920).[108] In any event the meaning of 'Beelzebul' for the NT is clear. He is the (not 'a', despite the lack of an article) prince of demons (cf. 12.24 par.), the commander in charge of demonic hordes (cf. T. Sol. 3.6; Origen, *C. Cels.* 8.25). In the Testament of Solomon he is said to have once been 'the highest-ranking angel in heaven' (6.1–2). This suggests identification

---

[106] A hybrid form, from Aramaic *bĕʿēl*, Hebrew *zĕbūl*.

[107] Cf. 4 Βασ 1.2 Sym. Some NT mss. have Βεεζεβουλ (so א, B), others *Beelzebub* (so c vg sy[s,p]; this is assimilation to 2 Kgs 1.2–6). Lit.: W. E. M. Aitken, 'Beelzebul', *JBL* 31 (1912), pp. 34–53; SB 1, pp. 631–4; W. Foerster, *TWNT* 1, pp.605–6; T. H. Gastor, *IDB* 4, s.v.; L. Gaston, 'Beelzebul', *TZ* 18 (1962), pp. 247–55; M. Limbeck, 'Beelzebul—eine ursprüchliche Bezeichnung für Jesus?', in *Wort Gottes in der Zeit*, ed. H. Feld and J. Nolte, Düsseldorf, 1973, pp. 31–42; E. C. B. MacLaurin, 'Beelzebul', *NovT* 20 (1978), pp. 156–60; Schenk, *Sprache*, pp. 157–58.

[108] It is possible that the 'Beelzebub' of 2 Kgs 1 is a play upon 'Beelzebul': 'such a use of corrupted names conveying more of the writer's or speaker's opinion of the character than its proper meaning is common in the OT . . .'; so T. R. Hobbs, *2 Kings*, Word Biblical Commentary 13, Waco, 1985, p. 8. See further G. A. Rendsburg, 'The Mock of Baal in 1 Kings 18.27', *CBQ* 50 (1988), pp. 414–7.

with Satan, and Rev 12.9 arm has 'Beelzebul' for διάβολος. It seems likely that by NT times 'Beelzebul' was one of Satan's several names, along with 'Asmodeus' (Tob 3.8; contrast T. Sol. 5, where Beelzebul and Asmodeus are separate beings), 'Belial' (Jub 1.20; 2 Cor 6.15), and 'Mastemah' (Jub. 10.8; 11.5). Still, this is not certain, and Hippolytus, *Haer*. 6.34.1, and the Gospel of Nicodemus distinguish the two. (Dante identified Satan and Beelzebul, Milton did not.)

(iv) *Concluding Observations*

(1) In his justly famous book on *The Quest of the historical Jesus*, A. Schweitzer made Mt 10 the edifice for his reconstruction of the Jesus of history (see pp. 358–64). In Schweitzer's estimation, that chapter 'is historical as a whole and down to the smallest detail' (p. 363), and it discloses that Jesus, when he sent out the twelve, expected the messianic woes and then the *Parousia* to arrive in the very near future (so already Reimarus). Schweitzer's conclusions on this matter have been contradicted from all sides. On literary grounds alone, Mt 10, being a conflation of Markan and Q material, can hardly be the floodlight that forever banishes the shadows from the pre-Easter stage.[109] Nevertheless, Schweitzer's observations on the eschatological character of Matthew's discourse on mission were right on target. The chapter is indeed 'a prediction of the events of the "time of the end", events . . . in which the supernatural eschatological course of history will break through into the natural course' (p. 363). Matthew's words to missionaries are permeated by eschatological motifs which show that Christian suffering belongs to the 'messianic woes' and will only be ended when—and this will be sooner rather than later—the Son of Man comes on the clouds of heaven (10.16–23). All of this follows from a plain reading of the text and a knowledge of the eschatological expectations of Judaism and Christianity. For Matthew, the missionary endeavour takes place in the latter days, and the sufferings of Christian missionaries are to be interpreted as a manifestation of the birth pangs which herald the advent of God's new world.

(2) Although Mt 10 scarcely scores the polemical points that 23 does, it is nonetheless not free of animosity towards the Jewish leaders. The scribes and Pharisees are not, it is true, named. But if one interprets Matthew by Matthew, much in chapter 10 would seem to implicate them as the chief opponents of the Christian mission (cf. on 9.36). When Jesus' messengers go forth into Israel,

---

[109] See further Beasley-Murray, pp. 286–7.

they, as sheep in the midst of wolves, are handed over to councils, flogged in synagogues, persecuted from town to town, and maligned by those who called the master Beelzebul. The implicit subjects of all these actions are the Jewish leaders (see on 10.16, 17, 25). This means, first of all, that the afflictions of Mt 10 are more than hypothetical: the evangelist has in mind the concrete actions of Jewish authorities. Then, secondly, the same fact also requires that in the First Gospel the Pharisees are more than just opponents. They are *eschatological* opponents. Because 10.16–23 is about the latter days, the Jewish leaders are clearly channels through which the eschatological sorrows afflict the followers of Jesus.

(3) The *imitatio Christi* runs like a bright thread throughout 10.5–25. The disciples, like Jesus, go only to the lost sheep of the house of Israel (10.5; 15.24). They preach the same message Jesus preached (10.7; cf. 4.17). They heal the sick, raise the dead, cleanse lepers, and cast out demons (10.8)—all of which Jesus did (8.2–4, 14–17, 28–34; 9.18–26). They wander from town to town, just like Jesus (10.11; cf. 4.23–5); and, like their master, they stay in the homes of others (10.11; cf. 8.14–16; 9.10?). The apostles also suffer like Jesus. They flee (see on 10.23), are delivered up before councils, are flogged, and are dragged before governors (10.17–19; cf. 26.57–27.31).[110] They in addition are betrayed by those closest to them, which recalls the betrayal of Jesus by one of the twelve (10.21; cf. 26.47–56).

That Matthew was conscious of these parallels is clear from two facts. The first is 10.25, which concludes our section: it is enough for the disciple to be like the master. This makes the imitation of Christ explicit. Equally telling is the arrangement of chapters 5–10. Before the apostles are told what to say and do (10), the narrative recounts what Jesus said (5–7) and did (8–9). Thus 5–9 is the hermeneutical key to 10. The acts of the apostles are given meaning by the acts of Jesus. In him the words of the SM have become flesh. The Christian Lord is, for Matthew, the incarnation of proper Christian behaviour and therefore its model. His words and deeds supply an example that demands and fortifies at the same time.[111]

---

[110] Cf. Farmer, *Jesus*, p. 158: 'Jesus had not only died "for us", as Paul taught, but he died to show those who confess him before the world . . . how to make their confession and, when necessary, *how to die* while making their confession'.

[111] McKnight, 'Matthew 10.23' (v), p. 507, is correct: 'christology provides the substructure for ecclesiology'. See further Davies, *COJ*, pp. 231–45. One recalls in this connexion Jn 13, where Jesus washes the feet of the disciples and tells them to do likewise. One also recalls the rabbinic texts in which the student copies or imitates his rabbi; on this see Davies, *SSM*, pp. 455–7. Precept and example go hand in hand; the teacher is living Torah. The emphasis in the First Gospel upon the imitation of Christ harmonizes well both with the author's possible rabbinic training (see vol. 1, p. 133) and with his concern to interpret Christian discipleship as an act of learning (cf. 11.29; 13.52; 28.19).

(v) *Bibliography*

B. Ahern, 'Staff or no Staff?', *CBQ* 5 (1943), pp. 332–7.

D. C. Allison, Jr., 'Paul and the Missionary Discourse', *ETL* 61 (1985), pp. 369–75.

E. Bammel, 'Matthäus 10.23', *ST* 15 (1961), pp. 79–92.

R. Bartnicki, 'Das Trostwort an die Jünger in Mt 10.23' *TZ* 43 (1987), pp. 311–19.

idem, 'Der Bereich der Tätigkeit der Jünger nach Mt 10.5b–6', *BZ* 31 (1987), pp. 250–56.

G. Baumbach, 'Die Mission im Matthäus-Evangelium', *TLZ* 92 (1967), pp. 889–93.

F. W. Beare, 'The Mission of the Disciples and the Mission Charge: Matthew 10 and Parallels', *JBL* 89 (1970), pp. 1–13.

M. E. Boring, 'Christian Prophecy and Matthew 10.23—a Test Case', in G. MacRae, ed. *Society of Biblical Literature 1976 Seminar Papers*, Missoula, 1976, pp. 127–33.

Brooks, pp. 47–54.

S. Brown, 'The Matthean Community and the Gentile Mission', *NovT* 22 (1980), pp. 193–221.

idem, 'The Mission to Israel in Matthew's Central Section (Mt 9.35–11.1)', *ZNW* 69 (1978), pp. 73–90.

idem, 'The Two-fold Representation of the Mission in Matthew's Gospel', *ST* 31 (1977), pp. 21–32.

G. B. Caird, 'Uncomfortable Words II. Shake off the dust from your feet', *ExpT* 81 (1969), pp. 40–3.

L. Cerfaux, 'La mission apostolique des Douze et sa portée eschatologique', in *Mélanges Eugène Tisserant*, volume 1, Rome, 1964, pp. 43–66.

idem, 'La mission de Galilée dans la tradition synoptique', *ETL* 27 (1951), pp. 369–89; 28 (1952), pp. 629–47.

R. Clark, 'Eschatology and Matthew 10.23', *RestQ* 7 (1963), pp. 73–81; 8 (1965), pp. 53–68.

H. J. B. Combrink, 'Structural Analysis of Mt 9.35–11.1', *Neotestamentica* 11 (1977), pp. 98–114.

Crossan, *Aphorisms*, pp. 268–72.

D. L. Dungan, *The Sayings of Jesus in the Churches of Paul*, Philadelphia and London, 1971, pp. 3–80.

J. Dupont, 'La persécution comme situation missionaire (Marc 13.9–11)', in Schnackenburg, *Kirche*, pp. 97–114.

idem, '"Vous n'aurez pas achevé les villes d'Israël avant que le Fils de l'homme ne vienne" (Mt 10.23)', *NovT* 2 (1958), pp. 228–44.

M. S. Enslin, 'The Samaritan Ministry and Mission', *HUCA* 51 (1980), pp. 29–38.

J. C. Fenton, 'Raise the Dead', *ExpT* 80 (1968), pp. 50–1.

A. Feuillet, 'Les origens et la signification de Mt 10.23b: Contribution à l'étude du problème eschatologique', *CBQ* 23 (1961), pp. 182–98.

H. Frankemölle, 'Zur Theologie der Mission im Matthäusevangelium', in Kertelge, *Mission*, pp. 93–129.

Geist, pp. 227–37.

C. H. Giblin, 'Theological Perspective and Matthew 10.23b', *TS* 29 (1968), pp. 637–61.

J. A. Grassi, 'The Last Testament-Succession Literary Background of Matthew 9.35–11.1 and its Significance', *BTB* 7 (1977), pp. 172–6.

M. Gruenewald, '"It is enough for the Servant to be like his Master"', in *Salo Wittmayer Baron Jubilee Volume*, Jerusalem, 1974, vol. 2, pp. 573–76.

Hahn, *Mission*, pp. 26–46, 120–8.

V. Hampel, '"Ihr werdet mit den Städten Israels nicht zu Ende kommen"', *TZ* 45 (1989), pp. 1–31.

Hare, pp. 96–114.

A. E. Harvey, '"The Workman is worthy of his Hire": Fortunes of a Proverb in the Early Church', *NovT* 24 (1983), pp. 209–21.

P. Hoffmann, 'Lk 10.5–11 in der Instruktionsrede der Logienquelle', in *Evangelisch-Katholischer Kommentar*, Vorarbeiten 3, Neukirchen, 1971, pp. 37–53.

Hoffmann, *Logienquelle*, pp. 235–334.

M. D. Hooker, 'Uncomfortable Words: X. The Prohibition of Foreign Missions (Mt 10.5–6)', *ExpT* 82 (1971), pp. 361–5.

A. D. Jacobson, 'The Literary Unity of Q: Lk 10.2–16 and Parallels as a Test Case', in Delobel, pp. 419–23.

Jeremias, *Promise*, passim.

idem, *Theology*, pp. 231–40.

Jülicher 2, pp. 44–50.

H. Kasting, *Die Anfänge der urchristlichen Mission*, Munich, 1969.

Kloppenborg, pp. 192–7.

M. Künzi, *Das Naherwahrtungslogien Matthäus 10.23*, BGBE 9, Tübingen, 1970.

Laufen, pp. 201–301.

L. Legrand, 'Bare foot Apostles? The shoes of St Mark (Mk 6.8–9 and parallels)', *IndTS* 16 (1979), pp. 201–19.

Levine, pp. 225–75.

J. M. McDermott, 'Mt 10.23 in Context', *BZ* 28 (1984), pp. 230–40.

S. McKnight, 'New Shepherds for Israel: An Historical and Critical Study of Matthew 9.35–11.1', unpublished Ph.D. dissertation, University of Nottingham, 1986.

idem, 'Jesus and the End-Time: Matthew 10.23', in *Society of Biblical Literature 1986 Seminar Papers*, ed. K. H. Richards, Atlanta, 1986, pp. 501–20.

G. Mangatt, 'Reflections on the Apostolic Discourse (Mt 10)', *BuL* 6 (1980), pp. 196–206.

T. W. Manson, *Only to the House of Israel? Jesus and the Non-Jews*, FBBS 9, Philadelphia, 1964.

R. E. Morosco, 'Redaction Criticism and the Evangelical: Matthew 10 as a Test Case', *JETS* 22 (1979), pp. 323–32.

E. Power, 'The Staff of the Apostles', *Bib* 4 (1923), pp. 241–66.

J. Radermakers, 'La Mission, engagement radical. Une lecture de Mt 10', *NRT* 93 (1971), pp. 1072–85.

B. Reicke, 'A Test of Synoptic Relationships: Matthew 10.17–23 and 24.9–14 with Parallels', in Farmer, *Studies*, pp. 209–29.

B. Rigaux, 'Die Zwölf in Geschichte und Kerygma', in Ristow, pp. 468–86.

L. Sabourin, '"You will not have gone through all the towns of Israel, before the Son of man comes" (Mt 10.23b)', *BTB* 7 (1977), pp. 5–11.

Schlosser 2, pp. 541–69.

S. Schulz, 'Die Gottesherrschaft ist nahe herbeigekommen (Mt 10.7/Lk 10.9)', in H. Balz and S. Schulz, eds., *Die Wort und die Worter*, Stuttgart, 1973, pp. 57–67.

idem, *Q*, pp. 404–19, 442–4, 449–51.

H. Schürmann, 'Mt 10.5–6 und die Vorgeschichte des synoptischen Aussendungsberichtes', in *Untersuchungen*, pp. 137–49.

idem, 'Zur Traditions- und Redaktionsgeschichte von Mt 10.23', in *ibid*, pp. 150–6.

A. Strobel, *Untersuchungen zum eschatologischen Verzögerungsproblem*, Leiden, 1961, pp. 278–86.

Trilling, pp. 99–105.

W. Trilling, 'Zur Entstehung des Zwölferkreises: Eine geschichtskritische Überlegung', in Schnackenburg, *Kirche*, pp. 201–22.

C. M. Tuckett, 'Paul and the Synoptic Mission Discourse?', *ETL* 60 (1984), pp. 376–81.

R. Uro, *Sheep Among the Wolves: A Study on the Mission Instructions of Q*, Helsinki, 1987.

Wanke, pp. 21–5.

Wenham, *Rediscovery*, pp. 243–51.

J. Wilkinson, 'The Mission Charge to the Twelve and Modern Medical Missions', *SJT* 27 (1974), pp. 313–28.

Zumstein, pp. 429–35, 443–53.

XXII

THERE IS NO NEED TO FEAR
(10.26–31)

(i) *Structure*

Three negative injunctions mark the beginning, middle, and end of 10.26–31. The first two imperatives introduce arguments while the third serves as a conclusion:

26a   General admonition: 'Do not fear' (μὴ οὖν)
26b–c   Statement about revelation in compound parallelism: 'Nothing is hidden . . .'
27a–b   Command to preach in compound parallelism: 'What I say to you in the dark . . .'

28a–b   Command not to fear the executioner: 'Do not fear those who kill . . .'
28c   Command to fear God: 'Fear rather the one able . . .'

29a   Observation about nature in interrogative form: 'Are not two sparrows . . .'
29b   Interpretation of observation: 'Not one of them falls . . .'
30   Proverb: 'All the hairs of your head . . .'
31a   Inferential negative imperative: 'Do not fear' (μὴ οὖν)
31b   Conclusion of argument *a fortiori*: 'You are worth more . . .'

The occurrence of μὴ οὖν in both v. 26a and v. 31a creates an *inclusio* that marks the boundaries of the section.

The themes of the three subsections differ, although each one is intended to reassure. 10.26f., with its contrasts between covered and revealed, hidden and made known, darkness and light, whispering and proclamation, is concerned with the eschatological revelation of God's truth; 10.28 with the real meaning of death; and 10.29–31 with God's sovereignty over the present.

On the place of 10.26–31 within Mt 10 as a whole see Excursus VIII and section (iv).

(ii) *Sources*

10.26–31 is, on the two-source theory, a block from Q. See Lk 12.2–7.

But because, in our judgement, most of the differences between 10.26–31 and its Lukan parallel are readily explicable in terms of Lukan redaction, it would be possible, all else being equal, to regard Matthew's text as Luke's source. 10.26 = Lk 12.2 has a parallel in Mk 4.22 = Lk 8.17 (see on 10.26). Two-source theorists postulate Markan/Q overlap, and this is our verdict. Certainly one can in this way easily account for Lk 8.17 and 12.2: one verse depends upon Mark, the other upon Q. Yet we must admit that nothing about 10.26 par. palpably militates against the Griesbach hypothesis[1] or the view that Luke used Matthew.

(iii) *Exegesis*

The primary function of 10.26–31 is manifest. The passage is surrounded on all sides by difficult commands and ominous prophecies. These our evangelist wishes to put in perspective by offering encouragement (cf. the function of 6.25–34 and 7.7–11).[2] Despite rejection, persecution, and even the prospect of death, the true follower of Jesus will know that he need not fear. God is the sovereign Lord, and what befalls God's own must somehow be within his will. The course of discipleship may seem to be a mighty maze, but it is not without a plan. Beyond this, earthly life is not what ultimately matters. The things of eternity are what count. What will it profit a man if he gains the whole world yet forfeits his soul?

10.26–31, which probably incorporates four originally separate logia (10.26–7; 28; 29 + 31b; 30) is we think a faithful record of words of Jesus.[3] (i) Both the form and the content of at least vv. 28–31 are strongly reminiscent of 6.25–34, whose core can be accepted as dominical (see on 6.25). (ii) Signs of a Semitic substratum are visible (see on vv. 26, 28, 31). (iii) V. 26 is attested in both Mark and Q. (iv) Vv. 26–7 have a natural *Sitz im Leben Jesu*. Certainly Jesus sought to encourage and exhort those he sent out to preach. (v) The whole paragraph is permeated by eschatology. 10.26 anticipates the revelation of the last day, and v. 28 gains its force from belief in the resurrection and final judgement. (vi) The prospect of suffering and even death (vv. 28–31) is consistent with Jesus' conviction that the messianic tribulation had entered the present with the death of John the Baptist (11.12) and would fall upon the saints. (vii) Jesus was fond of parallelism (vv. 26–8), of arguments *a fortiori* (v. 31), and of the divine passive (vv. 26, 30). (viii) Jesus surely possessed a proclivity for

---

[1] Theoretically, Lk 12.2 could depend upon Matthew, Lk 8.17 could be Lukan redaction, and Mk 4.22 could depend upon Lk 8.17.

[2] Cf. the way in which many prophetic books balance warnings with consolation and see on this L. Finkelstein, *New Light from the Prophets*, London, 1969.

[3] While we see no reason to regard 10.26 and 27 as originally separate sayings, many would disagree; see Wanke (v) and Gnilka, *Matthäusevangelium* 1, p. 390.

exercising what Hugh of St.-Victor meant by *cogitatio*, this being the soul's perception of God in the things of this world (cf. vv. 29–30). Moreover, characteristic is the emphasis upon God working directly in the world (vv. 29–30). No thought is given to angels or other intermediaries.

26. μὴ οὖν φοβηθῆτε αὐτούς. Compare 1 Pet 3.14; Rev 2.10. This redactional line[4] sets the theme: notwithstanding all appearances, there is no need to have fear or suffer despair. The imperative is repeated three times (see above).[5] This recalls the very similar threefold use of μὴ μεριμνᾶτε/-ήσητε in 6.25–34. The οὖν of 10.26 is clearly not inferential. It probably has either intensive force (as often in exhortations) or it may be adversative.[6] Who are 'they' (αὐτούς)? They must be those who have called the master Beelzebul and maligned the disciples (10.25). That is, they must be the scribes and Pharisees (see on 10.25). Matthew probably had in mind the rabbis and synagogue leaders of his day who made life difficult for the Jewish Christians they perceived as contumacious.

οὐδὲν γάρ ἐστιν κεκαλυμμένον ὃ οὐκ ἀποκαλυφθήσεται καὶ κρυπτὸν ὃ οὐ γνωσθήσεται. Compare 1 Cor 4.5[7] and 2 Bar. 83.3.[8] Lk 12.2 has δέ for γάρ,[9] ἐστίν before the first ὅ, and συγκεκαλυμμένον. Given Luke's fondness for συν-compounds,[10] the simplex is presumably original. Jesus now backs off from the frightening scenes he has just painted and directs the mind's eye towards the grand eschatological future. He thereby puts everything in perspective and gives the true interpretation of the disciples' predicament. It is not just that 'time brings all to light'.[11] Rather, on the last day God will see to it that the truth will be victorious (cf. the targum on Eccles 12.14). The eschatological judgement will be public and all lies exposed (cf.

---

[4] Compare 6.8, 31, 34; 10.31. There is no parallel in Luke. μὴ οὖν* is Matthean; and 'Do not fear' is redactional or at least has no parallel in 1.20; 17.7; 28.5, 10.

[5] The aorist subjunctive—used for categorical imperatives—appears in v. 26. Vv. 28 and 31 have the present tense.

[6] See H. E. Dana and J. R. Mantey, *A Manual Grammar of the Greek New Testament*, New York, 1927, pp. 255–8.

[7] 'Therefore do not pronounce judgement before the time, before the Lord comes, who will bring to light the things now hidden in darkness and will disclose the purposes of the heart.'

[8] 'He will certainly investigate the secret thoughts and everything which is lying in the inner chambers of all their members which are in sin. And he will make these manifest in the presence of everyone with blame'. This is followed by 'Therefore, nothing of the present things should come into your heart'. As in Mt 10.26, the thought of the apocalyptic revelation brings comfort. Contrast Ecclus 12.14.

[9] γάρ is probably from Q; cf. Mk 4.22.

[10] See Jeremias, *Lukasevangelium*, pp. 86–7. Cf. Schulz, *Q*, pp. 461–2.

[11] Diogenes Laertius 1.35 (attributed to Thales).

2 Esdras 16.64–6). Therefore those on the side of the truth need have no fear.

A second version of the saying preserved in Mt 10.26 = Lk 12.2 (Q) appears in Mk 4.22[12] = Lk 8.17. Because there is between the two no sign of literary dependence, the hypothesis of translation variants seems reasonable.[13] As to the precise application on Jesus' lips, we remain in the dark. The words do envisage 'the eschatological reversal of the situation'.[14] But whether this situation was the need for esoteric teaching[15] or the presence of the hidden kingdom of God[16] or something else again[17] we do not know, for the original context has been lost.[18]

27. Although that which is hidden will be revealed (v. 26), this is something the disciples should not simply wait for or expect. They themselves are called to bring it about proleptically, that is, to make known the truth and those who belong to it. They do this by preaching the gospel of Jesus (cf. Zahn, p. 409). As in the previous verse so here too Jesus makes his point through compound parallelism. The repetition gives added force to the commands and makes them more memorable.

ὃ λέγω ὑμῖν ἐν τῇ σκοτίᾳ εἴπατε ἐν τῷ φωτί. Lk 12.3 has ἀνθ' ὧν ὅσα before ἐν and ἀκουσθήσεται after φωτί: 'Therefore whatever you have said in the dark shall be heard in the light'. ἀνθ' ὧν (Mt: 0; Mk: 0; Lk: 3) is Lukan redaction. But has Matthew turned a statement of fact into a command (and accordingly dropped ἀκουσθήσεται)?[19] This would be consistent with his desire to encourage the missionary to preach the gospel in season and out of season, under all circumstances. Still, it seems more likely that Luke has here altered Q.[20] (i) Matthew's words better fit the Q context, which has to do with fearless confession (cf. 10.32–3 = Lk 12.8–9). (ii) Luke's wording could be the result of

---

[12] 'For there is nothing hid, except to be made manifest; nor is anything secret, except to come to light'. The final form (ἵνα) may be Markan (cf. Mk 4.21).

[13] Detailed discussion in Laufen (v). According to Black, p. 114, Mark's ἐὰν μή and ἀλλά, both meaning 'except', are best explained as translation Greek. On the variant in Gos. Thom. 5 (cf. P. Oxy. 654.4) see Fitzmyer, *Background*, pp. 381–4.

[14] Jeremias, *Parables*, p. 221, n. 6.

[15] Cf. Cadoux, p. 55.

[16] Cf. W. Manson, p. 60.

[17] According to Käsemann, *Questions*, p. 99, and *Essays*, p. 41, 10.27 reinterprets the proverbial 10.26: in the end-time caution must be thrown overboard; silence is no longer possible.

[18] The version in On the Origin of the World 125.17–18 is not independent of the synoptics; see Tuckett, *Nag Hammadi*, p. 30.

[19] So many, including Schweizer, *Matthew*, p. 246; Polag, *Fragmenta*, pp. 58–9; and Gundry, *Commentary*, p. 196.

[20] So also F. Horst, *TWNT* 5, p. 554, and Laufen, pp. 160–3; pace Schulz, *Q*, p. 462.

assimilation to 12.1, where the theme is hypocrisy. (iii) The Markan doublet of 10.26 = Lk 12.2 (Mk 4.22) probably shows that the theme of apocalyptic revelation was traditionally associated with preaching the gospel (cf. Nineham, p. 141). (iv) If in Q 10.27 was already about missionary proclamation, then Matthew's placement of 10.26–31 in a missionary discourse would find a ready explanation.

What does the 'I word' in 10.27a mean for Matthew? Christian missionaries, no matter what situation they find themselves in, are not to keep quiet but must plainly declare all that they have learned from and about Jesus. The gospel is not to be hid under a bushel. The truth must be fully served even now, even if its full revelation belongs only to the future. (The contrast between light and darkness is simply the contrast between the pre- and post-Easter periods.)

καὶ ὃ εἰς τὸ οὖς ἀκούετε κηρύξατε ἐπὶ τῶν δωμάτων. Lk 12.3 has this: 'What you have whispered in private rooms shall be proclaimed upon the housetops'. The Third Evangelist has radically altered the sense. Instead of being an injunction to preach (proclaim what is whispered), Jesus' word has become a warning that what one whispers will be preached abroad. With εἰς τὸ οὖς ἀκούετε, which has no exact parallel, compare Gen 50.4; Exod 11.2; Acts 11.22; and Josephus, *Ant*. 6.165. With ἐπὶ τῶν δωμάτων compare Josh 2.6, 8; 2 Βασ 16.22; Mt 24.17; Acts 10.9; Josephus, *Ant*. 6.49; *Bell*. 2.611; *b. Šabb*. 35b. Roofs were typically flat and used for various activities.

Gos. Thom. 33 reads: 'That which you will hear in your ear (and) in the other ear, that preach from your housetops'. This is much closer to Mt 10.27 than to Lk 12.3. Dependence upon the synoptic tradition can hardly be demonstrated, for it is Luke's version that is editorial (see above).[21]

28. The subject now switches from eschatological revelation to the meaning of death. But the underlying thought remains the same: all is not what it appears to be. God's eschatological future will reveal the true meaning of earthly events.

καὶ μὴ φοβεῖσθε ἀπὸ τῶν ἀποκτεννόντων τὸ σῶμα. So Lk 12.4, with φοβηθῆτε[22] and ἀποκτεινόντων and without καί.[23] A situation of possible martyrdom is presupposed. For the sense compare 4 Macc. 13.14 ('Let us not fear him who thinks he

---

[21] On Gos. Thom. 33 see further M. Marcovich, 'Textual Criticism on the Gospel of Thomas', *JTS* 20 (1969), pp. 54–5. He finds the saying to be remodelled along Gnostic interests: one hears a saying in one ear and interprets it with the other.

[22] So B D N W Θ *f*¹ for Matthew.

[23] Luke, following Q, introduces the saying with 'But I tell you my friends'.

kills'); Sextus, *Sent.* 363b ('As a lion has power over the body of a sage, so too does a tyrant, but only over the body'); T. Job 20.3 (the devil has authority over Job's σῶμα but not his ψυχή); and Asc. Isa. 5.10. One is also reminded of the first chapter of Epictetus' *Dissertationes*. φοβέω + ἀπό could reflect LXX usage, the Hebrew *yārē'* + *min*, or the Aramaic *dĕḥal* + *min*.

τὴν δὲ ψυχὴν μὴ δυναμένων ἀποκτεῖναι. Lk 12.4 ('and after that have no more that they can do') is very different and secondary.[24] Matthew's parallelism is in this instance not redactional but preserves Q.

ψυχήν is here the disembodied 'soul' which can survive bodily death and later be reunited with a resurrected body.[25] The conception, whether due to the influence of Hellenism[26] or whether a faithful continuation of OT thought,[27] is 'dualistic'.[28] Ambrose, *De Isaac* 8.79, rightly conveys the sense: 'We do not fear him who can carry off our clothing, we do not fear him who can steal our property but cannot steal us'.

φοβεῖσθε δὲ μᾶλλον τὸν δυνάμενον καὶ ψυχὴν καὶ σῶμα ἀπολέσαι ἐν γεέννῃ. Compare Heb 10.31; Jas 4.12; Hermas, *Mand.* 12.6. ἀπό (cf. v. 28a) is dropped because in the MT *min* is rare when the object of fear is God; and ἀπό would imply an avoidance improper for the believer's relationship to his Father (cf. Lagrange, p. 208). 'Soul' and 'body' form a *chiasmus* with the 'body' and 'soul' of vv. 28a–b. καί ... καί means 'both ... and'. Lk 12.5 has: 'I will show you whom to fear. Fear him who after he has killed, has power to cast into Gehenna. Yes I tell you, fear him' (cf. Justin, *1 Apol.* 19.7; 2 Clem. 5.4; Ps.-Clem. Hom. 7.5). Matthew is again closer to Q,[29] although μᾶλλον* could be redactional; and our evangelist may have dropped 'Yes etc.' as redundant. The disciples should fear[30]

---

[24] Cf. Schulz, *Q*, p. 158, and Jeremias, *Lukasevangelium*, p. 212.

[25] For belief in a disembodied, conscious interim state combined with belief in bodily resurrection many texts could be cited; see D. S. Russell, *The Method and Message of Jewish Apocalyptic*, London, 1964, pp. 357–85.

[26] Cf. E. Schweizer, *TWNT* 9, p. 645.

[27] See R. E. Gundry, *Sōma in Biblical Theology*, SNTSMS 29, Cambridge, 1976.

[28] Cf. F. Godet, *A Commentary on the Gospel of St. Luke* (trans. of *Commentaire sur l'évangile de saint Luc*, 1888–89), 4th ed., Edinburgh, 1889, vol. 2, p. 91: 'This saying of Jesus distinguishes soul from body as emphatically as modern spiritualism ...'. Tertullian, *De res. carnis* 35, found in Mt 10.28 evidence for 'the natural immortality of the soul.' While this goes too far, our text does stand in the way of those such as O. Cullmann (*Immortality of the Soul or Resurrection of the Dead?*, London, 1958) who have argued for a profound contradiction between disembodied immortality in Hellenism and resurrection in biblical religion.

[29] See Jeremias, *Lukasevangelium*, p. 212; also Marshall (v), p. 277.

[30] φοβεῖσθε κ.τ.λ. enjoins not the intellectual reflection called for by Proverbs but fearful reverence and humble submission. Cf. Schniewind, p. 133.

God,[31] not men (cf. Isa 8.12f.), for only the former has any real
power. Further, the fear of God will eliminate the fear
of all else. As Augustine put it: 'Let us fear prudently that we may
not fear vainly' (*Hom.* 15.1; cf. 2 Macc 6.30).

Mention of the death of both body and soul in Gehenna may allude
to the universal resurrection, when all, both good and evil, will stand
before the throne of God (cf. Rev 20.11–5). See further 5.29f., where
the whole body goes into Gehenna; also C. Milikowsky, 'Which
Gehenna? Retribution and Eschatology in the Synoptic Gospels and in
Early Jewish Texts', *NTS* 34 (1988), pp. 238–49.

The aorist ἀπολέσαι[32] is usually translated 'destroy' (so e.g. RSV);
and there are some Jewish texts in which the wicked are in fact
annihilated (e.g. *t. Sanh.* 13.3; *b. Roš. Haš.* 16b–17a). It would appear,
however, that the author of Matthew shared the prevalent view that
the wicked would suffer for ever; see on 5.29.

29. 10.26f. offered encouragement by invoking eschatological
revelation, 10.28 by calling to mind the deathless soul. 10.29–31
now offers, by means of an *a fortiori* argument, a third means
of consolation: God is sovereign, so whatever happens must,
despite appearances, somehow be within his will. 'Nothing
happens without God' (Origen, *De prin.* 3.2.7). (This disallows
the false supposition that God's will is done only in the future,
as 10.26–8 might be taken to imply. The heavenly Father is not
just the guarantor of the fantastic dream which is the
eschatological future but is also the sovereign Lord of the trying
and mundane present.)

οὐχὶ δύο στρουθία ἀσσαρίου πωλεῖται; 'Are not five sparrows
sold for two pennies' appears in Lk 12.6. 'The difference between
the two versions is practically quite unimportant, although the
equation 2:5 = 1:2 does not hold mathematically. On the
purchaser's taking a large number of birds the proportional
price may well have been reduced; as we should say nowadays,
they came cheaper by the half-dozen'.[33]

An ἀσσάριον (= Latin *assarius*; *'îssār* in the Mishnah) was a small
copper Roman coin worth about 1/16th of a denarius (a day's wage;
cf. 20.1–16). 'Half-penny' gives the sense. For its proverbial lack of
value see *m. Ḥul.* 12.5. Sparrows[34] were part of the diet of the poor
and were of all birds the cheapest. See Deissmann, *Light*, pp. 272–5.
For the sparrow's insignificance see Ps 84.3.

[31] τὸν δυν. is not the devil (against Olshausen, Stier, Grundmann, Stendahl,
Meier); see Zahn, p. 409, n. 47, and Alford 1, pp. 109–10. Tertullian, *De res.* 35,
identifies τὸν δυν. with God.

[32] With ψυχή also in Barn. 20.1 and Hermas, *Sim.* 9.26.3.

[33] Deissmann, *Light*, p. 273. Schweizer, *Matthew*, p. 246 speculates: 'Perhaps
the great devaluation of silver under Nero intervened between the earlier form
in Matthew and the later form in Luke'.

[34] στρουθίον most frequently translates *ṣippôr* in the LXX.

καὶ ἓν ἐξ αὐτῶν οὐ πεσεῖται ἐπὶ τὴν γῆν ἄνευ τοῦ πατρὸς ὑμῶν. Compare *Gen. Rab.* on 33.18: 'Not even a bird is caught without the will of heaven; how much less the soul of a son of man'.[35] After αὐτῶν Lk 12.6 continues with: οὐκ ἔστιν ἐπιλελησμένον ἐνώπιον τοῦ θεοῦ. Perhaps Q had: οὐ πεσεῖται ἄνευ τοῦ θεοῦ. Matthew's 'on the earth' could be influenced by Amos 3.5: 'Does a bird fall in a snare on the earth when there is no trap for it?' πεσεῖται and ἄνευ also have parallels in LXX Amos 3.5.[36] ἄνευ τοῦ πατρὸς ὑμῶν is rightly translated by the RSV as 'without your Father's will' (cf. the addition of τῆς βουλῆς in Irenaeus, *Adv. haer.* 2.26.2; Ps.-Clem. Hom. 12.31; and many of the Latin mss.). For ἄνευ meaning 'without the knowledge and consent of' when used of persons see BAGD, s.v. Our verse is not to be interpreted in terms of God's presence. Nor, *pace* Cook (v), is God the active cause of the sparrow's fall. On the problem of providence in the synoptics see on 6.32. Whether we are to envisage a nestling falling from its nest or an adult bird dropping dead during flight, or whether 'falls to the earth' is just a figurative way of speaking of death is unclear.

30. This is probably an interpolation made by the compiler of Q or by some tradent of that source (cf. the interpolation in 6.26).

ὑμῶν δὲ καὶ αἱ τρίχες τῆς κεφαλῆς πᾶσαι ἠριθμημέναι εἰσίν. So Lk 12.7, with ἀλλά for ὑμῶν δέ,[37] ὑμῶν after κεφαλῆς,[38] ἠρίθμηνται instead of ἠριθμημέναι, and without εἰσίν. For the genitive separated from its noun see also 13.16 (ὑμῶν δέ; diff. 10.23). The καί is ascensive and means 'even'. According to Schlatter, p. 348, τῆς κεφαλῆς corresponds to Palestinian usage: because naked corpses were often seen, the unqualified expression, 'your hairs', was not sufficiently precise.[39] But the Testament of Job, which was probably penned in the Diaspora, uses the expression (23.7–8), and Schlatter himself observes its use in Philo.

The question, How many hairs does a man's head have?, was probably proverbial and at home in Jewish wisdom (cf. Apoc.

---

[35] Additional texts in SB 1, pp. 582–3. On *m. Meg.* 4.9 see on 6.26. Ancient Jews were, as compared with other ancient peoples, much less cruel towards animals (cf. Montefiore and Loewe, pp. xci–xcii); and Mt 10.29 reflects a genuine sympathy for the animal world. Only one who cared for animals would be inclined to speak of God's care for them. On animals in the synoptic tradition see Goulder, pp. 101–2.

[36] The similarities with Amos 3.5 explain why some patristic texts have εἰς (τὴν) or ἐν παγίδι; see e.g. Ps.-Clem. Hom. 12.31; Origen, *C. Cels.* 8.70; Chrysostom, *Hom. on Mt.* 34.2.

[37] So also Mt 10.30 D.

[38] So also Mt 10.30 D.

[39] To his references add 1QapGen 20.3.

Sed. 8.6: 'Since I created everything, how many people have been born, and how many have died and how many shall die and how many hairs do they have?'). Like so many Jewish wisdom texts which contrast God's omniscience with human ignorance through the naming of things only God can count,[40] Mt 10.30 implies that only God can count hairs ('are numbered' is the divine passive; cf. Ps 40.12; 69.4 and recall the biblical statements about 'the sands of the sea'). The effect is intellectual consolation. One may not understand the events that befall humanity and how they can be permitted by the divine will; but if one does not even know the number of concrete hairs on one's own mundane head, how can one presume to judge the Creator, who is beyond comprehension?[41] 4 Ezra 4.10–1 puts it this way: 'You cannot understand the things with which you have grown up; how then can your mind comprehend the way of the Most High?' (cf. T. Job 38.5). Similarly, Mt 10.30 reminds readers that while they cannot understand the trying events that befall believers and how they can be permitted by the divine will, comfort may be found in this, that God knows what his people do not.

Our verse is usually understood to be about God's watchfulness and care (cf. Gnilka, *Matthäusevangelium* 1, pp. 388–9, citing 1 Sam 14.45; 2 Sam 14.11; and *b. B. Bat.* 16a). Certainly the notion that God takes care of human hairs was proverbial. See, in addition to 1 Sam 14.45 and 2 Sam 14.11, 1 Kgs 1.52; Lk 21.18; and Acts 27.34. But all these texts take up a well-known proverb which includes mention of 'a' hair or 'one' hair as well as falling to the ground or perishing. Neither one of these elements is to be found in Mt 10.30. The verse is not about one hair but all the hairs (plural) of one head, and nothing is said about them falling or perishing. What is asserted rather is the fact that hairs are numbered. Moreover, the pertinent OT texts all have to do with deliverance from physical evil. But it is manifest that Mt 10.30 is about something very different: escape from danger is not being promised. The point about the sparrow is not that it will not fall to the ground but rather that when it does the event will somehow be within God's will. One thus wonders how 10.30 can have the same import as a proverb which promises rescue from tribulation.[42]

31. This verse does not exclude the prospect of martyrdom but rather implies that, if it comes, it will be in accord with

[40] Job 38.37; Ecclus 1.2; 4 Ezra 4.7; 1 En. 93.14; Apoc. Sed. 8.7, 9; *b. Sanh.* 39a. Full discussion in Allison, 'Hairs' (v).

[41] Cf. Origen, *De prin.* 2.11.5, where Mt 10.30–1 is cited in a discussion which relegates the understanding of providence to the future state.

[42] In a memorable example of using a text with complete disregard for its original intention, Clement of Alexandria, *Paed.* 3.3, cites Mt 10.30 to argue that men should not be hairless.

God's will.[43] Although God may not nip evil in the bud, ultimately good will out.

μὴ οὖν φοβεῖσθε. So Lk 12.7b, without the conjunction, which is here inferential.

πολλῶν στρουθίων διαφέρετε ὑμεῖς. Compare 12.12. God who, in the words of St. Basil the Great, 'lives in the highest and cares for the humblest', cares even for the sparrow. How much more deeply then must he feel for those made in his image? They must be of incomparable value.

Wellhausen, *Matthaei*, p. 49, may have been correct in detecting a mistranslation from the Aramaic. The reference to 'many sparrows' is odd, and one instead expects something like 'you are of much more value than sparrows'. Wellhausen proposed an Aramaic sentence in which 'saggi' could have been taken either with 'sparrows' (many sparrows) or with the verb ('you are of much more value').[44]

(iv) *Concluding Observations*

(1) Because the prophecies of affliction in Mt 10 are mostly stock items borrowed from Jewish apocalyptic, one might infer that they are doctrinal and unhistorical, removed from the concrete reality of Matthew's experience. 10.26–31 gives the lie to such a notion. One does not offer consolation for hypothetical suffering. If the tribulation depicted throughout chapter 10 were only theoretical and not painful in fact, our evangelist would not have interrupted his discourse with what amounts to encouraging words. As it is, the text shows a concern that missionaries not lose heart and faint in the day of adversity. Just as 6.25–34 and 7.7–11 function to encourage the listener or reader overwhelmed by the sermon on the mount, so does 10.26–31 serve to hearten and cheer the missionary whose experience is so bad that it can be interpreted as belonging to the messianic birth pangs. In sum, 10.26–31, with its gemaric thrust, reveals both the reality of Christian suffering in Matthew's world and the pastoral concern generated by that suffering.

(2) 10.26–31 poses the problem of evil in a most acute fashion. A theodicy is first attempted by means of eschatology. What matters is not the pain of the present but one's fate in the

---

[43] Chrysostom rightly continues the thought: 'Deliverance from death is not near so great as persuading men to despise death' (*Hom. on Mt.* 34.2).

[44] The sense of 10.31 can also be improved by interpreting πολλῶν as 'all'; so Jeremias, *Theology*, p. 184. Certainly πολλοί has inclusive meaning elsewhere in the NT. See Jeremias, *TWNT* 6, pp. 536–45.

world to come: 'Fear him who can destroy both soul and body in Gehenna.' But lest the reader falsely infer that God's will is to be done only in the future, vv. 29–31, through the illustration of the sparrow and an argument *a fortiori*, assert that God is sovereign even now, so whatever happens must, despite all appearances, somehow be within his will. This, however, poses the unanswerable problem. How can God be the sovereign Lord of this world with all its ills and wrongs? If our analysis of 10.30 is correct, the question is responsible for the placement of v. 30. This sentence, which awkwardly interrupts the lines about the sparrow, is what J. Wanke has called a *Kommentarwort*. Perhaps proverbial, with the meaning that God's knowledge admits no rival, it has been inserted in order to qualify the eschatological solution to the problem of evil: that solution— which Matthew fully accepts (see below)—does not solve all the difficulties. One must, in the end, follow the path taken by Job and confess human inability to fathom the depths. God is a mystery, and he knows what his creatures do not. In that should lie solace. 'But indeed all the hairs of your head are numbered.'

(3) 10.26–31 concerns itself neither with human integrity nor with the truth as such. The passage is instead an appeal to the handmaiden of faith's certainty, which is the imagination, the faculty that looks beyond the present to the future and beyond the temporal to the eternal. Faith judges the here and now by pondering what is to come (so vv. 26–8). It sets itself upon the divine outcome and from there surveys the ache and doubt and turmoil that history hands the faithful. And from that anticipated conclusion it gains boldness for the moment and confidence even in the face of death. Hope engenders freedom, above all freedom from fear (cf. the last two beatitudes). Furthermore, faith, seeing not 'with but through the eyes' (Blake), has the ability to see beneath the surface or face of the world (so vv. 29 and 31), which ability it uses to seek the secreted reality that casts its shadow upon the cave wall. One may never be able to 'find bottom in the uncomprehensive deeps' (cf. our discussion of v. 30), but it is sometimes given to human beings to glimpse the heavenly in the earthly, which permits faith to make its unlikely extrapolation: God cares even for the sparrow. There is, therefore, no need to fear. The hand of God, although invisible, is always there.

(v) *Bibliography*

D. C. Allison, 'Matthew 10.26–31 and the Problem of Evil', *SVTQ* 32 (1988), pp. 293–308.

idem, "The hairs of your head are all numbered," *ExpT* 101 (1990), pp. 334–36.

J. G. Cook, 'The Sparrow's Fall in Mt 10.29b', *ZNW* 79 (1988), pp. 138–44.

Dautzenberg, pp. 138–53.

P. Doncoeur, 'Gagner ou perdre sa ψυχή', *RSR* 35 (1948), pp. 114–19.

Jülicher 2, pp. 91–7.

Laufen, pp. 156–73.

Manson, *Sayings*, pp. 106–8.

I. H. Marshall, 'Uncomfortable Words VI. "Fear him who can destroy both soul and body in hell" (Mt 10.28 RSV)', *ExpT* 81 (1970), pp. 276–80.

H. S. Pappas, 'The "Exhortation to Fearless Confession"—Mt 10.26–33', *GOTR* 25 (1980), pp. 239–48.

Riesner, pp. 464–7.

Schulz, *Q*, pp. 157–61, 461–5.

G. Schwarz, 'Matthäus 10.28: Emendation und Rückübersetzung', *ZNW* 72 (1981), pp. 277–82.

Wanke, pp. 66–70, 76–81.

Zeller, *Mahnsprüche*, pp. 94–101.

XXIII

CONFESSION, CONFLICT, COMPENSATION
(10.32–42)

(i) *Structure*

As urged in Excursus VIII, the third portion of the second major discourse falls into three paragraphs: 10.32–3, 34–9, 40–2. It is distinguished by a total dearth of imperatives. Every sentence describes either a particular circumstance or the consequence of a particular activity.

(ii) *Sources*

Mt 10.32–42 is, on the two-source theory, an amalgam of Q, Mark, and Matthean redaction.

The evangelist opened the section by taking up where he had left off in Q (in that source 10.32–3 followed upon 10.26–31; cf. Lk 12.2–9). He next moved forward in Q, passing over material already used (cf. Lk 12.22–34, on earthly cares) and material yet to be used (cf. Lk 12.35–46, watchfulness) until coming to a group of sayings on familial strife (cf. Lk 12.51–3). Having reproduced this, he moved forward again, looking for *logia* which would continue the theme. This took him to Q's equivalent of Lk 14.26–7. He then also tacked on 10.39 = Lk 17.33, probably under Markan influence; for Mk 8.34–5 joins the saying about taking up the cross to the saying about losing one's life. Finally, Matthew returned to the conclusion of the missionary discourse in Q (cf. Lk 10.16). Determined to close with a subsection treating of the reception of missionaries, he rewrote a sentence from Q or M (10.40), added a redactional line (10.41), and ended with Mk 9.41.

(iii) *Exegesis*

CONFESSION AND DENIAL BEFORE MEN (10.32f.)

Matthew, following Q (cf. Lk 12.2–9), now returns to the task of exhortation. The demand is for courage. One must confess Jesus in public no matter what the result. The motivation is the thought of eschatological consequences. One wants to be acknowledged by Jesus, not denied by him.

10.32–3 is composed of two complementary parts. V. 32 is about confession, v. 33 (its antithesis) about denial. V. 32a stands in parallel to v. 33a, v. 32b to 33b. That is, protasis matches protasis and apodosis matches apodosis:

a   Whoever confesses . . .
b   I will confess . . .
a   Whoever denies . . .
b   I will deny . . .

This is the parallelism of the eschatological *ius talionis* (cf. 6.14–15).[1]

10.32f. = Lk 12.8f., which is independently attested in Mk 8.38[2] (cf. Mt 16.27 = Lk 9.26), probably rests upon an authentic dominical word,[3] and it finds no better background than that provided by Dan 7. Like Dan 7 the saying has to do with the last judgement, it has as its central figure the Son of man,[4] and it makes this figure an instrument of judgement.[5] Both texts also set the stage with heavenly hosts or angels. Further, Dan 7 is the Tanach's most detailed, most colourful, and most powerful picture of the great assize, and presumably any allusion to the heavenly court and the last judgement might have sent Jewish hearers, steeped as they were in the Bible, back to the *locus classicus*. Moreover, ἔμπροσθεν appears in Mt 10.32f. and has its parallel in Dan 7.13 (*qŏdām*). As the one like a son of man comes before the Ancient of days and his host, so Jesus will confess and deny men before (ἔμπροσθεν) the angels of God (cf. Rev 3.5). Finally, as Pesch (v), p. 47, has remarked, 10.32–3 par. envisages a situation of persecution: 'The "forensic" stamp of the saying is significant (ὁμο-

---

[1] Cf. also 1 Sam 2.30; Mk 4.24; 8.35; and *Sipre* on Deut 11.28 ('Everyone who confesses to idolatry denies the entire Torah and everyone who denies idolatry confesses to the entire Torah').

[2] Cf. Mt 16.27; Lk 9.26. The Markan saying is secondary; see Higgins, *JSM*, pp. 57–60, and Pesch (v), pp. 40–1; although note the caution of Beasley-Murray, pp. 291–6. Other citations of or allusions to the saying Lk 12.8–9 par. include 2 Tim 2.12; Rev 3.5; Ignatius, *Smyr.* 10.2; 2 Clem. 3.2. In each case the context concerns the persecution of Christians.

[3] See Pesch (v), pp. 35–9, and Lindars, *Son of Man*, pp. 48–58. Cf. Perrin, *Rediscovering*, pp. 190–1. For Pesch, Jesus identified himself with the apocalyptic Son of man. For Lindars, 'son of man' was an idiomatic circumlocution. (This interpretation results in a sentence very much like *m.* '*Abot.* 4.11: 'He that performs one precept gets for himself one advocate; but he that commits one transgression gets for himself one accuser'.) For Perrin, the original saying referred only to 'me'; 'the Son of man' was added by a Christian hand. This last alternative is the least probable; see F. H. Borsch, *The Christian and Gnostic Son of Man*, SBT 2/14, London, 1970, pp. 16–20; also Marshall, pp. 515–16. But then the positions of Lindars and Pesch are also not free of difficulty. See Excursus VI. For the proposal that Lk 12.8–9 par. does not go back to Jesus but instead to an early Christian prophet see Käsemann, *Questions*, pp. 77–8.

[4] To be precise, Daniel refers to 'one like a son of man'.

[5] Although the one like a son of man is in Daniel 'not explicitly said to be given the task of judging, this is implicit in the rule committed to him'; so J. G. Baldwin, *Daniel*, Tyndale Old Testament Commentaries, Leicester, 1978, p. 150.

λόγεω, ἀρνέομαι, ἔμπροσθεν), and the invitation to the personal confession of Jesus and the warning of denying him plainly speak to a situation in which Jesus was rejected, a situation with which his disciples met'. Thus, 'only within the situation of "martyrdom" in which personal testimony is advanced is the invitation to "confession" and the warning of "denial" understandable'. All this matters because Dan 7 also deals with persecution; see 7.21 and 25. There is, accordingly, one more point of correlation between the saying about confessing and denying the Son of man and Dan 7. It would appear, therefore, that 10.32f. par. is in all probability based upon Daniel's apocalyptic vision.

Mt 10.32f. par. is so important for the quest of the historical Jesus not solely because of its service for the 'Son of man' problem. The text also tells us much about Jesus' soteriology. For it makes Jesus and his proclamation the deciding factors in the coming judgement. Rejection of Jesus by those who hear him entails exclusion from the kingdom; acceptance of him brings salvation. Jesus is thus not just a revealer but the focus of God's eschatological saving action and the criterion of judgement. The implicit Christology is unmistakable as is the implicit claim to a finality beyond that of the law and its covenant.[6] In sum, Mt 10.32f. par. is one of the signs of significant theological continuity between the preaching of Jesus and the proclamation of the post-Easter community.

32. πᾶς οὖν ὅστις ὁμολογήσει ἐν ἐμοὶ ἔμπροσθεν τῶν ἀνθρώπων. So Lk 12.8, with ὃς ἄν instead of οὖν ὅστις and the aorist subjunctive instead of the future indicative. οὖν*[7] and ὅστις* are Matthean favourites. Luke preserves Q.[8] ὁμολογέω[9] is often regarded as a legal expression,[10] and Jesus may have been speaking metaphorically when he first uttered 10.32a par.: one must make the good confession in all trial-like situations. But in Matthew a more literal reading is in order. For in chapter 10 the disciples are on trial: they appear in councils and synagogues, and before governors and kings (cf. 10.17–20). So confession takes place in a legal setting. For ἔμπροσθεν—a word which underlines the public character of the disciples' confession—in connexion with standing before a judge see Sus 29; Mt 25.32; 27.11; Lk 21.36; 2 Cor 5.10. Our evangelist probably identified the 'men' of vv. 32a and 33a with the hostile

[6] Cf. D. C. Allison, Jr., 'Jesus and the Covenant: A Response to E. P. Sanders', *JSNT* 29 (1987), pp. 57–78.

[7] The conjunction is intensive, not inferential; cf. 12.12 and BAGD, s.v., 3. Some commentators (e.g. Bonnard, p. 153) have wanted to see 10.32–3 as climactic, as bringing to a conclusion 10.26–31. This seems artificial. 10.26–31 is an interruption with which 10.32–3 has nothing more than a formal connexion.

[8] See Pesch (v), p. 28. In Luke our saying is introduced with 'I say to you'. This or 'Amen, I say to you' may very well have stood in Q; see Pesch (v), pp. 30–5.

[9] Which means 'acknowledge' or 'declare allegiance to'. Cf. the Hebrew *hôdâ + bĕ* and the Aramaic *'ôdî + bĕ*.

[10] See esp. O. Michel, *TWNT* 5, pp. 207–8. Cf. Mt 7.23; Acts 24.14; 1 Tim 6.12. But note Catchpole, 'Son of Man' (v), pp. 257–9.

authorities before whom accused missionaries were forced to speak (cf. 10.19–20).

ὁμολογήσω κἀγὼ ἐν αὐτῷ ἔμπροσθεν τοῦ πατρός μου τοῦ ἐν οὐρανοῖς.[11] This promise, which sets forth the condition of entrance into the kingdom, is Matthew's revision of Lk 12.8b = Q: 'also the Son of man will acknowledge before the angels (of God)'.[12] κἀγὼ (Mt: 9; Mk: 0; Lk: 6) is Matthean, as is 'my Father in (the) heavens' (cf. Mk 8.38).[13] Matthew will probably have thought of Jesus sitting on a throne at the last judgement (cf. 19.28; 25.31–46).[14]

33. Promise (v. 32) now becomes warning (v. 33), and it is upon this last that most of the weight falls.

ὅστις δ'ἄν ἀρνήσηταί με ἔμπροσθεν τῶν ἀνθρώπων.[15] Compare Lk 12.9: ὁ δὲ ἀρνησάμενός με ἐνώπιον τῶν ἀνθρώπων. Q probably began with ὅς (cf. Lk 12.8) and continued with what Matthew has preserved.[16] For denial[17] elsewhere in Matthew see 26.34, 35, 69–75.

ἀρνήσομαι κἀγὼ αὐτὸν ἔμπροσθεν τοῦ πατρός μου τοῦ ἐν οὐρανοῖς.[18] Compare 7.23; 25.12. Lk 12.9b (ἀπαρνηθήσεται ἐνώπιον τῶν ἀγγέλων τοῦ θεοῦ) has probably been assimilated to v. 9a, just as Mt 10.33b has been assimilated to v. 32b. Q may have had this: 'also the Son of man will deny him before the angels (of God)'.[19]

TRIBULATION AND FAMILIAL DIVISION (10.34–9)

In 10.34–9 the evangelist returns to two themes already

---

[11] τοις after εν appears in B f[13] 565 892 al. HG omits. NA[26] prints in brackets. The data is much the same for 10.33, where HG and NA[26] again disagree.

[12] Cf. Catchpole, 'Son of Man' (v), pp. 255–6. 'Me' replaces 'the Son of man' in Mt 5.12 = Lk 6.23. Perhaps 'of God' is Lukan redaction; see Jeremias, Lukasevangelium, pp. 208–9, 213.

[13] Both Rev 3.5 and 2 Clem. 3.2 have πατρός μου. This would seem to indicate Matthean influence, although this has been disputed (cf. Donfried, pp. 60–1). πατρός also appears in Mk 8.38: 'when the Son of man comes in the glory of his Father with the holy angels'.

[14] In Mk 8.38 Jesus is the judge. In Q he may have been thought of as an advocate (= pĕraqlîṭ in the rabbis) or accuser (= qāṭêgôr in the rabbis).

[15] So HG and NA[26]. B L 1424 pc omit αν.

[16] See Pesch (v), pp. 28–9.

[17] Note H. Riesenfeld, 'The Meaning of the Verb ἀρνεῖσθαι', ConNT 11 (1947), pp. 207–19, and C. K. Barrett, 'I am not ashamed of the Gospel', in New Testament Essays, London, 1972, pp. 116–43.

[18] HG, following C L f[13] Maj, prints αυτον καγω. NA[26], on the authority of P[19] ℵ B D W Δ Θ f[1] 33 892 al, is probably correct to print the opposite order, for it maintains the perfect parallelism with v. 32b.

[19] So Pesch (v), p. 30. Mk 8.38 has 'the Son of man' in both the protasis and apodosis of the denial saying.

introduced: eschatological tribulation and division within families. The effect is two-fold. First, the eschatological nature of suffering is emphasized. Secondly, the priority of Jesus and his way over against all earthly ties, including the strongest, family ties, is inculcated.

The section falls into two parts. 10.34–6 is declarative, 10.37–9 paraenetic; and the one is the basis for the other. 10.34–6 sets forth the character of Jesus' coming. He came not to bring peace but a sword, and his arrival brings to fulfilment the eschatological prophecy of Mic 7.6: a man's enemies can be those of his own household. 10.37–9 then draws out the implications of 10.34–6: one must not love father or mother more than Jesus. One must be prepared to face domestic strife, to take up the cross, to lose one's life in this world (cf. Deut 33.9; Philo, *De praem.* 17).

10.34–9 contains, like so many other Matthean passages, several triads. The first half (vv. 34–6) contains three 'I came' sentences as well as three pairs of family members (κατά being used in each case, that is, three times). And the second half (vv. 37–9) is comprised of three lines whose parallelism makes their triadic arrangement unmistakable:

37a καὶ ὁ φιλῶν . . .
37b καὶ ὁ φιλῶν . . .

38   καὶ ὃς οὐ λαμβάνει . . .

39a   ὁ εὑρών . . .
39b καὶ ὁ ἀπολέσας . . .

Note also that 'he is not worthy of me' appears three times in vv. 37–8.

34. This and the following verse, which Matthew took from Q (cf. Lk 12.51, 53[20]), form an indissoluble unit that faithfully preserves words of Jesus.[21] Their dominical intention has been rightly understood by the First Evangelist.

μὴ νομίσητε ὅτι ἦλθον βαλεῖν εἰρήνην ἐπὶ τὴν γῆν. Contrast 5.9.[22] Lk 12.51a has the same sense but different wording:

[20] Note also Mk 13.13. Lk 12.52 ('for henceforth in one house there will be five divided, three against two and two against three') is probably Lukan; cf. Schulz, *Q*, pp. 258–9. On ἀπὸ τοῦ νῦν and chiasmus see Jeremias, *Lukasevangelium*, pp. 60, 224.

[21] See Allison (v) and Mussner (v), pp. 165–7.

[22] The evangelist has done nothing to indicate how he harmonized 5.9 and 10.39. How could Jesus praise peacemakers and then announce that he did not come to bring peace but a sword? And what about the command to speak peace upon entering a house? Although these questions were raised by later exegetes (see e.g. Chrysostom, *Hom. on Mt.* 35.1), the text is silent. Yet perhaps 10.12–15 holds an answer. The missionary should send forth a blessing of peace when he enters a lodging; but if the place rejects the gospel, then the blessing of peace must be retracted. Thus the disciple, though a peacemaker, does not purchase peace at any price. When Jesus and his messengers are not received, there cannot but be conflict and division.

δοκεῖτε ὅτι εἰρήνην παρεγενόμην δοῦναι ἐν τῇ γῇ; μὴ νομίσητε may be Matthean; otherwise Mt 10.34a would seem to reproduce Q.[23] On 'I came' sentences see on 5.17.[24] 'To cast peace'—which sounds so strange in English—is a Semitism which means 'to bring peace' (cf. the Hebrew idiom, *hiṭṭîl šālôm*).[25] ἐπὶ τὴν γῆν in its Matthean context must mean 'on the earth'. On Jesus' lips it could have meant 'on the land (of Israel)'.

οὐκ ἦλθον βαλεῖν εἰρήνην ἀλλὰ μάχαιραν. Compare Ezek 38.21 and 2 En 52.14.[26] Lk 12.51b has this: 'No, I say to you, but rather division (διαμερισμόν)'. Although one can hardly decide whether Matthew has increased the parallelism (cf. 5.17) or whether Luke has changed the sentence structure, Luke's 'division' for 'sword' does appear to be secondary.[27] For the sword within prophecies of eschatological affliction see Isa 66.16; Wisd 5.20; Ecclus 39.30; Jub. 9.15; 1 En 62.12; 63.11; 90.19; 91.11–12; 4QPsDanA[a];[28] Ps. Sol. 15.7; Sib. Or. 3.797–9; 4.174; 2 Bar. 27.5; 40.1; Lk 21.24; Rev 6.4. It involves both strife and persecution and embraces the thought of martyrdom. For a retranslation of 10.34b into Aramaic see Albright and Mann, p. 130. (*Pace* Tertullian, *Adv. Marc.* 3.14, and others, the sword of which Jesus speaks is not, despite Eph 6.14–17 and Rev 1.16, the divine word.)

10.34 is about the proper interpretation of the present, and the main point is this: the time of Jesus and his church is not, despite the presence of the kingdom of God, the messianic era of peace. Jesus has not come 'to turn the hearts of fathers to their children and the hearts of children to their fathers' (Mal 4.6).[29] As Hahn has written, 'with the coming of Jesus the ultimate age of peace has not yet dawned, but instead the last struggle has broken out. In what way this struggle is to be

[23] So Harnack, pp. 86–7; *pace* Gundry, *Commentary*, p. 199. παραγίνομαι is a Lukan favourite: Mt: 3; Mk: 1; Lk: 8; Acts: 20. Against Jeremias, *Lukasevangelium*, p. 193, δοκέω + ὅτι is probably Lukan (Mt: 2; Mk: 1; Lk: 4); cf. Lk 19.11 and see Jeremias, *ibid.*, pp. 277–8. ἦλθον βαλεῖν ἐπὶ τὴν γῆν appears in Lk 12.49 (which has no parallel in Matthew). So that verse, whether or not it stood in Q, shows knowledge of the form of expression used in Mt 10.34a.

[24] To the prophetic texts there cited add 2 Bar. 3.1.

[25] See Schlatter, p. 349, and SB 1, p. 586, for texts. For possible Aramaic equivalents see Arens, p. 84.

[26] This last surely depends upon Matthew: 'there is no peace but a sword in his heart'.

[27] So rightly Mussner (v), pp. 165–6. Cf. Black (v), p. 116: 'a deliberate softening of the harsher expression in Matthew'.

[28] On this see Fitzmyer, *Aramean*, pp. 90–3, 102–7.

[29] McNeile, p. 147, raised an interesting possibility: the saying may have meant, in effect, 'I am not Elijah, since Elijah's work includes reconciliation and the bringing of peace'.

carried on is not stated, but the fact that now more than ever is the time of confrontation, is decisive. μάχαιρα in its antithesis to εἰρήνην must denote every kind of dispeace'.[30] In other words, the advent of the kingdom must not lead to a utopian view of the here and now: the enthusiastic extremes of 'over-realized eschatology' must be avoided, for all has not yet come to pass. Tribulation is still the believer's lot. One is reminded of Paul's rebuke of the Corinthians: the present is not the time to be filled or rich; it is not the time for strength or honour. Rather is it the time for suffering, for hunger, for homelessness, for being reviled (1 Cor 4.8–13).

35. This sentence is based upon Mic 7.6, which was not an important text for the early church. Apart from our passage and Mk 13.12 = Mt 10.21 (which may be a later development of the more original Q form), it is nowhere cited or alluded to in any extant Christian literature of the first century.

ἦλθον γὰρ διχάσαι ἄνθρωπον κατὰ τοῦ πατρὸς αὐτοῦ καὶ θυγατέρα κατὰ τῆς μητρὸς αὐτῆς καὶ νύμφην κατὰ τῆς πενθερᾶς αὐτῆς. Compare Philo, *De praem.* 134. As the sword splits in half, so does Jesus divide families. Lk 12.53 is similar.[31] νύμφη, which usually means 'bride', comes in the LXX to mean 'daughter-in-law', and that is its meaning here.[32] 'Note that there is no mention of son-in-law, since it was the new wife who moved into her husband's house, not the husband into the wife's family. The daughter mentioned in the saying would probably be the unmarried daughter, since she is still around to conflict with her mother.'[33]

The meaning of 10.35 is determined by the Jewish parallels. The verse is based upon Mic 7.6, which was drawn upon to describe the discord of the latter days (cf. Grelot (v)). *m. Soṭa* 9.15 reads as follows: with the footprints of the Messiah, 'children shall shame the elders, and the elders shall rise up before the children, for the son dishonoureth the father, the daughter riseth up against her mother, the daughter-in-law against her mother-in-law: a man's enemies are the men of his own house'. Similar statements are to be found in Jub. 23.16, 19; 1 En. 56.7; 100.1–2; Mk 13.12; 4 Ezra 5.9; 6.24; 2 Bar. 70.3,

---

[30] *Titles*, p. 153. While Hahn writes of the historical Jesus, his words are equally applicable to Matthew's viewpoint. Attempts to relate Jesus to the Zealots or to political revolutionaries by way of the saying about the sword should be dismissed: there is too much clear evidence pointing in the other direction. See also Davies, *Land*, pp. 336–344.

[31] Luke has ἐπί instead of κατά. Cf. LXX Mic 7.6.

[32] Cf. J. Jeremias, *TWNT* 4, pp. 1092–99.

[33] B. J. Malina, *The New Testament World: Insights from Cultural Anthropology*, Atlanta, 1981, p. 101.

7; LAB 6.1; *b. Sanh.* 97a. The conviction that the great tribulation would turn those of the same household against one another was clearly widespread. It follows that 10.35, like 10.34, comprehends the ministry of Jesus and the time of the church in terms of the eschatological woes. Jesus came not to bring peace but a sword, that is, division (cf. Justin, *Dial.* 35.3). His appearance coincides with—or, rather, causes—a crisis that divides even the members of one household, separating the faithful from the unfaithful (cf. 1 Cor 11.18–19). So the eschatological trial, the time of the fulfilment of Mic 7.6, has broken in with the appearance of Jesus; and before the messianic age of peace establishes itself, all must pass through affliction and suffer pain (cf. Acts 14.22; Barn. 7.11). As chaos and darkness came before the first creation (Gen 1.2), so division and strife must come before the second creation: the last things are as the first (cf. on 1.1). Thus, for the present, conflict, not concord, reigns. Rev 6.4, which also contains the antithesis, peace/sword, offers a good parallel. Here the time of tribulation and judgement has come, which means the giving of a sword and the taking of peace. 'And another horse came forth, bright red; its rider was permitted to take peace from the earth, so that men should slay one another; and he was given a great sword'. The absence of peace and the presence of the sword is a sign of the great tribulation. And it is in this great tribulation that the Matthean church must carry on its mission.

36. This line continues the quotation of Mic 7.6. It has no parallel in Luke and is probably editorial.

καὶ ἐχθροὶ τοῦ ἀνθρώπου οἱ οἰκιακοὶ αὐτοῦ. Compare 10.25. The τοῦ is generic. The οἰκιακοί are not slaves but household relatives (so BAGD, s.v.). LXX Mic 7.6 is very different from Matthew's text. 10.36 is closer to the MT: 'ōyĕbê 'iš 'anšê bêtô.[34] Has Matthew consulted or remembered the Hebrew?

Gos. Thom. 16 reads: 'Men possibly think that I have come to cast peace on the world and they do not know that I have come to cast divisions upon the earth: fire, sword, war. For there shall be five in a house: three shall be against two and two against three, the father against the son and the son against the father, and they will stand as solitaries'. If our tradition-history is correct, this shows Lukan influence ('divisions', 'three against two, two against three', 'father against son, son against father'). One might also detect Matthean influence in the use of 'sword', but this is far less certain (since 'sword' was in Q).

37. The subject now shifts slightly, from Jesus' effect upon families to what the disciple should do.

---

[34] See further Stendahl, *School*, pp. 90–1; Gundry, *OT*, pp. 78–9.

ὁ φιλῶν πατέρα ἢ μητέρα ὑπὲρ ἐμὲ οὐκ ἔστιν μου ἄξιος· καὶ ὁ
φιλῶν υἱὸν ἢ θυγατέρα ὑπὲρ ἐμὲ οὐκ ἔστιν μου ἄξιος. Lk 14.26 is
distinctly different: 'If any one comes to me and does not hate
his own father and mother and wife and children and brothers
and sisters, yes, and even his own life, he cannot be my disciple'
(cf. the list of accusatives in Mk 10.29 par.). With the exception
of ἔτι δὲ καί, this contains nothing characteristically Lukan.[35]
Mt 10.37 is probably a heavily redacted version of what appears
in Luke. The perfect parallelism is a sign of Matthew's hand (cf.
10.39), and the vocabulary is editorial.[36] The major motivation
for rewriting 10.37 was the desire to create two parallel clauses
that would match the two parallel clauses in v. 39. Note also
that Q's very Semitic 'does not hate'[37] has been altered to the
less offensive but still accurate 'love more'.

10.37 is all but universally credited to Jesus. The saying requires that
family ties, if they in any way become a hindrance to discipleship, must
be broken. 'The verse is not an attack on family relationships and
natural attachments, but is a clear insistence that following Jesus is
more important than family ties; if it is necessary to choose between
the two loyalties, then a man ought to choose to follow Jesus'.[38]
Compare m. B. Meṣ. 2.11: service to one's teacher comes before service
to one's father.

Gos. Thom. 55 shows in turn agreements with both Matthew and
Luke: 'Whoever does not hate his father and his mother will not be
able to be a disciple to me, and (whoever does not) hate his brethren
and his sisters and (does not) take up his cross in my way will not be
worthy of me' (cf. 101). 'Hate' and 'brethen' and 'sisters' appear in
Luke and probably belonged to Q. But 'will not be worthy of me' is,
we have urged, Matthean redaction. So the text of Thomas would
appear not to be free of canonical influence.

38. For Matthew, the cross is, as 10.39 makes plain, the
outstanding symbol of self-denial. The connexion with v. 37 is
patent: to break with the family is to take up the cross and lose
one's life in this world.

The saying about the cross appears five times in the synoptics: Mt
10.38; 16.24; Mk 8.34; Lk 9.23; 14.27. Mt 16.24 and Lk 9.23 derive
from Mk 8.34. Mt 10.38 and Lk 14.27 are from Q. The Markan

[35] See Jeremias, Lukasevangelium, p. 241.

[36] φιλέω: Mt: 5; Mk: 1; Lk: 2. ἤ: Mt: 60; Mk: 33; Lk: 45. ὑπέρ + accusative: Mt: 4;
Mk: 0; Lk: 2. ἄξιος: the word appears seven times in chapter 10. Pace Manson,
Teaching, pp. 237–8, there is no need to regard 'he is not worthy of me' and 'he is not
able to be my disciple' as translation variants. For ἄξιος used of martyrs see 2 Macc
7.29; Rev 3.4; 16.6.

[37] On this Semitic idiom see on 6.24. Matthew never uses 'hate' in a positive
sense.

[38] So Hill, Matthew, p. 195. For obvious reasons, 10.37 has been important
for Christian monasticism (cf. Vita Pachomii Gr. 37).

version ('If any man would come after me, let him deny himself and take up his cross and follow me'), which issues a challenge instead of declaring a negation, would appear to be more primitive.[39]

καὶ ὃς οὐ λαμβάνει τὸν σταυρὸν αὐτοῦ καὶ ἀκολουθεῖ ὀπίσω μου, οὐκ ἔστιν μου ἄξιος. Compare Jn 12.26.[40] Lk 14.27 has the same sense but different words: ὅστις οὐ βαστάζει[41] τὸν σταυρόν ἑαυτοῦ καὶ ἔρχεται ὀπίσω μου, οὐ δύναται εἶναί μου μαθητής. 'He is not worthy of me' is Matthean (cf. 10.37), as is the first verb (λαμβάνω*). ἔρχεται is Lukan (cf. Mk 8.34; Lk 9.23). On 'following' Jesus see on 8.19. Matthew's second καί probably equals οὐδέ, although some would translate 'and yet' (so BDF § 445.3).

The interpretation of the original meaning of 'take up his cross' has been much discussed, without any consensus emerging.[42] These are the major alternatives: (i) The expression was a pre-Christian catch-phrase, perhaps associated with political revolutionaries. When Jesus applied it to his followers he was exhorting them to ready themselves for punishment by the Romans.[43] (ii) Jesus, foreseeing the fate that did in fact befall him, demanded of his followers preparation for the same or a similar fate.[44] Or the church, after the event, formulated the saying with a view towards martyrdom.[45] (iii) Jesus originally spoke of 'taking up his yoke' (cf. Mt 11.29). After Easter 'yoke' became 'cross'.[46] (iv) Jesus, whose audience was familiar with the sight of a condemned man carrying his cross,[47] asked his listeners to take up their crosses only in a metaphorical manner: taking the road of discipleship and self-denial is like carrying a cross to the site of execution.[48] (v) The saying, understood metaphorically, had to do with the mark of the *Taw*, the last letter of the Hebrew alphabet (ת), sometimes represented by X or T,[49] and which in Ezek 9.4–6 is God's signature (cf. Job 31.35), a sign

[39] So also Pesch 2, p. 61; Laufen, pp. 304–8; for another view see Schürmann, *Lukasevangelium* 1, pp. 541–2.

[40] This is presumably an abbreviated version of our saying; cf. Lindars, *John*, p. 430.

[41] Cf. Jn 19.17: βαστάζων ἑαυτῷ τὸν σταυρόν.

[42] For a survey of opinion see Schneider (v), pp. 578–9.

[43] Cf. Schlatter, pp. 350–1; and Griffiths (v). But 'take up his cross' is not attested in pre-Christian Semitic sources. (There also appear to be no profane examples of λαμβάνειν or αἴρειν τὸν σταυρόν.)

[44] So Chrysostom, *Hom. on Mt.* 35.3, and Manson, *Sayings*, p. 131.

[45] This view is taken by many who deny that Jesus foresaw for himself a terrible end.

[46] Cf. Fitzmyer, *Luke* 1, pp. 785–6; also Schwarz (v). The rabbis often spoke of taking up the yoke of the law or the yoke of the kingdom. (Schwarz (v) proposes an Aramaic original in which Jesus said, 'Every one who wants to come after me, must know himself and carry my yoke'.)

[47] Or, more exactly, the cross-beam (*patibulum*). See on 27.32, also Hengel, *Leader*, p. 58, n. 76.

[48] Cf. Hill, *Matthew*, p. 195; Fletcher (v).

[49] See J. Finegan, 'Crosses in the Dead Sea Scrolls', *BAR* 5 (1979), pp. 40–9. The Greeks turned the Hebrew ת into a vertical cross, T.

of those who belong to Yahweh, a cultic seal that protects from judgement (cf. Ps. Sol. 15.8–10; Rev 7.2–3; 14.1; Odes Sol. 8.13). Only after the passion did the *Taw* come to be interpreted as a cross. Jesus himself only intended to call people to dedicate themselves to God and to prepare themselves for the coming assize.[50] (vi) The saying originally referred to the sufferings of Isaac (who carried wood on his shoulders) and intended these to be paradigmatic: Jesus' followers must, like Abraham's son, be prepared to offer themselves up as a sacrifice.[51]

Whatever the original meaning of 10.38, and whether or not it goes back to Jesus himself, Matthew's intention is plain enough. 10.38 is interpreted by its context. 'Cross' is in the first instance a vivid metaphor which stands for utter self abnegation (cf. the exposition of Calvin, *Inst.* 3.8). The disciples must voluntarily deny themselves (10.39). That is, they must selflessly engage in Christian service—even if it ruins their families. At the same time, in some cases the afflictions attendant upon self-denial will include suffering and death (cf. 10.17–25)—with the result that the cross as metaphor may give way to the cross as literal object. But then the disciple can ask for nothing better. Jesus himself took up his cross both figuratively and literally.[52] (What personal agonies and tensions are involved in all this Matthew does not allude to; but that he, who is so pastoral elsewhere, was aware of them we do not doubt; see section (iv).)

39. Again we have a Markan/Q overlap. Mt 10.39 = Lk 17.33 represents Q[53] while the doublet Mt 16.25 = Lk 9.24 depends upon Mk 8.35. There is also a variant in Jn 12.25.[54]

Because the sayings about self-denial (10.39) and taking up one's cross (10.38) are joined in Mark and appear to have been joined also in Q and in the tradition behind the Fourth Gospel (cf. Jn 12.26), the connexion must have been very early indeed. Perhaps the link was even forged by Jesus himself. Perhaps he interpreted his enigmatic saying about cross-bearing in terms of losing one's life. The authenticity of 10.39 par. is widely—and rightly—accepted. The saying has multiple attestation; Mk 8.35 and its Q counterpart could easily be translation variants;[55] the theme of self-denial was surely part and parcel of Jesus' message (and took on flesh in his actions); and Jesus was fond of riddles or paradoxes.[56]

[50] See the works of Dinkler cited in the bibliography. Several church Fathers identified the sealing of Rev 7.2–3 and 14.1 with the sign of the cross (e.g. Cyprian, *Ad Quirinum* 2.22).

[51] So O'Neill (v), who stresses the willingness of Isaac in Jewish tradition. Cf. Irenaeus, *Adv. haer.* 4.5.4: 'Righteously also do we, possessing the same faith as Abraham, and taking up the cross as Isaac did the wood, follow Him' (the Word).

[52] Cf. 20.23 and Zumstein, pp. 228–9.

[53] See Laufen, pp. 315–8.

[54] This may well be independent of the synoptics; so Dodd, *Tradition*, pp. 338–43. The saying is closest to Mt 10.39.

[55] See McNeile, pp. 148–9, and Black, pp. 188, 195–6.

[56] See Jeremias, *Theology*, pp. 30–1.

ὁ εὑρὼν τὴν ψυχὴν αὐτοῦ ἀπολέσει αὐτήν, καὶ ὁ ἀπολέσας τὴν ψυχὴν αὐτοῦ ἕνεκεν ἐμοῦ εὑρήσει αὐτήν. Compare b. Tamid 32a.[57] Matthew has made the sentence conform to the structure of 10.37 (ὁ εὑρών instead of ὃς ἐάν + aorist subjunctive, ὁ ἀπολέσας instead of ὃς ἐὰν ἀπολέσῃ) and added 'for my sake' (cf. 16.25; Mk 8.35). For his part, Luke (17.33) has added ζητήσῃ … περιποιήσασθαι and ζῳογονήσει and omitted as redundant the second appearance of 'his life'.[58] On the whole, therefore, Matthew is closer to Q and in this instance preserves Q's parallelism.

The emphasis in v. 39 is not upon literally losing one's life (martyrdom) but upon rigorous self-denial. Yet given the broader context, martyrdom is not, for Matthew, altogether out of view (cf. our comments on 10.38). Certainly 10.39 could be fittingly applied to such a situation: those who save their lives by dissociating themselves from Jesus will lose eternal life while those who lose their lives for Jesus' sake will find eternal life. For εὑρίσκω meaning 'win' or 'preserve' see BAGD, s.v. On the meaning of ψυχή see Dautzenberg (v). It does not here mean 'soul' (contrast 10.28) but 'life', perhaps even 'self.' Compare Gen 19.17; 1 Sam 19.11. Matthew probably saw in 10.39 a pronouncement about eschatology: he who loses his life in this world—because he looks only to God (cf. 6.25–34)—will win it for the world to come; and he who wins his life for this world—that is, seeks to secure his earthly existence (cf. Lk 12.16–21)—will lose it in the world to come (cf. Jn 12.25).[59] Unbounded faith in God courageously looks beyond this world and the boundary of death to the eschatological future which God will give to his own. (Does our saying not presuppose the resurrection?)[60]

ON WELCOMING MISSIONARIES (10.40–2)

The missionary discourse winds down with promissory words in which the disciples are not active but passive: they are received and served (contrast the thrust of vv. 37–9). One is reminded of the opening section, 10.5–15, which also treats of the reception

---

[57] 'What shall a man do to live? They replied: Let him mortify himself. What should a man do to kill himself? They replied: Let him keep himself alive'. Note also the parallel in Epictetus, Diss. 4.1.165 ('saved by death').

[58] Cf. Jeremias, Lukasevangelium, pp. 269–70; Polag, Fragmenta, pp. 78–9.

[59] So too Jesus himself; cf. Pesch 2, p. 62.

[60] Is it possible that Paul's frequent references to being 'crucified with Christ' have anything to do with the saying about cross – bearing?

of the gospel and its emissaries. 10.40–2, however, broaches a theme absent from 10.5–15, namely, that of compensation. Those who welcome the eschatological messengers of Jesus in effect welcome Jesus himself and gain for themselves reward. With this thought, which makes the decision for or against the missionaries equivalent to the decision for or against Jesus, chapter 10 comes to its close.

Once again Matthew's love of the triad is on display. 10.40–2 contains three sentences. μισθός* is used three times, as are εἰς ὄνομα*, προφήτης, and δίκαιος*. Three clauses begin with (καὶ) ὁ δεχόμενος. And after the general introductory statement (10.40), the subject is first prophets, then the just, then 'little ones'.[61]

40. Lk 10.16 has this: 'He who hears you hears me, and he who rejects you rejects me, and he who rejects me rejects him who sent me'.[62] Clearly Q's missionary discourse ended with a statement equating rejection or reception of Christian missionaries with rejection (so Luke; cf. 1 Thess 4.8[63]) or reception (so Matthew) of Jesus himself. Perhaps the positive formulation is due to Matthew's desire to give both thematic and formal consistency to vv. 40–2.[64] But if so, then Jn 13.20 ('he who receives any one whom I send receives me; and he who receives me receives him who sent me'; cf. 12.44–5)[65] almost certainly shows the influence of Matthew. The alternative is to suppose that the positive formulation (Mt 10.40) already appeared in Q[mt] or that for Lk 10.16 = Q Matthew substituted a similar saying known from the oral tradition (M).[66]

---

[61] The repetition of words in 10.40–2 does not justify the assertion of Fenton, p. 166: 'The paragraph is made up of separate sayings, which have been placed side by side because of words or phrases which are common to them . . .'. The sayings have been redacted so that they have a thematic unity; and the common vocabulary is largely due to the editor's own hand.

[62] This probably concluded Q's missionary discourse. So also Bultmann, *History*, p. 143; Manson, *Sayings*, p. 78. Against Hoffmann, *Logienquelle*, pp. 285–6, who finds Luke's form to be secondary as compared with Mt 10.40, see Schmid, *Verhältnisses*, pp. 278–9; Catchpole, 'Poor' (v), pp. 357–8; Riesner, p. 462.

[63] 'Whoever disregards this, disregards not man but God, who gives his Holy Spirit to you'. This could very well reflect Paul's knowledge of a missionary discourse close to that in Q; see Allison, 'Paul' (in the bibliography to 10.5–25).

[64] Mk 9.37 might also have influenced the formulation. Cf. Mt 18.5; Lk 9.48. Catchpole, 'Poor' (v), pp. 357–8, sees 10.40 as a conflation of Mk 9.37 and Lk 10.16 = Q.

[65] On 12.44–5 see P. Borgen, 'The Use of Tradition in John 12.44–50', *NTS* 26 (1979), pp. 23–6. He argues for independence from the synoptics.

[66] Cf. Bultmann, *History*, p. 143: 'The relationship of Lk 10.16 to the Mark – Matthew saying seems to me to be this: Matthew and Luke found the saying at the end of the missionary commission. Luke reproduced it, while Matthew replaced it with a passage from another tradition in vv. 40, 42, and so the version of v. 40 was influenced by the Q saying (Lk 10.16)'. In favour of the

ὁ δεχόμενος ὑμᾶς ἐμὲ δέχεται. Compare Jn 13.20; Ignatius, *Eph.* 6.1–2; Justin, *1 Apol.* 63. This is a statement of the *sālîaḥ* principle: the apostles are as the one who sends them (see on 10.2). Similar formulations can be found in rabbinic literature (e.g. *Mek.* on Exod 14.31 and *Sipre* on Num 12.8). It is presupposed that the apostles have been sent by Jesus (cf. 10.5 and 16). For δέχομαι see on 10.14. 'The one who receives you receives me' has two effects. To begin with, it magnifies the apostolic mission. It is not just that the cause of Jesus and his demands live on in the Christian missionaries. Rather, behind the ever-changing faces of the preachers of the gospel there stands the Son of God himself, and behind him God the Father. The authority of the exalted Jesus and his presence have been given to the disciples (cf. 28.16–20), with the result that they have become, to use a Pauline metaphor, members of his body. Master and servant are, in a sense, one. Secondly, if the missionaries are truly persuaded that those who receive them—reception involves both hospitality and faith in their message—truly receive Jesus, then it would hardly be thinkable to give up the missionary task, no matter how great its pains (cf. Schlatter, p. 352). The work, by its very nature, requires perseverance.

καὶ ὁ ἐμὲ δεχόμενος δέχεται τὸν ἀποστείλαντά με. Compare 1 Clem. 42.1–2. *Mek.* on Exod 18.12 contains a similar thought: 'everyone who welcomes (*qibbēl*) his fellow man is as though he had welcomed the Shekinah'. Particularly close is Jn 13.20: ὁ δὲ ἐμὲ λαμβάνων λαμβάνει τὸν πέμψαντά με. This could, obviously, be a translation variant of Matthew's line. On the other hand, John's wording could be explained as due to word preference. δέχομαι occurs only once in John, λαμβάνω over forty times. And while the Fourth Evangelist hardly avoids ἀποστέλλω (Jn: 28), he is fond of πέμπω (Jn: 32).

41. ὁ δεχόμενος προφήτην εἰς ὄνομα προφήτου μισθὸν προφήτου λήμψεται. A redactional origin for this verse seems likely.[67] It has no canonical parallel. The vocabulary is editorial.[68] On prophets in Matthew's community see on 7.15. They should be thought of as itinerant teachers. On the concept of eschatological reward see on 6.21. εἰς ὄνομα is a Semitism meaning 'because he is' (cf. *lĕšēm* and the Greek idiom, εἰς

pre – Matthean origin of 10.40 is the possibility that Matthew's 'receiving' and Luke's 'hearing' are translation variants of the Aramaic *qĕbal*; see Manson, *Sayings*, p. 78. See further Dodd, *Tradition*, pp. 343–7, for a detailed argument against the literary dependence of Jn 13.20 upon Matthew.
[67] Cf. Catchpole, 'Poor' (v), pp. 360–1; Gundry, *Commentary*, p. 202; Brooks (v).
[68] εἰς + ὄνομα*, μισθός*, λαμβάνω.*

λόγον). It makes the reward depend not upon the deed itself but its intention.

The 'reward' of 10.41a is usually taken to be eschatological: to receive a prophet is to share in his work and therefore to share in his reward on the last day (cf. the 'reward' in 10.42). The genitive (προφήτου), however, could be one of origin, in which case those who receive a prophet will be rewarded by the prophet, that is, will hear his words—just as the reward δικαίου would be hearing the words of a just man.[69]

καὶ ὁ δεχόμενος δίκαιον εἰς ὄνομα δικαίου μισθὸν δικαίου λήμψεται. This reproduces the redactional vocabulary of the previous line, which it parallels perfectly. There is on the literal level tension with 9.13, where Jesus does not call the righteous but sinners. Here δίκαιος is unequivocally positive. It probably denotes one who teaches righteousness.[70] 'Prophets' and 'just men' will again be paired in 13.17 and 23.29.

It would be hazardous to divine in 10.40–2 conclusions about Matthean church order. Some have seen a descending gradation of offices: 'you' refers to the apostles, 'prophets' to itinerants, 'just men' to community leaders, the 'little ones' to lay members.[71] But the parallelism in 10.41 is probably synonymous parallelism: the prophet and just man are one and the same.[72] Does not the context imply that both are itinerants? And were not both John the Baptist and Jesus simultaneously prophets and just men (cf. 3.15; 11.9; 13.57; 21.11, 32; 27.19)? And has not the entirety of chapter 10 had one group of people—the apostolic missionaries and their spiritual successors—in mind? We are also persuaded that the 'little ones' of v. 42 are likewise Christian missionaries and are therefore identical with those named in vv. 40 and 41. Chapter 18, it is true, seemingly demonstrates that μικροί can refer to Christians in general (cf. Barth, in TIM, pp. 121–2). If, however, 'sons of the kingdom' can mean one thing in 8.12, another in 13.38; if 'son of David' can mean one thing in 1.20, another in 1.1; if δίκαιος can mean one thing in 9.13, another in 13.43, 49—then why cannot

[69] Cf. Hill, Matthew, p. 196.

[70] So Hill (v) and Gundry, Commentary, p. 202. Cf. Dan 12.3; Mt 5.19; 1 Cor 12.28; Did. 13.2. One recalls the 'teacher of righteousness' of the Dead Sea Scrolls.

[71] So, with variations, Grundmann, pp. 301–2; Gaechter, Kommentar, p. 352. According to Käsemann, Questions, p. 91, the prophets are the leaders, the righteous the community. One could also propose a salvation–history interpretation: from OT prophets to post–biblical just men to the little ones of the church.

[72] Cf. Allen, p. 112; Hill (v); Cothenet (v). For the apostles as prophets compare 21.35–36 with 22.6.

the μικρῶν of 10.42 have slightly different connotations from the μικρῶν of 18.10 and 14? Further, if 10.42 does not refer to itinerant missionaries, then it has no real thematic connexion with its immediate context. But it is difficult to believe that our careful writer brought his second discourse to so awkward a conclusion. Certainly the other four major discourses have fitting conclusions that gather together the threads of what has preceded.

42. The form of the preceding clauses is abandoned for the final member of the series: ὁ + participle gives way to ὅς ἐὰν ποτίσῃ (cf. 1, p. 430, on the irregularity of the final beatitude).

καὶ ὃς ἂν ποτίσῃ ἕνα τῶν μικρῶν τούτων ποτήριον ψυχροῦ μόνον εἰς ὄνομα μαθητοῦ.[73] Compare Jer 16.7; Mt 25.35, 37, 42, 44; T. Isaac 6.21; T. Jacob 2.23.[74] For rabbinic parallels see SB 1, pp. 589–90. Matthew has adapted Mk 9.41 ('For whoever gives you a cup of water ἐν ὀνόματι, ὅτι Χριστοῦ ἐστε').[75] He has dropped 'for', turned 'you' into 'one of these little ones',[76] substituted the more vivid 'cold (water)'[77] for 'water', and simplified the awkward and peculiar 'in (the) name because you are Christ's', assimilating it to the similar expressions in 10.41.

'Because you are Christ's' has a Pauline ring (cf. Rom 8.9; 1 Cor 1.12; 3.23). This and the fact that the synoptics nowhere else use 'Christ' as a proper name without the article indicate that our saying has, at the very least, been influenced by Christian speech habits. This circumstance, however, does not eliminate the possibility that a dominical word has been revised by the tradition. The thrust of 10.42 harmonizes well with 25.31–46 (which we would attribute to Jesus); and 'in (the) name because you are Christ's' may suffer from textual corruption and/or be a post-Easter insertion.[78]

'Little ones'[79] was probably a term Jesus applied to his dis-

---

[73] HG, in agreement with Maj, prints εαν. NA[26] has ἄν, which better fits the string of ἄν's in chapter 10: see vv. 11 (bis), 14, 33 (bis).

[74] This reads: 'Blessed be the one who will perform acts of mercy in honour of your several names, and will give someone a cup of water to drink . . .'.

[75] Against O. Michel, TWNT 4, p. 654; and Jeremias, Theology, pp. 258–9, 10.42 does not preserve a non – Markan tradition. Cf. Catchpole, 'Poor' (v), pp. 359–60.

[76] Cf. 18.6, 10, 14; Mk 9.42. μικρός indicates firstly smallness of size not shortness of years. LSJ, s.v., gives examples of its use as a reproach.

[77] Cf. m. Ned. 8.7. ψυχρός is a synoptic hapax legomenon. As an adjective the word means 'cold', as a substantive it means 'cold (water)'.

[78] Cf. Taylor, Mark, p. 408, citing Ps. Sol. 9.16; also Catchpole, 'Poor' (v), p. 369.

[79] Lit.: O. Michel, '"Diese Kleinen"—eine Jüngerbezeichnung Jesu', TSK 108 (1938), pp. 401–15; Barth, in TIM, pp. 121–5; Schweizer, in Stanton, Matthew, pp. 138–9; G. N. Stanton, '5 Ezra and Matthean Christianity in the Second Century', JTS 28 (1977), pp. 67–83. In the rabbis the equivalents of μικρός designate either a child or an immature scholar; cf. SB 1, pp. 591–2, on qāṭān, zĕ'êr, and zĕ'êrā'.

ciples.[80] He may have picked it up from apocalyptic circles (cf. Zech 13.7; 1 En. 62.11; 2 Bar. 48.19; note that Zech 13.7 is cited in Mk 14.27). Its background is unclear. The appellation could be a natural development of characterizing faithful Israelites as God's sons or children. Or it may have something to do with king David, who, despite being ὁ μικρός (1 Βασ 16.11) and the 'least' of his brethren (LAB 59.2), became the exalted king. In any case the appropriateness of 'little ones' on Jesus' lips cannot be missed. He stressed God's fatherhood, said positive things about children,[81] promised that the lowly would be exalted (cf. Isa 60.22), treated his disciples as those with much to learn (cf. m. 'Abot 4.20), and knew that his followers were, by worldly standards, of little account. See further on 18.6.

ἀμὴν λέγω ὑμῖν, οὐ μὴ ἀπολέσῃ τὸν μισθὸν αὐτοῦ.[82] So Mk 9.41b, with ὅτι before οὐ. Note that an 'amen' saying earlier concluded the first and second paragraphs of the discourse (10.15, 23). Note also the frequency with which Matthew uses 'amen' to introduce sayings about reward or punishment: 5.26; 6.2, 5, 16; 19.28; 23.36. 10.42 illustrates 10.40f. by citing a concrete example. The hospitable but hardly extraordinarily generous[83] act of giving a cup of cold water to a hot and thirsty missionary simply because he is a missionary brings reward. The thought, which focuses on one's motive, not the size of one's deed,[84] fittingly closes chapter 10 by showing that even those who do not set out for the mission field can still participate in the Christian mission. By supporting the messengers of the gospel, they truly share in the great task that is the topic of chapter 10. In this way Matthew demonstrates his desire to make every part of his gospel relevant to every reader. Some

[80] Against Bultmann, History, p. 142, we do not find it necessary to infer that 10.42 originally had to do with children; cf. Riesner, pp. 462–3. Cf. the use of 'babes' in 11.25 and the 'children' of Mk 10.24. Admittedly, 'the early Church was more interested in the original disciples than in children; and we should expect the tendency of the tradition to be to transfer sayings concerning "children" or "little ones" to the disciples' (so Manson, Sayings, p. 138); but the image of giving water to the thirsty does not naturally call to mind a child but rather a man wandering away from his home; cf. 1 Kgs 17.10; 18.4.

[81] Some have even thought that Jesus' call to 'become as little children' meant, in essence, 'consider God your Abba'; cf. Manson, Teaching, p. 331; Jeremias, Theology, p. 156. In any case there is nothing in the Jesus tradition like the rabbinic statements in m. 'Abot 3.11 and b. B. Bat. 12b. Jesus never uses a child to illustrate foolishness or ignorance. Further discussion on 18.3.

[82] D it sy[s.c] bo Cyp have ἀπόληται ὁ μισθός: 'his reward will not be lost'. See Black, p. 245. Zahn, p. 416, n. 60, thought this pristine.

[83] In fact, giving a cup of water was the least work of hospitality; cf. L. Goppelt, TWNT 6, p. 160; 7, pp. 317, 323.

[84] Cf. b. Ber. 17a: 'It matters not whether you do much or little, so long as your heart is directed to heaven'. See also Sipre on Lev 5.17 and the texts cited in SB 2, p. 46.

might be tempted to pass over 10.1–42 on the grounds that it is addressed to missionaries only. But 10.42 is an invitation for all the faithful to involve themselves in whatever way they can with the apostolic mission. And if the invitation is accepted, then chapter 10 cannot but become meaningful even to those who stay at home.

(iv) Concluding Observations

(1) In Excursus VIII we proposed that the entirety of chapter 10 is chiastic. Whatever one thinks of that suggestion, it cannot be denied that 10.32–42 addresses topics already addressed by 10.5–25. For instance, the themes of familial division, eschatological trial, endurance in suffering, and the reception of missionaries are treated in both sections. It is for this reason that the Concluding Observations made in the commentary on 10.5–25 also apply, *mutatis mutandis*, to 10.32–42, and we accordingly refer the reader to pp. 196–197. Matthew's repetition, however, is hardly redundancy. Repetition is the key to learning, and if 10.32–42 reiterates previous paragraphs, it is because the evangelist is trying to underline without a pencil. Certain points need to be driven home, certain themes highlighted, certain lessons not forgotten. Now it is not coincidence that the majority of these points or themes or lessons common to 10.5–25 and 32–42 have to do with suffering and persecution. Matthew knows that the most troublesome side of his faith is the painful difficulties it brings—the persecution by authorities, the ridicule by friends, the disapproval by families. This is why 10.26–31 functions as it does to proffer comfort and encouragement (see pp. 210–11). The same pastoral motivation also explains why 10.32–42 exhorts the believer to make the good confession and warns him about the hatred that may come from those nearest. Suffering foreseen (cf. 10.34–6) is more easily endured, and pain is lessened when beyond it lies reward (cf. 10.32, 39).

(2) There is a second notable way in which 10.32–42 makes a contribution beyond 10.5–25, although the commentators have been blind to it. 10.5–25 is explicitly addressed to itinerants, and it is largely specialized instruction: the missionary should do this, the missionary should do that. But, to state the obvious, not all Christians were missionaries, and concrete advice on where to go and not to go, on what to take and not to take, would not have been of pressing relevance for many of Matthew's readers. So 10.5–25 would seem to have a smaller potential audience than, say, the sermon on the mount. 10.32–

42 is different. Although still ostensibly directed to the missionary, the whole section could be heeded equally by each and every believer. All must confess Jesus, take up the cross, and put faith above family. Thus 10.32–42 is, much more than 10.5–25, appropriate for everyone, without consideration of status or office. That Matthew was in fact concerned to make his discourse pertinent to all is shown by the very last verse: 'And whoever gives to one of these little ones even a cup of cold water only because he bears the name of Christ, truly I say to you, he will not lose his reward'. The 'little ones' are, we have shown, to be identified with Christian missionaries (see on 10.41). Thus 10.42 is not a word for them but for others—those who, although not itinerants, may, if they will, share in and further the Christian mission by supporting the heralds of the gospel. What the verse reveals, therefore, is Matthew's attention to the non-missionary. It is our proposal that such attention has helped form the entire section, beginning with 10.32. Although firstly addressed to the missionary, others are, in 10.32–42, hardly out of the picture.[85]

(v) *Bibliography*

For additional bibliography see section (v) for 10.5–25.
Allison, pp. 118–20, 128–37.
Arens, pp. 63–90.
J. B. Bauer, '"Wer sein Leben retten will ..." Mk 8.35 Parr.', in *Neutestamentliche Aufsätze*, ed. J. Blinzler et al., Regensburg, 1963, pp. 7–10.
W. A. Beardslee, 'Saving One's Life by losing It', *JAAR* 47 (1979), pp. 57–72.
M. Black, 'Uncomfortable Words. III: The Violent Word', *ExpT* 81 (1970), pp. 115–18.
idem, 'Not Peace but a Sword', in Bammel and Moule, pp. 287–94.
D. R. Catchpole, 'The Angelic Son of Man in Luke 12.8', *NovT* 24 (1982), pp. 255–65.
idem, 'The Poor on Earth and the Son of Man in Heaven: A Reappraisal of Matthew xxv. 31–46', *BJRL* 61 (1979), pp. 355–97.
Cope, pp. 77–81.
É. Cothenet, 'Les prophètes chrétiens dans l'Évangile selon saint Matthieu', in Didier, pp. 281–308.
Crossan, *Aphorisms*, pp. 88–94, 104–19.
Dautzenberg, pp. 51–82.
J. D. M. Derrett, 'Taking up the Cross and Turning the Cheek', in Harvey, *Approaches*, pp. 61–78.

---

[85] Our discussion raises the issue of whether there is not a *corps élite* in Matthew's thought. On this see on 19.16–22.

E. Dinkler, 'Jesu Wort vom Kreuztragen', in *Signum Crucis*, Tübingen, 1967, pp. 77–98.

idem, 'Das Kreuz als Siegeszeichen', in *ibid.*, pp. 55–76.

idem, 'Kreuzzeichen und Kreuz. Tav, Chi und Stauros', in *ibid.*, pp. 26–54.

idem, 'Zur Geschichte des Kreuzsymbols', in *ibid.*, pp. 1–25.

P. Doncoeur, 'Gagner ou perdre sa ψυχή', *RSR* 35 (1948), pp. 113–19.

H. Fleddermann, 'The Q Saying on Confessing and Denying', in *Society of Biblical Literature 1987 Seminar Papers*, ed. K. H. Richards, Atlanta, 1987, pp. 606–16.

D. R. Fletcher, 'Condemned to Die: The Logion on Cross-Bearing: What does it mean?', *Int* 18 (1964), pp. 156–64.

A. Fridrichsen, '"Sich selbst verleugnen"', *ConNT* 2 (1936), pp. 1–8.

Geist, pp. 294–300.

A. George, 'Qui veut sauver sa vie la perdra; qui perd sa vie la sauvra', *BVC* 83 (1968), pp. 11–24.

O. Glombitza, 'Das Kreuz', in *Domine, dirige me in verbo tuo*, Berlin, 1961, pp. 60–7.

J. G. Griffiths, 'The Disciple's Cross', *NTS* 16 (1970), pp. 358–64.

P. Grelot, 'Michée 7.6 dans les évangiles et dans la littérature rabbinique', *Bib* 67 (1986), pp. 363–77.

A. J. B. Higgins, '"Menschensohn" oder "ich" in Q: Lk 12.8–9/Mt 10.32–3?', in Pesch, *Menschensohn*, pp. 117–23.

D. Hill, 'ΔΙΚΑΙΟΙ as a Quasi-Technical Term', *NTS* 11 (1965), pp. 296–302.

K. Köhler, 'Zu Mt 10.37f.', *ZNW* 17 (1916), pp. 270–2.

W. G. Kümmel, 'Das Verhalten Jesu gegenüber und das Verhalten des Menschensohns: Markus 8.38 par und Lukas 12.8f. par Matthäus 10.32f.', in Pesch, *Menschensohn*, pp. 210–14.

J. Lambrecht, 'Q-Influence on Mark 8.34–9.1', in Delobel, pp. 277–304.

Laufen, pp. 302–42.

H. Leroy, 'Wer sein Leben gewinnen will . . .', *FZPT* 25 (1978), pp. 171–86.

B. Lindars, 'Jesus as Advocate: A Contribution to the Christological Debate', *BJRL* 62 (1980), pp. 476–97.

W. Michaelis, 'Zeichen, Siegel, Kreuz', *TZ* 12 (1956), pp. 505–25.

F. Mussner, 'Wege zum Selbstbewusstsein Jesu', *BZ* 12 (1968), pp. 161–72.

J. C. O'Neill, 'Did Jesus teach that his death would be vicarious as well as typical?', in Horbury, pp. 9–27.

Perrin, *Rediscovering*, pp. 185–91.

R. Pesch, 'Über die Autorität Jesu: Eine Rückfrage anhand des Bekenner- und Verleugnerspruchs Lk 12.8f. par.', in Schnackenburg, *Kirche*, pp. 25–55.

Riesner, pp. 454–75.

T. A. Roberts, 'Some Comments on Matthew x. 34–6 and Luke xii. 51–3', *ExpT* 69 (1958), pp. 304–6.

J. Schneider, *TWNT* 7, pp. 572–84.

Schulz, *Q*, pp. 66–76, 258–60, 430–3, 444–9, 457–9.

A. Schulz, *Nachfolgen und Nachahmen*, SANT 6, Munich, 1962, pp. 79–97.

E. Schweizer, *TWNT* 9, pp. 640–3.

G. Schwarz, 'Der Nachfolgespruch Markus 8.34b.c. Parr. Emendation und Rückübersetzung', *NTS* 33 (1987), pp. 255–65.

D. P. Seccombe, 'Take Up Your Cross', in *God Who is Rich in Mercy*, ed. P. T. O'Brien and D. G. Peterson, Grand Rapids, 1986, pp. 139–51.

P. Sellew, 'Reconstruction of Q 12.33–59', in *Society of Biblical Literature 1987 Seminar Papers*, ed. K. H. Richards, Atlanta, 1987, pp. 631–53.

Wanke, pp. 76–81.

Zimmermann, pp. 189–94.

Zumstein, pp. 225–31.

EXCURSUS IX

THE STRUCTURE OF MATTHEW 11–12[1]

Beare, p. 255, divides Mt 11 into three separate units: vv. 1–19 (Jesus and John the Baptist), vv. 20–4 (the verdict of Jesus on the cities of Galilee), and 25–30 (thanksgiving, proclamation, invitation). We endorse the analysis. Although his first unit, 11.1–19, is often divided into three separate sections (vv. 2–6, 7–15, 16–19),[2] the unity of 1–19 is manifest. Vv. 1–6, 7–15, and 16–19 all concern John the Baptist, and there is no break at all between vv. 15 and 16: both belong to the one speech of Jesus. Thematically there are slight differences between vv. 2–6 (where John inquires about Jesus' eschatological office), vv. 7–15 (where Jesus reveals who John really is), and vv. 16–19 (where the response of 'this generation' to Jesus and John is recorded); but these differences only mark the subsections of a unified paragraph.[3] There is near universal agreement that vv. 20–24 (the Galilean woes) constitute one pericope, vv. 25–30 (the revelation of the Son) another. We observe only that just as vv. 1–19 are made up of three subsections, so vv. 20–24 concern three cities (Chorazin, Bethsaida, Capernaum), and vv. 25–30 are typically divided into (a) thanksgiving (vv. 25–6), (b) revelation (v. 27), and (c) invitation (vv. 28–30).[4]

As regards chapter 12, while it is not possible to speak of a scholarly consensus, a good number of commentators, on the basis of both transitional sentences (see vv. 1, 9, 15, 22, 38, 46) and topical

---

[1] Lit.: Gaechter, *Kunst*, pp. 26–9; B. C. Lategan. 'Structural interrelations in Matthew 11–12', *Neotestamentica* 11 (1977), pp. 115–29.

[2] E.g. by Gnilka, *Matthäusevangelium* 1, pp. 405–26, and Rigaux, *Testimony*, p. 48.

[3] Cf. Beare, p. 255, and France, *Matthew*, pp. 192–7.

[4] Cf. Gnilka, *Matthäusevangelium* 1, pp. 426–42, and Meier, *Vision*, p. 78.

considerations, discern six paragraphs: vv. 1–8 (a Sabbath controversy), vv. 9–14 (another Sabbath controversy), vv. 15–21 (the servant of Yahweh), vv. 22–37 (the Beelzebul controversy), vv. 38–45 (request for a sign), vv. 46–50 (Jesus' true family).[5]

One may, then, divine nine sections in Mt 11–12: 11.2–19, 20–4, 25–30; 12.1–8, 9–14, 15–21, 22–37, 38–45, 46–50. A closer examination reveals that these should be divided into three triads. We have already observed how the narrative sections in chapters 1–4 and 8–9 so arrange themselves (see 1, pp. 66–7). That such is likewise the case here follows from reflection on the themes being treated. Gnilka, *Matthäusevangelium* 1, p. 470, has rightly seen that 11.25–30 and 12.46–50 serve similar functions: both, following warnings and words of judgement, concern not the rejection of Jesus but his acceptance; both, that is, are about the opportunity to join the new family of God. What needs to be added is that 12.15–21 is about the same opportunity. Its subject is not hostility or rejection or unbelief but Jesus as God's humble servant (cf. the πραΰς of 11.29), and the passage concludes with a declaration about the eschatological people of God: 'in him will the Gentiles hope.' Further, 12.15–21 is preceded by two controversy stories and in this also resembles both 11.25–30 and 12.46–50. The pattern that thus emerges is this:

		1	2	3
Unbelief/rejection	1	11.2–19	12.1–8	12.22–37
Unbelief/rejection	2	11.20–4	12.9–14	12.38–45
Invitation/acceptance	3	11.25–30	12.15–21	12.46–50

Our discussion leads to the outline presented on p. 69 of vol. 1.

[5] So e.g. Gnilka, *Matthäusevangelium* 1, pp. 442–72; Meier, *Vision*, pp. 84–9; and Rigaux, *Testimony*, p. 48 (with vv. 1–21 and 22–50 rightly grouped together). Exceptions include P. F. Ellis, p. 54 (who sees an a b a′ pattern in 11.2–27 + 11.28–12.21 + 12.22–50), and Gundry, *Commentary*, pp. 220–50 (who divides chapter 12 in this fashion: 12.1–21, 22–27, 28–45, 46–50).

XXIV

THIS GENERATION: INVITATION AND RESPONSE
(11.1–30)

(i) *Structure*

11.1–19 brings together three pericopae which are thematically related in that each has to do with John the Baptist: 11.2–6, 7–15, 16–19. Introducing the three pericopae are three questions: 'Are you the Coming One?', 'What did you go out into the wilderness to see?', 'To what shall I liken this generation?' Jesus answers the queries himself, twice quoting Scripture (11.5, 9), once quoting a proverbial couplet (11.17). In 11.2–6 and 7–15 the questions concern, respectively, the identity of Jesus and the identity of John. 11.16–19 then answers the third question by registering the response of 'this generation' to Jesus the Messiah and to John who is Elijah. The whole section is united by an *inclusio*: the ἔργα of the Christ (11.2) are identical with the ἔργα of Wisdom (11.19).

As to how 11.2–19 is structurally and thematically related to the remainder of chapter 11, Allen long ago summed up the facts with admirable clarity: in Mt 11 'the editor gives a survey of Christ's work. It falls into three sections. Christ's work is considered (a) in relation to that of the Baptist, 2–19; (b) in view of its apparent failure, 20–4; (c) in view of its real success, 25–20' (p. 113). 11.2–19 is thus a triad within a triad (cf. Beare, p. 255). The same is also true of 11.25–30, for it too is triadic. See further Excursus IX.

(ii) *Sources*

(i) Mt 11.2–19 very closely resembles Lk 7.18–35. Verbatim agreement is extensive, and the ordering of the sentences is the same. The only major differences are these: Matthew has nothing corresponding to Lk 7.20f. and 29f., Luke has nothing corresponding to Mt 11.14–15, and the Lukan parallel to Mt 11.12–13 appears in Lk 16.16. These facts are consistent with the Q hypothesis: Mt 11.2–19 = Lk 7.18–35 by and large reproduces a large block of Q material. That Lk 7.20f. and 29f. lack synoptic parallels is to be explained either by Matthew's tendency to abbreviate (manifest in his treatment of Mark) or by the possibility that the verses in Luke are redactional. That the Third Gospel lacks a counterpart to Mt 11.14f. may be put down to its editorial genesis. And that Luke's parallel to Mt 11.12f. appears not in Lk 7 but in Lk 16 has for its cause Matthew's desire to bring together into one place all of Q's statements about John the Baptist.

(2) There are no Markan parallels to the material in Mt 11.20–4. The Lukan parallels are as follows:

Mt 11.20	Lk——
21	10.13
22	14
23a	15
23b	——
24	12

Several problems pose themselves. In Q, did the woes appear after the mission discourse (so Matthew) or as part of that discourse (so Luke)? Whose order is original, Matthew's or Luke's? Are Mt 11.20 and 23b redactional, or did Luke omit them? In sorting through these issues, the following observations are the most pertinent. (a) On pp. 163–64 we have explained why the present placement of Lk 10.13–15 is probably due to Lukan redaction or an editor of Q^{lk}. To repeat the main point, Lk 10.13–15 awkwardly interrupts the address on mission with a soliloquy on Chorazin, Bethsaida, and Capernaum, and it breaks the natural connexion between 10.12 and 16. One infers that Lk 10.13–15 was placed (by Luke or a predecessor) after 10.12 because of the catchword connexion (ἀνεκτότερον ἔσται ... ἀνεκτότερον ἔσται). This in turn implies that Lk 10.13–15 par. did not originally belong to Q's mission discourse. (b) This conclusion is strongly reinforced by a second consideration. If the order of Lk 10.13–15 and 16 is reversed, thereby restoring what we have argued was the original sequence of Q, Luke's Q material from 10.12 through 10.24 appears in precisely the same order as it does in the First Gospel: mission discourse—woes—the great thanksgiving. This is not likely to be coincidence. (c) Concerning Mt 11.20 and 23b, the latter must be suspected of having an editorial origin. It completes the parallelism between 10.21–2 and 23–4, and our evangelist's proclivity for parallelism is firmly established. 11.20 may also be redactional. A transition is required after 11.16–19. Further, the vocabulary of 11.20 is either characteristic of Matthew (τότε ἤρξατο) or elsewhere redactional (πλεῖστος), or it is drawn forward from 11.21–3a (ἐγένοντο, δυνάμεις, μετενόησαν). (d) With regard to the difference in order between Mt 11.20–4 and Lk 10.12–15 (Mt 11.24 = Lk10.12), it is really illusory. Matthew has not one but two parallels to Lk 10.12: Mt 10.15 and 11.24. The first of these two verses occurs in Matthew precisely where it does in Luke (cf. Lk 10.2–12 par.). So the other verse, Mt 11.24, is best judged a redactional addition inspired by 10.15 = Lk 10.12. Matthew was moved to add it because it increases the parallelism between the words addressed to Chorazin and Bethsaida and the oracle of doom directed at Capernaum.

To sum up, then: in Q, Lk 10.13–15 appeared between the missionary discourse and the great thanksgiving (Lk 10.21–4). Matthew retained Q's order (mission discourse, woes, thanksgiving). He did not, however, simply reproduce Q. He inserted much material between the words on mission and the woes (including the section on John the Baptist). And he supplied the woes with an introduction (11.20) and expanded the speech spoken against Capernaum (originally only 11.23a) so that it would mirror the denunciation of Chorazin and Bethsaida.

(3) 11.25–30 does not take us very far upon the road to the solution to the synoptic problem. There is no parallel in Mark, and the parallel in Luke (10.21–2) agrees to such an extent with Mt 11.25–7 that the differences are scarcely very instructive. The only points to be made are (a) that the word-for-word agreement between Mt 11.25–7 and its Lukan parallel strongly suggests a common written source, Q^1 and (b) that the Griesbach hypothesis must come up with some explanation for Luke's hypothetical omission of 11.28–30.

The main issue concerning 11.25–30 is the origin of its third part, vv. 28–30. There is no Lukan parallel. Are the verses from Q?[2] Are they from M?[3] Or are they editorial?[4] A place in Q is unlikely because, to quote T. W. Manson, 'it is hardly credible that Lk. would have omitted a saying so entirely after his own heart'.[5] What of an origin in M?[6] This is implausible because, as we shall see, v. 27 draws upon Exod 33.12–13 while vv. 28–30 draw upon Exod 33.14, and both are permeated by Mosaic motifs. So 11.27 and 28–30 belong together. That they came into existence independently of each other is exceedingly doubtful. What then, finally, of a redactional genesis? Several observations speak against this. (a) Most of the vocabulary is not characteristic of the redactor. Indeed, several words occur nowhere else in Matthew.[7] (b) If vv. 29b–c, which for more than one reason must be suspected of being Matthean (see section (iii)), are excised, the result is two sentences which stand in perfect synonymous parallelism:

A   Come to me all you who are weary and burdened,
B   and I will give you rest.
A¹   Take my yoke upon you
B¹   and you will find rest for yourselves

---

[1] Against 11.25–7 being a Matthean composition that was copied by Luke, there are just too many words uncharacteristic of our author (cf. Gundry, *Commentary*, p. 216): ἐξομολογέω: Mt: 2; Mk: 1; Lk: 2; σοφός: Mt: 2; Mk: 0; Lk: 1; συνετός: Mt: 1; Mk: 0; Lk: 1; ἀποκαλύπτω: Mt: 4; Mk: 0; Lk: 5; νήπιος: Mt: 2; Mk: 0; Lk: 1; ἐδοκία Mt:1; Mk: 0; Lk: 2; βούλομαι: Mt: 2; Mk: 1; Lk: 2.

[2] So Norden (v), p. 301; Crossan (v), pp. 191–3. Cf. Harnack, *Sayings*, p. 307 ('the question . . . must remain open').

[3] So most; cf. Manson, *Sayings*, pp. 185–7; Schönle (v), pp. 54–6.

[4] So Bacon, p. 290; Frankemölle, p. 290, n. 74.

[5] *Sayings*, p. 185. According to Dibelius, *Tradition*, p. 279, n. 2, the situation in which Luke set the logion, namely, the return of the seventy, excludes quoting 11.28–30. Even if accepted, this objection would not explain why Luke did not insert the verses elsewhere.

[6] Strecker, *Weg*, p. 172, notes that 11.28–30 is located between Q material (11.25–7) and Markan material (12.1ff.), which is consistent with its being from M.

[7] φορτίζω, ζυγός, χρηστός, ἐλαφρός.

This suggests Matthean redaction of a pre-Matthean unit (cf. Stanton, 'Creative Interpreter' (v)). (c) There are possible Semitisms, and an Aramaic origin is conceivable (see Black, pp. 183–4).

In the Introduction, p. 121, we judged it unlikely that Q was known to the First and Third Evangelists in precisely the same form, that there is occasional cause for referring to Q^{mt} and Q^{lk} as slightly different versions or editions of the same sayings source. Here is an instance where the hypothesis has explanatory power. If vv. 28–30, which presuppose v. 27, were not known to Luke (and therefore not in his copy of Q), and if the verses did not come from M, and if they were not invented by Matthew, then an origin in Q^{mt} suggests itself. We conjecture the following. A tradent of Q^{mt}, recognizing the dependence of 11.27 upon Exod 33.12–13, composed 11.28–30 in order to further the Exodus allusion and the comparison/contrast between Jesus and Moses and their two revelations. To what extent he took up already formed material we do not know, although it is not implausible that he adopted traditional lines attributed to Wisdom or perhaps a saying ascribed to Jesus. In any case his purpose was to elaborate on the subject matter of 11.27.

(iii) Exegesis

THE BAPTIST'S QUESTION (11.1–6)

Following a transitional sentence (11.1), Matthew records a pronouncement story which looks back on the whole of Jesus' public ministry to date (cf. Lk 7.18–23). The pronouncement itself is occasioned by a question. Thus 11.2–6 belongs to the class of synoptic pronouncement stories in which Jesus responds to a sceptical or hostile inquiry. Other examples include Mt 12.38–42; 16.1–4; 22.34–40; Mk 10.2–9; 11.27–33; 12.13–17; Lk 10.25–37.

1. This redactional verse simultaneously concludes the preceding discourse and resubmerges the reader in the narrative flow.

καὶ ἐγένετο ὅτε ἐτέλεσεν ὁ Ἰησοῦς διατάσσων τοῖς δώδεκα μαθηταῖς αὐτοῦ. Compare 7.28; 13.53; 19.1; 26.1; and see on 7.28. διατάσσω,[8] a Matthean *hapax legomenon*, means more than 'teach' or 'instruct'. The sense is: 'When Jesus finished giving orders to his twelve disciples . . .'. On 'the twelve disciples', which creates an *inclusio* with 10.1, see on 10.1.

μετέβη ἐκεῖθεν τοῦ διδάσκειν καὶ κηρύσσειν ἐν ταῖς πόλεσιν αὐτῶν. See our comments on 4.23 and 9.35. Both μεταβαίνω*

---

[8] Cf. Lk 3.13; 8.55; 17.9, 10. The word occurs over twenty times in the LXX, for various Hebrew equivalents.

and ἐκεῖθεν* are Matthean favourites, and they appear together
also in 12.9 and 15.29 (cf. 17.20). The combination does not occur
in the LXX. αὐτῶν is not linked to the twelve disciples but hangs
in the air (cf. the use of 'their synagogues' in 4.23 and 13.54).

According to Fenton, p. 174, 'to heal' is omitted from 11.1 because
'Jesus is beginning to withdraw his miraculous power from Israel,
because their unbelief is becoming apparent'. 12.9–14, 22–3; 15.30–1;
17.14–18; 20.29–34; and 21.14, though cited by Fenton himself, cast the
shadow of doubt on this thesis. Equally doubtful is the opposite
proposal, namely, that 'Matthew mentions only teaching and preaching
in 11.1, and not healing as he does in 4.23 and 9.35, so as to call
attention to the fact that Jesus' teaching and preaching are rejected and
cease . . . [while] the healing ministry continues, even after the rejection
of Jesus by the Jews'.[9] See on 4.23. It is scarcely accurate to speak,
without qualification, of 'the Jews' rejecting Jesus.

Immediately following Jesus' charge to the twelve it is odd to read
that Jesus 'went on from there to teach and preach in their cities'.
The disciples' pre-Easter mission is never recounted, and they do not
make another appearance until chapter 12 (contrast Mk 6.7, 12, 30;
Lk 9.1–6, 10; 10.1–20). The omission is striking and has called forth
several explanations. For Gundry, the focus on Christology simply
overshadows all else (*Commentary*, p. 203; cf. Schlatter, p. 355). For
Wellhausen, *Matthaei*, p. 51, the disciples go out only after Easter
(cf. Argyle, p. 84). For Hare, p. 97, the evangelist is interested solely
in Jesus' instructions, not in the disciples' actions. For Hill, *Matthew*,
p. 196, the reader should perhaps assume that the disciples have in
fact been sent out: this is why they are not mentioned in chapter
11.[10] From our point of view, while the missionaries are commanded
to go out (10.5–6), they are never said to return because such a
notice might (i) lead to seeing in 10.23 an unfulfilled prophecy and
(ii) be taken to imply an end to the Jewish mission (see further on 10.23).

2–3. John the Baptist, though in prison, hears about 'the
deeds of the Christ'. His curiosity is piqued, and he sends
messengers to Jesus. His question, in its Matthean context, must
reflect waning faith, for John has already perceived Jesus'
identity (3.13–17). If, however, the query be judged historical, it
must have sprung from rising hope or genuine bewilderment.

ὁ δὲ Ἰωάννης ἀκούσας ἐν τῷ δεσμωτηρίῳ τὰ ἔργα τοῦ Χριστοῦ.
Compare 1 Kgs 13.11 and Josephus, *C. Ap.* 2.157 (τῶν ἔργων
αὐτοῦ [sc. Moses]). Lk 7.18 reads: 'And his disciples
announced to John all these things'.[11] Q cannot be recovered.

[9] J. A. Comber, 'The Verb Therapeuō in Matthew's Gospel', *JBL* 97 (1978),
p. 433.
[10] Cf. E. Bammel, *TWNT* 6, p. 903: the disciples were sent out, and their
success is perhaps the basis for John's question and Jesus' answer in 11.2–6.
[11] If 'all these things' appeared in Q, then one would naturally think of the
words spoken in the great sermon, Lk 6.20–49.

Both Mt 11.2a and Luke's line are redactional.[12] On John the
Baptist in Matthew see on 3.1.

δεσμωτήριον[13] is used only once in the First Gospel. Its meaning is
'jail' or 'prison' (cf. 14.3; Mk 6.17). The reference is back to 4.12
('John was handed over').

'The deeds of the Christ'[14] (cf. 11.19) is a key phrase. Being
defined in 11.4 as what has been heard and seen, and being
described in 11.5 as healing and preaching, it refers back not
only to the miracle chapters, 8–9, but also to the sermon on the
mount, 5–7, interpreting both Jesus' authoritative words and his
mighty deeds as messianic[15] (τοῦ Χριστοῦ).[16] The phrase,
therefore, is comprehensive and summarizes the content of
4.23ff. Even chapter 10 is included in so far as the disciples'
words and deeds are in effect a re-enactment or continuation of
their master's words and deeds.[17] In sum, 11.2 makes a closure
(4.23–11.2) and prepares for the following chapters, whose theme
is the response of people to 'the deeds of the Christ'. Compare
G. Barth's analysis: 'the question of the Baptist has a double
function: on the one hand it clearly expresses the decisive
question which comes out of what has gone before and so forms
a conclusion which once again illuminates the Christological
theme of the preceding chapters. On the other hand, the chapters
which follow must be understood even more in the light of this
question and the negative or positive answers to it' (*TIM*,
p. 251).

πέμψας διὰ τῶν μαθητῶν αὐτοῦ εἶπεν αὐτῷ.[18] If, as it seems,
Lk 7.18–19a ('And John, calling two[19] of his disciples, sent
them to Jesus, saying') is closer to Q[20], then Matthew's text is
an abbreviation for the sake of brevity.

[12] For Luke see Jeremias, *Lukasevangelium*, p. 160. Concerning Matthew,
ἀκούσας/-σαντες (Mt:21; Mk:10; Lk: 9), ἔργον*, and χριστός* are not infrequently redactional. Cf. also 12.24.
[13] Cf. LXX Gen 39.22; 40.5 (both times for *bêt hassōhar*); Acts 5.21, 23;
16.26; Josephus, *Bell.* 4.385; Hermas, *Sim.* 9.28.7.
[14] Cf. Josh 24.31; Judg 2.7; Job 37.15; Ps 28.5; Jn 6.28, 29; 9.3; Rom 14.20;
1 Cor 15.58; 16.10; Phil 2.30; Heb 4.4.
[15] *Pace* Gundry, *Commentary*, p. 204, who, referring to 23.2, restricts ἔργα
to deeds.
[16] One should translate: 'of the Messiah'. The usage is titular. Cf. on 1.1.
[17] Cf. Barth, in *TIM*, pp. 251–2; Gerhardsson, *Acts*, pp. 31–2; Verseput,
pp. 64–5.
[18] C³ L *f*¹ Maj aur ff¹ g¹ l vg sy^hmg bo Or read δυο, not δια. This is
probably assimilation to Lk 7.18. Note also the δύο's in Jn 1.35 and 37. Whether
πέμψας διά would have been considered an awkward Semitism is unclear; cf.
Black, p. 115.
[19] Cf. Mk 6.7; 11.1; J. Jeremias, 'Paarweise Sendung im Neuen Testament', in
Abba, pp. 132–9.
[20] Cf. Jeremias, *Lukasevangelium*, p. 161; Polag, *Fragmenta*, p. 40.

John's disciples are mentioned only twice in Matthew, in 11.2 and 14.12. Both texts are from the tradition. Matthew shows little interest in the Baptist's followers. The polemical situation some have detected behind John's Gospel and elsewhere in the NT cannot be discerned in our book.[21]

σὺ εἶ ὁ ἐρχόμενος, ἢ ἕτερον προσδοκῶμεν; So Lk 7.19, with ἄλλον for ἕτερον.[22] The placement of the pronoun is emphatic: 'Are *you* . . .?' On the Coming One see on 3.11. On John's lips the title referred either to Elijah or—more probably—to the Messiah. In Matthew the reference is to the Messiah. For προσδοκάω used of messianic expectation see 24.50; 2 Pet 3.12–14. The usage is Christian. Perhaps Matthew expected his audience to assume that Jesus did not meet the normal expectations associated with messianic figures. Certainly Jesus' deeds do not match those of the somewhat judgemental figure portrayed by John in Mt 3.10–12. And the Messiah was hardly expected to be a wonder-worker.

It is surprising enough that the John who, in 3.14, confesses his need to be baptized by Jesus, now asks about the Coming One. But matters are even more problematic if the emphatic testimony given by the Baptist to Jesus in Jn 1 be taken into account. One can understand why Christian exegetes have traditionally not been able to accept Mt 11.2 at face value. Tertullian, *Adv. Marc.* 18, was the exception. According to him, John's doubts were genuine, for the Spirit had been taken from him (cf. *De bapt.* 10). Most of the Fathers[23] convinced themselves that John was inquiring for the sake of his disciples. Others have held that John asked in order to lure Jesus into making a public declaration (cf. Plummer, p. 160), or that John did not doubt Jesus' identity but only his way of manifesting himself.[24]

4. καὶ ἀποκριθεὶς ὁ Ἰησοῦς εἶπεν αὐτοῖς. This is from Q, as Lk 7.22 (without 'Jesus') demonstrates. εἶπεν answers εἶπεν (v. 3).

Between his version of Mt 11.3 and 4 Luke has this: 'And when the men had come to him, they said, 'John the Baptist has sent us to you, saying, "Are you he who is to come, or shall we look for another?"' In that hour he cured many of diseases and plagues and evil spirits, and

---

[21] Contrast Schweizer, *Matthew*, p. 255: in 11.2–6 Matthew is showing adherents of the Baptist sect how the Holy Spirit is at work among the Christians. —For the problem of the Baptist movement and its relation to early Christianity see the helpful survey of Brown, *John* 1, pp. lxvii–lxx.

[22] For ἕτερος as involving a pronounced qualitative distinction see H. W. Beyer, *TWNT* 2, p. 700. Note also BDF § 306 and J. K. Elliot, 'The Use of ἕτερος in the New Testament', *ZNW* 60 (1969), pp. 140–1.

[23] See the names listed in ANF 3, p. 375, n. 15, the earliest being Origen.

[24] For further references see Alford 1, pp. 112–14; Strauss, pp. 219–21; and Dupont, 'Ambassade' (v), pp. 806–13.

on many that were blind he bestowed sight' (7.20–1). These two verses, which insure a literal interpretation of the words that follow, are permeated by Lukan style and vocabulary[25] and may be redactional.[26] If, instead, they are based upon Q,[27] Matthew has again abbreviated.

πορευθέντες ἀπαγγείλατε Ἰωάννῃ ἃ ἀκούετε καὶ βλέπετε. Lk 7.22 has εἴδετε καὶ ἠκούσατε. Matthew may have created a chiastic connexion with v. 5: ἀπαγγείλατε ... ἀκούετε ... βλέπετε/ἀναβλέπουσιν ... ἀκούουσιν ... εὐαγγελίζονται. But note the use of βλέπω and ἀκούω in 13.16–17 = Lk 10.23–4 (Q).

5. Borrowing the language of several passages in Isaiah (cf. 26.19; 29.18; 35.5–6; 42.7, 18; 61.1[28]), Jesus answers John by calling attention to the marvellous events that have been happening: the blind see, the lame walk, and so on (cf. Sib. Or. 8.205–7). The list consists of six items which are, in typical Matthean fashion, arranged in three pairs: a and b, c and d, and e and f.[29] (Luke has the six items but not the triad.) The reader's thoughts inevitably turn back to what has gone before. Jesus healed blind men in 9.27–31. He cured a lame man in 9.1–8. A leper was cleansed in 8.1–4. A deaf man regained his hearing in 9.32–4. 9.18–26 recounts a resurrection. And 4.17, 23; 5.3; 9.35; and 10.7 record preaching to the poor. Our gospel is, manifestly, arranged so that the various threads of chapters 4–10 are woven together in 11.2–6. The passage thus interprets 4–10 as a whole: Jesus is the Coming One of John's preaching, the Messiah of prophecy who, through his proclamation to the poor and his miraculous and compassionate deeds, brings to fulfilment the messianic oracles uttered so long ago by Isaiah the prophet. All of 4–10 is prophecy come to pass.

The influence of the Isaianic texts upon 11.5 is not, we should observe, confined to the vocabulary: it extends to the very form or structure of the sentence. Isa 29.18–19; 35.5–10; and 61.1–2 are lists. So is Mt 11.5.

τυφλοὶ ἀναβλέπουσιν καὶ χωλοὶ περιπατοῦσιν. So Lk 7.22, without 'and'. LXX Isa 61.1 has: τυφλοῖς ἀνάβλεψιν.[30] Compare

---

[25] See Jeremias, *Lukasevangelium*, pp. 161–2.

[26] So Manson, *Sayings*, p. 66; Hoffmann, *Logienquelle*, pp. 192–3.

[27] A possibility suggested by Matthew's 'what you see and hear'. Does this presuppose something like Lk 7.20–1?

[28] On the use of Isa 61 in Jewish and Christian sources see 1, p. 438.

[29] The καί before νεκροί does not (against Gundry, *Commentary*, p. 206) mean that 'the dead are raised' and 'the poor have good news preached to them' are not paired. In Greek, as in English, the last item in a series may be introduced with a conjunction. See e.g. Mt 12.44; 15.30; 19.18f.

[30] The MT has *wĕlaʾăsûrîm pĕqaḥ-qôaḥ*: 'and to those bound the opening'. Matthew's text might depend upon the LXX, which has misunderstood the Hebrew. But the meaning of *pĕqaḥ-qôaḥ* is disputed (see the commentaries), and BDB suggests 'opening (of the eyes)'. Moreover, the targum renders: 'to those bound, show yourselves to the light'. See further Chilton, *Strength*, pp. 161–3.

also 29.18; 35.5; and 42.7, 18. 'The lame walk' alludes to Isa
35.6: 'the lame man shall leap like a hart'. Note also Clement of
Alexandria, *Paed.* 1.9, quoting from the lost Apocryphon of
Ezekiel: 'And the lame I will bind up'.

λεπροὶ καθαρίζονται καὶ κωφοὶ ἀκούουσιν. Again Luke agrees
but without 'and'.[31] Compare Isa 35.5: 'The ears of the deaf
unstopped' (LXX: ὦτα κωφῶν ἀκούσονται); also 29.18 (ἀκούσονται . . . κωφοί) and 42.18 (οἱ κωφοί, ἀκούσατε). There is no
mention of lepers in Isaiah. Perhaps one is to infer that Jesus'
works go even beyond what the OT anticipates. Or maybe an
Elisha typology lies in the background (cf. 2 Kgs 5).

καὶ νεκροὶ ἐγείρονται καὶ πτωχοὶ εὐαγγελίζονται.[32] 'The dead
are raised' probably alludes to Isa 26.19 ('thy dead shall live,
their bodies shall rise'[33]). 'And the poor are evangelized' (cf.
1QH 18.14; Lk 4.18) draws upon LXX Isa 61.1: εὐαγγελίσασθαι
πτωχοῖς (MT: *lĕbaśśēr 'ănāwîm*). εὐαγγελίζομαι[34] (cf. *bśr*)
appears only here in Matthew. For 'the poor' see on 5.3. The
proclamation to the poor comes at the end because it gives
meaning to—that is, interprets—the miracles done by Jesus.
Moreover, the miracle that heals only the body does not
accomplish as much as the word that heals mind and heart and
brings eschatological salvation.

John has, according to 11.2, already heard of 'the deeds of the
Christ'. What then is the function of v. 5? Being a summary of
what is already known to both John and the reader, is it not
superfluous? The answer is No, for the verse contains more
than a list of miracles: it also supplies a hermeneutical
suggestion. Jesus' language directs one to Isaiah and is therefore
an invitation to put Jesus' ministry and Isaiah's oracles side by
side. Are not the promises of salvation being fulfilled? Is not
eschatology in the process of being realized?[35]

6. Jesus concludes with a beatitude (see Excursus II). In the
judgement of some, it once circulated independently of v. 5.[36]
But the connexion between Isa 61 and the makarism form is
attested in the dominical beatitudes.

[31] Lk 7.22 P[75] ℵ B D *f*[13] has καὶ before κωφοι, and this is printed by
NA[26]. HG omits, following Maj lat sy[h].
[32] The last three words are missing in k sy[s] Clem. Did a tired eye pass from
εγειρονται to ευαγγελιζονται? On the variant in sy[c] ('the poor are sustained')
see Black, pp. 250–1.
[33] LXX: ἀναστήσονται οἱ νεκροί, καὶ ἐγερθήσονται οἱ ἐν τοῖς μνημείοις.
[34] Lit.: G. Friedrich, *TWNT* 2, pp. 705–35; P. Stuhlmacher, *Das paulinische
Evangelium: I. Vorgeschichte*, FRLANT 95, Göttingen, 1968. The use of Isa
61.1–2 in the dominical beatitudes is indirect evidence that Jesus himself may
have used *bśr*.
[35] On the healing of the sick in messianic times see SB 1, pp. 593–6.
[36] E.g. Beare, p. 258. Contrast Bultmann, *History*, p. 110.

καὶ μακάριός ἐστιν ὃς ἐὰν μὴ σκανδαλισθῇ ἐν ἐμοί. This agrees word for word with Lk 7.23. Compare 13.57; 26.31; Jn 6.61; 16.1. On the transitive use of σκανδαλίζω see on 5.29. Exactly why John might be scandalized is not stated, although one thinks first of the discord between Jesus and popular messianic expectation.

'Blessed is he who is not offended in me' makes explicit the christological presupposition of 11.5: the works of eschatological salvation are being done through the speaker; and neither those works nor the gospel can be separated from him. Recognition of Jesus makes one blessed. The saying thus harmonizes with 10.32–3 par. ('He who confesses me, etc.') and 12.38–42 ('a greater than Jonah is here', 'a greater than Solomon is here').[37] If Jesus did indeed utter it (see below), it is hard to avoid speculation about his so-called 'messianic consciousness'. (In 11QMelch 2 it may be—the text is fragmentary—Melchizedek, a heavenly king, who fulfils Isa 61 and proclaims liberty to the captives.)

The dominical origin of 11.5–6, which characteristically proclaims the presence of the kingdom,[38] is usually granted by modern scholars.[39] What is not always granted is the authenticity of the setting.[40] Were Jesus' words in fact occasioned by John's wonder about his identity? If not, then the scholar is free to interpret 11.5–6 par. as proof only that Jesus viewed his work in terms of Isa 35 and 61: the new age had dawned. There are, however, very sound reasons for accepting the narrative framework supplied by Matthew and Luke, and before them by Q.[41] (i) John did, as we have argued when discussing 3.11, look forward to a messianic figure of some sort. (ii) Would not a Christian construction have made John testify to Jesus? As it is, the Baptist does not know Jesus' identity and we are not even told that he believed or accepted Jesus' words.[42] Mt 11.2–6 would scarcely score points against followers of John. (iii) If John associated the Coming One primarily or even exclusively with judgement, then Jesus' deeds and the rumours about his identity (cf. Mk 8.27) might have set the Baptist to thinking. How can this man be what people say he is? Can he be sent by God? What does he think of himself? As Dunn has written: 'As soon as the presence of the kingdom was proclaimed, the Baptist's camp would

---

[37] Cf. Beasley-Murray, p. 83: 'The beatitude thus implies that in his word and deed Jesus is the revelation of God's kingdom operative in the present and that to come under that sovereignty for salvation one must recognize his authority and submit to his way'.

[38] See Jeremias, *Theology*, pp. 103–5; Beasley-Murray, pp. 80–3.

[39] Cf. Bultmann, *History*, pp. 126, 128, 151. Contrast Pesch (v).

[40] Cf. Bultmann, *History*, pp. 23–4. Especially influential has been the scepticism of Strauss (v): Did prisoners have access to the outside world? Was it not polemic which led to the creation of the story in 11.2–6?

[41] With what follows see esp. Dunn (v).

[42] According to Hoffmann, *Logienquelle*, p. 201, there is no response because the chosen form (apophthegm) disallows it.

inevitably ask, Where is the judgement proclaimed by the Baptist as the chief mark of the end-time? This question could be expressed in the form, "Are you the Coming One, or should we look for another?", for the Coming One was to bring in the end-time, and Jesus' proclamation clearly implies that *his* works, particularly of exorcism, prove the presence of the end-time' (*Spirit*, p. 59). To which we can add: the way in which 11.4–6 seems studiously to avoid alluding to judgement (see below) makes it a very appropriate answer to the question, Where is the judgement? Jesus is in effect saying: that comes later, other things come first. (iv) If Christians formed 11.2–6 in order to persuade others of Jesus' messiahship, they chose an odd method. The Messiah was not, despite texts such as 2 Bar 29.6, thought of as a miracle-worker. Likewise, if 11.2–6 was produced in order to prove that Jesus was the eschatological prophet, why not *Mosaic* miracles? (v) If 11.2–6 was first formulated precisely to identify Jesus with John's dispenser of fire,[43] then why is our text not about Jesus as the Son of man or eschatological judge? (vi) If it is unwise to separate v. 5 from v. 6 (see above), it is also unwise to divide v. 6 from v. 4; for in 13.16, which goes back to Jesus, the seeing and hearing formula is linked to a makarism, as it is here: 'tell John what you see and hear. . . . And blessed is he . . .'. This is some reason for maintaining the unity of vv. 4–6. In addition, v. 4 in turn requires something close to 11.2–3 par. (vii) The parallels common to 5.3–6; 11.2–6; and 13.16–17 may be illustrated in this manner:

5.3–6	11.2–6	13.16–17
Isa 61	Isa 61	
makarism	makarism	makarism
	see and hear formula	see and hear formula

One can see that 11.2–6 shares certain features with *logia* generally regarded as uttered by Jesus. The joining of an allusion to Isa 61 with a beatitude is attested outside 11.2–6, as is the use of a see and hear formula in connexion with a makarism. Surely this speaks in favour of giving 11.2–6 the same status as 5.3–6 and 13.16f.

If our conclusions concerning the essential veracity of 11.2–6 be accepted, then the text becomes a key witness to Jesus' self-consciousness. To be sure, the reference in 11.2 to 'the Christ', which makes 11.2–6 directly address Jesus' messiahship, is, from the vantage point of history, obviously secondary. Furthermore, Jesus gives no name to himself. Is he the Messiah? Is he the suffering servant? Is he the Mosaic prophet? Is he Elijah? The questions are not answered. The relation of Jesus to the conventional titles remains elusive. Strongly implicit, however, is the identification also implicit in the beatitudes (see 1, pp. 438–9). The man through whom the poor have good news preached to them and through whom miracles have come[44] can only

[43] So Hoffmann, ibid., pp. 214–15; Schulz, *Q*, pp. 195–6.
[44] Given Jesus' undoubted success as a healer, it is arbitrary to hold, as does Jeremias, *Theology*, pp. 103–5, that Jesus originally intended to describe the time of salvation, not his own miracles. The antithesis is false.

be the anointed one of Isa 61.1, the bearer of the Spirit, who, in the
latter days, comforts the mourners and thereby brings promise to
fulfilment.

11.2–6 is also very instructive with regard to Jesus' eschatological
outlook. One must not miss the selective character of the scriptural
allusions in 11.4–6. Jesus draws upon Isa 29.18–19; 35.5–6; and 61.1.
Each of these texts, in its OT context, is closely associated with
judgement (cf. 29.20; 35.4; 61.2). It is not coincidence that Jesus picks
up only the promises of salvation. The central message for him, in
contrast with the Baptist, is not the prospect of judgement—although
that is hardly negated—but the presence of eschatological salvation.[45]

JESUS' TESTIMONY TO THE BAPTIST (11.7–15)

This passage consists of material taken from two different
sections of Q (cf. Lk 7.24–8; 16.16) plus Matthean redaction
(vv. 14–15). It opens with Jesus asking three questions. The first
question (v. 7c) is answered by another (v. 7d). The other two
questions (vv. 8a, 9a) are answered initially by a question
(vv. 8b, 9b), then by a clarifying declaration (vv. 8c, 9c). Because
the second clarifying declaration (v. 9c) identifies John as 'more
than a prophet', the way is cleared for a precise statement of
John's identity. Four points are made. John is the figure foretold
by Mal 3.1 (so v. 10); he is the greatest of those born among
women (v. 11); he is the turning point in salvation-history
(vv. 12–13); and he is Elijah (v. 14). The section ends with the
exhortation, 'He who has ears, let him hear' (v. 15).

11.7–9 par. probably represents the original unit, to which 11.10, a
citation of Scripture, and 11.11, an independent logion, were
subsequently added by the pre-Matthean tradition. 11.12–15 was then
added by Matthew himself. Against Beare, p. 259, there seems to be no
good reason for denying 11.7–9 a setting in the life of Jesus.[46] So far
from there being polemic against the Baptist, the pericope exalts him.
And of Jesus there is no mention at all.

7. τούτων δὲ πορευομένων. Compare 28.11. The words,
inspired by Q,[47] are redactional and serve to introduce a new
paragraph: when John's followers exit the stage the scene
changes. The crowd appears (v. 7b) and the subject of discourse
is different. The question is no longer, Who is Jesus? It is,
rather, Who is John?

---

[45] Lk 4.18–19, whatever its origin, offers a parallel: Jesus breaks off reading
the OT right at the point at which the theme becomes judgement.
[46] For Bultmann, *History*, p. 165, 11.10 and 11b are secondary additions; but
the rest perhaps preserves a genuine saying of Jesus. Cf. Theissen (v).
[47] Lk 7.24a reads: ἀπελθόντων δὲ τῶν ἀγγέλων Ἰωάννου.

ἤρξατο ὁ 'Ιησοῦς λέγειν τοῖς ὄχλοις περὶ 'Ιωάννου. Lk 7.24 lacks the subject[48] and has πρὸς τοὺς ὄχλους.[49] The agreement is proof of a narrative seam in Q. On the crowd(s) in Matthew see on 4.25.

τί ἐξήλθατε εἰς τὴν ἔρημον θεάσασθαι;[50] Lk 7.24 differs only in the verb form: ἐξεληλύθατε (cf. 11.8 diff. Lk 7.25; 11.9 diff. Lk 7.26).[51] On John and the wilderness see on 3.1. One wonders whether the crowds in the wilderness are intended to evoke messianic expectation (cf. 24.26).[52]

κάλαμον ὑπὸ ἀνέμου σαλευόμενον; So also Lk 7.24. Compare 1 Kgs 14.15; Isa 7.2 (ὑπὸ πνεύματος σαλευθῇ); Wisd 4.4 (ὑπὸ ἀνέμου σαλευθήσεται); Josephus, Ant. 4.51 (ἐξ ἀνέμου βίας σαλευομένου); b. Ta'an. 20a; and Lucian, Herm. 68 (ἐοικώς ... καλάμῳ ... πρὸς πᾶν τὸ πνέον καμπτομένῳ). κάλαμος[53] occurs most often in the LXX for qāneh and means 'reed'. It is not linked with σαλεύω (= 'shake') in the OT. 'A reed shaken by the wind' is best taken literally or as 'a metaphor for a commonplace event'.[54] The people did not go to the Jordan banks to gaze upon an everyday sight (cf. Job 40.21; Isa 19.6; 35.7).

One should not, however, altogether exclude the possibility that Jesus or Matthew had something very different in mind. To one steeped in the Hebrew OT, the image of reeds[55] blown by the wind might have recalled Exod 14–15, where God sends forth a strong wind to drive back the Sea of Reeds (sûp). The meaning of Jesus' query would then be: Did you go out into the wilderness to see a man repeat the wonders of the exodus? Certainly people at a later time did just that: Josephus, Ant. 20.97–9. Moreover, the royal attire in the question in 11.8 could conceivably, in Stendahl's words, 'refer to Davidic-messianic expectations' ('Matthew', p. 783). Which is to say: both 11.7 and 8 can be connected with popular messianic expectation.

[48] Matthew probably added it.

[49] Matthew is here original. See Jeremias, Lukasevangelium, pp. 33, 163.

[50] As with the ἰδεῖν in 11.8 and 9, it is possible that 'to see' should be taken not with what precedes but with what comes after: Why did you go into the wilderness? To see . . .? The sense is not altered. Cf. Gos. Thom. 78.

[51] So HG. NA[26] prints εξηλθατε in Lk 7.24–6; but is this not assimilation to Matthew?

[52] See Davies, SSM, pp. 114–16, and S. Talmon, King, Cult, and Calendar, Jerusalem, 1980, p. 215.

[53] Cf. 12.20; Isa 42.3; and the rabbinic qālāmôs.

[54] Allen, pp. 114–15. Because people were sometimes compared to reeds (cf. SB 1, pp. 596–7), some commentators have seen in the shaken reed an allusion to John's character—either to his weak faith (cf. 11.2–6) or, on the contrary, to his strength. This doubtless reads too much in the text. Theissen (v) thinks of Herod Antipas, whose personal symbol on coins was, until A.D. 26/27, the reed.

[55] The singular, κάλαμον, could easily be collective; cf. McNeile, p. 152, who cites Job 40.16; Ps 67.30; Isa 19.6; 35.7.

8. ἀλλὰ τί ἐξήλθατε ἰδεῖν; Luke again has the perfect instead of the aorist. On ἀλλά in multiple questions see BDF § 448.4. The word could be rendered: 'But if not that . . .' (cf. the Aramaic *'ellā*'). The shift from θεάσασθαι (11.7) to ἰδεῖν (cf. also 11.9) does not seem significant.

ἄνθρωπον ἐν μαλακοῖς ἠμφιεσμένον; Luke has this with ἱματίοις after μαλακοῖς.[56] μαλακός here means 'soft [i.e., luxurious] clothing'. John, of course, wore camel's hair and a leather girdle. The point—barring the suggestion made above—is that when people went to see John they were not expecting to feast their eyes upon worldly splendour. (Some would see an implicit depreciation of Herod's courtiers.)

ἰδοὺ οἱ τὰ μαλακὰ φοροῦντες ἐν τοῖς οἴκοις τῶν βασιλέων εἰσίν. Compare 2 Sam 11.8; 15.35; 2 Kgs 7.11; Gos. Thom. 78. This is probably very close to Q. Luke has made certain revisions: 'Behold, those in glorious apparel (ἐν ἱματισμῷ ἐνδόξῳ)[57] and having luxury (τρυφῇ ὑπάρχοντες)[58] are in kings' courts' (βασιλείοις).

9. ἀλλὰ τί ἐξήλθατε ἰδεῖν;[59] So Lk 7.26, with the perfect tense.

προφήτην; So Luke. In Lk 1.76 John is a 'prophet of the Most High'. Compare Mt 21.26.

In the first century, the word 'prophet' was not unambiguous.[60] It could refer to a diviner, that is, one able to tell the future (cf. 1 Sam 9.5–11; Josephus, *Ant.* 13.311; 15.373–8; *Bell.* 2. 159) or to an oracular prophet, one who, like the biblical prophets, interpreted the contemporary social-political situation, usually with an emphasis upon God's judgement (cf. Josephus, *Bell.* 6.300–9). 'Prophet' could also call to mind certain eschatological figures—either Elijah (cf. Mal 3; Ecclus 48.10; Mk 9.11[61]) or the prophet like Moses (cf. Deut 18.15–18; 1QS 9.11; 4Q175; Jn 1.45). And from Josephus we learn about men such as Theudas, the Egyptian, and others—self-proclaimed prophets—who led

---

[56] So also Mt 11.8 C L W Θ 0233 *f*[1.13] Maj b f h l sy co Chr. We have followed both HG and NA[26] in regarding this as assimilation to Luke. But a scribal slip is also a possibility: the endings of μαλακοῖς and ἱματίοις are identical.

[57] ἱματισμός: Mt: 0; Mk: 0; Lk: 2/Acts: 1; cf. Mk 9.3 diff. Lk 9.29. ἔνδοξος: Mt: 0; Mk: 0; Lk: 2.

[58] ὑπάρχω: Mt: 3; Mk: 0; Lk: 15/Acts: 25. See Jeremias, *Lukasevangelium*, p. 163.

[59] So NA[26]. HG moves ιδειν, placing it after προφητην. So ℵ* B¹ W Z 892 *pc* bo eth Or. This wrongly disturbs the parallelism, although one might argue for assimilation to Luke. See further Metzger, p. 29.

[60] For what follows see R. A. Horsley, '"Like One of the Prophets of Old": Two Types of Popular Prophets at the Time of Jesus', *CBQ* 47 (1985), pp. 435–63. See also Davies, *SSM*, pp. 115ff.

[61] Note also the papyrus fragment from Qumran cave 4 mentioned by J. Starcky, 'Les quatre étapes du messianisme à Qumran', *RB* 70 (1963), p. 498.

large movements and sought to perform acts of (eschatological) deliverance similar to those performed by Moses and Joshua (cf. Acts 5.36; 21.38).[62] John was no doubt thought of by many as not only an oracular prophet but also an eschatological figure (Elijah).[63]

ναὶ λέγω ὑμῖν, καὶ περισσότερον προφήτου. So also Lk 7.26. ναί is employed instead of 'amen' because it does not introduce a new thought but answers to what has just been said. The Baptist is not simply a seer or an oracular prophet. John is an eschatological prophet and himself the object of prophecy, for he is the messenger foretold by Malachi, Elijah (11.10, 14).[64]

10. οὗτός ἐστιν περὶ οὗ γέγραπται.[65] So also Lk 7.27. Compare Jn 5.46; 1 Cor 7.1. On 'it is written' see on 2.5. The formula used here ('This is . . .') reminds one of certain texts in the Dead Sea Scrolls (e.g. CD 1.13; 10.16; 16.15; 4QFlor. 1.16; 4QCatena[a] 1–4.7; 5–6.11; 1QpHab. 3.2, 13–14; 11QMelch. 2.15). For rabbinic parallels see Schlatter, p. 363.

ἰδοὺ ἐγὼ ἀποστέλλω τὸν ἄγγελόν μου πρὸ προσώπου σου. There is no ἐγώ in Lk 7.27. LXX Exod 23.20 agrees exactly with Matthew (cf. Gen 24.7; Isa 45.1–2). LXX Mal 3.1 is similar: 'Behold, I will send out my messenger'. In the OT, Exod 23.20 refers not to Moses but to God's angel, who led Israel safely to the promised land. So when the text is applied in the NT to eschatological preparation, one inevitably sees a typology: entrance into the kingdom is like the entrance into Canaan. ἄγγελον in Mt 11.10 means 'messenger' and designates a prophet, as sometimes in the LXX (see 2 Chr 36.15; Isa 44.26; Hag 1.13; Davies, *JPS*, pp. 86–7).

ὃς κατασκευάσει τὴν ὁδόν σου ἔμπροσθέν σου. Lk 7.27 agrees. Dependence upon LXX Mal 3.1 (καὶ ἐπιβλέψεται ὁδὸν πρὸ προσώπου μου) seems unlikely. The MT has *ûpinnâ-derek lĕpānāy*, which is a more likely source for our line.

Perhaps, when Q was translated into Greek, someone who was more familiar with Exodus than Malachi managed to conform v. 10b (quoting Exod 23.20) to the LXX but not v. 10c (quoting Mal 3.1). The issue, however, is complicated by Mk 1.2b. It too contains a

[62] Lit.: P. W. Barnett, 'The Jewish Sign Prophets—A.D. 40–70', *NTS* 27 (1981), pp. 679–97; D. Hill, 'Jesus and Josephus' "Messianic Prophets"', in Best, *Text*, pp. 143–54; R. A. Horsley, 'Popular Messianic Movements around the Time of Jesus', *CBQ* 46 (1984), pp. 471–95.

[63] On John as a prophet see Aune, pp. 129–32.

[64] According to Tertullian, *De mon.* 8, John is more than a prophet because he did more than prophesy: he baptized.

[65] C L W Θ 0233 *f*[1.13] Maj lat sy[p.h] co add γαρ (cf. 4.6, 10; 26.31). This plainly attributes John's status as 'more than a prophet' to the fact that he was himself the object of prophecy (cf. Cyril of Alexandria, *Comm. on Lk* 38). The interpretation is correct, but that is not proof of originality. א B D Z 892 b g¹ k sy[s.c] bo[mss] omit (so also HG and NA[26]).

composite quotation of Exod 23.20 and Mal 3.1, and it agrees precisely with Mt 11.10 save in omitting ἐγώ (cf. Lk 7.27) and ἔμπροσθέν σου. If one excludes coincidence and the possibility that Mk 1.2b is a post-Markan interpolation dependent upon Mt 11.10 or its parallel in Luke,[66] one must either postulate a link between Greek Q and Mark's tradition (for which the evidence is scanty indeed) or accept Plummer's statement: 'The passage was one of the commonplaces of messianic prophecy, and had been stereotyped in an independent Greek form before the Evangelists made use of it'.[67]

The combination of Exod 23.20 with Mal 3.1 was not a Christian innovation. It can also be found in Jewish texts (see Stendahl, *School*, p. 50). The connexion was perhaps made under the influence of the synagogal *haphtaroth* (Mal 3 being read with Exod 23).[68]

Mal 4.5–6 interprets Mal 3.1 as a prophecy about Elijah. Our text does the same (cf. 11.14). It thus makes John the Baptist (= Elijah) the messenger preparing the way for Jesus. (The OT has 'my messenger before me', 'me' being Yahweh. Matthew's σοῦ is Jesus. So Jesus has replaced Yahweh: 'the way of God is the way of Christ' (Schlatter, p. 363).)

11. In our judgement, 11.11 was at one time an isolated *logion*. In favour of this, the verse could stand on its own (cf. Gos. Thom. 46); its addition to 11.7–9(10) par. would be natural; the '(And) I say to you' is rather awkward coming so soon after 'Indeed, I say to you' (11.9 par.); and v. 11b creates tension with the high, unqualified praise expressed in 11.7–9 par.

There are good reasons for holding to both the unity and authenticity of the saying (cf. Schlosser 1, pp. 159–61). Since v. 11a did not originally follow upon v. 9 or v. 10 (see above), and since v. 11b could not have circulated by itself, and since vv. 11a and b are in antithetical parallelism, the two halves of our line must have come into being at the same time. As to an origin with Jesus, one has great difficulty supposing that a Christian decided to put John in his place by first proclaiming his exceeding greatness.

ἀμὴν λέγω ὑμῖν· οὐκ ἐγήγερται ἐν γεννητοῖς γυναικῶν μείζων Ἰωάννου τοῦ βαπτιστοῦ. Compare Lk 7.28: perhaps Matthew has changed οὐδείς ἐστιν to the more Semitic οὐκ ἐγήγερται[69] and moved it to the front, displacing μείζων; he has almost certainly added 'the Baptist'. Q otherwise has only 'John', and Matthew has tacked on the qualification elsewhere (in 17.13; cf. also 3.1 diff. Mk 1.4; 14.2 diff. Mk 6.14). Whether 'amen'* is redactional or whether Luke omitted it, who could say? 'Born

---

[66] So Taylor, *Mark*, p. 153, citing Holtzmann, Lagrange, and Rawlinson.

[67] A. Plummer, *St. Luke*, ICC, Edinburgh, 5th ed., 1922, p. 204.

[68] See J. Mann, *The Bible as read and preached in the Old Synagogue*, 1, Cincinnati, 1940, p. 479.

[69] ἐγείρω* is characteristic. Does the perfect tense function to exclude John from those (heretofore) born of women?

of woman' (cf. *yĕlûd 'iššâ*) is a Semitism.[70] That it here connotes frailty or the distance between mortals and the celestials is doubtful (cf. Schlosser 1, p. 161). μείζων equals *gādôl + min*. For ἐγείρω of prophets see 24.11, 24; Jn 7.52 (cf. the use of *qûm* in Jer 29.15; Amos 2.11).

ὁ δὲ μικρότερος ἐν τῇ βασιλείᾳ τῶν οὐρανῶν μείζων αὐτοῦ ἐστιν. Compare Zech 12.8. Lk 7.28 has 'kingdom of God' (so Q). μικρότερος probably has superlative sense (cf. 13.32; Lk 9.48; BDF §§ 60, 244). ἐν ... οὐρανῶν can carry local sense and go with 'least' ('least in the kingdom of Heaven'; so most modern translations). But the phrase can also be causal (cf. the Hebrew *bĕ*) and be taken with 'is greater than he' ('greater than he because of the kingdom' or 'greater than he when the kingdom comes'; cf. 6.7). The parallelism with v. 11a ('there has not arisen ἐν those born of women'; cf. 5.19) argues for the local sense.

Although Mt 11.11 is a secondary addition, this should not blind us to how it functions in its present context. 11.7–11a heaps praise upon John the Baptist, making him indeed the greatest among those born of women—and then v. 11b turns around and makes John less than the least. In this way John's greatness, which is no longer the subject, becomes a foil for the surpassing greatness of the kingdom.

The meaning of v. 11b is disputed. The problem concerns 'the least in the kingdom of Heaven'. These are the three major options: (i) Jesus, with reference to his humility, to his being younger than John, or to his being John's disciple, was speaking of himself.[71] Chrysostom, while observing that some identified 'the least' with angels or the apostles,[72] adopts this interpretation and writes of Jesus' 'condescension' (οἰκονομικῶς; *Hom. on Mt.* 37.3; cf. Tertullian, *Adv. Marc.* 4.18). (ii) 'The least in the kingdom of Heaven' really means 'anyone in the kingdom of Heaven (when it comes)'. On this view, 'Jesus is not contrasting all begotten (*sic*) of women, with John at their head, and some other group of men, the least of which is greater than John; he is contrasting the present state of the greatest of men with the future state of the least in the coming kingdom'.[73] In

---

[70] Cf. Job 11.12 LXX; Ecclus 10.18; 1QH 13.14; 18.12–13, 16, 23–4; Apoc. Mos. 33.2; Gal 4.4; 3 En. 6.2. See Schlatter, p. 364; SB 1, pp. 597–8; Black, p. 298.

[71] So F. Dibelius (v); Cullmann, *Christology*, p. 32. Cf. Origen, PG 17.293B; Hilary, PL 9.981A; Jerome, PL 26.74A.

[72] Ambrose was one who identified 'the least' with angels (*Comm. on Lk* 7.27).

[73] So J. C. O'Neill, *Jesus the Messiah: Six Lectures on the Ministry of Jesus*, London, 1980, pp. 10–11. Cf. Allen, pp. 115–16; McNeile, p. 154; Verseput,

other words: 'the least in the kingdom will be greater than the greatest is now'. This interpretation does not exclude John from the kingdom. (iii) 'The least in the kingdom' means 'anyone now in the kingdom of Heaven'. 'Just as Moses led the children of Israel to the borders of the Promised Land, but could not himself enter, so John led his followers up to the verge of the new order initiated by Jesus, but could not himself enter' (Manson, *Sayings*, p. 70). This understanding, which excludes John from the present kingdom, is the most popular with modern commentators.[74] In some of the Fathers it is combined with NT texts according to which Christians are born not of the flesh but of God, this making a contrast with John, who was only 'born of woman' (see e.g. Cyril of Jerusalem, *Comm. on Lk.* 38, citing Jn 1.12–13).

Interpretation (ii) or (iii) would seem the best for the redactional level. Matthew is not likely to have thought of Jesus as 'the lesser' or 'the least'.[75] As for the choice between (ii) and (iii) one can hardly be dogmatic. In the First Gospel the kingdom of Heaven is both present and future. But perhaps (ii) makes the most sense; for 11.12 (q.v.) would seem to include John, the herald of the kingdom, in the kingdom.[76]

As to what Jesus himself meant, (i) strikes us as out of character. Such a strong statement about his own greatness is hardly expected. And where else does Jesus call himself 'the lesser' or 'the least'? We are left, again, with (ii) and (iii). The former is the choice if 11.11 was uttered before John's death. Since Jesus included the Baptist in the kingdom, he could hardly have demoted him, were he alive, beneath 'the least in the kingdom'. If, however, 11.11 was spoken after Herod had John killed, one could hold interpretation (iii), for the saying might very well have been about the presence of the kingdom: those who are now alive and who submit themselves to the rule of God are the greatest, that is, the most blessed and privileged, of all men (cf. 12.38–42; 13.16–17). (The place of John, as well as of all the other dead saints, would in this case just simply not be addressed.)

12. Mt 11.7–11 par. was, in Q, joined to the equivalent of

pp. 87–9. O'Neill is writing about Jesus, not about Matthew. Against Gundry, *Commentary*, p. 208, we do not believe that 'Jesus would hardly have needed to say that the least in the future kingdom will surpass the greatest at the present time'.

[74] Cf. Wellhausen, *Matthaei*, p. 52. Those who regard v. 11b as secondary, a Christian demotement of John, usually adopt this opinion. A variation of this interpretation is proposed by Meier (v): John belongs to the kingdom but not to the new stage of the kingdom present in the church.

[75] And our gospel tells us neither that Jesus was John's disciple nor that he was younger than John.

[76] 11.9 might also put John in the kingdom, for he is 'more than a prophet'. Does he not then come after 'the prophets and the law' (11.13)?

11.16–19 = Lk 7.31–5. Mt 11.12–13 stood elsewhere (cf. Lk 16.16).[77] Matthew has brought the verses forward for thematic reasons: he wants Jesus' words about the Baptist to be in one place.

In Luke the equivalent of Mt 11.13 appears before the equivalent of 11.12. Luke, not Matthew, has preserved the order in Q. The statement about the old order naturally comes before the statement about the new order.[78]

ἀπὸ δὲ τῶν ἡμερῶν Ἰωάννου τοῦ βαπτιστοῦ ἕως ἄρτι ἡ βασιλεία τῶν οὐρανῶν βιάζεται καὶ βιασταὶ ἁρπάζουσιν αὐτήν. Lk 16.16b is very different: ἀπὸ τότε ἡ βασιλεία τοῦ θεοῦ εὐαγγελίζεται καὶ πᾶς εἰς αὐτὴν βιάζεται.[79] Matthew has replaced 'of God' with 'of the heavens', and ἀπό ... ἄρτι may be an expansion of the simple ἀπὸ τότε.[80] Beyond this, our evangelist appears to have been more faithful to Q than Luke. In the First Gospel the kingdom of Heaven βιάζεται while in Luke the kingdom of God is preached. Because εὐαγγελίζομαι is a Lukan favourite[81] most scholars have judged Lk 16.16b to be a rewriting of the more obscure phrase preserved by Matthew.

Matthew's 'From the days of John the Baptist', like Luke's 'From then', should be read inclusively (cf. 2.16; 24.21), not exclusively (cf. 26.29).[82] In other words, John belongs in the kingdom. As Trilling (v), pp. 277–8, has demonstrated, in

[77] So most. Against Lührmann, pp. 24–31, 11.12–13 was not already joined in Q to 11.7–11. Also to be rejected are the following proposals: that neither 11.12–13 nor Lk 16.16 is now linked to the material that surrounded it in Q (so Kümmel, *Promise*, pp. 121–2); that 11.12–13 and Lk 16.16 are not variants of the same *logion* (so Bammel, 'Luke 16.16–18' (v), p. 104); that Lk 16.14–18, together with Mt 5.19, constituted a unit in Q (so Schürmann, *Untersuchungen*, pp. 126–36; for criticism see Hoffmann, *Logienquelle*, pp. 53–6); that Mt 11.12–13 is informed by Q as well as an M variant (so Chilton, *Strength*, p. 222).

[78] Cf. Schulz, *Q*, p. 261. Justin, *Dial.* 51, although he clearly draws upon Matthew, has Luke's order.

[79] Though the suggestion that the sense of Lk 16.16b may not be very different from that of Mt 11.12, since the Lukan εὐαγγελίζεται does not rule out the possibility that the kingdom also βιάζεται, and the Lukan πᾶς εἰς αὐτὴν βιά-ζεται might perhaps be translated 'Every one uses violence against it', may be noted. The Gospel of the Nazaraeans had: the Kingdom of heaven διαρπά-ζεται (cf. Hennecke 1, p. 147).

[80] So Schulz, *Q*, p. 262; against Hoffmann, *Logienquelle*, p. 52. Cf. 22.46. For 'the days of X' see 2.1; 23.30; 24.37. The phrase is Semitic; cf. Gen 26.18; Judg 5.6; 2 Sam 21.1; Esra 9.7; Isa 1.1.

[81] See Jeremias, *Lukasevangelium*, pp. 39, 176. Yet the passive form is not so obviously Lukan. It does not occur in Acts. In Luke it occurs only twice, once with a parallel (7.22 = Mt 11.5).

[82] For Luke see Wink, pp. 51–7, and Kümmel, 'Lukas 16.16'(v). For Q see Hoffmann, *Logienquelle*, pp. 60–5. For Matthew see Catchpole 'Violence' (v), pp. 78–9, and Schweizer, *Matthew*, pp. 258–9.

Matthew ἀπό much more often than not is inclusive (cf. Wink, pp. 29–30). Further, would one not expect reference to a *point* in time rather than to a *span* of time ('the days of John') if the purpose were exclusion? And, since Jesus and John were alive at the same time, must not the time of Jesus, the time of the kingdom, include 'the days of John'? Moreover, throughout Matthew, the activities of John and Jesus are set in close parallelism. This is best explained by the supposition that the two men are thought of as belonging to the same period of salvation-history (see on 3.1). Finally, 11.9 makes John more than a prophet and therefore hints at his inclusion in a new period, the period after the law and the prophets (cf. 11.14–15). In short, then, the Baptist is to be considered 'the first herald of the kingdom' (John of Damascus, *De fide orth*. 4.15).

Most authorities have rightly treated this verse and the next as stemming from Jesus.[83] Lk 16.17 ('It is easier for heaven and earth to pass away than for one dot of the law to be void') is surely an attempt to soften the radical implications of Lk 16.16. So 16.16 was, at least for Luke, potentially too extreme or at least in need of qualification; and if Lk 16.17 was joined to 16.16 in Q (a disputed issue), the same holds true for Luke's tradition. It is difficult to harmonize this fact with the claim—sometimes made—that Lk 16.16a = Mt 11.13 is a product of a Hellenistic-Christian church; for Luke, himself a Hellenistic Christian, or his tradition (which must have been Hellenistic-Christian or pre-Hellenistic-Christian) found it expedient to dampen the potential force of the saying and thereby eliminate one possible (mis)interpretation. In addition, we observe that it is John who is presented as marking the shift in salvation-history. A later formulation would almost certainly have made Jesus the centre of reference.[84]

Mt 11.12 par. is, without a doubt, one of the NT's great conundrums. The differences between the two canonical versions show us that, even at the beginning, Matthew and Luke probably found contrary meaning in Jesus' words. Clearly any interpretation will have to be offered with appropriate modesty. Out of the wealth of proposals the following deserve mention.[85]

(i) According to R. Otto, p. 111, 'on the one side, the kingdom comes and works and affects and seizes and grows of itself, without man's being able to do anything to help. And yet on the other side, only by summoning all one's power, and with the most strenuous determination, does one press into it'. 'The law and the prophets could

[83] Cf. Jeremias, *Theology*, pp. 46–7. For doubts see Bultmann, *History*, pp. 164–5; Braumann (v).
[84] We have assumed, against Barth, in *TIM*, p. 63, and Hoffmann, *Logienquelle*, pp. 50–1, the original unity of 11.12–13. See Catchpole, 'Violence' (v), p. 87, Schlosser 2, pp. 516–17.
[85] For a history of interpretation see the survey of Cameron (v).

only prophesy it, John could only prepare the way for it, but now one could seize it, gain it, come to participate in it'.[86] This understanding is not far from that of the Greek Fathers, who tended to think in particular of asceticism (cf. Clement of Alexandria, *Paed.* 3.7.39).

(ii) A. Schweitzer (p. 357) offered this suggestion: 'The saying has nothing to do with the entering of individuals into the Kingdom; it simply asserts, that since the coming of the Baptist a certain number of persons are engaged in forcing on and compelling the coming of the Kingdom ... it is the host of penitents which is wringing it from God, so that it may now come at any moment'.

(iii) N. Perrin, speaking for many, finds in 11.12 par. a reference 'to the death of the Baptist and the prospective suffering of Jesus and his disciples'. Further, 'In Matt. 11.12 the use of kingdom of Heaven ... evokes the myth of the eschatological war between God and the powers of evil and interprets the fate of John the Baptist, and the potential fate of Jesus and his disciples, as a manifestation of that conflict'.[87] In other words, the suffering of John and of the saints after him is interpreted in terms of the messianic woes or the eschatological tribulation of the latter days.

(iv) F. W. Danker (v) has proposed that 'the violent ones' was a name given to Jesus and his disreputable followers by their opponents. Jesus then took up the critical appellation and used it in a positive fashion: the sinners, the 'violent ones', are indeed now storming the kingdom (cf. Jeremias, *Theology*, pp. 111–12; Wink, p. 20).

(v) Some scholars have suggested that the Pharisees or Jewish antagonists in general are the violent ones who attack the kingdom by keeping people out of it (cf. 23.13).[88]

(vi) Others have thought of demons as the violent ones: it is the spiritual forces of wickedness which do violence to the kingdom by attacking those who belong to it (cf. 13.19).[89]

(vii) An interpretation very popular in the twentieth century has it that the violent ones should be identified with the Zealots or some other fanatical group of political revolutionaries bent upon the task of forcing God to bring the kingdom. Such men wrongly do violence to the kingdom.[90]

In order to choose—albeit with hesitation—between the various interpretations, one must carefully consider the exact meaning of βιάζεται which can be read either as a middle or a passive. The middle is here, we think, excluded because,

---

[86] Otto, p. 111. Cf. Irenaeus, *Adv. haer.* 4.37.7; Clement of Alexandria, *Quis div. salv.* 21; Gregory Nazianzen, *Orat.* 40.24; Manson, *Sayings*, pp. 133–35. Chilton, *Strength*, p. 229, positing a use of the Aramaic *tĕqap*, offers this translation: 'The kingdom of God avails itself, and everyone avails himself of it'.

[87] *Language*, p. 46. Cf. Perrin, *Rediscovering*, pp. 74–5. For similar statements see Hahn, *Titles*, pp. 152–3; Allison, pp. 120–4; Kloppenborg, pp. 114–15.

[88] Cf. Schlatter, p. 368; Ellis, *Luke*, p. 203.

[89] Cf. Kümmel, *Promise*, p. 123.

[90] Cf. Manson, *Teaching*, p. 124, n. 2; Klausner, p. 206; Cope, pp. 75–76.

although 'the kingdom of God breaks in with power, with force', may be a possible translation, βιάζεται is naturally taken as parallel to βιασταὶ ἁρπάζουσιν, and the latter clearly refers to action of which the kingdom is the object. (We assume that the parallelism is roughly synonymous.)

As Schrenk (v) has shown, βιάζεται is best taken as a passive *in malam partem*: the kingdom of God is violently hampered or opposed or attacked. This corresponds with the current extra-biblical usage of βιάζομαι[91] and with the second half of the logion. The natural signification of βιαστής is violent one or violator (cf. BAGD, s.v.), and ἁρπάζω means to take something forcefully.[92] Mt 11.12 thus declares that violent men forcibly take the kingdom, which permits the second half of the saying to explicate the first: the kingdom of God is violently attacked because violent men forcibly seize it.

But what can that mean? Three considerations move us to suggest that both Jesus and Matthew understood the saying along the lines of interpretation (iii): the subject is the eschatological trial and those who, through their opposition to the heralds of the kingdom, close that kingdom to others. First, both Jesus and Matthew interpreted their time as belonging to the eschatological birth pangs (Allison, pp. 40–50, 115–41). Secondly, the hymnist who authored 1QH 2 described himself as being oppressed at the hands of the violent ones in the eschatological period of distress (see 2.10–11, 21–2). This is, as O. Betz (v) has observed, the closest parallel to our enigmatic synoptic saying. At Qumran, the time immediately before the new age was one of conflict and struggle, the time when violent ones oppressed the pious and their leaders. Thirdly, elsewhere the synoptic tradition uses violent images to depict the messianic woes, which are already being experienced (see on 10.34–6 and cf. Lk 12.49–50). To sum up, then: for Jesus and for Matthew, as for the apocalyptic literature in general, the great redemption must be preceded by a conflict between the forces of good and the forces of evil (cf. 1 En. 91.5–6). Further, this conflict has already been joined, from the days of John the Baptist until now.

13. πάντες γὰρ οἱ προφῆται καὶ ὁ νόμος ἕως Ἰωάννου ἐπροφήτ-ευσαν. Lk 16.6a reads: ὁ νόμος καὶ οἱ προφῆται μέχρι Ἰωάν-νου. Matthew's 'the prophets and the law' is exceedingly unusual,[93] Luke's 'the law and the prophets' being the normal

---

[91] See the evidence cited and discussed by Schrenk (v) and Moore's articles (v).

[92] See W. Foerster, *TWNT* 1, p. 472, and Moore (v).

[93] We have found no parallel.

and natural expression (see on 5.17). The First Evangelist has probably reversed the order to underline the prophetic side of the Scriptures.[94] πᾶς + γάρ* is also to be attributed to Matthew's hand[95] as is the verb, which excludes an antinomian interpretation: the law and the prophets have not lost their imperatival force, it is simply that their prophecies have come to pass in Jesus. Whether ἕως or μέχρι comes from Q there is no way to tell. On the one hand, the tradition shows a slight tendency away from μέχρι (cf. 24.34 = Lk 21.32 diff. Mk 13.30), and ἕως* is frequent in the First Gospel. On the other hand, the prepositional use of ἕως but not μέχρι is clearly attested for Q in 11.23 = Lk 10.15 and 23.35 = Lk 11.51.

It would seem that, if 11.12 includes John the Baptist in the time of the kingdom (see above), then 11.13 places him outside the time of the law and the prophets; for 11.13 supplies the explanation (γάρ) for v. 12, and, if the latter statement includes John in the new time, then evidently the latter must exclude him from the old time. ἕως will then be inclusive in v. 12 but exclusive in v. 13 (cf. Gundry, *Commentary*, p. 210).

Many have detected in Mt 11.13 par. a denigration of the law. Indeed, it has been common for Christian interpreters to assume that Jesus was implicitly abolishing the authority of Moses when he said 'the law and the prophets were until John'. According to Tertullian, *De pud.* 8, the burdens of the law ceased with John; and in another place the same author informs us that some early Christians used our verse as reason for disregarding OT legislation (*De ieiunio* 2). Similar views have been held by many modern scholars. Perhaps this explains the words of Catchpole 'Law' (v), p. 87: 'No one with traditional Jewish theological reflexes would have generated the saying in question'. It is, to be sure, admitted by all that Matthew's text relegates only prophecy to the past and that Lk 16.16b is qualified by 16.17; but it is thought that Jesus' statement was just too radical for many early Christian ears and was therefore some toned down. There is no doubt some truth in this position. The presence of the kingdom did, for Jesus, displace the Mosaic law from centre stage: the Torah was no longer the criterion for salvation. But this in itself involved neither abolition of Moses nor any sort of antinomianism. 11.12–13 is about the kingdom, not the law and the prophets. Moreover, if Jesus himself had set aside the law, the heated debates on the topic in the primitive community are hard to fathom. In our judgement, 'the law and the prophets were until John' is simply another way of saying that the End or the kingdom of God has entered the present. One dispensation has given way to another.

---

[94] Cf. the addition of 'or the prophets' to 5.17. Note also that in 11.9 John is a prophet. On the law as a prophetic corpus on 5.18.

[95] γάρ is added because of the new order of the clauses; cf. Klostermann, p. 98.

What that means for the Mosaic Torah is an open question not answered by Mt 11.12–13 par.

14. This redactional addition[96] draws out the implication of the citation in 11.10 and discloses what Matthew thinks is most important about John: he is Elijah *redivivus*.

καὶ εἰ θέλετε δέξασθαι. εἰ + θέλω* in the second person singular or plural is Matthean.[97] θέλω combined with δέχομαι recalls the use in Hebrew of *mā'an* + *lāqaḥ*, as in Jer 5.3 and 25.28. 'If you are willing to accept (it)' does not convey doubt or hesitation or unimportance. Nor are the words an appeal for faith or a call to take especial care. The conditional indicates either that what Jesus is about to say is new or that not all accept its truth.[98]

αὐτός ἐστιν Ἠλίας ὁ μέλλων ἔρχεται. Compare 17.12–13. 'The Coming One' (3.11; 11.3) is certainly a title for Matthew. On the function of Elijah in Jewish eschatological expectation see on 3.11 and 17.9–13.

That John thought of himself as one like Elijah is quite possible (see on 3.3–4). That he identified himself with Elijah seems doubtful (cf. Jn 1.21).[99] But the equation may have been made by Jesus (see on 17.9–13).

The mention of 'Elijah, the Coming One' would almost certainly have sent Matthew's readers back to Malachi's paragraph about Elijah. This is fitting. If 11.12–13 tells us that the old dispensation of the law and the prophets concluded with John, 11.14 conjures up the final passage in the prophetic corpus.

Some early Christians used 11.14 as one of their proof texts for reincarnation (cf. Tertullian, *De anima* 35). Matthew, one is confident, would not have accepted their interpretation. For one thing, Elijah, according to Jewish tradition, had not died but ascended. For another, reincarnation was foreign to early Jewish tradition. How then did Matthew understand the equation, John = Elijah? Given that stories about the Baptist's infancy seem to have circulated in the early church (cf. Lk 1–2), the First Evangelist is not likely to have thought of a man descending from heaven. Perhaps, then, he thought of the Baptist as holding Elijah's *office*, so that John came 'in the

[96] Cf. Manson, *Sayings*, p. 185; Gundry, *Commentary*, p. 211. In the judgement of Schönle (v), pp. 53–4, Matthew took vv. 14–15 from the oral tradition. This seems an unnecessary postulate.
[97] Cf. 16.24; 17.4; 19.17, 21; 27.43.
[98] Perhaps originally the trouble with seeing John as Elijah was his death; cf. 17.9–13.
[99] Contrast Klausner, pp. 243–4.

spirit and power of Elijah' (cf. Lk 1.17).[100] See further Origen, *Comm. on Mt.* 13.1–2; Jerome, *Comm. on Mt.* 1.222–4.

15. ὁ ἔχων ὦτα ἀκουέτω.[101] This imperative, which is found often in the Jesus tradition, apparently floated from one context to another. It typically functions as a hermeneutical warning and/or to mark the conclusion of a paragraph or other literary unit.[102] Here the words serve notice that one subsection (11.7–15) has ended and that another (11.16–19) is about to begin. The phrase harks back to those prophetic texts which refer to people who have ears but hear not (Isa 6.9; Jer 5.21; Ezek 12.2). The point is that it takes more than an ear in order to hear with understanding.   What   is   required   is   inner   attention, concentration, discernment. Words, unless heeded, go in one ear and out the other. That Jesus himself exhorted those with ears to hear need not be denied (it would be consistent with his prophetic vocation); but recovering the original contexts in which he so spoke is an impossible task.

'TO WHAT SHALL I LIKEN THIS GENERATION?' (11.16–19)

With this paragraph Matthew closes the discussion on John the Baptist. There is logic in the arrangement. The identity of Jesus (11.2–6) makes his estimation of John (11.7–15) authoritative. So the reader has been confronted first by the truth about Jesus and then by the truth about John. What then follows is a record of how their contemporaries responded to those truths.

The unity of 11.16–19 is, despite many, more probable than not.[103] Also more probable than not is its dominical origin (cf. Perrin, *Rediscovering*, pp. 120–1). (i) John the Baptist and Jesus are placed side

---

[100] If not, would one not be forced to suppose that for Matthew the story of the transfiguration is really about Jesus and Moses and John?

[101] HG and NA²⁶, following B D 700 *pc* k sy^s, omit απουειν. The verb is found in ℵ C L W Z Θ *f*.¹³ Maj lat sy^{c.p.h} co, and although it could easily have been passed over (ακουε ... ακουε), its omission in other witnesses at 13.9 and 43 cannot be coincidence.

[102] Cf. Mt 13.43; 25.29 v. 1.; Mk 4.9, 23; 7.16 v. 1.; Lk 8.8; 12.21 v. 1.; 14.35; Rev 2.7, 11, 17, 29; 3.6, 13, 22; 13.9; Gos. Thom. 8, 21, 24, 64, 65, 96; Gos. Mary BG 1.7.8–9; Clement of Alexandria, *Strom.* 5.14. See further Crossan, *Aphorisms*, pp. 68–73; also M. Dibelius, 'Wer Ohren hat zu hören, der höre', *TSK* 83 (1910) pp. 461–71 (who calls the formula a 'Weckruf'), and J. M. Robinson, 'Gnosticism and the New Testament', in *Gnosis*, ed. B. Aland, Göttingen, 1978, pp. 135–6.

[103] This follows from its finely balanced structure. Cf. Mussner, 'Kairos' (v), pp. 605–6. With Suggs, p. 34, 11.19d may be a secondary addition. But, *pace* Zeller (v), p. 252, we do not think 11.18f. commentary added by the community. Could 11.16–17 ever have stood by itself?

by side. No attempt is made to exalt one over the other. (ii) Christians certainly did not invent the insult about Jesus being a glutton and drunkard.[104] (iii) Jesus seems to have had a habit of taking up his opponents' accusations and doing something positive with them (see on 19.12). In this he stands in the line of the OT prophets, who often quoted in order to refute.[105] (iv) There are probable Semitisms (ἄνθρωπος = τις, τὴν γενεὰν ταύτην, 'Son of man' = 'one', parataxis in v. 17).[106]

16. τίνι δὲ ὁμοιώσω τὴν γενεὰν ταύτην;[107] Lk 7.31 has οὖν (so Q?) for δέ and τοὺς ἀνθρώπους followed by τῆς γενεᾶς ταύτης. The Third Evangelist has added 'the men'[108] while Matthew has omitted Q's redundant second question: 'and what are they like?'[109] τίνι δὲ ὁμοιώσω[110] means 'to what shall I compare' or 'how is it with'. The formula appears only four times in the synoptic tradition (Mt: 1; Mk: 0; Lk: 3), but it recalls the similar uses of ὁμοίοω and ὅμοιος to introduce many parables. For rabbinic parallels see Schlatter, p. 372, and Jeremias, *Parables*, p. 100. ἡ γενεὰ αὕτη (cf. Gen 7.1 and the rabbinic *haddôr* (*haz*)*zeh*) occurs often in the NT, but only twice outside the synoptics (Acts 2.40; Heb 3.10; cf. Phil 2.15). It is a *terminus technicus* which refers neither to the Jewish people (*pace* Lührmann, p. 30) nor to mankind in general (cf. Jerome, PL 26.180) but to Jesus' or Matthew's contemporaries, their 'generation'.[111] The expression has its roots in the OT, where the generation in the wilderness is called 'faithless', 'evil', 'sinful', 'perverse', 'crooked' (cf. Deut 1.35; 32.5, 20). In the rabbis that particular generation (*dôr hammidbār*) came to be seen, along with the generation of the flood (*dôr hammabbûl*), as especially corrupt (cf. *m. Sanh.* 10.3; *Mek.* on Exod 15.1; *b. Nid.* 61a). This is the spirit in which 'this generation' is used in the gospels. The term refers firstly not to chronological duration but to

[104] Later Christians, in fact, felt compelled to assert that the privilege of keeping bad company was reserved only for Jesus, who alone was above being lowered to the level of others; see e.g. Cyril of Alexandria, *Comm. on Lk.* 39.

[105] See A. Graffy, *A Prophet Confronts his People*, AnBib 104, Rome, 1984.

[106] The Peshitta and Old Syriac both contain a wordplay that could be original; see Black, p. 161.

[107] In Clement of Alexandria, *Paed.* 1.5.13, 'this generation' becomes 'the kingdom of Heaven'.

[108] Cf. 12.42 diff. Lk 11.31 and see Jeremias, *Lukasevangelium*, p. 204.

[109] Cf. Isa 40.18; Mk 4.30 diff. Mt 13.31; Lk 13.18. So Polag, *Fragmenta*, p. 42.

[110] Cf. Lam 2.13; Isa 40.18, 25; Ezek 31.2. Only here in Matthew is ὁμοιόω active and transitive. In 13.31 diff. Mk 4.30 and 13.33 diff. Lk 13.20 Matthew has changed actives to ὁμοία.

[111] For what follows see the excellent article of E. Lövestam, 'The ἡ γενεὰ αὕτη Eschatology in Mk 13.30 parr.', in Lambrecht, *Apocalypse*, pp. 403–13. The post-placed αὕτη is Semitic. See BDF § 292.

character, and it is pejorative (cf. Josephus, *Bell.* 5.442). Further,
Lk 17.22–37 and Mt 24.34–44 compare Jesus' time with the
days of Noah, and the vocabulary used in Mk 8.38; 9.19; 12.39;
and Mt 17.17 = Lk 9.41 (ἄπιστος, διεστραμμένη, ἁμαρτωλός) is
clearly taken from OT descriptions of the generation in the
wilderness (cf. Deut 1.35; 32.5, 20). Thus, as E. Lövestam has
urged, a typological perspective may very well inform the
synoptic usage. Is not Jesus' generation like that of the flood, in
so far as God's judgement fell—unexpectedly—upon the one
and will fall—unexpectedly—upon the other? And is not Jesus'
generation like that of the wilderness in that just as God's
mighty acts of salvation did not prevent grumbling and rebellion
in the wilderness, so is it with Jesus' deeds and his generation?
What in any case distinguishes the NT application of the phrase,
'this generation', is its christological context: it is the rejection
of Jesus that makes 'this generation' so sinful (cf. 11.16–19;
12.38–42; 16.1–4).

ὁμοία ἐστὶν παιδίοις καθημένοις ἐν ταῖς ἀγοραῖς ἃ
προσφωνοῦντα τοῖς ἑτέροις.[112] Lk 7.32, which has ὅμοιοί εἰσιν
τοῖς ἐν ἀγορᾷ after παιδίοις, and καὶ προσφωνοῦσιν ἀλλήλοις at
the end, reflects Luke's fondness for following an anarthrous
substantive with an article + participle (cf. Jeremias,
Lukasevangelium, p. 166). ἑτέροις could be Matthean, for our
evangelist dislikes ἀλλήλων (Mt: 2; Mk: 5; Lk: 11). Did Q
perhaps have ἄλλοις? The plural, 'in the market-places', is
probably redactional. Matthew often prefers plural forms (Allen,
p. 83) as well as more general statements.

In this and subsequent clauses one sees children sitting in the
market-place, that is, in a public location. They are playing a
game or games in which girls playing flutes invite boys to dance
the wedding dance and in which wailing boys call upon girls to
sing a funeral dirge (see on 9.23). But the boys do not respond
to the flutes, the girls to the wailing. Both groups refuse to play
the game. This brings the response: 'We piped to you and you
did not dance. We wailed and you did not mourn'.[113] The
situation is obviously supposed to parallel the situation of John
and Jesus. But in what way? Most commentators, identifying
the children who call with John and Jesus, have put forward
some such interpretation as this: John, the ascetic and herald of
judgement, called for mourning and repentance. Jesus
announced joy and the presence of the kingdom and invited
others to enter it with him. Both invitations fell upon deaf ears.

[112] So HG and NA²⁶. On the variants see Linton (v), pp. 167–71.
[113] Cf. Jeremias, *Parables*, pp. 160–2, citing E. F. F. Bishop, *Jesus of Palestine*,
London, 1955, p. 104.

Instead of repenting or rejoicing, people chose to ignore God's messengers. So it did not matter how or in what guise God made his appeal. As T. W. Manson put it: 'The way of John is too strait and the way of Jesus too lax for their taste' (*Sayings*, p. 70).

There are serious problems with this understanding of our parable. (i) 11.16 likens 'this generation' to the children who reproach others for not joining their game.[114] (ii) 'We piped to you and you did not dance' (usually taken to refer to Jesus) comes before 'We wailed and you did not mourn' (usually taken to refer to John). Yet John made his appeal before Jesus appeared on the scene.[115] (iii) The parallelism between 11.17 and 18 naturally inclines one to associate John with the line, 'We piped to you and you did not dance', Jesus with the line, 'We wailed and you did not mourn'. (iv) Those who speak (λέγουσιν) their complaint in v. 17 (the children) are like those who speak (λέγουσιν) their complaint in vv. 18 and 19 ('He has a demon', 'Behold, a glutton . . .'). For these reasons, then, we reject the standard interpretation and follow the minority which has identified the piping and wailing children with 'this generation'.[116] On this approach to the passage, the contemporaries of John and Jesus are like disagreeable children who complain that others will not act according to their desires and expectations. The Baptist came neither eating nor drinking but sternly demanded repentance in sackcloth and ashes. People instead wanted to play at making merry: 'We piped to you and you did not dance'. Jesus came, preaching good news and entering into joyous fellowship with others. But people demanded that he fast (cf. 9.14–17) and exclude 'sinners' from his company: 'We wailed and you did not mourn'.[117]

17. λέγουσιν· ηὐλήσαμεν ὑμῖν καὶ οὐκ ὠρχήσασθε, ἐθρηνή-σαμεν καὶ οὐκ ἐκόψαθε.[118] Luke has altered the first word (λέ-

---

[114] This explains why Klostermann, p. 99, postulates corruption of the present text. Others appeal to the imprecise character of the introductions to parables (cf. Marshall, p. 300). But in the present instance the words are crystal clear.

[115] The force of this observation is somewhat lessened by the possibility that Jesus was quoting a traditional rhyme.

[116] Cf. R. C. Trench, *Studies in the Gospels*, 2nd ed., London, 1867, pp. 148–57 (citing Euthymius and Stier); Zahn, p. 432; Jeremias, *Parables*, pp. 161–2; Marshall, pp. 300–1; Linton (v).

[117] A third interpretation, put forward in the twentieth century in order to avoid any hint of allegory, refuses to identify John and Jesus with any of the parable's characters. The point is simply that the two groups of bickering children accomplish nothing. See Verseput (v), pp. 112–13, criticizing Jülicher 2, pp. 30–3.

[118] υμιν appears before the second και in C L W Θ *f*¹³ Maj it sy. It increases the parallelism between 17a and b. This could explain its omission. By the same token, one could regard the parallelism as characteristically Matthean,

γοντες) and the last word (ἐκλαύσατε[119]). So also Polag, *Fragmenta*, p. 42.

αὐλέω (LXX: 0) and θρηνέω (mostly for a form of *yll* in the LXX) are *hapax legomena* for Matthew. The former means 'play the flute', the latter 'sing a dirge'. ὀρχέομαι (= 'dance') also appears in 14.6 = Mk 6.22 (of Herodias' daughter), κόπτω (= 'beat (one's breast)', 'mourn') in 21.8 = Mk 11.8 and 24.30. On the game indicated by these words see above. For θρηνέω with κόπτω see LXX Mic 1.8; Josephus, *Ant.* 6.377; 8.273.

Matthew's sentence[120] seems to have been proverbial. Compare Eccles 3.4; Herodotus 1.141; Aesop, *Fab.* 27 (Halm); *Midr. Rab.* on Lamen., Proem 12.[121]

18. ἦλθεν γὰρ Ἰωάννης μήτε ἐσθίων μήτε πίνων. Compare 3.4. Lk 7.33 reads: 'For John the Baptist came (ἐλήλυθεν[122]) neither (μή) eating bread nor drinking wine' (cf. Deut 29.6).[123] 'The Baptist' (cf. Lk 7.20) and 'neither bread nor wine' (cf. Lk 1.15) are probably Lukan additions. Matthew's μήτε ... μήτε increases the parallelism. (Q evidently had the anomalous μή ... μήτε, which Luke has reproduced.).

'Neither eating nor drinking' is, of course, not to be taken literally. It is simply the antithesis of 'eating and drinking', a phrase which often in the biblical tradition connotes carefree excess (cf. Isa 22.13; Mt 24.38, 49; 1 Cor 15.32).

καὶ λέγουσιν· δαιμόνιον ἔχει. So Lk 7.33, with λέγετε. Nowhere else do we learn that John was thought by some to be possessed. But the charge is historically likely. Jesus himself was similarly smeared (cf. 12.22–32), and the Baptist's ragged appearance and unconventional behaviour would have been consistent with a diagnosis of possession.

19. ἦλθεν ὁ υἱὸς τοῦ ἀνθρώπου ἐσθίων καὶ πίνων. ἐλήλυθεν (cf. 11.18 diff. Lk 7.33) appears in Luke. On the Son of man see Excursus VI. This is an instance in which those who argue that Jesus used 'Son of man' in an idiomatic fashion have much in their favour.[124] 'Son of man' could here simply be a modest

the omission as due to an eye skipping from αμεν to υμιν.
[119] This better harmonizes with non-Palestinian custom. κλαίω: Mt: 2; Mk: 3; Lk: 9–10.
[120] For a suggested Aramaic original see Jeremias, *Theology*, p. 26.
[121] See further A. A. T. Ehrhard, *The Framework of the New Testament Stories*, Manchester, 1964, pp. 50–3. Bultmann, *History*, 202, n. 1, cites an Arabic proverb: 'If he claps you, then you are to cheer him'. On the possibility that some of Aesop's fables were known to first-century Jews see on 7.15.
[122] Matthew has changed the Ἠλίας ἐλήλυθεν of Mk 9.13 to Ἠλίας ἤδη ἦλθεν (17.12).
[123] Bread in all probability simply means food, wine drink; cf. Gen 14.18 with 1QapGen. 22.15.
[124] Cf. Lindars, *Son of Man*, pp. 31–4; M. Black, 'Aramaic Barnāshā and the "Son of Man"', *ExpT* 95 (1984), p. 205.

periphrasis or self-referent ('one')—although Matthew himself will have understood the phrase as a christological title. For other sayings in which the Son of man comes see 18.11 v. 1.; 20.28 = Mk 10.45; Lk 9.56 v. 1.; 19.10.

καὶ λέγουσιν· ἰδοὺ ἄνθρωπος φάγος καὶ οἰνοπότης. Lk 7.34 has λέγετε (cf. 11.18 diff. Lk 7.33). For the pairing, 'glutton and drunkard', see the targums on Deut 21.20 and Gundry, OT, pp. 80–1.

τελωνῶν φίλος καὶ ἁμαρτωλῶν. Compare 9.11. Luke has the order, 2, 1, 3, 4. On 'toll-collectors' see on 5.46. On 'sinners' see on 9.10. Clement of Alexandria, Strom. 3.6, has the striking phrase: φίλος τελωνῶν καὶ ἁμαρτωλός. It may well be that 'glutton and drunkard' stands in synthetic parallelism with 'friend of toll-collectors and sinners'.[125] If the first phrase has in view Jesus' well-known habit of holding festive table-fellowship, then the second phrase could refer to the disreputable company typically imagined to participate.

καὶ ἐδικαιώθη ἡ σοφία ἀπὸ τῶν ἔργων αὐτῆς.[126] Lk 7.35 has τέκνων αὐτῆς πάντων (so HG). Q probably had τέκνων αὐτῆς (cf. Polag, Fragmenta, p. 42). Matthew has gained an allusion to 11.2, thus forming an inclusio: τὰ ἔργα τοῦ Χριστοῦ/τῶν ἔργων αὐτῆς. Matthew's καί is probably adversative (cf. on 1.19). The aorist, if not to be explained as the translation of a Semitic perfect, must be either prophetic (expressing the certainty of a future event) or gnomic (the line does have a proverbial ring).

If, as it appears, the ἔργα of Sophia are the ἔργα of the Messiah (11.2), then Matthew has gone beyond Q and identified Jesus with Wisdom.[127] So it is Jesus who is vindicated[128] by[129]

[125] Cf. Perrin, Rediscovering, pp. 105–6. Stauffer's attempt (p. 16) to equate 'glutton and drunkard' with 'bastard' (he cites Tg. Yer. to Deut 20.18ff.) and thereby find an indirect testimony to the virgin birth does not persuade.

[126] So HG and NA[26], following ℵ B* W pc sy[p.h] sa[ms]bo. τ. τεκνων (assimilation to Luke) is the reading of B[2] C D L Θ f[1] Maj lat sy[s.c.hmg] sa[mss] Chr Aug Hil mae. Jerome knew both readings and preferred εργων. For the exceedingly remote possibility that the text originally read, 'For Sodom is justified by Jerusalem', see R. Maddox, 'The Function of the Son of Man according to the Synoptic Gospels', NTS 15 (1968), pp. 65–6.

[127] Cf. Suggs, pp. 57–8; Künzel (v); Burnett, pp. 88–93. The equation appears elsewhere in early Christianity; see Davies, PRJ, pp. 147–76; Dunn, Christology, pp. 163–212. Whether or not Matthew saw any link between Jesus as the Son of man and Jesus as Wisdom is hard to determine; see Suggs, pp. 48–55; Kim, pp. 90–1.

[128] ἐδικαιώθη should not be taken in a negative sense ('judged', 'condemned'); cf. Schlatter, pp. 374–5.

[129] For instrumental or causal ἀπό see LXX Isa 45.25. If the preposition be understood to mean 'over against' (cf. Wellhausen, Matthaei, p. 53, proposing translation of the Aramaic min qodām), one would have to accept 'children' as the original reading (or at least the reading of Q).

his[130] works. What does that mean? Despite the poor response of people, the works of God in Jesus have made plain to all Jesus' identity (cf. 11.2–6) and the need to respond to him favourably (cf. the following pericope, 11.20–4). If people still disbelieve, that is not Wisdom's fault, that is not Jesus' doing: the blame lies with those who have ears but do not hear. Were Wisdom to be brought to trial with the crime of not stirring Israel to faith, she would be acquitted. Her works, that is, Jesus' works, exonerate her by bearing testimony to her labour for others.

WOES ON THE CITIES OF GALILEE (11.20–4)

The passage consists of (i) a transitional sentence which sets the scene and serves as heading, (ii) a prophetic oracle of doom addressed to Chorazin and Bethsaida, and (iii) a prophetic oracle of doom addressed to Capernaum.

The two oracles, which so strongly resemble each other, share a common form:
A. Address (21a, 23a)
B. Indictment (hypothetical condition, hypothetical response; 21b–c, 23b–c)
C. Verdict (comparison with the fate of other cities; 22, 24)
The pattern is taken from the OT. See, for instance, Isa 5.11–17; 29.15–21; 33.1; Mic 2.1–5; Hab 2.9–11 (cf. *1 En.* 94.8; 95.7; 96.4, 8; 98.9–11; 100.7–9). The woes in chapter 23 are a bit different. They consist only of Address and Indictment. There is no Verdict (cf. Isa 5.18–23).[131]

In Q, the woes immediately trailed the mission discourse (see above). Perhaps the purpose of the juxtaposition was to prepare missionaries for rejection. But if so, Matthew has not followed Q's interpretative lead. In the First Gospel the woes belong to a large complex whose theme is the decision for or against Jesus. Thus 11.20–4 carries forward the disappointment registered at the end of 11.16–19, a unit whose subject is the rejection of John and Jesus by 'this generation';[132] and it makes for a contrast with the following pericope, which concerns those who accept Jesus (11.25–30).

[130] *Pace* Trilling (v), p. 284, ἔργα probably does not include the works of John the Baptist, at least as regards the redactional perspective.
[131] On prophecies of doom and woe oracles see Aune, pp. 96–7, 116–17, 179–81, and the lit. he cites; also below, n. 137.
[132] Cf. Strauss, p. 345: 'The description of the ungracious reception which Jesus and John had alike met with, leads very naturally to the accusations against those places which had been the chief theatres of the ministry of the former'.

20. τότε ἤρξατο ὀνειδίζειν τὰς πόλεις ἐν αἷς ἐγένοντο αἱ πλεῖσται δυνάμεις αὐτοῦ, ὅτι οὐ μετενόησαν. Compare Jn 12.37 and *Mek.* on Exod 15.6 ('Thou didst give an extension of time to the men of Sodom, that they might repent . . . but they did not repent'). τότε ἤρξατο (Mt: 4; Mk: 0; Lk: 0) is characteristic of Matthew, and πλεῖστος, which here means 'numerous' (BDF § 245.1), is redactional in 21.8. Both ἐγένοντο[133] and μετενόησαι foreshadow the next verse, where they occur again. ὀνειδίζω (usually for the piel of *ḥārap* in the LXX) means 'reproach'. δύναμις (cf. the Hebrew *gĕbûrâ*) is drawn forward from 11.21 = Lk 10.13 (cf. Mt 11.23, where the word is again editorial). It recalls the 'deeds' of 11.2 and 19 and refers to a sensational event beyond normal human abilities, an event which has religious meaning and therefore should garner a religious response. The 'cities' are obviously Jewish cities (cf. 10.5–6) and the subject is *Jewish* rejection of Jesus. On 'repentance' see on 3.2. Since Jesus himself called for repentance (4.17), those who fail to repent are guilty of disobedience to him.[134]

21. What follows is, in Bengel's words, 'a prelude to the last judgement'.

οὐαί σοι, Χοραζίν· οὐαί σοι, Βηθσαϊδάν.[135] So Lk 10.13, although there is some doubt as to the ending of 'Bethsaida'.[136] On the eschatological woe (the antithesis of the eschatological beatitude) see Excursus II.[137] For οὐαί σοι (=ʾôy-lĕkā, lāk)+ place name see LXX Num 21.29 (Moab); Jer 13.27 (Jerusalem). Whereas 'woe to me' or 'woe to us' expresses fear or anguish, woes not in the first person convey a threat or warning.

Chorazin,[138] which is to be identified with the ruins called Khirbet Kerâzeh, two miles from Capernaum (= Tell Hum), is mentioned only here in the NT. Bethsaida[139] (= 'house of the fisher', *bêt-ṣaydāʾ*), a city located close to the northern tip of the Sea of Galilee and identified

---

[133] Jesus is the implicit subject of the passive; it is not a divine passive.

[134] This failure to repent is one of the reasons we cannot see a Galilean idyll in the First Gospel; cf. Davies, *GL*, pp. 240–1.

[135] So HG. NA[26] prints Βηθσαϊδά. Neither supplies an apparatus.

[136] Βηθσαιδαν appears in P45 ℵ W *f*1.13 28 700 *al*, Βηθσαιδα in B Maj, and there are other variants.

[137] See also W. Janzen, *Mourning Cry and Woe Oracle*, BZAW 125, Berlin, 1972, and H.-J. Zobel, *TDOT* 3, pp. 359–64.

[138] *b. Menaḥ* 85a refers to a certain *Karzayum*; this might be Chorazin, although Jastrow, s.v., puts the place 'near Jerusalem'. For archaeological details see Z. Yeivin, 'Ancient Chorazin comes back to Life', *BAR* 13 (1987), pp. 22–36.

[139] Cf. Mk 6.45; 8.22; Lk 9.10; Jn 1.44; 12.21. It is often identified with 'Julias', the city named by Philip after the daughter of Augustus; see Josephus, *Ant.* 18.28, and Schürer 2, pp. 171–2.

today with the ruins of et-Tell,[140] is named nowhere else in Matthew. Our evangelist has done nothing to make the reader ready for the mention of Chorazin and Bethsaida. He has not, for example, told us of any miracles done in those two places;[141] nor has he told us that some of Jesus' disciples hailed from Bethsaida (cf. Jn 1.44; 12.21).[142]

ὅτι εἰ ἐν Τύρῳ καὶ Σιδῶνι ἐγένοντο αἱ δυνάμεις αἱ γενόμεναι ἐν ὑμῖν, πάλαι ἂν ἐν σάκκῳ καὶ σποδῷ μετενόησαν. This must come very near to reproducing Q. Lk 10.13 disagrees only in having ἐγενήθησαν and καθήμενοι before the final verb. But this last difference does apparently change the image. In Matthew the penitents wear sackcloth and put ashes on their heads. In Luke they sit on sackcloth (cf. Isa 58.5; Josephus, Ant. 19.349) in the place of ashes (cf. Schlatter, p. 379).

For motivating clauses (kî, ὅτι) after 'ôy/οὐαί see 1 Sam 4.7; Ps 120.5; Isa 3.9; 6.5; Jer 4.13, 31; 48.1; Hos 7.13; Mt 23.13, 15, 23, 25, 27; Jude 11.

Tyre and Sidon[143] were both important coastal cities on the Mediterranean. In Isa 23 the former is denounced in a prophetic oracle, and in Ezek 28 both are rebuked and the certainty of divine judgement upon them is proclaimed. Thereafter it evidently became common for the two cities, which were thought of as arrogant centres of wealth, to be spoken of together—like Sodom and Gomorrah—, and sometimes in warnings of judgement (cf. Jer 25.22; 27.3; 47.4; Joel 3.4; Zech 9.1–4; 1 Macc 5.15; Jud 2.28).[144]

σάκκος[145] (= śaq) is a dark (cf. Rev 6.12; 1 Clem. 8.3) hair cloth used as a garment of mourning and penitence (cf. Gen 37.34; 2 Kgs 19.2; Isa 37.1–2; Jon 3.5; Rev 11.3; Josephus, Bell. 2.237; m. Taʿan. 2.1). σποδός (= 'ēper) means 'ashes', which were also an element in mourning rituals (cf. 2 Sam 13.19; Job 42.6; Jer 25.34; m. Taʿan. 2.1; cf. on 6.16). The combination, 'sackcloth and ashes', became a fixed phrase betokening sincerity (cf. Esra 4.3; Isa 58.5; Dan 9.3; Barn. 7.5).

The declaration in 11.21 gains in force because, while Chorazin and Bethsaida were Jewish cities, Tyre and Sidon were not. Thus Jesus, with the hyperbole of a prophet, is exclaiming that Jews failed to respond to phenomena which would have persuaded even pagans—and, what is more, even notorious pagans.

---

[140] See B. Pixner, 'Searching for the New Testament Site of Bethsaida', BA 48 (1985), pp. 207–16.

[141] The Gospel of the Nazaraeans reportedly narrated fifty-three miracles done in the two places; see Hennecke 1, p. 151.

[142] According to Chrysostom, Hom. on Mt 37.6, Jesus mentions Bethsaida precisely because it was the home of several of his apostles: this shows that the city was not unrepentant 'by nature'.

[143] Is the assonance between Βηθσαιδαν and Σιδωνι intentional?

[144] The two cities are also joined in Mt 15.21; Mk 3.8; 7.24; Lk 6.17; Acts 12.20; Josephus, Ant. 8.320; 15.95.

[145] See H. Stählin, TWNT 7, pp. 56–64. The English 'sack' comes from the same root.

22. πλὴν λέγω ὑμῖν, Τύρῳ καὶ Σιδῶνι ἀνεκτότερον ἔσται ἐν ἡμέρᾳ κρίσεως ἢ ὑμῖν. Having delivered the indictment (v. 21), Jesus now utters the verdict. For discussion see on 10.15, where Jesus avows that it will be easier for Sodom and Gomorrah in the day of judgement than for the city that rejects the apostles. Lk 10.13 lacks 'I say to you'[146] and has the dative, τῇ κρίσει (so Q), instead of ἡμέρᾳ κρίσεως.[147]

While πλὴν λέγω ὑμῖν introduces 11.22, ἀμὴν λέγω ὑμῖν introduces the nearly identical 10.15. This suggests that Matthew saw πλήν as the equivalent of 'amen', in which case πλήν would not be adversative ('but'; cf. Mt 18.7) or exceptive ('except that', 'only'; cf. Acts 20.22–3) but asseverative ('indeed', 'surely'); see Thrall, pp. 73–4. The LXX sometimes uses πλήν to translate the Hebrew *'ak* with asseverative meaning (e.g. Judg 20.39; Zeph 3.7).

23. καὶ σύ, Καφαρναούμ, μὴ ἕως οὐρανοῦ ὑψωθήσῃ;[148,149] Lk 10.15 differs only in having the article (τοῦ) before οὐρανοῦ. The line alludes to Isa 14.13, although verbal agreement with the LXX is lacking: 'You (the King of Babylon) said in your heart: I will ascend to heaven' (MT: *haššāmayim 'e'ĕleh*; LXX: εἰς τὸν οὐρανὸν ἀναβήσομαι; cf. Ezek 26.20; Amos 9.2; Obad 4; Ps. Sol. 1.5; *t. Soṭa* 3.19). On Capernaum see on 4.13 and 8.14. It was, according to Matthew, Jesus' 'own city' (9.1). This makes its lack of repentance all the more terrible, and also proves the truth of the proverb: 'A prophet is not without honour except in his own country' (13.57). Yet note that Jesus' harsh words do not prevent him from returning to Capernaum (see 13.54; 17.24).[150]

The commentators have discussed at some length the meaning of 'would you be exalted unto heaven?' Most have thought of Jesus' presence: he exalted Capernaum by residing there (cf. the reading in Maj.: ἡ ἕως τοῦ οὐρανοῦ ὑψωθεῖσα). Others have referred the expression to the city's geographical situation, to its prosperity, or to its pride. Of the various proposals, the last has

---

[146] Matthew could have added this (cf. 10.15). But omission by Luke for contextual reasons is also credible. See Marshall, p. 425.

[147] Cf. *běyôm dînā'*. The expression occurs only four times in the synoptics, all of these being in Matthew.

[148] If this is not to be punctuated as a question, it could conceivably be continued by the next clause: 'Lest you be exalted unto heaven, you shall be cast down to Hades' (Wellhausen, *Matthaei*, p. 55).

[149] So HG and NA[26], following א B* D W Θ lat syᶜ co. η εως (του) ουρανου υψωθεισα /υψωθης is the reading in *f*[13] Maj f h q syˢ·ᵖ·ʰ. See Metzger, pp. 30–1. The secondary readings can be easily accounted for on the supposition that Καφαρναουμ μη became Καφαρναουμ η when the first letter of μη was accidentally dropped.

[150] One can only wonder whether Jesus, when he uttered the woes against Chorazin, Bethsaida, and Capernaum was washing his hands of them utterly or whether he still cradled for them some faint glimmer of hope.

the most to commend it, for pride is the subject in Isa 14.13.
Yet even this may read too much into the text. The phrase
under discussion might be wholly rhetorical; that is,
Capernaum's exaltation may not be concrete but rather
hypothetical, serving simply to introduce her abasement: 'You
shall be brought down to Hades'.

ἕως ᾅδου καταβήσῃ.[151] Luke has καταβιβασθήσῃ.[152] The
phraseology again depends upon the OT, and Matthew this
time is at one with the LXX (Isa 14.15; cf. also 14.11; Ezek
31.14–15). ᾅδης is used by Matthew only two times, in 11.23 and
16.18. The word frequently translates šĕʾ ôl in the LXX and its
first meaning is 'netherworld', the place where the dead reside.
But by the first century 'Hades' seems to have merged, at least
in some minds, with 'Gehenna', the place of damnation and
punishment for the wicked (see the discussion on 16.18). In Mt
11.23, however, 'Hades' is not, any more than the 'heaven' of
the same verse, to be taken literally. It functions rather as part
of a figure of speech. So far from scaling the heights, Capernaum
is poised for a catastrophic fall and the deepest abasement.

ὅτι εἰ ἐν Σοδόμοις ἐγενήθησαν αἱ δυνάμεις αἱ γενόμεναι ἐν σοί,
ἔμεινεν ἂν μέχρι τῆς σήμερον. Compare Josh 4.9; Mt 10.11;
27.8; 28. 15. The line is without Lukan parallel and is
presumably editorial (see p. 236). On Sodom see on 10.15.
Perhaps 'would have remained until this day' alludes to Sodom's
complete obliteration.[153]

In the first century Sodom was no longer a city. Tyre and Sidon, on
the other hand, although they had in the past been sacked and burned
to the ground, were still inhabited (cf. Acts 12.20; 21.3). One wonders,
therefore, whether 11.20–4 does not intentionally bring together the
living wicked and the wicked dead. Chrysostom so mused (*Hom. on
Mt*. 37.6).

24. πλὴν λέγω ὑμῖν, ὅτι γῇ Σοδόμων ἀνεκτότερον ἔσται ἐν ἡμέρᾳ
κρίσεως ἢ σοί. This is the Matthean equivalent of Lk 10.12 (the
differences are slight) and it largely reproduces Mt 10.15 (q.v.).

---

[151] So NA²⁶. HG prints καταβιβασθησῃ, which is found in ℵ C L Θ f¹³
Maj syᵖ·ʰ mae bo. One has to decide whether assimilation to the LXX or to
Luke is more probable.
[152] So HG. NA²⁶ disagrees, but Metzger, p. 151 assigns to καταβηση the
status of D, indicating a very high degree of doubt. It is difficult to follow
NA²⁶ in accepting καταβηση in both Mt 11.23 and Lk 10.15. If the two texts
agreed with each other and the LXX from the beginning, how does one explain
the variant reading?
[153] Comber (v), p. 500 asks: 'Could it be that the destruction of Sodom
would remind Matthew's readers of the devastation of Capernaum in the Jewish
War?' On the stereotyped expression, 'until this day', see B. S. Childs, 'A Study
of the Formula, "Until this Day"', *JBL* 82 (1963), pp. 279–92.

But the line most closely resembles 11.22, the conclusion to the oracle spoken against Chorazin and Bethsaida.

According to Bultmann, *History*, p. 112, the woes on the cities of Galilee are 'a community formulation'. According to Hahn, *Mission*, p. 36, n. 2, the authenticity of at least Mt 11.21–2 is 'not ... open to dispute'. Hahn's evaluation, although unwisely apodictic, is the more judicious (cf. Sabourin, p. 556). Bultmann's case is as follows: 'The sayings look back on Jesus' activity as something already completed, and presuppose the failure of the Christian preaching in Capernaum. Moreover it would have been difficult for Jesus to imagine that Capernaum could be exalted to heaven by his activity (Wellhausen)'. The last point rests upon overinterpretation, and why the passage requires that Jesus' activity be completed is anybody's guess. (Certainly Matthew would not have concurred. He puts 11.20–4 in the middle of the Galilean period.) In addition, if the failure of the Christian preaching in Capernaum is presupposed (and how does one determine this?), does it not follow that failed Christian preaching in Chorazin and Bethsaida is also presupposed? But then the NT nowhere refers to a post-Easter mission in any of these cities (cf. Freyne, p. 361). It seems to us more prudent to receive the Galilean woes as dominical. Especially indicative is the focus on 'mighty works'. On the one hand, if Jesus did not perform healings in and around Capernaum, then about him we know nothing at all. On the other hand, where is the evidence for a Christian mission near the northern tip of the Sea of Galilee, a mission which had as its chief characteristic δυνάμεις? The judgement called down upon Chorazin and Bethsaida and Capernaum results in part or even largely from a hardheartedness towards miracles. Certainly this has a more natural setting in Jesus' ministry than in that of the early church (cf. Dunn, *Spirit*, pp. 70–1).

What does Mt 11.21–3a tell us about Jesus? We can be fairly certain that Jesus first preached his gospel in the hope that he would be heard and heeded. He can hardly have launched a mission and sent forth messengers fully persuaded that all the effort would be wasted and that 'this generation' would by and large disbelieve him. What follows? When Jesus' inspired preaching and mighty deeds did not generate a corporate repentance, disappointment must have been acute. The presumption is confirmed by Mt 11.21–3a par. The text is a testimony to dashed expectations. Chorazin and Bethsaida and Capernaum are condemned because something was expected of them, something which they failed to produce. Now whether, as many once confidently held, the data justify speaking of a 'Galilean crisis',[154] Jesus presumably hoped for a national revival or renewal which did not eventuate. One can only speculate as to how this unwelcome fact affected his eschatological ideas. But that it did in some way influence them seems inescapable. How could the failure of Israel not have had, in Jesus' mind, an impact upon God's actions? Throughout the OT, including the prophets, judgement and salvation hinge upon the people's

---

[154] For a helpful discussion of the subject see F. Mussner, 'Gab es eine "galiläische Krise"?', in Hoffmann, *Orientierung*, pp. 238–52.

repentance.[155] And many rabbis, at a later time, went so far as to affirm that the time of the Son of David's coming wholly depended upon Israel's moral condition.[156] Related notions are found earlier in the Pseudepigrapha;[157] and if Acts 3.19–21[158] be trusted, at least some early Christians proclaimed that the sending of the Messiah waited upon the people's positive response to the apostolic preaching (cf. 2 Pet 3.11–12; 2 Clem. 12). That Jesus himself did not accept a rigid eschatological determinism would seem to follow from such texts as Lk 13.6–9[159] and 18.1–9,[160] for in these places the time of salvation and the time of judgement are conceived of as contingent. Unfortunately, we cannot venture much more than this. Jesus may have believed in the power of repentance to hasten the end, or he may have believed in its power to put off the end.[161] But what he is not likely to have believed in was a firmly fixed eschatological scenario and a *Naherwartung* or 'near expectation' that were completely immune to the vicissitudes of historical experience. In our judgement, Mt 11.21–3a par. is a witness not only to unbelief but to a belief undone. The pathos the passage conveys has its source in the distance between promise and fulfilment, and the sound it records is that of the waves of hope crashing against the hard rocks of reality. If Jesus, fired with eschatological optimism, once anticipated that the Jewish people living in Capernaum and neighbouring cities would collectively join his cause, then 11.21–3a is the proof that he later came, however sadly or reluctantly, to change his mind. The future Jesus must have originally envisaged for the people of Galilee is not the future he foresaw—or, better, feared—when he opened his mouth and said: 'Woe to you, Chorazin! Woe to you, Bethsaida!'

THE GREAT THANKSGIVING (11.25–30)

Mt 11.25 is tripartite. It consists of three closely related strophes. The first strophe is an exultant thanksgiving which offers praise

[155] Note esp. Jer 4.1–4; 7.5–7; 12.14–17; 17.24–7; 18.5–11; 22.5; 26.1–6; Joel 2.12–14; Zech 1.3.

[156] Cf. *b. Sanh.* 97b, 98a; *b. Šabb.* 118b; *b. B. Bat.* 10a; *b. Yoma* 86b.

[157] See the texts cited by D. C. Allison, 'Romans 11.11–15: A Suggestion', *PRS* 12 (1985), pp. 23–5.

[158] 'Repent, therefore, and turn again, that your sins may be blotted out, that times of refreshing may come from the presence of the Lord, and that he may send the Christ appointed for you, Jesus . . .'. These words are widely regarded as preserving a pre-Lukan tradition.

[159] The parable of the barren fig tree. See our comments on 3.10 and Jeremias, *Parables*, pp. 170–1.

[160] The parable of the unjust judge. It seems to teach that 'God can *shorten* the time of distress for the sake of the elect who cry out to him day and night' (so Jeremias, *Theology*, p. 140; cf. Mk 13.20).

[161] For God delaying the end see Sib. Or. 4.162–78; 5.357–60; Gk. Apoc. Ezra 3; Tertullian, *Apol.* 39. Closely related is Paul's idea of the eschatological forbearance of God; see Rom 2.4.

for the revelation that God has hidden from the wise and made known to 'babes' (vv. 25–6). This is followed by a christological declaration: the revealed *gnosis* resides in Jesus (v. 27). The passage then ends with an invitation: 'Come to me, all you who are weary and burdened, and I will give you rest' (vv. 28–30).

The thematic connexion between 11.25–30 and 11.2–24 is clear enough. 11.2–19 culminated in a parable about the rejection of John and Jesus, and 11.20–4 declared judgement against Galilean cities for their failure to repent. 11.25–30 continues the theme of response. Its three stanzas, however, go beyond the refrain of failure. Rejection is not the whole story. If 'this generation' did not follow after John and Jesus, and if Chorazin and Bethsaida and Capernaum did not acknowledge Jesus' miracles, there are still the 'babes' who perceive what is happening.[162]

In 11.19 Matthew identified Jesus with Wisdom. The same equation is apparently implicit in the present passage.[163] There are, in any case, some very intriguing parallels between the Jesus of 11.25–30 and Sophia in Wisdom literature. Only the Father knows the Son, just as only God knows Wisdom (Job 28.12–27; Ecclus 1.6–9; Bar 3.32). Only the Son knows the Father, just as only Wisdom knows God (Wisd 8.4; 9.1–18). Jesus makes known hidden revelation, just as Wisdom reveals divine secrets (Wisd 9.1–18; 10.10). And if Jesus invites others to take up his yoke and find rest, Wisdom issues precisely the same call: Ecclus 51.23–30 (cf. Prov 1.20–3; 8.1–36; Ecclus 24.19–22; Odes Sol. 33.6–13; Ps.-Justin, *Or. Graecos* 5). For further parallels see on 11.30.

For Matthew, however, the primary background of Mt 11.25–30 is to be found in Jewish traditions about Moses (cf. Allison (v)). As we shall argue, the declaration about Father and Son knowing each other is grounded in Exod 33.12–13, where God knows Moses and Moses prays that he might know God; and the promise of rest in Mt 11.28 is modelled upon Exod 33.14. Further, in deeming himself to be 'meek' (v. 29), Jesus is taking up a chief characteristic of Moses (see on v. 29); and in referring to his 'yoke' (v. 29) he is using a term often applied to the law which was given through Moses. Thus what we have in Mt 11.25–30 is a presentation of Jesus in Mosaic

---

[162] In Q, 11.25 and what follows may have been subjoined to the woes against Galilean cities because the idea of truth being inaccessible to the wise and understanding helped make explicable the rejection of Jesus. Cf. the function of Mk 4.10–13.

[163] So most recent commentators. In Q (= 11.25–7) Jesus was probably conceived only as Wisdom's envoy and perhaps as Israel's representative (cf. Dunn, *Christology*, pp. 199–200). But for a different opinion see Crossan (v), who urges that Jesus became Sophia only in the last stage in the development of the Q tradition.

colours; and it is the similarities as well as the differences between the Messiah and the law-giver which clarify our evangelist's authorial intent.

25. Following 11.20–4 one might expect a complaint. Jesus instead offers a prayer of thanksgiving. Like the prayer in Jn 11.41–2, it is uttered aloud for the sake of those standing nearby.

ἐν ἐκείνῳ τῷ καιρῷ ἀποκριθεὶς ὁ Ἰησοῦς εἶπεν.[164] Both this and Lk 10.21 (ἐν αὐτῇ τῇ ὥρᾳ ἠγαλλιάσατο τῷ πνεύματι τῷ ἁγίῳ καὶ εἶπεν)[165] show signs of editorial reworking. The less precise 'at that time'[166] and (probably) 'answering he said'[167] are Matthean. 'In that hour'[168] and (probably) 'in the Holy Spirit'[169] are Lukan. Did Q have ἐν ἐκείνῃ τῇ ὥρᾳ ἠγαλλιάσατο καὶ εἶπεν? Matthew might have substituted ἀποκριθεὶς for 'rejoiced' because the latter did not follow well upon 11.20–4.

ἀποκρίνομαι usually means 'answer', 'reply'. That cannot be so here. Jesus is not answering, nor (*pace* Sand, *Matthäus*, p. 251) is he exactly reacting to what has preceded. So ἀποκριθεὶς ... εἶπεν is best explained as the equivalent of *wayyaʿan wayyōʾmer*, aś in 15.15; 17.4; 22.1; and 28.5 (cf. BAGD, s.v., ἀποκρίνομαι, 2). As so often in the LXX, the words are simply 'an enlarged equivalent for "said"' (Plummer, p. 165). Their appearance here adds a touch of solemnity (Zahn, p. 437). See further BDF § 140.

ἐξομολογοῦμαί σοι, πάτερ, κύριε τοῦ οὐρανοῦ καὶ τῆς γῆς.[170] The agreement with Lk 10.21 is perfect.[171] For 'heaven and earth' see also 5.17; 24.35; 28.18. ἐξομολογέω + σοι and ἐξομολογέω + κύριε are both common in the LXX.[172] Here the verb[173] means 'praise' (cf. LXX usage), not 'confess' (cf. 3.6). It covers the entirety of 11.25–30. It would hardly be prudent to restrict the compass to the hiding of revelation from the wise and understanding.[174] Jesus offers thanks for the giving

[164] C L W Θ f¹·¹³ Maj Or have απεκριθεις.

[165] So NA²⁶ and HG, but the mss. show many variants.

[166] Mt: 3; Mk: 0; Lk: 0. It is a Semitism; see vol. 1, p. 82.

[167] Mt: 44; Mk: 5; Lk: 25. This is also a Semitism.

[168] Mt: 0; Mk:0; Lk: 4; see Jeremias, *Lukasevangelium*, pp. 98, 189.

[169] πνεῦμα ἅγιος: Mt: 5; Mk: 4; Lk: 13; Acts: 42–43.

[170] According to the Zion Gospel edition, variant to Mt 11.25, the *Gospel of the Nazaraeans* had: ευχαριστω σοι. Other variants in Klijn (v).

[171] Marcion, for obvious reasons, omitted 'and the earth'.

[172] Cf. Gen 29.35; 2 Βασ 22.50 (ἐξομολογήσομαί σοι, κύριε); 1 Chr 16.34; 23.30; 29.13; 2 Chr 5.13; 30.22; Tob 13.10; Ps 7.17; 9.2 (ἐξομολογήσομαί σοι, κύριε); 17.49; 21.25; 32.2; 34.18; 70.22; 137.1 (ἐξομολογήσομομαί σοι, κύριε); Ecclus 51.1 (ἐξομολογήσομαί σοι, κύριε). Note also Ps 135. 26: ἐξομολογεῖσθε τῷ θεῷ τοῦ οὐρανοῦ.

[173] See esp. O. Michel, *TWNT* 5, pp. 199–220; also Robinson (v).

[174] Indeed, Chrysostom, *Hom. on Mt* 38.1, may not have been wide of the mark when he wrote: 'And while His being revealed to these (the 'babes') was fit matter of joy, His concealment from those ('the wise and understanding')

and hiding of revelation, for the *gnosis* given to the Son, and for the possibility of rest. On 'Father' (= 'abbā') see on 6.9.[175] The unqualified πάτερ appears in a prayer in 3 Macc 6.3, 8. It is quite rare in old Jewish texts.

'Lord of heaven and earth'—a phrase which recalls God's act of creation (Gen 1.1)—is used only three times in the NT: Mt 11.25; Lk 10.21; and Acts 7.24. In the LXX the appellation appears in Tob 7.17. Jth 9.12 has the similar δέσποτα τῶν οὐρανῶν καὶ τῆς γῆς (cf. Josephus, *Ant.* 4.40), T. Benj. 3.1 v. 1 Κύριον τὸν Θεὸν τοῦ οὐρανοῦ καὶ τῆς γῆς, Par. Jer. 5.32 ὁ Θεὸς τοῦ οὐρανοῦ καὶ τῆς γῆς.[176] Compare also Jub. 32.18: 'the Lord who created heaven and earth' (the Greek equivalent is in T. Job 2.3). The Aramaic translation of the synoptic address would be *mārēh šĕmayyāʾ wĕʾarʿāʾ*, and this is found in 1QapGen. 22.16 and 21. There does not seem to be any true rabbinic parallel.[177] It is possible, as Jeremias has argued, that Jesus was using an address he knew from the *Tefilla: qōnēh šāmayim wāʾāreṣ* (the first benediction, quoting Gen 14.19, 22; see Jeremias, *Theology*, p. 187).

ὅτι ἔκρυψας ταῦτα ἀπὸ σοφῶν καὶ συνετῶν καὶ ἀπεκάλυψας αὐτὰ νηπίοις. God has, in effect, 'made wise the simple' (Ps 19.7). Compare Wisd 10.21 ('because wisdom opened the mouth of the dumb, and made the tongues of babes (νηπίων) speak clearly'); Dan 1.17 (where the four youths —νεανίσκοι—are full of wisdom and understanding); and Ecclus 3.19 (v. 1.: 'Many are lofty and renowned, but to the meek (πραέσιν) he reveals his secrets'). Lk 10.21 has ἀπέκρυψας,[178] which increases the assonance with ἀπεκάλυψας. Note that the Qumran Hodayot (1QH) regularly has *kî* after introductory 'ôdekkâ 'ădônāy (e.g. 2.20, 31; 3.19; 5.20; 7.6). Compare Ps 118.21; 139.14. For giving thanks for revelation see 1QH 7.26–7; 1 En. 39.9–11; 69.27; The Prayer of Thanksgiving (Nag Hammadi: 6.7).

was no more of joy but of tears. Thus at any rate He acts, where He weeps for the city. Not therefore because of this doth He rejoice, but because what wise men knew not, was known to these. As when Paul saith, "I thank God, that ye were servants of sin, but ye obeyed from the heart the form of doctrine which was delivered to you".'

[175] Significantly, never in the canonical gospels does Jesus say, 'my Lord'.

[176] Par. Jer. 5.32 as a whole reads: εὐλογήσω σε, ὁ θεὸς σοῦ τοῦ οὐρανοῦ καὶ τῆς γῆς, ἡ ἀνάπαυσις τῶν ψυχῶν τῶν δικαίων ἐν παντὶ τόπῳ. This resembles Mt 11.25–30 in several respects. It opens with a thanksgiving to or blessing of God. It employs the title, 'God of heaven and earth'. And it draws upon Jer 6.16: 'rest for your souls'. One is not happy assigning these similarities to coincidence, but dependence of Par. Jer. 5.32 upon Matthew is improbable. For full discussion see Allison, 'Key Text' (v).

[177] SB 1, p. 607, cites only *ribbônô šel ʿôlām*.

[178] ἀποκρύπτω is a synoptic *hapax legomenon*. Matthew preferred the simplex (Mt: 7; Mk: 0; Lk: 4), especially in view of the following ἀπό.

'The wise and understanding'[179] (cf. 2 Bar 46.5) also appear
together Isa 29.14 and 1 Cor 1.19.[180] One is to think of the
worldly wise, men of secular sophistication who, though
sagacious in their own eyes and crafty in their own devices, are
yet far from true wisdom.[181] Already in the OT there is a
tendency to apply 'wise' and 'understanding' in a pejorative
context: it is recognized that those who profess to be devoted to
Wisdom often neglect her, and that they are sometimes the
most insensitive of all (Job 5.13; Isa 5.21; Jer 8.8; 9.23–24; 49.7;
Obad 8; Bar 3.23; Ecclus 37.16–26; cf. 1QH 3.14–15; Josephus,
Bell. 6.313). As for the present verse, Matthew—and Jesus?—
may well have thought of the scribes and Pharisees in particular
(so Chrysostom)—and of the 'babes', conversely, as those
unlearned in the (oral) law. This would fit well with the use of
παραδίδωμι: Jesus has his own tradition which is not that of
the scribes and Pharisees. In any event, Judaism itself had to
fight against the temptation to turn faith into an intellectual and
esoteric discipline; thus the sages ardently discussed the relative
merits of doing and studying (cf. *m. 'Abot* 1.17).[182]

νήπιος means 'infant', 'child', and in the LXX (cf. *'ōlē(ā)l*) it
often carries the literal meaning. But the LXX also makes the word a
technical term for the righteous (cf. Ps 18.7; 114.6; 118.130).[183] This
usage—which reminds one of the status of the *pĕtāyyim* at Qumran[184]—
is assumed in the gospel saying. The 'babes' are those who, in the eyes
of the world, are weak and simple, but before God they are the elect.

Mt 11.25 may well be based upon Isa 29.14, a verse Paul
quotes in 1 Cor 1.19: 'the wisdom of their wise men shall perish,
and the discernment of their discerning men shall be hid' (LXX:
ἀπολῶ τὴν σοφίαν τῶν σοφῶν καὶ τὴν σύνεσιν τῶν συνετῶν κρύ-
ψω). But the thought is common enough in Jewish texts.
Revelation does not come to all. It comes only to those who
have prepared themselves to receive it—to the pure in heart and
the poor in spirit (cf. Job 28.28; Ps 25. 14). This is because
religious knowledge is a function of being and has a moral

[179] σοφῶν καὶ συνετῶν is chosen over σοφῶν καὶ φρονίμων because the
emphasis is upon wholly theoretical, not practical, knowledge.
[180] Cf. also Prov 16.21; Dan 2.21; 1QH 1.35; Josephus, *Ant.* 11.57–8; 2 Bar
46.5. Schlatter, p. 381, cites two passages from *Sipre* on Deuteronomy (13, 305).
σοφία and σύνεσις were also regularly joined.
[181] But there could also be a pejorative glance at the apocalyptic seers, who
were full of learning and speculative wisdom; see C. Rowland, *The Open Heaven*,
London, 1982; *CHJ*, 3, forthcoming.
[182] See B. T. Viviano, *Study as Worship*, SJLA 26, Leiden, 1978, and L.
Finkelstein, in *CHJ* 2.
[183] For discussion see G. Bertram, *TWNT* 4, pp. 913–25; also Cerfaux,
'Sources' (v); Grundmann, 'Paränese' (v); and Dupont, '"Simples"' (v).
[184] Cf. 1QpHab. 12.4 and 4QpNah. 3–4.3.5, 7; and see Dupont, '"Simples"'
(v).

dimension. Such knowledge cannot be grasped either by dispassionate, neutral observers or by those who have no thirst for 'the things above'. Spiritual things are only discerned by the spiritual (1 Cor 2.14–15); and only those who love God can know him (cf. 1 Jn 4.8). Revelation, it follows, is necessarily hid from self-seeking savants and the vain exemplars of worldly reason, of however a devout demeanour. The doors to true wisdom remain closed to them. While knowledge, like wealth, 'puffs up' (1 Cor 8.1), the quest for God requires the annihilation of all pride. And in any case, 'if you understand it, it is not God' (Augustine). So strength of mind does not wrest spiritual blessings. In God's presence one must not only be humble of heart but lowly of mind (as the book of Job demonstrates so well). Divine truths are, therefore, revealed only to 'babes', that is, to the truly meek and humble. As Paul put it, in a passage closely akin to ours:[185] 'Has not God made foolish the wisdom of the world? For since, in the wisdom of God, the world did not know God through wisdom, it pleased God through the folly of what we preach to save those who believe' (1 Cor 1.20–1; the entire context should be consulted).[186] As with so much else, so too is it here true that the first shall be last, the last first (cf. Gos. Thom. 4).[187] (Our text, we should add, scarcely extols stupidity. There is in it no criticism of intellectuals as such, only of the proud and arrogant. Piety is not ignorance, faith is not obscurantism. Recall especially that the parables challenge to understanding.)

But what, we must now ask, is meant by ταῦτα, 'these things'?[188] What is it that is hidden from the wise and understanding and revealed to the elect? With regard to Jesus himself it is impossible to be precise,[189] although one presumes that the reference was to the awareness of the eschatological nature of certain events (cf. 16.17). As for Luke, the immediate context is Lk 10.17–20: the falling of Satan, the authority of the

[185] Suggs (v), p. 86, following Harnack, suggests that Paul knew Mt 11.25–7 par. Cf. Hunter (v), p. 244. It has also been urged that 11.25–6 and 1 Cor 1–4 might both draw upon a lost sapiential writing; cf. Crossan (v), pp. 193–4. 1 Cor 1–4 and Mt 11.25–30 share five key words in common: 'hidden', 'wise', 'understanding', 'revealed', 'babes'. Further discussion in Richardson (v).

[186] Compare also Josephus, *Ant*. 2.222 and 11Qps^a 154 4–7.

[187] The divine reluctance to reveal certain truths to every person has as its corollary the injunction to the faithful not to speak spiritual secrets before outsiders; see the texts cited in the commentary on 7.6.

[188] An unconnected ταῦτα may at one time also have introduced Mk 11.27–33 ('by what authority do you do *these things?*').

[189] From time to time it has been suggested that the occasion for 11.25–6 was the messianic confession at Caesarea Philippi, or some time shortly thereafter; cf. Manson, *Teaching*, p.110.

disciples, and the writing of their names in heaven. In Matthew one thinks rather of the ἔργα of Jesus (11.2, 19), especially his miracles (11.20–1; cf. 11.5–6). 'This generation' and the Galilean cities of 11.20–4 have not understood 'these things'. That is, they have missed the revelation conveyed by Jesus' speech and actions. Only the 'babes' have discerned the christological truth, that the kingdom is present in Jesus. Thus the knowledge is eschatological. Its content is the same as 'the secret of the kingdom of God' (Mk 4.11 par.).[190]

However one judges the importance of Isa 29 for Mt 11, Mt 11.25 is most illuminated when viewed against the background of Jewish eschatological expectation. It was widely anticipated that the End would bring unprecedented knowledge and wisdom for the elect (cf. Dodd, *Interpretation*, pp. 163–4) As Jer 31.34 expresses it: 'And no longer shall each man teach his neighbour and each his brother, saying, "Know the Lord", for they shall all know me, from the least of them to the greatest, says the Lord; for I will forgive their iniquity, and I will remember their sin no more.' Note also Hab 2.14: 'For the earth will be filled with the knowledge of the glory of the Lord, as the waters cover the sea' (cf. LXX Hos 6.2–3). Moreover, many Jews believed that the great redemption would be heralded by revelations concerning the time of the Messiah's coming and other secrets 'hidden since the foundation of the world' (Mt 13.35, quoting Ps 78.2; cf. 1QpHab. 7.1–5; 11.1–2).[191] This idea is fundamental for the apocalyptic literature. It also underlies Mt 11.25. But in our verse the eschatological revelation is not about the time of the consummation or, in fact, about any other future event. Instead, as 11.27 makes plain, the revelation is about the present: eschatological *gnosis* can even now be found in Jesus, who in his person and ministry has unveiled the end-time secrets (cf. 13.16–17). In brief, Mt 11.25–7 announces the realization of an eschatological hope.[192, 193]

[190] Cf. Christ, p. 81. See further Davies, *COJ*, p. 142, who finds the Matthean and Lukan contexts to be less dissimilar than often alleged. 'The total context, if we may so express it, is much the same. Especially does the context in both Matthew and Luke deal with events which are eschatological in their significance'. Cf. Suggs, pp. 88–9.—Gnilka, *Matthäusevangelium* 1, p. 435, identifies 'these things' with Jesus' sonship (v. 27).

[191] See also the texts cited by R. E. Brown, *The Semitic Background of the Term 'Mystery' in the New Testament*, FBBS, Philadelphia, 1968, pp. 1–30.

[192] Cf. 1 En. 93 + 91.12–7, the so-called 'Apocalypse of Weeks'. The writer of this placed himself in a very special time. He believed that the time of apostasy was fast coming to its close, that the 'righteous of the eternal planting' had already been elected, and that to them the Holy One was *presently* giving 'sevenfold instruction concerning all His creation' (93.10). Here the community already enjoys eschatological wisdom.

[193] For the suggestion, based in part upon an analysis of Mt 11.25–7, that

26. ναὶ ὁ πατήρ, ὅτι οὕτως εὐδοκία ἐγένετο ἔμπροσθέν σου.[194]
Compare 1 Cor 1.21: 'For since, in the wisdom of God, the
world did not know God through wisdom, it pleased (εὐδόκησεν) God through the folly of what we preach to save those
who believe'. In Lk 10.21 ἐγένετο is placed before εὐδοκία;[195]
otherwise there is agreement.

ναί effectively repeats the thanksgiving of the previous verse. ὅτι
κ.τ.λ. is comparable to the common targumic *ra'ăwâ min qŏdam
Adonai* (e.g. Tg. Neof. on Num 22.13 and 23.27, and the targum on
Isa 53.6) and to the rabbinic formula, *yĕhē' ra'â miqqammêh* (cf.
Schlatter, p. 383; SB 1, p. 607).[196] On ἔμπροσθέν σου (here a
Semitism) see 1, p. 82. For εὐδοκία/-έω as the ground for revelation see
Gal 1.15–16 and Eph 1.9 (cf. 1 En 37.4).

Bultmann, *History*, p. 160 wrote: 'Matt. 11.25f./Lk.10.21 is . . . in my
opinion, a saying originally Aramaic'; 'it is different from the sayings
of Jesus; yet, on the other hand, I see no compelling reason for denying
it to him'.[197] We would go further and, with Bousset (v), p. 85, Mussner
(v), and the majority of scholars, pronounce in favour of authenticity.
The saying is Semitic and thoroughly Jewish (note the thanksgiving,
with its parallels in 1QH, the designation of God as 'Lord of heaven
and earth', the untypical use of ἀποκαλύπτω,[198] and the reverential
circumlocution, εὐδοκία ἐγένετο ἔμπροσθέν σου). The simple ὁ πατήρ
(= *'abbā'*) and the poetic parallelism are characteristic of Jesus, as is
the implicit criticism of the worldly wise. The comparable 13.16f. par.
is usually considered dominical. Most significantly of all, the
christological presuppositions remain inchoate, and our verses are alone
in the NT in using νήπιος in a positive fashion, a fact which satisfies
the criterion of dissimilarity.[199] The arguments could hardly be
stronger.

27. This makes explicit the christological dimensions of
11.25f.: the revelation to 'babes' has come through Jesus.

In contrast with some Jewish apocalyptic texts, eschatological
revelation is here not handed on through angels.[200] It is instead

Jesus held a critical view of the type of apocalypticism found in Daniel, see
Grimm, *Danielbuch* (v). We find his argument unconvincing, in part because we
deem it more likely that when Jesus uttered Mt 11.25 he had Isa 29.14, not Dan
2.20–3, in mind.

[194] According to Irenaeus, *Adv. haer.* 1.20.3, the Marcosians knew Mt 11.26
in this form: οὐά, ὁ πατήρ, ὅτι ἔμπροσθεν σου εὐδοκία μοι ἐγένετο.

[195] So HG. Lk 10.21 NA[26] agrees with Matthew's order. But assimilation to
the First Gospel seems likely.

[196] Note also perhaps 1 Macc 3.60 and Lk 12.32.

[197] Cf. Hahn, *Titles*, p. 309: 'We shall have to adjudge this aphorism to the
Palestinian primitive church and to reckon with an originally Aramaic
rendering'.

[198] See on this A. Oepke, *TWNT* 3, p. 568.

[199] Cf. Mussner, 'Wege' (v), and see Rom 2.20; 1 Cor 3.1; 13.11; Gal 4.1, 3;
Eph 4.14; Heb 5.13.

channelled directly through a man, Jesus. Perhaps the closest parallel is to be found in the Dead Sea Scrolls. The author of 1QH 4.27–9 (the Teacher of Righteousness?) could write: 'Through me Thou hast illuminated the face of the Congregation and hast shown Thine infinite power. For Thou hast given me knowledge through Thy marvellous mysteries, and hast shown Thyself mighty within me in the midst of Thy marvellous Council. Thou has done wonders before the Congregation for the sake of Thy glory, that they may make known Thy mighty deeds to all the living' (Vermes).[201]

Did 11.27 and 25f. belong together from the beginning? Although far from certain, we are inclined to think not.[202] V. 27 is probably, to use Wanke's term, a 'Kommentarwort', perhaps added by a compiler of Q (note the catchword connexions: πατήρ/πατρός; ἀπεκάλυψας/ἀποκαλύψαι). Not only could both vv. 25f. and 27 stand on their own, but whereas in the former Jesus speaks to God in the second person ('I thank thee'), in the latter he uses the third person ('my Father').

πάντα μοι παρεδόθη ὑπὸ τοῦ πατρός μου. So Lk 10.22 (perhaps without μου). Compare 28.18; Jn 3.35 ('the Father loves the Son and has given all things into his hand'; cf. 13.3; 17.2); Gos. Thom. 61 ('to me was given from the things of my Father'); and Corp. Herm. 1.32 (εὐλογητὸς εἶ, πάτερ . . . παρέδωκας αὐτῷ τὴν πᾶσαν ἐξουσίαν).

πάντα (cf. MT Deut 18.18) refers firstly to the ταῦτα of 11.25; but it goes beyond that to include the whole revelation of God in Jesus, which is eschatological revelation.[203] (Dan 7.14 and Mt 28.18, although formally close, are instead about authority and power.) Embodied in the Jesus event are the eschatological

[200] For angels as intermediaries of revelation see Zech 4; Dan 8.15–26; 9.22–7; 10.18–12.4; 1 En. 1.2; Acts 7.53 (the law was delivered by angels); Gal 3.19 (the law came through angels); Heb 2.2; Rev 7.13–17; 17.7–18; 4 Ezra, passim; 2 Bar. 55–74; Apoc. Abr. 11ff.; 2 En. 3ff.; Josephus, Ant. 15.136 (on this see Davies, JPS, pp. 84–8); ARN B 2 (rejecting the notion that the law was handed down by angels); Pesiq. R. 21 (103b) (the angels descended with God at Sinai).—There is also a contrast between Jesus' unmediated revelation and the rabbinic chain of tradition (as in m. 'Abot 1.1): there are no links between Jesus and God the Father.

[201] The church for Matthew was an eschatological community dedicated to a perfection based on a revealed knowledge of the purposes of God and of his true intent in the law, as was the sect at Qumran, except that Jesus was even more central for the former than was the Teacher of Righteousness for the latter.

[202] So also Schulz, Q, p. 215; Légasse (v), pp. 247–9; pace Dunn, Spirit, p. 30.

[203] We cannot concur with those—see the list of names in Marshall, p. 436—who interpret 11.27 in the light of Dan 7.13–14 and Mt 28.18. The reasons have been given by Hunter (v), p. 246: '(a) Jesus proceeds to speak, and to speak exclusively, of the knowledge of God; (b) since Jesus was not yet "glorified", the idea of universal power is not yet relevant; (c) the verb παρεδόθη suggests a contrast with the paradosis of the Scribes (Mark vii. 3, 9) who are clearly in view in the first and last strophes'.

truths which heretofore have only been longed for in prophecy. This means, to speak concretely, that the First Gospel, which purports to be a record of Jesus' words and deeds, itself by implication lays claim to being revelatory. That is, in so far as it makes known the truth of and about Jesus, Matthew's gospel is, on its own terms, a vehicle of eschatological revelation.[204]

In the NT παραδίδωμι (cf. *msr*) more often than not is used in connexion with either the handing on of tradition or the delivering up of someone to prison, court, punishment, or death. Here the idea of passing down tradition is employed, but in a metaphorical manner. Just as one person transmits tradition to another, so does God the Father entrust his knowledge to the Son. There is in this both comparison and contrast. The Son, like others, has a tradition. Unlike others, however, his tradition is directly from God, not men (cf. Gal 1.11–12; contrast the chain of tradition in *m.* '*Abot* 1.1). As to what event or point in time might be indicated by the aorist (παρεδό-θη), the text is mute.[205] But this only enhances the atmosphere of mystery.

Is there implicit a contrast between Jesus' revelation and that of Moses? There was abroad in first-century Judaism a tradition that the law was given to Moses by angelic intermediaries (see n. 200). Considered from that point of view Jesus' revelation would be unprecedented. Moses, who was given tablets of stone, did not in any case receive the Torah as God's 'Son'.

καὶ οὐδεὶς ἐπιγινώσκει τὸν υἱὸν εἰ μὴ ὁ πατήρ, οὐδὲ τὸν πατέρα τις ἐπιγινώσκει εἰ μὴ ὁ υἱός. Compare Jn 10.15 and Dial. Sav. 134.14–15. This is one of the few instances in which Luke's text exhibits more parallelism than Matthew's: καὶ οὐδεὶς γινώσκει τίς ἐστιν ὁ υἱὸς εἰ μὴ ὁ πατήρ, καὶ τίς ἐστιν ὁ πατὴρ εἰ μὴ ὁ υἱός.[206] The small differences do not change the

---

[204] For pertinent reflections on this theme in early Christianity see O. Cullmann, 'The Tradition', in *The Early Church*, London, 1956, pp. 59–75.

[205] Some have surmised a reference to the Baptism; cf. Jeremias, *Theology*, p. 61. Allen, pp. 122–3, took the verb to imply pre-existence; cf. Plummer, p. 168. This opinion was common among older exegetes.—One wonders whether the aorist should not be considered constative: it 'treats an act as punctiliar which is not in itself point-action' (Robertson, p. 832).

[206] On the basis of patristic evidence Harnack (v), pp. 292–5, proposed that neither Luke nor Q had 'no one knows the Son except the Father'. Winter (v) agrees and also opines that the phrase was not present in the autograph of Matthew (cf. J. C. O'Neil, in Bammel, *Trial*, pp. 76–7). For a review and rejection of Harnack's view see Chapman (v). Also helpful is Suggs (v), pp. 71–7, who criticizes Winter. In the following patristic texts 'no one knows the Father . . .' is placed before 'no one knows the Son . . .': Justin, *Dial.* 100; *1 Apol.* 63; Irenaeus, *Adv. haer.* 1.20.3; 2.6.1; Tertullian, *Adv. Marc.* 4.25; Ps.-Clem. Hom. 17.4; 18.4, 13, 20; Origen, *De prin.* 2.6.1; Eusebius, *Dem. ev.* 149b,

sense. ἐπιγινώσκει and γινώσκει (cf. Jn 10.15) are not far apart in meaning (cf. on 6.32). Luke's καί (for Matthew's οὐδέ; so Q) is a natural stylistic improvement[207] (not a translation variant);[208] and his omission of the verb in the second clause is also a small improvement.[209] τίς ἐστιν for the accusative is likewise Lukan (cf. Lk 13.25 diff. Mt 25.11; Lk 22.60 diff. Mk 14.71) and does not bear on interpretation.

ἐπιγινώσκει has frequently been taken to mean 'chooses',[210] and certainly the Hebrew *yāda'* often means just that (cf. Gen 18.19; Jer 1.5; Hos 13.5; Amos 3.2). But the parallelism in Mt 11.27 strongly implies that the verb should mean the same thing in both its occurrences; and while 'no one chooses the Son except the Father' makes good sense, 'no one chooses the Father except the Son' would be difficult. It therefore seems better to give ἐπιγινώσκει a more common NT meaning, this being personal, concentrated experiential knowledge.[211] The Father acknowledges, takes account of, and concerns himself with the Son; the Son acknowledges, takes account of, and concerns himself with the Father. Thus they know each other.[212] One may compare the sentence in Tob 5.2 א (cited by Jeremias): αὐτὸς οὐ γινώσκει με, καὶ ἐγὼ οὐ γινώσκω αὐτόν. This is simply a roundabout way of describing a reciprocal relationship: 'We do not know each other'. Such a way of putting things was apparently characteristic of Semitic languages.[213]

It is a bit peculiar to read that 'no one knows the Son except the Father'. Perhaps it is assumed—as in 16.13–20 and Gal 1.15–16—that the identity or nature of the Son can only be known through divine

216d; Letter of the Council of Antioch to Alexander of Thessalonica. This cloud of witnesses is impressive. But (i) in the ms. tradition the clauses are reversed only in Mt 11.27 N X and Lk 10.22 U N b. (Also, Lk 10.22 1216 1579a omit the first clause.) (ii) Some of the patristic authorities cited knew both orders (e.g. Irenaeus, *Adv. haer.* 4.6.1; 4.6.7; Origen, *De prin.* 1.1.8; *Ps.-Clem. Rec.* 2.47). (iii) Jn 10.15 accords with the traditional arrangement. (iv) The inverted order makes the connexion with the last part of the verse (καὶ ᾧ κ.τ.λ.) awkward. (v) The tendency of the Fathers would have been to put God's unknowability first; and the human memory is not a Zerox machine. One can find the inverted order in later and even modern Christian lit. (cf. John of Damascus, *De fide orth.* 1.1).

[207] Although, admittedly, Luke never alters a Markan οὐδέ to καί.

[208] Did the Aramaic original have *lêt . . . 'ēllā'/lêt . . . 'ēllā'*? Cf. Beyer, p. 105.

[209] The repetition is more typical of Hebrew and Aramaic than Greek.

[210] See esp. Fuller, *Achievement*, p. 92.

[211] See further Gundry, *Commentary*, p. 217.

[212] It is worth remembering that in the biblical tradition 'to know' can refer to that most intimate of unions, sexual union.

[213] See further Jeremias, *Theology*, p. 58, n. 2, who cites also Gen 45.14; Jub. 23.19; 1QS 4.17; Frg. Tg. to Exod 15.2; Frg. Tg. to Num 21.15; T. Naph. 7.3; *m. Sanh.* 3.1.

revelation. Or perhaps the words in question are rhetorical overstatement, occasioned by the need to balance 'no one knows the Father' (a literary desideratum) and by the failure of so many people to recognize Jesus (a historical circumstance).[214] It is also possible to consider that no one knows the Son except the Father because only the Father completely knows the πάντα delivered to the Son. We leave the issue open.

The unqualified 'the Son'—which Matthew will probably have understood as 'the Son of God'[215]—is striking. Although common in the Gospel and Epistles of John, it occurs elsewhere in the NT only in Mt 11.27 par.; 28.19; Mk 13.32 par.; 1 Cor 15.28; and Heb 1.8. Whether Jesus ever spoke of himself as 'the Son' is, as one might expect, hotly disputed.[216]

καὶ ᾧ ἐὰν βούληται ὁ υἱὸς ἀποκαλύψαι.[217] This reproduces Q exactly, as Lk 10.22 proves. The mutual knowledge of Father and Son is for the benefit of others. The Son, by grace, makes known to others what the Father has made known to him. We are not far from Jn 1.18 ('No one has ever seen God; God the only Son, who is in the bosom of the Father, he has made him known') and Jn 14.9 ('He that has seen me has seen the Father'). To quote Origen, Jesus 'reveals the Father by himself being understood; for whoever has understood him understands as a consequence the Father also' (*De prin.* 1.2.6).

The authenticity of Mt 11.27 par. has been much discussed, with mixed results. Perhaps most have contended that the absolute use of 'the Son' cannot be attributed to Jesus and that the verse, which has a Johannine ring,[218] bears all the hallmarks of post-Easter reflection.[219] Others have used 11.27 par. to claim that Jesus himself had a high Christology and spoke of himself as 'the Son' who dispensed revelation.[220] Still others have claimed that 11.27 par. was originally a

[214] Cf. Suggs, pp. 93–5, who compares the rejection of prophetic figures and the elect in Wisdom literature and Qumran.

[215] Cf. Kingsbury, *Structure*, p. 42. Little is to be said for Hahn's view that, in earliest Christianity, 'the Son' and 'the Son of God' had different associations; cf. Marshall (v), pp. 87–8.

[216] For relevant considerations see Harvey, *Jesus*, pp. 154–73. He accepts the authenticity of Mt 11.27 and Mk 13.32 ('that hour no one knows, not even the angels in heaven nor the Son, but only the Father'), and makes a good case that Jesus understood his own sonship in terms of obedience, acquired knowledge, and authorisation as empowered agent.

[217] On the present tense, βουλεται (W L al), see BDF § 380.3. Wellhausen, *Matthaei*, p. 56, conjectured, without benefit of external attestation, that the original might have been αποκαλυψει.

[218] Cf. the famous description of Mt 11.25–30 as 'a thunderbolt from the Johannine sky' (Karl von Hase, *Die Geschichte Jesu*, 2nd ed., Leipzig, 1876, p. 422). This in all likelihood stands the truth on its head. Mt 11.25–7 par. was probably one of the vital seeds from which Johannine theology sprouted.

[219] Cf. Bultmann, *History*, p. 160; Norden (v); Arvedson (v), pp. 229–30; Hahn, *Titles*, p. 310.

[220] Cf. Otto, pp. 235–56; Marshall (v).

parable. In Aramaic, so it is urged, the definite articles were generic ('a son', 'a father'; cf. Lk 11.11), and Jesus was simply illustrating his situation by calling to mind a common feature of rural life, namely, the passing on of trade knowledge from father to son (cf. the similes in Jn 5.19–20;[221] As. Mos 11.12; 3 En. 45.1–2 E; 48C.7): just as only a father (really) knows his son, so only a son (really) knows his father.[222] We, regrettably, have not been able to make up our minds on this most important issue. While we see no certain signs of a post-Easter genesis,[223] we also fail to detect any truly telling signs of an origin with Jesus.[224] Of one thing, however, we are fairly sure. Mt 11.27 par. need not be described as 'Hellenistic'. According to Norden (v) and others, our passage belongs to the same world of thought as the Hermetic texts. It is about the unknown God who must be revealed by an otherworldly envoy. Further, it is alleged that the ideal of mutual religious knowledge is not native to Judaism but at home in the Hellenistic world at large and comes to expression in such statements as this: οἶδά σε, Ἑρμῆ, καὶ σὺ ἐμέ.[225] We are persuaded, however, that this text about Hermes and others like it from the Hermetic literature (see n. 255) take us too far afield. For there is a very important OT Scripture in which religious knowledge is both mutual and exclusive, and it is clearly the inspiration for Mt 11.27 par.

In Exod 33.12f. God 'knows' Moses by name, and Moses in turn prays that he may 'know' God. The full text is: 'Moses said to the Lord, "See, thou sayest to me, 'Bring up this people'; but thou hast not let me know whom thou wilt send with me. Yet thou hast said, 'I know you by name (yĕdaʿtikā bĕsēm; LXX: οἶδά σε παρὰ πάντας), and you have also found favour in my sight'. Now therefore, I pray thee, if I have found favour in thy sight, show me now thy ways, that I may know thee (wĕʾēdāʿĕkā; LXX: γνωστῶς ἴδω σε) and find favour in thy sight"'. As in Mt 11.25–30, we here have the notion of

[221] On this see C. H. Dodd, 'A Hidden Parable in the Fourth Gospel', in *MNTS*, pp. 30–40.

[222] See esp. Jeremias, *Prayers* (v); *Theology* (v). For criticism see Marshall (v), pp. 91–3; Dunn, *Spirit*, p. 32; Gundry, *Commentary*, p. 217. We do wonder with Dunn whether the conjectured proverb is in fact generally true.

[223] One might have expected anything from the man who could utter Mt 11.5–6, and Jesus probably did think of himself as an envoy of Wisdom. On the other side, the link between Jesus as Son and Jesus as revealer was a Christian theme; see e.g. Jn 1.14–18 and Heb 1.1–5.

[224] One possible pointer in this direction is 'no one knows the Son except the Father'. These words stand in tension with the Christian formulations in Jn 14.7; 17.3; 2 Cor 5.16; Phil 3.10; 2 Tim 1.12; and 1 Jn 2.3. And in a post-Easter word would one expect so much attention to the Father?

[225] See F. G. Kenyon, *Greek Papyri in the British Museum, I* (1893), number cxxii.49. For related formulations see Corp. Herm. 1.31; 10.15a. See also Davies, *COJ*, pp. 119–44, esp. 134–38.

reciprocal[226] knowledge.[227] Further, one assumes that ancient Jews would have supposed the mutual knowledge to be exclusive. Not only is this implicit from the context (cf. 33.7–11, 17–23), but Deut 34.10 has this to say: 'And there has not arisen a prophet since in Israel like Moses, whom God knew (yĕdāʿô; LXX: ἔγνω) face to face'. The words, 'face to face', imply a reciprocal knowledge. It is not just that God knows Moses but that God has revealed himself to Moses, face to face. Normally one approaches God not face to face but with head bowed, just as a subject approaches an earthly king with bowed face, looking to the ground, out of respect. Moses has such an intimate relationship with the Divine that he encounters him face to face.[228] So the act of knowing is, as in Exod 33.12–13, mutual: God knows Moses and Moses knows God. In addition, the knowledge is exclusive: 'And there has not arisen a prophet since in Israel like Moses . . .'. Only Moses has experienced God face to face; only his is a 'knowing' encounter with God in that sense. This takes us a long way towards our synoptic text. The parallel is even more impressive when one realizes that in Judaism Moses was the revealer *par excellence*. The knowledge he was given became, in the Torah, knowledge for others. So Moses, like Jesus, shared his revelation.

Strongly supportive of our contention for the influence of Exod 33.12f. upon Mt 11.25–30 is 1 Cor 13.12. In this verse Paul writes: 'For now we see in a mirror dimly, but then face to face. Now I know in part; then I shall understand fully even as I have been fully understood'. The Greek is: βλέπομεν γὰρ ἄρτι δι᾽ ἐσόπτρου ἐν αἰνίγματι, τότε δὲ πρόσωπον πρὸς πρόσωπον· ἄρτι γινώσκω ἐκ μέρους, τότε δὲ ἐπιγνώσομαι καθὼς καὶ ἐπεγνώσθην. This differs from Mt 11.27 in that (i) eschatology is no longer realized (full understanding belongs to the future) and (ii) knowledge is no longer exclusive (Paul assumes that all the elect will fully understand). Nonetheless, Mt 11.27 and 1 Cor 13.12 are conceptually very close. Furthermore, the latter contains an allusion to Moses. Paul has introduced his remarks about knowing and being known with a contrast between seeing in a mirror dimly and seeing face to face. The apostle is, as the commentators generally perceive, alluding to Num 12.8, where God speaks 'mouth to

---

[226] Cf. the paraphrase in Philo, *Poster C.* 13: τοῦ ὁρᾶν καὶ πρὸς αὐτοῦ ὁρᾶσθαι, 'to see (God) and to be seen by him'.—Note also Gos. Truth 19.32–3: 'they knew, they were known'. This probably depends upon the First Gospel; see Tuckett, *Nag Hammandi*, pp. 57–68.

[227] According to Philo, *Poster C.* 13, and *Spec. leg.* 1.42–3, Moses' prayer was not answered, so he did not in fact 'know' God. But this is not the natural reading (cf. Exod 33.14–16; 34.3–9; *Midr. Rab.* on Ps 25.4; Gregory of Nyssa in PG 44. 1025).

[228] Cf. P. J. Budd, *Numbers*, Waco, 1984, p. 137, commenting on the 'mouth to mouth' of Num 12.8: 'a unique immediacy and directness about revelation to Moses seems to be the point'.

mouth'[229] with Moses, 'not in dark speech' (wĕlōʾ bĕḥidōt; LXX: οὐ δι' αἰνιγμάτων)[230] but rather, according to the unpointed Hebrew, mrʾh. This last is usually read as marʾeh, as in BDB, s.v. This is the vocalization which underlies the RSV: 'clearly'. Similarly, the NEB has 'openly'. There are, however, rabbinic passages which understand mrʾh to mean marʾâ, 'mirror' (see SB 3, pp. 452–4). This probably explains 1 Cor 13.12: the passage presupposes the exegetical tradition according to which Num 12.8 means that God spoke to Moses '(as) in a mirror'.[231] Thus δι' ἐσόπτρου ἐν αἰνίγματι is the antithesis of bemarʾā wĕlōʾ bĕḥidōt: Paul has borrowed the OT phrase about Moses and simply dropped the negation (wĕlōʾ; cf. Tertullian, Adv. Praxean 14). That this is indeed the truth of the matter is strongly suggested by what immediately follows. For when Paul goes on to speak of the future and of how believers will then know God 'face to face',[232] his words again remind one of OT texts about Moses; see Exod 33.11; Num 14.14; Deut 5.4; and 34.10. Admittedly, all this would seem to imply that the special, direct mode of communication which Moses alone once had should be understood as a pointer to or anticipation of the intuitive knowledge Christians will have only at the eschaton, and one may well doubt, especially in the light of 2 Cor 3, whether Paul could really have thought that Moses, notwithstanding his undeniable greatness, enjoyed a revelatory experience Christians have as of yet been denied. Perhaps the proper conclusion is that the scriptural allusions noted do not reflect a consistent interpretation of OT passages but are more fittingly thought of as rather free, *ad hoc* adaptations of certain key phrases. But however one resolves that issue, the crucial fact for our purpose is quite plain. When ruminating upon the subject of knowing God and being known by him, Paul turned his thoughts to the law-giver. This lends great weight to the proposal that Mt 11.27 has a firm parallel in Jewish convictions about Moses, and that Exod 33.12f. and Deut 34.10 should be considered in relation to the synoptic text.[233]

Four further considerations confirm us in the judgement that Mt 11.25–30 is directly related to Exod 33.12f. First, both texts are immediately followed by a promise of rest. Exod 33.14 has this: 'And he said, "My presence will go with you, and I will give you rest"' (LXX: καὶ καταπαύσω σε). This is the LXX's closest parallel to Mt 11.28: 'Come to me, all who labour and are heavy laden, and I will give you rest' (κἀγὼ ἀναπαύσω ὑμᾶς). In view of the similarities between Mt 11.27 and Exod

---

[229] Paul changes 'mouth to mouth' to 'face to face' because his subject is sight, not speech. Note that the figure of the mirror is also present in 2 Cor 3.18, again in connexion with Moses.

[230] BDB, s.v., defines ḥîda as 'riddle, enigmatic, perplexing saying or question'.

[231] See further G. Kittel, *TWNT* 1, pp. 177–9.

[232] The phrase occurs seven times in the OT, four with reference to Moses and God's revelation to him (cf. Ecclus 45.5).

[233] Philo, it should be remarked, associated Num 12.8 with both Exod 33.12–13 and Deut 34.10; see *Rer. div. her.* 267; *Leg. all.* 3.100–3. Cf. Ps.-Clem. Hom. 17.18 and Chrysostom, *Hom. on Mt.* 78.4.

33.12f., this can hardly be coincidence. Secondly, both Mt 11.28 and Exod 13.12f. notably belong to *prayers*. In one place Moses is praying, in the other Jesus. (The difference is that whereas Moses must ask for knowledge, Jesus already has such. The contrast is no doubt deliberate.) Thirdly, the order of the first two clauses in Mt 11.27 has always been thought a bit peculiar: only the Father knows the Son, and only the Son knows the Father. One's natural tendency is to put the subject of God's unknowability first: it is the greater mystery (cf. the textual variants). But Exod 33.12f. can here shed some light. In it God's knowledge of Moses is mentioned before Moses' knowledge of God: 'Yet thou hast said, "I know you by name ...". Now therefore I pray thee ... show me thy ways, that I may know thee ...' This explains Matthew's order. The assertion about God's knowledge of Jesus comes before the assertion about Jesus' knowledge of God because in Exod 33.12f. the statement about God's knowledge of Moses precedes that about Moses' knowledge of God. That is to say, the arrangement of Mt 11.27 reflects the arrangement of Exod 33.12f. Fourthly, into 11.29 Matthew has inserted the characterization of Jesus as 'meek'. As we have shown in the commentary on that verse, Moses was for Judaism the exemplar in meekness. So when Jesus speaks of being meek he is claiming for himself one of the outstanding qualities of Moses. This is yet one more reason for viewing the Jesus of Mt 11.25–30 as the counterpart of Moses, the eschatological complement of the man in whose 'utterances one seemed to hear the speech of God himself' (Josephus, *Ant.* 4.329).

Although the preceding remarks are sufficient to establish the thoroughly Jewish character of Mt 11.27, there are a few additional observations which may also be relevant.

(i) 11.27 contains possible Semitisms (introductory asyndeton and the repetition of (ἐπι)γινώσκει), and the nearest verbal parallel is Tob 5.2 א (cited above)).

(ii) In Mt 11.27 par. the knowledge the Son has of the Father is *revealed* knowledge. Jesus 'knows' God because God has given him a revelation. This circumstance is illuminated not only by certain passages about Moses (see above) but could also be considered a prophetic conception. Thus, in 1 Sam 3.7 there is this: 'Now Samuel did not yet know (*yāda'; LXX:* γνῶναι) the Lord, and the word of the Lord had not yet been revealed (*yiggāleh*; LXX: ἀποκαλυφθῆναι) to him'. In this line, to 'know' God is to be the recipient of his prophetic and revelatory word (cf. Num 12.6).

(iii) In several OT passages (e.g. Hos 5.3; Amos 3.2) God 'knows' Israel. In other places Israel 'knows'—or should 'know'—God (e.g. LXX Isa 1.2–3; 26.13; Jer 9.1–6; Hos 8.2). It is noteworthy that the Tanak nowhere brings the two notions—of God knowing Israel and

Israel knowing God—together; and full knowledge of God by Israel is reserved for the future, as we saw. Still, a reader of the OT could justifiably assert that God had especially known Israel and that Israel especially has—or should have—known God in a particularly intimate way, and that the revelation of God to the world comes or should come through his 'son', Israel.

(iv) In context, Mt 11.27 par. speaks not only about mutual and exclusive knowledge but also about eschatological knowledge. The explanation for this is not to be found in 'Hellenism'. It is the OT which makes the knowledge of God an eschatological expectation. Moreover, the Dead Sea Scrolls more than once mingle the mysteries of eschatology with the theme of the intimate knowledge of God. For full details the reader is referred to the study of Davies (v). Pertinent texts include 1QS 4.22; 9.17–18; 11.3, 15–18; 1QSb 4.25–8; 1QH 2.13; 4.26–9; 10.27–8.

(v) Finally, the Jewish wisdom traditionally furnishes several parallels to Mt 11.27 par. While these parallels do not have the eschatological orientation or the stress upon mutual, exclusive knowledge, they do associate intimate knowledge of God with the father/son paradigm. Particularly noteworthy are these lines from Wisdom: 'the righteous poor man' 'professes to have knowledge (γνῶσιν) of God, and calls himself a child (παῖδα) of the Lord'; he 'boasts that God is his father (πατέρα)'; 'and if the righteous man is God's son (υἱός), he will help him, and will deliver him from the hand of his adversaries' (Wisd 2.10, 13, 16, 18).

In the light of all we have written, one can and probably should seek an understanding of Mt 11.27 without calling upon 'Hellenism' or even 'syncretistic Judaism'. The verse rather represents the confluence of certain OT affirmations about Moses as well as the prophets, Israel, and the wise man. One could put it like this: in a manner strongly reminiscent of Moses, Jesus, who is the perfect wise man and prophet, knows and reveals God, his Father, thereby fulfilling the calling of Israel while at the same time bringing to pass the prophecies of eschatological knowledge.

28. δεῦτε πρός με πάντες οἱ κοπιῶντες καὶ πεφορτισμένοι, κἀγὼ ἀναπαύσω ὑμᾶς. As Augustine somewhere has it, 'Christ is the true Sabbath'. Compare Gen 8.9; Ecclus 24.19 (Wisdom says: 'Come to me', προσέλθετε πρός με); Josephus, *Ant.* 3.61 ('Moses gave rest (ἀναπαύσας) to the Hebrews for a few days'); Pistis Sophia 95 ('All ye who are heavy under your burden, come hither unto me, and I will quicken you; for my burden is easy and my yoke light'). The closest OT parallel is Exod 33.14, where God says to Moses: 'and I will give you rest' (*wahănihōtî lāk; LXX:* καὶ καταπαύσω σε). This is being alluded to by our text, as the clear dependence of Mt 11.27 upon Exod 33.12f. shows. Note that whereas in the OT text it is God, not Moses, who gives rest, in the NT Jesus gives it. Once more, then, Jesus is greater than Moses.

Who precisely are the weary[234] and the burdened?[235] Leaving aside the interpretation of Ps.-Clem. Hom. 3.52 (those seeking the truth and not finding it), there would seem to be three options: those suffering under the burdens imposed by the Pharisaic establishment (cf. 23.4), those suffering from the costly demands of discipleship (so Stanton (v); cf. 10.16–39), or those suffering under the weight of sin (so most of the Fathers; cf. Chrysostom, *Hom. on Mt.* 38.3; Eusebius, *Dem. ev.* 88d). Most modern commentators favour the first option (cf. Künzel, p. 92): even though they may rest and not carry physical burdens on the sabbath, those under the Pharisaic yoke labour and bear a heavy load. Yet we wonder whether it is really necessary to be so exclusively specific. 11.28 may simply assume that the yoke of Christ alone brings true rest, and that therefore all (note the πάντες) who have not come to Jesus must be deprived of rest, that is, must be weary and burdened.

What is meant by 'I will give you rest'? According to Dibelius, *Tradition*, p. 280, we meet in Mt 11.28 'the totally unevangelical idea of "rest"'. He unfortunately did not elaborate. Presumably he was thinking about Gnostic ideas of 'rest'. Certainly ἀνά-παυσις came to be a loaded term in Gnostic circles.[236] But whether this should influence the interpretation of Mt 11.28 is far from obvious, and 'totally unevangelical' strikes us as injudicious overstatement. Mt 11.28 depends in the first instance upon an OT text, Exod 33.14. Beyond that, 'rest' has OT wisdom affinities,[237] and an eschatological interpretation lies near to hand. The messianic age was to be a time of rest (4 Ezra 7.36, 38; 8.52; SB 1, p. 607), and it was sometimes conceived of as a great sabbath (Heb 4.9; LAE 51.2; 2 En. 33.1–2; Barnabas, *Ep.* 15; SB 3, p. 687).[238] Also, in Jewish eschatology the End is as the beginning, the first creation is as the last (see on 1.1)—and after the first creation God rested (Gen 2.2). So given the NT's 'realized eschatology' or 'eschatology in the process of realization', one might only have anticipated that eschatological 'rest' would become a present reality. It is in Heb 4.1–13: 'we who have believed *enter into that*

[234] Cf. 6.28. Like the Hebrew *yāga'*, κοπιάω can mean 'be tired' or 'toil', 'strive'.

[235] φορτίζω (LXX:1) occurs in the NT only here and in Lk 11.46. For the related φορτίον see Mt 11.30 and 23.4.

[236] See e.g. Gos. Thom. 50, 60, 90; Gos. Truth 22.4–12; 37.19–21; 42–3; Dial. Sav. 120.1–8; Auth. Teach. 35.3–18; Acts Thom. 52. For discussion see P. Vielhauer, "Ανάπαυσις", in *Apophoreta*, BZNW 30, Berlin, 1964, pp. 281–99.

[237] Ecclus 6.28: 'For at last you will find the rest she gives'; 51.27: 'I have laboured little and found for myself much rest'.

[238] Discussion of texts in O. Hofius, *Katapausis: Die Vorstellung vom Endzeitlichen Ruheort im Hebräerbrief*, Tübingen, 1970, esp. pp. 59–74.

rest'. The presence of the kingdom means the presence of 'rest'. (Note that 2 Clem. 5.5 speaks of the ἀνάπαυσις of the kingdom.) We should like to propose that Mt 11.28 is kindred to Heb 4.3: Jesus, the Messiah and bringer of the kingdom, offers eschatological rest to those who join him and his cause (cf. Bacchiocchi (v)). This rest is not idleness but the peace and contentment and fullness of life that come with knowing and doing the truth as revealed by God's Son, who is always with his people.[239] Our interpretation is supported by the broader context. For 11.27 comes at the end of a chapter whose content is thoroughly eschatological while it immediately precedes debates about the sabbath (12.1–14). In other words, the context of 11.27 encourages one to think in terms of the sabbath and eschatology.

29. ἄρατε τὸν ζυγόν μου ἐφ᾽ ὑμᾶς. This imperative is synonymous with the summons 'Come to me' (28), for the same promise (rest) is attached to each. The literal meaning of ζυγός is 'balance', 'pair of scales' (cf. T. Abr. A 12) or 'yoke' (the wooden frame placed upon the necks of two draft animals, joining them together).[240] The word came to be a metaphor for obedience, subordination, servitude;[241] and Jewish teachers commonly spoke of the yoke of the Torah ('*ôl tôrâ*) and the yoke of the commandments ('*ôl miṣwōt*). But no Jewish teacher ever told another: Take up my yoke. This, however, is precisely what Jesus does. He is, therefore, playing not only the part of Wisdom (see p. 264) but also the part of Torah; or, rather, he is Wisdom, he is Torah.[242] How very significant this is should not be missed. For Judaism 'Torah' is 'all that God has made known of his nature, character and purpose, and of what he would have man be and do' (Moore 1, p. 263); it is the

[239] In Exod 33.14 the promise of rest is in effect a promise of God's presence. Perhaps our evangelist thought of Mt 11.28–30 along similar lines: true rest is made possible by the presence of Jesus with his people; cf. 28.20.

[240] In the NT ζυγός is never used of a literal yoke.

[241] Cf. Jer 5.5 (of the Torah); Ecclus 6.30 Hebrew (of Wisdom); 51.26 (of Wisdom); Ps. Sol. 7.9; 17.30 (the yoke of the Messiah); Acts 15.10 (of the law); Gal 5.1 (of the law); Did 6.2 (the teaching of Jesus); 2 Bar. 41.3 (of the law); Liv. Proph. Dan. 6; 2 En. 48.9 (of written revelation); 3 En. 35.6 (the yoke of the kingdom); *m. 'Abot* 3.5 (of the Torah); *m. Ber.* 2.2 (of the commandments); *b. Ber.* 10b (of the kingdom of Heaven). Note Ps.-Titus, *Ep.* ('to bear the yoke' is 'to observe God's order'); Hennecke 2, p. 152. Lit.: SB 1, pp. 608–10; A. Büchler, *Studies in Sin and Atonement in the Rabbinic Literature of the First Century*, London, 1928, pp. 52–118; and G. Bertram and K. H. Rengstorf, *TWNT* 2, pp. 898–904.

[242] Cf. Hamerton-Kelly, *Pre-Existence*, p. 70. The identification of Wisdom with Torah was a commonplace; cf. Bar 3.9, 37–4.1; Ecclus 24.3–25; 2 Bar. 38.4; T. Levi 13.1–9. Discussion in Davies, *PRJ*, pp. 163–76, and E. J. Schnabel, *Law and Wisdom from Ben Sira to Paul*, WUNT 2/16, Tübingen, 1985.

full revelation of God and of his will for man. So the identification of Jesus with Torah makes Jesus the full revelation of God and of his will for man. But this is precisely what 11.27 has already done, for there the Son declares that he knows the Father and has been given a complete revelation. Hence Jesus, in both 11.27 and 29, and in contrast to Moses, is the perfect embodiment of God's purpose and demand and the functional equivalent of Torah. Law-giver and law are one.[243]

There is another important contrast implicit in 11.29 between Jesus and Moses. The latter gave to Israel God's law. Jesus gives *his own* law (note the μου; cf. 7.24). It is telling that we have not been able to find the phrase, 'the yoke of Moses'. Jesus is like Moses in that he hands down a law. But he is unlike him in that what he hands down is his own.

καὶ μάθετε ἀπ' ἐμοῦ ὅτι πραΰς εἰμι καὶ ταπεινὸς τῇ καρδίᾳ. Compare 2 Cor 10.1 ('the meekness and gentleness of Christ') and T. Dan. 6.9. The line is Matthean. Not only is the vocabulary redactional,[244] but the words wreck the synonymous parallelism of vv. 28ab and 29ad and, unlike the surrounding clauses, contain no catchword to tie them to their context:

28a   Come to me all you who are weary and *burdened*,
28b   and I will give you *rest*.

29a   Take my *yoke* upon you
29d   and you will find *rest* for yourselves.

30a   For my *yoke* is easy,
30b   and my *burden* is light.

For μανθάνω with ἀπό see 24.32 = Mk13.28 and Josephus, *Ant.* 8.317. ὅτι can be either causal ('because') or explicative ('that'). Either sense seems fitting. On πραΰς see on 5.5. Moses was, for Judaism, the exemplar in meekness. According to Num 12.3, 'Now the man Moses was very meek (LXX: πραΰς σφόδρα), more than all men that were on the face of the earth'. The idea is picked up by Philo, for whom Moses is πρᾳότατος (*Vit. Mos.* 2.279; cf. 1.26). Similar assertions may be found elsewhere in Jewish literature, including Ecclus 45.4 and the rabbinic corpus (e.g. *b. Ned.* 38a). We do not doubt that Matthew's redactional reference to Jesus' meekness is yet one more clue that in 11.25–30 Jesus is being compared and contrasted with Moses.

[243] This is one of the many ways in which Jesus is superior to Moses; see further the discussion in Davies, *SSM*, pp. 93–108, on the transcending of Mosaic categories by Matthew's Jesus.

[244] μανθάνω: Mt: 3; Mk: 1; Lk: 0; πραΰς*; (ἐν) τῇ καρδίᾳ: Mt: 8; Mk: 1; Lk: 5. Five times Matthew follows (ἐν) τῇ καρδίᾳ with something other than a genitive personal pronoun; Mark and Luke never do this.

'Learn of me'—which is yet one more indication that in 11.25–30 Jesus is the functional equivalent of Torah: the Sages learned Torah, the disciples learn Jesus—has as its immediate antecedent the revelation spoken of in 11.25–7. But because that revelation encompasses Jesus' sayings and acts (cf. 11.2, 19, 20), one inevitably thinks of all that Jesus has said and done.[245] καὶ εὑρήσετε ἀνάπαυσιν ταῖς ψυχαῖς ὑμῶν. This is a quotation from Jer 6.16 (cf. also Gen 8.9; Isa 28.12). The LXX has: καὶ εὑρήσετε ἁγνισμὸν ταῖς ψυχαῖς ὑμῶν. The MT has: ûmiṣ'û margôaʿ lĕnapšĕkem. Matthew agrees with the LXX against the MT in both the verbal form and the plural ψυχαῖς; but ἀνάπαυσις is not from the Greek OT. Matthew or his source exchanged Jeremiah's ἁγνισμὸν for ἀνάπαυσις in order to gain a link with 28b (ἀναπαύσω). On the concept of 'rest' see on 11.28. ψυχαῖς here means 'selves', not 'souls'; see on 6.25, also Dautzenburg, pp. 134–7.

30. ὁ γὰρ ζυγός μου χρηστὸς καὶ τὸ φορτίον μου ἐλαφρόν ἐστιν. The words are paradoxical. What yoke is comfortable,[246] what burden[247] light?[248] But just as the pious Jew found the commandments not burdensome but liberating (cf. Deut 30.11; Philo, *Spec. leg.* 1.55),[249] so too should the disciple of Jesus be able to say: 'his commandments are not grievous' (1 Jn 5.3; cf. Jn 1.17: 'the law was given through Moses; grace and truth came through Jesus Christ').

While 11.30 helps explain the promise of rest in 28–9, the text neglects to tell us exactly why Jesus' yoke is comfortable, or how his burden can be light. There are several alternatives. (i) Love for God and neighbour (cf. 5.43–4; 19.19; 22.37) makes keeping the commandments easier. Compare Gen 29.20: 'Jacob served seven years for Rachel, and

[245] Cf. 1 Clem. 16, where 'the yoke of his grace' is used not in connexion with Jesus' teaching but with his humility in living out the rôle of the suffering servant of Isaiah.

[246] Or: 'easy (to wear)'. χρηστός: a Matthean *hapax legomenon*. Compare Josephus, *Ant.* 8.213: 'So the leaders of the people and Jeroboam went to him and urged him to lighten their bondage somewhat and to be more lenient (χρηστότερον) than his father, for, they said, the yoke (ζυγόν) they had borne under him had been heavy'.—The 'light yoke' of Testim. Truth 37.22–3 probably comes from Matthew. For 'heavy yoke' see 11QTemple 59.2; Ecclus 40.1.

[247] φορτίον; cf. 23.4 and the use of φορτίζω in 11.28. One recalls the 'heavy burdens' which the Egyptians put upon the children of Israel (Exod 1.11; 2.11; etc.). But the LXX does not use φορτίον to translate *siblâ*.

[248] ἐλαφρός: in the NT only here and 2 Cor 4.17.

[249] S. Schechter, *Some Aspects of Rabbinic Judaism*, London, 1909, pp. 148–69; also Urbach 1, pp. 390–3. Note *m. 'Abot* 6.2: 'No man is free but he who labours in the Torah'. For the law as bringing rest see *Sipre* on Deut 33.2. Only a few Jews seem to have experienced the law as a burden; cf. Acts 15.10; Gal 5.1; LAB 16.1.

they seemed to him but a few days because of the love he had for her'.
(ii) 'The yoke of Jesus is easy and light because Jesus acts for sinners,
because the yoke of Jesus does not throw a man upon his own efforts
but rather brings him into fellowship with the πραΰς' (Barth, in *TIM*,
p. 148, n. 2). (iii) What is burdensome is the Pharisaic oral tradition
(cf. 15.1–9; 23.4). Since Jesus' followers are free to throw that
overboard, their load is lightened. (iv) The fulfilment of Jesus' demands
will bring future reward, and this makes lighter the burdens of the
present. Slavery to the words of Jesus in this world will bring treasure
in the world to come (cf. *b. B. Meṣ.* 85b); and 'the sufferings of this
present time are not worth comparing with the glory that is to come'
(Rom 8.18). (v) Jesus' yoke is easy because in the midst of frightful toil
it is possible to know eschatological rest (vv. 28, 29). Just as one may
rejoice in suffering (5.10–12), so may one experience refreshment while
striving after the better righteousness. (vi) Maybe 11.30 hangs in the
air without explanation because it simply records the voice of
experience. Although the imperatives of Jesus must appear very harsh
to the uninitiated (cf. Ecclus 6.10), the truth is usually grasped only in
the living. Who else but the slave can confess: 'thy service is perfect
freedom'?

Of the six options just listed, we lean towards the last, although (iii)
is also plausible. It would not, however, be wise to be too insistent
upon one particular answer. The text does not explain itself, so the
exegete can do no more than make an educated guess.

In Gos. Thom. 90 Jesus says: 'Come to me, for easy is my yoke and
my lordship is gentle (*rmraš*), and you shall find rest for yourselves'.
One might contend for independent tradition since the order of the
clauses does not agree with Matthew's order. But *rmraš* probably
betrays knowledge of 11.29b–c, Matthew's redactional addition.

Discussion of Mt 11.25–30 has often taken as its point of departure
Ecclus 51.23–7, which reads as follows: 'Draw near to me, you who
are untaught, and lodge in my school. Why do you say you are
lacking in these things, and why are your souls (ψυχαί) very thirsty? I
opened my mouth and said, Get these things for yourselves without
money. Put your neck under my yoke (ζυγόν), and let your souls
(ψυχή) receive instruction; it is to be found (εὑρεῖν) close by. See
with your eyes that I have laboured (ἐκοπίασα) little and found
(εὗρον) for myself much rest (ἀνάπαυσιν)'. Beyond the vocabulary and ideas common to Mt 11.25–30 and Ecclus 51.23–7, E. Norden
(v), in an influential study, also observed a similar sequence of thought,
which he considered typical of the 'mystical philosophical literature of
the East':

Thanksgiving to God	Mt 11.25; cf. Ecclus 51.1–12
The revelation of a mystery	Mt 11.27; cf. Ecclus 51.13–22
The appeal to men	Mt 11.28–30; cf. Ecclus 51.23–30

It is not surprising, in view of the common words, common themes,
and common structure, that many have been sufficiently impressed to
assume the dependence of Mt 11.25–30 upon Ecclus 51 (although

Norden himself did not go so far).[250] We cannot count ourselves among their number (cf. Davies, *PRJ*, pp. 156–8). Of the five shared words, Matthew's ψυχαῖς and εὑρήσετε are taken from Jer 6.16, as is the concept of 'rest'. Further, Norden's analysis stands on thin ice. Both Mt 11.25–30 and Ecclus 51 are composites. The latter is the combination of a thanksgiving hymn and an acrostic poem (now independently attested in the Dead Sea Scrolls: 11QPsᵃ). And concerning the former, 11.25–7 did not originally introduce 11.28–30 (cf. Luke). So the neat parallelism pointed out by Norden is an artifact of a secondary combination and with that the case for direct dependence upon Ecclus 51 falls to the ground. The correct conclusion would seem to be this: Mt 11.25–30 and Ecclus 51 exhibit certain similarities because they both incorporate Torah and Wisdom motifs.[251]

Turning, finally, to the question of the origin of 11.28–30, can we trace the saying to Jesus? Although some have affirmed this,[252] we have serious reservations. The implicit identification of Jesus with Wisdom and Torah is more at home in the early church than the teaching of Jesus. Also standing in the way of a dominical origin is this fact: nowhere else does Jesus speak of his 'yoke' or make the promise of 'rest'. Some have conjectured that Mt 11.28–30, with its general invitation and rhythmic, balanced structure, had its *Sitz im Leben* in Christian liturgy, that it was part of a hymn, sung maybe at the Eucharist or at baptismal services.[253] Our own suspicion is that it was composed as an extension of 11.25–7. See further section (ii).

(iv) *Concluding Observations*

On 11.1–19—

(1) We urged, in the commentary on 3.1, that Matthew's understanding of John the Baptist can be fittingly summarized by three basic assertions: John is Jesus' forerunner; John is subordinate to Jesus; John's words and career run parallel to Jesus' words and career. We have already seen how strongly these three ideas colour the material in 3.1–17. They are no less prominent in 11.2–19. To begin with, 11.2–19 is in great measure a statement about John's rôle as forerunner. John looks for the

---

[250] So e.g. Allen, p. 124; W. Manson, p. 73; Rist (v); Goulder, pp. 360–3.

[251] We are confirmed in this by another consideration. Norden's attention to Ecclus 51 has kept many scholars from recognizing that the parallels in Ecclus 6.18–31 are even more impressive. Here again is Wisdom's invitation and the yoke metaphor (6.30, Hebrew). And the Greek text has several key words and phrases reminiscent of Mt 11.25–30. It seems that we are dealing with a natural coalescence of themes.

[252] Cf. Hunter (v); Bacchiocchi (v).

[253] For some interesting suggestions along this line see Rist (v) and Suggs, pp. 77–83, although they assign the whole of 11.25–30 to liturgy. Some have surmised that Mt 11.28–30 was first spoken by a Christian prophet; see e.g. Farmer, *Jesus*, p. 66. But against this see Boring, p. 212.

Coming One (11.3). He prepares the way for Jesus (11.10). And he fulfils the office of Elijah, which is the prelude to the Messiah's coming (11.14). Hence the Baptist is no independent figure. He is instead wholly Christianized. Everything he does points ahead to Jesus. Secondly, 11.2–19 makes John's subordination perfectly clear. The least in the kingdom is greater than he (11.11). Moreover, by making inquiry of Jesus and wondering whether he might not be the Coming One, the Baptist acknowledges Jesus' authority and his superior status. Finally, not only does 11.12f. place John and Jesus in the same era of salvation-history, but 11.2–19 puts the lifework of John and Jesus side by side and calls attention to the similarities or parallels amidst the differences. Both fulfilled prophecy (11.5–6, 10). Both were out of step with 'this generation' (11.16–17). Both were rejected (11.16–19). Both were called names (11.18–19).

(2) Taking a bird's eye view of the First Gospel, 11.1–19 marks a turning point in the plot. 1.1–4.22, conceived as a whole, is a preface or prologue to the public ministry. The genealogy, the infancy stories, the material on the Baptist, the temptation, the return to Galilee, and the call of the first disciples—all serve to establish Jesus' identity as Son of God and Messiah. Following 4.22, the next three chapters, which make up the sermon on the mount, give us Jesus' authoritative and revelatory words (5.1–7.29). After that, 8.1–9.34 recounts Jesus' marvellous and salvific acts. And then, subsequent to the missionary discourse, in which the apostles are commanded to do what Jesus has done and to preach what Jesus has preached (9.35–10.42), there is 11.1–19. The passage opens with a reference to τὰ ἔργα τοῦ Χριστοῦ. The comprehensive phrase, which summarizes the basic content of the public ministry up to chapter 11 (see p. 240), belongs, in effect, to a question: What does one make of τὰ ἔργα τοῦ Χριστοῦ? Is Jesus the one who is to come, or should we expect another? The all-important question brings Mt 1–10 to a close and introduces the rest of the gospel. The issue now becomes *response to Jesus*. The subject is explored in various ways in chapters 11–12 (the woes on Galilee, the great invitation, the controversy dialogues), and also in chapter 13, where the mysteries of faith and unbelief are pondered by means of parables. What then comes after chapter 13? Because, tragically, the questions posed by Jesus' person and work do not meet with a satisfactory response from corporate Israel, because, that is, as 11.1–12.50 demonstrates, Israel fails to fall in as one behind her Saviour, chapters 14–18 go on (a) to relate the founding of the church (see esp. 16.13–20) and (b) to offer instruction for its operation (18.1–35). Moreover, since Israel's negative response will lead not only to

forfeiture of the kingdom (cf. 21.43) but also to Jesus' crucifixion, 19.1–27.66 is a passion narrative. In a nutshell, then, Mt 1–10 records the offer, Mt 11–27 the refusal. And in this scheme 11.1–19 introduces the moment of decision for the people of God. The verses constitute one of the crucial switching points in the circuits of Matthew. 11.1–19 is Israel's fork in the road.

(3) 11.19 seems to be sufficient evidence that Matthew identified Jesus with Wisdom, with Sophia. 11.25–30 should, we think, also be cited in this connexion, and some would add 23.34–6. Nonetheless, we have not found Matthew's Wisdom Christology to be of great aid in coming to terms with his gospel or his theology. There are, to be sure, some scholars—Suggs and Burnett being the most prominent—who have found Wisdom motifs to be of prime importance for understanding portions of the First Gospel. Most of their conclusions, however, appear to us to be based upon uncertain inferences. Not once does the evangelist come right out and explicitly affirm that Jesus is Wisdom. This is why there are some scholars who can deny that the identification occurs even once.[254] They go too far. But their position is instructive. Matthew's Wisdom Christology is so quiescent that it can be entirely missed and altogether denied. Equally telling is Mt 23.34–6 par. If Q, as many believe, began with, 'Therefore the Wisdom of God said: I said ...' (so Lk 11.49), then Matthew's substitution ('Therefore, behold, I send ...') was, despite claims to the contrary, hardly designed to further a Wisdom Christology. One can, of course, argue that Mt 23.34 identifies Jesus with Wisdom. Yet this fact—if fact it is—could not be known without a knowledge of Q, and one seriously doubts whether Matthew would have permitted such an allegedly key christological fact to be obscured to all save those nurtured on Q. Moreover, and decisive for our evaluation, is this consideration: reflection upon Jesus as Wisdom does not much illumine the major Matthean themes. Suggs has not convinced us that Matthew's approach to the law owes much to Wisdom conceptions, and Burnett is not persuasive in contending that in chapter 24 Jesus speaks firstly as Wisdom incarnate. So while it may be a mistake when Kingsbury, in his discussion of Matthean Christology (*Structure*, pp. 40–127), fails to include Wisdom as even a minor christological title, it would be a greater mistake to consider Wisdom a major title. The equation of Jesus with Wisdom is at the periphery of Matthew's major concerns.

On 11.20–5—

κρίσις, a word which appears twice in 11.20–4, is a Matthean favourite. In seven instances it refers to the last judgement. Six of these belong to chapters 10–12 (10.15; 11.22, 24; 12.36, 41, 42; the exception is 23.33). The fact merits attention. Chapters 5–7 and 8–9 recount, respectively, Jesus' words and deeds.

[254] See esp. M. D. Johnson, 'Reflections on a Wisdom Approach to Matthew's Christology', *CBQ* 36 (1974), pp. 44–64.

Chapter 10 next instructs the apostolic missionaries on what they, following Jesus' example, should say and do. Then follows Mt 11–12, which, as urged above, largely has to do with the *response* of others to Jesus and to those associated with him (including John the Baptist). This is why the theme of judgement (κρίσις) suddenly becomes so prominent. The Jewish people have not responded properly to 'the deeds of the Christ' (11.2; cf. 11.19). They have not, *en masse*, turned to their messianic saviour. They have not, as a corporate body, acknowledged the meaning of Jesus' miracles. From Matthew's point of view this means that Israel has brought judgement upon herself. Thus the primary function of 11.20–4 in its present context is to serve notice that Jesus' mission to Israel has not achieved its first goal (corporate repentance) and that the nation will suffer the consequences.

On 11.25–30—

(1) It has been asserted that 'the Gospel of Matthew as a whole is simply a commentary on the crucially important passage 11.27–30' (Blair, p. 108). We would prefer to put it this way: 11.25–30 is a capsule summary of the message of the entire gospel. In this passage, Jesus reveals that he is the revealer. That is, he reveals that, as the meek and humble Son of the Father, he fulfils the calling of Israel, embodying in his own person Torah and Wisdom and thus making known the perfect will of God.

(2) There runs throughout Mt 1.1–8.1 a developed Mosaic/exodus typology (see on 5.1–2 and 8.1). The circumstances of Jesus' birth and early life resemble those of Moses' birth and early career. The baptism and the temptation recall the crossing of the Red Sea and the desert wanderings. And the mount of Jesus' great sermon corresponds to Mount Sinai. The purpose of all these parallels is in the first instance bound up with eschatology. The last things are as the first (see on 1.1). As it was in the beginning, so shall it be at the End. This is why the church, the eschatological people of God, is called into being by a series of events so reminiscent of the history which saw God call forth his 'son' Israel. Eschatology is being fulfilled. But there is more. In the narrative of the transfiguration, 17.1–8, Jesus is presented as the one prophesied by Moses in Deut 18.15 and 18: 'The Lord your God will raise up for you a prophet like me from among you . . .'. So it is not just that certain events in Jesus' life correlate with certain events in the Pentateuch. Rather, Moses himself looked into the future, beheld Jesus, and spoke of him. Our evangelist's Mosaic typology is accordingly in part a logical outworking of the fulfilment of

Deut 18.15 and 18: Jesus is the 'prophet like me'. But there is still more. Moses is above everything else the law-giver, the mediator of the divine Torah. That is his glory and that is his office. But it is a glory and an office he shares with another. For Jesus the Messiah is also the law-giver, the mediator of divine revelation, as 11.25–30 expresses so memorably. It is this fact, we submit, which is the real key to Matthew's interest in Moses. The evangelist is interested in comparing and contrasting Moses and his revelation with Jesus and his revelation. In other words, how do the first Torah and the eschatological Torah impinge upon and relate to one another? That this is indeed the heart of Matthew's concern is evident from the three places where the Mosaic motifs are most concentrated. In chapters 1–7 those motifs lead up to and surround a discourse in which the revelation to Moses is repeatedly cited (5.17–48). And in 11.25–30 Jesus, in speaking about his own revelation, draws upon an OT text about Moses (Exod 33.12–14); and he implicitly contrasts his yoke with the yoke of the law. Finally, in chapter 17 the Sinai typology evokes what Moses experienced after he received the commandments. So in those places where Matthew compares and contrasts Jesus and Moses, the law is always in mind.

The point of this is clear. Matthew is interested in Moses in large part because he is interested in the law. The Mosaic motifs are, that is, the product of studied reflection on the relationship between the Mosaic law on the one hand and the revelation of Jesus Christ passed on in the church on the other. Furthermore, the similarities between Moses and Jesus as well as the manifest differences between them leave no doubt as to Matthew's point of view, a point of view which has shaped and informed the entire gospel. Three convictions sum up everything. (i) The new revelation is like the old revelation (cf. chapters 1–8; 17.1–8). (ii) The new revelation does not contradict the old revelation (cf. 5.17–19; 13.51–2). (iii) The new revelation surpasses the old revelation (cf. 5.20–48). Accordingly the new law-giver is like Moses—in having a law which should be learned and studied (cf. 11.29; 28.20), in being meek (cf. 11.29), in being transfigured (17.1–8), etc.—yet is at the same time incomparably greater.[255]

(v) *Bibliography*

Abrahams 2, pp. 4–41.
Allison, pp. 120–4.

[255] On Jesus' superiority to Moses see n. 243.

D. C. Allison, 'Two Notes on a Key Text: Matt. XI.25–30', *JTS* 39 (1988), pp. 472–80.

Arens, pp. 221–43, 288–324.

T. Arvedson, *Das Mysterium Christi*, Uppsala, 1937.

S. Bacchiocchi, 'Matthew 11.28–30: Jesus' Rest and the Sabbath', *AUSS* 22 (1984), pp. 289–316.

E. Bammel, 'Is Luke 16.16–18 of Baptist's Provenience?', *HTR* 51 (1958), pp. 101–6

P. W. Barnett, 'Who were the "Biastai" (Mt 11.12–13)?', *RefTheoRev* 36 (1977), pp. 65–70.

J. B. Bauer, 'Das milde Joch und die Ruhe, Mt 11.28–30', *TZ* 17 (1961), pp. 99–106.

H. D. Betz, 'The Logion of the Easy Yoke and of Rest (Matt 11.28–30)', *JBL* 86 (1967), pp. 10–24.

O. Betz, 'Jesu heiliger Krieg', *NovT* 2 (1957), pp. 116–37.

Bousset, pp. 83–9.

G. Braumann, '"Dem Himmelreich wird Gewalt angetan" (Mt 11.12 par)', *ZNW* 52 (1961), pp. 104–9.

M. Brunec, 'De legatione Ioannis Baptistae (Mt 11.2–24)', *VD* 35 (1957), pp. 193–203, 262–70, 321–31.

F. C. Burkitt, 'Phares, Perez and Mt 11.12', *JTS* 30 (1929), pp. 254–8.

P. S. Cameron, *Violence and the Kingdom: The Interpretation of Matthew 11.12*, ANTJ 5, Frankfurt, 1984.

D. R. Catchpole, 'The Law and the Prophets in Q', in Hawthorne, pp. 95–109.

idem, 'On doing Violence to the Kingdom', *IBS* 3 (1981), pp. 77–91.

L. Cerfaux, 'L'Évangile de Jean et "le logion johannique" des Synoptiques,' in *L'Évangile de Jean*, ed. F. Braun, Bruges, 1958, pp. 147–59.

idem, 'Les sources scripturaires de Matth. xi. 25–30', *ETL* 30 (1954), pp. 740–6; 31 (1955), pp. 331–42.

J. Chapman, 'Dr Harnack on Luke 10.22: no Man knoweth the Son', *JTS* 10 (1909), pp. 552–66.

C. Charlier, 'L'Action de grâces de Jésus (Luc 10.17–24 et Matth. 11.25–30)', *BVC* 17 (1957), pp. 87–99

Chilton, *Strength*, pp. 203–30.

Christ, pp. 63–119.

J. A. Comber, 'The Composition and Literary Characteristics of Matt 11.20–24', *CBQ* 39 (1977), pp. 497–504.

W. J. Cotter, 'The Parable of the Children in the Marketplace, Q (Lk) 7.31–5', *NovT* 29 (1987), pp. 289–304.

J. J. C. Cox, '"Bearers of *Heavy* Burdens", A Significant Textual Variant', *AUSS* 9 (1971), pp. 1–15.

Crossan, *Fragments*, pp. 191–7.

Dalman, *Words*, pp. 280–7.

C. Daniel, 'Les Esséniens et "Ceux qui sont dans les maisons des rois" (Matthieu 11.7–8 et Luc 7.24–5)', *RevQ* 6 (1967), pp. 261–77.

F. W. Danker, 'Luke 16.16—An Opposition Logion', *JBL* 77 (1958), pp. 231–43.

W. D. Davies, '"Knowledge" in the Dead Sea Scrolls and Matthew 11.25–30', in *COJ* pp. 119–44.

F. Dibelius, 'Zwei Worte Jesu: II', *ZNW* 11 (1910), pp. 190–2.

De Kruijf, pp. 65–76.

C. Deutsch, *Hidden Wisdom and the Easy Yoke: Wisdom, Torah and Discipleship in Matthew 11.25–30*, Sheffield, 1987.

Dunn, *Spirit*, pp. 27–34, 55–60.

J. Dupont, 'L'ambassade de Jean-Baptiste (Matthieu 11.2–6; Luc 7.18–23)', *NRT* 83 (1961), pp. 805–21, 943–59.

idem, 'Les "simples" (*petâyim*) dans la Bible et à Qumran: À propos des νήπιοι de Mt. 11.25; Lc. 10.21', in *Studi sull' Oriente e la Bibbia offerti al P. Giovanni Rinaldi nel 60° compleanno de allievi, colleghi, amici*, Geneva, 1967, pp. 329–36.

R. A. Edwards, 'Matthew's Use of Q in Chapter Eleven', in Delobel, pp. 257–75.

A. Feuillet, 'Jésus et la Sagesse divine d'après les Évangiles synoptiques', *RB* 62 (1955), pp. 161–96.

Fiedler, pp. 136–47.

W. Foerster, *TWNT* 1, pp. 471–4.

H. Frankemölle, *Biblische Handlungsanweisungen*, Mainz, 1983, pp. 80–108.

A. Fridrichsen, 'Eine unbeachtete Parallele zum Heilandsruf', in *Synoptische Studien*, Munich, 1953, pp. 83–5.

idem, 'Zu Matth. 11.11–15', *TZ* 2 (1946), pp. 470–1.

Fuller, *Achievement*, pp. 89–95.

Geist, pp. 256–63.

A. George, 'Paroles de Jésus sur ses miracles (Mt 11.5, 21; 12.27, 28 et par.)', in Dupont, *Jésus*, pp. 283–301.

J. M. Gibbs, 'The Son of God as Torah Incarnate in Matthew', in *Studia Evangelica* 4/1, TU 102, ed. F. L. Cross, Berlin, 1968, pp. 38–46.

W. Grimm, 'Der Dank für die empfangene Offenbarung bei Jesus und Josephus', *BZ* 17 (1973), pp. 249–56.

idem, *Jesus und das Danielbuch. Band I: Jesu Einspruch gegen das Offenbarungs-system Daniels (Mt 11.25; Lk 17.20–1)*, ANTJ 6/1, Frankfurt am Main, 1984.

idem, *Weil ich dich liebe*, pp. 102–10, 124–30, 171–7.

W. Grundmann, 'Die νήπιοι in der urchristlichen Paränese', *NTS* 5 (1959), pp. 188–205.

idem, 'Matth. 11.27 und die johanneischen "der Vater—der Sohn"—Stellen', *NTS* 12 (1965), pp. 42–9.

Hahn, *Titles*, pp. 308–13.

Harnack, *Sayings*, pp. 272–310.

S. Hirsch, 'Studien zu Matt. 11.2–26', *TZ* 6 (1950), pp. 241–60.

Hoffmann, *Logienquelle*, pp. 50–79, 102–42, 196–231.

P. Hoffmann, 'Die Offenbarung des Sohnes. Die apokalyptischen Voraussetzungen und ihre Verarbeitung im Q-Logien Mt 11.27 par Lk 10.22', *Kairos* 12 (1970), pp. 270–88.

R. Hoppe, *Der theologische Hintergrund des Jakobusbriefes*, FB 28, Würzburg, 1977, pp. 45–52.

A. Houssiau, 'L'exégèse de Matthieu XI. 27B selon Saint Irenée', *ETL* 29 (1953), pp. 328–54.

A. M. Hunter, 'Crux Criticorum—Matt. 11.25–30', *NTS* 8 (1962), pp. 241–9.

Jeremias, *Prayers*, pp. 45–52.

idem, *Theology*, pp. 56–61.

Jülicher 2. pp. 23–36.

A. F. J. Klijn, 'Matthew 11.25/Luke 10.21', in *New Testament Textual Criticism: Its Significance for Exegesis*, ed. E. J. Epp and G. D. Fee, Oxford, 1981, pp. 1–14.

J. S. Kloppenborg, 'Wisdom Christology in Q', *Laval Théologique et Philosophie* (Quebec) 34 (1978), pp. 129–47.

H. Koester, 'Gnostic Writings as Witnesses for the Development of the Sayings Tradition', in *The Rediscovery of Gnosticism: Vol. 1: The School of Valentinus*, Studies in the History of Religions 41, Leiden, 1980, pp. 238–61.

D. Kosch, *Die Gottesherrschaft im Zeichen des Widerspruchs: Traditions- und redaktionsgeschichtliche Untersuchung von Lk 16.16, Mt 11.12f. bei Jesus, Q und Lukas*, Frankfurt am Main, 1985.

N. Krieger, 'Ein Mensch in weichen Kleidern', *NovT* 1 (1956), pp. 228–30.

W. G. Kümmel, *Jesu Antwort an Johannes den Täufer*, Wiesbaden, 1974.

Künzel, *Studien*, pp. 84–93.

G. Lambert, '"Mon joug est aisé et mon fardeau léger"', *NRT* 77 (1955), pp. 963–9.

J. Lambrecht, '"Are you the one who is to come, or shall we look for another?"', *Louvain Studies* 8 (1980), pp. 115–28.

S. Légasse, 'Le logion sur le Fils révélateur', in *La Notion biblique de Dieu*, ed. J. Coppens, Leuven, 1976, pp. 245–74.

idem, 'Le révélation aux ΝΗΠΙΟΙ', *RB* 67 (1960), pp. 321–48.

O. Linton, 'The parable of the children's game', *NTS* 22 (1976), pp. 159–79.

H. Ljungmann, 'En Sifre-text till Matt. 11.18f. par.', *SEÅ* 22–3 (1957–8), pp. 238–42.

U. Luck, 'Weisheit und Christologie in Mt 11.25–30', *WD* 13 (1975), pp. 35–51.

Lührmann, pp. 24–31, 60–8.

M. Maher, '"Take my yoke upon you" (Matt. xi. 29)', *NTS* 22 (1975), pp. 97–102.

W. Manson, pp. 71–6.

I. H. Marshall, 'The Divine Sonship of Jesus', *Int* 21 (1967), pp. 89–103.

J. P. Meier, 'John the Baptist in Matthew's Gospel', *JBL* 99 (1980), pp. 383–405.

P.-H. Menoud, 'Le sens du verbe BIAZETAI dans Lc 16.16', in Descamps, *Mélanges*, pp. 207–12.

H. Mertens, *L'hymne de jubilation chez les synoptiques*, Gembloux, 1957.

E. Meyer, *Ursprung und Anfänge des Christentums*, vol. 1, Stuttgart, 1924, pp. 280–91.

W. E. Moore, ·BIAZΩ, ΑΡΠΑΖΩ and Cognates in Josephus', *NTS* 21 (1975), pp. 519–43.

idem, 'Violence to the Kingdom', *ExpT* 100 (1989), pp. 174–7.

A. R. Motte, 'La structure du logion de Matthieu 11.28–30', RB 88 (1981), pp. 226–33.

F. Mussner, 'Der nicht erkannte Kairos (Mt 11.16–19; Lk 7.31–5)', Bib 40 (1959), p. 599–612.

idem, 'Wege zum Selbstbewusstsein Jesu', BZ 12 (1968), pp. 167–9.

Norden, pp. 277–308.

Percy, pp. 108–10, 187–202, 231–3, 251–3, 259–71.

Pesch, Taten, pp. 36–44.

A. E. J. Rawlinson, The New Testament Doctrine of the Christ, London, 1926, pp. 251–64.

M. Rist, 'Is Matt. 11.25–30 a primitive baptismal Hymn?', JR 15 (1935), pp. 63–77.

P. Richardson, 'The Thunderbolt in Q and the Wise Man in Corinth', in From Jesus to Paul, ed. P. Richardson and J. C. Hurd, Waterloo, 1984, pp. 91–111.

J. M. Robinson, 'Die Hodajot-Formel in Gebet und Hymnus des Frühchristentums', in Apophoreta, ed. W. Eltester, Berlin, 1964, pp. 194–235.

M. Sabbe, 'Can Mt 11.25–7 and Lc 10.21–2 be called a Johannine Logion?', in Delobel, pp. 363–71.

Schlosser 2, pp. 509–39.

V. Schönle, Johannes, Jesus und die Juden: Die theologischen Position des Matthäus und des Verfassers der Redenquelle im Lichte von Mt 11, BBET, Frankfurt am Main, 1982.

H. Scholander, 'Zu Mt 11.12', ZNW 13 (1912), pp. 172–5.

G. Schrenk, TWNT 1, pp. 608–13.

Schürmann, Untersuchungen, pp. 126–36.

Schulz, Q, pp. 190–203, 213–36, 261–7, 360–6, 379–86.

G. N. Stanton, 'Matthew as Creative Interpreter of the Sayings of Jesus', in Stuhlmacher, Evangelium, pp. 283–5.

idem, 'Matthew 11.28–30: Comfortable Words?', ExpT 94 (1982), pp. 3–9.

K. G. Steck, 'Über Matthäus 11.25–30', EvTh 15 (1955), pp. 343–9.

C. Stratton, 'Pressure for the Kingdom', Int 8 (1954), pp. 414–21.

Strauss, pp. 219–30.

A. Strobel, Untersuchungen zum eschatologischen Verzögerungsproblem, Leiden, 1961, pp. 265–77.

P. Stuhlmacher, Das paulinische Evangelium 1, FRLANT 95, Göttingen, 1968, pp. 218–25.

Suggs, pp. 31–58, 71–108.

G. Theissen, 'Das "schwankende Rohr" in Mt 11.7 und die Gründungsmünzen von Tiberias', ZDPV 101 (1985), pp. 43–55.

B. E. Thiering, 'Are the "Violent Men" False Teachers?', NovT 21 (1979), pp. 293–7.

W. Trilling, 'Die Täufertradition bei Matthäus', BZ 3 (1959), pp. 271–89.

Van Iersel, pp. 146–61.

Verseput, pp. 55–153.

A. Vögtle, 'Wunder und Wort in urchristlicher Glaubenswerbung (Mt 11.2–5/Lk 7.18–22)', in Evangelium, pp. 219–42.

M. Völkel, '"Freund der Zöllner und Sünder"', ZNW 69 (1978), pp. 1–10.

Wanke, pp. 31–40, 45–51.

J. Weiss, 'Das Logion Mt 11.25–30', in *Neutestamentliche Studien für Georg Heinrici zum 70. Geburtstag*, Leipzig, 1914, pp. 120–9.

Wink, pp. 18–41.

P. Winter, 'Matt. xi.27 and Luke x.22 from the first to the fifth Century', *NovT* 1 (1956), pp. 112–48.

D. Zeller, 'Die Bildlogik des Gleichnisses Mt 11.16f./Lk 7.31f.', *ZNW* 68 (1977), pp. 252–7.

Zumstein, pp. 130–52.

XXV

TWO SABBATH CONTROVERSIES AND THE SERVANT
OF DEUTERO-ISAIAH
(12.1–21)

(i) *Structure*

This section is composed of three subsections, each of which is introduced by a notice of Jesus' movements: 'At that time Jesus went through the grain-fields' (12.1); 'And going on from there' (12.9); 'Jesus, aware of this, withdrew from there' (12.15). The first two subsections (12.1–8, 9–14) recount sabbath incidents which involve conflict with the Pharisees. The third subsection contains a short summary of Jesus' activities and a long formula quotation from Isa 42.1–4, 9.

The arrangement of 8.1–17 supplies an interesting parallel. In this last we have two similar stories (two healings: 8.1–4, 5–13) which are then followed by 8.14–17, a paragraph which narrates a healing, offers a summary statement of Jesus' healing ministry, and cites a Scripture from Deutero-Isaiah.

(ii) *Sources*

Mt 12.1–21 is, according to the two-source theory, based upon Mk 2.23–8 (plucking grain on the sabbath), Mk 3.1–6 (the healing of the man with the withered hand), and Mk 3.7–12 (a Markan summary of Jesus' healing ministry). Beyond stylistic alterations and other minor changes, Matthew has added arguments to the first and second pericopae (see 12.5–7, 11–12a) and made Mark's lengthy summary (3.7–12) the opportunity for inserting the key formula quotation.

There are several minor agreements between Mt 12.1–8 and Lk 6.1–5, Luke's version of Mk 2.23–8. See Allen, p. 128, and Fitzmyer, *Luke* 1, pp. 605–6. Against Gundry, *Commentary*, p. 222, these do not imply Luke's knowledge of Matthew. (See Aichinger (v), though he finds it necessary to appeal to the hypothesis of a Proto- or Deutero-Mark.) There is also insufficient reason to follow Hübner, pp. 113–23, who has conjectured that Matthew and Luke have been influenced by a Q version of Mk 2.23–8, or Benoit (v), who argues that Matthew's text makes use of Mark as well as more primitive tradition.

303

(iii) *Exegesis*

THE SON OF MAN IS LORD OF THE SABBATH (12.1–8)

The tradition-history of Mt 12.1–8 is much like a snowball rolling down a hill. The core would seem to be 12.1–4 par., a simple pronouncement story consisting of (i) description of or allusion to circumstances, (ii) critical question, (iii) dominical counter-question.[1] To this the pre-Markan tradition added Mk 2.27: 'And he said to them: the sabbath was made for man, not man for the sabbath.'[2] Mark himself then evidently added 2.28, on the Son of man being Lord of the sabbath (see on 12.8). Finally, Matthew expanded the story by adding three verses which are intended to reinforce the single argument found in Mark (see Mt 12.5–7).

As it stands, Mt 12.1–8 falls into three parts. There is the setting (12.1), the Pharisees' criticism (12.2), and Jesus' response (12.3–8), which in turn is composed of three questions (introduced with ὁ δὲ εἶπεν αὐτοῖς) followed by three statements (introducted with λέγω δὲ ὑμῖν; cf. Gnilka, *Matthäus-evangelium* 1, p. 443).

E. P. Sanders has objected that our story is not likely to rest upon historical reminiscence: 'Pharisees did not actually spend their sabbaths patrolling cornfields'.[3] This common-sense observation is not as forceful as Sanders seems to suppose. In Matthew the Pharisees see (ἰδόντες) the plucking of grain and immediately respond. In Mark, however, the connexion between the reported action and the reported response is much looser. We are not actually told when the Pharisees raised their protest. Perhaps they only heard later about what had happened (although note *b. Šabb.* 127a, where Rabbi is in a field on the Sabbath). In any event, the stereotyped form of the story and the concentration, for brevity's sake, on the one thing needful, more than suffice to explain the appearance of artificiality; so Sanders' argument is not decisive (cf. Marshall, p. 231; Casey (v), pp. 4–5).

Pesch 1, p. 183, has put forward these arguments to support his assertion that our sabbath story is based on concrete tradition from the life of Jesus.[4] (i) Mark (2.23–8; 3.1–6), Luke's special tradition (13.10–17; 14.1–6), and the Gospel of John (5.1–18; 9.1–41) agree that

[1] So those cited in Hultgren, p. 139, n. 61. The same pattern occurs in Mk 2.15–17 par.; 2.18–22 par.; 3.1–6 par.; 3.22–30 par.; 6.1–6 par.; 7.1–15 par.; 9.9–13 par. All these represent one type of pronouncement story, namely, the objection story. For other analyses see Guelich, *Mark*, p. 119.
[2] See Taylor, *Mark*, p. 218. The authenticity of this saying seems more probable than not; cf. Lohse (v), pp. 84–5. For a review of the discussion of this verse see Neirynck (v).
[3] E. P. Sanders, 'Jesus and the Constraint of the Law', *JSNT* 17 (1983), p. 20. Others who regard Mk 2.23–6 as a community product include Lohse (v) and Beare, p. 272.
[4] Cf. Gnilka, *Markus* 1, p. 122; Borg, p. 152; Casey (v).

Jesus' sabbath practice made for conflict with certain Jewish authorities. Further, Mk 2.23–6 contains possible Semitisms[5] and concerns a situation (the plucking of grain on a sabbath) which cannot, without further ado, be considered typical of early Christian practice.[6] (ii) Jesus and his disciples were in fact poor, itinerant preachers as the story assumes. (iii) That Jesus was made responsible for the actions of his disciples (Mk 2.24) is historically plausible (cf. Mk 2.18; 7.5).[7] (iv) Jesus answers his critics with a scriptural proof in other conflict stories (Mk 7.1–13; 12.18–27); and the use of 1 Sam 21.2–10 presupposes a situation of hunger,[8] not a problem of Christian theology. (v) The implicit 'Sendungsbewusstsein' cannot be denied to Jesus; and in Mk 12.35–7 he again compares himself to David.

These five points are, in our estimation, forceful and support Pesch's estimate of the historicity of our story. To them we should like to add one other consideration. Even if the conflict stories about the sabbath were remembered in order to explain and defend the church's practice of observing the first day of the week, it is hard to perceive in Mk 2.23–6 any really helpful answer to Christian questions about the sabbath. Jesus' reasoning does not open itself up to easy generalisations. The argument hinges largely upon the parallel between David and Jesus. But where exactly does that leave the ordinary Christian? Is the situation depicted normative or exceptional? And is the sabbath abrogated or only modified? Even Mk 2.27–8 does not clear up these questions. It would seem to follow that Mk 2.23–6 was not freely created for the sole purpose of instructing Christians on how to treat the sabbath. Hard cases make bad law, as the saying goes. Would not an early Christian, seeking only to commend Christian practice, have created a story whose implications are a little more patent?

1. ἐν ἐκείνῳ τῷ καιρῷ ἐπορεύθη ὁ ᾽Ιησοῦς τοῖς σάββασιν διὰ τῶν σπορίμων. Before διά Mk 2.23 has: καὶ ἐγένετο αὐτὸν ἐν τοῖς σάββασιν παραπορεύεσθαι. On 'at the time' see on 11.25. The phrase is not intended to supply chronological information but to serve as a thematic bridge: it helps associate 11.25–30 (which is introduced by 'at that time' and which proclaims Jesus as the giver of rest) with 12.1–8 (where Jesus is the Lord of the sabbath). As is his wont, Matthew has omitted Mark's καὶ ἐγένετο and made the subject ὁ ᾽Ιησοῦς*. On the plural, 'sabbaths', see on 12.12. σπόριμος means 'sown', τὰ σπόριμα[9] 'standing grain', 'grain fields' (BAGD, s.v.; cf. LXX Gen 1.29; Lev 11.37;

---

[5] Pesch lists: τί in Mk 2.24 (see Black, p. 122), εἰ μή in 2.26 (see Beyer, pp. 31ff., 104ff.), and redundant ἄρχομαι (see Taylor, *Mark*, p. 63).

[6] Cf. Haenchen, *Weg*, p. 122, n. 4: Did the early Christians typically go through the fields on the sabbath in order to pluck grain?

[7] See D. Daube, 'The Responsibilities of Master and Disciples in the Gospels', *NTS* 19 (1972), pp. 1–15. Contrast Bultmann, *History*, p. 16, who has been cited by many.

[8] The narrative element was hardly added to supply a setting for the scriptural proof.

[9] In the NT only in Mk 2.23 par. Cf. 1 Kgs 8.15 Sym.

Ecclus 40.22). On the paths for Peah ('gleanings') see Casey (v), pp. 2–3.

οἱ δὲ μαθηταὶ αὐτοῦ ἐπείνασαν καὶ ἤρξαντο τίλλειν στάχυας καὶ ἐσθίειν. Compare Mk 2.23. Matthew has changed Mark's δέ to καί, added the remark on hunger, which anticipates v. 3 and thereby increases the parallelism between the situation of David and the situation of Jesus,[10] eliminated 'to make their way',[11] changed τίλλοντες to the infinitive, eliminated the article[12] before στάχυας, and added 'to eat' (cf. 12.4).

τίλλω[13] is 'pick' or 'pluck, στάχυς[14] 'head' or 'ear of grain'. Evidently, some grains were eaten without being cooked. Because grain ripened a few weeks after Passover (sometime between April and June), our text probably implies that Jesus' public ministry lasted at least one year.[15]

2. The Pharisees object to the disciples' action. Are not Jesus' followers neglecting a fundamental demand of the decalogue, one of the obligations of the covenant? Are they not breaking a commandment God himself kept (Gen 2.2; Jub. 2.16–18)? Are they not doing away with one of the signs that separates Jew from Gentile?[16]

οἱ δὲ Φαρισαῖοι ἰδόντες εἶπαν αὐτῷ. Compare 12.3a. Mk 2.24 has ἔλεγον, lacks ἰδόντες, and is introduced by καί.

ἰδοὺ οἱ μαθηταί σου ποιοῦσιν ὃ οὐκ ἔξεστιν ποιεῖν ἐν σαββάτῳ. Matthew has turned a question into an accusation by eliminating the interrogative form of Mk 2.24. This heightens the note of conflict. The substitution of ἰδού* for ἴδε is attested elsewhere (cf. 12.49 = Mk 3.34; 24.23 = Mk 13.21). οὐκ ἔξεστιν (cf. Mk 2.26; 6.18; Jn 5.10; Josephus, Ant. 13.252) recalls the rabbinic 'āsûr.

---

[10] Cf. Hummel, p. 41. Some have added—less plausibly—that the reference to hunger also supplies a reasonable motive—necessity—for the disciples' action (cf. the rabbinic apologetic for David in the texts cited by SB 1, pp. 618–19) or prevents the disciples from behaving in a wanton fashion.

[11] Cf. Judg 17.8 LXX and the Latin iter facere. The Greek could also mean 'to make a road' or 'to journey'. The Markan ms. tradition shows that scribes had difficulties with the words; see Taylor, Mark, p. 215. Casey (v), p. 2, conjectures mistranslation from an Aramaic source: 'br was misread as 'bd.

[12] Which is restored in (D) W 28 700 pc sa bo.

[13] LXX: 3, never with στάχυς as object. NT: only in Mk 2.23 par.

[14] Most often in the LXX for šibbōlet. In the NT: Mt 12.1; Mk 2.23; 4.28; Lk 6.1.

[15] But see Lane, p. 114, n. 79, quoting M. Smith: 'While Passover marks the official beginning of the harvest, grain is ripe sometimes earlier in sheltered places, not to mention the Jordan Valley'.

[16] Pertinent texts include Gen 2.2; Exod 20.8–11; Deut 5.12–15; Neh 13.15–22; Isa 56.6; Jub. 2.17–23; Tacitus, Hist. 5.4; Martial 4.4; Juvenal, Sat. 14.96–106.

The law permitted the poor to glean from the corners of the fields (Lev 19.9f.; Deut 23.24f.; cf. 4Q159; Josephus, *Ant.* 4.231–9; *m. Pe'a* passim; *b. B. Meṣ.* 92a). Exod 34.21, however, commands, 'Six days you shall work, but on the seventh day you shall rest; in ploughing time and in harvest you shall rest' (cf. *Jub.* 50.12; *m. Šabb* 7.2). The action of Jesus' disciples was, in accordance with the strictness of the times,[17] interpreted by the Pharisees as a violation of this statute.[18] For rabbinic legislation on the sabbath see SB 1, pp. 615–18, 623–9; Schürer 2, pp. 467–75. According to *m. Šabb.* 7.2, thirty-nine classes of work—including reaping—were prohibited. How many of these were in fact in force in the first century—and who would have enforced them—is debatable. NT scholars often assume that the laws codified later in the Mishnah were more or less already fixed by Jesus' time. But as Sanders has written, 'Josephus repeatedly says that the priests were the administrators of the law (e.g. *Ap.* II.187; cf. *AJ* XX.251), and few priests were Pharisees. We may recall, for example, that Ananus, a Sadducee, convened the Sanhedrin and had James and others executed (*AJ* XX.197–203). The ancestors of those who codified Mishnah Sanhedrin, which makes execution virtually impossible, were clearly not in charge of the court'.[19] Fortunately, we need not resolve the issue here and now. What matters is, first, that Exod 34.21 was certainly considered by Jews to be the law of the land and, secondly, that Jewish tradition had long recognized that exceptional circumstances sometimes allowed the non-observance of the Torah.[20] So the question for Jesus and Matthew and for their opponents was not, Can there be exceptions to the sabbath halakah? It was rather, What constitutes a legitimate exception? It was over this—a question which different Jews answered differently—that Jesus and his followers found themselves at odds with others (cf. Schoeps (v)). So Mt 12.1–8 is not evidence that either Jesus or Matthew took himself to be leaving the paternal roof of the law. The text is not antinomian polemic. Rather, it intends to be an attack upon a perceived casuistic interpretation of God's will and word.

[17] Visible esp. in *Jub.* 2 and 50 as well as in the Qumran texts, for which see L. H. Schiffman, *The Halakhah at Qumran*, SJLA 16, Leiden, 1975, pp. 77–133; also S. T. Kimbrough, 'The Concept of Sabbath at Qumran', *RevQ* 5 (1966), pp. 483–502.

[18] Cf. Philo, *Vit. Mos.* 2.22 ('It is not permitted to cut any shoot or branch, or even a leaf, or to pluck any fruit whatsoever'); *y. Šabb.* 9c (plucking is reaping). Nothing is said about the disciples breaking the sabbatical travel limit. See *b. Šabb.* 127a for a rabbi in a field on the sabbath.

[19] E. P. Sanders, 'Jesus and the Constraints of the Law', *JSNT* 17 (1983), p. 19. Pertinent also is the fact that even later rabbis had disagreements over what was lawful on the sabbath (cf. e.g. *m. 'Uq.* 3.10).

[20] See Num 28.9–10; 1 Macc 2.39–41; *Jub.* 50.10–1; Justin, *Dial.* 27; *Mek.* on Exod 31.14; *m. Yoma* 8.6; *m. Pesaḥ.* 6.1–2; *m. 'Erub.* 6.1; 10.11–15; *m. Šabb.* 16.1–7; 18.3; 19.1–3; *t. Šabb.* 15.10–17; *b. Šabb.* 129b, 132b; *b. Yoma* 85b. Also relevant is *b. Yeb.* 90b: 'Come and hear: Unto him ye shall hearken (Deut 18.15), even if he tells you, "Transgress any of all the commandments of the Torah" as in the case for instance of Elijah on Mount Carmel (cf. 1 Kgs 18, where Elijah offers a sacrifice outside the temple), obey him in every respect in accordance with the needs of the hour'. Here the word of a true prophet may abrogate Pentateuchal law.

3–4. In a manner reminiscent of rabbinic debate Jesus answers the objection with a question and appeals to Scripture (see Bultmann, *Tradition*, pp. 41–6, for parallels). Specifically, Jesus appeals to David's breach of the law in 1 Sam 21. There are two obvious points of correlation. In both instances a righteous man breaks a commandment, and both times he does so out of hunger.[21] Also implicit is a third point of comparison: Jesus, the Messiah and descendant of David, is like his ancestor the king. It is even possible to find a fourth parallel. For there is some rabbinic evidence (albeit late) which places David's act on a sabbath, when the old showbread was being replaced by the new (*b. Menaḥ.* 95b; *Yalquṭ* on 1 Sam 21.5; SB 1, pp. 618–19; Casey (v), pp. 9–13, arguing that Mark's account assumes a sabbath dating.)

It is noteworthy that by affirming that he was in peril and near starvation, the rabbis sought to justify David's act (cf. SB 1, pp. 618–19; note also Josephus, *Ant.* 6.242–4, which omits mention of the bread of the Presence). Perhaps Jewish scholars in Jesus' day had already concerned themselves with the problem. If so, Jesus might have been appealing to a text whose implications were known to be controversial.

Does the argument in 12.3–4 accord with the canons of rabbinic debate? Cohn-Sherbok (v) has shown that they do not. The analogy is poor: David and his company were, according to Jewish tradition, in great need and danger while Jesus and his followers were not; and beyond that the argument is essentially haggadic in Mark and fails to cite any definite scriptural precept, something which Matthew has to supply. What is the conclusion? While Jesus seems to have been 'familiar with rabbinic hermeneutics' he was, according to Cohn-Sherbok, 'not a skilled casuist in the style of the Pharisees and Sadducees' (Cohn-Sherbok (v), p. 40). Although one could object that Cohn-Sherbok does not prove that the rabbinic standards which he brings to bear upon Mt 12.1–8 were taken for granted in the first century, his conclusion stands. Jesus was not an adept in rabbinic debate. He may well have learned much from the Scripture scholars of his day, but he apparently did not expend his energies trying to master their methods. Rather, as B. Gerhardsson has written, 'the pattern of Jesus' own attitude to the behavioural aspect of the Jewish mother-tradition is that he shows very little interest in halachic minutiae but a very strong interest in the central ethos of the mother-tradition, which may be summarized in formulas such as "the great and first commandment" (Matt 22.38), "the weightiest matters of the law" (Matt 23:23) or in some other way. His own "new teaching" is a radicalization of the central core within the verbal Torah'.[22]

---

[21] Scripture does not inform us that David was hungry; but this is implicit and therefore is supplied by later tradition.

[22] B. Gerhardsson, *The Gospel Tradition*, CB, NT 15, Lund, 1986, p. 26. We are reminded of what John Maynard Keynes said of Sir Isaac Newton: 'It was his intuition which was pre-eminently extraordinary ... He seemed to know

ὁ δὲ εἶπεν αὐτοῖς. Compare 12.2a. Mk 2.25 has: καὶ λέγει αὐτοῖς. Again δέ replaces καί and the historical present disappears.

οὐκ ἀνέγνωτε τί ἐποίησεν Δαυὶδ ὅτε ἐπείνασεν καὶ οἱ μετ' αὐτοῦ. Compare Mk 12.10, 26. As compared with Mk 2.25, Matthew has turned οὐδέποτε into οὐκ and, for the sake of reducing prolixity of expression, dropped the words on either side of ἐπείνασεν: χρείαν ἔσχεν καί . . . αὐτός;

πῶς εἰσῆλθεν εἰς τὸν οἶκον τοῦ θεοῦ. This agrees with Mk 2.26, except that Mark has these words at the end: 'when Abiathar was high priest'. Lk 6.4 also omits the remark about Abiathar. No doubt both the First and Third Evangelists realized, as did Jerome after them (*Ep.* 57.9), that Mark had simply made an error. The high priest in question was Abiathar's son, the lesser known Ahimelech (see 1 Sam 21.1).[23] Why both Matthew and Luke chose to correct the error through elimination rather than emendation cannot be answered. ὁ οἶκος τοῦ θεοῦ is the LXX name for the shrine of the sacred ark (cf. Judg 18.31). Solomon's temple had not yet been built.

καὶ τοὺς ἄρτους τῆς προθέσεως ἔφαγον.[24] So also Mk 2.26, with ἔφαγεν. Compare 4QSam[b] frags. 3–4.3, which, unlike the MT, has David tell his companions that they may eat (if they have kept themselves from women).

'The bread of the Presence' (*leḥem happānîm*) has several equivalents in the LXX, including οἱ ἄρτοι τῆς προθέσεως (cf. Exod 40.23; 1 Βασ 21.6). The words refer to the 'showbread', the twelve loaves of bread which were arranged in two rows upon the table before the Holy of Holies. The loaves were baked on Friday, taken into the temple the morning of the sabbath, and offered as a thank offering.[25]

ὃ οὐκ ἐξὸν ἦν αὐτῷ φαγεῖν. Mk 2.26 has the same sense but is more compact: οὓς οὐκ ἔξεστιν φαγεῖν. See Lev 24.9: 'And it shall be for Aaron and his sons, and they shall eat it in a holy place, since it is for him a most holy portion out of the offering . . . .'

more than he could have possibly any hope of proving. The proofs were dressed up afterwards; they were not the instrument of discovery.' See also Davies *SSM*, pp. 423–4.

[23] A similar error occurs in Eupolemus, frag. 2B (= Eusebius, *Praep. ev.* 9.30.8), where Eli is erroneously said to have been the 'high priest' when David transferred his rule to Solomon. Cranfield, *Mark*, p. 116, notes there may be 'some confusion between Ahimelech and Abiathar in the O.T. itself—cf. 1 Sam xxii.20 with II Sam viii. 17, 1 Chr xviii.16, xxiv.6.'

[24] So NA[26]. εφαγεν is the reading of P[70] C D L W Θ *f*[1.13] Maj latt sy co; but it may be due to assimilation to Mark. ℵ B *pc* have εφαγον, which goes better with 12.1 (where the disciples eat).

[25] See Exod 25.23–30; 40.22–3; Lev 24.5–9; Num 4.1–8; 1 Sam 21.4–6; 1 Chr 9.32.

οὐδὲ τοῖς μετ' αὐτοῦ. This is a redactional addition (cf. 12.3). We do not know whether the legislation in Lev 24.9 was known or in force in David's time, though it seems unlikely.

εἰ μὴ τοῖς ἱερεῦσιν μόνοις; Mk 2.26, at least in א B 892 sa^mss bo^mss, has τοὺς ἱερεῖς and then this: 'and gave it to those who were with him?' Both Matthew and Luke have omitted this last as superfluous. The dative for the accusative is a stylistic improvement.

The precise force of Jesus' appeal to 1 Sam 21 has been debated.[26] Of the various proposals, the following deserve mention. (i) Jesus was simply reminding the Pharisees that a higher good (human need) takes precedence over a lesser good (ceremonial law). If the great king David could transgress the law when pressed by hunger and hardship, then so too may Jesus' disciples, when suffering hunger pangs, pluck grain on the sabbath.[27]

(ii) The rabbis permitted breach of the sabbath if life was in danger (SB 1, pp. 623–9), and Jesus and his disciples were, in a spiritual fashion, in the business of saving lives. Any delay in their mission would put others in peril.

(iii) If the plucking of grain took place on the 15th of Nisan, the first day of the Passover, when the sheaf offerings were prepared by the priests despite its being a sabbath, then Jesus might have been saying, in effect: just as David took to himself a priestly prerogative, so may I and my disciples (so M. Cohen (v), arguing that the σαββάτῳ δευτεροπρώτῳ of Lk 6.1 Maj. is historical and refers to the second sabbath of Nisan and the first in the pentecostal computation).

(iv) The urgency of the eschatological situation permitted the suspension of the law.[28] Just as a state of war might lead to violation of the sabbath, so too might the pressing needs of God's kingdom issue in exceptional behaviour. 'I must work while it is still day'.[29] Compare perhaps the attitude attributed to R. Joḥanan in b. Yeb. 79a: 'It is proper that a letter be rooted out of the Torah so that thereby the heavenly name shall be publicly hallowed'.

(v) Jesus could have been attacking the oral tradition, not the written Torah, to wit: 'the fact that scripture does not condemn David for his action shows that the rigidity with which the Pharisees interpreted the ritual law was not in accordance with scripture, and so was not a proper understanding of the Law itself'.[30]

(vi) Irenaeus, Adv. haer. 4.8.3, affirming that 'all the righteous possess the sacerdotal rank' (cf. 1 Pet 2.5, 9), argued that 'David had been appointed a priest by God', and that 'all the apostles of the Lord are priests'; and since, as 12.5–6 makes plain, priests could, when not

[26] See the survey of opinion in Banks, pp. 114–18.
[27] Cf. Allen, p. 127, and Nineham, pp. 105–6, who opines: 'many of the more liberal rabbis of the time would largely have agreed with Jesus'.
[28] See Borg (v) and Harvey (v).
[29] Cf. m. Ber. 9.5 (with Danby's comments) and b. Ber. 63a.
[30] Cranfield, Mark, p. 115. He does not explain how this view harmonizes with Mk 2.26b (only the priests may eat of the bread).

engaged in secular affairs, 'profane' the sabbath, so too may the priestly disciples of Jesus (cf. interpretation (iii)).

(vii) The example of David illustrates the possibility of breaking the law for the sake of some greater good, just as the following example of the priests in the temple (12.5–6) illustrates the possibility of observing one commandment at the expense of another. So the point is that one divine demand may overrule another; and since the commandment to love is the greatest commandment of all, observance of it may on occasion lead to disobedience to OT legislation (cf. Hummel, pp. 42–3, who urges that the meaning of 12.1–8 becomes clear only in the light of 12.9–14, where the theme of doing good to others—loving them— becomes explicit).

(viii) The point is christological. If David and his followers could break the Torah, how much more God's eschatological representative, the Messiah.[31]

Of the eight interpretations catalogued, (v) merits consideration since Matthew is not likely to have thought of Jesus as wantonly violating the Torah (5.17–20; see further below). But there is also probably truth in (viii) when taken in conjunction with (vii). Not only has Matthew emphasized the element of hunger and therefore the real need of the disciples, but both 12.5–6 and 8 make christological assertions, and 12.3– 4 supports a christological interpretation because, over against 1 Sam 21.1–6, it emphasizes David's active rôle and puts the priests in the background (cf. Pesch 1, pp. 181–2). So it seems that the basic issue of our text is this. Jesus' authority is illustrated by David's authority; and if David could act as he did, surely Jesus, in a manner of uncertain infringement (see below), could act similarly (cf. Sigal, p. 132).

That Matthew's understanding of the sabbath controversy is not far from Jesus' own understanding we think likely. But with regard to stage I of the tradition a few points need to be added. The gospels have Jesus coming into conflict with his contemporaries over sabbath observance on several occasions. The datum would seem to belong to the bedrock of the tradition (cf. Lohse (v), p. 84). If so, it appears altogether probable that Jesus sometimes flouted custom in part because he disputed the oral tradition and sought to get back to the original will of God as contained in the Torah (cf. interpretation (v)). In this connexion it is extremely important to note that the Pentateuch, which enters into almost no detail on the matter, plainly prohibits only two specific activities on the sabbath: the kindling of fires (Exod 35.3) and the gathering of sticks (Num 15.32–6). Exod 20.10 and Deut 5.14 prohibit 'work', but no definition is provided. Further, Scripture itself seemingly allows actions which later tradition would have frowned upon (e.g. 2 Kgs 11.4–8).[32] That Jews were aware that tradition had

[31] Cf. Schürmann, *Lukasevangelium* 1, pp. 303–4; Pesch 1, pp. 181–2.
[32] L. Finkelstein, 'Some Examples of the Maccabaean Halaka,' *JBL* 49 (1930),

added much to the written word in the matter of the sabbath is indicated by the Mishnah. In *m. Ḥag.* 1.8 we read: 'the rules about the sabbath ... are as mountains hanging by a hair, for the [teaching of] Scripture [thereon] is scanty and the rules many'. In addition, Exod 34.21, which is the basis for the accusation against Jesus and his disciples, was purportedly argued by no less an authority than Aqiba to have nothing to do with the sabbath (see M. Cohen (v)). It is therefore very hazardous to affirm, as has Goppelt, that Jesus 'suspended the sabbath commandment as such and by doing so suspended the Law, the very foundation of Judaism' (*Theology* 1, p. 94). On the contrary, Jesus—who, incidentally, was not arrested for breaking the sabbath—probably thought he was upholding the Torah against its false interpreters.[33] Why else would he defend himself by appealing to the Torah itself in the Hebrew Scriptures?[34] Against our contention, it might be asked, why then did not Jesus simply make a statement about the oral tradition and its failings? The answer is that while on some occasions he probably did just this (cf. Mt 15.1–20; 23.13–26), on other occasions he sought to be deliberately provocative in order to raise christological issues and to reveal the present as a time of crisis (see on 8.22 and cf. interpretation (iv)). In this he was like the OT prophets, who sometimes did outrageous things—including breaking the law—in order to proclaim God's will (see Harvey, *Jesus*, pp. 60–2).[35]

5. This and the next two verses are Matthew's own work,[36]

pp. 20–42. He writes: before the Maccabaean age, 'the observance of the sabbath was largely a matter of private conscience, every man desisting from his individual labor and resting as he thought proper. The only pressure was that of popular custom and public opinion, which probably changed from locality to locality, and perhaps even from generation to generation' (p. 27). The relevant biblical texts are Exod 16.23–30; 20.8–11; 23.12; 31.12–17; 34.21; 35.1–3; Lev 23.3; Num 15.32–6; Deut 5.12–15; Neh 10.31; 13.15–22; Isa 58.13; Jer 17.21–4; Ezek 22.8; Amos 8.5.

[33] Relevant here are the observations of Westerholm, p. 96, on the limitation of the scope of Jesus' conflicts with the Pharisees over the sabbath: 'With one exception (Mk 2:23–8 par.), they concern healing on the sabbath. Moreover, we do know that Jesus frequented the synagogue on the sabbath and often took part in the synagogue service ... There is thus no reason to believe that Jesus actively and systematically opposed sabbath regulations, be their origin scriptural or scribal, for their own sake. On the contrary, the lack of evidence for conflicts on other matters should probably be interpreted as indicating that his conduct was not found exceptionable'. Note should also be taken of Mk 16.1 and Lk 23.56. These texts imply that the women in Jesus' entourage kept the sabbath. Would they have done so if they had learned from Jesus not to observe it? Additional points in Davies, *COJ*, pp. 47–52.

[34] Cf. Irenaeus, *Adv. haer.* 4.8.3, who argues that Jesus both acted in accord with the law and justified himself by appeal to the law.

[35] Although we have not brought the fact into the discussion, fasting was traditionally forbidden by some Jews on the sabbath (cf. Jud 8.6; Jub. 50.12; SB 1, pp. 611–15), and this might have something to do with our pericope, to wit: at least Jesus' critics could not complain that his disciples should have fasted all day. But was the prohibition widespread? See Y. D. Gilat, 'On Fasting on the Sabbath', *Tarbiz* 52 (1983), pp. 1–15.

[36] Cf. Hummel, p. 44. These points may be made. (i) οὐκ ἀνέγνωτε (5a) is

without parallel in Mark or Luke. The point they make is this: 'if the priests who serve in the Temple on the Sabbath are innocent of wrong-doing (according to the rabbinic dictum that the "Temple service takes precedence over the Sabbath"), how much more innocent are the disciples, who are "serving" Jesus, "one greater than the Temple"?'[37]

The addition of 12.5–7 was perhaps motivated by the belief that the argument in 12.3–4 is of itself insufficient. Useful as was the reference to the conduct of David, it probably had no strict relevance to the question of the sabbath and was, moreover, merely of haggadic significance. To produce a strong argument such as Matthew desiderated for Jesus' justification of his disciples' conduct, more was needed. 'It was of the essence of the rabbinic system that any detailed rule, any halakha, must rest, directly or indirectly, on an actual precept promulgated in Scripture. It must rest on it directly or indirectly: that is to say, there was no need for a halakha to be laid down in so many words, so long as it could be derived from some precept by means of the recognized norms of hermeneutics. One of these norms, for example, was the inference a fortiori, or as the rabbis termed it qal wahomer, "the light and the weighty".'[38] This explains Matthew's addition to Mark: it makes Jesus' argument rest upon a definite precept and a recognized exegetical principle (*qal wāḥômer*). Thus Matthew's Jesus stands securely within the Jewish legal framework. It is not the authority of the law that is being debated but the obligations of the sabbath.[39]

ἤ οὐκ ἀνέγνωτε ἐν τῷ νόμῳ. Compare Neh 8.3 (ἀνέγνωσαν ἐν τῷ βιβλίῳ νόμου); Amos 4.5 (ἀνέγνωσαν ἔξω νόμον); Mt 21.42 (οὐκ ἀνέγνωτε ἐν ταῖς γραφαῖς); Mk 12.26 (οὐκ ἀνέγνωτε ἐν τῇ βίβλῳ Μωϋσέως); Josephus, *Ant.* 4.209 (ἀναγινωσκέτω τοὺς νόμους); and the synagogue inscription printed by Deissmann, *Light*, p. 440 (συναγωγὴν εἰς ἀνάγνωσιν νόμου). The addition of 'in the law' (contrast Mt 21.42) draws attention to the halakhic nature of the argument (cf. Daube, p. 71). On the rabbinic 'Have you not read?' (='You have read but not really understood'), see Daube, pp. 422–36. In the synoptics Jesus,

Matthean, as are ἤ and θέλω (5a, 7b). (ii) The quotation from Hos 6.6 has been inserted into a Markan passage in 9.13, where it is also immediately preceded by τί ἐστιν. (iiii) Neither 12.5 nor 6 is easily envisioned as an independent logion. Even when combined they demand a context. (iv) Q (see Mt 12.41–2) may have supplied the inspiration for 12.6.
[37] So D. J. Moo, 'Jesus and the Authority of the Mosaic Law', *JSNT* 20 (1984), pp. 16–17, citing *b. Šabb.* 132b.
[38] Daube, p. 68. Cf. Davies, *SSM*, pp. 103–4.
[39] Throughout the First Gospel the author is concerned to make it clear that the teaching of Jesus is not in antithesis to the written law of Moses, although it may be critical of the oral tradition: it is the full interpretation of the former, rather than its annulment; cf. Davies, *SSM*, pp. 103–5, and see on 5.17–20.

when addressing the crowds, says, 'You have *heard*'. When the leaders are being spoken to he says, 'Have you not *read*?' (cf. 5.21–48; 19.4; 21.16, 42; 22.31).

ὅτι τοῖς σάββασιν οἱ ἱερεῖς ἐν τῷ ἱερῷ τὸ σάββατον βεβηλοῦσιν καὶ ἀναίτιοί εἰσιν; For σάββατον βεβηλοῦν see LXX Isa 56.2, 6; Ezek 20.13; 1 Macc 1.43, 45; 2.34 (cf. *Mek.* on Exod 31.13). The assertion that the priests 'profane' the sabbath (cf. Zeph 3.4) was evidently a traditional way of phrasing the facts (cf. SB 1, p. 620). For other violations of the sabbath see Josephus, *Ant.* 14.63 (defensive fighting); *m. Ned.* 3.11 (circumcision); *m. Pesaḥ.* 6.1–2; *t. Pesaḥ.* 4.13 (passover sacrifice).

In order to fulfil Num 28.9–10 (cf. 11QTemple 13.17) the priests had to offer sacrifices on the sabbath and thereby violate the prohibition of sabbath work. But how is the activity of the disciples analogous to the service of the priests? The plucking of grain for hunger was not a religious observance; and if the priests were serving the temple by offering sacrifices, were the disciples serving Jesus by eating? Moreover, the priests were themselves subject to the sabbath ordinances as soon as they left the temple. So why does their action justify the disciples? First, the priests prove that Scripture allows at least one exception to the general sabbath rule. Secondly, since the violation of the sabbath is done for the sake of the temple, this shows that the temple service takes precedence over sabbath observance; if then there is something which is greater than the temple (as 12.6 asserts), it follows that it too may take precedence over observing the sabbath.

One could suppose that Mt 12.5 is not a reference to Num 28.9–10 but to the Pharisaic permission to reap the *'omer* on the sabbath.[40] In which case Matthew's analogy would be much tighter. But οὐκ ἀνέγνωτε κ.τ.λ. does not naturally call to mind the oral tradition. One thinks instead of the written Torah.

6. λέγω δὲ ὑμῖν ὅτι τοῦ ἱεροῦ μεῖζόν ἐστιν ὧδε. 'I say to you' underlines the theme of christological authority. μεῖζον is neuter, and although some have thought of the kingdom, others of love, Jesus' interpretation of the law, or the community of disciples, the reference must be to Jesus (cf. 12.8 and the reading in C L Δ 0233 *f*¹³ (1010) 1424 *pm* lat: μείζων). As Gundry writes, 'the neuter gender . . . stresses the quality of superior greatness rather than Jesus' personal identity' (*Commentary*, p. 223). Note that the words are 'greater than the temple', not 'greater than the law'.

---

[40] Cf. *m. Menaḥ.* 10.1, 3, 10; *t. Dem.* 1.28; *b. Menaḥ.* 65a; *b. Moʿed Qat.* 11b; and see Levine (v). The Sadducees and later Jewish tradition denied that the *'omer* could be reaped on a holy day (cf. the targum on Ruth 1.22).

7. Matthew now inserts Hos 6.6, a verse already cited in 9.13 (q.v.). The citation interrupts the continuity that otherwise obtains between 12.6 and 8: 'More than the temple is here . . . for the Son of man is Lord of the sabbath'. Perhaps, as Allen, p. 128, suggested, Mt 12.7 is 'of the nature of a parenthesis' (cf. McNeile, p. 169).

εἰ δὲ ἐγνώκειτε τί ἐστιν. Compare 12.3. The meaning is, 'Do you not know what this means?' (cf. Jn 13.12). Although the Pharisees read, they do not understand.

ἔλεος θέλω καὶ οὐ θυσίαν. The citation does not establish a moral law/ritual law antithesis; nor is Jesus asserting that the Pharisees should have mercy on the disciples. One also hesitates to find here a reference to the 'love commandment'. The point seems rather to be: 'It is ἔλεος which takes precedence over sabbath-law and not the demands of the sacrificial cult' (Hill (v), p. 115). Scripture shows that one commandment can outweigh another (cf. 12.5–6); and to this Jesus adds that the command to keep the sabbath, although it is worthy of observance, is subordinate to a greater law, which is his own person. That is, if Jesus' eschatological purposes come into conflict with sabbath law or custom, then sabbath law or custom will fare the worse.

οὐκ ἂν κατεδικάσατε τοὺς ἀναιτίους. Had the Pharisees understood the true meaning of the Scriptures, they would not have condemned the innocent disciples. (ἀναίτιος (cf. 12.5) is never used of persons in the LXX.)

8. This concluding line might be thought to have the effect of rendering much of the foregoing irrelevant. If Jesus the Son of man is Lord of the sabbath, if he stands not under but above the sabbath, then his dictate is law, and what is the need of argument? But 12.8 does help to complete the thought of 12.6. 'Something greater than the temple is here' is explained by 'the Son of man is Lord of the sabbath'.

Like Luke, Matthew has eliminated Mk 2.27: 'And he said to them, "The sabbath was made for man, not man for the sabbath."'[41] Matthew probably omitted the proverb-like line because it stands in tension with the christological conclusion in the next verse: the Son of man, not man in general, is Lord of the sabbath. Perhaps also Mark's statement was felt potentially too extreme.[42] (Mt 24.20 indicates continued observance of the sabbath in Matthean circles). Or just maybe Matthew was aware that the sentiment was used by his opponents (cf. *Mek.* on Exod 31.14; *b. Yoma* 85b).

κύριος γάρ ἐστιν τοῦ σαββάτου ὁ υἱὸς τοῦ ἀνθρώπου. Mk 2.28 introduces this sentence with ὥστε instead of γάρ* and has a

[41] On this see p. 304, n. 2.
[42] Does even Mark's gospel witness to this? Was 2.28 tacked on to tone down 2.27? Cf. Käsemann, *Essays*, p. 39.

different word order. Matthew's arrangement puts more emphasis upon the christological title ('Lord' coming in the first place).

Mt 12.8 is probably not an authentic saying of Jesus[43] or a Christian formulation attributed to Jesus.[44] Like 9.6 (q.v.), it is probably an editorial comment from Mark's hand.[45] Thus the quotation end in v. 7.

A SABBATH HEALING (12.9–14)

According to G. Theissen, *Miracle Stories*, pp. 106–12, Mt 12.9–14 par. should be classified as a 'rule miracle'. By this he refers to miracle stories which 'reinforce sacred prescriptions. They may be classified according as they justify rules, reward behaviour in accordance with the rules or punish behaviour contrary to the rules'.[46] Mt 12.9–14 par. is a 'justificatory rule miracle', for it justifies the divine prescription: it is lawful to do good on a sabbath. Other examples of the same type of miracle story include Mt 17.24–7 and Mk 2.1–12 par.

Mt 12.9–14 contains material from three sources. 12.9–10, 12b–4 is based upon Mk 3.1–6 (cf. Lk 6.6–11).[47] 12.11 comes from either M or Q (cf. Lk 13.15; 14.5). 12.12a is, as we shall argue, redactional.

The basic historicity of Mt 12.9–10, 12b–3(14), which Bultmann called 'an organically complete apophthegm' (*History*, p. 12), is generally conceded by most scholars (cf. Lohse (v), p. 84; Hultgren, pp. 82–4). There is no evidence that the primitive community was taken to task for healing on the sabbath. Additionally, the saying in Mk 3.4 ('Is it lawful on the sabbath to do good or to do harm, to save life or to kill?') is surely authentic, and it presupposes an encounter like what we now find in the gospels (cf. Bultmann, *History*, p. 12). Also relevant are these facts: (i) Mark's mention of the obscure Herodians (dropped by Matthew and Luke) is not easily assigned to ecclesiastical interests; (ii) there are Semitisms in Mk 3.1–6 (see Pesch 1, p. 195); (iii) certainly the conflict in the gospels between Jesus and the Pharisees has roots in the earthly ministry.[48]

Does Mt 12.11 (cf. Lk 13.15; 14.5) go back to Jesus? Everything would seem to point in that direction (cf. Lohse (v), pp. 86–9). The saying presupposes Jewish sentiment (cf. Deut 22.4), contains an

---

[43] So many, although there has been disagreement over the status of 'Son of man' in the original. See Excursus VI.

[44] So e.g. Tödt, pp. 130–2, and Beare (v).

[45] Cf. Cranfield, *Mark*, p. 118; Lindars, *Son of Man*, pp. 102–6.

[46] Cf. Dibelius, *Tradition*, p. 146, who referred to rabbinic 'theodicy legends' in this way: 'the miracle is not always told for its own sake, but for the benefit of the matter for which the Talmud stands, viz. *proclaiming a divine law* by which men must live'.

[47] This no doubt already followed Mk 2.23–7 in the pre-Markan tradition; cf. Pesch 1, pp. 187–8.

[48] See H. Merkel, 'Jesus und die Pharisäer', *NTS* 14 (1968), pp. 194–208. But for caution in this connexion see Davies, *COJ*, pp. 47–9, with reference to the work of W. L. Knox.

expression characteristic of Jesus (τίς ἔσται ἐξ ὑμῶν ἄνθρωπος; see on 7.9), is consistent with the several synoptic stories in which Jesus acts provocatively on the sabbath, and harmonizes with his tendency to exalt mercy over his contemporaries' understanding of holiness (see on 5.48).

9. Jesus leaves the outdoors for the indoors, entering a synagogue.[49] It is still the sabbath.[50]

καὶ μεταβὰς ἐκεῖθεν. This expands Mark's simple καί. μεταβαίνω* is Matthean, as is μεταβαίνω + ἐκεῖθεν* (Mt: 3; Mk: 0; Lk: 0).

ἦλθεν εἰς τὴν συναγωγὴν αὐτῶν. Mk 3.1 has εἰσῆλθεν[51] followed by πάλιν.[52] Matthew has added the personal pronoun. For its significance see on 4.23. In the First Gospel the synagogue is a place of confrontation.

10. **καὶ ἰδοὺ ἄνθρωπος χεῖρα ἔχων ξηράν.** This is a more economical version of Mk 3.1b. Compare Mk 3.3a. For καὶ ἰδού (cf. Lk 14.2) see on 1.20 and 3.16. ξηρός,[53] which replaces the rare ἐξηραμμένην of Mark, literally means 'dry' or 'dried up', but the word was used figuratively of diseased states (cf. LXX Hos 9.14; T. Sim. 2.12; Jn 5.3; also the use of ξηραίνω in LXX 3 Βασ 13.4; Zech 11.17). In our story one could translate either 'withered' or 'paralyzed', but there can hardly be a medical diagnosis in the modern sense. Luke adds that the hand in question was the right hand.[54] This accentuates the handicap.

καὶ ἐπηρώτησαν αὐτὸν λέγοντες. Mk 3.2 has παρετήρουν[55] and lacks λέγοντες.[56]

εἰ ἔξεστιν τοῖς σάββασιν θεραπεύειν;[57] Compare Lk 14.3. On εἰ introducing direct questions (cf. LXX Gen 17.17; Mk 10.2) see BDF § 440.3 (supposing a Hebraism). Matthew has added ἔξεστιν. This strengthens the link between 12.1–8 and 12.9–14 (cf. 12.2, 4). It also makes the Pharisees speak in the legal terminology of the rabbis (cf. the use of *nātar*) and increases the verbal correlation between question and answer. The other

---

[49] The Synagogue in Capernaum?

[50] In Luke it has become another sabbath.

[51] Which Matthew often turns into the simplex; see Allen, p. xxv.

[52] Which Matthew often drops from Mark: Mt: 17; Mk 28; Lk: 3. Luke has also here dropped the word. In Mark it may refer to Mk 1.21, a verse Matthew has omitted.

[53] Mt: 2; Mk: 1; Lk: 3. It occurs most often in the LXX for a form of *yābēš*.

[54] Cf. the reading in the Dutch gospel harmony noted by Black, pp. 290–91.

[55] Matthew never uses this verb (Mt: 0; Mk: 1; Lk: 3).

[56] ἐπηρώτησα(ε)ν + αὐτούς/αὐτόν (+ subject) + λέγοντες/λέγων: Mt: 5; Mk: 0; Lk: 3. ἐπερωτάω is redactional in 16.1 and 22.41.

[57] So HG, following B C Θ 0233 *f*[1.13] Maj. NA[26] has θεραπευσαι (cf. Lk 14.3); so ℵ D L W *pc*. One can only guess the original.

alteration Matthew has introduced—Mark's θεραπεύσει αὐτόν has become a simple infinitive—makes the issue more general. The question is no longer about Jesus in particular but about persons in general ('is it lawful on the sabbath to heal?').

Was it in fact permitted to heal on the sabbath?[58] Certainly the Essenes and the author of Jubilees would have answered in the negative (see n. 17). As for the Mishnah, it declares that life in immediate danger should be saved (e.g. *m. Yoma* 8.6; cf. *Mek.* on Exod 22.2). But this does not cover the gospel story, for the man could presumably have been healed at a later time. For a collection of the relevant rabbinic evidence see SB 1, pp. 623–9. Many rabbis thought it was permissible to carry the sick on the sabbath; and in *Eccles Rab.* 9.7, Abba Taḥnah raises the showing of mercy to a leper above correct sabbath observance (cf. SB 1, p. 391). Also pertinent is *m. Šabb.* 22.6, according to which healing on a sabbath is unobjectionable if consequent upon lawful actions. Nevertheless, the question in Matthew shows us that the dominant opinion in the Mishnah was held by many if not most teachers in Jesus' day: one should not heal on a sabbath.

How, then, does one explain Jesus' action? He undoubtedly took himself to be countering not God's will as declared in the written Torah[59] but rather 'the precepts of men'. Scripture nowhere prohibits healing on the sabbath, especially if nothing more is involved than asking a man to stretch forth his hand.[60] Yet one still wants to know why Jesus did not take the amenable route of compromise and wait a day (cf. Lk 13.14). Why not heal the man when all would applaud? It does not suffice to urge that Jesus was an itinerant who planned on being long gone by the morrow. There are too many controversy stories about healing on the sabbath to pass them off as anything but the result of intentional provocation. Jesus evidently sought opportunities to illustrate how the casuistry of the oral halakah could contradict the demands of love. This is why he played the rôle of the gadfly. Jesus' exaltation of the commandment to love, combined with his criticism of the oral tradition, often made for conflict with custom. Moreover, his eschatological message, which was about the world turned upside down, was well served by the disturbing or challenging of certain conventions. In fine, Jesus healed people on the sabbath in order to raise the fundamental issue of what God really wills.

ἵνα κατηγορήσωσιν αὐτοῦ. So Mk 3.2. κατηγορέω (cf. the rabbinic *qiṭrēg*) is a technical legal term meaning 'bring charges' or 'accuse'. A setting in court is presupposed.

---

[58] The question is Jewish, but Macrobius, *Sat.* 1.16.11, supplies a Roman parallel: Scaevola was asked to decide whether one could help an ox out of ditch on a holiday.

[59] It is worth observing that some OT sabbath legislation was intended to engender compassion for slaves, aliens, and other unfortunates; cf. Exod 20.10; 23.12; Deut 5.14.

[60] Thus we disagree with Dunn (v), p. 403, and many others: in our estimation, it is incorrect to state 'that Jesus was not willing to show even that fairly minimal level of respect for one of the fundamental laws regulating God's covenant with Israel'.

The Pharisees, who here as so often play a false part, question Jesus in order to entrap him. They are not honestly seeking another's halakhic judgement but an occasion to be used against Jesus in court (cf. BAGD, s.v. κατηγορέω). In view of 12.14, one thinks of the statute in Exod 31.14: 'Every one who profanes it [the sabbath] shall be put to death' (cf. Sipre on Num 15.33). One should note, however, that in the accounts of the trial of Jesus his perceived violations of the sabbath are not brought up at all (though note Jn 5.18 and Acts of Pilate 1.1).

11. At this point Matthew inserts a saying which allows Jesus to answer the question of his critics with a counter-question that appeals to human sentiment. The argument is once more *a fortiori*. One is reminded of the addition in 12.5–7 (also an argument *a fortiori*). Obviously Matthew is intent on sharpening Jesus' halakhic logic and making him a first-rate debater. Nonetheless, having made this observation it needs to be added that the First Gospel's legal debates remain relatively unsophisticated. This is because Matthew's Jesus always goes straight to the heart of the matter. His brevity and clarity focus on 'the weightier matters of the law' (23.23). This excludes long, drawn-out debate. It also explains why Jesus appeals more frequently to human instincts than to legal niceties (cf. Westerholm, p. 101).

Mt 12.11–12 has a close parallel in Lk 14.5 and a remote parallel in Lk 13.15. The last belongs to L material (Lk 13.10–17). Concerning Lk 14.5, it may come from Q, as may the Lukan context, Lk 14.1–6.[61] But there is no proving this, and Lk 14.1–6 could well be independent tradition (L) or even largely Luke's own composition. Perhaps the best solution is to regard Mt 12.11 as from Q and to leave the origin of Lk 14.5 open. In any case, Lk 14.5 and Mt 12.11 are variants of the same logion.[62]

ὁ δὲ εἶπεν αὐτοῖς. Lk 14.5 has: καὶ πρὸς αὐτοὺς εἶπεν. πρός + accusative is characteristic of Luke (cf. Jeremias, *Lukasevangelium*, p. 33).

τίς ἔσται ἐξ ὑμῶν ἄνθρωπος. Lk 14.5 has simply τίνος ὑμῶν. On Matthew's construction—a Semitism characteristic of Jesus—see on 7.9 and Black, pp. 118–19.

ὃς ἕξει πρόβατον ἕν. Compare 18.12–13. Whether ἕν simply means 'a' (sheep) or whether it is intended to reinforce the argument ('who has (only) one sheep') is not clear.

---

[61] So Schürmann, *Untersuchungen*, p. 213. He notes that Mt 12.10 has several items in common with Lk 14.2–3: καὶ ἰδού, ἔξεστιν + τῷ σαββάτῳ/τοῖς σάββασιν, θεραπεῦσαι/θεραπεύειν.

[62] *Gos. Truth* 32.18–20 ('Even on the Sabbath, he laboured for the sheep which he found fallen into the pit') is not independent of the synoptics.

Lk 14.5 has υἱὸς ἢ βοῦς[63] (cf. *m. B. Qam.* 5.6), which is probably original. Retranslation of his text into Aramaic results in paronomasia: *bĕrā* (son), *bĕʿîrā* (ox), *bêrā* (well; cf. Black, pp. 168–9; Black (v); Lohse (v), p. 87).[64] Matthew's text is explained by two considerations. First, the evangelist wished to make the argument *a fortiori* (cf. 12.12), and this excluded the use of 'son'. Secondly, in composing 12.9–14 he was probably reminded of the parable of the lost sheep (18.12–14; cf. Lk 15.4–7) and assimilated one passage to the other.[65]

καὶ ἐὰν ἐμπέσῃ τοῦτο τοῖς σάββασιν εἰς βόθυνον. Compare 15.14 (εἰς βόθυνον πεσοῦνται) and Lk 14.5 (εἰς φρέαρ πεσεῖται). The plural, 'sabbaths', is to be accounted for by the Aramaic *šabbĕtā*, which is an emphatic singular. It was wrongly understood here and elsewhere in the NT to be a plural (cf. Jeremias, *Theology*, p. 6, n. 10). For βόθυνος as a hazard see LXX Prov 26.27; Isa 47.11; Mt 15.14.

οὐχὶ κρατήσει αὐτὸ καὶ ἐγερεῖ; Compare 9.25 and Prov 12.10 ('A righteous man has regard for the life of his beast'). Perhaps Deut 22.4 is in the background: 'You shall not see your brother's ass or his ox fallen down by the way, and withold your help from them; you shall help him to lift them up again'. Lk 14.5c has καὶ οὐκ εὐθέως ἀνασπάσει αὐτὸν ἐν ἡμέρᾳ τοῦ σαββάτου;

Opinion probably differed as to whether one should help an animal out of a pit on the sabbath. CD 11.13–14 seems to exclude such action.[66] The rabbis discussed the issue and tended to agree that one could not pull an animal out of a pit or use instruments but that one could throw in food for the day or even toss in something which the animal could use to climb out (cf. *m. Beṣa* 3.4 and the texts cited in SB 1, pp. 629–30). Perhaps most first-century Galileans would have used normal means to extricate an animal from a pit on the sabbath, whatever the Pharisees or others may have taught. Compare Manson, *Sayings*, p. 189: 'The form of the question suggests that Jesus is not appealing to rule but to the actual practice of His hearers ... The question is addressed to men as men; and ordinary humanity is expected to supply the answer'.

12. The conclusion Jesus now draws illustrates 12.7: 'mercy' takes precedence over 'sacrifice'. Therefore, to use the rabbinic terminology, the 'commandments between man and man' take priority over the 'commandments between God and man' (cf. *m. Yoma* 8.9). Note that in *m. Yom.* 8.6 the treating of a sore throat on the Sabbath is permitted by at least one rabbi.

[63] But the textual tradition is confused; see Marshall, pp. 579–80.
[64] Black, who finds 'a son or an ox' unduly awkward, conjectures that Jesus originally said: 'Who of you shall have an ox (*bĕʿîrā*) or an ass (*bar ḥamrā*) fallen into a well (*bêrā*) ...'. But the text makes sense as it stands.
[65] Note the occurrence of τίς ἄνθρωπος ἐξ ὑμῶν in Lk 15.4. Also relevant to Matthew's fondness for πρόβατον*. βοῦς, on the other hand, is never used in the First Gospel.
[66] For discussion see Schiffmann (as in n. 17 on p. 307), pp. 121–2.

πόσῳ οὖν διαφέρει ἄνθρωπος προβάτου. The line, whose truth is self-evident, is redactional. Compare 6.26; 7.11; and 10.31. Both οὖν*[67] and προβάτον* are Matthean favourites.

ὥστε ἔξεστιν τοῖς σάββασιν καλῶς ποιεῖν. Compare Diognetus, *Ep.* 4.3: 'as if He forbade us to do any good thing on the sabbath day, is not this profane?' Matthew's legal rule derives from Mk 3.4: 'And he says to them: Is it permitted on the sabbath to do good (ἀγαθαποιῆσαι)[68] or to do evil, to save life or to kill?'[69] Matthew's ὥστε (the word is often inserted into Markan material)[70] turns Mark's words into a conclusion drawn from 12.11–12a: if one may do good to a sheep on the sabbath, and if human beings are of more value than sheep, then it is permitted on the sabbath to do good to a human being. In this way a question in Mark has become in Matthew a general rule. Thus Jesus has acted on principle. He has not overthrown the law. On the contrary, he has fulfilled it. For rabbinic texts which permit helping but not healing the sick on the sabbath see SB 1, p. 630. καλῶς ποιεῖν[71] is to do God's will. More concretely, it is to love one's neighbour, which is the chief commandment (cf. 7.12; 19.19; 22.39–40). And healing is an exercise of love. If it is lawful to do good, it must be lawful to heal.

13. Having justified his action beforehand, and having convicted his hearers of hypocrisy (for would they not help a beast?), Jesus now heals the disabled man. But note that Jesus does not stretch forth his hand, touch the man, or help him up (contrast 8.3, 15; 9.25; etc.). He simply speaks. Thus his act of healing is far less provocative than his words in vv. 11–12.

τότε λέγει τῷ ἀνθρώπῳ. So Mark, without τότε*.

ἔκτεινόν σου τὴν χεῖρα. Mark lacks the pronoun. For its placement before the noun see 22.13.

καὶ ἐξέτεινεν. The man obeys. Mark's text is the same.

καὶ ἀπεκατεστάθη ὑγιὴς ὡς ἡ ἄλλη. Compare the healings in 1 Kgs 13.1–10 (where Jeroboam's 'withered' hand is healed by

---

[67] Which may be either inferential or emphatic.

[68] So HG. NA[26] has ἀγαθὸν ποιῆσαι. In the LXX both καλῶς ποιέω and ἀγαθοποιέω translate the hiphil of *yāṭab*; cf. Lev 5.4; Zech 1.12.

[69] On this see Borg, p. 159, who takes the meaning to be: 'If it is lawful on the sabbath for the sake of Israel and the Torah to kill, how much more ought it to be permitted to heal this man, who is an Israelite, on the sabbath!' Since the Maccabees most Jews considered defensive war on the sabbath acceptable (cf. 1 Macc 2.39–41; Josephus, *Bell.* 2.517–18; *b. Šabb.* 19a; contrast Jub. 50.12; 2 Macc 15.1–5).

[70] ὥστε + indicative is relatively rare in the NT; see e.g. Mt 19.6; 23.31.

[71] Cf. Mk 7.37; Lk 6.27; Acts 10.33; 1 Cor 7.37–8; Phil 4.14; Jas 2.8, 19; 2 Pet 1.19. In the LXX the combination translates the hiphil of *ṭôb* or *yāṭab*, as in 2 Chr 6.8 and Jer 4.22.

the prayer of a prophet so that it becomes as it was before) and T. Sim. 2.11–14 (where Simeon prays to the Lord for the restoration of his 'withered' right hand). After the verb Mark has ἡ χεὶρ αὐτοῦ. ὑγιής is also redactional in 15.31.

14. Jesus has not, in Matthew's view, done anything to violate the sabbath. That the Pharisees thought otherwise is not clearly stated but is implied: they were sufficiently distraught to begin contemplating Jesus' death. Thus, by doing good to another, Jesus has put his own life in jeopardy.

ἐξελθόντες δὲ οἱ Φαρισαῖοι συμβούλιον ἔλαβον κατ' αὐτοῦ ὅπως αὐτὸν ἀπολέσωσιν.[72] Compare 22.15; Jn 5.18. As compared with Mk 3.6,[73] Matthew has changed καί to δέ (so often elsewhere), dropped εὐθὺς μετὰ τῶν Ἡρῳδιανῶν (did Matthew know the identity of the Herodians?),[74] and changed the peculiar συμβού-λιον ἐδίδουν[75] to συμβούλιον ἔλαβον (for 'to take counsel' Matthew always has συμβούλιον + λαμβάνω: Mt: 5; Mk: 0; Lk: 0). The most interesting change is the second, and one wonders whether our evangelist omitted mention of the Herodians here in order to concentrate on the opposition of the Pharisees and so focus on religion instead of politics.

JESUS THE SERVANT (12.15–21)

This paragraph is structurally reminiscent of 8.16–17. In both places we have a summary of Jesus' healing activity followed by a formula quotation from Isaiah. In both cases the OT text has to do with the suffering servant.

15f. constitutes yet one more summary of Jesus' ministry. For discussion see on 4.23–5.

ὁ δὲ Ἰησοῦς γνοὺς ἀνεχώρησεν ἐκεῖθεν. Compare 2.13, 22; 4.12; 14.13; 15.21; 22.18; and Mk 3.7 ('And Jesus with his disciples withdrew toward the sea') (cf. Lk 6.17). γνούς[76] highlights Jesus' (supernatural?) knowledge.

καὶ ἠκολούθησαν αὐτῷ πολλοί.[77] Compare 15.30; 19.2; Mk

---

[72] So both HG and NA[26], on the authority of ℵ B C f[1] 33 892 pc vg. D has introductory και instead of δε. For the first four words L Θ f[13] arm have the order 3 2 4 1, W Δ pc q the order 3 2 4, and Maj sy[h] have 3 2 4 with εξελθοντες moved immediately before οπως.

[73] Scholars do not agree whether Mk 3.6 is redactional; so Bultmann, *History*, p. 12; against Pesch 1, p. 188; Marshall, p. 234.

[74] On the Herodians (cf. Josephus, *Bell.* 1.319) see the review of opinion in Hoehner, pp. 331–42. Most take them to have been supporters of Herod Antipas and his policies. Matthew does mention them in 22.16 = Mk 12.13.

[75] On this see Taylor, *Mark*, p. 224. It appears to be a Latinism: *consilium capere* (so BDF § 5.3b).

[76] Cf. 16.8; 22.18; 26.10 (all of Jesus).

[77] So HG. NA[26] prints [οχλοι] after αυτω; so C D L W Θ f[1.13] Maj f h

3.7; Lk 6.17; and see on Mt 4.25. On 'following Jesus' see on 4.20 and 8.19. Here there is no thought of discipleship.

καὶ ἐθεράπευσεν αὐτοὺς πάντας. Compare 8.16; Mk 1.34; 3.10; Lk 4.40; 6.18; and see on Mt 4.24. The πάντας—Jesus healed *everybody*—is typically Matthean.

καὶ ἐπετίμησεν αὐτοῖς ἵνα μὴ φανερὸν αὐτὸν ποιήσωσιν. So Mk 3.12, with πολλὰ ἐπετίμα and αὐτὸν φανερόν(cf. Josephus, *Ant.* 2.10). On the messianic secret in Matthew see on 8.4. Note also 9.30; 16.20; and 17.9.

17. ἵνα πληρωθῇ τὸ ῥηθὲν διὰ Ἠσαΐου τοῦ προφήτου λέγοντος. See on 1.22; 3.3; and 4.14 (whose wording is identical).

18–21. The following formula quotation, from Isa 42.1–4, 9, is probably Matthew's independent translation of the Hebrew (cf. Jerome, *Ep.* 121), with some influence from the LXX[78] and the targum (cf. Stendahl (v),[79] Gundry (v)). It is the longest OT quotation in the First Gospel; and since 'Matthew is strictly economical in the length of his quotations, one need not suppose that he has included any irrelevant beginning or end' (Gerhardsson, *Acts*, p. 26).

Mt 12.18–21 has supplied ammunition for those contending that our evangelist drew upon a collection of testimonia.[80] The following points have been made. (i) The quotation contains several Matthean *hapax legomena*.[81] (ii) Papyrus Rylands Greek 460 is a Christian testimony collection which includes Isa 42.3–4 (folio 1, recto). (iii) Isa 42.1–4 was probably a messianic text in first-century Judaism (as it is in the targum). (iv) It is alleged that there is only one point of contact with the Matthean context—Jesus' silence (cf. Strecker, *Weg*, p. 69). Lindars even goes so far as to assert that 'the text owes nothing to its present context' (*Apologetic*, p. 145, n. 1). (v) It is possible to imagine Isa 42.1ff. being used in the pre-Matthean tradition in connexion with the resurrection, the baptism, Jesus' gentleness, and the Gentile mission (so Lindars, *Apologetic*, pp. 144–52).

Despite these five points, we strongly suspect that Mt 12.18–21 gives us Matthew's own original work (so also Gnilka, *Matthäusevangelium* 1, p. 453). Not only is the textual form not attested elsewhere, but it seems to us that the quotation is, from beginning to end, adapted to its present context (cf. Barth, in *TIM*, pp. 125–8). We would counter the claim of Lindars and others with these observations. (i) ὁ ἀγαπητός

(q) sy[p.h] sa[ms] bo. This could be pristine; see J. R. Royse, 'The Treatment of Scribal Leaps in Metzger's *Textual Commentary*', *NTS* 29 (1983), p. 547.

[78] Esp. 12.21.

[79] He writes (p. 115): 'it can only have a satisfactory explanation as a targumized text which is the fruit of reflection and acquaintance with the interpretation of the Scriptures'.

[80] See e.g. Strecker, *Weg*, pp. 67–70; Lindars (v); and R. Hodgson, 'The Testimony Hypothesis', *JBL* 98 (1979), p. 374.

[81] αἱρετίζω, ἐρίζω, κραυγάζω, συντρίβω, κατάγνυμι, τύφω, νῖκος.

κ.τ.λ. shows assimilation to Mt 3.17 and 17.5. (ii) 'I shall put my Spirit on him' not only recalls the baptism but links up nicely with the following pericope, where the theme is Jesus and the Spirit (12.22–37; see Cope, pp. 35–40). (iii) The double mention of the Gentiles (12.18d, 21) harmonizes with a major Matthean interest. (iv) The translation in 12.19 of yiṣ'aq by ἐρίσει is best explained by 12.15: Jesus did not choose to wrangle or quarrel with the Pharisees. (v) In 12.19 the rendering of the adverbial baḥûṣ by ἐν ταῖς πλατείαις (rather than, say, ἔξω) makes sense in the light of 12.16: Jesus was not heard 'in the streets'. He asked people not to make him known. (vi) For yôṣî' in Isa 42.1 the LXX has ἐξοίσει. Matthew's ἀπαγγελεῖ, though perfectly proper, is less natural and is due to his concern for preaching (cf. 8.33; 11.4; 28.8, 10). There may also be a link with 12.38–42, which concerns preaching to the Gentiles (to the men of Nineveh and the queen of the South; see Cope, pp. 40–4, and note the use of κρίσις in 12.41 and 42).

All in all, the entirety of Mt 12.18–21 serves Matthean themes and interests very well. Nothing is superfluous; everything fits. Matthew has evidently latched on to Isa 42.1–4 because it serves so remarkably to illustrate the nature of Jesus' ministry in Israel. Jesus is the unobtrusive servant of the Lord. God's Spirit rests upon him. He does not wrangle or quarrel or continue useless strife. He seeks to avoid self-advertisement and to quiet the enthusiasm that his healings inevitably create. He has compassion upon all, especially upon the 'bruised reed' or 'smouldering wick'. And he brings salvation to the Gentiles.

ἰδοὺ ὁ παῖς μου ὃν ᾑρέτισα, ὁ ἀγαπητός μου εἰς ὃν εὐδόκησεν ἡ ψυχή μου.[82] Compare Hag 2.23. Between Matthew's line and LXX Isa 42.1 ('Ιακὼβ ὁ παῖς μου, ἀντιλήμψομαι αὐτοῦ· 'Ισραὴλ ὁ ἐκλεκτός μου, προσεδέξατο αὐτὸν ἡ ψυχή μου) there is little verbal contact. Matthew's text would seem to be an alternative translation of MT Isa 42.1: hēn 'abdî 'etmāk-bô bĕḥîrî rāṣĕtâ napšî. ἰδοὺ ὁ παῖς[83] μου is the natural rendering of hēn 'abdî (and is the reading of Theodotion).[84] ὃν ᾑρέτισα for 'etmāk-bô is not too obvious; but the aorist indicative for the imperfect is due to the passage from promise (Isaiah) to fulfilment (Matthew); and the translation of tāmak by αἰρετίζω[85] is probably influenced by the use of bāḥar in Isa 41.8–9; 42.1; and 44.2. ὁ ἀγαπητός μου for bĕḥîrî is no doubt explained by

[82] If εν ω, which appears in C D f¹ 1 33 1424 lat vg Ir Hil be original, then the agreement with 3.17 would be increased.

[83] Jesus is called παῖς only five times in the NT: Mt 12.18; Acts 3.13, 26; 4.27, 30.

[84] παῖς is more easily associated with the υἱός of 3.17 than δοῦλος would be.

[85] Cf. LXX 1 Chr 28.6; Mal 3.17; Ps. Sol. 9.17; 17.5. The word can mean 'adopt' but here means 'choose'.

the baptismal tradition (see on 3.17 and cf. LXX Isa 44.2 and 2 Pet 1.17).[86] εἰς ὃν εὐδόκησεν[87] for rāṣĕtâ needs no explanation in view of 3.17 = Mk 1.9 (cf. Mt 17.5 and 2 Pet 1.17); and the LXX often renders rāṣâ by εὐδοκέω (as in Gen 33.10 and Lev 26.41). ἡ ψυχή μου naturally translates napšî.

In Mt 12.18 παῖς is not associated with Jesus' passion but has a much broader reference. Indeed, 'servant' is here a comprehensive title. It covers Jesus' entire ministry, all that Jesus says and does (cf. 8.17). Thus Jesus is the humble, suffering servant not only at the end but from the beginning.[88]

θήσω τὸ πνεῦμά μου ἐπ' αὐτόν. So LXX Isa 42.1, with ἔδωκα for θήσω. The verb in the MT is nātattî. Matthew's tense agrees with the targum (Gundry, OT, p. 113). τίθημι often does duty for nātan in the LXX.

καὶ κρίσιν τοῖς ἔθνεσιν ἀπαγγελεῖ. The LXX lacks καί and for the verb uses ἐξοίσει. The MT reads: mišpāṭ laggôyim yôṣî'. Matthew clearly preserves an independent translation of the Hebrew according to sense. In the hiphil yāṣā' can mean either 'bring out' (= ἐκφέρω) or 'spread abroad' (= ἀπαγγέλλω; cf. LXX Isa 48.20). Matthew again agrees with the targum (Gundry, OT, p. 113). The RSV translates the κρίσιν of Mt 12.18 as 'justice' (cf. 23.23). The assumption seems to be that 'judgement' would be inappropriate given the context (cf. BAGD, s.v., 3, and Gundry, Commentary, p. 229). If this be correct, the reference must be to the preaching of the post-Easter church: through his missionaries Jesus proclaims justice to the Gentiles (cf. Zahn, pp. 453–4). But 'judgement' remains a possible translation. Matthew may be thinking of Jesus as the judge of all nations and peoples (cf. 12.41–2; 25.31–46).[89]

οὐκ ἐρίσει οὐδὲ κραυγάσει. This is obviously free of LXX influence (οὐ κεκράξεται οὐδὲ ἀνήσει). Again we seem to have an independent translation of the Hebrew: lō' yiṣ'aq wĕlō' yiśśā'. ἐρίζω means 'quarrel, wrangle' while in Isa 42.2 ṣā'aq means 'clamour' (BDB, s.v.); and whereas κραυγάζω means 'cry (out)' or 'utter a (loud) sound', nāśā', even without qôl, can

---

[86] Note also that Luke turns Mark's ὁ ἀγαπητός to ὁ ἐκλελεγμένος in Lk 9.35 par. According to Grindel (v), pp. 110, ἀγαπητός 'is probably simply an exegetical reading of bᵉḥîrî prompted by early Christian vocabulary'.

[87] For εἰς with the accusative after εὐδοκέω see 2 Pet 1.17; Ps.-Clem. Hom. 3.53; cf. T. Jos. 17.3.

[88] Against Kingsbury, Structure, pp. 93–5, there is no good reason to subordinate Matthew's Servant Christology to his Son of God Christology; see D. Hill, 'Son and Servant: An Essay on Matthean Christology', JSNT 6 (1980), pp. 2–16.

[89] The Jerusalem Bible oddly enough has 'the truth.'

mean 'lift up a voice' (cf. Isa 3.7).[90] In the present context, the line from Isaiah means that Jesus, instead of quarrelling unprofitably with his opponents, goes on about his business, and instead of seeking publicity asks people not to make him known.

οὐδὲ ἀκούσει τις ἐν ταῖς πλατείαις τὴν φωνὴν αὐτοῦ. This differs considerably from the LXX: οὐδὲ ἀκουσθήσεται ἔξω ἡ φωνὴ αὐτοῦ. Matthew is much closer to the Hebrew: wĕlōʾ-yašmîaʿ baḥûṣ qôlô. ḥûṣ can mean 'the outside' (cf. the LXX's ἔξω) or 'a street' (especially in the plural; cf. Matthew's ταῖς πλατείαις, also LXX Ezek 7.19; 26.11; 28.23). Should one imagine a contrast with Mt 6.5, where the 'hypocrites' make themselves seen and heard in the streets?

κάλαμον συντετριμμένον οὐ κατεάξει καὶ λίνον τυφόμενον οὐ σβέσει. This differs in only three places from the LXX (κάλαμον τεθλασμένον οὐ συντρίψει καὶ λίνον καπνιζόμενον οὐ σβέσει). Both Matthew and the LXX are close to the Hebrew: qāneh rāṣûṣ lōʾ yišbôr ûpištâ kēhâ lōʾ yĕkabbennâ.

Do the 'bruised reed' and the 'smouldering wick' stand for any group of people in particular? The commentaries suggest several possibilities: the apostles, Gentiles, Christians, the poor in Israel. More probably one should think in general of the undistinguished—Jew and Gentile, Christian and non-Christian—at society's margin. They are paradigmatically represented by the toll collectors and sinners, harassed outcasts who were the objects of Jesus' tenderness and compassion. Jesus accepted the 'bruised reed' and the 'smouldering wick' as they were and bade them to lay aside the miseries of the past and to recognize the possibilities opened by the future. Implicit is the idea that there is always hope for human beings, however wretched or unremarkable they may seem.

ἕως ἂν ἐκβάλῃ εἰς νῖκος τὴν κρίσιν.[91] This appears to be a conflation of Isa 42.3c (MT: leʾĕmet yôṣîʾ mišpāṭ; LXX: ἀλλὰ εἰς ἀλήθειαν ἐξοίσει κρίσιν) and 4b (MT: ʿad-yāśîm bāʾāreṣ mišpāṭ; LXX: ἕως ἂν θῇ ἐπὶ τῆς γῆς κρίσιν).[92] εἰς νῖκος (often for lāneṣaḥ in the LXX) means not 'in' or 'unto victory' but 'successfully' (cf. LXX 2 Βασ 2.26; Jer 3.5; Amos 1.11; 8.7; and see Kraft (v)).

Many have suspected that Matthew's line has been influenced by Hab 1.4 MT (wĕlôʾ-yēṣēʾ lāneṣaḥ mišpāṭ ... ʿal-kēn yēṣēʾ mišpaṭ mĕʿuqqāl). This is a real possibility, especially since 1QH 4.25 seems to bring together Isa 42.3 and Hab 1.4 (see Grundel (v)).

[90] Stendahl, *School*, p. 111–12, notes that Matthew's ἐρίσει might be related to the OT Peshitta's 'to cry out;' for while the root (ryb) can mean 'cry,' in western Aramaic it means 'contend.' But see Gundry, *OT*, pp. 113–14.
[91] Irenaeus, *Adv. haer.* 3.11.6, has νεῖκος, 'contention.'
[92] Isa 42.4a ('He will not fail or be discouraged') is thus dropped.

'Until he successfully brings forth κρίσιν' probably refers to more than the Messiah's teaching. If κρίσιν means 'judgement', then the verse anticipates the universal judgement (25.31–46). If, on the other hand, the word means 'justice', then Jesus is being presented as the one who establishes God's will and righteousness in the world (cf. Barth, in *TIM*. p. 141). See further Davies, *SSM*, pp. 133–7. Has the choice of ἐκβάλῃ[93] been prompted by the use of ἐκβάλλω in the following pericope (12.24, 26, 27, 28, 35; cf. Stendahl, *School*, p. 114)? One can hardly decide. But the meaning must be 'bring forth', as in Jn 10.4 (cf. BAGD, s.v., 2).

καὶ τῷ ὀνόματι αὐτοῦ ἔθνη ἐλπιοῦσιν.[94] So LXX Isa 42.4, with ἐπί before τῷ (cf. Isa 11.10; Rom 15.12). The MT is altogether different: 'and the coastlands wait for his law'. Is the LXX reading due to an inner Greek corruption, νόμῳ having become ὀνόματι?[95] Or is our MT corrupt, Matthew and the LXX witnessing to a lost Hebrew text form (so Gundry, *OT*, pp. 115–16)?

(iv) *Concluding Observations*

(1) Mt 12.1–21 supplies strong corroborative evidence for our claim in the Introduction that the author of the First Gospel was a Jew. If one accepts, as we do, the theory of Markan priority (see section (ii)) and if one attributes the quotation from Isa 42 to the evangelist (see pp. 323–24), then all of the following must be attributed to Matthew's hand: ἐν ἐκείνῳ τῷ καιρῷ (12.1, a Semitism); the halakhic argument in 12.5–6 (which uses the *qal wāḥômer*); the citation in 12.7 of Hos 6.6 (a text made famous by Johanan ben Zakkai in the period after A.D. 70); εἰ to introduce a direct question (12.10, a Hebraism probably); and the citation of an OT text evidently translated fresh from the Hebrew (12.18–21; see pp. 323 ff.). Also pertinent are the omission of Mk 2.27 ('the sabbath was made for man, not man for the sabbath') and the elimination of Mark's faulty reference to Abiathar (Mk 2.26). The one may show a reluctance to say anything too radical about the sabbath, and the other underlines Matthew's knowledge of the OT. To all appearances, then, the author of Mt 12.1–21 was

[93] This translates the hiphil of *yāṣā'* in LXX 2 Chr 23.14; 29.5, 16; 2 Esdr 10.3. It never in the LXX renders *śûm*.

[94] It was once popular to consider this line an interpolation. It is missing in 33, and unlike the previous verses it is purely LXX. See Bacon, p. 475, and Kilpatrick, p. 94. But these are slender grounds indeed. Cf. Gundry, *OT*, p. 116.

[95] Cf. the LXX variants at Exod 16.4 and Ps 118.165.

influenced by Semitic patterns of speech, was thoroughly conversant with the OT, probably even in its original language, and was acquainted, at least to some extent, with the scholastic rabbinism of his day.

(2) The sabbath is mentioned in Matthew only four times, in 12.1–8 (plucking grain on the sabbath); 12.9–14 (healing on a sabbath); 24.20 (fleeing on a sabbath); and 28.1 ('Now after the sabbath, toward the dawn of the first day of the week, Mary Magdalene and the other Mary went to see the sepulchre'). While the last is of no theological significance, the other texts show us, first, that Matthew presupposed continued observance of the sabbath by Christians (24.20; cf. Bacchiocchi (v), pp. 69–71; note also Eusebius, *H.E.* 5.7) and, secondly, that he was concerned with what was 'lawful' on the sabbath (12.1–14). Unfortunately, our gospel does not spell out the differences between the sabbath observance of Jews and Christians in Matthew's area; and we also do not know whether the evangelist was familiar with (Gentile) Christians who honoured Sunday instead of Saturday. It does, however, seem reasonable to suppose, in view of Matthew's additions in 12.1–14, that there was conflict between Matthew's community and others over the nature of true sabbath observance. Furthermore, there would seem to be two tendencies detectable in the Matthean redaction. On the one hand, the concern with what is lawful (12.2, 4, 10) and the insertion of the halakhic argument in 12.5–6 evidence a desire to remain faithful to the sabbath and its OT legislation. Matthew has taken care to prevent his position from being interpreted as radical or antinomian. (Note also, perhaps, the omission of Mk 2.27: 'the sabbath was made for man . . .'.) On the other hand, there is a distancing of Jesus and his church from common Jewish sentiment. When Jesus quashes the objections of the Pharisees, he is attacking an over-developed casuistry. He is asserting that the 'commandments of men' can prevent faithful observance of the 'commandments of God' (cf. 15.3). God wills the sabbath to be honoured, but not at the expense of 'doing good' (12.10). In fine, Matthew has sought to find the middle ground between Christian antinomianism and Jewish legalism.

(3) Concerning the use of Isa 42 in Mt 12.18–21: the quotation is the longest in the gospel; it is linked in several intriguing ways with its present context (see pp. 323–24); and its 'targumized' text show it to be the product of much care and reflection. These facts give us to understand the great importance for Matthew of Jesus' rôle as servant. But why exactly is Jesus' status as God's παῖς (= '*ebed*) held up for so much emphasis? There can be little doubt. The reason is

Matthew's understanding of God's primary demand: love of neighbour (cf. 7.12; 19.19; 22.39). Such love is defined as unselfish service of others (cf. 5.43–8). To love is to serve and to serve is to love. Thus Matthew's emphasis upon the love commandment goes hand in hand with his desire to interpret Jesus with the christological category of servant. As the perfect embodiment of God's moral demand, Jesus the servant lives the commandment to love.

(v) *Bibliography*

H. Aichinger, 'Quellenkritische Untersuchung der Perikope vom Ährenraufen am Sabbat Mk 2.23–8 par Mt 12.1–8 par Lk 6.1–5', in *Jesus in der Verkündigung der Kirche*, SNTU A 1, ed. A. Fuchs, Linz, 1976, pp. 110–53.

S. Bacchiocchi, *From Sabbath to Sunday*, Rome, 1977, pp. 17–73.

Banks, pp. 113–31.

F. W. Beare, '"The Sabbath was made for man?"', *JBL* 79 (1960), pp. 130–6.

P. Benoit, 'Les épis arrachés (Mt 12.1–8 et par.)', *SBFLA* 13 (1962), pp. 76–92.

K. M. Bishop, 'St Matthew and the Gentiles', *ExpT* 59 (1948), p. 249.

M. Black, 'The Aramaic spoken by Christ and Luke 14.5', *JTS* 1 (1950), pp. 60–2.

Borg, pp. 145–62.

K. Bornhauser, 'Zur Perikope vom Bruch des Sabbats', *NKZ* 33 (1922), pp. 325–34.

P. M. Casey, 'Culture and Historicity: the Plucking of the Grain (Mark 2.23–8),' *NTS* 34 (1988), pp. 1–23.

B. Cohen, 'The Rabbinical Law presupposed by Matthew xii, 1 and Luke vi. 1', *HTR* 23 (1930), pp. 91–2.

M. Cohen, 'La controverse de Jésus et des Pharisiens à propos de la cueillette des épis selon l'Évangile de saint Matthieu', *Mélanges de science religieuse* (Lille) 34 (1977), pp. 3–12.

D. M. Cohn-Sherbok, 'An Analysis of Jesus' Arguments concerning the Plucking of Grain on the Sabbath', *JSNT* 2 (1979), pp. 31–41.

Cope, pp. 32–52.

J. D. M. Derrett, 'Christ and the Power of Choice (Mark 3.1–6)', *Bib* 65 (1984), pp. 168–88.

C. Dietzfelbinger, 'Vom Sinn der Sabbatheilungen Jesu', *EvTh* 38 (1978), pp. 281–98.

B. R. Doyle, 'A Concern of the Evangelist: Pharisees in Matthew 12', *AusBR* 34 (1986), pp. 17–34.

J. D. G. Dunn, 'Mark 2.1–3.6: a Bridge between Jesus and Paul on the Question of the Law', *NTS* 30 (1984), pp. 395–415.

Geist, pp. 307–16.

F. Gils, 'Le sabbat a été fait pour l'homme et non l'homme pour le sabbat (Mc II, 27)', *RB* 69 (1962), pp. 506–23.

J. A. Grassi, 'The Five Loaves of the High Priest', *NovT* (1964), pp. 119–22.

J. Grindel, 'Matthew 12.18–21', *CBQ* 29 (1967), pp. 110–15.

Gundry, *OT*, pp. 110–16.

Hendrickx, *Miracle Stories*, pp. 149–67.

J. M. Hicks, 'The Sabbath Controversy in Matthew: An Exegesis of Matthew 12.1–14', *RestQ* 27 (1984), pp. 79–91.

D. Hill, 'On the Use and Meaning of Hosea vi. 6 in Matthew's Gospel', *NTS* 24 (1977), pp. 113–16.

Chr. Hinz, ' "Jesus und der Sabbat" ', *KD* 19 (1973), pp. 91–108.

Hübner, pp. 113–41.

A. J. Hultgren, 'The Formation of the Sabbath Pericope in Mark 2.23–28', *JBL* 91 (1972), pp. 38–43.

R. Kraft, 'Εἰς νῖκος: Permanently/Successfully: 1 Cor 15.54; Matt 12.20', in *Septuagintal Lexicography*, ed. R. Kraft, Missoula, 1975, pp. 153–6.

J. W. Leitch, 'Lord also of the Sabbath', *SJT* 19 (1966), pp. 426–33.

E. Levine, 'The Sabbath Controversy according to Matthew', *NTS* 22 (1976), pp. 480–3.

Lindars, *Apologetic*, pp. 144–52.

A. Lindemann, ' "Der Sabbat ist um des Menschen willen geworden" ' *WD* 15 (1979), pp. 79–105.

E. Lohse, 'Jesu Worte über den Sabbat', in Eltester, pp. 79–89.

T. W. Manson, 'Mark 2.27f.', *ConNT* 11 (1947), pp. 138–46.

B. Murmelstein, 'Jesu Gang durch die Saatfelder', *Ἄγγελος* (Leipzig) 3 (1930), pp. 111–20.

F. Neirynck, 'Jesus and the Sabbath. Some Observations on Mark II.27', in Dupont, *Jésus*, pp. 227–70; reprinted in Neirynck, *Evangelica*, pp. 637–80.

E. Neuhäusler, 'Jesu Stellung zum Sabbat', *BuL* 12 (1971), pp. 1–16.

J. N. Neyrey, 'The Thematic Use of Isa 42.1–4 in Matthew 12', *Bib* 63 (1983), pp. 457–73.

H. Riesenfeld, 'The Sabbath and the Lord's Day in Judaism, the Preaching of Jesus and Early Christianity', in *The Gospel Tradition*, Philadelphia, 1970, pp. 111–38.

Roloff, pp. 52–62.

W. Rordorf, *Sunday* (trans. of *Der Sonntag*, 1968), Philadelphia, 1968, pp. 54–79.

J. Sauer, 'Traditionsgeschichtliche Überlegungen zu Mk 3.1–6', *ZNW* 73 (1982), pp. 183–203.

Schenke, *Wundererzählungen*, pp. 161–72.

H. J. Schoeps, 'Jésus et la Loi Juive', *RHPR* 33 (1953), pp. 1–20.

E. Schweizer, 'Der Sabbat—Gebot und Geschenk', in *Glaube und Gerechtigkeit*, ed. J. Kilunen et al., Helsinki, 1983, pp. 169–79.

Sigal, pp. 119–53.

Stendahl, *School*, pp. 107–15.

Trautmann, pp. 278–318.

H. Troadec, 'Le Fils de l'homme est maître même du sabbat (Marc 2.23–3.6)', *BVC* 21 (1958), pp. 73–83.

Tuckett, *Revival*, pp. 96–102.

Verseput, pp. 153–206.

K. Wegenast, 'Das Ährenrupfen am Sabbat (Mk 2.23–28)', in K. Wegenast and S. Wibbing, *Streitgespräche*, Gütersloh, 1968, pp. 27–37.

Westerholm, pp. 92–103.

XXVI

AN OBJECTION STORY, A TESTING STORY, A CORRECTION STORY
(12.22–50)

(i) *Structure*

As argued in Excursus IX, Mt 12.22–50 divides itself into three subsections. The first, 12.22–37, is an extended objection story, the second, 12.38–45, an extended testing story, the third, 12.46–50, a succinct correction story. Whereas the objection story and the testing story serve primarily to register Israel's unbelief, the correction story is about the family of God and holds forth the possibility of faith (cf. pp. 233–34).

12.22–37 and 38–45 both involve controversy with Pharisees. But in 12.46–50 Jesus simply addresses the crowds. The Pharisees have disappeared. Similarly, in 12.1–8 and 9–14 there is controversy and the Pharisees are present, but in 12.15–21 they play no rôle. There is thus a close structural parallel between 12.1–21 and 12.22–50. Both consist of two pericopae detailing conflict with Pharisess followed by one without conflict. The make-up of Jesus' audience clearly affects the character of the different paragraphs.

(ii) *Sources*

(1) *The account of the Beelzebul controversy, 12.22–32.* This text is a combination of Mk 3.22–30 and material from Q (cf. Lk 11.14–23; 12.10). Lk 11.14–23, which belongs to a portion of the Third Gospel showing little if any use of Mark, is, by contrast, wholly or almost wholly uninfluenced by the Second Gospel—as the divergence in vocabulary and syntax attests (cf. Hultgren (v); Marshall, p. 471). Hence, with Mark and Luke (= Q) before us, we can reconstruct Matthew's redactional procedure. The introduction (12.22–4) is based entirely upon Q.[1] So probably are 12.25–6 and 27–8, only the first of which has a parallel in Mark (Mk 6.25–6). So Markan influence in 12.22–8 is minimal or nil. In 12.29, however, Matthew reproduces the form of the strong man parable in Mk 3.27 (the form in Q—Lk 11.21–

---

[1] Matthew has already used this story in 9.32–4, so we have here a doublet. Probably both Matthew and Luke favoured Q's introduction because they found Mark's (in which Jesus' family declares him 'beside himself') to be disturbing.

2—is very different). In 12.30 Matthew returns to Q (cf. Lk 11.23). But having thus reached the end of Q's version of the controversy, our evangelist reverts again to Mark, in which the passage about blasphemy follows the parable of the strong man (Mk 3.28–9; cf. Mt 12.31–2). In adapting this text, Matthew also seems to have looked at the variant in Q (see Lk 12.10). In sum, then, 12.22–8 and 30 are from Q, 12.29 from Mark, and 12.31–2 draws upon both of Matthew's primary sources.[2]

(2) *The sayings on good and bad fruit, 12.33–7.* The first three verses are based upon a section in Q's great sermon (see Lk 6.43–5) from which Matthew has already drawn (cf. 7.16–20). The next two verses, which possess no synoptic parallel, must be assigned either to oral tradition (M) or to redaction. A firm decision one way or the other seems impossible.

(3) *The sign of Jonah, 12.38–42.* On the two-source theory, this is from Q (see Lk 11.16, 29–32), with perhaps some influence from Mk 8.11f. (see on 12.38). Two observations support or are consistent with this conclusion. First, Matthew has two versions of our story, one in 12.38–42, another in 16.1–4. The doublet is readily accounted for if he found the episode in two different sources, Mark and Q. Secondly, Mk 8.11–12 denies that any sign will be given to 'this generation'. So if the Griesbach hypothesis be embraced, the Second Evangelist went against both his sources, for both Matthew and Luke state that the sign of Jonah will be given (Mt 12.38–42; 16.1–4; Lk 11.16, 29–32). Is this probable? On the other hand, when one postulates Markan priority, both Matthew and Luke had two different versions in front of them, that of Q (a sign will be given) and that of Mark (a sign will not be given), and both simply followed Q.

(4) *The unclean spirit, 12.43–5.* This has its only synoptic counterpart in Lk 11.24f. Given the close verbatim agreement, one must suppose either a common written source (Q) or one evangelist's knowledge of the other.

(5) *Jesus' true family, 12.46–50.* This is Matthew's version of Mk 3.31–5. The priority of Mark is indicated by the introduction in Mk 3.20f., which the authors of Matthew and Luke were moved to drop. They were reluctant to pass on the information that Jesus' own thought him mad.

(iii) *Exegesis*

JESUS AND BEELZEBUL (12.22–37)

This is a drawn-out objection story (see on 9.1–8). It consists of an exorcism followed by three responses: the crowd's response to Jesus, the Pharisees' response to the crowd, and Jesus' response to the Pharisees. Whereas the response of the crowd (a question) and that of the Pharisees (an accusation) are narrated

---

[2] For a full list of the parallels and differences between Matthew and Luke and between Matthew and Mark in the Beelzebul controversy see Allen, pp. 132–3.

quite briefly, Jesus' response is extended. It consists of (i) three rebuttals followed by a warning (vv. 25–30): (ii) a passage on the unforgivable sin (vv. 31–2); and (iii) a little paragraph on fruits and words (vv. 33–7).[3]

Mk 3.22–27 and Lk 11.14–23 (Q) probably rest upon a primitive Aramaic account (Hultgren (v)). It consisted of Lk 11.14 (an exorcism) + Mk 3.22 = Lk 11.15 (accusation) + Mk 3.23–26 = Lk 11.17–18b (the divided kingdom) + Mk 3.27 = Lk 11,21–22 (the strong man). The charge and the two responses may be reckoned historical, although that they belonged to one occasion is usually doubted. Mark or his tradition added the isolated saying about blasphemy (3.28–29) and disturbed the beginning (cf. Bultmann, *History*, p. 13) while Q added the sayings in Lk 11.19–20 and 23.[3]

22. τότε προσηνέχθη αὐτῷ δαιμονιζόμενος τυφλὸς καὶ κωφός. Compare 4.24; 8.16; 9.32. Lk 11.14 (καὶ ἦν ἐκβάλλων δαιμόνιον καὶ αὐτὸ ἦν κωφόν) is probably closer to Q, for τότε*, προσφέρω*, δαιμονίζομαι (1, p. 418) and τυφλός* are all Matthean favourites. Also, the doublet in Mt 9.32 is closer to Lk 11.14 than to Mt 12.22. Why Matthew added the reference to blindness is unclear. Did he want to remind the reader of the parallel in 9.27–31 or prepare for 20.29–34? Or, more plausibly, did he desire to differentiate in some fashion between 12.22–4 and its doublet in 9.32–4? That a contrast between the blind man who comes to see and the Pharisees who cannot see is intended is perhaps a bit over-subtle.

καὶ ἐθεράπευσεν αὐτόν, ὥστε τὸν κωφὸν λαλεῖν καὶ βλέπειν.[4] Compare 9.33 and 12.15. ἐθεράπευσεν αὐτοὺς ὥστε τόν + object + infinitive is probably redactional, as it is in 15.30–1; and βλέπειν is needed because of the redactional τυφλός. So Matthew's line owes much to the redactor's hand. But Lk 11.14 (ἐγένετο δὲ τοῦ δαιμονίου ἐξελθόντος ἐλάλησεν ὁ κωφὸς) is no more likely to reproduce Q, for it bears all the hallmarks of Lukan redaction (see Jeremias, *Lukasevangelium*, p. 199).

23. καὶ ἐξίσταντο πάντες οἱ ὄχλοι καὶ ἔλεγον· μήτι οὗτός ἐστιν ὁ υἱὸς Δαυίδ; Matthew has expanded Q. Luke has simply: καὶ ἐθαύμασαν οἱ ὄχλοι. Of all the evangelists, ours shows the most interest in Jesus as the Son of David (see on 1.1 and 9.27). ἐξίσταντο[5] may have been suggested by Mk 3.21.

---

[3] See further Guelich, *Mark*, pp. 168–71, supplying a review of scholarly opinion on tradition-history.

[4] The readings, τον κωφον και τυφλον (so L W Δ Θ *f*[1.13] sy[p.h]) and τον τυφλον και κωφον (so C Maj q) are expansions in the interest of accuracy.

[5] ἐξίστημι: Mt: 1; Mk: 4; Lk: 3. In the biblical tradition the word often has the weakened sense of 'be astonished', 'be amazed', as here.

The crowds are presented in a relatively favourable light. If the Pharisees will shortly assert that Jesus casts out demons by the prince of demons, the crowds instead wonder whether Jesus might not be the Davidic Messiah.[6] The real enemies of Jesus are the Pharisees, who are sure of themselves, not the uncertain populace at large.

24. The Pharisees respond not so much to Jesus' exorcism as to the crowds. The narrative accordingly implies that what the Pharisees are interested in above all is keeping others from belief.

οἱ δὲ Φαρισαῖοι ἀκούσαντες εἶπον. Compare 9.34 and 11.2–3. In Lk 11.15 (τινὲς δὲ ἐξ αὐτῶν) the Pharisees are not named. Their appearance is most probably due to Matthew.[7] Mk 3.22 has 'scribes from Jerusalem'.[8]

οὗτος οὐκ ἐκβάλλει τὰ δαιμόνια εἰ μὴ ἐν τῷ Βεελζεβοὺλ ἄρχοντι τῶν δαιμονίων. The emphatic placement of οὗτος answers to 12.23 and implies contempt. As with 9.34 and Lk 11.15b, there is no need to suppose influence from Mk 3.22, where Jesus is accused of being possessed (Βεελζεβοὺλ ἔχει, καὶ ὅτι ἐν τῷ ἄρχοντι τῶν δαιμονίων ἐκβάλλει τὰ δαιμόνια).[9] Note that Matthew alone has the Semitic οὐκ ... εἰ μή.[10] It sharpens the charge. The Pharisees, we may observe, refer to Jesus not in the second person but in the third person. They are not arguing with the healer but with the onlookers.[11]

On Beelzebul see on 10.25. With 'prince of demons' compare 1QM 17.5–6 ('the prince of the kingdom of wickedness'); Jub. 48.15 ('the prince Mastema'; cf. 10.8); T. Dan. 5.6 ('your prince is Satan'); Jn 14.30 ('the ἄρχων of this world'; cf. 16.11); Eph 2.2 ('the prince of the power of the air'); b. Pesaḥ. 110a ('Ashmedai the king of the demons').

The attempt to discredit Jesus by claiming that he did his miracles through the agency[12] of an evil spirit was probably made on more than one occasion (cf. Jn 7.20; 8.48, 52; 10.20; Justin, Dial. 69; b. Sanh. 43a). There is a helpful collection of pertinent material on the subject

[6] Although μήτι usually assumes a negative response, it also occurs 'in questions in which the questioner is in doubt concerning the answer' (BAGD, s.v.). We may translate: 'Is this not perhaps . . ?' Cf. Lagrange, p. 241.

[7] Although this is not certain. See Marshall, p. 472, who observes that τις ἐκ is a Lukan favourite.

[8] Matthew often but not consistently omits 'the scribes' from Mark; see 9.11; 17.14; 21.23; 22.35, 41; 26.3, 47; and 27.1 with their Markan parallels. Perhaps this has something to do with Matthew's occasional positive use of 'scribe'.

[9] Perhaps these words were added to the primitive narrative (see p. 334) sometime before Mark.

[10] Cf. 13.57; 14.17; 15.24; 17.8; 21.19; and see BDF § 376 and Beyer 1, pp. 129–31.

[11] Pace Gundry, Commentary, p. 233, who claims that the Pharisees are speaking within themselves.

[12] On ἐν (cf. bĕ) of personal agency see BDF § 219.1. We doubt that Matthew or the tradition understood ἐν to mean 'by the power of the name'.

in Smith, *Magician*, pp. 21–80. It should be remarked that the charge of casting out demons by Beelzebul presupposes Jesus' undoubted success at exorcism. His opponents evidently did not deny his seemingly miraculous deeds but rather took the course of attributing them to a dark power (cf. Deut 13.1–5).[13]

25. εἰδὼς δὲ τὰς ἐνθυμήσεις αὐτῶν εἶπεν αὐτοῖς.[14] Lk 11.17 is very similar: αὐτὸς δὲ εἰδὼς αὐτῶν τὰ διανοήματα εἶπεν αὐτοῖς. ἐνθυμήσεις is probably Matthean (cf. 9.4 diff. Mk 2.8), αὐτὸς δέ probably Lukan. On the question of what stood in Q see Neirynck (v). On Jesus' supernatural knowledge of others' thoughts see on 9.4.

πᾶσα βασιλεία μερισθεῖσα καθ' ἑαυτῆς ἐρημοῦται. Compare Theod. Dan 2.41 (βασιλεία διῃρημένη ἔσται). Between βασιλεία and ἐρημοῦται Lk 11.17 has: ἐφ' ἑαυτὴν διαμερισθεῖσα. The δια– is Lukan (Jeremias, *Lukasevangelium*, p. 200), the κατά + genitive* Matthean.[15] The Q form (πᾶσα κ.τ.λ.) is more Semitic than the Markan form (καὶ ἐὰν κ.τ.λ.).

ἐρημόω[16] means 'lay waste' or 'depopulate'. Compare LXX Isa 6.11 ('until cities lie waste [ἐρημωθῶσιν]); Philo, *Decal.* 152 ('why great and populous countries are desolated [ἐρημοῦνται] by internal factions'); Rev 18.19; Josephus, *Bell.* 2.279; *Ant.* 11.24.

Jesus' words—which sound proverbial[17]—take for granted that Satan, like God, has a kingdom, a well-ordered and organized host of powers and influences that heed the beck and call of their dark Lord. Compare 4Q286 10 ii.1–13, where reference is made to the dominion(s) of Belial and his lot; also 4QAmram[b] frag. 2 and T. Dan. 6.1–4 (ἡ βασιλεία τοῦ ἐχθροῦ). Over against the kingdom of God is the kingdom of Satan.[18]

καὶ πᾶσα πόλις ἢ οἰκία μερισθεῖσα καθ' ἑαυτῆς οὐ σταθήσεται. For all practical purposes this is synonymous with the preceding clause. If Lk 11.17 (καὶ οἶκος ἐπὶ οἶκον πίπτει) is closer to Q,

[13] One wonders if, historically, the charge against Jesus was not stimulated in part by the comparative ease with which he cast out demons, or at least his refusal to employ much ritual. Might this not have suggested demonic co-operation?

[14] So NA[26] and HG, but the text is very uncertain. ειδως δε appears in ℵ*.2 B sa, ειδως δε ο Ιησους in C L W Θ 0106 *f*[1.13] Maj (lat) sy[p.h] mae, ιδων δε in P[21] ℵ1 D 892* k sy[s.c.] bo, ιδων δε ο Ιησους in 33 892[c] *pc* ff1 bo[mss]. Cf. the variants for 9.4.

[15] ἐπί + accusative (so also Mk 3.24) is here non-Lukan (Jeremias, *Lukasevangelium*, p. 200).

[16] Often for a form of ḥārēb in the LXX. In the NT the word is rare: Mt 12.25 par.; Rev 17.16; 18.16, 19.

[17] Similar sentiments appear in Sophocles, *Ant.* 672; Philo, *Decal.* 152; Cicero, *Lael.* 7.23. For (later) Jewish parallels see SB 1, p. 635.

[18] See on this the study of E. Langton, *Essentials of Demonology*, London, 1949.

then Matthew has increased the parallelism with v. 25b, perhaps under the influence of Mk 3.25 (καὶ ἐὰν οἰκία ἐφ' ἑαυτὴν μερισθῇ, οὐ δυνήσεται ἡ οἰκία ἐκείνη στῆναι[19]). Luke's text, however, may be an abridgement, and the agreement between Matthew and Mark a pointer to the agreement between Q and the pre-Markan tradition. It is also just conceivable that both Matthew and Luke may at this juncture depend upon Mark, in which case Q lacked any parallel to Mk 3.25. In favour of this last option there are no agreements between Matthew and Luke in Mk 3.25 par. Only Matthew has a triad of illustrations: kingdom, city[20], house (= family[21]). The effect is to make a more comprehensive statement: from the largest collective to the smallest, internal division wreaks havoc.

26. καὶ εἰ ὁ σατανᾶς τὸν σατανᾶν ἐκβάλλει, ἐφ' ἑαυτὸν ἐμερίσθη· πῶς οὖν σταθήσεται ἡ βασιλεία αὐτοῦ; Compare Mk 3.26. Lk 11.18 (εἰ δὲ καὶ ὁ σατανᾶς ἐφ' ἑαυτὸν διεμερίσθη, πῶς σταθήσεται ἡ βασιλεία αὐτοῦ;[22]) probably gives us Luke's abridged version of Q, which is more faithfully preserved by Matthew, although οὖν* is Matthean. Yet one could also argue that Matthew has assimilated his wording to Mk 3.26 (καὶ εἰ ὁ σατανᾶς ἀνέστη ἐφ' ἑαυτὸν καὶ ἐμερίσθη, οὐ δύναται στῆναι ἀλλὰ τέλος ἔχει).

On Satan see 4.1 and 10. We see no reason to think that the equation Matthew makes between Satan and Beelzebul was not also made by the primitive tradition; see further Fitzmyer, *Luke* 2, p. 921.

The Pharisees have charged Jesus with casting out demons by the prince of demons.[23] That is, they have assigned Jesus' power to evil forces, not God. Jesus responds by constructing a *reductio ad absurdum* which affirms Satan's rational behaviour.[24] Would

---

[19] So HG. NA[26] prints σταθηναι at the end, but this might be assimilation to the First Gospel.

[20] Matthew has added πόλις, a favourite of his. O. Michel, *TWNT* 5, p. 134, speaks of 'the favourite Hellenistic pair πόλις and οἰκία.' But 'house' and 'city' are also often paired in Jewish literature; see D. E. Fleming, '"House"/"City": An Unrecognized Parallel Word Pair,' *JBL* 105 (1986), pp. 689–93. Gnilka, *Matthäusevangelium* 1, p. 458, suggests that Matthew's use of πόλις in this context could reflect his personal experience of strife in a (large) city.

[21] οἰκία, like the Hebrew *bayit*, can mean both 'house' and 'family'.

[22] Luke continues: 'because you say that I cast out demons by Beelzebul'. If from Q, Matthew has dropped the words because they are redundant. But a Lukan origin cannot be excluded; cf. Schlosser 1, p. 129 (citing Bultmann, Lührmann, Boismard, Schulz).

[23] For a possible parallel see J. A. Montgomery, *Aramaic Incantation Texts from Nippur*, Philadelphia, 1913, pp. 253–4.

[24] This affirmation has troubled many Christian exegetes, who assume that demons fight against each other (cf. Eusebius, *Contra Hieroclem* 31 (530 A); note also Gos. Egyptians 3.61. 16–23 = 4.72.27–73.6).

it make sense for the devil to give a human being power if that power was in turn used to ransack the kingdom of demons? Once one grants that Jesus has in fact delivered souls from spiritual bondage and given them their health in body, mind, and spirit, it is foolhardly to see him in league with Satan. Satan would not knowingly and willingly destroy his own dominion.

27. καὶ εἰ ἐγὼ ἐν Βεελζεβοὺλ ἐκβάλλω τὰ δαιμόνια, οἱ υἱοὶ ὑμῶν ἐν τίνι ἐκβάλλουσιν; διὰ τοῦτο αὐτοὶ κριταὶ ἔσονται ὑμῶν. This is from Q. Lk 11.19 begins with εἰ δέ and ends with ὑμῶν ἔσονται; for the rest there is agreement.

Against Plummer, pp. 176–77, 'your sons' is not to be taken literally. Because Jesus is addressing the Pharisees, the phrase must refer to members of the Pharisaic sect or to Pharisaic sympathizers (cf. BAGD. s.v., υἱός, 1c). In Q the reference was simply to the 'sons' of the listeners, that is, to their own kind: in effect, 'an Oriental circumlocution for "you"' (Allen, p. 135).

'Your judges' alludes to the eschatological assize. Whether one should think of the Jewish exorcists as actively sharing the office of judgement is not impossible (see on 19.28). But perhaps it is best to imagine them as witnesses for the prosecution.

Jesus' reasoning in 12.27 is crystal clear. Two similar activities (Jesus' exorcisms, the exorcisms of others) are assigned by the Pharisees to two radically different sources (Beelzebul, God). Jesus brands this as irrational. Similar effects have similar causes; and good does not come from evil (cf. 12.33–7). When first uttered the argument may have been even more pointed if, as seems not improbable, the 'exorcism-rituals [of the sons of the Pharisees] looked much more like magic than Jesus' simple word and/or touch' (Meier, *Matthew*, p. 135).[25]

Ironically, when the tables were later turned and the church Fathers were required to account for the success of non-Christian exorcists and miracle workers, they responded precisely as the Pharisees in our story and referred to demons (see e.g. Justin, *1 Apol.* 54–8; Augustine, *Civ. dei* 10.16; 22.10). Furthermore, the difficulty of attributing genuine miracles to unbelievers, that is, to the 'sons' of the Pharisees, led to the untenable exegetical opinion that 'your sons' should be identified with the apostles (e.g. Chrysostom, *Hom. on Mt* 41.2). 'Your magic is my miracle, and vice-versa'[26] seems to have been the rule in the ancient world.[27]

[25] For stories of Jewish exorcists see 1 Sam 16.14–23; Tob 8.1–3; 1QapGen 20.29; Mk 9.38; Acts 19.13–14; Josephus, *Ant.* 8.45–9; *Bell.* 7.185; T. Sol. passim; Justin, *Dial.* 85; Irenaeus, *Adv. haer.* 2.6.2.

[26] R. M. Grant, *Gnosticism and Early Christianity*, rev.ed., New York, 1966, p. 93.

[27] See further E. V. Gallagher, *Divine Man or Magician? Celsus and Origen on Jesus*, Chico, 1982.

28. The authenticity of 12.28 would seem to be one of the assured results of modern criticism.[28] Jesus believed that the power of God was at work in him to overcome evil forces and that his success in fighting the devil and his minions was part of God's eschatological deliverance (cf. Dunn, *Spirit*, pp. 47–9). Scholars have been less sure as to how 12.27 should be handled. It is widely thought that it is illogical to refer to the successful exorcisms of others (12.27) and then to claim that Jesus' exorcisms are special signs of the presence of the kingdom.[29] For this reason the vast majority of exegetes have regarded 12.27 and 28 as sayings which did not belong together from the beginning.[30] We, however, think the consensus should be questioned. The standard opinion assumes a false exegesis. The inference made in 12.28 is not from exorcisms in general to the presence of the kingdom of God; it is rather from *Jesus'* exorcisms to the presence of the kingdom ('if *I* cast out demons'). How could Jesus ever have contended that the kingdom of God had come simply because a few demons had been cast out? If exorcisms were not exactly everyday affairs, they were hardly unknown until the wonder-worker from Nazareth came along. Therefore the force of Jesus' assertion must lie elsewhere, and that can only be in his very presence as the Christ. What matters is that *Jesus* cast out demons. In other words, the saying is a veiled testimony to Jesus' eschatological rôle. As so often in the genuine dominical materials, Jesus implicitly asserts the mystery and magnitude of his own person but gives to himself no title. He does not say that the kingdom has come because the Messiah or the Son of man is present and ransacking Satan's kingdom. He says simply, 'I cast out demons'. The listener should be moved to ask, 'Who then is this?' See further below.

εἰ δὲ ἐν πνεύματι θεοῦ ἐγὼ ἐκβάλλω τὰ δαιμόνια, ἄρα ἔφθασεν ἐφ' ὑμᾶς ἡ βασιλεία τοῦ θεοῦ. Lk 11.20 differs in only two respects: δακτύλῳ is in fourth place, and the ἐγώ is missing. The latter has probably been added by Matthew in order to increase the parallelism with v. 27. 'Kingdom of God'[31] fails to become 'kingdom of heaven' not because 'Matthew has hurried over the Q version of Mt 12.28 without stopping to modify it as he would normally have done' (Dunn, *Spirit*, p. 45), or because the evangelist sees some important distinction between 'kingdom of God' and 'kingdom of heaven' (see on 4.17); rather, βασιλεία τοῦ θεοῦ stands in conscious parallelism to πνεύματι θεου and in antithesis to βασιλεία αὐτοῦ (sc. Satan, v. 27).

As to whether Q had 'finger of God' or 'Spirit of God' there has

[28] Cf. Bultmann, *History*, p. 162; Käsemann, *Essays*, p. 39.
[29] Cf. Beare, pp. 278–9: 'this passage actually destroys the argument' and is 'wholly lacking in logic'.
[30] Cf. Bultmann, *History*, pp. 14, 162; Kümmel, *Promise*, pp. 105–6; Schlosser 1, pp. 130–2.
[31] In Matthew only here and 19.24; 21.31, 43.

been much discussion.[32] In favour of 'finger', these points have been made. (i) Luke, given his interests, would hardly have dropped 'Spirit' had it stood in his source. (ii) δάκτυλος appears only three times in the entirety of Luke-Acts, Lk 11.20, 46, and 16.24. 16.24 is from Luke's tradition, and 11.46 belonged to Q. So one can hardly detect in the word itself any special Lukan interest. (iii) The First Evangelist might have altered 'finger' to 'Spirit' because the former had magical connotations and because the latter linked up so well with the Matthean context, where πνεῦμα is a key word (12.18, 31, 32). Also, the desire to remove an anthropomorphism might have been a factor. On the other side, it has been argued (i) that Matthew, with his interest in comparing Jesus to Moses, would not have passed over an allusion to Exod 8.19[33], and (ii) that Luke, with his Exodus typology, might have added 'finger'. Balancing the several observations, we believe Q probably had 'finger'. Luke's Exodus typology is perhaps less obvious than many suppose,[34] and Matthew's interest in Moses may have been overridden by more important or immediate considerations. The conclusion, however, is really academic, for the OT equates 'finger of God' with 'hand of God' and 'Spirit of God'.[35]

ἔφθασεν[36] has also generated much discussion. The result would seem to be that the Greek implies the presence of the kingdom: it has already, in some sense, come. See further on 4.17. The other view[37] holds that, according to Mt 12.28, Jesus' exorcisms prepare for the kingdom by (1) defeating demons and (2) cleansing individuals from evil so that they may participate in that kingdom. On this less probable view, the kingdom is so close that its powers are already at work.

Mt 12.27–8 par. has been interpreted in several different ways.

(i) The juxtaposition of vv. 27 and 28 is simply illogical. If the exorcisms of Jesus prove the coming of the kingdom of God, then so do the exorcisms of others (see p. 339). Thus either v. 27 or v. 28 was not uttered by Jesus; or they were uttered by him on different occasions and from different perspectives. And in any event they cannot be harmonized.

[32] Barrett, *Spirit*, p. 63; Gnilka, *Matthäusevangelium* 1, p. 456; and Schlosser 1, pp. 132–4, all favour the originality of Luke's text. But the claim that Q probably had 'Spirit' is made by Rodd (v); Hamerton-Kelly (v); Van Cangh (v).

[33] Cf. also Exod 31.18; Deut 9.10; Ps 8.3; Eusebius, *Dem. ev.* 93c–d; *Sipre* on Num 8.4; *Mek.* on Exod 12.2 and 14.30; and *b. Menaḥ.* 29a.

[34] Cf. C. L. Blomberg, 'Midrash, Chiasmus, and the Outline of Luke's Central Section', in France 3, pp. 217–61. On the other hand, perhaps Jesus himself had a new exodus motif in mind. See also Manson, *Teaching*, pp. 82–83.

[35] Compare Ps 8.3 with 33.6 and note Ezek 3.14; 8.1–3; 37.1. Both 'Spirit' and 'finger' can mean, in effect, 'power'. Cf. Clement of Alexandria, *Strom.* 6.16: the finger of God is the power of God. Similarly, the *yad YHWH* of MT 2 Kgs 3.15 becomes, in the targum, *rûaḥ*. See further Hamerton-Kelly (v).

[36] φθάνω (Mt: 1; Mk: 0; Lk: 1) can mean 'come first', 'precede', 'anticipate'. This is the classical meaning of the Greek and is still found in 1 Thess 4.15. For φθάνω (+ ἐπί) meaning arrival and actual presence see LXX Cant 2.12; Theod. Dan 6.25; 7.13, 22 (all three translating *mĕṭā'*); Rom 9.31; 2 Cor 10.14; Phil 3.16; 1 Thess 2.16. Cf. BDF § 101; BAGD, s.v.; and note the RSV: 'has come upon you'. For reviews of the discussion see Kümmel, *Promise*, pp. 105–109; R. F. Berkey, 'ΕΓΓΙΖΕΙΝ, ΦΘΑΝΕΙΝ, and Realized Eschatology', *JBL* 82 (1963), pp. 177–87; G. Fitzer, *TWNT* 9, pp. 90–4; and Beasley-Murray (v).

[37] Held, e.g., by R. H. Hiers, *Jesus and the Future*, Atlanta, 1981, pp. 62–71.

(ii) It has been held that at least the Q community, which believed that Wisdom had sent many messengers to Israel, could have understood the kingdom of God to have come in the activities of non-Christian exorcists.

(iii) Sometimes it is urged that Jesus' exorcisms are different because they alone were the work of the Spirit or finger of God; and therefore only his exorcisms can be linked to the coming of the kingdom.

(iv) 12.27 par. is purely *ad hominem*. It is interested only in convicting Jesus' opponents of hypocrisy. It is not really implied that Jesus himself believed in the power of Jewish exorcists.

(v) Implicit is the supposition that Jesus' exorcisms were more abundant and of greater success than the exorcisms of others. Jesus' acts were qualitatively superior.

(vi) 'Your sons' should be equated with the apostles, so the question of exorcisms performed by unbelievers does not arise (see p. 338).

(vii) Jesus accepts the miracles of others but holds his own to be of different import because of his identity. What is decisive is not the exorcisms but the exorcist. See above.

We have already made clear our preference for interpretation (vii) with reference to the historical Jesus. We also think it is the best interpretation for the redactional level. (i) is no solution at all. (ii) would threaten Matthew's understanding of eschatology as bound to the person of Jesus. For (iii) there is not a tittle of evidence. How else but by God's power could Jewish exorcists cast out demons? As for (iv) it contradicts the literal sense of the text. (v) is a possibility (and is accepted by Verseput, p. 223), but requires that one read a great deal into the verse. (vi) is incredible. This leaves us with (vii), which is consistent with Matthew's redactional insertion of the emphatic ἐγώ. It also falls in nicely with one of the most fundamental Matthean themes: the coming of Jesus inaugurates the fulfilment of eschatology.

29. Jesus' third argument[38] takes the form of a parable. The point is that so far from belonging to Satan's kingdom and using Satan's power, Jesus has attacked that kingdom and overcome its power.

There are two different versions of the parable of the strong man, the version in Mt 12.29; Mk 3.27; and Gos. Thom. 35[39] on the one hand, and that in Lk 11.21–2 on the other. Some would regard the last as an allegorical expansion, Luke's own rewriting of Mk 3.27.[40] But

---

[38] Cf. Chrysostom, *Hom. on Mt* 41.3: 'Having then uttered His second refutation, He adds also a third, thus saying . . .'.

[39] 'Jesus said: It is not possible for one to enter the house of the strong man and take him by force unless he bind his hands; then he will ransack his house.' This might be independent of the synoptics. In fact, 'bind his hands' could be original over against 'binds the strong man'.

[40] E.g. Crossan (v), p. 189. Luke's text more clearly alludes to Isa 49.24–5 and 53.12.

the differences between Lk 11.21–2 and its Markan counterpart are sufficiently great to render it unlikely that the one was the source for the other. Beyond that, Jeremias, *Lukasevangelium*, p. 201, finds very little in Lk 11.21–2 to be characteristically Lukan. It seems best, therefore, to regard Lk 11.21–2 as reproducing Q.[41]

The authenticity of the parable of the strong man (in its Markan form) is little disputed, and rightly.[42] The logion has multiple attestation (Mark and Q). It has a good parallel in the dominical Lk 10.18. It is consistent with Jesus' conviction about the presence of the kingdom and the importance of his own person. And it has a credible setting in Jesus' ministry of successful exorcism. To all this it may be added that the church tended to put the decisive defeat of Satan not in the ministry itself but either at the cross[43] or in the future.[44]

ἢ πῶς δύναταί τις εἰσελθεῖν εἰς τὴν οἰκίαν τοῦ ἰσχυροῦ καὶ τὰ σκεύη αὐτοῦ ἁρπάσαι. Compare Isa 49.24 ('Can the prey be taken from the mighty, or the captives of a tyrant be rescued?') and Ps. Sol. 5.4 ('For a man will not take booty (σκῦλα) from a strong man' (ἀνδρὸς δυνατοῦ)).[45] Matthew has slightly re-written and simplified Mk 3.27 (ἀλλ᾽ οὐδεὶς δύναται τὰ σκεύη τοῦ ἰσχυροῦ εἰσελθὼν εἰς τὴν οἰκίαν αὐτοῦ διαρπάσαι). ἤ* makes what follows a variation of the previous argument (vv. 27–8). πῶς[46] increases the parallelism with 12.26 and 34. ἁρπάζω (Mt: 3; Mk: 0; Lk: 0) seems to be a word Matthew likes. The transformation of a statement (so Mark and Luke) into a question (so Matthew) makes for a better parallel with vv. 26 (which also has πῶς) and 27.

'The house of the strong man' is Satan's kingdom. 'His goods' or 'possessions' are the people he has under his sway: those possessed by demons.[47] Jesus frees them through his ministry of exorcism.[48]

ἐὰν μὴ πρῶτον δήσῃ τὸν ἰσχυρόν; Mark has the order, 1, 2, 3, 5, 6, 4. δέω, which means 'bind' or 'tie', was often used in

---

[41] Cf. Polag, *Fragmenta*, pp. 52–3, and Schweitzer, *Luke*, p. 195.

[42] See Pesch 1, p. 219.

[43] Cf. Jn 12.31; 14.30; 16.11; Col 2.14–5.

[44] Rev 20.1–15; Irenaeus, *Adv. haer.* 5.26.1. Jewish tradition tended to think of Satan's defeat as an eschatological event (cf. Jub. 23.29; 1 En. 10.4–7; 54.4–6; T. Zeb. 9.8).

[45] Note also Irenaeus, *Adv. haer.* 5.22.1: 'A strong man can be overcome neither by an inferior nor by an equal, but by one who is stronger.'

[46] For πῶς + δύναμαι (cf. ᾽êkâ + yākōl, as in Deut 7.17) see LXX Deut 1.12; 7.17; Tob 5.2; Est 8.6; Isa 36.9; Dan 10.17; 1 Macc 3.17, 53.

[47] Cf. T. Naph. 8.6: 'the devil will inhabit him as his own vessel' (σκεῦος). Contrast Basil, *Hom. Spir.* 8.18, who identifies the vessels with 'us, who had been abased in every manner of evil'.

[48] Patristic exegesis often discerned in 12.29 a reference to the harrowing of hell; cf. Asc. Isa. 9.16.

Jewish texts of binding Satan or evil spirits.[49] Just as demons may bind people (cf. Lk 13.16), so may people bind demons.

Whether Jesus himself or Matthew after him thought in terms of a specific time when the devil was overcome and bound is uncertain; but such an idea could well lie behind the synoptic temptation stories.[50]

καὶ τότε τὴν οἰκίαν αὐτοῦ διαρπάσει. Compare Josephus, *Bell.* 4.314 (πᾶσαν οἰκίαν διήρπαζον). Here Matthew follows Mark without alteration.

30. This is a warning which owes its present placement to Q (cf. Lk 11.23). It was tacked on at the end of the Beelzebul controversy to draw out the consequences of Jesus' battle with Satan.

ὁ μὴ ὢν μετ' ἐμοῦ κατ' ἐμοῦ ἐστιν, καὶ ὁ μὴ συνάγων μετ' ἐμοῦ σκορπίζει.[51] So Luke, thus the source is Q.[52] For a proposed Aramaic original see Jeremias, *Theology*, p. 27. The imagery seems to be that of gathering and scattering sheep,[53] though some commentators have thought of harvesting.[54] An allusion to the eschatological gathering of diaspora Jews seems improbable.

The words refer neither to the devil (*pace* Chrysostom, *Hom. on Mt* 41.4) nor to Jewish exorcists (*pace* Bengel, *ad loc.*). Jesus is speaking theoretically and in general of those who align themselves against God's kingdom. The gist is that there is no middle ground. One must either align oneself with God or with Satan. Compare Manson, *Sayings*, p. 87: 'the situation is one where no man can be neutral. It is war to the knife between the Kingdom of God and the kingdom of Satan. Jesus is God's chosen instrument for the waging of that war. He who takes his place by the side of Jesus, takes his place in the army of God. He who ignores the summons, is reckoned to the enemy'.

Mk 9.40 (cf. Lk 9.50) has Jesus say this: 'For he who is not against us is for us' (cf. *P. Oxy.* 1224 fol. 2r° col. 1). This is not a variant of Mt 12.30 par. but a different saying. Whether or not either was

---

[49] E.g. Tob 3.17; 8.3; Jub. 10.7; 1 En. 10.4, 11–13; 13.1; 69.28; T. Levi 18.12; Rev 20.2; Aramaic Incantation Bowls 7.15; 14.1–2; 37.5–6; 42.5 (see the edition of C. D. Isbell, *Corpus of Aramaic Incantation Bowls*, SBLDS 17, Missoula, 1975).

[50] Cf. Irenaeus, *Adv. haer.* 5.22.1; Zahn, p. 460; and see on 4.1–2. Reference to a pre-historical fall of Satan from heaven (cf. Otto, pp. 97–103) seems very doubtful.

[51] ℵ 33 *pc* sy^hmg Or Ath add με at the end; so also Lk 11.23 ℵ*·2 C² L Θ Ψ 33 892 *pc* sy^s bo.

[52] Against Gundry, *Commentary*, p. 235, who takes Mt 11.30 to be a re-writing of Mk 9.40, and Lk 11.23 to draw upon Matthew.

[53] Relevant texts for comparison include Isa 13.14; 40.11; Jer 23.2; Ezek 34.13; Zech 13.7–9; Mt 26.31 par.; Jn 10.12.

[54] Cf. Job 39.12; Mt 3.12; 13.28–30.

proverbial,[55] McNeile, p. 177, was correct in observing that the two utterances—whose authenticity should probably be left open—are 'not contradictory, if the one was spoken to the indifferent about themselves, and the other to the disciples about some one else'. Compare Schweizer, *Matthew*, p. 287: 'Ecumenical openness ... and the unambiguous demand for a clear confession of Jesus ... are certainly compatible'.

31f. The argument of 12.22–30 has ended. Jesus, however, continues to speak. He drops his defensive posture and takes up the offensive. His words are warnings to those who have not accepted the import of what has just been said.

In Mark the saying about blasphemy appears after the parable of the strong man. In Luke it appears in 12.10, in the middle of a Q block that is characterized by catchword connexions (Lk 12.8–12). It seems that Matthew has followed Mark's order, even though he has also drawn upon Q's form of the logion.[56]

The origin of 12.31f. par., which probably once circulated in isolation, is exceedingly complex, this because so many other questions are involved. Is Mark's version primary, or is Q's? Are the two translation variants? What might Jesus have meant by 'Son of man'? Different answers have been returned to all these queries, and the issue is made no easier by the perhaps independent parallels in Gos. Thom. 44[57] and Did. 11.7.[58] Many modern scholars have assigned the saying to a Christian prophet.[59] Part of the reason for this is that the exaltation of the spirit congenially fits a prophetic setting. On the other hand, we are doubtful of the ease with which so many now attribute sayings to early Christian prophets (cf. Hill, *Prophecy*, pp. 160–85; Aune, pp. 233–45). And our own interpretation of 12.31–2 par. (see below) is consistent with a setting in the ministry of Jesus.[60] We are

---

[55] Cf. Bultmann, *History*, pp. 98, 102. Cicero, *Pro Ligario* 11, preserves a close parallel to both (see Fridrichsen, 'Wer nicht mit mir ist, ist wider mich' (v)). Note also *m. 'Abot* 1.13: 'He who does not add takes away'. For the antithesis between scattering and gathering see the saying of Hillel in *t. Ber.* 7.14 and *b. Ber.* 63a: 'When men gather, scatter, and when they scatter, gather'.

[56] But Tödt, pp. 118–19; Higgins, *JSM*, p. 130 (although contrast his later thoughts in *SMTJ*, pp. 85–7); and Hultgren (v), p. 102, all argue that Matthew preserves the Q context.

[57] 'Jesus said: Whoever blasphemes against the Father, it shall be forgiven him, and whoever blasphemes against the Son, it shall be forgiven him; but whoever blasphemes against the Holy Spirit, it shall not be forgiven him, either on earth or in heaven'. This appears to be a secondary development of the Q tradition. 'Son of man' and 'Holy Spirit' have given way to 'Father', 'Son', and 'Holy Spirit'. On the other hand, there seems to be at least indirect influence from Mark (probably via Matthew); for 'neither on earth nor in heaven' is a development of 'neither in this age nor the age to come', which appears in Mt 12.32, in dependence on the formulation in Mk 3.29.

[58] 'And every prophet speaking in the Spirit do not tempt or judge; for every sin will be forgiven, but this sin will not be forgiven'. This is closer to the Markan tradition than Q.

[59] E.g. Käsemann, *Questions*, pp. 99, 102; Boring (v), pp. 159–64.

[60] Cf. Dunn, *Spirit*, p. 52. Recall that P. W. Schmiedel, in his famous article on the 'Gospels', in *Encyclopaedia Biblica*, ed. T. K. Cheyne and J. S. Black,

therefore inclined to accept a dominical origin. This, however, is now probably a minority position.

διὰ τοῦτο λέγω ὑμῖν. Mk 3.28 has ἀμὴν λέγω ὑμῖν ὅτι (which is probably more primitive; cf. Pesch 1, pp. 216–17). διὰ τοῦτο* (cf. 12.27) is a Matthean favourite.[61] Here it functions to link the saying about blasphemy with the previous verses.

πᾶσα ἁμαρτία καὶ βλασφημία ἀφεθήσεται τοῖς ἀνθρώποις, ἡ δὲ τοῦ πνεύματος βλασφημία οὐκ ἀφεθήσεται. Compare Lev 24.16 and Gos. Nicodemus 4.3. Mk 3.28 has this: πάντα ἀφεθήσεται τοῖς υἱοῖς τῶν ἀνθρώπων τὰ ἁμαρτήματα καὶ αἱ βλασφημίαι, ὅσα ἐὰν βλασφημήσωσιν. If, as seems likely, Lk 12.10 (which is very different) is close to Q, then Mt 12.31 must depend wholly upon Mark—in which case Matthew has revised Mark's text so as to increase the parallelism between 12.31 and 32. Thus 'will be forgiven men' comes at the end of the first clause (just as 'will be forgiven him' will in v. 32a); and 'but blasphemy against the Spirit, etc.' is added in anticipation of v. 32b ('but whoever speaks against the Holy Spirit . . .'). The result is that Matthew's text alone has two antithetical couplets which stand in near synonymous parallelism:

31a Every sin and blasphemy will be forgiven men
31b Blasphemy against the Spirit will not be forgiven

32a A word against the Son of man will be forgiven
32b A word against the Holy spirit will not be forgiven

Matthew's Greek is also an improvement over Mark's, and Matthew's substitution of 'men' for 'the sons of men' helps avoid confusion with v. 32a, where blasphemy against the Son of man will be forgiven.

'Sins' are offences against fellow human beings, 'blasphemies' (see on 9.3) offences against God. That 'all sins and blasphemies will be forgiven men' is to be taken literally and considered a revolutionary utterance is exceedingly doubtful. The statement, which looks forward to the last judgement, is simply a way of declaring God's readiness to forgive.

Mt 12.31a = Mk 3.28 demands comparison with Lk 12.10a = Q. According to the former, 'all sins will be forgiven the sons of men'[62]; according to the latter, 'every one who speaks a word against the Son of man will be forgiven'. These two statements are almost certainly variants of the same Aramaic original, which was read in two different

London, 1899–1903, contended that the authenticity of Mt 12.31–2 was unassailable because creation by a Christian was unthinkable.

[61] It is very common in the LXX, often for 'al-kēn, as in Gen 10.9; 11.9 and Exod 5.8.

[62] 'Sons of men', a Hebraism common in the OT, appears in the NT elsewhere only in Eph 3.5.

ways.[63] Lindars, *Son of Man*, p. 35, has explained things in this way. Jesus said something close to this: *wěkol dî yōʾmar millâ lěbar ʾěnāš yištěbêq leh*.[64] Mark's tradition took the meaning to be: 'Every thing which one blasphemes, to mankind there will be forgiveness for it'. Q's tradition, however, understood the words to mean: 'And everyone who says a word against the Son of man, there will be forgiveness to him'. Translated thus, 'Son of man' inevitably came to be understood as a title, a self-referent for Jesus. But Jesus himself may have used the term generically, with or without particular reference to his own person.

This account of things is probably close to the truth. Jesus, one imagines, declared that God could forgive men all sorts of blasphemies and slanders and offences; but those who opposed the eschatological work of God's Spirit were pushing God's inclination to forgive past its limit.[65] Such an interpretation is consistent with Mark's Greek. It also agrees with Q's text if one can believe that 'Son of man' was originally intended to be generic.

The preceding analysis entails that Mt 12.31a (cf. Mk 3.28) and 12.32a (cf. Lk 12.10a = Q) are in fact doublets, two different versions of one saying. Matthew, however, does not seem to have given them the same meaning. 12.31 he will have understood along the lines indicated for stage I of the tradition. But because the evangelist constantly uses 'Son of man' as a title and exclusive self-referent, he must have construed v. 32a differently. See further below.

The notion that some sins are more grievous than others was a common Jewish conviction; see Davies, *PRJ*, pp. 254–5, on the distinction between sins done unwittingly and those done with a 'high hand', that is, deliberate sins. Also well-attested is the notion of an unforgivable sin (cf. 1 Sam 3.14; *ARN* 39). But the rabbis, who wondered much about Exod 20.7 ('The Lord will not hold him guiltless who takes his name in vain'), disagreed as to whether blasphemy was such a sin (cf. *Mek.* on Exod 20.7).

καὶ ὃς ἐὰν εἴπῃ λόγον κατὰ τοῦ υἱοῦ τοῦ ἀνθρώπου, ἀφεθήσεται αὐτῷ. ὃς δ' ἂν εἴπῃ κατὰ τοῦ πνεύματος τοῦ ἁγίου, οὐκ ἀφεθήσεται αὐτῷ οὔτε ἐν τούτῳ τῷ αἰῶνι οὔτε ἐν τῷ μέλλοντι. Compare Lev 19.22 (ἀφεθήσεται αὐτῷ); Isa 22.14 (οὐκ ἀφεθήσεται ὑμῖν); Acts 6.13 (λαλῶν ῥήματα κατά); and Josephus, *Ant.* 15.81 (κατὰ τἀνδρὸς Ἰωσήπου λόγον εἶπεν). Matthew's line draws upon Q

---

[63] So also Wellhausen, *Matthaei*, pp. 60–1; Schippers (v); Lindars (v). Gundry, *Commentary*, pp. 238–9 is almost alone in positing two originally independent logia.

[64] For a slightly different suggestion see Casey, p. 230. Note that in LXX Dan 3.96, ὃς ἂν βλασφημήσῃ εἰς translates the Aramaic, *dî-yēʾmar šāluh ʿal*. Cf. also Acts 6.11 with 6.13.

[65] O'Neill (v) conjectures that Jesus was not speaking of the Holy Spirit but of 'this spirit', namely, the spirit of forgiveness. His case, though interesting, is unduly conjectural.

(see Lk 12.10) and Mk 3.29. κατά + genitive* is Matthean, as is the increased parallelism vis-à-vis Mark and Luke. It is nonetheless possible that εἴπῃ κατά[66] comes from Q and that Luke's βλασφημέω comes from Mark. Matthew's contrast between 'this world' and 'the world to come' (cf. Mk 10.30; Mk 3.29 has: εἰς τὸν αἰῶνα ἀλλὰ ἔνοχός ἐστιν αἰωνίου ἁμαρτήματος) reminds one of rabbinic style (cf. SB 4/2, pp. 799–976).[67] Schlatter, p. 409, cited a parallel from *Tanḥuma* and translated it into the following Greek: οὔτε ἐν τῷ αἰῶνι τούτῳ οὔτε ἐν τῷ αἰῶνι τῷ ἐρχομένῳ.

Scholars have differed over the meaning of the antithesis between forgiveness for speaking against the Son of man and the lack of forgiveness for those blaspheming the Holy Spirit. With regard to Q, the following interpretations have been offered.

(i) The word was first formulated by the post-Easter community. It stated that those who had rejected Jesus the Son of man in his earthly ministry would be forgiven for that sin, but that they would not be forgiven if they spoke against the activity of the Spirit in post-Pentecost days.[68] A variant of this view was put forward by Bousset, p. 39: 'One may perhaps blaspheme the remote (sojourning in heaven) Son of Man, but not the presently active Spirit!' (ii) Opposition to Jesus perceived as only a man is forgivable;[69] but opposition to the Holy Spirit and its workings is not forgivable. In other words, sin born of ignorance can be pardoned, but wilful sin cannot be (cf. Cope, p. 39; Hill, *Matthew*, p. 218). (iii) Opposition to the church's preaching is forgivable if one subsequently repents; but once one has entered the church and tasted of the Holy Spirit, subsequent unbelief will not be forgiven (cf. Heb 6.4; 10.36; this is close to much patristic interpretation; see further below).

Turning from Q to Matthew, the latter could not have endorsed interpretation (i). There is no distinction in tenses (past for the pre-Easter time, present for the post-Easter time), and for the evangelist 'Son of man' is not simply a designation of the earthly Jesus. Moreover, where else does Matthew let off so lightly those who opposed Jesus during the pre-Easter epoch? (ii) cannot be excluded. Yet what invites the reader to equate speaking against the Son of man with sin born of ignorance? And does not (ii) owe something to the outdated idea that 'Son of man' indicates Jesus' nature as a human being? Interpretation

[66] A Semitism; see Black, p. 195 ('probably Aramaic in origin'). Cf. Dan 7.25.
[67] Note also Mk 10.30; Lk 20.34–5; 4 Ezra 4.2, 27; 6.9; 7.12, 50, 113; 8.1–2, 52; 2 Bar 44.11–13.
[68] Cf. Fridrichsen, 'Le péché' (v); Tödt, p. 119; Schulz, *Q*, pp. 246–50.
[69] Cf. Bengel, *ad loc.*: 'This is said in accordance with our Lord's apparent condition, inasmuch as He was then conversing with them on an equal footing.'

(iii) involves two different groups (the converted and the unconverted), which is awkward. It also has nothing to do with the broader Matthean context.

As it stands, Mt 12.32 has no obvious meaning. Perhaps we have here an example of a saying whose Greek form (with 'Son of man' used as a title for Jesus) misrepresents the Aramaic original. Because the sayings of Jesus were regarded as authoritative, some of the more obscure ones just might have been passed on out of respect for the tradition, even when they were not comprehended. On the other hand, one wonders whether Matthew, who so consistently eliminated the obscurities of Mark, would have included such in his Gospel (cf. p. 192). We remain stumped.

Exactly how the two-age contrast was understood at the end of the first century is unclear. Systematic statements come only later.[70]

The history of the interpretation of Mt 12.31–32 is one of tragic misapprehension. Did. 11.7 is fairly faithful to the tradition as it is found in the synoptics: 'And every prophet speaking by the Spirit you will not tempt or condemn; for all sins shall be forgiven, but this sin shall not be forgiven'. Here blasphemy against the Spirit is opposition to the Spirit's inspiration. Similar is Ambrose, *De spiritu sancto* 1.3.54, where the sin against the Holy Spirit is identical with denying the Spirit's dignity and power and attributing to Beelzebub the casting out of demons. Other, less credible identifications of the unpardonable sin include rejection of the gospel (Irenaeus, *Adv. haer.* 3.11.9), slander of God's servants (Gos. Bartholomew 5.4), and denial of Jesus' divine nature (Athanasius, *Ep. Serap.* 4.17). But the dominant idea in church history is that the sin against the Holy Spirit is the 'sin unto death' of 1 Jn 5.16, that is, post-conversion relapse (cf. Origen, *De prin.* 1.3.7).[71] Novatian, for example, argued that those who recanted the faith under torture had sinned against the Holy Spirit and were lost for ever. As Jerome (*Ep.* 42) observed, this does not take the synoptic context very seriously, for there it is unbelievers (at least in Matthew and Mark) who are running the risk of damnation. But Jerome's exegesis did not, unfortunately, steer the course of Christian discussion on the matter. Augustine, in his attempt to uphold God's desire to forgive all everything, devoted a whole sermon to the subject (*Serm.* 71) and affirmed that the text has to do with impenitence lasting until death; it is resistance of the Spirit throughout one's life.[72] His interpretation, which made blasphemy against the Spirit not a specific act but a state of enmity, and one possible for Christians, became quite influential.[73]

---

[70] For full discussion see Vögtle, *Zukunft*, pp. 47–66; also Dalman, *Words*, pp. 147–56.

[71] For a list of patristic texts see Aquinas, *Summa theologica*, 2a2ae, question 14.

[72] Augustine went on thus to characterize the Donatists!

[73] For further discussion see B. Tipson, 'A Dark Side of Seventeenth-Century

Much later, John Bunyan's *Grace abounding to the Chief of Sinners* shows us how Jesus' word could come to haunt and torment sensitive and pious souls, who agonized over the possibility that they had committed the unpardonable sin. Sadly, there have even been individuals who have taken their own lives, evidently persuaded that they, for some wrong thought to be the sin against the Holy Ghost, were beyond the pale of mercy (e.g. the English Puritan John Child).[74]

Jesus' statement that a certain sin will not be forgiven in the world to come was later taken by some to imply the possibility of other sins that could be forgiven after death (an idea also found in rabbinic literature: *t. Sanh.* 13.3; *b. Roš. Haš.* 16b–17a). Our text was thus one of the proofs of purgatory (cf. Augustine, *De civ. dei* 21.24; Gregory the Great, *Dial.* 4.39). Theologians up through the nineteenth century continued to discuss the issue, usually in connexion with 1 Pet 3.18–22 (cf. Calvin, *Inst.* 3.5.7).

33. The possible supposition that blasphemy (see 12.31) cannot really have eternally evil consequences, because it consists only of words, is now seemingly countered by a statement on the connexion between words and the inner life (cf. Schlatter, p. 410). To speak evil is to be evil. Those therefore who have spoken evil of Jesus have revealed their true character.

12.33 heads a small subsection, reminiscent of 7.16–20, which is tripartite. Three subjects are treated: trees and fruit (v. 33), words and the heart (vv. 34–5), and words and the judgement (vv. 36–7). Each subunit of the subsection is characterized by an ἐκ γάρ statement and by a couplet in perfect antithetical parallelism.

ἢ ποιήσατε τὸ δένδρον καλὸν καὶ τὸν καρπὸν αὐτοῦ καλόν. Compare 7.17 ('Thus every good [ἀγαθόν] tree makes good [καλούς] fruit') and Lk 6.43 ('For there is not a good [καλόν] tree making rotten fruit'). Matthew's sentence can mean either 'make the tree good and its fruit (will be) good' or, less probably, 'regard (or: declare) the tree as good and its fruit as good' (cf. Black, pp. 202–3, 302; BAGD, s.v., ποιέω, I.1.e.B; Hutton (v)).

ἢ ποιήσατε τὸ δένδρον σαπρὸν καὶ τὸν καρπὸν αὐτοῦ σαπρόν. This has been formulated so as to make it perfectly parallel to the preceding line. Compare 7.17 ('But a bad [σαπρόν] tree makes evil [πονηρούς] fruit') and Lk 6.43 ('Nor again does a bad [σαπρόν] tree make good fruit'). For Matthew, the Pharisees are like a bad tree, and the bad fruit they have produced is their blasphemy against the Holy Spirit.

English Protestantism: The Sin against the Holy Spirit', *HTR* 77 (1984), pp. 301–30. For Calvin's rejection of Augustine on this see *Inst.* 3.3.22.

[74] For brief but helpful theological reflections see Cranfield, *Mark*, pp. 141–3. Note also Melanchthon, *Loci communes* 25, and recall Kierkegaard's father's experience.

ἐκ γὰρ τοῦ καρποῦ τὸ δένδρον γινώσκεται. Compare 7.20 ('Thus you will know them by their fruits') and Ignatius, *Eph.* 14.2 ('The tree is manifest from its fruit'). There is a close parallel in Ecclus 27.6: 'The fruit discloses the cultivation of a tree; so the expression of a thought discloses the cultivation of a man's mind.' Lk 6.44 has this: 'For each tree is known by its own fruit'. Note the parallel construction in Mt 12.37a: ἐκ γάρ + genitive (+ subject) + verb.

34. γεννήματα ἐχιδνῶν. This harsh address, which prefaces a new thought, appears again in 3.7 (q.v.) and 23.33.

πῶς δύνασθε ἀγαθὰ λαλεῖν πονηροὶ ὄντες. Compare Tabula of Cebes 40.2 ('no good thing comes from evils') and the texts cited in the commentary on 7.16. πῶς also follows 'generation of vipers' in 23.33. For πῶς before δύναμαι see on 12.29.

ἐκ γὰρ τοῦ περισσεύματος τῆς καρδίας τὸ στόμα λαλεῖ. Compare 15.18 and see on 12.33. For the heart as a treasure see on 6.21. Lk 6.45 lacks τοῦ and τῆς and at the end has λαλεῖ τὸ στόμα αὐτοῦ. 'The mouth speaks' is common in Jewish sources (cf. Gen 45.12; Isa 1.20; 40.5; Dan 7.8; Rev 13.5; *m. Ned.* 1.4).

35. ὁ ἀγαθὸς ἄνθρωπος ἐκ τοῦ ἀγαθοῦ θησαυροῦ ἐκβάλλει ἀγαθά. Compare Gos. Thom 45. After θησαυροῦ Lk 6.45 has τῆς καρδίας προφέρει τὸ ἀγαθόν. For ἐκβάλλει (redactional) with 'treasure' see also Mt 13.52. 'Good treasure' appears in Deut 28.12: 'the Lord will open to you his good treasury (*'ôṣārô haṭṭôb*; LXX: τὸν θησαυρὸν αὐτοῦ τὸν ἀγαθόν) from the heavens'. Note also T. Asher 1.6–9, which speaks of 'the treasure of the inclination'.

καὶ ὁ πονηρὸς ἄνθρωπος ἐκ τοῦ πονηροῦ θησαυροῦ ἐκβάλλει πονηρά. Compare Gos. Thom. 45. Observe again the parallelism with the preceding line. Luke lacks ἄνθρωπος and ends with προφέρει τὸ πονηρόν.

36. Whether this line and the next are redactional[75] cannot be decided. Perhaps Matthew took the verses from the oral tradition (M).

λέγω δὲ ὑμῖν ὅτι. This notifies the reader that a new thought follows.

πᾶν ῥῆμα ἀργὸν ὃ λαλήσουσιν οἱ ἄνθρωποι ἀποδώσουσιν περὶ αὐτοῦ λόγον ἐν ἡμέρᾳ κρίσεως. Compare 5.21–6. On anacoluthon after πᾶς see BDF § 466.3. Schlatter, p. 411, cites for comparison *Sipre* Num 112: *lîtēn 'et-haḥešbôn lĕyôm haddîn.* For the idea that every single word is known to God see on 6.4. On the 'day of judgement' see on 10.15.

ἀργός (= ἀ + ἐργόν; LXX: 5) means 'idle' or 'useless' or 'careless' (cf. 20.3, 6) and appears elsewhere with λόγος (cf.

---

[75] ἀποδίδωμι*, ἡμέρα κρίσεως*, and γάρ* are often redactional.

Chrysippus, *Stoic.* 2.277; Josephus, *Ant.* 15.224). Is Deut 32.47 (MT: *dābār rēq*) in the background of Matthew's sentence?

37. ἐκ γὰρ τῶν λόγων σου δικαιωθήσῃ, καὶ ἐκ τῶν λόγων σου καταδικασθήσῃ. Because words come from the heart, the judgement of an individual will be according to his or her words. Compare 11.19; 15.11; and Lk 19.22. The words sound proverbial, and the change from the third person plural in the previous verse to the second person singular here may indicate the use of tradition.

AN EVIL AND ADULTEROUS GENERATION (12.38–45)

12.38–45 is Q material (cf. Lk 11.16, 24–6, 29–32) which in Matthew constitutes a testing story.[76] After Jesus is asked by the scribes and Pharisees for a sign, he responds with a speech which takes up three points, the first being the sign to 'this generation' (the sign of Jonah; 39–40), the second being the sayings about past generations (41–2), the third being the fate of 'this generation' (vv. 43–5; cf. Gnilka, *Matthäusevangelium* 1, p. 463).

Into the Q material Matthew has introduced four major changes. First, he has supplied an introduction resembling Mk 8.11. This makes Mt 12.38–42a a testing or conflict story (contrast Lk 11.29–32). Secondly, Matthew has explained the meaning of the sign of Jonah by inserting 12.40, which compares Jonah's three day and night ordeal to the time of Jesus' stay in the tomb. Thirdly, he has reversed the order of the verses about the men of Nineveh and the queen of the south (cf. Lk 11.31–2) so as to gather in one place the sayings on Jonah (just as in 11.1–19 he gathers into one place most of the sayings on John the Baptist). Fourthly, the evangelist has added a conclusion (v. 45c: 'so shall it be also with this generation') which makes explicit the relevance of the parable of the evil spirit to the preceding logia. In Matthew's mind 12.38–45 is clearly a unity.

12.38–45 would seem to contain what were originally three separate complexes. The sayings about the men of Nineveh and the queen of the south (vv. 41f. par.), which belonged together from the beginning, did not, according to the consensus of scholarly opinion, originally follow the pericope on the sign of Jonah.[77] Also, 12.43–5, on the return of the evil spirit, must at one time have been isolated. This means that with regard to the earlier stages of the tradition, 12.38–40, 41f., and 43–5 must be considered individually.

The two most difficult questions concerning 12.38–45 are, first, the interpretation of the sign of Jonah in the tradition and, secondly, the

---

[76] For a review of research on the passage see Edwards (v), pp. 6–24.

[77] Cf. Vögtle (v), p. 240. But see Higgins, *SMTJ*, pp. 101–7, who takes Lk 11.29–32 to be a unity.

relationship between Q and its Markan parallel, Mk 8.11–12. Taking the latter problem first, in Mark Jesus says that no sign will be given whereas in Q he declares that the sign of Jonah will be given. It is unlikely that we here have two different stories or sayings from the life of Jesus, although some[78] have thought so. Either, therefore, the Markan tradition eliminated the reference to Jonah[79] or the Q tradition added that reference.[80] A decision is difficult. But (i) the sign of Jonah, whatever its precise meaning, in effect amounts to a denial of the request for a sign; so Mark's text ('No sign shall be given') is really at one with Q's: both just as definitely refuse the request for a miraculous demonstration. Hence Mark can be seen as an *interpretation* of the Q text.[81] (ii) The sign of Jonah *may*, on the lips of Jesus, have been a reference to Jesus' own person.[82] If so, there is an intriguing parallel in Lk 17.20–1, where, in response to a question about the time of the kingdom's coming, Jesus announces that no sign shall be given and then adds: 'the kingdom of God is in your midst', words which are sometimes taken to refer to Jesus himself (αὐτοβασιλεία; cf. Kümmel, *Promise*, pp. 32–6). So both Mt 12.38–40 par. and Lk 17.20–1 can be interpreted as having had originally the same meaning: Jesus rejected miraculous 'proofs' and adverted instead to his own person and work (cf. also Mt 11.2–4 par.). (iii) Q material reproduced in Mark quite often appears in a shortened form (cf. Gnilka, *Markus* 1, p. 305). For these three reasons, then, we think it more probable than not that Q's version is pristine.

If this is the right conclusion, then one must ask what 'the sign of Jonah' originally meant. The interpretation in terms of Jesus' death and resurrection (Mt 12.40) is Matthean and almost certainly *ex eventu*. As for Lk 12.30, which refers to 'the Son of man in his generation', it might likewise be a secondary addition. We are thus reduced to making educated guesses. Was Jesus himself (see above) or his preaching the sign?[83] Was Jesus' deliverance from death in view?[84] In the light of

---

[78] E.g. Gundry, *Commentary*, p. 243.

[79] So Vögtle (v), pp. 103–5; Bayer, pp. 124–6.

[80] So Bousset, pp. 38–9; Pesch 1, p. 409.

[81] Bultmann, *History*, p. 118, n. 1, raised the possibility that Mark omitted the sign of Jonah because its meaning was unknown to him. Cf. Gnilka, *Markus* 1, p. 305. And according to Perrin, *Rediscovering*, pp. 192–3, 'Mark puts great emphasis upon the mighty deeds of Jesus as the only, but complete, demonstration of his messiahship, and it would be natural for him to omit the reference to some other sign, however that reference was to be understood'.

[82] For people as signs see Isa 8.18; 20.3; Ezek 24.24.

[83] So many, including Manson, *Sayings*, p. 90; and Schulz, *Q*, pp. 255–6. But what of the future tenses? Why '*will* be given' and 'the Son of man *will* be'? Are the futures logical, that is, in relationship to Jonah; or are they translations of Aramaic imperfects used for indefiniteness; or are they reasons to doubt the interpretation in terms of Jesus' person or preaching? Full review in Bayer, pp. 121–4.

[84] So e.g. Schlatter, p. 416; and Bayer (v). This solution has the advantage of being in harmony with Matthew's interpretation and the universal judgement of the Fathers. And no doubt the miracle of the whale was the outstanding event associated with Jonah; cf. Vögtle (v), pp. 111–15. Also not to be ignored— though it seemingly has been—is the Jewish tradition that Jonah, identified with

Mt 24.30 ('the sign of the Son of man in heaven'), should one think of the Son of man coming as judge?[85] Should the sign of Jonah be identified with the destruction of Jerusalem (so Schmitt (v), citing Liv. Proph. Jon. 11, where Jonah prophesies the fall of Jerusalem)? Or was the reference to Peter (who was known as *bar Jona*), perhaps to his confession (cf. Gale (v))? Or was some error made in the transmission of the material, Ἰωνᾶ being a mistake for Ἰωάννης (John the Baptist[86]) or for the Hebrew *yônâ* ('dove', the reference being to the dove at the baptism; cf. Howton (v))? Our suspicion is that the interpretation in terms of preaching or Christology is correct; but demonstration is another matter. Truly we have here a 'dark saying' (Chrysostom, *Hom. on Mt.* 43.2).

Mt 12.38–42 has a parallel in Mt 16.1–4. The latter, however, depends firstly upon the apophthegm in Mk 8.11–13, not Q. Thus 12.38–42 and 16.1–4 are doublets, one with its source in Q, the other with its source in Mark.

38. Jesus' speech in 12.22–37 has not made converts. The scribes and Pharisees do not want words but a stupendous miracle, validation of Jesus' lofty claims. Of course the irony here, from Matthew's perspective, is that Jesus has already worked more than enough miracles to persuade an open mind (cf. 11.2–4).

τότε ἀπεκρίθησαν αὐτῷ τινες τῶν γραμματέων καὶ Φαρισαίων λέγοντες. Mt 16.1 refers to the Sadducees and Pharisees, Mk 8.11 to the Pharisees alone, Lk 11.16 to 'others'. Q probably had no introduction to the saying about the sign of Jonah: in it Mt 12.39–42 par. probably followed directly the paragraph about the unclean spirit, Mt 12.43–5 = Lk 11.24–6. On the scribes and Pharisees see on 2.4 and 3.7. The motivation for adding 'the scribes' cannot be discerned, although it may be observed that 'scribes and Pharisees' (in this order) is a Matthean favourite

the son of the widow of Zarephath, was resuscitated by Elijah (1 Kgs 17). This folk belief is attested already in L. Proph. Jonah; see also Ginzberg, *Legends*, 4, p. 197; 6, p. 318. But against equating the sign of Jonah with Jesus' death and resurrection, two points are usually made. (1) Q may not have contained any allusions to the death and resurrection of Jesus. (2) In Q, Lk 11.29–30 par. was probably understood in terms of preaching (cf. Lk 11.32). To these two objections a third may be added. The book of Jonah nowhere tells us that the Ninevites knew that Jonah had been saved from a sea monster (but note 3 Macc. 6.8); so how could his deliverance have been a sign to them? Nonetheless, one still wonders whether the tradition about Jonah being resurrected has not at least effected Matthew's interpretation of the sign of Jonah.

[85] Cf. Bultmann, *History*, p. 118; Edwards (v), p. 86. Cf. 24.30. For objections see Manson, *Sayings*, p. 90 (arguing that the analogy between Jonah's preaching and the Son of man's judgement is not close), and Bayer, p. 139.

[86] Cf. Michael (v) and Moxon (v). Has anyone proposed that the sign of Jonah was baptism (as practised by John and perhaps by Jesus and his disciples)? If baptism could be compared with Noah's ark (1 Pet 3.18–22) and passing through the Red Sea (1 Cor 10.1–5), why not also with Jonah's experience?

(1, p. 77). Note that ἀποκρίνομαι (finite) + participle occurs five times in Matthew, four times in 25.9–45 (Mk: 1; Lk: 1; cf. LXX Gen 23.5; Dan 2.7).

διδάσκαλε. This has no parallel in the other accounts. For its significance see on 8.19.

θέλομεν ἀπὸ σοῦ σημεῖον ἰδεῖν. This is Matthean.[87] Compare Jn 6.30: 'Then what sign do you, that we may see, and believe you?' Mt 16.1; Mk 8.11; and Lk 11.16 all have 'a sign from heaven'[88], and all use the word, πειράζω, 'tempt'. For εἶδον with σημεῖον see Lk 23.8; Jn 4.48; 6.14, 26, 30; Rev 15.1.

Because they lack faith, the scribes and Pharisees want to see a 'sign'.[89] Just as Moses and Aaron did signs which moved Israel to belief (Exod 4.30–1), so should Jesus now prove that God is on his side by performing some spectacular marvel. If the pericope preserves an authentic memory, then Jesus' healings and exorcisms were not considered by some sufficiently singular or spectacular to constitute proof of his claims; so he was asked to do something more, to provide a sign whose import could not be doubted.[90] It is even possible that the request was not motivated by hostility but by a genuine desire to discover if Jesus might not be able to supply definitive proof of his status as eschatological prophet. See further on 16.1.

39. ὁ δὲ ἀποκριθεὶς εἶπεν αὐτοῖς. So also Mt 16.2. The words are editorial.

γενεὰ πονηρὰ καὶ μοιχαλὶς σημεῖον ἐπιζητεῖ. Compare 16.4 and Lk 11.29 (ἡ γενεὰ αὕτη γενεὰ πονηρὰ ἐστιν· σημεῖον ζητεῖ[91]). On the phrase, 'evil and adulterous generation', see on 11.16. It recalls the descriptions of the generation in the wilderness in Deut 1.35 and 32.5. Note also Jub. 23.14 ('an evil generation'); 1QSb 3.7 ('a generation of wickedness'); and the targum on Isa 57.3 ('people of a generation whose deeds are evil ... they are adulterous'). μοιχαλὶς (= 'adulterous')

---

[87] θέλω* + ἀπό: Mt: 3; Mk: 0; Lk: 0.

[88] One is reminded of the rabbinic requirement that a sign, as opposed to a wonder, be 'from heaven'; see SB 1, pp. 726–7.

[89] On σημεῖον (cf. ᾿ôt) see Linton (v); K. H. Rengstorf, TWNT 7 (1964), pp. 199–261; H. Remus, 'Does Terminology distinguish Early Christian from Pagan Miracles?', JBL 101 (1982), pp. 531–51; Bayer, pp. 111–14; and P. Ciholas, 'The Socratic and Johannine ΣΗΜΕΙΟΝ as divine Manifestation', PRS 9 (1982), pp. 251–65. In the OT 'sign' often means a proof of God's word or a prophet's word (cf. Exod 3.12; 1 Sam 10.7, 9; 14.10; 1 Kgs 13.3, 5; 2 Kgs 19.29; 20.8–9; Isa 7.11, 14; 38.22; Jer 44.29).

[90] The request is historically plausible; cf. Deut 13.1–5; Lk 23.8; Jn 2.18; SB 1, pp. 640–1, 726–7. Paul could write, 'Jews seek signs' (1 Cor 1.22); and we know from Josephus that certain individuals promised their followers the sight of spectacular demonstrations (e.g. Ant. 18.85; 20.97, 170).

[91] Is Luke's line the result of stylistic improvement?

appears only three times in the synoptics, each time as a qualifier of 'generation' (Mt 12.39; 16.4; Mk 8.38). It is used in its OT sense: 'faithlessness (to Yahweh)' (cf. Isa 52.3; Jer 3.10; Ezek 23; Hos 1–3; 5.3–4). Luke may well have dropped the word from Q because his Gentile readers would not have understood its meaning as applied to 'generation' (a combination, incidentally, not found in the OT). For σημεῖον with (ἐπι)ζητέω see 16.4; Mk 8.11–12; Lk 11.16, 29; and Schlatter, p. 415. As in 16.4 = Mk 8.12, Matthew has compounded the verb (ζητεῖ→ἐπιζητεῖ): 'seeks' has become 'demands'. This underlines the hostility in the question.

καὶ σημεῖον οὐ δοθήσεται αὐτῇ εἰ μὴ τὸ σημεῖον Ἰωνᾶ τοῦ προφήτου. So Lk 11.29, without 'the prophet' (a Matthean addition which stresses the prophetic significance of what happened to Jonah). The genitive may be appositive (Jonah himself is the sign) or it may qualify the sign as that experienced by Jonah. For δίδωμι with σημεῖον see LXX Isa 7.14. Here the passive, δοθήσεται, has God as its unnamed subject.

In the Lives of the Prophets, a first century A.D. Jewish composition, we find this: Jonah 'gave a sign (ἔδωκε τέρας) to Jews and to all the land: when they should see a stone crying aloud in distress, the end would be at hand; and when they should see all the Gentiles gathered in Jerusalem, the city would be razed to its foundations' (L. Proph. Jonah 8). This would seem to provide the closest parallel in ancient Jewish sources to the synoptics' 'sign of Jonah'. (Pirqe R. El. 1.10, in which the sailors see the 'signs' God did to Jonah, is much later.) It is, however, very difficult to imagine that a crying stone can have had anything to do with Jesus' reference to the sign of Jonah.

40. The sign of Jonah is now explained: just as Jonah was in the belly of the sea monster three days and three nights, so shall the Son of man be in the belly of the earth three days and three nights. Matthew's text seems to make explicit what is implicit in the speeches in Acts, namely, that the resurrection is God's one great sign to Israel (cf. Acts 2.24, 32, 36; 3.15; etc.).

ὥσπερ γὰρ ἦν Ἰωνᾶς ἐν τῇ κοιλίᾳ τοῦ κήτους τρεῖς ἡμέρας καὶ τρεῖς νύκτας, οὕτως ἔσται ὁ υἱὸς τοῦ ἀνθρώπου ἐν τῇ καρδίᾳ τῆς γῆς τρεῖς ἡμέρας καὶ τρεῖς νύκτας.[92] This is an interpretation of Lk 11.30 = Q ('For just as Jonah became a sign to the Ninevites,

---

[92] Stendahl, School, pp. 132–3, proposed that this whole line is a post-Matthean interpolation. (i) The quotation is purely LXX. (ii) Justin, Dial. 107 does not cite it when we would expect him to do so. (iii) The text makes sense without 12.40 (iv) The addition of 'the prophet' at the end of 12.39 indicates that Matthew was thinking about Jonah's prophetic preaching, not his underwater adventures. Cf. Cope, pp. 41–2. These four reasons do give us cause for thought; but they are hardly decisive, and together they do not overturn the unanimous testimony of the mss. and versions. Cf. Bayer, pp. 115–16.

so shall also the Son of man be to this generation').[93] Matthew has (i) increased greatly the synonymous parallelism of the two clauses, (ii) assimilated to LXX Jon 2.1 (whence ἦν . . . νύκτας), and (iii) added redactional vocabulary (ὥσπερ*, γάρ*, γῆ*). Note that there is no explicit reference to the deliverance of Jonah or to Jesus' resurrection. But the figure of three days and nights posits an end to the time in the earth and so suggests the resurrection. With τῇ καρδίᾳ τῆς γῆς compare LXX Jon 2.3 (κοιλίας ᾅδου) and Ecclus 51.5 (κοιλίας ᾅδου). The phrase stands in contrast to σημεῖον ἰδεῖν (one cannot see things under the earth) and thereby 'highlights the fact that the "sign" demanded and "sign" to be given . . . are diametrically opposed in nature' (Bayer, p. 143).

12.40, which Christian interpreters have sometimes seen as an allusion to Jesus' descent to Sheol and the harrowing of Hades,[94] exhibits what has been called by R. A. Edwards the 'eschatological correlative'.[95] Its form is: Protasis: no ὥσπερ, ὡς + verb in past or present tense// Apodosis: οὕτως (κατὰ τὰ αὐτά)+ ἔσται + Son of man. This form occurs in 12.40; 24.27, 37, 38–9; Lk 11.30; 17.24, 26, 28–30. In Edwards' judgement, the eschatological correlative is closely related to what Käsemann called 'sentences of Holy law' and should be assigned to the Q community. This seems unduly speculative. There are parallels in the Pentateuch (e.g. Deut 28.63), in the prophetic books of the LXX (e.g. Jer 38.28; Amos 3.12), and in Paul (e.g. Rom 5.19; 1 Cor 15.22, 49). We do not find an origin with Jesus improbable (cf. Aune, p. 169).

Jesus did not, according to Matthew's own narrative, stay in the tomb three days and three nights. This is not, however, good evidence for either a pre-Matthean or dominical origin for 12.40. The 'three days and three nights' comes straight from Jonah, and can we not allow Matthew some poetic licence? Further, ancient Jews often counted parts of days as wholes.[96] Certainly our verse can hardly be turned into the key to setting the day of Jesus' death.[97]

---

[93] In favour of Matthew preserving Q, one could argue that Luke dropped an inaccurate chronology (as did the *Gospel of the Nazaraeans*, according to the Zion Gospel edition, variant to Mt 12.40; see Hennecke 1, p. 148). But nowhere else in Q is there any explicit reference to the death and resurrection of Jesus; and the more concrete interpretation (Matthew) seems secondary over against the less concrete interpretation (Luke).

[94] Which is why in certain paintings Hades is a mouth with teeth: the mouth of Jonah's whale has supplied the imagery.

[95] Lit.: R. A. Edwards, 'The Eschatological Correlative as a Gattung in the New Testament', *ZNW* 60 (1969), pp. 9–20; D. Schmidt, 'The LXX *Gattung* 'Prophetic Correlative''', *JBL* 96 (1977), pp. 517–22; Higgins, *SMTJ*, pp. 100–7; Aune, pp. 168–9.

[96] Cf. 1 Kgs 20.29; Est 4.16–5.1; SB 1, p. 649.

[97] Though this was done by no less an authority than B. F. Westcott. For the implausible suggestion that three days and three nights refers to time in an earthly prison see N. Walker, 'The Alleged Matthean Errata', *NTS* 9 (1963),

41f. In Luke the saying about the queen of the South comes before the saying about the men of Nineveh. Luke probably preserves the order of Q.[98] Luke's arrangement maintains the historical sequence, and the Matthean order can be put down to a redactional motive: by moving v. 41 to first place, the sayings about Jonah are brought together.

Mt 12.41f. par. has sometimes been attributed not to Jesus but to a Christian prophet.[99] Possibly supportive of a post-Easter origin are the following observations. (i) The Ninevites and the queen of the South were Gentiles, and it is more typical of the church than of Jesus to present Gentiles in a positive light. (ii) The mention of 'wisdom' betrays a special interest of the Q community. (iii) The theme of the impenitence of Israel no doubt characterised post-Easter theology. However, neither individually nor collectively do these three points add up to any sort of proof, and there is much evidence on the other side (cf. Mussner (v)). Not only is there a very good parallel in the authentic 11.20–4 (where unbelieving Jews are judged and found wanting *vis-à-vis* Gentiles[100]) but the christological implications are left unpacked. Both πλεῖον and ὧδε remain unexplicated, indeed enigmatic (cf. 13.16–17 par.). Further, as Perrin wrote, 'The double saying has no earlier history in the tradition; the point at issue is the question of repentance in face of a challenge, certainly a major concern of the message of the historical Jesus; the reference to the queen of the South and the men of Nineveh are vividly apposite and absolutely in accord with Jesus' use of unlikely good examples in his comparisons (the Good Samaritan); and the element of warning in the saying coheres with a major aspect of the message of the parables' (*Rediscovering*, p. 195; cf. Catchpole (v), pp. 100–1). Also typical of Jesus is the absence of any sentimental archaism: the best is at hand, now is the day of salvation.

ἄνδρες Νινευῖται ἀναστήσονται ἐν τῇ κρίσει μετὰ τῆς γενεᾶς ταύτης καὶ κατακρινοῦσιν αὐτήν· ὅτι μετενόησαν εἰς τὸ κήρυγμα Ἰωνᾶ, καὶ ἰδοὺ πλεῖον Ἰωνᾶ ὧδε. Compare Jon 3.2; Mt 12.6. Lk 11.32 has exactly the same thing, so the line has been taken without alteration from Q.

ἄνδρες Νινευη appears in LXX Jon 3.5, for the Hebrew ʾanšê nînĕwēh (cf. *m. Taʿan.* 2.1). Obviously, ἄνδρες must here have generic sense; it means not 'men' but 'people'.

ἀναστήσονται probably refers to the resurrection. Some would

---

p. 393. (He thinks Jesus was in custody from Tuesday to Thursday.) For how the early church Fathers handled the problem (there were many different solutions) see H. Drobner, 'Three Days and Three Nights in the Heart of the Earth: The Calculation of the Triduum Mortis according to Gregory Nyssa', in *The Easter Sermons of Gregory of Nyssa*, ed. A. Spira and C. Klock, Cambridge, Mass., 1981, pp. 263–78.

[98] Cf. Bultmann, *History* p. 112; Mussner (v), p. 169 Contrast Correns (v), p. 92. Fitzmyer, *Luke 2*, pp. 931–2, seems undecided.

[99] See e.g. Käsemann, *Beginnings*, pp. 95–6. Contrast Boring, p. 153.

[100] Cf. also the Gentile pair in Lk 4.25–7.

argue that it means no more than 'they will appear' (cf. Mk 14.57), others that the sense is, 'they will rise up to dispute' (Black, p. 134; cf. Isa 54.17). But the verb is in the future tense, and ἐν τῇ κρίσει[101] and γενεᾶς ταύτης both have eschatological content. In addition, the scene painted presupposes a universal judgement, for it involves the Ninevites and the Israel of Jesus' time, as well as the queen of the South (cf. Kümmel, *Promise*, pp. 44, 89).

κατακρινοῦσιν (cf. 20.18; 27.3) here means, in effect, 'they will be the standard by which this generation will be condemned by God' (cf. Wisd 4.16; Heb 11.7). εἰς[102] can be taken in two different ways. It might be causal: '*because of* the preaching of Jonah' (BAGD, s.v., 6a). 'At', however, is also a possible translation: '*at* the preaching of Jonah' (so most English translations).

Who or what is the πλεῖον that is ὧδε? In the light of 12.6, where Jesus is πλεῖον than the temple, one supposes that Matthew thought of Jesus himself (cf. Jn 4.12; 8.53). This the connexion between 12.40 and 41 makes plain, for since Jonah and Jesus have been compared in v. 40, one wants to make the same comparison in v. 41. But the question is not so easily resolved with regard to the pre-Matthean tradition and Jesus himself. For 12.6 is redactional, and the connexion between vv. 40 and 41 is secondary. Moreover, πλεῖον is neuter. These facts have encouraged some to depart from Matthew's interpretation. Thus C. H. Dodd found a reference to the kingdom: it was ὧδε, that is, already present (*Parables*, p. 31). And R. H. Fuller, calling attention to Jonah's κήρυγμα, equated πλεῖον with the preaching of the kingdom (*Mission*, pp. 34–5). Perhaps, however, the different interpretations are not profitably distinguished. In the synoptic tradition the kingdom and its preaching are never separated from the person of Jesus. So can we not understand πλεῖον to cover the 'Christ-event' in general? That is, can it not be equated with the coming of the kingdom and its herald, Jesus?

The contrast Jesus draws between Nineveh's repentance and the faithlessness of Israel was probably a traditional Jewish theme. In *Mek.* on Exod 12.1, Jonah leaves the land of Israel with this excuse: 'For since the Gentiles are more inclined to repent, I might be causing Israel to be condemned'. Put otherwise, if the Israelites were to hear Jonah, they would show badly, for they, unlike the pagans, would not repent in sackcloth and ashes.

---

[101] Cf. LXX Ps 1.5 (οὐκ ἀναστήσονται ἀσεβεῖς ἐν κρίσει) and *m. Sanh.* 10.3, where the resurrection is the subject: '*ômdîn baddîn* ('they will rise in the judgement'); also *m. Sanh.* 10.4, where *qûm + bĕmišpāṭ* is used with eschatological sense.

[102] Never after μετανοέω in the LXX.

βασίλισσα νότου ἐγερθήσεται ἐν τῇ κρίσει μετὰ τῆς γενεᾶς ταύτης καὶ κατακρινεῖ αὐτήν· ὅτι ἦλθεν ἐκ τῶν περάτων τῆς γῆς
ἀκοῦσαι τὴν σοφίαν Σολομῶνος, καὶ ἰδοὺ πλεῖον Σολομῶνος ὧδε.
For the event that this refers to see 1 Kgs 10.1–13; 2 Chr 9.1–
12; Josephus, *Ant.* 8.165–73. Lk 11. 31 departs from Matthew's
line in only two respects: τῶν ἀνδρῶν appears after μετά, and
αὐτήν is accordingly αὐτούς. In all likelihood, the differences
should be ascribed to the First Evangelist. His desire for perfect
parallelism will have led him to drop τῶν ἀνδρῶν, which has no
counterpart in 12.41. On the other hand, Luke often inserts
ἄνδρες (Jeremias, *Lukasevangelium*, p. 204), so one can hardly
be certain. (Schulz, *Q*, p. 252, assigns τῶν ἀνδρῶν to Luke.)

The 'queen of the South' is the queen of Sheba, whose story
is told in the OT (see above). The OT knows her only as 'the
queen of Sheba', but 'the queen of the south' does occur in T.
Sol. 19.3 and 21.1. Note that, according to 1 Kgs 10.1, the
queen of Sheba came to Solomon 'to test him with hard
questions.' So like the Pharisees she tested a king. But unlike
them, she could see the truth.

43–5. What is the proper interpretation of vv. 43–5? Several
suggestions have been made. (i) The verses constitute 'a warning about
the future: Jesus' own generation, now purified by his ministry, is
menaced by a greater power of evil' (Hill, *Matthew*, p. 221). (ii) It is
not enough to drive out a demon. The space it vacates must be filled
with God. If not, the last state will be worse than the first (so Manson,
Sayings, pp. 87–8; cf. Irenaeus, *Adv. haer.*1.16.3). (iii) According to
Gundry, *Commentary*, p. 246: 'The unclean spirit . . . [is] a figure of
the evil that characterizes the generation of the scribes and Pharisees.
Correspondingly, the period of the unclean spirit's absence . . . [is] a
figure of the apparent righteousness of the scribes and Pharisees; and
the return of the unclean spirit with seven others worse than himself
. . . represent[s] an outburst of multiplied evil on the part of the
scribes and Pharisees, an outburst that will falsify their righteousness
. . .'. (iv) In Fenton's judgement, 'the possessed man stands for *this
generation* of the Jews; the exorcism is the ministry of Jesus; the
emptiness of the man is the unbelief and unrepentance of the Jews; and
their *last state* is their condemnation at the last judgement'. (v) Jesus
defended his own success as an exorcist by remarking on the consistent
failure of other exorcists (cf. Harvey, *Jesus*, p. 109). (vi) Many of the
Church Fathers read the text as an allegory. For instance, Hilary of
Poitiers, in his commentary on Matthew, found a little three stage
history of the Jews. Equating the unclean spirit with the devil, he
argued that Israel was in Satan's power until the coming of the law,
that after Sinai Satan's power was broken and so he went to the
Gentiles, and that he finally returned to the Jewish people after they
rejected the Messiah.

In sorting through these and other interpretative possibilities, we
must distinguish the three stages of the gospel tradition. At stage I, the

life of Jesus,[103] 12.43–5 was not so much a parable as a straightforward warning to people who, although they had benefited from the ministry of healing and exorcism, had failed to embrace Jesus' teaching (cf. the parable of the ten lepers in Lk 17.11–19). Jesus surely helped many people who had doubts about much in his message; and from his point of view, they were enjoying the fruit (the healings and exorcisms) while rejecting the tree (his own person). Jesus saw fit to warn them that unless they entered the kingdom of which he spoke, they risked finding themselves back where they had been in the first place, subject to the prey of evil forces (cf. Jn 5.14).

With regard to the interpretation of Q, the one clue is the juxtaposition with the Beelzebul pericope. What does this imply? One could postulate a simple thematic connexion: both pericopae concern exorcism. But there may well be more. Lk 11.19 par. refers to the (successful) exorcisms of others besides Jesus. This fact has often troubled Christian exegetes, and it may have troubled a contributor to Q. If so, the story of the returning demon could have been put where it is in order to reflect the conviction that Jesus' exorcisms alone were truly efficacious: when others cast out demons, the demons typically returned.

Concerning Matthew's understanding of 12.43–5, the key, in our judgement, is the line, 'and the last things are worse than the first'. The wider context is Jesus' relationship to 'this generation', and what has happened is that unbelief has won out. Jesus has not converted Israel. What follows? From those to whom much has been given much will be required. Israel has had the opportunity to see and hear one greater than Jonah and one greater than Solomon. All to no avail. Therefore her judgement will be the harsher (cf. Heb 10.28–9). Indeed, given her response, she would have been better off in ignorance. So her last state will be worse than the first. The rejection of Jesus and his kindly deeds, his exorcisms, can only bring, in Matthew's eyes, unprecedented evil (cf. Zahn, p. 472; Hummel, pp. 126–7).

ὅταν δὲ τὸ ἀκάθαρτον πνεῦμα ἐξέλθῃ ἀπὸ τοῦ ἀνθρώπου, διέρχεται δι' ἀνύδρων τόπων ζητοῦν ἀνάπαυσιν καὶ οὐχ εὑρίσκει. τότε λέγει. Compare Josephus, *Ant.* 15.200 (ἄνυδρον διερχομένοις). Lk 11.24 lacks δέ[104] and has at the end μὴ εὑρίσκον λέγει. Matthew's τότε increases the parallelism with 12.45.

For 'unclean spirit' see on 10.1. ἐξέλθῃ is probably an Aramaism and serves for the passive: the demon has been driven out by an exorcist (cf. Lk 11.14). The articles before ἀκάθαρτον πνεῦμα and

---

[103] Bultmann, *History*, p. 164, observing that the passage 'does not seem to be a community construction', called attention to certain Arabic proverbs and suggested: 'perhaps it is taken from some Jewish writing'. But what stands in the way of attribution to Jesus?

[104] Matthew has probably added this in order to underline the contrast with the Ninevites and the queen of the South.

ἀνθρώπου are generic. ἄνυδρος[105], which means 'waterless', appears four times in the NT: Mt 12.43; Lk 11.24; 2 Pet 2.17; Jude 12. For spirits or demons in the desert or uninhabited places see on 4.1. The dislike of water by demons may be presupposed in 8.28–34 (q.v.).

The demon finds no rest in isolation because it is its nature to torment others. Evil always seeks to enlarge itself.

εἰς τὸν οἶκόν μου ἐπιστρέψω ὅθεν ἐξῆλθον. In Lk 11.24 ὑποστρέφω (Mt: 0; Mk: 0; Lk: 21) is used and appears in first place. For the possibility of a demon returning to the person he has been expelled from see Mk 9.25; Josephus, Ant. 8.47; Philostratus, VA 4.20; Acts Thom. 46. For a person as the home or house of Satan or a demon see T. Naph. 8.6; b. Giṭ. 52a. Caird, Luke, p. 155 comments: 'the spiritual world, like the natural, abhors a vacuum'.

καὶ ἐλθὸν εὑρίσκει σχολάζοντα σεσαρωμένον καὶ κεκοσμημένον.[106] So Lk 11.25, without σχολάζοντα,[107] a Matthean addition which stresses that, after the demon was expelled, nothing good took its place.[108] The heart, though swept[109] and decorated,[110] remained empty. As it stands, our text seems to make the demon's return and victory inevitable: 'and coming he finds, etc.' One expects a conditional. But the NT not infrequently substitutes parataxis for the conditional (BDF § 471.3), and this may well explain 44b. Perhaps one could translate: 'and if, upon coming, he finds ... then in that case he will go ...'.[111]

τότε πορεύεται καὶ παραλαμβάνει μεθ' ἑαυτοῦ ἑπτὰ ἕτερα πνεύματα πονηρότερα ἑαυτοῦ. Lk 11.26 lacks μεθ' ἑαυτοῦ and moves ἑπτά to the end.[112]

καὶ εἰσελθόντα κατοικεῖ ἐκεῖ. Lk 11.26 agrees.

καὶ γίνεται τὰ ἔσχατα τοῦ ἀνθρώπου ἐκείνου χείρονα τῶν πρώτων. Compare 2 Pet 2.20. This was taken without alteration from Q, as the perfect agreement in Lk 11.26 proves. The words sound proverbial (cf. 27.64; Jn 5.14).[113]

---

[105] Most often for ṣiyyâ in the LXX, where it never qualifies τόπος. But there is a parallel in Josephus, C. Ap. 2.25: ἀνύδρῳ τόπῳ.

[106] σχολαζοντα και is found in ℵ C* 565ᵛⁱᵈ 1424 al it.

[107] σχολάζω (Mt: 1; Mk: 0; Lk: 0) here means 'be unoccupied' (so BAGD, s.v.). In LXX Exod 5.8, 17 and Ps 45.10 it translates a form of rāpâ.

[108] Plummer, p. 185, n. 2: 'Matthew may have added it to make a triplet'.

[109] σαρόω is a late form of σαίρω. Cf. Lk 15.8.

[110] For κοσμέω with this sense see LXX 2 Chr 3.6; Philo, Deus Imm. 150; Lk 21.5; and Horsley 4, p. 15. The word can also mean 'set in order' (cf. Mt 25.7).

[111] Cf. syˢ·ᶜ and see Jeremias, Parables, pp. 197–8, citing Nyberg (v) and Beyer, pp. 259–86.

[112] The final placement of ἑπτά is Lukan; cf. Jeremias, Lukasevangelium, p. 202.

[113] Only here in the synoptic tradition are demons the cause of moral evil;

οὕτως ἔσται καὶ τῇ γενεᾷ ταύτῃ τῇ πονηρᾷ. Compare Lk 11.30. There is no true Lukan parallel. Although one could argue that the Third Evangelist dropped the words, their addition by Matthew seems more likely.[114] By recalling 12.39 ('an evil and adulterous generation'), our line links 12.43–5 to the pericope about the sign of Jonah and thus helps establish the unity of 12.38–45.

There is no reason to think that 12.45b should call any particular occurrence to mind, although interpreters have, from time to time, identified the last things that are worse than the first with the fall of Jerusalem and its aftermath or with the state of Judaism since the resurrection. It seems preferable to think less concretely of the sorry state of 'this generation' in general, that is, the sorry state of those who rejected the proclamation of Jesus and the proclamation of the church (cf. Gnilka, *Matthäusevangelium* 1, pp. 468–9).

JESUS' TRUE FAMILY (12.46–50)

At this point in his composition our author has exhausted most of Q, save (with a few exceptions) the saying he wants to use in chapters 18 and 23–5. So he now turns back to Mark. And having employed everything before Mk 3.31 which he wishes to use, he here naturally reproduces the correction story in Mk 3.31–5 (cf. Lk 8.19–21, which *follows* the parable of the sower). For its function in 11.1–12.50 as a whole see Excursus IX.

In Mark, the biographical apophthegm in 3.31–5 is introduced by this: 'and the crowd came together again, so that they could not even eat. And when his family heard it, they went out to seize him, for people were saying, "He is beside himself"' (3.20–21). Matthew has omitted these verses, probably because he found them potentially offensive. How could the Mary[115] of Mt 1.18–25 have thought Jesus mad? The omission reduces the tension between Jesus' physical family and his spiritual family; and this permits the presence of the family in 12.46–50 to serve 'more as a catalyst rather than a contrast' (Brown et al. (v), p. 99). Even if—and this is very far from certain—in Mark or the pre-Markan tradition, Mk 20f., 31–5 functioned as 'a polemic against a kind of caliphate' (Schweizer, *Mark*, p. 87), such an interpretation is far removed from Matthew's narrative, which is 'free from any harsh feelings' (John Climacus, *Scal.* 3).

---

[113] Demons typically cause only sickness or physical problems. But the idea that they cause moral evil seems to have been common enough in Judaism, being particularly prominent in the Testaments of the Twelve Patriarchs.

[114] Cf. Strecker, *Weg*, p. 103. οὕτως ἐστίν, ἦν, ἔσται: Mt: 13; Mk: 2; Lk: 3.

[115] Mary is not named in Mk 3.21; but when Mk 3.31–5 is brought into account, she most probably belongs to οἱ παρ' αὐτοῦ, 'his family'.

46. ἔτι δὲ αὐτοῦ λαλοῦντος τοῖς ὄχλοις. For similar formulations see LXX Dan 9.21; Mk 5.35; Josephus, *Ant.* 8.282. There is no parallel in Mark or Luke and the line is accordingly redactional. Compare 9.18 and 17.5 diff. Mk 9.7. ὄχλος appears in Mk 3.32. In Matthew the word has become plural (see on 4.25) and is moved forward so as to give notice from the beginning of a new audience. Jesus is no longer addressing the Jewish leaders (as he was in 12.22–45) but the crowds. Thus we pass from controversy narratives to what amounts to an invitation (cf. 11.25–30). Note the parallel with 12.1–21, where again two controversy stories are followed by a pericope about the crowds.

ἰδοὺ ἡ μήτηρ καὶ οἱ ἀδελφοὶ αὐτοῦ εἰστήκεισαν ἔξω ζητοῦντες αὐτῷ λαλῆσαι. Matthew has abbreviated Mk 3.31–2a, added ἰδού* (see on 1.18 and 3.16), placed 'mother' before 'brothers' (no doubt to increase the parallelism with vv. 47, 48, and 49), and, in general, rewritten Mk 3.31 so as to set Mt 12.46b and 47b in almost perfect parallelism.

It makes sense for Mk 3.31 to mention people 'standing outside', for Jesus is in a house (cf. 3.20f.). But Matthew has failed to tell us what Mark has told us (cf. Lk 8.20). That is, in abbreviating his source, he has neglected to inform us what 12.46 evidently assumes, namely, that Jesus is inside.[116] This is an example of imperfect editing, and evidence for the priority of Mark.

On the brothers and sisters of Jesus see on 13.55.

47. εἶπεν δέ τις αὐτῷ.[117] Instead of a crowd, as in Mk 3.32 (καὶ λέγουσιν αὐτῷ), here an individual speaks.

ἰδοὺ ἡ μήτηρ σου καὶ οἱ ἀδελφοί σου ἔξω ἑστήκασιν ζητοῦντές σοι λαλῆσαι. The differences from Mk 3.32 are accounted for by Matthew's desire to make vv. 46b and 47b analogous.

48. ὁ δὲ ἀποκριθεὶς εἶπεν τῷ λέγοντι αὐτῷ replaces Mark's καὶ ἀποκριθεὶς αὐτοῖς λέγει.

τίς ἐστιν ἡ μήτηρ μου καὶ τίνες εἰσὶν οἱ ἀδελφοί μου; So Mark, with either καί (so NA[26]) or ἤ (HG) for καὶ τίνες εἰσίν.

Pace Fenton, p. 206, there is no good reason to speculate that the relatives of Jesus stand for the whole of Israel.[118]

[116] Although one could conceivably argue that those standing ἔξω are not outside a house but outside the ring of people around Jesus. (But what of 13.1?)
[117] ℵ* B L T *pc* ff¹ k sy^{s.c} sa omit this and the rest of the verse. But it is not an interpolation (*pace* Verseput, p. 284). (i) There are differences between 12.47 and its synoptic counterparts. (ii) Accidental omission is a good hypothesis, given that both vv. 46 and 47 end with λαλῆσαι. (iii) V. 48 does not follow well upon v. 46: who is 'the one speaking to him'?
[118] Mt 12.48 was evidently exploited in the interests of a docetic Christology. 'Who is my mother and who are my brothers?' was used to affirm that Jesus

49. Jesus stretches forth his hand toward his disciples and declares that they are his mother and brothers. The words do not dissolve family bonds but rather relativize them. They do this by revealing that there are even stronger bonds.

καὶ ἐκτείνας τὴν χεῖρα αὐτοῦ ἐπὶ τοὺς μαθητὰς αὐτοῦ εἶπεν. This is rather different from Mk 3.34: 'And looking about at those sitting around him in a circle, he says'. Matthew likes ἐκτείνω (Mt: 6; Mk: 3; Lk: 3)[119] and he always omits Mark's use of περιβλέπομαι (Mt: 0; Mk: 6; Lk: 1). Further, in accordance with his ecclesiastical standpoint, the evangelist wants to make it perfectly clear that Jesus is referring to his disciples, not to the crowds.[120]

ἰδοὺ ἡ μήτηρ μου καὶ οἱ ἀδελφοί μου. So also Mk 3.34, with ἴδε. Compare 12.2 diff. Mk 2.24; 24.23 diff. Mk 13.21.

The elevation of one's spiritual family over one's physical family is found elsewhere in ancient Judaism. Already in Deut 33.9 Levi is commended for saying 'of his father and mother, "I regard them not"'. The Essenes in particular seem to have thought of their community as a replacement for the traditional family (cf. 1QS 1–9; Josephus, *Bell.* 2.120–58). For Jesus, the break with family was probably spurred on by both personal experience and eschatological expectation (see on 10.34–7). The kingdom demanded all of Jesus and those who followed him. This is why Jesus was 'a eunuch for the kingdom of heaven' (19.12). See further Hengel, *Leader*, pp. 13–15.

50. The relationship between 12.50 = Mk 3.35 to the pericope it concludes has been variously assessed. Dibelius, *Tradition*, pp. 57, 63–4, argued that Mk 3.35 should be considered a clarifying addendum to 3.31–4 (cf. Best (v), p. 315). Bultmann, on the other hand, proposed that Mk 3.35 was one of the sources from which 3.31–4 was spun, and that the saying could not be regarded as dominical (*History*, pp. 29, 143). But against Dibelius and Bultmann, it is not so obvious that Mk 3.35 could have circulated in isolation: most of its impact stems from the presence of Jesus' relatives (cf. Pesch 1, p. 222). Hence we cannot exclude the possibility that Mk 3.31–5 is more or less a unified pericope, perhaps with an historical basis (cf. Taylor, *Mark*, p. 245; Lk 11.27–8). Certainly 3.35 harmonizes with Jesus' eschatological outlook (cf. on 10.34–7) as well as with his hard sayings about the family (e.g. 8.22).

ὅστις γὰρ ἂν ποιήσῃ τὸ θέλημα τοῦ πατρός μου τοῦ ἐν οὐρανοῖς. So Mk 3.35, with ὅς and τοῦ θεοῦ. 'My Father in heaven' is characteristic of Matthew.

This is the only line in 12.46–50 in which 'father' is used. Some

---

was not born, that he had no parents or siblings; see Tertullian, *Adv. Marc.* 4.19; *De carne Christi* 7.

[119] Perhaps because it is so often used of Moses (and Aaron) in Exodus (cf. Exod 4.4; 8.16; 9.22, 23, etc.).

[120] *Pace* Gundry, *Commentary*, p. 249, who identifies the crowds with the disciples.

would take this to reflect an historical fact: by the time of his public ministry, Jesus' father, Joseph, was dead. While this inference is probably correct, the omission also makes a theological point. There is, as 23.9 states so plainly, only one father in the new Christian family, namely, God.

αὐτός μου ἀδελφὸς καὶ ἀδελφὴ καὶ μήτηρ ἐστίν. Compare Lk 11.28. Mk 3.35 begins with οὗτος ἀδελφός μου but otherwise agrees.

Mk 3.35 = Mt 12.50 is well attested outside the synoptics. It could lie behind Jn 15.14: 'You are my friends (φίλοι) if you do what I command you'. Note also 2 Clem. 9.11: 'For the Lord said: My brothers are those who do the will of my Father'.[121] This last is very close to Clement of Alexandria, *Ecl. proph.* 20: 'For my brothers, the Lord said, and fellow heirs are those doing the will of my Father'. While there is no reason to think that Jn 15.14; or 2 Clem. 9.11; or Clement of Alexandria, *Ecl. proph.* 20 must depend upon the synoptics, Gos. Eb. frag. 5 (= Epiphanius, *Haer.* 30.14.5) is different; for it contains a narrative setting which clearly recalls Matthew: 'Who is my mother and who are my brethren? And he stretched forth his hand towards his disciples and said: These are my brethren and mother and sisters, who do the will of my Father' (Hennecke 1, p. 158).

There is also a version of Mt 12.46–50 par. in Gos. Thom. 99: 'The disciples said to him: Your brothers and your mother are standing outside. He said to them: those who are here, who do the will of my Father, they are my brothers and my mother; these are they who shall enter the kingdom of my Father'. The last clause, which has no synoptic parallel, is an addition. It does, however, recall Clement of Alexandria, *Ecl. proph.* 20 ('fellow heirs'). For the rest, Thomas 99 (i) is shorter than its synoptic counterparts; (ii) has the disciples, not the crowd or an anonymous man, inform Jesus of his family's presence; (iii) agrees with Luke in lacking the question, 'Who is my mother and who are my brothers?'; (iv) agrees again with Luke in failing to mention Jesus' sister(s); (v) goes against all three synoptics in initially mentioning 'brothers' before 'mother'; and (vi) agrees with Matthew in having 'do the will of my Father' instead of 'do the will of God' (cf. 2 Clem. 9.11; Clement of Alexandria, *Ecl. proph.* 20; Gos. Eb. frag. 5). Only the last fact might cause one to raise the issue of dependence on the synoptics.

(v) *Concluding Observations*

(1) 12.22–50 tells us something about Matthew's understanding of faith. In 12.22–37 Jesus' ministry of exorcism is subject to two radically different interpretations. That is, the one undeniable fact is ambiguous and capable of bearing antithetical

---

[121] See Donfried, pp. 73–4, who thinks 2 Clement has used a source which was influenced by both Matthew and Luke.

meanings. How, then, does one get to the truth? The text implies that there are good reasons for embracing one view of Jesus rather than another (12.25–39). Yet Matthew also knows that rational persuasion has its limitations, as becomes clear in 12.33–7 and 38–45.[122] Thus, even though the sign of Jonah, which is the resurrection of Jesus, will be made known to 'this generation', people will not believe. Why not? The answer lies in Matthew's evaluation of Jesus' hearers. They belong to 'an evil and adulterous generation' (12.39). Now whether or not this be a fair estimation of Jesus' contemporaries, it remains true that faith for Matthew has a moral dimension. Faith cannot abide with ill-will and disagreeable natures; for good fruit cannot be found on a bad tree (12.33). In accordance with this, the confession of Jesus as the Messiah is in the last analysis not a question of right understanding but of a good heart (so Hummel, p. 127). Despite Socrates, sin is more than ignorance. Even scriptural knowledge will not save if the heart is corrupt. This is why the obstinate scribes and Pharisees, who refuse to accept Jesus on any but their own terms, cannot accept him at all. Blinded by their sin they cannot grope their way towards the truth. Made closed-minded by hard hearts they fail to recognize the Messiah when he meets them face to face.

(2) 12.22–45 proclaims the presence of salvation and underlines the unprecedented opportunity of the present time (cf. Gnilka, *Matthäusevangelium* 1, p. 468). The kingdom of God has come. The domain of Satan has been plundered. One greater than Jonah and Solomon has appeared. And a spectacular and unrivalled sign has been given to all—Jesus' resurrection. Hence God has, in his Son (cf. 11.25–30), spoken louder than ever before. It follows that *now* is the day of salvation in a sense untrue of any past moment. And it is not surprising that failure to hear and respond in the present means that 'the last things become worse than the first'. For the greater the opportunity missed, the greater the loss suffered.

(3) In 4.21–2 James and John leave their father when Jesus calls them to discipleship. In 8.22 Jesus tells a follower that he should not attend to his father's burial but should rather 'leave the dead to bury their own dead'. And in 10.34–7 it is foretold that those who further the gospel will find themselves opposed by their own family members. The picture drawn by these texts is rather disturbing. Faith in Jesus would seem to entail, at best, a loosening of family ties, at worst renunciation of one's parents

---

[122] Cf. Hummel, p. 127: Matthew is not, despite his love for proof texts, a rationalist.

and siblings.[123] Admittedly, this hard truth is understandable given Matthew's view of things. If faith matters above all else, then whatever hinders faith must be forsaken. Still, the circumstance is not a happy one, and just understanding its necessity might not bring much consolation. What will bring consolation, however, is the fact that the leaving behind of one's natural family will coincide with adoption into another family, and this is in large part the message of Mt 12.46–50. Although religious commitments may well weaken family ties, the disciple will not thereby be left alone, without a family. Rather, the Christian will join the household of faith, the church, in which there is a father (God) and in which there are many brothers and sisters (cf. 23.8). Thus Jesus' demand to forsake family is only made in view of the Christian family which awaits new members with open arms.[124] It is not a call to a solitary existence.

(v) *Bibliography*

Aune, pp. 240–2.

B. W. Bacon, 'What was the Sign of Jonah?', *Biblical World* (Chicago) 20 (1902), pp. 99–112.

Barrett, *Spirit*, pp. 53–65, 103–7.

Bayer, pp. 110–45.

Beasley-Murray, pp. 75–80, 108–11, 252–7.

E. Best, 'Mark iii. 20, 21, 31–35' *NTS* 22 (1976), pp. 309–19.

E. Boring, 'How may We identify Oracles of Christian Prophets in the Synoptic Tradition? Mark 3.28–29 as a Test Case', *JBL* 91 (1972), pp. 501–21.

idem, 'The Unforgivable Sin Logion Mark III 28–29/Matt XII 31–32/Luke XII 10: Formal Analysis and History of the Tradition', *NovT* 18 (1976), pp. 258–79.

C. R. Bowen, 'Was John the Baptist the Sign of Jonah?', *AJT* 20 (1916), pp. 414–21.

Brown, *Mary*, pp. 51–9, 98–9.

Carlston, pp. 16–21, 66–9, 129–36.

D. R. Catchpole, 'The Law and the Prophets in Q,' in Hawthorne, pp. 95–109.

B. Chilton, 'A Comparative Study of Synoptic Development: The Dispute between Cain and Abel in the Palestinian Targums and the Beelzebul Controversy in the Gospels', *JBL* 101 (1982), pp. 553–62.

---

[123] The complete break with one's family came to be the usual rule for monks and other religious; see e.g. Basil, *Reg. brev.* 190; Symeon the New Theologian, *Cat. Disc.* 7. Matthew's text does not go so far. One supposes that, for the evangelist, dissolution is required only when one's family opposes one's faith.

[124] Cf. Corp. Herm. 1.31–2, where God is the father and the enlightened are his sons and each others' brethren. Note also Rom 8.12–7. Sociologists would refer to a 'fictive kinship group'.

C. Colpe, 'Der Spruch von der Lästerung des Geistes', in Lohse, *Ruf*, pp. 63–79.

Cope, pp. 32–52.

L. Cope, 'Matthew 12.40 and the Synoptic Source Question', *JBL* 92 (1973), p. 115.

D. Correns, 'Jona und Salomo', in *Wort in der Zeit*, ed. W. Haubeck and M. Bachmann, Leiden, 1980, pp. 86–94.

Crossan, *Aphorisms*, pp. 47–50, 184–91.

B. R. Doyle, 'A Concern of the Evangelist: Pharisees in Matthew 12', *AusBR* 34 (1986), pp. 17–34.

Dunn, *Spirit*, pp. 44–53.

B. S. Easton, 'The Beelzebul Sections', *JBL* 32 (1913), pp. 57–73.

R. A. Edwards, *The Sign of Jonah in the Theology of the Evangelists and Q*, SBT 2/18, London, 1971.

O. E. Evans, 'The Unforgivable Sin', *ExpT* 68 (1957), pp. 240–4.

L. R. Fisher, '"Can this be the Son of David?"', in *Jesus and the Historian*, ed. F. T. Trotter, Philadelphia, 1968, pp. 82–97.

G. Fitzer, 'Die Sünde wider den Heiligen Geist', *TZ* 13 (1957), pp. 161–82.

A Fridrichsen, 'Le péché contre le Saint-Esprit', *RHPR* 3 (1923), pp. 367–72.

idem, *The Problem of Miracle in Early Christianity* (trans. of *Le problème du miracle dans le christianisme primitif*, 1925), Minneapolis, 1972, pp. 102–10.

idem, 'Wer nicht mit mir ist, ist wider mich', *ZNW* 13 (1912), pp. 273–80.

A. Fuchs, *Die Entwicklung der Beelzebulkontroverse bei der Synoptikern*, SUNT B5, Linz, 1979.

H. M. Gale, 'A Suggestion Concerning Matthew 16', *JBL* 60 (1941), pp. 255–60.

Geist, pp. 263–90.

O. Glombitza, 'Das Zeichen des Jona', *NTS* 8 (1962), pp. 359–66.

H. B. Green, 'Matthew 12.22–50 and Parallels', in Tuckett, *Studies*, pp. 157–76.

R. G. Hamerton-Kelly, 'A Note on Matthew 12.28 par. Luke 11.20', *NTS* 11 (1965), pp. 167–9.

R. Holst, 'Reexamining Mk 3.28f. and Its Parallels', *ZNW* 63 (1972), pp. 122–4.

J. Howton, 'The Sign of Jonah', *SJT* 15 (1962), pp. 288–304.

Hultgren, pp. 100–6.

Hummel, pp. 122–8.

A. M. Hutchinson, 'Christian Prophecy and Matthew 12:38–42: A Test Exegesis', in *SBL 1977 Seminar Papers*, ed. P. J. Achtemeier, Missoula, 1977, pp. 379–85.

W. R. Hutton, 'Make a Good Tree?', *ExpT* 75 (1964), pp. 366–7.

Jülicher 2, pp. 214–40.

Klauck, pp. 174–85.

Kloppenborg, pp. 121–34.

H. Kruse, 'Das Reich Satans', *Bib* 58 (1977), pp. 29–61.

J. Lambrecht, 'The Relatives of Jesus in Mark', *NovT* 16 (1974), pp. 241–58.

G. M. Landes, 'Matthew 12.40 as an Interpretation of "The Sign of Jonah" against its Biblical Background', in *The Word of the Lord Shall Go Forth*, ed. C. L. Meyers and M. O'Connor, Winona Lake, 1983, pp. 665–84.

Laufen, pp. 126–55.

S. Légasse, 'L' "homme fort" de Luc xi 21–22', *NovT* 5 (1962), pp. 5–9.

Lindars, *Son of Man*, pp. 34–44.

O. Linton, 'The Demand for a Sign from Heaven', *ST* 19 (1965), pp. 112–29.

E. Lövestam, *Spiritus Blasphemia*, Lund, 1968.

T. Lorenzmeier, 'Zum Logion Mt 12.28; Lk 11.20', in *Neues Testament und christliche Existenz*, ed. H. D. Betz and L. Schottroff, Tübingen, 1973, pp. 289–304.

Lührmann, pp. 32–48.

J. H. Michael, ' "The Sign of John" ' *JTS* 21 (1920), pp. 146–59.

V. Mora, *Le signe de Jonas*, Paris, 1983.

C. Moxon, 'Τὸ σημεῖον 'Ιωνα', *ExpT* 22 (1911), pp. 566–7.

F. Mussner, 'Wege zum Selbstbewusstsein Jesu', *BZ* 12 (1968), pp. 169–71.

F. Neirynck, 'Mt 12.25a/Lc 11.17a et le rédaction des evangiles', *ETL* 62 (1986), pp. 122–33.

W. Nestle, 'Wer nicht mit mir ist, ist wider mich', *ZNW* 13 (1912), pp. 84–7.

J. C. O'Neil, 'The Unforgivable Sin', *JSNT* 19 (1983), pp. 37–42.

C. S. Rodd, 'Spirit or Finger', *ExpT* 72 (1961), pp. 157–8.

P. Roulin, 'Le péché contre l'Esprit-Saint', *BVC* 29 (1959), pp. 38–45.

R. Schippers, 'The Son of Man in Matt. 12.32 = Luke 12.10 compared with Mark 3.28', in *Studia Evangelica IV*, TU 102, Berlin, 1968, pp. 231–5.

Schlosser, 1, pp. 127–53.

G. Schmitt, 'Das Zeichen des Jona', *ZNW* 69 (1978), pp. 123–9.

R. B. Y. Scott, 'The Sign of Jonah', *Int* 19 (1965), pp. 16–25.

R. Scroggs, 'The Exaltation of the Spirit by some Early Christians', *JBL* 84 (1965), pp. 359–73.

Schulz, *Q*, pp. 203–13, 246–50, 250–7, 476–80.

P. Seidelin, 'Das Jonaszeichen', *ST* 5 (1951), pp. 119–31.

R. Thibaut, 'Le signe de Jonas', *NRT* 60 (1933), pp. 532–6.

Tödt, pp. 118–20, 312–18.

Trautmann, pp. 258–77.

J. M. Van Cangh, ' " Par l'esprit de Dieu—par le doigt de Dieu" Mt 12.28 par. Lc 11.20', in Delobel, pp. 337–42.

Verseput, pp. 207–94.

A. Vögtle, 'Der Spruch vom Jonaszeichen', in *Evangelium*, pp. 103–36.

Wanke, pp. 26–9, 51–60, 70–6, 88–92.

J. G. Williams, 'A Note on the "Unforgivable Sin" Logion', *NTS* 12 (1965), pp. 75–7.

Witherington, pp. 85–92.

H.-Th. Wrege, 'Zur Rolle des Geisteswortes in frühchristlichen Traditionen (Lc 12.10 parr.)', in Delobel, pp. 373–7.

Wrege, pp. 156–80.

EXCURSUS X

THE STRUCTURE OF MATTHEW 13[1]

Our analysis of the structure of chapter 13 is based upon three observations. (i) Matthew elsewhere shows himself to be fond of triads, and that he is working with such here is demonstrated by the similar introductions in vv. 24, 31, and 33 on the one hand and by the introductory clauses in vv. 44, 45, and 47 on the other. (ii) If, as so many have done, one divides the chapter into two halves, so that one section is addressed to the crowds (13.1–35), the other to the disciples (vv. 36–52), then one must ignore 13.10 ('then the disciples came to him') as well as place in different sections the parable of the tares (13.24–30) and its interpretation (13.36–43) —something we hesitate to do, because on any analysis the parable of the sower and its interpretation belong to the same section. (iii) It would appear that 13.10–23 and 34–43 stand in conscious parallelism. Both contain a statement about the crowds and parables, a remark on the revelatory function of parables, a scriptural citation or allusion, and an extended interpretation of one relatively long parable.

These three observations lead us to propose that chapter 13 should

---

[1] Lit.: Cope, pp. 13–31 (the OT citations and allusions are the structural key); J. Dupont, 'Le point de vue de Matthieu dans le chapître des paraboles,' in Didier, pp. 221–59 (13.3–23 and 24–52 both consist of (a) parable(s) addressed to the crowds, (b) statement on the purpose of the parables, (c) interpretation); J. C. Fenton, 'Expounding the Parables. IV. The Parables of the Treasure and the Pearl (Mt 13.44–6)', *ExpT* 77 (1966), pp. 178–80 (the six units in 13.34–52 are chiastically organized); Gaechter, *Kunst*, pp. 14–15 (close to our own analysis); B. Gerhardsson, 'The Seven Parables in Matthew XIII', *NTS* 19 (1972), pp. 16–37 (the parable of the tares helps explain the first category of people described in 13.1–23, those represented by the seed which falls by the way; the parables of the mustard seed and leaven help explain the second category of people, those represented by the seed on stony ground; the parables of the treasure and of the pearl help explain the third category, the seed among the thorns; and the parable of the net helps explain those represented by the good seed; Gerhardsson offers this diagram:

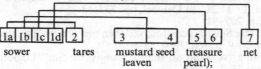

Gnilka, *Matthäusevangelium* 1, pp. 473–5 (critique of Lohmeyer and Dupont); W. S. Vorster, 'The Structure of Matthew 13', *Neotestamentica* II (1977), pp. 130–8; D. Wenham, 'The Structure of Matthew XIII', *NTS* 25 (1979), pp. 516–22 (the chapter is divided into two halves, each with four parables).

be divided into three parts. Section (1) contains the parable of the sower, the passage about the secrets of the kingdom, and the interpretation of the sower (13.1–23). Section (2) consists of the parable of the tares, the parable of the mustard seed, the parable of the leaven, the formula quotation in vv. 34–5, and the interpretation of the parable of the tares (13.24–43). Section (3) comprises the parable of the treasure, the parable of the pearl, the parable of the net (with interpretation), and, lastly, the saying about the scribe and his treasure (13.44–52). The result is that the first section is strikingly parallel to the second and that the second is strikingly parallel to the third. And the pattern of each is: parable or parables + added material, including interpretation. Pictorially—.

13.1–9	Parable of the *sower*
13.10–17	Discussion of parables (+ scriptural allusion)
13.18–23	Interpretation of the *sower*
13.24–30	Parable of the *tares*
13.32–2	Parable of the mustard seed
13.33	Parable of the leaven
13.34–5	Discussion of parables (+ scriptural citation)
13.36–43	Interpretation of the *tares*
13.44	Parable of the *treasure*
13.45–6	Parable of the pearl
13.47–8	Parable of the net
13.49–50	Interpretation of the net
13.51–2	Discussion of parables (saying on *treasure*)

According to this scheme, each section opens with a parable, and each begins and ends on the same note (*inclusio*). Further, no parable is separated from its interpretation. Our proposal also highlights the undeniable parallelism between 13.10–23 and 34–43 and explains why the interpretation of the parable of the tares is put off until after 13.34–5 (cf. the structure of the first section).[2] Finally, our three sections are very similar in that, after 13.3–9 the disciples ask Jesus a question, whereas after 13.24–33 they ask for an explanation of the parable of the tares; and in 13.44–52, after the third parable, Jesus asks, 'Have you understood all this?' In other words, a short conversation—introduced by a question—follows the parabolic part of each section.[3]

There is one further consideration which moves us to argue for a three-fold division. In chapter 24 Matthew follows Mark through 24.35. But thereafter the First Evangelist goes his own way. When he does, he gives us first three different paragraphs which underline the fact that no one knows the hour when the Son of man is coming (vv. 36–42, 43–

[2] Why, then, it may be asked is the interpretation of the parable of the net not the conclusion of 13.44–52? Probably because Matthew needed a paragraph which would not only fittingly close 13.44–52 but at the same time bring to an end all of chapter 13.

[3] Some scholars, admittedly, consider 13.52 a parable. But even if this is granted, it is different from all the other parables in the chapter, for it is not about the kingdom as such.

4, 45–51), and this is then followed by three more paragraphs, each of similar length and treating of the same theme, judgement: the parable of the maidens (25.1–13), the parable of the talents (25.14–30), and the depiction of the last judgement (25.31–46). In other words, as soon as Matthew leaves Mark he gives us six parables which are grouped into two triads. This is exactly what we find in chapter 13. Matthew follows Mark rather closely in 13.1–23. But when he sets out on his own course, beginning with 13.24, we have two triads: vv. 24–30 + 31–2 + 33 and 44, 45–6, 47–8 (cf. France, *Matthew*, p. 216). This is not coincidence. In both chapter 13 and chapters 24–5 we have to do with the same compositional technique.

XXVII

THE PARABLE OF THE SOWER AND ITS INTERPRETATION
(13.1–23)

(i) *Structure*

Mt 13.1–23 is readily divided into three subsections. There is, first, after the setting of the scene (13.1–3a), the parable of the sower (13.3b–9). Next comes a question and answer sequence in which Jesus explains why he speaks in parables (13.10–7). In the third place is 13.18–23, the interpretation of the parable of the sower.

(ii) *Sources*

All of the differences between Mt 13.1–23 and its Markan parallel can without difficulty be explained in terms of Matthean redaction, as the verse-by-verse analysis shows. This has not, however, prevented scholars from supposing Matthean priority[1] or from arguing that at least Luke knew Matthew[2] or from holding that the First and Third Evangelists had access to a non-Markan version of the parable of the sower and its interpretation.[3] The main reason for discontent with the view that Mt 13.1–23 and Lk 8.4–15 depend solely upon Mk 4.1–20 is the number of minor agreements against Mark. These include the following:

Common omissions—
4.1: 'and again he began to teach'
4.1: '(sat) in the sea'
4.2–3a: 'and he said to them in his teaching: Hear'
4.7: 'and it did not bear fruit'
4.8: 'growing up and increasing'
4.10: 'and when he was alone'
4.12c: 'lest they should turn again and be forgiven'
4.13: 'do you not understand this parable? How then will you understand all the parables?'

Common additions—

---

[1] E.g. Lohmeyer, *Matthäus*, pp. 190–212.
[2] E.g. Gundry, *Commentary*, pp. 250–61.
[3] E.g. Wenham, 'Synoptic Problem' (v). Cf. Marshall, p. 321.

Mt 13.3 = Lk 8.5:   article before the infinitive
Mt 13.11 = Lk 8.10:   'to know'
Mt 13.19 = Lk 8.12:   'heart'

Common alterations—
Mt 13.9 = Lk 8.8:   relative pronoun + present indicative becomes article + present participle
Mt 13.10 = Lk 8.9:   'those around him with the twelve' becomes 'the (his) disciples'
Mt 13.11 = Lk 8.10:   'mystery' becomes 'mysteries'

But should these minor agreements in fact perturb defenders of Markan priority? We believe not. The reader is referred to the commentary on 13.9–11 and 19 for our observations on most of the common additions and alterations. Here we address only the common omissions, concerning which the most important consideration is this: Luke is, on the two-source theory, abbreviating.[4] How then can it surprise when some of his omissions coincide with those of another reviser and abbreviator?[5] This is all the less remarkable when one examines the phrases that have been dropped. Some of them are grammatically or otherwise awkward (Mk 4.1, 8). Some are superfluous (4.2–3a, 7, 10). And some are theologically problematic or potentially unedifying (4.12c, 13). The independent excision of clauses such as these is nothing save wholly expected.

Given our interpretation of the minor agreements of Mt 13.1–22 = Lk 8.4–15 against Mark, it follows that, with the exception of Mt 13.12 (brought forward from Mk 4.25) and 16–7 (from Q; see Lk 10.23–4), the sole source of Mt 13.1–22 is Mk 4.1–20.[6]

(iii) Exegesis

THE PARABLE OF THE SOWER (13.1–9)

Jesus' famous parable of the sower, which is perhaps more fittingly designated the parable of the four soils, heads a chapter whose leading theme is the kingdom of heaven and its reception in the world. The subject comes up for treatment at this juncture in the gospel because of the rejection so far experienced by Jesus and his disciples. The pressing question is, Why has Israel not embraced her Messiah? Why has the good news of the kingdom engendered so much opposition? One answer to these questions is given in 4.3–9—the most important parable in chapter 13—and its interpretation: 'the kingdom of God is

[4] Mk: 349 words; Lk: 235 words.
[5] Matthew, excluding the vv. without Markan parallels, has 307 words, 42 less than Mark.
[6] For the convincing argument that Luke draws solely upon Mk 4.1–20 see Carlston, pp. 70–6.

present among men in a form which is not always effective. It is present in Jesus' person, in his deeds, even in his words, but the ministry of Jesus requires a human response' (Sabourin, p. 595). Put otherwise, the course of salvation-history is not predetermined, for while God may extend his love towards his people, he does not force them to respond. Hence if Jesus' ministry has not brought about what one might have anticipated, the fault lies neither with him nor with God but with human sin and hardened hearts. In this way, then, the parable of the sower comes to function as an apologetic, even a sort of theodicy, explaining the evil that has befallen Israel.

Over against Mk 3.3–9, Matthew has introduced the following significant changes. (i) It is explicitly mentioned that Jesus left 'the house' (cf. Mt 12.46). (ii) Mark's 'listen' (Mk 4.3) has been dropped. (iii) καὶ ἐγένετο (Mk 4.4) has been avoided. (iv) 'Seed' (collective singular) has become throughout 'seeds', with the corresponding verbal changes. (v) One word for 'choke' has been replaced by another (13.7). (vi) Several superfluous clauses have not been reproduced (Mk 4.2b, 7c, 8b, 9a). (vii) The order, thirtyfold, sixtyfold, and a hundredfold, has been reversed. (viii) Parallelism has been increased in several places (e.g., cf. 13.5a with 7a and 8a).

With regard to the meaning of the parable of the sower, Matthew like his fellow evangelists, gives us a detailed interpretation. Because, however, many regard the synoptic explanation as a product of the Christian community,[7] other interpretations have been tendered.[8] (i) In the judgement of Weder (v) the seed is a metaphor for the preaching of Jesus and its power. Jesus' word, while it may not be received, remains powerful and will inevitably do its work. Like the word of God, it will not return empty (cf. Isa 55.10–1). (ii) Very popular today is the notion that the main theme is the contrast between present and future. If the beginning of the kingdom is none too promising, or if Jesus' preaching has been largely ineffectual, the end will yet be glorious. On this view, the original purpose of the parable was encouragement or the assuaging of doubts.[9] (iii) According to C. H. Dodd, *Parables*, pp. 146–7, Mk 4.3–9 par. is a sort of résumé of salvation-history. The work of John the Baptist and the prophets had failed. 'True, says Jesus; but no farmer yet delayed to reap a good crop because there were bare patches in the field. In spite of all, the harvest is plentiful: it is only the labourers that are lacking. "Pray the Lord of the harvest to send labourers into His harvest."'[10] (iv) Some have affirmed that even if the synoptic

---

[7] Representative are Dodd (v) and Jeremias, *Parables* (v).

[8] Linnemann, *Parables*, p. 117, and a few others think that the original sense is now beyond our reach.

[9] Jeremias, *Parables*, pp. 149–51, and Perrin, *Rediscovering*, pp. 155–7, are typical. Dahl (v) and Hahn (v) also find the meaning to lie in eschatology but give more recognition to the element of growth than most modern scholars.

[10] Dodd, *Parables*, pp. 146–7. For criticism see Linnemann, *Parables*, pp.181–2.

interpretation does not derive from Jesus himself, it rightly catches his intention. The point is that people should hear and do the word Jesus speaks (cf. Mt 7.24–7).[11]

In reflecting upon the several interpretive options, the following considerations incline us to suppose that the last probably comes closest to grasping Jesus' intention. To begin with, Mk 4.13–20 favours this. Even if the passage is not from Jesus, it does preserve the earliest interpretation we have. Secondly, the sower is mentioned only at the beginning of the parable. This moves one to wonder whether there can be much emphasis upon christological themes. Thirdly, the detailed attention given to the various types of soil suggests that they are not without meaning and indeed that the differences in soil might be central to the message. Fourthly, *m. 'Abot* 5.10–15 contains six pericopae, each of which analyses four different types of people. One pericope in fact describes, very much like Mt 13.3–9 par., four different kinds of *hearers*—those who are slow to hear and swift to lose, those who are slow to hear and slow to lose, those who are swift to hear and slow to lose, and those who are swift to hear and swift to lose (5.12). It is not inconceivable that already in Jesus' time it was conventional to make a point by referring to four different classes of people (cf. *ARN* A 40), and this might be part of the background of the parable of the sower. Finally, why the different yields—thirty, sixty, a hundred—if the focus is the contrast between the present and the future? 'It is difficult to know in what sense it could be said that there is diversity in the coming of the kingdom of God' (Boucher, p. 50).

B. Gerhardsson, 'Sower' (v), has proposed that Mt 13.3–9 + 18–23 is to be understood in the light of the *Shemaʿ*, Deut 6.4–5. The seed that falls on the path and is devoured by birds represents those who do not love God with all their heart (cf. 13.19: 'snatches away what is sown in his heart'). The seed cast upon rocky ground represents those who do not love God with their souls. And the seed that is choked by thorns stands for those who fail to love God with all their might (or: mammon; cf. 13.22: 'the delight in riches choke the word'). This novel approach to our parable is somewhat strengthend by the ἀκούσατε of Mt 13.18 (cf. Deut 6.4: 'Hear, O Israel'). Nevertheless, we think Gerhardsson's proposal falls short of proof, in part because his analysis holds better for Matthew than for Mark and wrongly implies the priority of the former.

There have been other attempts to interpret the parable of the sower against an OT background. J. W. Bowker (v), for instance, regards Mk 4.1–20 par. as a midrash on Isa 6.13 ('a holy seed is its stump'). Isa 6.9–10 is paraphrased in Mk 4.10–12, and in rabbinic literature the 'holy seed' (*zeraʿ qōdeš*) is sometimes good seed that produces fruit. C. A. Evans, 'Sower' (v), partially endorses Bowker's proposal but maintains that Mk 4.1–20 is a midrash on Isa 6.9–13 *and* 55.10–1, the latter being associated with the former on the basis of the catchword, 'seed'. Evans futher argues that the parable of the sower and canonical Isaiah as a whole share a common theme: the efficacy of God's word despite all

---

[11] Cf. Marshall, pp. 323–4, and Beasley-Murray, p. 131.

obstacles. As with Gerhardsson's suggestion, we are not quite convinced. For one thing, Evans' thesis seems to require the original unity of Mk 4.1–20, and of that we are uncertain. For another, the verbal links with Isa 55.10–11 are not extensive.

1f. ἐν τῇ ἡμέρᾳ ἐκείνῃ ἐξελθὼν ὁ Ἰησοῦς τῆς οἰκίας ἐκάθητο παρὰ τὴν θάλασσαν.[12] Mk 4.1 (καὶ πάλιν[13] ἤρξατο[14] διδάσκειν παρὰ τὴν θάλασσαν) is more compact and less vivid. There is no Lukan parallel. On 'in that day' (a Septuagintism) see 1, p. 82. On 'the house', which may be Peter's, and which Jesus enters in 13.36, see on 9.10 (cf. 12.46). On 'he sat', which signals that Jesus is about to teach (cf. Newman (v)), see on 5.1. Jesus also sits when delivering two of his other major discourses (see 5.1 and 24.3). Did Matthew, as Gundry, *Commentary*, p. 251, asserts, use ἐξελθὼν in order to hint at Jesus' identity as the sower (who also 'goes out', 13.3: ἐξῆλθεν)?

καὶ συνήχθησαν πρὸς αὐτὸν ὄχλοι πολλοί. Mk 4.1b has συνάγεται (the historical present, which is often altered by the First Evangelist) and ὄχλος πλεῖστος (cf. Mt 21.8); otherwise there is agreement. On the ὄχλοι* in Matthew see on 4.25.

ὥστε αὐτὸν εἰς πλοῖον ἐμβάντα καθῆσθαι. So also Mk 4.1, with ἐν τῇ θαλάσσῃ at the end, a phrase our evangelist has let fall away as awkward and superfluous (he has already noted Jesus' posture in 13.1). Compare further 1 Macc 15.37 (ἐμβὰς εἰς πλοῖον) and *m. Ber.* 4.6, v. 1. (*yôsēb bispînâ*).

καὶ πᾶς ὁ ὄχλος ἐπὶ τὸν αἰγιαλὸν εἱστήκει. Compare Jn 21.4 (ἔστη Ἰησοῦς εἰς τὸν αἰγιαλόν). Mk 4.1 has πρὸς τὴν θάλασσαν after ὄχλος and τῆς γῆς ἦσαν after ἐπί. The standing of the crowds (cf. Exod 20.18) is probably intended to create a visual contrast: Jesus alone sits. αἰγιαλός (LXX: 2) means 'shore'. The word occurs only twice in the synoptics, both times in Matthew (13.2, 48).

3. καὶ ἐλάλησεν αὐτοῖς πολλὰ ἐν παραβολαῖς λέγων. Compare 3 Βασ 5.12 (καὶ ἐλάλησεν Σαλωμὼν τρισχιλίας παραβολάς). Mk 4.2 (καὶ ἐδίδασκεν αὐτοὺς ἐν παραβολαῖς πολλὰ καὶ ἔλεγεν αὐτοῖς ἐν τῇ διδαχῇ αὐτοῦ· ἀκούετε) is longer and less elegant, and Matthew has omitted the pleonasm. πολλά is not adverbial ('often') but accusative ('many things'; cf. BAGD, s.v., πολύς, I.1.b.a; so RSV; the NEB has 'at some length').

---

[12] ℵ Z 33 892 *pc* have εκ της οικιας, C E L W Maj απο της οικιας. D it sy[s], followed by Allen, p. 142, omit. της οικιας is the reading of B Θ *f*[1.13] 1424 *pc*.

[13] Only in Mark has Jesus already taught beside the sea; see Mk 2.13 and contrast Mt 9.9–13.

[14] Often omitted by Matthew.

EXCURSUS XI

THE PARABLES

Παραβολή, whose usual sense in Greek literature is 'comparison' (cf. Aristotle, *Rhet.* 2.20.2–4), has several meanings in the NT, including maxim or proverb (Lk 4.23), symbol or type (Heb 9.9; 11.19), comparison or similitude (Mk 3.23; 13.28), and story or tale embodying some truth (Mt 13.3, 10, etc.). Along with several others, each of these meanings is also attested for the Hebrew *māšāl*,[15] and the OT uses of this word are crucial for understanding the NT's use of παραβολή.[16] When Jesus spoke 'in parables', he was relating himself to a literary tradition firmly rooted in the OT, one which lived on in apocalyptic literature and the rabbis.

Unfortunately, throughout much of church history Jesus' parables have been understood as deliberately mysterious and involved allegories in which every character and action must be deciphered like a cryptogram.[17] If today things are different, if today the excesses of the old hermeneutical method are almost universally acknowledged, much of the credit must go to Adolf Jülicher and his massive, two-volume work, *Die Gleichnisreden Jesu* (originally published in 1888 and 1899). The book marked a dramatic turn in the discussion of Jesus' parables. Jülicher argued that there is a world of difference between an allegory on the one hand and a parable on the other. Whereas the latter is a narrative based on everyday life whose elements combine to make an instructive picture with simple or self-evident meaning, the former is a story whose features all stand for something extrinsic to the narrative. And Jesus, Jülicher contended, spoke in parables, not in allegories.

Despite the giant step forward it represents, *Die Gleichnisreden Jesu* was considerably marred by its adherence to the liberal theology of the day. Jülicher tended to interpret the parables as pedagogical

---

[15] Lit.: A. R. Johnson, '*Māšāl*', in *Wisdom in Israel and in the Ancient Near East*, VTSup 3, ed. M. Noth and D. Winton Thomas, Leiden, 1955, pp. 162–9; D. W. Suter, '*Māšāl* in the Similitudes of Enoch', *JBL* 100 (1981), pp. 193–212; and T. Polk, 'Paradigms, Parables, and *Měšālîm*', *CBQ* 45 (1983), pp. 564–83.

[16] Both words seem to have been used with little precision, of any speech that was strikingly unusual. But according to J. W. Sider, 'The Meaning of *Parabole* in the Usage of the Synoptic Evangelists', *Bib* 62 (1981), pp. 453–70, in the synoptics 'parable' consistently means 'illustration by analogy.'

[17] See Wailes, passim. Well known is Augustine's interpretation of the parable of the good Samaritan, in which the traveller is Adam, the thieves the devil and his minions, the inn-keeper Paul, etc. See *Quaest. ev.* 2.19. The seeds of this interpretation can be found already in Irenaeus, *Adv. haer.* 3.17.3. Note that both Tertullian, *De res. carnis* 33; *De pudic.* 9; and Chrysostom, *Hom. on Mt.* 47.1, found it necessary to set themselves against the excesses of parable interpretation.

illustrations of general moral and religious truths. For example, he took the parable of the labourers in the vineyard (Mt 20.1–16) to teach that all are equal in God's eyes and so equally treated by him. This approach gave both Christology and eschatology inadequate consideration. Jülicher also failed to take sufficiently into account the rabbinic corpus of parables, which often illuminates Jesus' words.[18]

Jülicher's first failing—his viewing the parables as little more than illustrations of religious and moral truisms—was probably most effectively countered and called into question by C. H. Dodd's influential book, *The Parables of the Kingdom* (first edition, 1935). In this Dodd tried to relate the parables not to religion in general but to Jesus' ministry in particular.[19] For Dodd, Jesus taught a realized eschatology which is consistently reflected in his parables. To illustrate: the parable of the sower implies that the ministry of Jesus is the time of the eschatological harvest, while the parable of the bridegroom (Mk 2.18–19 par.) teaches that the messianic time has commenced; and the parable of the pearl (Mt 13.45–6) means that the great treasure of the kingdom of God can be possessed even now. In fine, the parables proclaim the presence of the kingdom in the here and now and set forth the unprecedented opportunity afforded Jesus' hearers.

After Dodd the next major contribution to the study of the parables came from Joachim Jeremias: *The Parables of Jesus* (first published in German in 1947). Taking up where Dodd left off, Jeremias replaced 'realized eschatology' with 'eschatology in the process of realization' (*sich realisierenden Eschatologie*)—a phrase which perhaps the majority of NT scholars have found apt. Jeremias also made a contribution by underlining the fact that several of Jesus' parables seem to be variants of stories preserved in rabbinic texts and that one may sometimes discern the meaning of a synoptic parable by discovering the new twist Jesus evidently gave to an old tale. Even more importantly, however, was Jeremias' consistent attempt to interpret the parables in their *Sitz im Leben Jesu*. This was an emphasis begun by Dodd, but Jeremias carried it forward. Indeed, the entire first half of *The Parables of Jesus* is given over to uncovering ten 'laws of transformation'[20] which effected the shape of the parables in their transmission from Jesus to gospel. Jeremias' one goal was to get back to the historical Jesus.

In recent years scholars have built upon the foundations laid by Jülicher and Dodd and Jeremias. Among the more notable studies are those of Eta Linnemann, Dan Via, John Dominic Crossan, K. E.

---

[18] See esp. P. Fiebig, *Die Gleichnisreden Jesu im Lichte der rabbinischen Gleichnisse des neutestamentlichen Zeitalters*, Tübingen, 1912; also idem, *Altjüdische Gleichnisse und die Gleichnisse Jesu*, Tübingen, 1904. For a more recent attempt to relate Jesus' parables to a rabbinic background see D. Flusser, *Die rabbinischen Gleichnisse und der Gleichniserzähler Jesus. I. Teil: Das Wesen der Gleichnisse*, Bern, 1981.

[19] In this Dodd was largely anticipated by A. T. Cadoux, *The Parables of Jesus*, London, 1931.

[20] Jeremias' 'laws of transformation' owe much to B. T. D. Smith, *The Parables of the Synoptic Gospels*, Cambridge, 1937.

Bailey, Hans-Josef Klauck, Hans Weder, and Madeleine Boucher.[21] We need not here review their books. For this the reader may consult the surveys of Perrin, *Language*, pp. 113–17, 141–68, and C. E. Carlston, 'Parable and Allegory Revisited: An Interpretive Review', *CBQ* 43 (1981), pp. 228–42.[22] What we should like to stress here is that several common opinions and approaches are less than wholly satisfactory. To begin with, the emphasis of Dodd and Jeremias upon the *Sitz im Leben Jesu* has tended to direct attention away from the texts as they stand as well as away from the interpretations of the evangelists. While certainly understandable as part of the quest of the historical Jesus, the interpretation of the parables in their present literary contexts remains a legitimate concern. But redaction criticism of the parables has often not been given its due.[23]

Secondly, the meaning of the parables must not be too rigidly restricted to one point of comparison. Both Dodd and Jeremias, following in the footsteps of Jülicher, tended to confine the meaning of any given parable to a single application. Metaphorical language, however, has an affective component which goes beyond the straightforward imparting of information.[24] In addition, one cannot eliminate from the gospel parables every trace of allegory. In the first place, and as Klauck has made plain, allegory is not always obscure (cf. Quintilian, *Inst.* 8.6.44–59); and, further, one must draw a distinction between *Allegorie* (a compositional procedure which an author uses to add a symbolic dimension to his text) and *Allegorese* (an exegetical method which, without regard to authorial intention and situation, reads correlations into a text arbitrarily). The sweeping rejection of allegory must also be opposed because allegories are well-attested in ancient Palestinian literature[25] and because there are several synoptic parables which can only with great difficulty be

---

[21] Linnemann, *Parables*; D. Via, *The Parables: Their Literary and Existential Dimension*, Philadelphia, 1967; Crossan, *Parables*; idem, *Cliffs*; Bailey; Klauck; Weder; Boucher.

[22] Also helpful are W. Harnisch, ed., *Gleichnisse Jesu. Positionen der Auslegung von Adolf Jülicher bis zur Formgeschichte*, Darmastadt, 1982; idem, *Die neutestamentliche Gleichnisforschung von Hermeneutik und Literaturwissenschaft*, Darmstadt, 1982; and the review of research in M. S. Kjärgaard, *Metaphor and Parable*, Acta Theologica Danica 19, Leiden, 1986.

[23] See further J. W. Sider, 'Rediscovering the Parables: The Logic of the Jeremias Tradition', *JBL* 102 (1983), pp. 61–83. He argues that the interpreter's first task is interpretation of the text as it stands. See further Drury, *Parables*.

[24] In this lies the truth of the New Hermeneutic's 'language event'. Note that Dodd himself wrote that the parables of Jesus have a 'strangeness' about them which leaves 'the mind in sufficient doubt' about application 'to tease it into active thought' (*Parables*, p. 5).

[25] Pertinent texts include Gen 37.7; 41.14–36; 2 Sam 12.1–14; Ps 80.8–19; Isa 5.1–7; Ezek 17.1–24; Dan 2.31–45; 4.4–27, 4 Ezra 9.26–10.59; 11.1–12.39; and 2 Bar. 35.1–40.4. The rabbis traditionally understood all of Canticles to be an allegory; and one should recall that Paul, who had Pharisaic training, could occasionally resort to allegorizing, as in 1 Cor 9.8–12; 10.1–11 and Gal 4.21–31. See further L. Ginzberg, 'Allegorical Interpretation', in *Jewish Encyclopedia*, 1, 1901, cols. 403–11.

altogether purified of allegorical features.[26] This last is true in part because Jewish tradition, which is full of stock metaphors (like 'father' and 'fruit'), makes it almost inevitable that certain words be understood as tropic. Thus, as R. E. Brown has asked, using the terminology of Jülicher, 'Would a popular teacher be able to disassociate himself completely from familiar metaphor and speak in pure parables?'[27] This does not seem likely. It need only be added that the tension between allegory and parable becomes all but non-existent when, following Boucher and others, the latter is recognized as a *Gattung*, the former as a literary device which can appear in any one of several *Gattungen*, including the parable.

The third point we should like to make is that Dodd was probably incorrect to assert that in Jesus' parables 'all is true to nature and to life' (*Parables*, p. 9). There are quite a few texts which seem to give the lie to this generalization.[28] Indeed, their number is such that one is tempted to turn the tables and make the atypical features a key to interpreting a number of the parables. When a man who has worked one hour is paid the same as a man who has worked all day (Mt 20.1–16), when a lord girds himself and serves his slaves at table (Lk 12.37), and when a mustard seed becomes not a large plant but a *tree* (Mt 13.31–2 par.), is not the point precisely that God's ways are not our ways and that the workings of the kingdom do not always follow the laws of this world? Jülicher's justified attack upon allegorical extremism led him to stress the true-to-life character and realism of the events narrated in Jesus' parables. But he went too far. Anomalous elements must not be ignored or eliminated (on the grounds, for instance, that they are allegorical intrusions). They are instead to be understood as rhetorically appropriate, a method for stating surprising convictions about God and his transcendent ways. Everyday situations were not always enough to illustrate the radical nature of the kingdom, and Jesus on occasion imaginatively resorted to painting unlikely or impossible scenarios.

Lastly, one wonders whether it is not a mistake to insist that all of the synoptic parables be approached with one method or with one fixed set of expectations as to what a parable must be. Why is it impossible that Jesus on one occasion composed an allegory,[29] another time an exemplary story, and another time a true-to-life metaphor?[30] Furthermore, why is it implausible that the meaning of at least some of Jesus' parables were fully grasped only by those 'on the inside', by those who had been the recipients of special instruction?[31] The OT tradition of the *māšāl* as a mysterious word or riddle was certainly

[26] See further M. Black, 'The Parables as Allegory', *BJRL* 42 (1959–60), pp. 273–87, and J. W. Sider, 'Proportional Analogy in the Gospel Parables', *NTS* 31 (1985), pp. 1–23.

[27] *Essays*, pp. 323–4. See further M. D. Goulder, 'Characteristics of the Parables in the several Gospels', *JTS* 19 (1968), pp. 51–69.

[28] See esp. N. A. Huffman, 'Atypical Features in the Parables of Jesus', *JBL* 97 (1978), pp. 207–20.

[29] In this connexion it bears remarking that allegory need not be esoteric.

[30] See further the article of Black, as cited in n. 26.

[31] Cf. J. A. Baird, 'A Pragmatic Approach to Parable Exegesis', *JBL* 76 (1957), pp. 201–7.

available to Jesus.[32] And, as Morton Smith commented, the multitude of interpretations offered by modern scholars for various parables harmonizes well with the view that they are indeed mysterious things.[33] This is not to say that Jesus must have deliberately employed parables in order to obscure his meaning (cf. Nineham, pp. 127–8). The typical rabbinic use of the parable argues otherwise. Still, given that the parables of Jesus all involve two levels of meaning, need for clarification may sometimes have been in order (cf. Boucher, pp. 24–5). It is also not unthinkable that Jesus' parables, like so much of his other teaching, was intentionally infused with an implicit Christology which would be apparent only to some, and that Jesus purposely composed literary units whose depths could be reached only by the protracted pondering of those willing to explore beneath the surface (cf. Goppelt, *Theology* 1, p. 175). Jesus is recorded as uttering on more than one occasion, 'He who has ears to hear, let him hear!'; and many of his sayings about his ministry, the presence of the kingdom, and the fulfilment of prophecy are as much as anything else invitations to reflection.

ἰδοὺ ἐξῆλθεν ὁ σπείρων τοῦ σπείρειν. Compare 1 Clem. 24.5: ἐξῆλθεν ὁ σπείρων καὶ ἔκβαλεν[34] εἰς τὴν γῆν ἕκαστον τῶν σπερμάτων....[35] Matthew's line, which introduces the following parable, is from Mk 4.3, which has σπεῖραι without the article.

When the sower goes out in order to sow, has he already ploughed the field, or will that come later? The issue has been much discussed, with uncertain result.[36] One cannot reach a decision on the basis of presumed common practice for ancient texts reflect both orders, and it may, moreover, have been common to plough both before and after one sowed.[37] One also cannot base a decision upon the gospel text itself, for it can be read either way (cf. Payne, 'Order' (v)).

Tied in with the question about the order of sowing and ploughing is that concerning the sower's intention. If one presupposes that the task of ploughing has already been performed, then it is possible, though by no means necessary, to suppose that the seeds which fall on bad soil come to rest there through accident. But if one assumes that ploughing comes later, then it is more natural to think of the sower as throwing seed indiscriminately (cf. Ps.-Clem. Rec. 3.14). Those who accept the authenticity of the interpretation offered by Matthew and his fellow

[32] Note Ps 49.4; 78.2; Prov 1.5–6, Ezek 17.2; Hab 2.6; Ecclus 39.2–3; 1 En. 68.1.

[33] M. Smith, 'Comments on Taylor's Commentary on Mark', *HTR* 48 (1955), p. 31.

[34] Cf. Gos. Thom. 9.

[35] Hagner, pp. 164–5, regards literary dependence upon the synoptics as probable but not certain.

[36] See Essame (v); White (v); Jeremias, 'Palästinakundliches' (v); and Payne, 'Order' (v).

[37] For ploughing before sowing see Isa 28.24–6; Jer 4.3; Ezek 36.9; Gos. Thom 20; Apost. Const. 7.40.2; Columella, *De re rustica* 2.4.2; Pliny, *Nat. hist.* 18.176, 180–1; *t. Ber.* 7.2. For sowing before ploughing see Jub. 11.11, 24; *m. Šabb.* 7.2; *t. Šabb.* 4.12; *t.Neg.* 6.2; *b.Šabb.* 73a–b.

evangelists will also think not in terms of an accidental planting but purposeful procedure, for 'the word' is quite intentionally proclaimed to all.

4. καὶ ἐν τῷ σπείρειν αὐτὸν ἃ μὲν ἔπεσεν παρὰ τὴν ὁδόν. In Mk 4.4 ἐγένετο comes after καί, there is no αὐτόν and ὅ does duty for ἅ. Matthew's ἃ anticipates the plural in 13.8 = Mk 4.8 and thus adds consistency. Lk 8.5 agrees with Mt 13.4 in omitting Mark's ἐγένετο[38] and in adding αὐτόν (a natual addition; cf. Mt 13.25; 27.12; Lk 1.8; 2.6; etc.). ἐν τῷ σπείρειν is a Semitism (cf. BDF § 404).

ὁδόν here means '(foot)path'. According to *m. Pe'ah* 2.1, paths sometimes marked the boundaries of ownership. But paths also evidently ran through the middle of fields (cf. Mt 12.1?). Some have supposed that παρὰ τὴν ὁδόν is a mistranslation of the original Aramaic (cf. Black, p. 162). Jesus himself, it is urged, used the ambiguous *'al* and by it meant 'on';[39] but Mark's tradition wrongly took the word to mean 'beside'. παρά however, can, when followed by the accusative, mean 'on' (so BAGD, s.v. III.1.d). Even if that were denied, it is far from evident that 'beside' was not the meaning Jesus intended.

καὶ ἐλθόντα τὰ πετεινὰ κατέφαγεν αὐτά.[40] Compare LXX Gen 40.17 (καὶ τὰ πετεινὰ τοῦ οὐρανοῦ κατήσθιεν αὐτά) and Jub. 11.11 ('And the prince Mastema sent ravens and other birds to eat up the seed that had been sown in the land ...'). Mk 4.4 has ἦλθεν, καί before the second verb, and, in accordance with the earlier use of ὅ instead of ἅ, αὐτό at the end.

5–6. ἄλλα δὲ ἔπεσεν ἐπὶ τὰ πετρώδη ὅπου οὐκ εἶχεν γῆν πολλήν. Mk 4.5 opens with καί ἄλλο and has the singular, τὸ πετρῶδες. Matthew's τὰ πετρώδη anticipates the interpretation in 13.20 = Mk 4.16, where the plural is again used. Once more Matthew is increasing parallelism.

καὶ εὐθέως ἐξανέτειλεν διὰ τὸ μὴ ἔχειν βάθος γῆς. So Mk 4.5, with εὐθύς (see Allen, pp. xix–xx). The line has often been regarded as a Markan interpolation or a later gloss. It is missing in several Markan mss.

ἡλίου δὲ ἀνατείλαντος ἐκαυματίσθη. Compare Mk 16.2; Jas 1.11 ('the sun rises with its scorching heat and withers the grass'). Mk 4.6 has a ὅτε clause. Matthew's fondness for the genitive absolute is well known (cf. 1.18, 20; 6.3; 9.18; 18.25; etc.).

---

[38] Matthew usually drops this, and note that Luke has omitted all five uses of γίνομαι from Mk 4.1–20.

[39] Cf. Gos. Thom. 9; Justin, *Dial.* 125 (εἰς τὴν ὁδόν); Ps.-Clem. Rec. 3.14.7; Heiland 2388.

[40] So NA[26], following B Θ *f*[13] 1424 *pc.* ηλθεν+και after πετεινα (so HG) appears in ℵ C W *f*[1] Maj, ηλθον+και in D L Z *al.* Perhaps the readings in ℵ and D are due to assimilation to Mark.

καὶ διὰ τὸ μὴ ἔχειν ῥίζαν ἐξηράνθη. So also Mk 4.6. Compare Jn 15.6 ('If a man does not abide in me, he is cast forth as a branch and withers'). The seeds have sprouted but, because they have not sent down firm roots, they wither[41] and die; they can get no moisture (cf. Isa 53.2). Lk 8.6 is a bit different, simply explaining that the plant 'had no moisture' (cf. Jer 17.8?).

7. The reader is next informed that some seed will fall among thorns and be choked. This would appear to mark an advance over the fate of the first two groups of seed. If the seed on or beside the road never germinates, and if the seed on rocky soil springs up only for the briefest period, the seed among thorns grows some time before it is overcome. Thus the lifetime of the various seeds becomes greater as one moves toward the parable's climax.

ἄλλα δὲ ἔπεσεν ἐπὶ τὰς ἀκάνθας. Mk 4.7 begins with καὶ ἄλλο and has εἰς instead of ἐπί. Matthew's changes make for perfect parallelism with 13.5a (cf. 8a).

καὶ ἀνέβησαν αἱ ἄκανθαι καὶ ἔπνιξαν αὐτά.[42] Compare Hermas, Sim. 5.2.4 (ὁ ἀμπελὼν ... μὴ ἔχων βοτάνας πνιγούσας αὐτόν). Mk 4.7 differs in having συνέπνιξαν αὐτό.[43] Although Matthew reproduces Mark's συμπνίγω (LXX: O) in 13.22 = Mk 4.19, here he prefers the more common simplex, πνίγω.[44]

In the LXX ἄκανθα most often renders qôṣ, 'thorn'. It is futile to speculate on what species is envisaged in our parable. For ἀναβαίνω used of plants sprouting up see LXX Gen 41.5; Deut 29.23; Isa 5.6 (with ἄκανθαι).

8. ἄλλα δὲ ἔπεσεν ἐπὶ τὴν γῆν τὴν καλήν. The sentence in Mk 4.8 opens with καὶ ἄλλα and uses εἰς.[45] Once again Matthew has assimilated to 13.5a (cf. 7a).

καὶ ἐδίδου καρπούς.[46] Mk 4.8 has the singular (καρπόν) plus two participles ('growing and increasing'). No doubt Matthew thought the participles redundant and awkward (cf. Lk 8.8). διδόναι καρπόν (often in LXX) is Semitic.

ὃ μὲν ἑκατόν, ὃ δὲ ἑξήκοντα, ὃ δὲ τριάκοντα. This eliminates the Semitism[47] in, and the climactic order[48] of, Mk 4.8: καὶ ἔφερεν

---

[41] ξηραίνω (most often in the LXX for yābēš): Mt: 3; Mk: 6; Lk: 1. Unlike Mark, both Matthew and Luke reserve the verb for describing plant life.

[42] B C L W Z f¹ Maj read απεπνιξαν (assimilation to Luke?).

[43] Followed by καὶ καρπὸν οὐκ ἔδωκεν, a clause struck by both Matthew and Luke as awkward.

[44] LXX: 2; NT: 3 (Mt 13.7; 18.28; Mk 5.13).

[45] The textual tradition in Lk 8.8 is divided between ἐπί and εἰς. If the former is accepted, it constitutes a minor agreement with Matthew.

[46] So HG. NA²⁶ prints καρπόν. Neither supplies an apparatus.

[47] On this see Taylor, Mark, p. 254; also Maloney, pp. 150–2.

[48] An order which continues the progression discernible in the first three groups of seeds.

ἐν τριάκοντα καὶ ἐν ἑξήκοντα καὶ ἐν ἑκατόν. The motive for the change in order cannot be discerned. M. Pamment suggests: 'perhaps he deliberately avoids a climax to leave the emphasis of the parable in the description of individuals'.[49] That is, Matthew wants the stress to fall upon the variety represented by the harvest. This certainly seems a more likely explanation than that which divines an idealizing of earliest Christianity followed by downhill trends; but there is hardly room for certainty. For another suggestion see p. 402.

Is the estimation of the yield fantastic? According to Jeremias, a good harvest may yield up to tenfold, so the abnormal numbers—thirty, sixty, one hundred—witness to a true miracle (*Parables*, p. 150, n. 84). But according to Varro, *R.R.* 1.44.2, seed in Syria could yield a hundredfold; and other texts point in the same direction.[50] In trying to evaluate the issue one would like to know how the yield in the gospels is computed. Is it according to the number of seeds or grains on each stalk, or the proportion of stalks to grain planted, or the number of seeds produced for each seed planted, or something else again? Despite our desire to know, the text is mute. Perhaps, then, it is legitimate to look outside the NT for a solution. There are Jewish and Christian passages which refer to the exceedingly great harvests expected in the messianic age. Papias is quoted as having foretold that 'a grain of wheat shall bring forth ten thousand ears, and every ear shall have ten thousand grains . . .' (in Irenaeus, *Adv. haer.* 5.33.3–4). The fanciful descriptions in *b. Ketub.* 111b–112a are equally ludicrous (e.g. it will take a ship to carry one grape!). Compared to these texts, the numbers in the gospels do not seem obviously out of the ordinary. We therefore register our disagreement with Jeremias. The yield in our parable is probably not spectacularly overdone.

It is not coincidence that there are three different fruitful yields. These balance the three types of wasted seed. In fact, in Mark's version of the sower the two triads form a sort of chiasmus, with the worst seed and the best at the extremes, the best of the worst and the worst of the best in the middle. This makes for an orderly progression from the least fruitful to the most fruitful—

> seed which never sprouted because eaten by birds
> > seed which lasted only a while, until overcome with heat
> > > seed which grew up but was finally choked by thorns
> > > > thirtyfold yield
> > > sixtyfold yield
> > a hundredfold yield

[49] M. Pamment, 'The kingdom of Heaven according to the First Gospel', *NTS* 27 (1981), p. 218.

[50] E.g. Sib. Or. 3.263–4; Theophrastus, *Hist. Plant.* 8.7.4; Strabo 15.3.11; Pliny, *N.H.* 18.21.94–5.

It has even been proposed that the parable of the sower as spoken by Jesus was triadic throughout, and that the phrases or clauses which fall outside a triadic pattern are secondary.[51]

9. ὁ ἔχων ὦτα ἀκουέτω. This wandering imperative has the same form in 11.15 (q.v.) and 13.43. Mk 4.9 (καὶ ἔλεγεν· ὃς ἔχει ὦτα ἀκούειν ἀκουέτω) is not so succinct. That Luke, like Matthew, alters ὃς ἔχει to ὁ ἔχων is not remarkable. Both of them otherwise show a preference for this form of the saying (cf. Mt 11.15; 13.43; Lk 14.35). Gos. Thom. 9 fails to follow the parable of the sower with the saying about ears, and some have taken this as one indication that it draws upon tradition independent of the synoptics.

There is a variant of the parable of the Sower in Gos. Thom. 9: 'Jesus said: Behold, the sower went out, he filled his hand, he threw. Some fell on the way; the birds came, they gathered them. Others fell on the rock and did not strike root down into the earth and did not produce ears upwards. And others fell on the thorns. They choked the seed and the worm ate them. And others fell on the good earth; and it brought forth good fruit. It bore sixty per measure and one hundred twenty per measure'. Although one might infer Matthean influence from the consistent use of the plural for seeds (contrast Mark and Luke), one is hardly compelled to do so. At the same time, there are good reasons for doubting that, even if it is independent of the synoptics, Gos. Thom. 9 is closer to Jesus' original composition than the canonical versions. 'Sixty per measure and one hundred twenty per measure'[52] spoils the rhetorical balance between the three groups of bad seed and the three groups of good seed (see p. 385). Moreover, 'the worm ate them' (cf. Gos. Thom. 76) and 'per measure' (a helpful clarification) strike one as secondary additions; and 'he filled his hand, he threw' (cf. Gos. Thom. 17, 41) and 'did not strike root down into the earth and did not produce ears upwards' (ehrai etpe) might be influenced by Gnostic tendencies.[53] One could also argue that the treatment of Mk 4.3–9 by both Matthew and Luke reflects a predilection for abbreviating our parable, a predilection also manifest in Thomas.

THE REASON FOR SPEAKING IN PARABLES (13.10–17)

Although the disciples have, as shall soon be made clear,

---

[51] Cf. B. B. Scott, 'Essaying the Rock: The Authenticity of the Jesus Parable Tradition', *Forum* 2/1 (1986), pp. 10–11.

[52] Cf. perhaps Concept of our Great Power 43.19–21, where one hundred and twenty is 'the perfect number'.

[53] Cf. the Gnostic idea of the 'Pleroma' and Hipploytus, *Refut. omn. haer.* 5.3, which describes a Gnostic (Naassene) ritual in which corn is lifted towards heaven. For seed being cast to the earth cf. Corp. Herm. 14.10.

religious understanding, the parable of the sower moves them to ask a question. They want to know why Jesus speaks in parables. Why not instead teach in a straightforward manner? Their query gives Jesus the opportunity to discourse upon the differences between these who have been given the secrets of the kingdom of heaven and those who have not. The passage is based upon Mk 4.10–12 but has been augmented by a saying from Q (vv. 16–17 = Lk 10.23f.) and another from Mark (4.25; cf. Mt 13.12).

Mk 4.3–20 exhibits a pattern found in the OT, Jewish apocalypses, rabbinic literature, and Hermetic and Gnostic texts: a. teaching, (b. change of scene or audience,) c. question, d. reproach, e. interpretation/clarification (cf. Zech 4; Mk 7.14–23; 2 Bar 13–15; Gos. Thom. 42–43; Apocryphon Jas 6–7; Corp. Herm. 10.6–7; Daube, pp. 141–50). See E. E. Lemcio, 'External Evidence for the Structure and Function of Mark iv. 1–20, vii. 14–23 and viii. 14–21', *JTS* 29 (1978), pp. 323–38. In Matthew, however, the reproach has been dropped; compare 13.24–43 and contrast 16.5–12.

10. καὶ προσελθόντες οἱ μαθηταὶ εἶπαν αὐτῷ· διὰ τί ἐν παραβολαῖς λαλεῖς αὐτοῖς; Over against Mk 4.10 our text contains favourite Matthean vocabulary[54] and lacks 'And when he was alone' (perhaps because the point—that Jesus is speaking only to his disciples—is manifest from the context[55]). In addition, 'the twelve' has become 'the disciples'[56] and the ambiguous and difficult 'those who were about him' has been dropped (so also Luke), leaving a neater contrast between 'them' and 'the disciples'. But the main change *vis-à-vis* Mark is that the question directed to Jesus has been clarified. 'Asked him concerning the parables' is unclear. Is the subject the meaning of Jesus' parables (especially the sower) or the purpose behind parabolic teaching? Matthew opts for the second alternative: 'Why do you speak to them in parables?' (Contrast Luke, who chooses the other interpretation: 'And when his disciples asked him what this parable meant . . .').

11. Most interpreters now agree that Mt 13.11, 13 = Mk 4.11f. preserves an isolated saying which Mark or another inserted between the parable of the sower and its interpretation (see Ambrozic, pp. 47–53). The logion is also generally considered to be primitive. It contains Semitisms[57] and, more importantly, in the allusion to Isa 6.9 agrees

---

[54] προσέρχομαι*; διὰ τί (Mt: 7; Mk: 3; Lk 5); λαλέω (see on 13.13).

[55] Note the αὐτοῖς, which is pejorative. Are we to imagine that the disciples are in the boat with Jesus and that he now turns to talk to them alone?

[56] Similarly Luke ('his disciples'). Cf. Mt 18.1 diff. Mk 9.33–5. Matthew shows a tendency to turn Mark's 'the twelve' into 'the twelve disciples' (see with their Matthean parallels Mk 6.7; 10.32; 14.17). That is, Matthew is less inclined to use the unqualified 'the twelve'.

[57] Jeremias, *Parables*, p. 15, notes the antithetic parallelism, the redundant

with the targum over against both the MT and LXX.[58] Some would ascribe Mk 4.11f. to Jesus,[59] others to the early church.[60] But perhaps we are not confronted by such a clear-cut alternative. As Taylor conjectured, we could well have here 'an unauthentic version of a genuine saying' (*Mark*, p. 257). He suggested that before their adoption into Mark the words had nothing to do with the parables (cf. Jeremias, *Parables*, pp. 16–18). Before Mark ἐν παραβολαῖς (or its Semitic equivalent) meant simply 'in riddles', and the passage to which it belonged recorded Jesus' impression of 'the similarity between the results of his ministry and the experience of Isaiah' (*Mark*, p. 258). By alluding to the ironic words of Isa 6.9f., Jesus was in effect saying: 'To the disciples it had been given to know the secret of the Kingdom, but to those without everything happened in riddles!' (*ibid.*; cf. Mt 11.25f.). Chilton (v) has made a similar proposal. He finds Mk 4.12 to be dominical, 4.11, with its use of 'mystery' and 'those outside', to be influenced by post-Easter opposition to the gospel.[61] The former appears to be 'a characterization of those who refuse to see and hear, and not to reflect a deliberate banishment of the "outsiders"'; but the latter draws an exclusivist distinction between a closed community and those outside which is more characteristic of the post-Easter period (cf. Mk 9.38–40). Thus 4.11, according to Chilton, is the church's gloss on the authentic 4.12. Perhaps he is correct.

ὁ δὲ ἀποκριθεὶς εἶπεν αὐτοῖς. Mk 4.11 opens with καὶ ἔλεγεν αὐτοῖς. The minor agreement with Matthew in Lk 8.10 (ὁ δὲ εἶπεν) is nothing but coincidence.

ὅτι ὑμῖν δέδοται γνῶναι τὰ μυστήρια τῆς βασιλείας τῶν οὐρανῶν Compare the agraphon in Clement of Alexandria, *Strom.* 5.10.63 ('For the prophet says: Who shall understand a parable of the Lord save he that is wise and knowledgeable and loveth his Lord? For it is given to few to contain all things; for it is not as grudging that the Lord commanded in a certain gospel: My mystery for me and for the sons of my house') and Ps.-Clem. Hom. 19.20 ('And Peter said: "We remember that our Lord and teacher, commanding us, said, 'Keep the mysteries for me and the sons of my house'. Wherefore also he explained to His disciples privately the

demonstrative ἐκείνοις, and the threefold use of circumlocution for divine activity (δέδοται, γίνεται, ἀφεθῇ).

[58] Mark and the targum agree is using the third person, in having participles (partial agreement with the LXX) and the divine passive, and in ending with the phrase, 'and it be forgiven them'. See further Gnilka, *Verstockung*, pp. 13–17.

[59] E.g. Manson, *Teaching*, pp. 75–80; Jeremias, *Parables*, pp. 13–18. In a famous argument Manson contended that Mark mistranslated the ambiguous Aramaic *dĕ* by ἵνα. *dĕ* was intended as a relative: '*who* indeed see, etc.' (cf. the targum). For criticism see Black, pp. 212–14.

[60] E.g. Pesch 1, pp. 238–9; Carlston, pp. 105–9.

[61] μυστήριον appears in the synoptics only here. For οἱ ἔξω see 2 Macc 1.16; 1 Cor 5.12–13; 1 Thess 4.12.

mysteries of the kingdom of Heaven"'); also Hermas, *Sim.* 5.4. Matthew's wording is based on Mk 4.11: ὑμῖν τὸ μυστήριον δέδοται τῆς βασιλείας τοῦ θεοῦ. Our evangelist has replaced 'the kingdom of God' with his favourite 'the kingdom of Heaven' and underlined the element of knowing (γνῶναι; cf. the use of συνίημι in 13.13, 19, 23 and 51).

Pace McNeile, p. 189, and others, ὅτι is here not recitative but means 'because'. It answers to the διὰ τί of 13.10. The disciples ask, 'Why ...?' Jesus answers, 'Because ...' (cf. the use of διά after διὰ τί in 17.19–20).

μυστήριον(ια) appears in the gospels only in Mk 4.11 and its parallels. Its content, according to the consensus of modern scholarship, is the *presence* of the kingdom in Jesus and his ministry.[62] This mysterious presence is a truth which is recognized only by the minority, by those who, because they follow Jesus, understand his words. The background for the term as it is found in the gospels would therefore seem to be supplied not by Hellenistic religion but the Dead Sea Scrolls and Jewish apocalyptic literature.[63] In the Jewish sources *rāz* and its equivalents are often used in connexion with God's purposes for the last days, as in Dan 2.27–8: 'Daniel answered the king, "No wise men, enchanters, magicians, or astrologers can show to the king the mystery (*rāzâ*; μυστήριον) which the king has asked, but there is a God in heaven who reveals mysteries (*rāzîn*; μυστήρια), and he has made known to King Nebuchadnezzar what will be in the latter days"'.[64] Jewish sources also supply abundant parallels to the notion that God's secrets are made known only to a handful.[65]

One aspect of Mt 13.10ff. should not be missed. In their preoccupation with wondering how God can justly give knowledge to only a select group, some commentators have failed to see that the emphasis of the text lies not on privation but on God's gift. This 13.16f. and the remainder of the chapter make manifest. The normal state of humanity is ignorance of God's eschatological secrets. Human beings as human beings do not know the truth about the kingdom of heaven. If therefore some have come to know that truth, it can only be because of God's gracious dealings with them. Compare 1QH 1.21: 'these

---

[62] See the scholars cited by Ambrozic, p. 92, n. 198, and Beasley-Murray, p. 364, n. 169. This interpretation holds for the pre-Markan tradition as well as for Mark and Matthew. (We can detect no significant difference in meaning between the plural, 'mysteries' (Matthew, Luke) and the singular, 'mystery' (Mark).)

[63] For discussion see esp. J. A. Robinson, pp. 234–40; G. Bornkamm, *TWNT* 4, pp. 809–34; and R. E. Brown, *The Semitic Background of the Term 'Mystery' in the New Testament*, FBBS, Philadelphia, 1968.

[64] See further 1 En. 68.5; 103.2; 4 Ezra 10.38; 14.5; 2 Bar. 81.4; Par. Jer. 9.29; *b. Meg.* 3a; Tg. Ps.-Jn. to Gen 49.1; SB 1, pp. 659–60. Cf. Rom 11.25–6; 2 Thess 2.7; Rev 10.7; 17.5–7.

[65] Cf. Num 12.8; 1QS 9.17; 4 Ezra 12.36–7; 2 Bar. 48.2–3.

things I know by the wisdom which comes from thee, for thou hast unstopped my ears to marvellous mysteries'. Mt 11.25 ('revealed them to babes') and 16.17 ('flesh and blood has not revealed this to you but my Father who is in heaven') make the same point: eschatological knowledge is the gift of God. Thus 13.10ff. is a testimony to God's kindness. If one nonetheless still wants to ask how God can grant his eschatological revelation to only a few, we may answer for Matthew that it was the mission of the disciples after Easter to *share* through proclamation much that was theretofore kept secret (cf. 17.9), and further that if revelation has not come to all, the fault must lie not with God but with human sin and moral failing. 'Seek and ye shall find' (7.7) means that the truth is there for all those who search for it. The converse is that those who do not seek will not find. This is why there must be an economy of truth, that good may be rewarded and evil deprived. In addition, Matthew, who has passed down the warning about not giving dogs what is holy and not casting pearls before swine, almost certainly believed that it would be nothing less than blasphemous were certain divine mysteries to be made known without discrimination; and the tradition which traced the disaster of Noah's flood to the uncovering of heavenly secrets by people unworthy of them (1 En. 6–11; cf. 65.6) would not have been foreign to his world of thought.[66] In short, our author was probably persuaded that esoterism, so far from being arbitrary, was a moral necessity, and he would quite likely have been happy with Chrysostom's exegesis: 'This [Mt 13.10ff.] He said, not bringing in necessity, or any allotment made carelessly and at random, but implying them to be the authors of all their own evils, and wishing to represent that the thing is a gift, and a grace bestowed from above' (*Hom. on Mt* 45.1).

Lk 8.10b agrees with Matthew against Mark in three particulars: δέδοται after ὑμῖν, γνῶναι after δέδοται, and τὰ μυστήρια for τὸ μυστήριον. But it is unwarranted to hold that Matthew and Luke must preserve a non-Markan tradition.[67] Streeter, p. 313, handled the problem in this way: 'The phrase "the mystery is given to you" is obscure; the verb γνῶναι (to understand) is the most natural one for two independent interpreters to supply. But note the singular μυστήριον is read in Matthew by *k c, a ff*² Syr. S. and C., Clem. Iren.' To this we only need add that Matthew often prefers plurals (Allen,

---

[66] Note also 1QS 5.11–12; 2 Bar. 38.1; 51.4; *Exod. Rab.* on 12.50.

[67] *Pace* Cerfaux (v), among others, Mark's singular ('mystery') is probably not due to Pauline influence, and the priority of Matthew cannot be argued for on the basis of the common use of the plural ('mysteries') in Semitic sources (including the Dead Sea Scrolls).

p. 83) and that γινώσκω or a cognate is frequently associated with μυστήριον in early Christian literature.[68]

ἐκείνοις δὲ οὐ δέδοται. Mk 4.11 reads: 'But to those outside (τοῖς ἔξω) everything is in parables'. Matthew has split this line in two, a procedure which permits him to use the first half for the couplet in 13.11 and the second half for 13.13.

12. This verse, which is taken from Mk 4.25 (cf. Mt 25.29 = Lk 19.26: Q), has been inserted into its present Matthean context in order to illustrate further the differences between the disciples and those who do not understand the mysteries of the kingdom. It accentuates the distinction between those who perceive and those who do not. 'To him who has will more be given' refers to the disciples, who have understanding and will be given more understanding.[69] 'To him who has not, even what he has will be taken away' refers to those not privy to be secrets of the kingdom: they do not and will not understand. Thus it is explained why the parables hide and reveal at the same time. Their effect—illumination or darkness—depends upon the status of the hearer. Knowledge is rewarded with knowledge, ignorance with ignorance. Like begets like.

Mt 13.12 par. is presumably an authentic utterance of Jesus. It has multiple attestation (Mark, Q, Gos. Thom. 41), other antithetical proverbs are to be assigned to Jesus,[70] and retranslation into Aramaic is no problem.[71] Nevertheless, an impenetrable darkness would seem to cloak the original intention, for the pre-Easter context is unknown. We can guess that Jesus took up a secular sentiment or proverb whose meaning was, life is unjust, the rich get richer and the poor get poorer,[72] in order to a make some religious point. But beyond that no sound inferences can be drawn.

ὅστις γὰρ ἔχει. Mk 4.25 has ὅς. On the interchange between ὅς and ὅστις in the NT see BDF § 293.

δοθήσεται αὐτῷ. So Mk 4.25. God is the implicit subject of the passive.

καὶ περισσευθήσεται. This is a redactional addition,[73] perhaps suggested by Mk 4.24 ('and still more will be given you'). The same words will again be inserted in 25.29.

ὅστις δὲ οὐκ ἔχει. Mark has καὶ ὃς οὐκ ἔχει. Matthew's ὅστις* increases the parallelism with v. 12a, and δέ (which

---

[68] E.g. Rom 11.25; Eph 1.9; 3.3; 6.19; Col 2.2.

[69] Cf. 2 Bar. 38.1: 'O Lord, my God, you are the one who has always enlightened those who conduct themselves with understanding.'

[70] E.g. Mt 8.20; 12.35; 15.11; 23.12.

[71] See Jeremias, *Theology*, p. 23.

[72] For this sentiment in the rabbis see Schlatter, p. 430, and SB 1, pp. 660–62.

[73] περισσευω: Mt: 5 (redactional in 5.20; 13.12; 25.29); Mk: 1; Lk: 4. The passive of this verb does not occur in the LXX or classical Greek.

sharpens the contrast) is also redactional in the doublet in 25.29.

καὶ ὃ ἔχει ἀρθήσεται ἀπ' αὐτοῦ. This was found in both Mark and Q, and Matthew has not seen fit to introduce any alterations. Compare 4 Ezra 7.25; Gos. Thom. 41; and b. B. Qam. 92a.[74]

13. διὰ τοῦτο ἐν παραβολαῖς αὐτοῖς λαλῶ. Compare Mk 4.11c: 'but to those outside everything is in parables'. διὰ τοῦτο* is Matthean; and of twenty-six occurrences of λαλέω, exactly half belong to chapters 12 and 13.

ὅτι βλέποντες οὐ βλέπουσιν. Compare Mk 8.18 (quoting Jer 5.21).[75] Mk 4.12 (ἵνα βλέποντες βλέπωσιν καὶ μὴ ἴδωσιν) is more obviously an allusion to the Scriptures (LXX Isa 6.9: βλέποντες βλέψετε καὶ οὐ μὴ εἰδῆτε). Luke, like Matthew, has replaced Mark's Semitism with the sentence structure: verb + negative particle + verb (βλέποντες μὴ βλέπωσιν). All the synoptics agree against the OT in putting the clause on seeing before the clause on hearing.

Regardless of how one understand's Mark's troublesome ἵνα,[76] Matthew's ὅτι makes the parables a *response* to unbelief: they are uttered *because* people see and do not see, because they hear and do not hear. This puts the emphasis unambiguously on human responsibility. More particularly, it makes the parables a consequence of the unbelief that has withstood Jesus' gracious teaching and salvific ministry (see Mt 8–12). For Matthew, Jesus did not speak in parables to outsiders until hostility raised its ugly head.

καὶ ἀκούοντες οὐκ ἀκούουσιν οὐδὲ συνίουσιν. Mk 4.12 (καὶ ἀκούοντες ἀκούωσιν καὶ μὴ συνίωσιν) is a bit closer to the LXX (Isa 6.9: ἀκοῇ ἀκούσετε καὶ οὐ μὴ συνῆτε).

The use Matthew makes of συνίημι, which occurs here for the first time in our gospel, has been examined in detail by Held, in *TIM*, pp. 106–112. He demonstrates that 'understanding' is one of the chief characteristics of the disciples and that the evangelist's focus on this has led to significant modification of Mark's so-called 'messianic secret'. Thus, if by and large the disciples in the Second Gospel cannot 'understand' much before Jesus rises from the dead, in Matthew they can, at least with Jesus' aid (cf. 13.51; 15.15–20; 16.9–12; 17.10–13;

---

[74] Cf. b. B. Bat. 174b; b. Ḥul. 105b.

[75] Note also Heraclitus, frag. 107: 'Eyes and ears are evil witnesses for men if they have barbarian souls.' One must use discernment and imagination to see with more than the physical senses.

[76] It could be telic (so most). It could be the equivalent of ὅπως or ὅτι or even ὅτι πληρωθῇ. It could misrepresent the Aramaic dĕ, the meaning being 'who' (see p. 388, n. 59). Or it could be imperative: 'let them, etc.' See the commentaries on Mark.

note also Matthew's treatment of Mk 4.13 and 6.52). In this way Matthew blurs the line between the pre- and post-Easter periods. The result is that the Christian reader may identify more readily with the disciples. Also, the stress on understanding well serves Matthew's view of the apostles as the authoritative bearers of Jesus' teaching.

Isa 6.9–10 was a very important text for the early church.[77] In the NT it is cited or alluded to in Mt 13.13 par.; Jn 12.40; Acts 28.26–7; and Rom 11.8. And the use of πωρόω or πώρωσις in Mk 3.5; 6.52; 8.17; Rom 11.7, 25; 2 Cor 3.14; and Eph 4.18 has sometimes been traced to the influence of the passage from Isaiah. However that may be, Isa 6.9–10 offered itself as a convenient aid to explaining unbelief, and on more than one occasion it was employed to justify missionaries turning from an obdurate Israel to the Gentiles.

Lindars (v) has argued that the apologetic use of Isa 6.9–10 passed through three stages. In the first, the text was concerned with the negative response to the church's message (cf. Acts 28.25–7). In the second, it was associated with Jesus' ministry in particular and used to explain why he was rejected by his people (Mk 4.11–12). In the third stage, Isa 6.9–10 became applied specifically to Jesus' healing ministry and to people's refusal to accept it (Jn 12.40). Perhaps, however, it is better to combine the second and third stages and to regard them as the first stage, for Jesus himself probably used Isa 6.9–10 to interpret his own situation (see p. 388). If so, then Lindars' first stage would have to be moved to second place. One may also add a third stage, for the OT passage later came to be discussed in connexion with the problem of free will and providence (cf. Irenaeus, *Adv. haer.* 4.29.1; Origen, *De prin.* 3.1.7).

Matthew has omitted the final clause of Mk 4.12: 'lest (μήποτε) they turn again and be forgiven'. This probably sounded too harsh. Matthew did not want to leave the impression that Jesus intended from the beginning to leave sinners in their plight.[78] On the contrary, the gospel as a whole makes it plain that spiritual blindness is the effect of wickedness, not the result of some arbitrary, prior action of God or Jesus. That is to say, unbelief is rooted not in Jesus' words but in hardened hearts. If few are chosen, it is not because many have not been called.

HG and NA[26] both print the following after Mt 13.13: καὶ ἀναπληροῦται αὐτοῖς ἡ προφητεία Ἠσαΐου ἡ λέγουσα· ἀκοῇ ἀκούσετε καὶ οὐ μὴ συνῆτε, καὶ βλέποντες βλέψετε καὶ οὐ μὴ ἴδητε (or: εἰδῆτε). ἐπαχύνθη γὰρ ἡ καρδία τοῦ λαοῦ τούτου, καὶ τοῖς ὠσὶν βαρέως ἤκουσαν καὶ τοὺς ὀφθαλμοὺς αὐτῶν ἐκάμμυσαν, μήποτε ἴδωσιν τοῖς ὀφθαλμοῖς καὶ τοῖς ὠσὶν ἀκούσωσιν καὶ τῇ καρδίᾳ συνῶσιν καὶ ἐπιστρέψωσιν καὶ ἰάσομαι αὐτούς. With only minor and insignificant variants this is the

---

[77] Lit.: Dodd, *Scriptures*, pp. 36–9; Lindars, *Apologetic*, pp. 154–67; Gnilka, *Verstockung*, passim; C. A. Evans, 'The Function of Isaiah 6.9–10 in Mark and John', *NovT* 24 (1982), pp. 124–38.

[78] Cf. the careful introductions to the formula quotations in 2.17 and 27.9: in order to avoid the idea that God planned and carried out evil, the usual ἵνα πληρωθῇ is dropped.

text of all mss. and versions.[79] Along with many others, however, we think it slightly more likely than not that the lines are a (very early) post-Matthean interpolation.[80] These are the reasons: (i) ἀναπληροῦται and προφητεία are not found in the other formula quotations and indeed are Matthean *hapax legomena*. (ii) The gospel text runs smoothly if 13.14–15 is omitted. Indeed, 13.14–15 interrupts the antithetical parallelism between vv. 13 and 16: αὐτοῖς/ὑμῶν; οὐ βλέπουσιν/ βλέπουσιν; οὐκ ἀκούουσιν/ ἀκούουσιν. (iii) Only here is a formula quotation placed on Jesus' lips. (iv) The text is almost purely LXX, which runs against the Hebraizing tendency of the other formula quotations. (v) The citation seems superfluous because Isa 6.9 has just been alluded to so clearly (13.13). (vi) Acts 28.26–7 agrees exactly with Mt 13.14–15. Both reproduce the LXX except that they lack αὐτῶν after the first ὠσίν. Thus it has been suggested, and not implausibly, that Acts 28.26–7 was the source for the gospel quotation. (vii) λέ-γουσα in the nominative qualifying προφητεία (so that the prophet himself speaks the word) is unexpected. Matthew otherwise has *God himself speak, through* the prophet (cf. 1.22; 2.15, 17; etc.).

16f. In contrast with others (13.11), the disciples truly see and hear. In thus accurately perceiving they are, Jesus boldly proclaims, beholding what the prophets and the righteous of old only longed to see, namely, the eschatological revelation of God—which for Matthew includes Jesus' parables.

The close parallel in Lk 10.23–4 means that Mt 13.16–17 belonged to Q. In Luke the lines follow the great thanksgiving (Lk 10.21–2 = Mt 11.25–7), and that probably preserves the Q sequence.

The saying, whose original context is uncertain, is almost universally assigned to Jesus.[81] It is an important witness to the fact that he believed the powers of the eschatological age to be already present and accessible to human experience. Worth comparing are the beatitudes in Ps. Sol. 17.50 ('Blessed be they that *shall* be in those days, in that they *shall* see the good fortune of Israel which God *shall* bring to pass in the gathering of the tribes') and 18.7 ('Blessed *shall* they be' that *shall* be in those days, in that they *shall* see the goodness of the Lord which he *shall* perform for the generation that is to come'). In these two texts those who *shall* see the messianic age are blessed. Jesus, however, declares that salvation has come *now*. As T. W. Manson wrote: 'The point of the saying is that what for all former generations lay still in the future is now a present reality. What was for the best of the past only an object of faith and hope is now a matter of experience'.[82]

---

[79] But D opens with this: και τοτε πληρωθησεται επ αυτοις η προφητεια του Ησαιου λεγουσα· πορευθητι και ειπε τω λαω τουτω (cf. it).

[80] Cf. S. E. Johnson, 'The Biblical Quotations in Matthew', *HTR* 34 (1943), p. 137; Stendahl, *School*, pp. 129–32; Rothfuchs, pp. 23–4; Soares-Prabhu, pp. 31–5. For the other side see F. Van Segbroeck, 'Le scandale de l'incroyance', *ETL* 41 (1965), pp. 349–51; Gundry, *OT*, pp. 116–18.

[81] Cf. Bultmann, *History*, p. 126; Chilton, *Rabbi*, p. 135.

[82] *Sayings*, p. 80; see further Kümmel, *Promise*, pp. 112–13. – – *Pace* Grimm (v), we do not find Isa 52.13-15 to be the key to our text.

ὑμῶν δὲ μακάριοι οἱ ὀφθαλμοὶ ὅτι βλέπουσιν. Compare the makarism in *b.Ḥag.* 14b ('blessed are my eyes that have seen thus'). Matthew's ὑμῶν is emphatic. The line was much cited during the iconoclastic controversy (e.g. John of Damascus, *Imag.* 3.12).

Lk 10.23 has: μακάριοι οἱ ὀφθαλμοὶ οἱ βλέποντες ἃ βλέπετε. The differences between this and Matthew's version need not be traced to the ambiguity of the Aramaic *dî*, which could be read either as a relative pronoun or a subordinating conjunction (a proposal supported by Black, pp. 70–1, 215–16). Matthew has probably rewritten Lk 10.23 = Q (cf. Schulz, *Q*, pp. 420–1). For ἃ appears in Mt 13.17 = Lk 10.24; and one strongly suspects that Mt 13.16 has been assimilated to 13.13 (ὅτι βλέποντες), with the result that there is a shift from the content of what is seen (cf. Luke) to the topic of perception itself (which better fits 13.10–17).

καὶ τὰ ὦτα ὑμῶν ὅτι ἀκούουσιν.[83] There is no parallel in Luke. Matthew may have added the line so as to increase the parallelism with 13.13 and 17.[84]

ἀμὴν γὰρ λέγω ὑμῖν ὅτι πολλοὶ προφῆται καὶ δίκαιοι ἐπεθύμησαν ἰδεῖν ἃ βλέπετε καὶ οὐκ εἶδαν. Compare and contrast Jn 8.56 ('Your father Abraham rejoiced that he was to see my day; he saw it and was glad'); Heb 11.13 ('These all died in faith, not having received what was promised, but having seen it and greeted it from afar'); and 1 Pet 1.10 ('The prophets who prophesied of the grace that was to be yours searched and inquired about this salvation'); also Eph 3.4–5. Jewish parallels include the Palestinian targums to Num 24.3 and 15, where it is said that mysteries hidden from the prophets were revealed to Balaam. 'Righteous men' is here an inclusive term which covers all the just who looked forward to the coming of the Messiah. It is therefore broader than 'prophets' (cf. Josephus, *Ant.* 10.38).

Lk 10.24 lacks ἀμήν*, puts γάρ after λέγω, and has βασιλεῖς ἠθέλησαν before ἰδεῖν and ὑμεῖς after ἃ. Evidently Matthew has replaced 'kings' with 'righteous men' (δίκαιος* being a Matthean favourite; cf. esp. 10.41 and 23.29) and dropped ὑμεῖς (thereby adding to the parallelism between 17a and b). Whether 'amen' belonged to Q cannot be determined. Whereas Matthew often adds the word to Mark, Luke often drops it. Also, whether Q had ἠθέλησαν or ἐπεθύμησαν (cf. *Gos. Thom.* 38) it is impossible to say.[85]

---

[83] υμων is absent from B 1424 *pc* it. Since it decreases the parallelism between vv. 16a and b, it might be secondary.

[84] Omission by Luke is favoured by Marshall, p. 438, citing Bultmann, Schürmann, Kümmel, and W. Michaelis.

[85] That the words are translation variants (ἐπεθ. for *’āwâ*, ἠθέλησαν for *’ābâ*) is an unnecessary hypothesis.

καὶ ἀκοῦσαι ἃ ἀκούετε καὶ οὐκ ἤκουσαν. So Lk 10.24b.

While references to 'seeing' the Messiah or the world to come are common in Jewish literature, the reference to 'hearing' in connexion with eschatology recalls not Jewish parallels but rather Mt 11.4–5; 'Announce to John what you see *and hear* . . . the deaf *hear* . . . and the poor have good news preached to them'. The emphasis upon *hearing* eschatological events seems to have been characteristic of Jesus, the preacher and teacher. (Cf. his use of 'He who has ears to hear, let him hear'.)

Two texts from the *Mekilta* may shed some light on Mt 13.16f. *Mek.* on Exod 15.2 reads as follows: 'R. Eliezer says: Whence can you say that a maid-servant saw at the sea what Isaiah and Ezekiel and all the prophets never saw? It says about them: "And by the ministry of the prophets have I used similitudes" (Hos 12.10)'. *Mek.* on Exod 19.11 has this: 'Another interpretation: *In the sight of all the people.* This teaches that at that moment the people saw what Isaiah and Ezekiel never saw. For it is said: "And by the ministry of the prophets have I used similitudes" (Hos 12.10)'. In these passages the witnesses of the Exodus and the people at Sinai are said to have seen what the prophets did not see. Not only that, but those who did not see are associated with 'similitudes'. If Matthew knew this tradition or something similar, it may have encouraged him to bring together the saying about prophets and wise men with Jesus' words on parables. This would have been all the more natural given the *Urzeit = Endzeit* equation: if the prophets did not witness God's great miracles at the beginning of salvation-history, neither did they apprehend the consummation; rather, their visions of God were unclear; they saw only 'parables'.

Gos. Thom. 38 reads: 'Jesus said: Many times you have desired (ἐπιθυμεῖν) to hear these words which I say to you, and you have no other from whom to hear them. There will be days when you will seek me and you will not find me' (cf. *P. Oxy.* 655 IIa; Gos. Thom. 17). There is an interesting parallel to this in Irenaeus, *Adv. haer.* 1.20.2: 'I have often desired to hear one of these words, and I had no one who could utter it' (cf. Epiphanius, *Haer.* 34.18.13). Clearly we have to do with a tradition independent of the synoptics. Whether the saying is a secondary creation based upon Lk 10.23f. par. or upon some other word of Jesus cannot be decided with any conviction.

THE INTERPRETATION OF THE PARABLE OF THE SOWER (13.18–23)

Matthew's allegorical interpretation of the parable of the four soils agrees in all essentials with Mk 4.13–20, from which it was taken (cf. also Lk 8.11–15). The seed which was sown beside or upon the path and which was eaten by birds stands for those who do not understand the word of the kingdom. The evil one comes and snatches the word out of their hearts. The seed sown on rocky ground represents those who receive the word with joy but soon fall away when hard times come. The seed sown among thorns stands for those who receive the word but prove unfruitful because they give themselves over to the cares of the world and its riches. Finally, those sown in good soil are those who understand the word. They produce much fruit.

The tendency of twentieth-century scholarship has been to regard the interpretaion of the sower as secondary, 'a sermon upon the parable as text' (Dodd).[86] The reasons are several. (i) Jesus, it is urged, did not use allegory. (ii) The allegorical interpretation allegedly misses the eschatological thrust of the parable, that is, the contrast between the present and God's future. (iii) The vocabulary is said to be characteristic of the post-Easter period.[87] (iv)The style, many claim, is not Semitic,[88] and ἄκαρπος and πρόσκαιρος do not have Semitic counterparts.[89] (v) Mk 4.13–20 is not entirely consistent with either itself or with 4.3–9.[90] While in the latter the different soils stand for individuals, in 4.13–20 the seed represents individuals (as well as the word).[91] (vi) Gos. Thom. 9 offers no interpretation.

Of these several points, (i) carries little weight with us, in view of what was said on pp. 378–82. Moreover, it is not true that every detail of the parable receives an allegorical meaning; the sower, for example, is not identified, and the different yields are not explained.[92] As for (ii), it simply begs the question. (iii) has more force, although the studies of Cranfield[93] give reason for caution. The most obvious post-Easter expression, ὁ λόγος, could conceivably have had some equivalent in Jesus' speech. Note Lk 11.28: 'Blessed rather are those who hear the word of God and keep it.' Also making for caution is the

[86] *Parables*, p. 145. Cf. Bultmann, *History*, p. 187; Weder pp. 111–13.

[87] Dodd, *Parables*, p. 3, n. 1: 'πρόσκαιρος, ἀπάτη are not found in the Synoptics outside this passage; ἐπιθυμία is found elsewhere only in Lk xxii. 15, in a different sense; διωγμός and θλῖψις are found only in Mk. x. 30, and in the Synoptic Apocalypse (Mk. xiii.), passages which are for other reasons suspected of being secondary.' For further discussion see Jeremias, *Parables*, pp. 78–9.

[88] Payne, 'Authenticity' (v), however, calls attention to the fourfold parallelism, the redundant definite articles, the possibility that 'these are those who were sown' can be explained as an imperfect translation of Aramaic, the striking parataxis, and the threefold ἐν; see p. 180.

[89] But Cranfield refers to the Syriac adjective *zabnaya* (='temporary', 'transient'; see *Mark*, p. 162); and the Aramaic *quṣra* might also fit the bill.

[90] This can be taken to indicate the use of more than one source (cf. Albright and Mann, p. 178) or imperfect editing (cf. Brown (v), p. 328).

[91] One can avoid this by understanding the several uses of σπειρόμενοι as elliptical for 'sown (with seed)'; cf. NEB. This is not a natural way of reading the Greek. For the suggestion that the difficulty is due to misunderstanding Aramaic see Payne, 'Inconsistency' (v), pp. 173–7.

[92] The Fathers, by contrast, did allegorize the numbers. Brown (v), p. 328, n. 21, notes that for Jerome the one hundred percent=chaste women, the sixty percent widows, the thirty percent those married (PL 26.89); and that for Augustine 100=martyrs, 60=widows, 30=married (PL 35.1326). See also Theophylact in PG 123.532 and the texts in Wailes, pp. 100–1.

[93] Cranfield (v); also his commentary, *Mark*, pp. 161–3.

circumstance that the parable proper, Mk 4.3–9, which is accepted as dominical by almost all scholars, has several words which are not found elsewhere in the teachings of Jesus.[94] (iv), although not irrelevant, is not decisive, for it is hardly self-evident that a passage must be denied to Jesus simply because it has not been slavishly translated. Again, point (v) is of doubtful impact. One would be hard pressed to justify the supposition that folk literature must always be consistent in its details. Further, 4 Ezra in one place[95] identifies seed with the law, in another[96] with people. (Cf. also the similar shift of images in Col 1.5–10). Lastly, the failure of Thomas to reproduce the synoptic interpretation will carry weight only with those who think that source to be completely independent of the synoptics. And beyond that, one can make the argument that the author of Thomas systematically suppressed explanations of gospel material in order to keep them esoteric.

If the case against authenticity is not conclusive, what of the case for authenticity?[97] Its strongest claim is that once one grants that the parable has to do with preaching of the word, the Markan interpretation seems natural, and much of it inevitable. As Boucher puts it: 'There is nothing in the broad lines of ... [the] interpretation that strains the sense of the reference in the parable itself. Even a simple, uneducated hearer ... would have been able to supply [the] constituent meanings, once he had perceived the whole meaning to be about the word. There is yet further natural meaning that could have been suggested to a more sophisticated hearer, one who was willing and able to ruminate on the narrative. The birds who come and devour the first seed suggest an enemy, and one that is an outside agent, external to the earth. The rocky ground upon which the second seed falls suggests shallowness, a spontaneous but superficial response, the inability to survive hard times. The word "thorn" connotes something evil and injurious; thus the thorns among which the third seed falls suggest some pernicious thing in the very earth. The good soil in which the fourth seed falls and grows suggests the opposite of all these: resistance to attack from without, strength and endurance, the overcoming of difficulties from within. An intelligent hearer would be able to glean from the story such meanings as these, again if he initially understood the parable to be about the hearing of the word' (p. 49). Also favouring authenticity, or at least a Jewish Christian origin for the interpretation in Mk 4.13–20, is the passage in *m. 'Abot* 5.12 (see p. 376).

---

[94] πετρώδες, ἐξανατέλλω, καυματίζω, συμπνίγω, τριάκοντα, ἑξήκοντα.

[95] 9.31: 'For behold, I sow my law in you, and it shall bring forth fruit in you, and you shall be glorified through it forever.'

[96] 8.41–4: 'For just as the farmer sows many seeds upon the ground and plants a multitude of seedlings, and yet not all that have been sown will come up in due season, and not all that were planted will take root; so also those who have been sown in the world will not all be saved;' 'But man, who has been formed by thy hands and is called thy own image because he is made like thee, and for whose sake thou hast formed all things—hast thou also made him like the farmer's seed?'

[97] See Cranfield (v); Brown (v); Boucher, pp. 45–53.

So what, then, are we to conclude? It seems quite unreasonable to exclude dogmatically that Mk 4.13–20 rests upon an interpretation Jesus gave to the parable of the sower. At least the arguments against authenticity do not produce in us the tidal wave of doubt so often felt by others. At the same time, the case for a dominical origin, in our estimation, falls short of proof. And we remain troubled by the fact that the other extended interpretations of parables are not likely to come from Jesus (see on 13.37–43 and 49–50). See further Guelich, *Mark*, pp. 217–19, who believes that the parable of the sower was originally triadic (see above) and infers that the interpretation is secondary because it is not triadic.

18. ὑμεῖς οὖν ἀκούσατε τὴν παραβολὴν τοῦ σπείραντος.[98] ὑμεῖς is emphatic, τὴν παραβολήν elliptical ('(the meaning of) the parable'). Mk 4.13 ('And he says to them: Do you not understand this parable? How then will you understand all the parables?') would not have followed well upon the heels of the beatitude in 13.16f. So Matthew has toned down the passage; it is no longer so harsh on the disciples. Indeed, Matthew's Jesus clearly assumes that his closest followers have the ability to hear and understand. Compare Gundry, *Commentary*, p. 258: 'The typically Matthean οὖν ... helps turn Mark's question into an authoritative command based on the foregoing beatitude, as though to say, "Since you are so blessed to hear, hear!"'

19. The seed is identified with 'the word of the kingdom' and its fate now considered. Interestingly enough, nowhere in what follows is the sower clearly identified. The broader Matthean context, however, as well as 13.37 ('he who sows ... is the Son of man'), encourage one to think of Jesus.[99] The issue is Israel's response to Jesus and his proclamation.

παντὸς ἀκούοντος τὸν λόγον τῆς βασιλείας καὶ μὴ συνιέντος ἔρχεται ὁ πονηρὸς καὶ ἁρπάζει τὸ ἐσπαρμένον ἐν τῇ καρδίᾳ αὐτοῦ. The First Evangelist has simplified Mk 4.13, changed the plurals to singulars (cf. 13.20, 22, 23), added a reference to 'not understanding',[100] turned 'Satan' into 'the evil one' (see on 6.13), altered 'in them' to 'in his heart' (see below), introduced anacoluthon (cf. BDF § 466.3), and added typical Matthean vocabulary.[101] The expression 'word of the kingdom'[102] is

---

[98] σπειροντος appears in ℵ² C D L θ *f*¹·¹³ Maj co, σπειραντος in ℵ* B W X 33 *al* Or.

[99] Cf. Chrysostom, *Hom. on Mt* 44.4; Kingsbury, *Parables*, p. 34; Bonnard, p. 191.

[100] συνίημι is a key word in chapter 13; see vv. 13, 19, 23, 51. In fact, when Jesus has finished all his parables, he asks the disciples, 'Have you understood (συνήκατε) all these things?'

[101] πᾶς*, πονηρός*, ἁρπάζω*.

[102] On this and its relationship to other early Christian uses of λόγος see J. A. Baird, 'The Holy Word', *NTS* 33 (1987), pp. 585–99. Cf. the prophetic *dĕbar YHWH*.

unattested in ancient Jewish literature. It seems to mean 'the preaching of the kingdom' (cf. BAGD, s.v. λόγος 1.b.β). Lk 8.11 has 'the word of God' (cf. Lk 5.1; 8.21).

It is not to be overlooked that birds are frequently associated with the devil or demonic beings in Jewish tradition. In Jub. 11.11 Mastema sends ravens and birds to devour seed sown in the land. In Apoc. Abr. 13 Azazel manifests himself to Abraham in the form of an unclean bird. In b. Sanh. 107a Satan is seen by King David in the likeness of a bird. These texts (cf. also Rev 18.2) make the allegorical equation of birds with Satan less artificial than it otherwise might seem. Recall also Satan's status as the 'prince of the power of the air' (Eph 2.2; cf. T. Benj. 3.4 v.1.; 2 En. 29.5).

Lk 8.12 has the devil come to take the word 'from their hearts' (ἀπὸ τῆς καρδίας αὐτῶν). Some would detect here Matthean influence or a sign of a non-Markan source, for Matthew has 'in his heart', Mark only 'in him'.[103] But coincidental editing is no less likely. Mark's 'in them' could have prompted both Matthew and Luke to be more concrete, especially as the OT associates God's word with the heart (Deut 30.14) and as καρδία (Mt 16; Mk: 11; Lk: 22) is often redactional in both the First and Third Gospels. Note also that Luke will again add the word in 8.15 diff. Mk 4.20.

οὗτός ἐστιν ὁ παρὰ τὴν ὁδὸν σπαρείς. This is Matthew's version of Mk 4.15a. Whereas Mark's line introduces the account of the fate of the seed on or beside the path, Matthew's serves as the conclusion. This makes for a contrast with 13.20a: 'This is what was sown beside [or: on] the path. But as for that which was sown on rocky ground . . .'. Compare the contrast in vv. 22–3: 'This is the one who hears the word . . . But as for that which was sown on good soil . . .'.

20f. ὁ δὲ ἐπὶ τὰ πετρώδη σπαρείς Mk 4.16 again has plurals.

οὗτός ἐστιν ὁ τὸν λόγον ἀκούων καὶ εὐθὺς μετὰ χαρᾶς λαμβάνων αὐτόν. Mk 4.16b begins with οἱ ὅταν ἀκούσωσιν and uses λαμβάνουσιν. Matthew has assimilated to 13.19 (οὗτός ἐστιν ὁ), changed the plurals to singulars, but otherwise followed Mark. οὗτός ἐστιν κ.τ.λ. would seem to equate the hearer of the word with the seed, this in contrast to v. 19, where the seed is the word and the soil represents an individual. Sabourin, pp. 594–5, however, argues that the meaning really is: 'When I spoke about the seed sown on rocky ground, among thorns, on good soil, I had in mind him who hears the word . . .' This translation is permissible (cf. the Jerusalem Bible). But we prefer to endorse Allen, p. 147: Matthew 'follows Mk.'s confusion between the seed sown and the people amongst whom it is

---

[103] See e.g. Gundry, *Commentary*, p. 259.

sown'. The interpretation of the parable of the sower is simply not consistent in all its details.

οὐκ ἔχει δὲ ῥίζαν ἐν ἑαυτῷ ἀλλὰ πρόσκαιρός ἐστιν. So Mk 4.17, with introductory καί for δέ and plurals ('and they do not have root in themselves but last only for a while'). πρόσ-καιρος[104] means 'temporary, lasting only for a time' (cf. 2 Cor 4.18; Heb 11.25; Diognetus, *Ep.* 10.8). The word occurs only three times in the LXX, in 4 Macc. 15.2, 8, and 23. Luke explains with πρὸς καιρὸν πιστεύουσιν.

γενομένης δὲ θλίψεως ἢ διωγμοῦ διὰ τὸν λόγον εὐθὺς σκανδαλίζεται. Mk 4.17b opens with εἶτα, lacks δέ, and concludes with the plural, σκανδαλίζονται. For σκανδαλίζω[105] see on 5.29. It appears in an eschatological context in 24.10, again in close connexion with θλῖψις and the theme of persecution (cf. 24.9).

22. ὁ δὲ εἰς τὰς ἀκάνθας σπαρείς. Compare Mk 4.18: καὶ ἄλλοι εἰσὶν οἱ ἐπὶ[106] τὰς ἀκάνθας σπειρόμενοι.

οὗτός ἐστιν ὁ τὸν λόγον ἀκούων. In accordance with the singular subjects in vv. 19, 20, and 23, Mk 4.18 has been altered.

καὶ ἡ μέριμνα τοῦ αἰῶνος τούτου καὶ ἡ ἀπάτη τοῦ πλούτου συμπνίγει τὸν λόγον.[107] Compare Hermas, *Vis* 3.6. καὶ αἱ opens Mk 4.19, which also differs in having μέριμναι and συμπνί γουσιν and in lacking τοῦτο;[108] also, after 'wealth' Matthew has omitted as superfluous 'and the desire for other things enter in'.

ἀπάτη (= 'deceitfulness', 'pleasure')[109] is a Matthean *hapax legomenon* and appears in the synoptics only here and in Mk 4.19. It is used five times in the NT epistles (Eph 4.22; Col 2.8; 2 Thess 2.10; Heb 3.13; 2 Pet 2.13) and could be considered characteristic of the church's vocabulary. On the other hand, the word is joined with πλοῦτος only in the gospels.

καὶ ἄκαρπος γίνεται. So Mk 4.19. Lk 8.14 has: καὶ οὐ τελεσφοροῦσιν.

ἄκαρπος[110] is another Matthean *hapax legomenon* and yet one more word that is more characteristic of the epistles than the gospel tradition.[111]

---

[104] NT: 4 (Mt 13.21; Mk 4.17; 2 Cor 4.18; Heb 11.25).

[105] LXX: Prov 11.19; Lam 3.19; 2 Macc 12.23.

[106] So HG. NA[26] prints εις.

[107] So HG. NA[26] omits τουτο on the authority of ℵ* B D it sa^ms Eus. But the word is found in ℵ¹ C L W θ f^1.13 Maj lat sy sa^mss mae bo Or. Cf. also 12.32.

[108] On 'this aeon' see on 12.32. Cf. Lk 16.8; 20.34; Rom 12.2; 1 Cor 1.20; 2 Cor 4.4; Tit 2.12; etc.

[109] BAGD, s.v., notes that both meanings are here appropriate.

[110] LXX: 3 (for *ṣalmāwet* in Jer 2.6).

[111] NT: Mt 13.22; Mt 4.19; 1 Cor 14.14; Eph 5.11; Tit 3.14; 2 Pet 1.8; Jude 12.

23. ὁ δὲ ἐπὶ τὴν καλὴν γῆν σπαρείς, οὗτός ἐστιν ὁ τὸν λόγον ἀκούων καὶ συνίων.¹¹² The differences between this and Mk 4.20 (καὶ ἐκεῖνοί εἰσιν οἱ ἐπὶ τὴν γῆν τὴν καλὴν σπαρέντες, οἵτινες ἀκούουσιν τὸν λόγον καὶ παραδέχονται) can all be put down to Matthew's desire to increase parallelism with previous clauses. ὁ δέ + preposition + article + object + σπαρείς + οὗτός ἐστιν ὁ τὸν λόγον ἀκούων appears also in vv. 20 and 22, and συνίων makes for an antithetical *inclusio* with 13.19, which has μὴ συνιέντος.

ὃς δὴ καρποφορεῖ καὶ ποιεῖ ὃ μὲν ἑκατόν, ὃ δὲ ἑξήκοντα, ὃ δὲ τριάκοντα. Mk 4.20 has been rewritten so as to increase the parallelism with 13.8, whose last nine words are reproduced here without alternation. Although Matthew has inserted δή¹¹³ it occurs only here in his gospel. The usage is classical: 'he is just the man who' (BDF § 451.4).

καρποφορέω, found in the synoptics in Mt 13.23; Mk 4.20, 28; and Lk 8.15, occurs also in Rom 7.4, 5; and Col 1.6 and 10. The literal meaning ('bear fruit') is attested in the LXX (e.g. Hab 3.17; Wisd 10.7). The figurative meaning ('bear good works'; cf. Philo, *Cher.* 84) is not. The typical, early Christian usage, which is figurative, probably goes back to Jesus (cf. 12.33–5; Lk 6.43–5). Here, in Mt 13.23, one thinks of fruit brought forth in this world as well as fruit made manifest in the world to come (cf. Gnilka, *Matthäusevangelium* 1, p. 487). In addition to the possibilities already mentioned (see on 13.8), Matthew might have reversed the Markan sequence of thirty, sixty, one hundred, in order to lay emphasis upon failure rather than success. After all, the main function of Mt 13.1–22 in its broader context is to help explain Israel's cool response to Jesus.

(iv) *Concluding Observations*

When Mt 13.1–23 is preached today it is usually for the purpose of exhorting believers. While such an application is far from hermeneutically unlawful, it does inevitably miss the main point for Matthew. His version of the parable of the sower is not aimed at exhortation. Its purpose is rather to offer an explanation. The passage has to be understood within its wider context, this being chapters 11–12. These two chapters relate in some detail the failure of Jesus' ministry to effect repentance in corporate Israel. A difficult question is thus engendered, a

¹¹² So HG, following C L W *f*¹·¹³ Maj. NA²⁶ has συνιεις, the reading of ℵ B D θ 892 *pc* Or. A firm decision one way or the other seems impossible.
¹¹³ While frequent in the LXX, this word is rare in the NT (6–7).

question not unlike that addressed in Rom 9–11: how does one explain the failure of the Jews as a body to come to faith? Matthew, to be sure, knew of Jews who believed in Jesus. (He himself was one.) Yet their number was comparatively small. So Matthew was, like Paul before him, faced with the dilemma of a Messiah rejected by his people—in opposition to all Jewish eschatological expectation. What was his response? Just as Paul believed that God would, in the end, redeem his people, so too did the First Evangelist probably hope for Israel's eschatological redemption (1, pp. 22–4). But this conviction by itself hardly explained the unexpected response to Jesus himself or the unbelief of so many Jews in Matthew's day—and it is precisely to these failures of faith that Mt 13.1–23 is intended to speak. Although the word of the kingdom is preached to all, all do not respond in the same way. Some believe, some do not. The reason? Opportunity does not guarantee response, proclamation does not abolish sin. This is the main message of 13.1–23, which in effect offers something similar to the free will defence for the problem of evil. For Matthew, Israel's failure, the root of her trouble, does not lie with God. It lies rather with people who are free to harden their hearts. Therefore, unless or until God overrides wills, the gospel will meet a mixed reception.

(v) *Bibliography*

Ambrozic, pp. 46–106.

Boucher, passim.

J. W. Bowker, 'Mystery and Parable: Mark iv. 1–20', *JTS* 25 (1974), pp. 300–17.

Brown, *Essays*, pp. 321–33.

S. Brown, 'The Secret of the Kingdom of God (Mark 4.11)', *JBL* 92 (1973), pp. 60–74.

R. Bultmann, 'Die Interpretation von Mk 4, 3–9 seit Jülicher', in Ellis, *Jesus*, pp. 30–4.

Carlston, pp. 3–9, 21–5, 55–7, 70–6, 97–109, 137–49.

C. H. Cave, 'The Parables and the Scriptures', *NTS* 11 (1965), pp. 374–87.

L. Cerfaux, 'Le connaissance des secrets du royaume d'après Matt. xiii. 11 et parallèles', *NTS* 2 (1956), pp. 238–49.

Chilton, *Rabbi*, pp. 90–8.

C. E. B. Cranfield, 'St. Mark 4.1–34', *SJT* 4 (1951), pp. 398–414; 5 (1952), pp. 49–66.

Crossan, *Cliffs*, pp. 25–64.

idem, *Parables*, pp. 39–44.

J. D. Crossan, 'The Seed Parables of Jesus', *JBL* 92 (1973), pp. 244–66.

N. A. Dahl, 'The Parables of Growth', *ST* 5 (1951), pp. 132–66; reprinted in Dahl, *Jesus*, pp. 141–66.

G. Dalman, 'Viererlei Acker', *Palästina-Jahrbuch* 22 (1926), pp. 120–32.

M. Didier, 'La parabole du semeur', in *Au service de la Parole de Dieu*, Gembloux, 1969, pp. 21–41.

C. Dietzfelbinger, 'Das Gleichnis vom ausgestreuten Samen', in E. Lohse, ed., *Der Ruf Jesu und die Antwort der Gemeinde*, Göttingen, 1970, pp. 80–93.

Dodd, *Parables*, pp. 3–5, 144–7.

J. Drury, 'The Sower, the Vineyard, and the Place of Allegory in the Interpretation of Mark's Parables', *JTS* 24 (1973), pp. 367–79.

J. G. Du Plessis, 'Pragmatic Meaning in Matthew 13.1–23', *Neotestamentica* 21 (1987), pp. 33–56.

J. Dupont, 'Le chapitre des paraboles', *NRT* 89 (1967), pp. 800–20.

idem, 'La parabole du Semeur', *FV* 66 (1967), pp. 3–25.

idem, 'Le point de vue de Matthieu dans le chapitre des paraboles', in Didier, pp. 221–59.

W. G. Essame, 'Sowing and Plowing', *ExpT* 72 (1960), p. 54.

C. A. Evans, 'A Note on the Function of Isaiah vi. 9–10 in Mark iv', *RB* 88 (1981), pp. 234–5.

idem, 'On the Isaianic Background of the Sower parable', *CBQ* 47 (1985), pp. 464–8.

H. Frankemölle, 'Hat Jesus sich selbst verkündet? Christologische Implikationen in den vormarkinischen Parabelen', *BuL* 13 (1972), pp. 184–207.

V. Fusco, 'L'accord mineur Mt 13.11a/Lc 8.10a contre Mc 4.11a', in Delobel, pp. 355–61.

P. Garnet, 'The Parables of the Sower: How the Multitudes understood It', in *Spirit within Structure*, ed. E. J. Furcha, Allison Park, 1983, pp. 39–54.

H.-J. Geischer, 'Verschwenderische Güte. Versuch über Markus 4.3–9', *EvTh* 38 (1978), pp. 418–27.

A. George, 'Le sens de la parabole des semailles (Mc 4.3–9 et parallèles)', *SacPag* 2 (1959), pp. 163–9.

B. Gerhardsson, 'The Parable of the Sower and Its Interpretation', *NTS* 14 (1968), pp. 165–93.

Gnilka, *Verstockung*, passim.

idem, 'Das Verstockungsproblem nach Matthäus 13.13–15', in *Antijudaismus im Neuen Testament?*, ed. W. P. Eckert et al., Munich, 1967, pp. 119–28.

W. Grimm, 'Selige Augenzeugen, Luk. 10.23f.', *TZ* 26 (1970), pp. 172–83.

K. Haacker, 'Erwägungen zu Mc 4.11', *NovT* 14 (1972), pp. 219–25.

F. Hahn, 'Das Gleichnis von der ausgestreuten Saat und seine Deutung (Mk iv. 3–8, 14–20)', in Best, *Text*, pp. 133–42.

G. Haufe, 'Erwägungen zum Ursprung der sogenannten Parabeltheorie des Markus 4.11–12', *EvTh* 32 (1972), pp. 413–21.

J. Horman, 'The Source of the Version of the Parable of the Sower in the Gospel of Thomas', *NovT* 21 (1979), pp. 326–43.

M. Hubaut, 'Le "mystère" révélé dans les paraboles (Mc 4.11–12)', *RTL* 5 (1974), pp. 454–61.

P. H. Igarashi, 'The Mystery of the Kingdom (Mark 4.10–12)', *JBR* 24 (1956), pp. 83–89.

J. Jeremias, 'Palästinakundliches zum Gleichnis vom Sämann (Mark iv. 3–8 Par.)', *NTS* 13 (1966), pp. 48–53.

Jeremias, *Parables*, pp. 11–18, 28, 77–9, 149–53.

Jülicher 2, pp. 514–38.

Kingsbury, *Parables*, pp. 22–63.

J. R. Kirkland, 'The Earliest Understanding of Jesus' Use of Parables: Mark iv. 10–12 in Context', *NovT* 19 (1977), pp. 1–21.

Klauck, pp. 186–209, 239–55.

G. E. Ladd, 'The *Sitz im Leben* of the Parables of Matthew 13: the Soils', in *Studia Evangelica II*, ed. F. L. Cross, TU 87, Berlin, 1964, pp. 203–10.

M.-J,. Lagrange, 'Le but des paraboles d'après l'Évangile selon Saint Marc', *RB* 19(1910), pp. 5–35.

Lambrecht, *Parables*, pp. 85–109.

P. Lampe, 'Die markinische Deutung des Gleichinesses vom Sämann, Mk 4.10–12', *ZNW* 65 (1974), pp. 140–50.

X. Léon-Dufour, 'La parabole du semeur', in *Études*, pp. 255–301.

Lindars, *Apologetic*, pp. 154–67.

W. Link, 'Die Geheimnisse des Himmelreiches', *EvT* 2 (1935), pp. 115–27.

Linnemann, *Parables*, pp. 114–19.

G. Lohfink, 'Das Gleichnis vom Sämann (Mk 4.3–9)', *BZ* 30 (1986), pp. 36–69.

idem, 'Die Metaphorik der Aussaat in Gleichnis vom Sämann', in *À Cause de l'Évangile: Études sur les Synoptiques et les Actes offertes au P. Jacques Dupont*, LD 123, Paris, 1985, pp. 211–28.

U. Luck, 'Das Gleichnis vom Sämann und die Verkündigung Jesu', *WuD* 11 (1971), pp. 73–92.

W. Manson, 'The Purpose of the Parables: A Re-examination of St. Mark iv. 10–12', *ExpT* 68 (1957), pp. 132–5.

J. Marcus, 'Mark 4.10–12 and Markan Epistemology', *JBL* 103 (1984), pp. 557–74.

idem, *The Mystery of the Kingdom of God*, SBLDS 90, Altanta, 1986.

Marguerat, pp. 415–23.

L. Marin, 'Essai d'analyse structurale d'un récit-parabole: Matthieu 13.1–23', *ETR* 46 (1971), pp. 35–74.

C. F. D. Moule, 'Mark 4.1–20 yet once more', in *Neotestamentica et Semitica*, ed. E. E. Ellis and M. Wilcox, Edinburgh, 1969, pp. 95–113.

W. Neil, 'Expounding the Parables: II. The Sower (Mk 4.3–8)', *ExpT* 77 (1965–6), pp. 74–7.

B. M. Newman, 'To Teach or not to Teach (A Comment on Matthew 13.1–3)', *BT* 34 (1983), pp. 139–43.

Oakman, pp. 103–9.

P. Patten, 'The Form and Function of Parable in select apocalyptic literature and their Significance for Parables in the Gospel of Mark', *NTS* 29 (1983), pp. 246–58.

P. B. Payne, 'The Authenticity of the Parable of the Sower and Its Interpretation', in France 1, pp. 163–207.

idem, 'The Order of Sowing and Ploughing', *NTS* 25 (1978), pp. 123–9.

idem, 'The Seeming Inconsistency of the Interpretation of the Parable of the Sower', *NTS* 26 (1980), pp. 564–8.

Percy, pp. 202–15.

G. A. Phillips, 'History and Text: The Reader in Context in Matthew's Parables Discourse', *Semeia* 31 (1985), pp. 111–38.

H. Räisänen, *Die Parabeltheorie im Markusevangelium*, Helsinki, 1973.

Schulz, *Q*, pp. 419–21.

E. Schweizer, 'Marc 4.1–20', *ETR* 43 (1986), pp. 256–64.

G. Sellin, 'Textlinguistische und semiotische Erwägungen zu Mk 4.1–34', *NTS* 29 (1983), pp. 508–30.

E. F. Siegman, 'Teaching in parables (Mk iv. 10–12; Lk viii. 9–10; Mt xiii. 10–15)', *CBQ* 23 (1961), pp. 161–81.

D. O. Via, 'Matthew on the Understandability of the Parables', *JBL* 84 (1965), pp. 430–2.

Weder, pp. 99–117.

T. J. Weeden, 'Recovering the Parabolic Intent in the Parable of the Sower', *JAAR* 47 (1979), pp. 97–120.

D. Wenham, 'The Interpretation of the Parable of the Sower', *NTS* 20 (1974), pp. 299–319.

idem, 'The Synoptic Problem Reconsidered: Some Suggestions about the Composition of Mark 4.1–34', *TynB* 23 (1972), pp. 3–38.

K. D. White, 'The Parable of the Sower', *JTS* 15 (1964), pp. 300–7.

A. N. Wilder, 'The Parable of the Sower: Naïveté and Method in Interpretation', *Semeia* 2 (1974), pp. 134–51.

W. Wilkens, 'Die Redaktion des Gleichniskapitels Mark 4 durch Matthäus', *TZ* 20 (1964), pp. 305–27.

Zumstein, pp. 206–12.

XXVIII

THREE MORE PARABLES
(13.24–43)

(i) *Structure*

The basic structure of Mt 13.24–43 is this: three parables + additional material (cf. 13.44–52). Each parable is introduced with ἄλλην παραβολήν (13.24, 31, 33)—this in contrast to all the other parables in the chapter—, and each closely follows this with the formula, ὡμοιώθη (or: ὁμοία ἐστὶν) ἡ βασιλεία τῶν οὐρανῶν + dative. Following the three parables there is, first, a general statement about Jesus' parables (13.34f., a formula quotation), and, secondly, an interpretation of the section's first parable, 13.24–30. In this way the opening and closing sections of 13.24–43 correspond to each other as parable and interpretation (cf. 13.1–23), forming an *inclusio*. See further Excursus X.

(ii) *Sources*

The synoptic parallels to the units in Mt 13.24–43 are these:

	Matthew	Mark	Luke
The tares	13.24–30		
The mustard seed	13.31f.	4.30–2	13.18f.
The leaven	13.33		13.20f.
On parables	13.34f.	(4.33f.)	
The tares interpreted	13.36–43		

If the two-source theory is accepted, then 13.24–30 and 36–43 are either from M or redactional,[1] 13.31f. is from Q with some Markan influence, 13.33 is from Q, and 13.34f. is a redactional adaptation of Mk 4.33f. Thus Mt 13.24–43 is a collection of material drawn from all three of Matthew's major sources.

On the Griesbach hypothesis, Mk 4.30–2 is a product of Mt 13.31f. and Lk 13.18f. We think this problematic. The thesis entails that Mark was at some pains to avoid reproducing his sources when they gave concurrent testimony. If his sources were the First and Third Gospels, Mark has rewritten κόκκῳ σινάπεως ὃν λαβὼν ἄνθρωπος, replaced αὔξω with another verb, and dropped both δένδρον and ἐν τοῖς κλάδοις αὐτοῦ—all of which are common to Matthew and Luke. This is strange procedure. Moreover, while both Matthew and Luke have ὁμοία ἐστίν + dative, Mark has ὡς + dative[2] and lacks a main verb. The textual tradition witnesses to attempts to repair the broken construction (cf. Taylor, *Mark*, p. 270). So on the proposal of Markan posteriority, Mark has, for seemingly no good reason, neglected the joint agreement of his sources and also gone off on his own to produce a rather awkward sentence. How likely is this? Much more probable, as the commentary shows, is conflation of Mark and Q (= Lk 13.18f.) by Matthew.

One objection made to Markan priority in the section at hand is the common omission by Matthew and Luke of Mk 4.26–9, the seed growing secretly. Why would the two evangelists, working independently, choose to reject the same parable? Streeter, p. 171, held that they in fact did not: a scribal eye passed from the καὶ ἔλεγεν of Mk 4.26 to the καὶ ἔλεγεν of 4.30, and therefore in some early copies of Mark the parable of the seed growing secretly was not found. The difficulty with this solution is that the Markan textual tradition is unanimous in favouring inclusion. A much more satisfactory explanation makes appeal to the redactional interests of Matthew and Luke. Matthew probably omitted or replaced Mk 4.26–9 because retention of it would have destroyed the structure of the chapter, which requires three parables and only three parables in 13.24–43 (see pp. 000–00).[3] As for Luke, in chapter 13 he has long since left his

---

[1] Our own judgement is that 13.24–30 should be assigned to M, 36–43 to Matthean redaction.

[2] See Taylor, *Mark*, p. 270. Some Markan mss. have the accusative.

[3] Hill, *Matthew*, p. 230, writes: 'The reason for Matthew's omission of the Marcan parable may have been the fact that it gives the impression of

Markan source, so we can hardly anticipate the parable of the seed growing secretly here. One might expect it, however, in chapter 8, a chapter in which Luke draws extensively from Mark 4. But Luke does not in fact use any of Mk 4.26–34, for the good and simple reason that it is 'not relevant to his . . . purpose [in chapter 8] of presenting Jesus' teaching on the importance of hearing the word of God aright' (Marshall, p. 330).

(iii) *Exegesis*

THE PARABLE OF THE WEEDS (13.24–30)

In several respects the parable of the tares carries forward themes already treated in 13.1–23. It is not just that certain motifs—sowing, seeds, soil, kingdom, obstacles to growth, the devil or evil one—are repeated. Rather, and beyond this, both parables make it plain that while the victory of God's kingdom is sure, *the way from here to there is hampered by unbelief and its effects*. In other words, both address the same problem of evil,[4] which is the failure of the gospel to win the hearts of all, and both answer in a similar fashion. More precisely, and taking into account the broader context, the first two parables in Matthew 13 help explain unbelief in Jesus and the dilemma of a rejected Messiah. Just as seed may fall upon different types of soil, and just as weeds may be sown among wheat, so too is it with Jesus' ministry: the good comes with the evil. The one major difference between the sower and the tares is that while the former focuses on human responsibility, the latter points to the evil one: the devil must share the responsibility for the apparent failure of God's word.[5]

Most modern commentators assume that 13.24–30 and its interpretation address a situation in Matthew's community. Either that community was concerned with opposition to the gospel in its own day or it was worried about the character of some of its members and what to do about them.[6] Neither idea,

uninterrupted progress and growth on the part of the Kingdom, whereas Matthew is concerned at this point to affirm the eventual harvest of the Kingdom *in spite of* disappointments, setbacks and loss.' This complements our explanation.

[4] Schweizer, *Matthew*, p. 304, is correct: 'the two questions asked by the servants underline the incomprehensibility of evil.'

[5] 13.1–23 does, to be sure, recognize the devil and his activity; but in the parable of the sower and its interpretation the evil one is only one factor among others in explaining unbelief. It is different in 13.24–30, for here all without faith are 'sons of the evil one', and every weed that comes up has been planted by the enemy.

[6] Typical are Minear, p. 85, and Meier, *Matthew*, pp. 147–8. But according to

however, is expounded in the interpretation in 13.36–43—which in fact quite plainly identifies the field with the world, not the church; and we are persuaded that instead of conjuring up some hypothetical Matthean *Sitz im Leben* the text itself and its literary context should be the key to interpretation. When this natural requirement is observed, 13.24–30 can be seen to relate to the plot of the gospel as a whole. It is part of the answer to the difficult situation depicted in chapters 11–12. Confirming us in this judgement is 18.15–20, which shows us that Matthew's church practised excommunication; that is, the community pulled up Christian weeds when it was necessary. It did not wait for the eschaton to sort the good from the bad.[7]

Beginning with Jülicher, many scholars have argued that Mt 13.24–30 was composed by Matthew himself.[8] In support of this, the major themes harmonize well with Matthean interests, many words are clearly redactional, and Mk 4.26–9, which shares much vocabulary with Mt 13.24–30,[9] could have been the inspiration for a new composition (certainly this would explain its omission by Matthew). On the other hand, the word statistics are consistent with Matthew's having rewritten an oral tradition.[10] Furthermore, much of the vocabulary is more characteristic of M than of Matthean redaction.[11] When one adds that an origin with Jesus is possible (see below), that Gos. Thom. 57 may not depend upon the First Gospel (see p. 415), that it was not Matthew's habit to compose parables, and that the very similar Mt 13.47–8 (the parable of the tares) came from the tradition, presumption would seem to be against a redactional genesis. Compare Beare, p. 303: 'It is probable that Matthew has elaborated a parable which was given to him in the tradition, but that it was not the Markan parable' (so also Gnilka, *Matthäusevangelium* 1, pp. 489–90).

Those who regard Mt 13.24–30 as preserving pre-Matthean tradition often see it as the product of a complex tradition history. Kingsbury takes only vv. 24b–6 to come from Jesus and attributes the rest to the community and Matthew (*Parables*, p. 65). E. Schweizer suggests that the original consisted only of vv. 24b + 26 + 28b–9 (*Matthew*, p. 303). According to Weder, pp. 123–4, Jesus uttered vv. 24b + 26 + 30b. To this was added vv. 25, 27, and 28a, and then, at a later stage, vv. 28b, 29, and 30a. Matthew himself (stage 4) inserted

Barth (v), the parable was only a reaction against church discipline for the pre-Matthean tradition. Matthew himself understood it otherwise.

[7] Cf. Hill, *Matthew*, p. 232.

[8] Jülicher 2, pp. 555–63. Manson, *Sayings*, p. 192, conjectured that 13.24–30 is based upon Mk 4.26–9 but was produced by Matthew's tradition. Cf. Klauck, pp. 226–7.

[9] ἡ βασιλεία, ἄνθρωπος, καθεύδω, βλαστάνω, χόρτος, σῖτος, καρπός, θερισμός. Mark's βάλῃ τὸν σπόρον ἐπὶ τῆς γῆς also recalls Matthew's σπείραντι καλὸν σπέρμα ἐν τῷ ἀγρῷ αὐτοῦ.

[10] Cf. the situation in Mt 1–2.

[11] See J. H. Friedrich, 'Wortstatistik als Methode am Beispiel der Frage einer Sonderquelle im Matthäusevangelium', *ZNW* 76 (1985), pp. 29–42.

v. 24a and revised v. 30b. There would seem to be three arguments generally employed in attempts to reconstruct our text's growth. First, Weder thinks the parable should be pared down so that it is the perfect twin of 13.47–8 (cf. Catchpole (v)). Secondly, all agree that the Matthean redaction must be removed. Thirdly, it has been claimed that the reference to an enemy is awkward and intrusive, so one must reconstruct an original without 13.25 and whatever depends upon it. Concerning these three points, the first may or may not be valid. The parallels between 13.24–30 and 47–8 are admittedly intriguing; but surely Jesus could have composed two similar parables that were not structurally identical. As for eliminating Matthean redaction, the use of vocabulary statistics to expose the editor's contribution can be a fairly reliable guide; but in the present instance the inferences are not obvious. Perhaps, to repeat a point, the parable contains so much redactional vocabulary and style because Matthew was taking up oral tradition. Finally, we must admit, with reference to the sower of weeds, that 13.25 may well be secondary. It is not hard to imagine someone adding a transparent allusion to the devil and modifying the text accordingly. Thus the solution of Schweizer—vv. 25, 27, 28a, and 30 are secondary—could well be correct. Yet in the nature of the case one can scarcely be confident.

What of authenticity? The arguments against this boil down to two: the alleged dependence upon Mk 4.26–9, and the possibility of a post-Easter setting: the parable records the church's attempt to explain what should be done with evil in its midst (cf. Beare, pp. 304–5, citing 1 Cor 4.5). We have already disputed the first claim. With regard to the second, it is not manifest that 13.24–30 must have come into existence in order to deal with the problem of evil in the church. This is not to deny that it could have been employed to address that issue—as it was later on in church history.[12] Nevertheless, and as many have observed, a situation in the life of Jesus is far from unthinkable. In the words of E. Schweizer, 'If the nucleus of the parable went back to Jesus, it would represent a strong protest against the tendency of the Pharisees, the Qumran community, and the Zealots to delimit a sect of devout believers. Jesus rejected this practice and kept his circle open. He therefore avoided giving his group a new name, did not adopt a definite title for himself, did not even establish a fixed meeting place or any organization, however loose, for his followers.'[13] This interpretation gains credence because it can be equally maintained for the parable of the net (see Jeremias, *Parables*, pp. 224–7). It should also be added that 13.24–30 is in harmony with Jesus' remark that God sends his rain on the just and the unjust, and causes his sun to rise upon good and bad

---

[12] E.g. Augustine used the parable of the tares to argue against the Donatists that heretics or the lapsed should not be cut off from the church. Note also Hippolytus, *Haer.* 9.12.22, giving the view of bishop Callistus: 'Let the tares grow along with wheat; or, in other words, let sinners remain in the church.' The parable was again important for debates at the time of the Reformation and was discussed with reference to Erastians and Arminians; see A. B. Bruce, *The Parabolic Teaching of Jesus*, 9th ed., London, 1900, pp. 42–63.

[13] *Matthew*, p. 304. Cf. Dahl, *Jesus*, pp. 158–60; Weder, pp. 125–6.

alike (5.45). For the present God is forbearing; his judgement belongs to the future (cf. on 11.6). In conclusion, then, the origin of the parable of the tares should be left open.

24. ἄλλην παραβολὴν παρέθηκεν αὐτοῖς λέγων. Compare 13.31, 33; 21.33. The words are redactional (cf. Kingsbury, *Parables*, pp. 12–13).

ὡμοιώθη ἡ βασιλεία τῶν οὐρανῶν. The same words appear in 18.23 (introducing the story of the unmerciful servant) and 22.2 (introducing the parable of the marriage feast). They may be redactional, given the statistics on the verb (Mt: 8; Mk: 1; Lk: 3). But Lk 13.20 indicates that ὁμοιώσω τὴν βασιλείαν τοῦ θεοῦ appeared at least once in Q (cf. also Lk 6.47–9; 7.32; 12.36; 13.18, 19, 21, all with ὅμοιος + dative introducing a parable). Note also Gos. Thom. 57: 'The kingdom of the Father is like . . .'. Perhaps Matthew's source had ὁμοία ἐστὶν ἡ βασιλεία τοῦ θεοῦ or something similar (cf. vol. 1, pp. 125–6).

In the NT the passive of ὁμοιόω is deponent, and the meaning is 'become' or 'be like.' One should nonetheless not translate 13.24 as 'the kingdom of heaven is like a man . . .'. The formulae introducing the parables reflect the Aramaic *lĕ*,[14] and the meaning of this is not 'it is like' but 'it is the case with . . . as with . . .' (cf. Kingsbury, *Parables*, p. 67). That this is so can be inferred from the content of the parables themselves. For example, in Mt 13.45 the kingdom is not like the merchant but the pearl, and in 22.2 the kingdom is like the marriage feast, not the king.[15]

Why does Matthew sometimes introduce a kingdom parable with the aorist passive (13.24; 18.23; 22.2) and at other times use the future passive, ὁμοιωθήσεται (7.24, 26; 25.1)? In Black's judgement, the aorist represents a Semitic perfect, indicating a general truth (p. 129). But it seems more likely that the aorist is used when the main emphasis is upon what the kingdom has already become, the future when the consummation is the principle focus.[16] In the present case, although 13.24–30 culminates in the harvest (= the judgement), the parable is firstly a picture of how matters are at present: tares and wheat stand side by side.

ἀνθρώπῳ σπείραντι καλὸν σπέρμα ἐν τῷ ἀγρῷ αὐτοῦ. Compare the σπέρμα πονηρόν (= *zera* *mĕrē'îm*) of LXX Isa 1.4. καλόν[17]

[14] Which is an elliptical form of 'I will tell you a parable. To what can the affair be likened? To a . . .'. Cf. SB 2, pp. 7–8; note also the fuller form in the gospels: Mt 11.16; Mt 4.30–1; Lk 7.31–2; 13.18–19.
[15] See further Jeremias, *Parables*, pp. 100–2.
[16] Cf. D. A. Carson, 'The ὅμοιος Word-Group as Introduction to some Matthean Parables', *NTS* 31 (1985), pp. 277–82.
[17] καλός*. καλὸν σπέρμα Mt: 4; Mk: 0; Lk:0.

and ἐν τῷ ἀγρῷ[18] might be redactional. But Gos. Thom. 57, which might be independent of Matthew here, also has 'good seed' (čroč + nanou).

25. ἐν δὲ τῷ καθεύδειν τοὺς ἀνθρώπους. The meaning is, 'while men were sleeping.' According to BDF § 404.1, 'Attic does not use ἐν τῷ in this way,' and the construction is a Hebraism; see further 1, p. 82.

Against most patristic interpreters (e.g. Jerome, *Comm. on Mt.*, *ad loc.*), the men's sleep, which is not mentioned in Gos. Thom. 57, and which is passed over in the interpretation in 13.36–43, should not be given paraenetic significance.[19] ἐν δὲ κ.τ.λ. does not refer to the sower's servants but simply means, 'while people were sleeping'; in effect, 'while it was night' (cf. Gos. Thom. 57). The article τούς is thus generic, and the notice serves to underline the sinister character of the enemy: he belongs to the darkness instead of the light.

ἦλθεν αὐτοῦ ὁ ἐχθρὸς καὶ ἐπέσπειρεν ζιζάνια ἀνὰ μέσον τοῦ σίτου καὶ ἀπῆλθεν. None of these words or phrases is easily assigned to Matthean redaction.[20] The article before ἐχθρός could be a Semitism (so Jeremias, *Parables*, p. 224); or it might simply be motivated by the identification in 13.39 (the enemy is the devil). Note that there is no article in v. 28 (ἐχθρὸς ἄνθρωπος).

ζιζάνιον* (cf. Apoc. Mos. 16.3; Gos. Thom. 57) is presumably a Semitic word (BAGD, s.v.). It does not occur in the LXX or in the NT outside of Matthew. Compare the Syriac *zizōnē* and the rabbinic *zônîn*. Translated 'tares' by the KJV, it is usually taken to mean darnel (cf. Virgil, *Georg.* 1.154; *Gen. Rab.* on 6.7), but the identification is uncertain. Is one to think of a noxious weed that resembles wheat?

13.39 will identify the enemy with the devil.[21] One is reminded of 13.19, which took the birds of the air to symbolize the evil one. In both instances God's work of sowing is countered by Satanic opposition. Note that in 13.25 the devil does what the Son of man does: he sows. Thus the devil is made out to be an imitator, a maker of counterfeits. The result is that just as there are wolves in the midst of sheep (7.15), so too are there weeds in the midst of wheat.

[18] This is editorial in 13.31 diff. Mk 4.31 and Lk 3.19 (Q).

[19] *Pace* Gundry, *Commentary*, p. 263. Slumber can, of course, be a symbol of apathy and therefore of moral sloth (e.g. Rom 13.11).

[20] ἐχθρός: Mt: 7 (3 in 13.24–30, 36–43); 2 in OT citations: 10.36; 22.44); Mk: 1; Lk: 8. σπείρω: the word appears only four times outside 13.1–30, 36–43 and is in each instance from the tradition. ζιζάνιον: Mt: 8 (all in 13.24–30, 36–43); Mk: 0; Lk: 0. ἀνὰ μέσον (cf. 1 Cor 6.5; Rev 7.17; BDF § 204): Mt: 1; Mk: 1; Lk: 0. σῖτος: Mt: 4 (3 in 13.25–30); Mk: 1; Lk: 4.

[21] Some have thought Paul 'the enemy' (cf. Ep. Pet. ad Jac. 2); see H. J. Holtzmann, *Einleitung in das Neuen Testament*, 3rd ed., Freiburg im Breisgau, 1892, p. 381. Criticism in Davies, *SSM*, p. 336.

It is unclear whether the situation envisaged by 13.25 can be considered realistic. W. O. E. Osterley cited an example from Roman law which treats of the practice of sowing weeds in another's field;[22] and in the opinion of Jeremias, 'since a similar occurrence is reported from modern Palestine, the parable of the Tares among the Wheat may spring from an actual event.'[23] Others have held that the introduction of an enemy sowing weeds is an artificial touch which ruins an otherwise naturalistic parable.[24]

26. ὅτε δὲ ἐβλάστησεν ὁ χόρτος καὶ καρπὸν ἐποίησεν, τότε ἐφάνη καὶ τὰ ζιζάνια. Compare LXX Gen 1.11; also Ignatius, *Eph.* 10.3 ('plant of the devil'). ὅτε δέ + verb + ὁ + subject[25] is probably redactional, καρπὸν ἐποίησεν,[26] τότε*, and ἐφάνη (φαίνομαι*) might be. For the rest, βλαστάνω is a Matthean *hapax legomenon*, χόρτος is otherwise from the tradition,[27] and ζιζάνιον is confined to the parable of the tares and its interpretation.

27. προσελθόντες δὲ οἱ δοῦλοι τοῦ οἰκοδεσπότου εἶπον αὐτῷ. προσελθόντες is probably redactional (προσέρχομαι*); but οἰκοδεσπότης[28] is clearly Matthean only in 21.33.[29] And δοῦλος is common in the parables of Jesus.

The householder—Jesus has already been pictured as a 'householder' in 10.24f.—is the same person as the sower. The slaves, however, are not identified, and they are not mentioned in the interpretation (cf. Chrysostom, *Hom. on Mt.* 47.1).

κύριε, οὐχὶ καλὸν σπέρμα ἔσπειρας ἐν τῷ σῷ ἀγρῷ; This summarizes the action of 13.24b, from whence the vocabulary derives. 'Lord' is implicitly christological because in 13.37 the householder (who, we must assume, sowed the seed) will be identified as the Son of man.

πόθεν οὖν ἔχει ζιζάνια; πόθεν (Mt: 5; Mk: 3; Lk: 4) is redactional in 13.56 (although cf. 13.55 = Mk 6.2) and 21.25 diff. Mk 11.30; and οὖν* is a Matthean favourite.

28. ὁ δὲ ἔφη αὐτοῖς. Compare 13.29; 22.37; 27.23. Matthew is

---

[22] *The Gospel Parables in the Light of their Jewish Background*, London, 1936, p. 60.

[23] *Parables*, p. 224, citing H. Schmidt and P. Kahle, *Volkserzählungen aus Palästina*, I, Göttingen, 1918, p. 32. Alford 1, p. 143, cites a nineteenth century example from England. Note also R. C. Trench, *Notes on the Parables of our Lord*, 14th ed., London, 1882, p. 86.

[24] E.g. Schweizer, *Matthew*, p. 303, and Weder, p. 120.

[25] Mt: 3 (9.25; 13.26; 21.34): Mk: 0; Lk: 0.

[26] καρπός + ποιέω: Mt: 11 (redactional at least in 21.43); Mk: 0; Lk: 6.

[27] Mt: 3; Mk: 2; Lk: 1. Cf. 6.30 = Lk 12.28; 14.19 = Mk 6.39.

[28] Mt: 7; Mk: 1; Lk: 4. Cf. the rabbinic *ba'al habbayit* and see SB 1, pp. 667–8.

[29] *Pace* Weder, p. 121, n. 121, it cannot be said that the word is often redactional.

more fond of φημί* than the other evangelists; and ὁ δὲ ἔφη+ dative is editorial in 22.37 diff. Mk 12.29.

ἐχθρὸς ἄνθρωπος τοῦτο ἐποίησεν. Compare LXX Est 7.6 (ἄνθρωπος ἐχθρός) and Mt 13.52. On ἄνθρωπος as a substitute for the indefinite pronominal adjective (a Semitism) see 1, p. 81. It is, however, possible that ἐχθρός is here an adjective meaning 'hostile' (see BAGD, s.v.).

οἱ δὲ δοῦλοι αὐτῷ λέγουσιν· θέλεις οὖν ἀπελθόντες συλλέξωμεν αὐτά;[30] θέλεις, οὖν*, and ἀπελθόντες might be considered redactional on the basis of word statistics (see 1, pp. 77–8). συλλέγω*[31] is, with the exceptions of 7.16 (=Lk 6.44: Q) and 13.48 (M), confined to the parable of the tares and its interpretation.

29. The servants are instructed not to pull up the weeds, lest the wheat also be pulled up. The assumption seems to be that the number of weeds is so great that their roots have entwined with the roots of the wheat, with the result that one could not pull up the one without pulling up the other. (Or, less likely, the weeds have been discovered too late in the season, so their roots have had opportunity to mingle with the wheat.)

ὁ δέ φησιν. Compare 13.28.

οὔ, μήποτε συλλέγοντες τὰ ζιζάνια ἐκριζώσητε ἅμα αὐτοῖς τὸν σῖτον. The vocabulary is not clearly redactional.[32] On ἅμα+ dative see BDF § 194.3. Gos. Thom. 57 has μήπως. Already in the LXX, ἐκριζόω,[33] which means 'uproot', is used figuratively, of rooting out or destroying evil (e.g. Zeph 2.4; Ecclus 3.9). The word thus helps prepare for the interpretation in vv. 37–43.

30. ἄφετε συναυξάνεσθαι ἀμφότερα μέχρι τοῦ θερισμοῦ.[34] ἀφίημι* is sometimes redactional, ἀμφότεροι (Mt: 3; Mk: 0; Lk: 5) is redactional in 9.17, and Matthew likes μέχρι (Mt: 3; Mk: 1; Lk: 1).[35] But συναυξάνομαι is a biblical hapax legomenon, and θερισμός (Mt: 6; Mk: 1; Lk: 3) is confined to 9.37–8 (cf. Lk 10.2: Q) and to 13.24–30 + 36–43. For an interesting parallel to the idea that good and evil must stand side by side until the end see T. Abr. A 10.[36]

καὶ ἐν καιρῷ τοῦ θερισμοῦ ἐρῶ τοῖς θερισταῖς. Compare Rev

---

[30] NA[26] has λεγουσιν αυτω (so ℵ (D) 33[vid] 892 1241 1424 pc). HG prints the reverse order, following B C 1010 pc. ειπον αυτω is the reading of L W Θ f[1.13] Maj. A firm decision is scarcely possible.

[31] The word's use with 'weeds' is unusual.

[32] οὔ: Mt: 3; Mk: 1; Lk: 2. μήποτε: Mt: 7; Mk: 2; Lk: 2. συλλέγω*, ζιζάνιον*. ἐκριζόω: Mt: 2 (13.29; 15.13); Mk: 0; Lk: 1. ἅμα: Mt: 2 (13.29; 20.1); Mk: 0; Lk: 0. σῖτος: Mt: 4; Mk: 1; Lk: 1.

[33] See also LXX Dan 4.14, 26; Lk 17.6; Jude 12. Cf. the rabbinic 'āqar.

[34] So HG. NA[26] prints εως on the authority of B D 695 892 1424 pc. μεχρι(ς) is the reading of ℵ¹ C W Θ 0233 f[1.13] Maj.

[35] As well as ἕως if that is the correct reading.

[36] Note also Hermas, Sim. 3.

14.15. While Matthew likes ἐρῶ*, θεριστής (Mt: 2; Mk: 0; Lk: 0) appears only in 13.30 and 39.

συλλέξατε πρῶτον τὰ ζιζάνια καὶ δήσατε αὐτὰ εἰς δέσμας πρὸς τὸ κατακαῦσαι αὐτά. Compare 3.12 = Lk 3.17. There is nothing distinctively Matthean in this line except πρὸς + articular infinitive*. δέσμη is a NT *hapax legomenon*.

There is disagreement as to whether it was normal to gather weeds and to use them for fuel (so Jeremias, *Parables*, p. 225[37]) or whether the custom was to burn the whole field after the wheat stalks had been cut off (so Gundry, *Commentary*, p. 265). Texts from antiquity do not resolve the issue, and both practices are known from modern times.

τὸν δὲ σῖτον συναγάγετε εἰς τὴν ἀποθήκην μου. συνάγω* + ἀποθήκη is probably Matthean (see on 6.26). Gos. Thom. 57 lacks the clause. Perhaps it is a redactional addition modelled on 3.12.

Gos. Thom. 57 contains this version of the parable of the tares: 'Jesus said: the kingdom of the Father is like a man who had [good] seed. His enemy came by night, he sowed a weed among the good seed. The man did not allow the weed to be pulled up. He said to them: Lest perhaps you go to pull up the weed and pull up the wheat with it. For on the day of harvest the weeds will appear, they will be pulled and burned.' Whether or not this depends upon our gospel, it does seem to be an abbreviated version of something like Mt 13.24–30. If instead of taking *mpeprōme koou ehōle mpzizanion* in the third line as a false passive (so our translation) one rather understands the meaning to be, 'The man did not allow *them* to pull up the weeds,' then 'them' has no antecedent and presupposes the servants of Matthew's gospel. Further, the same line in Thomas also assumes both that weeds have sprung up (cf. Mt 13.26) and that a request to pull them up has been made (cf. Mt 13.28). Thomas' brevity is therefore not a sign of originality but of secondary compression. This fact should be kept in mind when evaluating Thomas' relationship to the synoptics.

THE PARABLE OF THE MUSTARD SEED (13.31f.)

This is a parable of contrast. It illustrates, by reference to the growth of a mustard seed, a vital truth about God's kingdom: a humble beginning and secret presence are not inconsistent with a great and glorious destiny. It is important to grasp that the focus is neither on the smallness or insignificance of a present circumstance nor on the greatness of God's future. (On both points instruction was unnecessary.) Rather, the emphasis for Matthew falls upon the juxtaposition of two seemingly

---

[37] He also asserts that the seeds of tares were fed to chickens.

incongruent facts, the one being the experience of Jesus and his followers in the present (cf. the mustard seed), the other being their expectations of the future (cf. the tree in which the birds of heaven nest). Our parable is an invitation to contemplate these two things—the present and the expected future, reality and hope—in the light of the mustard seed's story. The point is this: despite all appearances, between the minute beginning and the grand culmination there is an organic unity (cf. Lohmeyer, *Matthäus*, p. 218). Indeed, the one (the tree/the eschatological climax) is an effect of the other (the seed/God's activity in Jesus and his disciples). The end is in the beginning.

Mt 13.31–2 is a conflation of Mk 4.30–2 and Q (=Lk 13.18–19).[38] As to whether Mark's version, with its present tense, or that in Q, with its past tenses, is more faithful to the original, scholars do not agree.[39] Usually those favouring Mark do so because it seems more true to life: the mustard seed does not become a tree, and birds are not said to nest in its branches. But might not the overdone hyperbole be original, an attempt to stretch imaginations, a way of underlining how miraculous God's kingdom is?[40] Certainly Matthew must have understood matters thus, and we are inclined to think Jesus may have also. Compare the words of N. A. Huffman: 'He selected one of the greatest naturally occurring contrasts and carried it forward, creating an unforgettable hyperbole. The Q version is a true parable (not simile), narrated in the past tense, about a particular mustard seed which—*mirabile dictu*—became a tree!'[41] Supporting the judgement that Q is less touched by post-Easter influence are (i) the probably secondary nature of Mark's explicit contrast between μικρότερον and μεῖζον (see below) and (ii) the fact that Q is likely to be more original in using the past tense (cf. most of Jesus' parables, including that of the leaven).[42]

The parable in one form or the other is universally reckoned to Jesus.[43]

---

[38] So Bultmann, *History*, p. 172; Schulz, *Q*, p. 299, and most two-source critics. Q and Mark might go back to independent translations of the Semitic original. Certainly the common Greek vocabulary is quite small.

[39] For Q: Jülicher 2, p. 571; Schulz, *Q*, p. 301. For Mark: Pesch 1, p. 264, n. 20.

[40] Cf. *b. Ketub.* 111b: 'It once happened to a man at Shiḥin to whom his father had left three twigs of mustard that one of these split and was found to contain nine ḳab of mustard, and its timber sufficed to cover a potter's hut'. Here an obvious exaggeration serves to make a point about the miraculous possibilities in the land of Israel.

[41] N. A. Huffman, 'Atypical Features in the Parables of Jesus', *JBL* 97 (1978), pp. 211–12.

[42] We do not argue for Q's priority on the ground that Mark offers a parable of contrast, Q one of growth. Lk 13.18–19 is no less about contrast than Mk 4.30–2. What else can the transformation from mustard seed (proverbially small) to *tree* mean?

[43] Cf. D. Polkow, 'Method and Criteria for Historical Jesus Research', in *Society of Biblical Literature 1987 Seminar Papers*, ed. K. H. Richards, Atlanta, 1987, pp. 336–56. For suggestions concerning the Aramaic original see Black, pp. 165–6. He finds alliteration and wordplays.

What did he mean when he composed it? According to Dodd, 'the prevailing idea is that of growth up to a point at which the tree can shelter birds,' and its meaning is that 'the time has come when the blessings of the Reign of God are available for all men' (*Parables*, p. 153). This ignores the *contrast* between the seed's smallness and the resulting plant or tree (cf. Theophilus of Antioch, *Ad Autolycum* 2.14). Most modern scholars would argue that the theme is not growth but contrast—the contrast between the veiled kingdom in the present and its glorious future. In the words of C. Hunzinger, 'behind the parable there clearly lies the claim that the βασιλεία is already present in sign in the contemporary work of Jesus, even though it is now concealed and inconspicuous. The aim of the parable is that this inconspicuous presence should not be an offence but a guarantee of confidence. In the concealment of present demonstrations of God's power lies the promise of an imminent victorious exercise of His dominion. God has already made a beginning; this is the pledge that He will carry through His cause to the end.'[44] But see further below.

31. ἄλλην παραβολὴν παρέθηκεν αὐτοῖς λέγων. Compare 13.24 (q.v.) and 33.

ὁμοία ἐστὶν ἡ βασιλεία τῶν οὐρανῶν κόκκῳ σινάπεως. Compare Dial. Sav. 144.6–8: 'What is this mustard seed like? Is it from heaven or from the earth?' ὁμοία ἐστὶν κ.τ.λ. + dative is a formula which also appears in 13.33, 44, 45, 47; and 20.1.[45] It may derive from a pre-Matthean parable collection (perhaps with τοῦ θεοῦ); see 1, pp. 125–6.

Mk 4.30 ('With what can we compare the kingdom of God, or what parable shall we use for it? It is like a grain of mustard seed . . .') and Lk 13.18 ('What is the kingdom of God like? And to what shall I compare it? It is like a grain of mustard seed . . .') are closer to each other than to Matthew. Luke probably comes near to reproducing Q (cf. Jeremias, *Lukasevangelium*, p. 230). Matthew has probably assimilated to the formula he uses so often (see above). This makes for comparative brevity.

κόκκος[46] means 'grain' or 'seed' (cf. Jn 12.24; 1 Cor 15.37). σίναπι[47] means 'mustard.' Together the two words denote the 'mustard seed' (cf. 17.20; Lk 17.6; it is unnamed in the OT). The seed of the black mustard (*Sinapis* or *Brassica nigra* L), an annual plant, is probably meant. Another possibility is the closely related white mustard (*Sinapis alba* L).

ὃν λαβὼν ἄνθρωπος. This reproduces Q, as Lk 13.19 shows. Mk 4.31 has the less Semitic ὃς ὅταν. Perhaps the Q tradition

---

[44] *TWNT* 7, p. 290. Contrast Weder, pp. 131–3; he finds the point to be the *certainty* of God's good future.

[45] Similar formulations occur in 11.16; 13.52; 22.39; Lk 6.48–9; 13.18, 19, 21.

[46] LXX: 2: Lam 4.5; Ecclus 45.11.

[47] See SB 1, pp. 668–9; Clark (v); I. Löw, *Die Flora der Juden*, vol. 1, Berlin, 1928, pp. 516–27; C.-H. Hunzinger, *TWNT* 7, pp. 286–90.

added the reference to a man in order to increase the parallelism with the next parable, in which a woman puts leaven in bread.

ἔσπειρεν ἐν τῷ ἀγρῷ αὐτοῦ. This differs from both Mk 4.31 (σπαρῇ ἐπὶ τῆς γῆς) and Lk 13.19 (ἔβαλεν εἰς κῆπον ἑαυτοῦ). Because κῆπος is a Lukan *hapax* and because the reflexive is not typical of Luke,[48] the text of the Third Gospel probably preserves Q. Matthew has assimilated his line to other verses in chapter 13 (e.g. 3, 24, 27, 44).[49]

Is there any connexion between Matthew's 'in his field' and the Mishnaic legislation which permits mustard to be sown only in fields, not gardens (*m. Kil.* 2.8–9; 3.2)? If Matthew knew this ruling, it would help explain his revision of Q.

32. ὃ μικρότερον μέν ἐστιν πάντων τῶν σπερμάτων. This depends upon Mk 4.31, which lacks ὅ,[50] has ὄν instead of μέν ἐστιν, and ends with τῶν ἐπὶ τῆς γῆς. Matthew has improved the construction and omitted unnecessary words.

The entire line was probably added by Mark or by the pre-Markan tradition[51] in order to make explicit what Jesus and the compiler of Q took for granted, namely, the proverbial smallness of the mustard seed (cf. Mt 17.20 = Lk 17.6; *m. Nid.* 5.2; *m. Ṭohar.* 8.8; *b. Ber.* 31a; *Lev. Rab.* on 24.2). Comparative μικρότερον—which is only dubiously connected with the disciples' status as 'little ones'[52]—does duty for the superlative (cf. on 5.19), even though there are other seeds (e.g. the orchid seed) which are in truth smaller than the mustard seed. Absolute accuracy in popular literature is hardly to be expected.

ὅταν δὲ αὐξηθῇ μεῖζον τῶν λαχάνων ἐστὶν καὶ γίνεται δένδρον. This combines Mk 4.32 (whence ὅταν, μεῖζον, and τῶν λαχάνων) and Q = Lk 13.19 (whence αὐξηθῇ—Luke has ηὔξησεν—and καὶ ... δένδρον—Luke has καὶ ἐγένετο εἰς δένδρον). Compare Hermas, *Sim.* 8.3.

According to Pliny, *N.H.* 19.170, the mustard seed 'germinates at once'. Certainly a seed that grows into a ten foot herb in one season, as some mustard plants do, has a very rapid growth rate. λάχανον means 'vegetable' or 'garden herb' (cf. Lk 11.42; Rom 14.2). In the LXX it does duty for *yereq* and *yārāq* (e.g. Gen 9.3; Prov 15.17). Note that Theophrastus, *Hist. plant.* 7.1.1–3, includes the mustard in the category of λάχανα.

[48] Cf. Jeremias, *Lukasevangelium*, p. 230; contrast Schulz, *Q*, p. 299.

[49] But some have claimed that εἰς κῆπον ἑαυτοῦ is unPalestinian and to be explained by Luke's Hellenism; cf. Theophrastus, *Hist. plant.* 7.1.1–2.

[50] Matthew's ὅ, although it logically qualifies the masculine κόκκῳ, is neuter by attraction of σπερμάτων.

[51] Cf. Jülicher 2, p. 580; Dodd, *Parables*, p. 153; Crossan, 'Seed Parables' (v), pp. 256–7.

[52] Against Chrysostom, *Hom. on Mt.* 46.2.

The use of the verb, αὐξηθῇ, raises the issue of growth. Throughout church history exegetes have understood the parable of the mustard seed to depict more than a simple contrast. They have also urged that because the seed *grows*, there is a process between beginning and end. But modern interpreters in part reacting against the optimistic liberalism of the nineteenth century have tended to think otherwise, and Jeremias is sometimes quoted: 'in the Talmud (*b. Sanh.* 90b), in Paul (1 Cor. 15.35–38), in John (12.24), in 1 Clement (24.4–5), the seed is the image of the resurrection, the symbol of mystery of life out of death. The oriental mind sees two wholly different situations: on the one hand the dead seed, on the other, the waving corn-field, here death, there, through the divine creative power, life. . . . The modern man, passing through the ploughed field, thinks of what is going on beneath the soil, and envisages a biological development. The people of the Bible, passing through the same plough-land, look up and see miracle upon miracle, nothing less than resurrection from the dead. Thus did Jesus' audience understand the parables of the Mustard seed and the Leaven as parables of contrast' (*Parables*, pp. 148–9). This, however, is not the whole story. Even if the *main* point of the parable of the mustard seed lies in the theme of contrast, that is no reason to think that the *only* point; and as N. Dahl has written, 'the growth of seed and the regularity of life in nature have been known to peasants as long as the earth has been cultivated'; 'the idea of organic growth was far from foreign to men of antiquity; to Jews and Christians organic growth was but the other side of the creative work of God who alone gives growth' (*Jesus*, pp. 149–50). To this it should be added that if the kingdom is a reign, it has subjects (cf. Cadoux, p. 111; Mt 11.11; 23.13); and, in Boucher's words, 'since the ancients probably did not make a neat conceptual distinction between the kingdom of God and the people who would inhabit the kingdom, they could speak of the growth of the eschatological community as though it were the growth of the kingdom itself' (p. 55). Boucher is also correct in observing that 'Jesus surely hoped for increasing numbers of those who would hear the word and repent, and thus become members of the people who would enter the kingdom when it came in its fullness' (ibid.). These words could also be referred to our evangelist—although we must caution that he did not simply identify the kingdom with the church. For Matthew, the kingdom exists now; and it is 'an eschatological sphere of salvation, which breaks in, makes a small, unpretentious beginning, miraculously swells, and increases; as a divine "field of energy" it extends and expands ever farther' (Otto, p. 124; cf. Carlston, pp. 27–8).[53]

ὥστε ἐλθεῖν. Luke has καί, Mark ὥστε δύνασθαι.

τὰ πετεινὰ τοῦ οὐρανοῦ καὶ κατασκηνοῦν ἐν τοῖς κλάδοις αὐτοῦ. Luke 13.19 differs in lacking καί and in having a diffferent verb form (κατεσκήνωσεν). Mark, who agrees with Luke in not having καί but with Matthew in the verb form,

[53] For a much later Jewish parallel to the idea that the kingdom of God can grow see Scholem, pp. 220–1.

has this: ὑπὸ τὴν σκιὰν αὐτοῦ τὰ πετεινὰ τοῦ οὐρανοῦ κατασκηνοῦν. All three synoptics are drawing upon scriptural phrases, but it is impossible to speak of a citation. Compare Dan 4.10–12, 20f. The gospel text also recalls LXX Ps 103.12 (ἐπ᾽ αὐτὰ τὰ πετεινὰ τοῦ οὐρανοῦ κατασκηνώσει); Ezek 17.23 and 31.5–6. Note in addition that ἐν τοῖς κλάδοις and κατασκηνοῦν appear in Dan 4.12 and 21 Theod. It seems to us possible that Jesus himself may have alluded in his parable to the eschatological world tree[54] without having any particular Scripture in mind[55] and that the tradition subsequently, with the help of scriptural phrases, expanded his words in two different directions (Mark and Q).

The image of a large tree with birds resting in it or under it was a traditional symbol for a great kingdom. In addition to the passages already cited see Judg 9.7–15 (cf. Ps 80.8–13). Jewish tradition could also think of the messianic community as a planting, one which would spread throughout the earth; see Ps. Sol. 14.2–3; 1QH 6.14–16; 8.4–8[56] (cf. Isa 61.3; Acts of Thomas 146).

The meaning of κατασκηνοῦν[57] is probably 'to nest,' not 'to perch' (so BAGD, s.v.; cf. RSV; NEB has 'roost'). Compare LXX Ps 103.12. When used of persons the word means 'to dwell' (cf. 1 Clem. 58.1). Today, however, while mustard plants[58] in Palestine grow up to ten feet, and while birds eat their seeds and sometimes use their leaves for shelter, the plants do not provide nesting places for birds. Once again, therefore, the unrealistic nature of our parable is manifest. Mt 13.31f. is not a simple collection of observations about mustard seeds and plants.

Did Matthew think of the birds of heaven as standing for Gentiles?[59] One guesses that he did, in view of 21.43: 'the kingdom of God will be taken away from you and given to a nation producing the fruits of it.'

[54] Crossan, *Parables* (v) tries to eliminate from the original all traces of the world tree and argues that it was inserted later on in the interests of a post-Easter eschatology. He suggests that Ps 104.12 was the Scripture Jesus himself referred to. This is unconvincing; see Beasley-Murray, p. 123.

[55] Perhaps he said only, 'so that the birds of heaven may nest'.

[56] On the Qumran texts see esp. Mussner (v).

[57] Which is not (against Jeremias, *Parables*, p. 147) a technical term for the incorporation of Gentiles into the people of God. He cites only Jos. Asen. 15; but even this citation is doubtful; see C. Burchard, *Untersuchungen zu Joseph und Aseneth*, WUNT 8, Tübingen, 1965, pp. 118–19. Cf. Sabourin, p. 601.

[58] *Pace* Royale (v), our parable is not about the mustard tree (*Salvadora Persica* L). It did not evidently grow in Galilee and its seeds are not that small.

[59] Manson, *Teaching*, p. 133, n. 1, citing Ezek 17.23; 31.6; Dan 4.9, 18; 1 En 90.30; and *Midr. Ps.* 104.13, and Jeremias, *Parables*, p. 147, citing Jos. Asen. 15, assert that Jesus himself was thinking of Gentiles.

Gos. Thom. 20 contains this version of the parable of the mustard seed: 'The disciples said to Jesus: Tell us what the kingdom of heaven is like. He said to them: It is like a mustard seed, smaller than all seeds. But whenever it falls onto the worked earth, it produces a large branch and becomes a shelter for the birds of heaven.' This may show synoptic influence.[60] 'Kingdom of Heaven'—a phrase Thomas uses only three times (vv. 20, 54, 114)—recalls Matthew. Further, 'the smallest of all seeds', 'produces a great branch', and 'whenever' (the Coptic has *hotan*) all reflect the Markan tradition, which in these particulars is probably secondary.[61]

THE PARABLE OF THE LEAVEN (13.33)

This parable is much like the preceding. The introductions (vv. 31a–b, 33a–b) are very similar. Both parables recount the story of someone hiding something which then becomes great. And both have to do with an organic process. These similarities signal an identity of theme for Matthew. Both parables teach that the coming of the kingdom begins not with a grand, public spectacle but with a hidden presence. In this way the character and nature of Jesus' ministry, including its failure in Israel, can be understood. Eschatology commences not with a bang but with something unspectacular.

13.33, which has no Markan parallel, is from Q, where it followed directly the parable of the mustard seed (cf. Lk 13.18–21). Excepting the introduction, Matthew and Luke differ only in a few minor details.

Some have suggested that the parables of the mustard seed and leaven were originally spoken together.[62] But Mark has only the former, and the Gospel of Thomas separates the two. Further, 'the sharp break [between the two parables in Q] would seem to indicate that the similitude of the leaven is a secondary accretion to that of the mustard seed, even if Luke's shorter form (καὶ πάλιν εἶπεν) is the original Q form. We should expect ἤ alone if it were a more original form; cf. Lk. 14³¹; Matt. 7⁹, ¹⁶' (Bultmann, *Tradition*, p. 172; cf. Beasley-Murray, p. 122; contrast Dupont, 'Couple' (v)).

What did Jesus intend when he compared the kingdom to the working of leaven?[63] One can, as did the editor of Q, see the point in

[60] So C. M. Tuckett, 'Thomas and the Synoptics', *NovT* 30 (1988), pp. 148–53; against C. H. Hunzinger, 'Aussersynoptisches Traditionsgut im Thomas-Evangelium', *TLZ* 85 (1960), pp. 843–6.

[61] On the related parable in Acts of Thomas 146 see R. J. Bauckham, 'The Parable of the Vine: Recovering a Lost Parable of Jesus', *NTS* 33 (1987), pp. 84–101.

[62] E.g. Kümmel, *Promise*, p. 132. On double parables in the Jesus tradition in general see Jeremias, *Parables*, pp. 90–1. More often than not, the pairing of parables must be assigned to the tradition rather than Jesus.

[63] The authenticity of 13.33 par. has not been a subject of debate, although Schulz, *Q*, p. 309, expresses doubt.

the contrast between a small beginning and a magnificent end (cf. the parable of the mustard seed).[64] But the parable can also be understood as teaching a lesson about the inevitability of certain eschatological events (cf. Weder, p. 133) or, in accordance with most of the Fathers, about the projected pervasiveness and transforming influence of Jesus' gospel or his followers.[65] There is in addition the view that it means that little causes (Jesus and his ministry) can have great effects (cf. Jas 3.3–5).[66] It has even been submitted that 13.33 'was originally a warning against the dangerous contagion of evil. It would be understood as an illustration of the warning against "the leaven of the Pharisees"' (Beare, p. 309). Which view is correct? We are inclined to second the tradition in associating the parables of the mustard seed and leaven and in interpreting both as parables of contrast. Yet we admit that the two parables probably did not belong together from the first and that they could have been spoken on very different occasions and hence for different ends.

33. ἄλλην παραβολὴν ἐλάλησεν αὐτοῖς.[67] Compare vv. 24 (q.v.) and 31; also 3, 10, and 13. The words are redactional. Lk 13.20 has: καὶ πάλιν εἶπεν.[68]

ὁμοία ἐστὶν ἡ βασιλεία τῶν οὐρανῶν ζύμῃ.. This is probably Matthew's revision of Q. Lk 13.20f. ('To what shall I liken the kingdom of God? It is like leaven . . .'), presumably comes closer to Q. Compare Lk 13.18–19a.

In ancient sources leaven[69] (we are to think of old, fermented dough) is used figuratively of either a corrupting influence[70] or—much less frequently—of a beneficial influence[71] (cf. Abrahams, pp. 51–3).[72] See further on 16.6.

ἣν λαβοῦσα γυνὴ ἐνέκρυψεν εἰς ἀλεύρου σάτα τρία, ἕως οὗ ἐζυμώθη ὅλον. Lk 13.21 differs only in having the simplex,

---

[64] So e.g. Jeremias, *Parables*, pp. 148–9, who thinks that the emphasis lies upon the moment the dough is uncovered.

[65] Cf. Allen, p. 152. Note 5.13 ('You are the salt of the earth') and 14 ('You are the light of the world').

[66] Cf. Dodd, *Parables*, p. 155: 'When the Kingdom of God is compared to leaven, the suggestion is that the ministry of Jesus is itself such an influence.'

[67] The reading of C 1241 *pc* sa^mss—παρεθηκεν αυτοις λεγων—is probably assimilation to vv. 24 and 31.

[68] Probably Q; cf. Schulz, *Q*, p. 307.

[69] See H. Windisch, *TWNT* 2, pp. 904–8. The Mishnah contains directions for its use in *m. Menah.* 5.1–2. On the different types of leaven in the ancient world see Pliny, *N.H.* 18.26.102–4.

[70] E.g. Exod 12.15–20; 34.25; Lev 2.11; Mt 16.6; Lk 12.1; 1 Cor 5.6; Plutarch, *Quaest. Rom.* 289F; Ignatius, *Mag.* 10; Justin, *Dial.* 14.2; Ps.-Clem. Hom. 8.17. For rabbinic texts see SB 1, pp. 728–9. Some have surmised that Jesus' positive use of leaven would have been striking, even shocking; cf. Weder, p. 134.

[71] E.g. Philo, *Spec. leg.* 2.184–5.

[72] Lampe, s.v., lists texts from the Fathers under two headings: 'of sin', 'of grace'.

ἔκρυψεν.[73] For ἐγκρύπτω[74] + εἰς see LXX Prov 19.24; Amos 9.3. On pleonastic λαμβάνω (a Semitism) cf. p. 83. See BDF § 474.4 for the subject of prepositional dependent anarthrous nouns coming after genitives they govern (here σάτα after ἀλεύρου).

ἐγκρύπτω can mean either 'hide' or 'put into'. ἄλευρον[75] means 'wheat flour' (cf. Josephus, Ant. 3.142; Sib. Orac. 8.14). As for σάτον,[76] which refers to a Jewish dry measure, it is a loanword; compare the Hebrew sĕ'â and the Aramaic sā'tā' and see SB 1, pp. 669–70. According to Josephus, Ant. 9.85, 'the saton is equal to one and a half Italian modii' (= one and a half pecks); and according to Ant. 9.71 and 85, 'a saton of fine flour would be bought for a shekel'. A comparison of Ruth 2.17 ('an ephah of barley') with the targum ('three sata of barley') implies that three sata = an ephah. The same equation is presupposed in Tg. Onq. on Exod 16.36 (cf. b. Menaḥ. 77a).[77] ζυμόω[78] means 'ferment' or 'leaven'. For the passive see Philo, Vit. Con 81.

The woman in our parable is not herself a symbol although, in the past some have equated her with the Holy Spirit, wisdom, Mary, or the church; see Wailes, pp. 113–17. She is no more symbolic than 'the man' of v. 31.

Why is the measure specified? Why three measures? The quantity is excessive. Jeremias, Parables, p. 147, claims it would provide a meal for over a hundred people.[79] Has Gen 18.6 ('And Abraham hastened into the tent to Sarah, and said, "Make ready quickly three measures of fine meal, knead it, and make cakes"') influenced the text?[80] According to Jeremias, Jesus was probably unspecific (cf. Gos. Thom. 96); the tradition then added an allusion to Scripture (Parables, pp. 31–2). But it is unclear why, if indeed we have here a scriptural allusion (which is not at all certain), Jesus himself could not be responsible, or why Jesus could not have broken the bounds of actuality in order to make a point about God's supernatural kingdom. This is the more so as 'three measures' would suggest a feast, and Jesus often spoke of the kingdom as a great banquet.[81]

[73] So B K L N U Π 892 al. P75 ℵ A D W Θ Ψ f1.13 Maj Ath have ενεκρυψεν, which is probably assimilation to Matthew.

[74] A NT hapax legomenon. LXX: 7.

[75] LXX: 12 (always for qemaḥ); NT: 2 (Mt: 13.33; Lk 13.21).

[76] LXX: 2 (Hag 2.16 [bis]); NT: 2 (Mt 13.33; Lk 13.21).

[77] For the use of saton (sata) on a recently discovered Greek inscription see I. L. Merker, 'A Greek Tariff Inscription from Jerusalem', IEJ 25 (1975), pp. 238–44.

[78] NT: 4 (Mt 13.33; Lk 13.21; 1 Cor 5.6; Gal 5.9).

[79] Other commentators supply even larger numbers. Whatever the precise amount, a large quantity is indicated.

[80] Cf. also Judg 6.19; 1 Sam 1.24; Pap? Ḥev C ar recto 2 ('three seahs').

[81] Cf. Gundry, Commentary, p. 268: 'Is Jesus hinting at the messianic banquet?' The Fathers tended to allegorize the numbers. Theodore of Mopsuestia saw the three as representing Greeks, Jews, and Samaritans, Augustine heart, soul, and spirit. See McNeile, p. 199. Bengel, ad loc., refers to the three sons of Noah! Chrysostom, Hom. on Mt. 46.2, had sounder instincts when he wrote: 'But by "three measures" . . . He meant many, for He is wont to take this number for a multitude'.

With this verse should be compared 1 Cor 5.6: 'Do you not know that a little leaven leavens the whole lump?' It is not impossible that this reflects a knowledge of Jesus' parable. But most commentators regard the words (which also appear in Gal 5.9) as proverbial. Perhaps, then, one should consider the possibility that Jesus' parable was based upon the proverb preserved in Paul. If this were in fact the case, it would be one more instance of Jesus using a negative image in a positive fashion. (The negative associations of leaven are so prominent in Scripture and other ancient sources that some earlier exegetes understood the parable of the leaven to predict the corruption of the church in the world. While this exegesis can hardly be sustained, some modern scholars have tried to retain the negative connotations of leaven by proposing that Jesus intended it to reflect the disreputable character of many of the members of the kingdom.[82])

Gos. Thom. 96 ('Jesus says: the kingdom of the Father is like a woman who has taken a little leaven and hidden it in dough and made large loaves of it') is probably inferior to Mt 13.33 par. as a witness to Jesus. The introduction ('the kingdom of the Father is like a woman') could reflect knowledge of Mt 13.33b, for the sentences have the same structure, and Lk 13.20–1a (= Q) is rather different. However that may be, the contrast between a 'little' leaven[83] and 'large' loaves is probably a secondary clarification (cf. Mk 4.31–2; Gos. Thom. 8, 107). Also secondary is 'the kingdom of my Father'.

THE USE OF PARABLES (13.34–5)

Drawing upon Mk 4.33–4 and Ps 78.2, Matthew now composes a formula quotation which makes a general statement about Jesus' use of parables. Two ends are thereby served. First, Jesus' parabolic manner of speaking is grounded in OT prophecy. Just as Jesus' birth, childhood, ministry, and death are all foretold in the Scriptures, so too does the OT look forward to the Messiah uttering in parables mysteries hidden from the foundation of the world. Secondly, vv. 34f. serves, in a manner reminiscent of vv. 10–17, as a transition which notifies the reader of a switch in audience. Jesus at this juncture speaks not to the crowds and the disciples but to the disciples alone. He is turning away from those who do not understand and turning towards those who do.

34. ταῦτα πάντα ἐλάλησεν ὁ Ἰησοῦς ἐν παραβολαῖς τοῖς ὄχλοις. Compare Mk 4.33: 'And with many such parables he spoke to them the word, as they were able to hear (it).' ταῦτα πάντα*, Ἰησοῦς* and ὄχλοι* are Matthean favourites. And Mark's 'as

---

[82] Cf. Lohmeyer, *Matthäus*, pp. 220–1.
[83] Cf. 1 Cor 5.6; Gal 5.9, both of which have 'a little leaven'.

they were able to hear (it)' is not used probably because it would decrease the parallelism with the following clause and also because it would blur the contrast between the understanding disciples and the unenlightened masses. Further, 'in parables' prepares for the occurrence of this phrase in the following OT citation. Thus all the differences between Mt 13.34a and Mk 4.33 can be readily explained in terms of Matthean redaction.

καὶ χωρὶς παραβολῆς οὐδὲν ἐλάλει αὐτοῖς.[84] Mk 4.34 has δέ instead of καί, and οὐκ. Note the chiasmus with v. 34a.

35. This is a redactional formula quotation taken from Ps 78.2. A knowledge of both the LXX and the Hebrew seems to be presupposed. The verse replaces Mk 4.34b ('but privately to his own disciples he explained everything'), perhaps because Matthew wants to leave the impression that the disciples required explanations only on occasion.

Ps 78, which tells the story of Israel's early history, seems to have been an important text in early Christianity. It is quoted twice in the NT (Mt 13.35; Jn 6.31) and alluded to maybe ten times or more.[85] Lindars (v), with attention directed primarily to Mt 13.35 and Jn 6.31, has tried to trace the apologetic usage of the psalm through several stages—application to the resurrection, then to the teaching of Jesus in general, then to the parables. His analysis fails in part because he assumes that Mt 13.35 reflects a pre-Matthean application of Ps 78.2, whereas there is no good reason for not ascribing the citation to the redactor himself.

ὅπως πληρωθῇ τὸ ῥηθὲν διὰ τοῦ προφήτου λέγοντος.[86] On this standard formula see on 1.22. The evangelist probably understood the psalms to be largely prophetic. He may also have identified the Asaph of the title of Psalm 78 with the prophet named in 1 Chr 25.2 and 2 Chr 29.30 (cf. on 1.7).

ἀνοίξω ἐν παραβολαῖς τὸ στόμα μου, ἐρεύξομαι κεκρυμμένα ἀπὸ καταβολῆς.[87] Compare 5.1–2. The first six words agree

---

[84] Although א‎² D L Θ 0233 f¹ Maj lat bo Eus Or have ουκ instead of ουδεν, this is due to assimilation to Mark.

[85] NA²⁶, pp. 754–5, lists these parallels: Ps 78.15–16/1 Cor 10.4; Ps 78.18/1 Cor 10.9 and Rev 20.9; Ps 78.23/Rev 4.1; Ps 78.24/Rev 2.17; Ps 78.24–5/1 Cor 10.3; Ps 78.31/1 Cor 10.5; Ps 78.35/Acts 7.35; Ps 78.36–7/Mt 15.8; Ps 78.37/Acts 7.21; Ps 78.44/Rev 16.4; Ps 78.45/Rev 16.13; Ps 78.70/Rom 1.1; Ps 78.71–2/Jn 21.16.

[86] א* Θ f¹·¹³ 33 pc add Ησαιου; and, following the title of Ps 78 ('A Maskil of Asaph'), Hierᵐˢˢ have Asaph. See Zahn, pp. 479–81; Van Segbroeck (v), pp. 360–5; Gundry, OT, p. 119, n. 2; Metzger, p. 33.

[87] κοσμου is added at the end in א*·² C D L W Θ 0233 f¹³ Maj lat syᵖ·ʰ co Eus. NA²⁶ prints it in brackets. The addition would have been natural; cf. 25.34; Lk 11.50; Jn 17.24; Eph 1.4; Heb 4.3; 9.26; 1 Pet 1.20; Rev 13.8; 17.8; As. Mos. 1.14. For the absolute καταβολή = 'foundation (of the world)' see Ep. Arist. 129.

perfectly with the LXX. The MT has: *'eptĕḥâ bĕmāšāl pî.*[88] But the last five words differ from the LXX (φθέγξομαι προβλήματα ἀπ' ἀρχῆς) and seem to be an independent rendering of the Hebrew: *'abbîʿâ ḥîdôt minnî-qedem.* ἐρεύγομαι[89] is used for the hiphil of *nābaʿ* in LXX Ps 18.3 (cf. 1 Clem 27.7). Both words can mean 'belch forth' or 'declare'. Similarly, while κρύπτω never does duty for *ḥîdâ* in the LXX, κεκρυμμένα[90] means 'things hidden' while *ḥîdôt* means 'riddles', 'enigmas';[91] further the LXX's προβλήματα is not the best translation of *ḥîdôt*, and Matthew may have preferred a form of κρύπτω because of its significant use in 11.25 and 13.44 (*bis*). Finally, ἀπὸ καταβολῆς—a popular expression in early Christian literature[92]—is a satisfactory rendering of *minnî-qedem*, which means 'of old', 'from ancient times'.

Matthew was attracted to Ps 78.2 because of the phrase, 'in parables'. That he paid much attention to the verse's broader context is not manifest, and it could be claimed that in this verse Matthew has misused the OT, especially as Ps 78.1–4 is clearly about an open revelation, not mysteries revealed to a select few. On the other hand, it can be urged that since Ps 78 is about the history of Israel, and since for Matthew that history is recapitulated in Jesus' life (see on 5.1–2), the novel application of Ps 78.2 is not arbitrary (cf. our discussion of the use of Hos 11.1 in Mt 2.15; see 1, p. 263; Carson, 'Matthew', *ad loc.*).

For Matthew the meaning of Ps 78.2 is not, despite 13.12-13, that Jesus speaks in parables in order to hide things from the crowds. Rather, his parables are revelatory (cf. 13.52), even when others cannot grasp them.

THE INTERPRETATION OF THE PARABLE OF THE WEEDS (13.36–43)

Returning to a private location, Jesus now answers his disciples' request for an interpretation of the parable of the weeds. He complies by giving them a list of allegorical equations (vv. 37–9), by reciting a short account of the last judgement (vv. 40–3a), and by uttering a general admonition (v. 43b).

It is generally agreed that Mt 13.36–43 is a free Matthean composition. The word statistics are decisive.[93] Some indeed have

---

[88] Note the singular. The OT Peshitta and the Vulgate both have the plural, in agreement with the LXX and Matthew.

[89] A NT *hapax legomenon.*

[90] Cf. 2 Macc 12.41.

[91] Aquila translates with αἰνίγματα.

[92] Usually with κόσμου. See Gundry, *OT*, p. 119. Cf. Mt 25.34; Lk 11.50; Heb 4.3; 9.26; Rev 13.8; 17.8.

[93] See esp. Jeremias, *Parables*, pp. 82–5.

thought it possible that the text rests upon an interpretation Jesus gave.[94] And Weder, pp. 122–4, thinks only vv. 36, 40–3 redactional: vv. 37–9 preserve a pre-Matthean catalogue of equations (cf. Schweizer, *Matthew*, p. 309; also Gnilka, *Matthäusevangelium* 1, pp. 499–500). But we remain sceptical. 13.36–43 shows so many signs of Matthew's hand that the quest to discover behind it something pre-Matthean seems hopeless.

36. τότε ἀφεὶς τοὺς ὄχλους ἦλθεν εἰς τὴν οἰκίαν. Compare 26.44. Jesus moves to a house. Esoteric teaching demands a private setting. τότε*, ἀφίημι*, and ὄχλοι* are all redactional favourites, and ἔρχομαι + εἰς τὴν οἰκίαν is more characteristic of Matthew than the other evangelists (Mt: 7; Mk: 1; Lk: 1). On 'the house' (cf. 13.1) see on 9.10.

καὶ προσῆλθαν αὐτῷ οἱ μαθηταὶ αὐτοῦ λέγοντες.[95] προσέρχομαι* is beloved by Matthew; and προσέρχομαι + αὐτῷ + οἱ μαθηταί* is also patently redactional.

διασάφησον ἡμῖν τὴν παραβολὴν τῶν ζιζανίων τοῦ ἀγροῦ.[96] Compare 4.18: 'Then hear the parable of the sower' (redactional); also 15.15 diff. Mk 7.17. διασαφέω[97] (= 'explain') occurs only one other time in the NT: Mt 18.31 (cf. Acts 10.25 D). And Matthew alone of NT writers uses the adjectival genitive τοῦ ἀγροῦ (6.28, 30; 13.36). The title, 'the parable of the weeds', shows us that Matthew is thinking primarily not of the salvation of the righteous but of the wicked and their terrible fate. The subject is not reward but punishment.

37–9. Matthew's Jesus meets with the disciples' request by first compiling a list of seven allegorical equations.[98] After the first equation, each thereafter begins with ὁ δέ or τὸ δέ. The parallelism is typically Matthean, and the vocabulary is either redactional or taken from 13.24–30.

ὁ δὲ ἀποκριθεὶς εἶπεν. ἀποκριθείς + finite verb* is often redactional.

ὁ σπείρων τὸ καλὸν σπέρμα ἐστὶν ὁ υἱὸς τοῦ ἀνθρώπου. Compare 13.24 (q.v.). 'The Son of man'—Matthew's favourite christological title—is chosen because it is in this rôle that Jesus will act as the judge on the final day (see p. 51).

ὁ δὲ ἀγρός ἐστιν ὁ κόσμος. 'The field' is from 13.24 (q.v.), and κόσμος* is a Matthean favourite.

---

[94] E.g. M. de Goedt (v); Beasley-Murray, p. 135 (listing others like-minded). For objections see Jeremias, *Parables*, pp. 81–2.

[95] So HG. NA[26] prints προσηλθον.

[96] So HG and NA[26]. φρασον appears in ℵ² C D L W 0106 0233 0250 f[1.13] Maj it Or. It might be original (cf. 15.15); so Jeremias, *Parables*, p. 83, n. 60.

[97] LXX: 11, for *bāʾar* in Deut 1.5, for *ḥāwâ* in Dan 2.6.

[98] For rabbinic parallels see Schlatter, pp. 444–5.

R. C. Trench could write, concerning the phrase, 'the field is the world': 'over these few words, simple as they may seem, a battle has been fought, greater, perhaps, than over any single phrase in the Scripture, if we except the consecrating words at the Holy Eucharist.'[99] The reason is that the parable of the tares has often been viewed as treating of church discipline, as being instruction to refrain from trying to create a church purified of sinners. Augustine championed this view in fighting the Donatists, and the text has been similarly used down through the centuries (see n. 12). But it seems unlikely that our text should have much bearing on properly ecclesiastical issues, for (i) Matthew equates the field with the world, not the church; (ii) the Matthean context has nothing to do with church discipline (contrast chapter 18); and (iii) chapter 18 does not shy away from offering firm instructions on excommunication.

τὸ δὲ καλὸν σπέρμα, οὗτοί εἰσιν οἱ υἱοὶ τῆς βασιλείας. 'The good seed' has already been used in 13.24 (q.v.), 27, and 37. 'Sons of the kingdom' is an expression Matthew employed in 8.12. And the unqualified 'the kingdom' is clearly editorial (Mt: 6; Mk: 0; Lk: 1). *Casus pendens* is, in addition, found more often in Matthew than in Mark or Luke (Mt: 13; Mk: 4; Lk: 8–9).

In 8.12 'the sons of the kingdom' is an ironic appellation for Jews who will be cast out into the darkness. Here the phrase describes the faithful. The antithetical applications are striking (see on 8.12 for discussion). It has been suggested that the use of the one title to tag two different groups should warn church members that they, like unbelieving Jews, can lose their privileged status (cf. Ogawa, p. 208). The point would certainly be consistent with Matthew's own view of things; but we wonder whether to infer it from a comparison of 8.12 with 13.38 is to read into the text what is not there.

τὰ δὲ ζιζάνιά εἰσιν οἱ υἱοὶ τοῦ πονηροῦ. 'The weeds' is taken from 13.25 (cf. 26, 27, 29, 30, 36), and 'the sons of the evil one'[100]—a Matthean creation?[101]—is formulated on analogy with 'the sons of the kingdom.'[102] Matthew likes ὁ πονηρός/τὸ πονηρόν.* 'The sons of the evil one' helps underline the power of the devil in the world and the responsibility he bears for human

---

[99] R. C. Trench, *Notes on the Parables of Our Lord*, 14th ed., London, 1882, pp. 87–8.

[100] *Pace* McNeile, p. 201, του πονηρου is a proper name, 'the evil one'; see on 6.13. For similar formulations see 4QFlor. 1.8 ('sons of Belial'); Mt 23.15 ('sons of hell'); Acts 13.10 ('sons of the devil'); 1 Jn 3.10 ('children of the devil'); Irenaeus, *Adv. haer*. 3.3.4 ('first-born of Satan'); cf. Jn 8.44.

[101] The expression is apparently unattested in sources not influenced by the First Gospel.

[102] One is reminded of the two main groups in the Dead Sea Scrolls: the 'sons of light' and the 'sons of darkness'. For other parallels between the parable of the tares and its interpretation and the Dead Sea Scrolls, see Davies, *SSM*, p. 232.

failing, two themes Matthew wishes to bring out at this point in
his story, for he is still largely concerned with coming to grips
with Israel's response to Jesus.

ὁ δὲ ἐχθρὸς ὁ σπείρας αὐτά ἐστιν ὁ διάβολος. See on 13.25.
διάβολος (Mt: 6; Mk: 0; Lk: 5) seems to be redactional in 4.5
and 8. On 'the devil' see the discussion on 4.1.

ὁ δὲ θερισμὸς συντέλεια αἰῶνός ἐστιν. 'Harvest' is from 13.30,
and συντέλεια* + αἰῶνος is redactional no less than five times:
13.39, 40, 49; 24.3; 28.20.

The expression, 'end of the age', is frequent in Jewish apocalyptic
literature[103] and so Matthew's fondness for it shows his kinship with
those writings. See further Vögtle, Zukunft, pp. 151–6.

οἱ δὲ θερισταὶ ἄγγελοί εἰσιν. 'Harvesters' appeared in 13.30,
and it is characteristic of Matthew to associate the Son of man
with angels (13.41; 16.27; 25.31).

For eschatological judgement as a harvest see on 9.37–8. For angels
as instruments of that judgement see 1 En. 54.6; 63.1; Mt 24.31; Rev
14.15–19; SB 1, pp. 672–3, 974.

40. 13.24–30 told a story. 13.37–9 then supplied a lexicon of
sorts explaining the meanings of seven figures in that story.
13.40–3 now takes those meanings and with them constructs a
second narrative. In other words, the story in 13.24–30 uses the
figures on one side of the equations in 13.37–9 while 13.40–3
uses the figures from the other side:

13.24–30	13.37–9	13.40–3
sower	sower = Son of man	Son of man
field	field = world	world
good seed	good seed = sons of the kingdom	sons of the kingdom
weeds	weeds = sons of the evil one	sons of the evil one
enemy	enemy = the devil	the devil
harvest	harvest = judgement	judgement
harvesters	harvesters = angels	angels

The result is two stories with one meaning. (Note that as a
matter of fact the story in vv. 40–3 only takes up the separation
of the wheat and tares, recounted in 13.30; it passes over the
verses leading up to this.)

ὥσπερ οὖν συλλέγεται τὰ ζιζάνια καὶ πυρὶ καίεται, οὕτως ἔσται

---

[103] Cf. 1 En. 16.1; T. Levi 10.2; T. Benj. 11.3; As. Mos. 12.4; 4 Ezra 7.113;
2 Bar. 13.3; 19.5; 21.8; 27.15. Note also Trimorphic Protennoia 44.33–4; m.
Sanh. 4.5; SB 1, p. 671. Discussion in G. Delling, TWNT 8, pp. 65–7. Matthew
alone of NT writers has συντέλεια τοῦ αἰῶνος. And συντέλεια occurs only
once outside the First Gospel, in Heb 9.26: ἐπὶ συντελείᾳ τῶν αἰώνων.

ἐν τῇ συντελείᾳ τοῦ αἰῶνος.[104] Compare 12.40 (ὥσπερ . . . οὕτως ἔσται). In addition to the vocabulary borrowed from 13.29 and 39 (συλλέγεται τὰ ζιζάνια, συντελείᾳ τοῦ αἰῶνος), Matthew uses both ὥσπερ* and οὕτως* more than his fellow evangelists;[105] and οὖν* and πῦρ* are often editorial.

41f. ἀποστελεῖ ὁ υἱὸς τοῦ ἀνθρώπου τοὺς ἀγγέλους αὐτοῦ. See on vv. 37 and 39 and compare 24.31 = Mk 13.27.

καὶ συλλέξουσιν ἐκ τῆς βασιλείας αὐτοῦ πάντα τὰ σκάνδαλα καὶ τοὺς ποιοῦντας τὴν ἀνομίαν. Compare 7.23 and 1 Jn 3.4. The verb and βασιλείας are from 13.28–30 and 38. τὰ σκάνδαλα κ.τ.λ. borrows the language of LXX Ps 140.9b (καὶ ἀπὸ σκανδάλων τῶν ἐργαζομένων τὴν ἀνομίαν) and perhaps MT Zeph 1.3 (*'āsēp 'ādām . . . wĕhammakšēlôt 'et-hārĕšā'îm*).[106] Both σκάνδαλον (Mt: 5; Mk: 0; Lk: 1; see on 16.23) and ἀνομία* are recognizably Matthean.

'His kingdom'[107] is most naturally equated with the church; but 13.38 equates the field with the world. How does one resolve this seeming contradiction? There appear to us to be two plausible answers. Schweizer may be right in claiming that 'the Kingdom of the Son of Man encompasses the entire world, to the extent that it is proclaimed everywhere' (*Matthew*, p. 311; cf. Gundry, *Commentary*, p. 275). No less probable is Allen's proposal: 'When the Son of Man has come, then the kingdom also will have come. Hence at that future date the tares can be said to be gathered out of His kingdom' (p. 153). (If one rejects these two solutions and identifies 'his kingdom' with the church, then one must hold that Matthew believed that the church was peopled with 'sons of the evil one' and also, at the same time, that the church could be fitly described as the Son of man's kingdom. We deem this unlikely. The identification of 'his kingdom' and the church is also problematic because it presupposes that our text has to do with false disciples; but at this point in the gospel the issue is the unbelief of Israel, not unbelief in the ecclesia.)

καὶ βαλοῦσιν αὐτοὺς εἰς τὴν κάμινον τοῦ πυρός. This phrase is borrowed from Dan 3.6 (LXX: ἐμβαλοῦσιν[108] αὐτὸν εἰς τὴν κάμινον τοῦ πυρὸς τὴν καιομένην; Theodotion: ἐμβληθήσεται εἰς τὴν κάμινον τοῦ πυρὸς τὴν καιομένην). It is used again in 13.50.

ἐκεῖ ἔσται ὁ κλαυθμὸς καὶ ὁ βρυγμὸς τῶν ὀδόντων. On this Matthean refrain (Mt: 6; Mk: 0; Lk: 1) see on 8.12.

---

[104] κατακαιεται (cf. 3.12; 13.20) is the reading of ℵ B *f*[1] 892 1010 *al* Or Cyr, followed by NA[26] (with κατα in brackets). HG prints καιεται, which is found in C L W X Θ 0199 0233[vid] 0242[vid] 0250 *f*[13] Maj. A firm decision is impossible. D has κατακαιονται.

[105] Note also the statistics on οὕτως ἔστιν, ἦν, ἔσται: Mt: 12; Mk: 2; Lk: 3.

[106] We are not inclined to see MT Zeph 1.3 as the starting-point for the original parable; but this possibility is defended by Hill, *Matthew*, pp. 235–7.

[107] Cf. 16.28; 20.21; Lk 1.33; 12.31; 23.42; Jn 18.36.

[108] So 700 *pc* for Mt 13.42.

43. τότε οἱ δίκαιοι ἐκλάμψουσιν ὡς ὁ ἥλιος ἐν τῇ βασιλείᾳ τοῦ πατρὸς αὐτῶν. τότε*, δίκαιος*, and πατήρ + personal pronoun are Matthean* while βασιλεία + πατρός is redactional in 26.29.[109] Also, although ἐκλάμπω is a Matthean and NT *hapax legomenon*, ἔλαμψεν τὸ πρόσωπον αὐτοῦ ὡς ὁ ἥλιος appears in 17.2 diff. Mk 9.2–3. It is altogether probable that Matthew had that scene in mind here: the transfiguration of Jesus shows forth the eschatological glory which all the saints will share. Compare Dan 12.3 Theod.: οἱ συνιέντες ἐκλάμψουσιν ὡς ἡ λαμπρότης τοῦ στερεώματος.[110] See further p. 696.

ὁ ἔχων ὦτα ἀκουέτω.[111] Compare 13.9 and see on 11.15. The injunction announces a division in the narrative: a paragraph has ended.

(iv) *Concluding Observations*

(1) The parable of the tares and its interpretation cannot, if one is seeking the redactional viewpoint, be seen in isolation. This is because the discourse in chapter 13 naturally arises out of the opposition narrated in 11.1–12.50. How so? The problem posed by Israel's unexpected behaviour is the mystery of unbelief, and this is a theme addressed in the parable chapter. Specifically, and with respect to 13.24–30 and 36–43, the text first of all suggests that human failure is part of a wider problem, namely, the cosmic struggle between God and Satan. Those who oppose the Messiah are 'sons of the devil', that is, they are his planting. Thus their (from Matthew's perspective) irrational lack of faith is part and parcel of an even greater mystery, that of transcendent or non-human evil. Secondly, the parable of the tares addresses the question of theodicy by putting evil in eschatological perspective, by reminding one that the bad endures only for a season. If the sun now shines on the just and unjust alike, if 'until now the spirits of truth and falsehood struggle in the hearts of men and they walk in both wisdom and folly' (1QS 4.23–4), it shall not always be so. The tares will eventually be plucked up, the wheat gathered. It is therefore history's end which will give the answers to the difficult theological questions history, including the history of Jesus, raises.

[109] 'Kingdom of the Father' occurs in the NT only in Matthew. It is, however, common in the Gospel of Thomas; see 57, 76, 96, 97, 98, 99. Is this a sign of Matthean influence?

[110] Cf. also Judg 5.31; 2 Sam 23.3–4; Ep Jer 67; Ecclus 50.7; 1 En. 39.7; 104.2; Apoc. Adam 83.2–4; SB 1, pp. 673–4.

[111] ακουειν is added after ωτα in ℵ² C D L W 0119 0233 0250 *f*[1.13] Maj lat sy co Eus Or. See on 11.15.

(2) The parables of the mustard seed and leaven, cut from the same cloth, stand in continuity with the parable of the tares in that they too place God's triumph only in the future. For the present the kingdom is a mysterious, hidden entity, whose chief feature seems to be weakness. But according to our similitudes what matters is not the beginning but the end. The kingdom of God may not begin with success, but success is its divinely ordained destiny. If leaven leavens the whole lump, and if a little mustard seed becomes a tree, similarly will the kingdom, however obscure now, become, in the end, the measure of all things.

(v) *Bibliography*

Ambrozic, pp. 122–34.

P. Bacq and O. Ribadeau Dumas, 'Reading a Parable', *LumV* 39 (1984), pp. 181–94.

G. Barth, 'Auseinandersetzung um die Kirchenzucht im Umkreis des Matthäusevangeliums', *ZNW* 69 (1978), pp. 158–77.

H.-W. Bartsch, 'Eine bisher übersehene Zitierung der LXX in Mk 4.30', *TZ* 15 (1959), pp. 126–8.

Beasley-Murray, pp. 122–5, 132–5.

S. P. Brock, 'An Additional Fragment of 0106?', *JTS* 20 (1969), pp. 226–8.

L. H. Bunn, 'The Parable of the Tares', *ExpT* 38 (1927), pp. 561–4.

Carlston, pp. 26–8, 157–62.

D. R. Catchpole, 'John the Baptist, Jesus and the Parable of the Tares', *SJT* 31 (1978), pp. 557–70.

J. D. Crossan, 'The Seed Parables of Jesus', *JBL* 92 (1973), pp. 244–66.

Crossan, *Parables*, pp. 45–9.

Dahl, *Jesus*, pp. 155–60.

Dodd, *Parables*, pp. 147–50, 152–5.

J. Dupont, 'Le couple parabolique du sénevé et du levain', in Strecker, *Jesus*, pp. 331–45.

idem, 'Les paraboles du sénevé et du levain', *NRTh* 89 (1967), pp. 897–913.

R. W. Funk, 'Beyond Criticism in Quest in Literacy', *Int* 25 (1971), pp. 149–70.

idem, 'The Looking-Glass Tree is for the Birds', *Int* 27 (1973), pp. 3–9.

Geist, pp. 75–104.

M. de Goedt, 'L'explication de la parabole de l'ivraie (Mt. xiii, 36–43)', *RB* 66 (1959), pp. 32–54.

Grässer, pp. 141–9.

F. Jehle, 'Senfkorn und Sauerteig', *NKZ* 34 (1923), pp. 713–19.

J. Jeremias, 'Die Deutung des Gleichnisses vom Unkraut unter dem Weizen (Mt xiii. 36–43)', in *Neotestamentica et Patristica*, ed. H. Baltensweiler, Leiden, 1962, pp. 59–63.

Jeremias, *Parables*, pp. 31–2, 81–5, 146–9, 224–7.

Jülicher 2, pp. 546–63, 569–81.

Kingsbury, *Parables*, pp. 63–110.

Klauck, pp. 210–18.

Kümmel, *Promise*, pp. 124–40.

Künzel, pp. 125–34.

O. Kuss, 'Zum Sinngehalt des Doppelgleichnisses vom Senfkorn und Sauerteig', *Bib* 40 (1959), pp. 641–53.

idem, 'Zur Senfkornparabel', *TGI* 41 (1951), pp. 40–9.

Laufen, pp. 174–200.

R. Laufen, 'ΒΑΣΙΛΕΙΑ und ΕΚΚΛΗΣΙΑ: Eine traditions- und redaktionsgeschichtliche Untersuchung des Gleichnisses vom Senfkorn', in *Begegnung mit dem Wort*, ed. J. Zmijewski and E. Nellessen, Bonn, 1980, pp. 105–40.

Lindars, *Apologetic*, pp. 156–9.

H. K. McArthur, 'The Parable of the Mustard Seed', *CBQ* 33 (1971), pp. 198–201.

D. Marguerat, 'L'église et le monde en Matthieu 13.36–43', *RTP* 110 (1978), pp. 111–29.

Marguerat, pp. 436–47.

F. Mussner, '1QHodajoth und das Gleichnis vom Senfkorn (Mk 4.30–2 Par.)', *BZ* 4 (1960), pp. 128–32.

Oakman, pp. 114–28.

É. Pousset, 'Le sénevé et le levain', *Vie Chrétienne* 174 (1975), pp. 13–16.

J. F. Royale, 'On the Identification of the Mustard Tree of Scripture', *Journal of the Royal Asiatic Society* 8 (1846), pp. 113–37.

Schulz, *Q*, pp. 298–309.

B. Schultze, 'Die ekklesiologische Bedeutung des Gleichnisses vom Senfkorn (Matth 13.31–32; Mk 4.30–2; Lk 13.18–19)', *Orientalia christiana periodica* 27 (1961), pp. 362–86.

Scott, pp. 67–77.

C. W. F. Smith, 'The Mixed State of the Church in Matthew's Gospel', *JBL* 82 (1963), pp. 149–68.

L. Szimonidesz, 'Eine Rekonstruktion des Senfkorngleichnisses', *Nieuw Theologisch Tijdschrift* 26 (1937), pp. 128–55.

F. Van Segbroeck, 'Le scandale de l'incroyance. La signification de Mt XIII. 35', *ETL* 41 (1965), pp. 344–72.

E. Waller, 'The Parable of the Leaven: A Sectarian Teaching and the Inclusion of Women', *USQR* 35 (1979–80), pp. 99–109.

Weder, pp. 120–38.

D. R. Wickes, 'Note on Matthew 13.30 and Matthew 6.30 = Luke 12.38', *JBL* 42 (1923), p. 251.

Zumstein, pp. 187–95.

XXIX

THREE MORE PARABLES AND THE CONCLUSION OF THE DISCOURSE
(13.44–52)

(i) *Structure*

Mt 13.44–52 opens with a group of three parables. Each parable begins in a similar fashion:

44   ὁμοία ἐστὶν ἡ βασιλεία τῶν οὐρανῶν + dative
45   πάλιν ὁμοία ἐστὶν ἡ βασιλεία τῶν οὐρανῶν + dative
47   πάλιν ὁμοία ἐστὶν ἡ βασιλεία τῶν οὐρανῶν + dative

Following the third parable (vv. 47–8), there is, first, an interpretation of that parable (vv. 49–50) and, secondly, a dialogue between Jesus and his disciples (vv. 51–2). The dialogue not only brings 13.44–52 to a close (note the *inclusio* with v. 44 created by the key word, 'treasure'); it also winds up the whole discourse, 13.1–52, for the ταῦτα πάντα of v. 51 includes all the parables of chapter 13. See further Excursus X.

(ii) *Sources*

None of the material in 13.44–52 has a parallel in the canonical gospels.[1] This makes it possible to view the section as a whole as a purely Matthean composition.[2] But a redactional origin is only plausible for vv. 49–50 (the interpretation of the parable of the net) and vv. 51–2 (the conclusion of the discourse). The three parables in vv. 44–8 are to be assigned to Matthew's special tradition (M). They may in fact have come from a pre-Matthean parable collection, either oral or written (see further 1, p. 125).

(iii) *Exegesis*

In contrast with the surrounding verses, which speak of dread judgement (vv. 40–3, 49–50), the two parables which open our

---

[1] On the parallels in Gos. Thom. 8 (= Mt 13.47–8), 76 (= Mt 13.45–6), and 109 (= Mt 13.44) see below.
[2] So e.g. Gundry, *Commentary*, pp. 275–82, who quite implausibly thinks of Prov 2.1–9 and Mt 13.24, 36–43 and 22.1–14 as Matthew's main inspiration.

section—vv. 44 and 45–6—have to do with finding the kingdom and giving all one has to obtain it. Thus the focus of vv. 44–6 is definitely on the present, not on the future, and the reader is led to envision the actions of believers, not the deeds and fate of unbelievers.

THE HIDDEN TREASURE (13.44)

Finding the kingdom of Heaven is like finding a treasure hidden in a field, for the sake of which one will sell everything.

There is hardly any doubt concerning the origin of the parable of the hidden treasure: Jesus was its author. With regard to his intention, there is also general agreement. The parable, by reference to a once-in-a-lifetime discovery, to an event one only dreams about, expresses the incomparable worth of the kingdom and the necessity to do all one can do to gain it. One gladly risks everything to take advantage of the unexpected opportunity presented by the presence[3] of God's salvific kingdom with all its blessings. (While some exegetes stress the value of the kingdom, others put the emphasis upon the appropriate reaction. We prefer to see them as equally important. The two go hand in hand.[4])

The most thorough examination of Jesus' treasure parable, and certainly the most creative, is that of Crossan, *Finding* (v). In this Mt 13.44 is imaginatively discussed against the background of Jewish parables as well as trove folktales from around the world. Several interesting points emerge, such as that Jesus' narrative does not teach typical folktale morality (e.g. Do not take another's property), that it is unique in having a man sell all that he has, and that it distinguishes itself from Jewish parallels by its muteness on moral and legal matters (e.g. Who has the right of ownership when a treasure long hidden is discovered?). Crossan's own judgement is that Jesus' parable would have created 'moral shock' in a Jewish audience, for it sets the kingdom above traditional moral interests: the finder of the treasure schemes to possess property found on another man's land. But for reasons to be given below, it is not clear that this is the correct interpretation.

ὁμοία ἐστὶν ἡ βασιλεία τῶν οὐρανῶν.[5] Compare 13.45, 47, 52, and see on 13.24.

---

[3] Most scholars now recognize that the parable of the treasure implies the presence of the kingdom; cf. Linnemann (v); for dissent see Kümmel, *Promise*, p. 125, n. 75.

[4] Against the objection that Jewish hearers hardly needed to be persuaded of the value of the kingdom, it suffices to observe that what people most often require is not revelation but prompting to do what they already know they should yet do not.

[5] C L W Θ 0119 0233 0250 *f*[1.13] Maj f h q sy[p.h] Or have παλιν before και, which increases the parallelism with 45 and 47. Although omitted by א B D 0242 892 1241 *pc* lat sy[s.c] co the adverb could be original. Cf. the threefold use of ἄλλην in 13.24, 31, 33. On the other hand, no obvious explanation for the omission of πάλιν is forthcoming.

θησαυρῷ κεκρυμμένῳ ἐν τῷ ἀγρῷ.[6] Compare 25.25 (ἔκρυψα ... ἐν τῇ γῇ). The article is a Semitism.

In a day before safe-deposit boxes it seems to have been common enough for people to bury valuables in the ground, especially in times of political instability and crisis.[7] One is reminded of the Copper Scroll found in a cave at Qumran (3Q15), which gives directions for the recovering of caches of gold, silver, and other precious items.[8] Virgil, Aen. 1.358–9, refers to 'ancient treasure in the earth, a hoard of gold and silver known to none'.

Origen, Comm. on Mt. 10.5, equated the field with the Scriptures (cf. De prin. 3.11). But the parable does not open itself to this sort of allegorizing.

ὃν εὑρὼν ἄνθρωπος ἔκρυψεν. Compare 13.46. Our parable presupposes that the kingdom is hidden, that it is not yet revealed to everyone. This fits well with the thrust of the rest of the chapter. The revelation of God in Jesus is not perfectly vivid to all; it can only be perceived by those with ears to hear and eyes to see.

Commentators have long discussed whether the finder of the treasure acts immorally or unlawfully when he covers it up and seeks to make it his own. Some have defended his actions as above reproach. Others have thought him to behave immorally.[9] It is not easy to assess the issue. The story does not inform us on certain key points.[10] What is the status of the finder? What is he doing in the field? How is the treasure discovered? How did it come to be where it is? What kind of treasure is it? Who owns the field? How did the owner come to own the field? Without knowing such details one is hesitant to evaluate the legal or moral situation and even uncertain as to the value of discussing such. Certainly Jesus' failure to remark on them makes one wonder how important they can be. Further, whether or not 13.44 was originally associated with 13.45f., the parable of the pearl, it seems altogether likely that both texts were composed in order to make the same point. There is, however, nothing at all scandalous or illegal about the merchant's purchase of the magnificent pearl. When he goes and sells all that he has, he may be acting strangely, but he is not being immoral. Can it really be so different with the finder of the treasure?

---

[6] BDF § 255.1: τω (C Chr omit) is incorrect.

[7] Cf. Ecclus 20.30; Josephus, Bell. 7.114–15; 2 Bar. 6.7–9; Par. Jer. 3.6–11. Note also R. de Vaux, Archaeology and the Dead Sea Scrolls, London, 1973, pp. 34–5.

[8] Scholars have debated whether the treasures described were imaginary or real; for discussion see B. Pixner, 'Unravelling the Copper Scroll Code', RevQ 11 (1983), pp. 323–65.

[9] Cf. the parable of the unjust steward. Rabbinic texts sometimes thought relevant include m. Qidd. 1.5; Mek. on Exod 14.5; and m. B. Bat. 4.8–9. See further SB 1, p. 674.

[10] For an attempt to fill in Matthew's silence see Derrett (v).

καὶ ἀπὸ τῆς χαρᾶς αὐτοῦ ὑπάγει καὶ πωλεῖ πάντα ὅσα ἔχει καὶ ἀγοράζει τὸν ἀγρὸν ἐκεῖνον.[11] Compare Mk 10.21. χαρά, ὑπάγω (a Matthean favourite; see 1, p. 518, n. 14), πωλέω,[12] ὅσος,[13] ἀγοράζω, and ἀγρός* all occur in other M parables (13.24, 27, 46; 20.4, 7, 14; 25.9, 10, 21, 23). The historical present is not typical of Matthew. Since it takes all that he has for the man discovering the treasure to procure the field, it is often concluded that he is poor. If this is a correct inference,[14] there would be a contrast with the next parable, in which the main figure, the pearl merchant, is presumably well-to-do. (Cf. the contrast in 13.31–3: one parable has to do with a man, the other with a woman.)

The longer version of the parable of the hidden treasure in Gos. Thom. 109 is about ignorance; it avoids the possible objection that the finder acted illegally and seems to be influenced by a parable that is preserved in *Midr. Cant.*on 4.13.[15] In every way then it is secondary to Matthew's version.

THE PEARL OF GREAT PRICE (13.45–6)

As with the parable of the treasure, that of the pearl of great price is generally received as an authentic parable of Jesus. Further, its meaning on Jesus' lips must have been the same as that of 13.44:[16] 'when the truth is encountered, a choice has to be made, a decision, and it must be acted on immediately, whole-heartedly. And a price must be paid, amounting to all that one has'.[17] To these words of Vermes we need add only that 'kingdom' would be a better word than 'truth' and that the price paid is not a sacrifice but an exchange of something lesser for something greater (cf. Phil 3.7–8): the kingdom is a joy waiting to be discovered. Beare, p. 315, cites Lk 14.33 ('Any of you that does not take leave of all his possessions cannot be my disciple') and then adds: 'Anyone who counts the cost of discipleship has completely failed to grasp the greatness of the reward'.

J. D. Crossan has made an interesting and largely convincing case for seeing the parable of the pearl, the parable of the hidden treasure,

[11] B (28) *pc* bo Or omit παντα.

[12] With ὑπάγω also in 19.21 = Mk 10.21.

[13] For ὅσος + ἔχειν see also 13.46 and 18.25 (both M parables).

[14] But we do not know anything about the size of the field or what it was used for, etc., so how do we know what it cost?

[15] Cf. L. Cerfaux, 'Les Paraboles du Royaume dans l'Évangile de Thomas', *Le Muséon* 70 (1957), p. 314.

[16] Whether the two were originally spoken together—so Sabourin, p. 607; against Bultmann, *History*, p. 173—we have no way of determining. But one suspects that the two were at least joined in Matthew's source. (The parables are separated in Thomas; see 76 and 109.)

[17] Vermes, *World*, p. 52. Cf. T. Job 18.6–7.

and the parable of the great fish (Gos. Thom. 8)[18] as of fundamental importance for understanding all the other parables of Jesus.[19] In his judgement, the three parables are about advent, reversal, and action, and these three themes are the three rubrics under which all the parables are most profitably classified. By 'advent' Crossan means the coming of the kingdom, with its new world and new possibilities.[20] By 'reversal' is meant the undoing of the past and all its values.[21] By 'action' Crossan signifies expression of the new possibilities brought about by the kingdom's advent.[22] All this is neatly encapsulated in the main verbs of vv. 44 and 45f.: finds—sells—buys. A man finds a pearl or a treasure which shatters the normalcy of life and invalidates all previous plans for the future. The result is a new set of values, expressed in both vv. 44 and 45f. by the selling of all one's old possessions: these no longer mean anything. Finally, the person finding the treasure or pearl happily obtains the one thing needful. The kingdom now determines the course of one's existence. Advent, reversal, action: these words paradigmatically express the coming of the kingdom and its experience among human beings.

45. πάλιν ὁμοία ἐστὶν ἡ βασιλεία τῶν οὐρανῶν. See on 13.44. That these words are followed by 'a man, a merchant' rather than 'a pearl, which a merchant ...' (cf. 13.44: ὁμοία ... θησαυρῷ) demonstrates not only the inexactitude of the formulae introducing parables (see on 13.24): it is perhaps also a sign of pre-Matthean tradition. Had our evangelist freely composed vv. 44 and 45f., we would expect, given his predilection for parallelism, to find the introductions in perfect parallelism.[23]

ἀνθρώπῳ ἐμπόρῳ ζητοῦντι καλοὺς μαργαρίτας. ἔμπορος (= 'merchant', 'wholesale dealer'; cf. the rabbinic 'impôrîn) is a synoptic *hapax legomenon* while καλός* is a Matthean favourite. μαργαρίτης appears elsewhere only in the next verse and 7.6 (M). On the pleonastic ἀνθρώπῳ see 1, p. 80.

[18] On this see p. 443. We disagree with Crossan on its originality.
[19] See Crossan, *Parables*, pp. 26–36.
[20] Under this rubric he places these parables: the fig tree (Mk 13.28); the leaven (Mt 13.33); the sower (Mk 4.3–8); the mustard seed (Mk 4.30–2); the lost sheep (Mt 18.12–13); the lost coin (Lk 15.8–9).
[21] See the good Samaritan (Lk 10.30–7); the rich man and Lazarus (Lk 16.19–31); the Pharisee and the publican (Lk 18.10–14); the wedding guest (Lk 14.7–11); the proper guests (Lk 14.12–14); the great supper (Mt 22.1–10); the prodigal son (Lk 15.11–32).
[22] Parables of action: the wicked husbandman (Mk 12.1–12); the doorkeeper (Mk 13.37); the overseer (Lk 12.42–6); the talents (Mt 25.14–30); the throne claimant (Lk 19.12b, 14–15a, 27); the unmerciful servant (Mt 18.23–8); the servant's reward (Lk 17.7–10); the unjust steward (Lk 16.1–7); the workers in the vineyard (Mt 20.1–13).
[23] Gos. Thom. 76 (the pearl) and 109 (the tares) have similar introductions: both compare the kingdom to a person; but this is the tendency of Thomas throughout.

'Pearls' (see on 7.6) were more valued by the ancients than they are by us, and several commentators have suggested that pearls once held the place that diamonds do now. For ancient beliefs about pearls see Origen, *Comm. on Mt.* 10.7. One should recall that the author of the Hymn of the Pearl chose the pearl to symbolize the most valued possession of all, the original soul (see Hennecke 2, pp. 498–504). For pearls coupled with gold see 1 Tim 2.9; Rev 17.4; 18.12, 16; T. Jud. 13.5.

For Matthew's purposes ζητοῦντι is a key word. Its appearance here implies that the kingdom does not manifest itself to all but only to those who search it out. 'Seek and ye shall find'.[24] The lesson in context may be that Israel has not welcomed the Messiah because she has not sincerely sought the kingdom. (This interpretation does not, of course, exclude a paraenetic application for Matthew's Christian readers.)

The pearl is surely to be identified with the kingdom. Those exegetes who have equated the costly pearl with Jesus are therefore incorrect.[25] Nonetheless, their mistake is a small one. Matthew's gospel makes it plain enough that to find the kingdom is to find Jesus and that to find Jesus is to find the kingdom. (Cf. Origen's application of αὐτοβασιλεία to Jesus: *Comm. on Mt.* 14.7.)

46. εὑρὼν δὲ ἕνα πολύτιμον μαργαρίτην ἀπελθὼν πέπρακεν πάντα ὅσα εἶχεν καὶ ἠγόρασεν αὐτόν. Compare *b. Šabb.* 119a: 'He went, sold all his property, and bought a precious stone with the proceeds'. εὑρών, πάντα ὅσα εἶχεν,[26] and ἠγόρασεν have their counterparts in the previous parable, 13.44; and πιπράσκω[27] appears in another M parable, 18.25. πολύτιμος[28] is a Matthean *hapax*. Thus the vocabulary would seem to point to Matthew's tradition. ἕνα is probably an over-literal translation of the Aramaic *ḥad*. The proper translation is not 'the one precious pearl' but 'a specially valuable pearl' (see Jeremias, *Parables*, p. 200).

The parallel in *Gos. Thom.* 76 reads thus: 'The kingdom of the Father is like a man, a merchant, who possessed merchandise and found a pearl. That merchant was prudent. He sold the merchandise and bought the one pearl for himself.' Whether or not this depends in

---

[24] Origen, *Comm. on Mt.* 10.9: 'Now you will connect with the man seeking goodly pearls the saying, "Seek and ye shall find" . . .'.
[25] Cf. Acts of Pet. 20; Clement of Alexandria, *Paed.* 2.13; Origen, *Comm. on Mt.* 10.8–9; Fenton, p. 227. Similarly, the treasure in the field was often identified with Christ (cf. Acts of Pet. 20; Irenaeus, *Adv. haer.* 4.26.1)—as was the grain of mustard-seed of 13.31 (cf. Clement of Alexandria, *Paed.* 1.11; Simeon the New Theologian, *Cat. Disc.* 34.305–42).
[26] Cf. the rabbinic *kōl-mâ šeyyēš lô*.
[27] Mt: 3; Mk: 1; Lk: 0. On the perfect for the aorist see BDF § 343, 344.
[28] Cf. Jn 12.3; 1 Pet 1.7. LXX: 0.

any way upon Matthew is a question we have found no way to answer. But the secondary character of Gos. Thom. 76 *vis-à-vis* Mt 13.45–6 is manifest.[29] 'The kingdom of the Father' is a favourite of Thomas (see p. 431, n. 109). 'Who possessed merchandise' is probably an addition designed to stress the merchant's worldly ties. And the intrusive and unnecessary 'that merchant was prudent' (or: 'wise'; the Coptic is *sabe*) helps open the parable for esoteric or Gnostic interests. Note that the phrase has a parallel in Gos. Thom. 8 and is therefore probably redactional.[30]

THE DRAG-NET AND ITS INTERPRETATION (13.47–50)

The third and final parable of 13.44–52, a parable which in so many ways recalls the tares, returns the reader's thoughts to the last judgement, a topic already treated at length in vv. 36–43. The main point is quite simple: the wicked will, in the end, be separated from the righteous and suffer due punishment. Note that the fate of the righteous is not contemplated at all; rather is attention directed towards what becomes of the unrighteous. Thus vv. 47–50 makes known the tragic end of those who reject Messiah Jesus. (That our parable has anything to do with the mixed state of Matthew's church—so Smith (v), Sabourin, p. 610, and many others—is not apparent to us.)

The parable of the net is usually, although not universally, attributed to Jesus. There is no consensus at all concerning its original meaning. Once vv. 49–50 are subtracted as Matthean interpretation, the interpreter is only too free to speculate.[31]

47. πάλιν ὁμοία ἐστὶν ἡ βασιλεία τῶν οὐρανῶν. See on 13.44. The meaning of this and the following is: 'The kingdom of heaven may be compared to what happens when a net is cast into the sea'.

σαγήνῃ βληθείσῃ εἰς τὴν θάλασσαν. The σαγήνη[32] is a drag-net. It was either pulled between two boats or drawn to

[29] *Pace* B. B. Scott, 'Essaying the Rock', *Forum* 2/1 (1986), pp. 15–16. He argues that Matthew has assimilated the parable of the pearl to the parable of the treasure.

[30] Dehandschutter (v) points out that Gos. Thom. 76 is followed immediately by a saying about treasure (cf. Mt 6.19–21); and he suggests that the association reflects a knowledge of Mt 13, where the parable of the treasure is linked with the parable of the pearl. This is certainly possible.

[31] For various suggestions see Dodd, *Parables*, pp. 151–2; Otto, pp. 126–8; Jeremias, *Parables*, pp. 224–7; Beasley-Murray, pp. 135–8; Kümmel, *Promise*, pp. 136–8; H. Conzelmann, 'Present and Future in the Synoptic Tradition', in *God and Christ, Existence and Province*, JTC 5, ed. R. W. Funk and G. Ebeling, Tübingen and New York, 1968, p. 34.

[32] With βάλλω in LXX Isa 19.8.

land by ropes after being dropped offshore (cf. Lk 5.4–7). In the LXX σαγήνη occurs for *ḥerem* in Ezek 26.5, 14; 47.10; Hab 1.16. The word is used only here in the NT.

βάλλω + εἰς τὴν θάλασσν* is redactional in 4.18, from M in 17.27, and from Mark in 21.21 (cf. Mk 11.23).

καὶ ἐκ παντὸς γένους συναγαγούσῃ. Compare 22.9–10. γένος (cf. the rabbinic *gěnîsāʾ*), which is used of species of fish in Josephus, *Bell.* 3.508, appears only once in the First Gospel; but συνάγω* is often editorial. 'Of all kinds' (cf. Ezek 47.10)[33] underlines for Matthew the universality of the judgement and perhaps also hints at the Gentile mission. For Jesus the words may well have alluded to his disregard for traditional social boundaries. (For different kinds of fish representing different kinds of people see *ARN* 40.)

48. ἦν ὅτε ἐπληρώθη.[34] Only here in Matthew does πληρόω not have theological content. (Some, however, would find such even here: the verb to them suggests the fulfilment of time at the judgement.)

ἀναβιβάσαντες ἐπὶ τὸν αἰγιαλόν. ἀναβιβάζω, although common in the LXX, is a NT *hapax legomenon*. The word means 'bring up'. Here one should translate: 'pulling (it) up'. αἰγιαλός appears elsewhere in Matthew only in 13.2 (q.v.), where it is redactional. It is doubtful that it was intended to suggest an *inclusio* between the beginning and end of chapter 13.

καὶ καθίσαντες συνέλεξαν τὰ καλὰ εἰς ἄγγη, τὰ δὲ σαπρὰ ἔξω ἔβαλον. This line has been retouched by Matthew's hand. For συλλέγω* appears six times in chapter 13, σαπρός*[35] is often editorial, and ἔξω with βάλλω* is redactional in 5.13.

Would Matthew and his readers have thought of 'good' and 'bad' fish as clean and unclean fish (cf. Lev 11.9–12)? Or are we to think of edible and inedible fish? Or does 'bad' refer to 'non-edible marine creatures, such as crabs, which were regarded as worthless' (so Jeremias, *Parables*, p. 226)? Or are the various possibilities compatible? Is the reference to sitting supposed to allude to the fact that at the last judgement the judge or judges will be seated (cf. 19.28; 25.31)?

49. An interpretation of vv. 47–8—really of only v. 48b—is

[33] There are reportedly at least two dozen different types of fish in the Sea of Galilee.
[34] D Θ 1424 *pc* have οτε δε, which is in accord with Matthean style; cf. 9.25; 13.26; 21.34.
[35] Lit. 'rotten', which is inappropriate here (the fish are fresh from the water). But Matthew elsewhere uses the word with the meaning of 'worthless'. See on 7.17 (of false Christians: but that does not imply that our parable concerns false Christians, *pace* Gundry, *Commentary*, p. 280).

now offered. As most modern commentators recognize,[36] everything points to Matthean composition—word statistics, style, content. Moreover, of the four sentences in vv. 49–50, three are taken verbatim from 13.36–43 (which in part explains why the parable and its interpretation are not perfect mates; see below). Compare v. 49a with v. 40b, v. 50a with v. 42a, v. 50b with v. 42b.

οὕτως ἔσται ἐν τῇ συντελείᾳ τοῦ αἰῶνος. These exact words appeared earlier in 13.40b (q.v.).

The interpretation which follows is rather artificial, and even if Jesus' parable originally had to do with the eschatological judgement (a disputed issue), his meaning could hardly have matched Matthew's (cf. Beare, p. 315). For one thing, whereas in vv. 47–8 it is fishermen who cast, gather, and sort, in 49–50 the angels sort, which implies also that they cast and gather, for their rôle is allegorically that of the fishermen. But in what sense angels can be said to cast and gather is mystifying. Furthermore, while 'and throw them into the furnace' made sense in connexion with tares (13.42), fish were not fired but rather tossed back or used as fertilizer.

ἐξελεύσονται οἱ ἄγγελοι καὶ ἀφοριοῦσιν τοὺς πονηροὺς ἐκ μέσου τῶν δικαίων. This restates 13.41 (q.v.): 'the Son of man will send forth his angels, and they will gather out of his kingdom all causes of sin and those doing wickedness'. Compare also 13.39: 'the harvesters are the angels'. The vocabulary is drawn largely from chapter 13: ἐξέρχομαι* appeared in vv. 1 and 3 (of Jesus and the sower), ἄγγελος in vv. 39 and 41 (see above), πονηρός* in vv. 19 and 38 ('the evil one', 'the sons of the evil one'), μέσος[37] in v. 25 (weeds in the midst of good wheat), and δίκαιος* in vv. 17 and 43 ('prophets and just men', 'the righteous will shine like the sun'). Only ἀφορίζω (Mt: 3; Mk: 0; Lk: 1) is left unaccounted for. It, however, is used in 25.32, with reference to the last judgement, so Matthew's tradition had already connected the verb with the separation of good and bad on the final day.[38]

50. The final fate of the wicked is next related. In contrast with 13.36–43, the fate of the righteous is left unremarked. This shows, as already stated, where Matthew's interest lies. He is concerned with the problem of evil and its ultimate solution as well as with delivering a warning.

[36] Cf. Weder, p. 143. But Grundmann, pp. 355 and 356, n. 10, thinks it possible that parable and interpretation belonged together from the beginning, and that 13.47–50 may have been the starting point for the interpretation of the parable of the tares.

[37] On ἐκ μέσου (= mittôk) see BDF § 215.3.

[38] For ἀφορίζω with ἐκ μέσου see also 2 Cor 6.17. Compare Lev 20.25 LXX: ἀφοριεῖτε . . . ἀνὰ μέσον.

καὶ βαλοῦσιν αὐτοὺς εἰς τὴν κάμινον τοῦ πυρός. So also 13.42a, q.v.

ἐκεῖ ἔσται ὁ κλαυθμὸς καὶ ὁ βρυγμὸς τῶν ὀδόντων. See 13.24b.

Gos. Thom. 8 has this: 'The man is like a wise fisherman who cast his net into the sea, he drew it up from the sea full of small fish; among them he found a large and beautiful fish; and that wise fisherman threw all the small fish down into the sea and chose the large fish without regret'. The relation of this to Mt 13.47–50 can be explained in four ways: the two parables are independent;[39] or Matthew's parable is a secondary version of what we find in Thomas;[40] or Gos. Thom. 8 is a secondary version of what we find in Matthew;[41] or both are independent developments of the same original.[42] Our own, very tentative conclusion, is that Thomas, whether or not directly or indirectly dependent upon Matthew, passes on a secondary version of the text more faithfully preserved by the First Gospel. First, Gos. Thom. 8 shows signs of redaction: the intrusive 'wise' (bis) has its parallel in 76; the contrast between large and small recalls Gos. Thom. 96; and 'the man' makes sense only as a reference to Gos. Thom. 7 ('Blessed is the lion which the man eats and the lion will become man . . .'). Secondly, whether or not Thomas' text is about the redeemer choosing the Gnostic[43] or the Gnostic choosing gnosis, it can be explained partly as assimilation to the parables of the treasure and the pearl (both in Thomas). Thirdly, the structure of Mt 13.47–8 is in several particulars very close to the structure of 13.24–30, which in one form or another may go back to Jesus. Finally, while one can understand Jesus telling a story about a man who gave all he had in order to obtain a very valuable pearl or a great treasure, why would any fisherman keep only one fish, no matter how large? The story line seems contrived. The explanation may lie in the fact that the parable was rewritten in order to avoid a conventional understanding of the eschatological judgement (cf. Matthew's text): this would probably not have been congenial to the author of Thomas.

CONCLUSION: THE DISCIPLED SCRIBE (13.51f.)

Matthew concludes 13.44–52 and chapter 13 as a whole with a

---

[39] So evidently Jeremias, *Parables*, pp. 201, 224–7.

[40] So Crossan, *Parables*, pp. 33–4.

[41] So Sabourin, pp. 610–11, and C. L. Bloomberg, in Wenham, *Tradition*, p. 192. According to J. B. Bauer, 'The Synoptic Tradition in the Gospel of Thomas', in *Studia Evangelica* III, ed. F. L. Cross, Berlin, 1964, pp. 314–17, Gos. Thom. 8 depends upon the parable of the pearl in Mt 13.45 and the proverb preserved in Clement of Alexandria, *Strom.* 1.16 ('Among many small pearls will be a large one, and in a fishing net with many fishes will be the beautiful fish').

[42] Cf. B. B. Scott, 'Essaying the Rock', *Forum* 2/1 (1986), p. 16: 'The beginning of Matthew and the conclusion of Thomas may represent the originating structure'.

[43] Cf. perhaps Auth. Teach. 29.3–30.25, where Gnostics are like fish.

little dialogue which contains a comparative proverb. The major point is that the disciples have indeed understood Jesus' discourse and therefore qualify as skilled scribes.

Bultmann, *History*, p. 75, speculated—without citing evidence—that 13.51f. might rest upon a proverb: 'As a father brings out of his treasure things new and old, so is a scribe, who is wise unto heaven'. This was made into a dominical saying by Matthew (*ibid.*, p. 103). McNeile, pp. 205–6, on the other hand, argued that Matthew's text incorporates a dominical statement which in its original context explained that the Jewish scribe who followed Jesus would be able to bring forth the new as well as the old. Others have held that Mt. 13.51f. incorporates a Jewish-Christian tradition (e.g. Manson, *Sayings*, pp. 198–9), or a Jewish wisdom saying (Zeller (v)), or that a dominical parable about the kingdom has been transformed into something else (so Becker (v)). For ourselves, we are strongly inclined to regard the passage as an editorial production, as something new which Matthew brought out of his own storehouse.[44] Both the word statistics and the links with other passages in the chapter make this quite likely.

51. Even if v. 52 be assigned to the tradition, v. 51 must be considered an editorial transition, for it looks back upon all of chapter 13.

συνήκατε ταῦτα πάντα; The verb recalls vv. 13, 19, 23 and in the light of these indicates that the disciples are among those who hear the word and bear much fruit. ταῦτα πάντα* harks back to v. 34 ('all these things Jesus spoke in parables to the crowds') and anticipates v. 56 ('from where then did this man get all these things?'). The words are accordingly comprehensive and refer not just to vv. 36–50 but to everything spoken by Jesus beginning with 13.3 (cf. Cope, p. 25).

Given Matthew's tendency to purge his tradition of the interrogative form in sayings of Jesus (see 1, pp. 104–5), the question here is unexpected.[45] But perhaps we are to view it as simply rhetorical. Jesus is not asking for information but creating an opportunity to deliver a commendation.

λέγουσιν αὐτῷ· ναί.[46] Compare 9.28 (redactional). Gundry, *Commentary*, p. 281, observes that the asyndetic use of λέγουσιν in the historical present typifies Matthew's style and is often redactional in Markan contexts.

52. Jesus responds to the disciples' affirmation by declaring them to be scribes discipled for the kingdom of heaven, men who will bring forth from their storehouses things new and old.

[44] So also Gundry, *Commentary*, pp. 280–2; cf. Gnilka, *Matthäusevangelium* 1, p. 509.
[45] Origen, *Comm. on Mt.* 10.14, observed that some Christians even took the words to be not a question but an affirmation, to which the disciples added their 'yes'.
[46] C L W 0137 0233 Maj it sy^{p.h} co add κυριε. Cf. 9.28; 15.27; Mk 7.28 v. 1.; Jn 11.27; 21.15, 16.

Matthew probably thought of the words as including himself,[47] his Lord,[48] the twelve, and all Christian scribes or teachers. One also supposes that he thought of all these together as forming some sort of counterpart to the Jewish rabbinate.

ὁ δὲ εἶπεν αὐτοῖς. This phrase is redactional in 12.3, 11; and 19.11.

διὰ τοῦτο. The expression* means 'therefore' (cf. 12.27, 31; 13.13). It is a bit troublesome here. Are we to think that because the disciples have understood, they are scribes who may be compared to a householder who brings forth out of his treasure things old and new (so most commentators)? More probably one should give the words a weakened sense and view them as simply transitional ('so then', 'well'; cf. 18.23).

πᾶς γραμματεὺς μαθητευθεὶς τῇ βασιλείᾳ τῶν οὐρανῶν ὅμοιός ἐστιν ἀνθρώπῳ οἰκοδεσπότῃ. Compare 7.24, 26; Lk 12.36; Gos. Thom. 8; also 1QM 10.10 ('schooled in the law and learned in wisdom'). The positive use of 'scribe' is editorial (cf. 23.34) as are the verb, μαθητεύω,[49] and 'the kingdom of heaven'*. ὅμοιός ἐστιν calls to mind the similar uses of ὁμοία in vv. 31, 33, 44, 45, 47; and to both the dative ἀνθρώπῳ (cf. vv. 24, 45) and οἰκοδεσπότῃ (cf. v. 27) have parallels in earlier verses. There are thus good reasons for considering v. 52a redactional. If tradition has been taken up, Matthew has thoroughly recast it.

On Jewish and Christian scribes see on 2.4.[50] It is altogether probable that Matthew belonged to a 'school' of Christian scribes, who perhaps carried on their activities in a Christian synagogue. They were no doubt prominent leaders of Matthew's church. ('Every scribe' is taken by Gundry, *Commentary*, p. 281, to apply to all Christians. But the use of μαθητεύω in 28.19 does not prove this; and 13.51f. is clearly about *teachers*, which cannot include all. Cf. 1 Cor 12.29: 'Are all teachers?')

Given that his gospel is so much concerned with the last things, it may well be that Matthew thought of himself and his fellow Christian scribes as holding an office whose members had been entrusted with eschatological secrets. The authors of several apocalypses, including 1 Enoch, 4 Ezra, 2 Baruch, 2 Enoch, and 3 Enoch, were held to have been scribes.[51] Ecclus 39.1–3 is also pertinent: 'He who devotes himself

[47] Many have found in 13.52 the author's self-portrait; see e.g. Gnilka. *Matthäusevangelium* 1, p. 511. According to R. H. Fuller, *The New Testament in Current Study*, London, 1962, p. 83, 'Matthew betrays his method in Matt. 13:52.'

[48] So Origen, *Comm. on Mt.* 10.15; cf. Klostermann, p. 125. Certainly Jesus brought forth things old and new; cf. 5.17–20; 7.28–9. Further, he is an οἰκοδεσπότης in 10.25 and 13.27.

[49] Elsewhere in the NT only in Acts 14.21. Cf. Ignatius, *Eph.* 3.1; 10.1; *Rom.* 5.1.

[50] To the lit. there cited add Hengel, *Mark*, pp. 78–81, and Orton (v).

[51] See Ezra 7.11; Jer 36.26, 32; 1 En. 12.3–4; 15.1; 4 Ezra 14.50; T. Abr. B 11.3; 2 En. 64.5.

to the study of the law of the Most High will seek out the wisdom of all the ancients, and will be concerned with prophecies; he will preserve the discourse of notable men and penetrate the subtleties of parables; he will seek out the hidden meanings of proverbs and be at home with the obscurities of parables'.[52] See further Orton (v).

μαθητευθείς—either 'has become a disciple' or, more probably, 'discipled' (=instructed)—is striking.[53] Perhaps one key to understanding the verb in Matthew is this: the transitive use of μαθητεύω is confined to the NT, a fact which may be determined by 'the insight that one can become a disciple of Jesus only on the basis of a call which leads to discipleship'.[54] This notion at any rate seems to hold for Matthew, for in his gospel Jesus calls his disciples to himself and separates them from the crowd (4.18–22; 5.1) before he delivers his teaching (5.3ff.). Thus Christian discipleship is not a response to Jesus' teaching but is rather engendered by his call: 'follow me'. At the same time, the *content* of discipleship is indicated by 28.19f., where the making of disciples is defined primarily as 'teaching them to observe whatsoever I have commanded you'. In other words, discipleship means learning from Jesus and acting upon what one has learned.

What exactly does τῇ βασ. κ.τ.λ. mean?[55] If μαθητευθείς means 'has become a disciple', one could equate the kingdom with Jesus (cf. 27.57: ἐμαθητεύθη τῷ Ἰησοῦ) or take the meaning to be: 'having accepted (Jesus' teaching about) the kingdom'. But, following McNeile, p. 205, it is better to translate: 'instructed in (the truths of) the kingdom of heaven'. This suits the broader context.

It has on occasion been suggested that just as Mk 14.51f. (the flight of the naked young man) might be an autobiographical insertion, so too may Mt 13.51–2 be the author's signature: he was a scribe, and his name was 'Matthew' (cf. μαθητευθείς). Although we have not been able to persuade ourselves that the name of the man who wrote our gospel was in fact 'Matthew' and so cannot find here a wordplay, it remains true that 13.51–2 is probably something like a self-portrait (cf. n. 47 and Bacon, p. 131: 'an unconscious portrait').

ὅστις ἐκβάλλει ἐκ τοῦ θησαυροῦ αὐτοῦ καινὰ καὶ παλαιά. The picture painted is evidently of a householder bringing forth—for guests?—food, articles of clothing, and other necessities from his storehouse. Or should we think of MT Lev. 26.10 (which seems to be conflated with our line in Basil, *Ep.* 28)?

ἐκβάλλω*+ἐκ is Matthean (Mt: 6; Mk: 1; Lk: 1); and the combination occurs with treasure in 12.35 (*bis*): 'The good man out of

---

[52] Given Matthew's interest in Moses it may not be irrelevant to observe that Moses was considered by many to have been the scribe *par excellence*; see Vermes, *Tradition*, pp. 44–55.

[53] Dodd, *NTS*, p. 65, suggested on the basis of Syriac parallels that μαθ. here means 'converted.' Cf. Carson, *Matthew*, pp. 332–33, who speaks of a transformed allegiance.

[54] K. H. Rengstorf, *TWNT* 4, p. 465.

[55] D 700 *pc* add εν before τη. L Γ Δ (0233) 28 (33) 892ᶜ *pm* have εις την βασιλειαν.

his good treasure brings forth good, and the evil man out of his evil treasure brings forth evil' (perhaps redactional). Observe also that in both 12.35 and 13.52 there are two things brought forth: in the one instance good and bad things, in the other new and old. When one adds that ὅστις* is often redactional and that the καινός/παλαιός contrast was to hand in Matthew's tradition (see 9.17–18 = Mt 2.21–2), once again one is invited to infer an editorial origin.

θησαυροῦ forms an *inclusio* with the first verse in the final section of 13; see v. 44 and p. 434. In this way the beginning and end are matched in 13.44–52 just as they are in 13.1–23 and 24–43; see Excursus X.

The characterization of the scribe as one who brings forth new and old was probably a traditional Jewish *topos*, although our evidence for this is later than Matthew. Cant 7.13 ('The mandrakes give forth fragrance, and over our doors are all choice fruits, *new as well as old*, which I have laid up for you, O my beloved') is interpreted in *b*. '*Erub*. 21b in this manner: 'the old' are the commandments derived 'from the words of Torah' while 'the new' are those derived 'from the words of the scribes'. While this interpretation is not attested elsewhere, there is a very similar contrast between old and new in *m. Yad*. 4.3; and already in Jub. 45.15 Levi is said to preserve books as well as to renew them. Further, the idea that the scribes bring forth the new was evidently proverbial.[56] Hence it would appear that 13.51–2 is yet one more indicator of Matthew's first-hand acquaintance with Jewish tradition.[57]

What is meant by 'new' and 'old' in Mt 13.52? The suggestions can be represented thus:

The old—	The new—
the old revelation (Torah, OT)	the new revelation in Jesus[58]
Jewish tradition (teaching)	Christian tradition (teaching)[59]
Jesus' teaching	the teaching of Christians[60]
Jesus' parables	Matthew's interpretations[61]
the OT	Christian interpretation of the OT[62]
eschatological revelation (hidden)	eschatological revelation (revealed)[63]
observations about the world	Jesus' parabolic teaching
Jewish Christian tradition	Gentile Christian tradition
understanding before hearing the parables	understanding after hearing them

[56] Cf. *m. T. Yom*. 4.6; *t. T. Yom*. 2.14.
[57] *Pace* Betz (v), Isa 43.18–19 is not likely to lie behind our text.
[58] Cf. 5.17–48 and note Gnilka, *Matthäusevangelium* 1, p. 511.
[59] Cf. 9.14–17 and recall the mixing of traditions in the Didache.
[60] See Trilling (v), p. 34.
[61] 13.36–43, 49–50.
[62] Cf. the formula quotations.
[63] Note Ps 78.2, which is quoted in 13.35: 'I will open my mouth in parables, I will utter what has been hidden since the foundation of the world'. On this interpretation one could translate, 'things that are new and yet old'.

Although we have ranked these options in what we perceive to be the order of their probability (the most probable first, the least probable last), it must be confessed that the contrast remains cryptic (cf. Zeller (v)). All we can say with certainty is that the ability to teach things new and old rests upon the ability to understand Jesus' teaching. (The Fathers, who tended to see in 13.52 a reference to the OT (= παλαιά), found the verse useful in combating depreciation of the OT; cf. Irenaeus, *Adv. haer.* 4.9.1; Origen, *Comm. on Mt.* 10.15; Chrysostom, *Hom. on Mt.* 47.4. Note also *Ps.-Clem. Rec.* 4.5. We deem this a legitimate application.)

According to Meier, *Antioch*, p. 59, the order, new—old, is unexpected and points to the fact that 'Matthew, the Christian scribe, understands the old order by the criterion of the new order, which is accordingly mentioned first. Such a hermeneutic is displayed perfectly in the formula quotations, where at times the OT text is manipulated according to the measuring rod ('canon') of the Christ-Event' (cf. Gnilka, *Matthäusevangelium* 1, p. 511). Whether this reads too much in it is hard to say. Could one not also claim that 'new' comes before 'old' and therefore receives the emphasis because while the latter is what the Christian scribe shares with others, the former is what sets him apart and is thus his outstanding characteristic?[64]

(iv) *Concluding Observations*

Commentators of an earlier time were often encouraged to divine in the seven parables of Mt 13 a prophetic outline of church history. The approach remained popular until the present century (cf. Alford 1, p. 151). One has no difficulty understanding the reason. The opening parable (the sower) has to do with the beginning of the gospel in the preaching of Jesus and the apostles, the last (the net) with the great assize, and in between are parables which describe the kingdom with metaphors of growth (the tares, the mustard seed, the leaven). So the sequence is: beginning—growth—culmination.

If scholars nowadays do not take chapter 13 to be an allegorical representation of ecclesiastical history, this is in part because the interpretation is inevitably anachronistic: it must read into the text events which could not possibly have been on

[64] For other texts in which the new is mentioned before the old see 9.16–17; 2 Cor 5.17; Heb 8.13; 1 Jn 2.7.

the minds of a first-century author and his readers. Nonetheless, the old interpretation is to be commended for its recognition of two facts, the first being that the discourse—like the other major discourses—exhibits a thematic unity, the second being that it—again like the other major discourses—winds up on an eschatological note (cf. 1, p. 728). It is particularly important to recognize that, with regard to the first point, no parable in Mt 13 is out of place. The subject of the chapter as a whole is the kingdom and its fate in the world. The sower describes the initial proclamation of the gospel and its mixed reception. The tares continues in the same vein, emphasizing the mysterious rôle of transcendent evil (the devil). The mustard seed and the leaven then follow, making plain the certainty of the kingdom's ultimate victory despite all appearances. It is subsequent to this that we have the twin parables of the hidden treasure and the pearl and, lastly, that of the net. The first two appropriately succeed 13.1–43 by offering paraenesis: buy, sell, seek. Granted the kingdom's value and its sure eschatological triumph, one must strive to overcome every obstacle in the way of obtaining it. One must not respond as did the people denounced in Mt 11 and 12 or be like the unfruitful seeds described in 13.1–23 (cf. Dupont (v)). Rather, one must, recognizing the truth about the kingdom, do all to gain the one thing needful. The necessity for such action is, in turn, underlined by 13.47–50: judgement will come upon those who reject the kingdom (cf. the function of 7.24–7; 18.23–35; 25.1–46). There is, accordingly, a shift of emphasis between 13.1–43 and 13.44–50. Whereas the passages in the former are more descriptive, those in the latter are more paraenetic.

(v) *Bibliography*

Beasley-Murray, pp. 111–13, 135–8.
J. Becker, 'Erwägungen zu Fragen der neutestamentlichen Exegese', *BZ* 13 (1969), pp. 99–102.
O. Betz, 'Neues und Altes im Geschichtshandeln Gottes. Bemerkungen zu Matthäus 13.51f.', in *Wort Gottes in der Zeit*, ed. H. Feld and J. Nolte, Düsseldorf, 1973, pp. 69–84.
J. D. Crossan, *Finding is the First Act: Trove Folktales and Jesus' Treasure Parable*, Philadelphia, 1979.
idem, 'Hidden Treasure Parables in Late Antiquity', in *Society of Biblical Literature 1976 Seminar Papers*, ed. G. MacRae, Missoula, 1976, pp. 359–79.
J. Dauvillier, 'Le parabole du trésor et les droits orientaux', *Revue Internationale des Droits de l'Antiquité* 3/4 (1957), pp. 1071–5.
B. Dehandschutter, 'La parabole de la perle (Matt. 13.45–46) et l'Évangile selon Thomas', *ETL* 55 (1979), pp. 243–65.

Derrett, *Law*, pp. 1–16.

J. Dupont, 'Les paraboles du trésor et de la perle', *NTS* 14 (1968), pp. 408–18.

J. C. Fenton, 'Expounding the Parables. IV. The Parables of the Treasure and the Pearl (Mt 13.44–46)', *ExpT* 77 (1966), pp. 178–80.

O. Glombitza, 'Der Perlenkaufmann', *NTS* 7 (1960), pp. 153–61.

C. W. Hedrick, 'The Treasure Parable in Matthew and Thomas', *Forum* 2/2 (1986), pp. 41–56.

J. Hoh, 'Der christliche γραμματεύς', *BZ* 17 (1926), pp. 256–69.

Jeremias, *Parables*, pp. 32–3, 198–202, 224–7.

Jülicher 2, pp. 128–33, 563–9, 581–5.

Kingsbury, *Parables*, pp. 110–29.

J. Kremer, '"Neues und Altes"', in *Neues und Altes*, J. Kremer *et al.*, Freiburg, 1974, pp. 11–33.

Linnemann, *Parables*, pp. 97–105.

W. Magass, '"Der Schatz im Acker"', *LB* 21–2 (1973), pp. 2–18.

W. G. Morrice, 'The Parable of the Dragnet and the Gospel of Thomas', *ExpT* 95 (1984), pp. 269–73.

D. E. Orton, *The Understanding Scribe*, JSNTS 25, Sheffield, 1989.

R. Schippers, 'The Mashal-character of the Parable of the Pearl', in *Studia Evangelica II*, ed. F. L. Cross, Berlin, pp. 236–41.

C. W. F. Smith, 'The Mixed State of the Church in Matthew's Gospel', *JBL* 82 (1963), pp. 149–68.

T. Schramm and K. Löwenstein, *Unmoralische Helden*, Göttingen, 1986, pp. 42–9.

W. Trilling, 'Amt und Amtsverständnis bei Matthäus', in Descamps, *Mélanges*, pp. 29–44.

R. Waelkens, 'L'analyse structurale des paraboles. Deux essais: Luc 15.1–32 et Matthieu 13.44–46', *RTL* 8 (1977), pp. 160–78.

Weder, pp. 138–47.

D. Zeller, 'Zu einer jüdischen Vorlage von Mt 13.52', *BZ* 20 (1976), pp. 223–6.

Zumstein, pp. 159–63.

XXX

THE REJECTION AT NAZARETH
(13.53–8)

(i) *Structure*

At this juncture in the First Gospel our author ceases to group his narrative material in thematic triads and instead begins to follow Mark.[1] For this reason the remaining narrative sections, that is, 13.53–17.27; 19.1–23.39; and 26.1–28.20, do not exhibit any architectonic arrangement. They simply by and large reproduce the Markan sequence. Thus the various paragraphs cannot be discussed as parts of larger thematic units and are accordingly, for the purposes of this commentary, best discussed in isolation. (Contrast our procedure in 1.18–4.22; 8.1–9.34; and 11.1–12.50).

13.53–8, like its Markan source, Mk 6.1–6a, narrates (i) actions on the part of Jesus (53–4a), (ii) the (negative) reaction of others to those actions (54b–7a), and (iii) Jesus' behaviour subsequent to that reaction (57b–8). Unlike Mk 6.1–6a, however, Matthew's text would appear to have a chiastic blueprint (cf. Segbroeck (v)):

I. Jesus' overture: after finishing the parables, Jesus came to his own πατρίς and taught in the synagogue (53–4a)
II. The people's response (54b–7a)
   A. They were amazed (54b)
   B. They asked, 'From where did this man (πόθεν τούτῳ) . . .' (54c)
   C. 'Is not (οὐχ) this . . .' (55a)
   D. 'Is not (οὐχ) his mother . . .' (55b)
   E. 'And his sisters, are they not (οὐχί) . . .' (56a)
   F. 'From where then did this man (πόθεν . . . τούτῳ) . . .' (56b)
   G. They were scandalized (57a)
III. Jesus' response: after uttering a word about his πατρίς, Jesus did only a few miracles (57b–8)

The symmetry is obvious, and there can be little doubt that Matthew has reworked Mark so as to produce a chiastic pattern

---

[1] Cf. Allen, p. 157: 'From this point . . . the grouping of material taken from Mk and elsewhere under subject-heads ceases to be observable'.

with three οὐχ(ί) questions at the centre. Perhaps Matthew was stimulated to create the chiasmus by the presence of πατρίς at the beginning and end of the Markan pericope.

(ii) *Sources*

Matthew left Mark at 13.34 = Mk 4.34. He now returns to his source. But having already made use of all the material in Mk 4.35–5.43, this brings him to Mk 6.1; see further 1, pp. 102–3.

There is no reason to think that Mt 13.53–8 is anything other than a revised and abbreviated version of Mk 6.1–6a. Further, one may perhaps cite Mk 6.5f. = Mt 13.58 as evidence for Markan priority (*pace* Schlatter, p. 457). Matthew's less awkward 'And he did not do many miracles because of their unbelief' is potentially less offensive than Mark's more bold and cumbersome 'And he could do no mighty work there, except that he laid his hands upon a few sick people and healed them. And he marvelled because of their unbelief'.

The Lukan parallel to Mk 6.1–6a is found in Lk 4.16–30, a lengthy and programmatic pericope which is placed at the outset of Jesus' ministry. It is sometimes taken to be a Lukan construction based solely on Mk 6.1–6a but more likely preserves an independent narrative,[2] a pre-Lukan expansion and variant of the tradition also attested in Mark.[3] If so, then the story in Mk 6.1–6a par. has two independent synoptic witnesses.

It is also probable that the Gospel of John should be considered yet another witness to it. G. Reim has directed attention to the rather large number of verses in John which in one way or another recall the synoptic accounts of the rejection of Jesus at Nazareth: Jn 4.43, 44, 45, 48; 6.30, 41f., 52, 59, 61; 7.5, 41f., 44; 8.59; 10.31, 33, 39; 11.8; 12.36.[4] Reim plausibly argues that John knew a story much like that in Mark which also included (a) a request for a miracle and Jesus' critical response (Jn 4.48; 6.30), (b) an attempt to lay hands on him and stone him (7.30, 32, 44; 8.20, 59; 10.31, 33, 39; 11.8, 57), and (c) Jesus' successful flight (Jn 8.59; 10.39; 12.36)—all of which are also attested in Luke's account of what happened in Nazareth. This proposal, of course, raises a question: why then does not the evangelist ever recount the episode as such? According to Reim, the author of John, perceiving in the rejection of Jesus by his own a paradigm for the entire ministry, scattered elements from the story of that rejection throughout his gospel, using them especially to set the speeches in a hostile context. Because we are persuaded by Reim's argument, we conclude that John too knew a tradition related to Mk 6.1–6a = Mk 13.53–8, probably in a form close to Lk 4.16–30.[5]

---

[2] Probably not from Q, although a few have thought this; see the commentaries.

[3] For a review of opinion and lit. see Marshall, pp. 178–81.

[4] G. Reim, 'John iv. 44—Crux or Clue?', *NTS* 22 (1976), pp. 476–80.

[5] J. W. Pryor, 'John 4.44 and the *Patris* of Jesus', *CBQ* 49 (1987), pp. 254–63,

(iii) *Exegesis*

Following the preceding parables, 13.53–8 illustrates that the failure to understand leads not to indifference but to hostility. Those who do not grasp the secrets of the kingdom of Heaven necessarily find Jesus offensive.

The pericope may be classified as an objection story (see pp. 96) —although it remains in many respects unique. That we in any case have before us not an ideal scene but the literary record of a concrete event seems highly probable.[6] Not only is there multiple attestation (Mark, Luke, John), but would a free Christian creation make Jesus a carpenter, put his family, including Mary and James, in a bad light, and tell us that Jesus was *not able* to work a miracle—a statement immediately qualified by Mark and rewritten by Matthew?[7, 8] We are prepared to affirm that Mk 6.1–6a contains genuine tradition. Jesus on one occasion at least encountered hostility in the synagogue at Nazareth; his words and deeds were considered extraordinary and in need of special explanation; he was known as a carpenter; his mother was named Mary; he had brothers with the names James, Joses, Judas, and Simon; he had sisters; he implicitly included himself among the prophets; and he was a faith-healer whose success depended in part upon the co-operation and faith of those who came to him.

The unity of the pericope is sometimes queried. Tension has been detected between 13.54 = Mk 6.2 (the people know of Jesus' miracles) and 13.58 = Mk 6.5f. (which is about Jesus' failure to perform miracles) as well as between 13.57 = Mk 6.4 (Jesus knows that a prophet is without honour in his own town) and Mk 6.6a (where Jesus marvels at the unbelief in Nazareth). It has in addition been remarked that while the saying in 13.57 = Mk 6.4 mentions relatives (Mark has ἐν τοῖς συγγενεῦσιν αὐτοῦ as well as ἐν τῇ οἰκίᾳ αὐτοῦ), the surrounding material does not. For these and other reasons, many have affirmed that 'A prophet is not without honour, etc.' is a secondary addition (so Gnilka, *Markus* 1, pp. 228–9), or that the story was originally about Jesus' success but was subsequently modified under the impact of later experience (cf. Bultmann, *History*, pp. 31–2), or that the entire narrative was awkwardly spun out of the proverb in 13.57 = Mk 6.4 (cf. Bultmann, *ibid.*), or that the synoptic narrative combines what were originally two different stories (6.2a, 3ab, 4 and 6.2b, 3c, 5, 6a; so Schmidt, pp. 155–6). In our estimation, none of these options is compelling, for the observations on which they are based have other

---

also argues that Jn 4.44 was known to the Fourth Evangelist as part of the Nazareth incident.

[6] Cf. Pesch 1, p. 322; Gnilka, *Markus* 1, pp. 229, 233; Smith, *Magician*, pp. 15–16.

[7] Bultmann, *History*, p. 31, n. 3, sees in the notice of Jesus' inability to work miracles a reflexion of Christian missionary experience. Is this credible?

[8] Some would add that the designation of Jesus as the son of Mary also points to historical tradition because it must be understood as a polemical barb; see on 13.55.

interpretations. The mention of relatives in 13.57 = Mk 6.4 could well be due to Markan redaction,[9] and the supposed tension between 13.57 = Mk 6.4 and Mk 6.6a is fanciful. Surely Jesus could have quoted the aphorism ascribed to him and still have been surprised and disappointed by the response given him! As for the perceived contradiction between Jesus doing no miracle and the question, 'Where did this man get these mighty works?', the latter may well refer to Jesus' reputation, which had preceded him; or, to offer another explanation, the former could simply concern Jesus' non-success after leaving the synagogue. We, therefore, do not see the cause for performing surgery on our pericope.

53. καὶ ἐγένετο ὅτε ἐτέλεσεν ὁ Ἰησοῦς τὰς παραβολὰς ταύτας. See on 7.28. The statement seemingly implies that the material in chapter 13 was spoken at one time; but Matthew, who put together the discourse from disparate sources, certainly knew otherwise, so his language should not be pressed.

μετῆρεν ἐκεῖθεν. Compare 11.1 (ὅτε ἐτέλεσεν ὁ Ἰησοῦς ... μετέβη ἐκεῖθεν) and 19.1 (ὅτε ἐτέλεσεν ὁ Ἰησοῦς ... μετῆρεν[10]); also Gen 12.8 Aq. Whenever Jesus finishes a major discourse he immediately moves on to a new location (see 8.1; 11.1; 13.53; 19.1; 26.6). Discourse and narrative do not share the same geographical space.

54. καὶ ἐλθὼν εἰς τὴν πατρίδα αὐτοῦ. So Mk 6.1, with ἔρχεται. As usual, Mark's historical present has been avoided. πατρίς, which is selected in anticipation of the proverb in 13.57 (cf. Mk 6.1 and 4), can mean 'homeland' (cf. Jn 4.44) but here means 'native place' or 'home town' (cf. Philo, *Leg. ad Gai.* 278; Josephus, *Ant.* 6.67; 10.114). In view of 2.22–3, the reader is to think of Nazareth, not Capernaum (cf. Lk. 4.16 and see on 2.23).

ἐδίδασκεν αὐτοὺς ἐν τῇ συναγωγῇ αὐτῶν. This is based upon Mk 6.2 ('And on the sabbath he began[11] to teach in the synagogue'). Matthew has abbreviated and left implicit what Mark makes explicit, namely, that the event took place on the sabbath (cf. Lk 4.16). On the significance of αὐτῶν after 'synagogue' see on 4.23. The imperfect is probably inceptive.

---

[9] Cf. Gnilka, *Markus* 1, pp. 229, 232. Note that Gos Thom 31 and *P. Oxy.* 1 do not mention Jesus' relatives or his house; and Lk 4.24 and Jn 4.44 mention only the πατρίς. Furthermore, both Gos. Thom 31 and *P. Oxy.* 1 have appended to the saying about the prophet this remark: 'no physician heals those who know him'. Thus the tradition attests a form without family and house (Luke, John, Gos. Thom 31, *P. Oxy.* 1) and also reflects a tendency towards expansion (Gos. Thom 31, *P. Oxy.* 1). (N.B.: if the δεκτός of Lk 4.24 is, as one suspects, due to Lukan redaction (cf. Lk 4.19: κηρύξαι ἐνιαυτὸν κυρίου δεκτόν), then *P. Oxy.* 1 almost certainly draws upon Luke, for it too has δεκτός).

[10] Whereas μετῆρεν replaces Mark's ἔρχεται in 19.1, it replaces ἐξῆλθεν (Mk 6.1) in 13.53.

[11] Matthew often omits Mark's ἄρχω; see Allen, pp. xxi–xxii. Here the imperfect substitutes.

This is the last notice of Jesus teaching in the synagogue. But this must not be misunderstood to mean a formal break with that institution. To begin with, Mk 6.1–6a also reports the last appearance of the Markan Jesus in the synagogue, so in this Matthew is just following his predecessor, not imposing a new scheme. More importantly, by placing the story of rejection where he has, that is, after chapters 11–13, the First Evangelist has made it plain that Jesus continued his ministry to the Jewish synagogue despite all opposition. That is, notwithstanding the fact that the need for a new religious institution has become obvious and will soon be realized (cf. 16.13–20), Jesus does not abandon his people. He still speaks to them and still heals their infirm (cf. 14.34–6; 15.1–20, 29–31; 26.55; etc.). (Perhaps Matthew saw his Lord's persistence in this matter—note the imperfect tense—as precedent for missionaries in his own day: the existence of the church and the hostility of Israel did not provide an excuse for abandoning the Jews.)

ὥστε ἐκπλήσσεσθαι αὐτοὺς καὶ λέγειν. Compare 15.31 and 27.14 (both with θαυμάζω); also Lk 4.22. Matthew's phrase slightly shortens Mk 6.2: καὶ [οἱ] πολλοὶ ἀκούοντες ἐξεπλήσσοντο λέγοντες. Has Matthew omitted 'hearing' because of 13.13 ('hearing they do not hear')? See further on 7.28–29, although here as opposed to there the amazement or perplexity appears to be negative.

πόθεν τούτῳ ἡ σοφία αὕτη καὶ αἱ δυνάμεις; Compare LXX Job 12.13; Isa 11.2; Jn 7.15: 'How is it that this man has learning, when he has never studied?' Matthew's sentence combines and shortens what are two or three separate questions in Mark: 'Where did this man get all this? And what is the wisdom given to him? And what mighty works are done through his hands?' For similar dovetailing of Markan sentences see Allen, p. xxiv. πόθεν[12] (= 'from where') is here used with reference to the source of Jesus' authority. Compare 21.23–7, where the question, 'The baptism of John, whence (πόθεν) was it?', has for its answer either 'from heaven' or 'from men'. In 13.54 another alternative is implicit, that set forth in 12.22–30: God or Beelzebul. Note also 9.34 and 10.24f. The question before the synagogue congregation is whether the inspiration for Jesus' words and deeds comes from God or Satan. While the sympathetic reader of Matthew knows the answer, the subject is an open one for the speakers. For δύναμις see on 11.20.

55. The crowd continues to ask questions which attempt to explain away the extraordinary by associating it with the familiar. How can Jesus' reputation be harmonized with his humble origins? (It is implied that Jesus' family was not extraordinary.)

[12] Cf. Jn 7.27–8; 8.14; 9.29–30; 19.9.

οὐχ οὗτός ἐστιν ὁ τοῦ τέκτονος υἱός; Compare Jn 6.42: 'Is not this Jesus, whose father and mother we know?' The Greek word, τέκτων, most commonly means 'mason', 'carpenter', 'woodworker'. Other attested meanings include 'artisan', 'contractor', 'builder', and in 1 Βασ 13.19 it is used of metal smiths who make swords and spears. Despite the dearth of wood in ancient Palestine, we are probably to follow the Greek Fathers in thinking of Jesus as the son of a carpenter. Compare Justin, *Dial.* 88 (Jesus 'made yokes and ploughs'). Most of the ancient versions translate τέκτων with words designating a worker of wood.[13]

Mk 6.3 differs significantly from Matthew: οὐχ οὗτός ἐστιν ὁ τέκτων;[14] We are here faced with two very different sentences. According to Matthew, Jesus was the son of a carpenter (cf. the phrasing in Lk 4.22 and Jn 6.42). According to Mark, Jesus himself was a carpenter. How are the two texts to be explained? There are several possibilities. (i) Jesus and his father were both carpenters: the son was his father's apprentice (cf. Jn 5.19–20?). Hence both Matthew and Mark are correct (cf. Gnilka, *Matthäusevangelium* 1, p. 515). (ii) Menial labour was thought degrading (cf. Origen, *C. Cels.* 6.36) and it was therefore unedifying to imagine Jesus as a carpenter; so his father was turned into such (so many commentators). (Against the objection that this does not explain why Matthew did not simply drop the reference altogether and write, 'Is not his mother called Mary ...?', it may be replied that there was a need for three οὐχ(ί) phrases; see p. 451.) (iii) Mark's text has υἱός but with Mary, not Joseph: 'Is this not the son of Mary?' Now the expression, 'the son of Mary', has been considered odd; and while some have accounted for it by supposing that Joseph was long since dead,[15] and while others have discovered in the phrase an allusion to the virgin birth, E. Stauffer has made the case that 'the son of Mary' might have been intended as a slur: the circumstances of Jesus' birth were known to have been

---

[13] Lit.: G. W. Buchanan, 'Jesus and the Upper Class', *NovT* 7 (1964), pp. 195–209 (arguing from 2 Cor 8.9 and other texts that Jesus belonged to the upper class); Furfey (v); Höpfl (v); Lombard (v); McCown (v). For the suggestion that Jesus worked not only in a wood-worker's shop in Nazareth but perhaps also in Sepphoris, helping to construct Herod's capital, see R. A. Batey, 'Is not this the Carpenter?', *NTS* 30 (1984), pp. 249–58. Batey also calls attention to the Jesus traditions which may reflect the experience of a builder (e.g. Mt 7.24–7; Lk 13.4–5; Jn 2.19). For the implausible conjecture that 'carpenter' was used of Jesus in a metaphorical sense to mean 'scholar' or 'learned man' see Vermes, *Jesus the Jew*, pp. 21–2. He cited *y. Yeb.* 9b; *y. Qidd.* 66a; and *b. 'Abod. Zar.* 50b. This interpretation requires dismissing the gospel context.

[14] So HG and NA[26]. P[45vid] and other authorities have ο του τεκτονος ο υιος της Μαριας or ο του τεκτονος υιος Μαριας or ο του τεκτονος υιος και (της) Μαριας. Assimilation to Matthew probably explains the readings, although Taylor, *Mark*, pp. 299–300, thinks otherwise; see Blinzler (v), pp. 28–30, and McArthur (v), pp. 47–52.

[15] In Prot. Jas 9 Joseph is an old man when Jesus is born.

unusual, for there was doubt as to the father, so people contemptuously referred to Jesus as the son of his mother, implying illegitimacy (cf. Mt 1.18–19; Jn 8.41).[16] Whether or not Stauffer is correct, Matthew might have found 'the son of Mary' potentially disturbing and therefore have rejected it. (iv) The evangelist, in accordance with his interest in Jesus' legal descent from David, wanted to mention Jesus' father, not just his mother, and the easiest way to do this was to turn 'the carpenter' into 'the son of the carpenter' (so Gundry, *Commentary*, p. 283). (But why not write instead, 'Is this not the carpenter, the son of Joseph?')

Of these four explanations, (iv) seems implausible, and (ii) is unlikely because Jews did not despise manual labour. (i) or (iii) or a combination of them could be correct.

οὐχ ἡ μήτηρ αὐτοῦ λέγεται Μαριὰμ καὶ οἱ ἀδελφοὶ αὐτοῦ Ἰάκωβος καὶ Ἰωσὴφ καὶ Σίμων καὶ Ἰούδας;[17] Compare 12.46, 48–9; Jn 2.12; and Acts 1.14 (all of which mention Jesus' mother and his brothers). Mk 6.3 has this: 'Is this not . . . the son of Mary and brother of James and Joses and Judas and Simon?' Matthew has introduced four major alterations. First, he has formulated a second question beginning with οὐχ, this so that he can have three such questions at the heart of the pericope. Secondly, he has put the superior, Jesus, in the genitive (αὐτοῦ); thus Mark's 'the son of Mary and brother of . . .' has become '*his* mother called[18] Mary and *his* brothers . . .'. (Matthew has thus avoided writing, 'the son of the carpenter and of Mary', a phrase which would not have been congenial to the author of Mt 1–2.) Thirdly, the Hellenized 'Joses' (LXX: 0) has become 'Joseph', the LXX form of *yôsēp* (cf. 27.56 diff. Mk 15.40 and note the textual variants for Mt 27.56 and Acts 4.36). Fourthly, the evangelist has reversed the order of the last two brothers: Simon now comes before Judas. It is possible that Matthew, through oral tradition, believed Simon to be older than Judas and therefore moved him up to third place. Certainly this is more plausible than the proposal that Matthew has assimilated to the order of 10.2–4 (the opinion of Gundry, *Commentary*, p. 283).

Besides James, who became a leader of the Jerusalem church, the brothers of Jesus are mentioned by name in the NT only in 13.55 par. and Jude 1.1. For James see Acts 12.17; 15.13; 21.18; 1 Cor 15.7; Gal 1.19; 2.9, 12; Jas 1.1; Jude 1 (all referring, we take it, to one and the same

[16] Stauffer (v). For further discussion see McArthur (v) and Brown *et al.* (v). Both question Stauffer's argument and evidence.

[17] Ιωσηφ is the reading of ℵ² B C N Θ *f*¹ 33 700ᶜ 892 *pc* lat sy^s.c.hmg mae bo^pt Or. Ιωση (so 700* 1010 *pc* bo^pt) and Ιωσης (so K L W Δ 0119 *f*¹³ 565 1241 *pm* k qᶜ sy^p.h? sa bo^mss) are due to assimilation to Mark. But what is the explanation for Ιωαννης (so ℵ*vid D Γ 28 1424 *pm* vg^mss)?

[18] λέγω + name (= 'call')* is often redactional.

person).[19] Paul refers to 'the brothers of the Lord' in 1 Cor 9.5 and implies that those besides James were itinerants (cf. Eusebius, *H.E.* 1.7.14). Jn 7.5 relates that before Easter even Jesus' brothers did not believe him, a fact which, if accepted, excludes any of the twelve from being 'brothers'.

There has been much discussion concerning the 'brothers' (and 'sisters') of Jesus. Later Christian belief in Mary as *semper virgo* rendered problematic the thought that Jesus had blood brothers and sisters. Thus it came to be widely imagined that James and the rest were either cousins, that is, Mary or Joseph's nephews and nieces (the Hieronymian view)[20] or half-brothers, that is, the children of Joseph by an earlier marriage (the Epiphanian view).[21] It is true that ἀδελφός, like the Hebrew *'āḥ* and Aramaic *'āḥā*, need not mean 'blood brother' but can have broader meaning: 'kinsman' or 'relative' (cf. Gen 29.12; 24.48).[22] The Greek word, however, normally means '(blood) brother', and one can explain the conviction that the 'brothers' and 'sisters' of Jesus were not the children of Mary by seeing it as a consequence of belief in Mary's perpetual virginity. In line with this, the manner of expression in Mt 1.25 (Joseph did not know Mary 'until she had borne a son') and Lk 2.7 (Jesus was Mary's 'first-born son') would probably have been avoided had the evangelists already thought Mary ἀειπάρ-θενος. Further, Tertullian could hold that Jesus' brothers and sisters were Mary's offspring without expressing any awareness that he was in this departing from catholic tradition.[23] Nevertheless, it must be confessed that the issue is not so simply resolved. If, as is not unnatural, one equates 'Mary the mother of James the younger and of Joseph/Joses' (Mk 15.40 = Mt 27.56) with 'Mary the wife of Clopas' (Jn 19.25), it would seem to follow that the brothers named in Mk 6.3 and Mt 13.55 were not the sons of Jesus' mother but another Mary.[24] The same inference is to hand if one doubts, for the reason that 'Mary the mother of James and of Joses' (Mk 15.40) is an unexpected circumlocution for Jesus' mother, that the Mary of Mk 15.40 can be the Mary of Mk 6.3. It is accordingly at least *possible* that Jesus' 'brothers' and 'sisters' were not the children of Mary and Joseph; but nothing more definite can be hazarded.

56. The hostile crowd continues to ask questions. Are we to think that the public's knowledge of Jesus' origins is at odds with the notion that 'when the Christ comes, no one will know where he comes from' (Jn 7.27; cf. Justin, *Dial.* 8)?

---

[19] Cf. Josephus, *Ant.* 20.200, which refers to James the 'brother' of Jesus.

[20] So Jerome, Pelagius, Augustine. This became the dominant Roman Catholic opinion. For criticism see J. B. Lightfoot (v), for defence see McHugh (v).

[21] So Prot. Jas 9.2, Clement of Alexandria (?), Origen (citing in support the Gospel of Peter), Eusebius, Hilary of Poitiers, Epiphanius. For criticism see McHugh (v), pp. 208–22.

[22] Note that ἀδελφός means 'step-brother' in Mk 6.17–18.

[23] *Adv. Marc.* 4.19; *De carn. Christi* 7; *De monag.* 8. For the view that these texts are ambiguous and do not indicate that Tertullian was at one with Helvidius see McHugh (v), pp. 448–52.

[24] See Brown *et al.* (v), pp. 68–72.

καὶ αἱ ἀδελφαὶ αὐτοῦ οὐχὶ πᾶσαι πρὸς ἡμᾶς εἰσιν; In Mk 6.3 οὐκ εἰσίν comes after καί, there is no πᾶσαι,[25] and ὧδε (omitted by Matthew as redundant) precedes πρός.

Only in Mt 13.56 and Mk 6.3 do we hear of the 'sisters' of Jesus. We know nothing about them at all, for after departing the synoptic stage they disappear into the back streets of history, where only ecclesiastical fable can henceforth trace them. The silence of the NT may imply that they never became Christians.[26]

πόθεν οὖν τούτῳ ταῦτα πάντα; This redactional addition balances 54c (q.v.); see further p. 451. On ταῦτα πάντα* see on 13.51. The expression is defined by 54c as Jesus' wisdom and mighty deeds.

57. καὶ ἐσκανδαλίζοντο ἐν αὐτῷ. Compare T. Jud 18.5 ('he does not obey the prophet when he speaks and he is offended by a pious word'). Contrast Mt 11.6 ('Blessed is he who takes no offence in me'). Mk 6.3 agrees with Matthew. For the verb see on 5.29. It here signifies a denial of faith which has eschatological importance. By being 'scandalized'[27] at Jesus, the eschatological prophet who has come among them to work wonders and share wisdom, the citizens of Nazareth have passed eschatological judgement upon themselves.

ὁ δὲ Ἰησοῦς εἶπεν αὐτοῖς. This exact phrase (Mt:4; Mk: 5; Lk: 0) recurs in 14.16 diff. Mk 6.37; 16.6 diff. Mk 8.15; and 19.28 diff. Mk 10.29. It here replaces Mk 6.4a: καὶ ἔλεγεν αὐτοῖς ὁ Ἰησοῦς ὅτι. On the omission of ὅτι see Allen, p. xx.

οὐκ ἔστιν προφήτης ἄτιμος εἰ μὴ ἐν τῇ πατρίδι καὶ ἐν τῇ οἰκίᾳ αὐτοῦ. So Mk 6.4, with αὐτοῦ καὶ ἐν τοῖς συγγενεῦσιν αὐτοῦ[28] after πατρίδι. Matthew has abbreviated, perhaps partly out of a reverence for the relatives of Jesus (cf. his toning down of Mk 3.20–35). οἶκος can mean 'city' (T. Levi 10.4; perhaps also LXX Jer 22.5; Mt 23.38) and that may be its meaning here; that is πατρίδι and οἰκίᾳ may stand in synonymous parallelism (contrast Mark). If so, Matthew's text has no reference at all to Jesus' family.

The saying about the dishonoured prophet appears also in Lk 4.24; Jn 4.44; Gos. Thom 31; P. Oxy. 1, recto. There are, further, parallels

[25] A word which implies more than two; but later tradition tended to name only two; cf. Hennecke 1, p. 418.
[26] Tradition associates the 'sisters' of Jesus with the women of Lk 8.2–3 and makes them deaconesses (e.g. Didascalia 13). For full discussion see Hennecke 1, pp. 418–32, on 'the relatives of Jesus'.
[27] Bengel, ad loc.: 'As happens with those who observe one thing, but neglect to observe another of yet more pressing importance'.
[28] This links up with Mk 3.20–35 and is probably a Markan expansion; cf. Guelich, Mark 1, p. 311.

outside the Christian tradition, including Dio Chrysostom 47.6 ('all the philosophers held life to be difficult in the πατρίδι'); Epictetus, *Diss.* 3.16 ('the philosophers advise us to leave our country'; 'we cannot bear that those who meet us should say, "Hey-day! such a one is turned philosopher, who was formerly so and so"'; 'physicians send patients with chronic disorders to another place and air'); and Apollonius of Tyana, *Ep.* 44 ('until now my own country [ή πατρίς] alone ignores me'); also Pindar, *Olym.* 12.13–16. Bultmann, *History*, p. 31, cites an Arabic proverb: 'the piper has no friends in his own town'. What we have in the gospels is probably a Jewish version of the common sentiment that great men are rejected by their own: 'A prophet is without honour in his own country'.[29] The variant in Gos. Thom 31 and *P. Oxy.* 1 is, *pace* Crossan (v), probably an expanded edition of the version in Luke. Matthew and Mark also probably represent expansions. Is Jn 4.44—which is independent of the synoptics (Dodd, *Tradition*, pp. 238–41)—the closest to the original?

For Matthew, the meaning of 'A prophet is not without honour, etc.' is that Jesus is not recognized for what he is, namely, a true prophet. One is reminded of the situation of Jeremiah. He was opposed by people from Anathoth, his home town (Jer 1.1; 11.21; cf. 12.6).

On οὐκ ... εἰ μή see BDF § 376, citing Wellhausen ('imitation of Aram.'); also Beyer, p. 304.

Because we accept the unity of Mt 13.53–8 as it stands, it follows that Jesus himself quoted the proverb in 13.57 par. If so, then the text testifies to Jesus' prophetic self-consciousness. For while the utterance is to be judged traditional, Jesus applied it to himself, thereby implicitly identifying himself as a prophet. This should not surprise. There are other texts which point in the same direction.[30] And certainly Jesus anticipated, especially after the Baptist's execution, that opposition would probably lead to martyrdom, a fate suffered in Jewish tradition by the prophets (see on 5.12).

58. καὶ οὐκ ἐποίησεν ἐκεῖ δυνάμεις πολλάς. This is a revised version of Mk 6.5: 'And he was not able there to do any mighty work, except that he laid his hands upon a few sick people and healed them'.[31] Matthew has abbreviated and thereby eliminated the possible thought that Jesus was less than master of the situation. See 1, pp. 104–105. Inability has become refusal; Jesus is indisputably in charge.

διὰ τὴν ἀπιστίαν αὐτῶν. Compare Josephus, *Ant.* 2.327: Moses the prophet was met with unbelief (ὑπὸ ἀπιστίας). Mk

---

[29] Cf. Zahn, p. 503, and Steck, pp. 213–14. On the rejected prophet motif see on 5.12.

[30] The material is collected and discussed in Schnider, *passim*; also Hill, *Prophecy*, pp. 48–69.

[31] 'Except, etc.' is obviously an addition, perhaps a Markan addition; cf. Pesch 1, p. 321.

6.6a ('And he marvelled because of their unbelief') has been turned into an explanation for Jesus' action: he did few miracles *because* of the people's unbelief. Thus just as unbelief effects the way Jesus speaks to people (see on 13.13), so too does it effect the work he does.

Note that unlike the disciples, who have ὀλιγοπιστία (see on 6.30), the congregation in Nazareth has ἀπιστία,[32] no faith at all.

(iv) *Concluding Observations*

Coming as it does after the episodes of rejection in chapters 11 and 12 and after the little 'theodicy' of seven parables in chapter 13, Mt 13.53–8, which supplies a concrete example of people hearing but not hearing and seeing but not seeing (cf. 13.13), shows us that unbelief does not correspond to any geographical pattern:[33] Jesus is rejected in the north as well as the south, in his home town as well as in the capital. Thus there is no safe haven, no sacred space uncontaminated by hostility; there is no one group of people that will, as a unit, embrace Jesus. Opposition is truly pandemic. The lesson neatly complements 12.46–50, the passage which immediately precedes 13.1–52. For if in 13.53–8 one learns that geographical and social ties are not what really matter, in 12.46–50 it is similarly taught that family ties may be relaxed by commitment to Jesus. Hence the great parable discourse is framed by two texts which relativize the significance of natural or earthly connexions.

13.53–8 links up not only with what precedes but also with what follows. In 13.57 Jesus implicitly proclaims himself a prophet, and in 14.5 the people (correctly) hold John to be a prophet. The upshot is clear. John's fate, which is recounted in 14.1–12, is that of a prophet, and it must therefore lie ahead for Jesus. To be a prophet means to suffer rejection, and to suffer rejection means, ultimately, to suffer death.

(v) *Bibliography*

J. Blinzler, *Die Brüder und Schwestern Jesu*, SBS 21, Stuttgart, 1967.
Brown *et al., Mary*, pp. 59–72, 99–103.

[32] Mt: 1; Mk: 2; Lk: 0. Cf. Wisd 14.25; 4 Macc 12.4 ℵ (διὰ γὰρ ἀπιστίαν); Rom 4.20; 11.20, 23. For the related ἄπιστος see Mt 17.17 = Mk 9.19.
[33] Contrast R. H. Lightfoot, *Locality and Doctrine*; and *History and Interpretation*: Criticism by Davies, *Land*, pp. 231–243, esp. 238–243.

Crossan, *Aphorisms*, pp. 281–5.

Davies, *GL*, pp. 236–9.

W. Eltester, ed., *Jesus in Nazareth*, BZNW 40, Berlin, 1972.

P. H. Furfey, 'Christ as *Tektōn*', *CBQ* 17 (1955), pp. 324–35.

M. Goguel, 'Le rejet de Jésus à Nazareth', *ZNW* 12 (1911), pp. 321–4.

E. Grässer, 'Jesus in Nazareth (Mark 6.1–6a)', *NTS* 16 (1969), pp. 1–23.

M.-J. Lagrange, *Évangile selon Saint Marc*, EB, Paris, 1929, pp. 79–93.

J. B. Lightfoot, *Saint Paul's Epistle to the Galatians*, 10th ed., London, 1890, pp. 252–91.

R. H. Lightfoot, *History and Interpretation in the Gospels*, London, 1935, pp. 182–205.

idem, *Locality and Doctrine in the Gospels*, London, 1937.

E. Lombard, 'Charpentier ou maçon?', *RTP* 36 (1948), pp. 161–92.

H. K. McArthur, 'Son of Mary', *NovT* 15 (1973), pp. 38–58.

C. C. McCown, 'ὁ τέκτων', in *Studies in Early Christianity*, ed. S. J. Case, New York, 1928, pp. 173–89.

J. McHugh, *The Mother of Jesus in the New Testament*, Garden City, 1975, pp. 200–54.

B. Mayer, 'Überlieferungs- und redaktionsgeschichtliche Überlegungen zu Mk 6.1–6a', *BZ* 22 (1978), pp. 187–98.

L. Oberlinner, *Historische Überlieferung und christologische Aussage. Zur Frage der 'Brüder Jesu' in der Synopse*, FB 19, Stuttgart, 1975.

F. Van Segbroeck, 'Jésus rejeté par sa patrie (Mt 13.54–58)', *Bib* 49 (1968), pp. 167–98.

Schmithals, *Wunder*, pp. 92–9.

E. Stauffer, 'Jeschua ben Mirjam', in *Neotestamentica et Semitica*, ed. E. E. Ellis and M. Wilcox, Edinburgh, 1969, pp. 119–28.

R. L. Sturch, 'The "Patris" of Jesus', *JTS* 28 (1977), pp. 94–6.

P. J. Temple, 'The Rejection at Nazareth', *CBQ* 17 (1955), pp. 229–42.

T. Zahn, *Forschungen zur Geschichte des neutestamentlichen Kanons und der altkirchlichen Literatur*, VI/2, Leipzig, 1900, pp. 227–372.

XXXI

THE DEATH OF JOHN THE BAPTIST
(14.1–12)

(i) *Structure*

This section should perhaps be divided into three subsections: vv. 1–2, Herod's opinion of Jesus; vv. 3–5, John's imprisonment; vv. 6–12, John's martyrdom (cf. NA[26]; note that Herod is named only in 14.1, 3, and 6, that is, in the opening sentence of each proposed subsection). But one can scarcely be sure. One may even wonder whether our evangelist gave much thought at all to the internal arrangement or structure of 14.1–12.

(ii) *Sources*

The previous paragraph, Mt 13.53–8, drew upon Mk 6.1–6a, and because what follows this last, namely, Mk 6.6b–13, has already been mined (see chapter 10), Mk 6.14–29 is the next pericope to serve Matthew. He greatly abbreviates it. (Matthew's account has 172 words, Mark's 302.)

Mt 14.1–12 would seem to stand in the way of the Griesbach hypothesis, for it strongly impresses one as a less than perfect condensation of the longer Markan account. Consider these points:

(i) Although both narratives begin as a flashback, Matthew's does not so conclude: it is a parenthesis which never closes (*pace* Cope (v)). See 1, p. 107.

(ii) In Mt 14.9 Herod grieves (cf. Mk. 6.26). For this emotion there is no explanation; indeed, it makes little sense given 14.5 (Herod wished to do away with the Baptist). In Mark, however, we read that Herod heard John gladly (6.20). Thus Mt 14.9 = Mk 6.26 fits well only the Markan story.

(iii) Mt 14.6–8 presupposes guests as the backdrop for Salome's dance and Herod's oath; but these are not mentioned until 14.9. In Mark, however, the guests are mentioned before the particulars of the banquet are recited (6.21).

(iv) Is 'Herod the tetrarch' (Mt 14.1) not a correction of Mark's strictly inaccurate 'Herod the king' (Mk 6.14)?

(v) If Matthew be supposed the source for Mk 6.14–29, as on the Griesbach hypothesis, we are faced with an author who, without apparent support from the tradition, sought to insert novelistic elements

463

at almost every turn. He also stands guilty of needless verbosity. Why expand Matthew to no obvious end?

The Third Gospel contains two parallels to Mt 14.1–12 = Mk 6.14–29, the first being Lk 3.19–20, the second being 9.7–9. Both appear to be Lukan compositions based solely upon Mk 6.14–29 (see the commentaries).

(iii) Exegesis

Having, in the parable discourse (13.1–52), examined the root causes of unbelief, the evangelist is now about the task of showing how the failure to gain faith will manifest itself. For this 14.1–12 is paradigmatic. Unbelief begets not only misunderstanding (vv. 1–2) but also violent opposition to Jesus and those on his side (vv. 3–12; cf. also 13.53–8).

Of the many changes Matthew has introduced into Mk 6.14–29, these are the most significant. (i) The story has been made less colourful through a drastic shortening (Matthew is shorter by more than 100 words), and the whole has been rewritten in the evangelist's own style. (ii) Herod 'the king' has been corrected to Herod 'the tetrarch' (see on v. 1). (iii) The opinions as to who Jesus might be (other than John risen from the dead) have been dropped (Mk 6.15–16). (iv) The parallelism between John and Jesus has been somewhat enhanced (cf. pp. 475–76). (v) Assimilation to 21.26 has taken place (see on v. 5). (vi) A new conclusion has been supplied: John's disciples tell Jesus what has happened (14.12). *Pace* Lohmeyer, *Matthäus*, p. 233, none of these nor any other changes need be traced to the influence of a non-Markan source.

Concerning the tradition-history of Mt 14.1–12 = Mk 6.14–29, two different pieces must be distinguished: Mt 14.1–2 = Mk 6.14–16 (on the identity of Jesus) and Mt 14.3–12 = Mk 6.17–29 (on John's imprisonment and execution). The former was probably formulated, either by Mark[1] or a pre-Markan tradent,[2] as an introduction to Mk 6.17–29. The partial parallel in Mk 8.28 is consistent with the supposition that the original core may be Mk 6.14b–5 (at one time attached to a miracle story?) and that vv. 14a and 16 are secondary.

As for the story in Mk 6.17–29, which is not a story about Jesus at all, its history can only be guessed.[3] Our own suspicion is that a pre-Markan and perhaps non-Christian story-teller combined an account of John the Baptist's martyrdom[4] with popular traditions about

---

[1] So Gnilka, *Markus* 1, pp. 244–5, regarding vv. 14a and 16 as redactional.

[2] This is the judgement of Pesch 1, p. 332.

[3] *Pace* Schenk (v), we do not think it a Markan construction on the basis of popular traditions about John the Baptist.

[4] Supporting this judgement is Gnilka (v), who finds several motifs common to Jewish martyrologies (e.g. opposition to a king, faithfulness to the Torah). One naturally imagines that the postulated account was initially passed on in Baptist circles.

Antipas' court[5] and then glossed the whole with OT motifs (cf. Mk 6.22 with Est 2.9 and Mk 6.23 with Est 5.3, 6; 7.2; the relations between Herod, Herodias, and John are remarkably similar to those between Ahab, Jezebel, and Elijah; see esp. 1 Kgs 17–18 and recall that the NT often associates John and Elijah).[6] The purpose of the *Novelle* was perhaps to criticize the Herodian court. What of its provenance? *Pace* Bultmann, *History*, p. 301, there is no necessity for postulating a Hellenistic Jewish milieu.[7] The narrative contains Semitisms (Hoehner, p. 118, n. 3) and, more importantly, takes for granted a knowledge of the named characters (Herod, Herodias, Philip, John). It may therefore just as well have been composed in Palestine.

The historicity of the story is problematic. At least four objections can be, and have been, raised. (i) Josephus' well-known recital of the events surrounding John's death[8] seems to contradict the synoptics at certain key points, including the name of Herodias' first husband, the place of John's imprisonment, and the motive for his murder. See on 14.3 and 4. (ii) The synoptics require one to believe historical improbabilities. For instance, would a Herodian princess have performed a sensuous dance before strangers? And how could Herod, who was under the Roman thumb, have promised anybody half of his 'kingdom'? (iii) OT influences cannot be denied (see above). (iv) There are parallels to the passion narrative (see p. 476), which implies a manipulation of the facts for theological ends.

Considerations such as these have led to a negative evaluation of the historical accuracy of Mt 14.1–12 par. (cf. Beare, pp. 323–5). Whether they are as telling as is often made out is another matter. Neither (iii) nor (iv) is very powerful, for the OT allusions and the parallels to the passion narrative do not really affect the substance of the tale. Furthermore, we have in the verse-by-verse commentary argued that none of the objections classified here under headings (i) and (ii) is *necessarily* on target: each one can be doubted. Nonetheless, to confess to uncertainty about some of the criticisms is hardly to make the case for authenticity. Beyond that there is our own—admittedly subjective—impression or feeling that Mk 14.17–29 enshrines a popular story which probably mingles fact with fancy.[9] So while

---

[5] Some have, however, suggested that instead of popular tradition we should think of Herodian officials or their relatives who became Christians: they were the source of Mk 6.14–29. Note Lk 8.3 and 24.10, which mention Joanna, whose husband was a financial steward of Antipas, and Acts 13.1, which includes in the church at Antioch a certain Manaen, 'a member of the court of Herod the tetrarch'.

[6] A similar analysis is proposed by Gnilka, *Markus* 1, pp. 245–6. On the OT motifs see de la Potterie (v), who goes so far as to speak of a 'midrash'. On the connexions with Esther in particular see Aus (v).

[7] He cites Herodotus 9.108–113, Livy 39.43; and Plutarch, *Artax.* 17—very imperfect parallels.

[8] *Ant.* 18.117–19; Origen, *C. Cels.* 1.47; Eusebius, *H.E.* 1.11; idem, *Dem. ev.* 9.5.15. Most modern scholars assume that if there is any discrepancy between Josephus' version and the gospels, it is the gospels which must be wrong: but note Knox, *Sources* 1, p. 50.

[9] We understand Nineham's comment: Mk 6.14–29 has 'something of the

keeping an open mind, we are disposed to endorse Rawlinson's evaluation: 'it is a mistake to try to harmonize' the accounts in Josephus and the gospels: 'Josephus' version will give the facts as they presented themselves to an historian who wrote sixty years later, and who was concerned to trace the political causes of war. The story in Mk will be an account, written with a certain amount of literary freedom, of what was being darkly whispered in the bazaars or market-places of Palestine at the time . . .'.[10]

1. ἐν ἐκείνῳ τῷ καιρῷ. On this connecting formula, which has no parallel in Mk 6.14 and which therefore adds precision, see on 11.25. It appears three times in our gospel, always followed by verb + subject and always introducing a new section (11.25; 12.1; 14.1; cf. LXX Deut 10.1, 8; Dan 3.8).[11]

ἤκουσεν Ἡρῴδης ὁ τετραάρχης τὴν ἀκοὴν Ἰησοῦ.[12] Compare Mk 6.14: καὶ ἤκουσεν ὁ βασιλεὺς Ἡρῴδης, φανερὸν γὰρ ἐγένετο τὸ ὄνομα αὐτοῦ. Matthew has omitted καί, substituted the more proper 'Herod the tetrarch' (so also Lk 9.7; cf. Josephus, Ant. 18.27) for 'Herod the king' (which helps distinguish Antipas from Herod the Great; see 2.1, etc.),[13] supplied τὴν ἀκοήν (= 'the fame') Ἰησοῦ (cf. 4.24) as the object of the main verb, and dropped Mark's parenthetical φανερόν κ.τ.λ..

Herod Antipas,[14] the son of Herod the Great and Malthace, was the tetrarch of Galilee and Peraea from 4 B.C. to A.D. 39. He was not, despite Mark, a king. In fact, Antipas died in exile after unsuccessfully petitioning the emperor Caligula for the royal title (Josephus, Ant. 18.240–56). Perhaps, however, Antipas was called 'king' out of courtesy or local custom (so many commentators; it is not irrelevant to observe that the Aramaic malkaʾ has a broader range of meaning than the Greek βασιλεύς).[15] In this connexion it is significant that Matthew,

character of the fairy tale' (p. 173). He adds in a footnote: 'Such themes as the banquet and the dance, the request and the sworn promise, are constantly recurring motifs in literature of a similar kind . . .'.

[10] A. E. J. Rawlinson, St Mark, 2nd ed., London, 1927, p. 82.

[11] Chrysostom inferred from 'at that time' the haughtiness and thoughtlessness of Antipas, who bothered to inform himself about Jesus only after a very long time (Hom. on Mt. 48.2).

[12] So NA[26]. HG has τετραρχης. See BDF § 124.

[13] Luke's minor agreement with Matthew on this particular is not a sign of literary dependence. Throughout Luke and Acts the Third Evangelist uses the correct titles for Herod the Great, Antipas, Philip, Agrippa I, and Agrippa II; see Lk 1.5; 3.1, 19; 9.7; Acts 12.1; 13.1; 25.13, 14, 24, 26; 26.2, 7, 13, 19, 26, 27, 30.

[14] Lit.: Schürer 1, pp. 340–53; Hoehner, passim; E. Gabba, in CHJ 3, forthcoming.

[15] For other texts in which Antipas is a 'king' see Justin, Dial. 49; Gos. Pet. 1.2; Gos. Eb. frag. 3 (= Epiphanius, Haer. 30.13.6); Acts of Pilate, prologue; Origen, Comm. on Mt. 10.21. Cf. Acts 4.26–7 and next note; also the usage in Cicero, Verr. 2.4.27.

who knows that Antipas was a tetrarch, can also call him a 'king' (14.9 = Mk 6.26; cf. 2.22: Ἀρχέλαος βασιλεύει—Archelaus was only an ethnarch[16]). τετραάρχης[17] occurs only once in Matthew. The word originally designated one who ruled a quarter of a region but by the first century was commonly used of any petty ruler of a dependent state. Although usage was fluid, the title 'tetrarch' seems to have been one step below 'ethnarch', which was in turn one step below 'king'. See further Schürer 1, p. 333, n. 12. Both Josephus and inscriptions agree that Antipas was only a tetrarch.

2. Antipas explained Jesus' mighty works by the conjecture that John the Baptist had come back to life.

καὶ εἶπεν τοῖς παισὶν αὐτοῦ. In Mk 6.14, καὶ ἔλεγον ὅτι probably goes with καί ... Ἡρῴδης: 'And king Herod heard ... because people were saying that ...'. In Matthew the statement about Jesus being John is placed on Herod's lips; it is no longer simply something people in general are saying. Did Matthew's copy of Mark have ἔλεγεν (ℵ f[1.13] Maj lat sy)? Or is the reading of Mk 6.14 Maj assimilation to Matthew? Compare 21.46 diff. Mk 11.32.

For παῖς[18] used of a ruler's attendants or courtiers see LXX Gen 41.10, 37–8; 1 Βασ 16.17; Jer 43.31; 44.2; 1 Macc 1.6, 8.

οὗτός ἐστιν. The evangelist has added this identification formula, which he uses often (cf. the formula quotations and the christological statements in 3.17; 17.5; 21.11; and 27.37 and note the repetition of οὗτός ἐστιν in chapter 13).

Ἰωάννης ὁ βαπτιστής. So Mk 6.14, with the participle βαπτίζων. Compare 3.1 (q.v.) diff. Mk 1.4; also 11.11–12 diff. Lk 16.16. Ἰωάννου τοῦ βαπτιστοῦ appears in 14.8 = Mk 6.25, so Matthew has made his usage consistent.

αὐτὸς ἠγέρθη ἀπὸ τῶν νεκρῶν. Compare Lk 9.7 (with ἠγέρθη, a minor agreement). Mk 6.14 (ἐγήγερται ἐκ νεκρῶν) is shorter. ἠγέρθη ἀπὸ τῶν νεκρῶν is found in M material in 27.64 and is redactional in 28.7 diff. Mk 16.7. Matthew was evidently fond of the phrase, which is unique to him in the NT. The usual and expected ἐκ (cf. Jn 2.22; Acts 3.15; etc.) appears in the First Gospel only in 17.9 = Mk 9.9.

καὶ διὰ τοῦτο αἱ δυνάμεις ἐνεργοῦσιν ἐν αὐτῷ. Compare Gal 3.5. Mk 6.14 agrees, with the verb in fourth place. Note the connexion with 13.54: 'Where did this one get this wisdom and these mighty works' (αἱ δυνάμεις)? But here in 14.2 δυνάμεις does not mean 'miracles' but '(miraculous) powers'. Interestingly enough, the

---

[16] Josephus, *Ant.* 18.93, calls Archelaus the ethnarch a king (cf. *Vita* 5).
[17] NT: Mt 14.1; Lk 3.19; 9.7; Acts 13.1. LXX: O.
[18] Added three times to Mark by Matthew.

NT does not relate any miracles done by John (cf. Jn 10.41).[19] On ἐνεργέω (a Pauline favourite) see J. A. Robinson, pp. 241–47. The report that some took Jesus to be John the Baptist risen from the dead (cf. 16.14 = Mk 8.28) has generated much speculation. Some have thought it evidence for a Jewish belief in a dying and rising eschatological prophet.[20] M. Smith, on the other hand, has interpreted the notice in terms of necromancy.[21] Still others have asked whether the idea of reincarnation may not have gained a foothold in first century Judaism.[22] The evidence for this idea in ancient Jewish circles is, however, rather scant; and, as for Smith's proposal, where else in early Christian texts does 'raised from the dead' have anything to do with necromancy? With regard to the *topos* of a dying and rising prophet, the evidence is quite controversial[23]; and in any case it would have been possible to think of Jesus as John resurrected only if one did not know that the two were alive at the same time (cf. Jn 4.1–2) or that one had baptized the other. Should one then suppose that the real meaning of our verse is more figurative, to wit: Jesus possessed the same supernatural inspiration that had been at work in John? On this interpretation, which makes Jesus, so to speak, John's alter ego,[24] one could appeal to 2 Kgs 2.9–15, where Elisha is given a 'double share' of Elijah's 'spirit' as well as to Lk 1.17, where John the Baptist is said to come 'in the spirit and power of Elijah.' Nevertheless, in view of Mt 16.24 = Mk 8.28 we are inclined to take the text more literally: some believed that John had come back to life and was now known as Jesus. But rather than detecting behind this strange conviction an eschatological belief about a dying and rising prophet we prefer to think more simply of 'a very ill-informed piece of popular superstition.'[25]

3. ὁ γὰρ Ἡρῴδης κρατήσας τὸν Ἰωάννην. This condenses Mk 6.17a (αὐτὸς[26] γὰρ ὁ Ἡρῴδης ἀποστείλας ἐκράτησεν τὸν Ἰωάννην). ἀποστείλας has fallen away, and ἐκράτησεν has become κρατήσας.

For κρατέω meaning 'arrest' or 'take into custody' see LXX

[19] But this does not, of course, eliminate the possibility that the Baptist's followers attributed miracles to him; Jn 10.41 might be polemical.

[20] E.g. K. Berger, *Die Auferstehung des Propheten und die Erhöung des Menschensohnes*, Göttingen, 1976; R. Pesch, 'Zur Entstehung des Glaubens an die Auferstehung Jesu', *TQ* 153 (1973), pp. 222–6. Cf. Mk 9.11–13; Rev 11.3–12; Apoc. Elijah 4.7–19.

[21] *Magician*, pp. 33–4; cf. Kraeling (v). Note 1 Sam 28; Ps. – Clem. Rec. 2.13; Sepher Ha – Razim, first firmament, lines 176ff.

[22] Note Origen's rejection of this view: *Comm. on Mt.* 10.20.

[23] See esp. J. M. Nützel, 'Zum Schicksal der eschatologischen Propheten', *BZ* 20 (1976), pp. 59–94; E. Schweizer, review of Berger's *Auferstehung*, in *TLZ* 103 (1978), pp. 874–8; and A. Vögtle, in A. Vögtle and R. Pesch, *Wie kam es zum Osterglauben?*, Düsseldorf, 1975, pp. 80–3.

[24] Origen, *Comm. on Jn.* 6.30, preserves the peculiar opinion that Jesus and John were similar in outward appearance.

[25] Marshall, p. 356. For further discussion see Cullmann, *Christology*, pp. 31–4.

[26] Is this an Aramaism? See Black, pp. 96–100. If so, Matthew's text is at this point less Semitic.

B Judg 16.21; Acts 24.6. The verb adds to the Jesus/John parallelism because it occurs several times in the passion narrative (21.46; 26.4, 48, 50, 55, 57).

Matthew, like Josephus, does not inform us of the precise date of John's arrest. It does not matter for his purposes. For full discussion of the possibilities see Hoehner, pp. 125–31, 170–1, who concludes that John was probably imprisoned in A.D. 30–31 and executed in 31 or 32.[27]

ἔδησεν αὐτὸν καὶ ἐν φυλακῇ ἀπέθετο.[28] Mk 6.17 has καί at the beginning, no καί before ἐν, and no concluding verb: 'and he bound him in prison'. The Matthean changes are due to the dependent character of the previous clause.

See Josephus, *Ant*. 18.119, for another account of John's imprisonment and execution. Josephus plainly states that the Baptist was 'brought in chains to Machaerus,' to the fortress-palace rebuilt by Herod the Great and located east of the Dead Sea, thirteen miles southeast of Herodium. For a description of the place see Josephus, *Bell*. 7.163–209. Ruins are still visible today. It is often claimed that the synoptic accounts assume that John was executed at the court in Tiberias, not at Machaerus. But this is not perfectly clear, and it can just as well be argued that 'Antipas resided at various times at Machaerus, and that the nobilities of Galilee may have sent him a deputation on his birthday. The fact that there is no mention of a Peraean delegation being sent may indicate that Antipas was already in Peraea' (so Hoehner, p. 148; cf. Schürer 1, p. 348, n. 27). On the dining rooms discovered in the fortress at Machaerus and their possible connexion with Mk 6.14–29 par. see Manns (v) and Riesner (v).

For ἀποτίθεμαι used of putting someone in prison see LXX Lev 24.12; Num 15.34; and 2 Chr 18.26, all with φυλακή.

διὰ Ἡρῳδιάδα τὴν γυναῖκα Φιλίππου τοῦ ἀδελφοῦ αὐτοῦ. So Mk 6.17, with 'because he married her' at the end.

Herodias was indeed Herod's niece, but she was, according to Josephus, the wife of Herod, son of Mariamme II, not Philip, the tetrarch who married Salome (Josephus, *Ant*. 18.136–7). Many modern commentators have accordingly not hesitated to attribute an

---

[27] Schenk (v) puts forward the suggestion that John actually died after Jesus died. It was, according to Schenk, the evangelist Mark who first moved forward the Baptist's death. But Josephus does not indicate that much time passed between John's arrest and death, and Q (cf. 11.2–6 par.) assumes that John was arrested while Jesus was still active.

[28] ℵ* B 700 *pc* ff¹ h q bo^mss omit αυτον and NA²⁶ puts it in brackets. Is the explanation for omission homoioteleuton? There is more doubt about the words after αυτον. We have, following HG and NA²⁶, reproduced the reading of ℵ* B* *f*¹³ 33 1424 *al* ff¹ h: και εν φυλακη απεθετο (so also B² Θ 892 with τη φ.). D *pc* a e k have εν τη φυλ., ℵ² (Z^vid) εν τη φυλακη και απεθετο, *f*¹ 700 *pc* και απεθετο εν τη φυλ., and C L W 0119* Maj sy^h και εθετο εν φυλακη.

understandable error to the evangelists[29]; and it may well be that the omission of 'Philip' from Mt 14.3 D lat Aug, Mk 6.17 P[45] 47, and the autograph of Lk 3.19 resulted from an awareness of the difficulty.[30] Of the various attempts to harmonize the gospels and Josephus on the point, the most plausible is that Herod, son of Mariamme II, was named Herod Philip; see Hoehner, pp. 131–36.

4. The reason for John's arrest is given: he rebuked Herod's illicit union. The Baptist thus illustrates 10.26–31: he spoke the truth aloud, fearing God instead of those who can kill only the body.[31]

ἔλεγεν γὰρ αὐτῷ ὁ Ἰωάννης.[32] Mk 6.18 has ὁ Ἰωάννης after γάρ and the longer τῷ Ἡρῴδῃ instead of αὐτῷ.

οὐκ ἔξεστίν σοι ἔχειν αὐτήν. In Mk 6.18 ὅτι is placed before οὐκ and 'the wife of your brother' (cf. Mt 14.3 = Mk 6.17) does duty for αὐτήν. Once again Matthew has abbreviated. For similar examples of our author avoiding Mark's repetition see Allen, pp. xxiv – xxv.

For instances of ἔχω meaning 'marry' see LXX Isa 54.1; Jn 4.17–18; 1 Cor 7.2, 13; Josephus, *Ant.* 7.151.

John presumably denounced Antipas not because he had divorced his first wife (the daughter of Aretas) or because he was guilty of polygamy but because he had married his (living) brother's wife (cf. Lev 8.16; 20.21; Josephus, *Bell.* 2.116; *Ant.* 17.341; Origen, *Comm. on Mt.* 10.21; Eusebius, *H.E.* 1.11).[33] And according to the gospels, this was the cause of his arrest. Josephus tells a different story. In his account, the Baptist was arrested because he incited the people to the point of sedition (*Ant.* 118.118–19). Some commentators have maintained that between the synoptics and John there is in this regard a contradiction. Yet neither source can be credited with passing on anything more than an outline of selected events, which makes it possible to see the two as being complementary on the matter (cf. Schürer 1, p. 346; Smallwood, p. 185). Indeed, given the political situation, a denunciation of Herod's marriage may well have been politically explosive.[34]

[29] Herod had a large family and there was much intermarriage. See the table in Schürer 1, p. 614.

[30] Zahn, p. 505, however, argues that in Matthew 'Philip' is an interpolation from Mk 6.17.

[31] It is natural that John became for many Christian exegetes an example of righteous resistance to the state; see Gnilka, *Markus* 1, p. 253 (citing texts from Luther and Calvin).

[32] So HG, following C L W Θ 0119 *f*[1.13] Maj (lat). NA[26] favours the reading of B Z: ο Ιωαννης αυτω. But this might be assimilation to Mark. ℵ[2] has Ιωαννης αυτου, D has αυτω Ιωαννης, 28 565 *pc* have ο Ιωαννης, and ℵ* has simply Ιωαννης.

[33] *Pace* Gundry, *Commentary*, pp. 286–7, who, observing that Matthew's narrative fails to mention Herod's marriage to Herodias, infers that John was (according to Matthew) opposing the contemplation of their union. But could not Matthew assume their marriage as common knowledge or at least assume a knowledge of Mk 6.17 ('he [Herod] married her [Herodias]')?

[34] See further Hoehner, pp. 136–46. Antipas eventually found himself at war

5. καὶ θέλων αὐτὸν ἀποκτεῖναι ἐφοβήθη τὸν ὄχλον, ὅτι ὡς προφήτην αὐτὸν εἶχον. Compare 21.26, which Matthew has here anticipated: 'But if we say, "From men", we are afraid of the multitude, for all hold that John was a prophet'. Mk 6.19–20 has this: 'And Herodias had a grudge against him, and wanted to kill him. But she could not, for Herod feared John, knowing that he was a righteous and holy man, and kept him safe. When he heard him, he was much perplexed; and yet he heard him gladly'. Besides contracting his source, Matthew has (i) made Herod, not Herodias, the subject of the sentence, a change which limits the number of active characters, makes Herod less ambiguous and more malevolent, and enhances the parallelism between Herod and the Jewish leaders of 21.26; (ii) traded 'feared John' for 'feared the crowd' (cf. 1 Sam 15.24), an alteration which makes for increased parallelism between the opposition to John and the opposition to Jesus (cf. again 21.26, also 46); and (iii) turned 'just man' into 'prophet', an exchange which brings 14.5 into line with 11.9 (John was a prophet and more than a prophet) and 21.26 (see above).

It should not be forgotten that ἀποκτείνω is used of those killing Jesus in 16.21; 17.33; 21.38–9; and 26.4. It is therefore one more item which helps correlate the fate of John with that of Jesus. The participle θέλων is best understood as concessive: 'And even though he wanted . . .'.

The crowd's opinion that John is a prophet is quite correct from Matthew's viewpoint. In fact, 'for they held him to be a prophet' is the key to the story, at least as it appears in the First Gospel. Matthew has just finished recounting an episode in which Jesus speaks only one sentence: 'A prophet is without honour . . .'. Thus 13.53–8 and 14.1–12 together depict the inevitable, tragic lot of the true prophet (cf. 23.29–39).

6. γενεσίων δὲ γενομένων τοῦ Ἡρῴδου ὠρχήσατο ἡ θυγάτηρ τῆς Ἡρῳδιάδος ἐν τῷ μέσῳ καὶ ἤρεσεν τῷ Ἡρῴδῃ.[35] Compare Est 2.9. All the vocabulary with the exception of ἐν τῷ μέσῳ (cf. bĕʾemṣa),[36] is taken from Mk 6.21–2: 'But an opportunity came when Herod on his birthday gave a banquet for his

with Aretas of Nabataea, whose daughter he divorced in order to marry Herodias.

[35] NA[26] has γενεσιοις δε γενομενοις (so also Zahn, p. 506, n. 79), on the authority of ℵ B D L Z 1010 pc; see BDF § 200.3. HG prints γενεσιων δε γενομενων; so C K N Θ 565 892 1241 1424 al. Either reading could be correct. W 0119 0136 f[13] Maj have γενεσιων δε αγομενων. Compare f[1] pc: γενεσιοις δε αγομενοις.

[36] Cf. 10.16 (from Q); 18.2 (from Mark), 20 (from M). None of these texts has the article τῷ; but see LXX Exod 36.30; Ezek 1.4, 5; Acts 4.7.

and officers and the leading men of Galilee. For when the daughter of Herodias herself[37] came in and danced, she pleased Herod and his guests . . .'. Obviously, all but the essentials have been excised. Our evangelist is not interested in telling a good story but in getting to the theological points with as little distraction as possible.

γενέσια (LXX: O; cf. the rabbinic *gînîsĕyā*, *gînîsîn*) is the equivalent of the Attic γενέθλια and means 'birthday celebration' (BAGD, s.v.; the reference is not to the anniversary of Herod's accession[38]; see Schürer 1, p. 346, n. 26). We do not know the date of Herod's birth. But that can hardly matter for our author. Is it relevant to observe that 'the birthdays of Herod' was a proverbial expression (Persius, *Satura* 5.180)[39] or that Matthew and his audience *may* have thought of birthday celebrations as pagan (cf. m. '*Abod. Zar.* 1.3; SB 1, pp. 680–1; Origen, *Comm. on Mt.* 10.22)?

The 'daughter of Herodias' is to be identified with Salome (cf. Josephus, *Ant.* 18.136–7). But a difficulty has been detected in the unparalleled notice that a Herodian princess danced before Herod's court. Could the king really have been pleased by Salome's presumably shameless dance before strangers? Although this is the sort of question that the critical scholar must ask, we do not see that it can be answered. For our sources are silent on the considerations which might lead us to an informed judgement. What sort of dance was performed? Was it lewd or unseemly?[40] And what about Antipas' character? Were his scruples such that he would have been troubled by an indecent spectacle? Or should we hesitate to put anything past a man whose father and example was Herod the Great?[41]

7. ὅθεν μεθ' ὅρκου ὡμολόγησεν αὐτῇ δοῦναι ὃ ἐὰν αἰτήσηται. This summarizes Mk 6.22d–23 ('and the king said to the girl, "Ask me for whatever you wish, and I will grant it." And he vowed to her, "Whatever you ask me, I will give you, even half of my kingdom"'). Matthew has untypically eliminated the OT allusion (see Est 5.3, 6; 7.2[42]).

---

[37] On 'the daughter of Herodias herself' see, in addition to the Markan commentaries, Hoehner, pp. 151–4. Matthew's interpretation is consistent with the reading of Mk 6.22 A C W Θ *f*[13] Maj vg sy[h]: θυγατρος αυτης της Ηρωδιαδος (cf. Justin, *Dial.* 49.4).

[38] Josephus, *Ant.* 15.423, speaks of Herod the Great's 'accession, which they were accustomed to celebrate'.

[39] For Agrippa I celebrating a birthday see Josephus, *Ant.* 19.321. —Some Christian exegetes have used the depiction of Antipas' party to decry secular dancing and celebrations; see e.g. Chrysostom, *Hom. on Mt.* 48.4–10.

[40] Schlatter, p. 460, uses the phrase, 'die wilde Erotik'.

[41] Additional discussion in Hoehner, pp. 156–7.

[42] Cf. also 1 Kgs 13.8; Lk 19.8. Justin, *Dial.* 49, agrees with Matthew in not having the OT allusion. —For the motif of the drunken king doing the bidding of a woman (in this case a courtesan) to later regret see Plutarch, *Alex.* 38. Note also Josephus, *Ant.* 18.289–304.

ὅθεν is from Q in 12.44 = Lk 11.24 and without parallel in 25.24 and 26. Here it means 'therefore' or 'hence' (cf. Wisd 12.23; Acts 26.19; Heb 2.17). ὅρκος* is used in anticipation of its appearance in 14.9 = Mk 6.26. μετὰ ὅρκου (cf. LXX Lev 5.4; Num 30.11; Josephus, *Ant.* 2.3) is redactional in 26.72. For ὁμολογέω* meaning 'promise' see LXX Jer 51.25; Acts 7.17; Josephus, *Ant.* 6.40. On the aorist infinitive after this verb see BDF§ 350.

8. ἡ δὲ προβιβασθεῖσα ὑπὸ τῆς μητρὸς αὐτῆς· δός μοι, φησίν, ὧδε ἐπὶ πίνακι τὴν κεφαλὴν Ἰωάννου τοῦ βαπτιστοῦ. The last eleven words are taken from Mk 6.25b with little alteration while the first seven are a compact version of Mk 6.24–25a.

δέ is in this verse a purely transitional particle. No contrast is intended. 'Now' would be a correct translation. προβιβάζω (LXX: 2; Exod 35.34; Deut 6.7) is a NT *hapax legomenon*. Here one is uncertain how it should be rendered. ἡ δὲ προβιβασθεῖσα κ.τ.λ. could mean 'Now she, being put forward by her mother' or 'Now she, being urged on by her mother' (cf. Acts 19.33). More probably, however, the translation should be, 'Now she, being instructed by her mother'. This is consistent with LXX usage and with Mark's account. See BAGD, s.v., citing LXX Exod 35.34 and Deut 6.7. πίναξ (cf. the rabbinic *pîněqēs, pinqēs*) means 'platter' or 'dish', ἐπὶ πίνακι 'on a platter' or 'dish'—a hideous touch. The word does not appear in the LXX. For the head as a trophy of death see Josephus, *Ant.* 18.115. And for slaughter at a banquet see Josephus, *Ant.* 13.380. For the redactional addition of ὧδε, 'here', see 8.29 diff. Mk 5.7; 12.6 (without parallel); 14.17 diff. Mk 6.38; 14.18; 17.17 diff. Mk 9.19; 20.6 (?; there is no parallel); 22.12 (?; there is no parallel); 24.2 diff. Mk 13.2.

9–10. Having invoked his honour by taking an oath, and being unwilling to lose face before his guests, Antipas obliges the girl and has the Baptist beheaded (without a trial).[43]

καὶ λυπηθεὶς ὁ βασιλεὺς διὰ τοὺς ὅρκους καὶ τοὺς συνανακειμένους ἐκέλευσεν δοθῆναι, καὶ πέμψας ἀπεκεφάλισεν τὸν Ἰωάννην ἐν τῇ φυλακῇ.[44] Mk 6.26f is a bit longer. In addition to abbreviating and turning three sentences into one, Matthew has (i) replaced περίλυπος γενόμενος (Mk 6.26a) with the simpler and less forceful λυπηθείς; (ii) added (for stylistic reasons?) συν- to ἀνακειμένους[45] (cf. 9.10 = Mk 2.15 and esp. Mk 6.22); (iii) substituted the shorter

---

[43] Origen, *Comm. on Mt.* 10.22, finds in Herod's horrible action the edifying lesson that one should on occasion break an oath: the lesser of two evils is preferable.

[44] So NA[26], with τον (omitted by ℵ* B Z *f¹*) in brackets. —HG follows ℵ (L) W Z^vid 0106 0136 Maj lat sy co in printing ελυπηθη ο βασιλευς· δια δε. But NA[26] is to be followed: λυπηθεις ο βασιλευς δια (so B D Θ *f*¹·¹³ 700 1424 *pc*). See Carson, 'Matthew', p. 339.

[45] Because συνανακειμενους is read in Mk 6.26 ℵ A C² (* illeg.) D Θ *f*¹·¹³ Maj latt sy^h, it may also have stood in Matthew's copy of Mark.

ἐκέλευσεν⁴⁶ δοθῆναι (cf. 27.58) for οὐκ ἠθέλησεν ἀθετῆσαι αὐτήν (Mk 6.26b; cf. LXX Ps 14.4) —thus compensating for the omission of most of Mk 6.27a (which refers to the king's orders); (iv) replaced ἀποστείλας (Mk 6.27a) by his favourite πέμψας* and (v) turned αὐτόν (Mk 6.27b) into Ἰωάννην.

According to McNeile, p. 211, although beheading was common in the Greek and Roman worlds (cf. Rev 20.4; Josephus, *Ant.* 14.125), it was not sanctioned by Jewish law and custom—an assertion which, if true, would make John's execution all the more grotesque. But rabbinic sources recognize beheading as a standard mode of execution (e.g. *m. Sanh.* 7.1, 3), and it was employed by OT kings (e.g. 1 Sam 16.9; 2 Kgs 6.30–3). This is not to lessen the horror of being beheaded, nor to deny the importance of John's mode of execution. The Sages in facing martyrdom were concerned not so much with their suffering as with the peculiar form that their deaths assumed. See *Mek.* on Exod 22.23 and A. Büchler, *Studies in Sin and Atonement in the Rabbinic Literature of the First Century*, London, 1928, pp. 189–211. John died a shameful death (cf. *m. Sanh.* 7.3), the death of a criminal, which implied a grievous sin. In this he was like Jesus. Here then is one more parallel between forerunner and Messiah. Furthermore, one wonders whether John's scandalous end might not have served to lessen the scandal of Jesus' death. If even the great John the Baptist was beheaded by the government . . . .

The plural, ὅρκους (which suggests either repeated oaths or the several words of a single oath⁴⁷), is borrowed from Mark even though Matthew himself previously used the singular (14.7). Similarly, Matthew reproduces Mark's 'the king' despite having earlier substituted the correct title, 'tetrarch' (14.1); and the reference to Herod grieving makes sense only in Mark, where Herod hears John gladly; contrast Mt 14.5, where Herod wants to kill John. In section (ii) we called attention to these facts as well as to others and urged that they show Matthew's dependence upon Mark. Here, however, we should like to observe that at least the reference to grief may have been retained for a very good reason. Throughout 14.1–12 the fate of John foreshadows that of Jesus. It is not beside the point, therefore, to recall that in Matthew Pilate is Jesus' *reluctant* executioner, and he finally orders the crucifixion only after pressure is brought to bear upon him; see 27.1–26. So just as Pilate is disinclined to do away with Jesus, so is Herod Antipas disinclined to do away with John.

11. καὶ ἠνέχθη ἡ κεφαλὴ αὐτοῦ ἐπὶ πίνακι καὶ ἐδόθη τῷ

⁴⁶ κελεύω*. On verbs of commanding with passive infinitive see BDF § 392.4.
⁴⁷ Cf. LXX Num 5.21; 2 Macc 4.34; 7.24; 14.32; Josephus, *Ant.* 3.272; 7.294; BDF § 142.

κορασίῳ. Compare 14.8. Matthew has changed the active to the passive (Mk 6.28 has: ἤνεγκεν τὴν κεφαλήν . . . ἔδωκεν αὐτὴν τῷ . . .).

For κοράσιον,[48] the diminutive of the classical κόρη, 'girl', see also 9.24–5 = Mk 5.41–2. According to Hoehner, pp. 154–6, Salome could have been born between A.D. 15 and 19, which would make her between twelve and fourteen years old at the time of the incident recorded. She was in any event not yet married to Philip (who died in A.D. 34; cf. Josephus, *Ant.* 18.106, 136).

καὶ ἤνεγκεν τῇ μητρὶ αὐτῆς. Matthew has condensed Mk 6.28f. and increased the parallelism with the previous clause.

12. καὶ προσελθόντες οἱ μαθηταὶ αὐτοῦ ἦραν τὸ πτῶμα καὶ ἔθαψαν αὐτόν.[49] Compare 9.14 (οἱ μαθηταὶ Ἰωάννου); also Acts 8.2. Matthew has replaced Mark's ἀκούσαντες . . . ἤλθα(ο)ν καί with the more compact προσελθόντες,[50] dropped the superfluous αὐτοῦ[51] after πτῶμα, and let ἐν μνημείῳ fall away at the end. He has also preferred the more precise and descriptive ἔθαψαν (cf. 8.21–2) to ἔθηκαν.

πτῶμα (cf. 24.28, without parallel) is 'corpse'. The word was often used of those who had died violently (cf. LXX Ezek 6.5; Rev 11.8–9; and the rabbinic *pîṭûmā'*). The variant reading, σῶμα,[52] is, according to BAGD, s.v. πτῶμα, 'more dignified'.

καὶ ἐλθόντες ἀπήγγειλαν τῷ Ἰησοῦ. Compare Josephus, *Ant.* 10.62. This redactional conclusion (cf. 8.33; 11.4) artificially creates an inner logic between 14.1–12 and 14.13–21: the execution of John in the former supplies the motive for Jesus' withdrawal in the latter. On the inconcinnity this produces see 1, p. 107.

(iv) *Concluding Observations*

Although it stands out from the rest of the gospel by being a story about someone other than Jesus, the episode of John's imprisonment and martyrdom is not simply an interesting aside, an odd, slack moment in Matthew's narrative. This is because

---

[48] Most of the time in the LXX for *naʿărâ*, a word which, according to BDB, s.v., often refers to women of marriageable age.

[49] HG reads αυτο; so ℵ¹ C D L W Θ 0136 *f*[1.13] Maj lat bo. NA²⁶ prints αυτο[v]. Metzger, p. 36, urges that the external evidence favours αυτο but that 'it is much more likely that copyists would conform the personal pronoun to the impersonal for the sake of grammatical accord with πτῶμα (or σῶμα), than vice versa'.

[50] προσέρχομαι* is often editorial.

[51] Added again by ℵ*.² D L 565 *al* it vg^el sy^s.c.p. Cyr.

[52] W 0106 0136 Maj lat sy^h sa mae bo^mss.

the Baptist is no independent character. He is instead a passenger on the vessel of Jesus' career, an accessory whose words and life are in the service of another.[53] Such was the case in chapters 3 and 11, and so is it here. Mt 14.1–12 is, in fact, a christological parable. On its surface the passage is about John; but its organic connexion with Jesus' story is unmistakable. First of all, by illustrating the fate of a true prophet (martyrdom), John's sad end foretells what is in store for Jesus. Hence the juxtaposition with 13.53–8, where Jesus the prophet is rejected by his own, is hardly accidental. 14.1–12 discloses the true meaning of the previous pericope: the Messiah will surely die. Secondly, 14.1–12 not only sheds light upon what has gone before (13.53–8), it also portends in some detail exactly what is to happen in the passion narrative. The following parallels between John's passion and that of Jesus are to be observed:

John	Jesus
Herod the tetrarch was responsible for John's death	Pilate the governor was responsible for Jesus' death
John was seized (κρατέω, 14.3)	Jesus was seized (κρατέω, 21.46; etc.)
John was bound (δέω, 14.3)	Jesus was bound (δέω, 27.2)
Herod feared the crowds because they held John to be a prophet (14.5)	The chief priests and Pharisees feared the crowds because they held Jesus to be a prophet (21.46)
Herod was asked by another to execute John and grieved so to do (14.6–11)	Pilate was asked by others to execute Jesus and was reluctant so to do (27.11–26)
John was buried by his disciples (14.12)	Jesus was buried by a disciple (27.57–61)

That our evangelist was conscious of these parallels is established by his redactional work in 14.5 (see also on 14.10) as well as by his marked tendency elsewhere to increase the similarities between John and Jesus (see vol. 1, pp. 289–90). Thus, as in chapters 1–2, where the opposition to Jesus at his entry into the world foreshadows the opposition at his departure, so too in 14.1–12 is the end again anticipated: the fate of the forerunner is that of the coming one (cf. 17.12).

---

[53] Cf. Chrysostom, *Hom. on Mt*. 48.2, speaking of the evangelists: 'all their labour entirely was to tell what related to Christ, and they made themselves no secondary work besides this, except it were again to contribute to the same end. Therefore neither now would they have mentioned the history were it not on Christ's account, and because Herod said, "John is risen again".'

(v) *Bibliography*

R. Aus, *Water into Wine and the Beheading of John the Baptist*, Atlanta, 1988.

O. Böcher, 'Johannes der Täufer in der neutestamentlichen Überlieferung', in *Rechtfertigung Realismus Universalismus in Biblischer Sicht*, ed. G. Müller, Darmstadt, 1978, pp. 46–52.

O. L. Cope, 'The Death of John the Baptist in the Gospel of Matthew', *CBQ*, 38 (1976), pp. 515–19.

J. D. M. Derrett, 'Herod's Oath and the Baptist's Head', *BZ* 9 (1965), pp. 49–59, 233–46; reprinted in *Law*, pp. 339–62.

M. Dibelius, *Die urchristliche Überlieferung von Johannes dem Täufer*, Göttingen, 1911.

J. Gnilka, 'Das Martyrium Johannes des Täufers', in Hoffmann, *Orientierung*, pp. 78–92.

Hoehner, pp. 110–71.

F. Manns, 'Marc 6.21–29 à la lumière des dernières fouilles du Machéronte', *SBFLA* 31 (1981), pp. 287–90.

J. P. Meier, 'John the Baptist in Matthew's Gospel', *JBL* 99 (1980), pp. 383–405.

I. de la Potterie, 'Mors Johannis Baptistae', *VD* 44 (1966), pp. 142–51.

R. Riesner, 'Johannes der Täufer auf Machärus', *BK* 39 (1984), p. 176.

W. Schenk, 'Gefangenschaft und Tod des Täufers', *NTS* 29 (1983), pp. 453–83.

R. Schütz, *Johannes der Täufer*, ATANT 50, Zürich, 1967.

W. Trilling, 'Die Täufertradition bei Matthäus', *BZ* 3 (1959), pp. 271–89.

Wink, pp. 27–41.

XXXII

THE FEEDING OF THE FIVE THOUSAND
(14.13–21)

(i) *Structure*

The text has the same structure as 15.29–39. See p. 561.

(ii) *Sources*

Dependence upon Mk 6.30–44 is indicated, this in part because Mt 14.13–21 reads as though it has been displaced from some other context. There is, for example, the awkward link with the previous paragraph (which begins as a flash-back but does not so end; see p. 475), the unlikely repetition of ὀψίας γενομένης in adjacent paragraphs and the striking circumstance that Jesus gets into a boat although the narrative would seem to have him at Nazareth, which is not a coastal village (cf. 13.53–8). When one turns to Mark, however, none of these difficulties is felt; in that gospel they disappear and all is as it should be. The Markan context seems original.

If Mk 6.30–44 is the source for Mt 14.13–21, it follows that Matthew has abbreviated, introduced stylistic changes, and made the narrative more reminiscent of the Lord's Supper (see below). But the minor agreements with Lk 9. 10–17—exceptionally numerous[1]—raise the possibility that the First and Third Evangelists had access to a second source[2] or that Luke knew and used Matthew.[3] Neither possibility can be dogmatically excluded. Nonetheless, as the following shows, all the minor agreements can be readily explained in terms of redactional tendencies (cf. Neirynck (v), Pettem (v)).

Minor agreement	Explanation
ἀν/ὑπεχώρησεν (14.13 = Lk 9.10).	ἀναχωρέω* is a Matthean favourite; and Luke's use of ὑποχωρέω (Mt: 0; Mk: 0; Lk: 2) harks back to Mk 1.45 diff. Lk 5.16, where the word is editorial and used of Jesus retiring for privacy.

[1] Streeter, p. 313: 'The Feeding of the Five Thousand is a section in which there are more minor agreements than in any other of the same length'.
[2] Cf. Cerfaux (v). Marshall, p. 348, refers to the possible 'existence of continuing oral traditions of a familiar story'.
[3] Cf. Gundry, *Commentary*, pp. 291–5.

Minor agreement	Explanation

Minor agreement
οἱ ὄχλοι ἠκολού-
θησαν (14.13 = Lk
9.11).

Explanation
Matthew is fond of ὄχλος + ἀκολουθέω
(Mt: 6; Mk: 1; Lk: 2), and the expression is
redactional in Lk 7.9 (so Jeremias,
Lukasevangelium, p. 155); further, 'since the
subject of εἶδον (Mk. vi. 33) is different from
that of the previous verb ἀπῆλθον, grammar
and sense in Greek, as in English, demand
that the subject of εἶδον be expressed'
(Streeter, p. 314; cf. Taylor, *Mark*, p. 320).[4]

Common omission of
'they were like sheep
without a shepherd'
(Mk 6.34).
Jesus heals the
crowds (14.14 = Lk
9.11).

Matthew has moved this to 9.36; Luke has
omitted all of Mk 6.34a–c for the sake of
abbreviation.

In Mk 6.34 ἐσπλαγχνίσθη is followed by a
notice that Jesus taught. But throughout the
synoptic tradition the verb is more typically
and naturally associated with healings and
miracles (e.g. Mt 9.36; 14.14; 15.32; 20.34; Mk
1.41 v. 1.; 8.2; 9.22; Lk 7.13). No doubt this is
what moved Matthew and Luke to think of
healings. In addition, the similar sentiments in
Matthew and Luke are expressed quite
differently, and it is not irrelevant to record
that Matthew and Luke elsewhere add
generalized statements about Jesus healing
people.

omission of ὅτι
from Mk 6.35
(14.15 = Lk 9.12).

'ὅτι *recitativum* is most common in Mk ...
less in Lk, and still less in Mt' (BDF § 470).

τοὺς ὄχλους/τὸν
ὄχλον for αὐτούς
(14.15 = Lk 9.12).
βρώματα (14.15 =
Lk 9.13).

The clarification is natural and is paralleled
elsewhere (see on 14.15 and cf. 14.19 = Lk
9.16).
This 'is such an obvious word to use in this
context that, seeing that it does not occur in
verses in other respects verbally parallel, it is
of no real significance' (Streeter, p. 315).
Matthew and Luke independently make this
change often.[5]

οἱ δέ for καί in
Mk 6.37 (14.17 = Lk
9.13).
The dialogue in Mk
6.37–8 is similarly
omitted.

Both evangelists may have been less than
pleased with the sarcasm of the disciples
('Shall we go and buy two hundred denarii
worth of bread, and give it to them to eat?').

[4] According to Tagawa (v), p. 126, ἀκολουομθέω in Matthew betrays a
non-Markan source because it is impossible to see how the crowds could follow
Jesus since he went by sea, they by land. But must the verb be given the literal
meaning Tagawa supposes?
[5] *Pace* Gundry, *Commentary*, p. 291, οἱ δέ is hardly dependent upon Matthew
because out of place in Luke.

οὐχ ἔχομεν ὧδε εἰ μὴ πέντε ἄρτους καὶ δύο ἰχθύας/οὐκ εἰσὶν ἡμῖν πλεῖον ἢ πέντε ἄρτοι καὶ ἰχθύες δύο (14.17 = Lk 19.15).	The omission of Mk 6.37d–8d (see above) requires that the narrative resume with a statement about inability, and given the mention of five loaves and two fish in Mk 6.38, the agreement—far from perfect—is not surprising.
τὸ περισσεῦσαν (14.20 = Lk 9.17).	The Markan parallel is admittedly clumsy, and both Matthew and Luke have corrected in the light of Mk 6.8 (cf. Jn 6.12); see Streeter, p. 315.
ὡσεί (14.21 = Lk 9.14).	Compare Mk 8.9; Jn 6.10. Note also that ὡσεί is redactional in Mt 3.16 and 9.36 and often so in Luke (3.23; 9.28; 22.41, 59; 23.44; 24.11).

Our conclusion is that the minor agreements do not require modification of the standard two-source theory.

(iii) *Exegesis*

As it stands in Matthew the story of the feeding of the five thousand is above all about the compassionate Jesus and his supernatural ability to meet the lack of those in physical need. Theissen, *Stories*, pp. 103–6, rightly classifies it as a 'gift miracle' (*Geschenkwundergeschichte*), the chief characteristic of which is the making available of material goods in surprising ways. Examples include 1 Kgs 17.8–16 (Elijah and the jar of meal); 2 Kgs 4.1–7 (Elijah and the vessels of oil); 4.42–4 (Elijah feeds one hundred men); Mk 6.32–44 par.; 8.1–10 par. (the synoptic feeding stories); Lk 5.1–11 (the miraculous draught of fish); Jn 2.1–11 (the wedding at Cana); 21.4–8 (a miracle draught of fish); and *b. Ta'an.* 24b–25a (a bread miracle). Typically such miracles are not initiated by requests but by the spontaneous act of the miracle-worker. Further, the miracle itself is usually left undescribed, its facticity inferred from subsequent circumstances. Also, there is no acclamation or expression of wonder at the end.

If Mt 14.13–21 is a gift miracle which is firstly about the compassionate Christ making physical provisions, there are also important secondary themes. In the order of their significance these are as follows:

(i) 'Since gift miracles do not arise out of any ordinary activity, they are also not transmitted to provide a narrative background to such an activity (as may be presumed to have happened with exorcisms and healings). Since in the case of gift miracles there is no such activity to give them a meaning, deeper meanings are very soon found in them: they are allegorized' (Theissen, *Stories*, p. 106). This is so here. *Pace*

Gnilka, *Matthäusevangelium* 2, pp. 8–9, the feeding of the five thousand was for Matthew, as already for Mark and the pre-Markan tradition,[6] an allegory of the Eucharist. This can be seen from the following parallels:

14.13–21	26.20–9
ὀψίας δὲ γενομένης	ὀψίας δὲ γενομένης
ἀνακλιθῆναι	ἀνέκειτο
λαβών	λαβών
ἄρτους	ἄρτον
εὐλόγησεν	εὐλογήσας
κλάσας	ἔκλασεν
ἔδωκεν τοῖς μαθηταῖς	δοὺς τοῖς μαθηταῖς/ἔδωκεν αὐτοῖς
ἔφαγον	φάγετε
πάντες	πάντες

While these parallels can and have been dismissed as simply due to the common features of Jewish meals, influence from the Eucharist on 14.13–21 is assuredly to be reckoned with. First, the parallels occur in precisely the same order in the two passages. Secondly, the parallels extend beyond typical motifs or themes associated with Jewish meals (e.g. ὀψίας δὲ γενομένης, ἔδωκεν τοῖς μαθηταῖς, πάντες). Thirdly, Matthew has introduced certain changes which increase the parallelism. These include (a) the addition of ὀψίας δὲ γενομένης in 14.15 diff. Mk 6.35 (cf. Mt 26.20), (b) the changing of ἐδίδου (Mk 6.41) to ἔδωκεν (Mt 14.19; cf. 26.27), and (c) the omission of fish from 14.19 = Mk 6.41. It seems to us evident that Matthew intended 14.13–21 to be closely related to the institution of the Eucharist.

(ii) According to A. Schweitzer, pp. 376–80, Jesus intended the feeding to be a proleptic realization of the messianic banquet and in that sense a 'veiled eschatological sacrament'. Whatever one's verdict on the historical issue, it seems safe to suppose that Matthew, like Mark and Luke, understood Jesus' compassionate provision of bread and fish to prefigure the coming eschatological feast. To begin with, the Eucharist itself, with which our story has striking parallels, was thought to be a foretaste of the meal in the kingdom of God.[7] In addition, both bread (or manna) and fish (or Leviathan) are associated with the messianic feast in many Jewish texts (cf. 2 Bar. 29.3–8; 4 Ezra 6.52; and see on 6.11). That our text was susceptible of Schweitzer's interpretation at a very early time is suggested both by Jn 6.1–59, where the feeding of the five thousand is understood by the people as a *messianic* miracle of the prophet like Moses (cf. 6.14) as well as by Mark's reference to green grass (6.39), for this last is seemingly an

[6] And also for John and his tradition; see Brown, *John* 1, pp. 246–9. For Mark's text and the Eucharist see Tagawa, pp. 134–8; he effectively counters the arguments of Booby er (v). For the case that the story originally contained no Eucharistic allusions and that such were added only later see van Iersel (v).

[7] Cf. esp. Mk 14.25 par. The parallel here with the community of the Dead Sea Scrolls is notable; see esp. 1QSa, where the community meal and the eschatological banquet are seen to correspond to one another.

allusion to Ps 23, and that psalm received an eschatological interpretation in the early church.[8]

(iii) Tertullian, *Adv. Marc.* 4.21, and most commentators after him have observed the parallels between the gospel miracle and the story in 2 Kgs 4.42–4: 'A man came from Baalshalishah, bringing the man of God bread of the first fruits, twenty loaves of barley and fresh ears of grain in his sack. And Elisha said, "Give to the men, that they may eat." But his servant said, "How am I to set this before a hundred men?" So he repeated, "Give them to the men, that they may eat, for thus says the Lord, 'They shall eat and have some left'"'. So he set it before them. And they ate, and had some left, according to the word of the Lord.' This story is so close to the synoptic accounts of the feeding of the five thousand, especially Mark's version, that it has even been taken to be its inspiration. However that may be, there is no denying the similarities.

Elisha takes (barley) bread and ears of grain	Jesus takes bread and fish
Elisha commands, 'Give to the men, that they may eat'	Jesus commands: 'Give to them something to eat'
The people eat and food is left over	The people eat and food is left over

Given Matthew's knowledge of the OT, he can hardly have been oblivious of the correlations between 2 Kgs 4.42–4 and Mt 14.13–21. Moreover, given that in the broader context of the First Gospel (13.53–14.12) Jesus is interpreted in the category of prophet, Matthew may well have understood 14.13–21 to depict Jesus as the eschatological prophet.[9]

(iv) Readiness to see in Mt 14.13–21 a new Moses motif is natural. In Jn 6.25ff. the same event is represented as the counterpart of and antithesis to the gift of manna under Moses, and we might expect Matthew to reveal the same awareness of the theme, especially in the light of the typology in chapters 1–5 (see on 5.1) and the Mosaic motifs in such key texts as 11.25–30 and 17.1–8: 'as the first redeemer, so the last'. There are the further facts that (a) patristic interpreters of the synoptic account frequently direct attention to the parallel with Moses and the manna (e.g. Cyril of Alexandria, *Comm. on Lk.* 48, citing Ps 78.24); (b) *Sipre* on Num 11.22 records the tradition that the wandering Israelites ate fish in their desert wanderings (cf. Wisd 19.12); and (c) Mt 14.13–21 anticipates the messianic banquet, and in the Jewish texts in which manna or bread is the food for this last a new exodus theme is undeniable. Nonetheless, with the possible exception of his work in v. 21 (q.v.), Matthew reveals no accentuation of an exodus motif in this passage.[10] First, he speaks not of 'the desert' but only of a 'lonely place'. There is no concern to make manifest any parallelism with the

[8] D. C. Allison, 'Psalm 23 in Early Christianity: A Suggestion', *IBS* 5 (1983), pp. 132–7.

[9] For the gospel texts which have parallels in the Elisha cycle see the suggestive article of R. E. Brown, 'Jesus and Elisha', *Perspective* 12 (1971), pp. 85–99.

[10] Cf. Davies, *SSM*, pp. 48–9. The same is true of Mark; see Tagawa (v), pp. 148–50; contrast Stegner (v).

wilderness of the exodus. Next, whereas in the synoptics care is taken to gather all the leftovers after the eating, in the OT strict injunctions are given that the manna not be hoarded. Thirdly, by rejecting Mk 6.34, with its echo of Num 27.17, the evangelist has rejected an element which might be taken to point to a new Moses (on Moses as a shepherd see on 9.36). Finally, although the five fish have sometimes been taken to represent the five books of Moses and the twelve baskets the twelve tribes of Israel, it is hardly necessary to accept these symbolic interpretations. In conclusion, we remain uncertain whether Mt 14.13–21 reflects an interest in Mosaic motifs. (As explanation for this surprising result does it suffice to remark that clearer allusions to the exodus would have detracted from the parallels to the Eucharist, and that it is these last which Matthew wishes to accentuate?)

Matthew's revisions of Mk 6.30–44 include the following. (i) The text has been abbreviated. The result is a story with fewer details (e.g. the notice about groups of fifties and hundreds finds no place in the First Gospel). (ii) The return of the disciples from their missionary endeavours (Mk 6.30) has been eliminated. It would not fit the Matthean context. (iii) The activities of the disciples have been accentuated (see on v. 19); and their fault is no longer incomprehension but deficiency of faith (see on v. 17). (iv) Jesus now heals the crowd instead of teaching them (cf. p. 487). (v) Some OT allusions have been weakened or eliminated (see on vv. 17 and 19). (vi) A question of the disciples (Mk 6.37) and one of Jesus (Mk 6.38) have been dropped. (vii) The possible links to the institution of the Eucharist have perhaps been strengthened (cf. pp. 480–81). (viii) The parallels with the second feeding story (in 15.32–9) have been enhanced. (ix) The shepherd motif (Mk 6.34) has been moved to 9.36 (x) There is no longer any mention of fish in vv. 19–20 = Mk 6.41, 43. (xi) There may be an allusion to the exodus in Matthew's reworked conclusion (see on v. 21). (xii) In many ways the new account bears the imprints of Matthew's style (e.g. ἀνεχώρησεν ἐκεῖθεν, the parallelism of v. 13, ὀψίας δὲ γενομένης).

The origin of the story of the feeding of the five thousand has been a matter for much conjecture. The following proposals have been put forward:

(1) H. E. G. Paulus, in his *Das Leben Jesu* (1828), offered that Jesus, upon seeing the multitudes without food, distributed his own provisions and those of his disciples as an example to others who in turn did likewise, so there was enough for all.[11] Paulus even argued that the evangelists saw nothing miraculous in their feeding narratives.

(2) A second rationalizing interpretation was defended by E. Renan in his very popular *Vie de Jésus* (1863): Jesus retreated to a deserted area with a large company and, by the exercise of extreme frugality, found it possible to live there; and in this circumstance later piety discovered a miracle. (For Renan, 'no evidence in favour of a miracle which an historian could accept as conclusive has ever been produced'; S. Neil, *The Interpretation of the New Testament 1861–1961*, Oxford, 1964, p. 193, n. 3. This was his starting point for understanding all of the miracle stories about Jesus.)

---

[11] Despite incisive criticism by Strauss (v), this notion still has defenders—e.g. A. Nolan, *Jesus before Christianity*, London, 1977, pp. 51–2.

(3) Yet a third way of explaining away the miracle has been to postulate that it is only the inflated number—five thousand—which renders the story incredible (cf. Taylor, *Mark*, p. 321, citing Wellhausen). It was not Jesus who multiplied bread but the tradition which multiplied numbers.

(4) From time to time a scholar has conjectured that some figurative discourse of Jesus on bread was later misunderstood as historical narrative. Most significant and initiatory of this was David Friedrich Strauss, who wrote: 'If, in figurative discourses, Jesus had sometimes represented himself as him who was able to give the true bread of life to the wandering and hungering people, perhaps also placing in opposition to this, the leaven of the Pharisees: the legend, agreeably to its realistic tendency, may have converted this into the fact of a miraculous feeding of the hungry multitude in the wilderness by Jesus' (Strauss, p. 516). (Strauss' treatment of the feeding of the five thousand is typical of the 'mythical' interpretation he gave to the early Christian tradition. See Neil, *op. cit.*, pp. 12–19, for a critique.)

(5) Given the extensive parallels between the synoptic record and 2 Kgs 4.24–4 (see above), it is possible to regard the feeding of the multitude as a legend inspired by the OT.[12]

(6) A. Schweitzer, accepting the hypothesis that Jesus in fact distributed very small pieces among a crowd of people, went on to interpret this action in terms of Jewish eschatological expectation: 'The significance lies in the giving of thanks and in the fact that they had received from Him consecrated food. Because He is the future Messiah, this meal becomes without their knowledge the Messianic feast. With the morsel of bread which He gives His disciples to distribute to the people He consecrates them as partakers in the coming Messianic feast, and gives them the guarantee that they, who had shared His table in the time of His obscurity, would also share it in the time of His glory' (Schweitzer, p. 376).

(7) R. Eisler, in *ΙΗΣΟΥΣ ΒΑΣΙΛΕΥΣ ΟΥ ΒΑΣΙΛΕΥΣΑΣ*, Heidelberg, 1929–30, submitted that Jesus led people into the wilderness in order to repeat the miracle of the manna and incite a political revolt reminiscent of the exodus from Egypt.

In our estimation, the feeding of the five thousand probably rests upon an important episode of the pre-Easter period. Certainly no other gospel miracle has the attestation this one does—Mk 6.32–44 par.; Mk 8.1–9 par.;[13] Jn 6.1–13.[14] Admittedly, the several versions of the one event raise more questions than they answer and do not resolve the critical problem of what induced the conviction that food had been miraculously provided.[15] But we can reasonably hold that behind the

[12] Cf. M. S. Enslin, *The Prophet from Nazareth*, New York, 1961, pp. 155–6; Pesch 1, pp. 355–6.

[13] On this see the commentary on Mt 15.32–9. Knackstedt (v), however, argues for two different events in the life of Jesus.

[14] On the independence of this from the synoptics see Brown, *John* 1, pp. 236–50, also Dodd (v); Johnston (v); Barnett (v).

[15] For what it is worth, miracles of multiplication are not uncommon in the Bible; see e.g. Exod 16; 1 Kgs 17.8–16; 2 Kgs 4.1–7, 42–4; Jn 2.1–11. For other parallels see Liv. Proph. Ezek. 10; T. Zeb. 6.6; *b. Ta'an.* 24b–25a; *b. Yoma* 39a;

different acounts lies a meal shared by a large gathering in a deserted place which Jesus and possibly others interpreted as symbolic— probably along the lines suggested by Schweitzer. It is also likely that Jn 6 preserves important clues as to what went on, Jn 6.14–15 being especially crucial in this regard: 'When the people saw the sign which he had done, they said, "This is indeed the prophet who is to come into the world!" Perceiving then that they were about to come and take him by force to make him king, Jesus withdrew again to the mountain by himself'. E. Bammel (v) may well be correct in surmising that the event in the wilderness should be viewed as the occasion when Jesus made a definite and public break with popular messianism (cf. Manson, *Servant-Messiah*, pp. 70–1; also Dodd, *Founder*, pp. 139–42).

It is impossible to reconstruct the pre-Markan form of either Mk 6.32–44 or 8.1–9, and the primitive narrative beneath both also escapes anything more than general reconstruction. One presumes, however, that the story was first told in the Palestinian church,[16] and also that the narrative has been much shaped by 2 Kgs 4.24–4 and the tradition of the Eucharist.

13. ἀκούσας δὲ ὁ Ἰησοῦς. This redactional phrase[17] replaces the much lengthier Mk 6.30f. ('The apostles returned to Jesus, and told him all that they had done and taught. And he said to them, 'Come away by yourselves to a lonely place and rest a while.' For many were coming and going, and they had no leisure even to eat'). Because Matthew has narrated the sending of the twelve in chapter 10, and because so much has transpired since then, it is impossible for him to make the twelve's return coincide with the withdrawal of 14.13. Note also that because the motive for withdrawal has become John's execution, the reader no longer thinks of Jesus and his disciples as seeking rest in a spiritual corner: they rather are going into hiding (cf. 10.23).

ἀνεχώρησεν ἐκεῖθεν ἐν πλοίῳ εἰς ἔρημον τόπον κατ' ἰδίαν. Compare 2 Macc 5.27; Josephus, *Ant.* 8.348 (of Elijah). As

---

PGM 1.103–4. Christian saints (e.g. Seraphim of Sarov and John Bosco) have sometimes been reported to have miraculously produced food. For a strange, modern report on the supposed replication of food through psychic means see P. S. Haley, *Modern Loaves and Fishes—and Other Studies in Psychic Phenomena*, rev. ed., privately printed, 1960. Further parallels in Bultmann, *History*, p. 236; also E. Haraldsson, *Modern Miracles: An Investigative Report on Psychic Phenomena associated with Sathya Sai Baba*, New York, 1987, pp. 108, 117–18, 136–7, 220–2, 234–5.

[16] Gnilka, *Markus* 1, p. 258, calls attention to the OT background, to Jesus' rôle as Jewish host, and to the Semitisms in Mk 6.32–44. It is also significant that the allusions to 2 Kgs 4.42–4 do not appear to depend upon the LXX. — — Fowler's proposal (v), that Mk 6.30–44 is a redactional doublet of the tradition preserved in Mk 8.1–10, is unconvincing.

[17] ἀκούσας δέ: Mt: 6; Mk: 1; Lk: 5; followed by ἀνεχώρησεν: Mt: 3; Mk: 0; Lk: 0. Compare esp. Mt 4.12, which is the model for the present verse.

compared with Mk 6.32, Matthew has (i) replaced the plural ἀπῆλθον with the singular ἀνεχώρησεν[18] (cf. 4.12; Luke has the singular ὑπεχώρησεν); (ii) added the frequently redactional ἐκεῖθεν* (cf. 12.15; 15.21, both with ἀναχωρέω*; here the adverb most naturally refers to Nazareth, even though it was not on the shore); (iii) dropped the article before πλοίῳ (cf. 9.1; 13.2) and tacked on ἐν (cf. 4.21; 14.33); and (iv) reversed the order of 'to a lonely place' and 'in a boat' (which increases the parallelism with the next clause, where 'by land' precedes the geographical note, 'from the cities').[19]

On ἔρημος see on 3.1. The word is often linked with τόπος as in 14.15 = Mk 6.35; Rev 12.14; and Par. Jer. 8.11. Here ἔρημος is used adjectivally (cf. Mk 1.35) and one may translate the two together as 'a desolate' or 'lonely place' (cf. BAGD, s.v.). The traditional identification of eṭ-Ṭâbghah on the northwestern shore of the Sea of Galilee as the site of Jesus' miracle just might be correct. On the area and the archaeology of its churches see Pixner (v). But Luke's account (9.10) would seem to imply a location on the northeast shore of the lake, near Bethsaida—an area outside the jurisdiction of Herod Antipas. For other possibilities see Taylor, Mark, p. 319.

κατ' ἰδίαν, a fixed expression (= classical καθ' ἑαυτόν) which appears often in the synoptics,[20] means 'privately'. It is quite appropriate here. For with the death of John the curtain has begun to fall down upon Jesus too, so he must turn his immediate attention towards his disciples, towards those who will carry on after he is gone (cf. Soares Prabhu, pp. 126–8).

καὶ ἀκούσαντες οἱ ὄχλοι ἠκολούθησαν αὐτῷ πεζῇ ἀπὸ τῶν πόλεων. Compare Lk 9.11; Jn 6.2. Although the last four words are from Mk 6.33 ('Now many saw them going, and knew them, and they ran there on foot from all the towns, and got there ahead of them'), the first six are editorial. The changes can be ascribed to a desire to assimilate to vv. 13a–b. Both vv. 13a–b and 13c have basically the same structure: ἀκούσας/ἀκούσαντες + subject (Jesus, the crowds) + aorist verb ('he withdrew', 'they followed') + adverbial phrase of locomotion ('by boat', 'by land') + geographical notice ('to a desert place', 'from the cities').

---

[18] Gundry, Commentary, p. 290, infers from this word that Jesus had gone in the boat alone, and that the disciples followed by land as part of the crowd. Does Matthew's text really lend itself to this sort of literalism?

[19] We have followed the HG text for Mark. The reading printed by NA[26]— απηλθεν εν τω πλοιω εἰς ερημον τοπον—is probably the result of assimilation to Matthew.

[20] Mt 14.23; 17.1, 19; 20.17; 24.3; Mk 4.34; 6.31–2; 7.33; 9.2, 28; 13.3; Lk 9.10; 10.23. It is also found in the LXX, Hellenistic Greek, Philo, Josephus, and Paul; see LSJ, s.v., ἴδιος, VI.3; BAGD, s.v., 4; Schlatter, p. 463.

πεζῇ, which stands in contrast with ἐν τῷ πλοίῳ, means 'by foot' or, more generally, 'by land' (cf. 2 Βασ 15.17; Josephus, *Bell.* 4.659). Compare the meaning of πεζεύω, as in Acts 20.13. ἀπὸ τῶν πόλεων means 'from the towns (in the area)'. On the inexact use of πόλις (= 'village' as well as 'city') see on 2.23.

14. καὶ ἐξελθὼν εἶδεν πολὺν ὄχλον καὶ ἐσπλαγχνίσθη ἐπ' αὐτοῖς. So Mk 6.34, with 'because they were like sheep without a shepherd' at the end (also missing from Luke). The Markan clause, which gives the reason for Jesus' compassion,[21] is struck because it has already been used in 9.36 (q.v. for σπλαγχνίζομαι).

καὶ ἐθεράπευσεν τοὺς ἀρρώστους αὐτῶν. Compare Mk 6.13; also Jn 6.2. This replaces Mk 6.34c: 'And he began to teach them much'. For the reason see p. 479, on the minor agreement with Lk 9.11.

θεραπεύω is often redactional (cf. 4.23–4; 9.35; etc.). ἄρρωστος, on the other hand, is a Matthean *hapax legomenon*; but it does appear in Mk 6.5 and 13.[22] The word means 'powerless', then 'ill'.

15. In the evening Jesus' disciples, little knowing what is soon to happen, ask the master to dismiss the crowd. Their request is rooted in common sense and perhaps even compassion;[23] it is not a sign of lack of faith. It in any case makes the need of the entire crowd—and not just the sick[24]—known to the reader: they have no food. Compare the similar notices in the gift miracles in 1 Kgs 17.12; 2 Kgs 4.2; Jn 2.3; and *b. Taʿan.* 24b–25a.

ὀψίας δὲ γενομένης. Compare 8.16; 14.23; 20.8; 26.20 (part of the setting for the last supper); 27.57. The phrase (Mt: 6; Mk: 1; Lk: 0) replaces the uncommon καὶ ἤδη ὥρας πολλῆς γενομένης of Mk 6.35. πολύς of time (cf. 25.19) is again dropped in 14.15d = Mk 6.35d.

προσῆλθον αὐτῷ οἱ μαθηταὶ λέγοντες.[25] This phrase is

---

[21] The reference to sheep without a shepherd recalls certain scriptural texts, including Ezek 34.5–6; see on 9.36. For the doubtful suggestion that Ezek 34 is of fundamental importance for the feeding story see Bammel (v).

[22] Cf. also LXX Ecclus 7.35; Mal 1.8; 1 Cor 11.30; Josephus, *Bell.* 5.526. For the spelling see BDF § 11.1. ἀρρωστέω appears in Mt 14.14 D. For further discussion and references see Horsley 3, p. 63.

[23] Cyril of Alexandria, *Comm. on Lk.* 48: 'not so speaking as though they were themselves at all annoyed, and considered that the proper time had gone by; but seized with love towards the multitudes, and beginning to have a concern for the people, as being already intent upon their pastoral office . . .'.

[24] Cf. Chrysostom, *Hom. on Mt.* 49.2: 'Thus, since the sick were constantly the subject of His miracles, He works also a general benefit, that the many might not be spectators only of what befell others, but themselves also partakers of the gift'.

[25] So NA[26]. HG prints προσηλθαν. C D L W Θ 0106[vid] *f*[1.13] Maj lat sy add αυτου after μαθηται, and this could be pristine; see J. K. Elliott, 'Textual Criticism, Assimilation and the Synoptic Gospels', *NTS* 26 (1980), pp. 236–7.

editorial in 13.36 (q.v.). Mk 6.35b opens with προσελθόντες and follows μαθηταί with αὐτοῦ ἔλεγον ὅτι. On the omission of ὅτι see Allen, p. xx. He observes that Matthew deletes forty-two Markan occurrences of the word.

ἔρημός ἐστιν ὁ τόπος καὶ ἡ ὥρα ἤδη παρῆλθεν. Compare 14.13. After καί Mk 6.35 has ἤδη ὥρα πολλή; for the rest there is agreement. For παρέρχομαι of time see BAGD, s.v., 1.β. Here, with ὥρα, the meaning is: 'the hour (of the evening meal) has passed'.

ἀπόλυσον τοὺς ὄχλους.²⁶ Compare 15.39, where ἀπολύσας τοὺς ὄχλους is redactional. In Mk 6.36 αὐτούς is the object. Lk 9.12 has ἀπόλυσον τὸν ὄχλον. Both Matthew and Luke have assimilated to 14.13 = Lk 9.11. For ἀπολύω meaning 'dismiss' see Mk 6.45; 8.3, 9–10.

ἵνα ἀπελθόντες εἰς τὰς κώμας ἀγοράσωσιν ἑαυτοῖς βρώματα. Matthew has omitted τοὺς κύκλῳ ἀγροὺς καί from Mk 6.36 and changed τί φάγωσιν to βρώματα, which is grammatically smoother. ἀγρός is also omitted in 8.33 = Mk 5.14 and 14.35 = Mk 6.56; and Mark's κύκλῳ (Mk 3.34; 6.6, 36) is never taken over by the First Evangelist.

16. ὁ δὲ Ἰησοῦς εἶπεν αὐτοῖς. So Mk 6.37a, with ἀποκριθείς instead of Ἰησοῦς.

οὐ χρείαν ἔχουσιν ἀπελθεῖν. This is a redactional addition without parallel in the other accounts. ἔχω + χρεία (cf. ḥāšaḥ) is also editorial in 3.14 and 6.8. The combination prefaced by οὐ was a fixed expression (cf. Mt 9.12; also LXX Prov 18.2; Ecclus 3.22; Jn 2.25; 1 Thess 4.9; 1 Jn 2.27).

δότε αὐτοῖς ὑμεῖς φαγεῖν. So Mk 6.37 and Lk 9.13; compare Jn 6.5. The pronoun is clearly emphatic, and the sentence is obviousy modelled upon the command of Elisha in 2 Kgs 4.42 and 43: 'Give to the people that they may eat'. It is striking that the allusion does not show assimilation to the LXX (which has: δότε τῷ λαῷ καὶ ἐσθιέτωσαν; the MT reads: tēn lāʿām wĕyōʾkēlû). But the reader who catches the allusion will be prepared for what follows.

17. οἱ δὲ λέγουσιν αὐτῷ. Matthew has substituted δέ for Mark's καί, as often (cf. Lk 9.13).

οὐχ ἔχομεν ὧδε εἰ μὴ πέντε ἄρτους καὶ δύο ἰχθύας. Compare Jn 6.9; also 1 Kgs 17.12 ('I have nothing baked, only a handful of meal in a jar, and a little oil in a cruse'); 2 Kgs 4.2 ('Your maidservant has nothing in the house, except a jar of oil'); 4.42 ('twenty loaves of barley and fresh ears of grain'). On οὐκ . . . εἰ

²⁶ ℵ C Z f¹ 892 1241 pc syʰᵐᵍ saᵐˢˢ bo add ουν, which might be original (so Gundry, *Commentary*, p. 292).

μή (a Semitism) see on 13.57 and Schlatter, p. 464. On ὧδε see on 14.8. ἔχομεν (cf. Lk 9.13) was suggested by the ἔχουσιν of 14.16. Mk 6.37–8 has this: '"Shall we go and buy two hundred denarii worth of bread, and give it to them to eat?" And he said to them, "How many loaves have you? Go and see." And when they had found out, they said, "Five, and two fish."' Matthew, who is more circumspect about the disciples' honour, and who tends to drop questions by Jesus, has seen fit to abbreviate (cf. Lk 9.13). In doing so, he has weakened the allusion to 2 Kgs 4.42f., where, as in Mark, an impossible command is followed by a sarcastic rejoinder: 'How am I to set this before a hundred men?' (cf. also Num 11.13, 21–2). Another result of Matthew's surgery on Mark is that, whereas in the Second Gospel the disciples initially fail to understand what Jesus has in mind— which is why they ask about buying bread—, in Matthew's gospel they do understand—which is why they count the loaves and fish. Thus their deficiency is no longer in comprehension but in faith (cf. Held (v), p. 183; contrast Carson, 'Matthew', p. 341).

Bread and fish were the staples of the majority of Galileans (cf. 7.9– 10; Jn 21.9–10, 13; SB 1, pp. 683–4; *RAC* 2, pp. 611–12; 7, pp. 1014– 15). In John's gospel the word for fish is not ἰχθύς but ὀψάριον (6.9; cf. 21.9), a word which by the first-century had come to be used exclusively of fish, especially dried or preserved fish, the standard condiment for bread. It is doubtful whether one should interpret the fish as a spiritual food[27] or associate it with Num 11.22 ('Shall all the fish of the sea be gathered together for them, to suffice them?') or 11.31 ('quail *from the sea*'; cf. Wisd 19.12); but a connexion with the messianic banquet is possible (see p. 481). Also, while bread may have been a standing symbol for the Torah (see n. 29), we fail to see the relevance of this for our text.

The Fourth Gospel differs from the synoptics in having 'barley loaves' (ἄρτους κριθίνους), bread for the poor.[28] Compare 4. Βασ 4.42, where the man from Baalshalishah brings Elisha twenty loaves of barley (ἄρτους κριθίνους).

The numbers 'five' and 'two' have often been given symbolic import. The most common interpretation has it that the five loaves stand for the five books of Moses,[29] the two fish for the psalms and the prophets

---

[27] Bread and fish together are symbols of the Eucharist from a very early time, appearing as such in the catacombs and on frescos. See F. J. Dölger, ΙΧΘΥΣ, 5 vols., Münster, 1910, 1922–40; also R. H. Hiers and C. A. Kennedy, 'The Bread and Fish Eucharist in the Gospels and Early Christian Art', *PRS* 3 (1976), pp. 20–47. But the symbolism is probably due to the feeding stories.

[28] Chrysostom, *Hom. on Mt.* 49.1: the barley bread teaches 'us to trample under foot the pride of costly living'.

[29] For the Torah as bread see Prov 9.5 and SB 2, pp. 483–4.

or the apostles and the gospel (= the NT); see Quesnell (v). Matthew's text, however, does nothing, as far as we can determine, to foster such an approach.

18. ὁ δὲ εἶπεν· φέρετέ μοι ὧδε αὐτούς. There is no parallel in Mark or Luke. Compare 17.17 diff. Mk 9.19: φέρετέ μοι αὐτὸν ὧδε. The remark adds to Jesus' authority.

19. After directing the crowd to sit down, Jesus, acting like the host at a regular Jewish meal, takes the bread and fish, looks up to heaven, offers a blessing, and distributes the food to his disciples who in turn distribute it to the crowd.

καὶ κελεύσας τοὺς ὄχλους ἀνακλιθῆναι ἐπὶ τοῦ χόρτου. Compare Jn 6.10. This is the parallel to Mk 6.39–40: 'And he commanded them, that all should sit down by companies upon the green grass. So they sat down in groups by hundreds and by fifties'. Matthew has (i) abbreviated; (ii) made Jesus the one who instructs the crowd directly (cf. Gundry, *Commentary*, pp. 293–4); (iii) dropped ἐπέταξεν (ἐπιτάσσω: Mt: 0; Mk: 4; Lk: 4) in favour of κελεύσας (κελεύω*); (iv) replaced αὐτοῖς with τοὺς ὄχλους (cf. 14.15 diff. Mk 6.36); (v) turned the active infinitive (ἀνακλῖναι) into the passive (ἀνακλιθῆναι); (vi) removed the apparent allusion to Ps 23.2 ('he makes me lie down in green pastures'); (vii) changed the case after ἐπί (cf. Allen, p. xxviii); and (viii) neglected to refer to the symmetrical arrangement of the groups.[30]

λαβὼν τοὺς πέντε ἄρτους καὶ τοὺς δύο ἰχθύας, ἀναβλέψας εἰς τὸν οὐρανὸν εὐλόγησεν. Compare 1 Esdr 4.58 (ἄρας τὸ πρόσωπον εἰς τὸν οὐρανὸν ἐναντίον Ἰερουσαλημ εὐλόγησεν τῷ βασιλεῖ τοῦ οὐρανοῦ); also Jn 6.5, 11. Mk 6.41 has introductory καί and (perhaps) ηὐλόγησεν at the end.[31] The key parallel is 26.26: 'With them eating Jesus took bread, and blessed . . .' (cf. Acts 27.35). See further pp. 480–81.

For looking to heaven while praying—something relatively rare in Jewish texts (cf. SB 2, pp. 246–7)—see Ps 123.1; Philo, *Vit. Cont.* 66;[32] Josephus, *Ant.* 11.162; Mk 7.34; Lk 18.13; Jn 11.41; 17.1; *b. Yeb.* 105b (cf. Job 22.26). It is an outward sign of an inward dependence (cf. Pseudo-Hecataeus in Clement of Alexandria, *Strom.* 5.14).[33]

εὐλογέω used absolutely (cf. *bērak/bārî(ê)k*) is a Semitism

---

[30] Note that in 1QSa those taking part in the messianic celebration are arranged in camps (cf. Exod 18.25; Num 31.14).

[31] So HG. NA[26] prints ευλ. for Mk 6.41.

[32] The Therapeutae, according to Philo, 'take their stand in a regular line in an orderly way, their eyes and hands lifted up to Heaven, eyes because they have been trained to fix their gaze on things worthly of contemplation . . .'.

[33] The Roman Catholic practice of the priest looking up before the act of consecration supposedly comes from our text and its parallels.

meaning 'utter the blessing', 'bless (God)', 'give thanks (to God)'.³⁴ Matthew is not likely to have thought of the food itself as being blessed—although he may have understood the blessing to be the means of multiplication (so Origen, *Comm. on Mt.* 11.2). Did Matthew assume that Jesus uttered the traditional Jewish blessing: 'Blessed art Thou, O Lord our God, King of the world, who bringest forth bread from the earth' (*m. Ber.* 6.1)?

καὶ κλάσας ἔδωκεν τοῖς μαθηταῖς τοὺς ἄρτους. Compare 26.26: ἔκλασεν καὶ δοὺς τοῖς μαθηταῖς. Matthew has shortened Mk 6.41c–d (καὶ κατέκλασεν τοὺς ἄρτους καὶ ἐδίδου τοῖς μαθηταῖς αὐτοῦ) by (i) replacing two independent clauses connected by parataxis with a single clause consisting of participle + main verb (substituting an aorist for the imperfect; cf. Allen, p. xx); (ii) using the weaker simplex instead of κατακλάω (thus increasing the parallelism with the institution of the Eucharist; cf. also 15.36); and (iii) dropping the (unnecessary) personal pronoun.

οἱ δὲ μαθηταὶ τοῖς ὄχλοις. This replaces Mk 6.41e–f: 'in order to set before the people; and he divided the two fish among them all'. Compare the differences between 15.36 and Mk 8.6–7. Has Matthew made the disciples intermediaries in order to highlight the correspondence between the course of events and Jesus' command in 14.16 ('You give them something to eat')? Or did the author want us to think of the disciples as representatives of church leaders, through whose hands the Eucharist is given? See further on 15.36.

20. Matthew informs us that all ate and were satisfied; and then, as in many gift miracles, there is a remark on the overabundance of leftovers (cf. 1 Kgs 17.16; 2 Kgs 4.6–7, 44; 8.8–9; Lk 5.6–7; Jn 21.6, 11; *b. Ta'an.* 24b).

καὶ ἔφαγον πάντες καὶ ἐχορτάσθησαν. Compare Jn 6.11–12. This statement, which offers proof of the miracle, reproduces Mk 6.42 without alteration. χορτάζω in the fourth beatitude (5.6) is used in connexion with the hungry who will be satisfied in the eschatological kingdom. If one may link that verse to this, the satisfaction of the multitude may be thought of as foreshadowing the satisfaction of the messianic banquet (cf. Dodd, *Tradition*, p. 204, n. 2).

καὶ ἦραν τὸ περισσεῦον τῶν κλασμάτων. Compare Jn 6.12.

---

³⁴ Cf. 26.26; Lk 24.30; 1 Cor 14.16. In Mt 15.36 par. the verb used is εὐχαριστέω. Observe also the equation of εὐλογέω and εὐχαριστέω in Mk 8.6–7 and Mk 14.22 = Lk 22.19 = 1 Cor 11.24. In John's account of the feeding of the five thousand εὐχαριστέω is used (Jn 6.11). For further discussion see Jeremias, *Eucharistic Words*, p. 175.

The subject is probably the twelve, not the crowds. As in 15.37 diff. Mk 8.8, our evangelist has added τὸ περισσεῦον (so also Lk 9.17; cf. Jn 6.12) and the definite article before κλασμάτων.

κλάσμα means 'piece', 'fragment'. The word is used with ἄρτος in LXX Ezek 13.19 (κλασμάτων ἄρτου), and in Did. 9.3–4 it is used of the pieces of bread at the Lord's Supper (cf. Ps.-Athanasius in PG 28.529C).[35]

δώδεκα κοφίνους πλήρεις. Compare LXX Judg 6.38; Jn 6.13. Mk 6.43 ('twelve baskets full of the broken pieces and of fish') is longer. As in 14.19 = Mk 6.41, Matthew has dropped the mention of fish, perhaps because fish are not present in 26.26–9, the account of the Last Supper.

κόφινος (LXX: Judg 6.19 (for *sal*); Ps 80.7 (for *dûd*); cf. Latin *cophinus*, Hebrew *qûpā'*) is a 'basket', the usual LXX word for which is the Attic κανοῦν (always for *sal*, a cane basket). Juvenal, *Sat.* 3.14 and 6.542, writes of Jewish travellers with their κόφινοι. In the NT κόφινος occurs seven times, all but one (Lk 13.8 v. 1.) in connexion with the feeding of the five thousand. Interestingly enough, σπ(φ)υρίς is the word employed in the accounts of the feeding of the four thousand (see on 15.37; cf. 16.10). The distinction between the two words—maintained in 16.9–10 par.—is unclear. Was one basket larger than the other?[36] For bread in baskets see Exod 29.32; Num 6.15; 11QTemple 15.3; *b. Yoma.* 67a. That the baskets in our story belong to the disciples is left unsaid.

Our story does not, as might be expected, conclude by observing that the crowds marvelled (contrast Jn 6.14–15). Maybe the reader is to suppose that the people were ignorant of what had taken place. Maybe the epiphany was made known only to the disciples (so Held (v), p. 182; cf. Lohmeyer, *Markus*, p. 129).

Those who find symbolic significance in the numbers of 14.13–21 par. generally understand the twelve baskets to stand for the twelve apostles or the twelve tribes of Israel (cf. Origen, *Comm. on Mt.* 11.3 and see further Quesnell (v), pp. 229, n. 56, and 270–4).

21. οἱ δὲ ἐσθίοντες ἦσαν ἄνδρες ὡσεὶ πεντακισχίλιοι.[37] Compare Mk 6.44: καὶ ἦσαν οἱ φαγόντες τοὺς ἄρτους πεντακισχίλιοι ἄνδρες. Matthew has replaced καί with δέ as often elsewhere and slightly abbreviated. He has also moved forward the ὡς of Mk 8.9 (in the next feeding story) and turned it into ὡσεί (cf. the changes in 3.16 and 9.36).

[35] The related κλάσις was also used of the Eucharist; see e.g. the Acts of Paul and Thecla 5.

[36] In Acts 9.25 Paul is carried in a σπυρίς (contrast 2 Cor 11.33). For further discussion see F. J. A. Hort, 'A Note on the Words κόφινος, σπυρίς, σαργάνη,' *JTS* 10 (1909), pp. 567–71.

[37] ωσει is omitted in W 0106 *pc* lat sy[s.c.p] bo. ως is found in D Δ Θ 067 *f*¹ 33 700* *pc*. Cf. the variants for Mt 15.38. Perhaps there was no particle in the autograph.

χωρὶς γυναικῶν καὶ παιδίων. Compare LXX Num 17.14; Judg 20.15, 17. This editorial addition is also appended in 15.38. It may be just an interpretation of Mark which emphatically underlines the crowd's vastness. (χωρὶς κ.τ.λ. does not mean 'without women and children', as though the crowd were all male (cf. 2 Kgs 4.42–4), but 'besides woman and children'; cf. Origen, Comm. on Mt. 11.3; contrast Jerome, ad loc.).

But perhaps there is more. In Exod 12.37 one reads that the number of souls in the wilderness was 'six hundred thousand men on foot, lĕbad-miṭṭāp'. While the LXX translates the last two words πλὴν τῆς ἀποσκευῆς, the meaning is, as the RSV correctly renders, 'besides women and children' (cf. Philo, Vit. Mos. 1.147; Josephus, Ant. 2.317).[38] Moreover, when Moses, in Num 11.21, wonders how he is to feed the people that have come forth from Egypt, his words are these: 'the people among whom I am number six hundred thousand (men) on foot; and thou hast said, "I will give them meat. . . ."' As in Matthew, the number of individuals to be fed is not given but only the number of men (cf. Exod 12.37). One must consequently entertain the possibility that the concluding words of 14.13–21 were meant to allude to the way the people in the wilderness were counted.[39]

(iv) Concluding Observations

(1) The feeding of the five thousand was undoubtedly intended to echo the institution of the Eucharist (see p. 481). Concerning this fact, two observations are in order. First, there are other instances of Matthew using the literary device of foreshadowing. In chapters 1–2, for example, the story of the peril of the new-born Messiah clearly foreshadows the passion narrative, and the same is true of the account of the Baptist's martyrdom in 14.1–12. Thus the parallelism between 14.13–21 and 26.20–9 is hardly exceptional. Rather, Matthew consistently looks towards the end, and the conclusion colours all that comes before. Secondly, it is significant that both feeding stories (14.13–21; 15.32–9) appear in the section 13.53–17.27, the fourth major narrative section of the gospel. This is the section in which the stewardship of the kingdom is transferred from Israel to the church (see 16.13–20, the story of Peter's confession and its sequel). It is therefore most appropriate that 14.13–21 and 15.32–9, which are transparent symbols of a Christian service, should be told only after the need for a new religious community has become manifest, and precisely in the section in which that need is met.

---

[38] See further U. Cassuto, A Commentary on the Book of Exodus, Jerusalem, 1967, p. 125.

[39] Note also how often 'sons of Israel' occurs in Exod 16 (cf. LAB 20.8).

(2) As Gerhardsson has remarked, 'In Matthew's time the Eucharist had probably not yet been made fully distinct from the satiating common meals in the early Christian communities. Thus eucharistic symbolism does not exclude the possibility that the story is concerned with the satisfaction of elementary bodily hunger—and *vice versa*' (*Acts*, p. 57). In other words, the spiritualizing of 14.13–21 on Matthew's part does not discount the equal emphasis upon Jesus as the one who can meet mundane, physical needs. Our pericope therefore both shows Jesus' concern for such 'non-religious' needs and likewise demonstrates his ability (ἐξουσία) to act in accord with that concern. So the christological assertion that Jesus is Lord of all (cf. 28.18) seems implicit.

(v) *Bibliography*

E. Bammel, 'The Feeding of the Multitude', in Bammel and Moule, pp. 211–40.

P. W. Barnett, 'The Feeding of the Multitude in Mark 6/John 6', in Wenham and Blomberg, pp. 273–93.

G. H. Boobyer, 'The Eucharistic Interpretation of the Miracles of the Loaves in St. Mark's Gospel', *JTS* 3 (1952), pp. 161–71.

I. Buse, 'The Gospel Accounts of the Feeding of the Multitudes', *ExpT* 74 (1963), pp. 167–70.

L. Cerfaux, 'La section des pains', in *Recueil Lucien Cerfaux*, vol. 1, Gembloux, 1954, pp. 471–85.

H. Clavier, 'La multiplication des pains dans le ministère de Jésus', in *Studia Evangelica 1*, TU 73, ed. F. L. Cross, Berlin, 1959, pp. 441–57.

P. E. Cousins, 'The Feeding of the Five Thousand', *EvQ* 39 (1967), pp. 152–4.

J. D. M. Derrett, 'Leek-beds and Methodology', *BZ* 19 (1975), pp. 101–3.

Dodd, *Tradition*, pp. 196–222.

K. P. Donfried, 'The Feeding Narratives and the Marcan Community', in *Kirche: Festschrift für Günther Bornkamm zum 75. Geburtstag*, ed. D. Lührmann and G. Strecker, Tübingen, 1980, pp. 95–104.

A. M. Farrer, 'Loaves and Thousands', *JTS* 4 (1953), pp. 1–14.

R. M. Fowler, *Loaves and Fishes*, SBLDS 54, Chico, 1981.

G. Friedrich, 'Die beiden Erzählungen von der Speisung in Mark 6.31–41; 8.1–9', *TZ* 20 (1964), pp. 10–22.

R. M. Grant, *The Problem of Miraculous Feedings in the Greco-Roman World*, Berkeley, 1982.

A. Heising, *Die Botschaft der Brotvermehrung*, SBS 15, Stuttgart, 1966.

idem, 'Exegese und Theologie der alt- und neutestamentlichen Speisewunder', *ZKT* 86 (1964), pp. 80–96.

idem, 'Das Kerygma der wunderbaren Fischvermehrung (Mk 6.34–44 par.)', *BuL* 10 (1969), pp. 52–7.

H. J. Held, in *TIM*, pp. 181–4.

A. G. Hebert, 'History in the Feeding of the Five Thousand', in *Studia Evangelica 2*, TU 87, ed. F. L. Cross, Berlin, 1964, pp. 65–72.

E. D. Johnston, 'The Johannine Version of the Feeding of the Five Thousand—an Independent Tradition?', *NTS* 8 (1961), pp. 151–4.

Kertelge, *Wunder*, pp. 129–39.

J. Knackstedt, 'Die beiden Brotvermehrungen im Evangelien', *NTS* 10 (1964), pp. 309–35.

idem, 'De duplici miraculo multiplicationis panum', *VD* 41 (1963), pp. 39–51, 140–53.

H. J. Körtner, 'Das Fischmotiv im Speisungswunder', *ZNW* 75 (1984), pp. 24–35.

S. Masuda, 'The Good News of the Miracle of the Bread', *NTS* 28 (1982), pp. 191–219.

H. Montefiore, 'Revolt in the Desert?', *NTS* 8 (1961), pp. 135–41.

F. Neirynck, 'The Matthew-Luke Agreements in Mt 14.13–14/Lk 9.10–11 (par. Mk 6.30–34)', *ETL* 60 (1984), pp. 25–44.

F. Neugebauer, 'Die wunderbare Speisung (Mk 6.30–44 parr.) und Jesu Identität', *KD* 32 (1986), pp. 254–77.

H. Patsch, 'Abendmahlsterminologie ausserhalb der Einsetzungs-berichte', *ZNW* 62 (1971), pp. 210–31.

M. Pettem, 'Le premier récit de la multiplication des pains et le problème synoptique', *SR* 14 (1985), pp. 73–83.

B. Pixner, 'The Miracle Church at Tabgha on the Sea of Galilee', *BA* 48 (1985), pp. 196–206.

I. de la Potterie, 'Le sens primitif de la multiplication des pains', in Dupont, *Jésus*, pp. 303–29.

Q. Quesnell, *The Mind of Mark: Interpretation and Method through the Exegesis of Mark 6.52*, AnBib 38, Rome, 1969.

A. Richardson, 'The Feeding of the Five Thousand', *Int* 9 (1955), pp. 144–9.

Roloff, *Kerygma*, pp. 237–54.

Schenke, *Wundererzählungen*, pp. 217–37.

E. Stauffer, 'Zum apokalyptischen Festmahl in Mc 6.34ff.', *ZNW* 46 (1955), pp. 264–6.

W. R. Stegner, 'Lukan Priority in the Feeding of the Five Thousand', *BR* 21 (1976), pp. 19–28.

idem, *Narrative Theology in Early Jewish Christianity*, Louisville, 1989, pp. 53–81.

Strauss, pp. 507–19.

Tagawa, pp. 123–53.

van Cangh, J.-M., 'La multiplication des pains dans l'évangile de Marc', in Sabbe, pp. 309–46.

idem, *La multiplication des pains et l'euchariste*, Paris, 1975.

idem, 'Le thème des poissons dans les récits évangéliques de la multiplication des pains', *RB* 78 (1971), pp. 71–83.

Van der Loos, pp. 619–37.

B. van Iersel, 'Die wunderbare Speisung und das Abendmahl in der synoptischen Tradition', *NovT* 7 (1964), pp. 167–94.

P. G. Ziener, 'Die Brotwunder im Markusevangelium', *BZ* 4 (1960), pp. 282–5.

XXXIII

THE LORD OF THE SEA WALKS ON THE WAVES
(14.22–33)
AND HEALS THE SICK AT GENNESARET
(14.34f.)

(i) *Structure*

Following (a) the introduction (vv. 22–23), the story of Jesus on the waves falls into three parts: the encounter of the sea-striding Jesus with (b) the disciples (vv. 24–27) and (c) Peter (vv. 28–32);[1] then follows (d) the conclusion (v. 33). Verse 24 (the description of the storm) correlates with v. 32 (the subsiding of the storm), vv. 25 and 29 resemble each other (see on v. 29), and εὐθέως/εὐθύς appears in vv. 22, 27, and 31, which correspond roughly to the beginning, middle, and end of the section. Thus the structure is characterized by symmetry, and it may be by deliberate design that the key words, 'Take courage, it is I; have no fear' appear precisely at the centre of the episode.[2]

(ii) *Sources*

(i) As we shall see, Mt 14.22–33 can be easily explained as an adaptation of Mk 6.45–52 into which the material about Peter walking on the water has been inserted (Mt 14.28–31). One wonders, on the other hand, whether Mk 6.45–52 can be plausibly viewed as a revision of Mt 14.22–33. In the first place, on the Griesbach hypothesis one must give some explanation for the omission of the tale about Peter, and what that might be escapes us. Secondly, the confession of Jesus as the Son of God in Mt 14.33 (missing from Mk 6.51–2) reduces the dramatic tension of the Matthean narrative by making the scene at Caesarea Philippi a bit anticlimactic. When Jesus asks the all-important question, But who do you say that I am?, Peter simply *repeats* the acclamation of 14.33: You are the Son of God. In Mark, however, the answer returned—You are the Christ—has not been uttered before, so the scene retains its dramatic impact. This seems to us original and Matthew's text by comparison secondary. Thirdly, the priority of Mark seems upheld by the parallel in Jn 6.16–21, for in the Johannine account of the walking on the water,

---

[1] Vv. 24–27 and 28–32 are closely knit: 'If it is you', which opens the latter, depends upon 'It is I', which closes the former.
[2] Cf. Gerhardsson, *Acts*, p. 57.

which is to all appearances independent of the synoptics,[3] the peculiarly Matthean material finds no counterpart. In other words, John witnesses to the shorter, Markan form of the story, not the longer, Matthean form.

(ii) If, as we think, Mt 14.22–33 is in truth based upon its Markan parallel, this leaves unaccounted for the material about Peter. Where did it come from? Gundry, *Commentary*, p. 300, argues that it is 'haggadic midrash', and Matthew's own creation (cf. Beare, p. 330). Whether 'haggadic midrash' is the appropriate label or not, the case for a redactional genesis is strong (cf. Kratz (v)). In addition to Matthew's special interest in Peter, two points in particular weigh in its favour—the redactional vocabulary (κύριε, κέλευσόν με, verb of perception + φοβέομαι, κράζω + λέγων, καταποντίζομαι, ἐκτείνας τὴν χεῖρα, ὀλιγόπιστε, ἐδίστασας; see section (iii)) and the catchword links with the surrounding verses (εἰ σὺ εἶ in v. 28 harks back to the ἐγώ εἰμι of v. 27; the ἐλθεῖν πρός σε ἐπὶ τὰ ὕδατα of v. 28 recalls the ἦλθεν πρὸς αὐτοὺς περιπατῶν ἐπὶ τὴν θάλασσαν of v. 25; v. 29's περιεπάτησεν ἐπὶ τὰ ὕδατα καὶ ἦλθεν πρὸς τὸν Ἰησοῦν stands in chiastic relation to v. 25's ἦλθεν πρὸς αὐτοὺς περιπατῶν ἐπὶ τὴν θάλασσαν; in v. 30, ἄνεμον, ἐφοβήθη, and ἔκραξεν have parallels in vv. 24 and 26; and the εὐθέως of v. 31 has its counterpart in v. 22). We are, nevertheless, inclined to believe that the data are also consistent with a derivation from oral tradition.[4] Certainly the author of Matthew seems to have had access to non-Markan traditions about Peter (see e.g. 16.17–19 and 17.24–7). Further, there may be some justice in the supposition that 14.28–31 is a displaced resurrection story.[5] It is strikingly similar in several respects to the post-resurrectional scene in Jn 21, and the theme of faith versus doubt is a key element of the resurrection tradition (cf. 28.17; Mk 16.14; Lk 24.41; Jn 20.24–9). However, given the nature of our sources and our fragmentary knowledge, the proposal that the story of Peter walking on the water is Matthew's adaptation of a tradition recounting an appearance of the risen Lord to Peter can be nothing more than exceedingly tentative, and it may be that the tale is purely redactional, that is, the creation of Matthew.

(iii) The pericope about healings at Gennesaret, Mt 14.34–6 is, on the two-source theory, Matthew's edition of Mk 6.53–6 (there is no Lukan parallel). But there is admittedly nothing in the passage or its Markan relative that excludes the possibility of Matthean priority.

(iii) *Exegesis*

This passage, which is rich in both its christological implications

---

[3] See Brown, *John* 1, pp. 252–4, arguing that John's account is more primitive than Mark's. For a different opinion see Barrett, *John*, p. 279. Chrysostom thought the Johannine and synoptic pericopae to be sufficiently distinct as to record two different events.

[4] Cf. Kilpatrick, pp. 38–44; Schweizer, *Matthew*, p. 321.

[5] See esp. R. E. Brown, 'John 21 and the First Appearance of the Risen Lord to Peter', in *Resurrexit*, ed. E. Dhanis, Rome, 1974, pp. 246–65.

and its instruction on discipleship (see section (iv)), falls into two different form-critical categories. It can be regarded either as a rescue—specifically, sea rescue—story (cf. esp. T. Naph. 6.1–10 and Mt 8.23–7 par.) or as an epiphany, that is, an unexpected revelation of God or a divine being, which makes known some divine attribute or characteristic (cf. the transfiguration). Given the two alternatives, it is no surprise to learn that a penchant for form-critical purity has led some scholars to contend that our story is really an epiphany to which rescue motifs have been artificially tacked on[6] whereas others have made precisely the opposite case: the sea rescue story was contaminated by epiphany motifs.[7] Without denying that one of these reconstructions could in fact be correct, neither, it must be said, addresses the issue of the text as it stands. When this is done, it is hard not to agree that Mt 14.22–33 par. is properly labelled an epiphany which brings rescue (so G. Theissen) or a sea-rescue epiphany (J. P. Heil). As examples of texts in which an epiphany involves rescue Theissen cites h. Hom. 33.12; Euripides, *Ba.* 498; Aristides, *Hymn to Serapis* 33; Acts 5.17–25; 12.3–19.[8]

As compared with Mk 6.45–52, Matthew has introduced the following major changes into his account: he has (i) omitted Mark's reference to Bethsaida as the destination of the boat (14.22 diff. Mk 6.45); (ii) clarified the αὐτοῖς of Mk 6.46 (they are the crowds, not the disciples); (iii) assimilated the remark that Jesus went up to a mountain to 5.1; (iv) stressed that Jesus was alone on the mountain (κατ᾽ ἰδίαν; contrast Mk 6.46); (v) moved the μόνος of Mk 6.47c forward and omitted Mk 6.47c ('and he was alone on the land') as unnecessary; (vi) dropped the notice that Jesus saw (from the mountain) what was happening to the disciples (Mk 6.48); (vii) deleted the difficult remark that 'Jesus wanted to pass them by' (Mk 6.48); (viii) passed over Mk 6.50a ('For all saw him and were troubled') as adding nothing; (ix) inserted the incident involving Peter (14.28–31); and (x) completely altered the conclusion so that now the disciples, instead of not understanding, confess Jesus to be the Son of God (14.33; contrast Mk 6.51–2).

The possible historical basis for Mt 14.22–33 par. has engendered much discussion. There are, to be sure, those who remain content with the affirmation that the narrative simply records what happened: Jesus walked on the water. But, because of the modern reluctance to accept miracles at face value, there has been no dearth of other explanations. (i) Klausner, p. 269, supposed that the story goes back to a

[6] Cf. Bultmann, *History*, p. 216; Guelich, *Mark*, p. 346.
[7] This follows if one regards Mk 6.45–52 as a secondary development of the story in Mk 4.35–41 (cf. Jeremias, *Theology*, p. 87).
[8] *Stories*, p. 101. *Pace* T. Y. Mullins, 'New Testament Commission Forms, Especially in Luke-Acts', *JBL* 95 (1976), p. 605, Mt 14.22–33 is not an example of a commissioning story consisting of introduction, confrontation, reaction, commissioning, protest, reassurance, conclusion.

hallucinatory experience of the disciples—'simple, oriental village-folk and fishermen, for whom the whole world was full of marvels'. 'Mark actually says that they thought that it was "an apparition" . . . which is what it really was. But the appetite for miracles gradually implanted within them the belief that they had really seen Jesus and rowed together with him in the boat'. (ii) R. Otto (v), citing a tale about Simeon Stylites and calling attention to the studies of modern psychical research, offered that a genuine psychic experience gave rise to the NT accounts: Jesus was able to project his 'etherial double' in order to calm the troubled disciples.[9] (iii) Many have been attracted to the possibility that Jesus was walking on the shore or wading in the surf and, in the morning mist, was first thought to be a ghost, and then taken to be astride the waves (cf. Taylor, *Mark*, p. 327). A variant of this thesis holds that the error was not perceptual but philological: ἐπὶ τῆς θαλάσσης, which originally meant only 'by the sea' (cf. Jn 21.2), was mistakenly understood as 'on the sea', an error which proved decisive in the later telling of the story. This hypothesis is particularly associated with H. E. G. Paulus.[10] (iv) It is sometimes claimed that our text is displaced: at one time it was the story of a post-resurrectional encounter.[11] (v) Many today are satisfied to affirm that the story of Jesus walking on the water was the free creation of the Christian community; it was composed in order to teach a lesson about Jesus' power and presence (cf. Pesch 1, pp. 362–3).

We find it all but impossible to come to any definite conclusion on the issue at hand. In view of the solid connexion with the feeding of the five thousand[12] (which we think has an historical basis), it may be best to surmise some factual core. This would exclude options (iv) and (v). Of more than this we are hesitant. Does the story relate the exercise of some generally unrecognized human ability (so (ii)), or does it record the misinterpretation of a mundane occurrence (so (i) and (iii))? As

[9] The phenomenon of bilocation is reported of certain yogic masters and several Christian saints, including Anthony of Padua, Alfonso de Liguori, and Martin de Porres.

[10] See Strauss (v) for discussion and criticism.

[11] Cf. Kreyenbühl (v). But in opposition to this thesis, the tradition firmly links the sea walking with the feeding of the five thousand (so both Mark and John), and this last can hardly be regarded as a resurrection story. Moreover, Jesus praying alone on a mountain does not fit a post-Easter setting. Dodd, *MNTS*, pp. 119–21, seems to suggest that the incident had some historical basis but has been assimilated to post-resurrectional appearances.

[12] The link between the two stories cannot be explained as due to an exodus motif (cf. the crossing of the Sea of Reeds and the miracle of the manna). For then we would expect the order, walking on the water, feeding of the five thousand. Also unconvincing is Lindars' suggestion: 'The abiding presence of Jesus is a feature of the Church's eucharistic teaching (cf. Lk 24.13–35); this may explain why the walking on the sea was attached to the feeding at an early stage of transmission' (*John*, p. 245). Improbable too is influence from Ps 107.1–9, where God satiates the hungry and thirsty and saves those who cry to the Lord in trouble. It is worth noting that the feeding of the four thousand in Mk 8.1–10 par. is also followed by a sea crossing. If this is a pre-Markan doublet of the sequence in Mk 6, as many have been persuaded, it further testifies to the antiquity of the tie between the feeding and a water crossing (cf. Taylor, *Mark* pp. 628–32). May not the tie in fact be historical?

historians we know of no criterion by which to resolve the riddle. Perhaps it is wisest to confess that the truth lies undiscoverably hidden beneath the texts. We can observe, however, that in considering the problem at least two facts must be borne in mind. First, the history-of-religion parallels are both close and numerous. In 2 Kgs 2.14 and 6.6 Elisha defies the law of gravity in performing water miracles, and there are several places in the OT where reference is made to God walking on the waves or sea (see on v. 11). In *P. Berol.* 1.120 we read of a demon with the power to tread upon rivers and seas. Lucian, *Philops.* 13, refers to a magician who was imagined by people to march on the sea. *PGM* 1.121 contains instructions on how to pass over water without assistance. The Buddhist text, Jâtaka 190, tells the tale of a disciple who walked upon the water when he meditated upon the Buddha and who sank when he did not.[13] The Apophthegmata Patrum preserves the story of a certain hermit Bessarion crossing the river Chrysoroas on foot (PG 65, Bessarion 2). There is a similar story in Gregory the Great, *Dial.* 2.7. In the seventeenth century, according to Sabbatean sources perhaps influenced by the Gospels, Sabbatai Ṣevi, when to all appearances drowning, rose from the sea; and on another occasion he calmed a sea storm (Scholem, pp. 145–6, 446, n. 269). However one accounts for all the biblical and extra-biblical records, one wonders about the reasonableness of supplying one explanation for Mk 6.45–52, another for all the other narratives so much like it.[14]

Secondly, the tradition-history of our story seemingly indicates a development in the direction of the miraculous. Matthew, with its story of Peter sharing Jesus' power, and its confession of Jesus as the Son of God, patently represents an advance over the Markan account. Similarly, John's version of the story seems more primitive than Mark's.[15] Jn 6.15–21 is briefer, puts less emphasis upon the miraculous, and does not mention the stilling of the storm. All this indicates that, relatively speaking, John probably gives us the most undeveloped form of the story.

22. καὶ εὐθέως ἠνάγκασεν τοὺς μαθητὰς ἐμβῆναι εἰς πλοῖον καὶ προάγειν αὐτὸν εἰς τὸ πέραν.[16] Mark lacks αὐτόν and has εὐθύς instead of εὐθέως,[17] the unnecessary αὐτοῦ after μαθητάς, the definite article before πλοῖον (see on 14.13), and the specifying πρὸς Βηθσαϊδάν at the end (which finds no further mention in

[13] See further Stehly (v) and W. N. Brown, *The Indian and Christian Miracles of Walking on the Water*, London, 1928. *Pace* Stehly, there is no good reason to suppose that the story about Peter has been influenced by Buddhist tradition; see Gispert-Sauch (v).

[14] Note also Homer, *Od.* 5.54 (Hermes' sandals carry him over the water) and Virgil, *Aen.* 1.147 (Neptune glides over the waters). See further Bultmann, *History*, pp. 236–7.

[15] See n. 3. Contrast Pesch 1, p. 363, n. 20.

[16] So HG. NA²⁶ prints το before πλοιον, which is omitted by B Σ *f*¹ 33 565 700 892 *pc* bo^ms mae Eus.

[17] See on 4.20. On the textual variants for εὐθέως and εὐθύς in vv. 22, 27, and 31 see Smit Sibinga (v).

the Markan text).[18] ἀναγκάζω (= 'compel', 'force') is used only three times in the synoptics, in Mt 14.22 = Mk 6.45 and in Lk 14.23. It here has the weakened sense of 'urge' or 'invite' (so BAGD, s.v.).[19] Is the reader to presume that the disciples, anticipating the storm, are afraid to cross without Jesus and therefore need to be pressed? Or does Jesus' intention to perform and permit what follows suffice to explain his action (cf. Origen, *Comm. on Mt.* 11.5; Zahn, p. 513)?[20] Whatever the answer, there is an edifying lesson to hand: 'if it is as a result of obedience to Christ's command that the Church or the individual Christian is in a situation of danger or distress, then there is no need of fear' (Cranfield, *Mark*, p. 228).

ἕως οὗ ἀπολύσῃ τοὺς ὄχλους. Compare Mk 6.45: ἕως αὐτὸς ἀπολύει τὸν ὄχλον. ἕως οὗ (= 'while' in this context, an unclassical meaning; cf. 26.36 and the Aramaic *'ad dî*) is Matthew's preferred form of expression (Mt: 6; Mk: O; Lk: 4);[21] and the omission of the superfluous αὐτός, the substitution of the aorist for the historical present (see Allen, p. xx), and the replacement of 'the crowd' (singular) with 'the crowds' (plural) are all typical.

23. καὶ ἀπολύσας τοὺς ὄχλους. Matthew has assimilated Mk 6.46 (καὶ ἀποταξάμενος αὐτοῖς[22]) to Mt 14.15 and 22. The same words also appear in 15.39. We are given no clue as to why it was necessary to dismiss the crowd.

ἀνέβη εἰς τὸ ὄρος κατ' ἰδίαν προσεύξασθαι. Compare Lk 9.28 (ἀνέβη εἰς τὸ ὄρος προσεύξασθαι) and Jn 6.15 (ἀνεχώρησεν πάλιν εἰς τὸ ὄρος αὐτὸς μόνος). As can be seen from a comparison with Mk 6.46, Matthew has discarded ἀπῆλθεν for ἀνέβη (cf. 5.1) and added κατ' ἰδίαν (cf. 14.13 and esp. 17.1).

In his book on the mountain motif in the First Gospel, T. L.

---

[18] In Mt 14.34 = Mk 6.53 the boat arrives at Gennesaret. Did Matthew realize that Bethsaida and Gennesaret were on opposite sides of the Sea of Galilee and that therefore the geographical data in Mark are puzzling? See the Markan commentaries.

[19] See further H. Pernot, 'Greek and the Gospels', *ExpT* 38 (1927), p. 105.

[20] It has often been suggested that, as a matter of history, Jesus sent the disciples on because he did not want the crowd to stir up the disciples or the disciples to stir up the crowd; cf. Jn 6.14–15.

[21] According to Gundry, *Commentary*, p. 296, the change from ἕως + present indicative to ἕως οὗ with the aorist subjunctive 'implies that the disciples' going ahead has its limit: Jesus will rejoin his disciples shortly. As much as possible Matthew is protecting the terms of discipleship, according to which disciples follow rather than go ahead of their teacher, and the Christology of Immanuel, according to which Jesus is always with his people (1:23; 28:20)'. We doubt whether so much should be read into so little a change.

[22] In Mark the αὐτοῖς is just possibly ambiguous: it can be taken to refer to the crowds or (as Matthew has it) to the disciples. Thus Matthew has clarified.

Donaldson has argued that the mountain of Mt 14.23 'is not the setting for an extended event in the ministry of Jesus and the reference is just taken over from Mark with no apparent redactional interest' (p. 12). This may well be doubted. To begin with, Jesus' retreat to the mountain is not an indispensable part of its context: the story of Jesus walking on the sea would develop as well without a specific remark on Jesus' whereabouts before he takes to the water. So one might have expected Matthew, given his penchant for abbreviating miracle stories, to have omitted the mountain. That he has not done so perhaps indicates its significance for him. Next, 14.23 recalls both 5.1–2 and 17.1–8, and in these last a Moses typology is in evidence (τοὺς ὄχλους ἀνέβη εἰς τὸ ὄρος is common to 5.1 and 14.23, and ὄρος (. . .) κατ' ἰδίαν appears in 14.23 and 17.1). Thirdly, ἀνέβη + εἰς τὸ ὄρος is a phrase with Mosaic overtones (see on 5.2), and it occurs elsewhere in the NT in passages where Jesus is the counterpart of Moses (e.g. Lk 9.28; Jn 6.3, 15). Lastly, that Jesus is on the mountain alone recalls the situation of Moses on Sinai (cf. Exod 24.2); and the OT records that the law-giver prayed on Sinai (Exod 32.30–4). It is, therefore, quite possible that Matthew intended 14.23 to be part of his Moses typology. (That the mountain is in and of itself related to Matthew's Son of God Christology[23] or that it is to be thought of as an OT theophany motif[24] is unlikely.)

If one does not count 11.25–7, 14.23 is the first time we hear of Jesus praying. The content of his prayer is not indicated. What then is its function? For one thing, Jesus here embodies his own commandment: he prays to the Father in secret (cf. 6.5–6). For another, as Heil writes, Jesus' prayer 'indicates that the uniquely divine action of walking on the sea proceeds from Jesus' intimate union with his Father. It is after praying . . . that Jesus accomplishes the salvific will of his Father by rescuing his disciples from distress through his epiphanic action of walking on the sea. The fact that the motif of Jesus praying is directly oriented to his intimate relationship to God as manifested in the sea-walking action is confirmed by the conclusion of the story in which the disciples confess Jesus to be "truly the Son of God" (14:33)' (p. 33).

ὀψίας δὲ γενομένης μόνος ἦν ἐκεῖ. Compare Jn 6.15–16. Matthew's line depends upon Mk 6.47 ('And when evening came, the boat was out on the sea, and he was alone on the land'); but the First Evangelist has reversed the order of the clauses about Jesus' solitude and the boat on the sea (see v. 24a),[25] obliterated the contrast between sea and land, and underlined the mountain motif (ἐκεῖ). On ὀψίας γενομένης see on 14.15.

24. τὸ δὲ πλοῖον ἤδη μέσον τῆς θαλάσσης ἦν.[26] Compare Jn

---

[23] Contrast Kingsbury, *Structure*, p. 57.

[24] So Pesch 1, p. 360, citing Deut 33.2 and Hab 3.3.

[25] For other examples of inversion see G. Howard, 'Stylistic Inversion and the Synoptic Tradition', *JBL* 97 (1978), pp. 375–89.

[26] So HG and ℵ C L W 084 0106 f¹ Maj (lat) syʰ mae? ην (+εις D) μεσον της θαλασσης appears in D 1424 pc e ff¹ mae? απειχεν απο της γης σταδιους

6.17. Mk 6.47 is very similar: ἦν [πάλαι] τὸ πλοῖον ἐν μέσῳ τῆς θαλάσσης. ἤδη (cf. 14.15; it is redactional in 17.12) here has the sense, 'by this time' (cf. RSV). For μέσος/v with the genitive see also Lk 22.55; Jn 1.26; and Phil 2.15. The word need not be understood with mathematical strictness.

βασανιζόμενον ὑπὸ τῶν κυμάτων. Mk 6.48 reads: καὶ ἰδὼν αὐτοὺς βασανιζομένους ἐν τῷ ἐλαύνειν. Matthew has retained the verb (although it is now in the passive) but otherwise revised Mark completely. The reference to Jesus seeing the situation has been eliminated, the boat is now the object of the verb instead of the disciples,[27] and ὑπὸ τῶν κυμάτων comes forward from 8.24 to increase the parallelism between the stilling of the storm and Jesus' walking on the sea.

On water as representative of the powers of chaos and evil see p. 84. For theophanies in storms see Exod 19.16 and Ezek 1.4.

ἦν γὰρ ἐναντίος ὁ ἄνεμος. Mk 6.48 has the order: 1, 2, 4, 5, 3 + αὐτοῖς. ἐναντίος (= 'opposite', 'against') is a Matthean *hapax legomenon*. For the word with ἄνεμος see also Acts 27.4 and Josephus, *Bell.* 3.421.

It is exceedingly important to keep in mind that, in Jewish tradition, it is God alone who can rescue from the sea. Note especially Exod 14.10–15.21; Ps 107.23–32; Jon 1.1–16; and Wisd 14.2–4; also 1QH 6.22–5 and T. Naph. 6.1–10. As Heil, p. 36, expresses it: 'Since it is God who is master of the waters in the OT, distress at sea means distress oriented to a divine saving action through power over water.... In view of this OT background the disciples' distress in crossing the sea signifies, both from the meaning of the motif in itself and its function in a rescue story, distress specially oriented to a divine saving action. The distress implies rescue; the distress *at sea* implies rescue *by God*'.

25. τετάρτῃ δὲ φυλακῇ τῆς νυκτὸς ἦλθεν πρὸς αὐτοὺς περιπατῶν ἐπὶ τὴν θάλασσαν. Compare Jn 6.19. Mk 6.48c begins with the less precise περὶ τετάρτην φυλακήν (cf. Josephus, *Ant.* 18.356), uses the present ἔρχεται, and follows ἐπί with the genitive (cf. 13.2 diff. Mk 4.1; 15.35 diff. Mk 8.6).

The period between 6 p.m. and 6 a.m. was divided by the Romans

---

ικανους is the reading of Θ (700) sy^{c·p}? NA^{26} reproduces the text of B *f*^{13} *pc* sy^{c·p}? sa: σταδιους πολλους απο της γης απειχεν. But neither στάδιον nor ἀπὸ τῆς γῆς is attested elsewhere in the First Gospel, and ἀπέχω is not otherwise redactional. Further, the reading of B could be due to the influence of Jn 6.19 ('twenty-five or thirty *stadia*'; cf. Mt 14.24 bo: 'about twenty-five stadia'). Contrast Metzger, p. 37, and Gundry, *Commentary*, p. 297.

[27] βασανίζω is used in 8.6 of paralysis and in 8.29 of tormented demons.

into four equal periods or watches (cf. Mk 13.35; Lk 12.38; SB 1, pp. 688–9). So the fourth watch was the last (and the darkest), the time between 3 a.m. and 6 a.m. This implies that the disciples struggled without Jesus for quite some time.[28] Observe that the rescue from the Reed Sea took place 'in the morning watch' (LXX Exod 14.24: ἐν τῇ φυλακῇ τῇ ἑωθινῇ). For other precise indications of time in NT epiphany narratives see 28.1 par.; Lk 1.8, 26; 2.8; 24.36; Jn 20.1, 19, 26; 21.4; Acts 1.10. (Notwithstanding Exod 14.24; Ps 17.15; 143.8; Isa 17.14; Jos. Asen. 14.1–2; and LAB 42.3, rescue at or before morning does not appear to be a fixed Jewish motif.)

The crux to understanding the Christology of 14.22–33 is the fact that walking on the sea has its background in the OT, where Yahweh the omnipotent creator treads upon the waters. See Job 9.8 (MT: 'who trampled the waves (or: back) of the sea (monster)'; LXX: 'and walking (περιπατῶν) on the sea as if on ground');[29] MT Hab 3.15 ('Thou didst trample the sea with thy horses, the surging of many waters');[30] Ps 77.19 ('Thy way was through the sea, thy path through the great waters; yet thy footprints were unseen'); also Isa 43.16; 51.9–10; Frag. Tg. on Exod 15.11; and Pirqe R. El. 42 (on Ps 77.19).[31] By walking on the sea Jesus overcomes the powers of chaos and subdues them, like Yahweh in Job 9.8. And by crossing the sea so that his disciples may in turn cross safely, Jesus is again acting like Yahweh, who according to Ps 77.19 prepared the way for the Israelites to pass through the Sea of Reeds. In sum, Jesus' walking on the water demonstrates his domination of the sea and all it stands for and brings salvation to those in peril. Clearly the theophanic action of Yahweh has become the epiphanic action of Jesus (cf. Heil, pp. 56–7). The powers of the deity have become incarnate in God's Son.[32]

Mk 6.48 ends with this: 'And he wanted to pass them by'.[33] This strange notice, whose meaning is elusive, has been neglected by the

[28] Chrysostom, Hom. on Mt. 50.1: Jesus waited, 'instructing them not hastily to seek for deliverance from their pressing dangers, but to bear all occurrences manfully'.

[29] The targum has: 'and walked on the height of the strength of the sea'; see Heil, pp. 42–3.

[30] The targum has: 'You revealed yourself upon the sea in the chariot of your glory, in a heap of many waters'; see Heil, pp. 46–7.

[31] In Ecclus 24.5–6, Wisdom declares that she has walked in the depths of the abyss, and this followed by: 'In the waves of the sea, in the whole earth, and in every people and nation I have gotten a possession'.

[32] Eusebius, Dem. ev. 3.2, compares Jesus' walking on the water with Moses' actions at the Sea of Reeds, and several of the texts just cited do have to do with the exodus. Nonetheless, it must be emphasized that the parallels in our passage are between Jesus and Yahweh, not Jesus and Moses.

[33] For a survey of exegetical opinion see T. Snoy, 'Marc 6.48: "... et il voulait les dépasser"', in Sabbe, pp. 347–63.

First Evangelist because it seemingly states that Jesus was unable to do something he wished to do.

26. οἱ δὲ μαθηταὶ ἰδόντες αὐτὸν ἐπὶ τῆς θαλάσσης περιπατοῦντα ἐταράχθησαν.[34] Matthew has inserted μαθηταί and added ἐταράχθησαν, this last being moved forward from Mk 6.50a, which will be omitted. For ταράσσω see on 2.3. The word is also used of the human response to an epiphany in Lk 1.12 (cf. Lk 1.29); and it occurs notably in LXX Ps 76.16: 'The waters saw you, O God, the waters saw you and were afraid, the depths were troubled (ἐταράχθησαν) . . .'. For the seeing of Jesus coming on the sea there is a parallel in the targum on Ps 77.16: 'they saw your presence in the sea, O God, they saw your strength on the sea; the peoples trembled, even the depths were shaken'.

λέγοντες ὅτι φάντασμά ἐστιν. Mk 6.49 (ἔδοξαν φάντασμα εἶναι)[35] has been turned into direct speech (cf. 26.2 diff. Mk 14.1; etc.).

φάντασμα (LXX: 3, for ḥizzāyôn in Job 20.8) appears in the NT only in Mt 14.26 = Mk 6.49 (cf. Lk 24.37 D). The word means 'ghost' or 'apparition' (cf. Josephus, *Ant.* 1.331–3). Perhaps the disciples are perturbed because they think they see the ghost of a dead Jesus, or maybe an angel (cf. Josephus, *Ant.* 5.213) or a demon (cf. Ignatius, *Smyr.* 3.2). In any case the use of φάντασμα underlines the note of fear in the face of the extraordinary, the numinous. (Heb 12.21 uses the participial form of φαντάζω in a description of the theophany at Sinai.)

καὶ ἀπὸ τοῦ φόβου ἔκραξαν. Mark has simply καὶ ἀνέκραξαν, which entails that ἀπὸ τοῦ φόβου (cf. *miyyir'â*) is redactional, as also in 28.4. For fear as the typical response to an epiphanic encounter see Lk 2.9; 24.5, 37. One may also compare Ps 77.17: 'when the waters saw thee, they were afraid'.

27. εὐθὺς δὲ ἐλάλησεν αὐτοῖς ὁ Ἰησοῦς λέγων.[36] Mk 6.50b is less

---

[34] So NA[26]. C L W 0106 Maj f? sy[h] bo[pt] have και ιδοντες αυτον οι μαθηται (so HG). ℵ* Θ 700 *pc* sa read ιδοντες δε αυτον. 084 *f*[1] 1241 1424 *pc* bo[pt] have και ιδοντες αυτον. We have printed the text of ℵ[1] B D *f*[13] *pc* mae. Certainty is unobtainable.

[35] So HG. NA[26] follows ℵ B L Δ 33 892 *pc* in printing εδοξαν οτι φαντασμα εστιν; but this may well be assimilation to the First Gospel.

[36] The order of αυτοις and ο Ιησους is unclear. NA[26] follows ℵ[1] B *pc*: ο Ιησους αυτοις. HG follows C L W Θ 0106 *f*[1.13] Maj f q sy[h] with αυτοις ο Ιησους. ℵ* D 084 892 1010 *pc* ff[1] sy[c] sa bo Eus omit ο Ιησους. J. R. Royse, 'The Treatment of Scribal Leaps in Metzger's *Textual Commentary*', *NTS* 29 (1983), p. 547, reconstructs this plausible history: αυτοις ο ις became, through paraplepsis, αυτοις, and ο Ιησους was later reinserted, but before αυτοις (cf. the corrections of ℵ here). Finally, the late reading in 245 1195 1375 2145 *l*[47]—omit αυτοις—is accounted for by homoioteleuton on the ℵ[1] B variant.

compact: ὁ δὲ εὐθὺς ἐλάλησεν μετ' αὐτῶν καὶ λέγει αὐτοῖς. It is not surprising that Matthew has (i) decided to put εὐθύς in first position (cf. esp. 21.3); (ii) substituted αὐτοῖς for μετ' αὐτῶν (μετά never follows λαλέω in our gospel); (iii) added ὁ Ἰησοῦς (as often); and (iv) turned two independent clauses connected by καί into one sentence with the form, finite verb (ἐλάλησεν) + participle (λέγων; he generally prefers subordinate to co-ordinate clauses; see Allen, p. 75).

θαρσεῖτε. So Mark. For the verb, which occurs several times in the NT, all but once (Mk 10.49) on the lips of Jesus, see on 9.2. In Acts 23.11 the risen Lord appears to Paul and tells him to take courage (θάρσει).

ἐγώ εἰμι. So Mk 6.50 as well as Jn 6.20. The identification formula (= 'it is truly I'; cf. Lk 1.19; 24.39; Acts 9.5; 22.8; 26.15) is also probably here—as in Jn 18.2–9—a formula of revelation[37] intended to recall the mysterious, divine 'I am' of the OT (Exod 3.14; Isa 41.4; 43.10; 47.8, 10; in the Isaianic texts the LXX renders 'ănî hû' with ἐγώ εἰμι); for by walking on and subduing the sea Jesus has manifested the numinous power of Yahweh (see on 14.25). In the idiom of 11.27, the Son has made known the Father (cf. Lövestam (v)).

b. B. Bat. 73a attributes to Rabbah (b. Bar Ḥanah, third generation Amoraic) the tradition that clubs engraved with 'I am that I am, Yah, the Lord of Hosts, Amen, Amen, Selah' will subdue waves that would otherwise sink a ship. While certainly not directly comparable to the synoptic story, this rabbinic tradition does reflect the conviction that the inscrutable 'I am' contains within itself the power to make a stormy sea subside.

μὴ φοβεῖσθε. So Mk 6.50 and Jn 6.20. This is a standard entry in Jewish and Christian theophanies and epiphanies (cf. Mt 17.7; 28.5, 10; Lk 1.13, 30; 2.10; Rev 1.17; 2 En 1.8). For its use in connexion with the 'I am' formula see Isa 43.1–13 (an exodus context) and Apoc. Abr. 9.3 (God speaking to Abraham).[38]

28. This verse and the next three verses, which constitute a 'story within a story' (Heil), have no parallel in any of the other gospels. See section (ii) for discussion of source and origin.

---

[37] See esp. H. Zimmermann, 'Das absolute Ἐγώ εἰμι als die neutestamentliche Offenbarungsformel', *BZ* 4 (1960), pp. 54–69, 266–76; P. B. Harner, *The 'I am' of the Fourth Gospel*, Philadelphia, 1970; E. D. Freed, "Ἐγώ εἰμι in John viii. 24 in the Light of its Context and Jewish Messianic Belief', *JTS* 33 (1982), pp. 163–7.

[38] For detailed discussion of the formula in its OT contexts see E. W. Conrad, *Fear Not Warrior: A Study of the 'al tîrā' Pericopes in the Hebrew Scriptures*, Chico, 1985.

ἀποκριθεὶς δὲ αὐτῷ ὁ Πέτρος εἶπεν.³⁹ Compare 15.15; 26.33.
For Peter speaking after Jesus has addressed the disciples as a
unit see also 15.15; 16.16; 17.4; 18.21; 19.27; 26.33, 35.

κύριε. See on 8.6. Here the title seemingly reflects an
awareness that Jesus shares in the sovereign lordship of
Yahweh.

εἰ σὺ εἶ. This answers to the ἐγώ εἰμι of the preceding verse.
Does the εἰ mean 'if' or (as in 4.3) 'since'? Either sense would
be appropriate.

κέλευσόν με ἐλθεῖν πρός σε ἐπὶ τὰ ὕδατα. Compare 8.18 and
14.19; also Apoc. Jas. 2.25–8. κελεύω* is a Matthean favourite.
It is always followed by an infinitive in the First Gospel (8.18;
14.9, 19, 28; 18.25; 27.58, 64).

What motivated the change from θαλάσσαν/ης to ὕδατα?
Calling attention to Ps 69.14–15 and to Matthew's preference for ἐν
τοῖς ὕδασιν over ἐν τῇ θαλάσσῃ in 8.32 = Mk 5.13, Gundry,
Commentary, p. 299, proposes that 'waters' perhaps represents 'the
threat of death by persecution'. More likely is Heil's explanation: 'Jesus
walks across a long distance on the *sea*, as such, whereas Peter asks to
walk only on the *water* separating him from Jesus and not on the sea
as such' (p. 13, n. 9). It has also been thought that Matthew, in his own
composition, generally preferred ὕδατα over θάλασσα when writing
of the Sea of Galilee (1, p. 141).

29. Jesus bids Peter to come, and the apostle therewith begins
to walk towards Jesus on the waters. Thus even though Peter
will falter, Jesus has acknowledged the propriety of the disciple's
desire to act as his Lord acts (*imitatio Christi*).

ὁ δὲ εἶπεν· ἐλθέ. The imperative means 'come (here)' (cf.
BDF § 336.1).

Jesus not only has the ἐξουσία to walk on the sea but also
the ability to share his power and authority with others (cf.
11.27; 28.18). This is a crucial observation. For in Job 38.16
Yahweh asks Job, 'Have you come (LXX: ἦλθες) into the
springs of the sea (θαλάσσης) or walked (περιπάτησας) in the
recesses of the deep?' As Heil remarks, 'In the context Job had
challenged the divine rule over creation and now Yahweh
answers him, pointing out that it was He who created the earth
and seas (see Job 9.8). The implication is that if a man walks on
the sea, he does so only by divine authority' (p. 61). It follows
that if Peter walks on the sea at Jesus' bidding, then Jesus must
wield divine authority.

καὶ καταβὰς ἀπὸ τοῦ πλοίου ὁ Πέτρος περιεπάτησεν

---

³⁹ B 1424 *al* have αυτω at the end. This might be pristine because elsewhere
in Matthew ἀποκριθεὶς δέ is followed immediately by the subject (fifteen
times).

ἐπὶ τὰ ὕδατα καὶ ἦλθεν πρὸς τὸν Ἰησοῦν.⁴⁰ With the exception of καταβαίνω (with ἀπό in 8.1 [redactional]; 27.40, 42), the vocabulary is taken from earlier verses. Note the chiastic relationship with v. 25: ἦλθεν πρός ... περιπατῶν ἐπὶ/ περιεπάτησεν ἐπί ... ἦλθεν πρός. ...

30. Peter, suddenly perceiving the strength of the wind, takes the measure of his perilous situation and begins to waver: his faith has been wrecked by the force of the storm. This in turn prevents him from participating in Jesus' divine power and so he (like a πέτρος) starts to sink (so Ephrem the Syrian), crying out to the Lord for help. Compare with the entire verse Ps 69.1–3: 'Save me (LXX: σῶσόν με), O God! For the waters have come up to my neck. I sink in deep mire, where there is no foothold; I have come into deep water, and the flood sweeps over (κατεπόντισέν) me. I am weary with my crying (κράζων) ...'; also Ps 69.14f.

βλέπων δὲ τὸν ἄνεμον ἰσχυρὸν ἐφοβήθη.⁴¹ The word statistics⁴² do not clearly point to a redactional origin; but a verb of perception + φοβέομαι is editorial in 9.8 (ἰδόντες δέ ... ἐφοβήθησαν); 17.6 (ἀκούσαντες ... ἐφοβήθησαν σφόδρα); and 27.54 (ἰδόντες ... ἐφοβήθησαν σφόδρα).

καὶ ἀρξάμενος καταποντίζεσθαι ἔκραξεν λέγων. ἄρχω—here redundant and therefore an Aramaism; see MHT 4, p. 32—is redactional in 4.17; 11.20; and 12.1. καταποντίζομαι (= 'sink') is inserted by Matthew in 18.6 = Mk 9.42; and κράζω (cf. 14.26) + a participial form of λέγω (Mt: 9; Mk: 5; Lk: 1) is characteristic of the First Evangelist.

κύριε σῶσόν με. κύριε σῶσον also appears in 8.25, in the stilling of the storm pericope, and nowhere else in the NT. Clearly Matthew has assimilated the two sea rescue stories.

31. εὐθέως δὲ ὁ Ἰησοῦς. Compare 24.29.

ἐκτείνας τὴν χεῖρα ἐπελάβετο αὐτοῦ. Compare 2 Βασ 15.5 (ἐξέτεινεν τὴν χεῖρα αὐτοῦ καὶ ἐπελαμβάνετο αὐτοῦ); also Exod 4.4. ἐκτείνω + χείρ is redactional in 12.49 and 26.51; ἐπιλαμβάνομαι (= 'take hold of', 'grasp') is, however, a Matthean *hapax legomenon* (Mk: 1; Lk: 5).

In Ps 18.15–16 the taming of the sea by Yahweh is followed by this: 'He reached from on high, he took (LXX: ἔλαβεν) me, he drew me out (προσελάβετό) of many waters'. Similarly, in Ps 144.5–8 a request

⁴⁰ The o, bracketed by NA²⁶, is omitted by ℵ B D, and this reading is favoured by Smit Sibinga (v), arguing that o is assimilation to 14.28. So too HG.
⁴¹ NA²⁶ puts ισχυρον in brackets. The word is omitted (through homoioteleuton?) by ℵ B* 073 33 sa bo. See Metzger, p. 38.
⁴² βλέπω: Mt: 18; Mk: 14; Lk: 15. ἄνεμος: Mt: 9; Mk: 7; Lk: 4. ἰσχυρός: Mt: 4; Mk: 3; Lk: 4. φοβέομαι: Mt: 18; Mk: 12; Lk: 22.

for God to manifest himself publicly ('Bow thy heavens, O Lord, and come down! Touch the mountains that they smoke!') introduces a plea for deliverance from the waters of distress: 'Stretch forth thy hand (LXX: τὴν χεῖρα σου) from on high, rescue me and deliver me from the many waters ...'. So the pattern, theophany + deliverance from water, would have been familiar to readers of the psalms.

καὶ λέγει αὐτῷ· ὀλιγόπιστε. See on 6.30 and compare 8.26. The word, ὀλιγόπιστος, helps make the incident of 14.28–31 typical. Peter is an example of the believer who suffers from lack of faith in Jesus: after taking the first few steps of a difficult endeavour he falters when opposition begins to buffet. But— and this is what counts for the evangelist—Jesus is there to save *despite* inadequate faith. As Heil writes, 'Jesus does not "restore" a faith Peter once had; Peter never knew or believed that Jesus could save him from sinking in the waters. By rescuing Peter (and the disciples) Jesus calls Peter (and the disciples) to a greater faith—to a faith in the power of Jesus to save his people. Hence the fact that Jesus actually saves Peter is the climactic point of this incident of Peter walking on the water ...' (p. 64).

εἰς τί ἐδίστασας; Compare Apocryphon Jn 2.2.10–11. εἰς τί (='why?') appears also in 26.8, where it comes from Mk 14.4 (cf. also Wisd 4.17; Ecclus 39.16, 21; Mk 15.34). διστάζω (LXX: 0; NT: 2: Mt 14.31; 28.17) used absolutely means 'doubt' or (as here) 'not trust' (see Barth in *TIM*, pp. 113–14 and cf. 1 Clem 11.2; 23.3; 2 Clem 11.2). According to Black, pp. 128–30, the aorist (ἐδίστασας) is probably a Semitism (aorist for the Semitic perfect).

Bengel, *ad loc.*, commented: Peter 'is not blamed for leaving the vessel, but for not abiding in firm faith. He was right in exposing himself to trial; but he ought to have persevered'.

32. καὶ ἀναβάντων αὐτῶν εἰς τὸ πλοῖον ἐκόπασεν ὁ ἄνεμος. With this line Matthew returns to Mark, specifically Mk 6.51: καὶ ἀνέβη πρὸς αὐτοὺς εἰς τὸ πλοῖον καὶ ἐκόπασεν ὁ ἄνεμος. Two major changes have been introduced. First, the subject of the first clause has become Jesus *and Peter*. Secondly, two co-ordinate clauses connected by καί have been collapsed into one clause with the form, participle + finite verb (see on 14.27).

Just as walking on the sea is, in the OT, an attribute of Yahweh alone (see on 14.25), so too is the stilling of the storm a power the Scripture assigns only to God. See Job 26.11–12 ('The pillars of heaven tremble, and are astounded at his rebuke. By his power he stilled the sea; by his understanding he smote Rahab'); Ps 65.7 ('who dost still the roaring of the seas, the roaring of their waves, the tumult of the peoples'); 89.9–10 ('Thou dost rule the raging of the sea; when its waves rise, thou stillest them. Thou didst crush

Rahab like a carcass, thou didst scatter thy enemies with thy mighty arm'); 107.29 ('he made the storm be still and the waves of the sea were hushed'); Jon 1.15; Ecclus 43.23 ('By his counsel he stilled the great deep . . .'). Compare 4Q381 and Sepher Ha-Razim, first firmament, lines 226ff., fourth firmament, lines 31f. Once again, therefore, Matthew's story has christological implications. Jesus' action[43] makes him the channel of divine power and authority. And his epiphany means salvation.

33. The story ends with 'those in the boat'—that is, all the disciples save Peter[44]—worshipping Jesus, the Son of God. Compare the endings of the sea rescue narratives in Exod 14.31; Ps 107.31–2; and Jon 1.16.

οἱ δὲ ἐν τῷ πλοίῳ προσεκύνησαν αὐτῷ λέγοντες· ἀληθῶς θεοῦ υἱὸς εἶ. This replaces Mk 6.51c–2: 'And they were utterly astounded, for they did not understand about the loaves, but their hearts were hardened'. Mark's statement about the loaves is difficult, and when one also considers Matthew's habit of putting the disciples in a little better light (cf. Allen, pp. xxxiii–xxxiv), as well as, above all, his desire to depict them as men of understanding,[45] the omission does not surprise. Matthew has preferred to conclude the story with a christological affirmation, one which makes the reader focus more on Jesus and less on the disciples.

On προσκυνέω see on 2.2. 28.17 is the only other verse in which the disciples worship Jesus. ἀληθῶς (most often in the LXX for a form of the root 'mn) comes from the confession at the cross, 27.54: ἀληθῶς θεοῦ υἱὸς ἦν οὗτος (cf. Mk 15.39).

The title, 'Son of God', here refers to Jesus not in his capacity as a simple wonder-worker but in his status as revealer of the Father. What matters is not that Jesus has done the seemingly impossible but that he has performed actions which the OT associates with Yahweh alone (cf. Heil, p. 67, n. 89).

The reader of the First Gospel has been informed previously about Jesus' status as Son of God (cf. 2.15; 3.17; 4.3, 6; 8.29). But it is only in 14.33 that the disciples themselves come to make the confession of the church. Thus the unfolding of the gospel has witnessed a growth in their knowledge, a growth which will reach its pre-Easter maturity in 16.16. In short, the disciples are beginning to catch up with the readers of the gospel.

34. Subsequent to the walking on the sea we are informed, in

---

[43] The stilling of the storm is to be regarded as miraculous, not just a happy coincidence.

[44] Not the crew of the boat, as some have maintained.

[45] For this see esp. Barth, in *TIM*, pp. 105–12.

an independent pericope, that Jesus healed many in the area or city of Gennesaret. The passage—yet one more summary; see on 4.23—is based entirely upon Mk 6.53–6, probably a Markan composition[46] (cf. Jn 6.22–5; there is no Lukan parallel). It is characterized by brevity and lack of detail, especially when compared with the Markan counterpart. No names are named, no individual characters are introduced; we are simply told that Jesus healed the masses. This reinforces the impression, conveyed throughout Matthew, that Jesus did not neglect the common individual but rather identified with ordinary, and especially helpless, people. Maybe the most striking feature of 14.34–6 is that Jesus is represented 'as strongly influenced by the needs and expectations of the crowd. Jesus heals because he is asked to do so. To put it rather drastically, one can say that the crowd here "uses Jesus" as a source of health' (Gerhardsson, *Acts*, p. 29).

καὶ διαπεράσαντες ἦλθον ἐπὶ τὴν γῆν εἰς Γεννησαρέτ. This is taken from Mk 6.53, which lacks εἰς[47] and has καὶ προσωρμίσθησαν at the end. Matthew's text may be translated: 'And having crossed over they came unto land at Gennesaret'.

For διαπεράω see on 9.1. 'Gennesaret' (in the NT only in 14.34 = Mk 6.53 and Lk 5.1) is probably the name for the fruitful and well-forested valley on the northwest shore of the Sea of Galilee, south of Capernaum and north of Tiberias (modern El-Ghuweir). There is a glowing description of the place in Josephus, *Bell.* 3.516–21. 'Gennesaret', however, might also be taken to have been a town (cf. *y. Meg.* 1.70a?) which gave its name to the surrounding region as well as to the adjacent Sea of Galilee (which is called the Sea of Gennesaret in Lk 5.1). What our evangelist thought on the matter is unclear. The usual spelling of Gennesaret is Γεννησάρ (so 1 Macc 11.67; Josephus; Mt 14.34 D* 700 lat sy^{s.c.p}; Mk 6.53 D it vg^{mss} sy^{s.p} bo^{ms}). The rabbis have *Gînnêsar* and several other spellings (Jastrow, s.v.; Schlatter, pp. 473–4), but the feminine ending of the gospels remains unparalleled.

35. καὶ ἐπιγνόντες αὐτὸν οἱ ἄνδρες τοῦ τόπου ἐκείνου ἀπέστειλαν εἰς ὅλην τὴν περίχωρον ἐκείνην καὶ προσήνεγκαν αὐτῷ πάντας τοὺς κακῶς ἔχοντας. This is a revised, shortened version of Mk 6.54–6b. Matthew has, among other things, abbreviated, eliminated Jesus' movements from place to place, added a biblical phrase, 'the men of that place',[48] made the scene less graphic (e.g. by omitting 'when they go out of the boat' and 'on

---

[46] So Gnilka, *Markus* 1, pp. 271–2; contrast Pesch 1, p. 364.
[47] So at least HG. NA^{26} prints επι την γην ηλθον εις (so ℵ B L 33 sa^{mss} bo geo¹). ηλθον εις την γην and ηλθον επι την γην εις are also attested. The last is undoubtedly assimilation to Matthew, as are perhaps the other readings which have εις; so one is inclined to follow HG.
[48] Cf. ʾanšê hammāqôm (hahû), as in Gen 26.7.

their pallets'), and, as in the other healing summaries, added 'all', a little word which stresses Jesus' unbounded success as a healer.⁴⁹ The evangelist has also, in the interests of parallelism, refined v. 35a so that it resembles v. 34: καί + participle + finite verb + εἰς is used in both instances.

36. Given Matthew's dislike of magical practices (cf. Hull, pp. 116–41), it is surprising to find here no remark on faith or Jesus' teaching or preaching. But perhaps in this connexion it is worth noting that while the crowds are allowed to touch Jesus' garments, 'it appears as if this was something forced upon Him, rather than an opportunity which He sought. It is as if He had other work to do, and yet was too full of compassion to let this pass' (Plummer, p. 210).

καὶ παρεκάλουν αὐτὸν ἵνα μόνον ἅψωνται τοῦ κρασπέδου τοῦ ἱματίου αὐτοῦ. So also Mk 6.56, with κᾶν for μόνον and ἅψωνται at the end. The changes in Matthew are due to assimilation to the very similar 9.21 (q.v. for discussion), where μόνον ἅψωμαι τοῦ ἱματίου αὐτοῦ occurs.

καὶ ὅσοι ἥψαντο διεσώθησαν. Mk 6.56 has, after ὅσοι, ἂν ἥπτοντο⁵⁰ αὐτοῦ ἐσῴζοντο. διασῴζω (Mt: 1; Mk: 0; Lk: 0) is stronger than the simple σῴζω: the sick were *completely* healed (cf. Lk 7.3).

(iv) *Concluding Observations*

(1) In the First Gospel Jesus exercises powers and displays attributes traditionally connected with God alone. In the present pericope, Jesus both walks on the sea and subdues its rage, and these are acts which the OT assigns to Yahweh himself. In other words, Jesus here exhibits an authority which the Jewish Scriptures associate exclusively with the deity. The fact speaks volumes. In addition, Jesus is bold enough to refer to himself with the loaded and numinous 'I am'. In view of all this, it does not quite suffice to say that, for our author, God has acted through Jesus the Messiah. It seems more accurate to assert that, in Matthew's gospel, God actively shares attributes characteristic of himself with another, his Son. The step towards the later ecumenical creeds, which affirm Christ's deity, appears undeniable.

(2) So often the First Evangelist, while addressing

---

⁴⁹ The same motive explains the addition of μόνον in the next verse as well as the addition of δια- to σῴζω.

⁵⁰ So HG, following A Maj syʰ. NA²⁶ prints ηψαντο (so ℵ B D L W Δ Θ 0274 *f*¹·¹³); but is this not to be explained as due to Matthean influence?

christological issues with his right hand, is at the same time delivering teaching on discipleship with his left. And so is it here. If 14.22–33 is first of all about Jesus, his authority and identity (cf. Gerhardsson, *Acts*, p. 57), it is also, as most commentators, ancient and modern, have observed, also a little parable about Christian faith in the face of difficulties.[51] The stormy sea—so often a symbol of chaos and evil in the biblical tradition—represents the troubles in which believers will inevitably find themselves when they obey Jesus' commands (cf. 14.22). The boat, perhaps, represents the church. Jesus' walking on the water and coming to his disciples conveys the thought that he will not forget or abandon his own but will come to deliver them from evil. And Peter's actions, through which he displays his little faith, teach that what counts is Jesus' saving presence, not the Christian's strength of will or courage; and furthermore that faith is in fact participation in Jesus' divine power (cf. Held, in *TIM*, pp. 288–91).[52]

(3) 14.22–33 makes an important statement ˙about the continuity between the ecclesia and the Jewish past. The passage in part functions to demonstrate that, despite the broad front of resistance encountered in Israel, there nonetheless remained Jews who welcomed Jesus and believed, confessing him to be the Son of God. The harsh words about the Jews (e.g. 8.11–12 and 27.25) and the transcending of all ethnic limitations (e.g. 28.16–20) cannot overturn this fact and should not be permitted to obscure it. The church, according to Matthew, took root in a Jewish environment and began with nothing but Jewish members. In other words, it had its origin in a Jewish remnant.

(4) The part of Peter in 14.22–33 merits three remarks. First, there is here no portrait of a faultless hero: the apostle doubts and he sinks. Thus greatness and frailty go hand in hand. Secondly, it may well be, as commentators have often held, that 14.22–33 should be viewed partly as a rehearsal for Peter's rôle in the passion narrative. Just as other stories in chapter 14 point forward to the gospel's conclusion,[53] so too may Peter's bold entrance into the water, his subsequent sinking, and his eventual rescue by Jesus, foreshadow the apostle's overconfident confession (26.30–6), his denial of the Lord (26.69–75), and his

[51] Cf. Augustine, *Serm.* 25 and 26 (where he argues that Peter represents the common Christian condition).

[52] That one can move from the parabolic interpretation of Mt 14.22–33 to concrete assertions about Matthew's community—e.g. that miracles were on the wane, little faith on the rise—is, *pace* Braumann (v), not evident to us.

[53] E.g. John's martyrdom foreshadows the martyrdom of Jesus, and there are parallels between the feeding of the five thousand and the institution of the Eucharist.

final restoration (cf. 28.16–17). Thirdly, because the narrative section, 13.53–17.27, is dominated by the founding of the church (16.13–20), and because Peter is the rock on which that church is built (16.18), it is most fitting that, from this point on, Peter should begin to be singled out in various ways from the rest of the apostolic band (cf. 15.15; 16.22–3; 17.4, 24–5).

(v) *Bibliography*

P. Achtemeier, 'Person and Deed: Jesus and the Storm-Tossed Sea', *Int.* 16 (1962), pp. 169–76.

Barth, in *TIM*, pp. 113–14.

W. Berg, *Die Rezeption alttestamentlicher Motive im Neuen Testament dargestellt an den Seewandelerzählungen*, Freiburg, 1979.

G. Braumann, 'Der sinkende Petrus', *TZ* 22 (1966), pp. 403–14.

C. R. Carlisle, 'Jesus' Walking on the Water: A Note on Matthew 14.22–33', *NTS* 31 (1985), pp. 151–5.

A.-M. Denis, 'La marche de Jésus sur les eaux', in de la Potterie, pp. 233–47.

J. D. M. Derrett, 'Why and how Jesus walked on the Sea', *NovT* 23 (1981), pp. 330–48.

G. Gispert-Sauch, 'St Peter Walking on the Ganges?', *Vidyajyoti* 42 (1978), pp. 468–72.

Heil, passim.

Held, in *TIM*, pp. 204–6, 272.

D. F. Hill, 'The Walking on the Water', *ExpT* 99 (1988), pp. 267–9.

Kertelge, *Wunder*, pp. 35–6, 145–50.

R. Kratz, 'Der Seewandel des Petrus', *BuL* 15 (1974), pp. 86–101.

J. Kremer, 'Jesu Wandel auf dem See nach Mk 6.45–52', *BuL* 10 (1969), pp. 221–32.

J. Kreyenbühl, 'Der älteste Auferstehungsbericht und seine Varianten', *ZNW* 9 (1908), pp. 257–96.

H. Kruse, 'Jesu Seefahrten und die Stellung von Joh. 6', *NTS* 30 (1984), pp. 508–30.

P. Lapide, 'A Jewish Exegesis of the Walking on the Water', *Concilium* 138 (1980), pp. 35–40.

E. Lövestam, 'Wunder und Symbolhandlung: Eine Studie über Matthäus 14.28–31', *KD* 8 (1962), pp. 124–35.

Otto, pp. 368–74.

H. Ritt, 'Der "Seewandel Jesu" (Mk 6.45–52 par.)', *BZ* 23 (1979), pp. 71–84.

Schenke, *Wundererzählungen*, pp. 238–53.

J. Smit Sibinga, 'Matthew 14.22–33: Text and Composition', in *New Testament Textual Criticism*, ed. E. J. Epp and G. D. Fee, Oxford, 1981, pp. 15–33.

T. Snoy, 'Le rédaction marcienne de la marche sur les eaux (Mc., VI.45–52)', *ETL* 44 (1968), pp. 205–41, 433–81.

R. Stehly, 'Bouddhisme et Nouveau Testament—à propos de la marche de Pierre sur l'eau (Matthieu 14.28s)', *RHPR* 57 (1977), pp. 433–7.

Strauss, pp. 496–507.
Van der Loos, pp. 650–69.
H. Volk, 'Petrus steigt aus dem Boot', *Catholica* 14 (1960), pp. 49–55.
Zumstein, pp. 245–54.

XXXIV

THE PHARISAIC TRADITION; CLEAN AND UNCLEAN
(15.1–20)

(i) *Structure*

Mt 15.1–20, like its source, Mk 7.1–23, is a drawn-out objection story with three scenes. The first scene depicts Jesus with the Pharisees and scribes (vv. 1–9), the second Jesus with the crowds (vv. 10–11), the third Jesus with his disciples (vv. 12–20). Scenes I and III are similar in that each opens with a question directed to Jesus.

Note how the third scene helps knit the three sections together. In vv. 12 and 15 Jesus is asked about the Pharisees' response to the utterance in v. 11 and the meaning of that utterance. Thus vv. 12–20 elaborate upon the mid-point text 10–11; that is, scene III is a commentary upon scene II. At the very end of the whole passage, however, Jesus declares: 'But to eat with unwashed hands does not defile a man' (v. 20). This takes the reader back to the question posed at the beginning: 'Why do your disciples transgress the tradition of the elders? For they do not rinse their hands when they eat' (v. 2). This closure makes the unity of the whole manifest.

(ii) *Sources*

It is possible to contend that Mt 15.1–20 is more primitive than, and therefore not dependent upon, Mk 7.1–23 (so Sigal (v)). The First Gospel contains no explanation of Jewish handwashing (contrast Mk 7.2–4); it does not contain the sweeping, explicit remark that Jesus declared all foods clean (Mk 7.19c); and its teaching is probably closer to Jesus' teaching than Mark's account (cf. p. 531). Hence one might infer that Mk 7.1–23 is secondary, that it has been revised for Gentiles and reflects a more relaxed attitude towards the law. The inference, however, is not necessary. None of the observations made favour the Griesbach hypothesis if one believes that Matthew's Gospel was written by a Jew for a largely Jewish community and that its author was more conservative than Mark with respect to the law, for then the differences could all be readily explained by the interests of the First Evangelist (see section (iii)). Beyond this, there are several pointers to Matthew's dependence upon Mark in the passage at hand. (i) Peter's question in Mt 15.15 (concerning 'this parable') refers to the saying in v. 11. Vv. 12–14 interrupt the natural sequence. Matthew's account presupposes one without vv. 12–14—which is exactly what we find in Mark. (ii) With the exception of 15.1, which speaks of 'Pharisees and scribes', Matthew always refers to the 'scribes and Pharisees', in that order. Why the exception to the rule? One could surmise that the unusual order is due to Matthew following his source at this point. Again Mark satisfies on that account: he has 'the Pharisees . . . with some of the scribes' (7.1). (iii) In Matthew Jesus summons a crowd to give new teaching (15.10). The same is true in Mk 7.14, where the device is usually considered a trait of Markan redaction (see the commentaries). (iv) εἰσπορεύομαι appears in Mt 15.17 and Mk 7.18. The word is used eight times in Mark, only once in Matthew. So do we not have in Matthew's text a feature of Markan redaction? For further discussion see Tuckett (v), from whose discussion we have drawn.

(iii) *Exegesis*

Matthew continues to follow the Markan sequence. There is no obvious thematic link between 15.1–20 and the surrounding material (cf. Cope, p. 53).[1]

15.1–20 serves three major functions. It is first an attack on the Pharisaic tradition: that tradition does not have the same authority as Scripture, so it must be judged by Scripture, and where necessary condemned (vv. 1–9). There is secondly the attack on the Pharisees themselves: their lives exhibit hypocrisy and they cannot be followed (vv. 12–14; cf. 16.5–12). The third major thrust of 15.1–20 is the teaching on purity: what matters above all is the defilement effected by the human heart (vv. 10f., 15–20).

Against Meier (v) and others, we do not find in Mt 15 an abolition of OT purity laws. Not only would such an interpretation run afoul of other Matthean texts (e.g. 5.17–20), but the decisive statement in Mk 7.19 ('thus he declared all foods clean') has been omitted. Further, the redactional insertion of vv. 12–14 (a discussion of the Pharisees) as well as the editorial conclusion (v. 20: 'but to eat with unwashed hands does not defile a man') reveal that the evangelist's concern is not with the OT but with the Pharisees and their *paradosis*.[2]

Several major changes have been introduced into Mk 7.1–23. In addition to those mentioned in the previous paragraph the following

[1] Because we doubt that Mt 15.1–20 abolishes OT food laws we do not think it serves as an introduction to 15.21–8, where Jesus heals a Gentile. Some have proposed a connexion with 14.34–6: Jesus mingles with the crowds and this raises the issue of purity. (But the crowds are not said to be unclean).

[2] In 14.34–6 people grab the κρασπέδον (= ṣîṣit; cf. Num 15.38) of Jesus' garment. Does this not encourage the reader to think him a law-observant Jew?

may be remarked: (i) The explanation of the custom of washing the hands (Mk 7.3–4) is not reproduced, presumably because Matthew's largely Jewish community already knew the facts. (ii) The parallelism between several sentences has been enhanced, as one might have anticipated (see 1, pp. 94–5, and cf. v. 2a with v. 3, v. 4 with v. 5, v. 11a with v. 11b). (iii) Many of Mark's sentences have been abbreviated, much of his redundancy eliminated (see e.g. on vv. 10, 17, 19). (iv) The word κορβᾶν (Mk 7.11) has been dropped (see 1, p. 20). (v) Mark's section on *qorbān* (7.9–12) has been placed before the sentences from Isaiah (7.6–8). The inversion gives a smoother, more logical progression and puts the teaching of the law before the teaching of the prophets (cf. 5.17; 7.12; 22.40). (vi) The list of vices in Mk 7.21–2 has been cut from thirteen items to seven (see on v. 19).

The tradition-history of Matthew's source, Mk 7.1–23, is much disputed. Bultmann, *History*, pp. 17–18, held 7.1–8 to incorporate a pericope produced by the Palestinian church to which the Second Evangelist added vv. 9–13 ('a piece of community polemic'), the dominical 7.15, the pre-Markan interpretation of this last in vv. 18b–19, and the possibly redactional vv. 20–3 (these verses being 'Hellenistic'). According to Dibelius, *Tradition*, pp. 200–1, the core is 7.9–13. In the pre-Markan tradition this grew through the addition of 7.15, then vv. 17–19 and 20–3, then 7.6–8. Mark himself composed 7.1–5. For Hübner (v), 7.1–2, 5, 9, 10a, 11–13a represents a pre-Markan pericope of historical value while 7.15 (whose original form may be found in 18c + 20) is an independent logion. Pesch 1, pp. 368, 376, while agreeing about 7.15, thinks that 7.1, 5–13 should be treated as a unit stemming from the life of Jesus. Yet another possibility comes from Booth (v), who finds behind 7.1, 5, and 15 an historical kernel which has been expanded by Markan redaction (vv. 2–4, 8, 13, 23), a piece of Christian apologetic (vv. 6–8), the *qorbān* complex (vv. 9–13), and two pre-Markan interpretations of 7.15 (vv. 18–19, a medical explanation, vv. 20–2, an ethical explanation).[3]

Although full of uncertitude, we reckon Bultmann's analysis probably closest to the truth. Minus the Markan redaction (vv. 2–4), 7.1–8 was at one time an independent pericope to which Mark or a predecessor added vv. 9–13, a conflict story which lost its introduction when inserted into its present context. We disagree with Bultmann only in thinking it probable that the *qorbān* section records teaching Jesus gave on the subject of Pharisaic tradition[4] and in not excluding the possibility (we do not say probability) that 7.1–8 is based on an historical encounter,[5] for it is not obvious that the question about handwashing has a *Sitz im Leben* in the early

---

[3] Berger (v) also thinks vv. 1, 5, and 15 once formed a unit.

[4] See Booth (v), pp. 94–6, citing the closely related Mt 23.16–19.

[5] Isa. 29.13 was otherwise certainly cited by early Christians (see on vv. 8–9), and our text quotes the LXX, not MT. But the Hebrew does refer to a 'human commandment' (*miṣwat 'ănāšîm*) which has been memorized or taught, and the general subject is superficial loyalty; also, Isa 29.14, the next verse, refers to the failure of the wisdom of the wise and the learning of the learned. So Jesus *could* have cited Isa 29.13 in attacking a Pharisaic tradition. But see further p. 525.

church.[6] As for 7.15, we concur that it was originally an independent logion which came to Mark with Christian interpretations already attached.[7] Finally, whereas the material in vv. 1–13 seems to have been passed on in order to aid Christians in debate with Jewish opponents,[8] v. 15 and its attachments appear, because of the list of vices, to have been employed as moral instruction, perhaps in a catechetical situation.

1. τότε προσέρχονται τῷ Ἰησοῦ ἀπὸ Ἱεροσολύμων Φαρισαῖοι καὶ γραμματεῖς λέγοντες. This is a severe abbreviation of Mk 7.1–4. Matthew's revision has avoided possible exaggeration ('all the Jews') and eliminated information presumably well-known to his audience.[9]

Both τότε* and προσέρχομαι* are Matthean. On the Pharisees—only here in Matthew are they named before the scribes—see 1, pp. 301–2, and on the scribes p. 240. Whereas Mk 7.1 can be taken to mean that the Pharisees are from Galilee, the scribes alone from Jerusalem (cf. Taylor, *Mark*, p. 334), in Matthew both groups must be from the capital. On Jerusalem (which has not been named for ten chapters) see 1, pp. 232, 238–9, and J. K. Elliott, 'Jerusalem in Acts and the Gospels', *NTS* 23 (1977), pp. 462–9. Its appearance here reinforces its hostile character (it is home to Jesus' opponents) and points ahead to the passion narrative.

2. Jesus is asked by the Pharisees and scribes, who seem to be acting like inspectors,[10] why his followers transgress the tradition of the elders, in particular why they do not wash their hands before eating. Unlike the situation in Mark, there is here no immediate instigation for the question; that is, we are not informed that the Jewish leaders have witnessed the behaviour of Jesus' disciples.

διὰ τί οἱ μαθηταί σου παραβαίνουσιν τὴν παράδοσιν τῶν πρεσβυτέρων; Matthew has substituted the more judgemental παραβαίνω (= 'transgress'; cf. v. 3)[11] for the more general οὐ περιπατοῦσιν (cf. *hălākâ*) + κατά of Mk 7.5.

---

[6] Booth (v), p. 65, is relevant: 'It seems unlikely that either Mark or the early church should have created a question about handwashing, for it can hardly have been the most conspicuous or contentious example of a legal system which covered comprehensively almost every aspect of Jewish daily life. Handwashing is not specifically referred to again in our passage, so it has not been mentioned in the Question in order to 'link up' conveniently with a Jesus logion'.

[7] Mk 7.14, the end of 19, and 23 are probably Markan. That Mark has had a hand in formulating 7.14–23 is probably indicated by the structural parallels it shares with Mk 4.1–20; see E. J. Mally, 'The Gospel according to Mark', *JBC*, p. 37.

[8] Cf. U. B. Müller, 'Zur Rezeption Gesetzeskritischer Jesusüberlieferung im frühen Christentum', *NTS* 27 (1981), p. 182.

[9] It is just possible that Mk 7.3–4 is an early interpolation and that it was not in Matthew's copy; cf. Taylor, *Mark*, p. 335.

[10] Is it possible that certain Jerusalem authorities did in fact send representatives to Galilee to find out what the uproar concerning Jesus was about?

[11] Elsewhere in the NT only in Acts 1.25. In the LXX, for several Hebrew

παράδοσις¹² refers to the Pharisees' extrabiblical traditions. These later came to be codified in the Mishnah.¹³ Compare Josephus, *Ant.* 13.297: 'the Pharisees had passed down (παρέδοσαν) to the people certain regulations handed down by former generations and not recorded in the law of Moses, for which reason they are rejected by the Sadducaean group, who hold that only those regulations should be considered valid which were written down, and that those which had been handed down (παραδόσεως) by former generations need not be observed'. Because παράδοσις describes the Pharisaic tradition in Paul (n. 12), in the gospels, and in Josephus, it was clearly a technical term. It probably translates the Hebrew *massôret*.¹⁴

The tradition of the Pharisees had a controversial status before A.D. 70. The Sadducees repudiated it. So did those responsible for composing the Dead Sea Scrolls (we take them to have been Essenes). Note 1QH 4.14–15: 'Teachers of lies and seers of falsehood have schemed against me in a devilish scheme, to exchange the law engraved on my heart by Thee for the smooth things (which they speak) to Thy people'. In the Scrolls the seekers of smooth things are the Pharisees. Also noteworthy in this regard is Josephus, *Ant.* 17.41, which probably preserves a criticism of Nicolas of Damascus (cf. the note in the Loeb edition): the Pharisees pretend (προσποιεῖν) to observe the laws of which God approves. Behind this accusation may well lie the polemic that the laws which they *do* observe are of their own making¹⁵—in which case Mt 15.1–20 would in part contain a conventional criticism. However that may be, Jesus and the gospel writers were not alone in rejecting the Pharisaic *paradosis* as a later innovation. (That the Pharisees themselves were sensitive to the criticisms directed against them is apparent from the fact that they used such expressions as 'tradition of the elders' (Mk 7.3; Josephus, *Ant.* 10.51) and 'tradition of the fathers' (Gal 1.14; Josephus, *Ant.* 13.408). These ground the tradition in the authoritative past, which is just what we might expect from a Hellenistic school (cf. Davies, *JPS*, pp. 27–48). Recall *m.* '*Abot* 1.1, where the tradition is passed down from Moses to Joshua to the elders to the prophets and then to the men of the great synagogue: this is apologetical history.)

οὐ γὰρ νίπτονται τὰς χεῖρας αὐτῶν ὅταν ἄρτον ἐσθίωσιν.¹⁶ Compare LXX Lev 15.11 (τὰς χεῖρας οὐ νένιπται). The

equivalents, it is used of transgression of God's ῥῆμα, λόγος, διαθήκη, νόμος, and ἐντολή.

¹² Mt: 3; Mk: 5; Lk: 0. Paul uses the word both of Christian tradition (1 Cor 11.2; 2 Thess 2.15; 3.6) and Pharisaic tradition (Gal 1.14).

¹³ See SB 1, pp. 691–5; Davies, *JPS*, pp. 8–17; A. I. Baumgarten, 'The Pharisaic *Paradosis*', *HTR* 80 (1987), pp. 63–77 (our discussion owes much to this last).

¹⁴ Cf. the use of *māsar* in *m.* '*Abot*.

¹⁵ See Baumgarten (as in n. 13), pp. 70–1. —Modern scholarship has in fact increasingly come to observe that laws in the Mishnah often bear little relation to the written Torah. See Davies, *JPS*, 10–14, 306–7. In a way the NT anticipated polemically the results of modern study of the Mishnah.

¹⁶ NA²⁶ puts αυτων in brackets. It is missing from ℵ B Δ 084 *f*¹ 700 892 1424 *pc* f g¹.

observation, intended to substantiate the charge just delivered, combines Mk 7.5c ('but eat bread with hands defiled') with the gist of 7.2–4, which refers to the habit of washing hands. For 'eat bread' (=ʾākal leḥem) see Gen 31.54; Exod 2.20; b. Sanh. 100b. The expression simply means 'eat food' (cf. SB 1, pp. 704–5). But are we here to recall 14.15–21?

The custom of washing the hands with water was not primarily hygienic, although that aspect should not be entirely ignored.[17] The primary purpose of the washing was the removal of ceremonial defilement and ritual impurity. Already in Exod 30.17–21 the Aaronic priesthood is instructed to wash hands and feet before going into the tent of meeting; and in Lev 15.11 uncleanness is not transmitted by one with a discharge if he has rinsed his hands with water. Presumably the case of priests washing hands before eating consecrated food came to be adopted by members of the Pharisaic party because they 'held that even outside of the Temple, in one's own home, the laws of ritual purity were to be followed in the only circumstance in which they might apply, namely, at the table. Therefore, one must eat secular food (ordinary, everyday meals) in a state of ritual purity *as if one were a Temple priest*. The Pharisees thus arrogated to themselves—and to all Jews equally—the status of the Temple priests, and performed actions restricted to priests on account of that status. The table of every Jew in his home was seen as being like the table of the Lord in the Jerusalem Temple. The commandment, "You shall be a kingdom of priests and holy people" was taken literally: Everyone is a priest, everyone stands in the same relationship to God, and everyone must keep the priestly laws'.[18] Something similar happened at Qumran, but there total immersion was required before each meal.[19]

It is unfortunately very difficult to know to what extent if any the developed legislation in the Mishnah, which covers such topics as what sort of water can be used for purification, what vessels are appropriate, and so on (see esp. *m. Yad.*, passim), was observed in first-century Palestine. Also problematic is the extent of the custom before A.D. 70. Although Mark's statement, 'For the Pharisees, and all the Jews, do not eat unless they wash their hands' (7.3), is usually regarded as exaggerated, some see no difficulty in supposing that the habit was widespread.[20] But the evidence from rabbinic sources can be rejected

---

[17] For hygienic washing see Gen 43.24; 2 Kgs 3.11; Jer 2.22; Jn 13.1–5; *b. Ber.* 50b, and for washing hands as a symbol of innocence see on 27.24. Discussion in L. E. Goodman, 'The Biblical Laws on Diet and Sex', in *Jewish Law Association Studies II*, ed. B. S. Jackson, Atlanta, 1986, pp. 17–57. On p. 18 he observes that in the realm of clean and unclean 'intensity of experience fosters and can therefore be expressed by a muddling of categories'.

[18] J. Neusner, *From Politics to Piety*, Englewood Cliffs, 1973, p. 83.

[19] Cf. Josephus, *Bell.* 2.129, 138; 1QS 3.8–9; 5.13; CD 10.10–13. See M. Newton, *The Concept of Purity at Qumran and in the Letters of Paul*, Cambridge, 1985, pp. 26–40.

[20] See e.g. S. Safrai, in *CRINT*, section 1, vol. 2, pp. 801–2, citing *m. Ḥag.*2.5; *b. Šabb.* 13b–14a; *y. Šabb.*1.3d; *b. Yoma* 87b.

because of doubt concerning its antiquity; and the other texts usually cited—Jud 12.7; Ep. Arist. 305–6; Sib. Orac. 3.591–3—do not prove what many have imagined.[21] Booth (v) has even contended that there is no good reason to think handwashing before meals was widely practised before A.D. 70: in Jesus' time only the so-called *ḥăbērîm* (he identifies them as a type of Pharisee) rinsed their hands prior to eating *ḥullîn*, everyday food. But perhaps he has gone too far. Could Mark (whom perhaps most scholars take to have been Jewish) have written what he did if in his time or only shortly before none but members of a branch of Pharisaism washed before meals? Jn 2.6 is also pertinent: 'there were there six stone jars of water standing there, according to the purification of the Jews, each holding twenty or thirty gallons'. This is another first-century text which presupposes that handwashing was widely practised before A.D. 70 (see also perhaps Lk 11.38–9). Then there is the question whether the *ḥăbērîm* would have criticized non-Pharisees for neglecting a custom which (according to Booth) even many Pharisees neglected. Booth has, we think, probably underestimated the prevalence of ritual handwashing in Jesus' time.

3. ὁ δὲ ἀποκριθεὶς εἶπεν αὐτοῖς. So Mk 7.6, perhaps without the first verb (the mss. differ).

διὰ τί καὶ ὑμεῖς παραβαίνετε τὴν ἐντολὴν τοῦ θεοῦ διὰ τὴν παράδοσιν ὑμῶν; Compare 2 Chron 24.20; T. Levi 14.4 ('you want to destroy the light of the law which was granted to you for the enlightenment of every man, teaching commandments which are opposed to God's just commandments'); T. Asher 7.5 ('heeding not God's law but human commandments'). Matthew's sentence replaces Mk 7.9: καλῶς ἀθετεῖτε τὴν ἐντολὴν τοῦ θεοῦ, ἵνα τὴν παράδοσιν ὑμῶν τηρήσητε (or: στήσητε). Our evangelist has put the substance of Mark's ironical sentence into a question which mirrors v. 2: question answers question. Both have this form: διὰ τί + subject (in v. 3 ὑμεῖς is emphatic) + παραβαίνω + τὴν παράδοσιν/ἐντολήν + τῶν πρεσβυτέρων/τοῦ θεοῦ. The author's love of parallelism has once more expressed itself.

There are Jewish texts in which transgression of the law is a mark of the latter days.[22] This theme, however, does not seem to have anything to do with our present passage.

4. ὁ γὰρ θεὸς ἐνετείλατο λέγων.[23] Compare Mk 15.10: 'For Moses said'. Matthew's alteration (cf. 22.31 diff. Mk 12.26),

---

[21] Discussion in Booth (v), pp. 159–60.
[22] E.g. Jub. 23.19–21; CD 4–5; T. Levi 4.4; 10.3; 16.2; T. Iss. 6.1; *m. Soṭa* 9.13. (The passage that concludes *m. Soṭa* 9.13 shows how cultic and moral categories were related.)
[23] So HG and ℵ*·2 C L W 0106 Maj f syʰ. NA²⁶ and ℵ¹ B D Θ 084 f¹·¹³ 700 892 pc lat syˢ·ᶜ·ᵖ co Irˡᵃᵗ Cyr have ειπεν after θεος (assimilation to Mark?).

which heightens the antithesis with v. 5, shows that Jesus is not
attacking the Torah. The commandment of Moses is the
commandment of God (cf. Davies, *SSM*, pp. 105–6).

τίμα τὸν πατέρα καὶ τὴν μητέρα. Mark, in agreement with
LXX Deut 5.16, has σου twice (cf. MT Exod 20.12: ʾābîkā,
ʾimmekā). LXX Exod 20.12 has σου only after πατέρα.
Matthew has excised the possessive pronouns, which makes for
abbreviation and increased parallelism with the next line. From
what follows the imperative to 'honour' parents clearly includes
financial assistance (cf. Prov 28.24; 1 Tim 5.4).

καί· ὁ κακολογῶν πατέρα ἢ μητέρα θανάτῳ τελευτάτω. So
Mark. LXX Exod 21.17 (cf. Lev 20.9; Deut 27.6) has αὐτοῦ
(*bis*), and some mss. have τελευτήσει θανάτῳ at the end.[24] The
MT is accurately rendered by the LXX except that ἤ renders
wĕ. The citation of Exod 21.17[25] serves the purpose of stressing
the seriousness of breaking the fifth commandment. To dis-
honour one's parents[26] is a crime meriting severe punishment.

5. ὑμεῖς δὲ λέγετε. So also Mk 7.11. This stands in antithesis
to 'For God said' (v. 4).

ὃς ἂν εἴπῃ τῷ πατρὶ ἢ τῇ μητρί. Mark has ἐάν[27] before the
verb and ἄνθρωπος (strictly unnecessary) after it.

δῶρον. This is a substitution for Mark's longer κορβᾶν, ὅ
ἐστιν δῶρον (cf. Josephus, *C. Ap.* 1.167; throughout the LXX
δῶρον renders qorbān). The word qorbān[28] (Aramaic qûrbānāʾ,
qorbānāʾa) originally meant 'sacrifice' or 'offering' (BDB, s.v.).
In time it came to refer to a ban which involved the withdrawing
of something from profane or common use, the treating of it as
though it were dedicated to the temple.[29] From the Mishnah
(where the synonyms qônâ, qônām, and qônās are often used)
we learn that a qorbān vow formula could function as a legal
fiction which entailed no actual sacrifice (cf. *m. Ned.* 5.6, etc.)
and also that the word qorbān itself was sometimes used as a
secular word of protestation (e.g. *m. Ned.* 3.11). Scholars debate
to what extent these facts as well as the Mishnah's various
rulings on qorbān vows (see esp. *m. Nedarim*) are useful for
studying the first century. Particularly discussed, because of its

---

[24] Reverse order, in agreement with the synoptics, in A F Luc.
[25] Is this Markan redaction?
[26] κακολογεῖν means 'to speak evil of'. This seems an infelicitous translation
of the Hebrew mĕqallēl, 'he that curses' or 'repudiates'. Cf. H. C. Brichto, *The
Problem of 'Curse' in the Hebrew Bible*, Philadelphia, 1963, pp. 132–5.
[27] Matthew is fond of ὃς ἄν*.
[28] See the lit. cited in Fitzmyer (v), to which add Vermes, *World*, pp. 78–9,
and Baumgarten (v). —In Mt 27.6 κορβανᾶς means the temple treasury.
[29] See Josephus, *Ant.* 4.72–3; *C. Ap.* 1.166–7. Cf. also CD 16.14–15 (although
here the word qorbān is not used).

bearing on the gospels, is the question: When did the rabbis come to make allowances for ill-considered vows and permit alleviation? In *m. Ned.* 9.1 it is implied that by reason of the honour due father and mother, one can repent of a *qorbān* vow, and other mitigating circumstances are considered elsewhere (*m. Ned.* 4.7–8). But it seems safe to assume, in the light of Mark's account, that at least some first-century teachers held a *qorbān* vow to be binding regardless of the circumstances of its utterance (cf. Num 30.2–3; Deut 23.21–3), or at least binding in the situation presupposed by Matthew and Mark (see Baumgarten (v)).

ὃ ἐὰν ἐξ ἐμοῦ ὠφεληθῇς. The meaning is: 'what you would have gained from me (is *qorbān*).' Compare Gos. Naz. frag. 12 (κορβᾶν ὃ ὑμεῖς ὠφεληθήσεσθε ἐξ ἡμῶν) and the Jebel Ḥallet eṭ-Ṭûri inscription ('All that a man may find-to-his-profit in this ossuary (is) *qorbān* to God from him who is within it'[30]). This last evidently represents 'a dedicatory formula in common use among the Jews of the last few centuries B.C. and well into Christian times' (so Fitzmyer). There are also close rabbinic parallels: *qônām šeʾatâ nehĕnêtâ lî: konam*, if I have any benefit from thee (*m. Ned.* 8.7). The Mishnah plainly reveals how common it was, at least at the time of its composition, to pronounce a *qorbān* vow for the purpose of not sharing property with others (cf. Philo, *Spec. leg.* 2.16–17); and it contains texts in which the vow deprives one's relatives (e.g. *m. Ned.* 5.6).

6. οὐ μὴ τιμήσει τὸν πατέρα αὐτοῦ.[31] 'He need not honour his father'. This revision of Mk 7.12 improves upon Mark's Greek (Allen, p. 164), enhances the antithetical parallelism with the Scripture cited in v. 4a, and puts the statement about not honouring on the lips of the opponents themselves, which heightens the correlation between commandment and transgression[32] (cf. Gundry, *Commentary*, p. 304: 'Matthew makes the Pharisees and scribes issue a commandment ("... shall not honor ...") contrary to God's commandment ("Honor ...")'). On οὐ μή before the future (or aorist) as 'the most definite form of negation regarding the future' see BDF § 365.

καὶ ἠκυρώσατε τὸν λόγον τοῦ θεοῦ διὰ τὴν παράδοσιν ὑμῶν.[33]

[30] See Fitzmyer (v) for full discussion. We have reproduced his translation.
[31] So NA²⁶. HG prints η την μητερα αυτον; so C L W Θ 0106 *f*¹ Maj aur f ff vgᶜˡ syᵖ·ʰ. Other witnesses have και την κ.τ.λ. One cannot determine the original. The temptation for a scribe to add 'or (and) his mother' would have been great. But accidental omission (passing from αυτου to αυτου) is also easily envisioned. See Metzger, p. 38.
[32] Matthew is fond of such formal correlations; see e.g. 1, p. 218.
[33] την εντολην (L W *f*¹ Maj lat syʰ) and τον νομον (ℵ*·² C *f*¹³ *pc*) replace τον λογον in some authorities.

Mk 7.13 opens with a participle (ἀκυρούντες, continuing the previous sentence). Also, instead of διά κ.τ.λ. (cf. Mt 15.3) Mark has τῇ παραδόσει ὑμῶν ᾗ παρεδώκατε³⁴ and additional words which Matthew reckons superfluous ('And many such things you do'). ἀκυρόω³⁵ means 'make void' (cf. Gal 3.17; Josephus, *Ant.* 18.304, with ἐντολάς). The *qorbān* vow is supposed to be service to God. Such service, however, can never be isolated from service to fellow human beings. If the *qorbān* vow does nothing save deprive the needy, then it is not in accord with service to God, which demands as its invariable corollary love of neighbour.

7. Returning to Mk 7.6, Matthew once more quotes Scripture, this time to illustrate the Pharisees' hypocrisy, their inconsistency. 'The delay of the quotation till now makes it the climax of Jesus' counter accusation' (Gundry, *Commentary*, p. 305).

ὑποκριταί. For the meaning of 'hypocrite' and its usage in Matthew see 1, pp. 580–1; also Schenk, *Sprache*, pp. 451–52. Here the introductory vocative (so frequent in chapter 23) is a shortening of Mark's 'concerning you hypocrites'.

καλῶς ἐπροφήτευσεν περὶ ὑμῶν Ἡσαῖας. Matthew has moved περὶ ὑμῶν forward (it follows the prophet's name in Mark) and omitted τῶν ὑποκριτῶν (see above). καλῶς here means 'truly' (cf. Mk 12.32; Jn 4.17). Compare its use to introduce Scripture in Acts 28.25, again prefacing a passage from Isaiah, again in connexion with failings in Israel. On 'Isaiah' in the First Gospel see 1, pp. 292–3, and Schenk, *Sprache*, pp. 151-2.

λέγων. This replaces ὡς γέγραπται (cf. 3.3 diff Mk 1.2).

8f. ὁ λαὸς οὗτος τοῖς χείλεσίν με τιμᾷ. So Mk 7.6, with οὗτος in first place. Matthew's word order is closer to LXX Isa 29.13. LXX A reads: ἐγγίζει μοι ὁ λαὸς οὗτος τοῖς χείλεσιν αὐτῶν τιμῶσιν με. LXX B, which is nearer the MT, adds ἐν τῷ στόματι αὐτοῦ καὶ ἐν after οὗτος (this is also supplied in some Matthean mss.). See Stendahl, *School*, pp. 56–8; Gundry, *OT*, pp. 14–16.

ἡ δὲ καρδία αὐτῶν πόρρω ἀπέχει ἀπ' ἐμοῦ. So both Mark and the LXX, accurately translating the MT.

μάτην δὲ σέβονταί με διδάσκοντες διδασκαλίας ἐντάλματα ἀνθρώπων. Mark agrees. 'Their fear of me is (just) a human commandment which has been memorized' is the meaning of the Hebrew, and although Taylor, *Mark*, pp. 337–8, may be right in claiming that the MT could have been quoted by Jesus to make the charge in the synoptics (cf. n. 5), it is no less likely

³⁴ Matthew's omission of the redundancy is typical.
³⁵ Mt: 1; Mk: 1; Lk: 0. In the LXX only in 1 Esdr 6.32 and 4 Macc.

that the Scripture was quoted precisely because of what it says in the LXX: 'teaching the commandments and doctrines of men' (διδάσκοντες ἐντάλματα ἀνθρώπων καὶ διδασκαλίας). LXX Isa 29.13 and surrounding verses were much cited by early Christians (cf. Rom 9.20; 11.8; 1 Cor 1.19; 1 Clem 15.2; 2 Clem 3.5) and appear to have been used polemically against Jewish tradition and perceived Jewish hypocrisy, as in Mt 15.8–9; Mk 7.6–7; Col 2.22; *Pap. Eg.* 2 fol. 2ʳ (see Hennecke 1, p. 97); and Justin, *Dial.* 78.11.

10. Jesus now ceases to address his opponents and turns to the crowd. This coincides with a change in his argument. In vv. 3–9 he has responded to the charge about his disciples not keeping Pharisaic tradition. The issue there is authority. Beginning with v. 10 the broader issue of defilement becomes the subject.

καὶ προσκαλεσάμενος τὸν ὄχλον. Compare 15.32. Mark's πάλιν (in third position) has been dropped, perhaps because it is awkward (this is not a second gathering of the crowd). On ὄχλος see 1, pp. 419–20, and Allen, p. lxxxvi.

εἶπεν αὐτοῖς. In Mark the verb is ἔλεγεν. For the disagreement between the plural (αὐτοῖς) and the singular (ὄχλον) see BDF § 134.

Jesus proceeds to give the crowd teaching. But, as in chapter 13, he interprets or explains his teaching only to insiders (cf. vv. 15ff.).

ἀκούετε καὶ συνίετε. Compare 2 Sam 20.16; Isa 6.9; Mt 13.9, 18, 23, 43, 51. In Mark the call to attention has μου πάντες before καί, and the verbs are in the aorist.

Jesus' invitation to the crowd to hear and understand should caution those who refer to Matthew's attitude towards 'the Jews'. In the present passage Jesus rebukes only the Pharisees. He treats the crowd differently. It is not reprimanded but instead given teaching. Clearly the Pharisees and the Jewish masses are for Matthew two different groups; they should not be lumped together as one entity.[36]

11. This antithetical proverb or wisdom saying is the crucial declaration in 15.1–20. Perrin, *Rediscovering*, p. 150, thinks the saying 'perhaps the most radical statement in the whole of the Jesus tradition'. But see below.

οὐ τὸ εἰσερχόμενον εἰς τὸ στόμα κοινοῖ τὸν ἄνθρωπον ἀλλὰ τὸ ἐκπορευόμενον ἐκ τοῦ στόματος τοῦτο κοινοῖ τὸν ἄνθρωπον. Compare Menander, frag. 540 ('all that brings defilement comes from within'); Philo, *Spec. leg.* 3.209 ('for the unjust and impious

---

[36] Contrast Carlston, *Parables*, p. 29: the Pharisees are 'symbolic of the people as a whole, a kind of negative ideal of Judaism'.

man is in the truest sense unclean'); Sextus, *Sent.* 110 ('a person is not defiled by the food and drink he consumes but by those acts which result from an evil character': this depends upon Matthew); Pseud.-Phoc. 228 ('purification of the soul, not of the body, makes atonement': there are textual variants). The grammatically awkward Mk 7.15 has this: οὐδέν ἐστιν ἔξωθεν τοῦ ἀνθρώπου εἰσπορευόμενον εἰς αὐτὸν ὃ δύναται κοινῶσαι αὐτόν, ἀλλὰ τὰ ἐκ τοῦ ἀνθρώπου ἐκπορευόμενά ἐστιν τὰ κοινοῦντα τὸν ἄνθρωπον. Matthew has cut and changed a number of words, increased the parallelism of the two clauses, added 'the mouth' (*bis*), and smoothed out the grammar (although his τὸ ... τοῦτο is more Semitic than Mark's related construction; cf. MHT 4, p. 37). The result is a shorter, less cryptic, more explicit statement.

Why the addition of 'mouth' (also added in vv. 17 and 18)? The supplement not only adds clarity. It also recalls the Q saying in 12.34: 'For out of the abundance of the heart the mouth speaks'. Perhaps Mark's 'things which go out of a man' (7.15) and 'out of the heart of man' (7.21; cf. also the use of 'heart' in Isa 29.13) reminded Matthew of the earlier logion and he formulated and interpreted 15.11 accordingly. (The outcome is a bit infelicitous, for it is not just words which defile. So do actions; cf. v. 19.) That which goes into the mouth is, as the following will elucidate, food and drink, that which comes out the evil things produced by an evil heart. It would probably be pushing the text too far to include the making of a *qorbān* vow as one of the things which coming out of the mouth defiles a man.

Although κοινόω[37] means 'make common' or 'share', it here means 'defile' (cf. 4 Macc 7.6—the only LXX occurrence). This special meaning is to be explained by the transformation of κοινός, 'common': this word is used in 1 Macc 1.47, 62 'in the sense "ritually unclean", for which the Hebrew would be *ṭāmēʾ*, and it has this sense in the N.T. in this passage [Mk 7.2] and also in Acts x. 14, 28, xi. 8, Rev xxi, 27. The explanation of this use would seem to be that first κοινός came to be used among Jews as an equivalent for *ḥōl* (which denotes "that which is free for general use" as opposed to that which is *ḳādōš* ("holy"))— a not unnatural extension of the use of κοινός, as is illustrated by the fact that A.V., R.V. use "common" to render *ḥōl*, e.g. in 1 Sam xxi 4f.—though this usage, which is seen in the NT in Heb x.29, is not found in the LXX, which renders *ḥōl* by βέβηλος, e.g. in 1 Sam xxi 4f. From this use of κοινός to translate *ḥōl* it was an easy step to use it for *ṭāmēʾ*, since the two pairs of opposites, *ḳādōš* ("holy") and *ḥōl* ("free for general use"), and *ṭāhôr* ("ritually clean") and *ṭāmēʾ* ("ritually unclean"), though they are quite clearly to be distinguished, are obviously closely related' (Cranfield, *Mark*, p. 232; see further Booth (v), pp. 120–1).

Mk 7.15 = Mt 15.11 is accepted as a genuine saying of Jesus by most

---

[37] Cf. Acts 10.15; 11.9; 21.28; Heb 9.13.

critical scholars.[38] Furthermore, most endorse the Markan interpretation—Jesus declared all foods clean—as good interpretation: Jesus did in fact annul the food laws of Leviticus.[39] In agreement with these positions, Paul seems to have known our saying and to have understood it as did Mark (Rom 14.14),[40] and later Jewish history certainly knows of messianic enthusiasm leading to antinomian declarations.[41] There are, however, grave difficulties with the standard opinion. The criterion of dissimilarity does not favour the logion's authenticity. There are close early Christian parallels.[42] There are also, as we shall see, striking Jewish parallels. More significantly, if Jesus did in fact dispense with Scriptural food laws, the heated debates in the early church on that very issue just do not make sense.[43] There is additionally the striking fact that while in the canonical gospels Jesus' opponents accuse him of much, including blasphemy and sabbath breaking, they do not accuse him of speaking against cultic purity or food laws. Yet if he did so, surely, given the importance of those laws for first-century Judaism,[44] the inevitable violent outcry would have left some deposit in our sources.

In view of all this, one may reasonably deny that Mk 7.15 goes back to Jesus.[45] While we do not wish to exclude this possibility, another also merits consideration. Could not the saying have been known from the beginning but only understood later to bear on the concrete matters of ritual impurity? Mark, followed by Matthew, calls Jesus' sentence a 'parable', a *mashal*. Does this not indicate an awareness that its

---

[38] Bultmann, *History*, p. 105; Booth (v), pp. 96–114. Merkel (v), however, traces only 7.15a to Jesus.

[39] There is, however, a growing tendency to doubt this; see e.g. Jeremias, *Theology*, p. 210; Booth (v); Dunn (v).

[40] *Pace* Räisänen, 'Herkunft' (v). Note C. H. Dodd, *Gospel and Law*, New York, 1951, p. 49: 'the Greek term which is used for "unclean" (*koinos*) is an unusual and peculiar word to use in that sense, and Paul and Mark agree in using it. We may, I think, take it that Paul was acquainted with this saying of the Lord . . .'.

[41] See Scholem, pp. 242–3, on Sabbatai Ṣevi. It is sometimes suggested that Jesus 'sought the complete purity corresponding to the *eschaton*'. 'He pushed aside the Old Testament distinction between pure and defiled because he was after complete purity and total sanctification. This complete sanctification was, according to Old Testament voices like Num. 14.21 and Zech 14.21, to find realization in the *eschaton*.' So Goppelt, *Theology* 1, p. 92.

[42] Cf. Acts 10.15, 28; Rom 14.14, 20; 1 Cor 20.23; 1 Tim 4.4; Tit 1.15.

[43] See esp. Räisänen, 'Food Laws' (v). —One wonders whether Luke's omission of Mk 7.1–23 had anything to do with the perception that it could not be harmonized with the history of Acts 10ff.

[44] See Dan 1.8–16; Tob 1.10–13; 1 Macc 1.47–8, 62–3 ('many in Israel stood firm and found the courage to refuse unclean food. They chose death rather than contamination by such fare or profanation of the holy covenant . . .'); 2 Macc 6.18–31; 7.1–2; 3 Macc 3.4; Jub 22.16; Acts 10.14, 28; 15.20, 29. Food laws were part of Israel's distinct identity: Philo, *Leg. Gaj.* 361–2; Tacitus, *Hist.* 5.4–5.

[45] So Räisänen, 'Food Laws' (v).—Another suggestion is that the original behind Mk 7.15 was a bit different. But none of the proposals has yet proved persuasive; see Räisänen, *ibid.*, pp. 80–1.

interpretation was less than obvious?[46] We should like to suggest that Mk 7.15 was composed as a moral pronouncement or exhortation, not halakah. It was aimed at people perceived as preoccupied with the literal observance of Torah and tradition to the neglect of the weightier matters of the law (cf. 23.23). Assuming the continuing validity of the cult, its gist was that the disposition of the heart determines all else (cf. our exegesis of 6.22–3). There is a certain parallel with the OT prophets, who 'not only stressed the primacy of morality over sacrifice, but even proclaimed that the worth of worship, far from being absolute, is contingent upon moral living, and that when immorality prevails, worship is detestable'.[47] It was once fashionable to read the prophets as enemies of the Jerusalem cult. Now it is understood that declarations such as Hos 6.6—'I desire mercy, not sacrifice'—were never intended to set aside the Mosaic commandments. Despite their extreme formulation, they must be interpreted as rhetorical injunctions to upright behaviour. So too perhaps Mk 7.15.[48] Is its antithesis really absolute? Or do we rather have here the Semitic idiom of relative negation[49] in which all the emphasis lies on the second limb of the saying (cf. BDF § 448)? Did Jesus not address himself to Jews, not early Christians involved with the Jew/Gentile problem, and so take for granted the truth of the Torah and its observance by his contemporaries and *within that context* utter his words about what defiles and what does not?

Before proceeding it is necessary to scrutinize the use of κοινόω in Mk 7.15. It is often thought that in the first half it refers to cultic defilement, in the second to ethical defilement; see Booth (v), pp. 206–13. It is preferable, however, to adopt a different interpretation, one which assigns to the verb the same meaning in both lines.[50] According to this interpretation, food cannot really defile because true defilement is a function of morality.[51] What matters before God is the heart (cf. 5.21–8; 23.16–26). This does not make one indifferent to actions or all

---

[46] E. P. Sanders, 'Jesus and the Constraints of the Law', *JSNT* 17 (1983), p. 20: Mk 7.15 is 'too riddling to be understood'. We are not so sceptical, but he has a point. The meaning is not obvious.

[47] A. J. Heschel, *The Prophets*, vol. 1, New York, 1962, p. 195.

[48] Cf. Vermes, *World*, p. 11: Jesus 'felt free rhetorically to overemphasize the ethical as compared with the ritual—like certain of the prophets before him . . .'.

[49] See H. Kruse, 'Dialektische Negationen als semitisches Idiom', *VT* 4 (1954), pp. 385–400.

[50] Cf. B. F. Meyer, p. 148; R. H. Gundry, review of Booth (v), in *JBL* 107 (1988), p. 327.

[51] There is yet another, possible interpretation we do not wish to exclude: 'On one level the saying states the obvious fact that it is not food, but excrement, that defiles physically; on another level it teaches that it is not food, but evil thoughts, words, and deeds, that defile religiously. The implied trope changes the antithesis in the two lines from a contrast between material and material thing (food *vs.* bodily waste) to a contrast between material and spiritual thing (food *vs.* immorality). The saying is thus an exceptionally well constructed one, and the shift from the material to the spiritual reference in its two lines, far from being a flaw . . . is an intended and brilliant play or turn (*tropos*) on meaning'. So Boucher (v), p. 65.

external circumstances (we hardly have here a mandate for the Quietism of a Molinos or Guyon!). Rather, the meaning of such must be determined by its relationship to what is internal. Nothing which goes into a person can of itself defile, for true defilement is effected by intention. Such teaching, while it relativizes the ritual law, does not of necessity set it aside.

Our argument thus far is consistent with Jesus' characteristic focus on inward religion and with the fact that the language of purity and defilement had already long before him come to be used of moral and immoral behaviour.[52] Also supportive are the Jewish parallels. Beyond the prophetic corpus (see above), there is the oddly neglected 2 Chron 30.18–20: 'For a multitude of the people, many of them from Ephraim, Manasseh, Issachar, and Zebulun, had not cleansed themselves, yet they ate the passover otherwise than as prescribed. For Hezekiah had prayed for them, saying, "The good Lord pardon every one who sets his heart to seek God, the Lord the God of his fathers, even though not according to the sanctuary's rules of cleanness." And the Lord heard Hezekiah, and healed the people'. Here the efficacy of the heart which seeks God is such that it overrules cultic defilement. Without rejecting the cult, the lesson that purity of heart matters above all else is clearly taught. Also pertinent is Num Rab 19.18, where Joḥanan b. Zakkai is reported to have said: 'It is not the dead that defiles nor the water that purifies. The Holy One, blessed be He, merely says: "I have laid down a statute, I have issued a decree. You are not allowed to transgress my decree;" as it is written, "This is the statute of the law"'. Joḥanan is saying, as did Maimonides later, that defilement 'is a matter of scriptural decree and dependent on the intention of the heart'. It does not inhere in objects. While the cultic commands remain valid, they are translated into ethics: one becomes unclean only through a deliberate choice to disobey God's declared will (= Scripture). Here we are near the gospels. Defilement is caused not by what is external but by disposition, intent.[53]

In Mt 5.27–8 we read: 'You have heard that it was said: "You shall not commit adultery." But I say to you that everyone who looks at a woman lustfully has already committed adultery with her in his heart.' Mk 7.15, we suggest, could have been formulated similarly. 'You have heard that it was said: "It is what goes into a man that defiles a man." But I say to you: what comes out of a man defiles a man.' Just as the condemnation of lust does not mean indifference to the physical act of adultery, so too does the branding of the heart as the source of defilement not mean the dismissal of the laws of Leviticus. Jesus'

---

[52] E.g. in the Psalms (18.26; 24.4) and the Dead Sea Scrolls (1QS 5.13–14). Cf. Josephus, *Ant.* 18.117; Heb 10.22. In 1QS 3.6–9 internal purification comes before external purification, and it worth nothing that the Qumran sect 'is the first group within Judaism of whom we know that moral failure . . . incurred ritual defilement'; so A. R. C. Leaney, *The Rule of Qumran and its Meaning*, London, 1966, p. 139.

[53] Booth (v), p. 105, exaggerates the distance between Joḥanan's declaration and Mk 7.15. For ben Zakkai the cultic is construed in terms of the ethical and so has no independent meaning.

fondness for rhetorical excess in the posing of alternatives and his historical context (he was speaking to law-observant Jews!) must be given their due. Consider a passage from the *Mekilta*: 'It is not the place which honours (*mĕqabbēd*) the man but the man who honours (*mĕqabbēd*) the place'. If this were found not in a rabbinic document but in the gospels and regarded as an isolated saying of Jesus, would some scholars not consider it a radical attack on the temple and OT conceptions of sacred space? The lesson is obvious.

If our understanding of Mk 7.15 is correct, one can understand why the saying played little if any rôle in the early debates over Gentiles and food laws. The logion was simply not thought to imply a cancellation of the Levitical ordinances. It was rather construed as an exhortation (cf. the list of vices). The Jesus tradition did not determine the purity issue precisely because it was silent on the subject. If later on Jesus' utterance came to be viewed in a different light, that was only because subsequent experience (cf. Gal 2) and revelation (cf. Acts 10–11) had forged a situation which enabled believers to discern in Mk 7.15 confirmation of circumstances which had already come to be.[54]

Turning finally to Matthew's Gospel, its view is close to Jesus. The immediate literary context does nothing to encourage an interpretation in terms of OT food laws (cf. p. 517); and the Gospel as a whole, with its emphasis upon the continuing validity of the law and the prophets (5.17–20), certainly discourages any such notion. So the First Evangelist must have understood 15.11 in a relative, not absolute sense: what counts above all is the heart.

'For what goes into your mouth will not defile you, but what comes out of your mouth, that will defile you' is found in Gos Thom 14. If, as we think, Mt 15.11 does not depend upon extra-Markan tradition but is simply a redactional version of Mk 7.15, then Matthew influenced Thomas or his tradition, for Matthew's στόμα (*bis*, redactional) is matched by Thomas' *ro* = 'mouth'.[55] Contrast Dunn (v), pp. 263–64.

12. τότε προσελθόντες οἱ μαθηταὶ λέγουσιν αὐτῷ.[56] Compare 9.14; 15.1; 17.19; 18.21; 20.20. This and the next line are redactional.[57] (In Mark Jesus withdraws from the crowd and

---

[54] Cf. the situation with regard to the NT texts about human equality: the bearing of these on the issue of slavery came only later.

[55] Sometimes the story in *P.Oxy.* 5.840 of Jesus viewing the temple's utensils and his words there about the inability of water to cleanse impurity are considered authentic and thus reckoned pertinent to consideration of Mk 7.15 and the issues it raises. But against D. R. Schwartz, 'Viewing the Holy Utensils (P.Ox. V, 840)', *NTS* 32 (1986), pp. 153–9, we do not accept the tradition as ancient; see Booth (v), pp. 211–13.

[56] א B D Θ *f*¹³ 700 892 *pc* e omit αυτου after μαθ; so also NA²⁶ and HG. But see J. K. Elliott, 'Textual Criticism, Assimilation and the Synoptic Gospels', *NTS* 26 (1980), pp. 236–7.

[57] τότε* + προσέρχομαι*: Mt: 7; Mk: 0; Lk: 0. Φαρισαῖος: Mt: 29; Mk: 12; Lk: 27. σκανδαλίζω: Mt: 14; Mk: 8; Lk: 2.

goes into a house where the disciples ask him about his parable.)

οἶδας ὅτι οἱ Φαρισαῖοι ἀκούσαντες τὸν λόγον ἐσκανδαλίσθησαν; Compare v. 1 (where the Pharisees are named) and v. 6 (where τὸν λόγον appears). There is no Markan parallel. On σκανδαλίζω see on 5.29. 'The verb [in the passive] may mean "shocked", or "offended", but has often the force of "led into sin" (cf. 13.21; 24.10). There is a touch of that here—the saying causes the Pharisees to sin in that they reject Jesus' (Beare, p. 338).

Unlike the disciples, who must ask Jesus for his meaning, the Pharisees[58] evidently think they comprehend. At least their reaction reflects a conclusion about what has been said.[59] Note well that it is not 'the Jews' who are offended. Matthew's Jesus is not attacking Judaism as a whole but only the Pharisaic tradition.

13. The general effect of vv. 13–14 is to make it plain that the Pharisees are not just wrong about hand-washing and *qorbān*. There is much else in their tradition that must be rejected. In view, however, of 23.2–3 and 23 there can be no rejection of the tradition *in toto* (cf. Hummel, pp. 46–9).

ὁ δὲ ἀποκριθεὶς εἶπεν. Compare v. 3a.

πᾶσα φυτεία ἣν οὐκ ἐφύτευσεν ὁ πατήρ μου ὁ οὐράνιος ἐκριζωθήσεται. Compare 3.10; Lk 17.6;[60] Jn 15.1–8; Ignatius, *Trall.* 11; *Phil.* 3.1. Although φυτεία (the reference is to the Pharisees, not their teaching) is a NT *hapax legomenon*, ὁ πατήρ μου ὁ οὐράνιος is clearly editorial. For ἐκριζόω see on 13.29. Isa 60.21 reads: 'Your people shall all be righteous; they shall possess the land for ever, the shoot of my planting, the work of my hands . . .' (cf. 61.3). This is one of many texts in which the people of God are spoken of as God's planting.[61] But what we have in Mt 15.13 is the polemical proposition that not all in Israel are God's planting. The Pharisees, offended by the Messiah, show themselves not to be God's own. Hence they will be uprooted (cf. 13.29) at the final judgement.[62]

---

[58] The scribes mentioned in v. 1 have dropped out.

[59] λόγον probably refers to v. 11, but it could encompass earlier verses, even the entire complex.

[60] *Pace* Gundry, *Commentary*, pp. 306–7, the Q saying in Lk 17.6 is not Matthew's source for 15.13.

[61] E.g. Jer 32.41; 1 En 10.16; 84.6; 93.2, 5, 10; Jub 1.16; 7.34; 1QS 8.5; 11.8; CD 1.7; 1QH 6.15; Ps Sol 14.3 (ἡ φυτεία αὐτῶν ἐρριζωμένη . . . οὐκ ἐκτιλή-σονται). Cf. Asc. Isa 4.3.

[62] Schweizer, *Matthew*, p. 327, writes: 'It would be hard to frame a sharper attack on Israel's faith in its own election: Israel and its ruling class of Pharisees is not the vineyard planted by God but a wild thicket!' What is the justification for interpreting a reference to the Pharisees as a reference to all Israel?

Mt 15.13 'is one of those general statements that are capable of
many applications. It may be a genuine saying of Jesus; but we have
no guarantee that its present application in Mt is the original
application' (Manson, *Sayings*, pp. 199–200). Given that Isa 60.21 (see
above) is used in *m. Sanh.* 10.1 to support the teaching that 'all Israelites
have a share in the world to come', and given that Jesus, following
John the Baptist, queried this widely held notion (1, pp. 307–9), maybe
the saying about plants being uprooted is (if genuine) one more
indication that Jesus rejected what E. P. Sanders has called 'covenantal
nomism', which holds that salvation is a consequence of being born
into the covenant. Not every plant in Israel will stand. Those not
planted by the Father will be removed.

14. This verse was once joined to something close to 10.24–5;
see Lk 6.39–40, and Wanke (v). In Lk the saying about the
blind refers to the disciples, not the Pharisees. Because we do
not know the setting in the historical ministry of Jesus its
original intent escapes us (cf. Davies, *SSM*, p. 458).

ἄφετε αὐτούς. Compare 2 Kgs 23.18 (*hannîḥû lô*; LXX: ἄφετε
αὐτό); Mk 14.6; Lk 13.8; Acts 5.38; *t. Pesaḥ* 4.2. ἀφίημι* (cf.
Mk 7.12, omitted by Matthew) is often redactional. Gundry's
comment that 'these words reflect the church's break from the
synagogue' (*Commentary*, p. 307) may read too much into the
text.

τυφλοί εἰσιν ὁδηγοὶ τυφλῶν.[63] Compare 23.16 and 24.
Apparently certain religious authorities made themselves out to
be 'guides to the blind'.[64]

τυφλὸς δὲ τυφλὸν ἐὰν ὁδηγῇ, ἀμφότεροι εἰς βόθυνον
πεσοῦνται.[65] Compare Lk 6.39: 'He also told them a parable:
"Can a blind man lead a blind man? Will they not both fall into
a pit?"' Matthew's text is about blind *men* (plural) because it is
about the Pharisees. Also, Q's interrogative form has been
altered: Matthew's Jesus is not asking a question but passing a
judgement. For falling into a pit as a symbol of misfortune or
calamity see Ps 7.15; Prov 26.27; Isa 24.18; Jer 48.44; T. Reuben
2.9 (the spirit of intercourse 'leads the young person like a blind
man into a pit ...'); Ep. Apost 47 (quoting Matthew). Does
βόθυνον (cf. 12.11) here allude to Sheol, which is sometimes
called a 'pit' (*šaḥat*)?[66]

[63] So both NA[26] and HG, but the reading is doubtful. See Metzger, p. 39.
Maj has the order 3, 2, 1, 4; K *pc* sy[s.c] 3, 2, 4; ℵ*.2 Epiph 3, 2, 1; B D 0237 1, 2,
3. We have printed the text of ℵ[1] L Z Θ *f*[1.13] 33 700 892 1241 1424 *al* lat
sy[p.h].
[64] Cf. Rom 2.19; also Plato, *Rep.* 554b.
[65] So NA[26] and ℵ B Maj. HG, for the last three words, prints the order 3, 1,
2; so L Z. The two different orders also occur with the verb εμπεσουνται, and
there are other variants.
[66] Cf. Job 33.18; Ps 16.10; 30.9; Isa 38.18; etc.

15. ἀποκριθεὶς δὲ ὁ Πέτρος εἶπεν αὐτῷ· φράσον ἡμῖν τὴν παραβολὴν ταύτην.[67] Compare 13.36. This is the third time ἀποκριθείς + εἶπεν has been used in this section (cf. vv. 3, 13). In Mark we read that 'his disciples' (in the house[68]) asked Jesus about 'the parable'. But in Matthew Peter is the sole speaker. For the meaning of 'parable' see pp. 378–82. The word is here fitting because Jesus' declaration is extraordinary speech which is difficult to understand (cf. Boucher (v), p. 66).

Pace Schweizer, *Matthew*, p. 326, Peter's question harks back to v. 11, not vv. 12–14. Yet the rejection of Pharisaic teaching in vv. 12–14 does help explain why our evangelist has here introduced Peter. As soon as Jesus has discredited the teaching passed on by the guardians of the old tradition, he goes on to transmit teaching to Peter, the guardian of the new tradition. So later, in the post-Easter period, when the rock of the church will declare what to bind and loose (16.19), he will do so on the basis of instruction received from Jesus.

In Acts 10–11, 15 and Gal 2 Peter is involved in debates over the meaning of ritual impurity and its bearing upon the Gentile question. One must wonder whether Matthew's tradition associated the apostle with this topic and whether this encouraged his being mentioned precisely here. Was Peter remembered by Matthew's community as having issued teaching on the matter of clean and unclean?

16. ὁ δὲ εἶπεν. Compare 14.18, 29; 26.18. Mk 7.18 has: καὶ λέγει αὐτοῖς (cf. 26.18 diff. Mk 14.13).

ἀκμὴν καὶ ὑμεῖς ἀσύνετοί ἐστε; So Mark, with οὕτως instead of ἀκμήν. This last, a late word, is used nowhere else in the Greek Bible (cf. Heb 5.13 v. 1.). The adverbial accusative is the equivalent of ἔτι: 'even yet, still' (cf. Josephus, *Ant.* 19.118 and see BDF § 160). ἀσύνετοί harks back to v. 10: 'hear and understand'.

17. Jesus asks a second question, this about things entering the mouth. He is here expounding the first part of the saying in v. 11 (on what does not defile). In the next verse (v. 18) he will turn to the second part (on what does defile). 'The point of the passage is that the belly is not the real man, so that food which enters the former cannot affect the latter' (McNeile, p. 228).

οὔπω νοεῖτε ὅτι πᾶν τὸ εἰσπορευόμενον εἰς τὸ στόμα εἰς τὴν κοιλίαν χωρεῖ καὶ εἰς ἀφεδρῶνα ἐκβάλλεται;[69] Compare T. Job 38.5: καταβῇ ... εἰς τὸν ἀφεδρῶνα. ἀφεδρών (LXX: O) means 'latrine'. Matthew has revised Mk 7.18–19 ('"Do you not see that whatever goes into a man from outside cannot defile him, since it enters, not his heart but his stomach, and so

---

[67] ταυτην is missing from ℵ B *f*[1] 700 892 so bo and may be secondary.
[68] Matthew omits the mention of a house on several occasions.
[69] οὐ (so NA[26]) is found in B D Z *f*[13] 33 565 *pc* lat sy[s.c.p] sa mae Or; but is this not assimilation to Mark and Mt 16.11? So HG.

is evacuated?" Thus he declared all food clean') by shortening it, adding a reference to the mouth (as in v. 11), and excising Mark's concluding editorial comment: the First Evangelist could not abide such a sweeping dismissal of OT law.[70]

18. Having explained what does not defile a man, Jesus now declares what does, affirming that 'the treasuries of evil things are in ourselves' (Philo, *Fug.* 79).

τὰ δὲ ἐκπορευόμενα ἐκ τοῦ στόματος ἐκ τῆς καρδίας ἐξέρχεται, κἀκεῖνα κοινοῖ τὸν ἄνθρωπον. Compare Rom 10.8 for the close connexion between heart and mouth. Compare also v. 11b; Mk 7.20; Jas 3.6. Matthew has added 'out of the mouth' (cf. vv. 11, 17) and also, in anticipation of v. 19 = Mk 7.21, 'out of the heart'. And Mark's singular ('that going out') has been turned into the plural ('the things which go out'), in view of the following list.

19. The evils sown by the heart in the subterranean regions of human nature are now catalogued. They are seven in number (in Mark, thirteen).

Lists of vices are common in the NT.[71] They are not so characteristic of the OT (although note the Decalogue and Hos 4.2). It is usually thought that lists of virtues and vices, which are common in Hellenistic philosophy (especially Stoicism), entered Christianity via Hellenistic Judaism.[72] This may well be so, but caution is in order because the lists in 1QS 4 may be free of Greek influence (note also T. Reub. 3.3–6; T. Levi 17.11; As. Mos. 7.3–10); and there are also Iranian parallels. Probably early Christians used virtue and vice lists—largely taken over with little alteration from their environment—in catechetical instruction. But secondary uses are well-attested, such as the description of heretics or pagans.

ἐκ γὰρ τῆς καρδίας ἐξέρχονται.[73] Mk 7.21 opens with the longer ἔσωθεν γὰρ ἐκ τῆς καρδίας τῶν ἀνθρώπων.

διαλογισμοὶ πονηροί. Compare Ezek 38.10 (LXX: λογισμοὺς

---

[70] *Pace* Gundry, *Commentary*, p. 308, who attributes the omission simply to maintenance of antithetical parallelism. —We note the possibility that Mark originally wrote καθαρίζον, not καθαρίζων: 'decontaminating all foods' (meaning excrement is neither clean nor unclean); see Malina (v), pp. 22–5. In this case Mark's text would not clearly dismiss the Mosaic food ordinances.

[71] Examples include: Mt 15.19 = Mk 7.21–2; Rom 1.29–31; 1 Cor 6.9–10; 2 Cor 12.20; Gal 5.19–20; Eph 5.3–5; Col 3.5, 8; 1 Tim 1.9–10; 2 Tim 3.2–5; Tit 3.3; 1 Pet 4.3; Rev 9.20–1; 21.8. Cf. Did 5.1; 1 Clem 35.5; Barn 18–20; Hermas, *Mand.* 8.5; Polycarp, *Phil.* 2.2; 4.3; 5.2; 6.1; Teach. Silvanus 84.20–6; 2 En 10.4–5; 3 Bar 4.17; 8.5; 13.4. Allen, p. 167, cites an interesting Buddhist parallel (cf. Deissmann, *Light*, p. 315, n. 8).

[72] Cf. Wisd 14.25–6; Philo, *Sac.* 32; *Rer. div. her.* 173; *Conf. ling.* 117; 4 Macc 1.26–7.

[73] These words and those after ἐξέρχεται in v. 18 are omitted through homoioteleuton in ℵ* W bo^ms.

πονηρούς); Jas 2.4. οἱ διαλογισμοὶ οἱ κακοὶ ἐκπορεύονται appears in Mk 7.21. πονηρός* is a Matthean favourite, and the omission of the definite articles increases the resemblance with the following items. Although the list opens with 'evil designs' (the only double-membered entry) it goes on to cite six concrete actions. Perhaps implicit is the truth that behind every public evil there lurk the sinful, wicked thoughts which are its roots (cf. Gen 6.5). Indeed, maybe διαλογισμοὶ πονηροί is Matthew's Greek equivalent for the *yēṣer hārāʿ*, the evil impulse, which the rabbis generally located in the heart.[74]

φόνοι, μοιχεῖαι, πορνεῖαι. Mark has a different order: 2, 3, 1.[75] φόνος (= 'murder') and μοιχεία (= 'adulterous acts') occur only here in the First Gospel. For the meaning of πορνεία see on 5.32.

κλοπαί, ψευδομαρτυρίαι, βλασφημίαι. Only the first and last items are from Mark; the other, which reflects Matthew's interest in evil speech, is redactional (cf. 26.59–60). Mark has a much longer list here: 'theft, coveting, wickedness, deceit, licentiousness, the evil eye, blasphemy, pride, foolishness'. On the meaning of 'blasphemy' (it here means more than 'slander') see on 12.31.

Matthew's list has (for mnemonic or catechetical reasons?) been influenced by the second table of the decalogue (as have the lists in 1 Cor 5.9–10; 1 Tim 1.9–10; and Barn 19). After 'evil devices', the catalogue refers to murder, adultery, unchastity, theft, bearing false witness, and blasphemy. This resembles the sixth through ninth commandments, which concern murder, adultery, theft, and bearing false witness—commandments which immediately follow the injunction to honour father and mother (cf. Mt 15.4). The differences are two: Matthew has two words for sexual sins (cf. Mk 10.19; 1 Cor 6.9; Heb 13.4; Did 5.1; Barn 19.4) and two words for sinful speech (cf. the pairs in Rom 13.13). He has, in other words, slightly expanded the inventory while staying close to both the content and order of Exod 20.13–17. Perhaps the evangelist wanted a total of seven entries, seven being the number of completeness.[76] Or is there some connexion with the fact that most rabbinic authorities came to recognize seven Noachic commandments (four of these being: do not blaspheme, do not kill, do not commit adultery, do not rob; see Davies, *PRJ*, pp. 113–17)? Note also that in Matthew every item ends with -οι or- αι. This feature, which exemplifies the evangelist's love for parallelism, is absent from Mark.

Matthew's list of vices is thoroughly conventional. Following the

[74] See Davies, PRJ, pp. 20–35. Cf. 4 Ezra 3.21.
[75] So HG, but the text is uncertain and NA[26] prints πορνεῖαι, κλοπαί, φόνοι, μοιχεῖαι.
[76] On this see K. H. Rengstorf, *TWNT* 2, pp. 623–31; M. Pope, in *IDB* 4, pp. 294–5.

general διαλογισμοὶ πονηροί, all the entries are related to the decalogue, appear often in the OT, and show up in other early Christian vice lists: φόνος (cf. Rom 1.29; Rev 9.21; 22.15; Did 5.1; Barn 20.1), μοιχεία (cf. 1 Cor 6.9; Did 5.1; Barn 19.4), πορνεία (cf. 2 Cor 12.21; Gal 5.19; Eph 5.3; Col 3.5; Rev 9.21; Did 5.1; Barn 19.4), κλοπή (cf. 1 Cor 6.10; Rev 9.21; Did 3.5; 5.1), ψευδομαρτυρία (cf. Did 5.1; Polycarp, *Phil.* 2.2; 4.3), βλασφημία (cf. Eph 4.31; Col 3.8; 1 Tim 6.4). Next to Mk 7.21–2, the list most closely related to Mt 15.19 is, to our knowledge, Did 5.1. It contains five of the vices cited in Matthew—in precisely the same form and order: φόνοι, μοιχεῖαι ... πορνεῖαι, κλοπαί ... ψευδομαρτυρίαι. Is this a coincidence, evidence of a shared tradition, or a sign of literary dependence?

20. ταῦτά ἐστιν τὰ κοινοῦντα τὸν ἄνθρωπον. Cf. v. 18b and Mk 7.23: 'All these things come from within and they defile a man'.

τὸ δὲ ἀνίπτοις χερσὶν φαγεῖν οὐ κοινοῖ τὸν ἄνθρωπον. This, which refers back to v. 2 (τό is anaphoric: BDF § 399), is redactional. Note the parallelism with the previous clause.

Matthew's closing words have the effect of making the whole discussion turn around the question of the Pharisaic tradition rather than the written law, for the washing of hands before meals was not enjoined in the latter, only the former.

(v) *Concluding Observations*

(1) Matthew believed that the law and the prophets were still valid (5.17–20). He also believed that the Gentiles had come to a full share in God's salvation (28.16–20). In holding together these two beliefs the evangelist exhibited the qualities which Edmund Burke considered characteristic of the sound statesman: the disposition to preserve and the ability to reform (cf. 13.52). There was preservation because, despite acceptance of the Gentile influx, the Jewish Torah was not abandoned (cf. 15.4–9). There was reformation because, in the light of the Messiah's teaching, Jewish tradition had to be critically evaluated and in some measure rejected.

We unfortunately do not know very much about the everyday, concrete realities of Matthew's community. For example, how did law-observant Jews relate to uncircumcised Gentiles? We can only guess. Perhaps, however, we can make a good guess. Notwithstanding the fact that many—not all—pious, non-Christian Jews refused to eat with Gentiles,[77] we detect in our Gospel no evidence of segregated groups. This makes the existence of separate fellowships (cf. Gal 2) improbable. On the other hand, that there was a total disregard of traditional law, so that Jewish Christians had no scruples at all concerning what they

[77] See the texts cited in n. 44.

ate, is most unlikely.[78] Unlikelier still is a scenario in which Gentile Christians observed all the laws of Judaism (Matthew nowhere mentions circumcision). We are left, then, with the likelihood that Gentile believers kept a minimum number of OT commandments, sufficient to allow fellowship with Jews. Such *may* have been the situation in Antioch before the crucial debate between Peter and Paul.[79] More importantly, one is put in mind of the so-called 'Apostolic Decree' (Acts 15.20, 29; 21.45; cf. Rev 2.15, 20). This decree, which, according to the best mss., prohibited four things—eating meat sacrificed to idols, eating blood, eating strangled animals, and intercourse with near kin—recalls the Holiness Code of Lev 17–18, which lays down rules not only for Israelites but also for the 'strangers that sojourn among them' (Lev 17.8).[80] The decree was clearly designed to allow Gentiles and law-abiding Jews to share a common religious life. Whether or not Matthew's community knew and observed the 'Apostolic Decree' we do not know, although we incline to think so.[81] The First Gospel was probably composed in Antioch, and Acts has the decree being taken there (Acts 15.23, 30). Yet even if the decree was not followed by Matthew's church, a similar rule of compromise probably was.[82]

(2) The insertion of 15.12–14 (on the Pharisees as blind leaders) is a clue to Matthew's historical context. Why were these verses added if the Pharisees or their spiritual descendants were not participants with the evangelist in a real and urgent *Auseinandersetzung*? Why the mention of the Pharisees being offended? Why the command to separate from them? Why the remarks on their failings as leaders? Surely 15.12–14, like chapter 23, manifests Matthew's concern with the emergent rabbinism of his day. For him the question of the authority of late first-century rabbis was no dead issue. This can only mean that he knew of Christians whose loyalties were not wholly unambiguous, and that he felt bound to direct them away from the Jewish synagogues.

(3) 'What comes out of the mouth proceeds from the heart, and

---

[78] Matthew's omission of Lk 10.8 ('eat whatever is set before you') says much; see p. 174. —The social consequences of giving up all the law would, among other things, have borne heavily upon them. See A. E. Harvey, 'Forty Strokes Save One: Social Aspects of Judaizing and Apostasy', in Harvey, *Approaches*, pp. 79–96.

[79] So J. D. G. Dunn, 'The Incident at Antioch (Gal 2.11–18)', *JSNT* 18 (1983), pp. 3–57.

[80] Was the decree a version of the Noachian commandments (see p. 536), perhaps abbreviated or in the form current in the first century?

[81] The decree was observed elsewhere, including the circles in which Revelation (cf. 2.15, 20) and the Preaching of Peter (a source of the Pseudo-Clementines) were composed; see E. Molland, 'La circoncision, le baptême et l'authorité du décret apostolique (Actes 15.28sq.) dans les milieux judéo-chétiens des Pseudo-Clémentines', *ST* 9 (1955), pp. 1–39.

[82] Whether this puts Paul at odds with Matthew depends largely on whether one thinks the apostle accepted or could have accepted the Apostolic Decree. For different opinions see Davies, *PRJ*, pp. 117–9; R. N. Longenecker, *Paul, Apostle of Liberty*, New York, 1964, pp. 254–60; D. R. Catchpole, 'Paul, James and the Apostolic Decree', *NTS* 23 (1977), pp. 428–44.

that defiles a man' (15.18). This line reminds one of so much in the SM, which refers several times to the καρδία and demands that it be pure and focused in intent. This stress on the heart, on the interior life of religion, on intention and attitude, is indeed found throughout Matthew and is a chief characteristic of the whole of his Gospel. The evangelist must have believed that typical of Jesus' moral teaching and at its centre was the demand for integrity, for harmony between thought and act. In this he was, we think, correct. This is not to say that here we have something unique. The Psalms, the prophets, and the rabbis all attest the necessity of cleansing the heart and purifying interior disposition. In the First Gospel, however, there is a regular and emphatic dwelling on the theme, so that Matthew remains a constant reminder that Jesus 'laid an extraordinary emphasis on the real inner religious significance of the commandments' (Vermes, *World*, p. 47).

(v) *Bibliography*

Banks, pp. 132–46.

G. Barth in *TIM*, pp. 86–9.

A. I. Baumgarten, '*Korban* and the Pharisaic Paradosis', *Journal of the Ancient Near Eastern Society* (New York) 16 (1984), pp. 5–17.

S. Belkin, 'Dissolution of Vows and the Problem of Anti-social Oaths in the Gospels and Contemporary Literature', *JBL* 55 (1936), pp. 227–34.

Berger 1, pp. 461–507.

R. P. Booth, *Jesus and the Laws of Purity*, JSNTS 13, Sheffield, 1986.

Boucher, *Parable*, pp. 64–8.

G. W. Buchanan, 'Some Vow and Oath Formulas in the New Testament', *HTR* 58 (1965), pp. 319–26.

A. Büchler, 'The Laws of Purification in Mark 7.1–23', *ExpT* 21 (1909), pp. 34–40.

C. E. Carlston, 'The Things that Defile (Mark 7.15) and the Law in Matthew and Mark', *NTS* (1968), pp. 75–96.

idem, *Parables*, pp. 28–35, 162–7.

Cope, pp. 52–65.

Crossan, *Aphorisms*, pp. 250–5.

Daube, pp. 141–57.

J. D. M. Derrett, 'ΚΟΡΒΑΝ, Ο ΕΣΤΙΝ ΔΩΡΟΝ', *NTS* 16 (1970), pp. 364–8.

J. D. G. Dunn, 'Jesus and Ritual Purity', in *À cause de l'Évangile*, LD 123, Paris, 1985, pp. 251–76.

Fiedler, pp. 249–55.

M. Fitzpatrick, 'From Ritual Observance to Ethics: the Argument of Mark 7.1–23', *AusBR* 35 (1987), pp. 22–7.

Fitzmyer, *Essays*, pp. 93–100; reprint of 'The Aramaic Qorban Inscription from Jebel Hallet et-Turi and Mk 7.11/Mt 15.5', *JBL* 78 (1959), pp. 60–5.

Hübner, *Gesetz*, pp. 176–82.
Hultgren, pp. 115–19.
Jülicher 2, pp. 50–67.
E. Käsemann, 'Matthäus 15.1–14', in *Exegetische Versuche und Besinnungen* 1, Göttingen, 1960, pp. 237–42.
Klauck, pp. 260–72.
H. Krämer, 'Eine Anmerkung zum Verständnis von Mt 15.6a', *WuD* 16 (1981), pp. 67–70.
W. G. Kümmel, 'Äussere und innere Reinheit des Menschen bei Jesus', in *Das Wort und die Wörter*, ed. H. Balz and S. Schulz, Stuttgart, 1973, pp. 35–46.
idem, 'Jesus und der jüdische Traditionsgedanke', *ZNW* 33 (1934), pp. 105–30; reprinted in *Heilsgeschehen und Geschichte*, Marburg, 1965, pp. 15–35.
J. Lambrecht, 'Jesus and the Law: An Investigation of Mark 7.1–23', *ETL* 53 (1977), pp. 24–82.
D. Lührmann, '. . . womit er alle Speisen für rein erklärte (Mk 7.19)', *WuD* 16 (1981), pp. 71–92.
N. J. McEleney, 'Authenticating Criteria and Mark 7.1–23', *CBQ* 34 (1972), pp. 431–60.
B. J. Malina, 'A Conflict Approach to Mark 7', *Forum* 4/3 (1988), pp. 3–30.
C. Margoliouth, 'The Tradition of the Elders', *ExpT* 22 (1911), pp. 261–3.
Meier, *Vision*, pp. 100–4.
H. Merkel, 'Markus 7.15. Das Jesuswort über die innere Verunreinigung', *ZRG* 20 (1968), pp. 340–63.
Montefiore, *Synoptic Gospels* 1, pp. 152–66.
W. Paschen, *Rein und Unrein*, Munich, 1970.
H. Räisänen, 'Jesus and the Food Laws: Reflections on Mark 7.15', *JSNT* 16 (1982), pp. 79–100.
idem, 'Zur Herkunft von Markus 7.15', in Delobel, pp. 477–84.
Riches, pp. 112–43.
H. J. Schoeps, 'Jésus et la loi juive', *RHPR* 33 (1953), pp. 1–20.
P. Sigal, 'Aspects of Mark pointing to Matthean Priority', in Farmer, *Studies*, pp. 195–205.
R. Smend and U. Luz, *Gesetz*, Stuttgart, 1981.
Tuckett, pp. 103–10.
Westerholm, pp. 62–91.
S. Zeitlin, 'The Halaka in the Gospels and its Relation to the Jewish Law at the Time of Jesus', *HUCA* 1 (1924), pp. 357–73.

XXXV

THE CANAANITE WOMAN
(15.21–8)

(i) *Structure*

Although one could analyse the text as exhibiting a pattern common to many other healing stories—(i) the scene, (ii) appearance of supplicant, (iii) dialogue, with appeal and word of healing, and (iv) recovery of sick individual—the pericope is, we deem, more profitably divided into three main sections—setting (vv. 21–2a), extended conversation (vv. 22b–8c), conclusion (v. 28d). This analysis emphasizes that the heart or centre of the piece is the conversation or exposition[1] and that the rest is frame.

The most distinctive structural feature of 15.21–8 is the arrangement of the dialogue. It is made up of four dyadic units, each of which consists in turn of words addressed to Jesus followed by his reaction:[2]

22	The woman's request
23a	Jesus' response (ὁ δέ + ἀποκρίνομαι)
23b	The disciples' request
24	Jesus' response (ὁ δέ + ἀποκρίνομαι)
25	The woman's request
26	Jesus' response (ὁ δέ + ἀποκρίνομαι)
27	The woman's request
28	Jesus' response (τότε + ἀποκρίνομαι)

It is only in the last verbal exchange that Jesus favours the Gentile woman with her request. In the three preceding exchanges, in which Jesus' response is consistently introduced with δέ, his words only constitute an obstacle for faith to overcome. In this way the dramatic tension is heightened and Jesus' eventual acquiescence, introduced by τότε, made all the more surprising.

---

[1] On Matthew's tendency to enlarge conversations between Jesus and supplicants see Held, in *TIM*, pp. 233–7.

[2] Mk 7.24–30 also consists of setting + conversation + conclusion; but its conversation contains only two dyadic units: vv. 26f. and 28f.

(ii) *Sources*

Seemingly solid reasons can be adduced to support the notion that Mt 15.21–8 (which is without Lukan parallel)[3] draws upon some source besides or in addition to Mark.[4] Matthew's text differs from Mk 7.24–30 to a surprising degree (cf. Beare, p. 340; of 140 words in Matthew and 130 in Mark, fewer than forty are held in common). Further, Mt 15.21–8 is more Jewish than its parallel (note esp. v. 24b: 'I was sent only to the lost sheep of the house of Israel'), it is more potentially offensive to non-Jews (Mark's 'let the children first be fed'[5] is missing), and it contains Semitisms not found in Mk 7.24–30 (see on vv. 23, 24, 28). Notwithstanding these facts, good cause remains for the judgement that Matthean redaction explains the differences between our two texts.[6] The First Evangelist has elsewhere added logia to miracle stories and expanded the conversational element.[7] Moreover, as several authorities have demonstrated (e.g. Trilling and Meier), he seems to have deliberately set out to show that the pre-Easter mission was confined to Israel. When to this one adds that so much of the vocabulary of Mt 15.21–8 can be regarded as editorial,[8] that several of the phrases in the passage have parallels in 8.5–13[9] (which is about another Gentile) and 9.27–31[10] (which is a redactional creation), and that there are satisfying explanations for the omissions of the unparalleled Markan material,[11] the words of Allen, p. 169, merit assent: 'the editor had rewritten Mk's narrative with a view to explaining how it was that Christ, in spite of such sayings as 10^{5.6}, should have extended His compassion to a heathen woman. He did not enter into a house on heathen soil. Rather the woman came out to Him. At first He paid no attention to her entreaty, conscious that His mission concerned only the lost sheep of the house of Israel. When she still importuned Him, He told her that the children's bread, *i.e.* privileges intended for the Jews, should not be cast to dogs, *i.e.* to heathen women like herself. She, inspired by her misery, was quick to turn the analogy in her own favour. It was quite true, yet dogs fed from the crumbs of their master's table. Therefore mercy shown to her might be justified by the metaphor. Thus, as in the previous case of

---

[3] For discussion of the reasons which might have led Luke to omit the pericope of the Syrophoenician woman see Russell (v), pp. 282–6.

[4] Cf. Streeter, p. 260 (suggesting a conflation of Mark and M); Lohmeyer, *Matthäus*, p. 252; Hahn, *Mission*, p. 32, n. 1.

[5] The sentence can be understood as a secondary addition designed to tone down the surrounding material—and it is found only in Mark, not Matthew.

[6] So also Allen, p. 169; Held (v); Donaldson, p. 263, n. 62.

[7] See Held, as in n. 1.

[8] ἐξέρχομαι in nominative participle*, ἀναχωρέω*, ὁ Ἰησοῦς*, ἰδού*, ἐλεέω*, υἱὸς Δαυίδ*, προσέρχομαι*, προσκυνέω*, γάρ*, ἀποκριθείς + finite verb*, θέλω*, τότε*, temporal ἀπό*, and ἐκείνη ὥρα all qualify as characteristic of Matthew.

[9] See further section (iv).

[10] Cf. 15.22 with 9.27 and 15.28 with 9.29.

[11] E.g. on the omission of 7.24b ('And he entered a house, and would not have any one know it; yet he could not be hid') see on 15.21.

condescension to a heathen (8^{5-13}), faith forced the barrier of Christ's rule of working only amongst His own people.' That Allen has rightly expressed the truth of the matter, and that Mt 15.21–8 in all its parts can in fact be explained as a Matthean revision of Mk 7.24–30, is the view we have adopted in what follows.[12]

(iii) *Exegesis*

Chrysostom, *Hom. on Mt.* 52.1, compared the sequence, debate with scribes and Pharisees over food laws (15.1–20) followed by the story of Jesus and the Canaanite woman (15.21–8), with the sequence in Acts 10: following Peter's vision about clean and unclean things, the apostle visits the Gentile Cornelius and welcomes him into the faith. Is the comparison apt? It assumes that both 15.1–20 and 21–8, in different ways, treat the same theme, namely, the place of Israel and the place of the Gentiles in salvation-history. Although many exegetes, ancient and modern, would concur, we harbour reservations. If, as we have urged, 15.1–20 does not clearly abolish OT laws, then it is difficult to see how it bears on the Gentile problem. Indeed, one could perhaps even argue that the trailing of 15.1–20 by 21–8 guarantees that the former will not be interpreted in any antinomian fashion, for in the latter the primacy of the Jews and of God's covenant with them are unequivocally upheld. There is in any event nothing in 15.1–20 or 21–8, considered by themselves, to indicate that God has rejected his people or introduced a new way of salvation.

We must also demur from those commentators who suppose that Matthew and his church would have found 15.21–8 useful in their relations with Gentiles (cf. e.g. Hill, *Matthew*, p. 253). As it stands, that is, taken in isolation, our passage does not really resolve anything. It in fact raises more questions than it answers (cf. p. 545). It does show that, despite the priority of Israel, Jesus was, on an exceptional occasion, willing to share messianic blessings with a non-Jew because of her faith. But the tension, which is almost a general principle, between Matthew's particularism and his universalism, remains unresolved and unclarified. Should Christian missionaries follow Jesus' example and confine themselves to Israel? Or should they preach to Gentiles in the hope that they will come to faith? And what is required of Gentiles once they have come to faith? Must they keep the law or are they free of all Jewish legislation?[13] These questions are not

---

[12] See further Dermience (v). For an attempt to show that the data are consistent with the Griesbach hypothesis see Russell (v).

[13] In Ps.-Clem. Hom. 2.19 we read that the Canaanite woman 'changed what she was .... For she, being a Gentile, and remaining in the same course of life,

addressed by 15.21–8, a text which recounts a quite exceptional situation and which leaves the status of the Gentiles hanging in the air (cf. Donaldson, p. 134). It is only with 28.16–20, which sheds its light on all that has come before, that any clarity is achieved (cf. Donaldson, pp. 133–4, and note Tertullian, *Praescr. Haer.* 8). Not until his conclusion does Matthew's commitment to the law-free Gentile mission become explicit, and not until the end do the differences between pre- and post-Easter praxis become plain. Thus 15.21–8 can only be rightly grasped when it is interpreted within its broader context, which is the gospel as a whole.

The various attempts to classify Mt 15.21–8 according to form criticism illustrate the limitations of the method. According to Bultmann, *History*, p. 38, it 'belongs to the apophthegms' but also 'proves to be a controversy dialogue of a sort' (cf. Taylor, *Mark*, p. 347: 'more akin in form to the Pronouncement-story'). In Derrett's estimation, the pericope is midrash. Gnilka, however, classifies Mk 7.24–30 as a 'Streitgespräch' (*Markus* 1, p. 291), and Nineham, *Mark*, p. 198, calls it a miracle story. The problem, of course, is that 15.21–8 does not exhibit any pure form. One can, to be sure, remedy the untidy situation by performing surgery, excising either the miracle framework[14] or the extended conversation[15] as secondary. But such procedure is arbitrary. Early Christians were not ruled by iron-clad form-critical laws. Further, in the present instance Gnilka, *Markus* 1, p. 290, appears correct in affirming that while the miracle is subordinate to the dialogue, the dialogue at the same time is not viable without the surrounding history. We therefore conclude that Mt 15.21–8 stands as a unit and is an example of a mixed type: it is a miracle story which contains elements characteristic of both pronouncement stories and controversy dialogues.

Does the story of the Syrophoenician or Canaanite woman go back to an event in the life of Jesus? Beare, pp. 342–4, speaks for many when he takes the pericope to be a retrojection of post-Easter debates (cf. Klauck (v)). For the following reasons we have our doubts. (i) 'The authenticity of the passage as a piece of original Palestinian tradition is attested by its obvious unpalatableness to Gentile Christian taste, for such a story could not conceivably have arisen gratuitously in a Gentile environment' (Brandon, p. 33). (ii) As the passage indicates, Jesus did in fact confine his ministry to Israel (cf. Rom 15.8). (iii) Only in Mk 7.24–30 par. is it possible to think of Jesus as being bested in argument. (iv) 'The question of the original use of the story in the Palestinian Church is ... difficult to answer. Two interpretations appear to be possible, namely either that it was invoked first by the Jewish Christians

---

He would not have healed had she remained a Gentile, on account of its not being lawful to heal her as a Gentile'. This well represents one possible interpretive extreme.

[14] Cf. Dibelius, *Tradition*, p. 261, n. 1, and Lohmeyer, *Markus*, pp. 144–5. Burkill, 'Development' (v), outlines this history: (i) Mk 7.27b (the product of strict Jewish Christianity); (ii) the creation of a miracle story (showing the possibility of Gentiles being accepted on the basis of their faith); (iii) Mark's additions (vv. 24, 31, and perhaps 27a); (iv) Matthew's additions.

[15] So Kertelge (v).

to justify isolated admissions of Gentiles to a qualified membership of the Church and later gained currency as an established ruling, or that it was originally employed to express disapproval of the extension of Christian privileges to the heathen' (Brandon, p. 34; cf. Nineham, *Mark*, p. 200). One wonders whether a story whose import is so ambiguous could have been created for the express purpose of granting instruction on the Gentile problem. Surely an author unconcerned to record a pre-Easter episode would have done a better job of making his intentions clearly known. Does it not make more sense to conclude that Mt 15.21–8 par. is based on an historical incident in which Jesus made plain his exclusive commitment to Israel and yet was compelled also to acknowledge the faith of a Gentile woman (cf. Hahn, *Mission*, p. 32)? See further Theissen (v).

It has, from time to time, been thought that Mt 15.21–8 and its Markan parallel have been influenced by 1 Kgs 17.8–24 (see e.g. Derrett (v)). In this last Elijah encounters a Gentile woman, the location is Sidon, the woman's sick son is miraculously healed, there is reference to 'a morsel of bread', and we find a sentence reminiscent of Mark's 'let the children first be fed': 'But first make me a little cake of it and bring it to me, and afterward make for yourself and your son' (1 Kgs 17.13). Moreover, Christian tradition turns the Syrophoenician woman into a widow (so Mk 7.26 sy^{s.c}; Ps.-Clem. Hom. 2.19), just like the woman in 1 Kgs 17.8–24. On the other hand, it must be said that the verbal agreements are quite minimal, that the story in 1 Kings does not focus on the Jewish/Gentile question, and that in the OT a resurrection is recounted whereas in the NT there is an exorcism. Perhaps Matthew and other early Christians would have perceived the similarities we have delineated, but signs of literary dependence are not apparent. Thus the relationship (if any) between Mt 15.21–8 par. and the tale about Elijah remains obscure.

21. Following his debate with the scribes and Pharisees (15.1–20) Jesus heads for the region of Tyre and Sidon. Whether he actually arrives there is unclear. But that his motivation is escape from danger is, as Origen, *Comm. On Mt.* 11.16, noted, made probable by the verb used, ἀναχωρέω; see on 4.12.

καὶ ἐξελθὼν ἐκεῖθεν ὁ Ἰησοῦς ἀνεχώρησεν εἰς τὰ μέρη Τύρου καὶ Σιδῶνος. This is a revised version of Mk 7.24a ('And from there[16] he arose and went away to the region of Tyre'). Matthew has altered Mark's sentence so as to obtain a favourite construction (participle[17] + ἀναχώρησεν[18]). He has also changed

---

[16] καὶ εκειθεν is the reading of Mk 7.24a A Θ f^{1.13} Maj sy^h. εκειθεν δε appears in ℵ B L Δ 892 1241 1424 pc sy^{hmg}. If Matthew had the text of ℵ B before him, then he altered δέ to καί, against his usual custom, because he wanted to save the particle for the dialogue in vv. 23–7 or because use of a δέ in 21 would have lessened the impact of the δέ in 20. *Pace* Gundry, *Commentary*, p. 310, καί is probably not a pointer to a thematic link between 15.1–20 and 21–8.
[17] Matthew's ἐξελθών is less Semitic than Mark's ἀναστάς.
[18] Cf. 2.22; 4.12; 12.15; 14.13; 27.5; Mk: 0; Lk: 0.

(μεθ)όρια to μέρη (cf. 2.22: ἀνεχώρησεν εἰς τὰ μέρη[19]) and added καὶ Σιδῶνος (which creates a traditional, biblical phrase; see on 11.21). ἐκεῖθεν* either refers to Gennesaret (14.34) or has no antecedent. In Mark the reference could be to the house of 7.17. Although εἰς can mean 'to' with the connotation of arrival, as in 16.13 and Mk 7.24, the preposition can also mean 'towards' or 'up to' or 'near;' and as this sense is attested elsewhere in the First Gospel (e.g. 17.27; 21.1), and as 10.5–6 lays down the rule that the pre-Easter mission should be confined to Jewish territory, one might suppose that here Jesus does not enter Gentile lands.[20] But this is far from obvious. Matthew could have thought of Jesus as going to a pagan region so long as no missionary work was done there (cf. Chrysostom, *Hom. on Mt.* 52.1, and we may recall the sojourn to Egypt in 2.13–21 as well as, perhaps, 8.28–34). So the text is not unambiguous (see further below).

Matthew has omitted from Mark the following: 'And he entered a house, and would not have any one know it; yet he could not be hid.' The omission of 'and he entered a house' (cf. 15.12–15 diff. Mk 7.17) is perhaps due to the house being inevitably thought of as belonging to a Gentile: Jesus does not offend Jewish sentiment by entering a non-Jewish dwelling (cf. Acts 10.28). It is also possible that Matthew moves Jesus outdoors in order to generate a parallel with 8.5–13: in both instances Jesus heals a Gentile from a distance. As for the dropping of a sentence in which Jesus fails to accomplish what he wills, that is only to be expected (cf. Allen, p. xxxi).

As a matter of history, Jesus himself probably never left the boundaries of Jewish population.[21] The Markan note that he entered the region of Tyre, if not a redactional invention (so Gnilka, *Markus* 1, p. 290), is probably to be understood thus: 'at that time the territories of Tyre and Sidon extended far east into the interior: that of Tyre stretched over the whole of the northern district of upper Galilee as far as the basin of Lake Huleh, while that of Sidon extended as far as the territory of Damascus. If Jesus wished to pass from Galilee to the region of Caesarea Philippi, he would of necessity have to touch Tyrian territory. This region lying between Galilee and Caesarea Philippi had once been part of the kingdom of Israel, and talmudic statements about the boundaries of those parts of Palestine with an Israelite population prove that in the time of Jesus it was still mainly inhabited by the descendants of the northern Israelite tribes' (Jeremias, *Promise,*

---

[19] The use of μέρη may have been motivated in part by a desire to save ὅριον for the following verse.

[20] Cf. Allen, p. 168, and those named in n. 25. Note Ambrose, *De interp. Job et David* 4.14: 'the Canaanite woman went out from the territory of the pagans and found Christ'.

[21] See esp. A. Alt, 'Die Stätten des Wirkens Jesu in Galiläa territorialgeschichtlich betrachtet', *ZDPV* 68 (1951), pp. 15–72; reprinted in Alt's *Kleine Schriften,* vol. 2, Munich, 1953, pp. 436–55.

p. 36). Jesus as a Jew confined his energies to reaching his own people (cf. Rom 15.8, and on the data of the Fourth Gospel Jeremias, ibid., pp. 37–8).

22. καὶ ἰδού. This is redactional. See on 1.20 and 3.16. Here ἰδού retains its sense of surprise. Jesus is encountering a Gentile.

γυνὴ Χαναναία ἀπὸ τῶν ὁρίων ἐκείνων ἐξελθοῦσα ἔκραζεν λέγουσα. This draws upon both Mk 7.25a ('But immediately a woman ... coming [ἐλθοῦσα]') and 26a ('Now the woman was a Greek, a Syrophoenician by birth'); and ὁρίων may derive from 7.24, (μεθ)όρια. Matthew likes κράζω + λέγω (see on 9.27) as well as ἐκεῖνος* and ἐξέρχομαι as a nominative participle*, and his predilection for direct speech has long been noted (cf. Bultmann, *History*, p. 312).

The major question concerning 15.22a is why our evangelist has turned Mark's Syrophoenician woman[22] into a Canaanite.[23] The following proposals are among the possible answers. (i) Matthew was simply following a non-Markan tradition (see section (ii)). (ii) He wished to fashion a wordplay: Χαναναία/κυνάρια. (iii) Χαναναία and Συροφοινίκισσα are translation variants of the Aramaic *kĕna'ănîtā'* (so Schwarz (v)). (iv) According to Kilpatrick, p. 132, 'Canaanite' was, around Matthew's time, used in Semitic circles to mean 'Phoenician'; and Matthew, being himself a Phoenician, used the terminology of his environment. (v) Bengel, *ad loc.*, recalling Gen 9.25—Canaan will be a slave of slaves—, implies that 'Canaanite' connotes the woman's subordination to the Jews. (vi) Most modern exegetes have supposed the change to 'Canaanite' was made because of its OT associations: one automatically thinks of Israel's enemies. Thereby is evoked 'Israel's deeply-engrained fear of and revulsion towards Gentile ways' (Donaldson, p. 132)—which in turn allows one to see in Jesus the overcoming of such fear and revulsion.

In our judgement, solution (vi) is most satisfactory. It is consistent with Matthew's addition of 'and Sidon' in v. 21. This creates a phrase ('Tyre and Sidon') which has negative connotations in the biblical tradition. Thus 'Tyre and Sidon' and 'Canaanite' work together to recall traditional prejudices. We concur with Chrysostom, *Hom. on Mt.* 52.1: 'the evangelist speaks against the woman, that he may show forth her marvellous act, and celebrate her praise the more. For when thou hearest of a Canaanitish woman, thou shouldest call to mind those wicked nations, who overset from their foundations the very laws of nature.[24] And being reminded of these, consider also the power of Christ's advent.'

[22] Who in later tradition is given the name 'Justa' (Ps.-Clem. Hom. 2.19; cf. 3.73; 4.1; 13.7). Ps.-Clem. Hom. 2.20–1 goes on to relate other legends about her.

[23] Χαναναῖος is a NT *hapax legomenon*. The spelling agrees with the LXX, Philo, and Josephus.

[24] The negative connotations of 'Canaanite' are manifest in the striking phrase of Gregory Nazianzen, *Orat*. 33: 'Canaanite soul'.

A second question raised by 15.22a is how the woman's movements are to be perceived. Whereas in Mark it is manifest that Jesus has gone into the province of Tyre, this is not the case in Matthew. γυνή ... ἀπὸ τῶν ὁρίων ἐκείνων ἐξελθοῦσα is usually translated: 'a woman ... from that region came out' (RSV, assuming ἀπό to denote place of origin, as in 4.25). It is, however, possible to render the phrase as 'a woman ... came out from that region',[25] which would make the situation similar to that in 8.5–13: a Gentile is on Jewish territory and seeks out Jesus. But just as the εἰς of 15.21 is of uncertain meaning, so too here: one can hardly decide whether Jesus has or has not departed from Jewish territory. In short, the grammar is ambiguous, and Matthew's theology does not clarify the matter, for it allows for either reading.

ἐλέησόν με, κύριε υἱὸς Δαυίδ. This has no parallel in Mark and, in view of Matthew's interest in confessions of faith, is redactional (cf. Held, in *TIM*, p. 235). For discussion see on 9.27, and for the cry for help as a standard element in miracle stories Theissen, *Stories*, pp. 53–4.

Whether or not 'Son of David' is taken to be a messianic title or to allude to Jesus as healer (see on 9.27), it remains surprising that the appellation is spoken by a non-Jew. Is one to infer that already the woman is acknowledging that Jesus is the Jewish saviour, his mission to Israel?

Note that all three times the woman addresses Jesus she calls him 'Lord' (which here lies somewhere between 'sir' and the informed Christian confession). This helps keep her boldness in check. She may debate with Jesus, but that does not diminish her recognition of his superiority.

ἡ θυγάτηρ μου κακῶς δαιμονίζεται. Compare 8.6; Mk 7.25b ('whose little daughter was possessed by an unclean spirit'); and 26b ('and she begged him to cast out the demon from her daughter'). For the verb and adverb see on 4.24. κακῶς δαιμονίζεται appears only here in the Greek Bible. Has Mark's θυγάτριον (diminutive) become θυγάτηρ for the sake of consistency (so Gundry, *Commentary*, p. 311)? See v. 28.

Jews were not, it hardly needs be said, the only ancient people to believe as a matter of course in evil spirits.[26] Here the substitution of 'severely possessed by a demon' or 'demonically sick' for Mark's 'possessed by an unclean spirit' allows the woman to speak as a Gentile instead of a Jew ('unclean spirit' is Jewish terminology). Note also that the omission of Mark's ἀκάθαρτον is consistent with Matthew's unconcern with any thematic connexion between 15.1–20 and 21–8 (cf. p. 543).

---

[25] Cf. Bengel, *ad loc.*; Allen, p. 168; Lagrange, p. 308; against Klostermann, p. 134; Gundry, *Commentary*, pp. 310–11.
[26] See G. Luck, *Arcana Mundi*, Baltimore and London, 1985, pp. 163–225.

23. Jesus reacts to the cries of the woman for her child with stone silence, as though he has not heard anything. Why? He is not mulling over her words, nor is it beneath him to talk with a woman (cf. *m. 'Aboth* 1.5). Rather, he is either turning her down or trying her faith. The disciples, then, in view of Jesus' tacit refusal, take it upon themselves to ask their master to dismiss the woman.[27] Perhaps they want to avoid contact with a Gentile, or maybe the woman has become a bother (note the imperfect tense of ἔκραζεν in v. 22: it intimates persistence). Whatever the answer, the entire verse is redactional and serves primarily to set the stage for the declaration in v. 24.

ὁ δὲ οὐκ ἀπεκρίθη αὐτῇ λόγον. Compare LXX 3 Βασ 18.21; 1 Chr 21.12; Isa 36.21 (καὶ οὐδεὶς ἀπεκρίθη αὐτῷ λόγον, for *wělō'-'ānú 'ōtô dābār*); and Mt 22.46 (redactional). ἀποκρίνομαι appears four times in our pericope, each time introducing Jesus' response to what has just been said (see p. 541).

καὶ προσελθόντες οἱ μαθηταὶ αὐτοῦ ἠρώτουν αὐτὸν λέγοντες. Compare 9.14; 13.10; 14.12; 15.12; 17.19; 24.1, 2. προσέρχομαι* is often editorial, and ἐρωτάω (Mt: 4; Mk: 3; Lk: 16) is redactional here and in 16.13 (cf. Mk 8.27: ἐπερωτάω); 19.17; and 21.24 (cf. Mk 11.29: ἐπερωτάω). Although the latter usually means, in the LXX and elsewhere, 'ask a question', it can also, when followed by λέγων, introduce a request in direct discourse (cf. *šā'al* and note Jn 4.31; 12.21; Allen, p. 168, cites Fayum Towns 132.1 and SIG 328.5; 930.56).

ἀπόλυσον αὐτήν, ὅτι κράζει ὄπισθεν ἡμῶν. Compare the disciples' request in the story of the feeding of the five thousand (14.15). κράζω + ὄπισθεν[28] (cf. *qārā' + 'aḥărê*, as in 1 Sam 20.37; 24.8; Jer 12.6; and *t. Šabb.* 7.13) is not otherwise attested in biblical Greek, but the improper use of ὄπισθεν as a preposition followed by the genitive is found in the LXX (cf. from the NT Lk 23.26; Rev 1.10 v. 1; and see BDF § 215.1). 'The implication of "she crieth after us" is that Jesus and the disciples are walking on and paying no heed to the woman' (Manson, *Sayings*, p. 201).

Légasse (v), p. 28, and several others have taken ἀπόλυσον to mean not 'send away' or 'dismiss' but 'set free'.[29] On this interpretation, the disciples want Jesus to favour the woman's request. Some support for this can be found in the seeming absence of a connexion between

---

[27] On the motif of obstacles in miracle stories see Theissen, *Stories*, pp. 52–3.

[28] Which here scarcely denotes discipleship, against Gundry, *Commentary*, p. 312.

[29] In a footnote the Jerusalem Bible claims that the verb here means 'let her go with her request granted'.

vv. 23 and 24 if the former be understood to invite a simple dismissal. Why respond to the disciples with 'I was sent only to the lost sheep of the house of Israel' if they have just asked Jesus to get rid of the woman? Nonetheless, one wonders whether it is natural to read so much into ἀπόλυσον, and Jesus' words in the next verse can constitute a general declaration which simultaneously upholds the disciples' request and discourages or tests the woman.

24. Although he does not dismiss the woman as requested, Jesus declares unequivocally the absolute priority of Israel for his mission: 'I was sent only to the lost sheep of the house of Israel.' The words would seem to exclude the Gentile petitioner from the benefits of Jesus' healing ministry. At best she has been challenged to show that her request is grounded in an authentic faith and is more than a self-seeking hope in magic. Again there is no parallel in Mark.

ὁ δὲ ἀποκριθεὶς εἶπεν. So also v. 26a. Whether Jesus is speaking to the woman or to the disciples or to both is unclear.

οὐκ ἀπεστάλην εἰ μὴ εἰς τὰ πρόβατα τὰ ἀπολωλότα οἴκου Ἰσραήλ.[30] Compare 10.6. In favour of the line being a Matthean creation, one could urge that it depends upon 10.6,[31] observe that it has no parallel in Mk 7.24–30, and note that some of the vocabulary might be considered redactional;[32] see further Gundry, *Commentary*, pp. 312–13. What can be said on the other side, that is, for thinking 15.24 to preserve a traditional utterance? First, the saying could have floated independently of any context. Certainly its presence here does not necessitate a redactional genesis (cf. Bultmann, *History*, p. 38). Secondly, there are striking Semitisms—οὐκ ... εἰ μή meaning 'only' (cf. BDF § 376), ἀποστέλλω εἰς + indication of circle concerned,[33] and οἴκου Ἰσραήλ without the definite article. Thirdly, the similar 10.5–6 is probably not redactional. Fourthly, elsewhere Matthew has ἀποστέλλω + πρός τινα (cf. 21.34, 37; 23.34, 37; 27.19), not εἴς τινα.[34]

Taking everything into account, we find the evidence almost

[30] sy^s contains this interesting variant, which Streeter, p. 260, n. 1, considered 'even more Judaistic': 'I have not been sent save after the flock, which hath strayed from the house of Israel.' The Judaistic flavour of this is not evidence for originality. The variant of D (εἰς τὰ πρόβατα ταῦτα τὰ ἀπολωλότα) is also more Semitic than the text we have printed; see Black, p. 304.
[31] So E. von Dobschütz, in Stanton, p. 20. For a survey of opinion on 10.5–6 and 15.24 see H. Frankemölle, 'Zur Theologie der Mission im Matthäusevangelium', in Kertelge, *Mission*, pp. 100–2.
[32] πρόβατον*; Ἰσραήλ: Mt: 12; Mk: 2; Lk: 12; also, the divine passive is ubiquitous in the First Gospel.
[33] See Jeremias, *Promise*, p. 26, n. 2.
[34] Although Matthew does use ἀποστέλλω + εἰς redactionally (8.31; 14.35; 20.2).

perfectly balanced. That Matthew created 15.24 on the basis of 10.5–6 has much to be said for it, but there are also reasons for thinking otherwise. A firm verdict, therefore, is not possible. We simply do not know whether Matthew received 15.24a as an isolated saying or whether he himself minted it.

Two additional points concerning tradition-history. (i) *If* 15.24 came to Matthew from the tradition, it is possible, as many have argued, that it was invented by a Jewish-Christianity resistant to the Gentile mission.[35] (The objection that the woman's request is in fact granted does not militate against this, for the present context is almost certainly secondary.) (ii) If, on the other hand, Jesus himself spoke 15.24—a possibility not to be excluded—, he *might* have been speaking of his ministry to the outcasts *within* Israel (cf. Fuller, *Christology*, p. 128). In this case the genitive, οἴκου Ἰσραήλ, could be understood not as Matthew understands it (as explanatory: see below) but as a partitive genitive ('I was sent to the lost sheep *within* Israel'), and the meaning would be very close to Mk 2.17: 'I did not come to call the righteous but sinners' (on which see pp. 105–107).

'The lost sheep of the house of Israel', a phrase which anticipates and so interprets the 'children' of v. 26, can be interpreted in at least four different ways. (i) Origen (citing Rom 9.8 and disparaging the Ebionites) and a few exegetes since have thought of spiritual Israel, Israel according to the spirit (*De prin.* 4.3.8). But nothing in Matthew justifies anything save an ethnic understanding of 'Israel'. (ii) One might think of the ten lost tribes.[36] This, however, renders 10.5–6 senseless, for there the lost sheep of Israel are located in Jewish territory: they are not scattered abroad. (iii) Some have taken the phrase to refer only to the lost within Israel, the assumption being that many or most were not lost (partitive genitive: see above). (iv) The most popular and surely most credible interpretation has it that 'the lost sheep of the house of Israel' was intended by Matthew to characterize the Jewish nation as a whole. It was by and large lost (with the emphasis probably not on sinfulness but lack of leadership). See further on 10.6.

25. Instead of letting Jesus' first pronouncement still her desire, the woman simply ignores what has been said and, kneeling,[37] again asks for help. To what the woman owes her enormous faith so quickly acquired we are not told; but her tenacity, like that of the widow of Lk 18.1–8, has,

---

[35] Cf. Bultmann, *History*, pp. 155, 163. But his argument that 'I was sent' requires a post-Easter setting is not persuasive; see Jeremias, *Promise*, p. 27.

[36] See A. S. Geyser, 'Some Salient New Testament Passages on the Restoration of the Twelve Tribes of Israel', in Lambrecht, *Apocalypse*, pp. 305–10.

[37] On this motif see Theissen, *Stories*, p. 53.

understandably, often been taken by expositors to be an instructive example of perseverance in faith;[38] and more than one commentator has recalled the tale of Jacob wrestling with the angel. (We assume that the woman has heard the conversation of 15.23–4; but some exegetes have pictured Jesus and the twelve being out of her hearing, so that v. 25 is a response not to the words of v. 24 but to the silence of v. 23a.)

ἡ δὲ ἐλθοῦσα προσεκύνει αὐτῷ λέγουσα· κύριε, βοήθει μοι. Compare v. 22a. Matthew's line is an abbreviated version of Mk 7.25b–6. Our evangelist has dropped the reference to the woman's ethnic status because he has already called her a Canaanite; and the description of the daughter's affliction is superfluous in view of v. 22. For the rest, a form of (προσ)-έρχομαι + a form of προσκυνέω + αὐτῷ is distinctly Matthean (Mt: 6; Mk: 0; Lk: 0), and 'Lord, help me'[39]—which has a biblical ring[40]—recalls v. 22b.

26. 'The more urgent she makes her entreaty, so much the more doth He also urge His denial' (Chrysostom, *Hom. on Mt.* 52.3). Jesus responds to the Canaanite woman by uttering a little parable which, totally devoid of conciliatory overtones, almost inevitably strikes the modern Christian as too off-putting, even cruel, as designed to wound a human heart: it is not good to take the bread of the children and to throw it to the dogs.[41]

ὁ δὲ ἀποκριθεὶς εἶπεν. So also v. 24a. Mark has: καὶ ἔλεγεν αὐτῇ. The omission of the pronoun need not, pace Gundry, *Commentary*, p. 314, be understood to mean that Jesus is addressing not the woman but only the disciples. It is simply assimilation to v. 24a. (Gundry's interpretation forces him to imagine that the woman's response in v. 27 is possible only because she has overheard Jesus talking to his disciples.)

οὐκ ἔστιν καλὸν λαβεῖν τὸν ἄρτον τῶν τέκνων καὶ βαλεῖν τοῖς κυναρίοις. Compare Jesus' initial, negative response to the nobleman's request in Jn 4.46–54; also our comments on Mt 8.7. Mk 7.27b begins with 'let the children first be fed' (cf. Rom

---

[38] See further Gnilka, *Markus* 1, pp. 294f., to which add Chrysostom, *Hom. on Mt.* 52.2.

[39] βοηθέω: Mt: 1; Mk: 2 (Mk 9.22, 24); Lk: 0.

[40] Cf. LXX Ps 40.3; 43.27; 85.17; 93.17, 18; 108.26; Isa 50.9.

[41] We wonder whether Beare, pp. 342–43, is not too extreme in his evaluation. For him, Mt 15.26 is 'atrocious,' and it exhibits 'the worst sort of chauvinism' and 'incredible insolence'. Does this not overlook the biblical doctrine of election, which by definition involves a stubborn point of singularity? And might not Jesus, burdened by the needs of his own people, have shunned a Gentile woman in the belief that if he were to heal her he would be besieged by a superstitious throng?

1.16) and follows with this: οὐ γάρ[42] καλόν ἐστιν κ.τ.λ. (with βαλεῖν—note the metathesis with λαβεῖν—at the end). The γάρ naturally falls away because 'let the children first be fed' has been dropped; but the reason for the absence of the statement about Israel's priority is far from obvious, for it seemingly accords with Matthew's own view of things.

Some critics have entertained the notion that the Markan line is a post-Markan interpolation and therefore was not in Matthew's copy.[43] There is, however, no need for this expedient, which has no textual support. Mark's πρῶτον may have been omitted because it could imply that the pre-Easter Jesus himself would some day turn to the Gentiles, or that once the Gentiles have begun to be fed, the Jews should henceforth be excluded—two thoughts the evangelist could not have countenanced. It is also possible that Matthew detected an inconsistency between 'let the children first be fed' and the story line: the woman is in fact fed at the same time as the children.[44] Whatever the solution, Munck (v) is correct to observe that in Mark 'the question . . . is how far the time has come for the Gentiles to be helped, and not, as in Matthew, how far Jesus is to help them at all' (cf. Held (v), p. 200).

The parable,[45] at least as it stands in the First Gospel,[46] implicitly assumes that Jesus is a Jew, the woman a Gentile, and probably further that the word 'dog' was sometimes used as an appellation for Gentiles (see on 7.6). 15.26 also, as v. 24 leaves no doubt, presupposes the equation, 'the children' = Israelites;[47] and it may even be that the bread should be considered a symbol of salvation (cf. the feeding stories). That the table too is symbolic, intended to allude to the Lord's table (cf. 1 Cor 10.21), is, however, too much.[48]

[42] After γάρ NA[26] prints ἐστὶν καλόν. But HG, perhaps rightly, suspects this of being under Matthean influence.

[43] E.g. Bultmann, *History*, p. 38; Held (v), p. 198.

[44] We find it difficult to accept Gundry's explanation of the omission: Matthew 'wants to play up the woman's faith by casting another obstacle in its way, here by transforming a reference to sequential priority into a flat refusal. This magnifying of the woman's faith makes a better justification of the mission to Gentiles than a "first", which narrow-minded Jewish Christians might use to argue for a delay till all Israel is saved and the rule of God takes over the earth . . .' (*Commentary*, p. 314).

[45] As a curiosity and specimen of exegetical ingenuity it may be recorded that F. Spitta, *Jesus und die Heidenmission*, Giessen, 1909, pp. 41–9, took Jesus' words about the dogs literally: he wanted to eat and the dogs to be fed before he left the table to perform a miracle!

[46] For the proposal that in Mark 'dogs' does not stand for Gentiles see Tagawa (v).

[47] Cf. Exod 4.22; Deut 14.1; Isa 1.2; Hos 11.1; Mt 3.9; 17.25–26; Lk 15.31; Rom 9.4; etc. Bengel, *ad loc.*, commented: 'Jesus spoke severely to the Jews, but honourably of them to those without.'

[48] Despite Ps.-Clem. Hom 2.19, which refers to 'the table in the kingdom', it

κυνάριον is the diminutive of κύων, the word used in 7.6. The distinction is that the former ('small dog'), connoting familiarity, probably refers to a pet or house-dog (for which see 1, p. 675, n. 14) as opposed to a stray or wild dog (cf. BAGD, s.v.; full discussion in Horsley 4, pp. 157–9). According to McNeile, p. 231, 'the Aram. would have no diminutive; Jesus may have meant dogs in general, and the woman first introduced the thought of pet dogs—"the dogs under the table" (Mk.).' This is far from certain. Jesus, if he did not speak Greek in this instance, could have used either the Aramaic *gûrā*[49] or perhaps a form of *kalbā* (so Gundry, *Commentary*, p. 315, citing GKC § 86.g, esp. n. 1). On the other hand, if Jesus did not use a diminutive, as McNeile argues, then, despite the circumstance that Hellenistic writers were often inexact in their use of diminutives,[50] the tradition may have tried to soften Jesus' words by using κυνάριον (just as many modern interpreters have tried to lessen offence by finding in the diminutive reason to infer that the dogs Jesus speaks of, being pets and not strays, are also members of the household; cf. O. Michel, *TWNT* 3, pp. 1103–4).

Was Jesus, in his response to the Syrophoenician woman, taking up a traditional maxim or proverb? Attention has been called to a parallel in Tg. Neof. on Exod. 22.30 (cf. also the Frag. Tg. on the same verse); and Burkill, 'Development' (v), has proposed that, as an isolated saying, Mt 7.26 par. could have meant something like 'charity begins at home'. While remaining doubtful of this last conjecture (cf. p. 544), we accept that it is possible that Jesus' words were influenced by a traditional saying.[51] See esp. Theissen (v), who stresses the economic situations in the Tyre-Galilee region.

27. Despite Jesus' discouraging words, the woman, so far from displaying resentment or becoming sullen, remains insistent and offers a riposte: the dogs eat the crumbs that fall from their masters' table. Her words take up Jesus' parable and extend it.[52] The woman dutifully recognizes both the priority of Israel and Jesus' obligation in that regard. 'She does not want to diminish Israel's privileges, but desires only a superfluous crumb' (Cranfield, *Mark*, p. 249). She accepts her secondary status among the house-dogs. At the same time, she raises the possibility of being fed even now, at the same time as the children are fed.

is also doubtful that Jesus or the evangelists had the messianic banquet in mind; contrast Jeremias, *Eucharistic Words* p. 234.

[49] SB 1, p. 722, suggests *gûryāytā qĕtannĕyāytā*.

[50] For discussion see D. C. Swanson, 'Diminutives in the Greek New Testament', *JBL* 77 (1958), pp. 134–51.

[51] On the targumic parallel see R. Le Déaut, 'Targumic Literature and New Testament Interpretation', *BTB* 4 (1974), p. 247. Tertullian, *De orat.* 4.6 ('Doth a father take away bread from his children and hand it to the dogs?') is not independent of the gospel tradition but rather a conflation of Mt 7.9 and 15.26.

[52] Cf. W. Schadewaldt, 'The Reliability of the Synoptic Tradition', in Hengel, *Mark*, p. 97.

ἡ δὲ εἶπεν. The string of ὁ δέ's or ἡ δέ's (cf. vv. 23, 24, 25, 26) continues: the woman is debating. Mark has: ἡ δὲ ἀπεκρίθη καὶ λέγει αὐτῷ. According to Gundry, *Commentary*, p. 315, 'Because Matthew shifted the address of Jesus' saying from the woman, she can no longer be said to answer Jesus. Therefore "she said" substitutes for Mark's "she answered and says to him."' A better explanation is this: ἀποκρίνομαι here would break the pattern outlined on p. 541.

ναί, κύριε. Compare 9.28 (redactional). So most mss. for Mk 7.28.[53] For the third time the woman addresses Jesus as Lord. This places her spirited exchange within the confines of faith: she confesses Jesus' lordship even as she argues her case with him.

ναί* either means 'Yes, certainly, that is true' (cf. BAGD, s.v., 2) or it denotes an urgent repetition of the woman's request (BDF § 441.1; cf. Rev 14.13; 16.17; and note Zahn, pp. 525–6). The word is not intended to contradict Jesus' οὐκ, as though the woman were saying: 'Yes it is!'

καὶ γὰρ τὰ κυνάρια ἐσθίει ἀπὸ τῶν ψιχίων τῶν πιπτόντων ἀπὸ τῆς τραπέζης τῶν κυρίων αὐτῶν. Compare Judg 1.5–7;[54] Gos. Phil. 82.21–3;[55] Philostratus, *V.A.* 1.19; and *b. B. Bat.* 8a. Allen, p. 168, paraphrased: 'It is neither good to give the children's food to the dogs, nor is it necessary; for they eat of the crumbs.' Mk 7.28 lacks γάρ*, qualifies κυνάρια with 'under the table',[56] uses ἐσθίουσιν, and follows ψιχίων simply with τῶν παιδίων.

πιπτόντων makes plain what Mark assumes: the food the dogs eat consists of the small scraps that have fallen (by accident) to the floor— although some interpreters have thought of the bread with which the hands were wiped after a meal.[57]

Matthew has presumably substituted τῶν κυρίων αὐτῶν for Mark's τῶν παιδίων because the former alone creates a verbal link with the surrounding narrative: the Gentile woman has called Jesus Lord and then gone on to state that dogs can feed on the fallen crumbs of their lords. But it can also be argued that the change is due to a desire to stress even more the superiority of the Jews. (While most commentators, from Chrysostom on down, have held the κυρίων to be the Jews, one

---

[53] P45 D W Θ f13 565 700 it sys omit ναι. Has it been borrowed from Matthew?

[54] On this see Storch (v). He raises the possibility of a conscious allusion to this text.

[55] This probably depends upon Matthew; see Tuckett, *Nag Hammadi*, p. 75.

[56] Gundry, *Commentary*, p. 315, is too subtle in explaining the omission of 'under the table' as due to a desire to avoid giving a handle to those wishing to press Gentile inferiority.

[57] Cf. SB 1, p. 726; Jeremias, *Parables*, p. 184.

could argue that the word stands in effect only for Jesus, explaining the plural as required by the logic of the preceding parable. The one plural, 'dogs', demands the other plural, 'masters'.)

28. Jesus, although he has not really changed his mind about anything—his mission is still only to the lost sheep of Israel, and the priority of Israel in salvation-history remains uncontested—finally gives in to the woman. The reason is not her wit, which has entangled Jesus in his own words, but rather her great faith—the real miracle of our story—, along with her recognition of the divinely ordained division between Jew and Gentile.

τότε ἀποκριθεὶς ὁ Ἰησοῦς εἶπεν αὐτῇ. Mark has simply καὶ εἶπεν αὐτῇ. As in Jesus' three previous responses, a form of ἀποκρίνομαι is employed; but the ὁ δέ is replaced by τότε* and ὁ Ἰησοῦς* added. The first change breaks the string of δέ's begun in v. 23 and shows that the woman has persuaded Jesus to do her will: he will now act in accord with her wishes. The second change adds a sense of closure. Jesus is named only at the beginning and end of the narrative.

ὦ γύναι. There is no parallel in Mark. The interjection, ὦ (Mk: 2; Mk: 1; Lk: 2), here expresses emotion (cf. BDF § 146.1b) and reminds one of the comparable ὦ ἄνθρωπε of Rom 2.1, 3; 9.20; 1 Tim 6.11; and Jas 2.20. Compare also 4 Macc 15.17; Josephus, *Ant.* 1.252; 6.305; 17.74.

μεγάλη σου ἡ πίστις· γενηθήτω σοι ὡς θέλεις. Compare Josephus, *Ant.* 15.87 (μεγάλης . . . πίστεως) and *Mek.* on Exod 14.31 (gĕdôlâ haʾămānâ). Matthew's wording is rather different from Mark's: 'For this saying you may go your way' (Mk 7.29b). Although one might argue that our evangelist is here following a non-Markan source, especially as nowhere else in Matthew does μεγάλη qualify πίστις, it is to be noted that γίνομαι + the dative is characteristic of our gospel (Mt: 5; Mk: 2; Lk: 1); that Matthew's phrase recalls 8.13 (ὡς ἐπίστευσας γενηθήτω σοι—spoken by Jesus to a Gentile) as well as the redactional 9.29 (κατὰ τὴν πίστιν ὑμῶν γενηθήτω ὑμῖν); and that the τοσαύτην πίστιν of 8.10 is the conceptual equivalent of 'great faith'. There is thus no reason not to assign v. 28b to Matthean redaction.

καὶ ἰάθη ἡ θυγάτηρ αὐτῆς ἀπὸ τῆς ὥρας ἐκείνης. This editorial remark does duty for the longer and much more vivid Mk 7.30 ('And she went home and found the child lying in bed, and the demon gone'). Matthew's sentence resembles 8.13 (ἰάθη ὁ παῖς ἐν τῇ ὥρᾳ ἐκείνῃ); and ἀπὸ τῆς ὥρας ἐκείνης—probably a Semitism (1, p. 81)—is elsewhere redactional (9.22; 17.18). Note that the exorcism—which at this point is really incidental—is described as a healing, and that there is no trace of any exorcism ritual.

(iv) *Concluding Observations*

(1) Writing of Mt 15.24, Jeremias (v), p. 27, gave it as his judgement that 'Matthew's only reason for preserving the logion in spite of its repellent implications was that it bore the stamp of the Lord's authority.' We must register our disagreement. It is understandable that a man like Marcion, with his estimation of the OT, would have found Mt 15.24 unpalatable (cf. Tertullian, *Adv. Marc.* 4.7). But the fact that Matthew has *two* sayings limiting Jesus' mission to Israel (10.5–6; 15.24) and that at least one of them has been redactionally inserted into a Markan pericope (15.24) strongly suggests that 15.24 had special meaning for and was congenial to him. (Of what other doublet could one possibly make the case for its being 'repellent'?) Quite simply, the verse makes it abundantly plain that the biblical doctrine of Israel's election must be taken seriously. God in Christ, according to our gospel, kept his covenant with his people. The Messiah was, in accordance with the Scriptures, sent first of all to the Jews, God's chosen people. Even in the face of opposition and disbelief, and even after prolonged conflict, Jesus continued to direct his mission to the leaderless sheep of Israel. What does all this say about our author? Despite his knowledge of the post-Easter Gentile mission and his experience of Jewish opposition in his own time, Matthew remained faithful both to the intent of the historical Jesus and to the particularism of the OT. He unequivocally granted, indeed strenuously upheld, the central place of Israel in God's dealings with humanity.

(2) According to Trilling, Matthew insisted so stridently upon Jesus' dedication to Israel largely in order to present the Jews as guilty and to leave them without excuse. According to Frankemölle, the point was rather to demonstrate God's covenantal faithfulness: the promises of the OT had to be fulfilled. We freely concede that there is probably a measure of truth in both analyses. But there is also another side of the picture. Just as Paul, in Romans, had to argue vigorously, in combating Gentile arrogance, for the continuing importance of Israel in God's plan, so too may it have been for our evangelist. Although 28.16–20 extends the missionary horizon to all peoples, it does not shut out Israel: the πάντα τὰ ἔθνη almost certainly includes the Jews (cf. on 28.19). If so, the missions to Jew and Gentile are to be carried on at the same time. Some confirmation for this can perhaps be gleaned from this, that although in chapter 10 missionaries are commanded to go forth into Israel, they are never said to return; that is, their mission is never made out to be over—which would be more than consistent with the

existence of a continuing mission to Israel in Matthew's place and time (see further on 11.1). It is also noteworthy that 15.24 comes as late as it does. Even after he has met opposition from so many Jewish quarters, Jesus remains preoccupied with his people. His persistence in this regard cannot but be exemplary. It is true that in 21.43 we read of the kingdom passing from the Jews; but it is delivered into the hands of the church, made up of Gentiles *and Jews*. Thus the Jewish element is hardly a thing of the past. Beyond this, the First Gospel—and in this it is in harmony with Paul—seems on occasion to foresee a special rôle for Israel in the eschatological drama (see e.g. on 19.28 and 23.39). One should not, therefore, come away from Matthew with the notion that Israel's election no longer counts for anything. Notwithstanding the rejection of the Messiah, the Jews, in some mysterious way, remain divinely advantaged. In the church there is, to use a Pauline phrase, neither Jew nor Greek, and yet there is a continued place for the Jewish people as such (cf. Davies, *JPS*, pp. 143–50, on Paul, whose position we take to be close to Matthew's; see further below).

(3) The parallelism between Mt 8.5–13 and 15.21–9 is truly striking. Both pericopae are about Jesus encountering a despised Gentile (in the one case a military officer, in the other a Canaanite woman). In both the Gentile comes to Jesus and asks for the healing of his or her child. In both the supplicants call Jesus 'Lord'. In both the focus is not on the healing itself but the preceding conversation, which in each instance contains a general statement by Jesus about Israel. In addition, both passages record initial hesitation on the part of Jesus (we took Jesus' words in 8.7 as a question: see note *in loc.*), relate that the Gentile won Jesus over by surprising words demonstrating great faith, and recount that the healings, accomplished from a distance, transpired 'from that hour'. Finally, there are also a few verbal parallels (see on 15.28). How are all these similarities to be explained? One can hardly follow Bultmann, *History*, p. 38, according to whom 'the two stories are variants' (cf. p. 64). The differences make that nearly inconceivable. One is also disinclined to attribute the similarities to the stories' being examples of the same *Gattung* or *Untergattung*. More likely is the possibility that, in the oral tradition, the two stories, because of their similar subjects, were to some extent assimilated to one another. But whatever the answer, Matthew himself, it is important to observe, has added to the catalogue of semblances (just as he enhanced the similarities between the two feeding stories). Thus the verbal parallels, the emphasis upon faith in 15.21–8, and the discussion of Israel in 8.10–12 are all due to his redaction.

When one inquires into the motivation behind extending the parallels between 8.5–13 and 15.21–8 it may be noted in the first instance that our author displays a tendency, visible in his treatment of verbal doublets, to assimilate like to like (cf. 1, p. 91). There is, however, more at work here than a stylistic habit. Matthew's contributions to the list of parallels by and large focus on two themes: faith, and the place of Israel. The reason is not hard to figure. There are only two episodes in our gospel in which Jesus clearly helps a Gentile: 8.5–13 and 15.21–8. Given Matthew's understanding of salvation-history, he cannot let these exceptional episodes go by without making it perfectly clear that when Gentiles are granted salvation it is solely on the basis of their faith: they are not expected to become Jews. On the other hand, he cannot permit Jesus to extend a hand to the Gentiles without letting the reader know (a) about Israel's special election (15.24, 26) and (b) about Israel's failure to live up to her election (8.10–12). In sum, Mt 8.5–13 and 15.21–8 are so very much alike in part because they tell similar stories which moved Matthew in each case to reflect upon the same themes.

(v) *Bibliography*

T. A. Burkill, 'The Historical Development of the Story of the Syrophoenician Woman', *NovT* 9 (1967), pp. 161–77.
idem, 'The Syrophoenician Woman: the Congruence of Mark 7.24–31', *ZNW* 57 (1966), pp. 23–37.
idem, 'The Syrophoenician Woman: Mark 7.24–31', in *Studia Evangelica 4*, TU 102, ed. F. L. Cross, Berlin, 1968, pp. 166–70.
A. Dermience, 'Tradition et rédaction dans la péricope de la Syrophénicienne', *RTL* 8 (1977), pp. 15–29.
Derrett, *Studies* 1, pp. 143–69.
Donaldson, pp. 132–4
B. Flammer, 'Die Syrophoenizerin. Mk 7.24–30', *TQ* 148 (1968), pp. 463–78.
R. A. Harrisville, 'The Woman of Canaan: A Chapter in the History of Exegesis', *Int* 20 (1966), pp. 274–87.
Held, in *TIM*, pp. 197–200.
J. Jeremias, *Promise*, pp. 25–39.
Jülicher 2, pp. 254–9.
Kertelge, *Wunder*, pp. 151–6.
Klauck, pp. 273–80.
S. Légasse, 'L'épisode de la Cananéenne d'après Mt 15.21–8', *BLE* 73 (1972), pp. 21–40.
Levine, pp. 82–116.
D. S. Margoliouth, 'The Syro-Phoenician Woman', *Exp* 22 (1921), pp. 1–10.
Munck, *Paul*, pp. 261–4.
J. H. Neyrey, 'Decision Making in the Early Church: The Case of the Canaanite Woman', *ScEs* 33 (1981), pp. 373–8.
E. A. Russell, 'The Canaanite Woman and the Gospels (Mt 15.21–8; cf. Mk 7.24–30)', in Livingstone, pp. 163–200.
Schenke, *Wundererzählungen*, pp. 254–67.
G. Schwarz, ΣΥΡΟΦΟΙΝΙΚΙΣΣΑ—ΧΑΝΑΝΑΙΑ (Markus 7.26/ Matthäus 15.22)', *NTS* 30 (1984), pp. 626–8.
F.-J. Steinmetz, 'Jesus bei den Heiden. Aktuelle Überlegungen zur Heilung der Syrophönizierin', *GuL* 55 (1982), pp. 177–84.

A. Stock, 'Jesus and the Lady from Tyre', *Emmanuel* 93 (1987), pp. 336–9, 358.

W. Storch, 'Zur Perikope von der Syrophöniziern. Mk 7.28 und Ri 1.7', *BZ* 14 (1970), pp. 256–7.

Tagawa, pp. 117–21.

G. Theissen, 'Lokal- und Sozialkolorit in der Geschichte von der syrophönikischen Frau (Mk 7.24–30)', *ZNW* 75 (1984), pp. 202–25.

Trilling, pp. 103–5, 133–4.

K. M. Woschitz, 'Erzähler Glaube. Die Geschichte vom starken Glauben als Geschichte Gottes mit Juden und Heiden', *ZKT* 107 (1985), pp. 319–32.

XXXVI

THE FEEDING OF THE FOUR THOUSAND
(15.29–39)

(i) *Structure*

The passage should be compared with 14.13–21, the other feeding story. Both pericopae contain three main parts: (i) an introduction which sets the scene (14.13–14; 15.29–31—in both places Jesus shows his compassion by healing the sick), (ii) a dialogue between Jesus and the disciples (14.15–18; 15.32–34), and (iii) the miracle itself, consisting of the blessing and distribution of bread (14.19; 15.36), the result (the crowd ate and was satisfied—14.20a–b; 15.37a), and a demonstration of the miracle and its greatness (remarks on the leftovers and the number of people—14.20c–21; 15.37b–8).

(ii) *Sources*

The introduction to the feeding of the four thousand (vv. 29–31) is a new redactional creation and only one of two pericopae in 13.53–17.27 not from Mark (the other being 17.24–7). In its place in Mark, that is, between the story of the Syro-Phoenician woman and the miracle of multiplication, stands Mk 7.31–7, which records the healing of a deaf man. Matthew's omission of this is easy to comprehend. His dislike of everything savouring of magic is well known (cf. Hull, pp. 116–41), as is his relative lack of interest in the so-called 'messianic secret' (see on 8.4); and he would not have been happy either with Jesus' groaning (cf. pp. 104f.) or with Jesus' being disobeyed (cf. Allen, p. 170); and why include notice of a long and circuitous journey during which nothing happened? Still further, by offering a healing summary at this juncture rather than the story of one man's recovery, the evangelist increases the parallelism between the two feeding stories: both are introduced similarly (cf. 14.13–14 with 15.29–31).

Although Matthew has omitted Mk 7.31–7, it has not failed to exert some influence on Mt 15.29–31. Not only has Mark's vocabulary affected the First Gospel,[1] but the arrival at the Sea of Galilee, the bringing of a sick man or sick persons to Jesus, the healing of a dumb

---

[1] Markan influence may be detected in the following: ἦλθεν, τὴν θάλασσαν τῆς Γαλιλαίας, ἀνα(−), αὐτῷ, ὄχλοι, κωφούς, λαλοῦντας.

man or dumb individuals, and the astonishment and acclamation of a crowd are all common elements.[2]

Verses 32–9, which record the miracle, depend, in our estimation, solely upon Mk 8.1–10. Granted the truth of the two-document hypothesis, no other source need be postulated. But is there any evidence in 15.32–9 par. itself to indicate that the two-document hypothesis is indeed true, that Mark is here anterior in time to Matthew? There may well be. Matthew's two feeding stories are more closely assimilated to one another than are those in the Second Gospel. What follows? To judge by the textual history of the synoptics, the proclivity of the tradition was, as might be expected, towards assimilation of our two stories to one another.[3] Thus if Mark is primary, one can see the textual tradition and the redactional tendencies of Matthew moving in the same—and it seems to us perfectly natural—direction. If, however, one accepts the priority of Matthew, then some reason must be given for Mark's decision to decrease the similarities between Mk 6.32–44 and 8.1–10.

(iii) *Exegesis*

The meaning for Matthew of 15.29–39, another 'gift miracle' (see p. 480), is in great measure the same as the meaning of 14.13–21. The story first of all speaks about the compassionate Christ making physical provision for his own. At the same time, it also points forward to both the Eucharist and the eschatological banquet. The story may also be intended to present Jesus as the eschatological prophet. See further p. 482. The one major difference between the account of the feeding of the five thousand and that of the four thousand is that the latter alone is intended to express the conviction that the coming of Jesus began to fulfil the eschatological promises associated in Jewish tradition with Mount Zion (see below).

Despite the many formal similarities, accentuated by Matthew, and the overlaps in meaning, there are several important differences between the two multiplication miracles, at least in the details. The most significant of these are: (i) only the second story takes place on a mountain; (ii) whereas in 14.13–21 the miracle is occasioned by words of the disciples, here the initiative lies wholly with Jesus (cf. Jn 6.5); (iii) the allusions to 2 Kgs 4.24–4 (see p. 482) are not nearly so pronounced in 15.29–39 as in 14.13–21; (iv) only in chapter 15 is the crowd said to have been with Jesus three days; (v) the words of blessing are different: the εὐχαριστήσας ἔκλασεν κ.τ.λ. of 15.36 is closer to

---

[2] *Pace* Lange, *Erscheinen*, pp. 408–10, influence from Mk 3.10–13 is dubious; cf. Donaldson, pp. 123, 257, n. 4.

[3] E.g. τοῖς ὄχλοις in 15.35 (cf. 14.19), δύο and ἔδωκεν in 15.36 (cf. 14.19). See further HG, pp. 124–5.

the traditional formulations in Lk 22.17, 19 and 1 Cor 11.24 while the εὐλόγησεν καὶ κλάσας of 14.19 is closer to the words of institution in Mt 26.26 = Mk 14.22;[4] (vi) Jesus looks towards heaven only in 14.19; (vii) the numbers are not the same: in 14.13–21 the disciples have five loaves and two fish, twelve baskets are later filled, and the number of men is estimated at five thousand; but in 15.29–38 there are seven loaves and a few little fish, seven baskets are left over, and the crowd is numbered at four thousand, not counting women and children; (viii) the word for basket in 14.20 is κόφινος, in 15.37 σπυρίς. All but the first of these eight disagreements were to hand in the tradition (= Mark). So Matthew has contributed little in this connexion.

The major changes which the author of our gospel has introduced into Mk 8.1–10 may be gathered under four headings: he has, first, increased the parallelism with the first feeding (see on vv. 34, 36, 37, and 38; also Allen, p. 172); secondly, certain irrelevant details have been omitted and the entire paragraph slightly abbreviated (see on vv. 32, 33, and 36); thirdly, stylistic improvements and revisions have been made (see on vv. 34 and 39); and, finally, the whole has been prefaced not with the story in Mk 7.31–7 but with a general statement about Jesus healing many (see p. 561).

Going back to Hilary and Augustine, many commentators on the gospels have held that whereas the crowd at the first multiplication miracle was predominately Jewish, the crowd at the second was predominately Gentile. The reasons for this are several: Mk 8.1 seems to place what follows in the Decapolis; while the numbers in the first story—five and twelve—can be associated with Israel (the twelve tribes, the five books of the law), the number seven—there are seven fish and seven baskets in 15.29–38—can be associated with Gentiles (cf. the seven Noachic commandments and the seven deacons in Acts 6; also, the number four thousand has sometimes been taken to allude to the four corners of the world); in Mt 15.29 the Sea of Galilee is named, and the only other time it is named in the First Gospel is 4.18, which follows a paragraph in which Galilee is the land of the Gentiles; in the feeding of the five thousand the pieces left over are gathered in κόφινοι, a word which some texts seem to link especially to Jews (see on 14.20), whereas in the feeding of the four thousand an altogether different word is used (see on 15.37); and, lastly, only after the second multiplication story do the crowds praise 'the God of Israel'—a term which, it is affirmed, indicates that the speakers are non-Jews. So it is often maintained that Jesus first feeds the Jews and then the Gentiles.[5] (Note Mk 7.27: 'let the children *first* be fed.') It is unnecessary for us

---

[4] Some have found in this reason to suppose that the feeding of the four thousand was passed on in an environment influenced by the eucharistic tradition common to Luke and Paul while the feeding of the five thousand was passed on in circles familiar with the tradition in Matthew and Mark.

[5] Donaldson, p. 261, n. 42, cites the following scholars holding this position: J. Wilkens, McNeile, S. E. Johnson, Rienecker, Lohmeyer, Schniewind, Schmid, Gaechter, Tasker, Fenton, Hill, Gundry, and Davies; to which we may add Zahn and Bacon.

to render a verdict on this interpretation as it pertains to Mark.[6] With respect to Matthew, however, we must give it as our judgement that it is probably off the mark.[7] On the one hand, Matthew's text does nothing to indicate that Jesus is in the Decapolis, all speculation as to the symbolic significance of the various numbers is quite uncertain, there is nothing in the unqualified phrase, 'the Sea of Galilee', to indicate Gentile territory, the precise meanings of both κόφινος and σπυρίς are unknown, as are the exact differences between them, and 'the God of Israel' is most commonly found in the biblical tradition as an acclamation on the lips of Jews. On the other hand, nowhere else in Matthew are οἱ ὄχλοι Gentile, our evangelist has edited Mark so as to remove Jesus' trip through non-Jewish territory (contrast 15.29 with Mk 8.1), and the Zion typology (see on 15.29) makes more sense if the crowd that is fed is Jewish. In sum, then, 15.29–39 continues Jesus' ministry to the lost sheep of the house of Israel.

The most obvious fact about the feeding of the four thousand is its close resemblance to the feeding of the five thousand. Three explanations are possible: two similar events took place in the pre-Easter period, the tradition doubled one event, or Mark duplicated a story found in one or more of his sources. Most modern scholars have opted for the second or third alternative: we are dealing with a doublet.[8] There are sound reasons for their consensus. The phenomenon of doublets is well-attested in the biblical tradition;[9] the two multiplication miracles are told in very much the same way; Jn 6.1–15 has parallels to both synoptic feedings (Brown, *John* 1, pp. 236–44); and the two stories appear in what have been taken to be parallel sequences.[10] There is in addition the problem of the disciples' question before the second feeding: 'Is it conceivable that the disciples, after they had themselves witnessed how Jesus was able to feed a great multitude with a small quantity of provision, should nevertheless on a second occasion of the same kind, have totally forgotten the first, and have asked, Whence should we have so much bread in the wilderness as to feed so great a multitude?' (Strauss, p. 508). Still, it is not wholly out of the question that two separate but like events led to the two stories now found in Matthew and Mark. Strauss answered his own objection with this: 'if Jesus on two separate occasions fed a multitude with disproportionately small provision, we must suppose, as some critics have done, that many features in the narrative of the one incident were transferred to the other, and thus the two, originally unlike, became in the course of oral tradition more and more similar; the incredulous question of the disciples especially having been uttered only on the first occasion, and

[6] For discussion see Tagawa, pp. 140–8 (opposed); Nineham, *Mark*, pp. 207–8 (noncommittal); Gnilka, *Markus* 1, p. 304 (opposed); Pesch 1, pp. 400–2 (favourable).

[7] Cf. Trilling, pp. 133–4, and Donaldson, p. 261, n. 42.

[8] See the commentaries on Mark. Usually the feeding of the four thousand is taken to be less original.

[9] E.g. the quails in Exod 16 and Num 11, the water from a rock in Exod 17 and Num 20, the story of Goliath in 1 Sam 17 and 2 Sam 21.

[10] For the details see esp. Taylor, *Mark*, pp. 628–32.

not on the second' (Strauss, p. 509).[11] Moreover, there is the difficulty that if Mt 15.29–39 par. be a doublet, the differences in details—especially the numbers (see p. 563)—have no obvious explanation. One also wonders whether the similarities of the broader contexts might not in part be due to Mark's hand: certainly they cannot in any usual sense of the term be considered true doublets.[12] What, then, is one to conclude? The case made by those who believe that the tradition or Mark mistakenly[13] multiplied one fact into two is strong enough we think to merit our assent; but the rejoinders prevent our conviction on the matter from approaching certainty. (For discussion of the historicity of the feeding(s) of the multitude see pp. 483–5.)

29. καὶ μεταβὰς ἐκεῖθεν ὁ Ἰησοῦς ἦλθεν παρὰ τὴν θάλασσαν τῆς Γαλιλαίας. Compare Mk 7.31, which follows the story of the Syro-Phoenician woman. For μεταβαίνω* + ἐκεῖθεν* (Mt: 3; Mk: 0; Lk: 0) see also 11.1 and 12.9 (both of Jesus, the last with ἦλθεν). 'The Sea of Galilee' (see on 4.18, also with παρά) is from Mk 7.31. Despite 4.15 ('Galilee of the Gentiles'), the phrase, 'the Sea of Galilee', does not in itself bring Gentiles to mind (cf. Trilling, p. 133).

καὶ ἀναβὰς εἰς τὸ ὄρος ἐκάθητο ἐκεῖ. Compare 5.1–2; 14.23; 23.2. Note the parallelism with the previous clause: καί + aorist participle (μεταβάς and ἀναβάς, both verbs of movement ending in -αβάς) + reference to place of departure or arrival + finite verb + concluding location. Should we suppose that the following story takes place where the sermon on the mount was delivered?

There are two important questions concerning 15.29b. The first is its relationship to Jn 6.3: ἀνῆλθεν δὲ εἰς τὸ ὄρος Ἰησοῦς καὶ ἐκεῖ ἐκαθέζετο (or: ἐκάθητο) μετὰ τῶν μαθητῶν αὐτοῦ. Both Matthew and John introduce their feeding stories with the notice that Jesus went to a mountain and there sat down, and there is common vocabulary (εἰς τὸ ὄρος, ἐκάθητο, ἐκεῖ). The parallels are the more interesting because in both instances the contexts mention the healing ministry of Jesus.[14] What does one conclude? There would seem to be three possibilities: coincidence, John's knowledge and use of Matthew, independent use

[11] For additional discussion see Taylor, *Mark*, p. 359; also Knackstedt, as on p. 495.

[12] The parallels are as follows: (i) Mk 6.30–44, feeding of five thousand; 8.1–9, feeding of four thousand; (ii) 6.45–56, sea crossing; 8.10, sea crossing; (iii) 7.1–23, controversy dialogue; 8.11–13, dispute over signs; (iv) 7.24–30, on food; 8.14–21, on leaven; (v) 7.31–6, a healing; 8.22–6, a healing. It is very difficult to know what one should make of these similarities, especially when the parallels in Jn 6 are also brought in for consideration. But surely only the two feeding stories could count as doublets of the same event. The other analogous episodes are hardly variants of one another.

[13] *Pace* Fowler (as on p. 494) and Donfried (as on p. 494), we find it difficult to imagine that Mark deliberately duplicated the story.

[14] Cf. Mt 14.14 and Lk 9.11. There is no reference to healing in either Mk 6.30–44 or 8.1–10.

of tradition. Donaldson (v), in his review of the issue, opts for common oral tradition. This was also the conclusion of Dodd, *Tradition*, pp. 208f. We scarcely wish to exclude this option, but it does appear to us that both gospel texts can be easily explained in other terms. Matthew, as we shall argue, seems to have introduced the mountain motif in order to connect Jesus' ministry with the eschatological hopes centred around Mount Zion. In other words, a redactional interest is all that need be postulated for the appearance of the mountain in Mt 15.29. The same is true with John. The author of Jn 6 was clearly intent upon depicting Jesus as one like Moses, and he could readily have placed Jesus on a mountain in order to further the correlation between the last redeemer and the first.[15] So the striking agreements do not require a common, non-Markan tradition. (As for the possibility that John depends upon the First Gospel, it suffices to refer to the investigations of those several scholars who have shown that John's version of the feeding of the five thousand probably does not draw upon any of the synoptics.[16])

The second question regarding 15.29 is its OT and Jewish background. The mountain of our pericope is a place of gathering, healing, and feeding. In addition, the story that follows anticipates the messianic banquet while the subsequent two verses (15.30f.) recall both the prophecy of Isa 35.5f. (cf. Ryan (v)) and the pregnant clauses of Mt 11.5; thus the broader context has to do with eschatological fulfilment. All this suggests a Mount Zion typology. For in Jewish expectation Zion is the eschatological gathering site of scattered Israel,[17] a place of healing,[18] and the place of the messianic feast.[19] Furthermore, it is worth remarking that if there is in fact an allusion to Isa 35.5–6 in Mt 14.30–1 (see on v. 31), that OT passage is part of a prophecy about the pilgrimage of Israel to Mount Zion. We are therefore led to endorse the exposition of Donaldson, pp. 130–1: 'All the elements in this passage—the gathering of the crowds; the healing of the lame, maimed, blind and dumb; the allusion to Is 35.5f.; the feast of plenty; echoes of the pastoral metaphor, the eschatological activity of the "God of Israel" and, above all,

---

[15] Esp. as John has Jesus *sit* on the mountain; see on 5.1–2.

[16] See esp. Dodd, *Tradition*, pp. 199–211, and Brown, *John* 1, pp. 236–50; also Donaldson, pp. 123–6.

[17] Cf. Jer 31.10–12 and Ezek 34.14 and see further Donaldson, pp. 42–3. On pp. 129–30, Donaldson argues that the crowds of 15.29–31 are anticipated by 15.24: 'the lost sheep of the house of Israel'.

[18] E.g. Isa 35.5–6; Jer 31.8; Mic 4.6–7; and Clement of Alexandria, *Paed.* 1.9 (quoting the lost Apocryphon of Ezekiel). In the light of conclusions to be drawn below, it may not be irrelevant to point out that in rabbinic tradition Sinai is a place of healing; see *Mek.* on Exod 20.18 and the other texts cited by SB 1, pp. 594–6.

[19] Isa 25.6–10; Jer 31.12–14; Ezek 34.26–7; 5 Ezra 1.38–48; *Exod. Rab.* on 25.8; *Pesiq. R.* 41.5.

the mountain setting—are part of the Zion complex of ideas. Moreover, Matthew combined these elements into an event whose shape conforms closely to the pattern of Zion eschatology: a gathering of the lost sheep of Israel to "the mountain" where the Messiah of the God of Israel heals their infirmities and feeds them plentifully. The centre of the pattern, of course, has been transformed, for it is the presence of Christ and not the restoration of the temple that gives the event its eschatological foundation. Nevertheless, the formative influence of Zion eschatology is apparent, for the care with which Matthew has constructed the setting for 15.29–31 is evidence of its theological importance for the evangelist, and such a configuration of elements would call to mind no other theological background than that of Zion eschatology'.

Having concurred so far with Donaldson, we have yet one more issue to address. How is it that τὸ ὄρος can here be interpreted in terms of a Zion typology while elsewhere we have insisted on a Sinai background (see on 5.1–2; 14.23; and 17.1)? The answer, we suggest, is straightforward. Already in the OT, Sinai and Zion motifs are merged: see, for instance, Ps 68. Later examples of conflation may be found in Tg. Neofiti on Exod 4.27[20] and *Midr. Rab.* on Ps 68.9.[21] Decisive above all else in this connexion is the expectation in Isa 2.2–3: 'law will go forth out of Zion'.[22] Here Mount Zion functions as the eschatological Sinai, the mountain of law-giving. The upshot for us is that by associating τὸ ὄρος with Sinai and Zion at the same time, that is, by making Jesus the new Moses in whose coming the promises made concerning Zion have begun to find fulfilment, the First Evangelist was not entering virgin territory. Rather he was simply following a path laid out already by Jewish tradition.

30. καὶ προσῆλθον αὐτῷ ὄχλοι πολλοὶ ἔχοντες μεθ' ἑαυτῶν τυφλούς, χωλούς, κυλλούς, κωφούς, καὶ ἑτέρους πολλούς.[23] προσ-

[20] Horeb (= Sinai) is given a title of Zion: 'the mountain of the sanctuary of the Lord'.

[21] According to this, Mount Sinai was created out of Mount Moriah (= Mount Zion).

[22] Cf. Jub. 1.15–29; Sib. Or. 3.715–19.

[23] The textual tradition is exceedingly confused. χωλους, τυφλους, κυλλους, κωφους is found in ℵ *pc* a b ff² syˢ and NA²⁶. HG prints the reading of P Γ Θ *f*¹·¹³ 700 *pm* f syᶜ·ᵖ saᵐˢˢ bo: χω., τυ., κω., κυ. B *pc* saᵐˢˢ mae have χω., κυ., τυ., κω., C K 565 1010 *pm* χω., κω., τυ., κυ., L W Δ *al* l ꝗ vg syʰ κω., χω., τυ., κυ., 33 892 1241 *pc* aur ff¹ vgᶜˡ κω., τυ., χω., κυ., 1424 κω., τυ., κυ., χω., D *pc* χω., τυ., κυ. (omitting κω), Or τυ., χω., κω., κυ. There is no way to sort out such confusion with any degree of certainty. We have printed a conflated reading: τυ., χω. (so Or) followed by κυ., κω. (so ℵ *pc* a b ff² syˢ). Our reason is two-fold. First, 11.5 mentions the blind before the lame and both before the deaf or dumb (cf. 12.22; 21.14). We might expect some consistency in this regard. Secondly, Matthew's fondness for chiasmus might incline one to expect the list in v. 31 to reverse the order of v. 30: deaf or dumb, maimed, lame, blind.

ἔρχομαι* is a redactional favourite, as is the construction, προσέρχομαι + αὐτῷ (= Jesus) + subject.[24] ὄχλοι πολλοί (Mt: 5; Mk: 0; Lk: 1; cf. Mk 8.1) is also recognizably editorial and recalls 14.13.

Of the four types of sick people here listed, three are found elsewhere in the gospel. For the blind see 9.27f.; 11.5; 12.22; 20.30; and 21.14; for the lame 11.5 and 21.14; and for the deaf (or dumb; see on 9.32f.) 9.32f.; 11.5; and 12.22 (cf. also Mk 7.32). κυλλός (= 'crippled'; LXX: 0) is the exception. The word appears nowhere else in the NT save 18.8 = Mk 9.43, where it refers to the possibility of entering the kingdom of heaven with injured limbs. καὶ ἑτέρους πολλούς serves to increase the range of illnesses and makes continued iteration of specifics unnecessary.

καὶ ἔρριψαν αὐτοὺς παρὰ τοὺς πόδας αὐτοῦ.[25] Compare Josephus, Bell. 2.625 (soldiers τὰ ὅπλα παρὰ τοῖς ποσὶν ἔρριψαν αὐτοῦ); Ant. 2.159 (Judas ῥίπτει πρὸ τῶν Ἰωσήπου ποδῶν ἑαυτόν); T. Job 39.3 (ἔρριψεν ἑαυτὴν παρὰ τοὺς πόδας αὐτῶν). ῥίπτω (9.36; 15.30; 27.5) is redactional all three times Matthew uses it (Mk: 0; Lk: 2). Here it has a weakened sense: not 'they flung' but 'they put' (cf. LXX Gen 21.15; 2 Macc 3.15). One wonders, given the statements about feet in 5.35; 22.44; and 28.9, whether or not position at Jesus' feet implies his lordship (so Gundry, Commentary, p. 318).[26] There is in any event no allusion to the foot being an instrument of healing; and that there is a glance at Isa 52.7 ('How beautiful upon the mountains are the feet of him who brings good tidings . . .') is, against Schweizer, Matthew, p. 331, rather doubtful (even though the OT context concerns Zion). But Donaldson, p. 130, could be right in associating ἔρριψαν with 9.36, where the Jewish crowds are designated as ἐρριμμένοι. Might not the appearance of the verb in 15.30 indicate that the evangelist has in mind the scattered sheep of Israel?

καὶ ἐθεράπευσεν αὐτούς. So 4.24 (q.v. for the verb); 12.15 (with πάντας); 19.2 (with ἐκεῖ at the end); and 21.14. The statement is 'absolute and general', to quote Gerhardsson (v). Compare 14.14, which introduces the feeding of the five thousand.

31. ὥστε τὸν ὄχλον θαυμάσαι.[27] Compare 8.27; 9.33 ('and the crowds marvelled'); and 27.14 (ὥστε θαυμάζειν . . .).

[24] 5.1; 8.5; 9.14; 9.28; 13.36; 14.15; 15.30; 17.14; 19.3; 20.20; 21.14, 23; 22.23; 24.3; 26.7, 69; Mk: 1; Lk: 0.
[25] D b have υπο.
[26] Perhaps relevant here is the enthronement motif connected with Zion speculation; see Donaldson, pp. 46–7, citing, among other texts, Isa 24.23; 52.7; Ezek 17.22–4; 34.23–31; Mic 4.6–7.
[27] The plural, τους οχλους, found in B L W Maj lat sy^{c.p.h} mae, might be original: 'It is very improbable that Mt. in this non-Marcan passage would have the singular' (Allen, p. 171). Cf. Schenk, Sprache, p. 351

βλέποντας κωφούς λαλοῦντας, κυλλοὺς ὑγιεῖς καὶ χωλοὺς
περιπατοῦντας καὶ τυφλοὺς βλέποντας. Compare 11.5; also Isa
35.5f.; *Mek.* on Exod 20.18 (where it is recorded that at Sinai
there were no blind, dumb, deaf, or lame individuals); Sib. Or.
8.206f.; and Mk 7.37 ('And they were astonished beyond
measure, saying, "He has done all things well; he even makes
the deaf hear and the dumb speak"'). It is quite possible that
the use of the rare μογιλάλος in Mk 7.32 ('And they brought
to him a man who was deaf and had an impediment in his
speech (μογιλάλον)') led Matthew back to LXX Isa 35.5f.[28]
('then the eyes of the blind shall be opened and the ears of the
deaf shall hear; then the lame shall leap as a hart, and the
tongue of the dumb leap for joy . . .') and so encouraged him to
compose a list of miraculous healings.[29] Certainly Origen and
many others since have cited Isa 35.5f. when discussing Mt
15.31 (cf. *Comm. on Mt.* 11.18).

καὶ ἐδόξασαν τὸν θεὸν Ἰσραήλ. So also 9.8, without Ἰσραήλ
(which is, obviously, the Jewish people, not the patriarch).

'The God of Israel' (only here in Matthew) is a conventional title
which occurs often in the OT and books inspired by it. The following
may be cited: Exod 5.1; 1 Kgs 1.48; 1 Chr 16.36; Ps 41.13; 59.5;
68.35; 69.6; 72.18; 106.48; Isa 29.23;[30] 1QM 13.2; 14.4; Lk 1.68; T.
Sol. 1.13; *t. Ḥag.* 2.1.[31] In all these texts the appellation, 'the God
of Israel', is on the lips of Jews; and, with few exceptions, it is used
in acclamations (it was clearly liturgical). *Pace* Jeremias, *Promise*,
p. 29, n. 1, and many others, the use of the title is not evidence for a
Gentile crowd. (The name, 'Israel', was popularly understood to
mean 'one who sees God'.[32] One accordingly wonders whether the
emphasis upon sight in our text (βλέποντας . . . βλέποντας) led to the
use of 'Israel'.)

32. ὁ δὲ Ἰησοῦς. This replaces Mk 8.1a: 'In those days,
when again a great crowd had gathered, and they had nothing
to eat'. Matthew's δέ helps link vv. 32–9 with its introduction,
vv. 29–31.

προσκαλεσάμενος τοὺς μαθητὰς αὐτοῦ εἶπεν. Matthew has

---

[28] μογιλάλος occurs only here in the LXX.
[29] See further Donaldson, p. 127.
[30] Against Gundry, *Commentary*, p. 319, the similarities between Isa 29.18–19
and Mt 15.30–1 are not sufficient reason to imagine that Matthew had Isa 29.23
in particular in mind.
[31] Cf. also Apost. Const. 8.15.7, which probably preserves a Hellenistic
synagogal prayer.
[32] E.g. Philo, *Leg. all.* 3.186; *De fuga* 208; Clement of Alexandria, *Paed.* 1.9;
Origen, *De prin.* 4.3; Eusebius, *Praep. ev.* 11.6; On the Origin of the World
105.24–5.

added the possessive pronoun,[33] changed the historical present (λέγει) to an aorist (as frequently), and dropped the superfluous, concluding αὐτοῖς. Note that in Jn 6.5, as here, the scene opens with a declaration of Jesus; contrast Mt 14.15 and Mk 6.35.

σπλαγχνίζομαι ἐπὶ τὸν ὄχλον. So Mk 8.2a. For the verb, which also appears in the introduction to the feeding of the five thousand (14.14 = Mk 6.34), see on 9.36.

In Mk 8.1–2 there is both a change of audience and a change of time ('In those days, when again a great crowd had gathered . . .'): the multitudes of Mk 7.31–7 and 8.1–10 are not the same. In Matthew, by way of contrast, the hungry crowd is that of the previous paragraph: the sick and those with them. The change makes for one scene instead of two and thus enhances the parallelism with 14.13–21.

ὅτι ἤδη ἡμέραι τρεῖς προσμένουσίν μοι καὶ οὐκ ἔχουσιν τί φάγωσιν. This reproduces Mk 8.2b without alteration. For 'three days'—here a parenthetical nominative[34]—as an approximate period of time see on 16.21. Here the expression, while it can hardly be evidence for a one-time post-resurrectional setting, could have tied into some pre-Markan context which the Second Evangelist disturbed (cf. Taylor, *Mark*, p. 357). Or should the words be thought of in connexion with the biblical tradition that God helps or saves people after three days (see on 16.21)? Whatever the answer, the notice makes it manifest that if any brought provisions, they have by now been spent. As Schweizer writes: 'the power of attraction which proceeds from Jesus is made more impressive and the situation more urgent by the mention of three days' (*Matthew*, p. 156).[35]

καὶ ἀπολῦσαι αὐτοὺς νήστεις οὐ θέλω, μήποτε ἐκλυθῶσιν ἐν τῇ ὁδῷ. Mk 8.3 follows καί with a conditional (ἐὰν ἀπολύσω) and therefore, instead of μήποτε[36] + the aorist subjunctive ἐκλυθῶσιν, has simply ἐκλυθήσονται. The only other difference is that Matthew has replaced the needless εἰς οἶκον αὐτῶν with the authoritative οὐ θέλω (which 'heightens the note of mastery

---

[33] Its presence in Mk 8.1 A B W Θ *f*¹³ Maj sy^{s.p} sa bo^{ms} is probably due to harmonization to Matthew; but note J. K. Elliott, 'Textual Criticism, Assimilation and the Synoptic Gospels', *NTS* 26 (1980), pp. 236–7.

[34] Cf. BDF § 144. Allen, p. 171, commented: 'the accusative would be so much more natural, that the nominative in Mt. and Mk. must be regarded as a proof of dependence of one Evangelist upon the other'. Cf. Plummer, p. 220. The phrase could be a Semitism; see Doudna, pp. 74–6; but there are parallels in the papyri; see MHT 2, p. 447.

[35] Beare, p. 347, rightly observes the possibility 'that this mention of so long a time may have prompted Matthew to elaborate the single healing of Mark [7.31–7] into the mass healings of the remodelled introduction [Mt 15.29–31]'.

[36] Mt: 8; Mk: 2; Lk: 7.

and dignity of Christ's words'; so Allen, p. 171). The effect of the editing is to make vv. 32d–e parallel to vv. 32b–c: in both a main clause with Jesus as subject is trailed by a subordinate clause with the crowd as subject (cf. Gundry, *Commentary*, p. 320).

ἐν τῇ ὁδῷ (= *bĕderek*) is a fixed expression favoured by Mark (Mk 8.3, 27; 9.33, 34; 10.52). Matthew has it in 5.25; 15.32; 21.8 (*bis*), and 32. He does not seem to lend it any symbolic significance. 'On the way' and 'on the journey' would be adequate translations. Mark's comment, 'and some of them have come a long way' (8.3c), falls away because it would add little to Matthew's purposes[37] as well as disrupt the parallelism with v. 32c.[38]

33. καὶ λέγουσιν αὐτῷ οἱ μαθηταί. Matthew has substituted λέγουσιν for ἀπεκρίθησαν and dropped αὐτοῦ at the end[39] (contrast 15.32 = Mk 8.1). One wonders whether both changes were not made in order to create a chiastic structure within the dialogue in vv. 32–3:

32	ὁ δὲ Ἰησοῦς . . . εἶπεν·		
33	καὶ λέγουσιν αὐτῷ	οἱ μαθηταί·	πόθεν . . .
34a	καὶ λέγει	αὐτοῖς	ὁ Ἰησοῦς· πόσους . . .
34b	οἱ δὲ	εἶπαν·	

πόθεν ἡμῖν ἐν ἐρημίᾳ ἄρτοι τοσοῦτοι ὥστε χορτάσαι ὄχλον τοσοῦτον; This is a revision of Mk 8.4: 'How (πόθεν; cf. Jn 6.5) can one feed these (τούτους; cf. Jn 6.5) with bread here in the desert (ἐπ' ἐρημίας)?' Our evangelist has made the question a little more concrete ('us' for 'one', 'this crowd' for 'these', 'enough bread' for 'bread'), and his ἐν ἐρημίᾳ is an improvement. Also, his formulation underlines the disciples' rôle as mediators (cf. Held (v)). Against Gundry, *Commentary*, p. 320, and a few others, we are unable to see that whereas in Mark the disciples fail to understand, in the First Gospel their question has been revised 'so as to imply that only the disciples are unable—for Jesus *is* able—and that they understand their responsibility to give bread to the crowd, as Jesus commanded them previously . . .'.

ἐρημία (cf. 2 Cor 11.26; Heb 11.38; and the rabbinic *'ĕrîmîn*) appears in the gospels only in 15.33 = Mk 8.4. It designates an

---

[37] But according to Danker (v), Mark's text may here allude to Josh 9.6, 9 or Isa 60.4. Did Matthew miss the allusion, or is Danker incorrect?

[38] If one imagines that ἀπὸ μακρόθεν (cf. Eph 2.13, 17) and ἥκω (cf. Isa 39.3; 60.4; Tob 13.11) would have called to mind Gentiles (so Pesch 1, pp. 402–3), then Matthew's omission of the words is consistent with our claim that he was thinking of Jews.

[39] Its appearance in 15.33 C D L W Θ *f*¹ Maj may be put down to Markan influence.

uninhabited region and often stands in contrast to πόλις (as in Josephus, *Ant.* 2.24; *Vit.* 11). Here the thought is: there are no nearby villages in which to buy food. For the related ἔρημος of the first feeding see on 14.13 and 15. For χορτάζω see on 14.20.

34. καὶ λέγει αὐτοῖς ὁ Ἰησοῦς. Mk 8.5a has this: καὶ ἐπηρώτα[40] αὐτούς. Other places where a form of λέγω has been substituted for a form of ἐπερωτάω (Mt: 8; Mk: 25; Lk: 17) include 15.12 diff. Mk 7.17; 16.15 diff. Mk 8.29; 17.19 diff. Mk 9.28; 19.3 diff. Mk 10.2; 19.16 diff. Mk 10.17; 26.63 diff. Mk 14.61; 27.13 diff. Mk 15.4 (cf. 16.13 diff. Mk 8.27: ἠρῶτα for ἐπηρώτα). Here the exchange makes for greater parallelism with v. 33 (see above).

πόσους ἄρτους ἔχετε; In Mk 8.5 the verb is in second place. It is unusual for Matthew to leave Jesus asking a question; contrast 14.17 diff. Mk 6.37–8 and see 1, p. 105.

οἱ δὲ εἶπον.[41] Mk 8.5 uses εἶπαν.

ἑπτά, καὶ ὀλίγα ἰχθύδια. Mk 8.5 has only ἑπτά, so the reference to fish has been added, as also in 15.36 diff. Mk 8.6. The source for the addition in both instances is Mk 8.7 (καὶ εἶχον ἰχθύδια ὀλίγα). The motive would seem to be assimilation to 14.17 and 19. In addition, the mention of fish here permits the omission of Mk 8.7[42] and thus contributes to compression of the narrative.

ἰχθύδιον (cf. *dāgâ*, as in *b. Ned.* 51b), which appears twice in the NT, in Mt 15.34 and Mk 8.7 (cf. Barn. 10.5), is the diminutive of ἰχθύς (cf. *dāg*) and means 'little fish' (BAGD, s.v.). One might argue that the word makes the miracle all the greater. But the use of ἰχθύας in 15.36 would appear to discredit such an interpretation. More plausible is Bengel's suggestion: by referring to 'a few small fish', the disciples are disparaging their provisions: 'we have nothing except seven loaves and some small fish'.

35. καὶ παραγγείλας τῷ ὄχλῳ ἀναπεσεῖν ἐπὶ τὴν γῆν.[43] As in 14.19, Jesus, obviously in charge, once again orders the crowd to recline on the ground.[44] Instead of the aorist participle, Mark

[40] So HG, following A D Θ 0131 *f*[1.13] Maj. NA[26] follows ℵ B: ηρωτα.

[41] So HG, without apparatus. NA[26] prints ειπαν, without apparatus. See further BDF §§ 80–1.

[42] 'And they had a few small fish; and having blessed them, he commanded that these also should be set before them'.

[43] εκελευσε for παραγγειλας (followed by και λαβων in C L W Maj sy[h] and by και ελαβε in 700 (892[c]) *pc* sy[s.c.p]) could very well be pristine. Although one can dismiss it as assimilation to 14.19, Matthew himself exhibits a strong tendency to assimilate the two feeding stories. See further J. O'Callaghan, 'Consideraciones críticas sobre Mt 15.35–36a', *Bib* 67 (1986), pp. 360–2.

[44] Even if it was early Christian practice to receive the Eucharist while standing (cf. Dix, p. 137), the tradition that Jesus reclined with his disciples at the Last Supper was well-known (cf. 26.20; Mk 14.18; Lk 22.14; Jn 13.4).

has the present παραγγέλλει and, in place of the accusative after ἐπί, the genitive (cf. 13.2 diff. Mk 4.1; 14.25 diff. Mk 6.48; and Allen. p. xxviii).[45]

ἀναπίπτω (only here in Matthew; LXX: 6) is also used in the feeding stories in Mk 6.40 and Jn 6.10. It regularly describes the reclining that accompanies eating (BAGD, s.v.). Compare *m. Sanh.* 2.3: 'When they make for him the funeral meal all the people sit on the ground . . .'.

36. ἔλαβεν τοὺς ἑπτὰ ἄρτους καὶ τοὺς ἰχθύας. Mark has καὶ λαβών and lacks 'and the fish'. This last difference is accounted for by Matthew's assimilation to 14.19 (q.v. for discussion).

καὶ εὐχαριστήσας ἔκλασεν καὶ ἐδίδου τοῖς μαθηταῖς. Matthew has tacked on the last καί and again omitted αὐτοῦ after μαθηταί (cf. 15.33 diff. Mk 8.4). See 14.19 for discussion, including the variation between εὐλογέω (14.19) and εὐχαριστέω (15.36). The use of the latter gives the text a perfect parallel in the eucharistic tradition preserved in Lk 22.19 and 1 Cor 11.24 (καὶ εὐχαριστήσας ἔκλασεν).

οἱ δὲ μαθηταὶ τοῖς ὄχλοις. So 14.19 (q.v.). Mk 8.6 reads: ἵνα παρατιθῶσιν, καὶ παρέθηκαν τῷ ὄχλῳ. Once more Matthew's desire to assimilate the feeding of the four thousand to the feeding of the five thousand is patent.

The notice that Jesus gave the food to his disciples who in turn handed it on to the crowd could well have been intended as an allusion to the Eucharist. In early practice the elements were given to the deacons for distribution.[46] On the omission of Mk 8.7 (which strikes one as an awkward addition), see on 15.34. See also Held (v), who stresses that by dropping the separate meal of fish Matthew has come closer to the celebration of the Lord's Supper.

37. καὶ ἔφαγον πάντες καὶ ἐχορτάσθησαν. So also 14.20a (q.v.) = Mk 6.42. Matthew has added πάντες.

καὶ τὸ περισσεῦον τῶν κλασμάτων ἦραν ἑπτὰ σπυρίδας πλήρεις. Compare 16.10. Mk 8.8 reads: καὶ ἦραν περισσεύματα κλασμάτων ἑπτὰ σπυρίδας. Mt 14.20 is the source for τὸ περισσεῦον, τῶν, and πλήρεις. On the meaning of σπυρίς and its difference from κόφινος see on 14.20. The evidence is insufficient for the claim that the latter might have been firstly associated with the Jews. But perhaps the difference in the numbers of baskets—twelve in chapter 14, seven in chapter 15—reflects the fact that the σπυρίς (or: σφυρίς; see BDF § 34.5) was larger than the κόφινος (cf. Chrysostom, *Hom. on Mt.* 53.2).

---

[45] On the interchange between ἐπί with the accusative and ἐπί with the dative in NT Greek see BDF § 233.
[46] See Dix, pp. 135–6.

38. οἱ δὲ ἐσθίοντες ἦσαν τετρακισχίλιοι ἄνδρες χωρὶς γυναικῶν καὶ παιδίων.⁴⁷ Compare Mk 8.9: 'There were about four thousand'. Matthew's sentence reproduces 14.21 (q.v.) save that ἄνδρες ὡσεὶ πεντακισχίλιοι has become τετρακισχίλιοι ἄνδρες.

39. καὶ ἀπολύσας τοὺς ὄχλους ἐνέβη εἰς τὸ πλοῖον. Compare 14.22 and the sentence structure of 5.1. Mk 8.9–10 (καὶ ἀπέλυσεν αὐτούς, καὶ εὐθὺς ἐμβὰς εἰς τὸ πλοῖον μετὰ τῶν μαθητῶν αὐτοῦ) has been rewritten in accordance with Matthew's love for subordinate clauses, his habit of omitting Mark's nearly omnipresent εὐθύς, his desire to recall the feeding of the five thousand (where ἀπολύω + τοὺς ὄχλους occurs thrice: 14.15, 22–3), and his proclivity for dropping the superfluous (here Mark's 'with his disciples').

καὶ ἦλθεν εἰς τὰ ὅρια Μαγαδάν.⁴⁸ This differs substantially from Mk 8.10 ('he came into the district of Dalmanutha').⁴⁹ Why the geographical alteration? Μαγαδάν is a NT *hapax legomenon*, as is Mark's Δαλμανουθά. Indeed, both names are otherwise unattested. The location of the latter remains unknown, although it must have been near Lake Gennesaret. If Magadan is not to be identified with Magdala (the modern Tarichaeae; cf. 27.56: Mary Magdalene), a town which the Talmud puts near Tiberias on the west side of the Sea of Galilee (see SB 1, p. 1047; Schlatter, p. 495), then its identity is also unknown. It is possible that Matthew and Mark accurately present us with two different names for some small, insignificant hamlet, in which case Matthew's knowledge of Galilee might be reckoned considerable. One should also not discount the possibility that Mark's text is corrupt⁵⁰ and that Matthew, recognizing this, substituted an educated guess.

(iv) *Concluding Observations*

In view of the many similarities in both Matthew and Mark between the feeding of the five thousand and the feeding of the four thousand, one must ask, Why the repetition? Why tell a story about Jesus which, in all essentials, has already been told, and quite recently at that? In addressing the issue as it touches

---

⁴⁷ After ησαν, B Θ *f*¹³ 33 892 1010 *pc* add ως, ℵ 1241 *pc* ωσει. Cf. 14.21.

⁴⁸ Μαγαδαν is the reading of ℵ* B D (so both NA²⁶ and HG). Μαγεδαν appears in ℵ² lat (sa) Eus, Μαγδαλα in L Θ *f*¹·¹³ Maj syʰ, Μαγδαλαν in C N W 33 565 *al* q mae bo. Cf. the variants for LXX Josh 15.37.

⁴⁹ But D has Μελαγαδα, D* Μελεγαδα, Dᶜ Μαγαιδα, P⁴⁵(?) Μαγεδαν, Θ *f*¹·¹³ it Μαγδαλα, 28 Μαγεδα. However one unravels the textual mess, the influence of Matthew seems certain (cf. the το ορος of Mk 8.10 W).

⁵⁰ For the various conjectures see Taylor, *Mark*, pp. 360–1.

Mark, two complementary points appear pertinent. The first
has to do with Mark's sources. It seems quite likely that the
Second Evangelist's tradition contained two slightly different
feeding narratives and that therefore the duplication was not his
doing. So the presence of Mk 6.30–44 and 8.1–10 in the same
book may be ascribed first of all to faithful reproduction of the
tradition. The second point concerns Markan theology. By
making the disciples ask, after witnessing the first feeding, 'How
can one feed these men with bread here in the desert?', the
important Markan theme of misunderstanding is furthered (cf.
esp. 6.52 and 8.14–21). Matters are not quite the same when it
comes to Matthew. The source-critical situation is, to be sure,
similar: the two feeding stories were to hand in Mark, so their
presence in Matthew reflects faithfulness to the tradition. On
the other hand, it cannot rightly be affirmed that the First
Evangelist was much interested in emphasizing or exploring the
disciples' misunderstanding, at least not in the almost systematic
way it is emphasized and explored in Mark's gospel. Is there,
then, some other theme which 15.29–39 advances? Or does it
suffice to say that 15.29–39 is told by Matthew just because it
was also told by Mark? Persuaded that an affirmative response
to this last question would probably underestimate Matthew's
editorial freedom to omit for one reason or another Markan
passages, one might be content to affirm that, as repetition
makes for emphasis, the major themes of 14.22–33 (for which
see pp. 480–3) are underlined in 15.29–39 by way of
reiteration; that is, their recurrence calls attention to their
importance. And there is indeed truth in such an observation. It
is, however, far from being the whole story. For 15.29–39 does
more than repeat 14.22–33 and its motifs. The pericope has an
independent contribution to make. This is manifest from the
redactional introduction (15.29–31), which makes the feeding of
the four thousand the vehicle of an idea not found in the feeding
of the five thousand, namely, that in Jesus the Messiah the
eschatological promises surrounding Zion have begun to be
fulfilled (cf. Donaldson (v)). As argued in the commentary on
15.29, the gathering of the Jewish crowds, the healing of the
sick, the allusion to Isa 35.5–6, the feeding of many, and the
mountain setting are all at home in Jewish texts about Mount
Zion. Perhaps it is even fair to infer from 15.29–39 that Jesus
has, for Matthew, *replaced* Zion as the centre of God's dealings
with his people.[51] However that may be, it is in 15.29–39, not

---

[51] Cf. Donaldson, p. 200. This would be consistent with Matthew's awareness,
apparent elsewhere, that the story of Jesus shattered the geographic dimensions
of Jewish expectation, both Galilean and Judean; see Davies, *GL*, pp. 221–43.

14.22–33, that Matthew's interest in the prophecies made to Zion
and his conviction that they have found their fulfilment in Jesus
come to the surface of our gospel.

(v) *Bibliography*

In addition to what follows see section (v) for 14.13–21

F. W. Danker, 'Mark 8.3', *JBL* 82 (1963), pp. 215–16.
Donaldson, pp. 122–35.
Gerhardsson, *Acts*, pp. 28, 55–7.
Held, in *TIM*, pp. 185–7.
Kertelge, *Wunder Jesu*, pp. 139–45.
E. Repo, 'Fünf Brote und zwei Fische', in *Probleme der Forschung*,
     SUNT A 3, ed. A. Fuchs, Munich, 1978, pp. 99–113.
T. J. Ryan, 'Matthew 15.29–31: An Overlooked Summary', *Horizons* 5
     (1978), pp. 31–42.
Schenke, *Wundererzählungen*, pp. 281–307.

XXXVII

REQUEST FOR A SIGN FROM HEAVEN
(16.1–4)

(i) *Structure*

This pericope narrates first the actions of the Pharisees, secondly Jesus' response to those actions, and thirdly Jesus' abrupt departure. The focus is all upon the words of Jesus' response, which seem to have been purposely arranged into three dyadic units (vv. 2–3a, 3b–c, 4a–b). Pictorially—

  I. The Pharisees come, tempt Jesus, and question him (1)
 II. The Response of Jesus (2–4b)
    A. On the reading of the weather (2b–3a)
      1. You can predict fair weather (2b)
      2. You can predict foul weather (3a)
    B. On the signs of the times (3b–c)
      1. You can interpret the sky (3b)
      2. You cannot interpret the signs of the times (3c)
    C. On this generation and its fate (4a–b)
      1. It seeks a sign (4a)
      2. None save that of Jonah will be given it (4b)
III. The departure of Jesus (4c)

(ii) *Sources*

16.1 depends upon Mark (cf. Mk 8.11) just as 16.4 follows Q (cf. 12.39 = Lk 11.29). Vv. 2–3 are problematic. There is a parallel of sorts in Lk 12.54–56. Some have thought this sufficiently close to Mt 16.2–3 to permit a common origin in Q.[1] The differences, however, appear too excessive for this: the shared vocabulary is minimal (six words out of forty-seven or forty-eight are the same), the clauses are in different orders (the storm comes first in Luke, secondly in Matthew), and the topics are not exactly the same (prediction based on clouds and wind in Luke, upon the colour of the sky in Matthew). Still, the similarities are such as to demand some connexion, especially in view of the closeness of Mt 16.3b–c to Lk 12.56. The best hypothesis seems to be this. Matthew's text is from M, Luke's text from L or Q. (It is also just possible that Q^{mt} and Q^{lk} here differed greatly.) However that may be,

---

[1] E.g. Gundry, *Commentary*, pp. 322–5, and März (v).

both texts probably go back to the same saying of Jesus; one which incorporated an old weather proverb[2] and rebuked people for their failure to perceive the significance of Jesus' ministry. The dissimilarities are then presumably to be explained by a modification in the course of transmission. Since Luke's logion corresponds to a Palestinian environment (clouds from the west are from the sea and so bring rain, winds from the south are from the desert and so herald heat), perhaps someone in Matthew's tradition altered the saying to accord with observations about weather in another area.

(iii) *Exegesis*

Continuing his close following of the Second Gospel, Matthew next gives us a pronouncement story, of the inquiry type,[3] which relates that, despite everything Jesus said and did, the Jewish leaders remained unmoved and sought to trip Jesus up by making a request he could not fulfil. The account in the first instance paints a telling picture of sad men who, professing to want evidence, in fact refuse to see the proofs right in front of their noses. In the second place, because no sign is to be given except that of Jonah, the story teaches that God's way is not to force belief through stupendous miracles. His persuasion is roundabout, that it may beget an authentic faith (cf. p. 583–4).

One should not overlook the possibility that a thematic connexion may be discerned not only between 15.32–9 (the feeding of the four thousand) and 16.5–12 (on the leaven of the Sadducees and Pharisees) but also between 15.32–9 and 16.1–4. The miraculous feeding harks back to the similar miracle performed by Elijah in Kings while 16.1–4 mentions Jonah. This is interesting because the two prophetic figures were linked in Jewish tradition. According to 1 Kgs 17 Elijah healed the son of a widow, and this son was later identified with Jonah.[4] Further, the healing of the widow's son by Elijah was in fact a resurrection, and for Matthew the sign of Jonah is the resurrection of Jesus. Perhaps, then, a typology lies behind the sequence in 15.32–16.4, the thought being that while 'this generation' vainly asks for a sign, it has been sent one no less remarkable than Elijah and will even be favoured with a sign reminiscent of what Jonah experienced.

To be dismissed is the thesis that the sign of Jonah is Peter's confession.[5] To be sure, Peter is called *bar Jonah* in 16.17, and his

---

[2] For Greek weather proverbs see G. Hellmann, in *Sitzungsberichte der Preussischen Akademie*, Physikalisch-Mathematische Klasse (1923), p. 159. A Jewish example may be found in *b. Yoma* 21b; and according to *b. B. Bat.* 84a, 'the sun is red at sunrise and at sunset'.

[3] See R. C. Tannehill, 'Varieties of synoptic Pronouncement Stories', *Semeia* 20 (1981), pp. 114–16.

[4] See L. Proph. Jon. 4–5 and Ginzberg 4, p. 197; 6, p. 138.

[5] *Pace* H. M. Gale, as in the bibliography for 12.22–50.

revelation from heaven could be likened to a sign from heaven. But in 12.40 the sign of Jonah is identified with the resurrection of Jesus, and the same equation must hold in chapter 16.

Concerning the authenticity of our pericope, Matthew's source, Mk 8.11–13, may well be a Markan construction: it is unusually lacking in detail and the narrative context does nothing but introduce the saying about a sign. Yet the saying about Jonah—in its Q form—is dominical (see on 12.38), and it may well have been uttered in response to the demand for a miracle.

1. The Pharisees and Sadducees—an unlikely alliance united in common cause against a perceived enemy (cf. 3.7)—tempt Jesus, asking for a sign from heaven. (In 12.38 it was the scribes and Pharisees who did this.) Obviously they do not really want Jesus to give them a compelling sign.[6] What they seek is to make him stumble and lose face with the people. They are hypocritically asking for something they believe he cannot deliver. But to the sympathetic reader, who has just finished with the feeding of the four thousand, the request for a marvellous sign is ludicrous, a symptom of acute spiritual blindness.

καὶ προσελθόντες οἱ Φαρισαῖοι καὶ Σαδδουκαῖοι.[7] Mk 8.11 has ἐξῆλθον (cf. 12.14 = Mk 3.6; what is the reference?) and does not mention the Sadducees. προσέρχομαι* is often redactional. On the Pharisees and Sadducees see on 3.7. The latter have been added here (implausibly[8]) because the immediate discussion, being about 'this generation', is comprehensive, and also because, in the next paragraph, Matthew wants Jesus to speak about 'the leaven of the Pharisees and Sadducees' (16.16 diff. Mk 8.15).

πειράζοντες ἐπηρώτησαν αὐτὸν σημεῖον ἐκ τοῦ οὐρανοῦ ἐπιδεῖξαι αὐτοῖς. Compare LXX Exod 17.2 (Moses to Israel in the wilderness: τί πειράζετε κύριον; cf. 17.7); Ps 77.41 (ἐπείρασαν τὸν θεόν, again of the wilderness generation; cf. 77.56); Jer 10.2 (τῶν σημείων τοῦ οὐρανοῦ); Ep. Jer. 66 (of false gods: σημεῖα . . . ἐν οὐρανῷ οὐ μὴ δείξωσιν); and Lk 11.16; also Jn 6.26 (which occurs after a multiplication miracle). Mk 8.11b–d reads: καὶ ἤρξαντο συζητεῖν αὐτῷ, ζητοῦντες παρ' αὐτοῦ σημεῖον ἀπὸ τοῦ οὐρανοῦ, πειράζοντες αὐτόν. Matthew has, in accord with his stylistic proclivities, dropped the unnecessary καὶ ἤρξαντο and the infinitive dependent upon it (see Allen,

[6] Chrysostom, *Hom. on Mt.* 53.3: 'Had they believed, they would not even have asked'.

[7] *f*[1] 33 565 *pc* mae Or omit οι.

[8] The two groups were not bedfellows, and the presence of Sadducees outside Judea—only here in the NT—is surprising. But see Schlatter, p. 496, for texts in which priests appear outside Jerusalem.

pp. xxi–xxii), moved πειράζοντες to first place (cf. 19.3 diff. Mk 10.2), replaced ζητοῦντες παρ' αὐτοῦ with ἐπηρώτησαν[9] αὐτόν ... ἐπιδεῖξαι[10] (ἐπιδείκνυμι: Mt: 3 (in each instance immediately followed by a pronoun); Mk: 0; Lk: 1), and substituted ἐκ for ἀπό (Matthew reserves ἀπὸ τοῦ οὐρανοῦ (cf. Lk 21.11) for movement from heaven to earth: 24.29; note also 17.9 diff. Mk 9.9).

On the nature of the sign requested see on 12.38. The assumption is that what Jesus has heretofore said and done—signs *on the earth* (cf. Acts 2.19)—is insufficient to compel belief. It is not likely that ἐκ τοῦ οὐρανοῦ is a periphrasis for 'from God' (although note 21.25). The object sought is rather some kind of sign in or from the heavens (such as a heavenly voice) as opposed to all the earthly signs Jesus has until now reportedly worked (cf. Origen, *Comm. on Mt.* 12.2; Chrysostom, *Hom. on Mt.* 53.3; Schlatter, pp. 496–7; certainly the mention of 'heaven' with the meaning of 'sky' in the next two verses hints that the author's thoughts were on the firmament itself). Probably one should think of an unambiguous, eschatological sign, one so dramatic or cosmic in scope as to preclude the need for interpretation; compare Mt 24.27, 30; Mk 13.24–5 (sun and moon are darkened, stars fall); Lk 21.11, 25; Rev 12.1, 3; 4 Ezra 5.4 (the sun shines at night, the moon during the day); 7.6 (a day without moon or stars). The point is not to demonstrate the nearness of the culmination. Instead, Jesus has made such grandiose claims for himself (cf. 7.21–3; 9.2; 11.4–6, 27; 12.28, 41f.) that his critics can challenge him to prove his power and eschatological office.[11]

2f. ὁ δὲ ἀποκριθεὶς εἶπεν αὐτοῖς. So also 12.39, there introducing Jesus' answer to the scribes and Pharisees, who have asked for a sign. The expression (Mt: 5; Mk: 2; Lk: 0) replaces Mk 8.12a ('And he sighed deeply in his spirit'), which has, as expected, been omitted because of our evangelist's tendency to make Jesus a less emotional figure (1, p. 104).

ὀψίας γενομένης λέγετε· εὐδία, πυρράζει γὰρ ὁ οὐρανός.[12] Compare Lk 12.54 and note the verbal link οὐρανός creates with v. 1. ὀψίας followed by γενομένης (Mt: 7; Mk: 5; Lk: 0) is also editorial in 14.15 and has no parallel in 20.8; and both γάρ* and οὐρανός* are redactional favourites. On the other hand, εὐδία (cf.

[9] It here means 'besought'; see on 15.23.
[10] Does Matthew prefer ἐπιδεῖξαι because of the similarity with ἐπηρώτησαν?
[11] On the expectation of signs to be performed in the latter days see SB 1, pp. 640–1; 4, pp. 977–1015. Also relevant are Josephus' descriptions of the sign prophets; see p. 249, n. 62.
[12] Vv. 2b–3 are omitted by ℵ B X Γ *f*[13] *al* sy[s.c] sa mae bo[pt] arm Or and the Gospel of the Nazaraeans (cf. Hennecke 1, p. 148); and Jerome claimed they were not found in *plerisque codicibus*. In addition, v. 4 follows v. 2 without any

Ecclus 3.15; Philo, *De gig.* 51—in parallelism with γαλήνη—; Josephus, *Ant.* 14.157; Ignatius, *Smyr.* 11.3), a word meaning 'fair weather', is a NT *hapax legomenon*; and πυρράζω, which is otherwise attested solely in Byzantine writers, means 'be (fiery) red'. (For the related πυρ(ρ) ίζω see LXX Lev 13.19, 42, 43, 49; 14.37.)

καὶ πρωΐ· σήμερον χειμών, πυρράζει γὰρ στυγνάζων ὁ οὐρανός. The same sign at a different time betokens a different future. Observe the close parallelism with the previous line (a Matthean trait). Save for γάρ* and οὐρανός*, the vocabulary cannot be said to be typical of the redactor.[13]

χειμών, while it means 'winter' in 24.20 par. and Jn 10.22, here obviously signifies 'stormy' or 'rainy weather' (cf. Acts 27.20; Josephus, *Ant.* 6.91). στυγνάζω (cf. στυγνός, used of the night in Wisd 17.5), here means 'dark, gloomy' (and is elsewhere descriptive of a sad countenance, as in *PGM* 13.177; cf. the mention of πρόσωπον in the next clause); but in the LXX the word is used only with the sense 'be shocked' (e.g. Ezek 27.35; 32.10; cf. Mk 10.22?). If the saying about the meaning of a red sky at dawn and dusk was proverbial, perhaps it was especially associated with sailors, for whom the question of what the day would bring held special meaning (cf. Schlatter, p. 497).

problem; εὐδία, πυρράζω and στυγνάζω are NT *hapax legomena*; and γινώσκω + infinitive occurs nowhere else in Matthew. These are very strong reasons for regarding the passage as secondary, and many have so deemed it; thus Zahn, p. 530, n. 45 (a gloss from Papias); McNeile, p. 235; Streeter, pp. 241–2 (arguing for an origin in Rome); Hirunuma (v); and Gnilka, *Matthäusevangelium* 2, pp. 39–40. But there have been those on the other side: Schlatter, pp. 497–8; Lagrange, pp. 315–16; Butler, pp. 141–2; Gundry, *Commentary*, p. 323; and März (v). With great hesitation we include ourselves with the second group of scholars, for these reasons. (i) Only πυρράζω can be claimed to be a late word. εὐδία and στυγνάζω are used in the LXX (as is πυρρίζω). (ii) If γινώσκω + infinitive is unparalleled in Matthew, it has LXX precedent (e.g. Isa 7.15; 8.4), and οἶδα + infinitive does occur in 7.11 (cf. BDF § 392.2). (iii) The parallelism of vv. 2–3 is typical of Matthean style (see 1, p. 94). (iv) ὀψίας γενομένης, γάρ and ὁ οὐρανός are frequently editorial (see the text), and Matthew likes πῦρ as well as κρίνω and associated words (see Gundry, *Commentary*, p. 645). Further, only Matthew among the evangelists has the plural of καιρός: here and 21.41 (v) One wonders whether Lk 12.54–6 can fairly be considered the source of Mt 16.2–3. Are not the differences (cf. p. 577) too great? (vi) Vv. 2–3 are attached to v. 1 by means of a catchword (οὐρανοῦ, οὐρανός). (vii) An explanation for the omission of vv. 2–3 is to hand: the lines 'were omitted by copyists whose climate the natural phenomena described did not very well suit, the rather as they did not occur in the parallel text, ch. xii. 38, 39' (F. H. A. Scrivener, *A Plain Introduction to the criticism of the New Testament*, 3rd ed., Cambridge, 1883, p. 572). The Markan parallel might also have contributed to excision. (viii) Finally, if vv. 2 and 3 are excised, 'we are left with a Matthean paragraph which is a sheer and otiose "repeat" of xii. 38f.' (Butler).

[13] πρωΐ: Mt: 3; Mk: 5; Lk: 0. σήμερον: Mt: 8; Mk: 1; Lk: 12. χειμών: Mt: 2; Mk: 1; Lk: 0. πυρράζω: Mt: 2; Mk: 0; Lk: 0. στυγνάζω: Mt: 1; Mk: 1; Lk: 0.

τὸ μὲν πρόσωπον τοῦ οὐρανοῦ γινώσκετε διακρίνειν. So Lk 12.56, with ὑποκριταί at the beginning, τῆς γῆς καί before τοῦ, and οἴδατε δοκιμάζειν for the last two words. If the saying in Lk 12.56 had been known to Matthew one would have no trouble explaining why 'of the earth' has fallen away: it is unrelated to Mt 16.2b–3a. But the omission of 'hypocrites' would be puzzling, as would the substitution of γινώσκετε διακρίνειν for οἴδατε δοκιμάζειν. We prefer to think that the saying in 16.3b–c = Lk 12.56 circulated in two different forms. (Do we perhaps have translation variants?)

'The face of heaven' (cf. the common biblical pĕnê hāʾădāmâ ['the face of the ground'], as in Gen 6.1, 7, etc.) means 'the appearance of the sky' (cf. the meaning of πρόσωπον in 1 Βασ 16.7; 2 Cor 5.12; Jas 1.11).

τὰ δὲ σημεῖα τῶν καιρῶν οὐ δύνασθε; Compare Lk 12.56b. καιρός (cf. ʿēt), which in secular usage indicates the favourable moment for an undertaking, often bears in the biblical tradition—in both the plural (cf. 21.41, redactional) and singular—an eschatological sense, as here.[14] Jesus is referring to 'the (last) times (set by God)' which demand personal decision.[15]

Gos. Thom. 91 ('You test the face of the sky and of the earth, and him who is before your face you have not known, and you do not know how to test this moment') shows no knowledge of Matthew. It must either depend upon the Third Gospel, or Luke and Thomas must independently attest the same logion.

4. Jesus concludes his response by cryptically denying the Pharisees and Sadducees their request and then departing. The sign of Jonah—to be given in the future—is enough. God will not be put on display, nor will he compel people to believe. (How one is to harmonize the statement that *only* the sign of Jonah will be given with Matthew's conviction that Jesus' miracles were signs (cf. 11.1–24; 16.3–4) is far from clear. Did he perhaps draw a distinction between signs in general and a sign from heaven, that is, between signs such as Jesus' exorcisms and the type of irresistible sign some wanted? Or did he think of Jesus' miracles as only δυνάμεις, not σημεῖα? Or do we have a genuine contradiction created by the saying about Jonah and the early Christian interpretation of Jesus' miracles as signs?)

[14] For the plural with eschatological meaning see LXX Ezek 12.27; Dan 7.25; 9.27; 11.14; Tob 14.5; Lk 21.24; Acts 1.7; 3.20; Eph 1.10; 1 Thess 5.1–2; 1 Tim 4.1; 6.14–15; Rev 12.14; Ignatius, *Eph.* 11.1; Barnabas, *Ep.* 4.3; 4 Ezra 4.37.

[15] For further discussion of καιρός see O. Cullmann, *Christ and Time*, rev. ed. (trans. of *Christus und die Zeit*, 1962), Philadelphia, 1964, pp. 39–44; G. Delling, *TWNT* 3, pp. 456–65; and J. Barr, *Biblical Words for Time*, SBT 33, rev. ed., London, 1969, passim.

γενεὰ πονηρὰ καὶ μοιχαλὶς σημεῖον ἐπιζητεῖ. Compare Mk 8.12: 'Why does this generation seek a sign?' (cf. Mt 12.38). Matthew has, as often, avoided placing a question in Jesus' mouth (cf. 1, p. 105). He has also carefully assimilated the entire line to 12.39 (q.v. for discussion). On the difference between ἐπιζητέω and ζητέω see on 6.32.

The switch from the direct, second person address ('you say', 'you know') in vv. 3 and 4 to the third person here ('this generation', 'given to it') is evidence for vv. 2–3 being an interpolation, whether Matthean or post-Matthean.

καὶ σημεῖον οὐ δοθήσεται αὐτῇ εἰ μὴ τὸ σημεῖον Ἰωνᾶ. The wholly negative Mk 8.12 ('Amen I say to you, no sign shall be given to this generation') has been brought into near perfect agreement[16] with the Q saying in 12.39 (q.v. for discussion). There is no significant link with the *bar Jonah* of 16.17 (see p. 578).

The resurrection of Jesus is, according to Matthew, the sign that shall be given to 'this generation' (cf. 12.38–9). Is there supposed to be irony in the circumstance that the Sadducees dogmatically denied the resurrection of the dead?

καὶ καταλιπὼν αὐτοὺς ἀπῆλθεν. So Mk 8.13, with ἀφείς after καί, πάλιν ἐμβάς after αὐτούς, and εἰς τὸ πέραν at the end. Matthew has abbreviated and moved εἰς τὸ πέραν to the following verse.

Jesus[17] leaves the Sadducees and Pharisees (who perhaps are to be thought of as uninterested in continuing the subject). He does not stay on in a vain attempt to persuade them of the truth but leaves the incorrigible to their own devices. And in the event, even the resurrection will not persuade them (cf. 28.11–5).

(iv) *Concluding Observations*

The chief lesson to be drawn from 16.1–4 is this: despite the proverb, seeing is not believing. If the Sadducees and Pharisees of our story were not persuaded by Jesus' δυνάμεις, neither would they have been won over by a spectacular sign from heaven (cf. Lk 16.31). The truth is that one does not see until one believes. For the faith that holds the soul also rules one's perception. It is therefore vain to expect hardened hearts and

---

[16] 'The prophet' is missing in 16.4 (but is restored in C W Θ *f*[1.13] Maj it vg[cl] sy mae bo).

[17] The disciples appear to enter the picture only in the next paragraph; see on 16.5.

firmly fixed minds to be melted by demonstrations of power. In our gospel, accordingly, miracles, while certainly pointers to God's presence in Jesus, are always therapeutic or salvific, that is, worked for the benefit of others. They are never straightforward, overpowering marvels aimed at convincing sceptics (cf. 13.56: 'he did not do any mighty works there because of their unbelief'). What our gospel demands of the individual is love of God and trust in his Messiah, not intellectual assent to the wonder-working abilities of Jesus. Thus the text makes the possession of faith a moral issue,[18] and it is altogether fitting that whereas miracles do not create faith,[19] faith does in fact work miracles (cf. 17.20; 21.21–2). It is God's habit to hide himself and keep silent before the challenges of unbelief, and his good pleasure to make himself known to a faith already held. 'To him who hath shall more be given' (13.12).

(v) Bibliography

In addition to what follows see the bibliography for 12.38–50.

T. Hirunuma, 'Matthew 16.2b–3', in New Testament Textual Criticism, ed. E. J. Epp and G. D. Fee, Oxford, 1981, pp. 35–45.
Kertelge, Wunder, pp. 23–7.
G. Klein, 'Die Prüfung der zeit (Lukas 12.54–56)', ZTK 61 (1964), pp. 373–90.
C.-P. März, 'Lk 12.54b–56 par. Mt 16.2b, 3 und die Akoluthie der Redenquelle', SNTU A 11 (1986), pp. 83–96.
P. Sellew, 'Reconstruction of Q 12.33–59', in Society of Biblical Literature 1987 Seminar Papers, ed. K. H. Richards, Atlanta, 1987, pp. 654–60.

---

[18] One recalls Dostoevsky's assertion that God denies us certainty so that we might have freedom, and that there would be no virtue in choosing the right path if no element of risk were involved.

[19] Comparable perhaps are those rabbinic texts, such as b. B. Meṣ. 59b, in which undisputed miracles are dismissed as of no argumentative worth. If one believes in the Torah, even a voice from heaven will not persuade otherwise. See Davies, PRJ, p.374.

XXXVIII

THE LEAVEN OF THE PHARISEES AND SADDUCEES
(16.5–12)

(i) Structure

This pericope has three major divisions. It opens with a narrative introduction (v. 5), continues with an extended conversation (vv. 6–11), and closes with an editorial remark: 'Then they understood . . .' (v. 12). The conversation, which has three short speeches (contrast Mark), two by Jesus and one by the disciples, is placed at the centre and begins and ends with the same wording (vv. 6b, 11b: *inclusio*; contrast Mark).

(ii) Sources

A cursory examination inclines one to concede that, concerning Mt 16.5–12 and its Markan parallel, [1] either text could be the source for the other. Apart from stylistic variations traceable to each redactor, the two accounts differ primarily in their portrait of the disciples. In Matthew the disciples momentarily misapprehend the purport of a saying of Jesus. In Mark, by contrast, they are wholly obdurate in understanding. One could with equal ease argue (i) that Matthew, in accord with tendencies discernible elsewhere, placed the disciples in a better light by giving them comprehension or (ii) that Mark, bent upon magnifying the disciples' lack of insight, modified his Matthean source accordingly. Both the Griesbach theory and the standard two-source theory adopted in this commentary would seem to work.

Closer attention, however, gives one second thoughts. Mt 16.5–12 has handed commentators few troubles. The meaning is not hard to make out, and the several pieces go together to make a coherent whole. Matters are altogether different with regard to Mk 8.14–21. Interpretations of the Markan passage vary greatly,[2] and the text bristles with problems.[3] What, for example, is the significance of the 'one loaf' (missing in Matthew)? And why exactly does Jesus rebuke

---

[1] Luke has no parallel to Mk 8.14–21, only a version of the saying in Mk 8.15 par. See Lk 12.1 (from Q or L).

[2] For a review of the discussion see Quesnell (v).

[3] See further J. C. Meagher, *Clumsy Construction in Mark's Gospel* (New York, 1979), pp. 74–81.

his disciples? If it is simply for a misunderstanding, his words seem excessively harsh. If, on the other hand, the disciples are rebuked for something else, why is this not explicit in the text?[4] Again, what is the meaning of the mention of Herod (who is replaced by the Sadducees in the First Gospel)? And what is the function of Mk 8.15? Does it not strike the careful reader as an awkward insertion (of Mark)[5] or as misplaced?[6] Is there any connexion between 8.15's warning about the leaven of the Pharisees and the leaven of Herod and the two miraculous feedings, or are we to suppose that vv. 17–21 simply record Jesus' response to the disciples' discussion in v. 16?[7] It is our conviction that, given the very real perplexities of Mk 8.14–21 as compared with the clarity of Mt 16.5–12, it makes more sense to think of the latter as an improvement upon the former. What could have possessed a man to turn the perfectly intelligible Mt 16.5–12 into a riddle? To what end, on the Griesbach hypothesis, could he have been working? Whatever the process of origination which lies behind Mk 8.14–21, surely it must have been something other than the clumsy rewriting of the straightforward story found in Matthew.

(iii) Exegesis

Granted the priority of Mk 8.14–21, the following major changes may be ascribed to the First Evangelist. (i) Mark's account has been abbreviated (see esp. 16.9–10 diff. Mk 8.17c–20). (ii) Stylistic improvements have been made (e.g. the substitution of ὁρᾶτε καὶ προσέχετε for ὁρᾶτε, βλέπετε). (iii) Herod (Mk 8.15) has been replaced by the Sadducees (Mt 16.6), giving rise to the fixed expression, 'the Pharisees and Sadducees'. (iv) The OT allusions in Mk 8.18 (cf. Jer 5.21; Ezek 12.2), which are applied to the dull disciples, have been dropped—not because our author missed the references but for the sake of consistency with 13.10–17 (see on 16.9). (v) The disciples' responses to Jesus' questions (Mk 8.19, 20) have been omitted. It is assumed that they must know the answers. (vi) The warning of 16.6 = Mk 8.15 is repeated at the end, forming an *inclusio* (see p. 585). (vii) Mark's conclusion—'And he said to them, "Do you not yet understand?"'—has been eliminated. In its place Matthew has added a sentence which leaves no doubt about the disciples' ability to apprehend: 'Then they understood . . .'.

---

[4] In the First Gospel, the use of ὀλιγόπιστοι in 16.8 shows that the disciples have let anxiety about food overcome them (cf. 6.30).

[5] Cf. Nineham, *Mark*, p. 215. But that the saying is not a Markan interpolation is argued by Taylor, *Mark*, p. 366, who comments: 'it is not Mark's habit to insert sayings into the body of a narrative, as Matthew does . . . but to append them at the end . . .'. It may also be observed that the questions in vv. 17 and 21 presuppose misunderstanding of a difficult saying. See further Ziener (v).

[6] See Pesch 1, p. 411, for the suggestion that a pre-Markan apophthegm consisted of vv. 14 (without 'in the boat'), 16, 17a–b, 15.

[7] In Matthew the warning is taken up again (16.11) and made the main point of the narrative (cf. 16.12).

Three themes dominate the Matthean understanding of 16.5–12: Jesus as provider of physical needs, Jesus as instructor of disciples, and the Jewish leaders as teachers of dangerous error. The last two motifs largely explain the significant alterations noted above. Jesus' status as pedagogue is enhanced by the softening of the disciples' misunderstanding and by the edifying conclusion: Jesus' speech leads to comprehension.[8] And the alteration to 'the leaven of the Pharisees and Sadducees' and the inclusion of the phrase in a warning repeated twice drive home the point that one must take care not to be fooled by the teachings of Jewish religious leaders.

The historical basis of Mt 16.5–12 par. is most uncertain. The Markan pericope could be a redactional composition. It not only presupposes the two feedings (which may be doublets) but presupposes them in their Markan wording (cf. Taylor, *Mark*, p. 363; Gnilka 1, pp. 309–10). The one reasonably sure fact is that the saying in 16.6 = Mk 8.15 (cf. Lk 12.1) is authentic (cf. Pesch 1, p. 413). It is attested in Mark and Q or L and does not sound like a post-Easter construction (especially notable in this regard is the mention of Herod). But what Jesus might have meant by the saying is another story. Was he, as Luke has it, alluding to hypocrisy? Or was Matthew right in equating leaven with teaching? Did Jesus have in view the demand for a sign (cf. 12.38; Lk 23.8)? or simply the evil tendencies in his opponents (cf. the use of leaven for the *yēṣer hāraʿ* in rabbinic sources: SB 1, 728–9)? Or was Jesus issuing a warning about a false messianism, or deriding political opportunism, or alluding to the dangers being laid by plotting enemies? All these possibilities have been upheld by one scholar or another. We regretably have discovered no criteria by which to judge between them.[9]

5. **καὶ ἐλθόντες οἱ μαθηταὶ εἰς τὸ πέραν ἐπελάθοντο ἄρτους λαβεῖν.**[10] Compare Mk 8.14: 'Now they had forgotten to bring bread; and they had only one loaf with them in the boat'. The first word and the last three of Mt 16.5 have been taken from Mk 8.14, εἰς τὸ πέραν (see on 8.18) from Mk 8.13.

Like the ἐξεβλήθη of 9.25 and the ἐνέπαιξαν of 27.31, ἐπελάθοντο, although an aorist, evidently has pluperfect sense: 'they had forgotten'[11] (so RSV; see Burton, pp 22–3). (The alternative is that the disciples forgot to get bread after their arrival; see Zahn, p. 532, n. 49.)

[8] Cf. Held, in *TIM*, p. 292.

[9] For the suggestion that a wordplay may have been intended between the Aramaic *ḥămîrāʾ* ('leaven', 'leavened bread') and *ʾămîrâ* ('speech') see Negōiţă and Daniel (v).

[10] L W *f*[1] Maj lat sy insert αυτου before εις. It could be original (see p. 570, n. 33). B K Π 892 1424 *al* sy reverse the order of αρτους λαβειν (assimilation to Mark's order?).

[11] While ἐπιλανθάνομαι usually implies wilful neglect in the LXX, there are quite a few exceptions (e.g. Gen 41.51 and Wisd 2.4; 19.20), and clearly the forgetfulness of Mt 16.5 is inadvertent.

On the infinitive as complement of the verb see BDF § 392.1.b. Allen, p. 173, correctly assessed the significance of the changes introduced by the First Evangelist into Mt 16.5: 'In Mk. the dialogue which follows presumably took place in the boat during the crossing of the lake. Mt. by inserting καὶ ἐλθόντες οἱ μαθηταί before εἰς τὸ πέραν in Mk v. 13 seems to wish to make it clear that the subject of ἐπελάθοντο did not include Christ. The disciples forgot, not the Lord. His insertion has the further effect that the whole of what follows took place, not during the crossing, but when they had reached the other side'.

6. ὁ δὲ Ἰησοῦς εἶπεν αὐτοῖς. This phrase (see on 13.57) replaces Mark's much stronger καὶ διεστέλλετο αὐτοῖς λέγων. Our evangelist has also eliminated or replaced διαστέλλομαι (Mt: 1 (16.20); Mk: 5; Lk: 0) in 13.26 diff. Mk 5.43 and 17.9 diff. Mk 9.9. The insertion of 'Jesus'* is typical.

ὁρᾶτε καὶ προσέχετε ἀπὸ τῆς ζύμης τῶν Φαρισαίων καὶ Σαδδουκαίων. Mk 8.15 lacks the first καί (Matthew's text is an improvement), uses βλέπετε[12] instead of προσέχετε (Matthew likes προσέχω + ἀπό*; see on 6.1; it is probably a Semitism: BDF § 149), repeats τῆς ζύμης (unnecessary for Matthew's purposes; see 1, p. 32), and has Ἡρῴδου[13] instead of Σαδδουκαίων. The last change is the most interesting. It stems from three causes, the first being Matthew's uncertainty as to Mark's meaning (an uncertainty one shares after looking at the various interpretations offered by commentators on Mark), the second being the equation of leaven with (false) teaching (what did Herod teach?), the third being a desire to associate the Sadducees and Pharisees so that together the two groups might represent the leadership of Judaism and its united opposition to Jesus (cf. 3.7; 16.1).

Leaven (cf. śĕʾōr), as will be explained shortly (v. 12), is, according to Matthew, a metaphor for teaching. Probably in the background is the common use of leaven to symbolize a corrupting influence, an evil tendency which, although insignificant to start with, quickly multiplies to corrupt the whole (see on 13.33).[14] But it is also possible to equate leaven

---

[12] βλέπετε (imperative): Mt: 1; Mk: 7; Lk: 2.
[13] So ℵ A B C D K L X Π Maj lat sy^s.p.h bo eth goth. Ηρωδιανων (so P[45] W Δ Θ f[1.13] pc i k sa arm geo) is influenced by Mk 3.6 and 12.13.
[14] Because leaven is proscribed during Passover week and explicitly excluded from certain sacrificial rituals (e.g. Exod 23.18; Lev 2.11; 6.16–17), 'it is likely that the process of fermentation was associated with decomposition and putrefaction, and so became emblematic of corruption' (so N. M. Sarna, *Exploring Exodus*, New York, 1986, p. 90; he adds: 'the ban on leaven during the Passover week signifies that natural liberation ... involves moral and spiritual rejuvenation, and must not be tainted by moral corruption'). Cf. Testim. Truth 9.29.9–21.

with the neutral idea of influence (cf. Schlatter, p. 499). On this view, 'leaven' only takes on negative connotations because of the preceding 'Take heed and beware' and the qualifying genitives, 'of the Pharisees and Sadducees'.

Lk 12.1 has the following: 'In the meantime, when so many thousands of the multitudes had gathered together that they trod upon one another, he began to say to his disciples first, "Beware of (προσ-έχετε ἑαυτοῖς ἀπό) the leaven of the Pharisees, which is hypocrisy"'. Schürmann, *Untersuchungen*, pp. 123–4, assigns this to Q.[15] His judgement may be tentatively accepted. For although the use of προσέχετε by both Matthew and Luke but not Mark need not point to a common source (both evangelists introduce it elsewhere[16]), the following material in Luke is from Q. Consequently we seem to have a Markan/Q overlap. Whether the clarifying conclusion, 'which is hypocrisy',[17] already stood in Q (so Marshall, p. 512) or is to be assigned to Luke himself (so Fitzmyer, *Luke* 2, p. 953) is uncertain; but perhaps the latter alternative is the more likely, for ἥτις can be considered redactional; see Jeremias, *Lukasevangelium*, pp. 43–4, 211.

7. οἱ δὲ διελογίζοντο ἐν ἑαυτοῖς λέγοντες ὅτι ἄρτους οὐκ ἐλάβομεν. Compare T. Job 2.3: διελογιζόμην ἐν ἑαυτῷ λέγων. Allen, pp. 173–4, translated: 'And they were reasoning in (or amongst) themselves, saying, (He says it) because we took no bread' (italics deleted). This assumes that ὅτι is causal (cf. Chrysostom, *Hom. on Mt.* 53.4, and the NEB) and that 'the disciples suppose that the Lord's warning against the leaven of the Pharisees had some reference to the fact that they were without sufficient provision, as though He were advising them to be on their guard against purchasing poisoned loaves' (Allen, *ibid.*). But ὅτι may simply introduce here direct discourse (ὅτι *recitativum*): 'And they were reasoning in (or amongst) themselves, saying, "We took no bread"' (cf. RSV).

Mk 8.16 opens with καί (which our evangelist often replaces with δέ), follows the first verb with πρὸς ἀλλήλους (this is consistently dropped by Matthew: Mt: 0; Mk: 4; Lk: 8; ἐν ἑαυτοῖς, by contrast, is several times inserted: Mt: 6; Mk: 2; Lk: 2), and ends with ἔχουσιν or ἔχομεν[18] (the First Evangelist has substituted ἐλάβομεν in order to enhance the parallelism with 16.5 (cf. v. 8) and, as often, avoided the historical present).

---

[15] For an origin in L see Manson, *Sayings*, p. 268, and Fitzmyer, *Luke* 2, p. 953.

[16] See on 6.1 for Matthew and, for Luke, Jeremias, *Lukasevangelium*, p. 211. Note esp. that Luke has changed the βλέπετε ἀπό of Mk 12.38 to προσέχετε ἀπό (Lk 20.46).

[17] Only here does Luke associate the Pharisees with hypocrisy (contrast Matthew!).

[18] Both N A[26] and H G print εχουσιν, the text of the P[45] B W f[1] 28 565 700 *pc* k co. But εχομεν appears in ℵ A C L Θ f[13] Maj vg sy[p.h]. Taylor *Mark*, p. 366, follows C. H. Turner in interpreting Mark's sentence in this

διαλογίζομαι + ἐν ἑαυτοῖς (LXX: 0; Mt: 3; Mk: 1 Lk: 0) is also redactional in 21.25 diff. Mk 11.31. In the present instance the expression could, as both Origen, *Comm. on Mt.* 12.5–7, and Chrysostom, *Hom. on Mt.* 53.4, thought, mean 'pondered in their minds' (so BAGD, s.v., διαλογίζομαι; cf. Gundry, *Commentary*, p. 326). This would entail that the object of Jesus' knowledge in v. 8 ('But Jesus, knowing . . .') is the content of the disciples' hearts (so NEB; see further on 9.4). 'Discussed (it) amongst themselves' (cf. Mk 8.17)[19] is also, however, a possible translation (so RSV; cf. Zahn, p. 532). On this alternative, the following words, 'But Jesus, knowing . . .', would hark back to v. 7 (Jesus knew what the disciples were discussing).

8. γνοὺς δὲ ὁ Ἰησοῦς εἶπεν. So Mk 8.17a, with introductory καί instead of δέ, the historical present λέγει in place of εἶπεν (cf. 16.6a diff. Mk 8.15), and the dative αὐτοῖς (strictly superfluous) at the end. The changes introduced by Matthew are all typical. (Matthew may also have added ὁ Ἰησους* for this is missing from Mk 8.17 א¹ B Δ 892* aur i saᵐˢˢ bo.)

τί διαλογίζεσθε ἐν ἑαυτοῖς. On the meaning of this see the discussion on the previous verse. The First Evangelist has added the last two words[20] in order to enhance the parallelism with v. 7.

ὀλιγόπιστοι. For the meaning of this redactional insertion[21] see on 6.30. The word is appropriate here because the disciples have done more than just misunderstand Jesus' saying. They have also—oddly enough, given all that they have witnessed—come to wonder about their provisions. (The reader infers that the reflection on or discussion about bread (v. 7) led to anxious thoughts.)

ὅτι ἄρτους οὐκ ἐλάβετε;[22] The supplanting of Mark's ἔχετε by ἐλάβετε brings the verse into line with vv. 5 and 7 (q.v.). ὅτι may mean either 'because' or 'that'.

fashion: 'And they were discussing with one another why they had no bread'. One could also, assuming ἔχουσιν to be original, translate: 'And they were discussing (it) with one another because they had no bread' or 'And they were discussing with one another (the fact) that they had no bread'. If ἔχομεν be judged the original reading, ὅτι may be taken as recitative ('And they were discussing with one another, saying, "We have no bread"') or causal ('And they were discussing with one another, "(He says this) because we have no bread"'). Because we do not know what was in Matthew's copy of Mark and because the possibilities for interpretation are so many, we cannot be precise about the changes made at this point.

[19] However, Mk 8.17 Θ 28 124 565 700 *pc* geo² arm have εν ταις καρδιαις υμων ολιγοπιστοι.

[20] They appear already in Mk 8.17 P⁴⁵—early evidence for Matthean influence on Mark's text.

[21] Which has been added to Mk 8.17 P⁴⁵. See also n. 19.

[22] NA²⁶ follows א B D Θ *f*¹³ 700 892 1241 *pc* lat mae bo arm in printing εχετε. ελαβετε (supported by HG) appears in C L W *f*¹ Maj f sy sa Or Eus Chr.

9f. οὔπω νοεῖτε, οὐδὲ μνημονεύετε τοὺς πέντε ἄρτους τῶν πεντακισχιλίων καὶ πόσους κοφίνους ἐλάβετε; This is a much abbreviated version of Mk 8.17c–19. With the exception of the concluding verb, ἐλάβετε (cf. vv. 5, 7, 8; Mark has ἤρατε), Matthew's vocabulary is all from Mark.

Aside from condensing and introducing stylistic alterations, the evangelist has dropped the remark that the disciples' hearts were hardened along with the interrogative allusion to scripture, 'Having eyes do you not see, and having ears do you not hear?' (cf. Isa 6.9–10; Jer 5.21; Ezek 12.2). These have no doubt fallen away for the sake of consistency. In 13.13–17 it is unbelieving Jews who are described as having dull hearts, closed eyes, and deaf ears; the disciples, by contrast, are blessed because their eyes see and their ears hear. It would be awkward indeed for Jesus to turn around just a few chapters later and reprimand the disciples for having hardened hearts and no spiritual perception. That this is indeed the truth of the matter follows from v. 12, where Matthew clearly tells us that the disciples came to comprehension: 'then they understood that he did not tell them to beware of the leaven of bread, but of the teaching of Pharisees and Sadducees'. (On one other occasion a Markan notice about the disciples' being hard-hearted has been omitted: Mk 6.52 finds no place in the First Gospel.) For further discussion see Barth (v).

The verb μνημονεύω (only here in Matthew) means, in v. 9, more than just 'remember', a purely intellectual activity. Like the Hebrew *zākar*, it connotes being mindful, paying heed.[23] The disciples should not just recall a miraculous fact but should responsibly engage its implications for the present.

οὐδὲ τοὺς ἑπτὰ ἄρτους τῶν τετρακισχιλίων καὶ πόσας σπυρίδας ἐλάβετε; As compared with Mk 8.20 ('"And the seven for the four thousand, how many baskets full of broken pieces did you take up?" And they said to him, "Seven"'), Matthew has introduced pretty much the same changes as in 16.9 diff. Mk 8.17c–19 (see above). The motivation is maintenance of parallelism: vv. 9 and 10 are twins. On the σπυρίδες and κόφινοι see on 14.20.

11. Jesus' concluding question—'How is it that you fail to perceive that I did not speak about bread?'—makes everything clear: leaven is not to be understood literally.[24] Thus Jesus can

---

While one can hardly be certain, influence from Mark could explain the text of ℵ B, and the switch to ελαβετε would be more than consistent with the change in 16.7 diff. Mk 8.16 (ἔχουσιν becomes ἐλάβομεν).

[23] BDB, s.v., *zākar*: 'remember, recall, call to mind, usu. as affecting present feeling, thought, or action'. See further Dahl, *Jesus*, pp. 11–29.

[24] For the metaphorical use of leaven see on 13.33; also Mitton (v); SB 1, pp. 728–9. According to SB, the only example of leaven being used for teaching in rabbinic literature is *y. Ḥag.* 2.76c, 37 = *Pesiq. R.* 121a.

restate his warning without any possibility of being misunderstood: Beware of the leaven of the Pharisees and Sadducees.

πῶς οὐ νοεῖτε ὅτι οὐ περὶ ἄρτων εἶπον ὑμῖν; Mark's account ends at this point with the following: 'And he said to them: Do you not yet understand?'[25] This could not be reproduced by Matthew because the disciples' answers have been omitted (making 'And he said to them' unnecessary) and because their coming to understanding is about to be recorded. Matthew's replacement functions as do the interpretations of the parables in chapter 13 and elsewhere: the meaning of an earlier parabolic utterance is clarified by plain speech.

πῶς οὐ (cf. Mk 4.40 Maj.; Lk 12.56 (πῶς οὐκ οἴδατε); Rom 8.32; 2 Cor 3.8) occurs only here in the First Gospel.

προσέχετε δὲ ἀπὸ τῆς ζύμης τῶν Φαρισαίων καὶ Σαδδουκαίων. This repeats the last part of 16.6 (q.v.) and is redactional.

12. τότε συνῆκαν ὅτι οὐκ εἶπεν προσέχειν ἀπὸ τῆς ζύμης τῶν ἄρτων ἀλλὰ ἀπὸ τῆς διδαχῆς τῶν Φαρισαίων καὶ Σαδδουκαίων.[26] Compare 13.51; 17.13. διδαχή (cf. LXX Ps 59.1; Mt: 3; Mk: 5; Lk: 1) is used two other times in Matthew, both with reference to Jesus' teaching. In each case the word may include manner or style as well as content (7.28; 22.33). Here content is the sole subject.

Mark uses the phrase, 'the leaven of the Pharisees and the leaven of Herod'; that is, τῆς ζύμης appears twice (Mk 8.15). Matthew, however, refers simply to 'the leaven of the Pharisees and Sadducees': τῆς ζύμης appears once. So in the First Gospel there is nothing to indicate that there were important differences between the teaching of the Pharisees and the teaching of the Sadducees: the two are grouped together. It has been claimed that this betrays an ignorance of the doctrinal conflicts between the two Jewish parties and, accordingly, makes it unlikely that our evangelist was a Jew. This is unconvincing (see further 1, pp. 31–2). Matthew does not here have doctrinal particulars in mind. He is simply thinking of the Jewish leaders as co-conspirators in the plot against Jesus and as partners in the attempt to put the church out of business. 'The teaching of the Pharisees and Sadducees' refers to all that the Jewish leaders say which blocks the avenue to faith in Jesus and causes people to remain in unbelief.

[25] Mark has συνίετε. Matthew replaces this with νοεῖτε because of 9a (οὔπω νοεῖτε).

[26] D Θ f[13] 565 pc a b ff[2] sy[s] omit των αρτων. Allen, p. 175, and McNeile, pp. 236–7, regard the omission as original. But it ruins the parallelism between τῆς ζύμης τῶν ἄρτων and τῆς διδαχῆς τῶν Φ. καὶ Σ (τῆς . . . τῶν in each instance). C E W Maj c f q sy[p.h] sa[ms] bo[mss] have the singular, του αρτου (which also wrecks the parallelism with the ending of the verse). ℵ* (33) ff[1] sy[c] have των Φ. και Σ. in place of των αρτων, which is probably due to a simple scribal error. We have followed both HG and NA[26] in printing the reading found in ℵ[2] B L 892 1241 (f[1] 1424) pc lat co Or.

(iv) *Concluding Observations*

(1) Matthew could have used 16.5–12 to emphasize either Jesus' miraculous ability to meet physical needs or his pedagogical skills or both. These two themes, however, remain subsidiary. What stands out in the passage is the admonition about the Pharisees and Sadducees. The warning is repeated twice, frames the discourse as an *inclusio* (p. 585), and is interpreted in the conclusion (leaven = teaching). It is clearly the main point for our evangelist. The explanation for this fact, we should like to suggest, is to be found in the Matthean *Sitz im Leben*. There was, evidently, still a need for Matthew to warn his readers about the Jewish leaders, that is, rabbis and synagogue authorities. Why? It is altogether likely that Matthew knew Christians who still attended Jewish synagogue. Moreover, we cannot doubt that he himself engaged Jewish intellectuals in theological discussion (cf. 1, pp. 133–8). There was, therefore, a practical need in Matthew's eyes to issue a clear admonition to be wary of what the learned and persuasive yet unbelieving Jewish leaders had to say. And he met that need effectively by having Jesus utter and repeat a warning about the leaven of the Pharisees and Sadducees.

(2) It has sometimes been asserted that 16.6 and 11 contradict 23.2–3, which reads: 'the scribes and Pharisees sit on Moses' seat; so practise and observe whatever they tell you, but do not do what they do; for they preach, but do not practise'. Jeremias cites this supposed example of 'the unconcerned juxtaposition of conflicting traditions' as 'one of the fundamental reasons why the redaction-critical analysis of the First Gospel cannot achieve success' (*Theology*, p. 307, n. 1; cf. our own comments in 1, p. 458). With this we must take issue. 16.6 and 11 can hardly imply that everything taught by the Jewish leaders was held to be false, just as 23.2–3 can scarcely mean that everything they said was held to be true. And whereas in one place the text is about what Christians and the Jewish teachers have in common (23.2–3), in the other it is about what divides the two groups (16.6, 11). When these facts are considered, the two passages made out by Jeremias to be antithetical can actually be considered complementary. Jewish Christians, Matthew implies, would do well to listen to the synagogue leaders in so far as their speech is grounded in the authoritative oracles of the OT. But believers must, at the same time, take heed, for those leaders are also interested in building up the synagogue, not the church, and one of their aims is to discourage belief in Jesus as the Messiah.

(v) *Bibliography*

Bacon, pp. 511–17.

Barth, in *TIM*. pp. 114–16.

N. A. Beck, 'Reclaiming a Biblical Text: The Mark 8.14–21 Discussion about Bread in a Boat', *CBQ* 43 (1981), pp. 49–56.

P. B. Emmet, 'St. Mark 8.15', *ExpT* 48 (1937), pp. 332–3.

Hoehner, pp. 202–13.

E. E. Lemico, 'External Evidence for the Structure and Function of Mark 4.1–20; 7.14–23; and 8.14–21', *JTS* 29 (1978), pp. 323–38.

J. Mánek, 'Mark VIII. 14–21', *NovT* 7 (1964), pp. 10–14.

T. W. Manson, 'Mark 8.14–21', *JTS* 30 (1928), pp. 45–7.

C. L. Mitton, 'Leaven', *ExpT* 84 (1973), pp. 339–43.

A. Negŏiṭṭā and C. Daniel, 'L'Énigme du levain', *NovT* 9 (1967), pp. 306–14.

Q. Quesnell, *The Mind of Mark*, AnBib 38, Rome, 1969.

Roloff, *Kerygma*, pp. 246–51.

Schenke, *Wundererzählungen*, pp. 289–94, 299–307.

D. H. Smith, 'An Exposition of Mark VIII. 14–21', *ExpT* 59 (1948), pp. 125–6.

G. Ziener, 'Das Bildwort vom Sauerteig Mk 8.15', *TTZ* 67 (1958), pp. 247–8.

EXCURSUS XII

JESUS AS MESSIAH[1]

Because of its crucial importance for understanding Jesus and for evaluating the continuity between the pre- and post-Easter periods, we must inquire whether the disciples did in fact acknowledge Jesus' messianic status during the earthly ministry and whether Jesus accepted such an acknowledgement. We begin with three sayings which are generally taken, in one form or another, to be authentic: 'And I tell you, everyone who acknowledges me before men, the Son of man also will acknowlege before the angels of God; but he who denies me before men will be denied before the angels of God' (Lk 12.8–9; see on Mt 10.32–3); 'If it is by the finger of God that I cast out demons, then the kingdom of God has come upon you' (Mt 12.28 par.); 'The men of Nineveh will arise at the judgement with this generation and condemn it; for they repented at the preaching of Jonah, and behold, something greater than Jonah is here. The queen of the South will arise at the judgement with this generation and condemn it; for she came from the ends of the earth to hear the wisdom of Solomon, and behold, something greater than Solomon is here' (12.41–2). There is no doubt

[1] Lit.: D. Aune, 'A Note on Jesus' Messianic Consciousness and 11QMelchizedek', *EvQ* 45 (1973), pp. 161–5; K. Berger, 'Die königlichen Messiastraditionen des Neuen Testaments', *NTS* 20 (1973), pp. 1–44; idem, 'Zum

that the genuine sayings of Jesus contain at least an 'implicit Christology'.[2] Certainly Jesus acted with 'the immediate authority of God'[3] and believed himself to be playing a decisive, even unique rôle in salvation-history.[4] Do we, however, have evidence that he thought of his function in traditional terms? or that he bestowed upon himself a conventional title? The issue can only be approached by considering Jesus' historical context. Here the words of O. Betz move one to reflection: 'The Qumran texts, and also the New Testament writings, show that a servant of God had to prove his credentials before the godly. He had to give a clear description of his commission in terms that met the requirements of scripture or tradition. The individual was not important; in Qumran he vanished entirely behind the office. The people who belong to the history of Israel are certainly named, as they are in the Bible. But ... this is true of none of the figures on the contemporary stage. They have titles describing an office or function: the Teacher of Righteousness, the Wicked Priest, the seekers of smooth things.... And John, the voice in the wilderness, bears a title which he certainly did not give himself—he was the Baptist. The Gospels show how people puzzled over who John and Jesus really were and what

Problem der Messianität Jesu', *ZTK* 71 (1974), pp. 1–30; idem, 'Zum traditionsgeschichtlichen Hintergrund christologischer Hoheitstitel', *NTS* 17 (1971), pp. 391–426; O. Betz, 'Die Frage nach dem messianischen Bewusstsein Jesu', *NovT* 6 (1963), pp. 20–48; idem, *Jesus*, pp. 83–112; Bornkamm, *Jesus*, pp. 169–78; Bultmann, *Theology* 1, pp. 26–32; Cullmann, *Christology*, pp. 111–36; N. Dahl, 'The Crucified Messiah', in *Messiah*, pp. 10–36; M. De Jonge, 'The Earliest Christian Use of *Christos*: Some Suggestions', *NTS* 32 (1986), pp. 321–43; idem, 'The Use of the Word "Anointed" in the Time of Jesus', *NovT* 8 (1966), pp. 132–48; D. Flusser, 'Two Notes on the Midrash on 2 Sam 7', *IEJ* 9 (1959), pp. 99–109; Fuller, *Christology*, pp. 109–14; Goppelt, *Theology* 1, pp. 167–72; W. Grundmann *et al.*, *TWNT* 9, pp. 482–576; Hahn, *Titles*, pp. 136–239; Harvey, *Jesus*, pp. 120–53; J. Klausner, *The Messianic Idea in Israel from Its Beginnings to the Completion of the Mishnah*, New York, 1955; Kümmel, *Promise*, pp. 109–21; idem, *Theology*, pp. 66–74; Leivestad; Longenecker, pp. 63–82; T. W. Manson, *Servant-Messiah*; W. Manson; I. H. Marshall, *The Origins of New Testament Christology*, Leicester, 1976, pp. 83–96; B. F. Meyer, pp. 174–202; Moule, *Christology*, pp. 31–5; J. Neusner, W. S. Green, and E. Frerichs, eds., *Judaisms and their Messiahs at the Turn of the Christian Era*, Cambridge, 1987; J. C. O'Neill, *Messiah*; idem, 'The Silence of Jesus', *NTS* 15 (1969), pp. 153–67; R. Pesch, 'Die Messiasbekenntnis des Petrus (Mk 8.27–30): Neuverhandlung einer alten Frage', *BZ* 17 (1973), pp. 178–95; 18 (1974), pp. 20–31; Riesner, pp. 298–352; G. Scholem, *The Messianic Idea in Judaism and Other Essays on Jewish Spirituality*, New York, 1971; M. Smith, 'What is implied by the Variety of Messianic Figures?', *JBL* 78 (1959), pp. 66–72; S. Talmon, 'Types of Messianic Expectation at the Turn of the Era', in *King, Cult and Calendar in Ancient Israel*, Jerusalem, 1986, pp. 202–24 and *The World of Qumran from Within*, Jerusalem, 1989, pp. 273–300; W. C. van Unnik, 'Jesus the Christ', *NTS* 8 (1962), pp. 101–16; Vermes, *Jesus the Jew*, pp. 129–59.

[2] Cf. Bultmann, *Theology* 1, p. 43 ('Jesus' call to decision implies a christology'), and Fuller, *Christology*, pp. 103–8.

[3] So Dunn, *Spirit*, p. 79 (original in italics). He appeals to Jesus' emphatic use of ἐγώ (cf. Jeremias, *Theology*, pp. 250–5), his novel use of 'amen' (see on 5.17), and Mk 11.27–33 par.

[4] Cf. Fuller, *Christology*, p. 104: 'in Jesus' ministry God is already beginning his eschatological action, and will shortly consummate it.'

they thought their mission was (John 1.19–23; Matt 11.3); Jesus himself asked his disciples what people thought of him (Mark 8.27–8 par.). In answer, the mention of a particular office was expected, or the name of a man who was a particularly worthy holder of such an office: a prophet like Elijah or Jeremiah, John the Baptist or the Messiah (Matth 16.14–16). It may be that one or [the] other of these enquiries is not historical. But the fact that they are reported at all shows much much emphasis was laid on the need to formulate the divine commission clearly—to describe and justify it in the light of already existing ideas and concepts. And we know how Paul fought for the recognition of his apostolic status.'[5] Given his Jewish environment, then, is it likely that Jesus could have completely avoided characterizing his own person in traditional categories? 'Would not a Jew in Jesus' time, exercising the sense of authority which many scholars believe the gospel data reveal, have most naturally sought to associate his ministry with some rôle bearing some kind of designation or descriptive reference?'[6] The question is the more pressing when one takes account of how often the question of Jesus' authority comes up in the gospels.

In some critical circles the possibility that Jesus thought of himself as Messiah is no longer seriously entertained. Nonetheless, the subject cannot be ignored. Jesus was executed as a political offender, and the gospels inform us that it was precisely as 'king of the Jews' that he was crucified. There is not much question about the genuineness of the inscription. How then does one explain it? Does it not push the messianic problem back into the pre-Easter period? One might respond that although such is indeed the case, it is quite probable that Jesus was misunderstood, that his activity gave rise to expectations he himself did not condone. One recalls Jn 6.15: 'Perceiving then that they were about to come and take him by force to make him king, Jesus withdrew again to the mountain by himself' (on this see esp. Dodd, *Tradition*, pp. 213–16). There was a lively expectation among the Jewish people of Palestine that a political saviour would break the Roman yoke. Stirred by Jesus' eschatological preaching and ministry of miracles, some could easily have hoped him to be the messianic deliverer. But if one thing is clear, it is that Jesus was not a political Messiah, that he did not seek to promote a political revolution against Rome. His aim was neither non-political nor directly political, and he seems to have left behind himself 'a movement of broken Messianic hopes'.[7] So was he not executed on false charges? Must we not credit misunderstanding as the ultimate cause for his arrest and crucifixion? Surely Jesus did not openly declare, 'I am the king of the Jews.'

Yet nagging questions remain. The category of messiahship was variegated in first-century Judaism. There was no unanimity concerning a coming anointed one.[8] While the idea of a 'nationalistic' Davidic

---

[5] Betz, *Jesus*, p. 81.

[6] F. H. Borsch, *The Christian and Gnostic Son of Man*, SBT 2/14, London, 1970, p. 2, n. 2.

[7] Bornkamm, *Jesus*, p. 172. See further Davies, *Land*, pp. 336–54.

[8] See the articles of De Jonge cited in n. 1. Yet according to Fitzmyer, *Essays*, pp. 119–20, 'it would be hypercritical to insist ... that one should simply speak

Messiah may have been dominant, it was not without competition. Several years ago W. C. van Unnik urged that the Messiah could have been thought of chiefly as the one possessed by God's Spirit, and that this was most important for early Christianity.[9] More recently K. Berger has maintained that the messianic hope was sometimes fixed after the model of the wise man (particularly Solomon).[10] It is also well to recall the expectation of a priestly Messiah at Qumran alongside a kingly Messiah (1QS 9.11; 1QSa 2.11–23). The issue of Jesus' messiahship is larger than the issue of Jesus and political messianism.

Beyond this, the confession of Jesus' messiahship is not fully explicable without some pre-Easter foundation. 'The resurrection by itself is inadequate to explain the origin of Jesus' messiahship. The exaltation of a martyr to God was by no means an indication of his eschatological and messianic, i.e. his unique, status.'[11] N. Dahl has sought to trace the origin of the confession of Jesus as Messiah to the inscription on the cross.[12] According to him Jesus was crucified as a political Messiah, and the resurrection, understood as vindication, was the confirmation of the crucified Christ. The Christians then took over the inscription of the cross, which means that the Roman authorities are indirectly responsible for the confession, 'Jesus is the Christ.' But why did the earliest believers, who knew that Jesus had rejected political messianism, feel obliged to adopt the verdict of the Romans? The resurrection was the vindication of Jesus, not his executioners. There were certainly other titles of honour—all of them less open to misunderstanding—available to convey the status of Jesus. Moreover, the title on the cross 'seems to have been framed in secular terms with "King" rather than "anointed one". . . . Besides, even if "Christ" had been written over the cross, Christians . . . would be unlikely to perpetuate, in a title, the idea that Jesus was crucified ostensibly as a revolutionary.'[13] Barring acceptance of Hahn's proposal that confession of Jesus as Messiah does not go back to the earliest period,[14] one is pressed into the pre-Paschal period for some explanation (cf. Harvey, *Jesus*, pp. 136–8). And with this our sources concur, for the synoptics contain two pericopae in which Jesus is directly confronted with the question of his messiahship (Mk 8.27–30 par.; 14.53–65 par.). In neither does he deny the proposal.

---

of "Anointed Ones". . . . A genuine Old Testament theme of an anointed agent of Yahweh had developed into the expectation of a Messiah . . .'. Cf. Moule, *Christology*, pp. 31–2, and see further L. H. Schiffman, 'The Concept of the Messiah in Second Temple and Rabbinic Literature', *RevExp* 84 (1987), pp. 235–46. By Jesus' time many if not most religious Jews could no doubt have intelligibly referred to the central figure of eschatological expectation as 'the Messiah' (cf. 2 Bar. 30.1; 4 Ezra 7.28).

[9] van Unnik, as in n. 1. For criticism see De Jonge, 'The Earliest Christian Use of *Christos*', pp. 335–6.

[10] See the articles cited in n. 1.

[11] Hengel, *Son*, p. 62. Cf. Jeremias, *Theology*, p. 255.

[12] See the article cited in n. 1. Note also the 'Postscript' to his book, *Messiah*, pp. 161–6.

[13] Moule, *Christology*, p. 33, citing F. Bovon, *Les derniers jours de Jésus*, Neuchâtel, 1974, p. 37.

[14] Hahn, *Titles*, pp. 161–8. Criticism in Marshall, *Christology*, pp. 91–4.

In attempting to go beyond the observations just made, it seems to us that the way forward may be found in two OT passages, Isa 61.1–4 and 2 Sam 7.4–17. These we now consider in some detail. The former lies behind the dominical beatitudes (see Excursus II) as well as 11.2–6 (see pp. 242–6). Moreover, Isa 61.1–4 'has so many points of contact with the gospel tradition as a whole' (see further below) that its presence in the synoptics cannot be put down to 'the invention of any one evangelist or even ... of the early church as opposed to Jesus or his disciples. Indeed it introduces us to a complex of ideas which pervade the whole gospel record and are bound up with the style of preaching and action adopted by Jesus' (Harvey, *Jesus*, p. 140). When it is further noted that in both pre-Christian Judaism and the NT Isa 61.1–4 is brought into connexion with both Isa 42.1–4[15] (which concerns the chosen servant who has the Spirit and a *tôrâ*) and Isa 52.7[16] (which is about the herald who brings good news and proclaims, 'Your God reigns'), we have here a group of passages which, to quote Harvey again, 'centre round a figure who is a servant and a son, a herald, and an anointed one. Moreover, as a herald he has a specific message to pronounce: he proclaims that God is king, he has good news for the poor and he comforts those who mourn. Now there can be no doubt that the heart of Jesus' message concerned the Kingdom of God, and that he laid great emphasis on preaching to the poor and the outcast; moreover his healing ministry was concentrated upon those manifestations of the new age—the cure of the blind, the deaf, the dumb and the lame—which are mentioned in related Isaiah-passages. That is to say, if one wished to offer a classic and concise description of the character of Jesus' work and message, it was to these passages that one would naturally turn' (*Jesus*, p. 141). We need only add that Matthew and Luke both did the latter (cf. Mt 12.18–21; Lk 4.18–19; Acts 4.27; 10.38).

Before drawing out the implications of Jesus' apparent use of Isa 61 as a sort of 'programme' for his work, we need to look at 2 Sam 7.4–17. The significance of this passage for the Jesus tradition has been particularly stressed by O. Betz. As we know from Qumran, 2 Sam 7.4–17, which was continually reinterpreted and reapplied in the OT,[17] was seen as an eschatological text in first-century Palestinian Judaism.[18] The earliest Christians also understood it thus, and the passage played its part in early Christology, as can be inferred from the ancient confession in Rom 1.3–4 as well as from Lk 1.32–3; Heb 1.5; and Rev

[15] The LXX adds 'sight to the blind' to Isa 61.1, taking the phrase from Isa 42.7, which describes the ministry of the servant introduced in 42.1–4. 1QH 17.26 ('Thou didst shed thy Holy Spirit upon thy servant', cf. Isa 42.1) is evidently part of the heading for a psalm which uses the *měbaśśēr* of Isa 52.7 in connexion with phraseology borrowed from Isa 61.1–2 (see 1QH 18.14–15).

[16] In 11QMelch 2.15–18 Isa 61.3 is used to interpret Isa 52.7. Note that whereas *měbaśśēr* (= 'herald') occurs in 52.7, *lěbaśśēr* is found in 61.1. Also, Acts 10.36 alludes to Isa 52.7, Acts 10.38 to Isa 61.1 (see the commentaries).

[17] J. Becker, *Messianic Expectation in the Old Testament* (trans. of *Messiaserwartung im Alten Testament*, 1977), Philadelphia, 1980.

[18] See D. Juel, *Messiah and Temple*, SBLDS 31, Missoula, 1977, pp. 169–97.

21.7.[19] Betz further contends that 2 Sam 7.4–17 (cf. 1 Chron 17.3–15) was a key text for Jesus and that he applied it to himself. This proposal sheds light on several facets of the Jesus tradition; in particular, it explains the confluence of the major motifs in the examination before the high priest (Mk 14.53–65 par.). The hearing begins with witnesses who claim that Jesus spoke of tearing down the temple and rebuilding it. Their testimony does not agree. The priest asks, 'Have you no answer to make? What is it that these men testify against you?' Jesus says nothing. The high priest then asks, 'Are you the Christ, the Son of the Blessed?' Jesus answers, 'I am, and you will see the Son of man seated at the right hand of Power and coming with the clouds of heaven.' Betz observes that 2 Sam 7 clarifies this entire sequence, which otherwise remains obscure.[20] In Nathan's prophecy, God promises David that his line will not fail: 'I will raise up your offspring after you, who shall come forth from your body, and I will establish his kingdom. He shall build a house for my name, and I will establish the throne of his kingdom for ever. I will be his father, and he shall be my son.' Betz comments: 'If the Nathan prophecy is given an eschatological interpretation, the building of the house of God is a messianic duty. Conversely, anyone who sets up to be a builder of the temple is indirectly claiming to be the Messiah and the Son of God. It is now clear why the high priest, when an examination of the witnesses to Jesus' statement about the temple is at a deadlock, puts the direct question as to the messianic claim and forces Jesus' confession.'[21] See further the commentary on 26.57–68.

To Betz's argument one might respond that all he has demonstrated is the influence of 2 Sam 7 upon a pericope formulated by the early Christian community. To move from Mk 14.53–65 par. to the historical Jesus is a non sequitur. We, however, do not believe that the issue of the historicity of the trial before the High Priest is closed. More importantly, the motifs of sonship, temple building, and kingship do not simply converge in one Markan paragraph: they also converge in the historical ministry of Jesus. That Jesus thought of himself as God's Son in some special or even unique sense is nearly certain (Dunn, *Spirit*, pp. 11–40). That he spoke of the end of the old temple and of a new eschatological temple is no less likely (Allison, pp. 152–3). And that Jesus conceived of himself as some sort of king would seem to be implicit in the fact that he evidently chose twelve disciples. What did he intend by such an act? He wanted to create a symbol for the eschatological restoration of Israel (cf. Sanders, *Jesus*, pp. 98–106). The important point is this: Jesus himself stood outside the symbolic group and was undeniably its leader. (Recall that he alone was arrested and

---

[19] Cf. Betz, *Jesus*, pp. 94–101; also Hengel, *Son*, p. 64. On the use of 2 Sam 7 in Acts see E. Schweizer, 'The Concept of the Davidic "Son of God" in Acts and its Old Testament Background', in *Studies in Luke-Acts*, ed. L. E. Keck and J. L. Martyn, Nashville, 1966, pp. 186–93.

[20] According to Anderson, *Mark*, p. 331, '"Are you the Christ, the Son of the Blessed?" is introduced somewhat abruptly in so far as it has no obvious connexion with the foregoing proceedings, certainly not with the alleged prediction on Jesus' part of the destruction of the Temple.'

[21] Betz, *Jesus*, p. 90. Cf. B. F. Meyer, pp. 179–80.

crucified—a not insignificant fact.) Who then did he take himself to be? It is hard to avoid the inference that he thought of himself as the leader-to-be of the restored people of God, a destined king. What follows for our purposes? When Mark, in Mk 14.53–65, and Matthew, in 16.13–20, made Jesus Son and Christ and builder of a new community or temple, they were not playing fast and loose with the tradition but rather being faithful to it.

If it is a correct judgement that both 2 Sam 7.4–17 and Isa 61.1–4 inspired Jesus to think, say, and do certain things, what may one infer? The key point is that *both texts have to do with a messianic figure, that is, an anointed one.* This is explicit in Isa 61.1: 'the Lord has anointed me' (cf. 42.1). It is implicit in 2 Sam 7, for the prophecy is manifestly about a king, and all Jewish kings were, at enthronement, anointed; indeed, the king was known by the title, 'the Lord's anointed' (1 Sam 24.6, 10; 26.16). In addition, 2 Sam 7 was, before Jesus' time, interpreted of the coming Davidic Messiah (see n. 18); and the targum on Zech 6.12 bestows upon the temple builder of 2 Sam 7 the title *měšîḥāʾ*. It appears, therefore, that what our two OT texts have in common, besides their influence on the gospels, is this: they were both messianic in the proper sense of the word. Thus if Jesus found his own person and work anticipated by them, he could scarcely have avoided a 'messianic consciousness'.

To sum up the argument to this point, most of the central themes or features of Jesus' ministry can be directly related to a handful of OT texts—2 Sam 7.4–17; Isa 42.1–4; 52.7; 62.1–4—which taken together would have been understood by first-century Jews as pertaining to eschatology and the (Davidic) Messiah:

—kingdom | *malkût*/βασιλεία appears three times in 2 Sam 7.12, 13, 16; and in Isa 52.7 the bringer of good tidings says to Zion, 'Your God reigns'

—ministry to outcasts, the poor | Isa 61.1: 'to bring good tidings to the poor', 'to bind up the brokenhearted', 'to comfort all who mourn'

—Jesus as bearer of the Spirit | Isa 61.1: 'the Spirit of the Lord is upon me' (cf. 42.1)

—Jesus as preacher of good news | Isa 52.7: 'How beautiful upon the mountains are the feet of him who brings good tidings, who publishes peace, who brings good tidings of good, who publishes salvation' (the LXX uses εὐαγγελίζομαι twice)

—Jesus as teacher and revealer | Isa 42.4: 'till he has established *mišpāṭ* in the earth; the coastlands wait for his *tôrâ*' (on this see Davies, *SSM*, pp. 130–7)

—Jesus as Davidid (see on 9.27) | 2 Sam 7.4–17 is about one of David's descendants

| —God as Jesus' Father in a special sense, Jesus as God's Son in a special sense | 2 Sam 7.14: 'I will be his father and he will be my son' |
| —the old temple replaced by a new temple | 2 Sam 7.13 'He shall build a house for my name' |

It is even possible to associate Jesus' exorcisms and healings with Isa 61 and 2 Sam 7. For one thing, the dominical Mt 11.4–6 links Isa 61.1 with other texts in Isaiah which are about eschatological healing (see on 11.2–6). For another, 2 Sam 7, originally a prophecy about Solomon, was naturally thought of as foretelling the coming of a king like Solomon, and Solomon was in Jewish tradition an exorcist and great healer (see on 1.1 and 9.27). It also bears mention that Isa 61.1 could have been viewed as pertaining to exorcism: 'to proclaim liberty to the captives, and the opening to those who are bound.' The possessed were often spoken of as having been 'bound' by demons.[22]

In view of all we have said, it may not be too much to say that Isa 61 and 2 Sam 7 provided Jesus with a large part of the blueprint for his ministry, understood as properly messianic. There is, however, one objection which must be faced. Why are there no undeniably authentic sayings in which Jesus clearly asserts that he is the Messiah? The answer to this is probably threefold. (i) Mk 14.62 par. may be a genuine logion despite the doubts of many (see on 26.64); (ii) Jesus may have been reticent to publish abroad his acceptance of a title so much open to misunderstanding: his self-conception did not harmonize with generally accepted notions of 'Messiah'; and (iii) it may have been 'understood that he who was to be enthroned as Messiah must not encroach on God's prerogative of making the announcement himself.'[23] Concerning this last, R. N. Longenecker, following the lead of D. Flusser, and with reference to the Teacher of Righteousness, Jesus, and Simeon ben Kosebah, has written of the following pattern: '(1) external acclamation, (2) reticence on the part of the individual to speak of himself in the terms others were using, yet (3) a consciousness on that person's part of the ultimate validity of the titles employed. . . .'[24] It cannot be said that Longenecker has conclusively proven that such a pattern existed in ancient Judaism. But the possibility cannot be denied, and the relevance for study of the gospels is obvious.[25]

---

[22] Cf. R. H. Hiers, '"Binding" and "Loosing:" The Matthean Authorizations', *JBL* 104 (1985), p. 245.

[23] J. C. O'Neill, 'The Charge of Blasphemy at Jesus' Trial before the Sanhedrin', in Bammel, *Trial*, p. 75.

[24] Longenecker, p. 73. See further the articles of D. Flusser and J. C. O'Neill cited in n. 1. Perhaps it is worth remarking that Sabbatai Sevi's messianic pretensions were not taken seriously until he was acclaimed by another, Nathan of Gaza; see Scholem, p. 207.

[25] We recall here words of C. K. Barrett: Jesus 'consistently permitted himself to be addressed by a term [Rabbi], that concealed rather than disclosed the true meaning and character of his mission. It was not false, for he did teach. . . . But if . . . he allowed himself to be addressed as Teacher, there was an element of secrecy, of concealment, about his work'; *Essays on John*, London, 1982, p. 31. See further Davies, *Invitation to the New Testament*, Garden City, 1965, p. 182 (on the reticence of Jesus to talk about himself).

XXXIX

JESUS, THE MESSIAH AND THE SON OF GOD, FOUNDS HIS CHURCH
(16.13–20)

(i) *Structure*

This pericope, which enshrines several triads, consists of a narrative introduction (v. 13a), a dialogue (vv. 13b–19), and a narrative conclusion (v. 20). In the dialogue itself, Jesus speaks three times, in vv. 13, 15 and 17–19. Furthermore, vv. 17–19 contain three sentences, each of which consists of three parts—a statement of theme plus an antithetical couplet.[1]

(ii) *Sources*

We suggest tentatively that Mt 16.13–20 is the product of conflation. Just as the First Evangelist has elsewhere combined Markan and Q accounts of the same incident (e.g. in 3.1–17 and 12.22–32), so here has he merged the Markan and M accounts of Peter's confession. Most proponents of the two-source theory have, to be sure, thought otherwise. Usually the judgement is this: vv. 13–16 and 20 derive from Mark, vv. 17–19—perhaps originally two or more isolated sayings—from M. But, as we shall soon see, there are reasons for surmising that vv. 17–19 came to Matthew as a piece and that they pre-suppose a christological confession of Peter; so it is natural to infer that Matthew knew a non-Markan version of Mk 8.27–30, one which included the blessing of Peter.

It must be conceded that, on our proposal, Mk 8.27–30 could reasonably be regarded as secondary *vis-à-vis* its Matthean parallel; for we shall contend that the Markan text is a truncated version of what we find in Matthew. Hence the Griesbach hypothesis would here seem to work; that is, Matthew may indeed have here the more primitive text (cf. Butler, pp. 131–3). If we nonetheless remain opposed to the theory of Matthean priority, it is because the evidence from the rest of the gospel points in another direction. What we discover in Mt 16.13–20 par is the exception, not the rule.

---

[1] Cf. Burney, p. 117; Jeremias, *Golgotha* (v), p. 69; Gnilka, *Matthäusevangelium* 2, p. 47.

(iii) *Exegesis*

The episode recounted in 16.13–20 takes the form of a pronouncement story, the two key elements of which are Peter's confession and Jesus' response to that confession. In its present, Matthean context the primary function is to record the establishment of a new community, one which will acknowledge Jesus' true identity and thereby become the focus of God's activity in salvation-history. The event has been occasioned by the rejection of Jesus by corporate Israel, a rejection chronicled in the previous chapters (see section (iv), point (2)).

As with so many other synoptic texts, the OT supplies the requisite background for a proper interpretation. What we appear to have before us is a passage whose major themes have their collective root in Davidic messianism, above all in Nathan's famous oracle to David, preserved in 2 Sam 7.4–16 and 1 Chron 17.3–15. In Mt 16.13–20 Jesus is confessed as both Christ and Son of God; he builds a new church or temple; and he gives to Peter the keys to the kingdom of Heaven. These are all Davidic motifs. In 2 Sam 7 and 1 Chron 17 it is promised that one of David's descendants will rule over Israel as king (and therefore as anointed one), that he will be God's son ('I will be his father, and he will be my son'), that he will build a temple ('he shall build a temple for my name'), and that 'his kingdom' will be forever. This oracle was, before Jesus' time, understood to refer not (just) to Solomon but to Israel's eschatological king (see p. 598). Mt 16.13–20 presupposes its fulfilment in Jesus.[2] Moreover, the giving of the keys of the Kingdom of heaven to Peter has its closest OT parallel in Isa 22.22: 'And I (God) will place on his (Eliakim's) shoulder the key of the house of David; he shall open, and none shall shut; and he shall shut, and none shall open'. Although this verse does not appear to have received a messianic interpretation in Judaism, 'the house of David' did have messianic associations,[3] and the text—which is applied to Jesus in Rev 3.7—is about the activity of a man second only to the king. That it lies behind Mt 18.19 is altogether likely (cf. Emerton (v)). In sum, therefore, Mt 16.13–20 records the eschatological realization of the promises made to David.

If 16.13–20 rests not only upon Mk 8.27–30 but also a second version of the confession of Caesarea Philippi, it is all but impossible to determine what non-Markan elements are due to redaction and what to tradition. Whatever conclusions one may reach on the issue, the

---

[2] Cf. O. Betz, *Jesus*, pp. 91–2; B. P. Robinson (v), pp. 90–1.
[3] Note Zech 12.7–13.1; Lk 1.27.

following are the major differences between Mt 16.13–20 and its Markan parallel: (i) 'His disciples' are mentioned twice in Mk 8.27, once in Mt 16.13 (this could be due to Matthew's desire to abbreviate). (ii) Mark's εἰς τὰς κώμας (8.27) has become εἰς τὰ μέρη (16.13). (iii) Mark's 'in the way' (8.27) has no counterpart in Matthew (cf. 20.34 diff. Mk 10.52). (iv) Whereas in the Second Gospel Jesus asks, 'Whom do men say that I am?' (8.27), in Matthew his words are these: 'Whom do men say that *the Son of man* is?' (16.13). (v) Mk 8.28 records only three popular opinions about Jesus: some say he is John the Baptist, others Elijah, others one of the prophets. Mt 16.14 adds a fourth possibility: he is Jeremiah. (vi) 'Peter' occurs in Mk 8.29, 'Simon Peter' in Mt 16.16. (vii) There is no Markan parallel to Mt 16.17–19. (viii) The concluding prohibition in Mk 8.30 is to 'say nothing concerning him'. In Matthew the command is more specific: the disciples are to 'tell no one that he was the Christ'. (ix) Mk 8.27–30 is preceded by the story of the healing of the blind man of Bethsaida, Mk 8.22–6. Matthew has omitted this. According to Gundry, *Commentary*, p. 328, he did this because the material had already been incorporated into 9.27–31. It is more probable that the First Evangelist found Jesus' use of saliva, and especially the fact that the cure is not from the first complete ('I see men, but they look like trees walking'), too problematic to reproduce.

There are basically three different approaches to the tradition-history of 16.13–20. (i) Some have held that the text as it stands represents a more primitive tradition than the Markan and Lukan parallels. This has been maintained not only by proponents of the Griesbach hypothesis but also by others who accept Markan priority. Bultmann, for instance, claimed that Mt 16.17–19 contains the original conclusion to Peter's confession, which was replaced in Mark's tradition by a passion prediction and the rebuke of Peter, Mk 8.31–3.[4] Similar proposals have been put forward by Meyer (v) and Nickelsburg (v).[5] (ii) Others have affirmed that vv. 17–19 contain pre-Matthean tradition(s) which originally had some other setting. Cullmann, for instance, in his important book on *Peter* (v), placed Mt 16.17–19a in the context of the Last Supper.[6] More popular has been the guess that the verses were at one time part of a resurrection story.[7] Robinson (v), on the other hand, isolates three separate sayings with three different origins (v. 17—from the primitive Palestinian community; v. 18— redactional; v. 19—dominical in an earlier form). His conclusions are

[4] *History*, pp. 258–9. Cf. J. Weiss and W. Bousset, *Die drei älteren Evangelien*, 3rd ed., Göttingen, 1917, p. 332; Lagrange, p. 321.

[5] According to Nickelsburg, Mt 16.13–19 is a commissioning story with formal similarities to the epiphanic commissioning stories in 1 En. 12–16 and T. Levi 2–7.

[6] Cf. Bonnard, p. 242. A setting at the last supper was already proposed in the nineteenth century by J. F. Blair, *The Apostolic Gospel*, London, 1896, pp. 328–31.

[7] Cf. Stauffer (v); Brown, *John* 2, pp. 1088–9 (Mt 16.16–19 is a composite of sayings which originally belonged to post-resurrection contexts); Strecker, *Weg*, pp. 206–7; Kähler (v). For earlier proponents of this view see Burgess (v), pp. 113–18.

in line with the recent tendency to doubt the unity of vv. 17–19. (iii) It is possible to regard the three verses as redactional.[8] In favour of this, 16.17–19 is triadic, it exhibits parallelism, and it contains redactional vocabulary[9]—all possible indications of Matthean composition.

— In our judgement, the third option is the least probable. 16.17–19 contains several words and expressions Matthew does not use elsewhere: Βαριωνᾶ, σὰρξ καὶ αἷμα, πύλαι ᾅδου, κατισχύω, κλείς. There is also a high number of Semitisms— a higher percentage than is normal for redactional material. Note the appearance of Βαριωνᾶ (= 'son of Jonah'), σὰρξ καὶ αἷμα with the sense of 'earthly' (see on v. 17), ὁ πατήρ μου ὁ ἐν τοῖς οὐρανοῖς (although this should perhaps be considered redactional), πύλαι ᾅδου (see on v. 18), δῆσαι ... λῦσαι (cf. SB 1, pp. 738–47), and asyndeton (v. 19).[10] All this moves one to suspect a Semitic original, especially when note is taken of the possibility of a wordplay in Aramaic: Kephā'/kephā' (see on v. 18). Furthermore, there are partial parallels to the content of vv. 17–19 in several NT texts, including Mk 3.16 (where Jesus is said to have surnamed Simon Peter); Jn 1.42 (where Jesus says to Peter: 'so you are Simon the son of John? You shall be called Cephas'); 20.23 ('If you forgive the sins of any, they are forgiven; if you retain the sins of any, they are retained'; cf. Mt 16.19); and Gal 1.15–18 (see below, p. 609). Finally, although Matthew loves parallelism and triads, nowhere else does he manufacture a triad consisting of three units with the form of thesis statement + antithetical couplet. For these reasons we reject the hypothesis of a redactional genesis.[11]

Also problematic is the second option, that vv. 17–19 originally had some other context, or that the three verses preserve two or more sayings which were at one time independent. In the first place, the unity of the section is a reasonable conclusion: the finely crafted structure (see p. 602) argues that we do not here have heterogeneous sayings unequally yoked; and the confluence of architectural images (gates, keys, building on a rock) as well as the background in Davidic messianism (cf. p. 603) reinforce this inference. We also wonder whether vv. 17 and/or 18 could ever have stood in isolation. Do they not demand a narrative context, one in which Peter has made an important statement about Jesus? In the second place we shall see below that the reasons for linking 16.17–19 with a resurrection appearance are quite

---

[8] So Goulder, pp. 383–93 and Gundry, *Commentary*, pp. 330–6.

[9] ἀποκριθεὶς ... εἶπεν*, Ἰησοῦς*, ὁ πατήρ μου ὁ ἐν τοῖς οὐρανοῖς*, κἀγώ (Mk:9; Mk:0; Lk:6), βασιλεία τῶν οὐρανῶν*, ἐάν*. See further Gundry, *Commentary*, pp. 331–3, for additional suggestions, although he stretches the evidence a good deal (e.g. μακάριος, Πέτρος, κατισχύω, and λύω are all quite questionable instances of editorial vocabulary).

[10] For the rendering of portions of 16.17 and 18 into Aramaic see Fitzmyer (v). For a rendering of v. 19 into Aramaic see Jeremias, *Theology*, p. 22. None of the proposed Semitisms demands a Semitic original. But, *pace* Kähler (v), pp. 38–40, they do strongly imply one. See esp. Grelot, 'Origene' (v). He translates all of 16.16–19 into Aramaic.

[11] Perhaps some weight should also be given to Trilling's observation (pp. 156–7) that Matthew prefers personal metaphors; architectural images are not characteristic of the redactor.

tenuous. The long-running popularity of this position among NT scholars is not justified by the evidence. What then, in the third place, of Cullmann's interesting conjecture? Although it cannot be disproved, we deem it less than probable. While there are certain parallels between Lk 22.31–4 and Mt 16.17–19, they are not so strong as to demand the same original setting. Probably the main motivation for Cullmann's hypothesis is his conviction that Mk 8.27–33 preserves the true historical sequence: confession of Jesus as the Christ followed by correction of a false idea of messiahship. Taking this as the starting point (which is less than certain because the primitive unity of Mk 8.27–33 is hardly guaranteed: see below), Cullmann directs attention to Mk 14.61–2 par. and to 15.2 par., where Jesus shows extreme reluctance towards the title, 'Messiah'. How can he have enthusiastically welcomed it on another occasion? The question overlooks the fact that in Mk 14.61–2 and 15.2 Jesus is addressing outsiders. In Mt 16.13–20, on the other hand, he is speaking to his inner circle, men who were with him constantly. There was ample opportunity to teach them, to show them how the word 'Messiah' might be filled with new content. And if Jesus, as we think, believed himself to be 'Messiah' and yet dissociated himself from many of the traditional connotations of that title, he could well have regarded Peter's messianic confession as a crucial breakthrough and then have gone on to affirm that he himself must suffer and die. In other words, we do not see that Mk 8.27–33 is inconsistent with Mt 16.17–19. The two traditions, *if* historical, need not be traced to two different occasions.

It remains to consider Bultmann's proposal, that Mt 16.17–19 preserves the original ending to the episode of Peter's confession. What considerations favour this possibility? Given the emotional debates in the early church surrounding Peter and his authority (cf. Acts 11.1–3; 1 Cor 1.12; Gal 1.18–2.21) and the NT's otherwise unanimous verdict that the foundation of the church is Jesus, not Peter, it requires very little imagination to conjure up a situation in which someone—Mark or a predecessor of his—could have found Mt 16.17–19 potentially problematic and therefore omitted it. (Certainly in the last two centuries there have been people who, on theological grounds, have wished to regard the verses as not belonging to the original text of the First Gospel; see Burgess (v.).) Beyond this, Mk 8.27–30 does strike one as an odd text. If 8.30 be thought to preserve tradition, we are asked to believe that early Christians passed on a pericope in which Jesus, after inviting discussion of the issue, responded to the church's confession— Jesus is the Christ—with an unexplained injunction to silence. Surely this is not what one would have anticipated. And yet, if Mk 8.30 be, on the contrary, held redactional (so most contemporary scholars), we are invited to suppose that the tradition handed down an account in which Peter's confession was, depending upon whether the story ended with v. 29 or vv. 31ff., met either by no response at all on Jesus' part or by an abrupt change of subject. Again, this is not what one would have expected. The only alternative is to postulate that the reaction of Jesus has been lost (cf. Kümmel, *Theology*, p. 69). But then why not consider the possibility that Mt 16.17–19 preserves that lost reaction? There is another factor to be considered. Vögtle, 'Problem' (v), has made the straightforward observation that our three verses find no better setting in the gospel history than the confession at Caesarea Philippi. While this fact might be taken to indicate a redactional composition (the material fits its present context so well because it was specially made for it), it is also more than consistent with Mk 8.27–30 being a truncated version of what is preserved in Mt 16.13–20.

At this point we must pause to consider an important objection. Jn 6.66–71, the Johannine parallel to Peter's confession, has nothing corresponding to Mt 16.17–19. Does this not support the priority of the Markan version? There is force in the question. Still, one might respond that the traditional ending (preserved in Matthew) was excised or dropped early enough so as to effect both the pre-Markan and pre-Johannine traditions. Also, the Fourth Evangelist might not have taken over the tradition behind Mt 16.17–19 even if he had known it, for there is in his gospel a consistent muting of Peter's prominence. Between 1.35–42, where it is *Andrew* who first follows and believes in Jesus, and the Last Supper, Peter does nothing save utter the confession of 6.68–9. After Jn 17, he does play a significant rôle in the narrative, but it is a rôle always overshadowed by the presence of 'the beloved disciple', who sits next to Jesus (13.23), is entrusted with the care of Mary (19.26–7), is the first disciple to discover the empty tomb (20.8), is the first disciple to believe in the resurrection (20.8), and is the first to recognize the risen Jesus when he stands on the shore of the Sea of Tiberias (21.7). There can be no doubt that John betrays a tendency to underplay Peter's pride of place, and this tendency could have led to the omission of the tradition about the church being founded on Peter.

Then too one must keep in mind one of the compositional methods of the Fourth Evangelist: he scatters throughout his gospel material which, in the tradition, was united.[12] To cite two examples: elements from the story of Jesus' rejection at Nazareth (Mk 6.1–6a par.) have been dispersed throughout the first part of John (see on 13.53–8) whereas elements from the episode in Gethsemane (Mk 14.32–42) have been strewn throughout the second half (see on 26.36–46). We should like to raise the possibility that in like manner John may have known something close to Mt 16.13–20 and that he drew upon it in more than one place. It is striking that the Fourth Gospel does not just have a parallel to Peter's confession. It also contains an account of Jesus giving to Peter the name 'Cephas' (= 'rock')—*and precisely in the context of a messianic confession*. In Jn 1.35–42, Andrew meets Jesus. He then informs Peter that Jesus is the Messiah. Next follows the renaming of Peter. In other words, confession of Jesus as Messiah (v. 41: 'we have found the Messiah') is juxtaposed with Peter being given the name Cephas (v. 42: 'You shall be called Cephas'), just as in Mt 16.13–20. Is this coincidence? Or is it a sign that Matthew's association of 16.18 ('and I tell you, you are Peter') with a messianic confession was given by the tradition?

The following is a list of the traditions common to Mt 16.13–20 and the Gospel of John (cf. Brown, *John* 1, pp. 301–2):

[12] Cf. E. C. Hoskyns, *The Fourth Gospel*, ed. F. N. Davey, London, 1947, pp. 81–2.

Mt 16.13-20	John
Following a messianic confession Simon is named Peter (= 'rock')	Following a messianic confession Simon is named Cephas (= 'rock') (1.35-42)
Some say Jesus is one of the prophets	'This is indeed the prophet who is to come into the world' (6.14)
Jesus asks his disciples a question about his identity	Jesus asks his disciples whether they wish to go away (6.67)
Simon Bar-Jonah, responding to a question addressed by Jesus to all the disciples, confesses Jesus to be the Christ and Son of God	Simon the son of John, responding to a question addressed by Jesus to all the disciples, confesses Jesus to be 'the Holy One of God'—a title closely associated with Son of God (6.69)[13]
'Flesh and blood has not revealed this to you but my Father in heaven'	'No one can come to me unless it be granted him by the Father' (6.65); 'the flesh is useless' (6.63)
Peter is the rock on which the church is built	Peter is made by Jesus to be the shepherd of the Christian flock (21.15-17)
Following the confession the subject turns to Jesus' passion (cf. Mk 8.31-3)	Following the confession the subject turns to Jesus' passion (6.70-1)
'Whatever you bind on earth shall be bound in heaven, and whatever you loose on earth shall be loosed in heaven'	'If you forgive the sins of any, they are forgiven; if you retain the sins of any, they are retained' (20.23)[14]

Our suggestion is that John knew the confession of Caesarea Philippi in a form close to that in Matthew and drew upon it at several junctures. That is to say, the material in the right-hand column represents the scattering of material originally belonging to the story represented in the left-hand column. Seen in this light, John's Gospel, so far from being a witness for the priority of Mk 8.27-30, buttresses our claim for the possible originality of Mt 16.13-20.

The discussion thus far inclines us to concur with Bultmann and the other scholars who have found in Mt 16.13-20 an early account of Peter's confession. But we cannot follow Bultmann's reckoning that 'the whole narrative' is in fact 'an Easter story, which had been (perhaps for the first time in Mark) carried back into the ministry of Jesus'. He argued this in part because he was persuaded that 'Peter's experience of Easter was the time when the early Church's messianic faith was born' (History, p. 259). This is a judgement we cannot share. As we have argued in Excursus XII, the messianic question was already raised and answered in the pre-Easter period. There are, however, other

[13] See on this Cullmann, Christology, p. 285.
[14] If one could accept the argument of J. L. Martyn, 'We have found Elijah,' in Jews, Greeks, and Christians, SJLA 21, ed. R. Hamerton-Kelly and R. Scroggs, Leiden, 1976, pp. 181-219, that a pre-Johannine tradition identified Jesus with Elijah, another parallel could be added (cf. Mt 16.14: 'others say Elijah').

resurrection story of Jn 21.15–12, where Peter is personally commissioned as an authority by the risen Lord, and his task is to take care of the church ('feed my lambs'). And in this same discussion the possibility of a disciple living until the *parousia* is brought up (vv. 22–3)—which matters because some have understood 'the gates of Hades will not prevail against αὐτῆς' (Mt 16.18) to promise Peter immortality. Lastly, there are resurrection traditions in which Jesus is called the Son of God (Jn 20.31; cf. Rom 1.4), in Jn 20.29 the risen Christ utters a beatitude (cf. Mt 16.17), and the closest parallel to Mt 16.19 is the post-resurrectional saying in Jn 20.22–3 (cf. p. 639). So all in all there would seem to be substantial similarities between Mt 16.13–20 and early Christian stories about the resurrection.

And yet we are not quite convinced. To begin with, the observations about 'Hades' and the beatitude form can carry no weight, for the historical Jesus certainly composed beatitudes (cf. Lk 6.20–2 par.), and 'Hades' appears in a Q saying whose authenticity is generally granted (see on 11.23). Next, we have already given reasons for thinking that Jn 20.29, the parallel to Mt 16.19, may very well owe its present placement to the evangelist (see pp. 607–8). If so, the verse's present location cannot help us in pinning down the origin of its Matthean counterpart. There is also the difficulty that Mt 16.17, which speaks of the Father revealing (ἀπεκάλυψεν) something to Peter does not remind one of any of the NT's appearance stories; and ἀποκαλύπτω, a verb attested in Q (10.26 = Lk 12.2; 11.25–27 = Lk 10.21–2), plays no part in the NT's resurrection traditions. But the decisive consideration seems to us to be this. 'There is no parallel in the accounts of the appearance of the Risen Christ for the pattern of confession followed by investiture'.[15] In other words, the major structural feature of Mt 16.13–20 is missing from the stories with which Bultmann would classify it. When one adds that so much else one would expect from a resurrection story is missing—there is no crisis situation, no unexpected appearance of Jesus, no failure to recognize him—there is justification for refusing to label Mt 16.13–20 an Easter narrative.

At this point we should like to raise the possibility that Mt 16.13–20 rests upon an event in the life of Jesus. Review of this opinion, however, involves so many disputed and difficult issues—for example, the place of the church in the thought of Jesus, the rôle of Peter in the early church, Jesus' messianic awareness—that we cannot herein do the subject justice: for that a monograph would be required. No less importantly, we ourselves remain uncertain and can hardly declare ourselves fully persuaded in our minds. What we wish cautiously to affirm is simply this: despite the dense cloud of witnesses, the issue of authenticity should not be considered closed. Our reasons for taking this position may be outlined as follows:

(1) *The evidence of Paul.* In Gal 1.11–1.21 Paul relates his own call

---

[15] Robinson (v), p. 88. He continues: 'John 21 contains an investiture, but it is preceded only by a recognition (v. 7) and by an assertion about the speaker (Peter) (vv. 15–17), not by a confession about Jesus. John 20 contains a confession (v.28) but no investiture. Matt. 28 has an investiture (vv. 18–20) but it is preceded only by an act of homage (v. 17) not by a confession'.

in terms reminiscent of Mt 16.13–20.[16] According to the apostle, Jesus Christ, God's Son, was 'revealed' (1.12: ἀποκαλύψεως Ἰησοῦ Χριστοῦ; cf. 1.16; 2.2) to him, and he did not confer with 'flesh and blood' (1.16). In the broader context it is precisely Paul's authority as opposed to the authority of Peter which is in dispute; that is, Paul is comparing himself with Peter. If one takes into consideration the additional facts that Paul shows knowledge of Peter's special commissioning (Gal 2.7–8), that Paul nowhere else either speaks of God 'revealing' Jesus to someone or uses 'flesh and blood' with the meaning 'human' or 'man as such' (cf. Gal 1.1, 12),[17] that the designation of James and Cephas and John as 'pillars' is conceptually close to Peter being the community's foundation rock,[18] and that only in Gal 2.7–8 does Paul call Cephas 'Peter' (which would make plain to Greek readers the meaning of his name), one must entertain the *possibility* that Gal 1–2 evinces knowledge of the tradition embedded in Mt 16.17–19. Proof, to be sure, is lacking. But one cannot overlook Gal 1–2 as a possible witness to the very early circulation of something very much like Mt 16.17–19.[19]

C. K. Barrett has argued that 1 Corinthians also shows Paul's knowledge of the gospel tradition about Peter. Commenting on 1 Cor 3.11 ('for no other foundation can any one lay than that which is laid, which is Jesus Christ'), Barrett has written: 'There is good (though not conclusive) reason to think that Peter had been at work in Corinth. . . . If he had not himself been present, others had, who represented him and pushed his claims. In either case use had probably been made of the tradition (Matt. xvi. 18) that Jesus had renamed Simon as Peter (*Kepha*, the rock), and given the promise that he would build his church on this rock. We may recall also the description (in Gal. ii. 9) of Peter, John, and James as "pillars" (cf. Eph. ii. 20). . . . It seems probable that (with or without his approval) Peter had been represented as the true foundation of the church'.[20] If Barrett is right, at least the primitive character of an important portion of Mt 16.13–20 would be established.

(2) *Semitisms*. Our passage as a whole has a number of Semitisms which give it a Semitic cast (see p. 605). This is consistent with its containing primitive tradition—although one fully concedes it does not prove such.

[16] Cf. Chapman (v); Dupont (v); Feuillet (v); Robinson (v), p. 89; Wenham (v)—all arguing for Paul's knowledge of the tradition preserved in Matthew. For the improbable judgement that Mt 16.17–19 betrays a knowledge of Gal 1 see F. Refoulé, 'Primauté de Pierre dans les évangiles', *RevScRel* 38 (1964), pp. 1–41.—Mt 16.17 and Gal 1.15–16 have often been linked together by Christian theologians, e.g. by Bullinger, *Decades* 1.21.

[17] See further Dupont (v), pp. 417–19.

[18] See C. K. Barrett, 'Paul and the "Pillar" Apostles', in *Studia Paulina in honorem Johannis de Zwaan*, ed. J. N. Sevenster and W. C. van Unnik, Haarlem, 1953, pp. 1–19, who shows that 'pillar' designates a major rôle in the eschatological temple.

[19] Brown et al. (v), p. 89, contend that the contrast between a revelation from God and a communication of 'flesh and blood' was a traditional way of describing resurrection appearances. This is speculation.

[20] *The First Epistle to the Corinthians*, New York and London, 1968, pp. 87–8.

(3) *The Dead Sea Scrolls.* Postulation of a Palestinian provenience for our pericope is supported by some parallels in texts found at Qumran (cf. esp. Betz (v)). In these last we find the notion of a new, eschatological community established on a rock foundation, safe from the ravages of evil (see 1QH 6.26f.; 7.8–9).[21] In addition, 4QPs[a] frags. 1–10, col. 3.15–16 refers to the Teacher of Righteousness, '[whom] God [ch]ose as the pillar. F[or] he established him to build for him a congregation of [his chosen ones in truth].'[22] Also pertinent is the observation that 4Q403 I.1.38–46 attests to belief in the animate nature of God's heavenly temple, and this may shed light on our passage's picture of the faithful as constituting a temple: the step from animate temple to community is much smaller than the step from inanimate temple to community.[23]

(4) *The criterion of consistency.* There are several features in 16.17–19 which are consistent or more than consistent with the teaching and actions of Jesus as recounted elsewhere in the synoptics.

a. Jesus uttered beatitudes (e.g. Lk 6.20–2 par., from Q). Indeed, in Mt 13.16–17 = Lk 10.23–4 (Q, and surely dominical) he speaks a blessing to those who are the beholders of eschatological revelation. The parallel with Mt 16.17 is undeniable.

b. In 16.18 Jesus speaks of building his community on a rock. This reminds one of Mt 7.24–7 = Lk 6.47–9, a dominical parable, where we read about the wise man who builds his house upon the rock.

c. The closest NT parallel to 16.16f. is the saying in 11.27 = Lk 10.22 (Q), which *may* go back to Jesus. The key terms common to both are πατήρ, υἱός, ἀποκαλύπτω.

d. Mt 16.17–19 draws upon 2 Sam 7.4–16 (cf. p. 603), a text which we on other grounds suspect that Jesus must have used (see Excursus XII).

e. Mk 14.58 par. is good reason to believe that Jesus envisaged the renewal of the people of God as the building of God's eschatological temple (see on 26.61).

f. The tradition that Jesus gave Simon the name *Kepha* is worthy of credence. It not only has multiple attestation (Mt 16.17: M; Mk 3.16; Jn 1.42), but there is also a tradition that he gave a new name to the sons of Zebedee, 'sons of thunder' (Mk 3.17). In addition, if the giving of a name is to be understood as a prophetic act (see on v. 17), this would be consistent with Jesus' self-conception as a prophet.

(5) *The criterion of dissimilarity.* According to this, any synoptic saying which is sufficiently distinct from both Jewish and Christian texts should have its origin with Jesus.[24] In the present case, a Jewish origin is clearly impossible and to our knowledge has never been

---

[21] Cf. Betz (v) and M. Delcor, *Les hymnes de Qumran* (*Hodayot*), Paris, 1962, pp. 53–4, 181.

[22] Trans. of M. P. Horgan, *Pesharim*, CBQMS 8, Washington, D. C., 1979, pp. 197–8.

[23] Cf. D. C. Allison, '4Q403 fragm. 1, col. I, 38–46 and the Revelation to John', *RevQ* 47 (1986), pp. 409–14.

[24] Discussion in M. D. Hooker, 'Christology and Methodology', *NTS* 17 (1971), pp. 480–7.

proposed: a promise to the apostle Peter cannot be traced back to Judaism. At the same time, certain elements of our narrative point away from a Christian origin. 'The gates of Hades', 'the keys of the kingdom', and 'bind and loose' are not distinctively Christian figures of speech.

(6) *The geographical setting.* According to Bultmann, *History*, p. 257, the naming of Caesarea Philippi does not 'ensure the historical character of what is told, since the note belongs to the previous section and corresponds to v. 22a' (that is, Mk 8.22a). This judgement is problematic. Mk 8.27a, with its naming of Caesarea Philippi, clearly introduces what follows.[25] Certainly this is how Matthew understood matters. Moreover, the naming of the district around Caesarea Philippi, an item not strictly necessary for the telling of the story, is striking. Why this area if the tradition were not firm on the point? Nothing stands in the way of thinking that Jesus, who certainly did at least visit Bethsaida (see on 11.21), could also have gone a bit further north to the villages of Caesarea Philippi.

(7) *Objections.* Of the several objections usually raised against the pre-Easter origin of part or all of Mt 16.13–20, the following may be mentioned.

a. According to Bultmann, *History*, p. 257, the historicity of our narrative is put in doubt by the fact that Jesus would not have initiated the action recounted, that is, he would not have asked his disciples a question—'Who do men say that I am?'—to which he surely knew the answer. Against this, the question could be just a literary device used to introduce otherwise accurate tradition. Further, perhaps John's gospel here sheds instructive light. In the words of J. A. T. Robinson: 'In the Synoptic account the question of the disciples' faith ... is presented without motive or explanation. This exercise in theology by Gallup poll ... has no obvious occasion or interpretation.... In John, however, we can see it as the consequence (rather than the climax) of an earlier turning-point or dangerous corner in the ministry. The Johannine setting, again, explains not only the need for forced withdrawal and the sharp rebuke of disciples, but the reiterated suppression by Jesus in the Markan narrative of all publicity (7.24, 36; 8.26, 30; 9.9, 30).... John also alone tells us of the background of disaffection among "disciples" at the time (6.66f.). This not only gives a reason for testing the loyalty of the Twelve but would explain the reference in Mark 8.38 and parallels (cf. Matt. 10.33 = 12.9) to those who are "ashamed" of Jesus, and the repeated language of the Gospel about those who are offended or do not stay the course (e.g. Mark 4.17 and pars.; Matt. 11.6 = Luke 7.23; Luke 9.62; 22.28; Mark 14.27–29 and pars.; John 16.1).'[26]

b. Perhaps the most common objection raised against Mt 16.17–19 is that Jesus could never have spoken of 'my church'. ἐκκλησία occurs only twice in the canonical gospels, both times in M material: Mt 16.18; 18.17. And the word was clearly popular among early Christians, so its presence in the gospels is suspect. While conceding the force of

[25] See the commentaries on Mark and Pesch (v), p. 180.
[26] *Priority*, pp. 207–8. See further Pesch (v), pp. 20–1.

this objection, we still do not find it decisive. For one thing, it is possible that the expression itself is secondary or even redactional,[27] and that the primitive narrative may have had 'temple' (cf. Mk 14.58; Jn 2.19–21) or some such. For another, there are possible Semitic equivalents, including Aramaic *kĕnîštā'*, *qĕhēlā'*, and *ṣibbûrā'*, and Hebrew *sôd*, *yaḥad*, *'ēdâ* and *('am) haqqāhāl*.[28] Although none of these terms is associated with messianic or eschatological expectation, Ps 74.2 (which is adopted in Acts 20.28) may take us a step in this direction: 'Remember thy congregation (MT: *'ēdâ*; LXX: συναγωγή), which thou hast gotten of old, which thou hast redeemed to be the tribe of thy heritage! Remember Mount Zion, where thou hast dwelt'. In addition, one can scarcely dismiss as incredible the idea that Jesus hoped for the eschatological restoration of Israel, for the renewal[29] of God's loyal people, or that he saw the beginnings of revival in the group around him, together with those who had embraced the preaching of the kingdom. Mk 14.58 par., if accepted as dominical, would seem to be decisive; for if Jesus could speak of building a temple not made with hands surely he could have spoken on some other occasion of the new eschatological community which he envisioned. (The objection, raised by many, including Beare, p. 353, that Jesus did not set out to form a sect, that he did not have a remnant mentality, overlooks two crucial facts.[30] First, John the Baptist presents us with the phenomenon of an 'open remnant', that is, 'a remnant of penitents to be saved on the day of judgement, but open to all who would produce "fruit that befits repentance"'.[31] This did not involve rigid particularism or intentional exclusivity. Indeed, in Deutero-Isaiah the remnant exists for the sake of all Israel: a remnant saves (cf. T. W. Manson, *Teaching*, pp. 175–88). Jesus' ministry may be interpreted along similar lines.[32] Secondly, 'if the ministry of Jesus relates to the judgement of Israel, the question of remnant is *ipso facto* posed. It is the eschatology of judgement and restoration that called Judaic remnant groups into being'. Jesus' 'summons to faith is combined with the demand for repentance and set under the sign of judgement. Faith saves from judgement. But faith is an option, an act freely placed, with the antecedent possibility of refusal. The alternative, the refusal of faith, is a real alternative, judgement, a real peril. It is in this perspective that the question of Jesus and the remnant is accurately posed'.[33] Once Jesus began to experience opposition to his person and message some

---

[27] Cf. 'his kingdom' (13.41; 16.28) and 'his angels' (13.41; 16.27; 24.31).

[28] The last four are found in the Dead Sea Scrolls.

[29] Cf. Hort (v), p. 11: 'What He declared that He would build was in one sense old, in another new. It had a true continuity with the Ecclesia of the Old Covenant; the building of it would be *re*building. Christ's work in relation to it would be a completion of it, a bestowal on it of power to fulfil its as yet unfulfilled Divine purposes'. Cf. Acts 15.16, citing Amos 9.11.

[30] For what follows we are indebted to B. F. Meyer, 'Jesus and the Remnant of Israel', *JBL* 84 (1965), pp. 123–30.

[31] Meyer, 'Remnant', p. 127.

[32] See further D. C. Allison, 'Jesus and the Covenant: A Response to E. P. Sanders', *JSNT* 29 (1987), pp. 57–78.

[33] Meyer, 'Remnant', p. 128.

sort of remnant idea was almost inevitable. The message which went out to all was, as the parable of the sower presupposes, only accepted by some—those known from the gospels as 'the poor', 'the babes', the 'few'. No doubt Jesus both hoped and expected that these last would increase in number[34] until 'all Israel' came to faith (cf. Rom 11.26). In the meantime, however, he found himself at the head of a group, however unstructured,[35] which was bound together by firm religious convictions, and we see no good reason to doubt that he could have thought of and referred to that group in remnant terms.)

c. But there is another problem. How could Jesus have spoken of building a community in the future (οἰκοδομήσω) or of giving Peter the keys to the kingdom in the future (δώσω)? Most contemporary interpreters assume that the future tenses reflect the perspective of the post-Easter period. But why is the assumption necessary? Why exclude the possibility that the original meaning was simply 'from this point on I will build'? Compare the future tense in Mk 1.17: 'Come follow me, and I will make you become (ποιήσω ὑμᾶς γενέσθαι) fishers of men'. There is also the possibility that Jeremias is right in interpreting the future tenses as modal imperfects with voluntative significance: 'I intend (from now on) to build', 'I intend (from now on) to give to you the keys of the kingdom of Heaven'.[36] In either case we do not sense a genuine difficulty.

d. Lastly, how can one reconcile the promise to Peter with his rôle in the early church? T. W. Manson was of the opinion that if Mt 16.17–19 were genuine, 'Peter must have enjoyed an authoritative position as ruler of the primitive Church, and that the earliest documents show that no such absolute status was accorded to him' (*Sayings*, p. 203). He goes on to refer to Acts 11 (where Peter has to justify his dealings with the Gentile at Joppa) and Gal 1–2 (where Paul opposes Peter) and affirms: 'there is no satisfactory answer to this objection'. We must demur. Matthew's text, rightly interpreted, neither says nor implies anything about Peter being a 'ruler' with 'absolute status'. Has Manson not allowed later use of the text by papal proponents to colour its meaning for him? Our own suggestion, set forth at various points in the commentary below, is that vv. 17–19, if they should be traced back to Jesus, probably had more to do with Peter's rôle as missionary than with anything else (cf. Cullmann's position). At the same time, one must not underestimate Peter's importance in the early church, an importance consistent with his having been singled out by Jesus for special tasks. Certainly in the

---

[34] Meyer, ibid., p. 130, raises an important point: 'In past discussion of the remnant question, the likely relationship between the theme of the remnant brought to fullness, found in Micah (2.12; 4.7), Isaiah (6.12 [LXX]; 37.31), Jeremiah (3.16) and Ezekiel (36.10–12) and, on the other hand, the gospel's contrast parables or parables of growth imaging the unprepossessing origins of the messianic community and its certain destiny as the vast assembly of the saved, has not yet been examined'.

[35] There is no thought of a separate, organized body with rituals of its own: that is a later development.

[36] J. Jeremias, *TWNT* 3, p. 749.—Note that 'will build' must refer to a process over time, not to an eschatological point in time.

synoptic gospels Peter is without question the most important disciple. He is a spokesman for the others (e.g. Mk 8.29, 23–3; 10.28; 11.21; 14.29; Lk 12.41; cf. Jn 6.68–71). Whenever a select group of disciples is mentioned, Peter is among them (e.g. Mk 1.29, 36; 5.37; 9.2; 13.3; 14.33). Also, only Peter's denial is recorded. What happened to the others we are not told.

When one turns from the gospels to Acts, the picture is much the same; that is, Peter is the outstanding disciple. According to Acts, he was in charge of the election of Matthias (1.15–26); he gave the sermon on the day of Pentecost (2.14–42); he healed a lame beggar in the temple gate called Beautiful and followed this with another sermon (3.1–26); he answered the questions of the Jewish authorities (4.1–22); and he dealt with the deceit of Ananias and Sapphira (5.1–11). Again, the multitudes besought Peter for healing (5.15); those in Jerusalem sent Peter, along with John, to bring the Holy Spirit to those in Samaria (8.14–25); the believers in Joppa requested Peter to come when Tabitha died (9.36–43); and Cornelius the Gentile was instructed by an angel to send for 'one Simon who is called Peter' (10.1–48; cf. 11.1–18). After the death of James the brother of John and his own subsequent arrest, Peter left Jerusalem (12.1–17). His words were these: 'Tell this (the story of Peter's escape from prison) to James and to the brethren'. How exactly James came to his leadership rôle is not for us important. What matters is that, according to Acts, James came to power only after Peter had begun to travel abroad. Before that, Peter was the central figure in the church. Galatians confirms this picture. Paul spoke of this first visit to Jerusalem in this way: 'Then after three years I went up to Jerusalem to consult with Cephas, and remained with him fifteen days. But I saw none of the other apostles except James the Lord's brother' (Gal 1.18–19). This seemingly presupposes that Peter was then the leading man among the apostles. But when writing about his second trip to Jerusalem, Paul used the phrase, 'James, Cephas, and John' (Gal 2.9). This points to James' ascendancy. It does appear to us in any case that Peter's place in the early church, as attested to in Acts and the Pauline epistles, is more than consistent with his having been given by Jesus a very special function.

To conclude the argument: with regard to the authenticity of Mt 16.17–19 there is no oasis of certainty in the sea of scholarly doubt. One can hardly affirm without hesitation that Mt 16.17–19 goes back to Jesus. But it does appear that many of the arguments against a dominical origin are not as persuasive as often thought, and there are weighty points to be made on the other side. The judicious course is to be undogmatic. Mt 16.17–19 *may* preserve the original conclusion to the incident at Caesarea Philippi, and the text *may* give us an important glimpse into the life of Jesus.

13. ἐλθὼν δὲ ὁ Ἰησοῦς εἰς τὰ μέρη Καισαρείας τῆς Φιλίππου.[37] Mk 8.27 begins with καὶ ἐξῆλθεν[38] (sc. from

---

[37] A few mss. have εξελθων, which is due to assimilation in Mark.
[38] Pace Gundry, *Commentary*, p. 328, Matthew's revision hardly gains an allusion to Jesus as the Coming One.

Bethsaida, which Matthew has dropped), has καὶ οἱ μαθηταὶ αὐτοῦ (strictly unnecessary in view of what follows) before εἰς, and reads τὰς κώμας instead of τὰ μέρη (cf. 15.21 diff. Mk 7.24). The last change does not make for any great difference in meaning, for κώμη in the plural and followed by the genitive can refer to 'a larger district, to denote the villages located within it' (BAGD, s.v., citing LXX usage).

Caesarea Philippi[39] was a Gentile town located on a terrace on the southern foot of Mount Hermon,[40] over twenty miles north of the Sea of Galilee. The city was named ἡ Πανεάς (cf. the rabbinic *Panyāys*, *Panyā's*, and *Pamyāys* as well as the modern Banyas) in honour of the god Pan, who there had a cave shrine. Augustus gave it to Herod the Great in 20 B.C. Herod's son, Philip, upon becoming tetrarch of the area, had the city enlarged and renamed, in honour of Augustus[41] and himself. (The double name served to distinguish the place from Caesarea (Maritima) on the coast.) As is indicated by the expressions in Mark and Matthew—'the villages of Caesarea Philippi', 'the district of Caesarea Philippi'—, the city ruled over its surrounding territory (cf. Sherwin-White, p. 127). See further Josephus, *Bell.* 1.404–6; 2.168; 3.509–15; *Ant.* 15.363–4.

For an attempt to link the geography of Caesarea Philippi with the contents of Mt 16.17–19 see Immisch (v). On his view, the rock, the building of the church, and the gates of Hades correspond to the area's rocky cliffs, the nearby temple, and the cave of Pan (cf. Nickelsburg (v), p. 598). For the hypothesis and its reception see Burgess (v).

ἠρώτα τοὺς μαθητὰς αὐτοῦ λέγων. Mk 8.27b begins with ἐν τῇ ὁδῷ (cf. 18.1 diff. Mk 9.34; 20.17 diff. Mk 10.32), continues with ἐπηρώτα (cf. Matthew's preference for the simplex in v. 13a diff. Mk 8.27a and 21.24 diff. Mk 11.29), and follows λέγων with a redundant αὐτοῖς (cf. 15.32 diff. Mk 8.1; 16.8 diff. Mk 8.17; etc.). The dropping of 'in the way' makes the story take place in the region or district of Caesarea Philippi. In Mark the discussion occurs on the way there. In other words, whereas in

---

[39] Lit.: Avi-Yonah, pp. 164–7; Baly, pp. 194–6; Schürer 2, pp. 169–71; G. A. Smith, pp. 303–6.

[40] For the suggestion that Mount Hermon was 'a place where one went for revelation' see Nickelsburg (v), p. 590, citing T. Levi 2.5 and 1 Enoch 6 and 13. Cf. Robinson (v), p. 100, n. 16, citing J. T. Milik, 'Le testament de Lévi en araméen', *RB* 62 (1955), p. 405. It is also possible that Mount Hermon plays a rôle in LAB 40.4, for 'Mount Stelac' could be Mount Hermon: in Tg. Onq. on Deut 3.9 Mount Hermon is 'the mount of snow', and 'Stelac' could represent either the Aramaic *tĕlag* or the Hebrew *šeleg*, words meaning 'snow'. One should note, however, that Mount Hermon may also have had negative connotations. According to 1 En. 6.6 (cf. 2 En. 18), it was the place of an angelic rebellion.

[41] On this Bengel, *ad loc.*, commented: 'Caesarea—this very name, which had not before been given to towns in Palestine, might have warned all that the Jews were subject to Caesar, the sceptre having departed from Judah, and that Messiah had come'.

Mark Jesus is still travelling, in Matthew he has arrived at his destination.[42] Is this just possibly because our evangelist perceived the possible links between Caesarea Philippi and this pericope (see above)?

τίνα λέγουσιν οἱ ἄνθρωποι εἶναι τὸν υἱὸν τοῦ ἀνθρώπου;[43] Mark has με after τίνα and ends with εἶναι.

Why has the First Evangelist substituted 'the Son of man' for 'me'? There are several possible explanations. (i) Perhaps he knew the idiomatic use in Aramaic of 'Son of man' as a self-referent and therefore for him 'the Son of man' and 'me' were for all practical purposes interchangeable (cf. 16.21 diff. Mk 8.31, where Matthew changes 'Son of man' to 'he').[44] (ii) One might simply claim that 'the Son of man' is from M's account of the confession and is not redactional (cf. Borsch, p. 378). (But that would still leave us with the question of why Matthew at this point chose to follow M rather than Mark.) (iii) Perhaps our evangelist wished to create an *inclusio* with 16.27–8, where 'the Son of man' is next used. This might be his way of marking the beginning and end of the section which consists of 16.13–20 + 21–3 + 24–8. (iv) There is also the possibility that the author simply wanted to create a wordplay: οἱ ἄνθρωποι ... τὸν υἱὸν τοῦ ἀνθρώπου. (v) According to Fenton, p. 267, 'the Son of man' by Matthew's time 'had almost ceased to be a title, and became a name, in the same way that Christ became another name for Jesus ...'. On this account, the question in 16.13 would be the equivalent of 'Who do men say that Jesus is?' (We, however, believe that 'the Son of man' was a sort of title for Matthew; see Excursus VI). (vi) Gnilka, *Matthäusevangelium* 2, p. 58, raises the possibility that the apocalyptic idea of the hidden Son of man (1 En. 48.7; 62.7; 69.26) lies in the background. 'The Son of man was concealed from the beginning, and the Most High ... revealed him to the holy and the elect ones'. (vii) Maybe the best guess is that Matthew desired in 16.13–20 to bring together three major christological titles: the Son of man, Messiah, the Son of God. (This might be combined with (vi); see further Meier, *Vision*, p. 110.)

14. In response to Jesus' query, the disciples observe that Jesus has been identified with John the Baptist, with Elijah, with Jeremiah, and with 'one of the prophets'. The common denominator is the prophetic office. No mention is made of the Messiah.

Mt 16.14 = Mk 8.28, which has a very close parallel in Mk 6.14,[45]

---

[42] In his account, Luke omits all mention of Caesarea Philippi.

[43] με follows τινα (again, assimilation to Mark) in D L Θ *f*[1.13] Maj it vg[mss] sy[(s.c).p.h] Ir[lat] Tert: 'Who do men say that I, the Son of man, am?'

[44] See Lindars, *Son of Man*, pp. 115–16.

[45] The relationship between Mk 6.14 and 8.28 is disputed. Theissen, *Stories*, pp. 170–1, argues for the originality of 6.14, Bultmann, *History*, p. 302, for the originality of 8.28. Pesch 2, p. 31, argues for literary independence. See further Guelich, *Mark*, p. 327.

probably presents us with information from the life-time of Jesus (cf. Pesch 1, pp. 335–6). Although there are passages in the gospels where Jesus reminds one of Elijah (see e.g. on 4.18–22), and while early Christians did sometimes think of Jesus as a prophet,[46] the primitive church was more occupied with other christological conceptions. And the conjecture that Jesus was a prophet of one sort or another is just what one would expect from sympathetic Jews of the pre-Easter period.

οἱ δὲ εἶπαν. This shortens the more Semitic Mk 8.28a (οἱ δὲ ἀπεκρίθησαν[47] αὐτῷ λέγοντες).

οἱ μὲν ᾽Ιωάννην τὸν Βαπτιστήν.[48] So Mark, without οἱ μέν. Matthew has added οἱ in order to increase the parallelism with what follows (ἄλλοι, ἕτεροι). μέν . . . δέ* is often redactional.

ἄλλοι δὲ ᾽Ηλίαν. Mark differs in having introductory καί. On Elijah in Jewish messianic speculation see on 3.11 and 17.10–12. John the Baptist was identified by some, including possibly Jesus himself, with Elijah (cf. 11.14; 17.12–13). But Jesus' miracles and his preaching of repentance no doubt reminded many of Elijah[49] and thus encouraged speculation that the Nazarene's ministry should be associated with expectations about the Tishbite.

ἕτεροι δὲ ᾽Ιερεμίαν. These words, which have no parallel in Mark, are either from M or they are a redactional addition. (In favour of the latter possibility, 'Jeremiah' is also redactional in 2.17 and 27.9, and Matthew is the only NT author to name him.)

There would seem to be three explanations for mentioning Jeremiah. (i) The text could be referring to a Jewish eschatological expectation, one which some connected with Jesus. Our sources, however, know nothing of an expected return of the prophet.[50] (ii) Is Jeremiah simply an example or specification for 'one of the prophets', chosen because his book stood at the head of the latter prophets?[51] (iii) More probable is the proposal that certain parallels between Jesus and Jeremiah were noticed by someone (perhaps Matthew). Both Jesus and

[46] For the evidence see Cullmann, *Christology*, pp. 13–50; Longenecker, pp. 32–8.

[47] So D (W) Θ 0143 *f*[13] 28 (33) 565 *pc* lat followed by HG. NA[26] prints οι δε ειπαν αυτω λεγοντες; so ℵ B C² L Δ 892 *pc* k. NA[26] also adds οτι (in brackets) at the end, on the authority of ℵ* B C*[vid] *pc*.

[48] οι μεν is omitted by D W a b d e ff[1,2] g[1] r[1,2]. αλλοι appears in Δ c g² vg[mss]. On the variant, τινες μεν (1 bo? sa? Or?) see Wright (v).

[49] See the commentary on 4.18–22 and 14.13–21; also now W. Roth, *Hebrew Gospel*, Oak Park, 1988.

[50] Cf. SB 1, p. 730. 2 Esdr 2.18 ('I will send you help, my servants Isaiah and Jeremiah') is Christian and probably from the second century.

[51] So Stendahl, 'Matthew', p. 787. Cf. *b. B. Bat.* 14b. Contrast Carmignac (v).

Jeremiah were prophets of judgement and spoke against the temple. Both were associated with Moses and were thought of as having Mosaic traits.[52] Both were figures of suffering, and both were martyrs (see on 23.37 and cf. Menken (v)). There are also several places in the First Gospel where Jesus borrows from the sayings of Jeremiah,[53] and the one prophesied the new covenant instituted by the other.

ἢ ἕνα τῶν προφητῶν. Compare Mk 8.28d: ἄλλοι δὲ ὅτι εἷς τῶν προφητῶν. Matthew's editorial work makes 'one of the prophets' an opinion put forward by those who think Jesus might be Jeremiah. That is, one group of people identifies Jesus with John the Baptist, a second group identifies him with Elijah, and a third group thinks he might be Jeremiah or one of the prophets. On prophets in first-century Judaism see on 11.9.

'Or one of the prophets' makes plain what the three previous identifications have in common. John the Baptist was a prophet (cf. 11.9). Elijah was a prophet. Jeremiah was a prophet. Thus the one fact upon which opinion reportedly concurred was that Jesus was a prophetic figure—an evaluation which Jesus himself evidently shared (cf. Mk 6.4; Lk 13.33).[54]

15. λέγει αὐτοῖς. This abbreviates Mk 8.29a (καὶ αὐτὸς ἐπηρώτα αὐτούς). Compare Lk 9.20a. Asyndetic λέγει (cf. the Aramaic participle 'āmar) is never used in Mark; Matthew, however, has inserted it several times (MHT 4, p. 31).

ὑμεῖς δὲ τίνα με λέγετε εἶναι; So also Mk 8.29b and Lk 9.20b. The 'you', which is in first place, is emphatic.

16. ἀποκριθεὶς δὲ Σίμων Πέτρος εἶπεν. Matthew's text differs from Mark's in having δέ (Mark has asyndeton), Σίμων (Mark has simply 'Peter'), no definite article before Πέτρος, and εἶπεν (Mark has λέγει αὐτῷ; cf. 16.14 diff. Mk 8.28). On 'Simon' and 'Peter' see on 4.18,[55] and on the phenomenon of double names Horsley 1, pp. 89–96. Here 'Simon' has probably been added in anticipation of the tradition cited in v. 17 ('Blessed art thou, Simon bar Jonah . . .').

Because Jesus has asked the disciples what they think, Peter, in his response, has been made out as their spokesman and representative (e.g. by Gundry, *Commentary*, p. 330). Certainly this is the situation in Mark, as well as in Luke. In Matthew, however, all the attention immediately becomes focused on Peter

[52] Cf. Jer 1.4–12 with Exod 3.7–4.17 and Deut 18.18. Note also Liv. Proph. Jer. 19, v. 1.: 'And God bestowed this favour upon Jeremiah . . . so that he might become a partner of Moses'.
[53] Cf. 7.22 with Jer 14.14 and 29.13–14; 11.29 with Jer 6.16; 21.13 with Jer 7.11; 23.34 with Jer 7.25–6; 26.28 with 31.31–4.
[54] Cf. Mk 6.4; Lk 13.33; Fuller, *Christology*, pp. 125–9.
[55] Also the article by Elliot (v).

(vv. 17–19). Note especially the singular μακάριος εἶ. Peter alone is said to be blessed, and he alone is named as the rock upon which the church is to be built. If he were just a spokesman we would instead have statements about the disciples as a group.

σὺ εἶ ὁ χριστός. So also Mark. Lk 9.20 has 'the Christ of God'. On χριστός, its background and meaning in Matthew, see on 1.1. The definite article and the entire context leave no doubt that we have here not a name but a title: 'the Messiah'. This is the first time in Matthew that the disciples have called Jesus 'the Messiah'. But the reader has known the truth from the beginning (1.1, 16–18; 2.4; 11.1–2).

ὁ υἱὸς τοῦ θεοῦ ζῶντος.[56] Compare 2 Βασ. 23.1 (χριστὸν θεοῦ); Mt 14.33; 26.63; 27.40, 43, 54; Mk 14.61; Lk 22.70; Jn 1.49 (where 'Son of God' stands in parallel to 'king of Israel'); 6.69 (see p. 608); and 11.27 (ὁ χριστὸς ὁ υἱὸς τοῦ θεοῦ). The phrase has no parallel in Mark's account of what happened at Caesarea Philippi and thus either comes from Matthew's special source (M) or is a redactional addition perhaps inspired by the tradition of the trial before the Sanhedrin, where Jesus is adjured 'by the living God' to say whether or not he is 'the Christ, the Son of God'.[57]

It has been debated whether 'Son of God', whose truth as applied to Jesus will be confirmed again by the voice at the transfiguration (17.4), is here intended to be a messianic title (in favour of this one could appeal to Hebrew parallelism) or whether it refers instead to the secret, personal relationship Jesus alone has with the Father (cf. 11.27; so the vast majority of commentators). But one is not, on the redactional level, faced with mutually exclusive alternatives. Surely Matthew could have seen in 'Son of God' both messianic associations (cf. 1, p. 263) and a reflection of the unique relationship reflected by 11.27 (cf. our remarks in 1, pp. 339–40).

Concerning the phrase, 'the living God', participial forms of ζάω are often used of God in the NT.[58] The usage, which is also well attested in the LXX[59] and non-canonical Jewish literature,[60] goes back to the Hebrew combination of 'ēl or 'ĕlōhîm with ha(ā)y (cf. the Aramaic 'elāhā' ḥayyā'). The meaning is not primarily that Israel's

[56] D* has του σωζοντος.

[57] On 'Son of God' in the First Gospel see vol. 1, pp. 263–4 and 339–40; also D. C. Allison, 'The Son of God as Israel: A Note on Matthean Christology', *IBS* 9 (1987), pp. 74–81; D. Verseput, 'The Role and Meaning of the "Son of God" Title in Matthew's Gospel', *NTS* 33 (1987), pp. 532–56.

[58] E.g. Acts 14.15; Rom 9.26; 2 Cor 3.3; 6.16; 1 Thess 1.9; 1 Tim 3.15; 4.10; Heb 3.12; Rev 7.2. Cf. Jn 6.57: 'the living Father'.

[59] E.g. 4 βασ 19.4, 16; Ps 41.3; Isa 37.4, 17; Hos 2.1

[60] E.g. Sib. Or. 3.763; T. Job 37.2; Jos. Asen. 11.10; T. Sol. 1.13; 5.12; Philo, *Decal.* 67; *P. Oxy.* 924.11; *PGM* 12.79; *t. Ber.* 7.13.

God alone is alive, pagan gods not alive (cf. 1 Thess 1.9); rather, '"living" is applied to God in the Old Testament and Judaism to stress that God has life in and of himself, and alone gives it to others' (Meier, *Vision*, p. 109). With respect to the present context, Mt 16.16, the 'Son, who stands on the side of God *vis-à-vis* man, shares this quality of "living" so completely that he can promise his community that the powers of death will not prevail against it' (so Meier, *ibid.*). Death has lost its power over the followers of the Son of God, for they are protected by 'the living God'.

Because all the disciples have already confessed Jesus to be the Son of God (14.33; cf. 11.27), one wonders why the present confession is treated as a break-through attributable only to divine revelation. Has Peter done anything more than just reiterate an insight already expressed? One way around the difficulty is to place all the emphasis upon the confession of Jesus as Messiah: Peter is not being praised for his confession of Jesus as the Son of God but for being the first to perceive Jesus' messianic identity (which would entail that the earlier confession was incomplete). But whether one should drive such a clear wedge between the two titles is far from obvious, and certainly most exegetes have not thought of Peter being praised only for part of his confession. A second way around the difficulty is to surmise that the earlier confession of Jesus as the Son of God was not borne of the fullest conviction. Yet of this the text says nothing. Perhaps, then, it is best to explain the inconcinnity in terms of sources. Maybe the fact that there are two confessions of Jesus as Son of God, the second of which is presented as though it were a new or fresh insight, is due to Matthew's imperfect assimilation of his sources, which presented him with two different Son of God confessions.

17. Peter's confession begets a beatitude: Jesus declares Simon blessed. The language recalls 11.27. But whereas there we read of the Son revealing the Father, here the Father has revealed the Son.

There is no reason to regard v. 17 and the two following verses, which have no parallel in Mark or Luke, as the product of post-Matthean interpolation, as some earlier scholars did; see Moffatt, pp. 252–3, and Burgess (v), pp. 42–9, 99–100, 108. The first to doubt the genuineness of the text was apparently F. A. Stroth, in an anonymous article published in 1781, in *Repertorium für biblische und morgenländische Literatur*. (Some of the Church Fathers explained the absence of 16.17–19 from Mark by appealing to Peter's modesty.)

ἀποκριθεὶς δὲ ὁ Ἰησοῦς εἶπεν αὐτῷ. Note the parallelism with v. 16a, upon which the words have been modelled.

μακάριος εἶ, Σίμων Βαριωνᾶ. Compare Deut 33.29; Eccles 10.17; Ps 128.2 (LXX, 127.2 has μακάριος εἶ, for *'ašreykâ*). On beatitudes in the Jesus tradition and elsewhere see Excursus II. For beatitudes directed towards recipients of revelation see also Mt 13.16 = Lk 10.23 (Q); Jn 20.29; 4 Ezra 10.57; and Jos. Asen. 16.14.[61]

---

[61] Discussion in Kähler (v), pp. 46–55. He also cites several late parallels: 3

βαριωνᾶ[62] is the Greek transliteration of the Aramaic *bar yônâ*, 'Son of Jonah'. But in Jn 1.42 Simon is said to have been ὁ υἱὸς Ἰωάν-νου, 'the son of John'. The Gospel of the Hebrews evidently had υἱὲ-Ἰωάννου (= *bar Yôḥānan*), in agreement with the Fourth Gospel. Cullmann, supposing Peter to have been a one-time Zealot, conjectured that Matthew's record is correct on the matter and (following R. Isler) that 'bar-Jonah' derives from an Akkadian word meaning 'terrorist' or 'rebel' (cf. the use of *baryônā'* in *b. Giṭṭ.* 56a and *b. Ber.* 10a). He has not convinced many. More probable is the supposition that Simon, perhaps because there was another Simon in the apostolic band, was called by Jesus 'son of John' or 'son of Jonah'[63] and that Matthew's tradition inadvertently turned 'John' into 'Jonah' (the name of a biblical prophet) or, alternatively, that John's tradition inadvertently turned 'Jonah' into the much more popular 'John'.[64] Certainly there is interchange between the two names in LXX mss.[65] (Whether 'Jonah' was sometimes used as an abbreviation of 'Johanan' is unclear; for discussion see J. Jeremias, *TWNT* 3, p. 410.)

Some have asserted that Matthew himself may have changed 'John' to 'Jonah'. This is Gundry's judgement.[66] He claims that our author desired to associate Simon with 'the sign of Jonah' (12.39; 16.4). There is also the possibility, once one entertains the notion that a redactional motive may be behind the alteration, that Matthew wanted to highlight Peter's status as a true prophet: his confession comes from divine inspiration. Recall that Matthew, in 1.10, may have changed 'Amon' to 'Amos' in order to create an allusion to that OT prophet (cf. 1, p. 77). Recall also that some have thought the Peter of Acts 10, who is at first reluctant to go to the Gentiles, to be modelled in part after the OT's Jonah.[67]

En. 4.9; Memar Marqah 2.9; Gos. Bartholomew 1.8; Apoc. Paul 48–51; Pistis Sophia 19; 38; Gos. Mary BG 10.14ff. He finds in these texts a common scheme involving the delivering of a beatitude by a heavenly figure to a figure from the sacred past and uses this to support the theory that Mt 16.16–19 was originally part of a resurrection story. One must, however, wonder about the date of the soruces noted and observe that the beatitude in Mt 13.16 concerns revelation and is not typically assigned to the risen Lord. Also, Mt 16.13–20 does not recount a vision (in contrast e.g. to 4 Ezra 10.57 and Jos. Asen. 16.14).

[62] Lit.: O. Cullmann, *The State in the New Testament*, New York, 1956, pp. 16–17; Hengel, *Zeloten*, pp. 55–7; H. Hirschberg, 'Simon Barionah and the Ebionites', *JBL* 61 (1942), pp. 171–91; R. Marcus, 'A Note on Bariona', *JBL* 61 (1942), p. 281.

[63] It should be observed that 'Simon son of John' or 'son of Jonah' occurs only three times in the NT, all three times on the lips of Jesus: Mt 16.17; Jn 1.43; 21.15–17; cf. Gos. Heb. frag. 9. Did the tradition rightly remember that this is what Jesus himself called Peter?

[64] 'Jonah' occurs in the OT as the name of the prophet Jonah, in Jub. 34.20 as the name for a woman, and in the Talmud as the name of a few rabbis (all post-Tannaitic; cf. Jastrow, s.v.). 'John', by contrast, was a very popular name. The NT knows five people by that name, and there are many in Josephus.

[65] See the variants for 4 Βασ 25.2; 1 Chron 26.3; 1 Esdr 9.1, 23.

[66] Cf. Goulder, p. 387; Robinson (v), p. 90.

[67] On the parallels between Peter and Jonah in Acts see R. W. Wall, 'Peter,

ὅτι σὰρξ καὶ αἷμα οὐκ ἀπεκάλυψέν σοι. Compare Gal 1.15–16; Ignatius, *Phil.* 7.2 ('I did not know from human flesh'). Note the plural subject ('flesh and blood') with singular verb ('has revealed').

Although *bāśār wādām* does not appear in the MT, 'flesh and blood' came to be a technical term in rabbinic texts meaning 'human agency' in contrast to divine agency. See SB 1, pp. 730–1. Such is its meaning here and in Gal 1.17 ('I did not confer with flesh and blood'). E. Schweizer has rightly written: 'In Mt. 16.17 "flesh and blood" ... denotes man in his limitation *vis-à-vis* God. The reference is not to his mortality but to his inability to know God.... Flesh and blood are not parts of man. They include his intellectual, religious and mystical capacities. The opposite is God' (*TWNT* 7, p. 123).

ἀποκαλύπτω (cf. 10.26; 11.25, 27), which has no object but whose general meaning is plain from the context, should probably here be given its full eschatological content. God has not simply unveiled a secret for Peter's benefit: he has unveiled an *eschatological* secret (cf. the use of the verb in 10.26; Lk 17.30; Rom 1.17–18; 8.18; 1 Cor 3.13; 1 Pet 1.5; 5.1; also Rom 2.5; Thess 1.7; Rev 1.1). Indeed, it may well be that in the background of Mt 16.17 lies the idea of a hidden Messiah (cf. Jn 7.27; Justin, *Dial.* 8.4; 100.1).

'My Father who is in heaven' is usually redactional in the First Gospel (1, p. 76.) But the phrase was almost certainly to hand in Matthew's tradition,[68] and here it provides a neat contrast with the mention of Hades in v. 18; so it may be from M's account of Peter's confession.

18. Jesus continues, giving Simon a new name (Peter, the rock) and speaking for the first time of 'my church', which will be built upon the rock against which the gates of Hades will not prevail. The verse is among the most controversial in all of Scripture. The literature it has generated is immense, and not a little of it rather polemical. For a helpful survey of the history of the discussion see Burgess (v).

There is an OT background to v. 18 which only a few scholars seem to have appreciated.[69] Of the OT figures to receive a second name, the most memorable are Abram and Jacob. The

"Son" of Jonah: the Conversion of Cornelius in the Context of Canon', *JSNT* 29 (1987), pp. 79–90.

[68] Cf. Jeremias, *Prayers*, pp. 30–2 (although not all of his points are persuasive).

[69] But see Ford (v) and the two articles of Chevallier (v). Note also Waetjen, p. 172.

former was given the new name Abraham to signify that he would be the father of a multitude (Gen 17.1–8). The latter was renamed Israel, by which the people that would spring from him would be known (Gen 32.22–32). We find particularly intriguing the parallels between Gen 17 and Mt 16. In both cases we are witnessing the birth of the people of God (the Jews in the one case, the church in the other). In both that birth is associated with one particular individual (Abraham, then Peter), and in both that individual has a name which symbolizes his crucial function (Abraham is taken to mean 'father of a multitude', Peter to mean the 'rock' on which the church is founded). Are we to conclude that the Peter of Mt 16 is the parallel to Abraham?

Strongly buttressing this inference is Isa 51.1–2: 'Hearken to me, you who pursue deliverance, you who seek the Lord; look to the rock from which you were hewn, and to the quarry from which you were digged. Look to Abraham your father and to Sarah who bore you; for when he was but one I called him and I blessed him and made him many': cf. LAB 23.4. Here Abraham, like Peter, is a rock (the MT has ṣûr, the LXX πέτραν). So just as the OT figure whose name was changed in order to signify the coming into being of the people of God was likened to a rock, so too in Matthew is the birth of the church accompanied by Simon gaining the new name, Πέτρος. In this we detect design.

It is crucial in this connexion to note that John the Baptist, in a saying preserved by Matthew, took up Isa 51.1–2 in order to issue a warning to the Jews: 'Do not presume to say to yourselves, "We have Abraham as our father"; for I tell you, God is able from these stones to raise up children to Abraham' (3.9, q.v.). In this saying the Baptist holds forth the possibility that God can bring forth a new people, not from the old rock or quarry (Abraham and Sarah) but from elsewhere. What we seem to have in Mt 16.17–19 is the realization of John's dire prophecy. Here the new people of God is brought into being, hewed not from the rock Abraham but instead founded on the rock Peter.[70]

Compare *Jalqut Shimon*, I § 766, on Num 23.9 (in SB 1, p. 733): when God 'saw Abraham who was going to arise, He said, Behold, I have found a rock (pîṭrāʾ) upon which to build and establish the world. Therefore he named Abraham a rock (ṣûr)' (cf. Isa 51.1–2). We suspect Christian influence because of the lateness of the text and the use of the loanword pîṭrāʾ. But if this supposition is correct, that only goes to show how the rôles of Peter and Abraham lent themselves to comparison.

κἀγὼ δέ σοι. These words do not require that v. 18 was first attached by Matthew to v. 17, for our evangelist never uses

[70] Is it relevant to note that just as Abraham was known not only as the Father of the Jews but also of proselytes (see on 1.1), so too Peter, at least according to Acts, was the first to preach the gospel to the Jews (Acts 2) and helped open the Gentile mission (Acts 10)?

κἀγώ to string together previously unconnected sayings.[71] On the combination καί . . . δέ see BDF § 447.9.

ὅτι σὺ εἶ Πέτρος, καὶ ἐπὶ ταύτῃ τῇ πέτρᾳ οἰκοδομήσω μου τὴν ἐκκλησίαν.[72] Compare 7.24; Eph 2.20; 1 Tim 3.15; Rev 21.14; Od. Sol. 22.12.

'You are Peter' matches 'you are the Christ' (σὺ εἶ in both cases). And just as Peter spoke revelation, so now does Jesus. But does this mean that Peter only now gets his new name? This is the judgement of perhaps most commentators. But Augustine thought otherwise (*De con. ev.* 2.53(109)). Gundry, *Commentary*, p. 335, concurs: 16.17 'probably implies a play on the name as already given rather than a giving of the name at this time. For the latter, we should have expected the future tense, "You will be called"; and repeated earlier references to Simon as "Peter", most of them Matthew's insertions, take away the point of a name-giving here. Otherwise we would have to suppose, doubtfully, that Matthew expects his readers to take all the earlier references as anachronisms'. We are not convinced. Gundry's comment on the future tense is scarcely decisive. Indeed, does not the present tense (σὺ εἶ) point to an event taking place as Jesus speaks? Such an interpretation would not, *pace* Gundry, involve an anachronism. For while Simon is called Peter before 16.17, *he is only called this by the narrator* (cf. the situation with regard to 'Christ'!) No one else in the story uses 'Peter' until 16.17. Furthermore, the first notice of Simon is followed by this: 'who is called Peter' (4.18). The note does not indicate when or why Simon received this name (cf. 10.4). Certainly he does not receive it in 4.18. It is most natural to think that 4.18 looks forward to 16.17, that 16.17 explains a fact 4.18 mentions but leaves unexplained. We are confirmed in this by the parallels between Mt 16.17–19 and Gen 17.1–8 (see above). These gain their full force only when one thinks of 16.17–19 as recounting the giving of a new name.

---

[71] See 10.32, 33 (redactional); 11.28 (M); 16.18; 18.33 (M); 21.24 (once from Mark, once redactional); 26.15 (redactional).

[72] Eusebius in a few places has επι την πετραν (see Zahn, p. 541, n. 65).—Harnack (v), basing his argument on Ephrem, wanted to excise καί . . . ἐκκλησίαν. Nowhere else in the NT is Peter made the church's foundation, and Harnack also thought the αὐτῆς at the end of v. 18 to be awkward. His solution was to conjecture that originally the tradition promised immortality to Peter: 'Thou art Peter, and the gates of Hades will not prevail against *you*'. After Peter died, the prophecy was falsified and was therefore modified by the addition of the clause on the church ('and on this rock I will build my church') and the alteration of σου (Peter) into αὐτῆς (the church). Although Harnack's hypothesis was at one time accepted by some, it no longer can claim many adherents. Cf. Burgess (v), pp. 97–99. For effective criticism see Zahn, pp. 725–30.

As we know from Jn 1.42 and the Pauline epistles,[73] behind Πέτρος (and also, probably, πέτρα) lies the Aramaic kephāʾ, a word which is usually said to mean 'rock'.[74] But it has been argued that the first meaning of the Aramaic kephāʾ was 'stone' (cf. λίθος and the first meaning of πέτρος). Lampe (v), with this as his starting point, claims that when Jesus gave Simon the nickname Kephāʾ, he could not have been thinking of a rock foundation. In his estimation, Jesus gave Peter the nickname 'stone' for reasons we can only guess, but which were probably not theological or religious. It was only in the post-Easter period, and only after Kephāʾ had already been translated by Πέτρος, that a wordplay was conceived with πέτρα, and the apostle made out to be the foundation of the church. All this falls far short of proof. For one thing, Lampe (who wrongly asserts that kephāʾ was not a personal name in pre-Christian times; see 1, p. 396), has evidently failed to consider the possibility that Jesus on one occasion gave Simon the name Kephāʾ and then, on a later occasion, used that name (with perhaps slightly different sense) to make a theological statement.[75] Even if the first meaning of kephāʾ was 'stone', it also, as the Dead Sea Scrolls and the targumim show, meant 'rock' (cf. Fitzmyer (v), p. 115); and this fact could have allowed Jesus to play upon kephāʾ in the manner Mt 16.18 recounts. No less importantly, Lampe (v) seems to assume that it would be awkward to speak of building upon a stone instead of a rock; but the image behind Mt 16.18 is of a temple being constructed, and in Judaism the temple was founded not upon a rock but upon a (foundation) stone, the ʾeben šĕtîyyâ (cf. the use of ʾeben/λίθον in Isa 28.16).

As we have just observed, Simon may, notwithstanding Matthew's point of view, have been given his nickname for purely secular purposes. This would line up with what we find in rabbinic sources, where certain teachers give their students nicknames that reflect character or appearance.[76] But it is no less probable that the name Kephāʾ was given to make a theological point (cf. Mt 16.18). In Jewish tradition the giving of a new name could mark an important event or a change in someone's status. Examples include the renaming of Abraham (Gen 17.5), Sarah (Gen 17.15), Jacob (Gen 32.28), Jerusalem (Isa 62.2–4; cf. Zech 8.3; Bar 5.4), the conquering saints (Rev 2.17; cf. Isa 65.15), and Aseneth (Jos. Asen. 15.7). Also not to be forgotten are the OT texts in which a prophet bestows a name in order to register publicly a theological conviction. See, for example, Isa 7.3; 8.3–4; Jer 20.1–6; and Hos 1.4–9. Prophets used names in parabolic fashion (note also Isa 7.14; 9.6; Jer 23.6; Zech 6.12). This matters because Jesus conceived of himself as, among other things, a prophet, and he not only uttered

[73] See 1 Cor 1.12; 3.22; 9.5; 15.5; Gal 1.18; 2.9, 11,14.

[74] Notwithstanding patristic writers there is no connexion between Kephāʾ and κεφαλή = caput; see on this Y. Congar, 'Cephas—Céphalè—Caput', Revue du moyen âge latin 8 (1952), pp. 5–42.

[75] Neither Jn 1.42 nor Mk 3.16 intends to say anything about the time or circumstance of Peter's getting a new name; and Matthew's point of view cannot answer the historical question.

[76] See SB 2, pp. 5–6; Lampe (v), p. 239.

parables but performed parabolic acts in the prophetic vein.[77] One must wonder whether the naming of Peter or the symbolic application of his name should not therefore be considered a prophetic act. (It is also possible that 'sons of Thunder', the name given to the sons of Zebedee, originally had some theological or prophetic significance now lost. This is made more likely by the fact that Peter and James and John, the only three to have received nicknames as far as we know, appear to have formed an inner circle during the earthly ministry.)

καὶ ἐπὶ ταύτῃ τῇ πέτρᾳ has been the object of much heated debate and much wasted ingenuity. 'This rock' has been identified variously with Peter's faith or confession,[78] with Peter's preaching office,[79] with the truth revealed to Peter,[80] with the twelve apostles,[81] with Jesus,[82] with Jesus' teaching,[83] and even with God himself.[84] All this is special pleading. The most natural interpretation is that of Roman Catholic tradition: the rock is Peter. 'The word-play, and the whole structure of the passage, demands that this verse is every bit as much Jesus' declaration about Peter as v. 16 was Peter's declaration about Jesus' (France, *Matthew*, p. 254). The only sound cause for objecting to this is that one might have expected Πέτρος ... πέτρῳ instead of Πέτρος ... πέτρᾳ. Why two different Greek words, one masculine, one feminine? An explanation probably lies in this, that *kephā'*, the Aramaic presumably behind both Πέτρος and πέτρᾳ, 'was used with different nuances. When translated into Greek, the masculine form *petros* would lend itself as a more likely designation of a person (Simon), and a literary variant, the feminine *petra*, for an aspect of him that was to be played upon.'[85]

It is possible that there is a mythological background to the imagery of the rock. 'My church', interpreted in the light of 2 Sam 7 (see p. 603), evokes the idea of a temple, and the conception of the people of God as a temple was well known in both Judaism and early Christianity.[86] This is important because in Jewish tradition the rock at the base of the temple on Zion, the so-called *'eben šětîyyâ*, is at the

[77] See Jeremias, *Parables*, pp. 227–9.
[78] So Ambrose, Chrysostom, the Nestorians generally, Calvin, Zwingli, and John Locke.
[79] So Melanchthon; see Cullmann, *Peter* (v), p. 168.
[80] So McNeile, p. 241.
[81] So Hort (v), pp. 16–17.
[82] So e.g. Origen, Augustine, and Luther; so also Wilcox (v), for the hypothetical pre-Matthean tradition he reconstructs.
[83] For this last see esp. Gundry, *Commentary* p. 334, making the most of the parallel with 7.24–7. Contrast Zahn, pp. 541–6.
[84] Knight (v) urges that the rock is God-in-Christ.
[85] So Fitzmyer (v), p. 119, citing Gander (v).
[86] See esp. Gärtner, passim.

centre of the world.[87] It links heaven and the underworld, being the
gate to the former as well as the portal to Hades, the realm of the
dead. Note that in 16.18c mention is made of the 'gates of Hades'.
Perhaps, then, the informed reader should imagine the church at the
centre of the cosmos, sitting on top of the powers of evil.

οἰκοδομέω, associated elsewhere in the NT with ἐκκλησία
only in 1 Cor 14.4,[88] is used again in both 26.61 (from Mk
14.58) and 27.40 (from Mk 15.29), where people claim that
Jesus threatened to tear down the temple (ναός) and then
rebuild it or raise it up (οἰκοδομέω). What is the relationship
between the three verses? The key is the evangelist's treatment
of Mk 14.58, from which he has omitted 'not made with hands'.
This last is usually, and rightly, taken to refer to the Christian
community.[89] Why its omission by Matthew? One can scarcely
maintain that he rejected the conception of the church as a
temple (it is implicit in 16.18). Rather, Mk 14.58, interpreted of
the church, might be thought to put its founding in the post-
Easter period ('after three days'), which would create tension
with Mt 16.18, which places the church's birth before the
resurrection.[90] The difficulty was solved by modifying Mk 14.58
so that one thinks more readily of Jesus alone being raised up
(cf. Jn 2.19–22) instead of the Christian community. (Perhaps
Matthew felt justified in his editing by the circumstance that
Mk 14.58 is attributed to false witnesses and could therefore
reasonably be held to be a misunderstanding or misrep-
resentation of something Jesus said.)

For other texts in which a community or group of people is spoken
of as being built see Jer 12.16; 18.9; 31.4 ('I will build you, and you
shall be built, O virgin Israel'); 33.7; 42.10; Amos 9.11 ('In that day I
will raise up the booth of David that is fallen and repair its breaches,
and raise up its ruins, and rebuild it as in the days of old'); 4QpPs[a]
frags. 1–10, col. 3.15–16 (God chose the teacher of righteousness as a
pillar and 'established him to build for him a congregation . . .');
4QpIsa[d] (= 4Q164); 1 Cor 3.9–15; Eph 2.19–20; SB 1, pp. 723–3. Such
usage was natural given the likening of the people of God to both temple[91]

---

[87] See Davies, *GL*, p. 8, n. 10, and lit. cited there.
[88] For οἰκοδομή with ἐκκλησία see 1 Cor 14.5, 12.
[89] See Juel, pp. 144–57.
[90] The future tense ('*will build* my church') might refer to the post-Easter
period; but the foundation for the building is already laid in the pre-Easter
period. 16.16–19 is not just a picture of things to come. Rather, it records an
inauguration.
[91] See esp. 1QS 5.5–7; 8.4–7; 8.8–10; 9.3–6; CD 3.18–4.10; 1QpHab 12.3 (in
this last Lebanon = temple). Discussion in Gärtner, passim, and G. Klinzing,
Das Umdeutung des Kultus in der Qumrangemeinde und im Neuen Testament,
Göttingen, 1971.

and house (cf. the phrase, 'house of Israel').[92]

ἐκκλησία[93] occurs only twice in the canonical gospels, here and in 18.18. It is disputed whether Jesus could have used some Semitic equivalent (on this see pp. 612–4). As the word is used in Matthew it has two slightly different meanings. In 16.18 the universal church is in view, in 18.18 the local assembly (cf. the apparent fluctuation in Acts and the Pauline epistles).[94] In the LXX, from Deuteronomy on, ἐκκλησία is the equivalent of *qāhāl*, which means according to BDB, s.v., 'assembly, convocation, congregation'. It never stands for *'ēdâ*, which is usually rendered by συναγωγή. It is doubted whether the background to early Christian usage is to be found in the LXX, and it must be conceded that the NT uses of ἐκκλησία sometimes lack LXX parallels. Still, most scholars would concur with Bultmann that 'in content "Church (of God)" ἐκκλησία (τοῦ Θεοῦ) corresponds ... with *qhl* (*YHWH*)', and 'in understanding themselves as Congregation or Church the disciples appropriate to themselves the title of the Old Testament Congregation of God, the *qĕhal-YHWH*' (*Theology* 1, p. 38).[95] In line with this, the early Christians— like the Qumran convenantors, who spoke of their community as the *qĕhal* (*'El*)[96]—thought of themselves as a counterpart to the Sinai-Congregation (cf. 1 Cor 10.1–5; Heb 12.18–24), which in Deuteronomy is called the ἐκκλησία (e.g. 4.10; 9.10; 18.16; 31.30; cf. Philo, *Ebr.* 213; *Decal.* 32). That Matthew himself perceived the connexion we need not doubt. The typology that runs through chapters 1–5 (see on 5.1–2) and the numerous parallels between Jesus and Moses entail that the church had its origin in a new exodus.[97]

Despite the previous paragraph, it should be observed that in Matthew the church is not characterized as being τοῦ Θεοῦ. Jesus

---

[92] For 'house' as community see 4QpPs[a] 1–10 ii 14; 1 Tim 3.15; Heb 3.1–6; 1 Pet 2.5; 4.17; Hermas, *Sim.* 9.13.9; 9.14.1; SB 3, pp. 683–84.

[93] Lit.: J. Barr, *The Semantics of Biblical Language*, Oxford, 1961, pp. 119–29; K. Berger, 'Volksversammlung und Gemeinde Gottes', *ZTK* 73 (1976), pp. 167–207; J. Y. Campbell, 'The Origin and Meaning of the Christian Use of the Word *Ekklesia*', *JTS* 49 (1948), pp. 130–42; N. A. Dahl, *Das Volk Gottes*, 2nd ed., Darmstadt, 1963; Hort (v); Johnson (v); Kümmel (v); Linton (v); O. Linton, *RAC* 4, pp.905–21; I. H. Marshall, 'New Wine in Old Wineskins: V. The Biblical Use of the Word Ἐκκλησία', *ExpT* 84 (1973), pp. 359–64; W. Schrage, '"Ekklesia" und "Synagogue"', *ZTK* 60 (1963), pp. 178–202.

[94] As to whether the universal or the particular meaning came first, perhaps most suppose the particular did; but a firm decision cannot in truth be reached.

[95] See further Linton and Berger, as in n. 93.

[96] 1QM 4.10; 1QSa 2.4; CD 7.17; 11.22; 12.6.

[97] The old view that ἐκκλησία should be understood according to its etymology and so means 'those called out' should probably be abandoned.

speaks rather of 'my church'. For Matthew the community belongs to God *through Jesus*.

καὶ πύλαι ᾅδου οὐ κατισχύσουσιν αὐτῆς. Compare Isa 28.15–19 (where the cornerstone laid in Zion will withstand the assault of water while those who have made a covenant with Sheol and death will be swept away) and 1QH 6.19–31 (here the speaker has journeyed to the gates of death but finds refuge in a city founded on a rock). The notion that the underworld or the realm of the dead was locked by gates was common in the Ancient Near East and appears already in the Epic of Gilgamesh. Note Homer, *Od.* 14.156, and Diogenes Laertius 8.34–5 (quoting Aristotle).[99]

The spectrum of opinion on these words, which in the early church were so often used against heretics, and which later came to serve as an apology for tradition,[100] is unusually broad. Among the various proposals we note the following:

(i) Harnack (v), holding 'on this rock I will build my church' to be an interpolation (see n. 72), argued that the original text had σου instead of αὐτῆς and thus took the whole line to be a promise of immortality to Peter. In favour of this, such an interpretation makes for a good connexion with 16.28 ('there are some standing here who will not taste death . . .'),[101] and it would go some way towards explaining why Mark or Mark's tradition dropped 16.17–19: the prophecy had been shown false by Peter's death (cf. Otto (v)). There is also the fact that Jn 21.20–3 reflects the conviction that one or more of Jesus' disciples would live to the consummation (see the commentaries). There is, however, no textual justification for the suggested emendation, and one does not wish to 'correct' the text unless it is otherwise unintelligible.[102]

(ii) B. P. Robinson (v), although he does not accept Harnack's textual reconstruction, follows Harnack in finding a promise of immortality: αὐτῆς refers back to Peter (ταύτῃ τῇ πέτρᾳ), not the church. That the apostle was dead when Matthew composed his gospel is no objection to this interpretation but rather proof that Matthew thought in terms of successors to Peter. The promise, in other words, is not spoken to Peter as such but to Peter as holder of a particular office.[103]

[98] That Matthew and other early Christians preferred ἐκκλησία over συναγωγή might be explained by the constant use of the latter in connexion with Jewish gatherings. And yet, despite the pejorative usage in Rev 2.9 and 3.9 ('synagogue of Satan') and elsewhere, συναγωγή could still be used of Christian gatherings (Jas 2.2; Ignatius, *Polyc.* 4.2; Hermas, *Mand.* 11.9; Lampe, s.v.).

[99] See further the texts and secondary lit. referred to by A. Cooper, 'Ps 24.7–10: Mythology and Exegesis', *JBL* 102 (1983), pp. 48–9.

[100] E.g. against the iconoclasts it was argued that if the use of images were wrong, then the gates of Hades had in fact prevailed against the church; cf. John V of Jerusalem, *Icon.* 16.

[101] Cf. Origen, *Comm. on Mt.* 12.33 (commenting on 16.28 he contends that Peter will be spared spiritual death and cites 16.18).

[102] See further Euringer (v), pp. 141–56, and above, n. 72.

[103] We note two possible objections. (i) It is not clear that the αὐτῆς of v. 18

(iii) Bousset, p. 65, associated 16.18 with the tradition of Christ's descent into hell: 'The company of the righteous who have fallen asleep also belongs to the ecclesia triumphans. The gates of Hades are opened and they no longer hinder passage to freedom'.[104] One must agree with Bultmann, *History*, p. 139, n. 2: 'apart from the fact that the descent into Hades is nowhere hinted at in the text, it is not possible to see any connexion between the bursting of the gates of Hades by Christ's descent into hell, and the phrase οὐ κατισχύσουσιν: the Church had not been imprisoned in Hades!'

(iv) McNeile, in his commentary, *ad loc.*, cites the first passion prediction (16.21) as well as Acts 2.24 and 31 and goes on to find an allusion to Jesus' resurrection: 'The *ecclesia* is built upon the Messiahship of her Master, and death, the gates of Hades, will not prevail against her by keeping Him imprisoned'. C. Brown (v) puts forward a similar view, stressing that Mt 16.19 is in truth a passion prediction. We wonder, however, whether the meaning can be so far beneath the surface of the text, which does not directly speak of Jesus himself.

(v) Schlatter, pp. 509–10, contends that the general resurrection is in view. The gates which, in the past, let people in and never out will, in the end, not hold those Christ has saved (cf. Ep. Apost. 28). The main difficulty with this interpretation is that it does not do justice to κατισχύσουσιν, which most naturally connotes an advancing force (see below).

(vi) Gero (v), following the textual tradition of certain Syriac mss., urges that our line was originally about the 'bars', that is, 'levers' of Hades. The verse simply promises that Peter, the rock, will not be dislodged from his place, even by the powers of Hades. The church's foundation is immovable. The consensus of the Greek textual tradition, however, is not to be disregarded unless there are truly compelling reasons. This is why we also cannot follow Köbert (v). He accepts the Syriac evidence but equates *mûklê* with prison bars.

(vii) Another suggested emendation has come from A. Pallis[105] and Eppel (v). They believe 'gatekeepers' (*šō'ărê*, πυλωροί; cf. LXX Job 38.17b; 2 En. 42.1; *b. Ḥag.* 15b) should be read instead of 'gates'.

(viii) According to Gundry, *Commentary*, p. 335, 'the gates of Hades' particularly represent 'death by martyrdom'. The promise is that the church will not be obliterated by persecution. But the equation of 'the gates of Hades' with 'death by martyrdom' is, *pace* Gundry, hardly established by the prominence of persecution in the First Gospel.

(ix) According to L. E. Sullivan (v), our text pictures the church on the attack, reaching into Hades to draw up its members. Is it, however, natural to see the church—which in this context is depicted as a building—as the aggressor?

refers to Peter himself instead of the church. (ii) If there is anything at all to our comparison of Peter with Abraham, the latter was not perceived as the holder of an office. His place in salvation-history was unprecedented and unique, without follower.

[104] For like-minded others see Burgess (v), pp. 105–6. Acts of Thomas 8 (p. 115) borrows from Mt 16.16 the title, 'Christ, Son of the living God', in the middle of a discussion of the descent *ad inferos*. Also relevant is Od. Sol. 42.

[105] A. Pallis, *Notes on St. Mark and St. Matthew*, London, 1932, *ad loc.*

(x) In Allen's words, 16.18c could mean that 'the organised powers of evil shall not prevail against the organised society which represents My teaching' (*Matthew* p. 176). This accords with the dominant trend in Roman Catholic interpretation and makes for a good connexion with v. 19, which can be taken to concern Peter's teaching authority.

(xi) Perhaps most contemporary expositors would concur with Schweizer, *Matthew*, p. 342: 16.18 simply 'states unequivocally that death with all its power cannot put an end to the Christian community'. The church will endure until the end of the world (cf. SB 1, p. 736). This interpretation has in its favour the OT equation of 'gates of Sheol' with 'gates of death' (the older expression);[106] and it can appeal to Prov 1.12 and Isa 5.14, where the image of Hades swallowing victims is an image of death: this is rather close to Mt 16.18's depiction of an active Hades. (Most exegetes holding this view remark that 'gates' is to be understood as an example of synecdoche, the part (the gates) standing for the whole (Hades). As to why then 'the gates of Hades' is used instead of 'the powers of Hades' or just 'Hades', the answer lies in v. 19, where the mention of 'keys' inevitably conjures up the image of gates or doors. In other words, both vv. 18 and 19 have to do with doors or gates.)

(xii) In the judgement of Jeremias, *TWNT* 6, pp. 923–7, 'the gates of Hades' refers not to the realm of the dead but to the ungodly powers of the underworld which will assail the church[107] in the latter days. Citing passages for comparison from Revelation (6. 8; 9.1ff.; 20.3, 7–8) and 1QH 5.20ff., he takes the text to mean that church will emerge triumphant from the eschatological assaults of evil. Compare Bultmann, *History*, p. 139: 'in the end, when the powers of the underworld overcome mankind, the Church will be saved'.[108]

In the attempt to come to a conclusion of our own, the following points are to be borne in mind. To begin with, we have already stated objections to interpretations (i)–(ix). These may be eliminated. Next, while it might be argued that the structure of vv. 17–19 requires that αὐτῆς refers to πέτρα and thus Peter, this is not a decisive observation: the rules about parallelism are nowhere carved in stone. Further, as Zahn, p. 548, noted long ago, the nearness of αὐτῆς to ἐκκλησία favours connecting the two, as does the common sense observation that the 'gates of Hades' must direct themselves against the whole church, not just a part of it. The RSV supplies the correct translation: 'prevail

---

[106] Pertinent texts include Job 17.16; 38.17; Ps 9.13; 107.18; Isa 38.10; Jon 2.7; Wisd 16.13; 3 Macc 5.51; Ecclus 51.9 (Heb.). Revelation couples 'Hades' with 'death' in 1.18; 6.8; 20.13–14; and in 2 Macc 5.51, πρὸς πύλαις ᾅδου καθεστῶτας means to stand at death's door (cf. 1QH 6.24; Ps. Sol. 16.2).

[107] He claims that while αὐτῆς formally refers to πέτρα, materially it refers to the church built upon the rock.

[108] For related analyses see Betz (v) (stressing the Qumran parallels); Hiers (v), pp. 242–3; and C. K. Barrett, *Church, Ministry, and Sacraments in the New Testament*, London, 1985, pp. 17–18. Dublin (v) came to a similar conclusion by positing an original *sa'ar* (= storm) instead of *ša'ar* (= gate).

against it' (sc. the church).[109] In the third place, although 'gates of Hades' is a fixed expression in the OT one must beware of reading the OT meaning into Matthew's text, for conceptions about Hades and Sheol changed over time. By the first century there was a tendency to think of Hades or certain sections of it as an underworld peopled not by the dead in general but by the *ungodly* dead, as well as by demons and evil spirits.[110] The simple equation of Hades with death probably does not hold for Mt 16.18. Fourthly, nothing stands in the way of viewing 'gates' as an instance of synecdoche: the 'gates' stand for the city and its inhabitants (cf. above). Furthermore, there are ancient texts which blur the distinction between 'gates'[111] and 'gate keepers'.[112] Lastly, πύλαι + κατισχύω[113] is not a recognized idiom (which is another reason for doubting that one can simply appeal to the OT usage of 'gates of Hades'). But in the LXX the verb is always active when followed by the genitive.[114] This means that the gates of Hades should be understood as *active*: the church on the rock is suffering an onslaught (cf. 7.24–7).

Taking everything into consideration, we do not wish to rule out interpretations (x) and (xi). But interpretation (xii) seems to us to be the best choice. One should probably think of the end-time scenario, when the powers of the underworld will be unleashed from below, from the abyss, and rage against the saints (cf. 1 En. 56.8; Rev 6.8; 11.7; 17.8). The promise is that even the full fury of the underworld's demonic forces will not overcome[115] the church. One may compare Rev 9.1–11, where the demonic hosts, under their king Abaddon, come up from the bottomless pit to torment humanity. They prevail against all save those with the seal of God. Also worth comparing is 1QH

[109] Cf. Lagrange, p. 327; Cullmann, *Peter*, p. 53.

[110] The NT is not alone in sometimes merging the idea of Sheol (=Hades, the realm of the dead) with the idea of Gehenna (the place of eschatological torment; see on 5.22). Cf. W. J. P. Boyd, 'Gehenna—According to J. Jeremias', in Livingstone, pp. 9–12. Relevant texts: 1 En. 22.1–14; 51.1; 103.5–8; Jub. 22.22; Luke 16.19–31; Josephus, *Bell.* 3.374–5. For the underworld as the home of fallen angels or evil spirits see Jub. 5.10; 2 Pet 2.4; Jude 6. Note that ἄβυσσος (cf. the Heb. *těhôm*) was used of both the realm of the dead (e.g. LXX Ps 70.20; 106.26; Rom 10.7) and the realm of the devil, demons, or evil spirits (e.g. 1 En. 21.1–10; 88.1–3; Lk 8.31; Rev 9.1–2, 11; 11.7; 17.18; 20.1–3).

[111] Gates are personified in Ps 24.7, 9 ('Lift up your heads, O gates!'); Isa 3.26 (Zion's gates lament and mourn); and Jer 14.2 (Judah's gates languish).

[112] For the gatekeepers or guardians see LXX Job 38.17b (a correct interpretation of the MT?); 2 En. 42.1; *b. Ḥag.* 15b. Cf. Sib. Or. 8.122.

[113] NT: 3, in Mt 16.18; Lk 21.36; 23.23. The word appears about a hundred times in the LXX, most often for a form of *ḥāzaq*.

[114] Cf. T. Dan. 5.2; T. Jos. 6.7; T. Reub. 4.11.

[115] In T. Reub. 4.11 κατισχύω is used of Belial, in Acts 19.16 of evil spirits. Recall also the description of Satan as ἰσχυρός in Mk 3.27 par.

6.22–9. In this the author faces the gates of death but is delivered by entering a fortified city founded on a rock: and the whole context is the great eschatological conflict.[116]

If Mt 16.18 be traced back to Jesus, it may have concerned Peter's rôle as eschatological missionary. By adding members one builds a community. Thus in making Peter the foundation of the emerging community, Jesus was announcing his pre-eminence as a 'fisher of men'. Congruent with such a proposal is, first, the fact that Peter was, to judge from Acts, the evangelist *par excellence* in the primitive community and, secondly, the fact that Peter felt impelled to live his life as a missionary, moving on from Jerusalem to other places.[117] As for the meaning of 'and the gates of Hades shall not prevail against it' (see above), these words harmonize with the other promises in which Jesus foresees at least some of his disciples survivng to the end, despite eschatological tribulation (see on 10.23 and 16.28).

19. καὶ δώσω σοι τὰς κλεῖδας τῆς βασιλείας τῶν οὐρανῶν.[118] Compare Isa 22.22 (on this see below); Rev 1.18 and 3.7 (Jesus has the keys of Death and Hades as well as the key of David); 3 Bar 11.2 (the angel Michael is the 'holder of the keys of the kingdom of Heaven'; cf. Par. Jer. 9.5); 3 En. 18.18 ('Anapi'el YHWH the prince keeps the keys of the palaces of the heaven of Arabot); 48 C 3 (Metatron has the keys to the treasure chamber of heaven); *PGM* 3.541 ('the keys of the triangular paradise of earth, which is the kingdom'). Heaven was conceived of as having gates or doors (cf. 1 En. 9.2).[119] It is not obvious, however, that we have in Mt 16.19 that image.[120] For in the synoptics 'the kingdom of Heaven' is not equated with the heavenly world. This is why Jeremias construes 'the βασιλεία τῶν οὐρανῶν, whose key Peter holds, as the royal dominion of God in the last time' and, in our judgement rightly, proposes tht 'if a concrete image lies behind the phrase τὰς κλεῖδας τῆς βασιλείας τῶν οὐρανῶν, we should think of the gates of the future city of God' (*TWNT* 3, pp. 748–9 and n. 55; cf. Rev 21.12–13, 15, 21, 25). (If 'kingdom of Heaven' has replaced an original

---

[116] See further Betz (v).

[117] Acts has Peter in Jerusalem, Samaria, in Lydda, in Joppa, and in Caesarea (1–5; 8.14; 9.32, 38–9; 10.23–4), and the tradition that he made it to Rome merits assent; see W. O'Connor, *Peter in Rome*, New York, 1969. Cf. also 1 Cor 9.5. Did Peter visit Corinth?

[118] καὶ (so HG) is found in B² C*.³ L W *f*¹³ Maj syʰ boᵖᵗ Eus. NA²⁶ omits, following ℵ B* C² D *f*¹ 33 *pc* ff¹ saᵐˢ mae. δε is supported by Θ 1424 *pc* saᵐˢˢ boᵖᵗ. There is also some disagreement as to the order of σοι and δωσω.—In Rev 1.18 the accusative plural of κλείς is κλεῖς instead of κλεῖδας; cf. Mt 16.19 ℵ² B² C D *f*¹·¹³ Maj.

[119] For the gates of paradise see T. Levi 18.10.

[120] An image which is behind the popular picture of Peter standing at the gates of heaven, deciding who should and should not be permitted entry.

'temple' (as perhaps in v. 18), then it would be pertinent to remark that 'keys of the temple' or 'sanctuary' was a known expression: 2 Bar. 10.18; Par. Jer. 4.4.)

Does v. 19a have the same sense as vv. 19b and c, so that to have the keys is simply to have the power to bind and loose, or are binding and loosing instead instances of the exercise of the wider authority indicated by 19a? If possession of the keys means the power to bind and loose, then one may urge that Peter is promised no more than the other disciples, for in 18.18 the power to bind and loose is clearly held by others. But if v. 19a is broader in scope, then one can make the case for Peter having a unique function (cf. Vatican II, Dogmatic Constitution on the Church, 3.22). In our estimation, it is most natural to think of v. 19a as being explicated by what follows: to have the keys is to have the power to bind and loose. Further, 19a and vv. 19b–c probably have to do with teaching authority (for the connexion between keys and teaching see Lk 11.52; *Sipre* on Deut 32.25; *b. Šabb.* 31a–b; for 'binding' and 'loosing' as metaphors for halakhic decisions see below). We do, however, still insist that Peter is not thereby put on the same level as his fellow disciples. It remains true that only he is explicitly said to have the keys. More significantly, v. 19 cannot be isolated from vv. 17 and 18, and in these last Peter is spoken of in terms not applicable to anyone else. Also, it should not be overlooked that whereas 18.18 concerns the local community or assembly, 16.19 is about the church universal (cf. v. 17); hence the authority bestowed in 16.19 is implicitly wider than that given in 18.18. For these reasons, then, we are not persuaded that the existence of 18.18, with its more general promise of the authority to bind and loose, diminishes Peter's prominence. If the power to bind and loose was also given to others, that does not entail that those others exercised their power in quite the same way as did Peter, or that they too held the keys of the kingdom. See further Excursus XIV, p. 650.

καὶ ὃ ἐὰν δήσῃς ἐπὶ τῆς γῆς ἔσται δεδεμένον ἐν τοῖς οὐρανοῖς, καὶ ὃ ἐὰν λύσῃς ἐπὶ τῆς γῆς ἔσται λελυμένον ἐν τοῖς οὐρανοῖς. Compare 18.18 and Jn 20.23; also Job 38.31 ('Can you bind the chains of the Pleiades, or loose the cords of Orion?'); Josephus, *Bell.* 1.111 ('the real administrators of the state, at liberty to banish and to recall, to loose and to bind': λύειν τε καὶ δεσμεῖν).

What, for Matthew, is the meaning of the juridic 19b–c? The giving of keys manifestly means the bestowing of authority; to have keys means to have power, to be in control (cf. Rev 1.18; 2 En. 40.9–11; *b. Sanh.* 113a). Beyond that, exegetical disagreement reigns. As with v. 18dc, one can list a host of competing interpretations.

(i) Because 'binding' and 'loosing' are, in intertestamental literature, most frequently associated with exorcism,[121] one might see 16.19 as

---

[121] E.g. T. Levi 18.12 and T. Sol. 1.14. See Hiers (v).

assigning to Peter power over demons (cf. 10.8; Lk 10.17–19). This can only be a suggestion with regard to the historical Jesus or a pre-Matthean stage (cf. Hiers (v)). As compared with Mark, Matthew is much less interested in Jesus' activity as exorcist.[122] More importantly, the Matthean context does not suggest exorcism; and in any case, while one can conceive of Jesus giving Peter the power to bind demons, can we think of him giving Peter the power to loose them? Or are we to take the binding clause to refer to the binding of demons, the loosing clause to the loosing or freeing of human beings?

(ii) One could contend that Peter is being told that his judgements about people in the present will determine their destiny at the last judgement (cf. Schweitzer, *Quest*, p. 371); or that he has the authority to determine who goes to heaven, who to hell (cf. Falk (v)). With this 19.28 might be held consistent. But where else is the terminology of binding and loosing used in connexion with the eschatological assize?

(iii) Some have taken 16.18 to give Peter the authority to forgive or not forgive sins (perhaps in a baptismal setting).[123] In favour of this, appeal has been made not only to Jn 20.23 but also to the targumic expression, 'loose and forgive'.[124] Already in the LXX λύω can mean—as it does so often in the church Fathers—'forgive' (e.g. Job 42.9–10). Particularly striking is a passage in Tg. Neof. Gen 4.7: 'If you perform your deeds well in this world, it shall be loosed and forgiven (*yeštĕrê wĕyeštĕbeq*) you in the world to come. But if you do not perform your deeds well in this world, your sin shall be retained (*nĕṭîr*) for the day of judgement'. We find no insuperable objection to interpreting Mt 16.19 in terms of forgiveness. If it were not for the fact that another interpretation has even more in its favour (see below), we should be moved to accept it.

(iv) Falk (v) has discussed the Talmudic evidence for sages binding and releasing vows, that is, deciding which vows must be kept and which could be absolved (the relevant terms are *'āsar* and *hittîr* or *pātaḥ*; note *m. Naz.* 5.1–4; *b. Ḥag.* 10a). But one is at a loss to fathom how 16.19 can have anything to do with vows.

(v) Many have thought in terms of the authority to release or enforce a ban, that is, exclusion from the community.[125] In support of this, 18.18 is clearly susceptible of such an interpretation; and in *b. Mo'ed. Qat.* 16a *'āsar* and *šĕrê* are used of issuing a ban and releasing a ban: 'A toot (from the horn blown at banning) binds and a toot releases'. According to SB 1, p. 739, however, only in *b. Mo'ed. Qat.* 16a does *'āsar* mean 'impose an excommunication'.

(vi) In the view of G. Lambert (v), 16.19 simply refers in general to all the powers given by Jesus to Peter. Citing Hebrew, Egyptian, Greek,

---

[122] D. C. Duling, 'The Therapeutic Son of David', *NTS* 24 (1978), pp. 392–410.

[123] So Schlatter, p. 511, arguing that 'bind' and 'loose' describe activities of a judge. Cf. Jeremias, *Theology*, p. 238, and Basser (v).

[124] See A. Diez Macho, 'The Recently Discovered Palestinian Targum', *VTSup* 7 (1960), p. 231, and Vermes (v).

[125] See esp. F. Büchsel, *TWNT* 2, pp. 59–60.

and Roman sources he claims that the opposites (binding and loosing) have no specific content but denote totality. This is simply too vague to satisfy and cannot cite any patristic support. It also leaves 'the keys of the kingdom of Heaven' unexplained.

(vii) 'Binding' and 'loosing' appear as technical terms in many magical texts from the ancient world. In *b. Šabb.* 81b, for example, there is this: 'R. Ḥsda and Rabbah son of R. Huna were travelling in a boat, when a certain matron said to them, "Seat me near you," but they did not seat her. Thereupon she uttered something and bound the boat. They uttered something and freed it'. The terms used are *'āsar* and *šěrā'*. There are parallels to this language in the magical papyri (Smith, *Magician*, p. 203) and elsewhere. F. C. Conybeare long ago tried to link Mt 16.18 to such magical usage.[126] As with interpretation (i), this is possible only for some pre-Matthean stage. Matthew's animus towards magical practices is established (Hull, pp. 116–41).

(viii) Allen, p. 177, affirmed that one must distinguish between the church and the kingdom: 'The Church was to be built on the rock of the revealed truth that Jesus was the Messiah, the Divine Son. To S. Peter were to be given the keys of the kingdom. The kingdom is here, as elsewhere in this Gospel, the kingdom to be inaugurated when the Son of Man comes upon the clouds of heaven. If S. Peter was to hold supreme authority within it, the other apostles were also to have places of rank ... The ἐκκλησία, on the other hand, was the society of Christ's disciples ...'. Although Allen is correct in affirming that church and kingdom are not simply identified by Matthew,[127] one can hardly see the sense of referring v. 19 to the consummation, to the time when God's will is done on earth as it is in heaven; for the contrast between earth and heaven (what is bound here will be bound there, what is loosed here will be loosed there) presupposes that heaven and earth have not yet been united under God's will, that the two spheres are still separate.

(ix) B. H. Streeter interpreted 16.19 by calling upon Lk 11.52 ('Woe to you lawyers! for you have taken away the key of knowledge; you did not enter yourselves, and you hindered those who were entering'). He wrote: 'To Peter, then, is given that *true insight into the nature of the righteousness* taught by Christ—a righteousness that will "exceed that of the scribes and Pharisees"—which is the indispensable qualification of one who is "to bind and to loose" (i.e. to expound the moral law) with such discrimination that what he shall "bind on earth, shall be bound in heaven."' Further, Peter had the authority to decide 'how much or how little of the Law the members of the new dispensation shall be required to observe'.[128]

---

[126] F. C. Conybeare, 'Christian Demonology', *JQR* 9 (1897), pp. 444–70.

[127] Yet they are more closely related than he supposes. The church is the custodian of the present kingdom: 21.43. See further on 13.42. (Confusion between the church and the kingdom is already apparent in Od. Sol. 22.12, if this alludes to Mt 16.18 or the tradition behind it: 'And the foundation of everything is thy rock, and upon it thou hast built thy kingdom'.)

[128] B. H. Streeter, *The Primitive Church*, New York, 1929, p. 63. Cf. Tertullian, *De pud.* 21.

(x) Streeter's solution is not far from the major opinion of modern exegetes, which has it that Peter, as a sort of supreme rabbi or prime minister of the kingdom, is in 16.19 given teaching authority, given that is the power to declare what is permitted (cf. the rabbinic *šĕrê/šĕrā'*) and what is not permitted (cf. the rabbinic *'āsar/'ăsar*). Peter can decide by doctrinal decision what Christians must and must not do.[129] This is the traditional Roman Catholic understanding, with the proviso that Peter had successors. Compare already Epist. Clem. to Jas. 5, in which Simon Peter speaks to the brethren about Clement as follows: 'Since, as I have been taught by the Lord and Teacher Jesus Christ, whose apostle I am, the day of my death is approaching, I lay my hands upon this Clement as your bishop; and to him I entrust my chair of discourse, even to him who has journeyed with me from the beginning to the end, and thus has heard all my homilies ... Wherefore I communicate to him the power of binding and loosing, so that with respect to everything which he shall ordain in the earth, it shall be decreed in the heavens. For he shall bind what ought to be bound, and loose what ought to be loosed, as knowing the rule of the Church'. This interpretation of binding and loosing in terms of teaching authority seems to us to be correct (see further below).

(xi) A variant of the preceding interpretation holds that the teaching authority which Jesus grants Peter in 16.19 is granted to other disciples or church leaders in 18.18, so stress should not be laid on Peter's uniqueness.[130]

(xii) Another variant has it that the perfect tenses (lit. 'will have been bound', 'will have been loosed') required that decisions made on earth follow decisions already made in heaven.[131] On this view, the movement is not from below to above but from above to below. Heaven does not ratify decisions made by Peter; rather, Peter declares what heaven has already determined. We are not convinced, for at least four reasons. (a) In 18.18 ὅσα ἐὰν δήσητε ... ἔσται δεδεμένα κ.τ.λ. is immediately followed by this: 'Again, I say to you, if two of you agree on earth about anything they ask, it will be done for them by my Father in heaven'. Here God's action is indisputably subsequent to human deicision. Is this not a clue to understanding 18.18, and near proof that the future perfects can be pressed too far? (b) The LXX, the *koine*, and the NT can use periphrastic future perfects as though they were simple future passives; see Cadbury (v) and BDF § 352. Examples include LXX 2 Βασ 22.3; Isa 8.17; Heb 2.13. In Mt 16.19 the future passives are probably emphatic futures (cf. Aristophanes, *Pl.* 1027). Or maybe we have here an Aramaism (Grelot, 'Origene' (v), pp. 96–7,

---

[129] E.g. Zahn, pp. 553–4; Hummel, p. 63; Beare, p. 335 (with this: 'the "keys" are probably not to be understood as entrance keys, as if to suggest that Peter is authorized to admit or to refuse admission, but rather to the bundle of keys carried by the chief steward, for the opening of rooms and storechambers within the house—symbols of responsibilities to be exercised within the house of God'); B. P. Robinson (v).

[130] E.g. J. D. Kingsbury, 'The Figure of Peter in Matthew's Gospel', *JBL* 98 (1979), p. 73.

[131] See esp. the articles of Mantey (v); also Albright and Mann, p. 197; Gundry, *Commentary*, p. 335; Marcus (v); Carson *ad loc.*

citing Dan 5.19). (c) There are a good number of synoptic (including Matthean) sayings in which the first clause describes a human action, the second a correlative divine action subsequent in time, and in which the verb is in both clauses the same (e.g. Mt 5.7; 6.14–15; 10.32–3). 16.19 belongs to this class. (d) One recalls that the rabbis had no difficulty affirming that their halakhic decisions could 'bind' God. See the many texts to this effect cited by SB 1, pp. 741–7. Further criticism in Porter (v).

(xiii) According to SB 1, p. 739, interpretations (v) and (x) are not mutually exclusive: both can be true at the same time. Does this not overload the terms?

We have already remarked on our preference for interpretation (x): Peter is the authoritative teacher without peer. This harmonizes with the dominant rabbinic usage[132] and, more importantly, with 23.13: 'But woe to you, scribes and Pharisees, hypocrites! because you shut the kingdom of Heaven against men; for you neither enter yourselves, nor allow those who would enter to go in.' Here, as the context proves, the scribes shut the door to the kingdom by issuing false doctrine. The image is closely related to 16.19, and the inference lies near to hand that just as the kingdom itself is taken from the Jewish leaders and given to the church (21.43), so are the keys of the kingdom taken from the scribes and Pharisees and given to Peter. Supportive of this is the broader context of Peter's confession. In the immediately preceding 16.5–12 Jesus warns: 'Beware of the leaven of the scribes and Pharisees'. Matthew takes this to be about the *teaching* of the scribes and Pharisees. It would make good sense for the evangelist, in the very next paragraph, to tell a story in which Jesus replaces the Jewish academy with his own 'chief rabbi'.

Additional considerations confirm us in our judgement, one being that revelation and doctrinal content are otherwise the major themes of our pericope, another being that if 16.19b and c refer to teaching authority, there is a possible connexion with 19a, for keys are associated with knowledge or teaching in both the synoptic and rabbinic traditions (see above). Lastly, Peter is not only called the 'first' of the twelve disciples who in chapter 10 are commanded to preach to Israel, but he, along with others, is in 28.16–20 instructed by the risen Lord to make disciples of all nations, 'teaching them to observe all that I have commanded you'. Thus the pre-eminent tasks our gospel envisages for Peter are those of proclamation and instruction. This too well suits our interpretation of 16.19.

There is a variant of 16.19b–c in 18.18 and Jn 20.23. With Bultmann, *History*, p. 141, we judge 18.18 to be secondary *vis-à-vis* 16.19.[133] As

---

[132] The texts are gathered in SB 1, pp. 738–41.

[133] So also Trilling, pp. 157–8, and Gnilka, *Matthäusevangelium* 2, p. 56, against Käsemann, *Questions*, pp. 106–7; Boring, pp. 213–14. Our position

for Jn 20.23, it does not depend upon the synoptics (Dodd (v)) and would appear to represent an independent translation from Aramaic (or perhaps Hebrew); which is to say, 16.19 and Jn 20.23 are translation variants of the same logion.

Emerton (v) has made the satisfying inference that the original saying drew upon Isa 22.22: 'And I (the Lord) will place on his (Eliakim's) shoulder the key of the house of David; he shall open (*pātaḥ*), and none shall shut (*sōgēr*); and he shall shut (*sāgar*), and none shall open (*pōtēaḥ*).' The pre-Matthean tradition, probably seeing a reference to teaching authority, rendered the Aramaic equivalent of *pātaḥ*—perhaps *pĕtaḥ* (cf. Tg. Isa 22.22)—with λύω[134] and the Aramaic equivalent of *sāgar*—perhaps *'ăḥad* (cf. Tg. Isa 22.22)—with δέω.[135] John's tradition, on the other hand, could have translated *pĕtaḥ* and *'ăḥad* with ἀφίημι and κρατέω respectively. Such a tradition-history, although certainly hypothetical, is supported by this, that keys are normally associated with opening and closing, not binding and loosing. (Only here in the Greek Bible is κλείς found with λύω.[136]) In other words, 'binding' and 'loosing' (19b–c) do not naturally go with keys (v. 19a), but they do go with 'opening' and 'closing'. For this reason one might maintain that v. 19a was not originally joined to vv. 19b–c. This is unnecessary. The close parallel in Isa 22.22, which refers to keys as well as to opening and closing, seems sufficient to indicate that we have in Matthew an interpretative translation which has resulted in an unusual juxtaposition of images. Another pointer in this direction is Mt 23.13 (quoted above). If, as we think, this, and not Lk 11.52, is the better witness to Q, we have here, in early tradition, the idea that people can shut (κλείω) others out of the kingdom. It is reasonable to suppose that the picture behind Mt 16.19 was originally the same—especially as this firms up the link with v. 18. Whereas the latter has to do with gates, things which open and close, v. 19, in its original form, would have been about things which open and close gates, namely, keys.[137]

One final point. Rev 3.7 has this: 'The words of the holy one, the true one, who has the key of David, who opens and no one shall shut, who shuts and no one shall close'. Here 'the key of David'—which 'must be the key that opens the door into the kingdom of God'[138]—is used for opening and closing, not binding and loosing. Once more then we are encouraged to conjecture that what must lie behind Mt 16.19 is a saying in which Jesus handed over the keys to the kingdom and with them the power to open and to close.

follows from our analysis of the unity and antiquity of 16.17–19. Another reason for our conclusion is the OT background. Isa 22.22, the inspiration for our text, is addressed not to a group but to an individual. See further on 18.18.

[134] Cf. the LXX at Gen 42.27; Job 39.5; Ps 101.20; Isa 5.27; 14.17; 58.6; Jer 47.4.

[135] Although δέω does not translate *sāgar* in the LXX, it does render *lo-yippātēaḥ* in Job 32.19.

[136] But for κλείς with δέω see Rev 20.1–2.

[137] Should one also entertain the possibility of a wordplay behind vv. 18–19? In the targums *pĕtaḥ* = open, *maptehîn* = keys, *pithā'* = 'opening' or 'gate'.

[138] So G. R. Beasley-Murray, *The Book of Revelation*, London, 1974, p. 100.

With regard to the original meaning on the lips of Jesus, Cullmann, *Peter*, pp. 210–12, has proposed that vv. 19a and 19b–c were spoken on different occasions and dealt with different subjects. V. 19a had to do with Peter opening the door to the kingdom through his preaching, 19b–c with the authority to forgive sins. We should like to suggest that consideration be given to the possibility that vv. 19a and 19b–c— emended in accord with our previous discussion—belonged together from the first and that both had to do with Peter's evangelistic mission. If certain Jewish teachers shut the door of the kingdom to others by what they said and did (Mt 23.13 par.), Peter was to open that door by his missionary activity. The apostle had the keys of the kingdom insofar as he proclaimed the good news. By his preaching did he not in effect open the kingdom for those who accepted the gospel, and by the same preaching did he not close the kingdom to those who rejected him and his message? One is reminded of Q's missionary discourse. The apostolic missionaries bring blessings upon those who receive them but judgement upon those who do not. The one eschatological message effects salvation for some, condemnation for others. It 'opens' and 'closes' at the same time.

20. With this verse Matthew presumably returns to Mark. Jesus commands his disciples not to tell anyone that he is the Messiah.

τότε διεστείλατο τοῖς μαθηταῖς ἵνα μηδενὶ εἴπωσιν ὅτι αὐτός ἐστιν ὁ Χριστός.[139] Mk 8.30 (which might be redactional) has this: καὶ ἐπετίμησεν αὐτοῖς ἵνα μηδενὶ λέγωσιν περὶ αὐτοῦ. In Matthew τότε* has replaced καί. τοῖς μαθηταῖς is necessary because of the focus on Peter since v. 15. Similarly, Mark's περὶ αὐτοῦ has become the explicit ὅτι αὐτός κ.τ.λ. because the reference is back to v. 15: silence is to be kept concerning Jesus' identity, not the words in praise of Simon Peter.

(iv) *Concluding Observations*

(1) *Christology.* 16.13–20 begins by moving the reader to draw a comparison between Jesus and great heroes from the past, Elijah, Jeremiah, John the Baptist. It at once becomes apparent that the contrasts are greater than the similarities. Even if Jesus is undeniably a prophet, he is greater than all other prophets. Indeed, even more than John the Baptist is he more than a prophet. Jesus is 'the Christ, the Son of the living God'. As such he is not one in a series. He rather stands alone. He is the realization of the messianic hopes of Judaism, the fulfiller of the Davidic promises, the culmination of salvation-history. He also builds the church, which is the eschatological temple, and he

[139] B* D e sy^c have επετιμησεν, which is assimilation to Mark and/or Luke.

speaks of the inability of the powers of Hades to overcome those who follow him. He also has the keys to the kingdom and the power to give them to another. Are we not dealing in 16.13–20 with a person who cannot adequately be described in purely human categories (cf. our comments on 14.22–33, where the term 'I am' appears)? Here we have Davidic messianism, but with a difference. As Jewish messianism had anticipated, the Messiah in Matthew is certainly a human figure. But he also stands in a special relation to God, as God's Son. Unfortunately, we do not know how the First Evangelist conceptualized this, how exactly he thought of the person of Jesus. Did he conceive of him as transcending the traditional messianic categories in such a way that Gundry's use of the term 'essential deity' (*Commentary*, p. 330) is justified? Or would 'functional deity' be better? The application of the word 'God' to Jesus is extremely rare in the NT, and it is not found in the First Gospel. Is it, however, there implied? Should one hazard that 'deity' was a significant implication of Matthew's Christology, as it was of John's? We only ask the question. We do not answer it.

(2) *Ecclesiology*. (a) 16.13–20 is the crucial pericope in Matthew's fourth narrative section. The first narrative section, 1.1–4.23, introduced us to Jesus. The second, 8.1–9.38, recounted Jesus' mighty acts and witness to Israel. The third section, 11.1–12.50, recorded the negative response of corporate Israel to her Messiah's activities. What we then have in the next narrative section, 13.53–17.27, is the consequence of the rejection of the Messiah: the people of God are founded anew. In other words, the birth of the ecclesia—of Jew and Gentile—is traced directly to the failure of Israel to live up to her eschatological calling. The underlying logic of the narrative is explicitly formulated in 21.43, which speaks of the kingdom being taken from its Jewish custodians and given to the church.

(b) Jesus is the Son promised in 2 Sam 7.4–16, the king who builds the eschatological temple. This temple is the church. Like the old temple, it is founded on a rock. But unlike the old temple, it has no geographical location. It is not in Jerusalem. The new, eschatological temple is a spiritual temple. It stands under the rule: 'Where two or three are gathered in my name, there am I in the midst of them' (18.20; cf. Jn 4.21). Matthew is thus at one with the rest of the NT in substituting for the holiness of place the holiness of a person: holy space has been Christified (see further Davies, *GL*, pp. 366–76).

(3) *Peter*. The parallels between 16.13–20 and Gen 17.1–8 indicate that Peter functions as a new Abraham. He is the first of his kind, and he stands at the head of a new people. Peter is, like Abraham, a rock (cf. Isa 51.1–2), and the change in his name

denotes his function. What follows? Peter is not just a representative disciple, as so many Protestant exegetes have been anxious to maintain. Nor is he obviously the first holder of an office others will someday hold, as Roman Catholic tradition has so steadfastly maintained. Rather, he is a man with a unique rôle in salvation-history. The eschatological revelation vouchsafed to him opens a new era. His person marks a change in the times. His significance is the significance of Abraham, which is to say: his faith is the means by which God brings a new people into being.

(v) *Bibliography*

E. L. Allen, 'On this Rock', *JTS* 5 (1954), pp. 59–62.

B. W. Bacon, 'The Petrine Supplements of Matthew', *Expositor* 13, Series 8 (1917), pp. 1–23.

H. W. Basser, 'Derrett's "Binding" Reopened', *JBL* 104 (1985), pp. 297–300.

J. Betz, 'Christus—petra—Petrus', in *Kirche und Überlieferung*, ed. J. Betz and H. Fries, Freiburg, 1960, pp. 1–21.

O. Betz, 'Felsenmann und Felsengemeinde (Eine Parallele zu Mt. 16.17–19 in den Qumranpsalmen)', *ZNW* 48 (1957), pp. 49–77.

K. Bornhäuser, 'Zum Verstandnis von Matth 16.18f.', *NKZ* 40 (1929), pp. 221–37.

G. Bornkamm, 'Die Binde- und Lösegewalt in der Kirche des Matthäus', in *Die Zeit Jesu*, ed. G. Bornkamm and K. Rahner, Freiburg, 1970; trans. into English as 'The Authority to "Bind" and "Loose" in the Church in Matthew's Gospel', in *Perspective* (Pittsburgh) 11 (1970), pp. 37–50.

C. Brown, 'The Gates of Hell and the Church', in *Church, Word, and Spirit*, ed. J. E. Bradley and R. A. Muller, Grand Rapids, 1987, pp. 14–43.

Brown et. al., *Peter*, pp. 83–101.

R. Bultmann, 'Die Frage nach dem messianischen Bewusstsein Jesu und das Petrus-Bekenntnis', *ZNW* 19 (1919–20), pp. 165–74; reprinted in *Exegetica*, ed. E. Dinkler, Tübingen, 1967, pp. 1–9.

idem, 'Die Frage nach der Echtheit von Mt 16.17–19', *ThBl* 20 (1941), pp. 265–79; reprinted in *Exegetica*, pp. 255–77.

V. Burch, 'The "Stone" and the "Keys" (Mt 16.18ff.)', *JBL* 52 (1933), pp. 147–52.

J. A. Burgess, *A History of the Exegesis of Matthew 16.17–19 from 1781 to 1965*, Ann Arbor, 1976.

H. J. Cadbury, 'The Meaning of John 20.23, Matthew 16.19, and Matthew 18.18', *JBL* 58 (1939), pp. 251–4.

J.-M. van Cangh and M. van Esbroeck, 'La primauté de Pierre (Mt 16.16–19) et son contexte judaïque', *RTL* II (1980), pp. 310–24.

J. Carmignac, 'Pourquoi Jérémie est-il mentionné en Matthieu 16.14?', in G. Jeremias, *Tradition*, pp. 283–98.

K. L. Carroll, 'Thou art Peter', *NovT* 6 (1963), pp. 268–76.

J. Chapman, 'St. Paul and the Revelation to Peter, Matt XVI. 17', *RBén* 29 (1912), pp. 133–47.

M.-A. Chevallier, '"Tu es Pierre, tu es le nouvel Abraham" (Mt 16/18)', *ETR* 57 (1982), pp. 375–87.

idem, 'A propos de "Tu es Pierre, tu es le nouvel Abraham" (*ETR* 57, 1982, p. 395ss)', *ETR* 58 (1983), p. 354.

H. Clavier, 'Πέτρος καὶ πέτρα', in *Neutestamentliche Studien*, BZNW 21, Berlin, 1954, pp. 94–109.

A. C. Cotter, 'Tu es Petrus', *CBQ* 4 (1942), pp. 304–10.

L. Crawford, 'Tu es Pierre, et sur cette pierre . . .', *Cahiers du Cercle Ernest Renan* (Paris) 33 (1985), pp. 13–16.

O. Cullmann, 'L'apôtre Pierre instrument du diable et instrument de Dieu', in *New Testament Essays*, ed. A. J. B. Higgins, Manchester, 1959, pp. 94–105; translated into German and published in *Vorträge und Aufsätze*, Tübingen/Zürich, 1966, pp. 202–13.

idem, *Peter: Disciple, Apostle, Martyr*, 2nd ed. (trans. of *Petrus*, 2nd ed., 1960), Philadelphia, 1962.

idem, *TWNT* 6, pp. 94–112.

B. T. Dahlberg, 'The Typological Use of Jeremiah 1.4–19 in Matthew 16.13–23', *JBL* 94 (1975), pp. 73–80.

A. Dell, 'Matthäus 16.17–19', *ZNW* 15 (1914), pp. 1–49.

idem, 'Zur Erklärung von Matthäus 16.17–19', *ZNW* 17 (1916), pp. 27–32.

J. D. M. Derrett, 'Binding and Loosing (Matt 16.19; 18.18; Jn 29 [*sic*].23)', *JBL* 102 (1983), pp. 112–17.

A.-M. Dubarle, 'La primauté de Pierre dans Matthieu 16.17–19. Quelques références à l'Ancient Testament', *Istina* (Paris) 2 (1955), pp. 335–8.

J. Dublin, 'The Gates of Hades', *Expositor* 11, Series 8 (1916), pp. 401–9.

D. C. Duling, 'Binding and Loosing', *Forum* 3/4 (1987), pp. 3–31.

J. Dupont, 'La révélation du Fils de Dieu en faveur de Pierre (Mt 16.17) et de Paul (Ga 1.16)', *RSR* 52 (1964), pp. 411–20.

P. Elbert, 'The Perfect Tense in Matthew 16.19 and Three Charismata', *JETS* 17 (1974), pp. 149–55.

J. K. Elliott, 'Κηφᾶς: Σίμων Πέτρος: ὁ Πέτρος: An Examination of New Testament Usage', *NovT* 14 (1972), pp. 241–56.

J. A. Emerton, 'Binding and Loosing—Forgiving and Retaining', *JTS* 13 (1962), pp. 325–31.

R. Eppel, 'L'interpretation de Mt 16.18b', in *Aux Sources de la Tradition Chrétienne*, Paris, 1950, pp. 71–3.

S. Euringer, 'Der locus classicus des Primautes (Mt 16.18) und der Diatessaron text des hl. Ephräm', in *Beiträge zur Geschichte der christliches Altertums und der byzantinischen Literatur*, ed. A. M. Königer, Bonn, 1922, pp. 141–79.

Z. W. Falk, 'Binding and Loosing', *JJS* 25 (1974), pp. 92–100.

A. Feuillet, '"Chercher à persuader Dieu" (Ga 1.10a). Le début de l'Épître aux Galates et la scène matthéenne de Césarée Philippe', *NovT* 12 (1970), pp. 350–60.

J. Fitzmyer, 'Aramaic *Kepha*' and Peter's Name in the New Testament', in *Advance*, pp. 112–24.

Flew, *Jesus and His Church*, pp. 89–98.

J. M. Ford, '"Thou art 'Abraham' and upon this Rock . . ."', *HeyJ* 6 (1965), pp. 289–301.

T. Fornberg, 'Peter—the High Priest of the New Covenant?', *EAJT* 4 (1986), pp. 113–21.

Frankemölle, pp. 220–47.

R. H. Fuller, 'The "Thou art Peter" Pericope and the Easter Appearances', *McQ* 20 (1967), pp. 309–15.

J. Galot, 'La première profession de foi chrétienne', *EspVie* 97 (1987), pp. 593–9.

idem, 'Le pouvoir donné à Pierre', *EspV* 98 (1988), pp. 33–40.

G. Gander, *La notion primitive d'Eglise d'après l'Evangile selon Matthieu chapitre 16, versets 18 et 19*, Aix-en-provence, 1966.

idem, 'Le sens des mots: Πέτρος—πέτρα/Kiphâ—kiphâ—Kyp'—kyp' dans Matthieu xvi. 18a', *RTP* 29 (1941), pp. 5–29.

Gaston, pp. 223–7.

Geist, pp. 127–62.

S. Gero, 'The Gates or the Bars of Hades? A Note on Matthew 16.18', *NTS* 27 (1981) pp. 411–14.

P. Grelot, 'L'origine de Matthieu 16.16–19', in *À Cause de l'Évangile*, LD 123, Paris, 1985, pp. 91–105.

idem, *Les paroles de Jésus Christ*, Desclée, 1986, pp. 174–205.

idem, '"Sur cette pierre je bâtirai mon Église" (Mt 16.18b)', *NRT* 109 (1987), pp. 641–59.

R. H. Gundry, 'The Narrative Framework of Matthew 16.17–19', *NovT* 7 (1964), pp. 1–9.

F. Hahn, 'Die Petrusverheissung Mt 16.18f.', in *Das kirchliche Amt im Neuen Testament*, ed. K. Kertelge, Freiburg, 1977, pp. 543–63.

A. von Harnack, 'Der Spruch über Petrus als den Felsen der Kirche', in *Sitzungsberichte der Preussischen (Deutschen) Akademie der Wissenschaften zu Berlin (Philosophisch-historische Klasse)* (1918), 1, pp. 637–54.

J. H. A. Hart, 'Cephas and Christ', *JTS* 9 (1907), pp. 14–47.

R. H. Hiers, '"Binding" and "Loosing": The Matthean Author-izations', *JBL* 104 (1985), pp. 233–50.

P. Hoffmann, 'Der Petrus-Primat im Matthäusevangelium', in Gnilka, *Kirche*, pp. 94–114.; reprinted in Lange, *Matthäus-Evangelium*, pp. 415–40.

Horstmanns, pp. 8–31.

F. J. A. Hort, *The Christian Ecclesia*, London, 1914, pp. 1–21.

G. Howard, 'The Meaning of Petros-Petra', *RestQ* 10 (1967), pp. 217–21.

O. Immisch, 'Matthäus 16.18', *ZNW* 17 (1916), pp. 18–26.

J. Jeremias, *Golgotha*, Leipzig, 1926.

idem, *Jesus als Weltvollender*, Gütersloh, 1930.

idem, *TWNT* 3, pp. 743–53; 6, pp. 920–7.

G. Johnston, *The Doctrine of the Church in the New Testament*, Cambridge, 1943.

C. Kähler, 'Zur Form- und Traditionsgeschichte von Math. xvi. 17–19', *NTS* 23 (1976), pp. 36–58.

J. Kahmann, 'Die Verheissung an Petrus', in Didier, pp. 261–80.

F. Kattenbusch, 'Der Spruch über Petrus und die Kirche bei Matthäus', *TSK* 94 (1922), pp. 96–131.

H. Klein, 'Das Bekenntnis des Petrus and die Anfänge des Christusglaubens im Urchristentum', *EvTh* 47 (1987), pp. 176–92.

G. A. F. Knight, 'Thou art Peter', *TToday* 17 (1960), pp. 168–80.

R. Köbert, 'Zwei Fassungen von Mt 16.18 bei den Syrern', *Bib* 40 (1959), pp. 1018–20.

W. G. Kümmel, 'Jesus und die Anfänge der Kirche', *StTh* 7 (1953), pp. 1–27.

J. Lambrecht, '"Du bist Petrus." Mt 16.16–19 und das Papsttum', *SNTU* 11 (1986), pp. 5–32.

P. Lampe, 'Das Spiel mit dem Petrus-Namen—Matt. 16.18', *NTS* 25 (1979), pp. 227–45.

H. Lehmann, 'Due bist Petrus: zum Problem von Mattheaeus 16.13–26', *EvTh* 13 (1953), pp. 44–67.

O. Linton, *Das Problem der Urkirche in der neueren Forschung*, Uppsala, 1932.

J. Ludwig, *Die Primatworte Mt. XVI, 18–19 in der altkirchlichen Exegeses*, Münster, 1952.

P. J. Maan, 'Die Exegesis von Matth. 16.18–19', *IKiZeit* 52 (1962), pp. 100–7.

F. Manns, 'La Halakah dans l'évangile de Matthieu. Note sur Mt 16.16–19', *BibOr* 5 (1983), pp. 129–35.

Manson, *Sayings*, pp. 201–5.

J. R. Mantey, 'Distorted Translations in John 20.23; Matthew 16.18–19 and 18.18', *RevExp* 78 (1981), pp. 409–16.

idem, 'Evidence that the Perfect Tense in John 20.23 and Matthew 16.19 is Mistranslated', *JETS* 16 (1973), pp. 129–38.

idem, 'The Mistranslation of the Perfect Tense in John 20.23, Matt 16.19, and Matt 18.18', *JBL* 58 (1939), pp. 243–49.

J. Marcus, 'The Gates of Hades and the Keys of the Kingdom (Matt 16.18–19)', *CBQ* 50 (1988), pp. 443–55.

W. Marxsen, 'Der Fels der Kirche', in *Der 'Frühkatholizismus' im Neuen Testament*, BS 21, Neukirchen, 1959, pp. 39–54.

Meier, *Vision*, pp. 106–21.

M. J. J. Menken, 'The References to Jeremiah in the Gospel according to Matthew (Mt 2.17; 16.14; 27.9)', *ETL* 60 (1984), pp. 5–24.

B. F. Meyer, pp. 185–97.

C. F. D. Moule, 'Some Reflections on the "Stone" *Testimonia* in relation to the Name Peter', *NTS* 2 (1955), pp. 56–8.

G. W. E. Nickelsburg, 'Enoch, Levi, and Peter: Recipients of Revelation in Upper Galilee', *JBL* 100 (1981), pp. 575–600.

F. Obrist, *Echtheitsfragen und Deutung der Primatsstelle Mt 16.18f. in der deutschen protestantischen Theologie der letzten dreissig Jahre*, Münster, 1961.

A. Oepke, 'Der Herrenspruch über die Kirche Mt 16.17–19 in der neuesten Forschung', *StTh* 2 (1948–50), pp. 110–65.

R. Pesch, 'Das Messiasbekenntnis des Petrus (Mk 8.27–30)', *BZ* 17 (1973), pp. 178–95; 18 (1974), pp. 20–31.

S. E. Porter, 'Vague Verbs, Periphrastics, and Matt. 16.19', *Filologia Neotestamentaria* (Cordoba) 2 (1988), pp. 155–73.

J. Ringger, 'Das Felsenwort', in *Begegnung der Christen*, ed. M. Roesle and O. Cullmann, Stuttgart, 1959, pp. 271–346.

B. P. Robinson, 'Peter and his Successors: Tradition and Redaction in Matthew 16.17–19', *JSNT* 21 (1984), pp. 85–104.

J. Schmid, 'Petrus "der Fels" und die Petrusgestalt der Urgemeinde', in *Begegnung der Christen*, ed. M. Roesle and O. Cullmann, Stuttgart, 1959, pp. 347–59.

K. L. Schmidt, *TWNT* 3, pp. 502–39.

R. Schnackenburg, 'Das Vollmachtswort vom Binden und Lösen', in *Kontinuität und Einheit*, ed. P.-G. Müller and W. Stenger, Freiburg, 1981, pp. 141–57.

O. J. F. Seitz, 'Upon this rock: A Critical Re-examination of Matt 16.17–19', *JBL* 69 (1950), pp. 329–40.

E. Stauffer, 'Zur Vor – und Frühgeschichte des Primatus Petri', *ZKG* 62 (1943/4), pp. 3–34.

A. Stock, 'Is Matthew's Presentation of Peter Ironic?', *BTB* 17 (1987), pp. 64–9.

L. E. Sullivan, 'The Gates of Hell (Mt 16.18s)', *TS* 10 (1949), pp. 62–4.

E. F. Sutcliffe, 'St. Peter's Double Confesion in Mt 16.16–19', *HeyJ* 3 (1962), pp. 31–41.

idem, 'St. Peter's Double Confession: An Additional Note', *HeyJ* 3 (1962), pp. 275–6.

Trilling, pp. 156–63.

G. Vermes, *Studies*, pp. 121–4.

A. Vögtle, 'Messiasbekenntnis und Petrusverheissung', *BZ* 1 (1957), pp. 252–72; 2 (1958), pp. 85–103; reprinted in *Evangelium*, pp. 137–70.

idem, 'Zum Problem der Herkunft von Mt 16.17–19', in Hoffmann, *Orientierung*, pp. 372–93.

D. Wenham, 'Paul's Use of the Jesus Tradition: Three Samples', in Wenham, *Tradition*, pp. 24–8.

M. Wilcox, 'Peter and the Rock: A Fresh Look at Matthew xvi. 17–19', *NTS* 22 (1975), pp. 73–88.

B. G. Wright III, 'A Previously Unnoticed Greek Variant of Matt 16.14', *JBL* 105 (1986), pp. 694–7.

EXCURSUS XIII

PETER IN MATTHEW[1]

A survey of the contemporary literature on Peter in Matthew reveals two major tendencies. Hummel represents one. For him Peter is a sort of chief rabbi, the guarantor of the Christian halakah. Jesus builds the church upon the apostle and gives to him the authority signified by the keys of the kingdom of heaven. Representative of the other tendency is Strecker, for whom Peter stands as the typical Christian, a symbol of

[1] Lit.: P. Batiffol, *Primitive Catholicism* (trans. of *Urkirche und Katholizismus*, 1910), Exeter, 1911; J. Blank, 'Neutestamentliche Petrus-Typologie und

every disciple (so already Origen). A third approach, an attempt to find the mean between two perceived extremes, comes from Kingsbury (whose conclusions resemble those of Hoffmann). Arguing that Strecker's position takes too modest a view of Peter's significance and that Hummel's interpretation flies in the face of 23.8 ('But you are not to be called rabbi, for you have one teacher, and you are all brethren') and 23.10 ('Neither be called master, for you have one master, the Christ'), Kingsbury finds the truth to be this: Peter is 'first' (10.1) because he is the first apostle to be called (4.18–22). His primacy therefore belongs to salvation-history, and one should not read more than this into it.

In order to make an informed judgement on the positions just introduced it is necessary to review the pertinent texts. Here are the places where Peter is mentioned in the First Gospel:

Text in Matthew	Text in Mark
4.18–22: Peter is called to be a disciple	1.16–20
8.14–15: Peter's mother-in-law is healed	1.29–31
10.2: Peter is the 'first' of the twelve apostles	Cf. 3.16: Peter is named first but is not so called
14.28–31: Peter walks on the water and sinks	6.45–52 lacks this episode
15.15: Peter asks a question	7.17: only the disciples ask a question (cf. Mt 15.12)
16.13–20: Peter confesses Jesus to be the Messiah and Son of God and is favoured with a beatitude which makes him out to be the church's foundation and recipient of the keys of the kingdom	8.27–30: Peter confesses Jesus to be the Messiah but there is no beatitude, nothing corresponding to Mt 16.17–19
16.21–3: Peter is rebuked by Jesus	8.31–3

Petrusamt', *Concilium* 9 (1973), pp. 173–9; Brown *et al.*, *Peter*; Cullmann, *Peter*; R. Feldmeier, 'Die Darstellung des Petrus in den synoptischen Evangelien', in Stuhlmacher, *Evangelium*, pp. 267–71; H. Frankemölle, 'Amtskritik im Matthäusevangelium', *Bib* 54 (1973), pp. 247–62; P. Hoffmann, 'Der Petrus-Primat im Matthäusevangelium', in Gnilka, *Kirche*, pp. 94–114, reprinted in Lange, *Matthäus-Evangelium*, pp. 415–40; Hummel, pp. 59–64, 103–6; J. D. Kingsbury, 'The Figure of Peter in Matthew's Gospel as a Theological Problem', *JBL* 98 (1979), pp. 67–83; Künzel, pp. 180–217; F. Mussner, *Petrus und Paulus*, QD 76, Freiburg, 1976; R. Pesch, *Simon-Petrus*, Stuttgart, 1980; Sand, *Matthäus*, pp. 327–35; W. Schenk, 'Das "Matthäusevangelium" als Petrusevangelium', *BZ* 27 (1983), pp. 58–80; R. Schnackenburg, 'Petrus im Matthäusevangelium', in *À Cause de l'Évangile*, LD 123, Paris, 1985, pp. 107–25; T. V. Smith, *Petrine Controversies in Early Christianity*, WUNT 2/15, Tübingen, 1985; Strecker, *Weg*, pp. 198–206; C. P. Thiede, *Das Petrusbild in der neueren Forschung*, Wuppertal, 1987; idem, *Simon Peter*, Exeter, 1986; W. Trilling, 'Amt und Amtsverständnis bei Matthäus', in Descamps, *Mélanges*, pp. 29–44; idem, 'Zum Petrusamt im Neuen Testament', *TQ* 151 (1971), pp. 110–33; H. Zimmermann, 'Der innere Struktur der Kirche und das Petrusamt nach Mt 18', *Catholica* 30 (1976), pp. 168–83.

17.1–9: Peter and James and John witness the transfiguration; Peter wants to build three booths	9.2–10
17.24–7: Peter is asked about the temple tax	No parallel
18.21: Peter asks how many times one should forgive a brother	No parallel
19.27: Peter says, 'Lo, we have left everything and followed you. What then shall we have?'	10.28: Peter says 'Lo, we have left everything and followed you'
26.31–5: Peter's denial foretold	14.27–31
26.36–46: Peter and James and John are witnesses of Gethsemane	14.32–42
26.58, 69–75: Peter's denial	14.54, 66–72

The passages in which Peter is mentioned in Mark but not Matthew are these: Mk 1.35–8 ('Simon and those with him' seek out Jesus in order to report to him on the people; Matthew has omitted the entire episode); 5.35–43 (Peter and James and John enter the ruler's house to witness a miracle; Matthew has abbreviated the story); 11.20–4 (Peter exclaims about the withered fig tree; in Matthew the disciples in general speak); 13.3 (Peter and James and John and Andrew ask about the temple; in Matthew disciples ask the question); 16.7 (the angel tells the women to announce what has happened to Peter and the others; in Matthew the message is simply for 'the disciples').

Several facts are immediately apparent. First, Peter does not really play much of a rôle before chapter 14, and after chapter 18 Matthew has added nothing of substance to the Markan portrait. The explanation undoubtedly lies in Matthean ecclesiology, for it is precisely in the fourth major narrative section, 13.53–17.27, and in the subsequent discourse in 18.1ff., that Jesus formally establishes the church and gives it instruction. Which is to say: Peter's prominence seems to be a function of ecclesiology. The chief apostle dominates the section which is dominated by the church. Secondly, Matthew has carried forward the Markan tendency to make Peter address questions to Jesus. Thirdly, most if not all of the omissions of Peter by Matthew seem readily explained by literary rather than theological reasons (e.g. simple abbreviation; cf. Brown *et al.*, *Peter*, pp. 76–7). One might, however, want to urge that the First Evangelist wished to weaken the notion of a special group of three or four disciples. Fourthly, Peter would seem, on the face of it, to stand out from the other disciples. He is called the 'first' (10.2), he is the recipient of a far-reaching makarism (16.17–19), and he is recognized by outsiders as possessing knowledge about Jesus (cf. esp. 17.24–7: 'Does not your teacher pay the tax?'). Should one not therefore conclude that Hummel's evaluation might well be correct?

But there are other factors to be considered. Hummel's position can be resisted by the claim that when Matthew writes of Peter he also writes of the other disciples (so Kingsbury). Peter is called along with others (4.18–22). He is not the only one to pose questions (15.12). He is not alone in confessing Jesus to be the Son of God (14.33), nor alone in having a beatitude spoken over him (13.16–17), nor in receiving divine revelation (13.11, 16–17). Further, if Peter has the authority to bind and loose, so have others (18.18). All this moves Kingsbury to write of 'Matthew's firm resolve to anchor Peter within the circle of the disciples'. The same observations can and have been called upon also by those who emphasize Peter's rôle as representative disciple or Christian. Finally, Hummel's interpretation has been thought weakened by the places in Mark but not Matthew where Peter is prominent (see above) as well as by 14.28–31, where the apostle fails to demonstrate sufficient faith.

What is one to make of the conflicting indicators? Notwithstanding the previous paragraph, we find ourselves siding with Hummel against Kingsbury. Peter's imperfections in our judgement do not qualify his primacy or unique status. Instead they serve to magnify his greatness, for they demonstrate how genuine were the obstacles he had to overcome in order to achieve what he did. Further, the parallels between Peter and the others do not prove what some imagine. An overlap in function does not entail an identify of status or office. To illustrate: the First Evangelist has done much to assimilate his portraits of John the Baptist and Jesus, and one can list many ways in which the two men are spoken of in identical fashion (cf. 1, pp. 289–90). Yet, to state the obvious, Jesus and John are hardly on the same theological plane. Again, there are many ways in which Jesus and his twelve disciples resemble one another (cf. p. 197). Once more, however, the similarities are consistent with tremendous differences. And so it may also be with the parallels between Peter and his fellow apostles, especially as what naturally sticks in the mind of the reader is not what Peter has in common with others but what sets him apart.

A further point is this: Peter, like Paul, seems to have been a controversial figure in early Christianity, one whose authority and function were subject to some debate. This the monograph of T. V. Smith has recently demonstrated with abundant materials (even if some of its details may be questionable). Granted Smith's broad conclusion—Peter's controversial status—, we tend to think that Strecker's interpretation of Peter as well as that of Kingsbury are probably theological abstractions unlikely to reflect the actualities of Matthew's historical situation. Passages such as Mt 10.2; 16.17–19; and 17.24–7 were not composed in a historical vacuum. These texts were first read in the light of beliefs already held about Peter. This is all the more certain as Peter was, according to Gal 2, at one time in Antioch, which we take to have probably been our evangelist's own city. Matthew's audience undoubtedly came to the gospel text with certain firm ideas about Peter and his place.

Continuing this line of thought, one should remember that, as a matter of history, Peter was, to judge by the body of NT evidence, generally recognized as the most important of Jesus' disciples. On this the synoptics, Acts, and the Pauline epistles concur. Peter was not simply remembered as the first apostle to be called; nor were his authority and influence in any way typical. We know next to nothing about Andrew and Philip, Matthew and Bartholomew, James the son of Alphaeus and Simon the Cananaean. Beside them Peter stands forth as the exception, a well-defined face in a faceless crowd. So one must ask, Were not Peter's record and achievements simply too well known[2] for him to be effectively used only as a type, or for his primacy to be effectively reduced to a one-time chronological circumstance? Can Matthew's text really be divorced from the history of early Christianity in such a way as to make either Kingsbury or Strecker appear very plausible on the issue at hand?

We would hasten to add that, despite our disagreement with Kingsbury, he is not entirely mistaken. There is a sense in which Peter's primacy reflects his rôle in salvation-history. But this has nothing to do with his having been the first disciple to be called—an assertion which in any case is not clearly established by the text, for was Andrew not called at the very same time? The key to Peter's primacy is to be found not in 4.18–22 but in 16.13–20. Peter is the rock on which the church is established. As we urged on pp. 623–4, Matthew seems to present Peter as one like father Abraham. He is the patriarch of the church, the man of faith whose name was changed, the man who became the rock on which the ecclesia came into being. If this be correct, then Peter's uniqueness in salvation-history lies in this, that just as Abraham stands at the beginning of the birth of the old people of God, Israel, so does Peter stand at the birth of the new people of God, the church.

But is there more to Peter's pre-eminence than his special status in salvation-history? We consider this likely. One should seriously entertain the notion that Matthew conceived of Peter as an authoritative link, perhaps *the* authoritative link, between Jesus on the one hand and the Matthean community on the other. If the First Gospel was composed in Antioch it is not implausible that some of the book's special material (M) was thought of—whether rightly or wrongly—as stemming from Peter. Moreover, if Matthew, like Papias after him, believed that Peter was in some sense a source for the Gopel of Mark, then in view of his adoption of most of that gospel our evangelist could have thought of his own composition as depending in no small way upon the great apostle. There is thus some reason to infer that the office of key-holder (16.19) may have included the passing down of tradition.

Also not impossible is the suggestion that Peter was thought of as holding some type of 'office' which others held after him. This would certainly go a long way towards explaining Matthew's interest in one who was, after all, long since dead. Further, shortly after Matthew penned his gospel, Ignatius of Antioch expounded a fairly developed view of the episcopal office. Was Peter perhaps already perceived by Matthew and his readers as having some relationship to that emerging institution?

Unfortunately, we cannot address the issue with great conviction. We know far too little about Matthew's church and its concrete situation to make confident assertions about either possible historical links to Peter or the relationship (if any) between that church's authorities or 'offices' and Jesus' chief apostle. But of a few things we can be reasonably sure. Peter was not simply a representative disciple for Matthew, and he was not just the first disciple to be called. He was

[2] It is highly significant that 'even the distant Gentile converts of Paul in Galatia know of Peter' (Brown *et al.*, *Peter*, p. 159, n. 337).

the pre-eminent apostle, which meant he held a significance and authority the other disciples did not hold. His rôle in salvation-history was pivotal, and probably his authority continued to make itself felt in the living tradition of Matthew's community.[3]

[3] We do not know whether Matthew's emphasis on Peter owes anything, by way of reaction, to a comparison with Paul. Was Peter in opposition to Paul in Matthew's tradition or in Matthew's mind? Did the evangelist elevate Peter in order to depreciate Paul? Gal 2 recounts a serious confrontation between the two apostles, and precisely at Antioch, where we locate the Gospel. One also recalls the fundamental opposition in the later Pseudo-Clementines. The problem, however, is that while a few Matthean texts have been thought to allude to Paul (see e.g. on 5.19 and 13.25), this is most uncertain. We remain in the dark concerning Matthew's views on Paul. Full discussion in Davies, *SSM*, pp. 316–41.

XL

THE PASSION AND RESURRECTION PREDICTED
(16.21–3)

(i) *Structure*

This paragraph has the standard triadic form of an objection story. Jesus (i) says and/or does something which (ii) results in a protest or remonstrance; then (iii) Jesus reacts by rebutting the objection (cf. 9.1–8, 10–13; 12.1–8).

(ii) *Sources*

16.21–3 is based upon Mk 8.31–3[1] (as is also Lk 9.22). This judgement is consistent with the observation that Mark's text lacks precisely those features of Mt 16.21–3 which one must consider characteristic of the First Evangelist: τότε* (v. 21), ἄρχω with ἀπό (v. 21, Mt: 3; Mk: 0; Lk: 4), ὁ Ἰησοῦς* (v. 21), ἀπέρχομαι* with εἰς (v. 21, Mt: 12; Mk: 8; Lk: 4), τῇ τρίτῃ (v. 21; Mt: 3; Mk: 0; Lk: 6), ἐγείρω* (v.21), and σκάνδαλον (v. 23; see on 13.41).

(iii) *Exegesis*

Once it has become evident that Israel as a corporate body is not going to welcome Jesus as the Messiah, two tasks remain for God's rejected servant. First, he must establish a new community, the church, and give her instruction. Secondly, he must give his life as a ransom for many. Having, in the previous passage, begun the first task, Jesus next turns his eyes towards the second.

Three very different verdicts on the tradition-history of Mt 16.21–3 par. are to be considered. (i) The unit could be regarded as of a piece with the preceding confession.[2] (ii) The confession and 16.21–3 par. may have been brought together by Mark or the pre-Markan tradition.[3]

[1] *Pace* Bayer, pp. 182–8, Mt 16.21–3 does not show the influence of non-Markan tradition.
[2] Cf. George (v), p. 40; and Bayer, pp. 154–66.
[3] The independence of Mk 8.27–30 is argued by R. Pesch, 'Das

(iii) Some have held the passion prediction to be a secondary insertion into a pericope in which the rebuke of Peter followed directly upon his messianic confession: originally Jesus rebuffed Simon for embracing a nationalistic messianism.[4] The third option is the least likely. If Jesus so clearly rejected the title 'Messiah', it is incomprehensible how it came to be so widely employed in the early church and indeed embedded in primitive formulas of faith.[5] Further, one is inclined to think that a story which recounted Jesus' direct contradiction of the community's own confession would not have been modified in transmission but simply rejected out of hand.

With regard to the two alternatives left, a decision is difficult. In favour of splitting our two texts is the ἤρξατο of Mk 8.31 par., for this could mark a traditional seam. In addition, Mk 8.27–9 (30) par. would be intelligible in isolation; and while Mk 8.31–3 par. as it stands could not have circulated as an independent piece, matters may have been different for an earlier form of the story. Nonetheless, despite these considerations there are also reasons for inferring that the first passion prediction and Peter's confession may have belonged together in the pre-Markan tradition, perhaps from the beginning. (i) Jn 6.25–71 contains a sequence which clearly parallels Mk 8.11–33:

	Mark 8	John 6
Request for a sign	11–13	25–34
Remarks on bread	14–21	35–9
Faith of Peter	27–30	60–9
Passion theme, betrayal	31–3	70–1[6]

If John is at this point independent of the synoptics, the common sequence may point to early tradition. (ii) The transition from talk about Jesus as 'Messiah' (Mk 8.29) to talk about Jesus as the 'Son of man' has a close parallel in Mk 14.61f., and we regard this last sequence as traditional and perhaps rooted in Jesus' own speech (cf. also Jn 12.34). (iii) There are possible catchword connexions between 8.27–9 (30) and 31–3: οἱ μαθηταὶ αὐτοῦ (vv. 27, 33), οἱ ἄνθρωποι (vv. 27, 33), ὁ Πέτρος (vv. 29, 32, 33). It must be confessed, however, that these three arguments are far from conclusive, and as they are balanced by the arguments on the other side, one can hardly reach a decision on the question of the unity of Mk 8.27–33 par.[7]

A judgement as to the possible historical basis of our scene—which, as just concluded, *could* have been joined from the first to Peter's confession—depends upon whether one can believe that Jesus, at least towards the end of his public ministry, sensed the direction the wind

Messiasbekenntnis des Petrus', *BZ* 17 (1973), pp. 179–85; cf. Kümmel, *Theology*, pp. 69–70, 90.

[4] Cf. E. Dinkler, 'Petrusbekenntnis und Satanswort', in *Zeit und Geschichte*, ed. E. Dinkler, Tübingen, 1964, pp. 127–53; Hahn, *Titles*, pp. 157–9; and Fuller, *Christology*, pp. 109–10. Ernst (v) makes a similar proposal. He reconstructs a pre-Markan paragraph consisting of Mk 8.27a, 31, 32, 29b, 33.

[5] E.g. Rom 6.4; 14.9; 1 Cor 15.3. Cf. Gnilka, *Markus* 2, p. 18.

[6] See further Brown, *John* 1, pp. 238–9, 301–2.

[7] For further discussion see Bayer, pp. 154–66.

was blowing and foresaw his fate. Because we are persuaded that he was in fact gifted with such foresight (see on v. 21), everything argues that a pre-Easter memory has been stored in 16.21-3 par. It has, admittedly, been proposed that Jesus' harsh rebuke of Peter reflects early Christian polemic;[8] but we find it more natural to sympathize with those scholars who have been impressed by the difficulty of imagining who in the early church would have been so bold as to create the allegedly pure fiction—which Luke felt moved to excise— that Jesus called Peter Satan. Perhaps also indicative of a pre-Easter origin is the phrase, 'after three days' (Mk 8.31). Matthew and Luke, in the light of the event, revise this to 'on the third day'. Would not a free post-Easter creation have made the change unnecessary in the first place? Lastly, Mk 8.31-3 contains several Semitisms.[9] The passage was presumably formulated by the Palestinian community.

Matthew's alterations of Mk 8.31-3 are relatively minor and serve largely to make explicit what remains implicit in Mark. Among other things, the First Evangelist has added a reference to Jerusalem (v. 21), changed 'after three days' to the more exact 'on the third day', given words to Peter's rebuke (v. 22b), and added 'you are a stumbling block to me' (v. 23).

21. ἀπὸ τότε ἤρξατο ὁ Ἰησοῦς.[10] This phrase also appears in 4.17 (q.v. for discussion). Mark has simply καὶ ἤρξατο.

δεικνύειν τοῖς μαθηταῖς αὐτοῦ. This replaces Mark's διδάσκειν αὐτούς. Only here in Matthew is δείκνυμι/δεικνύειν (Mt: 3; Mk: 2; Lk: 4–5) editorial. Has the word been chosen in order to emphasize private instruction (so Gundry, Commentary, p. 337; cf. 4.8; 8.4)? Or does it signal revelation (cf. Rev 1.1)?

ὅτι δεῖ αὐτὸν εἰς Ἰεροσόλυμα ἀπελθεῖν καὶ πολλὰ παθεῖν ἀπὸ τῶν πρεσβυτέρων καὶ ἀρχιερέων καὶ γραμματέων καὶ ἀποκτανθῆναι. The evangelist has (i) substituted αὐτόν for 'the Son of man' (cf. 5.11 diff. Lk 6.22); (ii) added 'to go to Jerusalem and'[11] (a change which makes explicit what is implicit in Mark,[12] increases the parallelism with the third passion prediction, 20.17–19 = Mk 10.32–4, and names the place where the Jewish leaders exercise the most power; see 1, p. 239); (iii)

---

[8] See Bultmann, History, p. 258, and J. B. Tyson, 'The Blindness of the Disciples in Mark', JBL 80 (1961), pp. 261–8.

[9] See Pesch 2, p. 55.

[10] So ℵ² C (B² D: -ο) L W Θ f^{1.13} Maj latt sy sa^{ms} bo^{mss}. ℵ¹ 892 pc Ir^{lat} have no subject. Ιησους Χριστος appears in ℵ* B* sa^{mss} mae bo (and is accepted by McNeile, p. 244, and Gundry, Commentary, p. 337). If Χριστος has not simply been imported from the previous verse, the reading may reflect the thought that 16.21 marks a major turning point in the gospel (cf. Kingsbury's analysis and Gnilka, Matthäusevangelium 1, p. 99). We have, however, expressed our doubts as to whether 4.17 and 16.21 can really be the keys to Matthew's structure; see on 3.1 and 4.17 and cf. J. Murphy-O'Connor, 'The Structure of Matthew xiv–xvii', RB 82 (1975), p. 366. Also Neirynck (v), p. 54.

[11] ἀπέρχομαι* is often redactional.

[12] The elders, chief priests, and scribes resided in Jerusalem.

omitted καὶ ἀποδοκιμασθῆναι[13]—either because it is superfluous[14] or because it does not occur in any of the other passion predictions;[15] (iv) traded ὑπό[16] for ἀπό[17] (so also Luke; contrast 17.12 and see MHT 1, p. 102); and (v) omitted the definite articles before 'chief priests' and 'scribes' (which makes the three groups named act as one; cf. Lk 9.22).

δεῖ[18] (cf. 17.10; 24.6; 26.54), which in Matthew is the functional equivalent of γέγραπται, expresses the conviction that Jesus' passion is the realization in time of a destiny stored up for and dictated to the Messiah by the Scriptures, which convey God's will.[19] In connexion with a prophecy of suffering and resurrection, the use of δεῖ could call to mind several OT texts, including Ps 22; 34.19–22; 89.38–45; 118.10–25; Isa 52–3; Dan 7; Hos 6.2; and Zech 13.7–9. Matthew himself, we suspect, will probably have had Isaiah in mind above all. With regard to Jesus himself, Isa 52–3 and Dan 7 seem equally likely candidates (cf. Cavallin (v)).[20] On the vexed issue of whether pre-Christian Judaism was familiar with the notion of a suffering Messiah see p. 38, n. 109.

πολλὰ παθεῖν[21] means 'to suffer many things'. Although the verb, which should be reckoned as belonging to the *passio iusti* tradition,[22] may by itself mean 'to die' (as in As. Mos. 3.11; Josephus, *Ant.* 13.268, 403), it here envisages the sufferings which lead up to the crucifixion (cf. Marshall, p. 370). What we have in Matthew is a clear chronological sequence: Jesus goes to Jerusalem, he there suffers at the hands of the Jewish leaders, and then finally he is killed.

LXX Ps 33.20 reads: πολλαὶ αἱ θλίψεις τῶν δικαίων, καὶ ἐκ πασῶν αὐτῶν ῥύσεται αὐτούς (cf. 4 Macc 18.15). According to Ruppert, p. 65, it is very possible that Jesus himself spoke of his suffering with reference to the Hebrew or Aramaic equivalent of this in mind (MT Ps 34.20

[13] Cf. LXX Ps 117.22; Mk 12.10.
[14] Cf. the omission of ἐξουδενηθῇ from Mk 9.12.
[15] The verb is retained in 21.42 = Mk 12.10, an OT citation.
[16] Cf. Josephus, *Ant.* 13.268.
[17] D retains ὑπό.
[18] Lit.: W. Grundmann, *TWNT* 2, pp. 21–5; E. Fascher, 'Theologische Beobachtungen zu δεῖ,' in *Neutestamentliche Studien*, BZNW 21, Berlin, 1954, pp. 228–54; Patsch, pp. 189–94; W. J. Bennett, Jr., 'The Son of man must . . .', *NovT* 17 (1975), pp. 113–29; Bayer, pp. 202–5. The word may here represent an Aramaic future.
[19] Cf. the βάπτισμα ἔχω βαπτισθῆναι κ.τ.λ. of Lk 12.50.
[20] Also, perhaps, Ps 34.19 (see text). If Dan 7 is in the background, then it should not be forgotten that δεῖ is often used in eschatological contexts (e.g. LXX Dan 2.28–9; T. Naph. 7.1; Mt 24.6; Rev 1.1).
[21] Lit.: W. Michaelis, *TWNT* 5, pp. 903–39; D. Meyer, 'Πολλὰ παθεῖν', *ZNW* 55 (1964), p. 132.
[22] See Ruppert, pp. 65–6.

has this: *rabbôt rāʿôt ṣaddîq ûmikkullām yaṣṣîlennû YHWH*). While this interesting conjecture cannot be proven, it seems more probable than direct inspiration from Isa 53.4 and 11.[23]

On the chief priests and scribes see on 2.4. The πρεσβύτεροι[24] (= *hazzĕqēnîm*, a lay group), together with the chief priests and scribes, made up the membership of the Sanhedrin in Jerusalem (see Schürer 2, pp. 210–18).[25] The order of the present verse—elders, chief priests, scribes—is unusual because unattested elsewhere. Two observations. First, the Pharisees are not mentioned here. This is because they play no rôle in the passion narrative. Secondly, Matthew does not speak of the Jews rejecting Jesus. Only the leaders are named.[26]

ἀποκτείνειν is elsewhere used of the fate of martyred prophets (e.g. 23.34; Mk 6.19; Rom 11.3, quoting 3 Βασ 19.10; 1 Thess 2.15; Rev 11.7). It also plays a rôle in the *passio iusti* tradition.[27]

καὶ τῇ τρίτῃ ἡμέρᾳ ἐγερθῆναι. Compare Mk 8.31: μετὰ τρεῖς ἡμέρας ἀναστῆναι. With one exception (27.63), Matthew consistently prefers 'on the third day' (the standard patristic expression) over 'after three days';[28] and ἐγείρω* (cf. *qûm*) is one of his favourites. It would be unwise to discern much difference between ἀναστῆναι and ἐγερθῆναι (cf. Bayer, pp. 208–11)—as though Jesus rises on his own in Mark but is raised (by God) in Matthew. Both formulations probably assume that God is the author of the resurrection.[29]

The contrast between Jesus being killed and then being raised (by

---

[23] *Pace* Michaelis (as in n. 21). —Attention should be called to the link maintained between δεῖ and πάσχω in Barnabas: 7.5, 11; 12.5.

[24] Lit.: G. Bornkamm, *TWNT* 6, pp. 655–61; Jeremias, *Jerusalem*, pp. 222–32.

[25] See 21.33; 27.41; 26.3, 47, 57, 27.1, 3, 12, 20; 27.41; 28.12; Mk 11.27; 14.43, 53; 15.1; Lk 9.22; 20.1; 22.52; Acts 4.5, 23; 6.12; 23.14; 25.15; cf. Josephus, *Ant.* 11.83; 12.406. See further Schürer 2, p. 212; also A. F. J. Klijn, 'Scribes, Pharisees, Highpriests, and Elders in the New Testament', *NovT* 3 (1959), pp. 259–67; and Schenk, *Sprache*, pp. 68–69.

[26] On rulers and authorities as the standard opponents of the righteous in Jewish literature and their rôle in the *passio iusti* tradition see L. Ruppert, *Der leidende Gerechte und seine Feinde*, Würzburg, 1973, pp. 81–5.

[27] See Ruppert, *ibid.*, pp. 118–24.

[28] Cf. 1 Cor 15.4. Luke consistently emends Mark's expression. Schlatter, pp. 525–6, shows that 'on the third day' and 'after three days' could be synonymous; see also Taylor, *Mark*, p. 378. Nevertheless, Matthew and Luke clearly prefer 'on the third day'. Is the reason chronological precision, or the establishing of an allusion to Hos 6.2, or the conforming of usage to a standard confession (cf. 1 Cor 15.3)?

[29] Further discussion in R. Schnackenburg, 'Zur Aussageweise "Jesus ist (von den Toten) auferstanden"', *BZ* 13 (1969), pp. 1–17. Mark can use intransitive forms of ἀνίστημι of people who are raised by Jesus or God (cf. 5.42; 12.23, 25). According to Lindars, *Son of Man*, p. 64, the use of ἀνίστημι in the Markan passion predictions goes back to a literal translation of *yĕqûm* (= 'stand'), 'a substitute for the passive of the causative stem (="be caused to stand") . . .'.

God) recalls several sentences in Acts: 2.22–4; 3.13–15; 4.10; 5.30–1; 10.39–40. The contrast scheme these verses enshrine was probably at the centre of the earliest Christian preaching in Jerusalem.[30] This does not, however, require that the passion predictions had their *Sitz im Leben* only in the post-Easter period (see further below).

There are three major passion predictions in Mark.[31] There are four in Matthew: the First Gospel reproduces the Markan three and adds another, 26.1–2. Some have held that one or two of the predictions in Mark, like the fourth in Matthew, should be considered editorial.[32] N. Perrin has even gone so far as to claim that all three passion predictions are creations of the Second Evangelist.[33] But it is worth noting that there are three statements about the Son of man being 'lifted up' in John's gospel: 3.14; 8.28; 12.32–4. These could contain primitive tradition (so Black (v)) and they do, interestingly enough, correspond roughly to the triadic series in Mark.[34] Perhaps, then, the Markan scheme is best thought of as traditional.

Another reason for judging Perrin mistaken is that Mk 8.31 and 9.31 appear to represent two different pre-Markan traditions.[35] Mk 8.31; 9.12b; and Lk 17.25 all contain δεῖ, πολλὰ παθεῖν, and either ἀποδοκιμασθῆναι or ἐξουδενηθῆναι.[36] Mk 9.31; 14.41; and Lk 24.7, on the other hand, have in common the key term, παραδίδωμι, and in Aramaic would involve a wordplay: 'the Son of man ... sons of men'. It is possible that both types circulated at one time without notice of the resurrection, but nothing compels such a conclusion;[37] in fact, there are

[30] Cf. Roloff (v), pp. 38–9; Goppelt 2, p. 6.

[31] 8.31; 9.31; 10.32–4: these become progressively more detailed. This is not so in Matthew, for the fourth prediction (26.1–2) is not as specific as the third (20.17–19).

[32] For the redactional origin of Mk 10.33–4 see Gnilka, *Markus* 2, pp. 95–6. For criticisms see Bayer, pp. 171–4. For the redactional origin of 9.31 or its secondary character *vis-à-vis* 8.31 see Strecker (v) and Hoffmann (v), pp. 171–5. For the redactional origin of 8.31 see Bultmann, *History*, p. 258.

[33] N. Perrin, 'Towards an Interpretation of the Gospel of Mark', in *Christology and a Modern Pilgrimage*, rev. ed., ed. H. D. Betz, Missoula, 1974, pp. 10–21.

[34] See Brown, *John* 1, pp. 145–6.

[35] Cf. Hahn, *Titles*, pp. 37–42; Roloff (v), pp. 39–40.

[36] This type probably had the Son of man as subject. Note that ἀποδοκ. and ἐξουδ. allude to Ps 118.22 and Isa 53.3.

[37] Concerning the παραδίδωμι logia, Mk 14.41 is most likely an abbreviation of the fuller 9.31: 'since the shorter form in Mk 14.41b appears in the immediate context of the betrayal of Jesus, a reference to the death and resurrection would exceed the contextual limits of the narrative surrounding 14.41b' (Bayer, pp. 197–8); also, Lk 9.44, which does not refer to the resurrection, is a Lukan abbreviation of Mk 9.31 (cf. Fitzmyer, *Luke* 1, p. 812). With regard to the πολλὰ παθεῖν tradition, Mk 9.12 is an abbreviated form which presupposes the resurrection (see 9.9); further, the fates of John the Baptist = Elijah and Jesus are set side by side, and as the former did not rise from the dead, mention of Jesus' resurrection would break the parallelism. Neither can Lk 17.25 be cited as evidence for a pre-Lukan *Kurzform* of Mk 8.31, for elsewhere Luke has clearly shortened a passion prediction (Mk 9.31 = Lk 9.44), and 17.25 is at the least a Lukan insertion; see R. Schnackenburg, 'Der eschatologische Abschnitt

points to be made against it (see below). In any event, the existence of at least two different prediction traditions seem probable.

Should one entertain the notion that the two traditions had their origin in words of the historical Jesus? One may begin to answer this very important question by observing that the tradition shows a tendency to become more and more concrete. Mk 10.32–4 supplies the clearest illustration. In these verses the δεῖ—πολλὰ παθεῖν—ἀποδοκιμασθῆναι/ἐξουδενηθῆναι tradition is expanded by details that are manifestly after the event: 'and deliver him to the Gentiles; and they will mock him, and spit upon him, and scourge him'. Other examples of the process include the following: the ἀποκτενοῦσιν of Mk 10.34 has become, in Mt 20.19, σταυρῶσαι; the 'after three days' of Mk 8.31; 9.31; and 10.34 has become, in Matthew and Luke, 'on the third day'; and the 'rejected by the elders and chief priests and scribes' of Mk 8.31 par. is no doubt a specification of what is preserved in Lk 17.25: 'rejected by this generation'. What all this means is that the early traditions were much less specific than what we now find in the gospels. This poses a question. Why were the predictions not specific, concrete, and full of details to begin with? An explanation would be to hand if Jesus himself spoke in an obscure or at least a generalized way of his coming death and vindication.

Beyond this consideration, it must be emphatically said that Jesus certainly sensed his coming troubles and foresaw for himself suffering and death.[38] To begin with, four observations made by C. H. Dodd and repeated by others after him merit our assent: 'We may observe (1) that the whole prophetic and apocalyptic tradition, which Jesus certainly recognized, anticipated tribulation for the people of God before the final triumph of the good cause;[39] (2) that the history of many centuries had deeply implanted the idea that the prophet is called to suffering as a part of his mission; (3) that the death of John the Baptist had shown that this fate was still part of the prophetic calling; and (4) that it needed, not supernatural prescience, but the ordinary insight of an intelligent person, to see whither things were tending, at least during the later stages of the ministry' (Parables, p. 40). When one adds that Mt 10.34–6 = Lk 12.51–3 (see the commentary); Mt 20.22–3 = Mt 10.38–9 (see the commentary); and Lk 12.49–50 (see Allison, pp. 124–8) preserve dominical material, there need not be any doubt about Jesus expecting an untimely and violent demise.[40] Yet even once this is fully granted, the passion predictions as we have them

Lk 17.20–37', in Descamps, Mélanges, pp. 222–3. To all of this we may add that the prediction about the temple in Mk 14.58 and Jn 2.19 is formally very similar to the synoptic passion and resurrection traditions. Both have this structure: destruction/death→(three days later) renewal/resurrection; see esp. Jeremias (v). If one can accept the essential authenticity of Mk 14.58 and Jn 2.19 (see Allison, pp. 153–4), this is reason to suppose that some of the passion predictions were from the beginning also resurrection predictions.
[38] See further Schürmann (v); Vögtle (v); also Schürmann's 'Jesu Todesverständnis im Verstehenshorizont seiner Umwelt', TGl 70 (1980), pp. 141–60.
[39] See further Allison, pp. 5–25.
[40] Also important is the enigmatic Lk 13.32–3; see the commentaries.

not only look forward to Jesus' death but also to his resurrection. Is it at all credible that a foundation for such two-membered predictions is to be discovered in the pre-Easter period?[41]

One may confidently hold that Jesus did not simply predict his own death and the dissolution of his movement. Surely he assumed that God would vindicate his cause notwithstanding the coming time of trouble. It would have been altogether natural for one who had faith in God's justice and power to look beyond present and expected troubles and hope for the Lord's favourable verdict. Such faith and hope in fact together mark the heart of Jewish eschatology, and we scarcely err in supposing that Jesus shared them. Just as the visionary group that spoke of its sufferings in Isa 61.1–3; 63.17; and 65.13–14 also boldly declared its confidence in a swift victory (Isa 57.13; 66.5–16), so Jesus will have believed in God as the one who would speedily rescue him from coming calamity. Moreover, if Jesus had sought to express the idea of vindication despite and subsequent to death, the category of resurrection would naturally have suggested itself, especially as (i) resurrection was closely tied to the thought of martyrdom; (ii) it was hoped that the kingdom of God was at hand; and (iii) Jesus, with the Pharisees and against the Sadducees, accepted the doctrine of the resurrection (cf. Mk 12.18–27 and see on 12.41–2). We therefore concur with C. K. Barrett: 'That Jesus should ... predict that, after dying in fulfilment of the commission laid upon him by God, he would be vindicated, and that he should give his vindication the form of resurrection, is ... in no way surprising' (*Jesus*, p. 78).

Predictions of death followed by resurrection would, we suspect, originally have been tied into the eschatological sequence. After the emerging of Easter faith, forecasts of suffering and resurrection would have been reinterpreted as realized in the exaltation of one man and filled out in the light of his historical passion (cf. above). But resurrection was primarily a collective category, and for Jesus himself, discussion of resurrection would almost certainly have been discussion about eschatological matters, about the vindication of all the saints— just as the prospect of suffering was, in Jesus' proclamation, a collective prospect[42] and part of the latter days. To be sure, Jesus alone is the focal figure of the passion and resurrection predictions as we know them. But the original horizon was presumably wider. The structure of the predictions, death—resurrection, coincides with the eschatological sequence, tribulation—vindication. Is the parallel fortuitous? Not if the passion predictions had their origin in dominical prophecies about the

[41] Bultmann, *Theology* 1, p. 29, could dismiss the predictions with a simple rhetorical question: 'Can there be any doubt that they are all *vaticinia ex eventu?*' This query gains force from the widespread literary habit of making leading characters prophesy their deaths; see e.g. Plato, *Apol.* 39c (Socrates); Philo, *Vit. Mos.* 2.291 (Moses); Acts 20.22 (Paul); Bede, *Vita Sancti Cuthberti* (Cuthbert). Against this, however, one may set the observation that 'men in hazardous occupations or involved in risky undertakings have predicted their deaths with a high degree of accuracy both with regard to mode and time. This can be seen especially during periods of persecution' (Borsch, pp. 330–1).

[42] Cf. esp. Mk 8.31–8 and 10.35–40 and see Barrett, *Jesus*, pp. 49–53.

final affliction and eschatological salvation; not if the picture originally painted was of Jesus and the community around him anticipating the messianic woes and, beyond that, the general resurrection.[43]

Three final points. First, one should keep an open mind even about the note of time in the passion and resurrection predictions.[44] Not only do the words, 'after three days', not correspond to the chronology of the canonical narratives, but 'three days' was the equivalent of 'a little while' or 'a few days'.[45] It is also possible that Hos 6.2, which the targums and the rabbis refer to the general resurrection, is pertinent background;[46] or that the well-attested motif of God not allowing the righteous to suffer beyond three days[47] has made itself felt here (cf. Ruppert, pp. 63–5). Secondly, concerning 'the Son of man', the subject of so many passion and resurrection predictions, there are good reasons for surmising that, on Jesus' lips, the phrase could on occasion possess a collective dimension (see Excursus VI). This is consistent with our claim that the passion predictions may have been formulated with more than the solitary fate of Jesus in view. Thirdly, if the pre-Easter predictions were eschatological in content, there is an intriguing parallel with Dan 7. Just as, in that important text, the saints of the Most High, who are identified with the one like a son of man, are delivered into the hands of their enemy, only to receive the kingdom after a time, two times, and half a time, so Jesus promises that the Son of man, the representative and head of the faithful community, will be delivered into the hands of men, only to be resurrected after three days. Do the passion predictions go back to Jesus' reflection upon Dan 7?[48]

22. Imagining that Jesus 'was the Christ as the generality of men supposed' (Irenaeus, *Adv. haer.* 3.18.4), Peter, playing the fool and not understanding the secret purposes of God (cf. Wisd 2.22), imprudently counters his Lord with these words: 'This will not happen to you!'[49] Perhaps emboldened by the promise that the gates of hades will not prevail against the church, the apostle does not yet recognize that the way to life is

---

[43] See further Allison, pp. 115–41.

[44] Cf. Jeremias (v) and K. Lehmann, pp. 181–5.

[45] See J. B. Bauer, 'Drei Tage', *Bib* 39 (1958), pp. 354–8. Cf. Acts 25.1; 28.7, 12, 17; Josephus, *Ant.* 8.408; LAB 56.7; T. Job 31.2; Par. Jer 9.14; T. Sol. 20.7.

[46] Discussion in H. K. McArthur, 'On the Third Day', *NTS* 18 (1971), pp. 81–6.

[47] See K. Lehmann, passim; also E. L. Bode, *The First Easter Morning*, AnBib 45, Rome, 1970, pp. 119–24.

[48] For this possibility see esp. Schaberg (v). She calls special attention to 7.13 and 25 as well as to 12.2 and observes that it is possible to find connexions between Dan 7.13 and 12.1 and the three Johannine 'lift up' statements (Jn 3.13–14; 8.28; 12.31–4). —Pace Hoffmann (v), p. 184, nothing indicates that the predictions of death and resurrection go back to a prophecy of death and *parousia*.

[49] Compare Apocryphon Jas 5.35–6.1: 'But I [James] answered and said to him, "Lord, do not mention to us the cross and death, for they are far from you"'.

through death.[50] This gives Matthew's Jesus the opportunity to stress, in the strongest way possible, the necessity of messianic suffering. 'Unless a grain of wheat falls into the earth and dies, it remains alone; but if it dies, it bears much fruit'. Peter's fancies and Jesus' subsequent rebuke (v. 23) also forcefully demonstrate the difficulty of apprehending the ways of God.

καὶ προσλαβόμενος αὐτὸν ὁ Πέτρος ἤρξατο ἐπιτιμᾶν αὐτῷ λέγων. So Mk 8.32b, without λέγων and (perhaps) with αὐτόν in the fifth, not third position. Compare *Gen. Rab.* on 22.7, where Samael 'rebukes' Abraham and tries to turn him away from the path of suffering and death, that is, from sacrificing his son Isaac. In the gospels, προσλαμβάνομαι (= 'take aside'; cf. Acts 18.26) appears only in 16.22 = Mk 8.32. 'The motive of the drawing aside was possibly, as Bede suggests, "in order that he might not appear to reprove the Master in the presence of his fellow-disciples": there is a suggestion of patronizing about it' (Cranfield, *Mark*, p. 279).

ἵλεώς σοι, κύριε. Compare LXX 2 Βασ 23.17 (ἵλεώς μοι, κύριε); 1 Chron 11.19 (ἵλεώς μοι ὁ θεός); Isa 54.10 (κύριος ἵλεώς σοι). There is no parallel in Mark.[51] ἵλεως, which is often followed in the LXX, where it is always used with reference to God, by a dative personal pronoun, is found also in Heb 8.12. ἵλεως is the Attic form and appears in the LXX, Philo, and Josephus (cf. also P. Oxy. 939). Homer has ἵλαος. Some Matthean mss. have ἵλεος. According to BAGD, s.v., the word means 'merciful', 'gracious' (cf. ἱλαρός); and one must here supply both a verb (εἴη) and a subject (ὁ θεός): '*may God be gracious* to you, Lord, i.e., may God in his mercy spare you this, God forbid!' (cf. F. Büchsel, *TWNT* 3, pp. 300–1; so RSV and NEB). It is more probable, however, that ἵλεώς σοι, κύριε means something like 'far be it from thee, Lord!' Several times in the LXX ἵλεως does duty for the Hebrew *ḥālîlâ*, an exclamation meaning 'far be it' (cf. BDB, s.v.); see 1 Βασ 14.45; 2 Βασ 20.20; 23.17; 1 Chron 11.19. And two of these texts have ἵλεως + dative personal pronoun + κύριε or ὁ θεός (see above). It is telling that *ḥālîlâ* is sometimes translated in the LXX by μὴ γένοιτο (e.g. Gen 44.7, 17; Josh 24.16). Thus the KJV—'Be it far from thee'—would appear to be the correct translation (cf. Vulgate: *absit a te*). See further BDF § 128.5 and note Liv. Proph. Dan. 18, where ἵλεώς μοι must mean 'far be it from me!'

---

[50] Some would see Peter's rebuke as evidence that the reference to the resurrection is secondary (e.g. Haenchen, *Weg*, p. 296). This seems hypercritical. The prospect of death remains unappealing and unexpected even when accompanied by the promise of resurrection.

[51] Taylor, *Mark*, 379, is not in much company in holding that Mk 8.32b lat and sy[s] contain readings which represent the original Markan text.

οὐ μὴ ἔσται σοι τοῦτο. Again there is no Markan parallel. The words restate for emphasis the protest just lodged: 'This shall not happen to you!' On the future indicative after οὐ μή see BDF § 365.

23. ὁ δὲ στραφεὶς εἶπεν τῷ Πέτρῳ. This abbreviates Mk 8.33a: 'Turning (ἐπιστραφείς[52]) and seeing the disciples he rebuked Peter saying'. The omission of 'rebuked' (ἐπετίμησεν, cf. v. 22) is not easily put down to a desire to spare Peter.[53] The harsh words that follow speak against that.[54]

ὕπαγε ὀπίσω μου, σατανᾶ. So Mark. Compare 4 Βασ 9.19 (ἐπιστρέφου εἰς τὰ ὀπίσω μου, for the MT's *sōb 'el-'aḥărāy*); Mt 4.10 (ὕπαγε, σατανᾶ—redactional).

ὕπαγε ὀπίσω μου is probably just a rebuke meaning 'get away from me' (cf. 4.10 Maj.; Lk 4.8 Maj.). But it is possible that Jesus is telling Peter to get back in line, to quit taking the lead, to become a follower so that he might once more learn what discipleship is all about.

The suggestion that 'μου is possibly an early mistake for σου, which would be a lit. rendering of an Aramaic idiom, equivalent to ὑπ. ὀπίσω or simply ὕπαγε' (so McNeile, p. 245; cf. Bussby (v); Black, p. 218), is quite uncertain. The idiom is attested in Syriac, not Aramaic. Further 4 Βασ 9.19 (see above) supplies a close parallel to the received text.

On 'Satan' see on 4.10. One needs to draw a distinction between playing the rôle of Satan and being possessed by Satan. Peter is doing the former; see Best, pp. 28–33. Contrast Elious in T. Job 41–2: he is 'filled with Satan' and the one speaking in him is 'not man but beast'. (The occasional attempt in church history (note e.g. *Sanc. Pachomi Vit. Gr.* 57) to understand Jesus' words as addressed to Satan *instead of* Peter should be dismissed as apologetics.)

Against Osborne (v), σατανᾶ is not here the equivalent of the evil impulse. Also, while Limbeck (v) might be correct in understanding σατανᾶ to mean not 'Satan' but 'accuser' or 'adversary'[55] (cf. esp. 2 Sam 19.22) as far as Mark or the pre-Markan tradition goes, this cannot be the right interpretation for Matthew. 4.10 is decisive.

σκάνδαλον εἶ ἐμοῦ.[56] Compare 2 Sam 19.22. This is an editorial insertion.

[52] Cf. 9.22 diff. Mk 5.30. Always in Matthew ἐπιστρέφω means 'return'.

[53] On the other hand, it is also impossible to see here a polemic against Peter or his followers. 'The intention is to display, in no less a person than Peter, at the high moment of his confession, the intense power of the Jewish messianic interpretation, which rejected the idea of suffering' (Hill, *Matthew*, p. 264).

[54] And make impossible Origen's attempt to construe ὕπαγε κ.τ.λ. as a mild rebuke (*Comm. on Mt.* 12.21–2). On the tendency of others to weaken Peter's disgrace throughout exegetical history see Gnilka, *Markus* 2, p. 19.

[55] So *śāṭān* often in the OT; cf. Origen, *Comm. on Mt.* 12.21; BDB, s.v.

[56] So ℵ B (C Θ) *f*¹³ 700 *pc*. For ει εμου, L W *f*¹ Maj sy^h have μου ει, 565 εμοι ει, D (*pc*) ει εμοι, ℵ^c C μου. There is no textual evidence for an original ειμι σοι.

σκάνδαλον (LXX: 21, most often for *môqēš* or *mikšôl*; the word is rare in pre-Christian secular Greek) is a Matthean favourite (see on 13.41). For the related verb, σκανδαλίζω, see on 5.29. The noun means 'trap', 'object of offense', or—as here—'temptation to sin' (cf. Wisd 14.11; 1 Macc 5.4; Ps. Sol. 4.23; Mt 18.7; Rom 16.17; Rev 2.14; Barn 4.9).[57] Peter, up against what Paul called 'the stumbling block of the cross' (cf. Gal 5.11; also 1 Cor 1.23), himself has become a stumbling block, an obstacle tempting Jesus to leave the path that goes through Gethsemane and Golgotha (cf. Bengel, *ad loc.*). Two observations need to be made. First, the connexion between Satan and σκάνδαλον is also found in 13.41. Secondly, while Peter is named a rock in 16.18, in 16.23 he is a σκάνδαλον. One wonders whether, as Schweizer, *Matthew*, p. 345, thinks, there is intended a wordplay on the πέτραν σκανδάλου or *ṣûr mikšôl* of Isa 8.14 (cf. Rom 9.33; 1 Pet 2.8).

ὅτι οὐ φρονεῖς τὰ τοῦ θεοῦ ἀλλὰ τὰ τῶν ἀνθρώπων. Compare 12.40 ('he who is not with me is against me') and the formulations in Rom 8.5; Phil. 3.19; and Col 3.2.[58] The words reproduce Mk 8.33c without change. The meaning is: 'because you do not concur with the ways of God (which include suffering and death for the Messiah) but instead concur with the ways of men (expecting the Messiah to triumph without pain)'. Compare Chrysostom, *Hom. on Mt.* 54.6: 'Let them hear, as many as are ashamed of the suffering of the cross of Christ. For if the chief apostle, even before he had learnt all distinctly, was called Satan for feeling this, what excuse can they have, who after so abundant proof deny His economy? I say, when he who had been so blessed, who made such a confession, has such words addressed to him; consider what they will suffer, who after all this deny the mystery of the cross'. For φρονέω τά τινος see Herodotus 2.162; LXX Est 8.13 (12b); 1 Macc 10.20 (other examples in LSJ, s.v. φρονέω, II.2.c.).

(iv) *Concluding Observations*

(1) Everything in our gospel takes its meaning from its relation to the events recounted in chapters 26, 27 and 28. It is therefore not surprising that 16.21–3, the first formal passion prediction,

[57] Lit.: A. Humbert, 'Essai d'une théologie du scandale dans le Synoptiques', *Bib* 35 (1954), pp. 1–28; J. H. Moulton, 'Σκάνδαλον', *ExpT* 26 (1915), pp. 331–2; G. Stählin, *Skandalon*, Gütersloh, 1930; idem, *TWNT* 7, pp. 338–58.

[58] The rabbinic parallels cited by SB 1, p. 748 (including *b. Šabb.* 114a: 'Who is a student of the scribes? He who leaves his business and makes God's business his concern') are not particularly close (cf. Bayer, p. 162, n. 66).

only makes explicit a fact previously foreshadowed and implied in a dozen different ways, namely, that Jesus must go to Jerusalem, be rejected by the Jewish establishment, die, and then rise from the dead. Already the reader knows of the opposition of Jerusalem and the Jewish leaders (2.1–6; 9.32–4; 12.1–8, 14), of Jesus' willingness to take up the rôle of the suffering servant of Isaiah (12.15–21), of his determination to die and redeem his people (1.21; 9.15), and of his coming triumph over death (12.40). 16.21–3 is, accordingly, a knot in the narrative where the various threads are drawn together.

(2) The divine δεῖ of 16.21 should not be taken to mean that Jesus viewed his fate as strictly inevitable, as something which would befall him whether he liked it or not. For the evangelist, Jesus' will and the divine will were one, and the rebuke of Peter shows plainly enough that the Messiah went to his death as a free man, that his destiny was one he chose for himself. He acted voluntarily.

(3) The jarring juxtaposition of 16.13–20, where Jesus congratulates Peter with a makarism, and 16.21–3, where Jesus rebuffs Peter as Satan,[59] is full of edifying lessons which exegetes throughout the centuries have rightly unfolded.[60] To begin with, Peter's pre-eminence makes his misunderstanding in effect universal: if even the favoured Simon, rock of the church and recipient of divine revelation, did not grasp the truth, then, we may assume, that truth was hid from all. God's intentions for Jesus were so dark and mysterious that they simply could not, before the event, be comprehended. This in large part explains why Jesus is such a lonely figure in Matthew and why he is trailed throughout the gospel by misapprehension and even opposition. God's ways are inscrutable. At the same time, the darkness of the pre-Easter period is only revealed to be such by the light diffused by Easter, so the readers of the gospel must know themselves to live in a special time, one no doubt demanding unprecedented responsibilities (cf. Chrysostom as quoted on p. 664). Another lesson is to be found in this, that Peter's fall from the heights shows him to be anything but an idealized figure. Like David and so many other biblical heroes, the apostle serves as a warning that privilege and even divine election will not keep a body from evil mischief. Finally, Peter must also, again like David and so many others, be intended to stand as a symbol of God's ever-ready willingness to bestow

---

[59] Meier, *Vision*, p. 118, prints a helpful diagram.

[60] For Augustine see A.-M. la Bonnardière, 'Tu es Petrus. La péricope Matthieu XVI, 13–23 dans l'oeuvre de S. Augustin', *Irénikon* 34 (1961), pp. 451–99.

forgiveness on the imperfect. For as soon as Peter has been quickly dismissed for words better left unsaid, Jesus selects him, along with two others, to be witnesses of the transfiguration. Thus Peter, so far from being punished for his misguided thoughts, is immediately granted a glimpse of the glorified Christ. Is the reader not expected to see in this a triumph of grace?

(v) *Bibliography*

Allison, pp. 137–40.

Aune, pp. 177–9.

M. Bastin, 'L'annonce de la passion et les critères de l'historicité', *RevScRel* 50 (1976), pp. 289–329; 51 (1977), pp. 187–213.

Bayer, pp. 154–66, 177–90, 199–218, 222–43.

M. Black, 'The "Son of Man" Passion Sayings in the Gospel Tradition', *ZNW* 60 (1969), pp. 1–8.

Borsch, pp. 329–53.

F. Bussby, 'Mark VIII.33: A Mistranslation from the Aramaic?', *ExpT* 61 (1950), p. 159.

P. M. Casey, 'General, Generic and Indefinite: The Use of the Term "Son of Man" in Aramaic Sources and in the Teaching of Jesus', *JSNT* 29 (1987), pp. 40–9.

H. C. Cavallin, 'Tod und Auferstehung der Weisheitslehrer', *SUNT* A5 (1980), pp. 107–21.

J. Ernst, 'Petrusbekenntnis—Leidensankündigung—Satanswort', *Catholica* 32 (1978), pp. 46–73.

A. Feuillet, 'Les trois grandes prophéties de la Passion et de la Résurrection des évangiles synoptiques', *RevThom* 67 (1967), pp. 533–60; 68 (1968), pp. 41–74.

Geist, pp. 127–62.

A. George, 'Comment Jésus a-t-il perçu sa propre mort?', *LumV* 20 (1971), pp. 34–59.

E. Haenchen, 'Die Komposition von Mk viii 27—ix 1 und Par.', *NovT* 6 (1963), pp. 81–109.

Hahn, *Titles*, pp. 37–42.

P. Hoffmann, 'Mk 8.31. Zur Herkunft und markinischen Rezeption einer alten Überlieferung', in Hoffmann, *Orientierung*, pp. 170–204.

M. D. Hooker, *The Son of Man in Mark*, Montreal, 1967, pp. 103–47.

Horstmann, pp. 21–31.

J. Jeremias, 'Die Drei-Tage-Worte der Evangelien', in G. Jeremias, *Tradition*, pp. 221–9.

idem, *Theology*, pp. 276–86.

Lindars, *Son of Man*, pp. 60–74.

I. H. Marshall, 'The Synoptic Son of Man in Recent Discussion', *NTS* 12 (1966), pp. 327–51.

O. Michel, 'Der Umbruch: Messianität=Menschensohn. Fragen zu Markus 8.31', in G. Jeremias, *Tradition*, pp. 310–16.

F. Neirynck, 'ΑΠΟ ΤΟΤΕ ΗΡΞΑΤΟ and the Structure of Matthew', *ETL* 64 (1988), pp. 21–59.

B. A. E. Osborne, 'Peter: Stumbling Block and Satan', *NovT* 15 (1973), pp. 187–90.

Otto, pp. 237–55.

Patsch, pp. 185–97.

R. Pesch, 'Die Passion des Menschensohnes', in Pesch, *Menschensohn*, pp. 166–95.

J. Roloff, 'Anfänge der soteriologischen Deutung des Todes Jesu (Mk.x. 45 und Lk xxii 27)', *NTS* 19 (1972), pp. 38–64.

Ruppert, pp. 60–71.

J. Schaberg, 'Daniel 7, 12 and the New Testament Passion-Resurrection Predictions', *NTS* 31 (1985), pp. 208–22.

W. Schmithals, 'Die Worte vom leidenden Menschensohn', in *Theologia Crucis*, ed. C. Andresen and G. Klein, Tübingen, 1979, pp. 417–45.

H. Schürmann, 'Wie hat Jesus seinen Tod bestanden und verstanden?', in Hoffmann, *Orientierung*, pp. 325–63.

G. Strecker, 'Die Leidens- und Auferstehungsvoraussagen im Markusevangelium', *ZTK* 64 (1967), pp. 16–39; English translation in *Int* 22 (1968), pp. 421–42 ('The Passion and Resurrection Predictions in Mark's Gospel').

V. Taylor, *Sacrifice*, pp. 85–91.

idem, 'The Origin of the Markan Passion Sayings', in *Essays*, pp. 60–71.

Tödt, pp. 141–221.

A. Vögtle, 'Todesankündigungen und Todesverständnis Jesu', in Kertelge, *Tod*, pp. 51–113.

N. Walker, '"After Three Days"', *NovT* 4 (1960), pp. 261–2.

B. Willaert, 'La connexion littéraire entre la première prédiction de la passion et la confession de Pierre chez les synoptiques', *ETL* 32 (1956), pp. 24–45.

XLI

THE COST OF DISCIPLESHIP
(16.24–8)

(i) *Structure*

This passage consists of the briefest narrative introduction (v. 24a: 'Then Jesus said to his disciples') followed by a short collection of logia (vv. 24b–8). The first few sayings focus on discipleship (vv. 24b–6). The last two move attention to the eschatological future, to the coming of the Son of man, when true disciples will be rewarded. The underlying logic is straightforward. Thought of God's future should encourage acts of discipleship in the present, for it is only the final judgement and the final state that count.

16.24–8 is a bit unusual in that all the sayings are connected by catchword. This is not the case for the Markan parallel, Mk 8.34–9.1.[1] It would appear that the First Evangelist has modified his source so as to forge artificial verbal links throughout:

24: θέλει
25: θέλῃ
    τὴν ψυχὴν αὐτοῦ/τὴν ψυχὴν αὐτοῦ
26: τὴν ψυχὴν αὐτοῦ/τῆς ψυχῆς αὐτοῦ
    δώσει
27: ἀποδώσει
    ὁ υἱὸς τοῦ ἀνθρώπου
28: τὸν υἱὸν τοῦ ἀνθρώπου

With few exceptions (e.g. some of the miracle stories[2] and chapter 18), Matthew usually eschews catchword connexions in favour of thematic relations (cf. 1, pp. 87–8). Perhaps the reason for his proceeding otherwise here was a desire for artistic consistency. Having found the first few verses joined by catchword he found it aesthetically appropriate to extend the verbal chain to the end.

There is one more significant structural difference between Mt 16.24–8 and Mk 8.34–9.1. In the latter four sentences are introduced with γάρ (vv. 35, 36, 37, 38). In the former there

---

[1] Only Mk 8.34–7 displays catchword links.
[2] See Held, in *TIM*, pp. 237–9.

are only three such sentences (vv. 25, 26, 27; the γάρ in Mk 8.37 has been dropped). This could have something to do with Matthew's fondness for the triad. The whole section can be set forth so that Jesus (i) utters a general declaration (v. 24) which is then (ii) explicated by three double-membered γάρ statements or questions (vv. 25, 26, 27) which are then (iii) followed by a concluding announcement prefaced by ἀμήν (v. 28).

(ii) *Sources*

Mt 16.24–8 par. is of no help in solving the synoptic problem. If it is not difficult to regard Matthew's text as a revision of Mk 8.34–9.1, nothing demands this, and proponents of the Griesbach hypothesis would have no problem explaining Mark's text as dependent upon Matthew. The differences are relatively slight and can reasonably be attributed to the editorial proclivities of either evangelist. If we, nonetheless, accept Mark's priority, it is only because this can be inferred from other texts and considerations.[3] (For the Lukan parallel, which also depends upon Mark, see Lk 9.23–7.)

(iii) *Exegesis*

In a series of (originally isolated) sayings which contains several doublets (v. 24 = 10.38; v. 25 = 10.39; cf. also v. 27 with 10.32–3 and v. 28 with 10.23)[4] Jesus instructs his followers on the nature of discipleship. The main thrust of the passage is that true discipleship is not easy of achievement because it is a 'following' (v. 24c) of the master's example. If Jesus endured both suffering and crucifixion (16.21–3), likewise must his disciples give up their lives and carry a cross (vv. 24–5). The passage furthermore teaches that following Jesus in such a manner is accomplished primarily through a surrender or denial of self—which, in the context of the gospel as a whole, means above all obedience to another's will. Hardly anything more difficult could be asked of human beings. The effort, however, shall prove more than worth-while, for what matters is not gain in this world (v. 26) but

---

[3] The minor agreements—all insignificant—between Mt 16.24–8 and Lk 9.23–7 against Mark are as follows: εἴ τις in 16.24 = Lk 9.23 diff. Mk 8.34; a form of ἔρχομαι in 16.24 = Lk 9.23 diff. Mk 8.34; αὐτοῦ after ψυχήν in 16.25 = Lk 9.24 diff. Mk 8.35; omission of 'and the gospel' in 16.25 = Lk 9.24 diff. Mk 8.35; use of a passive form of ὠφελέω + nominative ἄνθρωπος in 16.26 = Lk 9.25 diff. Mk 8.36; omission of 'and he said to them' in 16.28 = Lk 9.27 diff. Mk 9.1.

[4] Note that all the parallels belong to chapter 10 and are there also addressed to the disciples.

reward in the world to come (v. 27). Finally, the text underlines its eschatological perspective by proclaiming that the Son of man will come sooner rather than later (v. 28).

Matthew's pericope differs from Mk 8.34–9.1 in the following respects: (i) Jesus no longer speaks to the crowd and the disciples but to the disciples alone (cf. n. 4). (ii) All the sayings—not just some—have been linked by catchword (see above). (iii) The sayings in vv. 24 and 25 have, as one might have anticipated, been partly assimilated to their Q parallels (cf. 10.38 = Lk 14.27; 10.39 = Lk 17.33). (iv) Mk 8.38 (on being ashamed of Jesus in 'this generation') has been omitted (see p. 675). (v) A standard line about each being rewarded according to his deeds has been added (see on v. 27). (vi) The object of 16.28 = Mk 9.1 has, for several reasons, been changed from 'the kingdom of God' to 'the Son of man coming in his kingdom' (see on v. 28).

24. τότε ὁ 'Ιησοῦς εἶπεν τοῖς μαθηταῖς αὐτοῦ. τότε* and ὁ 'Ιησοῦς* are Matthean. Mk 8.34a has been altered so that the disciples alone hear Jesus' hard demands. It would not, in Matthew's eyes, be appropriate for Jesus to demand of the crowds, who have not decided for or against him, what he demands of his closest followers. The inference lies near to hand that the teaching is for the church, not the world at large.

εἴ τις θέλει ὀπίσω μου ἐλθεῖν. Compare 10.38 = Lk 14.27 (Q); also Jn 12.26. Mk 8.34 has ἀκολουθεῖν at the end, Lk 9.23 ἔρχεσθαι. The minor agreement of Matthew and Luke against Mark is probably due to coincidental editing.[5]

ἀπαρνησάσθω ἑαυτὸν καὶ ἀράτω τὸν σταυρὸν αὐτοῦ καὶ ἀκολουθείτω μοι.[6] Compare 10.38. Matthew has followed Mark without alteration. Luke has inserted καθ' ἡμέραν (Lk 9.23) and dropped the ἀπ- prefix. Note the homeophony of the three verbs: each begins with ἀ and ends with θω or τω.

On the verb, ἀπαρνέομαι, Fenton, p. 273, has this to say: 'The same word is used of Peter denying Jesus in 26.34f., 75, and a similar word is used in 10.33, 26.70ff. From these passages, it is clear that the word means "to disown somebody", "to disclaim any connexion with somebody". The condition of discipleship is therefore the breaking of every link which ties a man to himself; cf. *You are not your own*, 1 Cor 6.19' (cf. Bengel, *ad loc.*).

---

[5] Luke also evidently replaced a form of ἀκολουθέω with a form of ἔρχομαι in Lk 14.27 diff. Mt 10.30.

[6] Given its absence from all Greek mss. of Matthew, Mark, and Luke, the interesting Diatessaronic reading, 'take his cross upon his shoulders . . .', is probably secondary. According to W. L. Petersen, 'Romanos and the Diatessaron', *NTS* 29 (1983), pp. 491–2, it is to be explained by way of Isa 9.6 ('the government shall be upon his shoulders'); cf. Justin, *1 Apol.* 35.2. One wonders, however, whether an Isaac typology is not in the background. Isaac carried wood on his shoulders (so the Palestinian targums on Gen 22.3–6).

(According to Bultmann, *History*, p. 161, n. 1, ἀπαρνεῖθαι ἑαυτόν 'is foreign to Semitic usage'. On p. 414 he writes that the words are 'in all probability the Greek substitute for μισεῖν τὴν ψυχήν'.)

The first two verbs in v. 24b—ἀπαρνησάσθω and ἀράτω—are aorist, the third—ἀκολουθείτω—present. This suggests that the decision to renounce the self and to take up one's cross stands at the beginning of the disciple's journey and is to be followed by a continued determination to stick to the chosen path. One first picks up the cross and then one carries it, following the trail first walked by Jesus.

Marshall, p. 373, rightly catches the impact of v. 24 as a whole: the verse depicts the disciple as in 'the position of the man who is already condemned to death', and it enjoins a self-denial which 'regards its life in this world as *already finished . . .*'. For further discussion see on 10.38.

25. As the γάρ indicates, v. 25 elucidates v. 24: one must take up one's cross because it is only through the loss of life—that is, displacement of the ego from the centre of its universe and the accompanying willingness to give up personal ambition and even to suffer and, if need be, die for God's cause—that life—the eschatological life so well depicted by the beatitudes—is gained. Meier, *Matthew*, p. 187, aptly comments: 'The paradox of temporal loss for eternal gain is *the* law of Christian existence'. Maybe the best commentary is Gal 2.20: 'I have been crucified with Christ. It is no longer I who live . . .' (cf. Origen, *Comm. on Mt.* 12.25). For further discussion see on 10.39.

ὃς γὰρ ἐὰν θέλῃ τὴν ψυχὴν αὐτοῦ σῶσαι ἀπολέσει αὐτήν. So Mk 8.35 (also Lk 9.24, with the more correct ἄν[7]). The Q version (10.39 = Lk 17.33) differs slightly in wording but not in content. For σῴζω + ψυχήν see LXX Gen 19.17; 1 Βασ 19.11; Jer 31.6; Amos 2.14 (all four times for *mālaṭ* in niphal or piel + *nepeš*); Josephus, *Ant.* 9.240; 11.255; and T. Abr. A 11.10, 12. Note also 1Q27 1.3–4: 'They do not know what shall befall them, nor do they *save their life* from the mystery to come'. For the meaning of ψυχή see on 10.28 and 39.

ὃς δ' ἂν ἀπολέσῃ τὴν ψυχὴν αὐτοῦ ἕνεκεν ἐμοῦ εὑρήσει αὐτήν. Three changes have been made. Mark's ἑαυτοῦ after τήν[8] has been eliminated and replaced with αὐτοῦ after ψυχήν (cf. Jn 12.25); his 'and for the gospel' (after ἐμοῦ) and has fallen away (cf. 19.29 diff. Mk 10.29; did Matthew think 'on account of me' and 'on account of the gospel' synonymous?); and σώσει has given way to εὑρήσει (which makes an antithesis with

---

[7] ἐάν after relatives is found in the LXX and the papyri; see on 11.27.

[8] HG prints την εαυτου ψυχην (so B 28 Or). NA[26], preferring the preponderance of the external evidence, prints την ψυχην αυτου, but this reading could be due to harmonization.

ἀπολέσῃ). All three changes mark assimilation to the parallel in 10.39.[9]

The fixed expression, ἕνεκεν ἐμοῦ (cf. 5.11; 10.18, 39; see Satake (v)) here means in effect that the disciple is Jesus' possession: believers act for the sake of Jesus in obedience to his will. The lord of the self has become another.

26. The primacy or ultimate value of a person's life (ψυχή) as compared with all else is now proclaimed by two questions whose (negative) answers are too obvious to be made explicit. What good is even the greatest possession if there is no possessor to enjoy it (cf. Zahn, p. 560)? (The point is not the surpassing value of human beings as such but rather life as the prerequisite for enjoying anything; cf. Gnilka, *Markus* 2, p. 25). There is no value in gaining the (present) world if the cost is loss of life in the world to come (cf. 6.19–24).[10]

τί γὰρ ὠφεληθήσεται ἄνθρωπος ἐὰν τὸν κόσμον ὅλον κερδήσῃ τὴν δὲ ψυχὴν αὐτοῦ ζημιωθῇ; Compare Eccles 1.3 ('What does a man gain by all the toil at which he toils under the sun?') and 2 Bar. 51.15 ('For what then have men lost their life, and for what have those who were on the earth exchanged their soul?').

Matthew's line is based upon Mk 8.36 (cf. Lk 9.25), which has ὠφελήσει ἄνθρωπον (Matthew's nominative makes for a better parallel with v. 26b and improves the Greek—which is why the same change occurs in Luke), the second verb[11] in the sixth rather than the ninth place, and καὶ ζημιωθῇ[12] τὴν ψυχὴν αὐτοῦ for its conclusion. For τί before a form of ὠφελέω see also LXX Hab 2.18 (for *mâhô'îl*); Wisd 5.8; Ecclus 34.23–5; 1 Cor 14.6; and Ignatius, *Smyr.* 5.2.

κόσμος has the sense, 'the external considered as a counter attraction to the spiritual and eternal' (Swete, p. 184) or, more precisely, 'the prizes of business and social life' (Taylor, *Mark*, p. 382).

Schlatter, pp. 521–3, refers τὸν κόσμον ὅλον κερδήσῃ to the disciples' missionary work: while saving others, they are not to neglect their own salvation (cf. 1 Cor 9.27).[13] This is improbable with reference both to Jesus and to Matthew. It is much more natural, especially in view of the possible

[9] This is pertinent for evaluating two of the minor agreements listed in n. 3 (αὐτοῦ after ψυχήν and omission of 'and the gospel').

[10] Lines from 6.19–24 and 16.24–8 are naturally associated because of theme, and they are in fact brought together in patristic texts (e.g. Justin, *1 Apol.* 15; 2 Clem. 6).

[11] NA[26] prints κερδησαι without εαν (so ℵ B 0214[vid] 892 1424), but HG has κερδηση (so A (C) D (L) W Θ *f*[1.13] Maj latt).

[12] So HG. NA[26] prints ζημιωθηναι; see previous note.

[13] For κερδαίνω used of winning converts see D. Daube, 'κερδαίνω as a Missionary Term', *HTR* 40 (1947), pp. 109–20.

rabbinic parallels,[14] to think of 6.19–24 as well as of 4.8–9 (the devil's offer of the world): the temptation is to seek lordship over worldly situations and ownership of worldly goods (cf. H. Schlier, *TWNT* 3, p. 672).

The ψυχή (see on 10.28 and 39) is the true self, that part which can survive death. Luke can rightly replace τὴν ψυχὴν αὐτοῦ with ἑαυτόν. ζημιόω[15] (LXX: 7, six times for the qal or niphal of '*ānaš* = 'fine', 'punish') in the passive is the antithesis of κερδαίνω (cf. Phil 3.8) and means 'suffer loss' (cf. Prov 22.3; 2 Cor 7.9; Phil 3.8). For its use with the accusative (cf. Philo, *Spec. leg.* 3.143; Josephus, *Ant.* 11.214) see BDF § 159.2. Here the word calls to mind the final judgement: punishment[16] will be meted out when the Son of man comes at the end of the age (cf. 16.27). Yet Matthew must also have believed that even in this world those who do not live towards God forfeit their lives.

Whether or not 16.26a par. was based upon a proverbial sentiment,[17] its truth, if one believes God to be lord of the future, is patent. Those who gain this world at the cost of the next are dangers to their own souls, fools without peer. 'No mortal can in solid reality be lord of anything' (Philo, *De cherub.* 83). This life offers no certainties, no permanent security, no lasting inheritance. Nothing belongs to us in the end; rather, we belong to death (cf. Pesch 2, p. 63). To seek worldly possessions and power at the expense of repose in a place of everlasting treasure (6.19–21) is an unconscionable blunder, with sin as its only possible explanation. Recall Lk 12.16–21.

Mt 16.26a par. was evidently quite popular among early Christians. Variants appear in 2 Clem. 6.2;[18] Justin, *1 Apol.* 15.12 (Matthean influence is clear); and Clement of Alexandria, *Strom.* 4.6. Also, Ignatius, *Rom.* 6.1 ('The farthest bounds of the universe shall profit me nothing. ... It is good for me to die for Jesus Christ rather than to reign over the farthest bounds of the earth')[19] may presuppose our saying. In addition, Gos. Thom. 67 ('Whoever knows the all but fails (to know) himself lacks any place at all') just might be a reworked edition of the logion found in Mt 16.26a par.

ἢ τί δώσει ἄνθρωπος ἀντάλλαγμα τῆς ψυχῆς αὐτοῦ; Even if one

---

[14] See SB 1, p. 749, and Daube, as in previous note.

[15] See A. Stumpff, *TWNT* 2, pp. 890–4.

[16] ζημιόω often has a legal sense; see Stumpff, as in previous note.

[17] Beare, p. 360: 'This saying looks like a proverb of profane wisdom—what is the point of making millions if you kill yourself in the effort?' Cf. Bultmann, *History*, p. 97, citing Ecclus 11.18–19; Ps.-Phoc. 116–17; and SB 2, pp. 190–1, and arguing for a non-dominical origin. But would not the saying have taken on a new meaning in the context of Jesus' eschatological preaching?

[18] Donfried, p. 83, considers this possibly independent of the synoptics.

[19] Some mss. follow these words with Mt 16.26.

has gained the whole world, it cannot be returned in exchange for participation in eternal life. Worth comparing is Ps 49.7–9: 'Truly no man can ransom himself, or give to God the price of his life, for the ransom of his life is costly and can never suffice, that he should live forever . . .'. Perhaps our text was first formulated with (the Hebrew text of) this line from the Psalms in view.[20] If so, vv. 26a and b could well have originated together, and their basis would be the OT, not secular wisdom.

Mk 8.37 begins with τί γάρ; for the rest there are no differences.[21] Luke fails to supply a parallel. Matthew's ἤ τί is due to structural considerations. The revision stresses the continuity between vv. 26a and b and underlines the fact that the two questions go hand in hand. It also leaves 16.24–8 with only three γάρ statements (cf. p. 669). ἀντάλλαγμα (LXX: 10; NT: 2) is 'something given in exchange', 'recompense'.[22] Compare especially Ecclus 26.14: 'Nothing can be given in exchange (ἀντάλλαγμα) for a disciplined soul'.

Bultmann, *History*, pp. 97–8, is able to cite several secular parallels (e.g. Homer, *Il.*9.401–2 and passages from *A Thousand and One Nights*). He believes that we have here a proverb which the church took from folk-lore, a proverb which originally gave expression to the notion that life is itself the highest good. The saying is not to be attributed to Jesus (cf. *ibid.*, pp. 102–4). This verdict is not required. A background in the OT is near to hand (cf. above), and v. 26b (along with v. 26a) would fit well the eschatological preaching of Jesus (cf. n. 17 and Pesch 2, p. 63).

27. This is a doublet of the Q saying in 10.33 = Lk 12.9. See on 10.33 for questions of tradition-history, authenticity, and interpretation; and see Excursus VI on the Son of man question.

One may observe that if, as is natural, 16.13–28 be regarded as a unit,[23] then with vv. 27 and 28 the third major christological theme of the section is enunciated. 16.13–20 largely concerns Jesus' identity (he is the Messiah and the Son of God). 16.21–3 then tells of Jesus' upcoming passion and resurrection. Finally, 16.27–8 is about Jesus' future as the eschatological judge, the Son of man of Dan 7. The sequence is: identity, history, future.

μέλλει γὰρ ὁ υἱὸς τοῦ ἀνθρώπου ἔρχεσθαι ἐν τῇ δόξῃ τοῦ πατρὸς αὐτοῦ μετὰ τῶν ἀγγέλων αὐτοῦ. Compare 24.30f.; 25.31. Mk

[20] There is no dependence upon the LXX.

[21] NA[26] prints the vernacular δοι in Mk 8.37 (so ℵ* B). The future indicative δώσει of P[45] A C D W Θ *f*[1.13] Maj latt is more likely to be original (so HG).

[22] Beginning with Origen, *Comm. on Mt.* 12.28, Christian commentators have often elaborated the saying by asserting that only Christ or his blood could ransom a human soul.

[23] Cf. Schweizer, *Matthew*, p. 347, observing that 'Son of man' occurs both at the beginning (16.13) and the end (vv. 27–8).

8.38 reads: 'For whoever is ashamed of me and of my words in this adulterous and sinful generation, of him will the Son of man also be ashamed, when he comes in the glory of his Father'. Matthew has eliminated the first half of Mark's line. This enables him, with the addition of v. 27b, to continue the run of double-membered subunits (cf. vv. 25 and 26 and see p. 668).[24] Our evangelist has also added (in anticipation of v. 28; see below) μέλλει,[25] changed ἔλθῃ to ἔρχεσθαι (an alteration required by the addition of μέλλει), and replaced the concluding τῶν ἁγίων with the simple possessive, αὐτοῦ (Matthew never has 'holy angels', and ἀγγέλων αὐτοῦ—cf. 13.41; 24.31; 25.31— parallels both πατρὸς αὐτοῦ and πρᾶξιν αὐτοῦ).

Although μέλλω need not imply imminence (cf. 3.7; 11.14; 12.32), more often than not it does in the First Gospel (2.13; 17.12, 22; 24.6). That nearness is intended in 16.27, where the verb is editorial, is strongly suggested by what follows, v. 28, which is an assertion about the Son of man coming in the near future (see below). In fact, v. 28 can be viewed as explicating the μέλλει of v. 27.

ἐν τῇ δόξῃ τοῦ πατρὸς αὐτοῦ[26] (cf. 6.29—Solomon's glory; 25.31—the Son of man's glory; also Rom 6.4: διὰ τῆς δόξης τοῦ πατρός) means 'in the splendour'[27] (or: glory) of his Father'. The phrase, which takes up a major biblical concept,[28] makes its impact first from the immediately preceding lines (which are about suffering and death) and the earthly fate of the speaker (Jesus). The future will stand in stark contrast to the present. If now the Son of man and his followers are rejected, forced to suffer, and even executed, things to come will see the world turned upside down (cf. the beatitudes). The Son of man, once rejected and despised, will participate in God's eschatological kābôd.[29] Then, secondly, 'in the δόξῃ of his Father' gains meaning from what follows, the pericope about the transfiguration of Jesus before his three disciples. Clearly the appearance of Jesus bathed in light is presented as an anticipation

[24] It does not suffice to assert that Mk 8.38a is omitted because its content has been given before (cf. 10.33; 12.39; 16.4): the First Evangelist has a tendency to assimilate doublets to each other, not eliminate them.
[25] Cf. 17.12 diff. Mk 9.13; 17.22 diff. Mk 9.31; 20.22 diff. 10.38; 24.6 diff. Mk 13.7.
[26] Schlatter, p. 523, compares *t. Ḥag.* 2.1: 'the glory of our Father who is in heaven'.
[27] For δόξα as 'splendour' or 'radiance'—so often in the LXX—see Philo, *Spec. leg.* 1.45; Acts 22.11; 1 Cor 15.40–1; *PGM* 13.189; T. Job 33.2–3.
[28] On 'the glory of God' see R. Kittel, *TWNT* 2, pp. 235–58; also G. H. Davies, *IDB*, s.v., 'Glory', and the lit. cited there.
[29] In the Similitudes of Enoch, the Elect One or Son of man is frequently associated with glory—e.g. 1 En. 45.3; 55.4; 61.8; 62.2; 69.29 (always the 'seat' or 'throne of glory'; cf. Mt 19.28; 25.31).

of his eschatological glory (cf. Lk 9.32: 'they saw his δόξαν').[30] καὶ τότε ἀποδώσει ἑκάστῳ κατὰ τὴν πρᾶξιν αὐτοῦ. Following his beloved τότε*, Matthew continues with OT phraseology. There is no synoptic parallel. Compare LXX Ps 61.13 (σὺ ἀποδώσεις ἑκάστῳ κατὰ τὰ ἔργα αὐτοῦ); Prov 24.12 (ὃς ἀποδίδωσιν ἑκάστῳ κατὰ τὰ ἔργα αὐτοῦ); Ecclus 35.22 (ἕως ἀνταποδῷ ἀνθρώπῳ κατὰ τὰς πράξεις αὐτοῦ); T. Job 17.3 (ἀποδώσω αὐτῷ καθὰ ἔπραξεν); LAB 3.10. Very similar words also appear in Rom 2.6; 2 Tim 4.14; Rev 2.23; 22.12 (both sayings of the risen Lord); and Apoc. Pet. 1 (Ethiopic; cf. also Ps. Sol. 17.8–10; 2 Cor 11.15; 1 Pet 1.17; 1 Clem. 34.3; 2 Clem. 11.6; Hermas, Sim. 6.3.6; Acts Thom. 29). In view of all these texts, it seems more proper to speak of a stereotyped phrase or expression rather than a scriptural citation or allusion.[31]

On the singular, πρᾶξιν,[32] Bengel, ad loc., appropriately remarked: 'in the singular, for the whole life of man is one doing' (cf. Schweizer, Matthew, p. 347).

That there is any real contradiction between Mt 16.27b and Paul's doctrine of justification by faith would seem to be unlikely. For one thing, Paul himself, in Romans, could write that God 'will render to every man according to his works' (Rom 2.6; cf. 1 Cor 3.10–15; 2 Cor 5.10). For another, Matthew no less than Paul believed that salvation was God's gift (cf. Przybylski, pp. 106–7). If there is no antithesis between faith and works, then there need be no contradiction between justification by faith and judgement according to works.[33]

28. The section winds up with an asseveration whose interpretation has long divided exegetes.[34] ἀμὴν λέγω ὑμῖν. So also Mk 9.1 (after καὶ ἔλεγεν αὐτοῖς). For 'amen' see on 5.18. The omission of Mark's 'and he said to them' links v. 28 more closely to what precedes. On ἀμὴν λέγω ὑμῖν + οὐ μή + ἕως ἄν sentences see 1, pp. 487–9.

ὅτι εἰσίν τινες τῶν ὧδε ἑστώτων οἵτινες οὐ μὴ γεύσωνται θανάτου ἕως ἂν ἴδωσιν τὸν υἱὸν τοῦ ἀνθρώπου ἐρχόμενον ἐν τῇ βασιλείᾳ αὐτοῦ. Compare Jn 8.51–2;[35] Gos.

[30] The phrase, 'to come in (or: with) glory' was later taken up into the creeds: 'who shall come again in glory to judge the quick and the dead'.
[31] Pace M. Dibelius and H. Conzelmann, The Pastoral Epistles (trans. of Die Pastoralbriefe, fourth ed., 1966), Hermeneia, Philadelphia, 1972, p. 123, there is no real reason to suspect that ἀποδώσει κ.τ.λ. was 'perhaps a Jewish curse formula'.
[32] Cf. the Hebrew singulars in Ps 62.13 and Prov 24.12.
[33] See further Sanders, Paul, pp. 515–18. The rabbis taught that salvation was a gift while they at the same time spoke of judgement according to deeds.
[34] For a review of the history of interpretation see Künzi (v).
[35] This is clearly a variant of our saying, and probably independent of the synoptics; see B. Lindars, 'Discourse and Tradition: The Use of the Sayings of Jesus in the Discourses of the Fourth Gospel', JSNT 13 (1981), pp. 97–7.

Thom. 18 (see p. 681); *P. Oxy.* 654.5; also LXX 2 Esdr 15.3–4 (εἰσιν τινες + nominative participle). Through ἴδωσιν Matthew follows Mark[36] with only one deviation: ἑστώτων has replaced ἑστηκότων.[37] After ἴδωσιν the First Evangelist goes his own way. Mark has: τὴν βασιλείαν τοῦ Θεοῦ ἐληλυθυῖαν ἐν δυνάμει (cf. Jn 3.3). The substitution of τὸν υἱὸν τοῦ ἀνθρώπου κ.τ.λ., which switches attention from the kingdom to Jesus, continues the string of catchword connexions in 16.24–8 (see p. 668). It also makes for greater parallelism with v. 27: both vv. 27 and 28 have 'the Son of man' + a form of ἔρχομαι + ἐν τῇ + noun in the dative case + αὐτοῦ. For 'his kingdom'[38] (Mt: 2; Mk: 0; Lk: 0) see also 13.41 (cf. 20.21; Lk 22.29; also Mt 16.18: 'my church').

'Coming in his kingdom', a phrase which appears nowhere else in Matthew, is worthy of remark. Of believers it is said that they, at the end, will enter into the kingdom. But of Jesus it is said that he will come ἐν τῇ βασιλείᾳ αὐτοῦ. That is, instead of entering the kingdom he brings it with him (cf. Schlatter, pp. 524–5).

What does Mt 16.28 mean? These are the possibilities. (i) The reference could be to the transfiguration. When the disciples saw Jesus on the mountain with Moses and Elijah, they were in truth seeing the Son of man coming in his kingdom (cf. 2 Pet 1.16–18?). This was the interpretation of most of the Fathers, and it would also seem to have been Mark's understanding.[39] Further, there are significant links between 16.28 and 17.1–13. Both have to do with vision (16.28: ἴδωσιν; 17.2: μετεμορφώθη; v. 3: ὤφθη; v. 9: τὸ ὅραμα). Both involve only some of the disciples (16.28: τινες; 17.1: Jesus took Peter and James and John). And both contain eschatological motifs (16.28: the Son of man coming in his kingdom; 17.3: Moses and Elijah—cf. Rev 11.3–13;

[36] Both Zahn, p. 561, and Schlatter, p. 525, defend the priority of Mt 16.28. Against this see Chilton, *Strength*, pp. 253–5.

[37] There is some doubt as to the placement of ὧδε in Mark. See the commentaries and NA[26], p. 117.

[38] Gundry, *Commentary*, p. 341: 'In quick succession the first evangelist has written about the Father of the Son of man, the angels of the Son of man, and the kingdom of the Son of man—a Christological emphasis hard to overestimate'.

[39] Clement of Alexandria, *Exc. Thdot.* 4.3; Origen, *Comm. on Mt.* 12.31 ('some' refer 16.28 to the transfiguration); Ephraem the Syrian, *Comm. ev. con.* 14.57; Hilary, *De trin.* 11.37; Cyril of Jerusalem, *Comm. on Lk.* 51; Chrysostom, *Hom. on Mt.* 56–7; Augustine, *De con. ev.* 2.56; Cyril of Alexandria, *Comm. on Mt.* 16.18. For Mark's view see G. H. Boobyer, *St. Mark and the Transfiguration Story*, Edinburgh, 1942; Cranfield, *Mark*, pp. 287–8; Schierse (v); Nardoni (v). The identification of the transfiguration with the event foretold in Mk 9.1 lies behind the chapter division of Mk 8–9: 9.1 is joined not with 8.38 but with the following narrative. That this is the correct interpretation is suggested by the καὶ ἔλεγεν αὐτοῖς of Mk 9.1, which implies that the saying was originally isolated. Mark apparently placed the logion before the transfiguration because he understood the one to be promise, the other fulfilment. For another view of the matter see Ambrozic (v).

v. 5: the cloud—cf. Mt 24.30; 26.64; 1 Thess 4.17). The one objection is that 'the Son of man coming in his kingdom' is most naturally associated with the *parousia*. Particularly decisive in this regard is 16.27: 'The Son of man will come in the glory of his Father with his angels and then will render to each according to his work'. This is about the last judgement, and it would be quite odd if the very next verse, which is also about the Son of man coming, were about a different event.

(ii) Calvin took Mt 16.28 par. to be a prophecy not of the transfiguration but of the resurrection.[40] There is much to be said for this. In 28.16–20 the resurrected Jesus speaks the language of enthronement: ἐδόθη μοι πᾶσα ἐξουσία ἐν οὐρανῷ καὶ ἐπὶ τῆς γῆς (cf. Dan 7.14 and see our comments, *ad loc.*). Here there seems to be a sort of proleptic *parousia*.[41] Meier, *Matthew*, p. 188, could well be correct: 'Perhaps Mt makes a distinction between the Son of Man's coming in apocalyptic glory to judge on the last day and his coming to his church in an anticipated "parousia" at the end of the gospel (cf. 28:16–20). It is at that moment, after the turning point of the ages (the death-resurrection), that Jesus the Son of Man can proclaim for the first time that he has received all power over the cosmos (28 18). Then, for the first time, do his disciples see him coming with his royal power'.[42]

(iii) A few have identified the coming of the Son of man in 16.28 par. with the post-Easter outpouring of the Holy Spirit.[43] Pentecost, however, is nowhere mentioned in our gospel.

(iv) Gregory the Great (*Hom.* 32; see PL 76.1232–8) argued for fulfilment in the early triumph of Christianity (cf. Cotter (v)). Equating the kingdom with the church, Gregory claimed that at least some of the apostles lived long enough to see the ecclesia expanding vigorously into the world and overtaking its enemies (cf. Bede, in PL 92.215). Swete, *Mark*, p. 186, is a modern proponent of this view, which has had currency among Roman Catholics especially. But the criticism made against (i) applies here equally.

(v) Wettstein, *ad loc.*, connects Mt 16.28 par. with the destruction of Jerusalem in A.D. 70: this last was the Son of man's judgement of Israel (cf. Alford 1, p. 177). This position gains support from those who would affirm that 24.4–31 is not about the return of Jesus at the close of the age but about the Jewish war and the destruction of the temple.[44] We, however, in the commentary on chapter 24, have argued against this interpretation. It seems to us that the coming of the Son of man in 24.30 must be identified with the *parousia*.

(vi) According to Plummer, p. 236, Mt 16.28 'hardly admits of any other interpretation than the Second Advent'; and 'at the time when

[40] Calvin, *ad loc.*: 'By the coming of the kingdom of God we are to understand the manifestation of heavenly glory which Christ began to make at his resurrection . . .'.

[41] Cf. Meier, *Law*, pp. 35–7; Schaberg, pp. 111–30.

[42] Cf. Lindars, *Son of Man*, pp. 118–20.

[43] T. F. Glasson, *The Second Advent*, London, 1947, p. 112, argues that Jesus' prophecy looked forward to Pentecost but that Matthew mistakenly thought of the *parousia*.

[44] Cf. S. Brown, 'The Matthean Apocalypse', *JSNT* 4 (1979), pp. 2–27.

Mt. wrote, it was commonly believed that most of those who were then alive would live to see the Second Advent (1 Thes. iv. 15), and some of the Twelve were then alive' (cf. Schlatter, p. 524, citing Jn 21.20–3). Even though this entails that the First Gospel contains a false prophecy, probably a majority of modern commentators would endorse Plummer's words, or at least concur that the First Evangelist had in mind the *parousia*.[45] Compare 4 Ezra 4.26: 'If you are alive, you will see, and if you live long, you will often marvel, because the age is hastening swiftly to its end'.

(vii) It is possible to think of 'to taste death' as referring not to physical death but to a spiritual death. It suffices to quote Cranfield, *Mark*, p. 286: 'It is true that Jn viii. 51f. provides support for such a use of γεύεσθαι θανάτου, and that for the thought of a spiritual death from which believers will be exempt we may compare Jn xi. 26, and also that in this context (viii. 35) the idea of a life which can be retained even when one has lost one's life is present; but for this interpretation ἕως is difficult—would it be implied that after they have seen, they will "taste death"?'

(viii) One could conceivably argue that Matthew simply passed on 16.28 without himself giving it any particular interpretation. As a transmitter of Jesus' words, might he not have included in his gospel authoritative sayings which he did not understand (cf. Luz 1, p. 382, on 7.6)? The difficulty with this is twofold. First, Matthew certainly had the freedom to omit what he did not like, find useful, or comprehend (e.g. Mk 6.52; 14.51–2). Secondly, the substitution of 'the Son of man coming in his kingdom' for Mark's 'the kingdom of God has come in power' points to a definite understanding. Matthew has interpreted Mark.

Our choice concerning the redactional understanding of 16.28 would clearly seem to be between (ii) and (vi). As to which one of these is correct, one is hard pressed to say. But perhaps the two are in fact complementary. The resurrection is, for Matthew, an eschatological event (see esp.on 27.51–3). Moreover, both the resurrection and the *parousia* are associated with Danielic Son of man imagery; see, for example, on 24.30 and 28.18. Consequently, the resurrection is a foretaste of the second advent, a preview of what is to come. More than this, it is the first act in the eschatological instalment of Jesus. This makes it possible to suppose that, from Matthew's perspective, 16.28 looks forward at the same time to both the resurrection and the *parousia*. In other words, 16.28 foretells both because they are the two halves of one event, the eschatological glorification and vindication of the Son of man.

Turning from Matthew to the pre-Matthean tradition, we have already expressed our conviction that, in Mark, the saying should be linked first to the transfiguration. But what of the pre-Markan

[45] Cf. Sabourin (v); Gnilka, *Matthäusevangelium* 2, p. 89.

tradition? How was our saying understood, and how did it come into being? In addition to the explanations catalogued above, the following have been offered. (i) C. H. Dodd, stressing the past sense of the perfect participle (ἐληλυθυῖαν), contended that 'the meaning appears to be that some of those who heard Jesus speak would before their death awake to the fact that the Kingdom of God had come. The only open question is whether Jesus meant that the Kingdom had already, in His ministry, come "with power", and that His hearers would afterwards recognize the fact, or whether He intended to distinguish its partial coming at the moment of speaking from some subsequent coming "with power"' (*Parables*, pp. 37–8). Today this interpretation has few if any defenders.[46]

(ii) V. Taylor, *Mark*, p. 386, accepting the saying as dominical, wrote this: 'A visible manifestation of the Rule of God displayed in the life of an Elect Community is the most probable form of His expectation; but what this means cannot be described in detail because the hope was not fulfilled in the manner in which it presented itself to Him, although later it found expression in the life of the Church, as it still does in its life and its impact on human society'.

(iii) W. Michaelis, suggesting that ὧδε means 'thus', and that τῶν ἑστηκότων refers to 'those who stand' (as opposed to those who fall), finds a statement about the last generation (and not the generation of Jesus): 'Some (will) stand in such a way as not to taste death'.[47] This hypothesis has largely been neglected.

(iv) B. Chilton, pp. 251–74, reconstructs this original: 'Amen I say to you, there are those standing (by) who will not taste death until they see the kingdom of God in power'. Identifying those who will not taste death with immortals—such as angels, Enoch, Elijah[48]—, Chilton takes the meaning to be that God's revelation on behalf of his people is a reality; that is, Jesus is promising the kingdom in power, and the immortals are sureties of his promise. Chilton's work does not, we think, make his interpretation more than a novel conjecture, in part because it is unnecessary to equate those who will not taste death with immortals.[49] See further Carson, 'Matthew', pp. 380–82.

(v) Bultmann, *History*, p. 121, spoke for many: Mk 9.1 is 'a community formulation of consolation in view of the delay of the

---

[46] For critical discussion see the contributions cited by Beasley-Murray, p. 380, n. 151.

[47] W. Michaelis, *Der Herr verzieht nicht die Verheissung*, Berne, 1942, pp. 34–9.

[48] Cf. 4 Ezra 6.25–6; Tg. Ps.-J. on Deut 32.1. 'To taste death' is a Semitic idiom—not found in the OT—with parallels in literary Greek. In the synoptics it occurs only in Mt 16.28 par. Cf. J. Behm, *TWNT* 1, p. 672; SB 1, pp. 751–2. For the comparable 'to taste life' idiom see Horsley 4, p. 41.

[49] The '(not) to taste death' idiom is not connected with immortals in the following places: Jn 8.52; Heb 2.9; Gos. Thom. 1, 18, 19, 85; *IGA* 5.423; LAB 48.1; Aristides, *Apol.* 15. Compare Lk 2.26, of Simeon: 'it had been revealed to him that he would not see death before he had seen the Lord's Christ'. 'To see death' is here the equivalent of 'to taste death' (cf. T. Abr. A 19). Chilton, 'Usage' (v), argues that 4 Ezra 6.26 and Tg. Ps.-J. on Deut 32.1 represent first century Palestinian usage, but the evidence is much too meagre.

Parousia: at any rate some will still live to see it'.[50]

(vi) Others holding to a post-Easter genesis would claim that Mk 9.1 was formed on the basis of Mk 13.30, perhaps by Mark himself.[51]

(vii) Even if ὧδε is not a secondary addition to the synoptic textual tradition,[52] it is not likely to have belonged to an originally isolated saying, and it could be Markan redaction.[53] This raises the possibility that Jesus was originally speaking not of 'those standing here' but simply of 'those standing', and that he was using a common expression for withstanding persecution (see on 10.23). If so, the meaning would be almost identical to the meaning of 10.23: both logia foretell that before the disciples are overcome utterly, the kingdom of God or the Son of man will come. It is even possible, given the similarities in structure and vocabulary, that the two sayings are variants.[54] Very tentatively, we favour this solution. (Its acceptance creates a more direct bridge between Mk 9.1 and Jn 8.51–2 ('Truly, truly, I say to you, if any one keeps my word, he will never see death') as well as Gos. Thom. 18 ('Blessed is he who shall stand [ōhe] at the beginning, and he shall know the end and he shall not taste death'). Neither of these last two shows any trace of the synoptic ὧδε, and both, in their parallels to 'those standing', have clauses about faithful discipleship.)

(viii) It has sometimes been affirmed that, since we do not know the original context in which Mk 9.1 was uttered (by Jesus or someone else), its meaning inevitably escapes us.[55] We simply do not know what was intended.

(v) Concluding Observations

Our text drives home the point that the disciples—and, implicitly, all believers—must not passively observe their Lord and what he does. They are not to be seated spectators watching from the grandstand the actions foretold in 16.21–3. Rather must they themselves enter the arena after their Lord. For Matthew, Jesus is not a substitute but a leader. He does not do something for those who do nothing. Instead he commands, 'Follow me' (4.18–22; 9.9). This authoritative call leaves no room for considerations of convenience or even self-preservation. Discipleship is a doing of what is right, no matter how irksome the privations, no matter how great the dangers (cf. the missionary discourse). Faith means obedience, and

[50] Cf. Bornkamm (v). For criticism see Schlosser 1, pp. 343–6; also Ambrozic (v), who argues for authenticity while contending that 'some standing here' should be assigned to Mark or his tradition.

[51] E.g. Vögtle (v); Perrin (v)—the last claiming Markan creation.

[52] ωδε is missing in Mt 16.28 ff² Hil, Mk 9.1 i r, Lk 9.27 1355; and those witnesses which attest it do not agree on its placement.

[53] See Chilton, Strength, pp. 260–1.

[54] Cf. Gaston, Stone, p. 451, and see further on 10.23.

[55] Cf. R. Schnackenburg, God's Rule and Kingdom, 2nd ed. (trans. of Gottes Herrschaft und Reich, 1961), New York and London, 1968, pp. 205–7.

obedience is the grave of the will ('Not as I will, but as Thou wilt' (26.39)).

(v) *Bibliography*

For additional bibliography see section (v) for 10.32–42

Ambrozic, pp. 203–40.

Beasley-Murray, pp. 187–93.

Berger, *Amen*, pp. 62–7.

E. Best, 'An Early Sayings Collection', *NovT* 18 (1976), pp. 1–16.

G. Bornkamm, 'Die Verzögerung der Parusie', in *In memoriam E. Lohmeyer*, ed. W. Schmauch, Stuttgart, 1951, pp. 116–26.

Chilton, *Strength*, pp. 251–74.

B. Chilton, 'An evangelical and critical approach to the sayings of Jesus', *Themelios* 3 (1978), pp. 78–85.

idem, '"Not to Taste Death": A Jewish, Christian and Gnostic Usage', in Livingstone, pp. 29–36.

A. C. Cotter, 'Non gustabunt mortem', *CBQ* 6 (1944), pp. 444–55.

E. Fascher, 'Der unendliche Wert der Menschenseele', in *Forschung und Erfahrung*, Göttingen, 1961, pp. 44–57.

D. Gewalt, '1 Thess 4.15–17; 1 Kor 15.51 und Mk 9.1—Zur Abgrenzung eines "Herrenwortes"', *LB* 51 (1982), pp. 105–13.

H. Giesen, 'Mk 9.1—ein Wort Jesu über die nahe Parusie?', *TTZ* 92 (1983), pp. 134–48.

E. Haenchen, 'Die Komposition von Mk VIII, 27—IX, 1', *NovT* 6 (1963), pp. 81–109.

Hortsmann, pp. 34–69.

H. Kahlefeld, 'Jünger des Herrn. Eine Besinnung zur Perikope Mk 8.34–38', *GuL* 30 (1957), pp. 1–6.

R. Koolmeister, 'Selbstverleugnung, Kreuzaufnahme und Nachfolge', in *Charisteria Johanni Kopp*, Stockholm, 1954, pp. 64–94.

Kümmel, *Promise*, pp. 25–9.

W. G. Kümmel, 'Eschatological Expectation in the Proclamation of Jesus' (trans. of 'Die Naherwartung in der Verkündigung Jesu', in *Zeit und Geschichte*, ed. E. Dinkler, Tübingen, 1964, pp. 31–46), in *The Future of Our Religious Past*, ed. J. M. Robinson, New York, 1971, pp. 29–48.

M. Künzi, *Das Naherwartungslogion Markus 9.1 par.*, BGBE 21, Tübingen, 1977.

E. Nardoni, 'A Redactional Interpretation of Mark 9.1', *CBQ* 43 (1981), pp. 365–84.

N. Perrin, 'The Composition of Mark 9.1', *NovT* 11 (1969), pp. 67–70.

L. Sabourin, 'Matthieu 10.23 et 16.28 dans la perspective apocalyptique', *SciEsp* 37 (1985), pp. 353–64.

A. Satake, 'Das Leiden der Jünger "um meinetwillen"', *ZNW* 67 (1976), pp. 4–19.

Schlosser 1, pp. 323–71.

A. Schulz, *Nachfolgen und Nachahmen*, SANT 6, Munich, 1962, pp. 79–97, 161–72.

G. Schwarz, '"... ἀπαρνησάσθω ἑαυτόν ..."? (Markus VIII 34 Parr.)', *NovT* 17 (1975), pp. 109–12.

E. Trocmé, 'Marc 9.1: prédiction ou réprimande?', in *Studia Evangelica II*, TU 87, ed. F. L. Cross, Berlin, 1964, pp. 259–65.

A. Vögtle, 'Exegetische Erwägungen über das Wissen und Selbstbewusstsein Jesu', in *Gott im Welt*, ed. H. Vorgrimmler, Freiburg, 1964, vol. 1, pp. 642–7.

XLII

THE SON OF GOD TRANSFIGURED: A GREATER THAN MOSES
(17.1–8)

(i) *Structure*

One wonders whether the text does not reflect a chiastic arrangement. One can correlate the narrative introduction with the narrative conclusion, the transfiguration of Jesus with the words of Jesus, the response of Peter with the response of the disciples. Pictorially:

a. Narrative introduction (1)
   b. Jesus is transfigured (2–3)
      c. Peter's response (4)
         d. The divine voice (5)
      c. The disciples' response (6)
   c. Jesus speaks (7)
a. Narrative conclusion (8)

If this chiastic analysis is correct, it means that the voice from heaven is the structural centre of the pericope.

(ii) *Sources*

If one accepts the priority of Mark it is natural to see Mt 17.1–8 as a reworking of Mk 9.2–8. Among other things, it is more probable that Matthew substituted 'Lord' for 'rabbi' than that Mark substituted 'rabbi' for 'Lord' (17.4 = Mk 9.5), and more likely that Matthew added 'with whom I am well pleased' (17.5; cf. 3.17; 12.18) than that Mark dropped it. There are, however, a number of minor agreements between Matthew and Luke which have created doubts.[1] Such agreements have been understood to imply (i) that something is wrong with the theory of Markan priority,[2] (ii) that Matthew and Luke were, in telling the story of the transfiguration, influenced by a source other than Mk 9.2–8,[3] or (iii) that Luke knew and used

---

[1] For a list see Allen, pp. 185–6; also Neirynck (v).
[2] Dabrowski (v), e.g., accepts Matthean priority here.
[3] So Blinzler (v), pp. 32–62. Manson, *Teaching*, p. 32, suggested influence from a Q version of the event. For the view that Luke depends solely upon Mk 9.2–8 see Fitzmyer, *Luke* 1, pp. 791–2. There is no parallel in John.

Matthew.[4] We are not inclined to accept any of these options. It does not seem to us that the minor agreements are sufficiently numerous or exact to disallow the hypothesis of independent editing by Matthew and Luke of the same source, Mark. For discussion see on vv. 2, 3, 4, 5; also Neirynck (v).

(iii) Exegesis[5]

In the Second Gospel the transfiguration[6] is probably best understood in comparison with Mark's emphasis upon the passion and resurrection of the Son of man (cf. 8.27–9.1). This appears from the insistence on the cross (9.12); from the priority given to Elijah, who is identified with the Baptist, whose death was a premonition of that of Jesus himself (9.12); from the similarity between the transfiguration and Gethsemane, in that the witnesses are both identical (9.2; 14.33); and from the metamorphosis of Jesus in 9.2, which looks forward to the glory of the resurrection. In Matthew things are otherwise. The major theme of the epiphany story would seem to be Jesus' status as a new Moses, and Exod 24 and 34 would seem to be important influences.[7] Consider the following changes which the First Evangelist has introduced into the Markan narrative:

(i) Moses now comes before Elijah. This is not a triviality. It at least means that no priority of significance is given to Elijah, and probably that the reference to Moses is to be taken as emphatic.

(ii) While Mark only refers to 'the garments of Jesus', which became glistening, intensely white 'as no fuller on earth could bleach them' (9.3), Matthew adds: 'and his face shone like the sun' (17.2). This recalls Exod 34.29–35, where the Hebrew reads: 'the skin of [Moses'] face shone' because he had been talking to God. Matthew does not quote either the Masoretic text or the LXX exactly (the LXX reads: 'the appearance of the skin of his face was glorified:' δεδόξασται ἡ ὄψις τοῦ χρώματος τοῦ προσώπου αὐτοῦ, which is an attempt at 'refinement' or 'spiritualization'), so that there is no direct verbal allusion to Exod 34.29. And one might think it difficult to grasp why Matthew, did he have a direct reference to that passage in mind, has omitted all reference to the 'skin', unless he too is governed by a concern for an even greater refinement than the LXX. Nevertheless, the evangelist does bring out the essential force of the Hebrew text.

[4] So Allen, p. 186; Gundry, Commentary, p. 346.
[5] For a review of modern approaches and interpretations see Nützel (v), pp. 10–86, although his focus is not on Matthew.
[6] The term goes back to the Vulgate's transfiguratus est.
[7] See esp. Davies (v). Schweizer, Mark, p. 181, observes that LAB 11–12 closely associates Exod 24 and 34. It should also be noted that LAB 19.16 says that Moses' appearance 'became glorious' not just on Sinai but at his death (see Ginzberg 3, p. 93, for later tradition).

The shining of Moses' face was so unendurable, so the Exodus story implies, that Moses in his converse with the people had to put a veil on it. Furthermore, the skin of Moses is not mentioned in other accounts of the light from his face (e.g. 2 Cor 3.7–18 and LAB 12.1), and the likening of Moses' face to the sun, though not found in the OT, was evidently common (see on v. 2).

(iii) In describing 'the cloud' that appears, Matthew uses the same verb as Mark and Luke, ἐπισκιάζω. But he adds a significant adjective. The cloud is 'bright' (φωτεινή). He thereby expresses a paradox: a bright cloud overshadows. Can we detect why this adjective? Is it not to make it beyond doubt that the Shekinah is in mind, that presence of the Lord which used to fill the tabernacle in the wilderness, and which was often connected with depths of light 'more intense than the midsummer sun'?

(iv) In Mark the heavenly voice declares to the disciples, 'This is my beloved Son'. In Luke this becomes, 'this is my Son, my Chosen'. In Matthew we find this: 'This is my beloved Son, with whom I am well pleased.' These variants are interesting, especially that in our gospel. 'With whom I am well pleased' also occurs in the narrative of Jesus' baptism, but originally it is from Isa 42.1, where it refers to the suffering servant of Deutero-Isaiah. Matthew appears to have added the phrase in order to signify Jesus as the one who is destined to bring his law to the nations (Isa 42.4). Such a suggestion is supported by this, that the following words, 'listen to him', in their broader Matthean context point to Jesus as an ethical teacher, like Moses. Moreover, it is possible, even probable, that ἀκούετε αὐτοῦ is to be interpreted in the light of Deut 18.15: 'the Lord your God will raise up for you a prophet like me from among you, from your brethren—him you shall listen to . . .' (cf. 18.18; the Greek in 18.15 is, αὐτοῦ ἀκούσεσθε; note that many Matthean mss., against Mark, place the pronoun before the verb).

Pace Schweizer, *Matthew*, p. 349, there is scarcely room for doubt that Matthew has modified Mark for the deliberate purpose of presenting Jesus after the manner of Moses.[8] Yet it must be added that in this he was only drawing out what was already to hand in the tradition. Although Mark, as we have seen, does not appear to have stressed the Mosaic background of the transfiguration, the tradition he received was largely formulated with Sinai in mind.[9] This follows from the parallels between Mk 9.2–8 on the one side and Exod 24 and 34 on the other: in both (i) the setting is the same: a high mountain (Exod 24.12, 15–18; 34.3; Mk 9.2); (ii) there is a cloud that descends and overshadows the mountain (Exod 24.15–18; 34.5; Mk 9.7); (iii) a voice comes from the cloud (Exod 24.16; Mk 9.7); (iv) the central figures, Jesus and Moses, become radiant[10] (Exod 34.29–30, 35; Mk 9.2–3); (v)

---

[8] The same is true of Luke; note esp. the insertion of ἔξοδος in Lk 9.31.

[9] Cf. Gnilka, *Markus* 2, p. 32; Chilton (v).

[10] The issue of the original meaning of the story in Exodus is irrelevant for the interpretation of our gospel. Even if one contends that *qāran* means 'become horned' or 'disfigured', the LXX, the Peshitta, the targumim, and Pseudo-Philo all attest that the OT passage was widely understood to say that Moses was glorified or became radiant.

those who see the radiance of the central figure become afraid (Exod 34.30; Mk 9.6); (vi) the event takes place 'after six days' (Exod 24.16; Mk 9.2); and (vii) a select group of three people is mentioned (Exod 24.1; Mk 9.2). In addition to all this, it may be noted that Moses and Elijah, who both converse with the transfigured Jesus, are the only OT figures of whom it is related that they spoke with God on Mount Sinai. So their appearance on a mountain in the NT should probably evoke the thought of Mount Sinai.

Matthew, we may be certain, observed the influence of Sinai motifs on the story of Jesus' transfiguration and felt justified in increasing the parallels for his account. It must, however, be stressed that if Jesus is thus made out to be a new Moses, he is also clearly greater than Moses, just as he is greater than Elijah. At the last, Moses and Elijah disappear, leaving Jesus alone. This fact is underlined by Matthew (contrast Mark and Luke): αὐτὸν Ἰησοῦν μόνον. The pronoun is emphatic: 'Jesus himself alone.' Jesus, it would seem, takes Moses' place and supersedes him (cf. Heb 1.1–2; 3.1–6). Observe also that the voice from heaven addresses Jesus as 'my beloved Son'. This is a title Moses did not have, and the voice in the transfiguration says nothing at all about the law-giver: it passes over him in silence. In fine, therefore, Jesus is at the same time like Moses and greater than Moses.

While the transfiguration as it stands in Matthew is first of all a picture of Jesus as a new and greater Moses, this fact scarcely eliminates the presence of other important themes. For instance, 17.1–8 recalls the baptism and confirms Peter's confession, it foreshadows the resurrection and anticipates the *parousia*. Nonetheless, we remain persuaded that the Mosaic motifs are the key to Matthew's story, and attempts to give other themes pride of place do not persuade.

According to Schweizer, *Matthew*, p. 349, 'Matthew does not base his account on stories associated with Moses but on Old Testament passages that touch on the mystery of the eschaton and resurrection' (cf. Gnilka, *Matthäusevangelium* 2, p. 93). What is the evidence for this contention, for the affirmation that the transfiguration in Matthew is first of all eschatological revelation?[11] A number of items in 17.1–8 have parallels in eschatological expectation. Thus, the righteous will, in the end, undergo a transformation and become glorious and luminous, while their garments will glisten (see on v. 2). For his part, the Son of man will come on the clouds of heaven (see on 24.30). Beyond that, voices occur often in apocalyptic revelations (see on 3.16), as do mountains (see on 5.1); and it was believed that God would 'tabernacle' among his people at the end (see on 17.4). Schweizer also finds allusions to eschatological expectation in the use of προσῆλθεν (v. 7; cf. 28.18, of the risen Lord), ἐγέρθητε (cf. 9.25, of a resurrection), and μὴ φοβεῖσθε (frequent in apocalypses). But all this is open to question.

---

[11] This has been argued for Mark by Lohmeyer (v) and Kee (v).

προσῆλθεν, ἐγέρθητε, and μὴ φοβεῖσθε are not the loaded terms Schweizer seems to make them, and the Son of man is associated with clouds whereas 17.5 refers to one cloud, the Shekinah. When one adds that heavenly voices and mountains are not the peculiar properties of apocalyptic literature, the evidence for Schweizer's approach becomes meagre. In fact, it really consists only of the glorious transformation common to the pre-Easter Jesus and the saints at the consummation (see 13.43). Still, given that 17.1–8 immediately succeeds a *parousia* prediction (16.28) and that early Christians saw Jesus' resurrection glory as a harbinger of their own destiny, it would be imprudent to deny that 17.1–8 was in part intended to portray the eschatological glory of both the Messiah and his followers. The narrative provides a glimpse of what eschatological resurrection will mean.

Donaldson (v), while not rejecting the Sinai parallels and the eschatological undertones, favours the thesis that the mountain of Mt 17.2 is a mountain of enthronement.[12] 'This is my Son' is an enthronement formula in Ps 2.7 (cf. 2 Sam 7.14) and can be interpreted in messianic terms. Further, mountains are often associated with kingship and enthronement in Jewish tradition, and Donaldson detects in 17.1–8 a three-fold enthronement form: elevation, presentation, enthronement.[13] He also contends that the redactional introduction of 'his kingdom' in 16.28 means that 'the narrative to follow is no longer vaguely related to the coming of the kingdom with power; it is seen, rather, as the fulfilment of the promise that Jesus will appear in his kingly role. With this change, the enthronement character of the narrative is thrown into sharp relief' (p. 151). We are not convinced, however, that so much can be read into the modification of 16.28, and we further have doubts about the influence of the triadic enthronement form upon the First Evangelist (see on 28.16–20).

Closely related to Donaldson's interpretation is the earlier work of Riesenfeld (v), which connects the transfiguration with Tabernacles. Taking his start from Peter's proposal to build τρεῖς σκηνάς, from the Scandinavian thesis of an annual New Year festival during which the king was enthroned,[14] and from the link between Tabernacles and eschatology (see Zech 14), Riesenfeld maintains that the transfiguration portrays the eschatological enthronement of Jesus Messiah in a Tabernacles setting.[15] The reference to 'after six days' may be harmonized with this proposal (see on v. 1); and it may be observed not only that Ps 2.7 is an enthronement text but also that Ps 97.2, part of what has been claimed to be a psalm about Yahweh's enthronement, mentions clouds. There is, nonetheless, much doubt about the theory of a New Year enthronement feast;[16] and Riesenfeld's thesis, which to a great degree hinges upon the obscure request to build booths, leaves

[12] Cf. Borsch (v).
[13] Cf. O. Michel, in Stanton, *Matthew*, p. 36; Jeremias, *Promise*, pp. 38–9.
[14] See A. R. Johnson, 'The Rôle of the King in the Jerusalem Cultus', in *The Labyrinth*, ed. S. H. Hooke, London, 1935, pp. 71–111; N. H. Snaith, *The Jewish New Year Festival*, London, 1947.
[15] See also Daniélou (v); Roehrs (v).
[16] See de Vaux 2, pp. 504–6.

much in the text unilluminated. And certainly Matthew himself shows no tendency towards enhancing alleged Tabernacles motifs.

M. Sabbe (v) and others[17] have supposed that the First Evangelist modified his Markan source under the influence of LXX Dan 10. This last contains several words and phrases reminiscent of Mt 17.1–8: τὸ ὅραμα, ἦρα τοὺς ὀφθαλμούς μου, ἰδού, τὸ πρόσωπον αὐτοῦ ὡσεὶ ὅρασις ἀστραπῆς, φόβος, ἤκουσα, πεπτωκὼς ἐπὶ πρόσωπόν μου, ἤγειρέ με, μὴ φοβοῦ. None of these similarities seem to us substantial. We are confirmed in this by the fact that there are also a striking number of parallels between 17.1–8 and both Acts 1[18] and 1 En. 14.13–25.[19] Our conclusion is that parallels are not always what they seem to be.

Finally, Best, *Temptation*, pp. 169–73, urges a possible link with the binding of Isaac.[20] Gen 22.2 ('Take your son, your only son Isaac, whom you love . . .') is very close to Mk 9.7 par. Further, Abraham took Isaac up on a mountain, Jewish tradition puts a cloud on Mount Moriah,[21] and there are traditions about Abraham becoming luminous.[22] These last, however, are much too late, and the date of the Moriah cloud tradition is not established. We therefore think that any connexion between the transfiguration—in any of its synoptic or pre-synoptic versions—and the Akedah is unlikely.

Of the several attempts to uncover the tradition-history of our passage and pin down its origin, the following may be mentioned.

(i) Traditionally the story has been accepted as largely historical, and some modern scholars still agree with this.[23] The problems raised by such an approach were set forth by Strauss (v) and involve more than a simple rejection of all things supernatural. One wonders, for instance, how the disciples instantly recognized Moses and Elijah. (The tendency of the Fathers to attribute their knowledge to the Holy Spirit (e.g. Tertullian, *Adv. Marc.* 4.23) scarcely satisfies.) Also, although history does sometimes present astounding parallels, how can a factual episode exhibit so many similarities to an event in the life of Moses?[24]

[17] E.g. Murphy-O'Connor (v).

[18] For these see Albright and Mann, p. 206.

[19] Note the following: 'fear' (v. 13); 'I fell upon my face' (v. 14); 'I saw a vision' (v. 14); 'and behold' (v. 15); 'its appearance was . . . like the shining sun' (v. 18); 'the voice' (v. 18); 'his goun, which was shining more brightly than the sun, it was brighter than any snow' (v. 20); 'the face of the Excellent and Glorious One' (v. 21); 'prostrate on my face' (v. 24); 'the Lord called me' (v. 24); 'he lifted me up' (v. 25).

[20] Cf. D. Flusser, *Jesus*, New York, 1969, p. 97.

[21] See Donaldson, pp. 144, 268, n. 48.

[22] See Ginzberg 1, p. 307; 2, p. 188.

[23] E.g. Blinzler (v) and Cranfield, *Mark*, pp. 292–4. The latter regards the transfiguration itself (Mk 9.2b, 3) as 'factual', Mk 9.4–7 as recording a vision and audition 'miraculously brought about by God'.

[24] On the other hand, we do not find forceful the objection raised by many, including Murphy-O'Connor (v), p. 9: 'Having been a witness to the one moment when the divine power within Jesus blazed forth, could Peter then have denied him so firmly and callously in the courtyard of the high priest? Would we not expect Peter rather to proclaim his faith in Jesus, confident that no harm would come to him from such a proclamation? If things really happened as described in the Transfiguration story, Peter's later behaviour is inexplicable'. But the

(ii) Several commentators have found the origin of the story in a visionary experience of the disciples.[25] On this Taylor, *Mark*, p. 387, comments: 'Naturally, in hypotheses of this kind the recognition of the basic historical element varies, but it is their peculiar merit that, if the psychological assumptions are conceded, they are able to give a worthy explanation of the several elements in the narrative.' This leaves open the issue of whether one should think of a hallucination or a vision divinely bestowed or some third possibility.

(iii) It was once fairly popular, with reference to Lk 9.32 ('Peter and those who were with him were heavy with sleep, and when they wakened . . .'), to rationalize the text in this fashion: 'During or after a prayer offered by Jesus, or by themselves, in which mention was made of Moses and Elias, and their advent as messianic forerunners desired, the three disciples . . . slept, and (the two names mentioned by Jesus yet sounding in their ears) dreamed that Moses and Elias were present, and that Jesus conversed with them: an illusion which continued during the first confused moments after their awaking' (Strauss, p. 538, offering a critique and citing as proponents Rau, Gabler, Kuinöl, and Neander).

(iv) Even more implausible was the way in which Paulus and Schleiermacher rationalized the narrative: the disciples, after sleeping, awoke to see Jesus, in the first rays of morning, talking to two strangers, who then departed into a low hanging cloud.[26] Like the previous solution, this no longer maintains any appeal.

(v) Strauss (v), observing the parallels between Jesus on the mount of transfiguration and Moses on Mount Sinai, affirmed that the former was created whole cloth on the basis of the latter. Its purpose was to show that the Messiah was not inferior to the law-giver.

(vi) Bultmann, following J. Wellhausen, gave it as his verdict that the transfiguration is a displaced Easter narrative (*History*, p. 259).[27] But the reasons for this—the occurrence of ὤφθη (cf. 1 Cor 15.5–8), the use of μεταμορφόω in resurrection appearances (Narrative of Joseph of Arimathea 5; cf. Mk 16.12), the presence of a mountain (cf. Mt 28.16–20; Acts 1.12),[28] the element of fear (cf. Mk 16.8; etc.), the luminousness of Jesus,[29] the Son of God Christology (cf. Rom 1.4), the chronological notice ('after six days' = on the seventh day), the alleged post-Easter setting of the account in 2 Pet 1.16–18,[30] the fact that the Ethiopic Apocalypse of Peter and Pistis Sophia make

---

failure to act according to one's deepest convictions is common to human experience. In this respect the story of the murmuring Israelites in the desert is true-to-life.

[25] So, according to Taylor, *Mark*, p. 386, Ed. Meyer, Harnack, Schniewind, E. Underhill, Rawlinson, and Bartlet.

[26] Discussion in Strauss, pp. 539–40; also Schweitzer, *Quest*, pp. 52–3.

[27] So also those named by Stein (v), p. 79, n. 2.

[28] For other resurrection stories with mountains see Donaldson, p. 266, ns. 17–19.

[29] Cf. Acts 26.13; Rev 1.13–16; Ep. Pet. Phil. 134.9–13; Sophia Jesus Christ 91.10–13; and see J. M. Robinson, 'Jesus: From Easter to Valentinus (or to the Apostles' Creed),' *JBL* 101 (1982), pp. 5–37.

[30] Against this see Stein (v), pp. 88–9; Bauckham, pp. 210–11.

the transfiguration a resurrection appearance[31]—have all been effectively countered.[32] Especially telling are the form-critical differences between Mk 9.2–8 par. and canonical resurrection narratives.[33] Also, where else in resurrection stories do we find OT saints,[34] or a heavenly voice, or Jesus addressed as 'rabbi', or Jesus saying next to nothing at all?

(vii) Theissen, *Stories*, pp. 96–7, agrees with Bultmann in considering the transfiguration to be a former Easter appearance. But he goes on to find an ascension story. Originally, Jesus was first transfigured and then he disappeared. This theory is subject to the same criticisms as (vi).

(viii) Many scholars would agree with Strauss that the story has no foothold in history but would also stress that it was created out of Hellenistic epiphany motifs instead of OT texts. In Kümmel's words, here we find 'a conception, foreign to Judaism but familiar to Hellenism, of a natural, native gift of power, to which corresponds the epiphany, the becoming visible of the divine being before the eyes of certain men' (*Theology*, p. 123). This is also the judgement of Conzelmann, according to whom 'we have an account of a first appointment of Jesus to the rank of Son of God; the story originally competed with the narrative of the baptism' (*Theology*, p. 128). Kee's work (v), along with the fundamental dependence of the transfiguration on Pentateuchal motifs, however, would seem to lay this thesis to rest: the constitutive elements of Mk 9.2–8 par. are all very much at home in Jewish tradition (cf. Gerber (v)).

(ix) Lohmeyer (v), apparently rejecting any historical basis, distinguished two sources: Mk 9.4–5(6), 7–8, a legend based on eschatological expectation, and 9.3, a Hellenistic legend using the terminology of the mystery cults.[35]

(x) Fuller, *Christology*, pp. 171–2, arguing that υἱός μου has replaced an original '*abdî* = παῖς μου, contends that 'the basis of the story is the Palestinian Christology of Jesus as the eschatological prophet.' This was later developed in a Hellenistic direction, whence the metamorphosis.[36]

(xi) Murphy O'Connor finds in Lk 9.28–36 a tradition independent of Mark. It consisted roughly of Lk 9.28–33a (minus 'who were Moses

---

[31] But the Apocalypse of Peter shows knowledge of both Matthew and 2 Peter, so its value as an independent witness is dubious.

[32] See esp. the work of Stein (v).

[33] Cf. C. H. Dodd, 'The Appearances of the Risen Christ: An Essay in Form-Criticism of the Gospels', in *MNTS*, pp. 102–33.

[34] Bultmann, *History*, p. 260, concedes this when he speculates that in the original story Jesus appeared with two angels; only later were Moses and Elijah named.

[35] For criticism see Bultmann, *History*, p. 260, n. 5. In his commentary on Mark Lohmeyer seems to accept the story as a unity.

[36] Cf. Hahn (v); related analyses in Masson (v) and U. B. Müller (v). H.-P. Müller (v) is one more author who sees the canonical narratives as the result of the combining of two different traditions (in his case one in Mk 9.2c–6 + 8; the other in 2a–b + 7(+9)); but he assigns both stories to a Palestinian milieu.

and Elijah', 'Peter and those who were with him were heavy with sleep, but waking they saw his glory', and 'and his clothes became dazzling white') + 36b ('Jesus was found alone'): 'It happened after these words, about eight days, taking with him Peter and John and James, he went up the mountain to pray. And as he was praying, the appearance of his face was altered. And behold, two men talked with him, who appearing in glory spoke of his "exodus" which he was about to fulfil in Jerusalem. But Peter and those with him saw his glory and the two men standing with him. And when they parted from him, Jesus was found alone.' Affirming that the two men should be identified with angels and explained as a literary device, and also that 'the appearance of his face was altered' reflects only Jesus' emotional state, O'Connor surmises that Jesus, 'in a flash of insight', realized his death would be a saving event, and thus his face 'lit up'. Mark then inherited a 'somewhat garbled form' of this event and added the Sinai parallels. All this is quite unconvincing. The pre-Lukan character of 9.28–32a is not demonstrated, and the omission of 'and his clothing became dazzling white' arbitrary, as is the interpretation of 'the appearance of his face was altered'.

(xii) Chilton (v), p. 123, gives this account of the genesis of the transfiguration story: (a) the dominical Mk 9.1 swears by deathless witnesses that the kingdom is forceful (see on 16.28); (b) the witnesses were understood to be Moses and Elijah; (c) then developed a scene 'which emphasizes in visio-literary fashion the continuity of Jesus' disclosure with archetypal prophetic revelation (Exod 24).' This reconstruction comes to grief on Chilton's doubtful interpretation of Mk 9.1 (see on 16.28).

(xiii) According to Fitzmyer, *Luke* 1, p. 796, 'no real historical judgement can be made.'

What is one to conclude? Our own suspicion is that an unusual event in the life of Jesus lent itself to his being seen as some sort of counterpart to Moses on Sinai. There are at least two reasons for so thinking. First, no one has yet put forward a convincing theological or literary explanation for Peter's remarks about booths, and this raises the possibility of an historical kernel so intractable is it. Secondly, while the parallels between Jesus and Moses are striking, they are at points rather inexact (see e.g. our discussion of 'after six days' in v. 1). This implies that the Mosaic motifs cannot in themselves suffice to explain the story's origin. Thus the question becomes: what might have happened which would have caused someone to search for parallels in Exod 24 and 34? The answer can only be: a vision of a radiant Jesus. To this it may be replied that this too must be considered a legendary item. Does not Jewish tradition attribute radiance to Adam (*Gen. Rab.* on 2.4; *Lev. Rab.* on 16.1), Abraham (see n. 22), Aseneth (Jos. Asen. 18.–20), the Israelites at Sinai (LAB 12.7), the Rechabites (Hist. Rechab. 11–12), R. Eliezer (*ARN* B 13), and a host of others, including Sabbatai Sevi (Scholem, pp. 132, 142, 188–90, 222)—just as Christian tradition attributes the same to Montanus and Lucius (Mart. of Montanus and Lucius 11), Arsenius the Great (PG 65, Arsenius 27), Abba Pambo (PG 65, Pambo 1, 12), and the desert fathers Joseph of Panephysis (PG 65, Josephus of Panephysis 7), Sisoes (PG 65, Sisoes 14), and Silvanus

(PG 65, Silvanus 12)?[37] Perhaps. But it must be acknowledged that there are purported first-hand reports of people being surrounded by unnatural lights, and all these do not belong to the distant past. Several different witnesses claimed to see a glow around the nineteenth century Russian saint, Seraphim of Sarov;[38] and in our own century, the well-known British writer and mystic, Evelyn Underhill, was once, according to an eye-witnesses, transfigured by light.[39] Such reports persist.[40] There are also occasional accounts of people enveloped by light which have no religious context whatsoever.[41] We are accordingly encouraged to conjecture that, however the circumstance be understood, Jesus was seen by others to be surrounded by light, that this experience was subsequently interpreted in terms of Exod 24 and 34, that this in turn led to a searching for—and, later, creation of—further parallels between what had happened to Jesus and what had happened to Moses (whence the mention of three disciples, 'after six days', etc.), and that, finally, from all this there came into existence the narrative tradition ultimately behind Mk 9.2–8 par.[42] This hypothesis seems to us to do the most justice to all the data.

It remains to remark on the striking similarities between the transfiguration and the baptism (see 1, p. 320). One might explain these by postulating that the passages belong to the same literary *Gattung* or that they arose in the same community. No less probable is the possibility that the story of the baptism influenced the story of the transfiguration. (Perhaps the transfiguration did not originally have a voice, this being borrowed later from the baptism.)

1. This verse, in which Jesus takes all the initiative, sets the scene with motifs reminiscent of Exod 24: six days, three disciples, a high mountain (see pp. 685–7).[43]

καὶ μεθ' ἡμέρας ἕξ. So Mk 9.2, with μετά. Compare Jn 12.1. Luke has 'after eight days' (cf. Lev 23.36; Jn 20.26; Tg. Yer. I

---

[37] Many Christian saints reportedly appeared radiant at one time or another, including Saints Dominic, Francis of Assisi, Antony of Padua, Catherine of Siena, Francis of Paola, Francis Xavier, Philip Neri, and Bernadette.—Note also, from outside the biblical tradition, Marinus of Samaria, *Proclus* 23.

[38] See V. Zander, *St. Seraphim of Sarov*, Crestwood, 1975, pp. 10, 61, 64, 90–4, 110, 112, 126.

[39] See *The Letters of Evelyn Underhill*, ed. C. Williams, London, 1943, p. 37.

[40] See *The Skeptical Inquirer* 8/4 (1984), p. 306. The closest parallel we have found to the transfiguration of Jesus comes from modern India; see E. Haraldsson, *Modern Miracles: An Investigative Report on Psychic Phenomena associated with Sathya Sai Baba*, New York, 1988, pp. 251–7. Additional first-hand accounts in P. Treece, *The Sanctified Body*, New York, 1989, pp. 29–85.

[41] See *Nature* 22 (1880), p. 204; 32 (1885), pp. 316–17; also W. R. Corliss, *Rare Halos, Mirages, Anomalous Rainbows and related Electromagnetic Phenomena*, Glen Arm, 1984, pp. 82–91.

[42] One might object that in Mark it is Jesus' clothes which are lit up, not Jesus himself. But the clothes only shine because Jesus is shining *through* them. This is made plain by the use of μεταμορφόω and the parallels with Exod 24 and 34.

[43] The notion that the transfiguration occurred at night seems to have arisen from Luke's account of the disciples sleeping; Matthew and Mark do not speak to the issue one way or the other.

on Exod 24.11). The notice, 'after six days', is not only ambiguous—is the reference to 16.13? or to 16.21? or to 16.24?—but also quite anomalous for the synoptic tradition: chronological precision before the passion narrative is rare. An allusion to Exod 24.16 ('the glory of the Lord settled on Mount Sinai, and the cloud covered it six days; and on the seventh day he [God] called to Moses out of the midst of the cloud;' cf. Jub. 1.2) is probable (cf. Bonaventure, *Itin. mentis in Deum* 1.5). To this it has been objected that 'in Exod 24.15–18, in contrast to the Transfiguration Narrative, the six day period was the length of time during which Moses was on the cloud-covered mountain before he heard the voice of God' (Donaldson, p. 143). But this demands too much. The story of Jesus' transfiguration was interpreted by means of Sinai motifs, not simply created out of them. One cannot, therefore, expect all the parallels to be perfect. (Other explanations of the time notice—historical reminiscence,[44] an allusion to the interval between the Day of Atonement and Tabernacles,[45] an attempt to tie the transfiguration to the prophecy of Mk 9.1 par.,[46] a reference to the time between the first and sixth days of the Feast of Booths,[47] an anticipation of the passion week chronology,[48] or an allusion to the apocalyptic scheme of a seven-day world history[49]—are all less than satisfying.)

παραλαμβάνει ὁ Ἰησοῦς τὸν Πέτρον καὶ Ἰάκωβον καὶ Ἰωάννην τὸν ἀδελφὸν αὐτοῦ. So Mk 9.2, with the definite article before 'James' and (perhaps) before 'John' and without 'his brother'. For this last change see on 4.21. In Matthew the one article does duty for all three names; see BDF § 276. On 'Peter and James and John' (cf. 26.37; 2 Pet 1.16–18) see further p. 695, n. 56. In Exod 24.1 Moses separates himself from the people and takes with him seventy elders and a special group of three people whose names are given: Aaron, Nadab, and Abihu. One strongly suspects that the informed reader is to recall this OT text.

καὶ ἀναφέρει αὐτοὺς εἰς ὄρος ὑψηλὸν κατ' ἰδίαν. Compare Mt 4.8; 2 Pet 1.18 ('in the holy mountain'); Rev 21.10. Mk 9.2 has the redundant μόνους at the end. Matthew saves the word for v. 8, where it refers solely to Jesus (cf. p. 704).

---

[44] So Cranfield, *Mark*, p. 293. But why bother to record such a fact? If fact it is, the parallel with Sinai must explain its being mentioned.

[45] So Riesenfeld (v), pp. 276–7; Bonnard, p. 254.

[46] Origen, *Comm. on Mt.* 12.31, knows this interpretation but rejects it.

[47] So Baltensweiler (v), pp. 46–51. Cf. Jn 7.37.

[48] So Schnellbächer (v): the resurrection occurred after the sixth day of the passion week.

[49] Cf. Horstmann, p. 101; Gnilka, *Matthäusevangelium* 2, pp. 93–4. Origen, *Comm. on Mt.* 12.36, already puts forward a related interpretation.

On the mountain motif in Matthew see on 5.1 and 15.29. Here the mountain corresponds to Sinai. It has also been suggested that we should think of Mount Moriah or Carmel (cf. 1 Kgs 18), or that enthronement traditions are in the background,[50] or that the rôle of mountains in Jewish eschatology[51] has been influential. For reasons already given we are sceptical of all these proposals. ὑψηλός, often used of mountains,[52] literally means 'high'. Compare its use in 4.8 (redactional). Both Philo, *Mos.* 2.70, and Josephus, *Ant.* 3.76, have Sinai as the highest (ὑψηλότατον) mountain in its region. This fact supports our interpretation, which stresses the Mosaic parallels. None of the synoptic evangelists seems to have been interested in locating with any precision the mount of transfiguration, and none names it. Christian tradition from an early time pointed to Mount Tabor.[53] More recently, Mount Hermon has been favoured.[54] For a rejection of these two sites and a vote for Mount Meron see Liefeld (v), p. 167, n. 27.

2. καὶ μετεμορφώθη ἔμπροσθεν αὐτῶν. So also Mk 9.2. The language implies 'not a mere illumination from without, but an irradiation from within, a transient effulgence, so to speak, of the beams of divine glory through the veil of humanity' (Strauss, p. 535). The passive is presumably divine: God transfigures Jesus.

μεταμορφόω (cf. Ps 33.1 Sym.; Philo, *Mos.* 1.57—of Moses; *Leg. ad Gai.* 95), rare before NT times, means 'transform', 'change in form' (cf. Rom 12.2; Diognetus, *Ep.* 2.3). The verb—avoided by Luke, perhaps because of its associations with the mystery religions[55]—is used in 2 Cor 3.18, in a context where the splendour of Moses is a foil for the δόξα of Christians: 'We all, with unveiled face, beholding the glory of the Lord, are being changed into his likeness from one degree of glory to another . . .'. Unless one conjectures Pauline influence on Mark, it seems plausible that μεταμορφόω had, in Jewish and/or Christian tradition, come to be used of the story in Exod 34.[56]

[50] So Riesenfeld (v), p. 217, finding a connexion with Tabernacles; so Donaldson (v), without such a connexion. The allusion to Ps 2.7 ('this is my beloved Son'), which in the OT belongs to an enthronement text, is more than consistent with this interpretation, for in 2.4 there is this: 'I have set my king on Zion, my holy hill'. Note also the link between mountains and thrones in Jewish tradition (e.g. Ps 2.6; 48.2; Jer 8.19; Jub. 1.27–9; 1 En. 18.8).
[51] Cf. Ezek 40.2; Zech 14.4; Rev 21.10.
[52] Cf. LXX Gen 7.19, 20; Isa 14.13; 28.4; Ezek 40.2; T. Levi 2.5; Rev 21.10.
[53] So already Origen, in PG 12.1548, and Cyril of Jerusalem, *Cat.* 12.16. Tradition has it that Saint Helen built a church on Tabor; so Nicephorus Callistus, in PG 146.113.
[54] E.g. Swete, p. 187; Klausner, p. 303.
[55] For the association see J. Behm, *TWNT* 4, pp. 754–6.
[56] Chilton (v), pp. 123–4, commenting on 2 Cor 3.7–4.6, makes the interesting conjecture that Peter and James and John claimed 'a place akin to that of Aaron, Nadab and Abihu in their account of the Transfiguration and that Paul, who initially accepted their authority, later trumped their claim by comparing himself directly to Moses'.

Even though the primary background for the synoptic picture of
Jesus transfigured is to be found in the change Moses experienced
on Sinai, it may not be irrelevant to keep in mind the expectation
that the bodies of the righteous will, in the end, undergo a
transformation, for the transfigured Jesus is probably intended to
show forth what believers will become (cf. p. 688). See Dan 12.3;
1 En. 38.4 ('the light of the Lord of the Spirits has shined upon the
face of the holy, the righteous, and the elect'); 104.2; 2 Bar. 51.1–3
('the shape of their face will be changed into the light of their
beauty'), 10, 12; 4 Ezra 7.97 (the saints' faces will 'shine like the
sun'); and Davies, *PRJ*, pp. 303–8.[57]

καὶ ἔλαμψεν τὸ πρόσωπον αὐτοῦ ὡς ὁ ἥλιος. Compare
1 En 38.4; 4 Ezra 7.97; and T. Levi 18.40 (where the priestly
Messiah will 'shine forth as the sun on the earth'); also Rev 1.16
(ἡ ὄψις αὐτοῦ ὡς ὁ ἥλιος φαίνει ἐν τῇ δυνάμει αὐτοῦ);
and 10.1. The line has no parallel in Mark and must be
redactional (cf. the redactional 13.43: τότε οἱ δίκαιοι
ἐκλάμψουσιν ὡς ὁ ἥλιος). Although the OT does not compare
Moses' face to the sun, Philo, *Mos.* 1.70, says that dazzling
brightness flashed from Moses like 'rays of the sun' (ἡλιοειδοῦς
φέγγους). And Schlatter, p. 527, cites *Sipre Num.* 140: 'The face of
Moses was as the face of the sun.' Compare also LAB 12.1:
Moses' 'face surpassed the splendour of the sun and the moon'.
Clearly we are dealing here with a common motif and another
Mosaic parallel.

Lk 9.29a has this: καὶ ἐγένετο ἐν τῷ προσεύχεσθαι αὐτὸν τὸ εἶδος τοῦ
προσώπου αὐτοῦ ἕτερον. The minor agreement is hardly close: 'face'
and 'his' are the only common words, and they are from the LXX
(Exod 34.29). Furthermore, Streeter, pp. 315–16, was correct in
remarking that 'if we speak of a change in a person's appearance, the
first thing we think of and mention is the *face*. If, then, there is anything
that requires to be explained in this agreement ... it is not why both
Matthew and Luke use the word πρόσωπον, but how Mark managed
to avoid doing so. It reads a bit strangely to say a person was
transfigured, and then to go on and to speak of the difference in his
clothes without mentioning the face.'[58]

τὰ δὲ ἱμάτια αὐτοῦ ἐγένετο λευκὰ ὡς τὸ φῶς. Mk 9.3 opens
with καὶ and concludes with στίλβοντα λευκὰ λίαν. Matthew
has assimilated to the previous line (ὡς ὁ ἥλιος).

[57] The notion that the saints will shine with light in the future may be related
to the belief in the luminousness of angels (Dan 10.6; 1 En. 71.1; etc.), for it was
anticipated that the elect would be like the angels; see on 22.30. Recall also that
holy people or martyrs were sometimes said to have 'the face of an angel' (e.g.
Stephen in Acts 6.15; Paul in Acts of Paul and Thecla 3; SB 2, pp. 665–6). This
must refer to radiance (cf. Add Est. 15.13).
[58] Streeter also raised the possibility that πρόσωπον at one time stood in
Mark's text; cf. Taylor, *Mark*, p. 389.

The supernatural brightness of the clothes of divine or heavenly beings or of the resurrected just is a common motif in the biblical tradition; see Dan 7.9 LXX, Theod. (of the Son of man); 1 En. 14.20 (the gown of God); 63.15–16 (the garments of the righteous); Mk 16.5 (an angel's robe); Rev 3.4–5; 7.9 (white garments of the saints); T. Job 46.7–9 (supernatural shimmering cords to be worn around the waist); 2 En. 22.8–9 (clothes of glory); 3 En. 12.1 (Metatron's robe has luminaries in it); Sepher Ha-Razim 2.93 (angelic garments 'white as light'). Like God, who 'covers himself with light as with a garment' (Ps 104.2), those who belong to him are also destined to shine like the sun.

3. καὶ ἰδοὺ ὤφθη αὐτοῖς Μωϋσῆς καὶ Ἠλίας μετ' αὐτοῦ συλλαλοῦντες.[59] Mk 9.4 lacks ἰδού,[60] names Elijah before Moses (Ἠλίας σὺν Μωϋσεῖ; cf. p. 685 and note the order of 17.4 = Mk 9.5[61]), and, instead of μετ' κ.τ.λ., has the fuller καὶ ἦσαν συλλαλοῦντες τῷ Ἰησοῦ. One would not guess from Matthew that, as Luke has it, Moses and Elijah spoke with Jesus about his passion (Lk 9.31).

συλλαλοῦντες would seem to indicate that Jesus belongs to the same world as Moses and Elijah (cf. Apoc. Zeph. 9.5). But there may be more to the unrecorded conversation than this. συλλαλέω is used of Moses in LXX Exod 34.35, at the end of the account of his transfiguration, while 34.29 associates Moses' transfiguration with the act of 'talking with God'. Is this, then, one more OT detail which has affected our NT story?[62]

Why are Moses and Elijah mentioned?[63] Probably because they are the two OT figures who encountered God on Sinai/Horeb.[64] But Moses and Elijah have most often in Christian exegetical history been taken to represent, respectively, the law and the prophets—which leads to the conclusion that in Jesus the Messiah and Son of God the law and the prophets are surpassed[65] or fulfilled and

[59] So HG. NA[26] moves μετ αυτου to the end, following ℵ B W f¹ 892 ff¹ ff² q. But this could be due to assimilation to the order in Mark and Luke, so one inclines to accept the testimony of C D L Θ f¹³ Maj lat sy^h.

[60] Lk 9.30 agrees with Matthew in adding ἰδού. But the significance of this is not great, given the frequency with which both add the word to their sources (cf. 1, p. 78). Note that Matthew adds it soon again in 17.5 (bis) and cf. Exod 34.30.

[61] Luke also puts Moses before Elijah. But this is simply the more natural order. It has in fact often been suggested that the pre-Markan order must have named Moses first (e.g. Chilton (v), pp. 117–18, citing in agreement W. L. Knox, T. A. Burkill, and U. B. Müller).

[62] The NT text does not raise the issue of whether Jesus spoke to the heavenly beings in a human language or an angelic language.

[63] Review of opinion in Nützel (v), pp. 113–22; also Jeremias, TWNT 2, pp. 940–1.

[64] So also Gundry, Commentary, p. 343. Cf. Cyril of Jerusalem, Cat. 12.16.

[65] According to Smith, Magician, p. 121, 'if we suppose with Paul that the Law was "ordained by angels through an intermediary" (Gal 3.19; cp. Acts 7.53), and that Sinai is the symbol of slavery (Gal 4.25), we shall see the mountain of the transfiguration as opposed to Sinai, and the declaration to

confirmed.[66] Such an interpretation would help account for Matthew placing Moses before Elijah: this accords with the fixed formula, 'the law and the prophets' (cf. 5.17; 7.12). We cannot, however, be at all sure that this interpretation was intended by the author of our gospel, especially as Elijah was not a writing prophet. And there are still other suggested interpretations. Thrall (v), for instance, suspects that Moses and Elijah are mentioned in order to show that Jesus—the only one to rise from the dead—is greater than both (cf. vv. 5–6); and Pamment (v) has claimed that both Moses and Elijah, like Jesus, were rejected by the people but vindicated by God. Others have begun with the fact that Moses and Elijah are also paired in Jn 1.21 (Moses indirectly); Rev 11.3 (probably); and *Midr. Rab.* on Deut 10.1—all three times as eschatological figures. Even though the pairing is infrequent, the two figures are naturally associated.[67] They were both wonder-workers. Both suffered. Both were prophets. Both were connected with the law.[68] Both were, according to tradition, spared death,[69] and (perhaps) both were expected to return.[70] It has therefore seemed natural to many to discern their significance for the transfiguration by interpreting them together, sometimes as eschatological figures. But Liefeld (v), p. 173, may be correct to contend that whereas Moses' rôle is primarily typological, that of Elijah is primarily eschatological (cf. 17.9–13).[71] The appearance of Moses confirms the Exodus theme while the appearance of Elijah gives the whole scene an eschatological dimension. There is yet another possibility, seemingly neglected by exegetes. If, according to the Pentateuch, Moses' face became lit up on Sinai, Elijah was, in Jewish tradition, associated with fire and light. Not only did the prophet call down fire from heaven and ascend in a fiery chariot, but this is found in *Liv. Proph.* Elijah 2–3: 'When he was born, his father Sobacha saw that men of shining white appearance were greeting him and wrapping him in fire, and they gave him flames of fire to eat, and he went and reported this in Jerusalem and the oracle told him: "Do not be afraid, for *his dwelling will be with light* and his word judgement ..."'. Perhaps Elijah is named in Mt 17.3 par. because he,

which the gospel story leads, "this is My beloved Son", as a declaration of deliverance from the Law into the "liberty in which Christ has set us free"'. This goes much too far, whether with reference to Matthew, to Mark, or to the pre-Markan tradition.

[66] Cf. Cyril of Jerusalem, *Comm. on Lk.* 51; Augustine, *Serm.* 28 (78).4; 29 (79).1; Gnilka, *Matthäusevangelium* 2, p. 95.

[67] Cf. *Pesiq. R.* 4.2: 'Moses and Elijah are equal to each other in everything'.

[68] For Elijah as interpreter of the law in Jewish sources see Davies, *SSM*, pp. 158–61.

[69] Although Moses' death is recorded in the OT, this did not prevent the emergence of the belief that he must have ascended to heaven; see e.g. Josephus, *Ant.* 4.323–6; *Sipre* on Deut 34.5 (357); b. *Soṭa* 13b; *Memar Markah* 5.3. On the other hand, it has sometimes been argued that Moses represents the dead, Elijah the living; so Chrysostom, *Hom. on Mt.* 56.3; Ephraem Syrus, *Nat.* 1.35–6.

[70] Although the evidence for a return of Moses is scanty and quite debatable; see Jeremias, *TWNT* 4, pp. 860–1.

[71] Cf. Gnilka, *Markus* 2, p. 34: Moses is the 'Vorbild', Elijah the 'Vorläufer'.

like Jesus and Moses, also had had his appearance transfigured into light.

4. ἀποκριθεὶς δὲ ὁ Πέτρος εἶπεν τῷ Ἰησοῦ. Mk 9.5 opens with καί and uses the historical present, λέγει.

κύριε. Mark has ῥαββί, Luke ἐπιστάτα.[72] See on 8.6. Because 'rabbi' is strange in a context where Jesus is transfigured into a divine being, the independent alterations of Matthew and Luke are natural improvements.

καλόν ἐστιν ἡμᾶς ὧδε εἶναι. Compare LXX Num 11.18. The words, which agree with Mk 9.5 as well as with Lk 9.33, prepare for the next clause. But it is unclear whether Peter is happy because of what he is experiencing or because he has an opportunity to serve Jesus and Moses and Elijah. On the accusative + infinitive after καλόν see BDF § 409.3

εἰ θέλεις. Compare 11.14 (redactional); 16.24; 19.17 (redactional), 21 (redactional). This is editorial and replaces Mark's simple καί.[73] Its purpose is to make Peter act with due deference (cf. the insertion of 'Lord'). BDF § 372.2(c) compares the French, *s'il vous plaît*.

ποιήσω ὧδε τρεῖς σκηνάς. Mark has the plural, ποιήσωμεν, lacks ὧδε (which Matthew has borrowed from v. 4b = Mk 9.5b), and puts τρεῖς after[74] σκηνάς. The first difference means that Peter no longer speaks for the others but of himself alone: he will build the tents or booths.

σοὶ μίαν καὶ Μωϋσεῖ μίαν καὶ Ἠλίᾳ μίαν. So also Mk 9.5d. What is the significance of the three σκηναί? We have not been able to come to any decision on the matter. Boobyer (v) and Riesenfeld (v) stress the connexion with the Feast of Tabernacles. They do so in order to highlight the eschatological thrust of the transfiguration, for in Jewish tradition Tabernacles is associated with eschatological themes. Others have simply surmised that Peter wished to prolong the blessed moment, or that his request arose from a desire to observe the feast that was at hand. But the background has also been found in the OT references to 'the tent of meeting' ('ōhel mô'ēd). The LXX quite frequently translates 'ōhel with σκηνή[75] (the word Peter uses), and the usual rendering of 'ōhel mô'ēd is σκηνὴ τοῦ μαρτυρίου (e.g. Exod 29.4, 10, 30, 32). The tent of meeting was,

---

[72] Which is redactional: Mt: 0; Mk: 0; Lk: 6.

[73] But we must consider the possibility that Matthew has simply added εἰ, for it is quite possible that the text of Mk 9.5 D Θ *f*[13] is correct: καὶ θέλεις κ.τ.λ.; cf. Cranfield, *Mark*, p. 291.

[74] So A D W Θ *f*[1.13] Maj sy[h]. Is not the order of P[45] ℵ B C L Δ 33 892 1424 *pc* (τρεῖς σκηνάς) the result of harmonization? So HG, against NA[26].

[75] The Greek word also renders *miškān* ('dwelling place') and *sūkkâ* ('booth'). Full discussion in O. Michaelis, *TWNT* 7, pp. 369–82.

according to the OT, near Mount Sinai, and it was where God spoke to Moses face to face (Exod 33.7–11; Deut 31.14–15). It was also where Moses went after being transfigured (Exod 34.34–5). When one adds that the tent of meeting was often surrounded by the cloud of God's presence (e.g. Exod 33.9–10; Lev 16.2; Deut 31.15), it is tempting to infer that Peter wanted to build booths because he wanted to recreate the conditions which obtained at Sinai. Yet would one not then expect a request to build *one* tent, not three?[76] So perhaps one should consider the interpretation of Cyril of Jerusalem, *Comm. on Lk.* 51: 'Peter, thinking perchance that the time of the kingdom of God was even now come, proposes dwellings on the mountain, and says that it is fitting there should be three tabernacles. . . . But he knew not, it says, what he was saying; for it was not the time of the consummation of the world, nor for the saints to take possession of the hope promised to them . . .'. Support for this reading may be garnered from those biblical texts in which God or his Messiah are foreseen as tabernacling among the saints at the end.[77] Lastly, it could be that Peter's proposal presupposes that the saints in heaven have dwellings,[78] and that, come to earth, dwellings need to be made for them (cf. Marshall, *Luke*, pp. 386–7).

Even though Matthew has not remarked upon Peter's error (contrast Mark), the apostle's proposal is inevitably thought of as inappropriate, this for two reasons: (i) Jesus still has to go his way to death, and (ii) Moses and Elijah must soon disappear. The transfiguration is only a fleeting moment, not a permanent state of affairs (cf. Pesch 2, pp. 75–6).

5. The proceedings are now interrupted by a cloud—which is 'the sign both of God's self-revelation and of his self-veiling' (Cranfield, *Mark*, p. 295)—and then by a heavenly voice which, repeating the divine declaration of the baptism, but here addressed to the disciples instead of Jesus, proclaims Jesus to be God's Son and the suffering servant. As so often happens in Jewish literature, interpretation follows revelation (cf. Sabbe (v), p. 84).

ἔτι αὐτοῦ λαλοῦντος. This is redactional (cf. 12.46, also redactional). There is, indeed, a parallel in Lk 9.34 (ταῦτα δὲ αὐτοῦ λέγοντος), but the only common word is αὐτοῦ.

ἰδοὺ νεφέλη φωτεινὴ ἐπεσκίασεν αὐτούς. Compare Mk 9.7: καὶ ἐγένετο νεφέλη ἐπισκιάζουσα αὐτοῖς; also Ezek 1.4

---

[76] Whether or to what extent the fact that the tabernacle, like Sinai itself, was divided into three gradations of holiness mitigates this objection is unclear.

[77] Cf. Ezek 37.27; 43.7, 9; Zech 2.10–11; 8.3, 8; 14.6–9; Rev 21.3.

[78] Cf. 1 En. 39.4–8; 41.2; 71.16; Jn 14.2; 2 En. 61.23; T. Abr. A 20.14.

('a great cloud with brightness round about it'); Rev 14.14 ('a
white cloud'); Liv. Proph. Jer. 14 ('a cloud as of fire'); T. Abr. A
9.8 ('a cloud of light'); Apoc. Adam 71.9–10 ('the cloud of great
light'); 75.19–20 ('great clouds of light'); Liv. Proph. Jer. 18 ('a
cloud like fire, just like the ancient one'). Matthew has added
ἰδού (as in vv. 3 and 5c) and, as usual, dropped Mark's καὶ
ἐγένετο. Luke also has the genitive absolute and the finite
verb instead of the participle. φωτεινή creates a parallel with v. 2
and makes the reference to the Shekinah, the cloud of God's
presence, unmistakable.[79]

At Exod 40.35 the LXX uses ἐπισκιάζω (= 'overshadow' or
'envelope'; cf. Lk 1.35) for *sākan*: Moses could not enter the tent of
meeting because ἐπεσκίαζεν ἐπ᾽ αὐτὴν ἡ νεφέλη καὶ δόξης κυρίου
ἐπλήσθη ἡ σκηνή. Is this text not in the background of Mt 17.5?

There seems to have been some expectation that the cloud of the
wilderness would return at the consummation (cf. Isa 4.5; 2 Macc 2.8).
Thus we may have here an eschatological motif: the Shekinah has once
again appeared. Whether αὐτούς refers to Jesus and Moses and Elijah
or to the disciples as well is uncertain; but, *pace* Gundry, *Commentary*,
p. 344, it seems most likely that we are to picture the cloud first
enveloping Jesus and the OT figures and then departing, leaving Jesus
alone.[80] For φωνὴ κ.τ.λ. readily implies a distance between the cloud
and the disciples. In this case the cloud would be the vehicle for
removing Moses and Elijah (see on v. 9). Luke agrees with Matthew
against Mark in using the accusative after ἐπεσκίασ(ζ)εν. This,
however, scarcely seems compelling evidence for Luke's knowledge of
Matthew.[81]

καὶ ἰδού. Mark has καὶ ἦλθεν or ἐγένετο. Matthew has
assimilated to Mt 3.17.

φωνὴ ἐκ τῆς νεφέλης λέγουσα. Matthew has added the verb
(cf. also Lk 9.35); this increases the parallelism with 3.17 (q.v.
for discussion). Compare 2 Pet 1.18: 'and this voice we heard
from heaven' (cf. Ps.-Clem, Hom. 3.53). The places in which
God speaks from a cloud are few and far between (cf. Exod
24.16—ἐκ μέσου τῆς νεφέλης—and T. Job 42.1–3). This
strengthens the Exodus connexion.

οὗτός ἐστιν ὁ υἱός μου ὁ ἀγαπητός, ἐν ᾧ εὐδόκησα. Compare

[79] Cf. esp. Exod 24.16–17; also Ezek 10.4; 2 Macc 2.8; *ARN* 2; *b. Sanh.*
39a.—Christian exegetes since Origen (cf. *Comm. on Mt.* 11.42) have often
identified the cloud with the Holy Spirit, which has led to interpreting the scene
as a revelation of the Trinity (cf. Bonaventure, *Lignum vitae* 12). One is reminded
of the rabbinic equation of the Shekinah cloud with the Spirit of God; see
Davies, *PRJ*, p. 211.
[80] So also A. Oepke, *TWNT* 4, pp. 910–11.
[81] See further C. M. Tuckett, 'On the Relationship between Matthew and
Luke', *NTS* 30 (1984), p. 136.

3.17 (q.v. for full discussion); also Ps 2.7; Isa 42.1; 44.2; 2 Pet 1.17. So Mk 9.7, without the last three words. The agreement with Mt 3.17, the voice at the baptism, is perfect. Our author has thus modified Mark's text so that in addition to drawing upon Ps 2.7 it also plainly alludes to Isa 42.1. The appropriateness of this cannot be missed. Not only does the modification make 3.17 and 17.5 say precisely the same thing (repetition for emphasis),[82] but it is fitting that Jesus should be presented as the *'ebed Yahweh* in a pericope so influenced by Mosaic motifs, for Moses was known as the *'ebed* or παῖς *par excellence* (cf. Exod 14.31; Num 12.7–8).

Instead of ὁ ἀγαπητός, Luke has ὁ ἐκλελεγμένος, an allusion to Isa 42.1 (MT: *běḥîrî*; LXX: ὁ ἐκλεκτός). This means that both the First and Third Evangelists have modified Mark by drawing upon the same OT text. Is this not reason to postulate literary contact between Matthew and Luke? We do not think so. First, Matthew and Luke allude to different clauses from Isa 42.1. Secondly, Mk 1.11 seemingly alludes to both Ps 2.7 and Isa 42.1 (see on 3.17), and because the voice of Mk 9.7 is so reminiscent of Mk 1.11, it would have been natural for both Matthew and Luke to have made the voice at the transfiguration allude to Isaiah as well as the Psalm.[83] Thirdly, one should also take account of 2 Pet 1.16–18, which contains a version of the transfiguration that many have considered independent of the synoptics (so e.g. Bauckham, pp. 205–12). For 2 Pet 1.17, in its version of the heavenly voice of the transfiguration, also echoes both Ps 2.7 and Isa 42.1: 'This is my Son, my Beloved, on whom I have set my favour.' Is this not additional evidence that the voice from the cloud was regularly associated with the voice at the baptism and therefore assimilated to Isa 42.1 (cf. also Ps.-Clem. Hom. 3.53; Apoc. Pet. E 17) and that the similarities between Mt 17 and Lk 9 do not demand knowledge by one of the other?

αὐτοῦ ἀκούετε.[84] Mark has the reverse order. The words presumably refer to Deut 18.15 and 18 and show Jesus to be the prophet like Moses (cf. p. 686). For other texts where Jesus is presented as the object of Moses' prophecy of a future prophet see Acts 3.22 and 7.37 (both embedded in pre-Lukan and perhaps primitive material); also Ps.-Clem. Hom. 3.53 and Ps.-Clem. Rec. 1.39–43.

---

[82] The continued assimilation of the baptism and transfiguration narratives in the tradition may be signalled by the presence of a light in certain accounts of the baptism; cf. 1, p. 330.

[83] The point has even more force if ὁ ἀγαπητός (Mk 9.7) was thought to depend upon Isa 42.1 (cf. Mt 12.18 and see on 3.17).

[84] So HG, following C L W Θ *f*[13] Maj lat sy Chr PsAug Cyp Hil Ephr mae. NA[26] has the reverse order, on the authority of ℵ B D *f*[1] 33 ff[1] r[2] Hip Or sa bo. One can hardly come to any decision, for Mark has one order, Luke another, and assimilation to either is possible.

The imperative, ἀκούετε, may here mean more than just 'hear'. The Hebrew *šāmaʿ* often means 'obey', as in Exod 6.12 and 2 Chron 28.11 (MT: *šĕmāʿûnî*; LXX: ἀκούσατέ μου); and the same holds true on occasion for ἀκούω in the NT (e.g. Mt 18.15–16; Lk 16.29, 31; Jn 5.25; 8.47; Acts 28.28).

The command to hear or obey Jesus—directed to the disciples, not Moses and Elijah[85]—probably pertains not solely to the future ('listen to him from now on') but also looks back to the episode at Caesarea Philippi, where Jesus' words about suffering were not easily digested.[86]

6. The verse has no parallel in either Mark or Luke and is editorial.[87]

καὶ ἀκούσαντες οἱ μαθηταὶ ἔπεσαν ἐπὶ πρόσωπον αὐτῶν καὶ ἐφοβήθησαν σφόδρα. Compare Exod 34.30 (those who saw Moses' face were afraid to come near) and Mk 9.6. The motif of falling on one's face in fear is a standard part of any heavenly ascent or revelation story. But here there is more, for there is a contrast between Jesus' face, which is shining, and the faces of the disciples, which are hidden. Mark places the awe felt by the disciples early in the narrative, immediately after the transfiguration and the vision of Moses and Elijah: not the fact that Jesus commands but his transfiguration itself is emphasized. Luke makes the descent of the cloud the occasion for fear (Lk 9.34). With Matthew it is otherwise. He reserves the experience of awe on the part of the disciples until immediately after the words, 'Hear ye him'. It is the divine word which is awesome.

7. Again there is no parallel in Mark or Luke, and again we may ascribe the verse to the First Evangelist.[88]

καὶ προσῆλθεν ὁ Ἰησοῦς καὶ ἁψάμενος αὐτῶν εἶπεν. On προσέρχομαι see on 4.3. Only here and in 28.18 does Jesus 'approach' anyone. In both cases he approaches his disciples, and in both cases he is in an exalted state.

ἐγέρθητε καὶ μὴ φοβεῖσθε. Like touching, the expression is common in epiphanies.[89]

8. ἐπάραντες δὲ τοὺς ὀφθαλμοὺς αὐτῶν. This replaces Mk

---

[85] *Pace* Origen, *Comm. on Mt.* 12.42, and Moiser (v).

[86] Chrysostom, *Hom. on Mt.* 56.5, sees the words as looking backwards whereas Schweizer, *Matthew*, p. 349, takes them to look forward. The two interpretations are not antithetical but complementary.

[87] Verb of perception + φοβέομαι: see on 14.30. μαθητής*. ἔπεσεν ἐπὶ πρόσωπον is redactional in 26.39 diff. Mk 14.35. σφόδρα*.

[88] προσέρχομαι*, ὁ Ἰησοῦς*, ἐγείρω*. ἅπτω is redactional in 8.15. μή + φοβέομαι is without parallel in 1.20; 10.26; 17.7; 28.5, 10. Gundry, *Commentary*, p. 345, is correct to call attention to the parallelism between vv. 6 and 7 'in the contrasts between hearing and touching, falling and getting up, fearing and not fearing'.

[89] Cf. Dan 10.11–12; Jos. Asen. 14.11; 23.16.

9.8a: καὶ ἐξάπινα περιβλεψάμενοι. Only here does Matthew use the verb ἐπαίρω, but 'lifting his/her/their eyes' is a common enough phrase (one favoured by Luke and John).[90]

οὐδένα εἶδον εἰ μὴ αὐτὸν Ἰησοῦν μόνον. Mk 9.8b has: οὐκέτι οὐδένα εἶδον ἀλλὰ τὸν Ἰησοῦν μόνον μεθ᾽ ἑαυτῶν. Evidently Moses and Elijah have been taken away to heaven by the cloud. This recalls other texts in which clouds serve as vehicles.[91] Compare Josephus, Ant. 4.326: while Moses 'was yet communing with them, a cloud of a sudden descended upon him and he disappeared in a ravine.'

The history of the interpretation of the transfiguration is rather interesting.[92] In 2 Peter the story is employed as an apologetic. It vindicates belief in Jesus as God's beloved Son and as the recipient of divine honour and glory. It also serves to uphold what 2 Pet 1.19 calls 'the prophetic word', which word, given the content of 2 Peter, probably refers to the promises of the second advent or, more precisely, to the transfiguration as an anticipation of and therefore prophecy of that advent. That is, Christ's glory at his first coming assures believers that his promise of a glorious second coming is most sure (cf. 3.1–18).[93] In the second-century Apocalypse of Peter (chapter 17) the transfiguration is recounted in response to the disciples' request that they behold the fate of the righteous ones after death. Furthermore, when Peter asks where the righteous ones dwell and inquires about their world, the scene expands to include the paradise of God, with its lights and flowers and trees and fragrances and fruits. So here the transfiguration is a preview of what heaven will be like and an illustration of the glory that awaits the Christian (cf. Proclus, in PG 65.763; Ps.-Dionysius, Div. nom. 1.4; Bede, in PL 92.217–19). Perhaps the most common interpretation in Christian history is that found in Acts of Peter 20 and Acts Thom. 143: the transfiguration is a revelation of Christ's heavenly or divine nature, a revelation of Jesus as he always was and is. On this view, Jesus was not really changed; rather, the disciples were enabled to perceive what was always the case (cf. the story in 2 Kgs 6.15–17). This interpretation has often been put forward with Phil 2.6–7 (ἐν μορφῇ θεοῦ) in mind (e.g. Leo of Rome, in PL 54.312).[94]

Most traditional approaches to the transfiguration can be assigned to one of two categories: either the emphasis is upon Christ's divinity

---

[90] Cf. LXX Gen 13.10; 2 Sam 18.24; Ezek 18.6; Lk 6.20; 16.23; Jn 4.35; 6.5; Par. Jer. 5.5.

[91] See Ps 104.3; Isa 19.1; Dan 7.13; Mk 13.26; 14.62; Acts 1.9; 1 Thess 4.17; Rev 11.12; 4 Ezra 13.1–4; T. Abr. A 10; 2 En. 3.1–3; 3 En. 24.3–4; b. Sanh. 98a.

[92] See further Boobyer (v) and McGukin, Transfiguration (v).

[93] See further Neyrey (v). For the view that the Transfiguration shows forth the glory of Jesus' parousia see Chrysostom, Hom. on Mt. 56.7; Theodoret, Ep. 145; Euthymius Zigabenus, in PG 129.476.

[94] It is interesting that Philo spoke of Moses being 'changed into the divine' on Sinai; see Quaest. Exod. 2.29. Note that Irenaeus, Adv. haer. 4.20.9, saw the transfiguration as God granting Moses his request to see God's glory (Exod 33).

or it is upon his humanity. In the latter case the transfiguration represents what all believers will experience at the resurrection. But in the Hesychiasts of Byzantium the two traditions are fused. Gregory Palamas identified the light of Tabor with the ineffable, uncreated light of Christ which bathes the whole cosmos and which can yet be seen in the chambers of the heart by those who say the Jesus Prayer and accomplish poverty of spirit, that is, by those in the process of being deified through participation in the divine life. So the light of the transfiguration belongs to Christ as God but at the same time transforms human beings into their divine destiny.[95]

(iv) *Concluding Observations*

(1) In 17.1–8 the great light of 4.16 becomes visibly radiant to those called, in 5.14, to be the light of the world. For Matthew the first purpose of the manifestation is to recall Exod 24 and 34 and certain events in the life of Moses. The point of this is not simply christological, although that is important: Jesus is the prophet like Moses (cf. Deut 18.15, 18) who, as the unique Son of God, surpasses Moses. Also significant is the closely related eschatological theme: 'as it was in the beginning, so shall it be in the end' (see on 1.1); 'as the first redeemer, so the last redeemer'. When Jesus, in circumstances strongly reminiscent of Exod 24 and 34, goes up on a mountain and is transfigured into light, the reader is to infer that history has come full circle, that the eschatological expectations of Judaism have begun to find their fulfilment. The eschatological prophet, the one like Moses and Elijah, has appeared, and the light of the resurrection and *parousia* has already shone forth. Israel's primal history is being recapitulated by her Messiah, God's Son, the eschatological embodiment of true Israel.[96]

(2) The transfiguration, with its wealth of theological associations, relates itself in diverse ways to the immediately preceding narrative. To begin with, the story illustrates 16.24–8 by first showing forth the glory of the *parousia* foretold in vv. 27

---

[95] The idea that the transfigured Christ represents human destiny is also sometimes combined with the idea that the transfiguration restores human nature to its original glory (cf. the Aposticha for the vespers service of the transfiguration in the Orthodox church: 'by thy transfiguration [thou] didst cause the dark nature of Adam to flourish, restoring its element to glory and splendour;' cf. the Jewish tradition about Adam's glory). Similar ideas apparently led to the belief, occasionally expressed (e.g. by Andrew of Crete, in PG 97.949), that the disciples were transfigured when Jesus was. Note that Ephraem Syrus, *De paradiso* 1.6, makes Moses' transfiguration on Sinai a picture of humanity's destiny.

[96] See further D. C. Allison, Jr., 'The Son of God as Israel: A Note on Matthean Christology', *IBS* 9 (1987), pp. 74–81.

and 28 (cf. 2 Pet 1.16–18 and Basil the Great in PG 29.400D) and secondly by making concrete the resurrection hope of those who follow the hard commands of Jesus issued in vv. 24–6. As for 16.21–3 (the prophecy of Jesus' passion and vindication), 17.1–8 illumines this by anticipating Jesus' exaltation as well as by interpreting the suffering which must come first as that of the servant written of by the prophet Isaiah. Moving backward yet one more pericope, there is also a close connexion with 16.13–20, for both at Caesarea Philippi and on the mount of transfiguration Jesus is proclaimed to be the Son of God. There is, to be sure, a major difference in that in the earlier story the Son of God confession comes from a man, Peter, whereas in the latter God himself speaks. But this only makes 17.1–8 set the divine seal of approval over Peter's pronouncement (cf. the baptismal story). Further, the two pericopae are alike in so far as both qualify sonship with suffering service: just as 16.13–20 is followed by 16.21–3, which holds forth the necessity for suffering, so 17.1–8 interprets Jesus' sonship in terms of Isaiah's servant ('in whom I am well pleased'; cf. Isa 42.1).

(3) The transfiguration narrative has a remarkable twin of sorts in the account of Jesus' execution, 27.32–54. In the one, a private epiphany, an exalted Jesus, with garments glistening, stands on a high mountain and is flanked by two religious giants from the past. All is light. In the other, a public spectacle, a humiliated Jesus, whose clothes have been torn from him and divided, is lifted upon a cross and flanked by two common, convicted criminals. All is darkness. We have here pictorial antithetical parallelism, a diptych in which the two plates have similar lines but different colours. If the two scenes were sketched on transparencies they could be superimposed. Consider the schema on the opposite page.

It is truly striking that in both pericopae those looking on are overcome by fear (17.6; 27.54, the only two places Matthew uses ἐφοβήθησαν σφόδρα), and that in both instances Jesus is confessed by others to be the Son of God (17.6; 27.54). In this confession—that is, in Christology—inheres the unity beneath the two radically disparate events, transfiguration and crucifixion. As God's Son, it is Jesus' lot to participate in the polarities, indeed the whole gamut, of human experience. This is because the Son of God is the Messiah (16.16), and that means the eschatological man, in whom the eschatological pattern of suffering-vindication, tribulation-salvation must play itself out. Therefore in fulfilling the prophets and their ancient oracles of doom and consolation, Jesus is humiliated and exalted, surrounded by saints and ringed by sinners, clothed with light and yet wrapped in a garment of darkness.

THE TRANSFIGURATION

light   Private epiphany   glorification

Moses   Jesus   Elijah

The mountain
Jesus takes others with him
There are onlookers (three disciples are named)
Jesus is confessed as the Son of God
Elijah is present
'they were afraid'
garments glisten
'after six days'

THE EXECUTION

darkness   Public spectacle   humiliation

thief   Jesus   thief

Elevation on the cross
Jesus is taken by others
There are onlookers (three women are named)
Jesus is confessed as the Son of God
'let us see whether Elijah will come'
'they were afraid'
garments torn and taken away
'from the sixth hour there was darkness'

(v) *Bibliography*

B. W. Bacon, 'After Six Days', *HTR* 8 (1915), pp. 94–121.

idem, 'The Transfiguration Story', *AmJTh* 6 (1902), pp. 236–65.

H. Baltensweiler, *Die Verklärung Jesu*, Zürich, 1959.

D. Baly, 'The Transfiguration Story', *ExpT* 82 (1971), p. 70.

J. B. Bernardin, 'The Transfiguration', *JBL* 52 (1933), pp. 181–9.

T. F. Best, 'The Transfiguration: A Select Bibliography', *JETS* 24 (1981), pp.157–61.

J. Blinzler, *Die neutestamentlichen Berichte über die Verklärung Jesu*, Münster, 1937.

G. H. Boobyer, *St Mark and the Transfiguration Story*, Edinburgh, 1942. Borsch, pp. 382–7.

G. B. Caird, 'The Transfiguration', *ExpT* 67 (1956), pp. 291–4.

C. E. Carlston, 'Transfiguration and Resurrection', *JBL* 80 (1961), pp. 233–40.

B. D. Chilton, 'The Transfiguration: Dominical Assurance and Apostolic Vision', *NTS* 27 (1980), pp. 115–24.

Cope, pp. 99–102.

E. Dąbrowski, *La transfiguration de Jésus*, Rome, 1939.

J. Daniélou, 'Le symbolisme eschatologique de la Fête des Tabernacles', *Irénikon* 31 (1958), pp. 19–40.

Donaldson, pp. 136–56.

R. Dunkerley, 'Jesus on Tabor', *ExpT* 36 (1925), pp. 523–5.

A. Feuillet, 'Les perspectives propres à chaque évangéliste dans les récits de la transfiguration', *Bib* 39 (1958), pp. 281–301.

R. Frieling, *Die Verklärung auf dem Berge*, Stuttgart, 1969.

A. Fuchs, 'Die Verklärungserzählung des Markus-Evangelium in der Sicht moderner Exegese', *TPQ* 125 (1977), pp. 29–37.

J. Galot, 'Révélation du Christ et liturgie juive', *EspV* 98 (1988), pp. 145–52.

W. Gerber, 'Die Metamorphose Jesu, Mk 9.2f. par.', *TZ* 23 (1967), pp. 385–95.

Hahn, *Titles*, pp. 334–46.

J. Höller, *Die Verklärung Jesu*, Freiburg, 1937.

Horstmann, pp. 72–103.

H. C. Kee, 'The Transfiguration in Mark: Epiphany or Apocalyptic Vision?', in *Understanding the Sacred Text*, ed. J. Reumann, Valley Forge, 1972, pp. 135–52.

A. Kenny, 'The Transfiguration and the Agony in the Garden', *CBQ* 19 (1957), pp. 444–52.

R. Le Déaut, 'Actes 7.48 et Matthieu 17.4 (par.) à la lumière du targum palestinien', *RSR* 52 (1964), pp. 85–90.

X. Léon-Dufour, 'La transfiguration de Jésus', in *Études*, pp. 83–122.

W. L. Liefeld, 'Theological Motifs in the Transfiguration Narrative', in *New Dimensions in New Testament Study*, ed. R. N. Longenecker and M. C. Tenney, Grand Rapids, 1974, pp. 162–79.

E. Lohmeyer, 'Die Verklärung Jesu nach dem Markus-Evangelium', *ZNW* 21 (1922), pp. 185–215.

F. R. McCurley, ' "And after six days" (Mk 9.2): A Semitic Literary Device', *JBL* 93 (1974), pp. 67–81.

J. A. McGuckin, 'Jesus Transfigured: A Question of Christology', *CR* 69 (1984), pp. 271–9.

idem, *The Transfiguration of Christ in Scripture and Tradition*, Lewiston, 1986.

C. Masson, 'La transfiguration de Jésus (Marc 9.2–13)', *RTP* 97 (1964), pp. 1–14.

U. W. Mauser, *Christ in the Wilderness*, SBT 39, London, 1963, pp. 110–19.

J. Moiser, 'Moses and Elijah', *ExpT* 96 (1985), pp. 216–17.

H.-P. Müller, 'Die Verklärung Jesu', *ZNW* 51 (1960), pp. 56–64.

U. B. Müller, 'Die christologische Absicht des Markusevangeliums und die Verklärungsgeschichte', *ZNW* 64 (1973), pp. 159–93.

J. Murphy-O'Connor, 'What really happened at the Transfiguration?', *Bib Rev* 3 (1987), pp. 8–21.

F. Neirynck, 'Minor Agreements Matthew—Luke in the Transfiguration Story', in Hoffmann, *Orientierung*, pp. 253–66.

J. H. Neyrey, 'The Apologetic Use of the Transfiguration in 2 Peter 1.16–21', *CBQ* 42 (1980), pp. 504–19.

J. M. Nützel, *Die Verklärungserzählung im Markusevangelium*, FB 6, Würzburg, 1973.

M. Pamment, 'Moses and Elijah in the Story of the Transfiguration', *ExpT* 92 (1981), pp. 338–9.

S. Pedersen, 'Die Proklamation Jesu als des eschatologischen Offenbarungsträgers (Mt. xvii.1–13)', *NovT* 17 (1975), pp. 241–64.

A. M. Ramsey, *The Glory of God and the Transfiguration of Christ*, London, 1949.

H. Riesenfeld, *Jésus transfiguré. L'arrière-plan du récit évangélique de la transfiguration de Notre-Seigneur*, Copenhagen, 1947.

W. R. Roehrs, 'God's Tabernacles among Men: A Study of the Transfiguration', *CTM* 35 (1964), pp. 18–25.

M. Sabbe, 'Le rédaction du récit de la Transfiguration', in *La venue du Messie*, ed. E. Massaux, Bruges, 1962, pp. 65–100.

W. Schmithals, 'Der Markusschluss, die Verklärungsgeschichte und die Aussendung der Zwölf', *ZTK* 69 (1972), pp. 379–411.

E. L. Schnellbächer, 'καὶ μετὰ ἡμέρας ἕξ (Markus 9.2)', *ZNW* 71 (1980), pp. 252–7.

M. Smith, 'The Origin and History of the Transfiguration Story', *USQR* 36 (1980), pp. 39–44.

R. H. Stein, 'Is the Transfiguration (Mark 9.2–8) a Misplaced Resurrection-Account?', *JBL* 95 (1976), pp. 79–96.

Strauss, pp. 535–46.

F. C. Synge, 'The Transfiguration Story', *ExpT* 82 (1970), pp. 82–3.

M. E. Thrall, 'Elijah and Moses in Mark's Account of the Transfiguration', *NTS* 16 (1970), pp. 305–17.

B. Trémel, 'Des récits apocalyptiques: Baptême et transfiguration', *LumV* 23 (1974), pp. 70–83.

A. A. Trites, 'The Transfiguration of Jesus: The Gospel in Microcosm', *EvQ* 51 (1979), pp. 67–79.

W. H. Williams, 'The Transfiguration—A New Approach?', in *Studia Evangelica 6*, ed. E. A. Livingstone, TU 112, Berlin, 1973, pp. 635–50.

XLIII

ELIJAH AND JOHN
(17.9–13)

(i) *Structure*

17.9–13 is a single scene with one conversation.[1] After a brief narrative introduction (v. 9a) there is a command of Jesus (v. 9b), next a question from the three disciples, Peter, James, and John (v. 10), and then, thirdly, a response from Jesus (vv. 11–12). An editorial comment (v. 13) serves as the conclusion.

(ii) *Sources*

Mk 9.9–13, which has no parallel in Luke,[2] is undoubtedly the source of Mt 17.9–13. This is because the Markan 'passage teems with confusion. Mark phrases v. 10 in such a manner that the disciples appear to be ignorant about the general resurrection. In v. 12 he completely loses track of the point about Elijah when he stumbles across the saying on the suffering of the Son of man, so that he has to complete the first idea in v. 13. Twice he cites Scriptures which are non-existent; this is especially bewildering since Mark is so little concerned with proof-from-prophecy elsewhere. Most puzzling of all is that Mark never . . . tells us what he means. Why does he not go on and say what we all know, that John was Elijah?' (Wink, p. 13). None of these difficulties is met with in Matthew. We find it well nigh impossible to fathom why anyone would revise Matthew's text to give us the perplexities of Mark. But that Matthew, faced with Mark's troublesome words, ironed out the difficulties and cleared everything up, is altogether natural. (*Pace* Lohmeyer, *Matthäus*, p. 269, there is no good evidence here of influence from a non-Markan source; see Gnilka, *Matthäusevangelium* 2, p. 100.)

---

[1] Contrast Mk 9.9–13, which can be divided into two scenes, vv. 9–10 and 11–13.

[2] Although Lk 9.36b shows a knowledge of Mk 9.9–10.

(iii) *Exegesis*

This objection story, which is clearly presupposed in its Matthean form by Justin, *Dial.* 49, accomplishes several purposes. It first of all deprives Jewish critiques of 'realized eschatology' of one forceful objection, namely, since Elijah has not yet come, the eschatological scenario cannot be unfolding. Beyond that, the passage emphasizes yet once more the parallels between Jesus and his forerunner, John, thus adding to that Matthean theme. Lastly, the command to keep silence until the Son of man is raised from the dead (v. 9) underlines not only the differences between the pre- and post-Easter epochs and the impossibility of preaching the whole truth about Jesus until he has completed his mission but also makes Peter and James and John authoritative bearers of the tradition about Jesus.

The First Evangelist has introduced three major changes into his Markan source. (i) He has omitted Mk 9.10 (see on v. 9). (ii) He has added a new conclusion (see v. 13). (iii) He has moved Mk 9.12b, so awkward in its Markan context, to a more appropriate location.

Bultmann, *History*, pp. 124–5, 332, seems to regard Mk 9.9–10 as Markan redaction, 9.11–12a + 13 as a traditional pericope, and Mk 9.12b as a post-Markan gloss.[3] Although there is general agreement that Mk 9.9–10, which cannot be separated from the transfiguration story (cf. Bayer (v)), is editorial[4] and that vv. 11 and 13 are traditional,[5] there is no consensus about v. 12. Conzelmann, *Theology*, p. 133, departs from his mentor in viewing the verse as redactional; but Tödt, p. 169, thinks that the dissimilarity of the verbs used in 8.31; 9.12b; and 12.10f. is 'intelligible only if it was caused by a previously formed text'. In our judgement, Bultmann was probably half-right. Mk 9.12b, which so clumsily interrupts the discussion of Elijah,[6] is indeed to be regarded as intrusive; but, *pace* Bultmann and others, it should be understood not as the product of a later scribe—a view which simply lacks evidence, textual or otherwise—but as an insertion made by the Second Evangelist himself (cf. Lk 24.26).[7, 8]

[3] For Bultmann, Mk 9.2–10 is a Markan interpolation into the original sequence, 9.1, 11–12a + 13.

[4] Cf. Gnilka, *Markus* 2, p. 40. Contrast Bayer (v).

[5] Gnilka, *Markus* 2, p. 40, however, regards 11a as redactional.

[6] Wink (v) suggests that 'the Son of man' in Mk 9.12b is a mistranslation of 'that son of man' (= Elijah). Acceptance of this proposal would radically alter one's reconstruction of the tradition-history of the passage.

[7] Another possibility is that v. 12b has been displaced, and several proposals have been made on this assumption; see Oke (v). Of these, the most plausible is that v. 12b once followed upon v. 10: 'So they kept the matter to themselves, questioning what the rising from the dead meant and how is it written of the Son of man, that he should suffer many things and be set at nought.' See C. H. Turner, *The Study of the New Testament, 1883 and 1920*, 3rd ed., Oxford, 1926, p. 61.

[8] Whether Mk 9.12b is to be regarded as an authentic saying of Jesus is disputed. Affirming authenticity are Taylor (v) and Black (v); denying it are Tödt (v) and Hahn (v).

Mk 9.11–12a + 13, which probably arose independently of the transfiguration story, appears to answer an objection to the proclamation of eschatological fulfilment. There was a Jewish expectation about Elijah which created problems: 'Elijah must come first'. It is usually held that the words in quotation marks allude to Elijah as forerunner of the Messiah. The evidence for this idea is, however, meagre,[9] and Elijah, expected to come 'before the great and terrible day of the Lord' (Mal 4.5), was assigned a number of different eschatological rôles (see on v. 11). What follows? The Christian claim that prophecies had been fulfilled, that the Messiah had come, that the resurrection of the dead had commenced (see on 27.51b–3) and so on could have called forth, among other protests, the retort that Elijah had not yet come—to which Mk 9.11–12a + 13, perhaps taking up a word of Jesus which identified John with Elijah,[10] answered by asserting that Elijah had in fact come, in the person of the Baptist, and further that, so far from being welcomed, he was treated with contempt (cf. Justin, *Dial.* 49).[11] It is, however, no less probable that Mk 9.11–12a + 13 par. should be thought of as stemming directly from the pre-Easter period. Jesus announced that the kingdom of God had come upon people and was in their midst, that Satan had been cast out of heaven and bound, that the time of fulfilment had dawned. This message could have been challenged by the non-appearance of Elijah. If the last days have arrived, where is the prophet? Jesus himself may have solved the difficulty by seeing in the ministry of John the Baptist the fulfilment of Elijah expectations.[12]

9. καὶ καταβαινόντων αὐτῶν ἐκ τοῦ ὄρους. Mk 9.9a begins with δέ[13] and uses ἀπό[14] instead of ἐκ (cf. 16.1 diff. Mk 8.11). In both Matthew and Mark the line, like Mt 8.1 (q.v.), recalls LXX Exod 34.29. It thus adds to the Sinai parallels.

---

[9] See Allison (v); Faierstein (v); Fitzmyer (v).

[10] Wink, pp. 15–16: 'the identification of John with Elijah was both an act of typological-prophetic confidence and at the same time a bold, utterly amazing affirmation which turns the tables on the Jewish expectations as radically as does the reinterpretation of messiahship involving Jesus. What is expressed is the quite offensive paradox that the heavenly Elijah should be this captive, murdered prophet: a *dead* Elijah. This identification cannot be said to be a simple apologetical retort to the Jewish protest that Elijah must first come, for this answer is just as offensive as the statement that the crucified Jesus is the messiah . . .'.

[11] Whether or not Mk 9.12a be taken as a question, v. 13 seems to affirm that although Elijah has come he has not restored all things, for the people rejected him; cf. Nineham, *Mark*, p. 241. In other words, Mk 9.9–13 depicts both the fulfilment and the non-fulfilment of eschatological expectation: Elijah has indeed come, but he was not permitted to restore all things.

[12] Those favouring a post-Easter origin for Mk 9.11–13 include Bultmann, *History*, pp. 124–5; Gnilka, *Markus* 2, p. 40; and Beare, p. 366. For attempts to set the passage in the ministry of Jesus see Otto (v); Taylor, *Mark*, p. 393; and Jeremias, *Theology*, p. 295.

[13] So A W Θ *f*[1.13] Maj f sy[h] followed by HG. NA[26] prints και; so ℵ B D Δ Ψ 33 892 *pc*; but is this not assimilation to Matthew?

[14] So ℵ A C L W Θ *f*[1.13] Maj and HG; εκ appears in NA[26] on the authority of B D Ψ 33 *pc*. Again, is this not assimilation to Matthew?

ἐνετείλατο αὐτοῖς ὁ Ἰησοῦς λέγων. Compare v. 10a. In Mk 9.9b the first word is διεστείλατο and αὐτοῖς is followed simply by ἵνα. Matthew is fond of ἐντέλλομαι (Mt: 5; Mk: 2; Lk: 1), a word he will later use of Moses (19.7) as well as of the risen Christ (28.20). He also often prefers direct speech (which here increases the parallelism with v. 10). διαστέλλομαι is dropped more than once (Mt: 1; Mk: 4; Lk: 0).

μηδενὶ εἴπητε τὸ ὅραμα ἕως οὗ ὁ υἱὸς τοῦ ἀνθρώπου ἐκ νεκρῶν ἐγερθῇ.[15] Compare 8.4; 9.30; 16.20; also Dan 8.26; 12.4, 9. Between μηδενί and ὁ Mark has ἃ εἶδον διηγήσωνται εἰ μὴ ὅταν and, for the last word, ἀναστῇ. The changes are readily understood. Matthew has conformed his line to 16.20; ἕως* οὗ is often editorial;[16] and ἐγείρω* is a Matthean favourite.

ὅραμα, used so often in Daniel[17] and Acts, is a synoptic *hapax legomenon*. The word itself may indicate either a vision or a solid manifestation or sight. That the latter may be intended here is perhaps indicated by Peter's request to build tents or booths. One does not make dwellings for intangible beings.

In Mark the command to silence proves the centrality of the passion for Markan theology. The glorious Christ is not to be preached before Easter, for without the cross there is no gospel.[18] What about Matthew's understanding of the injunction, the last such in his gospel? On the messianic secret in Matthew see on 9.30. The present verse, 17.9, makes the three apostles unique and authoritative bearers of the kerygma. They will proclaim after Easter things previously concealed. In the light of the resurrection and after the cross they will be able to tell the whole truth about Jesus the Son of man.

Mk 9.10 ('So they kept the matter to themselves, questioning what the rising from the dead meant') has been omitted by our gospel. The result is that the understanding of the disciples (cf. v. 13) is no longer doubtful (cf. the omission of Mk 6.52 and 8.17). See further the discussion on pp. 587–92. Matthew may also have been moved to excise 9.10 because he found it difficult to believe that the disciples could have wondered about the meaning of the (general) resurrection of the dead.[19]

---

[15] So NA²⁶. HG prints αναστη (so ℵ C L θ *f*¹·¹³ Maj) at the end, assuming that the other reading is due to Matthean influence. But εγερθη is in accord with Matthew's preferred usage; see on 16.21.

[16] It is redactional or without parallel in 1.25; 14.22; 17.9; 18.34; 26.36.

[17] Most frequently for *ḥāzôn*.

[18] The explanation that the command to secrecy functioned to explain why the pericope was not known in the early tradition is today much less popular than it once was.

[19] This only holds, however, if he had the text of B ℵ Maj before him. Mk 9.10 D W *f*¹·¹³ lat have οταν εκ νεκρων αναστη: 'They kept the matter to

10. καὶ ἐπηρώτησαν αὐτὸν οἱ μαθηταὶ λέγοντες.[20] Matthew has made the subject, 'the disciples', explicit, and changed Mark's imperfect to an aorist (see on v. 13). Otherwise there are no differences. Note that the redactional alterations of vv. 9b and 10a make for two parallel sentences: καί + finite verb + αὐτοῖς/αὐτόν + definite article (ὁ/οἱ) + subject ('Ιησοῦς/μαθηταί) + λέγων/λέγοντες.

τί οὖν οἱ γραμματεῖς λέγουσιν ὅτι 'Ηλίαν δεῖ ἐλθεῖν πρῶτον; Compare *m. Ber.* 1.1: *lāmmâ 'āmĕrû hăkāmim.* Mark opens with ὅτι λέγουσιν. οὖν* is Matthean, and our author has rightly interpreted Mark's ὅτι as meaning τί = 'why?' (cf. BAGD, s.v. ὅτι, l.c). On the scribes see 1, p. 240. On the expectation under discussion see below and 1, pp. 313–14. On δεῖ as a way of referring to Scripture see on 16.21. An allusion to LXX Mal 3.22–3 (ἐγὼ ἀποστέλλω ὑμῖν 'Ηλίαν τὸν Θεσβίτην πρὶν ἐλθεῖν ἡμέραν κυρίου τὴν μεγάλην καὶ ἐπιφανῆ, ὃς ἀποκαταστήσει καρδίαν πατρὸς πρὸς υἱόν . . .) seems certain.

11. Jesus begins his response to the disciples' question by agreeing with the scribal expectation: Elijah is to come and restore all things.

ὁ δὲ ἀποκριθεὶς εἶπεν. Mk 9.12a follows δέ with ἔφη αὐτοῖς. ἀποκριθείς/-θέντες + finite verb* is often redactional, and Mark's αὐτοῖς has been eliminated as otiose.

'Ηλίας μὲν ἔρχεται καὶ ἀποκαταστήσει πάντα. Compare Mk 9.12: 'Ηλίας ἐλθὼν πρῶτον ἀποκαθιστάνει πάντα. (This, unlike its Matthean parallel, could be a question.) The addition of μέν[21] (= 'it is true') is typical (μέν . . . δέ*), and ἀποκαταστήσει marks assimilation to LXX Mal 3.23 (for which see above).

ἀποκαθίστημι occurs only one other time in Matthew, in 12.13, of a hand being restored. But the passage in Malachi gave the word an eschatological connotation (cf. Acts 1.6; 3.21). In its present context, the future tense, ἀποκαταστήσει, is not likely to mean that Elijah is still to come or will come again. 'Will restore' simply agrees with what the OT and the scribes say. Many Christian interpreters, however, have taken Matthew's text to mean that Elijah has come and will come (so

themselves, questioning what "When he shall rise from the dead" means.'— Another possibility is that Mk 9.10 reflects a problem with which Matthew was no longer concerned. If Jesus did not distinguish between his vindication and the general resurrection of the dead, then, after Easter, his solitary resurrection would have been difficult to reconcile with the disciples' expectations and they might have concluded that they did not understand what Jesus meant by resurrection—a conclusion with its literary deposit in Mk 9.9–10.

[20] Perhaps αυτου, found in B C D *f*[13] Maj f ff[2] q sy mae bo[pt], should be added after μαθηται.

[21] NA[26] reads μεν for Mk 9.12b, but it is missing in D L W Ψ *f*[1] 28 565 892 pc latt and seems to have been taken over from Matthew.

e.g. Chrysostom, *Hom. on Mt.* 57.1, and Gundry, *Commentary*, p. 347). Historically this has been one way of avoiding the contradiction between the synoptic identification of John with the Tishbite and the Baptist's denial that he was Elijah (Jn 1.21): John the Baptist fulfilled the rôle of Elijah in preparation for the first advent, the historical Elijah will return to prepare for the second advent (cf. Rev 11.1–13).

The precise nature of Elijah's task of *apokatastasis* is left unstated and we cannot tell what Matthew had in mind, for there were differing notions. Mal 4.5–6 has Elijah reconciling families. The LXX (3.22–3) adds that the prophet will also reconcile 'the heart of a man with his neighbour'. In Lk 1.17 Elijah is thought of as one who will turn 'the disobedient to the wisdom of the just, to make ready for the Lord a people prepared' (cf. 4 Ezra 6.26). The idea that Elijah would preach repentance was presumably common (cf. Rev 11.1–13; *Pirqe R. El.* 43)—and probably did much to encourage the identification of John with Elijah. In Ecclus 48.10 the prophet is expected 'to restore the tribes of Jacob', which may mean ingathering the diaspora (cf. Tg. Ps.-J. on Deut. 30.4) or purifying a remnant (cf. *m. 'Ed.* 8.7). According to rabbinic texts he will explain points in the Torah which baffled or divided the rabbis (see Davies, *SSM*, pp. 158–61). There are also places where Elijah is expected to restore the bottle of manna, the bottle of sprinkling water, and the bottle of anointing oil (e.g. *Mek.* on Exod 16.33). Finally, already by Matthew's time Elijah—who in the OT raises the dead—may have been expected to inaugurate the resurrection or reawaken the dead.[22] (Note that in Mark the disciples' question about Elijah follows directly a discussion about the resurrection of the dead.)

12. Jesus next makes a claim for 'realized eschatology:' Elijah has in fact already come. But Jesus goes on to observe that Elijah's mission, to restore the people of God, was met with opposition, and that this same opposition will lead to the death of the Son of man.

λέγω δὲ ὑμῖν ὅτι. Mk 9.13a commences with ἀλλά.

Ἠλίας ἤδη ἦλθεν. Mark has: καὶ Ἠλίας ἐλήλυθεν. Compare 14.15 (ἤδη παρῆλθεν—diff. Mk 6.35). The reader of the gospel immediately equates Elijah with John the Baptist, for the equation has already been made (see on 11.14).

καὶ οὐκ ἐπέγνωσαν αὐτόν. This is redactional. It explains why Elijah was rejected: his identity was not recognized.

ἀλλ' ἐποίησαν ἐν αὐτῷ ὅσα ἠθέλησαν. Compare Dan 8.4; 11.3, 16; Jub. 2.29; Josephus, *Ant.* 10.103.[23] Mk 9.13 reads: καὶ ἐποίησαν αὐτῷ ὅσα ἤθελον. Matthew often substitutes the aorist for the imperfect (Allen, pp. xx–xxi). His ἐποίησαν ἐν αὐτῷ (cf.

---

[22] Relevant texts include Sib. Or. 2.187–8 (cf. Did. 16.6): 8.169–70 (?); *m. Soṭa* 9.15; *b. Sanh.* 113a; *y. Sabb.* 3c; *Ma'ase Daniel*, pp. 225–6.
[23] These texts appear to record a standard way of expressing ungodly tyranny.

716   COMMENTARY ON MATTHEW

LXX Gen 40.14; Theod. Dan 11.7) reminds one of the Hebrew ʿāśâ + bĕ and the Aramaic ʿăbad + bĕ. As with the previous clause the identity of the subjects ('they did') is not specified. Are they the Jewish people as a whole or their leaders or Herod and Herodias (cf. 14.1–12)? In view of the next line, where the Son of man also is done in by 'them' (αὐτῶν), one may do best to think of those in charge, that is, those with political and religious authority.

Matthew has omitted Mark's final clause ('as it is written of him'), perhaps because he knew that there is no OT text predicting Elijah's rejection. (1 Kgs 19.2, 10, and 14 scarcely qualify. They concern the historical Elijah.[24]) Still, it may not be irrelevant to point out that Mal 4.6 can be read as holding forth the *possibility* of Elijah's failure: 'And he will turn the hearts of fathers to their children . . . *lest* I come and smite the land with a curse'. Also, there may have been a tradition about Elijah = Phinehas[25] and other immortals who would taste death at the end (cf. 4 Ezra 7.29).

οὕτως καὶ ὁ υἱὸς τοῦ ἀνθρώπου μέλλει πάσχειν ὑπ' αὐτῶν.[26] This is a much revised version of Mk 9.12b: 'And how is it written of the Son of man, that he should suffer many things and be treated with contempt?' The First Evangelist has (i) moved the statement from its place in Mark (see section (ii)); (ii) characteristically added οὕτως* and ὑπ' αὐτῶν[27] in order to enhance the parallelism between the fate of John and the fate of Jesus (see pp. 475–6); (iii) made the Son of man the active subject; (iv) inserted μέλλει (see on 16.27), connoting necessity, as he will shortly again in another passion prediction (see 17.22; cf. 20.22); and (v) in general resolved the ambiguities of the Markan passage.[28] In the process the clear allusions to Isa 53— πολλὰ πάθη and ἐξουδενηθῇ[29]—have been passed over. Evidently the evangelist judged the parallelism between John and Jesus to be of greater moment in this context.

13. An editorial remark[30] on the disciples' understanding draws the paragraph to its close.

τότε συνῆκαν οἱ μαθηταὶ ὅτι περὶ Ἰωάννου τοῦ βαπτιστοῦ εἶπεν αὐτοῖς. Compare the redactional 16.12 (τότε συνῆκαν ὅτι . . .)—also concluding a paragraph. This is the second time

[24] Also dubious is the opinion that Rev 11.3–14 and related traditions are in the background.
[25] A. Zeron, 'The Martyrdom of Phineas-Elijah', *JBL* 98 (1979), pp. 99–100.
[26] The excision of this clause by Albright and Mann, p. 205, is groundless.
[27] Cf. Josephus, *Ant.* 7.209; 10.92.
[28] For these ambiguities see Allen, p. 187.
[29] See the Markan commentaries and Black (v) for details.
[30] τότε*, μαθηταί*, and βαπτιστής* are all typical. συνίημι: Mt: 7; Mk: 5; Lk: 4.

Matthew makes the equation of John with Elijah explicit (the first being 11.14). No other NT writer does so even once. (It is a characteristic of Matthew to make explicit what was only implicit in his tradition.)

(iv) *Concluding Observations*

17.9–13, which so thoroughly eliminates the obscurities of Mk 9.9–13, answers a Jewish objection against Christian claims, adds to the numerous parallels already drawn between John and Jesus, and marks out Peter and James and John as authorities for the Jesus tradition (cf. p. 711). The passage also, through the identification of John with Elijah, may be intended to form an *inclusio* with 11.14 ('he is Elijah who is to come'), indicating that the central section of the gospel is coming to its close. Lastly, one should consider the way in which vv. 9–13 balance vv. 1–12 and parallel 16.13–23. If the transfiguration presents Jesus as the glorified Son of God, the sequel announces the suffering of the Son of man. This mirrors 16.13–23, where the confession of Jesus as Son of God and the promise of his church's triumph are followed by a passion prediction concerning the Son of man (16.21–3). The pattern—the Son of God triumphant/the Son of man suffering—may be illustrated in this fashion:

	16.13–20	16.21–3	17.1–8	17.9–13
Son of God	Jesus is confessed as Son of God and his church is promised victory		A voice from heaven proclaims the glorified Jesus to be the Son of God	
Son of man		The Son of man must be killed		The Son of man must suffer

(v) *Bibliography*

D. C. Allison, '"Elijah must come first"', *JBL* 103 (1984), pp. 256–8.
Arens, pp. 243–8.
Bayer, pp. 166–9.

M. Black, 'The Theological Appropriation of the Old Testament by the New Testament', *JTS* 39 (1986), pp. 1–17.

M. M. Faierstein, 'Why do the Scribes say that Elijah must come first?', *JBL* 100 (1981), pp. 75–86.

J. A. Fitzmyer, 'More about Elijah coming first', *JBL* 104 (1985), pp. 295–6.

U. Holzmeister, 'Einzeluntersuchungen über das Geheimnis der Verklärung Christi', *Bib* 21 (1940), pp. 200–10.

Horstmann, pp. 106–36.

J. Louis Martyn, 'We have found Elijah', in *Jews, Greeks and Christians*, ed. by Robert Hamerton-Kelly and Robin Scroggs, Leiden, 1976, pp. 181–219.

C. C. Oke, 'The Rearrangement and Transmission of Mark ix, 11–13', *ExpT* 64 (1953), pp. 187–8.

Taylor, *Sacrifice*, pp. 91–7.

Tödt, pp. 152–221.

Wink, pp. 13–17, 30–3.

XLIV

JESUS HEALS AN EPILEPTIC

(17.14–20)

(i) *Structure*

The pericope falls into two parts, each of which falls into two sections:

I. The healing miracle (14–18)
  A. The request for healing (14–16)
  B. The words and actions of Jesus (17–18)
II. The discussion about faith (19–20)
  A. The disciples' question (19)
  B. Jesus' answer (20)

(ii) *Sources*

In all three synoptics the account of the healing of the epileptic child follows the transfiguration, although Luke has nothing corresponding to Mk 9.9–13. The two-source theory explains both Mt 17.14–20 and Lk 9.37–42 as secondary versions of the much longer Mk 9.14–29. But some have surmised that the First and Third Evangelists had access to a non-Markan source, this because of the several minor agreements[1] and because Matthew and Luke have shorter accounts which are close to what some think was the pre-Markan form of our story.[2] The minor agreements, however, are 'so minor that they cannot be regarded as indicative of anything more than coincidence' (so Fitzmyer, *Luke* 1, p. 806). Moreover, since both evangelists, according to the two-source theory, found it meet to abridge Mark's story, there will inevitably be common omissions. In our estimation, the redactional tendencies of Matthew and Luke adequately account for their differences *vis-à-vis* Mk 9.14–29.

---

[1] (κατ)ελθόντων (17.14; Lk 9.37), ἄνθρωπος/ἀνήρ (17.14; Lk 9.38), λέγων (17.15; Lk 9.38), ὅτι (17.15; Lk 9.38), ἠδυνάσθησαν/ἠδυνήθησαν (17.16; Lk 9.40), ὁ Ἰησοῦς (17.17; Lk 9.41), εἶπεν (17.17; Lk 9.41), ὧδε (17.17; Lk 9.41), καὶ διεστραμμένη (17.17; Lk 9.41), παῖς (17.18; Lk 9.42), and the common omission of Mk 9.15–16 and of most of Mk 9.20–6. From these Gundry, *Commentary*, p. 353, infers Luke's use of Matthew.
[2] So e.g. Schramm, pp. 139–40, and Schweizer, *Matthew*, p. 352.

(iii) *Exegesis*

This account of Jesus' successful exorcism of a demon of epilepsy, which is largely composed of standard miracle story motifs,[3] is in Matthew on its way to becoming a pronouncement story. The tale is told primarily for the sake of Jesus' provocative declaration in v. 20. (Vv. 19 and 20 constitute much more than an epilogue.) The focus—in complete contrast to Luke's presentation[4]—is not on Christology, that is, on Jesus as healer or any other christological theme,[5] but on discipleship and faith. In Matthew the lesson is not what Jesus can do but what his followers can do.

Matthew has altered his Markan source in a multitude of ways, including the following. (i) He has greatly shortened and simplified Mark's involved account. There are sixteen verses in Mark, seven in Matthew (cf. the compressing of Mk 5.1–17 in Mt 8.28–34 and of Mk 5.21–43 in Mt 9.18–26 and see Held, in *TIM*, pp. 165–92). (ii) He has not let the crowd play a significant rôle (contrast Mk 9.14–17). (iii) He has made the father of the epileptic fall on his knees and call Jesus 'Lord' (17.14f.). (iv) He has diagnosed the affliction as epilepsy (v. 15) and assimilated the description to 4.24. And of the three Markan summaries of the illness (9.18, 20, 22), he has kept only the third, moving it forward (Mt 17.15). (v) He has added καὶ διεστραμμένη to γενεὰ ἄπιστος (v. 17). (vi) He has omitted almost all of Mk 9.20–6, which vividly describes the boy's convulsions, contains a conversation between Jesus and the lad's father,[6] and recounts the violent exit of the demon. (vii) He has used a phrase— 'and the son was healed from that hour'—which he uses elsewhere in stories where one person pleads for the healing of another (cf. 8.13; 15.28). (viii) He has failed to mention the house of Mk 9.28. (ix) He has substituted for Mark's final sentence ('This kind cannot be driven out by anything but prayer (and fasting)') another, longer conclusion, the saying about faith moving mountains.

Several of these alterations help move the focus of the narrative to the disciples' failure and to the concomitant theme of faith. 'Matthew has succeeded in showing that there is no longer any question about whether and how Jesus can heal, but whether and how the disciples can. We are here concerned unequivocally with the faith of the wonder-worker, with exclusive reference . . . to the disciples' (Held (v), p. 191).

The tradition-history of Mk 9.14–29 is much disputed. Bultmann, *History*, pp. 211–12, detected two originally separate miracle stories,

---

[3] For these see Theissen, *Stories*, pp. 47–80.

[4] In Luke 'all the stress falls on the authority of Jesus himself', and the story 'is no longer, as in Mk, an example by which the disciples are taught about their own healing authority' (Marshall, *Luke*, p. 389).

[5] We fail to find compelling Gundry's attempt to argue that one of Matthew's major concerns is an emphasis upon 'Jesus as God' (*Commentary*, p. 349).

[6] The effect of this omission is to make the father's faith firm from the beginning; contrast Mark.

roughly vv. 14, 16–20 and 21–7 (15 and 28–9 are taken to be editorial; cf. Bornkamm (v)).[7] Taylor, *Mark*, p. 396, and Schweizer, *Mark*, p. 187, are also of the opinion that Mk 9.14–29 combines two different accounts—but they contend that these accounts were variants of the same story. According to Kertelge (v), the original core is deposited in vv. 20–7; this was reworked into an episode about the disciples, with its climax in vv. 28–9. On the analysis of Roloff (v), the primitive account, based on historical reminiscence, lies in vv. (14–17a), 17b–19a, 19c–20, 25–7. Petzke (v) finds the basic story, whose historicity he doubts, in vv. 17–19a, 19d–20, 25–7. Vv. 19b and 21–4 are then ascribed to a secondary rewriting of that, and vv. 14–16, 19c and 28–9 attributed to Markan redaction.

Whether any of these reconstructions is correct may well be doubted. But several conclusions do seem more probable than not. First, at least vv. 28–9 are, as most now concede, probably secondary (cf. Pesch 2, pp. 84–5). Next, the reason the story came to be placed after the transfiguration is that it presupposes a separation of Jesus from (some of) his disciples. Thirdly, if Jesus was in fact a successful exorcist who commanded his followers to carry on his work, our story could, although there is no way of proving this, be based upon a remembered failure of the disciples (see further Pesch 2, p. 95). Lastly, the story may have functioned in some sector of the early church to help explain a decline in miracles.

14. καὶ ἐλθόντων πρὸς τὸν ὄχλον προσῆλθεν αὐτῷ ἄνθρωπος γονυπετῶν αὐτόν. This, like Lk 9.37–8a, drastically abbreviates Mk 9.14–17a. Luke agrees with Matthew against Mark in opening with the genitive absolute and in omitting much of the same material. Allen, pp. 187f., satisfactorily explained Matthew's modification of Mk 9.14–17a: the question is omitted in order to guard against imputing any sort of ignorance to Jesus (cf. 1, p. 105); and the rest is passed 'over because it is ambiguously expressed. Who were the parties to the dispute—the scribes and the disciples, or the scribes and the multitude? Why should the people be astonished ... when they saw Christ?'[8]

The genitive absolute (with unexpressed subject; see BDF § 423.6) is Matthean (cf. vv. 9, 22, 24), προσέρχομαι* is frequently editorial, and γονυπετέω (= 'kneel down;' LXX: 0) is again redactional in 27.29.

15. The man asks Jesus to have mercy on his son, whose epileptic condition is described (cf. the pleas in 8.5–13; 9.18–26; and 15.21–8; see Theissen, *Stories*, pp. 54–5).

καὶ λέγων· κύριε. 'Lord' replaces 'teacher', as elsewhere. See

---

[7] Criticism in Petzke (v), pp. 187–8.

[8] Does the Markan crowd marvel, as some have thought, because Jesus is still outlined in radiance (cf. Exod 34.29–35)? For this and other opinions see Tagawa, pp. 105–7.

8.25 diff. Mk 4.38 and recall the substitution of 'Lord' for 'rabbi' in 17.4 diff. Mk 9.5 (Lk 9.38 agrees with Mark against Matthew in having 'teacher'.) ἐλέησόν μου τὸν υἱόν. Compare Mk 9.17b ('I brought my son to you') and Lk 9.38b ('I beg you to look upon my son'). Matthew favours ἐλεέω* and, like the LXX psalter, often links it with 'Lord', as in 15.22; 20.30, and 31 (all without synoptic parallel). ὅτι σεληνιάζεται καὶ κακῶς πάσχει.⁹ This replaces Mk 9.17c: 'having a dumb spirit' (cf. Lk 9.39). The First Evangelist has in effect correctly diagnosed the boy as having epilepsy (σεληνιά-ζεται: see on 4.24; also Lucian, *Philops.* 16 and Wilkinson (v)). One must keep in mind, however, that for Matthew there is no thought of a purely physical affliction. The problem is caused by a malign spirit (cf. Origen, *Comm. on Mt.* 13.6).¹⁰

On κακῶς see on 4.24. Only here in the NT is the adverb joined to πάσχω; but κακῶς πάσχουσιν does appear in the LXX, in Wisd 18.19 (cf. also Aeschylus, *Prom.* 759; Polybius 3.90.13).

πολλάκις γὰρ πίπτει εἰς τὸ πῦρ καὶ πολλάκις εἰς τὸ ὕδωρ.¹¹ Compare Mk 9.18, 22a; and Lk 9.39. Matthew has replaced Mk 9.18a with Mk 9.22a (which he will later omit) and, as so often, enhanced the parallelism (πολλάκις + εἰς τό, *bis*). That the child falls into the fire¹² and water¹³ indicates that his behaviour is self-destructive. That is, the epileptic demon is an imp which perversely attacks its host by causing him to act against his own well-being.

16. The man informs Jesus that his suffering son was laid before the disciples and that they were unable to heal him.¹⁴

⁹ So both NA²⁶ and HG. Given Matthean usage one expects ἔχει at the end (cf. 4.24; 8.16; 9.12; 14.35), and this is the reading of א B L Zᵛⁱᵈ Θ *pc* Chr Or. One can, however, argue that ἔχει, which results in a more idiomatic expression, is assimilation to the general Matthean or synoptic usage. πάσχει appears in C D W *f*¹·¹³ Maj lat syᶜ·ʰ. See further Gundry, *Commentary*, p. 349.
¹⁰ Early Christian expositors were concerned to blame epilepsy on evil spirits instead of the moon (cf. Chrysostom, *Hom. on Mt.* 57.3). While their judgement on this has been invalidated by modern medicine, one must recognize that their motive was the preservation of God's goodness: they did not want to attribute disease directly or even indirectly (via the moon in this case) to God. By assigning an illness to demons they were setting God against sickness.
¹¹ ἐνίοτε (cf. Ecclus 37.14), 'sometimes', replaces the second πολλάκις in Ɖ Θ *f*¹ *pc* it mae.
¹² 'The fire is that of the house or daily village life' (F. Lang, *TWNT* 6, p. 940). Note Vit. Pachomii 9.
¹³ On demons and water see on 8.32.
¹⁴ It has sometimes been thought by pious exegetes that the man's words insulted the apostolic dignity and should not have been spoken, and this verdict has gone hand in hand with the exhortation to place blame on oneself instead of others (cf. Cyril of Jerusalem, *Hom. on Lk.* 52). More recently, it has been supposed that, at some point in the tradition, the failed exorcists were not Jesus' disciples but the Jewish scribes (cf. Pesch 2, pp. 84, 90).

καὶ προσήνεγκα αὐτὸν τοῖς μαθηταῖς σου. Compare Mk 9.18:
'And I asked your disciples to cast it out' (Lk 9.40a is very
similar). προσφέρω* is an editorial favourite and is used of the
sick being brought for healing in 4.24; 8.16; 9.2, 32; 12.22; and
14.35 (all unparalleled).

καὶ οὐκ ἠδυνάσθησαν αὐτὸν θεραπεῦσαι[15]. Mark has simply
ἴσχυσαν after οὐκ, Luke ἠδυνήθησαν. Matthew's longer
phrase is required by his omission of Mark's ἐκβάλωσιν in the
previous line, and ἠδυνάσθησαν anticipates vv. 19 (ἠδυνήθημεν) and 20 (ἀδυνατήσει). Note that θεραπεύω is also
redactional in 17.18 diff. Mk 9.27.

One recalls the incident in 2 Kgs 4, where Gehazi, Elisha's disciple, is
unable to resurrect a dead child. Only Elisha himself can perform the
miracle. Whether one should here speak of an allusion to that OT
story is uncertain.

Note that the disciples' inability is all the more a failure given
that, in 10.1, Jesus gave them the authority to cast out unclean
spirits. The implication is that their lack of success stems not
from strict incapacity but from not exercising an authority they
in fact possess.

17. ἀποκριθεὶς δὲ ὁ Ἰησοῦς εἶπεν. So also Lk 9.41. Mk 9.19
has something a bit different: ὁ δὲ ἀποκριθεὶς αὐτοῖς λέγει.
The agreement between Matthew and Luke is inconsequential
given the frequency with which both gospels, as opposed to
Mark, have ἀποκριθείς/θέντες + δέ + subject + verb of speech
(Mt: 17; Mk: 0; Lk: 9) as well as the habit of both writers to
replace Mark's historical present.

ὦ γενεὰ ἄπιστος καὶ διεστραμμένη. Mk 9.19 lacks the last
two words. Lk 9.41 agrees with Matthew according to both HG
and NA[26]. But καὶ διε. is not found in Lk 9.41 e a Epiph
Mcion[Tert, Epiph] and should perhaps be considered secondary (cf.
Streeter, p. 317).[16]

The perfect passive participle of διαστρέφω (= 'pervert') also qualifies
γενεά in Phil 2.15.The link goes back to Deut 32.5: γενεὰ σκολιὰ καὶ
διεστραμμένη. In Mt 17.17 ἄπιστος—often used of heathen[17]—has
replaced σκολιά (cf. Acts 2.40; Phil 2.15) because the subject of the
pericope is faith. Perhaps Deut 32.20 has played a rôle in the change
also, for there the 'perverse generation' (γενεὰ ἐξεστραμμένη) is said to
have no πίστις or 'ēmūn. On γενεά in the synoptics see on 11.16.

[15] So HG. Against B, but following א C D Maj, NA[26] prints ηδυνηθησαν.
Is this not assimilation to Luke?
[16] Much less probable is the conjecture that και διε. stood in Mark, although
it is found in P[45vid] (W) f[13] pc and is accepted as authentic by Taylor, Mark,
p. 398.
[17] E.g. 1 Cor 6.6; 7.15; Ignatius, Magn. 5.2; 2 Clem. 17.5. But there are many
exceptions (e.g. Liv. Proph. Ezek. 15).

Who exactly is Jesus speaking of when he refers to an unbelieving and perverse 'generation' (not 'race')? The father is hardly to the fore (contrast Lk 9.41). According to Chrysostom, *Hom. on Mt.* 57.3, Jesus' words pertain to the crowd. Held (v), however, contends that only the disciples are thus rebuked. It seems best to conflate the two interpretations. Jesus is casting a mournful eye over his disciples who have, by their 'little faith', retrogressed to the spiritual level of the multitude.

ἕως πότε μεθ' ὑμῶν ἔσομαι; So Mk 9.19, with πρός + acusative (cf. Lk 9.41). Compare Jn 14.9: 'Have I been with you so long, and yet you do not know me?' For ἕως πότε—common in the LXX—see also Jn 10.24 and Rev 6.10 (cf. the Hebrew *admātay*). That there is any allusion to 1.23 (μεθ' ἡμῶν ὁ θεός) is improbable.

ἕως πότε ἀνέξομαι ὑμῶν; Mk 9.19 agrees. ἀνέχομαι (Mt; 1; Mk: 1; Lk: 1) means 'endure' or 'put up with' (compare 2 Cor 11.1). On its use with the genitive see BDF § 176.1. That the word cryptically alludes to LXX Isa 46.4, where Yahweh says, to Israel, ἐγὼ ἀνέχομαι ὑμῶν, is very far from obvious.

The words introduced by ἕως πότε, which recall the divine and prophetic complaints in Num 14.27 and Isa 6.11, express 'prophetic exasperation' (Hill) and function as a reprimand. It is almost as though Jesus has been wasting his time, and his task—soon to come to its end—is thankless. Whether the saying, which would be difficult to imagine standing alone, goes back to Jesus, is disputed.[18]

φέρετέ μοι αὐτὸν ὧδε. This is Matthew's version of Mk 9.19d: φέρετε αὐτὸν πρός με. Compare Mt 14.18. On the dative for the Semitic πρός[19] + accusative see Allen, p. xxix.

Lk 9.41 agrees with Matthew in inserting ὧδε. Streeter, p. 317, raised the possibility that the word did not originally belong to Luke. It is missing from Lk 9.41 D (r¹), and those mss. which have it do not agree on its precise placement. But Matthew and Luke add the word other times to Mark,[20] so coincidence is not an unreasonable inference, especially given ὧδε's natural placement after φέρετε[21]

18. καὶ ἐπετίμησεν αὐτῷ ὁ Ἰησοῦς, καὶ ἐξῆλθεν ἀπ' αὐτοῦ τὸ δαιμόνιον, καὶ ἐθεραπεύθη ὁ παῖς ἀπὸ τῆς ὥρας ἐκείνης. Compare 8.13; 9.22; 15.28. The tripartite sentence is, like Lk 9.42, a

[18] Dibelius, *Tradition*, p. 278, believes the saying is that of a divine being 'who appears in humiliation only for a time, and will soon return to heaven'. Cf. Bultmann, *History*, p. 157. But the background is to be found in the OT, and Taylor argues for authenticity (*Mark*, p. 398).—That there is any allusion to the Jewish Sophia myth may be doubted.

[19] Matthew often omits this word: Mt: 41; Mk: 63; Lk: 165.

[20] See Mt 8.29; 14.8, 17, 18; Lk 9.12; 23.5.

[21] Cf. LXX Josh 18.6; Judg 18.3; 2 Esdr 4.2; Mt 14.18; Jn 20.27.

radically shortened version of Mk 9.20–7. Clearly both evangelists regarded Mark's drawn out account as less than essential. And Matthew at least would not have liked the question Jesus asks ('How long has he had this?'),[22] the doubt about Jesus' ability ('if you are able' (*bis*)), or the narrative's violence (the description of the lunatic's paroxysm). Concerning this last, Jesus' healing word is always, in the First Gospel, instantly efficacious and there can be no resistance (see Hull, pp. 128–41, and note the omission of Mk 1.23–8 and 8.22–6).

19. The miracle completed, the disciples inquire about their earlier failure.[23]

τότε προσελθόντες οἱ μαθηταὶ τῷ Ἰησοῦ κατ' ἰδίαν εἶπον. In Mk 9.28 mention is made of a 'house': 'And with him going into the house his disciples asked him privately.' τότε* and προσέρχομαι* are characteristic of Matthew's diction, and several Markan references to 'the house' have already been dropped (Mk 2.1; 3.20–2; 7.17, 24; see also Mk 10.10). For κατ' ἰδίαν see on 17.1.

διὰ τί ἡμεῖς οὐκ ἐδυνήθημεν ἐκβαλεῖν αὐτό;[24] Mk 9.28 has ὅτι for διὰ τί (see BDF § 300; the same alteration was made in 9.11 diff. Mk 2.16).

20. ὁ δὲ λέγει αὐτοῖς. Mk 9.29 begins with καὶ εἶπεν αὐτοῖς.

διὰ τὴν ὀλιγοπιστίαν ὑμῶν.[25] From here on Matthew goes his own way. For 'little faith' and its meaning see on 6.30. Only here does Matthew have the substantive, ὀλιγοπιστία.

In Meier's words, 'the little faith of the disciples is a faith which *understands* and assents, but which does not *trust* God totally' (*Matthew*, p. 194). Such faith is always weak and ineffectual, its vigour constantly being enervated by doubt.

ἀμὴν γὰρ λέγω ὑμῖν. See on 5.17 and compare 21.21 = Mk 11.23.

ἐὰν ἔχητε πίστιν ὡς κόκκον σινάπεως, ἐρεῖτε τῷ ὄρει τούτῳ· μετάβα ἔνθεν ἐκεῖ, καὶ μεταβήσεται, καὶ οὐδὲν ἀδυνατήσει ὑμῖν.[26] Compare 21.21; Mk 11.23; Lk 17.6; Gos. Thom. 48,

---

[22] In Matthew 'Jesus does not ask questions, does not discuss, does not issue orders through intermediaries; he makes summary, firm decisions' (Theissen, *Stories*, p. 178).

[23] There is no parallel in Luke to this verse or the next. The Third Gospel ends with the healing and the crowd's reaction.

[24] So HG. Many Matthean mss. read ηδυν., and NA[26] follows their lead. For discussion see J. K. Elliott, 'Textual Variation involving the Augment in the Greek New Testament', *ZNW* 69 (1978), pp. 247–52.

[25] απιστιαν (cf. 17.17) appears in the third place in C D L W Maj latt sy[s.p.h]. *Pace* Zahn, p. 567, n. 14, and Klostermann, p. 144, this is not the original reading. See Allen, p. 190.

[26] D has μεταβηθι ενθεν, C L W Maj μεταβηθι εντευθεν, Θ *f*[13] *pc* μεταβα εντευθεν, ℵ B *f*[1] 700 μεταβα ενθεν.—At the end ℵ[2] C D L W *f*[1.13] Maj lat

106. Matthew's sentence replaces Mk 9.29: 'This kind cannot be driven out by anything but prayer (and fasting).' If by 'prayer' is intended 'not merely prayer as a pious exercise, but rather the sense of complete dependence on God from which sincere prayer springs,' then 'Mt's form of Jesus' answer gives the true point' of the Markan text (so Cranfield, *Mark*, p. 305).

The saying about faith, whose synoptic contexts are all secondary, seems to have been preserved in Q as well as Mark. The Lukan variant, Lk 17.6, differs significantly from Mark and cannot derive therefrom (cf. Zmijewski (v), pp. 82–3); and given that both Mt 17.21 and Lk 17.6, against Mark, use the phrase, 'faith as a grain of mustard seed', and the fact that Matthew repeats the saying on two different occasions, one naturally assigns the Lukan text to Q (so most).

Neither Mark nor Luke appears to have much altered the logion he received (see Zmijewski (v), pp. 86–93). It is otherwise with Matthew. Both Mt 17.20 and 21.21 are conflations of Mark and Q.[27] And both are assimilated to each other. With regard to 17.20, our present concern, Matthew has taken from Mark the introductory phrase with 'amen' and 'this mountain',[28] while the second person (ἔχητε, ἐρεῖτε, ὑμῖν), the conditional formulation (ἐάν), and the grain of mustard seed are from Q. There are also certain redactional corrections. The change from συκαμίνῳ (so Luke = Q) to ὄρει (so Mark) required the excision of Q's 'be rooted up and planted'. Matthew's replacement, μετάβα ἔνθεν[29] ἔκει, contains two of his favourite words (μετα-βαίνω*, ἐκεῖ*). Having made that modification, it was natural to follow with καὶ μεταβήσεται. Finally, the concluding words, 'and nothing will be impossible for you' (cf. Mk 9.23),[30] have no parallel in either Mark or Luke and should be credited to Matthean creativity. They make explicit the meaning of Jesus' saying on faith, and ἀδυνατήσει neatly recalls the ἠδυνάσθησαν of 17.16 and the ἠδυνήθημεν of 17.19.

On 'grain of mustard seed', a symbol of the smallest quantity, see 13.31. One wonders whether Jesus or Matthew intended the organic image to indicate that faith can grow (cf. Mt 13.31–2, a passage which has often been connected with 17.20 and so interpreted; cf. Origen, *Comm. on Mt.* 13.5). However that may be, Matthew's novel placement of the saying about faith moving mountains is, at first glance, problematic. The logion, taken by itself, seems to be calling for any faith at all, however small (see

---

(sy[p.h.]) (mae) bo[pt] Or add, from Mk 9.29, the following: τουτο δε το γενος ουκ εκπορευεται (εκβαλλ- ℵ[2]; εξερχ- *al*) ει μη εν προσευχη και νηστεια. See Aland and Aland, p. 296.

[27] *Pace* Manson, *Sayings*, p. 140, and Perrin, *Rediscovering*, pp. 137–8, who wrongly conclude that Mt 17.20 and Lk 17.6 preserve two independent traditions.

[28] 'This mountain' has not been added in order to gain an allusion to 17.1.

[29] NT: Mt 17.20; Lk 16.26. The word occurs about forty times in the LXX.

[30] Cf. also Job 42.2; Jer 32.17.

below), whereas in Mt 17 the disciples are rebuked not for being ἄπιστος but for having ὀλιγοπιστία. Perhaps we should postulate behind Matthew two competing notions of faith—the one being saving faith (whose antithesis is unbelief), the other the special faith required to perform great miracles (cf. Luz, in Stanton, p. 107). If so, the disciples have the former but not the latter.

'To move mountains' was, for obvious reasons, a proverbial expression for the impossible or improbable.[31] A literal interpretation is clearly ludicrous, although in Christian tradition the miracle of actually moving physical mountains has been attributed to certain saints (e.g. Gregory Thaumaturgus).[32]

If Lk 17.6 is close to Q, Mk 11.23 to the pre-Markan tradition, can both go back to one dominical saying? Most modern exegetes have affirmed this, convinced that Q's variant is the more primitive.[33] Their reasons are compelling. (i) The condition in Mark—'and does not doubt in his heart but believes that what he says will come to pass' (cf. Jas 1.6)—must be an edifying clarification and expansion of the simpler 'if you have faith'. (ii) 'Faith as a grain of mustard seed' is probably original. The connexion of faith with the mustard seed is unparalleled in Judaism, Jesus was fond of agricultural metaphors, and he composed a little parable about mustard seed (see on 13.31–2). (iii)'Sycamine'[34] probably became 'mountain' either because of the Markan passion narrative (where the Mount of Olives is mentioned) or because 'to move mountains' was a common idiom. No good explanation can be given for the change from 'mountain' to 'sycamine'.[35] (iv) Whereas in Mark the word about moving mountains is in the protasis, in Luke = Q the word about uprooting the sycamine is in the apodosis. Again Luke = Q is more primitive, for Mk 11.22b (ἔχετε πίστιν θεοῦ) betrays

[31] Cf. Isa 54.10; Josephus, *Ant.* 2.333; T. Sol. 23.1; *b. Sanh.* 24a; *b. Ber.* 64a; *b. B. Bat.* 3b. In Homer, *Od.* 5.480–5, the Cyclops literally casts a mountain into the sea.

[32] According to Jeremias, *Theology*, p. 165, 'the decisive feature for understanding' Jesus' saying about faith moving mountains 'is that the disappearance of mountains (Isa 40.4; 49.11; esp. Zech 14.10) and their reappearance to support the mountain of God (Isa 2.2 par. Micah 4.1) was expected as an eschatological event. Even the weakest kind of faith, as tiny as a grain of mustard seed, will—so Jesus promises—not primarily perform spectacular miracles, so much as have a share in the eschatological consummation.' This seems to us a good example of finding eschatology where there is none.

[33] Cf. Zmijewski (v) and Gnilka, *Markus* 2, p. 133. Pesch 2, p. 205, is unpersuasive in contending for Mark's originality.

[34] Is this the mulberry tree or the sycamore fig? Probably the latter. The LXX translates *šiqmâ* with συκάμινος, and the *šiqmâ* was known for its deep, firm roots (cf. *m. B. Bat.* 2.11; *Gen. Rab.* on 2.5–6); see Marshall, *Luke*, p. 644.

[35] *Pace* Hahn (v). Our conclusion entails that Paul already knew the saying in a secondary form; see 1 Cor 13.2. — One wonders whether 1 Cor 13.2 does not imply that Paul thought the saying had been misused by others for 'enthusiastic' ends.

a knowledge of Q's order. (v) Whether the paraenetic second person (Q) or the more formal third person (Mark) is original cannot be determined (cf. the problem of the Matthean and Lukan beatitudes, Mt 5.3–12 par.). But one could favour Q simply on the grounds that the Markan text has undergone so many other changes (cf. Zmijewski (v), pp. 94–5).

As a word of Jesus, Lk 17.6 par. takes its force from a paradoxical juxtaposition: the insurmountable is accomplished by the infinitesimal. To uproot a sycamine and plant it in the sea—a striking image and absurd task[36]—is utterly impossible. But it can be done by something as small as a grain of mustard seed, if that something is genuine faith in God. For with God the impossible is possible (cf. Mk 10.27 par.), and faith may share in God's power. Jesus' logion therefore is not about general faith in God's providence or even degrees of faith; rather, it is a bold invitation and challenge, a call for the individual to seek the God who is not far off but near at hand, the God who does miracles of all kinds for his own.[37]

Whether Jesus explicitly defined such faith as faith in God or in himself or intentionally used 'faith' absolutely is in the final analysis of little consequence. The concrete situation in which Jesus originally proclaimed his message would have given it reference to his own person and ministry. Further, in Jesus' preaching acceptance of God was acceptance of God's eschatological representative, and *vice versa* (cf. 10.32–3 par.).[38]

(v) *Concluding Observations*

The primary thrust of 17.14–20, which concerns discipleship much more than Christology, is highlighted by the three-fold repetition of certain words:

ἄπιστος, v. 17	ἠδυνάσθησαν, v. 16
ὀλιγοπιστία, v. 20	ἠδυνήθημεν, v. 19
πίστις, v. 20	ἀδυνατήσει, v. 20

The main theme is this: faith enables, lack of the same cripples. This is because πίστις is the pre-condition which God has set for his acting in the world. Compare 13.58: 'And he did not do many mighty works there, because of their unbelief.' The principle holds for disciples (who may be of 'little faith', that is,

---

[36] 'The idea of planting a tree in the sea is frankly absurd. It is a plain warning against taking the saying in a sense that was never intended. This word of Jesus does not invite Christians to become conjurers and magicians, but heroes like those whose exploits are celebrated in the eleventh chapter of Hebrews' (Manson, *Sayings*, p. 141).

[37] See further Bornkamm, *Jesus*, pp. 129–37.

[38] Compare *Mek.* on Exod 14.31: 'If you say they believed in Moses, is it not implied . . . that they believed in God? But this is to teach you that having faith in the shepherd of Israel is the same as having faith in Him who spoke and the world came into being.'

be believers without miracles) as well as for those outside the church.

It is crucial to observe that, in the First Gospel, πίστις is never a power in and of itself (it is not positive thinking or some active force), nor does it give its possessor power to wield. Faith, as trust and hope, instead calls upon God or Jesus to act on its behalf: 'Lord save, we perish!' One may therefore say that the eye of faith, like the physical eye, contemplates not itself but the object before it, which for Matthew should always be God in Christ. Above all, when faith, even faith the size of a mustard seed, passes beyond simple belief or assent, it becomes the opportunity for God, the mover of mountains, to enter his world in a fresh and surprising way.

(v) *Bibliography*

H. Achinger, 'Zur Traditionsgeschichte der Epileptiker-Perikope', in *Probleme der Forschung*, ed. A. Fuchs, SNTU A 3, Munich, 1978, pp. 114–43.

P. J. Achtemeier, 'Miracles and the Historical Jesus: A Study of Mark 9.14–29', *CBQ* 37 (1975), pp. 471–91.

G. Barth, 'Glaube und Zweifel in den synoptischen Evangelien', *ZTK* 72 (1975), pp. 269–92.

Berger, *Amen-Worte*, pp. 46–8.

G. Bornkamm, 'Πνεῦμα ἄλαλον. Eine Studie zum Markusevangelium', in *Gesammelte Aufsätze II*, Munich, 1971, pp. 21–36.

C. E. B. Cranfield, 'St. Mark 9.14–29', *SJT* 3 (1950), pp. 57–67.

J. Duplacy, 'La foi qui déplace les montagnes (Mt 17.20; 21.21 par.)', in *À la rencontre de Dieu*, Lyon, 1961, pp. 272–87.

F. Hahn, 'Jesu Wort vom bergversetzenden Glauben', *ZNW* 76 (1985), pp. 149–69.

Held, in *TIM*, pp. 187–92.

Howard, *Ego*, pp. 86–97.

Kertelge, *Wunder*, pp. 174–9.

X. Léon-Dufour, 'L'episode de l'enfant épileptique', in *La formation des évangiles*, Bruges, 1957, pp. 85–115.

D. Lührmann, *Glaube im frühen Christentum*, Gütersloh, 1976, pp. 17–30.

G. Petzke, 'Die historische Frage nach den Wundertaten Jesu', *NTS* 22 (1976), pp. 180–204.

Roloff, *Kerygma*, pp. 143–52.

W. Schenk, 'Tradition und Redaktion in der Epileptiker-Perikope Mk 9.14–29', *ZNW* 63 (1972), pp. 76–94.

Schenke, *Wundererzählungen*, pp. 314–49.

W. Schmithals, 'Die Heilung des Epileptischen', *ThViat* 13 (1976), pp. 211–34.

Schulz, *Q*, pp. 465–8.

G. Schwarz, 'πίστιν ὡς κόκκον σινάπεως', *Biblischen Notizen* (Bamberg) 25 (1984), pp. 27–35.

Strauss, pp. 431–4.

L. Vagany, 'Les accords négatifs de Matthieu-Luc contre Marc: L'episode de l'enfant épileptique', in *Le problème synoptique*, Tournai, 1954, pp. 405–25.

Van der Loos, pp. 397–405.

J. Wilkinson, 'The Case of the Epileptic Boy', *ExpT* 79 (1967), pp. 39–42.

Zeller, *Mahnsprüche*, pp. 131–3.

J. Zmijewski, 'Der Glaube und seine Macht: Eine traditionsgeschichtliche Untersuchung zu Mt 17.20; 21.21; Mk 11.23; Lk 17.6', in *Begegnung mit dem Wort*, ed. J. Zmijewski and E. Nellessen, Bonn, 1980, pp. 81–103.

Zumstein, pp. 435–43.

XLV

JESUS AGAIN PROPHESIES HIS DEATH AND RESURRECTION
(17.22–3)

(i) *Structure*

The short paragraph, 17.22–3, consists of a prophecy of Jesus which is sandwiched between a circumstantial introduction (v. 22a) and a brief narrative conclusion (v. 23c; cf. Thompson, p. 28). The prophecy itself foretells three separate events.

(ii) *Sources*

Matthew's source for this section is Mk 9.30–2, with the addition of μέλλει in Mt 17.22 perhaps coming from oral tradition (cf. 16.27; Lk 9.44). The several minor agreements of Mt 17.22–3 and Lk 9.43–5 against Mk 9.30–2—introductory genitive absolute, omission of Mk 9.30b–31a, δέ, εἶπεν for ἔλεγεν, μέλλει,[1] and παραδίδοσθαι instead of παραδίδοται—are due to independent editing. There is no good reason to infer that Matthew has here been influenced by a non-Markan source[2] or, *pace* Gundry, *Commentary*, p. 354, that Matthew has served Luke as a source.

(iii) *Exegesis*

For a third time,[3] and without adding any additional details, Jesus plainly prophesies his end: he will be handed over and killed, after which he will rise. Although there does not seem to be any firm link with the pericopae on either side (17.14–20 or 24–7),[4] the prophecy of Jesus' death and resurrection does hark back to 16.21, 27–8, and 17.12.

---

[1] But this word does not appear in the same place in Luke and Matthew. In the latter it is before 'the Son of man,' in the former it comes after the subject.

[2] Lk 9.43–5, however, could conceivably depend in part upon independent (oral?) tradition; see Taylor, *Mark*, p. 403; contrast Fitzmyer, *Luke* 1, p. 812.

[3] Many refer to 17.22–3 as the second passion prediction, 16.21 being the first; but this overlooks 17.13.

[4] For the suggestion that 17.22–3 raises the issue of one's attitude towards Rome, an issue addressed then in 17.24–7, see Davies, *SSM*, p. 391.

Apart from minor stylistic changes the only major alteration made by the First Evangelist on his Markan source is the omission of the references to the messianic secret and the disciples' misunderstanding in Mk 9.30b ('and he would not have any one know it') and 32 ('But they did not understand the saying and they were afraid to ask him'). This results in a slight paring back of length.

Matthew's source, Mk 9.30–2, has sometimes been thought a product of Markan redaction.[5] While it does seem that at least vv. 30 and 32 are probably editorial,[6] v. 31 must be traditional—and is even perhaps based on a dominical word (see on 8.31; it certainly has Semitic features).[7] Whether Mark knew the logion in isolation[8] or as part of a collection[9] is disputed. Also disputed is whether 9.31a ('The Son of man is delivered into the hands of men') was originally independent of one or both of the two clauses it now precedes. According to Hahn, *Titles*, p. 38, 'the repetitive passive participle [ἀποκτανθείς] is obviously intended to co-ordinate death and resurrection and marks this saying [9.31c] as being a more or less independent second member, distinct from the original expression which ended with the killing of Jesus.' Jeremias, however, claims that the switch from the present tense (παραδίδοται) to the future tense (ἀποκτενοῦσιν, ἀναστήσεται) is proof of a break after 9.31a; and this is said to be supported by Mk 14.41, which mentions only the handing over.[10] But the latter may be a truncated saying (see Bayer, pp. 197–8). In addition, 'the Son of man is delivered into the hands of men' almost demands something more. Could it really have stood by itself (cf. Lindars, *Son of Man*, p. 74)? We regard the evidence for a short form of Mk 9.31 as inconclusive.

22. συστρεφομένων δὲ αὐτῶν ἐν τῇ Γαλιλαίᾳ.[11] These words, which set the scene, depend upon Mk 9.30a ('they went on from there and passed through Galilee'), although 'Galilee' is the only common word. On the construction, participle + δέ + αὐτοῦ/αὐτῶν + prepositional phrase, which is often redactional, see on 8.5. On Galilee see on 4.12 and 15. Here 19.1 is being anticipated: Jesus is in Galilee for the very last time.

---

[5] E.g. by Strecker and Perrin (see the articles in the bibliography to 16.21–3).

[6] Gnilka, *Markus* 2, p. 53; against Pesch 2, pp. 98–100. Even Taylor, *Mark*, p. 402, speaks of Mk 9.30 and 32 as 'constructed by Mark,' even though he also wants to maintain some basis in the tradition.

[7] Bayer, pp. 169–70, lists the following: 'the Son of man;' παραδίδοται, representing an Aramaic participle (cf. Jeremias, *Theology*, p. 281); 'delivered into the hands of;' *bar 'ĕnāšā'/bĕnê 'ĕnāšā'*.

[8] Cf. Dibelius, *Tradition*, p. 226.

[9] So Jeremias, *Theology*, p. 281, assigning it to Mk 9.30–50.—Pesch 2, p. 98, proposes that Mk 9.30–2 either circulated in isolation or was bound to Mk 8.27–30.

[10] *Theology*, p. 281. So also Lindars, *Son of man*, pp. 63–7.

[11] C D L W Θ *f*[13] Maj c (e) ff[1] sa[mss] mae bo have αναστρεφομενων: 'as they were staying in Galilee.' Schlatter, p. 537, conjectures an original στρεφομενων. There is no doubt that the best reading, found in ℵ B *f*[1] 892 lat sa[mss], is a bit unusual. But is that sufficient cause for emending the text and substituting, as does Vara (v), λαλια ('talk,' 'discussion') for Γαλιλαια?

The verb, συστρέφω,[12] which in the LXX most often translates the qal of *qāšar*, means 'gather up' or (in the passive) 'come together,' also 'crowd around' (cf. Zahn, p. 569, n. 17). The RSV has 'as they were gathering in Galilee.' But McNeile's translation could also be correct: 'while they were moving about together' (cf. the NEB). If the precise meaning of the verb is difficult, so is the subject. Who are 'they'? Should we think of the twelve, of the twelve plus other disciples, or of the disciples plus outsiders? And is Jesus gathering together a group to go to Jerusalem for the Passover? 'Or are we to think in terms of popular messianic expectations (cf. Luke 9.43; John 6.15), which Jesus countered by announcing his Passion?' (Schweizer, *Matthew*, p. 354).

εἶπεν αὐτοῖς ὁ Ἰησοῦς. This replaces Mk 9.31a–b: 'For he taught his disciples, and said to them (ἔλεγεν αὐτοῖς) that.'

μέλλει ὁ υἱὸς τοῦ ἀνθρώπου παραδίδοσθαι εἰς χεῖρας ἀνθρώπων. Compare 26.45. So Mk 9.31, without μέλλει (for the addition of this see on 16.27; cf. Lk 9.44 and Mt 20.22 diff. Mk 10.38)[13] and with the present indicative passive παραδίδοται instead of the present passive infinitive.

παραδίδωμι[14] is in the NT frequently used in connexion with the passion of Jesus. According to N. Perrin, it is possible to reconstruct three stages in its development. It first arose as a descriptive term without theological connotation, as in Mt 10.4: 'Judas Iscariot, who betrayed him' (cf. Mk 14.42; Acts 3.13; Rom 8.32). Early Christian passion apologetic next created a group of παραδίδωμι sayings which stress the divine and scriptural necessity of the passion (e.g. Mt 26.2; Mk 9.31; 10.33; 14.41; Rom 4.25; 1 Cor 11.23). In these the verb is in the passive. Finally, Isa 53 came into play and thus was formed the (παρα)δίδωμι (in the active with reflexive object) + ὑπέρ statements (e.g. Gal 1.4; 2.20; 1 Tim 2.6; Tit 2.14). None of the reasons given for this historical reconstruction, however, amount to anything more than a convenient sorting of the material. Further, there is nothing to prohibit the supposition that, let us say, Perrin's second group (where παραδίδωμι is in the passive) goes back to Jesus and that from it there arose the first group (descriptive παραδίδωμι). And what of the possible background of the second group—which is dominated by the Son of man idiom or title—in Dan 7, where the saints of the Most High, identified with the Son of man, are delivered into the hands of their eschatological enemies, only to receive the kingdom after a time, two times, and half a time (see further on 16.21)?

Without prejudging the issue of historicity, it seems to us that the

[12] Elsewhere in the NT only in Acts 28.3.
[13] The addition is altogether natural because Mark's present tense, which may well represent an Aramaic participle with future meaning, is so striking.
[14] Lit.: F. Büchsel, *TWNT* 2, pp. 171–4; Tödt, pp. 156–61; Popkes, pp. 153–89; N. Perrin, 'The Use of *(Para)didonai* in Connection with the Passion of Jesus in the New Testament,' in *A Modern Pilgrimage in New Testament Christology*, Philadelphia, 1974, pp. 94–103.

background for the several statements with the form, 'the Son of man' + a passive form of παραδίδωμι + 'into the hands of men/sinners,' is to be found in Dan 7 or (less probably) Isa 53.[15] But one could also claim that no special background need be cited. Concerning the latter possibility, the Semitic idiom, 'deliver into the hands of' (Hebrew *nātan* + *běyad*, Aramaic *měsar* + *lîdê*), is well attested in Jewish literature and occurs in many different contexts.[16]

The meaning of παραδίδωμι + εἰς(τὰς) χεῖράς τινος is 'hand over to the power or authority of' (cf. BDF § 217.2 and note Aristobulus in Eusebius, *Praep. ev.* 8.10.8: 'it is possible for people speaking metaphorically to consider that the entire strength of human beings and their active powers are in their hand'). In the present context, the passive probably, *pace* Thompson, pp. 30–1, refers not principally to Judas (cf. 10.4; 26.21–5, 48) but points rather to God, as Origen already contended: 'as in the case of Job, the Father first delivered up the Son to the opposing powers, and ... then they delivered Him up into the hands of men, among which men Judas also was ...' (*Comm. on Mt.* 13.8).[17] 'Otherwise the addition [of ἀνθρώπων in v. 22] is superfluous' (Plummer, p. 243).

23. καὶ ἀποκτενοῦσιν αὐτόν. This agrees with Mk 9.31. Mt 16.21 = Mk 8.31 has the aorist passive infinitive, ἀποκτανθῆναι. The verb is used elsewhere both of the deaths of prophets (23.34, 37) and the deaths of Christian disciples (10.28; 24.9). Thus Jesus stands at the end of one line of martyrs and at the beginning of another.

καὶ τῇ τρίτῃ ἡμέρᾳ ἐγερθήσεται. Mark has: 'and having been killed after (μετά) three days he will arise' (ἀναστήσεται). The redundant participle, ἀποκτανθείς, has been dropped, and the more accurate 'on the third day' substituted, as in 16.21 (q.v.) diff. Mk 8.31.[18]

καὶ ἐλυπήθησαν σφόδρα. Compare 18.31; 26.22; also Jon 4.1; Dan 6.15 (*śaggî' bě'ēš*); Tob 3.10; 1 Macc 10.68; 14.16. The clause replaces 'and they were ignorant about the saying and feared to ask him' (Mk 8.32). Both λυπέω* and σφόδρα* are editorial favourites.

---

[15] Cf. Lindars, *Son of Man*, pp. 82–3. παραδίδωμι occurs in LXX Isa 53.6, 12 (*bis*), *měsar* in Tg. Isa 53.5, 7, 12. Even if Jesus or the tradition intended no allusion to Isa 53, it remains possible that Matthew, like J. Jeremias in our own time, perceived one.

[16] E.g. Deut 1.27; Josh 2.24; Judg 2.14; 11.32; 16.24; 18.10; 1 Sam 30.15; 2 Kgs 21.14; Job 9.24; Ps 106.41; Dan 11.11; 1 Macc 4.30; Josephus, *Ant.* 2.20; T. Job 20.3; Par. Jer. 1.6; 2.7; 3.8; *b. B. Qam.* 82b; *b. Ta'an.* 18b.

[17] Cf. Isa 53; Rom 4.25; 8.32; Josephus, *Ant.* 2.20.

[18] See further Thompson, pp. 34–5.

According to Hill, *Matthew*, p. 271, 'the deep sorrow of the disciples indicates that they did not understand the meaning of the announcement about the Resurrection.' This does not put the emphasis on the right spot. One must contrast 17.23 with 16.21–3. After the passion prediction at Caesarea Philippi the reaction on Peter's part is absolute refusal to accept Jesus' prospective end: 'Far be it from thee, Lord!' By 17.23 this is no longer the response. Now the disciples, having listened to Jesus (cf. 17.5), understand and are reconciled to the inevitable. They grieve precisely because they know all too well what the future holds (cf. Meier, *Matthew*, p. 195).

(iv) *Concluding Observations*

(1) The First Evangelist might have passed over Mk 9.30–2 as a doublet, a text not needed in view of 16.21–3 (=Mk 8.31–3). That he has not done so but has instead chosen to follow Mark and let Jesus speak once again of his coming passion and resurrection is consistent with the fact that the gospel's conclusion (26.1ff.) is Matthew's Rosetta stone, by which all else is deciphered. Repetition of the passion predictions does more than emphasize Jesus' prophetic powers and make plain the voluntary nature of his suffering. It also connotes necessity and destiny (cf. the δεῖ of 16.21) and, in terms of plot, pushes the reader forward in anticipation: the key to everything must lie in the end. To recall M. Kähler, Matthew, like Mark, is indeed a passion narrative with an extended introduction.

(2) If in 28.18 Jesus will declare, 'All ἐξουσία in heaven and on earth has been delivered to me (by God)' (cf. LXX Dan 7.14, where the one like a son of man is given eternal ἐξουσία), here, in 17.22–3, the Son of man speaks of being delivered into the hands, that is, authority of sinful men. The poles of experience represented by the two texts are worlds apart, a fact which holds much pathos for Matthew's readers. God gives the Son of man into the hands of others, and God gives the Son of man universal ἐξουσία. It is the burden of the gospel to demonstrate that these two opposing acts, so far from being contradictory, are, in God's hidden but sovereign will, the two complementary halves of the same divine purpose.

(v) *Bibliography*

In addition to what follows see section (v) on 16.21–3.

Bayer, pp. 169–71, 177–81, 188–90.
J. Brière, 'Le Fils de l'homme livré aux hommes. Mc 9.30–7,' *AsSeign* 56 (1974), pp. 42–52.
W. G. Thompson, pp. 27–49.
J. Vara, 'Dos conjeturas textuales sobre Mateo 25.21, 23 y Mateo 26.32/17.22 y par.,' *Salmanticensis* 33 (1986), pp. 81–6.

XLVI

THE TEMPLE TAX
(17.24–7)

(i) *Structure*

The pericope consists of two short scenes. In the first Peter is asked by certain tax collectors in Capernaum whether Jesus pays the temple tax. He answers, Yes. In the second scene Peter goes to Jesus and is given teaching about the temple tax and instructions on what to do.

The narrative exhibits a good deal of parallelism. The two scenes mirror each other. Both open with similar narrative introductions (ἐλθόντων/ἐλθόντα + εἰς + verb in aorist tense beginning with πρὸ + subject + εἶπαν/λέγων). And both have conversations which direct a question or questions to Peter. Further, the final four clauses all have the form: participle + aorist imperative:

going to the sea	—cast a hook
and the first fish coming up	—take
and opening its mouth	—you will find
taking that	—give it

This creates a pleasing rhythm.

(ii) *Sources*

There is no parallel in Mark or Luke or John. This raises the possibility of a purely redactional origin.[1] But the hypothesis that 17.24–7 preserves oral tradition retouched by Matthew[2] merits our assent.[3] The main reason for so concluding is that while the gospel was written after

---

[1] So Goulder, pp. 395–97, and Gundry, *Commentary*, pp. 355–7.

[2] For Matthean features see Kilpatrick, p. 40, and our own comments below.

[3] Cf. Schweizer, *Matthew*, p. 355, and most commentators. Several words or phrases occur only here in Matthew: δίδραχμον, τελέω with the meaning 'pay', προφθάνω, οἱ βασιλεῖς τῆς γῆς, τέλος, ἀλλότριος, ἐλεύθερος, ἄγκιστον, στατήρ. Possible Aramaisms include τὸν ἀναβάντα πρῶτον ἰχθύν, auxiliary λαβών, and ἀντὶ ἐμοῦ καὶ σοῦ (pronoun instead of reflexive). For a tentative rendering of portions of vv. 25 and 27 into Aramaic see Horbury (v), p. 283, ns. 91 and 95.

737

the destruction of the temple in A.D. 70 (cf. 1, pp. 127–38), 17.24–7, as we shall see, must have come into being while the temple was still standing.

(iii) *Exegesis*

This 'reasonably stylish passage', with its 'comparatively elaborate use of participles, a wide range of vocabulary, and a liveliness almost like Luke's at his most free and individual',[4] may be labelled what Theissen calls a 'rule miracle' (see p. 316). The miracle serves to justify and illustrate Jesus' teaching or ruling on a certain tax. The miracle itself, however, is not in fact recounted (see on v. 27), so one might contend that, form-critically considered, the episode has as much claim to be classified a scholastic dialogue.[5]

The paragraph is located at the end of chapter 17 primarily for two reasons. First, Matthew has just recounted a story which, in its Markan setting, is followed by notice that Jesus and his disciples went to Capernaum (see Mk 9.30–3), and the story about Peter and the coin in the fish's mouth was presumably set in that city before Matthew's telling of it. (The temple tax was collected in or near a person's place of residence, and both Jesus and Peter were officially residents of Capernaum.) Secondly, it is in the narrative section stretching from 13.53 to 17.27 that Peter comes into prominence, this because the section records the founding of the church on the chief apostle. Matthew has placed his other special passages about Peter in this section.[6]

Before one can proceed with the interpretive task, one must establish the identity of οἱ τὰ δίδραχμα λαμβάνοντες and the nature of the tax they collected. The broad consensus of modern commentators, a consensus enshrined in the paragraph headings of synopses and annotated Bibles, is that our text concerns the temple tax, the half-shekel levy believed to be prescribed by Exod 30.11–16 (see on v. 24). A few scholars, however, have

---

[4] Moule, *Birth*, pp. 278–9

[5] Bultmann, *History*, p. 35. Dibelius, *Tradition*, p. 106, classifies the miracle of the coin as a 'legend'. Bauckham (v), p. 225, compares the controversy stories which have a miracle as climax (e.g. Mk 2.1–12 par.; 3.1–6 par).

[6] Bauckham (v), p. 226, has suggested a third reason: 'The collection of the Temple tax in Palestine outside Jerusalem began four weeks before Passover (15 Adar). Admittedly, this allows an improbably short period for Jesus' journey through Perea to Jerusalem (Matt. 19–20), but if Matthew envisaged Jesus' ministry as lasting no more than a year, he had to place this pericope during Jesus' last visit to Capernaum'. This suggestion presupposes Matthew's knowledge of the Jewish calendar.

held a different view of the matter and thought of a secular tax imposed by the Romans. Their interpretation demands examination. Its chief merits are these:

(i) According to Cassidy (v), pp. 572–3, 'Jesus' reply invokes a civil frame of reference' (cf. Sherwin-White, p. 126). 'The kings of the earth' refers to civil rulers; κῆνσος is a Latin loanword which 'refers specifically to a category of Roman taxes based directly upon the provincial census'; and ἐλεύθερος 'frequently connotes freedom in the political and civil sense'.

(ii) On the basis of such texts as Philo, *Spec. Leg.* 14, and Josephus, *Ant.* 16.172 ('offerings which each of them makes of his own free will'), Cassidy (v), p. 574, concludes that 'the annual temple didrachma should not be considered a tax in the usual sense of the term, but rather should be regarded as a voluntary offering, an annual pledge. Given the certainty that the Matthean collectors are collecting a tax and given the high probability that they are collecting a civil tax, the traditional step of equating the didrachma tax with the annual temple offering seems invalid'. The point gains some force if one accepts the study of S. Mandell, 'Who Paid the Temple Tax when the Jews were under Roman Rule?', *HTR* 77 (1984), pp. 223–32. She claims that the temple tax was probably paid only by Pharisaic Jews, not the general population.

(iii) If, as is most likely, Matthew's gospel was composed after A.D. 70 and the destruction of the temple in Jerusalem, one could claim that 17.24–7, if about a temple tax, would have no direct bearing on Matthew's readers—many of whom were Gentiles anyway and therefore not subject to a specifically Jewish tax. (The force of this point is such that 17.24–7 has been taken by some scholars as good evidence for the First Gospel having been composed before A.D. 70.)[7]

(iv) When 17.24–7 is considered to be about civil taxes, one may think either of Roman capitation taxes or transit tolls. Although our knowledge about Roman tax practices is unfortunately minimal, we do know that in Egypt at least there were capitation taxes and transit tolls fixed at two drachmae or thereabouts (see Cassidy (v), calling attention to those scholars who have claimed that the Roman procedures in Egypt were paralleled in Judaea). Cassidy (v), p. 578, is able to assert: 'if Matt 17.24–27 referred to an Egyptian setting, there would be no great difficulty in concluding that the 2 drachmae tax described was a civil tax'. He goes on: 'Not only is a tax of this amount plausible for Egypt during this period, but Matthew's description of how it was collected and paid also agrees well with the patterns for collection and payment that [Sherman] Wallace had defended.[8] Wallace indicates that, in addition to receiving taxes at their banks, tax collectors also went out and located the more reluctant payers. He also indicates that it was desirable for the tax payments to be made in even tetradrachmae'.

(v) The instruction in 17.24–7 resembles the instructions given

---

[7] See Robinson, *Redating*, pp. 104–5; Gundry, *Commentary*, p. 357.
[8] S. Wallace, *Taxation in Egypt from Augustus to Diocletian*, Princeton, 1938.

elsewhere in the NT concerning secular taxes; see Mk 12.13–17 par.; Rom 13.1–7; 1 Pet 2.13–17.

(vi) Many of the church Fathers understood 17.24–7 to be about Roman taxation.[9]

(vii) If the half-shekel tax were the issue, Jesus' answer could be construed as contradicting the Torah, for many took the temple tax to be commanded by Exod 30.11–16. Neither Jesus nor Matthew, however, would simply have dismissed without further ado a Mosaic commandment.

These seven points would seem to constitute a formidable case. Still, we are not persuaded. It remains more probable than not that 17.24–7 concerns the temple tax. On (i)—The terms of the discussion are indeed drawn from civil discourse, but that is precisely because Jesus is arguing from a secular situation to a religious situation: it is with the earthly kings and their sons as it is with God and his children. On (ii)—The fact that not all paid the temple tax simply shows that the issue was open for discussion, and Jesus' opinion on the matter—does he side with the Pharisees or not?—may well have been sought. Moreover, it is not at all clear from Matthew's text that the collection under discussion was anything but voluntary. On (iii)—There are other pericopae in the First Gospel which could never have been *directly* relevant for Matthew's readers: such passages held meaning because of the principles they illustrated. Who would argue that the story of the plucking of corn on the sabbath would be relevant only to people who plucked corn on the sabbath? Similarly with 17.24–7: even if the text pertains to a situation before A.D. 70, its argument, as we shall discover, does have more general implications. See section (iv) and recall 5.23–4: 'If you are offering your gift at the altar . . .'. This last no doubt came into being when the temple was still standing. But the destruction of the temple did not render the substance of it obsolete. On (iv)—The sums *may* harmonize with a civil tax. But they *certainly* harmonize with the temple tax. Josephus, *Ant.* 18.312, and *Bell.* 7.218, states that the temple tax amounted to two drachma = one didrachmon. This fits Mt 17.24, which refers to the collectors of τὰ δίδραχμα.[10] It also fits v. 27, where Peter is to pay for himself and Jesus a στατήρ, for this was the equivalent of four *drachmas* or two *didrachma*, the exact amount for two people. Also, the *stater* of NT times was the Tyrian *tetradrachmon*, which was accepted by Jews as a 'shekel of the sanctuary' (Exod 30.13; cf. *t. Ketub.* 13.3: 'all money spoken of in the torah is Tyrian money'). On (v)—There is no good reason why Jesus and the early church may not have held similar ideas with respect to certain religious and civil taxes. On (vi)—Some of the Fathers took 17.24–7 to be about the temple tax[11]—which is

[9] Cf. Irenaeus, *Adv. haer.* 5.24.1; Clement of Alexandria, *Paed.* 2.1.14.1; Origen, *Comm. on Mt.* 13.10; Ambrose, *Comm. on Lk.* 4.73–5; Augustine, *De cat. rud.* 21; Gregory Nazianzen, *Orat.* 29.20.

[10] Is the plural explained by the fact that one was supposed to give every year? Or do we have here an Aramaism, as Black (v) thinks?

[11] Horbury (v), p. 265, n. 3, cites Melito, *Peri Pascha* 86; Hilary of Poitiers

particularly significant given their distance from the pre-70 situation. On (vii)—There were differences of opinion as to what the Torah demanded in connexion with a temple tax. Surely the Essenes, who evidently required only a once-in-a-lifetime payment (4QOrdinances), did not imagine themselves to be dismissing Moses when they acted otherwise than the Pharisees.

If the case against the usual interpretation does not stand up to scrutiny, what can be said on the other side? One observation is decisive. Jesus' words presuppose that the discussion is about a tax levied in the name of God (cf. Bauckham (v), p. 219, citing Josephus, *Ant.* 18.312). Kings are towards their sons as God is towards his sons. The whole point is that *God's children are free with respect to God their Father*: he does not tax them. Clearly the tax in question must be a religious one.

What is the origin of 17.24–7? There are those who accept the historicity of the passage as a whole[12] as well as those who dismiss it as entirely the product of the early church.[13] There are, however, many who think the issue is not so clear cut. According to Lindars, for example, 'the mention of Peter may be due to Matthew, and the question concerning payment of the tax may be an artificial setting for the saying, completed with a "fishing story" derived from a well known theme of folk-lore. But the saying itself is a parable, and has nothing to do with the temple tax: "From whom do kings of the earth take toll or tribute? From their sons or from others? (Do they not take it) from others? Then the sons are free"'.[14] Lindars calls attention to the possible parallel in Lk 12.32–4 (on selling possessions) and suggests that the reconstructed dominical parable lies behind the discussion in Jn 8.31–58.

Lindars' analysis resembles that of Kilpatrick, pp. 41–2. He suggests that the core is contained in vv. 25f., which were subsequently turned into a dialogue with Peter, that v. 27 was added after A.D. 70,[15] and that Matthew rewrote the introduction (v. 24).

We must number ourselves among those who doubt the historicity of the story as it stands. Although truth is stranger than fiction, the miracle of the fish almost certainly belongs to folklore. The story of the person who loses a piece of jewellery or a key in a lake or ocean, only to regain it later through catching a fish and cleaning it seems to

---

[12] See esp. Bauckham (v); also Derrett (v), affirming Jesus' 'sixth sense'.

17.10; Apollinarius, in Reuss, pp. 27–8; Cyril of Alexandria in Reuss, *ad loc.* Add Ambrose, *Ep. 7, ad Justum* 12, and Theodoret, *Quaest. in Num. Inter.* 9.

[13] E.g. Strauss, pp. 506–7 (judging the miracle 'extravagant and useless'); Flusser (v) (reckoning unpersuasively with Qumran influence); and Beare, p. 371.

[14] B. Lindars, 'Discourse and Tradition: The Use of the Sayings of Jesus in the Discourses of the Fourth Gospel', *JSNT* 13 (1981), pp. 92–3. Bultmann, *History*, p. 35, already surmised that vv. 25–6 'were originally connected with something quite different from the Temple tax'.

[15] It is quite common to regard v. 27 as a secondary addition; cf. e.g. Schweizer, *Matthew*, p. 356.

be at home in all times and places. There are Greek examples[16] as well as rabbinic examples.[17] Christian tradition is filled with variations on the theme,[18] and the modern press still publishes versions of the familiar plot.[19] In addition, the story of the co-operating fish who miraculously renders service for the holy man is widespread,[20] and the narratives about people finding much-needed money in unexpected places are without number.[21] So we are disinclined to accept Mt 17.27 as sober reporting. Nevertheless, it is only the conclusion which, as far as we can tell, should stand under suspicion. *Pace* Gnilka, *Matthäusevangelium* 2, p. 118, the rest of the pericope makes very good sense as a story from the pre-Easter period. Bauckham (v), p. 232, is persuasive: 'An argument against the Temple tax which is based, not on any criticism of the Temple or its worship, but on the character of God as Father and King, seems much more likely to come from Jesus than from the Jewish Christian church. The way in which Jesus here gives priority to God's fatherhood over his kingship, as a model for God's relationship to his people, coheres with a prominent and distinctive feature of Jesus' authentic teaching, i.e. the fact that, while Jesus repeatedly speaks of God's kingdom, his portrayal of the way God exercises his rule is usually in terms of fatherhood rather than kingship.'

Bauckham (v), p. 230, has raised the intriguing possibility that Paul may have known our pericope or its teaching. The apostle evidently modelled his collection for the poor in Jerusalem on the collection of the temple tax.[22] But he stressed that payment was purely voluntary: he was not collecting a tax (cf. Rom 15.25–7; 2 Cor 9.7). 'That Jesus was known to have objected in principle to theocratic taxation could partly explain this'. Bauckham also observes that such an attitude on the part of the historical Jesus would go some way towards explaining his overturning of the tables in the temple: he did not believe the temple should be supported by taxation.[23]

24. ἐλθόντων δὲ αὐτῶν εἰς Καφαρναούμ. Compare 17.22a and see 1, p. 90 (on repetition). Mk 9.33 (καὶ ἦλθεν εἰς Καφαρναούμ) explains the present placement of our story; see p. 738. Note that the text requires a location where fish can be readily obtained.

προσῆλθον οἱ τὰ δίδραχμα λαμβάνοντες τῷ Πέτρῳ καὶ εἶπαν.

---

[16] In Herodotus 3.39–42, Polycrates throws his ring into the sea to appease Fate; but a week later it comes back to him at dinner in a fish.

[17] E.g. *b. Šabb.* 119a. Additional examples in Bauckham (v), pp. 239–40.

[18] Miraculous fish stories are told about, among others, Cadoc, Kentigern (cf. Glasgow's heraldic arms), Arnolf of Metz, and Egwin.

[19] See Dodd, *Tradition*, p. 225, n. 7.

[20] In Liv. Proph. Ezek. 11 the fish come of their own accord to be eaten by hungry people. One also recalls the charming stories about fish raising their heads out of the water to hear Francis of Assisi's preaching!

[21] For one example see Augustine, *De civ. dei* 22.8 (another fish story).

[22] See K. F. Nickle, *The Collection*, SBT 48, London, 1966, pp. 74–93.

[23] An origin with Jesus is likewise consistent with Horbury's observation (v), p. 282, that vv. 25–6 have a 'primitive ring' because 'the antithetical question formally corresponds to synoptic sayings widely accepted as authentic'.

Compare 18.1; 26.17. Both προσέρχομαι* and λαμβάνω* are often editorial.

ὁ διδάσκαλος ὑμῶν οὐ τελεῖ τὰ δίδραχμα;²⁴ On 'teacher' as a christological title see on 8.19. 'Your teacher' also appears in 9.11 and 23.8 and is found in no other NT document. οὐ anticipates a positive answer (BDF § 427.2). τελέω (Mt: 7; Mk: 0; Lk: 4) might be considered redactional but only here in Matthew does it mean 'pay' (as in classical usage; cf. LSJ, s.v., and note Rom 13.6; Josephus, *Ant.* 2.192; 12.158).

The temple tax²⁵ was intended to support the sacrificial system in Jerusalem. For its local collection see Philo, *Spec. leg.* 1.78; *m. Šek.* 2.1. According to the Mishnah the tax was to be paid annually, in the month of Adar (February–March) by all adult Jewish males over twenty years of age (*m. Šek.* 1.1ff.). But the Dead Sea Scrolls (4QOrdinances) and a few rabbinic texts (e.g. *m. Šek.* 1.4; *Mek.* on Exod 19.1; *b. Menaḥ.* 65a) supply evidence that there was some dispute as to precisely who was to pay—for instance, are the priests liable?—and how often (the Essenes made a one-time contribution). (That the Galileans in particular were lax in making payment, as Freyne (as in n. 25) has proposed, seems, however, improbable; cf. Horbury (v), pp. 280–1.) Although apparently of post-Exilic origin, the temple tax was regarded by the Pharisees at least as firmly grounded in Scripture (Exod 30.11–16; cf. Neh 10.33–4). After A.D. 70 the tax, now known as the *fiscus iudaicus*, was diverted by the Romans to support the temple of Jupiter Capitolinus (cf. Josephus, *Bell.* 7.218; Dio Cassius 66.7.2; Smallwood, pp. 371–6).²⁶

25. λέγει· ναί. Compare 13.51; 15.27. ναί* also answers direct questions in 9.28; 13.51; and 21.16. On asyndetic λέγω (often in Matthew, never in Mark; is it an Aramaism?) see 1, p. 84 and Lagrange, pp. xcii–xciii.

καὶ ἐλθόντα εἰς τὴν οἰκίαν προέφθασεν αὐτὸν ὁ Ἰησοῦς λέγων.²⁷ Compare 2.11; 8.14; 9.23, 28; 13.36.²⁸ On 'the house'

---

²⁴ τα, missing in א* D 1010 mae bo, is placed in brackets by NA²⁶. W *pc* sa read το.

²⁵ Lit.: Freyne, pp. 277–81; Horbury (v); J. Liver, 'The Half-Shekel Offering in Biblical and Postbiblical Literature', *HTR* 56 (1963), pp. 173–98; Mandell (as on p. 739); Nickle (as in n. 22), pp. 74–87; and Schürer 2, pp. 270–2.

²⁶ Montefiore (v) contends that Mt 17.24–7 is precedent for dealing with the *fiscus iudaicus*. Cf. Davies (v). But we have here established (p. 741) that the tax must be one levied in God's name.—We also deem unlikely the alternative put forward by Thompson (v), that Matthew intended 17.24–7 to be advice about the Jewish *aurum coronarium*, the tax made to the patriarchate. The evidence for this tax is late (fourth century A.D.), and it is not at all clear that it was formally established before A.D. 135.

²⁷ So א¹ B *f*¹ 892 and HG and NA.²⁶ The reading is very uncertain. εισελθοντα appears in א*·² (D), εισελθοντων in Θ *f*¹³ (33) sy^c?, οτε ηλθον in C (*al*) sy^c?, οτε εισηλθεν in L W Maj.

²⁸ Thompson, p. 54: 'Matthew always describes movement into the house with the same expression.'

and its identity—is it Peter's house? Jesus' house? or what?— see on 9.10. For προφθάνω (= 'anticipate'), a NT *hapax legomenon* most often for *qādam* in the LXX, followed by the participle see BDF § 414.4. Josephus, *Ant*. 6.123, has ἔφθασε λέγων.

τί σοι δοκεῖ, Σίμων; Compare 18.12; 21.28; 22.17, 42; 26.66 (= Mk 14.64); Jn 11.56. Matthew seems to have been fond of τί + dative personal pronoun + δοκέω, a construction with good rabbinic parallels (Schlatter, pp. 539–40). On 'Simon' see on 4.18. Is he being addressed because it is his house?

οἱ βασιλεῖς τῆς γῆς ἀπὸ τίνων λαμβάνουσιν τέλη ἢ κῆνσον; 'The kings of the earth' (= *malkê hā'āreṣ*), here in emphatic position, is an old expression with pejorative connotations. It is antithetical to 'the king of heaven' (= God). The phrase is found often in the Psalms as well as in Revelation and apocalyptic literature in general.[29] It is inclusive, that is, it encompasses all earthly rulers (not just the Romans).

τέλος (cf. Rom 13.7 and the τελῶναι, the collectors of civil taxes) refers to '(indirect) taxes' or 'customs duties' (BAGD, s.v., citing 1 Macc 10.31; 11.35; Josephus, *Ant*. 12.141). κῆνσος (= Latin *census*) is found elsewhere in the NT in Mt 22.17, 19 and Mk 12.14 (in the pericope about paying taxes to Caesar). It means 'poll-tax'. See further Horsley 3, pp. 70–1. Together the two words cover indirect and direct taxes, that is, taxes of every kind (cf. Rom 13.7, where φόρος and τέλος perform this function).

ἀπὸ τῶν υἱῶν αὐτῶν ἢ ἀπὸ τῶν ἀλλοτρίων; ἀλλότριος (most often for *nākrî* = 'foreigner' in the LXX) occurs in Matthew only here and the following line. Note the chiastic order created by the next verse: sons—others—others—sons.

The opposition between 'sons' and 'others'—which, *pace* Gundry, *Commentary*, p. 356, does not seem to have an OT ring—has been understood to designate different groupings—a king's nation versus all other nations,[30] a king's household versus all outsiders,[31] or a king's immediate family versus everyone else.[32] The first option is unlikely because kings did in fact exact taxes from their own people. The second fails because the evidence that a king's household could be described as his 'sons' does not seem to exist. This leaves us with the third view: the son's are the king's family, the others those outside his family.

Who are the sons in the implicit interpretation of the parable?

[29] Josh 12.1; Ezra 9.7; Ps 76.12; Lam 4.12; Ezek 27.33; Rev 1.5; 6.15; 1 En 48.8; 4 Ezra 15.20.
[30] So Allen, p. 192; cf. the NEB ('from their own people or from aliens?')
[31] So Gundry, *Commentary*, p. 357.
[32] So Bauckham (v), pp. 221–2.

That is, who are God's sons? Most commentators assume that they must be equated with Jesus' followers or all Christians. But Horbury (v), pp. 282–4, and Bauckham (v), p. 223, have argued that we should think of the Israelites (cf. Mt 8.12). This seems the best interpretation both for level I (the historical Jesus) and for level III (the evangelist Matthew). God's sons are free and he does not tax them. 'Jesus takes up the common Jewish belief that God is both King and Father to his people, a belief which is everywhere presupposed in his own preaching, and points out an implication of this belief by making a comparison with earthly kings *who are also fathers.*' (Bauckham).

26. εἰπόντος δέ· ἀπὸ τῶν ἀλλοτρίων.[33] On the genitive absolute with implicit subject see BDF § 423.6. This passage is unique in the NT in using such a construction to introduce direct discourse.

ἔφη αὐτῷ ὁ Ἰησοῦς. Thompson, p. 57, citing 4.7; 19.21; 21.27; and 27.65, writes that asyndeton + ἔφη + αὐτῷ/οῖς + verbal content is in our gospel characteristic 'at the end of dialogues to introduce the climax or concluding statement'.

ἄρα γε ἐλεύθεροί εἰσιν οἱ υἱοί.[34] Compare Jn 8.33, 36. ἄρα γε (Mt: 2; Mk: 0; Lk: 0; cf. LXX Gen 26.9; Acts 17.27) is also used in 7.20, where it is redactional and again introduces a sentence. ἐλεύθερος is a synoptic *hapax legomenon*, but sonship and freedom are important and related concepts elsewhere in early Christian literature (e.g. Jn 8.31–8; Rom 8; Gal 3.23–5.1). The major thrust of Jesus' parable is this. The sons of earthly kings do not pay toll or tribute, and Jesus and his disciples are, as members of Israel, sons of God. They therefore should be exempt from any taxes levied in God's name. 'The sons are free'. What is thereby rejected is not the temple cult but instead the idea that taxation is the appropriate means of maintaining that divine institution.

27. In the narrative's conclusion Jesus gives Peter precise instructions for paying the tax.[35] Thus Peter not only receives halakah but acts upon it.

Jesus' command well fits the previous teaching. The tax will be paid

---

[33] So both NA[26] and HG, but there is no room for assurance. ο δε εφη· απο των αλλοτριων. ειπ. δε is found in ℵ bo[pt], λεγει αυτω ο Πετρος in W *f*[13] Maj (f) q sy[c.p.h] (mae), λεγ. αυ. ο. Π.· απο των αλλοτριων. ειποντος δε (+αυτου C) in C L, and λεγει αυτω in D sy[s]. Above we have printed the reading of B Θ *f*[1] 700 892* ([mg] + του Πετρ.) *pc* sa bo[pt] Or.

[34] 713 Ephr add, after v. 26, this: εφη Σιμων· ναι. λεγει ο Ιησους· δος ουν και συ ως αλλοτριος αυτων. This late addition assumes that the text centres around Jesus' sonship. Cf. Garland (v), p. 206.

[35] Cf. Acts Thom. 143: Jesus paid tribute and poll-tax for himself and for his disciples.

but not out of the money at hand. 'By using a lost coin rather than drawing on the common money box (John 12.6; 13.29) Jesus meets the demand without acknowledging it as a legitimate charge' (Horbury (v), p. 274). One can even go further and affirm that the miracle of the fish shows that God himself will provide for the upkeep of the temple; that is, he will supply his people with the funds which they may voluntarily offer.

ἵνα δὲ μὴ σκανδαλίσωμεν αὐτούς. Compare 1 Cor 8.9–13. δέ here has its full force: 'but', 'however'. αὐτούς refers not to the kings of the earth but to the tax collectors and to the authorities they represent.

What precisely does the verb (see on 5.29), which is used again shortly in 18.6–9, mean here? It obviously does not mean 'cause to sin'. Probably the best translation is 'give offence'. What Jesus and his followers should avoid, if at all possible, is offending the devout people who, in collecting the temple tax, believe themselves to be serving God. Voluntary payment should be made in order to prevent others from inferring that Peter or Jesus has rejected the temple cult. See further section (iv), part (3).[36]

πορευθεὶς εἰς θάλασσαν βάλε ἄγκιστρον. Compare 4.18; 13.47; 21.21; also LXX Isa 19.8; and Lk 5.4 (where Jesus commands Peter to let out fish nets; cf. Jn 21.6). πορευθείς (pleonastic) is perhaps redactional (cf. Thompson, p. 60). ἄγκιστρον (LXX: 5, three times for ḥakkâ) is an old Greek word meaning 'fish-hook' (Homer, Od. 4.369; Ignatius, Mag. 11). Although a metaphorical usage is exceedingly common in early Christian literature (Lampe, s.v.), our text is to be taken literally (see further below). Further, pace Homeau (v), the reference is not ironic and to the Dead Sea, in which there are no fish.

καὶ τὸν ἀναβάντα πρῶτον ἰχθὺν ἆρον. Compare LXX Dan 7.3. The vocabulary is not distinctive.[37] On the active intransitive for the passive (a possible Aramaism; cf. McNeile, p. 258) see 1, p. 81. The sense is: 'And the first fish being drawn up . . .'.

καὶ ἀνοίξας τὸ στόμα αὐτοῦ εὑρήσεις στατῆρα. For ἀνοίγω +στόμα (Mt: 3; Mk: 0; Lk: 1) see also 5.2 and 13.35. 'You will find' (cf. 21.2) expresses the certainty of Jesus' prophetic foreknowledge.

στατήρ (LXX: 0) is sometimes used for šeqel in Aquila and Symmachus. Rabbinic texts have 'istêrā' and 'isṭārā' (cf. Jastrow, s.v.).

---

[36] The use of σκανδαλίζω supplies another argument against a reference to civil taxes: the word is too weak for the refusal to pay an enforced Roman tax.

[37] ἀναβαίνω: Mt: 9; Mk: 9; Lk: 9. πρῶτος: Mt: 15; Mk: 8; Lk: 9. ἰχθύς: Mt: 5; Mk: 4; Lk: 6. αἴρω: Mt: 19; Mk: 19; Lk: 20.

The word designates a Greek silver coin worth four drachmas or two didrachmas; see p. 740 and 1, p. 144. The only other time it occurs in the NT is Mt 26.15 v. 1. (Judas and his thirty pieces of money).

ἐκεῖνον λαβὼν δὸς αὐτοῖς ἀντὶ ἐμοῦ καὶ σοῦ. On auxiliary λαμβάνω see 1, p. 83. It is a Semitism. Also Semitic is the use of the simple pronoun instead of the reflexive (cf. MHT 4, p. 36). For ἀντί with the meaning of ὑπέρ (cf. 20.28) see BAGD, s.v., 3.

Bengel, *ad loc.*, wrote: 'A manifold miracle . . . 1, Something shall be caught; 2, and that quickly; 3, there shall be money in a fish; 4, and that in the first fish; 5, the sum shall be just what is needed; 6, it shall be in the fish's mouth'. The story ends, however, without informing the reader that Peter went and did as Jesus commanded. No miracle is recorded. This striking fact, which has been taken to show that Matthew was interested only in the passage's halakhic content, has also led to the suggestion that Jesus' words were not intended to be taken literally: they 'were merely a playful comment' on the lack of ready money.[38] But the reader most naturally assumes that Peter, as a faithful disciple, did as the Lord commanded him. The proposed interpretation is really not much more satisfactory than the idea that 'and there you will find a *stater*' really meant 'and go to the market and there you will obtain a stater through sale of the fish'[39] or the supposition that Jesus was using a metaphor: as a fisher of men go out and get a rich convert![40]

This version of our story appears in Ep. Apost. 5: 'And when we, his disciples, had no denarii, we said to him, "Master, what should we do about the tax-collection?" And he answered and said to us, "One of you cast the hook, the net, into the deep and draw out a fish, and he will find a denarius in it. Give that to the tax-collector for me and for you' (Hennecke 1, pp. 193–4). The differences between this and Mt 17.24–7 are quite striking: there is only one scene, not two; Peter is no longer the central figure; and the disciples inaugurate the dialogue, not Jesus. Given that the *Epistula Apostolorum* is from the second century, it just might preserve tradition independent of Matthew, even though elsewhere the document clearly betrays a knowledge of the First Gospel.

[38] France, *Matthew*, p. 268.
[39] Jeremias, *Theology*, p. 87, conjectures that Jesus originally said, 'Cast your hook into the sea, sell your catch and pay the temple tax with the proceeds'—or something very similar. His words were subsequently altered by the introduction of the fairy-tale motif. For related suggestions see Strauss, pp. 506–7.
[40] Gerhardsson, *Acts*, p. 60, seems to entertain this possibility.

(iv) *Concluding Observations*

(1) 'From whom do the kings of the earth extract toll or tribute? From their sons or from others?' The answer is, From others, for the sons are free. Originally a parable about the relationship between God and Israel, in the post-Easter period the words have constantly been reinterpreted as equally descriptive of the relationship between God and the church. This is altogether natural. Although God has regularly been conceived of by Christians as an almighty king and stern judge, he has been primarily depicted as a loving father. The corollary of this is that those within the ecclesia have always thought of themselves as belonging to God's family ('the *sons* are free'). The roots of this theological concept—God as father, believers as sons—are to be found in the OT and Judaism. But the theme was given renewed emphasis by Jesus, who among other things instructed his followers to address God as 'abba'. Mt 17.24–7 is a faithful witness to this characteristic emphasis, as is Matthew's gospel as a whole, with its dozens of references to God 'the Father' (cf. 1, pp. 76, 79). Whether 'father/son' language should be retained by the modern church in its liturgical and theological speech is a serious question which continues to be much discussed. But the experience to which that language attests, an experience presupposed as fundamental by Mt 17.24–7, must somehow come to clear expression if one is not to make a decisive break with Matthew and his Lord.

(2) Whether the apostle Paul knew the tradition behind Mt 17.24–7 cannot be known (cf. p. 742). But his actions do illustrate our text's rejection of theocratic taxation. Paul asked for contributions for the poor in Jerusalem. But he was adamant about the voluntary nature of the work. It seems likely that, in an analogous fashion, the evangelist Matthew thought Jesus' words about the temple tax to be applicable to the church and so disclaimed legalism with respect to the gathering of ecclesiastical funds. God does not tax his children; rather does he supply benefits to them. For Matthew this must have meant that church giving should be a matter of charity dependent upon the free will of the people.

(3) 'Lest we offend them'. The temple tax is to be paid, not because it is something God requires but because refusal may cause offence. The lesson is clear. Personal freedom is delimited because it must be responsibly exercised, which means it must take into account the effect upon others (cf. Garland (v)). As Paul so plainly recognized, freedom does not mean licence. 'There is a negative legalism that is no better than positive legalism when it supposes that fundamental freedom must be

demonstrated at all costs (cf. 1 Cor 9:19ff.; also 8:1ff.; Rom 14)' (Schweizer, *Matthew*, p. 357). In our gospel the freedom of Christian sonship is not any sort of antinomianism; it is not the abnegation of tasks or responsibilities. The believer belongs not just to God but also to the church and to the world. Hence one's actions must always be weighed with regard to their broader consequences. 'None of us lives to himself' (Rom 14.7), and 'if food causes my brother to stumble, I will never eat meat, lest I cause my brother to fall' (1 Cor 8.13). 'We endure anything rather than put an obstacle in the way of the gospel of Christ' (1 Cor 9.12). Freedom is a task.

(v) *Bibliography*

R. Banks, 'Jesus and Custom', *ExpT* 84 (1973), pp. 265–9.

R. Bauckham, 'The Coin in the Fish's Mouth', in Wenham and Blomberg, pp. 219–52.

M. Black, "ΕΦΦΑΘΑ (Mk 7.34), [ΤΑ] ΠΑΣΧΑ (Mt 26.18 W), [ΤΑ] ΣΑΒΒΑΤΑ (Passim), [ΤΑ] ΔΙΔΡΑΧΜΑ (Mt 17.24 bis)', in Descamps, *Mélanges*, pp. 60–2.

Brown, *et al.*, *Peter*, pp. 101–5.

R. J. Cassidy, 'Matthew 17.24–7—A Word on Civil Taxes', *CBQ* 41 (1979), pp. 571–80.

D. Daube, 'The Temple Tax', in *Appeasement or Resistance and Other Essays on New Testament Judaism*, Berkeley, 1987, pp. 39–58.

J. D. M. Derrett, 'Peter's Penny: Fresh Light on Matthew xvii. 24–27', *NovT* 6 (1963), pp. 1–15; revised and reprinted in *Law*, pp. 247–65.

R. A. Eisler, *Orpheus—the Fisher*, London, 1921, pp. 91–106.

D. Flusser, 'Matthew 17.24–7 and the Dead Sea Sect', *Tarbiz* 31 (1961–2), pp. 150–6.

D. E. Garland, 'Matthew's Understanding of the Temple Tax (Matt. 17.24–7)', in *Society of Biblical Literature 1987 Seminar Papers*, ed. K. H. Richards, Atlanta, 1987, pp. 190–209.

H. A. Homeau, 'On Fishing for Staters: Matthew 17.27', *ExpT* 85 (1974), pp. 340–2.

W. Horbury, 'The Temple Tax', in Bammel and Moule, pp. 265–86.

R. A. Horsley, *Jesus*, pp. 279–84.

Hummel, pp. 103–6.

S. Légasse, 'Jésus et l'impôt du Temple', *ScEs* 24 (1972), pp. 361–77.

N. McEleney, 'Matthew 17.24–7—Who Paid the Temple Tax?', *CBQ* 38 (1976), pp. 178–92.

R. Meyer, 'Der Ring des Polykrates, Mt 17.27 und die rabbinischen Überlieferung', *OLZ* 40 (1937), pp. 664–70.

H. W. Montefiore, 'Jesus and the Temple Tax', *NTS* 10 (1964), pp. 60–71.

Thompson, pp. 50–68.

Van der Loos, pp. 680–7.

EXCURSUS XIV

THE STRUCTURE OF CHAPTER 18[1]

We follow McNeile, pp. 259–70, Bonnard, pp. 267–79, and HG in discerning six different paragraphs: 18.1–5, 6–9, 10–14, 15–20, 21–2, and 23–35.[2] The chapter naturally divides itself into these sections on the basis of both thematic and verbal considerations. Vv. 1–5, with their central assertion introduced by 'amen' in v. 3, feature παιδίον/παιδία (vv. 2, 3, 4, 5) and βασιλεία (vv. 1, 3, 4) and focus on the theme of imitating and receiving children. In vv. 6–9, σκανδαλίζω (vv. 6, 8, 9) and σκάνδαλον (v. 7, three times) are the key words and the passage is a warning about causing others or oneself to stumble. In this section the evangelist leaves behind παιδίον and βασιλεία for μικρός (v. 6) and ζωή (vv. 8, 9). That the third section, vv. 10–14, begins with v. 10, is shown by the first three words: ὁρᾶτε μὴ καταφρονήσητε. Here σκανδαλίζω gives way to a new verb, καταφρονέω, and the subject is no longer that of laying stumbling blocks. Vv. 10–14 are about God's love for the lost, illustrated by the parable of the lost sheep. The unity of the subsection is seen in the repetition in v. 14 of phrases found in v. 10:

10   ἑνὸς τῶν μικρῶν τούτων

   τὸ πρόσωπον τοῦ πατρός μου τοῦ ἐν οὐρανοῖς
14   ἔμπροσθεν τοῦ πατρὸς ὑμῶν τοῦ ἐν οὐρανοῖς
   ἓν τῶν μικρῶν τούτων

Thus the paragraph begins and ends in the same fashion.

With the fourth unit, 18.15–20, which gives instructions for communal discipline, we no longer read about 'children' or 'the little ones'. Instead the key word becomes ἀδελφός, 'brother'. In fact, this word occurs at least once in each of the three remaining paragraphs (in vv. 15, 21, and 35). In this way the six paragraphs of chapter 18 sort themselves into two triadic units.[3] In 18.1–5 + 6–9 + 10–14 Jesus

---

[1] Lit.: P. Bonnard, 'Composition et signification historique de Mt 18', in *De Jésus aux Évangiles*, BETL 25, Gembloux, 1967, pp. 130–40; Gaechter, *Kunst*, pp. 45–8; W. Pesch; idem, 'Die sogenannte Gemeindeordnung Mt 18', *BZ* 7 (1963), pp. 220–35; Thompson, pp. 238–52; W. Trilling, *Hausordnung*; Schweizer, *Matthew*, pp. 358–60; L. Vaganay, 'Le schématisme du discours communautaire à la lumière de la critique des sources', *RB* 60 (1953), pp. 203–44.

[2] Hill, *Matthew*, 272–7, combines 18.21–2 and 23–35 and so counts five units; so also Meier, *Vision*, pp. 127–35. Cf. Gnilka, *Matthäusevangelium* 2, pp. 119–49 (with v. 5 attached to vv. 6–9 instead of 1–4). Trilling proposes this division: 18.1–5, 6–14, 15–20, 21–35. Gundry, *Commentary*, p. 358, refrains from partitioning the chapter in order to 'honor Matthew's melding together' of topics.

[3] As also Gaechter recognizes. W. Pesch (as in n. 1), Beare, p. 373, and Gnilka, *Matthäusevangelium* 2, pp. 119–20, divide Mt 18 into two major parts, vv. 1–14 and 15–35.

issues instructions about 'children' and 'the little ones'. In 18.15–20 + 21–2 + 23–35 he speaks about one's 'brother'.

After 18.15–20, a paragraph dominated by ἐάν (vv. 15 (*bis*), 16, 17 (*bis*), 18 (*bis*) 19 (*bis*)), there follows 18.21–2, a short unit introduced by τότε. It contains Jesus' memorable saying about forgiving one's brother seventy-seven times. Lastly, serving as the chapter's conclusion, there is the parable of the unmerciful servant. The key words are several: δοῦλος/σύνδουλος (vv. 23, 26, 27, 28, 29, 31, 32, 33), ὀφείλω/ ὀφειλέτης (vv. 24, 28, 30, 34), ἀποδίδωμι (vv. 25, 26, 28, 29, 30, 34), and ἀφίημι (vv. 27, 32, 35). (Note that the first half of chapter 18 also concluded with a parable.)[4]

One final comment. 18.15–20 tackles a very difficult subject. Reproving one's brother is always a most delicate matter, and one must undertake the sad task in a spirit of love and humility. One can make the case that the three paragraphs before vv. 15–20 and the two that follow serve as buffers of a sort; that is, they emphasize the qualities which are required if one is going to be so bold as to carry out the directions of 18.15–20. Before talking about reproof Jesus goes on at length about humility (vv. 1–5), about not offending others (vv. 6–9), and about God's love for those who have gone astray (vv. 10–14). And as soon as he finishes the subject of disciplinary measures he turns to reconciliation and forgiveness. The effect is to strike a balance. Just as, in 7.1–6, the evangelist joins a logion about discernment to injunctions prohibiting judging and condemning others (7.1–5), so in chapter 18 he surrounds the material on fraternal correction with material promoting a spirit of generosity, humility, and forgiveness. In short, the way in which Matthew encircles vv. 15–20 is proof of his deep pastoral concern.

---

[4] It is also significant that both major sections terminate with redactional summary conclusions introduced by οὕτως (see vv. 14 and 35; the particle is not used elsewhere in chapter 18). Moreover, the two final sentences mention 'my Father in heaven' or 'my heavenly Father'.

XLVII

ON CHILDREN AND LITTLE ONES
(18.1–14)

(i) *Structure*

As argued in Excursus XIV, 18.1–14 consists of three subsections, vv. 1–5 (on greatness), vv. 6–9 (on offences), and vv. 10–14 (on the lost sheep). The first, which contains three key declarations (vv. 3, 4, 5), features the catchword παιδίον. The second subsection, which has three main parts (vv. 6, 7, 8–9), is united by the proverbial συμφέρει/καλόν form, which is used three times (vv. 6, 8, 9). The third subsection does not feature any catchword, but 'one of these little ones' and 'Father who is in heaven' both occur twice, in vv. 10 and 14, at the beginning and end.

(ii) *Sources*

The opening paragraph, 18.1–5, is based upon the dispute about greatness in Mk 9.33–7. The minor agreements with Luke are not impressive.[1] Matthew has treated his source rather freely. He has shortened the narrative introduction (so that it has become much less colourful), dropped the declaration in Mk 9.35 ('If anyone wants to be first, let him be last of all and servant of all;' cf. 20.26–7 = Mk 10.43–4; Mt 23.11), added the sayings in vv. 3 (from Mk 10.15 or, more likely, M) and 4 (based probably upon the Q saying in 23.12 = Lk 18.14), and omitted the end of Mk 9.37 ('and whoever receives me . . .'; cf. Mt 10.40). All of these changes can be explained in terms of Matthew's tendency to abbreviate and, above all, his desire to collect sayings about παιδία. This last accounts for the omission of Mk 9.35 and 37c–d as well as for the addition of vv. 3 and 4. The upshot is thematic unity and smooth catchword connexions.

---

[1] Wenham (v) lists the following: (1) the omission of Mk 9.35; (ii) the omission of ἐναγκαλισάμενος αὐτό, (iii) ὃς ἐὰν δέξηται, (iv) the introduction of a statement about the small being great (18.4; Lk 9.48). But the first is an improvement of the very awkward Markan sequence, the second the type of detail often omitted by Matthew and Luke on the theory of Markan priority, and the third the product of coincidental editing. As for the fourth agreement, it occurs at different locations in Matthew and Luke, there is no shared vocabulary except οὗτός ἐστιν, and the common inclusion of a saying about greatness may be ascribed to the stimulation of Mk 9.35.

Turning to 18.6–9, these are the synoptic parallels:

Matthew	Mark	Luke
18.6	9.42	17.2b, 2a
18.7	—	17.1
18.8	9.43, 45	—
18.9	9.47	—

The last two verses are Matthew's version of Mk 9.43–5 and 47. They have been partly assimilated to 5.29–30 (verses which also depend upon Mk 9.43–7). 18.7 is from Q, as Lk 17.1 shows. As for 18.6, we appear to have a Markan/Q overlap. This follows from the juxtaposition in Matthew and Luke (but not in Mark) with 18.7 = Lk 17.1 as well as from the fact that Lk 17.1–2—which lacks πιστευόντων (contrast Mt 18.6; Mk 9.42)—cannot simply be derived from Mark.[2] Thus Mt 18.6–7 is a mixture of Q and Mark, Lk 17.1–2 from Q (with perhaps a little Markan influence; see n. 2).

Concerning 18.10–14, this would seem to consist of a parable from Q (see Lk 15.3–7), an editorial introduction (v.10), and an editorial conclusion (v. 14). (That Luke might depend upon Matthew here seems quite implausible. Nothing characteristic of the First Gospel appears in Luke.) From time to time it has been thought that the differences between Mt 18.10–14 and Lk 15.3–7 are sufficiently great to disallow origin in a common source.[3] As we shall show, however, when the redactional tendencies of both evangelists are taken into account, one can without much trouble explain the deviations by way of editorial interests.[4]

(iii) *Exegesis*

18.1–14 is a block of moral teaching which has special bearing on relations among church members. Vv. 1–5 demand humility. Vv. 6–9 demand the elimination of all stumblingblocks, whether placed before others or before oneself. And vv. 10–14 demand exceptional kindness towards all believers, including—or especially—the 'least.'

παιδίον and μικρός are the key terms which hold the section together. How they relate to each other is disputed. While it is manifest that Jesus opens the chapter by referring to literal children (v. 2: 'and calling to him a child, he put him in their

[2] See further Schlosser, 'Lk 17.2' (v). It may be, however, that Lk 17.2b, ἢ ἵνα σκανδαλίσῃ ἕνα τῶν μικρῶν τούτων, derives from Mark, in which case Q would have had the equivalent of Lk 17.1–2a; so Fleddermann (v), pp. 67–8. Hence we cannot be certain that Q used the transitive form of σκανδαλίζω.

[3] Cf. Streeter, p. 265; Marshall, *Luke*, p. 600. Manson, *Sayings*, p. 283, assigned Mt 18.12–14 to M, Lk 15.4–7 to L. McNeile, p. 265: 'If the evangg. used a common source, it was in very different recensions.'

[4] See further Schmid, *Verhältnisses*, pp. 305–8, and Thompson, pp. 164–74.

midst'), by vv. 10–14 he is clearly using 'little ones' as a designation for believers. The problem is finding the point of transition. Where does the subject switch from children to believers? Some have thought v. 5 to be that point: 'Whoever receives one such child . . .' (so e.g. Zahn, pp. 575f.). According to Gundry, *Commentary*, p. 360, in v. 3 'the child already cuts the figure of a disciple.' It seems best, however, to identify the shift in subject with the shift in vocabulary. παιδίον is the key word in vv. 1–5, μικρός in vv. 6–14. In our judgement, then, the first paragraph, 18.1–5, concerns literal children while the next two paragraphs, 18.6–9 and 10–14, have to do with believers (so also Schlatter, p. 547). The use of πιστευόντων in v. 6 (borrowed from Mk 9.42) reinforces this conclusion. Only after v. 5 do we find explicit indication that believers are in the picture.[5]

Exegetes are divided over whether chapter 18 is addressed to all Christians equally[6] or first of all to ecclesiastical leaders.[7] Three considerations move us to side with those who see the discourse as aimed at every Christian disciple. First, the content of the directions does not demand a special audience. Humility, kindness, and a willingness to forgive others are required of every believer. Secondly, unlike chapter 10, where Jesus, addressing a special group, namely, missionaries, speaks to 'the twelve apostles,' his audience here is simply 'the disciples.' Thirdly, we have discovered elsewhere a tendency on Matthew's part to avoid as much as possible specialized instruction relevant for only a minority (see pp. 230–31).

ON CHILDREN (18.1–5)

This memorable pronouncement story, whose formal features we have considered on p. 750, offers moral counsel. One should turn and become like little children, for only by this means will one enter the kingdom (v. 3). One should humble oneself as a child, for in the kingdom the humble will be great (v. 4). And one should welcome children 'in my name', for to receive such a one is to receive Jesus himself (v. 5). The sequence is: entrance into the kingdom, greatness in the kingdom, service in this world.

As compared with its source, Mk 9.33–7, the following features mark

---

[5] The one objection to this is that the μικρῶν τούτων of v. 6 must take up the παιδία of v. 3. But the words are different, and μικρῶν τούτων is a fixed expression in the First Gospel which does not demand an antecedent; see 10.42; 18.6, 10, 14.

[6] So Bonnard, p. 267; Thompson, pp. 71–2.

[7] So Kilpatrick, p. 79; Martinez (v).

Matthew's account. (i) The narrative introduction (Mk 9.33f.) has been abbreviated, with the result that the rivalry between the disciples is not mentioned. (ii) The two parts of the story (vv. 1 and 2–5) have been assimilated to one another. The disciples act (v. 1a) and then speak (v. 1b). Similarly, Jesus first acts (v. 2) and then speaks (vv. 3–5). (iii) The episode commences with the disciples asking Jesus a question. In Mark they are silent. (iv) Mk 9.35 has been omitted, which makes for a smoother narrative. (The commentators on Mark are agreed that Mk 9.33–7, in large part due to Mk 9.35, is not skilfully arranged.) (v) The reference to Jesus taking the child into his arms (Mk 9.36) is missing. (vi) Two logia (vv. 3 and 4) have been introduced. (vii) Mk 9.37c–d has been eliminated.

The tradition-history of Mk 9.33–7 is complicated. Vv. 33f. probably represent either Markan redaction[8] or reproduce a narrative fragment.[9] As for 9.35–7, v. 35 is presumably a Markan insertion. Either it is based upon Mk 10.43f., or Mark has here preserved a floating logion. Is then 9.36f—often considered a duplicate of Mk 10.13–16—perhaps a pre-Markan unit? But it too has been broken down further. V. 36 could be redactional, v. 37a a saying of Jesus, and v. 37b community commentary.[10]

1. Whether, as Origen, *Comm. on Mt* 13.14, affirms, the disciples' question about greatness comes up because of the prominence of Peter in 17.24–7 (or in all of chapters 14–17 for that matter), is not clear.[11] (The ἄρα is not decisive.[12]) Matthew's text does not even reveal whether the disciples have themselves in mind or are simply speaking in general.

ἐν ἐκείνῃ τῇ ὥρᾳ.[13] For this redactional transition see on 8.13 and Thompson, p. 70. There is no parallel in Mark.

προσῆλθον οἱ μαθηταὶ τῷ Ἰησοῦ λέγοντες. Compare 5.1; 13.36; 14.15; 24.3; and 26.17 (all are distinctive, and two introduce major discourses).

τίς ἄρα μείζων ἐστὶν ἐν τῇ βασιλείᾳ τῶν οὐρανῶν; Compare Gos. Thom. 12. For other questions from the disciples see 13.10; 15.12; 17.19; 21.20; 24.3. 'In the kingdom of Heaven' has been added, as a comparison with Mk 9.34 proves. The phrase has become the cause of some contention. Is the reference to the future, that is, to who *will be* the greatest (μείζων: the comparative is used for the superlative; see on 5.19) in the

---

[8] So Fleddermann (v), pp. 58–9, and Thompson, p. 123.
[9] Cf. Taylor, *Mark*, p. 404.
[10] See further the Markan commentaries.
[11] Thompson, pp. 94–9, thinks that the parable about the kings of the earth in 17.24–7 suggests the question about the kingdom of heaven, for the doctrinal statement about the disciples' freedom 'makes them wonder about the criteria for greatness in the eschatological community . . .'.
[12] This can be a connective (see Thompson, pp. 73–4) or just a particle 'to enliven the question' (BAGD, s.v., 2).
[13] ημερα is found in Θ *f*¹ 33 700 1424 *pc* it sy^{s.c} Or. Cf. 13.1; 22.23.

coming kingdom?[14] Or are the disciples wondering about the present?[15] Have church and kingdom here become identified? ἐστίν (vv. 1, 4) scarcely solves the problem, for the futuristic use of the present is well attested in the NT (BDF § 323). As in 11.11, we side with those who adopt the eschatological interpretation, this largely because v. 3 uses οὐ μὴ εἰσέλθητε (οὐ μή with the aorist subjunctive, which is the most definite form of negation regarding the future). It should be stressed, however, that it may be unwise to set the two interpretations against one another and choose between them. Do not the disciples assume that any hierarchy in the future kingdom will be reflected in some way in the structure of the church and that greatness in the kingdom means greatness even now?

2. Jesus responds with a symbolic action, an enacted parable. He calls a child[16] and sets him in the disciples' midst. The verbal is here aided by the visual.

καὶ προσκαλεσάμενος παιδίον ἔστησεν αὐτὸ ἐν μέσῳ αὐτῶν. So Mk 9.36, with λαβών as the first verb. The presence of a child shows that our narrator was not thinking of the house in Capernaum as empty save for Jesus and the twelve.

3. καὶ εἶπεν. This shortens Mk 9.36, which has this: 'and taking him in his arms he said to them.'

ἀμὴν λέγω ὑμῖν, ἐὰν μὴ στραφῆτε καὶ γένησθε ὡς τὰ παιδία, οὐ μὴ εἰσέλθητε εἰς τὴν βασιλείαν τῶν οὐρανῶν. Compare 5.20, whose structure (λέγω . . . ὑμῖν . . . ἐὰν μή . . . οὐ μὴ εἰσέλθητε εἰς τὴν βασιλείαν τῶν οὐρανῶν) seems to have influenced or been influenced by the present verse. Our evangelist has either drawn upon M or jumped ahead to Mk 10.15 (which he will later omit: Mt 19.13–15). If the latter, Matthew has substituted ἐάν for ὃς ἄν, replaced δέξηται τὴν βασιλείαν τοῦ θεοῦ with στραφῆτε καὶ γένησθε, altered the singular παιδίον to the plural τὰ παιδία, supplanted εἰσέλθῃ by εἰσέλθητε, and finished the declaration with τὴν βασ. κ.τ.λ. instead of the simple αὐτήν. Because such changes do not seem to us to be convincingly explicable in terms of Matthean redaction,[17] we tentatively attribute Mt 18.3 to a non-Markan source.[18] It thus becomes an independent witness to the saying also known in Mk 10.15[19] (=

[14] So e.g. Zahn, p. 574.

[15] So Lagrange, p. 346, and Gundry, *Commentary*, p. 359.

[16] Sometimes in later Christian tradition identified with Ignatius of Antioch; see J. B. Lightfoot, *The Apostolic Fathers, Part II.*, 2nd ed., London, 1889, vol. 1, p. 27.

[17] *Pace* Dupont, 'Matthieu 18.3' (v), and Gundry, *Commentary*, p. 360.

[18] So also Crossan (v), p. 88, and Jeremias, *Theology*, pp. 154–5.

[19] Mk 10.15 probably circulated independently of its present synoptic context; see Ambrozic, pp. 136–8.

Lk 18.17); Jn 3.3, 5;[20] and Gos. Thom. 22 and 46.[21] In fact, it appears to be more primitive than Mk 10.15,[22] for 'to receive the kingdom' is probably a post-Easter expression,[23] and in any case it seems to be influenced by the use of δέχομαι in the surrounding verses. Jesus, as Matthew has it, probably spoke about becoming like little children.

The meaning of the saying for Matthew is plain enough. To become a child[24] has nothing to do with innocence or simplicity or sinlessness.[25] Rather, as v. 4 proves, the Matthean Jesus is calling for humility, for what Chrysostom called the 'mother, root, nurse, foundation, and centre of all other virtues' (*Hom. 1–55 in Acts* 30.3). The point, of course, is not that children are self-consciously humble but that they are, as part of society at large, without much status or position. The followers of Jesus, reflecting upon this illustration, are to rid themselves of all pride—'the root, the source, the mother of sin' (Chrysostom, *Hom. 1–88 in Jn* 9.2)—and forget about worldly standing.

But what did Jesus mean when he called his hearers to become like children?[26] A sampling of opinion includes the following: (i) He was calling for openness.[27] (ii) He was calling for trust in God.[28] (iii) He was calling for spontaneity.[29] (iv) 'To receive the kingdom as a little child is to allow oneself to be given it, because one knows one cannot claim it as one's right or attempt to earn it.'[30] (v) To be like a child is

[20] On the independence of this from the synoptics see Lindars (v).

[21] Cf. also Justin, *1 Apol.* 61.4 (a conflation of Mt 18.3 and Jn 3.3, 5?—so Robinson, *Priority*, p. 317); Hermas, *Sim.* 9.29; Ps.-Clem. Hom. 11.26; Clement of Alexandria, *Cohort. ad gent.* 9.82. On Gos. Thom. 22 and 46 see Crossan (v), pp. 90–3; and Robinson (v). Robinson shows how Jesus' saying came to be used in two different ways—one represented by the baptismal interpretation in Jn 3, the other by Gos. Thom. 22, where androgyny is the theme.

[22] So Lindars (v), with a convincing argument; see also Schweizer, *Matthew*, p. 361.

[23] Cf. J. Jeremias, 'Mc 10.13–16 parr. und die Übung der Kindertaufe in der Urkirche', *ZNW* 40 (1941), pp. 243–5. The expression occurs only here in the synoptics.

[24] In the Apocalypse of Paul from Nag Hammadi, the revealer is a little child. Is this circumstance the result of someone making Jesus a literal fulfilment of his own saying?

[25] For innocence or sinlessness in connexion with children see Hermas, *Sim.* 9.29; but the idea of the innocence of children is not often echoed in ancient Jewish texts. For this reason alone the occasional and bizarre use of Mt 18.3 as a proof text for Christian nudism (e.g. by the Adamites) is wildly off the mark.

[26] The authenticity of the saying is almost beyond question; see Bultmann, *History*, p. 105; Nineham, *Mark*, p. 269. However, Lohmeyer, *Markus*, pp. 205–6, attributes the logion to the community.

[27] So M.-F. Lacan, 'Conversion et royaume dans les évangiles synoptiques', *LumV* 9 (1960), p. 31.

[28] Cf. Perrin, *Rediscovering*, p. 146.

[29] So Neuhäusler, p. 136.

[30] Cranfield, *Mark* p. 324. This seems to be the view of most modern exegetes.

to be humble (so Matthew). (vi) According to Jeremias, *Theology*, pp. 155–6, picking up a suggestion of T. W. Manson, *Teaching*, p. 331, to become a child again means to learn to say *'abbā'* again. (vii) Schilling (v), accepting Mark's text as more original than Mt 18.3, has proposed that Jesus compared the kingdom itself to a child: receive the kingdom as you would receive a child, with affection.[31]

Our own suspicion is that when Jesus urged people to become as children he was, in effect, asking them to begin their religious lives afresh. In *b. Yeb.* 48b the convert to Judaism is 'like a new-born child.' The comparison is natural and occurs elsewhere, including Paul.[32] The point is that the sort of repentance Jesus demanded and its fruit, entrance into the kingdom, become no less significant than physical birth. The Fourth Gospel appears to have taken our saying in this fashion (ἐὰν μή τις γεννηθῇ ἄνωθεν), and Matthew's interpretation in terms of humility may also have grown from such an understanding, for the ability to go back and start one's spiritual life afresh requires above all courageous humility. We propose that just as John the Baptist, by exhorting Jews to be baptized, may have been telling them that they had to think of themselves as though they were pagan converts, so Jesus, by calling his hearers to become like children, may have been encouraging them to see their lives as being in need of a new beginning.

ἐὰν μὴ στραφῆτε may mean 'unless you are converted' (cf. Jn 12.40) or 'unless you change' (Dupont, 'Matthieu 18.3' (v)). But in Aramaic *tûb* is used alongside other verbs with the sense 'again', and the Hebrew *šûb* is employed similarly. This explains why the LXX contains 'a whole series of double expressions which paraphrase an "again" and are analogous in structure to the στραφῆτε καὶ γένησθε . . .'.[33] Thus, if a Semitic original lies behind Matthew's Greek, it would have meant 'become again like children'. Did our evangelist recognize the idiom?

'To enter the kingdom' (cf. the rabbinic 'to enter (the rule of) the future aeon': SB 1, pp. 252–3) has already appeared in 5.20 and 7.21 and will appear again in 19.23–4 and 23.13.[34] As a rule, the expression has, in the synoptics, a future sense, even when the verb is in the present tense. It is probably modelled on OT expressions about entering the promised land (1, p. 501) and on the Psalm passages about entering the temple gates (e.g. Ps 118.20).[35] It is erroneous to infer that a

[31] So also Robbins (v), p. 59.

[32] Cf. 2 Cor 5.17; Philemon 10. See Daube, p. 113; also J. Z. Smith, 'The Garments of Shame', *HR* 5 (1965), pp. 217–38.

[33] Jeremias, *Theology*, p. 155, appealing to R. Le Déaut, 'Le substrat araméen des évangiles', *Bib* 49 (1968), p. 390. He cites many texts, including LXX Deut 1.40; 2.1; Ps 84.7; 103.9; Ezek 47.6; Hos 2.11; Mic 7.19; Mal 1.4; 3.18. Contrast Schnackenburg, 'Grosssein' (v), pp. 277–79.

[34] See also Mk 9.47; 10.15, 23–5; Lk 18.17, 24–5; Jn 3.5.

[35] See further H. Windisch, 'Die Sprüche vom Eingehen in das Reich Gottes', *ZNW* 27 (1928), pp. 163–92, and J. Marcus, 'Entering into the Kingly Power of God', *JBL* 107 (1988), pp. 663–75.

spatial conception of the kingdom is implied by the notion of entrance. In the Psalms the procession of the faithful coincides with God's movement with or towards them, as in Ps 24.3–10 and 68.24–35 (cf. Isa 52.8–12). Thus, even in the phrase 'to enter the kingdom' the dynamic idea of God's kingly rule is dominant: one enters into the divine eschatological action (see further Marcus, as in n. 35; he calls attention to the Biblical texts in which people 'enter' into an action: e.g. Jn 4.38).

4. ὅστις οὖν ταπεινώσει ἑαυτὸν ὡς τὸ παιδίον τοῦτο, οὗτός ἐστιν ὁ μείζων ἐν τῇ βασιλείᾳ τῶν οὐρανῶν. For similar texts see on 23.12, also SB 1, p. 774. This is probably a Matthean creation dependent upon the Q saying in 23.12 = Lk 18.14: 'whoever humbles himself will be exalted.'[36] The evangelist has qualified 'humbles' with 'as this child' (cf. v. 3) and, in the light of v. 1 (where μείζων occurs), defined exaltation as greatness in the kingdom. ὅστις*, οὖν* (here just a simple connective), οὗτός ἐστιν*, and βασιλεία τῶν οὐρανῶν* are all Mattheanisms; and for other texts where Jesus' answer borrows the vocabulary of the disciples' question see Thompson, p. 80.

The words of v. 4 would probably have struck many first-century Jewish ears as surprising and peculiar. Even if, as we suspect, Christian exegetes have tended, for theological reasons, to overestimate the denigration of children in ancient Judaism,[37] one does not find Jewish texts in which children are examples or models to be imitated. Further, for those who took knowledge of and obedience to the law to be the essence of piety, the unlearned child would scarcely have been a natural illustration of religious greatness (cf. *m. 'Aboth* 3.11). Were then the synoptic declarations about children intended to provoke puzzlement and/or reflection? Were they even perhaps designed in part to contradict a perceived overemphasis upon a scholarly approach to faith?

5. Our pericope, like Mk 9.33–7, concludes with a promise about receiving children. The narrative logic is a bit awkward. The child is no longer a model to be imitated (as in vv. 3–4) but the object of one's action. One can argue that the inconcinnity has a source-critical explanation: vv. 3–4 are a Matthean insertion which disrupts the Markan train of thought. But perhaps this is an unfair judgement. Perhaps the evangelist saw the continuity between vv. 4 and 5 in this, that the reception of a child (v. 5) is really an illustration of the humility enjoined by v. 4.

---

[36] So also Gundry, *Commentary*, p. 360.
[37] Jeremias, *Theology*, p. 227, is typical of many when he writes that children 'were counted as things of little value'. See further the oft-cited article of A. Oepke, *TWNT* 5, pp. 636–53. France, *Matthew*, p. 270, goes so far as to proclaim that children were 'of no importance in Jewish society'.

καὶ ὃς ἐὰν δέξηται ἓν παιδίον τοιοῦτο ἐπὶ τῷ ὀνόματί μου, ἐμὲ δέχεται. Compare Jn 13.20, and for discussion of the Jewish idea of representation our commentary on 10.40–1. Matthew, working on Mk 9.37, has added καί, turned ἄν into ἐάν (so also Lk 9.48), reversed the verb and subject to give a more natural order (so also Lk 9.48; cf. Mt 10.40), and substituted παιδίον τοιοῦτο for τῶν τοιούτων παιδίων (Luke has τοῦτο τὸ παιδίον).

'In my name' is the key to this line. To receive a child in Christ's name (we take ἐπὶ κ.τ.λ. to go with the verb not the subject)[38] is to perceive Christ in that child and act accordingly (ἐμὲ δέχεται). We have here the same principle as in 25.31–46: the Son of man unites himself to others, especially the weak and insignificant, so that to show kindness to them is to show kindness to him. 'The Son of Man has made himself one with all those who objectively need help, whatever be their subjective dispositions.'[39]

We should not overlook the fact that if, in 18.5, Jesus commands the reception of children, it is not very long before he enacts his own words, for in 19.13–15 he does this very thing, that is, he receives children. Once more, therefore, Jesus unites word and deed in his own person and thereby becomes the model to be imitated.

ON OFFENCES (18.6–9)

This paragraph, which has three main parts (see section (i)), consists of sayings which use the verb σκανδαλίζω or the noun σκάνδαλον. The tone is no longer one of promise (cf. vv. 3–5) but of warning. Verse 6 demands that one not offend 'one of these little ones' and offers for motivation the spectre of severe divine punishment. The reference is no longer to literal children (as in vv. 1–5) but to certain members of the Christian community (see p. 754). Verse 7 next speaks of stumbling blocks in general and contains two woes. The subject is wider than the little ones. Finally, vv. 8–9 turn attention from others towards oneself: one must guard against one's own members and the spiritual damage they can wreak.

Mt 18.6–9 draws upon Mk 9.42–7, part of a pre-Markan collection

---

[38] Pace Hill, *Matthew*, p. 273, 'in my name' does not mean 'because I have commanded it'. Also doubtful is reference to an invocation.

[39] T. Preiss, *Life in Christ* (trans. of *La Vie en Christ*, 1952), SBT 13, London, 1957, p. 52. Cf. the parallel with Paul in Acts: 'why do you persecute *me*?' means 'why do you persecute Christians?'

of logia.[40] It was held together by catchwords: ὄνομα (vv. 37, 38, 39, 41), παιδίον-μικρός (vv. 37, 42), σκανδαλίζω (vv. 42, 43, 45, 47), πῦρ (vv. 43, 48, 49), ἁλίζω-ἅλας (vv. 49, 50). The repeated use of (ἐ)άν + the subjunctive (vv. 37, 41, 42, 43, 45, 47) also bound the sayings together. The precise shape of the pre-Markan sequence is disputed. But one has little hesitation affirming that, by means of catchword links, the complex probably grew out of the dominical triad in vv. 43, 45, and 47 (cf. Neirynck (v), p. 68, who senses in these three verses 'the rhythm of the spoken word').

The sayings in 18.6–9 would all seem to go back to Jesus (cf. Gnilka, *Matthäusevangelium* 2, p. 126). Concerning vv. 8–9, whose true meaning is not far from the parables of the pearl and treasure (13.44–6: one sacrifices all for the kingdom), 'the sharpness of the alternatives set out, as well as the form of expression, seem characteristic of Jesus' thought.'[41] With regard to vv. 6–7, Bultmann, *History*, p. 144, gave it as his judgement that their 'origin can no longer be determined.'[42] But the vividly memorable v. 6 has multiple attestation (Mark and Q; see Mk 9.42 and Lk 17.2) and was known to Paul.[43] V. 7 also has multiple attestation (Q and 1 Clem 46.8) and is in perfect accord with the proclamation of Jesus.

6. Switching from παιδίον to μικρός, and with that from literal children to the 'little ones' who believe, Jesus now warns, in the strongest possible language, against causing others to stumble.

ὃς δ᾽ ἂν σκανδαλίσῃ ἕνα τῶν μικρῶν τούτων τῶν πιστευόντων εἰς ἐμέ. So Mk 9.42a, with καί instead of δέ.[44] Lk 17.2b (from Q or Mark?) has this: ἢ ἵνα σκανδαλίσῃ ἕνα τῶν μικρῶν τού-των.[45] Note that this last lacks any reference to believing, which therefore may not have stood in Q. In any case πιστευ-όντων must be secondary.[46] Compare 1 Clem 46.8: ἢ ἕνα τῶν ἐκλεκτῶν μου διαστρέψαι. This is probably independent of the synoptics.[47] The verb (cf. 17.27 and see on 5.29) means to

[40] Discussion in E. Best, 'Mark's Preservation of the Tradition', in Sabbe, pp. 28–9; Descamps (v); Neirynck (v); Schnackenburg (v); Vagany (v).

[41] B. H. Branscomb, *The Gospel of Mark*, New York and London, n.d., p. 173.

[42] His sole reason seems to be the parallels listed by SB 1, p. 779, esp. *b. Sanh.* 55a.

[43] D. C. Allison, 'The Pauline Epistles and the Synoptic Gospels', *NTS* 28 (1982), pp. 13–15.

[44] HG on the authority of ℵ C*vid Δ it omits εις εμε from Mk 9.42. NA[26] and Taylor, *Mark*, p. 410, regard the two words as probably original. They are found in A B C² L W Θ Ψ *f*¹·¹³ Maj lat sy sa bo^pt. Certainty is impossible. Supporting HG is the possibility of assimilation to Matthew. Supporting retention is the fact that nowhere else does Matthew follow πιστεύω with εἰς. —HG also omits τούτων from Mk 9.42.

[45] The Lukan mss. disagree over the placement of ἕνα.

[46] οἱ πιστεύοντες is Christian terminology; cf. Acts 19.18; Eph 1.19; 2 Thess 1.10. So is εἰς μέ after 'to believe' (only here in the synoptics).

[47] Discussion in Hagner, pp. 152–64. The order of the clauses in 1 Clement agrees with the order in Luke.

pervert and mislead, intellectually and morally. Here, in view of the consequent punishment, it must signify causing others to lose their faith and fall away from God.

'One of these[48] little ones' appears four times in Matthew (10.42; 18.6, 10, 14), only once in Mark and Luke (Mk 9.42; Lk 17.2). The expression has, in its Matthean context, been taken to refer to missionaries (as in 10.42),[49] catechumens, recent converts, or lowly Christians, that is, those of little faith or those lightly esteemed by others. A firm decision one way or the other is impossible (see further below).

συμφέρει αὐτῷ ἵνα κρεμασθῇ μύλος ὀνικός εἰς τὸν τράχηλον αὐτοῦ καὶ καταποντισθῇ ἐν τῷ πελάγει τῆς θαλάσσης.[50] This differs from both Mk 9.42 and Lk 17.2a, which may be translation variants. 1 Clem 46.8 has this: κρεῖττον ἦν αὐτῷ περιτεθῆναι μύλον καὶ καταποντισθῆναι εἰς τὴν θάλασσαν. Matthew's words, which are based upon Mark's version, are explained by a preference for συμφέρει* as well as for the construction συμφέρει + dative + ἵνα + aorist subjunctive (cf. 5.29–30).[51] Also, κρεμάννυμι[52] is redactional in 22.40, καταποντίζομαι[53] (cf. 1 Clem 46.8) editorial in 14.30,[54] and ἐν τῷ πελάγει[55] before θαλάσσης (a fixed phrase meaning 'in the depths of the sea;' cf. BAGD, s.v., πέλαγος)[56] adds emphasis: to

[48] τούτων is found in both Matthew and Luke and may have stood in Q (but it also appears in Mk 9.42, at least according to most modern critical editions). Does a Semitic demonstrative pronoun stand behind the logion?
[49] That 10.42 need not be determinative for the meaning of 18.5 has been shown by Thompson, pp. 107–9. See our own discussion on 10.42.
[50] HG prints εις: so W Θ f¹·¹³ Maj. επι appears in D 565 1424 al. NA²⁶ accepts the reading of ℵ B L N Z 28 892 pc: περι. Is this last not due to Markan and/or Lukan influence?
[51] Note also Jn 11.50; 16.7.
[52] According to Gundry, Commentary, p. 361, 'because a millstone would not fit around a person's neck, Mark's "be placed around" requires readers to infer the use of a rope. To avoid taxing the reader ... Matthew substitutes "be hung".' We question this. The gospels sometimes require one to envisage the literally impossible (e.g. a camel going through the eye of a needle); that is precisely what makes certain sentences unforgettable. Why not here also? In both Matthew and Mark the picture could be of a millstone encompassing a neck.
[53] In Matthew the picture shifts slightly—from being thrown into the sea (Mark and Luke) to being drowned. Has the evangelist also shifted the scene from the lake (the Sea of Galilee) to the open ocean (the Mediterranean)? —For the verb cf. LXX Exod 15.4 (of Pharaoh at the Red Sea); Liv. Proph. Ezek. 10 (the drowning of Chaldeans by Ezekiel); Josephus, Ant. 14.450 (the drowning of partisans of Herod by certain Galileans).
[54] Nowhere else in the NT.
[55] πέλαγος: LXX: 2 Macc 5.21; 4 Macc 7.1; cf. Ep. Arist. 214. Cf. the rabbinic pīlāgôs.
[56] Schlatter, p. 549, cites Lev. Rab. 12.1: biplîgôs dĕyammā'.

offend one of the little ones is to commit a black sin deserving of the greatest punishment. The divine displeasure will be horrible.

μύλος means molar (cf. Ps. Sol 13.3?), mill (as in Mt 24.41), and millstone (cf. Judg 9.53—as an instrument of punishment), here the latter. ὀνικός (LXX: 0) means 'pertaining to a donkey.' Together the two words designate a large, heavy millstone worked by donkey power (cf. Ovid, *Fast.* 6.318) as opposed to a handmill millstone (cf. Origen, *Comm. on Mt* 13.17, citing Mt 24.41).[57] The picture of such a giant millstone being thrown into the sea, signifying a dark, eternal grave out of all reach, may have been common, for it occurs also in Rev 18.21 (cf. Jer 51.63–4). Moreover, the figure of a millstone around the neck was for Jews, like that of an albatross around the neck for us, proverbial (SB 1, p. 778; it referred to suffering or difficulty). The merging of the two images—millstone around the neck, millstone in the sea—is, however, something we have not found elsewhere.[58]

On the lips of Jesus, Mt 18.6 par. could have been about literal children,[59] the disciples (see on 10.42), or 'the poor' of the beatitudes.[60] In Matthew the general meaning is not in doubt: 'these little ones' are believers ('who believes in me'); and to harm them is to harm oneself, for one cannot cause others to stumble without causing oneself to stumble. Salvation is part of a social process, and there can be no thoughtlessness towards others: 'Our life and our death is with our neighbour; if we gain our brother, we have gained God, but if we scandalise our brother, we have sinned against Christ' (PG 65, Anthony 9).

Whether our evangelist had a particular group of believers—catechumens, recent converts, etc.—in mind cannot be determined (see above). One can, however, confidently state that the Pauline application of the σκανδαλίζω sayings in Rom 14.13 and 1 Cor 8.13—the apostle applies them to weak believers—is not foreign to the spirit of Mt 18.

7. οὐαὶ τῷ κόσμῳ ἀπὸ τῶν σκανδάλων. This has no parallel in Luke and appears to be editorial. It aids the transition from v. 6 to v. 7b. On οὐαί—untypically followed here by an impersonal subject—see on 11.21. κόσμος* is often redactional, as is σκάνδαλον, a word repeated three times in the present verse. On ἀπό + genitive of cause in interjections see BDF § 176.1 and 210.1. Rabbinic parallels (cf. 'ôy + lĕ + min) in Schlatter, p. 549. Rev 8.13

[57] See further SB 1, pp. 775–8. Pictures in P. J. Achtemeier, ed., *Harper's Bible Dictionary*, San Francisco, 1985, p. 636, and R. de Vaux, *Archaeology and the Dead Sea Scrolls*, rev. ed., London, 1973, plate xx (discussion on pp. 28–9).
[58] In Suetonius, *Aug.* 67, the emperor does away with several people by throwing them into a river with weights around their necks. But the weights are not said to be millstones.
[59] So Manson, *Sayings*, pp. 138–9, who has been followed by many.
[60] So Kümmel, *Promise*, pp. 93–4.

has οὐαὶ ἐκ (the closest LXX or NT parallel to Matthew's οὐαὶ ἀπό). On asyndeton see 1, p. 84, and for σκάνδαλον see on 16.23.

ἀνάγκη γὰρ ἐλθεῖν τὰ σκάνδαλα. Compare 24.6 (δεῖ γάρ ... ἀλλά); also 1 Cor 11.19 and Ps. -Clem. Hom. 12.29 (τὰ κακὰ ἀνάγκη ἐλθεῖν). Lk 17.1 reads: ἀνένδεκτόν ἐστιν τοῦ τὰ σκάνδαλα μὴ ἐλθεῖν. ἀνάγκη (= '(it is) necessary') is a Matthean *hapax legomenon* and probably from Q, although Luke's ἀνένδεκτον (= 'impossible') is a NT *hapax*. Because the infinitive + article in the genitive is characteristic of the Third Evangelist (Jeremias, *Lukasevangelium*, p. 262), Matthew has a better chance of preserving Q, although his γάρ* will be redactional.

Why is it necessary that there be σκάνδαλα? The text does not inform us. Marshall, commenting on Lk 17.1, returns this answer: 'presumably because of the evil influence of Satan in the world' (*Luke*, p. 641). While Matthew might have concurred, another response, which does not contradict that just cited, must be entertained. 24.10–11 foretells σκάνδαλα for the latter days, and these σκάνδαλα stand under the eschatological δεῖ: before the good triumphs, evil must flourish (cf. 24.6; Justin, *Dial*. 35). Thus σκάνδαλα are inescapable.[61]

πλὴν οὐαὶ τῷ ἀνθρώπῳ δι' οὗ τὸ σκάνδαλον ἔρχεται.[62] Luke, like Ps.-Clem. Hom. 12.29, lacks πλήν[63] (cf. Mt 11.22, 24), τῷ ἀνθρώπῳ[64] (cf. Mt 26.24), and τὸ σκάνδαλον (the word is editorial in v. 7a; is the singular due to the singular ἀνθρώπῳ?). All three may be redactional, and one strongly suspects that 26.24 = Mk 14.21 (οὐαὶ δὲ τῷ ἀνθρώπῳ ... δι' οὗ) has affected Matthew's formulation. Judas is in any event a perfect illustration of the tragic man through whom offence comes.

On πλήν as an adversative see Thrall, pp. 20–4, and Schenk, *Sprache*, pp. 411–12. Schlatter, p. 549, shows that *taqlā* (= 'stumbling block') followed by *'al + yād* is well attested in rabbinic sources.

If σκάνδαλα in general are inevitable and necessary (v. 7b), this does not entail that any particular individual is bound to commit them. One may, our passage assumes, exercise the will in such a way as not to lead others into sin. There is no escape from responsibility.

8–9. These two verses, variant expressions of the same theme,

[61] ἀνάγκη with the meaning of 'distress' was used of the latter days: LXX Zeph 1.15; Lk 21.23; 1 Cor 7.26.

[62] B Θ *f*[13] Maj it vg[el] sa[mss] add εκεινω after ανθρωπω.

[63] So HG, *pace* NA[26]. It appears (under Matthean influence) in P[75] ℵ B D *f*[1.13] 33 *pc* it sy[s.hmg] co. A W(*) Θ 063 Maj lat sy[p.h] read δε.

[64] The presence of this makes for a Semitic construction; Schlatter, p. 549, cites *t. Ber*. 3.20: *'ôy lô lā'ādām še*.

shift the subject and have been thought a bit disruptive (v. 10 would follow v. 7 nicely). The declaration in v. 6 has to do with offending others, that in v. 7 with offences in general. But the imperatives in vv. 8–9 demand that one rid the self of whatever in it leads to sin: response to temptation from one's members must be swift, sure, severe. Perhaps the connexion with vv. 6–7 is to be found in this, that occasions of sin in oneself lead to the stumbling of others; thus in order to avoid offending one's brother, one must first take care of oneself. (In this connexion, one wonders whether vv. 8–9 are not similar in function to 7.3–5, the parable of the log and splinter. In order to correct a brother one must first be free of his faults. Similarly here, before one undertakes to reprove a fellow believer (vv. 15ff.), one must be free of personal σκάνδαλα.)

These verses exhibit a good deal of parallelism with respect to each other. Both verses consist of a conditional clause with σκανδαλίζει followed by an imperative followed by a *Tobspruch* or 'better . . . than' saying (cf. 1, p. 525). 18.8–9 is a doublet of 5.29–30. Both passages depend on Mk 9.43–7. There is no evidence of a non-Markan source in either place. See on 5.29–30 and Thompson, pp. 117–18.

As remarked in the discussion of 5.29–30, Origen, *Comm. on Mt.* 13.24–5, argued that the body members of 18.8–9 are to be understood as metaphors and that the Pauline idea of the body of Christ is here present: the hand and eye and foot belong to the body of Christ, so the subject is excommunication. A few modern exegetes have thought this credible.[65] There is no doubting that the ecclesiological interpretation fits the context of 18.8–9, especially as the surrounding verses are about dealing with others, not oneself. But one hesitates to follow Origen for several reasons. Nowhere does our gospel refer to the church as the body of Christ; the use of the singular possessive σου after hand and foot and eye is more natural with the personal application; one presumes that 5.29–30 and 18.8–9 must have the same import, but the former in no way suggests Origen's interpretation; finally, we have argued above that the alternative approach in terms of personal virtue and vice is quite intelligible and suits the context.

εἰ δὲ ἡ χείρ σου ἢ ὁ πούς σου σκανδαλίζει σε. This line, which combines Mk 9.43a (καὶ ἐὰν σκανδαλίζῃ σε ἡ χείρ σου) and 45a (καὶ ἐὰν ὁ πούς σου σκανδαλίζῃ σε), is assimilated to 5.30 (q.v. for discussion), which has: καὶ εἰ ἡ δεξιά σου χεὶρ σκανδαλίζει σε. Our evangelist has turned the two separate Markan clauses about hand and foot—which are spoken of as though they were personified—into one clause, perhaps simply to save space. That the present indicative—one expects ἐάν + the subjunctive—'implies that scandal was a concrete problem in the Matthean community' (so Thompson, p. 112) is possible

---

[65] See esp. Via (v) and Pesch, *Seelsorger*, pp. 25–8.

but not certain. In a discussion of εἰ with the indicative of reality, BDF § 372.3 detects movement of εἰ into the sphere of ἐάν (they cite Mt 5.29), finding examples of 'encroachment on the domain of the unreal' (e.g. Mk 9.42).

σκανδαλίζει σε could mean here not 'scandalises you' but 'makes you an offence towards others'.[66] If so, then the link with vv. 6–7 would be very close: take care of yourself so that you do not become a stumbling block to your brother.

ἔκκοψον αὐτὸν καὶ βάλε ἀπὸ σοῦ.[67] So 5.30 (q.v.), with αὐτήν (sc. χεῖρα). Both Mk 9.43 and 45 have simply ἀπόκοψον αὐτόν, which is less forceful. Despite G. Stählin, *TWNT* 3, pp. 859–60, and 7, p. 352, as well as the fact that amputation was practised by ancient physicians (cf. Quintilian, *Inst. orat.* 8.3.75),[68] a literal interpretation is wholly improbable; see on 5.29 and Origen, *De prin.* 4.33. Mutilation of the physical body is no more the burden of this sentence than it is the point of the logion on eunuchs in 19.10–12.

καλόν σοί ἐστιν εἰσελθεῖν εἰς τὴν ζωὴν κυλλὸν ἢ χωλόν. Mk 9.43 has ἐστίν σε κυλλόν after the first word and lacks ἢ χωλόν; but Mk 9.45 uses χωλόν, so once more Matthew has combined the two verses. Mt 5.30 is rather different: 'For it is better (συμφέρει) for you that one of your members perish'.

καλόν followed by ἢ to denote comparison (cf. LXX Lam 4.9; Jon 4.3) is probably a Semitism.[69] On εἶναι with the dative + predicate adjective see BDF § 190.2. κυλλός (cf. 15.30–1) means 'maimed', χωλός (cf. 11.5; 15.30–1; 21.14) 'lame'. On the bizarre picture of a mutilated resurrection body (resurrection should mean no deformities; cf. Moore 2, pp. 380–87) see on 5.29. The rhetoric is unmistakably hyperbolic.

ἢ δύο χεῖρας ἢ δύο πόδας ἔχοντα βληθῆναι εἰς τὸ πῦρ τὸ αἰώνιον. Compare 5.29 (q.v. for discussion): 'than that all your body go in to Gehenna;' also Sextus, *Sent.* 13 ('Cast away every part of the body which leads you to intemperance; for it is better to live temperately without it than to perish whole'). Again Matthew has intermixed part of Mk 9.43 (ἢ τὰς δύο χεῖρας ἔχοντα ἀπελθεῖν εἰς τὴν γέενναν, εἰς τὸ πῦρ τὸ ἄσβεστον) with part of 9.45 (ἢ τοὺς δύο πόδας ἔχοντα βληθῆναι εἰς τὴν γέενναν). In doing so he has let two definite articles fall away

[66] Thompson, pp. 116–17, appealing to the causative force of verbs in -ίζω; see BDF § 108.3.

[67] W Maj syʰ bo improve by making the second word αυτα.

[68] Additional parallels in H. Hommel, 'Herrenworte im Lichte sokratischer Überlieferung', *ZNW* 57 (1966), pp. 1–23.

[69] See Black, p. 117, and Doudna, pp. 90–2. —For καλόν ἐστιν/ἦν see 15.26 = Mk 7.27; 17.4 = Mk 9.5; 26.24 = Mk 14.21.

(τάς, τούς) and preferred 'into eternal fire' (cf. 25.41)[70] to 'into Gehenna' or 'into the fire unquenchable.'

The text concerns the relation between present action and the future kingdom, signified by 'life'. The war with sin in the here and now determines one's final destiny. Every obstacle in the way of 'life' is to be eliminated, no matter what the personal cost. Nothing matters but the treasure of the kingdom (cf. 13.44). No sacrifice can be too great. The self must suffer what Symeon the New Theologian labelled ζωοποιὸς νέκρωσις, 'a life-giving mortification' (*Orat*. 57).

καὶ εἰ ὁ ὀφθαλμός σου σκανδαλίζει σε. So Mk 9.47 with ἐάν and the present subjunctive instead of the indicative (cf. 18.8 diff. Mk 9.43, 45). So also Mt 5.29 (q.v. for discussion), with δέ for καὶ and ὁ δεξιός after σου. καὶ is conjunctive and introduces a sentence synonymous with the previous one.

ἔξελε αὐτὸν καὶ βάλε ἀπὸ σοῦ. This agrees with 5.29. Mk 9.47 has simply ἔκβαλε αὐτόν. Plummer, p. 250, wrote: 'We sacrifice even the most valuable of our limbs, in order to avoid the death of the body by incurable disease. We ought to be ready to sacrifice things of still greater value, in order to avoid the death of the soul . . .'.

καλόν σοί ἐστιν μονόφθαλμον εἰς τὴν ζωὴν εἰσελθεῖν. Mk 9.47 has σέ, places the second verb after μονοφθ., and terminates the line with τὴν βασ. τοῦ θεοῦ. Matthew's 'enter into life'[71] increases the parallelism with 18.8. 5.29 has 'For it is better (συμφέρει) for you that one of your members perish' (cf. 5.30).

ἢ δύο ὀφθαλμοὺς ἔχοντα βληθῆναι εἰς τὴν γέενναν τοῦ πυρός. Compare 5.29 ('than that your whole body be thrown into Gehenna'). Matthew has reproduced Mk 9.47 but added τοῦ πυρός at the end (thus increasing the parallelism with 18.8).

Mt 18.8–9 may very well be directly alluded to in *Gen. Rab.* on 2.3: 'A philosopher asked R. Hoshaya: If the rite of circumcision is beloved why was it not given to Adam (by nature)? He replied: By the same token, why is it that you shave the corners of your head . . .? The philosopher replied: Because it grew about me in *šěṭût*. He said to him: By the same token you should have blinded your eye(s), cut off your hand(s), and broken your legs, for they grew around you in *šěṭût*.' Basser (v) has persuasively contended that *šěṭût* here means not 'foolishness' but 'offensiveness', and that the rabbinic text only makes sense with the gospel passage as its background. (R. Hoshaya was a third century Amora.)

---

[70] Cf. also 25.46 and see further Allen, pp. 195–6, and Thompson, pp. 113–14.

[71] Cf. 19.17; Tabula of Cebes 4, 5.

THE LOST SHEEP (18.10–14)

At this juncture Matthew turns to Q[72] and adopts the parable of the lost sheep (see Lk 15.3–7). He has supplied it with a new introduction (v. 10) and a new conclusion (v. 14).

In Luke, where the parable is paired with that of the lost coin, the meaning is rather different. The audience is the scribes and Pharisees, and Jesus is attempting to justify himself in the face of their criticism. Why does he associate with disreputable folk? In Lk 15.3–7 the lost sheep represents a lost sinner, and the joy of finding is God's joy at his conversion. In Matthew, by way of contrast, the parable of the lost sheep is addressed to disciples and oriented towards ecclesiastical concerns. All members of the church are specially cared for by God, who is eager to preserve his own, including 'the little ones'. Hence one should not despise 'the little ones'. Compare Argyle, p. 139: 'In Luke's version a sinner has been converted and won for Christ in an evangelical mission. In Matthew a lapsed member has been recovered for the Church and saved from destruction.'[73]

As it stands in Matthew our parable contains the theme of the *imitatio Dei* (see on 5.43–8). The shepherd recovering his lost sheep illustrates God's concern for his little ones, and his concern for such is the paradigm and illustration for a similar human concern (cf. 18.14): divine love for the lost invites human love for the lost.

The unit begins and ends with the phrase, 'one of these little ones'. So there is an *inclusio*. But is there also a chiasmus? Gaechter, *Kunst*, pp. 50f., has observed the following arrangement:

10a　one of these little ones
10b　　my Father who is in heaven
12b　　　has gone astray
12c　　　　the ninety-nine
12c　　　　the one that went astray
13b　　　the ninety-nine
13b　　　went astray
14　　my Father who is in heaven
14　one of these little ones

Is this coincidence or the result of Matthew's studied effort? (For a chiastic analysis of the Lukan parallel see Bailey (v).)

The parable is almost universally considered authentic.[74] Modern scholars are also in general agreement as to its meaning on Jesus' lips. Even though the Lukan setting (Lk 15.1–2) is perhaps editorial, it

---

[72] Gundry, *Commentary*, p. 366: 'Did children's tendency to get lost trigger importation of the parable concerning the lost sheep?'

[73] We fail to discern any good reason for Gundry's contention (*Commentary*, p. 365) that Mt 18.10–14 is a thrust 'against antinomian influences'.

[74] Cf. Lambrecht (v), p. 45; Weder, p. 173, n. 31.

seems overwhelmingly likely that Jesus composed the similitude in order to rebut criticism of his table fellowship with toll-collectors and sinners.[75] Jesus entered into close relations with certain individuals who were widely thought of as beyond the pale of proper piety and therefore fellowship, that is, as outside the flock of Israel (see on 9.10–13), and the parable of the lost sheep probably served as an apologetic for those who objected, its aim being not dissimilar to Mk 2.17: 'It is not the healthy who need a physician but the sick'.[76] (*Pace* Fitzmyer, *Luke* 2, p. 1073, the parable of the lost coin (Lk 15.8–10) probably stood in Q, immediately after the parable of the lost sheep.[77] It was rejected by Matthew because while a sheep going astray readily represents a Christian going astray, a lost coin does not.)

18.10–14 has several verbal contacts with the LXX of Ezek 34. Compare v. 12 with Ezek 34.10–11 (ἐκζητήσω τὰ πρόβατά μου) and 34.12 (ζητεῖ ... ἐκζητήσω τὰ πρόβατά μου), v. 12 with Ezek 34.13 (ἐπὶ τὰ ὄρη Ἰσραήλ), and vv. 12–13 with Ezek 34.16 (τὸ ἀπολωλὸς ζητήσω καὶ τὸ πλανώμενον). Thompson, p. 160, proposes that 'although the parable may be based on the prophecy in Ezekiel, the imagery has been modified and adapted to the Christian community'. We are not inclined, however, to suppose that the parable was composed with an eye on Ezek 34; rather, as the similitude was passed on, its lines came to be filled in by the OT text. Note well that it is Matthew alone who uses τὰ ὄρη and πλανάω. Did he perceive certain parallels and further the process of assimilation?

10. This redactional[78] introduction to the parable of the lost sheep makes for a smoother transition between paragraphs. 'One of these little ones' recalls the opening sentence of the previous paragraph (v. 6), as does 'see that you do not despise'. At the same time, the switch from σκανδαλίζω to καταφρονέω informs the readers that they have come to a new subsection. V. 10 therefore gathers up what has gone before while it also prepares for what follows.

ὁρᾶτε μὴ καταφρονήσητε ἑνὸς τῶν μικρῶν τούτων.[79] Again we have asyndeton (cf. v. 7). ὅρα/ὁρᾶτε μή* is Matthean, and 'one of these little ones'—to be repeated in v. 14, making an *inclusio*—is taken from v. 6. καταφρονέω (= 'despise', cf. 1 Cor 11.22) occurs in only one other place in the synoptics, in 6.24 = Lk 16.13, the parable of the two masters. According to Gundry,

---

[75] So e.g. Dodd, *Parables*, p. 92; Weder (v).

[76] If, behind Jn 10.1–6, there are in fact two dominical parables (as argued by Robinson, *Twelve Studies*, pp. 67–75), the second may originally have been 'on the mutual confidence between shepherd and sheep, suggesting the *rapport* between Jesus and the outcasts, which angered the Pharisees (cf. Mk 2.15–17)' (Lindars, *John*, p. 355). If so, the link with the synoptic parable is manifest.

[77] So also Polag, *Fragmenta, ad loc.* But that the two were composed at the same time by Jesus and passed on together—so Jeremias, *Parables*, p. 91—is not susceptible of proof.

[78] So also Gundry, *Commentary*, p. 364.

[79] D *pc* it vg^mss sy^c sa^mss add (from 18.6) των πιστευοντων εις εμε.

Commentary, p. 364, 'Despising connotes both an attitude of disdainfulness and injurious acts growing out of that attitude'.

λέγω γὰρ ὑμῖν ὅτι. Matthew is fond of γάρ*.

οἱ ἄγγελοι αὐτῶν ἐν οὐρανοῖς διὰ παντὸς βλέπουσιν τὸ πρόσωπον τοῦ πατρός μου τοῦ ἐν οὐρανοῖς.⁸⁰ Compare 5.8 (which promises the pure in heart that they will see God). While word statistics do not demonstrate a redactional genesis they are consistent with one.⁸¹

The motive for not despising little ones is that their angels always behold the face of the Father in heaven. It is assumed that the value of the little ones on earth is revealed by their having incorporeal representatives in heaven.

The belief that God, out of his love for mankind, has appointed for every person an angel, is well-attested in Jewish sources.⁸² It may ultimately derive from the Iranian idea of *fravašis* ('guardian spirits').⁸³ Or perhaps it is an individuation of the idea that each nation has its heavenly counterpart.⁸⁴ One assumes that the angels of Mt 18.10 are at least intercessors, mediators between God and the little ones.⁸⁵ Whether they are also to be thought of as creatures who come and go between heaven and earth ('ascending and descending') and perform the functions Raphael performed for Tobias (in the book of Tobit) is disputed, although that is the dominant tradition in Christian exegesis.⁸⁶

---

⁸⁰ B (33) *pc* sa^mss have εν τω ουρανω (assimilation to 22.30?), and N *f*¹ aur e ff sy^s sa^mss Cl Or Eus omit εν ουρ. At the end D L^c W 078^vid Maj lat sy^c.p.h bo^pt add what is traditionally v. 11: ηλθεν γαρ ο υιος του ανθρωπου (+ζητησαι και (L^mg) 892^c 1010 *al* c sy^h bo^pt) σωσαι το απολωλος. This is generally regarded as a gloss inspired by Lk 19.10 and is omitted in modern critical editions. It is not found in ℵ B L* Θ *f*^1.13 33 892* *pc* e ff¹ sy^s sa mae bo^pt Or. See Arens, pp. 180–93.

⁸¹ ἄγγελος, plural forms: Mt: 13; Mk: 4; Lk: 10. ἐν οὐρανοῖς*. διὰ παντός (sc. τοῦ χρόνου, a common idiom attested in the LXX): Mt: 1; Mk: 1; Lk: 1. βλέπω: Mt: 20; Mk: 15; Lk: 15. πρόσωπον: Mt: 10 (only here of God); Mk: 3; Lk: 13. πατήρ(= God the Father) + ἐν (τοῖς) οὐρανοῖς*.

⁸² Ps 34.7; 91.11; 1QH 5.20; 1 En 100.5; Jub 35.17; T. Levi 5.3; Philo, *De gig.* 12; T. Job 43.10; LAB 33.1; 59.4; 3 Bar. 12–13; T. Adam 4.1; T. Jacob 2.5 ('I am the angel who has been walking with you and guarding you from your infancy'); *b. Ta'an.* 11a (each person has two ministering angels); SB 1, pp. 781–3; 2, 707–8; 3, 437–40. Cf. Heb 1.14; On the Origin of the World 124.5.–17; CMC 3, 11, 12; Apoc. Paul 7–10. There are also Hellenistic parallels: Heraclitus, frag. 123; Plato, *Rep.* 620D; *Phaedo* 108B; Menander, frags. 550–1 (all people are assigned a spirit at birth); Marcus Aurelius Antoninus 5.27; Ammianus Marcellinus 21.14.3; Synesius of Cyrene, *Hymn* 4.264.

⁸³ There was a tradition that the names of angels came from Babylon (SB 2, p. 90).

⁸⁴ Dan 10.13; 12.1; Ecclus 17.17; cf. 2 Macc 11.6; 3 Macc 6.18–19; 1 En 20.5.

⁸⁵ Cf. Job 33.23; Tob 12.15; 1 En 40.6, 9; 104.1; T. Levi 3.5; 5.6; LAB 15.5.

⁸⁶ See Origen, *De prin.* 1.8.1. —Because in Jewish literature the angels are for the most part described as looking like human beings (e.g. Josh 5.13; Ezek 40.3; Dan 10.5; Mk 16.5), it was possible to develop the strange notion that an

Many modern Christian exegetes have sought to find some contrast between Mt 18.10 and traditional Jewish convictions. For example, O. Michel, *TWNT* 4, p. 653, n. 15, asserts that in Jewish sources the angels cannot see God's glory, so that when Jesus affirms that the angels of the little ones behold God, he is introducing the new idea that God's world government is for even the smallest. And Schweizer, *Matthew*, p. 367, finds highly significant the presence of guardian angels in heaven, for 'this idea is far from universal' and found only in later writings. We have serious reservations about these judgements. Schweizer is in error because in LAE 33.1 (first century) the guardian angels move back and forth between heaven and earth. And against Michel, the sources hardly allow his generalization. Our text does speak of angels seeing God.[87] But while this seemingly contradicts some texts,[88] it harmonizes with others.[89] Beyond this, v. 10b is not introduced as though it were revelation; it instead supplies a reason for the injunction in v. 10a.

Because the little ones of 18.10 are not literal children but believers, one may not infer that the angels see God because those in their care are innocents and that therefore such angels will gradually lose privileged access when those innocents grow up and grow into sin.[90] This idea would in any event not fit first-century Judaism because it did not see children as sinless. The presence of angels in heaven representing the little ones— who may even have strayed—is an expression of God's compassion for those in the ecclesia.

Following majority opinion, we have assumed that guardian angels are referred to in Mt 18.10. Because, however, one expects guardian angels to be not in heaven but on earth, close to their wards, other possibilities have been put forward. J. H. Moulton (*JTS* 3 (1902), pp. 514–27) thought there could be some connexion with the Zoroastrian notion that a part of every individual stands before the heavenly Ahura. In some texts this is a sort of heavenly Doppelgänger (cf. Mani's twin in *CMC*). More plausible (but still less than likely) is the possibility that 'their angels' is the equivalent of 'their souls' and refers to the state of the little ones in the after-life: they have become 'like angels in

individual's angel resembles him or her in appearance (cf. Acts 12.15; CMC 18–23, 32–3; SB 2, pp. 707–8).

[87] Admittedly, 'to see the face of the king' can refer to access to the king (as in LXX 2 Βασ 14.24); but such access obviously includes literal vision of the monarch.

[88] E.g. 1 En 14.21; Tg. Ps -Jon., Tg. Neof. 1, and Frag. Tg. on Gen 28.12; *Sipre* on Num 12.8. Cf. I Pet 1.12.

[89] There are quite a few texts which refer to 'the angels of the Presence' or 'ministers of the Presence' or angels who stand before God: Tob 12.15; 1QH 6.13; 4Q4001 i.4; 1QSb 4.25–6; Jub 2.2, 18; Lk 1.19; Rev 8.2; Irenaeus, *Adv. haer.* 1.14.1.

[90] For sin distancing guardian angels from God see Jerome, *In Jer.* 30.12; Basil the Great, *Hom. in Ps.* 33.5. —For the same reason our text is irrelevant for the debate on the baptism of infants.

heaven' (22.30; is it possible that in Acts 12.15 'Peter's angel' means Peter's disembodied spirit?; on people becoming angels see on 22.30).

The notion, often supported by appeal to Mt 18.10, that each individual Christian has a guardian angel, has been a not insignificant element in popular Christian piety, although it is true that the cult of the saints has worked to lessen the attention paid to angels.[91] In post-NT literature guardian angels are first attested in Hermas, *Vis.* 5.1–4 and *Mand.* 6.2 (along with angels of wickedness; cf. 1QS 3.17–25). The church Fathers discussed whether Mt 18.10 implies that every individual has an angel (Chrysostom said yes), whether adults or just children are guarded, whether wickedness can drive one's guardian angel away (Origen and Jerome so thought), whether evil individuals have over them evil angels or spirits, whether one's guardian angel was received at birth or baptism, and whether one could be looked after by more than one angel (Mt 18.13 seemed to imply an affirmative answer to this last question). The subject first received systematic treatment at the hands of the twelfth-century theologian Honorius Augustodunensis, who supposed each soul to be given an angel at the moment of conception. For Aquinas on the subject see Summa T. 1a.113. He taught that guardian angels come from only the lowest angelic ranks. Calvin, in his cautious discussion of the theme (*Inst.* 1.14.6–7), did not claim to know whether each believer has an angel; but, citing Mt 18.13 and Lk 16.22 (Lazarus is carried to Abraham's bosom by angel*s*), he held for certain 'that each of us is cared for not by one angel merely, but that all with one consent watch for our safety'. He took note in his analysis of the 'vulgar imagination', which assigns a bad angel as well as a good angel to every person. Schleiermacher, *Die christliche Glaube* §§ 42–3, regarded the Biblical references to guardian angels as incidental and affirmed that their existence is a matter of indifference for conduct and dogmatics. Later Bultmann, with his demythologization program, took the next step and denied altogether the existence of disembodied spirits. But his contemporary, K. Barth, devoted much energy to the subject of angels and regarded them as real beings created to serve God and his redemptive purposes; see CD III/3, pp. 426–608 (with many patristic citations). He nevertheless held the idea of individual guardian angels to be 'suspicious' and did not find it evidenced by Mt 18.10.

12. The parable proper begins with this verse, which poses two questions.[92] The first question serves to engage one's attention ('What do you think?'). The second question is rhetorical and presumes a positive response ('If a man has a hundred sheep . . .').

τί ὑμῖν δοκεῖ; Compare 17.25; 21.28; 22.17, 42; 26.66 (all

[91] Lit.: J. Turmel, 'Histoire de l'angélologie des temps apostoliques à la fin du Vᵉ siècle', *Revue d'histoire et de littérature religieuses* 3 (1898), pp. 533–52; J. Daniélou, *The Angels and their Mission* (trans. of *Les Anges et leur Mission*, 1953), Westminster, 1987; and P. Brown, *The Cult of the Saints*, Chicago, 1981, pp. 50–68.

[92] Questions commonly introduce parables; see Jeremias, *Parables*, p. 103.

without parallel); and Jn 11.56. The three words—by which 'the narrator shows how sure he is of the verdict of his listeners' (Linnemann (v), p. 65)—are redactional.[93] There is no Lukan parallel.

ἐὰν γένηταί τινι ἀνθρώπῳ ἑκατὸν πρόβατα καὶ πλανηθῇ ἓν ἐξ αὐτῶν. Compare Ps 119.176 ('I have gone astray like a lost sheep'); 1 Pet 2.25. Lk 15.4 reads: τίς ἄνθρωπος ἐξ ὑμῶν ἔχων ἑκατὸν πρόβατα καὶ ἀπολέσας ἐξ αὐτῶν ἕν. Luke's introduction ('What man among you having') is traditional (Jeremias, *Lukasevangelium*, pp. 197, 245), Matthew's ἐάν + γίνομαι (Mt: 3; Mk: 1; Lk: 0) redactional,[94] even though this is the only place he has τινι ἀνρθώπῳ. The Third Evangelist is also more likely to preserve Q in having ἀπόλλυμι here and later. πλανάω*[95] (cf. vv. 12c, 13b), a word the LXX uses with πρόβατον,[96] is several times due to Matthean redaction.[97] Here the word serves two ends. (i) It furthers the possible allusion to Ezek 34 (see p. 769). (ii) It emphasises that 'the disciple who goes astray can be saved from being lost through the pastoral concern of others' (Thompson, p. 157); in other words, πλανάω (instead of ἀπόλλυμι) lines up with the circumstance that 'the one sheep does not represent somebody lost (i.e., an unbeliever), but somebody in danger of becoming lost through straying (i.e., a professing disciple in danger of apostasy).'[98]

Throughout Christian history the man with the sheep has been identified with Jesus himself, and our parable has often been conflated with Jn 10 (e.g. by Bonaventure, *Lignum vitae* 13; cf. already the Gospel of Truth 31–2, where Mt 12.11 is also brought into the composite picture). One guesses that the First Evangelist likewise identified the shepherd with Jesus and took the logic of the parable to be this: God (v. 14) approves of the actions of the shepherd Jesus who set out for the lost little ones (vv. 13–14), and those who believe in Jesus must do what he did. Such an interpretation is natural in the light of 9.36; 15.24; and 26.31 (in these Jesus is likened to a shepherd) as well as early

[93] So Schulz, *Q*, p. 387; *pace* Bultmann, *History*, p. 171.

[94] Mt: 3; Mk: 1; Lk: 0. See further Schulz, *Q*, p. 387, who observes the frequency of ἐάν in Mt 18.

[95] Neither the verb nor its form addresses the issue of whether the one sheep is being led astray or simply wanders off.

[96] See Isa 53.6 and Jer 22.17.

[97] Schulz, *Q*, p. 387, and others, have asserted that Matthew's verb preserves Q: it was changed by Luke to make a link with Lk 15.8–9 and 24, where ἀπόλλυμι occurs. But Gundry, *Commentary*, p. 366, is correct: 'Luke's reference to lostness ... is not necessarily the result of assimilation to the associated parables of the lost coin and the lost son, for the association of all three parables with one another may hinge on the common element of lostness'.

[98] Gundry, *Commentary*, p. 365. Cf. Trilling, p. 112.

Christian tradition in general (e.g. Lk 12.32; Jn 10.1–21). It is also consistent with the memory that king David had been a shepherd (see esp. 2 Sam 7.7–8) and with Jesus' status as God's eschatological agent, for in Matthew Jesus is David's son, and in the OT the gathering of sheep on the eschatological mountain is prophesied (Isa 40.11; Jer 31.10; Ezek 34.11–16).

οὐχὶ ἀφήσει τὰ ἐνενήκοντα ἐννέα ἐπὶ τὰ ὄρη καὶ πορευθεὶς ζητεῖ τὸ πλανώμενον;[99] Compare 1 Sam 17.28 ('with whom have you left those few sheep in the wilderness?'). In Lk 15.4 the finding is certain: οὐ καταλείπει τὰ ἐνενήκοντα ἐννέα ἐν τῇ ἐρήμῳ καὶ πορεύεται ἐπὶ τὸ ἀπολωλός ἕως εὕρῃ αὐτό; πορεύομαι + ἐπί with accusative is Lukan.[100] For the rest the Third Gospel is probably very close to Q. If so, Matthew struck the last three words as superfluous, substituted οὐχὶ ἀφήσει for οὐ καταλείπει,[101] replaced τὸ ἀπολωλός with τὸ πλανώμενον (cf. the previous clause and LXX Ezek 34.16), and, *pace* Gundry, *Commentary*, p. 365, probably dropped ἐν τῇ ἐρήμῳ (cf. 1 Sam 17.28 and Lk 8.29 diff. Mk 5.5) in favour of ἐπὶ τὰ ὄρη (cf. LXX Jer 27.6; Ezek 34.13).[102] This last change, if such it be, may reflect Matthew's familiarity with the OT pastoral metaphor of Yahweh gathering and feeding his flock on the mountains (as in Jer 23 and Ezek 34).[103] But recall also the variation between mountain and plain in 5.1 par.

Commentators have not been at one over the question Jesus raises. Would a shepherd normally have taken the risk of leaving his flock to rescue a solitary beast? If not, then the point would be the great value of the one stray:[104] it is so valuable that the security of the others must be gambled. Attempts have been made to avoid this conclusion by postulating either mistranslation from Aramaic (e.g. Bussby (v) conjectures an original with 'walled compound') or circumstances not mentioned (Bishop (v) claims the mention of ninety-nine implies that they have just been counted and are therefore safe in the sheep-fold; Jeremias, *Parables*, pp. 133–4, supposes that the sheep would be left to the charge of others or driven into a

[99] ℵ W 078 *f*¹ Maj q sy^h have αφεις and omit και πορευθεις—which allows one to take ἐπί κ.τ.λ. with ζητεῖ and thus eliminate the problem of whether the ninety-nine were left. Other readings try to smooth out the difficulty of the future tense being following by the present tense; see Thompson, p. 156.

[100] Jeremias, *Lukasevangelium*, p. 245.

[101] ἀφίημι: Mt: 37: Mk: 34; Lk: 31. καταλείπω: Mt: 4; Mk: 4; Lk: 4.

[102] There is no suggestion that the mountains are dangerous.

[103] So Donaldson, p. 219, n. 50, rejecting Bussby's argument (v) that 'on the mountains' and 'in the desert' are translation variants. For a similar suggestion see Black, p. 133, n. 4, following, P. Joüon.

[104] See N. A. Huffman, 'Atypical Features in the Parables of Jesus', *JBL* 97 (1978), p. 211.

cave).[105] For ourselves, we think Jesus' parable presupposes assent from the hearer, which disallows finding untypical or strange behaviour. The point is not the taking of some unusual risk but the great joy at recovering the one stray. The failure to relate what happened to the ninety-nine is just a consequence of sticking to the point.

According to Linnemann (v), p. 66, 'The "1 = more than 99" is of course bound up with the situation. It is "correct" only at the moment of finding or of losing. The thing lost is an object of concern as long as it is lost; the thing found is an object of joy at the moment at which it is found. Our attitude to the object outside this setting is not an element in this general human situation which the similitude conjures up.' Compare the hyperbole in *Mek.* on Exod 19.21: 'If only one of them [the Israelites] should fall it would be to Me as though all of them fell . . . Every one of them that might be taken away is to Me as valuable as the whole work of creation.' Lauterbach comments: 'To God one Israelite is as valuable as all the tribes of Israel.'

13. καὶ ἐὰν γένηται εὑρεῖν αὐτό. Lk 15.5 has this: 'and finding (εὑρών) it he lays it on his shoulders' (cf. Isa 40.11). Matthew has probably assimilated his clause to v. 12a (ἐὰν γένηται) and maybe—although this is far from certain—eliminated the vivid image of the sheep on the shoulders (an image so important for later Christian art).[106]

ἀμὴν λέγω ὑμῖν ὅτι. Compare Lk 15.7. Has Matthew added 'amen' (see on 5.17)?

χαίρει ἐπ' αὐτῷ μᾶλλον ἢ ἐπὶ τοῖς ἐνενήκοντα ἐννέα τοῖς μὴ πεπλανημένοις. Lk 15.5–7 is very different. With the exception of μὴ πεπλανημένοις (see on 1.19 and cf. v. 12), Matthew probably comes closer to Q. Nowhere else does our author employ either ἐπί + dative to express rejoicing[107] or μᾶλλον . . . ἤ. Luke's longer and more picturesque line is full of redactional phrases[108] and has been influenced by Lk 15.9–10, the conclusion of the parable of the lost coin. In addition, 'conversion' is one of his favourite themes.

14. οὕτως οὐκ ἔστιν θέλημα ἔμπροσθεν τοῦ πατρὸς ὑμῶν τοῦ ἐν

---

[105] So also Marshall, p. 601. Cf. the modern story of the goatherd Muhammed ed-Deeb, who purportedly discovered Qumran Cave 1 while looking for a stray sheep. He had left the rest of his flock (fifty-five sheep) with two others.

[106] Linnemann (v), p. 67, regards the laying of the sheep on the shoulders as a 'decorative accretion', Matthew here being original. Cf. Perrin (v), p. 99. According to Fitzmyer, *Luke* 2, p. 1077, it may 'be a literary touch introduced by Luke, not only from the ancient Near Eastern art forms of the *kriophoros*, the figure known in ancient Assyria and Syria of the tenth-eighth centuries B.C., but in the Greek world as well . . .'.

[107] Cf. Jona 4.6 LXX; Josephus, *Ant.* 1.294; 3.32.

[108] See Jeremias, *Lukasevangelium*, p. 246.

οὐρανοῖς ἵνα ἀπόληται ἓν τῶν μικρῶν τούτων.[109] Compare Lk
15.7 (which probably comes closer to Q) and Jn 6.40 (τοῦτο γάρ
ἐστιν τὸ θέλημα τοῦ πατρός μου, ἵνα . . .). This is Matthew's
redactional conclusion to the parable of the lost sheep. οὕτως*
(cf. Lk 15.7), θέλημα + πάτρος (Mt: 4; Mk: 0; Lk: 0),[110]
ἔμπροσθεν* and πατήρ + ἐν οὐρανοῖς* are all
characteristic.[111] ἀπόληται is from Q (cf. Lk 15.4, 6, 8, 9), and
the final four words create an *inclusio* with v. 10.

The will of God concerning the little ones, that they should
not perish, becomes an imperative for the believer. The disciple
must be like God (cf. 5.48), that is, must act as God, the good
shepherd (Ps 23, etc.), acts and so share in his activity of saving
the lost.

θέλημα + ἔμπροσθεν instead of the genitive (cf. the
circumlocution in 11.26) is probably a Semitism (cf. BDF § 214.6). SB
1, p. 786, and Jeremias, *Parables*, p. 39, compare the common targumic
ra'ăwā' (min) qodam (as in Tg. Onk. Num 23.27; Tg. Isa 53.6, 10).
The RSV rightly translates: 'the will of'.

Gos. Thom. 107 contains a version of our parable: 'Jesus says: The
kingdom is like a shepherd who had a hundred sheep. One of them, the
largest, went astray. He left behind the ninety-nine and sought for the
one until he found it. Having suffered difficulty, he said to the sheep: I
love thee more than ninety-nine.' Although this is conceivably
independent of the synoptics,[112] it represents an interpretation even
further removed from Jesus' intent than Matthew's version (cf. also
Irenaeus, *Adv. haer.* 1.7.1; 1.8.4).[113] By making the one sheep the
largest, the text, from which the theme of joy has receded completely,
misses the point that 'it was not the high value of the animal that
caused the shepherd to set out on his search, but simply the fact that it
belonged to him, and without his help it could not find its way back to
the flock' (Jeremias, *Parables*, p. 134)[114]

[109] υμων (so ℵ D (*ημ.) K L W Δ f¹ 28 565 *pm* latt syᶜ·ᵖ·ʰᵐᵍ) is the
reading accepted by both HG and NA²⁶ as well as by Thompson, p. 160, n. 38.
μου appears in B N Γ Θ 078 f¹³ 33 700 892 1010 1241 1424 *pm* syˢ·ʰ co Or.
Metzger, p. 45, argues that the latter is assimilation to v. 10 ('rny Father'). But
Gundry, *Commentary*, p. 367, prefers μου on the basis of Matthew's love for
parallelism.

[110] Luke has simply 'in heaven', a respectful circumlocution which is surely
original; cf. Manson, *Sayings*, p. 209.

[111] Against Jeremias' attempt (v), p. 40, to find an Aramaic original for Mt
18.14, see Linnemann (v), p. 147, n. 8.

[112] So Petersen (v). Of the items in 18.10–14 which we have identified as
redactional, Gos. Thom. 107 agrees with two—the omission of 'Who among
you' and the use of πλανάω (= Coptic *sōrm*). There is agreement with Luke in
ἕως εὕρῃ αὐτό = *šantefhe erof* (but this stood in Q).

[113] Against Petersen (v), we cannot think that Gos. Thom. 107 is more original
than its synoptic counterparts. Cf. Perrin (v) and Fitzmyer, *Luke* 2, p. 1074.

[114] Cf. Schweizer, *Matthew*, p. 368, who writes that Gos. Thom. 107 'totally
perverts the meaning of the parable'.

(iv) *Concluding Observations*

(1) Mt 18.1–14 demands certain qualities requisite for the performance of God's will within the ecclesia. The passage is particularly concerned with those attributes and actions which will check the impulse to judge others and which will make brotherly correction, necessary as it will be (18.15–20), a true act of charity (cf. vv. 21ff.), so that there is a hedge around 18.15–20, a buffer of grace, which reflects deep pastoral concern. The way in which the evangelist has taken various sayings from different sources (Mark, Q, M) and skilfully edited them so that all is now directed to this one end justly excites our admiration. His mastery of the tradition is undeniable.

(2) Genuine humility (cf. vv. 3–4), special kindness towards children (v. 5), refraining from offending others, especially the weak or marginal (vv. 6–7), serious self-control (vv. 8–9), and heart-felt, loving concern for all fellow believers, including 'these little ones' (vv. 10–14)—all of these virtues are called forth in view of their communal relevance. In other words, Jesus' various imperatives have in view not the solitary individual but the one in relation to the many. Nothing could make clearer that the Matthean Jesus demands no flight from the world, if by that is meant a literal going out of it for the purpose of gaining solitude. The Christian lives for the common good. Indeed, there is no alternative to this, for salvation itself requires humility (vv. 3–4), and humility is, most concretely, service towards others (v. 5). Matthew we think would have agreed that 'we are members one of another' (Eph 4.25) and eagerly embraced the maxim that those who go to hell do so on their own, while those who go to heaven cannot but do so in the company of a multitude.

(3) The various injunctions delivered in 18.1–14 all centre upon either one or two related virtues: love of others and self-effacement. The two go hand in hand, not only because self-effacement without love is vain (1 Cor 13.3) but because Matthew associates both with the theme of imitation. Concerning love, Jesus commands the imitation of God (5.45–8), and this entails that one love others, for God is chiefly characterized by his unbounded love and mercy (cf. 5.43–8). In the present context God's love is clearly expressed in vv. 10–14, and no less clear is it that Jesus' disciples must follow suit as best they are able.[115] As for self-effacement (ταπείνωσις), this follows not so much from the imitation of God as from the imitation of Christ (a theme implicit in v. 5 and, more obviously,

---

[115] Cf. Theophan, *Philokalia*, Evagrius 5.6: 'Nothing so makes a man resemble God as doing good to others'.

in vv. 12–13, if one thinks of the shepherd as Jesus; see p. 773). Jesus was meek and lowly in heart (11.29), he did not wrangle or cry aloud (12.19), and he gave his life as a ransom for many (20.28). These facts become imperatives for the believer, who is to take up the cross as Jesus did (10.38; 16.24). The least becoming the greatest has no better illustration than Jesus himself (cf. 20.26–8).

(v) *Bibliography*

Ambrozic, pp. 136–58, 171–7.

S. Arai, 'Das Gleichnis vom verlorenen Schaf: Eine traditionsgeschichtliche Untersuchung', *AJBI* 2 (1976), pp. 111–37.

K. E. Bailey, pp. 142–56.

H. W. Basser, 'The Meaning of "Shtuth", Gen. R. 11 in Reference to Mt 5.29–30 and 18.8–9', *NTS* 31 (1985), pp. 148–51.

E. F. F. Bishop, 'The Parable of the Lost or Wandering Sheep', *ATR* 44 (1962), pp. 44–57.

M. Black, 'The Marcan Parable of the Child in the Midst', *ExpT* 59 (1947), pp. 14–16.

J. Blinzler, 'Kind und Königsreich Gottes nach Markus 10.14, 15', *Klerusblatt* 38 (1934), pp. 90–6.

R. Brown, 'Jesus and the Child as Model of Spirituality', *IBS* 4 (1982), pp. 178–92.

F. Bussby, 'Did a Shepherd leave Sheep upon the Mountains or in the Desert?', *ATR* 45 (1963), pp. 93–4.

Chilton, *Rabbi*, pp. 101–7.

J. D. Crossan, 'Kingdom and Children: A Study in the Aphoristic Tradition', *Semeia* 29 (1983), pp. 75–95.

Derrett, *Essays* 1, pp. 4–31.

J. D. M. Derrett, 'μύλος ὀνικός (Mk 9.42 par.)', *ZNW* 76 (1985), pp. 284–5.

idem, 'Cutting off the Hand that causes Offense', in *Jesus' Audience*, pp. 201–4.

idem, 'Fresh Light on the Lost Sheep and the Lost Coin', *NTS* 26 (1979), pp. 36–60.

A. Descamps, 'Du discours de Marc ix.33–50 aux paroles de Jésus', in *La formation des évangiles*, Bruges, 1957, pp. 152–77.

J. Dupont, 'La brebis perdue et la drachme perdue', *LumVie* (Supplément) 34 (1957), pp. 15–23.

idem, 'Les implications christologiques de la parabole de la brebis perdue', in Dupont, *Jésus*, pp. 331–50.

idem, 'Matthieu 18.3', in *Neotestamentica et Semitica*, ed. E. E. Ellis and M. Wilcox, Edinburgh, 1969, pp. 50–60.

idem, 'La parabole de la brebis perdue', *Gregorianum* 49 (1968), pp. 265–87.

H. Fleddermann, 'The Discipleship Discourse (Mark 9.33–50)', *CBQ* 43 (1981), pp. 57–75.

A. Göttmann, 'L'attitude fondamental du disciple d'après les Synoptiques', *BVC* 77 (1967), pp. 32–45.

R. C. Gregg, 'Early Christian Variations on the Parable of the Lost Sheep', *Duke Divinity School Review* 41 (1976), pp. 85–104.

J. Héring, 'Un texte oublié: Mt 18.10. A propos des controverses recentes sur le pedobaptisme', *Aux Sources de la Tradition Chrétienne*, Neuchatel and Paris, 1950, pp. 95–102.

Jeremias, *Parables*, pp. 38–40, 132–6.

Jülicher 2, pp. 314–33.

H. Koester, 'Mark 9.43–7 and Quintilian 8.3.75', *HTR* 71 (1978), pp. 151–3.

H. B. Kossen, 'Quelques remarques sur l'ordre des paraboles dans Luc XV et sur la structure de Matthieu XVIII 8–14', *NovT* 1 (1956), pp. 75–80.

Künzel, pp. 157–63.

Lambrecht, *Parables*, pp. 35–45.

R. Leaney, 'Jesus and the Symbol of the Child (Luke ix.46–8)', *ExpT* 66 (1954), pp. 91–2.

S. Légasse, *Jésus et l'enfant*, Paris, 1969.

B. Lindars, 'John and the Synoptic Gospels: A Test Case', *NTS* 27 (1981), pp. 287–94.

Linnemann, *Parables*, pp. 65–73.

E. R. Martinez, 'The Interpretation of οἱ μαθηταί in Matthew 18', *CBQ* 23 (1961), pp. 281–92.

J. Monnier, 'Sur la grâce, à propos de la parabole de la brebis perdue', *RHPR* 16 (1936), pp. 191–5.

F. Neirynck, 'The Tradition of the Sayings of Jesus: Mark 9.33–50', *Concilium* 20 (1966), pp. 62–74.

D. Patte, 'Jesus' Pronouncement about entering the Kingdom like a Child: A Structural Exegesis', *Semeia* 29 (1983), pp. 3–42.

W. Pesch, *Seelsorger*.

W. L. Petersen, 'The Parable of the Lost Sheep in the Gospel of Thomas and the Synoptics', *NovT* 23 (1981), pp. 128–47.

V. K. Robbins, 'Pronouncement Stories and Jesus' Blessing of the Children: A Rhetorical Approach', *Semeia* 29 (1983), pp. 43–74.

J. M. Robinson, 'The Formal Structure of Jesus' Message', in *Current Issues in New Testament Interpretation*, ed. W. Klassen and G. F. Snyder, New York, 1962, pp. 91–110.

F. A. Schilling, 'What means the Saying about receiving the Kingdom of God as a Little Child?', *ExpT* 77 (1965), pp. 56–8.

J. Schlosser, 'Lk 17.2 und die Logienquelle', *SNTU* 8 (1983), pp. 70–8.

W. Schmidt, 'Der gute Hirte: Biblische Besinnung über Lukas 15.1–7', *EvTh* 24 (1964), pp. 173–7.

R. Schnackenburg, 'Mk 9.33–50', in *Synoptischen Studien*, ed. J. Schmid and A. Vögtle, Munich, 1953, pp. 184–206; reprinted in *Schriften*, pp. 129–54.

idem, 'Grosssein im Gottesreich', in Schenke, *Studien*, pp. 269–82.

F. Schnider, 'Das Gleichnis vom verlorenen Schaf und seine Redaktoren', *Kairos* 19 (1977), pp. 146–54.

Schülz, *Q*, pp. 387–91.

Schweizer, *Gemeinde*, pp. 106–14.

G. Stählin, *Skandalon*, Gütersloh, 1930.

Thompson, passim.

Trilling, pp. 106–13.

Trilling, *Hausordnung*.

L. Vaganay, 'Le schématisme du discours communautaire à la lumière de la critique des sources', *RB* 60 (1953), pp. 203–44.

D. O. Via, 'The Church as the Body of Christ in the Gospel of Matthew', *SJT* 11 (1958), pp. 271–86.

Weder, pp. 168–77.

D. Wenham, 'A Note on Mark 9.33–42/Matt 18.1–6/Luke 9.46–50', *JSNT* 14 (1982), pp. 113–18.

Zumstein, pp. 396–405, 416–21.

XLVIII

RECONCILIATION AND FORGIVENESS
(18.15–35)

(i) *Structure*

As urged in Excursus XIV, Mt 18.15–35 falls into three sections of unequal length. The first paragraph runs from v. 15 to v. 20 and outlines the method for admonishing a brother who has sinned. This is followed by vv. 21–2, which call for a spirit of unbounded forgiveness. The whole unit ends with the parable of the unforgiving servant, vv. 23–35.

(ii) *Sources*

18.15 is reminiscent of Lk 17.3, 18.21–2 of Lk 17.4. The remainder of the material is without parallel. This means that the parable in vv. 23–35 is to be assigned to M (we reject the hypothesis of a redactional origin; see below). As for the heterogeneous logia gathered in 18.15–22, Streeter, pp. 257–8, 281–2, thought they also came from M. Gundry, *Commentary*, pp. 367–71, on the other hand, regards 18.15–22 as a Matthean expansion of the material more faithfully preserved in Lk 17.3–4 (= Q). Our own suggestion is that vv. 15–17 and 21–3 (without the narrative framework) were taken from Q^{mt} and that v. 18 is a redactional doublet of the saying in 16.19.[1] Only vv. 19–20 should be classified as M material (cf. Brooks, pp. 105–6). The evangelist probably knew them as oral tradition. Whether the two verses were already joined before Matthew cannot be determined.

REPROVING A BROTHER (18.15–20)

This paragraph sets down the community rules for dealing with trouble between Christian brothers. If one brother has sinned against another, the offended party should first seek reconciliation in private. If this initial attempt fails, the offended

---

[1] Catchpole (v) argues unpersuasively that Q had a portion consisting of something close to Lk 17.3 + Mt 18.16–17 + Lk 17.4. Gnilka, *Matthäusevangelium* 2, pp. 135–6, assigns 18.15–17 to M.

should next seek the aid of another brother, maybe two (cf. Deut 19.15), and try again. If that likewise does not produce results, the matter must be brought before the whole community. If, after that, and despite all the well-intentioned effort, the sinner remains recalcitrant, he should be treated as 'a toll-collector and Gentile'. Description of this whole procedure, recounted in vv. 15–17, is followed by three verses which ground the authority of the church in theological propositions.

15. How does a Christian respond to a personal offence committed by a fellow believer? One is to seek reconciliation by bringing the wrongdoer to penitence. In other words, the offended brother is to imitate the shepherd of vv. 10–14 and go after the one stray sheep (cf. Thompson, p. 187).[2]

This is the first of eight consecutive sentences or clauses which recount first a circumstance and secondly a (possible) result. Each circumstance is introduced with ἐάν, and each result clause is introduced by a verb (ὕπαγε, ἐκέρδησας, παράλαβε, εἰπέ, ἔστω, ἔσται, ἔσται, γενήσεται).

ἐὰν δὲ ἁμαρτήσῃ εἰς σὲ ὁ ἀδελφός σου.[3] Compare T. Gad. 6.3 (καὶ ἐὰν ἁμάρτῃ εἰς σέ). ἁμαρτάνω + εἰς + personal pronoun (cf. v. 21) is common in the LXX (e.g. Gen 20.6, 9; 43.9, etc.; cf. ḥāṭā̄ + lě). The meaning is: 'sin against someone'. The parallel in Lk 17.3 lacks δέ and εἰς σέ and uses the second aorist subjunctive (ἁμάρτῃ) instead of the first. ἐάν + the aorist subjunctive occurs nine times in vv. 15–20 and hence characterizes the unit (cf. Thompson, p. 176). On the use of 'brother' as a catchword in the last half of chapter 18 see p. 750. Here it clearly means 'Christian brother' (cf. 1, pp. 512–13).

Because we accept the reading εἰς σέ as original (see n. 3), the sin—which must be both serious and intentional to be subject to the following regulations—is specifically that committed against a Christian brother. Further, the offence is not of a public nature, otherwise the initial concern for privacy would be out of place.

ὕπαγε ἔλεγξον αὐτὸν μεταξὺ σοῦ καὶ αὐτοῦ μόνου. Compare Lev 19.17 (LXX: ἐλεγμῷ ἐλέγξεις τὸν πλησίον σου; on this and

---

[2] There is no real contradiction with the prohibition against judging in 7.1–5; see vol. 1, pp. 668–9, 673–4; Schlatter, p. 556.

[3] ℵ B f¹ pc sa bo^pt Or Cyr omit εις σε. NA²⁶ puts the words in brackets. Many modern commentators deny their authenticity and suggest influence from the εἰς ἐμέ of v. 21. But their omission can be explained as assimilation to Lk 17.3 (so HG) or as the product of a desire for a wider application (like that in *Regula S. Benedicti* 23). We concur with Gundry, *Commentary*, p. 367: the use of 'between you and him alone' in the next clause and the subject of the following paragraph, which is about a brother sinning against a brother, both favour the originality of εις σε.

on rebuke in Judaism see on v. 17). Matthew's line is longer
than the simple command in Luke: ἐπιτίμησον αὐτῷ. If Q had
ἐπιτιμάω instead of ἐλέγχω (but see below), then the First
Evangelist has conformed his text to LXX Lev 19.17. On the use
of a simple pronoun instead of the reflexive (cf. 17.27) see
1, p. 629.

Presumably the substance of Matthew's line comes from Qᵐᵗ. ὕπαγε
might be considered redactional (see on 4.10); but ἐλέγχω is a
Matthean *hapax*, and the only other appearance of μεταξύ (in 23.35)
is from Q. Also, μόνος is more often than not from the tradition
(4.4 = Lk 4.4; 4.10 = Lk 4.8; 14.23 = Mk 4.46–7; 17.8 = Mk 9.8). Its only
two clearly redactional uses (12.4; 24.36) belong to the construction, εἰ
μὴ μόνος (contrast 18.15).

The fundamental meaning of ἐλέγχω (most often in the LXX
for the *hiphil* of *yākah*) is 'to lay open, expose, uncover, reveal,
demonstrate the mistake or guilt of another'; and 'applied to
the guilty person, it means "to convince him of his objective
mistake by furnishing evidence of his culpability".... Therefore,
the individual disciple is commanded to approach his brother
and attempt to expose his guilt in such a way as to persuade
him of his sin'.[4]

ἐάν σου ἀκούσῃ, ἐκέρδησας τὸν ἀδελφόν σου. This line, not
v. 17, states the result hoped for. Lk 17.3 is rather different:
'and if he repents, forgive him' (cf. T. Gad. 6.3). Given Luke's
fondness for μετανοέω (Mt: 5; Mk: 2; Lk: 9), his version may
not be just a simple reproduction of Q (cf. Fitzmyer, *Luke* 2,
p. 1139).

ἀκούσῃ means more than 'he hears'. The verb has nearly the
connotation of 'obey'. 'He heeds' would be a good translation
(cf. 10.14). For κερδαίνω (only here in Matthew with personal
object) + τινά see also 1 Cor 9.19–22 and 1 Pet 3.1. The
combination does not occur in the LXX. Note that ἀδελφός (*bis*
in v. 15) underlines the familial character of the Christian
community (cf. 12.46–50) and strengthens the link to Lev 19.17,
where τὸν ἀδελφόν σου occurs. Concerning ἐκέρδησας, Bengel,
ad loc., aptly wrote: 'The healed body of a sick man does not
become the property of the physician; a house does not become
the property of him who extinguishes the fire in it.... But the
man whom I have *gained* becomes in some sense my own'.

16. ἐάν δὲ μὴ ἀκούσῃ. V. 15c (introduced by ἐάν δὲ
ἀκούσῃ) made one possible eventuality explicit (the offender
accepts reproof). Now, in v. 16a, we come to the other, less
happy alternative: persuasion has failed.

[4] So W. G. Thompson, p. 178.

παράλαβε μετὰ σεαυτοῦ ἔτι ἕνα ἢ δύο.[5] Compare LXX Gen 22.3: παρέλαβε δὲ μεθ' ἑαυτοῦ δύο παῖδας. Although παραλαμβάνω* is often editorial in the First Gospel, it is followed by μετά only here and in 12.45 = Lk 11.26 (Q). ἔτι is redactional in 12.46; 17.5; and 19.20.

There is a parallel of sorts in the Talmud: 'Samuel said: Whoever sins against his brother, he must say to him, I have sinned against you. If he hears, it is well; if not, let him bring others, and let him appease him before them' (y. Yoma 45c). In this, however, it is the offending person who takes the initiative, not the offended. Matthew's text is really much closer to what we find in the Dead Sea Scrolls.[6] In these reproof of an erring brother is made in front of witnesses (the number is not specified) before the leaders of the community are presented with the problem. See further below, on v. 17.

ἵνα ἐπὶ στόματος δύο μαρτύρων ἢ τριῶν σταθῇ πᾶν ῥῆμα. This alludes to Deut 19.15 (cf. 17.6) in perhaps a non-LXX version (see 1, p. 55; Luc. has: δύο μαρτύρων ἢ τριῶν, the LXX: δύο μαρτύρων καὶ ἐπὶ στόματος τριῶν μαρτύρων).

ἐπὶ στόματος (='al pî) means, by metonymy, what the mouth utters (cf. Lk 19.22; T. Job 38.2). 'Two or three' probably means 'two or more',[7] but not more than a few. ῥῆμα (=dābār) here means not 'word' but 'thing' or 'matter' (cf. BAGD, s.v.).

According to Beare, p. 379, the citation of Deut 19.15 is not pertinent because whereas the OT text has to do with witnesses of a crime, in Mt 18.15-17 'the others are brought along not to confirm the evidence that an offence has been committed but to make it unnecessary to bring a charge at all'. One wonders whether this is a fair criticism. Anyone familiar with the exegetical methods used in the Dead Sea Scrolls or the Talmud knows well enough that original context scarcely determined later application. And with reference to Deut 19.15 in particular, although its legal application was not lost sight of,[8] it was clearly thought of as enshrining a general principle with wide relevance. Thus, for example, Deut 19.15 no doubt played a rôle in the eschatological expectation of 'two witnesses' (Rev 11), and in T. Abr. 13, rec. A, the OT verse is cited as support for the strange idea that there will be three judges or groups of judges in the afterlife—Abel, the angels, God. In addition, some ancient and modern commentators have, perhaps rightly, claimed that the two or three witnesses of 2 Cor 13.1 are in fact not individuals but rather Paul's three visits to the

[5] Thompson, p. 180, n. 18 prefers σου after μετα (so P⁴⁴ᵛⁱᵈ B (both with a different word order) א D W Maj) on the ground that it is not classical. Cf. NA²⁶.

[6] Yet we caution that very little is known about how the synagogue dealt with offenders in the first century; see Davies, SSM, p. 224.

[7] Cf. B. S. Jackson, '"Two or Three Witnesses"', in Essays in Jewish and Christian Legal History, SJLA 10, Leiden, 1975, pp. 153–71.

[8] Cf. Num 35.30; Deut 17.6; 11QTemple 61.6–7; 64.8–9; Josephus, Ant. 4.219; SB 1, pp. 790–1.

community.[9] Whether that be so or not, Mt 18.16 is not the only ancient text to enlarge the original horizon of Deut 19.15; and both 2 Cor 13.1 and 1 Tim 5.19 prove that Matthew was not the first to draw on Deut 19.15 with reference to church discipline.[10]

17. ἐὰν δὲ παρακούσῃ αὐτῶν, εἰπὲ τῇ ἐκκλησίᾳ. Παρακούω[11] appears only twice in our gospel, both times in 18.15–17. On ἐκκλησία see on 16.18. The local community is here meant, not the church universal. Its 'rôle is not to rebuke or condemn, but rather to support the individual disciple in his final attempt to convince and reconcile his brother. For this larger assembly adds still more authority to his words' (Thompson, p. 184). παρακούω here means, as it does uniformly in the LXX, 'hear without heeding' (cf. Swete, p. 106). It expresses a deliberateness not so clearly conveyed by the μὴ ἀκούσῃ of v. 16.

ἐὰν δὲ καὶ τῆς ἐκκλησίας παρακούσῃ, ἔστω σοι ὥσπερ ὁ ἐθνικὸς καὶ ὁ τελώνης. Compare 5.37, and for the meaning of ἐθνικός and τελώνης see on 5.46–7. The definite articles (ὁ, *bis*) are generic.

Matthew likes ὥσπερ,* and ἐθνικός* may be reckoned among his favourite words. Probably, therefore, our line has been reformulated by him (cf. Brooks, p. 102).

To treat someone as a Gentile and toll-collector would involve the breaking off of fellowship and hence mean exclusion from the community—no doubt in hope that such a severe measure (it would have dire social and probably economic consequences) would convict the sinner of his sin and win him back (cf. 2 Thess 3.14; Titus 1.13; Calvin, *Inst.* 4.12.5). The passage is therefore about excommunication. Once a brother has refused to heed the whole church, there can be no appeal to a higher authority: the matter has been settled. (As against Thompson, p. 185, we find it difficult to think that an 'official' church censure is not the topic of this verse. In his judgement, since our text says only that the offended brother is to regard the sinner as a toll-collector and Gentile, the response of the community is not considered. But does it make sense to tell only one person to decline fellowship with another? 'The discipline of "shunning" a fellow Christian would not be effective unless all the other members agreed to implement the decision'.[12])

[9] See B. S. Jackson, '*Testes Singulares* in Early Jewish Law and the New Testament', in *Essays* (as in n. 7), pp. 172–201.
[10] See further H. van Vliet, *No Single Testimony: A Study on the Adoption of the Law of Deut. 19:15 Par. into the New Testament*, Utrecht, 1958.
[11] Mt: 2; Mk: 1 (5.36); Lk: 0; LXX: 6–7, for several Hebrew words.
[12] So J. P. Meier, in Brown and Meier, *Antioch*, p. 70.

The command to reprove a brother has a long history in Jewish literature.[13] The key text is Lev 19.15–18, which includes (v. 17) 'You shall not hate your brother in your heart, but you shall reprove your neighbour, lest you bear sin because of him'.

The second imperative in v. 17—'you shall reprove your neighbour'—has parallels in the wisdom tradition (cf. Prov 3.12; 25.9–10; 27.5–6; Ecclus 20.2), as does the command not to hate one's brother in the heart (cf. Prov 10.18; 26.24–5). The two themes are brought together in Ecclus 19.13–20.2, where reproving another is considered an antidote for anger (cf. Lev 19.17c: 'lest you bear sin because of him'). These themes are also taken up in T. Gad 4 and 6, where dependence upon Lev 19.15–18 is manifest. Again we find the need for reproof connected with the command to love. Particularly striking as background for the gospels is T. Gad 6.3–5: 'Love one another from the heart . . . and if anyone sins against you, speak to him in peace. Expel the venom of hatred, and do not harbour deceit in your heart. If anyone confesses and repents, forgive him. If anyone denies his guilt, do not be contentious with him, otherwise he may start cursing, and you would be sinning doubly. In a dispute do not let an outsider hear your secrets . . .'. The parallels to Mt 18.15–17 are remarkable and include mention of the possibility that the offender may not repent (cf. b. 'Arak. 16b). Note also the demand for secrecy: this recalls the first step of Mt 18.15–17, in which the offended party must first try to settle the dispute in private.

T. Gad 6 has nothing to do with a formal or judicial process. In the Dead Sea Scrolls it is otherwise. The rebuke commanded by Lev 19.17 becomes, presumably because of Lev 19.15 ('You shall do no injustice in mišpāṭ'), part of a formal procedure.[14] See 1QS 5.24–6.1 and CD 9.2–8 (discussion in Davies, SSM, pp. 221–4). If one has a complaint against another, one first takes up the matter with him; that is, one reproves him according to Lev 19.17. If this does not have its intended effect, then the matter must be brought before the community. This brings us very close to Matthew's text. Whether or not one should postulate sectarian influence upon Matthew's tradition is unclear (see further section (iv)). One cannot, however, doubt that Mt 18.15–17 has a long pre-history in Judaism and must have been composed by an individual heavily influenced by Jewish tradition. Here we have one of the many reasons for characterizing M material as Jewish, or as stemming from a Jewish-Christian community.

Beare, p. 380, speaks for many when he writes: 'It is striking that the action [recounted in Mt 18.17] is to be taken by the local community, with no hint of a council of elders, let alone an authoritative officer, like a bishop. Matthew insists on the equality of all members . . .'. This is an argument from silence, and whether 18.15–20 really implies a 'democratic' institution is problematic. Could one not just as easily assert that the presence of leaders is taken for granted? It is the better

---

[13] For what follows see esp. J. L. Kugel, 'On Hidden Hatred and Open Reproach: Early Exegesis of Leviticus 19.17', HTR 80 (1987), pp. 43–61.

[14] L. H. Schiffmann, Sectarian Law in the Dead Sea Scrolls, Chico, 1983, pp. 89–109.

part of wisdom to recognize with Thompson, p. 184, that 'Matthew's intention was not to describe the structure of the local community, but rather to emphasize its rôle in the final attempt at reconciliation'.

18. ἀμὴν λέγω ὑμῖν. See on 5.18.

ὅσα ἐὰν δήσητε ἐπὶ τῆς γῆς ἔσται δεδεμένα ἐν τῷ οὐρανῷ, καὶ ὅσα ἐὰν λύσητε ἐπὶ τῆς γῆς ἔσται λελυμένα ἐν τῷ οὐρανῷ.[15] In the discussion of 16.19 (q.v.) we outlined in detail the possible interpretations of 'binding' and 'loosing'. Our main conclusion there—namely, Peter has the authority to 'bind' and 'loose' by issuing authoritative halakah—leads us to affirm that here the meaning is this: the halakhic decisions of the community have the authority of heaven itself. In context the reference is to the church's verdict on the behaviour of an individual Christian. (We take v. 18 to follow v. 17 closely. It does not apply to the actions described in vv. 15 and 16).

The differences between 18.18 and 16.19 are minor: ὅσα (*bis*) in 18.18, ὅ (*bis*) in 16.19[16]; the plural δήσητε in 18.18, the singular δήσῃς in 16.19 (the reasons for this change are manifest); τῷ οὐρανῷ (*bis*) in 18.18, τοῖς οὐρανοῖς (*bis*) in 16.19 (the singular is probably original, the plural due to the τῶν οὐρανῶν of 16.19a); the plural λύσητε in 18.18, the singular λύσῃς in 16.19 (again, the reason for the difference is obvious). Because 16.19 has so many points of contact with the verses before it, and because 18.18, on the other hand, is more obscure and has no organic links with its present context (cf. Thompson, p. 194), we infer, with Zimmermann (v), that 18.18 is Matthew's own insertion, his revised edition of 16.19 (cf. p. 639, n. 133).

19. πάλιν ἀμὴν λέγω ὑμῖν ὅτι.[17] Compare 18.18; 19.23, 28; T. Job 37.8 (καὶ πάλιν λέγω σοι). Whether πάλιν here equals *ôd* and means 'again' (as in 19.24) or (as in 4.8) carries the sense of the Aramaic *tûb* = 'then' (so MHT, p. 32) is unclear. In any case πάλιν κ.τ.λ. links originally separate traditions. On 'amen' see on 5.18.

ἐὰν δύο συμφωνήσωσιν ἐξ ὑμῶν ἐπὶ τῆς γῆς περὶ παντὸς πράγματος οὗ ἐὰν αἰτήσωνται, γενήσεται αὐτοῖς παρὰ τοῦ πατρός μου τοῦ ἐν οὐρανοῖς. Compare Ignatius, *Eph.* 5.2 ('if the prayer of one or two has so much force'). The notion that the prayer of several outweighs the prayer of one was probably a commonplace (cf. SB 1, pp. 793–4).

---

[15] So HG. NA[26] omits τω both times, following B Θ f[13] *pc.*

[16] ὅσα/ὅσους ἐάν (Mt: 5) is less characteristic of Matthew's style than is ὅς/ὅστις ἐάν (Mt: 15).

[17] NA[26] puts αμην in brackets. It is missing from ℵ D L Γ f[1] 892 *al* lat sy[p] bo.

ἐπὶ τῆς γῆς and ἐν οὐρανοῖς (cf. 18.10, 14) should probably be ascribed to the redactor. They create catchword links to the preceding saying and belong to Matthew's favourite vocabulary (1, pp. 77–9). For the rest, δύο does not precisely match the δύο ἢ τριῶν of v. 17; only here in Matthew do we find συμφωνέω + περί (common classical usage); πρᾶγμα (cf. ῥῆμα in v. 16; also 1QS 6.1) is a Matthean *hapax legomenon*; αἰτέομαι (Mt: 6, Mk: 6; Lk 3) is not clearly redactional anywhere else;[18] and 18.19 is the only verse in Matthew with the construction, γίνομαι + dative + παρά. Perhaps the pre-Matthean tradition (M) had this: 'If two of you agree concerning anything which they ask, it will be done for them' (cf. 7.7 = Lk 11.9; Mk 11.24).

'On the earth' qualifies 'you', not 'agree', just as 'in the heavens' qualifies 'my Father' (cf. vv. 10, 14). On the connexion between omnipotent prayer and the forgiveness of one's brother (the topic of the next paragraph) see 1, pp. 616–17. That connexion holds here. The power of the community depends upon the spiritual harmony (συμφωνέω) of its members, a harmony which must include the practice of forgiveness (vv. 21–35). One is reminded of Gos. Thom. 48. 'If two make peace with each other in this one house, they will say to the mountain, "Move away" and it will move away' (cf. Mart. Montanus and Lucius 10).

Matthew has evidently added v. 19 and the next verse to the section on reproof. As it stands, v. 19 clarifies v. 18 by stating that agreement among believers on earth will have its sure effect in heaven. But v. 19, which, detached from its context, would concern communal prayer in general, originally had a wider scope than v. 18, which is about communal discipline in particular. It is likely that v. 19 at one time offered assurance or encouragement: even if only two agree on something, it will be done for them.

Whether the saying goes back to Jesus cannot be determined; but Jesus did make large promises about prayer (see e.g. 17.20), and our verse is conceivable as a promise to missionaries (which Jesus, according to Mk 6.7, sent out 'two by two'): take courage on your journeys, for God will hear your prayers.

Derrett (v), denies that vv. 19–20 concern prayer: the two in agreement are the offender and offended of vv. 15–17, αἰτήσωνται refers to pursuit of a judicial matter, γενήσεται κ.τ.λ. means God will ratify the outcome, and the 'two or three' of v. 20 are impartial judges to the dispute (cf. Sand, *Matthäusevangelium*, p. 374). But v. 17 refers to taking matters before the church, not judges. And is it not more natural to identify the 'two or three' of v. 20 with the 'two' of v. 19, as commentators throughout the ages have done?

20. The paragraph ends with a promise that the risen Christ

---

[18] In 27.20 it seems to be borrowed from Mk 15.8 (cf. Gundry, *Commentary*, p. 563).

will be present where two or three are gathered 'in his name'. Following upon v. 19 the meaning is that the community's prayer becomes Jesus' prayer, and his prayer cannot but be answered.

οὐ γάρ εἰσιν δύο ἢ τρεῖς συνηγμένοι εἰς τὸ ἐμὸν ὄνομα.[19] Compare Eccles 4.12; MT Jer 3.17 ('all the nations shall gather in the name of the Lord in Jerusalem'); Acts 4.31 (ἦσαν συνηγμένοι). 'Two or three' presumably means, as in v. 16, 'two or more', and given the broader context the verse does nothing to promote 'individualism' or an anti-ecclesiastical attitude (see R. Pesch (v)).

On the 'name' of Christ in the First Gospel see on 7.22 and 28.19 (cf. 10.41–2; 19.29). (Nowhere else in Matthew do we find εἰς τὸ ἐμὸν ὄνομα (cf. lišmî).) συνάγω (see on 2.4) + εἰς usually has reference to gathering in a place (cf. 3.12; T. Job 28.6). But Thompson, p. 197, citing Rev 16.14 and 20.7–8, where εἰς after συνάγω expresses the reason for gathering, argues that here the meaning is this: 'two or three disciples gather together to invoke the name of Jesus'. Most commentators seem rather to assume that 'gathered in my name' simply refers to the act of coming together as Christians: 'For where two or three are gathered with reference to me' (cf. H. Bietenhard, TWNT 5, p. 274). But it is worth considering whether 'in my name' is not here used as in 7.22: 'in the power of my name' (cf. 1 Cor 5.4).

ἐκεῖ εἰμι ἐν μέσῳ αὐτῶν.[20] Compare Ezek 43.7; Joel 2.27 (an eschatological promise); Zech 2.10–11 (an eschatological promise); 11QTemple 46.12 ('ăšer 'ānôkî šōkēn bĕtôkmâ, with reference to the temple sanctuary). This is the sole use of ἐκεῖ after οὗ in Matthew, but ὅπου ... ἐκεῖ does appear in 6.21 (q.v.).[21]

Just as the presence of the risen Christ[22] is not confined to any particular space or time, so is it independent of numerical considerations (cf. Schlatter, p. 558).

V. 20 especially recalls a saying in m. 'Abot 3.2, recorded in the name of R. Hananiah b. Teradion (who was killed in the Bar Kokba revolt), the father-in-law of R. Meier: 'But if two sit together and words of the

---

[19] D opens with ουκ εισιν γαρ and follows ονομα with παρ οις ουκ. This text lies behind g¹ and syˢ. 'It can be explained as an attempt to suppress ... possible confusion between οὐ and οὗ, in later Greek written and pronounced in an identical way—something which in a lectio solemnis could embarrass both the reader and the hearers' (Englezakis (v), p. 271).

[20] On the minor variants for this clause see Englezakis (v), pp. 271–2.

[21] Cf. 24.28; Mk 6.10; Lk 12.34; Jn 12.26; Jas 3.16.

[22] Despite Trilling, p. 42, we doubt that the presence of Christ in 18.20 (he thinks this static) is in any way different from the presence promised in 28.20 (he considers this dynamic). See further Frankemölle, pp. 32–4.

Law (are spoken) between them, the Divine Presence rests between them ...'. Similar is the saying attributed to R. Simeon ben Yoḥai (A.D. 100–70) in *m. 'Abot* 3.3: 'If three have eaten at one table and have spoken over it words of the Law, it is as if they had eaten from the table of God'. It is possible that the saying of R. Ḥananiah b. Teradion was called forth by the gospel saying as a kind of counterblast, but more probably it expresses what was a rabbinic commonplace—which would make Mt 18.20 a Christified bit of rabbinism. Compare also *Mek.* on Exod 20.24 and *m. 'Abot* 3.6: 'R. Ḥalafta b. Dosa of Kefar Hanania said: If ten men sit together and occupy themselves in the Law, the Divine Presence rests among them, for it is written, God stands in the congregation of God. And whence (do we learn this) even of five? Because it is written, And has founded his group upon the earth. And whence even of three? Because it is written, He judges among the judges. And whence even of two? Because it is written, Then they that feared the Lord spoke one with another: and the Lord hearkened and heard. And whence even of one? Because it is written, In every place where I record my name I will come unto thee and I will bless thee.' Again, although one might conjecture that this last was prompted by the saying preserved in Matthew, it seems more likely that the rabbinic texts cited are independent of Christianity, and that Mt 18.20 is a Christian reformulation of a rabbinic sentiment. Jesus, the 'effulgence' of God's glory (Heb 1.3; cf. Jn 1.14), has simply been substituted for the *shekinah*, and gathering together 'in my name' for study of the Torah. As in the Mishnah, so in Matthew: the zone of the sacred is not dictated by geography but is mobile.[23] The difference is that holy space is 'Christified' in the gospel and is entered into by gathering in Christ's name.

18.20 is almost universally regarded not as a saying of the pre-Easter Jesus but as an utterance of the risen Lord, this because it presupposes the 'spiritual' presence of Jesus among his disciples. While we concur with this judgement, we note that even here dogmatism has no place, for Paul could write in this fashion: 'For though absent in my body I am present in spirit, and, as if present, I have already pronounced judgement in the name of the Lord .... When you are assembled, and my spirit is present, with the power of our Lord Jesus, you are to deliver this man to Satan ...' (1 Cor 5.3–5).[24] Was Paul the only one capable of speaking of being spiritually present with others?

In church history Mt 18.20 has been employed in sundry ways. It has not only, for example, been cited as support for the authority of church councils (cf. Leo, *Ep.* 98.1: if Christ is with two or three, how much more with a whole company of bishops), but also quoted as a justification of Free Churches (Christ is present for any two or three gathered in his name: no institution is required). But the saying has also been for certain Christians a stumblingblock. The mention of 'two or three' troubled early Christian solitaries and was used against them

---

[23] See B. M. Bokser, 'Approaching Sacred Space', *HTR* 78 (1985), pp. 279–99.

[24] We recall also a saying of the last Guru of Sikhism, Gobid Singh (1675–1708): 'Where there are five, there am I.'

(cf. Ignatius, *Eph.* 5, long recension). Is not Christ also present with one? H. W. Attridge, on the basis of a re-examination of the text with ultraviolet light, has argued that the following originally stood in *P. Oxy.* 1.23–7: 'Where there are three, they are without God, and where there is but a single one I say that I am with him' (cf. Clement of Alexandria, *Strom.* 3.68; Gos. Thom. 30).[25] This is best interpreted as a response to Mt 18.20 by anchorite Christians (cf. Zahn, p. 583, n. 41).[26]

ON RECONCILIATION (18.21f.)

Following the instructions on excommunication we find a pronouncement story which serves as 'gemara'. 18.21f., which contains a correction of a suggestion of Peter, is a sort of safeguard. Its function is to be a hedge against rigidity and absolutism, to balance the hard teaching of the previous paragraph. The concern is to avoid any calculus of 'less and more' and to make explicit the attitude that is necessary if one is to undertake the hard task of correcting a brother. Forgiveness, like love, must be limitless. Without such forgiveness the community cannot correct the wayward, cannot pray as a united force, and cannot have Christ in its midst (cf. Schlatter, p. 558).

It is sometimes affirmed that vv. 21–2 stand in tension with what has gone before. How can one display unlimited forgiveness and yet undertake proceedings which may end in a brother's expulsion? The question overlooks the fact that 'the injured man who endeavours to reclaim his injurer must of course have forgiven him in his heart: otherwise it would be hopeless to seek reconciliation. He goes, not for his own sake, to seek for reparation, but for the wrong-doer's sake, to win him back from evil' (Plummer, p. 255). We would add two points. First, in the Jewish tradition reproof and love belong together and are not perceived as antithetical, this in part because the classic text on reproof, Lev 19.17, is followed immediately by the command to love one's neighbour as oneself (Lev 19.18). Then, secondly, for Matthew, membership in the Christian community clearly disallows certain types of behaviour. The community would cease to be if it did not insist that its members acknowledge in word and deed the lordship of Christ,

[25] See H. W. Attridge, 'The Original Text of Gos. Thom., Saying 30', *Bulletin of the American Society of Papyrologists* 16 (1979), pp. 153–7. The text continues: 'Lift up the stone and there you will find me; cleave the wood, and I am there.' Cf. Gos. Thom. 77. See further Fitzmyer, *Essays*, pp. 397–401.

[26] It should be noted that in *Mek.* on Exod 20.24 we find this: 'And how do we know that He is even with one? It is said: In every place where I cause My name to be mentioned I will come unto thee and bless thee'. Did this Jewish sentiment encourage the formulation of such statements as that found in *P. Oxy.* 1.23–7?

with its many moral demands. Thus the spirit of forgiveness cannot mean blindness and indifference to sin within the church (cf. Paul).

21. τότε προσελθὼν αὐτῷ ὁ Πέτρος εἶπεν.[27] Both τότε* and προσέρχομαι* are characteristic of the redactor, and Matthew's special interest in Peter is well known. The line may be ascribed to the redactor.

κύριε. See on 8.6. Peter also uses this title of Jesus in 14.28, 30; 16.22; 17.4. It is characteristic of Peter's speech in Matthew.

ποσάκις ἁμαρτήσει εἰς ἐμὲ ὁ ἀδελφός μου καὶ ἀφήσω αὐτῷ; ἕως ἑπτάκις; Compare 1 Cor 8.12. Aside from ἕως* and ἀδελφός*, the second of which links vv. 21–2 with the paragraphs on either side (cf. p. 750), the vocabulary is not clearly editorial.[28] For ἁμαρτάνω + εἰς see on 18.15. On 'brother' in the First Gospel see 1, pp. 512–13. Here fellow believers are obviously in mind. The parataxis is Semitic (BDF § 471.2).

In Lk 17.4 the repeat offender says 'I repent' on seven occasions. The passage is thus about forgiving those who ask for forgiveness. Matthew's text, however, says nothing about the offender's repentance. Is it simply assumed? This is evidently the opinion of Meier, *Matthew*, p. 207, who avers that in v. 21 'the focus shifts to the brother who is not recalcitrant, but who sins often and therefore needs forgiveness often'. Probably, however, vv. 21–2 should not be so neatly separated from what has gone before. Does not the appearance of key words or phrases common to 18.15–20 and 21–2 (ἁμαρτήσει εἰς, ὁ ἀδελφός + pronoun) point to some thematic connexion? Is not the effect of the juxtaposition to inculcate an attitude of forgiveness in the midst of the necessary but unpleasant proceedings just described?

With Peter's offer to forgive seven times one may compare the following: Gen 4.15 (sevenfold vengeance upon Cain's murderer); Lev 16 (there is a sevenfold sprinkling of blood for the sins of the people); Lev 26.18 ('I will chastise you again sevenfold for your sins'; cf. vv. 21, 24); 2 Βασ 12.6 (sevenfold satisfaction of guilt); Prov 24.16 ('a righteous man falls seven times, and rises again'); 4Q511 2, frag. 35 (God's avenging judgements, seven times refined); LAB 6.6 (a span of seven days given for repentance). Was there a traditional connexion between the the number seven and themes of vengeance, expiation, and forgiveness?

[27] NA[26] puts αυτω at the end; so B (D) 892 1424 *pc* Or. HG follows ℵ² L W Θ *f*¹·¹³ Maj aur q sy^{p.h} Lcf in printing the order we have. ℵ* sy^s omit αυτω altogether.

[28] ποσάκις: Mt: 2 (18.21; 23.37, the last from Q); Mk: 0; Lk: 1. ἁμαρτάνω: Mt: 3 (18.15, 21; 27.4, the first from Q); Mk: 0; Lk: 4. εἰς: nowhere else in Matthew after ἁμαρτάνω. ἐμέ: Mt: 9; Mk: 4–5; Lk: 9. ἑπτάκις: Mt: 2; Mk: 0; Lk: 2

The rabbinic texts gathered in SB 1, pp. 795–7, show that the sages were well-acquainted with the need to forgive an offender more than once. There are, however, passages which recommend limiting forgiveness, for example to three times (e.g. *b. Yoma* 86b–87a). The understandable assumption here is that justice demands that mercy be bounded. *If* the notion that one might forgive another three times was part of common wisdom (we can only guess this), then Peter's proposal might have seemed excessively generous, in which case Jesus' proposal would be doubly so.

22. λέγει αὐτῷ ὁ Ἰησοῦς. Compare 4.10; 8.4, 20; 9.28; 15.34; 19.21; 26.31, 52, 64. For asyndeton see 1, p. 84, and on the historical present p. 288.

οὐ λέγω σοι ἕως ἑπτάκις. This repeats Peter's suggestion only to negate it. οὐ probably goes with λέγω ('I do not say to you', so RSV); λέγω σοι is not, *pace* Schlatter, p. 559, and Zahn, p. 584, n. 43, parenthetical, as though the meaning were: 'Not (I say to you) up to seven times'. Jesus answers Peter's question by calling for what is in effect unlimited forgiveness.

ἀλλ' ἕως ἑβδομηκοντάκις ἑπτά. ἑβδομηκοντάκις is a NT *hapax legomenon*. For ἑπτά see 1, p. 87. ἑβδομηκοντάκις ἑπτά occurs in the LXX, in Gen 4.24: 'If Cain is avenged sevenfold, truly Lamech ἑβδομηκαντάκις ἑπτά' (the Hebrew is: *šibʿîm wĕšibʿâ*; note also T. Benj. 7.4). In exegetical history Gen 4.24 has often been associated with Mt 18.22,[29] and rightly. In the gospel Gen 4.24 is recalled because it refers to a blood-feud 'carried on without mercy and without limit. The reply of Jesus in v. 22 says: Just as in those old days there was no limit to hatred and vengeance, so among Christians there is to be no limit to mercy and forgiveness' (Manson, *Sayings*, p. 212).

Does the Greek number mean 'seventy times and seven' (70 + 7; so BDF § 248) or 'seventy times seven' (four hundred and ninety; so RSV)? In favour of the former, the Hebrew means seventy-seven (GK § 134r). In favour of the latter, the early versions (including the Vulgate) favour seventy times seven. Fortunately, there is no need to resolve the issue, for both numbers amount to the same thing. One is not being commanded to count but to forgive without counting. The quality of Christian forgiveness requires that it should not be conceived in quantitative terms.[30]

The Gospel of the Nazaraeans contained the following: 'If thy brother

---

[29] Cf. Tertullian, *De orat.* 7; Origen, *Comm. on Mt.* 14.5; Philoxenus, p. 128 (ed. Fox); Allen, p. 199.

[30] That the evangelist did not intend this radical teaching on forgiveness to justify acquiescence to all sorts of evil is proved by its link with vv. 15–20: the demand to forgive stands beside the demand to correct sin. The two must be held together.

has sinned with a word and has made thee reparation, receive him seven times in a day. Simon his disciple said to him: seven times in a day? The Lord answered and said to him: Yes, I say to thee, until seventy-seven times' (*usque septuagies septies*; Jerome, *Adv. Pelag.* 3.2). Notwithstanding some scholars,[31] this must be a conflation of Mt 18.21–2 and Lk 17.4.

Although Mt 18.21–2 clearly opposes Gen 4.23–4, this is not reason to speak of Jesus here revoking the Torah. The Pentateuch itself, by its institution of the *lex talionis*, had long before Jesus' times invalidated the unbridled vengeance countenanced in the song of Lamech.

THE PARABLE OF THE UNFORGIVING SERVANT (18.23–35)

Between the introduction (v. 23a) and the conclusion (v. 35), the parable consists of three scenes (vv. 23b–7, 28–30, 31–4), each having the same form: situation (vv. 23b–5, 28, 31) – – words (vv. 26, 29, 32–3) – – response/action (vv. 27, 30, 34).

Jeremias (v), p. 97, affirms that 18.23–35 is not an apt illustration of vv. 21f., for the king in our parable forgives only once, not seventy plus (or times) seven. This criticism, echoed by others, misses the mark. It was surely as obvious to Matthew—who after all was responsible for the present setting of the parable—as it is to us that 18.23–35 does not illustrate 18.21–2, and he did not join the two units because they teach precisely the same lesson. Rather, although both have to do with forgiving, they have different emphases. 18.21–2 is a memorable call for repeated forgiveness. 18.23–35 is a vivid reminder that the failure to forgive is failure to act as the heavenly father acts (cf. 5.48). Between the two themes there is scarcely any real tension.

Despite its being preserved only in Matthew, 18.23–35 is almost universally reckoned an authentic parable of Jesus.[32] Some have to be sure ascribed its composition to Matthew.[33] But their reasons are inadequate, especially as certain internal tensions all but prove that the parable, which probably came to Matthew as oral tradition, has at points been infelicitously altered (see below). There is no denying the presence of Matthean style and vocabulary, and there is good cause to think that the evangelist has created or reformulated the introduction (v. 23) as well as the conclusion (v. 35), and also that he has introduced other changes as well (see on vv. 23, 24, 26). Yet all this in no way prevents us from holding that the shape of the parable closely

---

[31] Jeremias, *Sayings*, pp. 83–5, argues for independence from Luke and thinks the tradition may be historical.

[32] Cf. Dietzfelbinger (v); Gnilka, *Matthäusevangelium* 2, p. 148.

[33] E.g. Gundry, *Commentary*, pp. 371–2 (positing dependence upon the parable in Lk 7.41–3); Drury, p. 92.

approximates the original composition.[34] In our judgement, although the alterations and additions have at points made the parable difficult to interpret, they have not produced any great change in the theological meaning. Jesus, like Matthew, was interested in moving people to imitate God the Father in his forgiveness and to warn them of the consequences of failing to do so.[35]

Much effort has been expended trying to show exactly what first-century situation our parable represents, and also that its details are true-to-life (e.g. Derrett (v)). But Beasley-Murray, p. 115, speaks for others when he declares: 'Everything in the parable is set on an astronomical scale. It is the nearest thing to a tale from the Arabian nights in the teaching of Jesus; it could have come from Scheherazade herself, had she been a disciple'. He continues: 'Surely those exegetes who want to cut down the figures (e.g., from ten thousand talents to ten) have locked their imaginations in their filing cabinets'. At the risk of being reckoned unimaginative, we beg to differ. De Boer (v) has persuaded us of the redactional origin of μυρίων ταλάντων (v. 24). Unless this astounding figure be considered editorial, certain questions remain unanswered. How, for example, can the sale of the unmerciful servant's family—this would bring only a fraction of the debt incurred—lead to repayment (καὶ ἀποδοθῆναι, v. 25)?[36] And how can the servant realistically ask the king for time to repay a debt of such magnitude? And is it plausible that 10,000 talents would ever have been given to anybody as a *loan* (this is what δάνειον means)? Again, how can putting the unmerciful servant in prison (v. 34) in any way effect the recovery of 10,000 talents (ἕως οὗ ἀποδῷ πᾶν τὸ ὀφειλόμενον)? All these problems evaporate immediately when one assumes that the story as first told involved a much smaller amount (De Boer suggests 10,000 *denarii*).[37] Then the situation becomes this. A servant is unable to pay a loan back to his

[34] Weder (v) suggests that the original parable consisted of only vv. 23–30. Contrast Broer (v), pp. 152–55. We agree with J. D. Crossan, 'The Servant Parables of Jesus', in *Society of Biblical Literature 1973 Seminar Papers*, vol. 2, ed. G. MacRae, Cambridge, 1973, pp. 99–100: 'The conclusion in 18.32–4 is especially appropriate from a dramatic and literary viewpoint.... Apart from the concluding 18.35 ... the dramatic unity of the parable is flawless'.— According to Gnilka, *Matthäusevangelium* 2, p. 147, the parable originally ended with v. 33 (so also Broer (v)) and was about failure to respond to the ministry of Jesus.

[35] R. A. Horsley, pp. 254–5, believes 18.23–33 was originally about literal, economic debt, that Jesus was calling his fellow Jews to release others from certain economic obligations. Cf. Oakman, pp. 149–56. But why abandon the earliest interpretation unless the evidence clearly demands it?

[36] Gundry, *Commentary*, p. 374, rightly uses the word 'absurdity' in this connexion, although he does not draw the correct conclusion.

[37] Manson, *Sayings*, p. 213, suggests the original may have had *ten* talents.

master. The master, upon being implored, decides not to recover his funds by selling the man and his family; instead he unexpectedly cancels the loan. Subsequently the servant fails to treat another as he has been treated: he demands immediate repayment of a debt. Upon hearing this, the master determines to revoke his kindness. He puts the wicked servant in prison, until he or his friends and family can arrange to have the original debt repaid.

The supposition that the sum of 10,000 talents is Matthew's own contribution is confirmed not only by the resulting clarity the text achieves when the sum is reduced. There is also the striking fact that in the parable preserved in 25.14–30 = Lk 19.11–27, Matthew's version refers to a servant with five talents, a second with two talents, a third with one talent. In Luke the three servants are each entrusted with one pound. Here, as the commentators generally recognize, Matthew has greatly inflated the monetary amounts (cf. Jeremias, *Parables*, pp. 28, 60, n. 41). There is thus precedent for the sort of change we have conjectured for 18.24. When one adds that the motivation for the alteration is perfectly clear—it underscores the greatness of God's mercy, which cancels incalculable debts—the inference is inevitable. We also remind the reader that there are other places in the First Gospel where an apparent redactional modification has left the exegetes confused (see e.g. 1, pp. 515–16, on 5.22). Sometimes sense can only be gained when the tradition-history is critically examined.

23. The introduction to the parable does several things. It tells us that the following has something to say about the kingdom of God, and it sets the stage for the opening scene: a king wished to settle accounts with his servants. Moreover, the reader, for whom 'king' and 'servant' are stock images for God and his people, immediately thinks in terms of theological truths. While this does not entail a one-to-one correspondence between the actions of the king and the actions of God, it does 'transpose the intent of the parable from the realm of human relationships to those of the human and divine'.[38]

διὰ τοῦτο. For this combination (a Matthean favourite[39]) as the introduction to a new paragraph see 6.25 and 12.31. As in 13.52 (again a parable concluding a major discourse), the words have a weakened sense: 'so then, well'.

ὡμοιώθη ἡ βασιλεία τῶν οὐρανῶν ἀνθρώπῳ βασιλεῖ. For kings in Matthean parables see also 17.25; 22.2, 7, 11, 13; 25.34, 40. For the fixed formula, ὡμοιώθη ... ἀνθρώπῳ, see on 13.24. Whether it is here redactional[40] or derives from a pre-Matthean source (cf. 1, pp. 125–6) cannot be determined. But 'king' is

[38] N. A. Huffman, 'Atypical Features in the Parables of Jesus', *JBL* 97 (1978), p. 213.
[39] See 1, p. 77. It occurs often in the LXX (cf. 'al kēn).
[40] See esp. De Boer (v), pp. 223–7.

probably redactional.[41] 'King' occurs only in the introductory verse, v. 23. Throughout the rest of the parable, which seems to be 'a story of a wealthy merchant and his slaves, rather than one of a king and his ministers' (so Allen, p. 201), the word used is 'lord'. In addition, in the parable of the wedding feast, Q's ἄνθρωπός τις (so Lk 14.16) has become in the First Gospel ἀνθρώπῳ βασιλεῖ (so Mt 22.2), and the tendency of rabbinic tradition to add 'king' to the beginning of a parable is documented (see Jeremias, *Parables*, pp. 28, 102, n. 59). De Boer (v), pp. 226–7, also observes, citing Mt 13.45; 20.1; 21.33 (diff. Mk 12.1); and 22.2 (diff. Lk 14.16), that 'it is a Matthean pattern to specify the ambiguous ἄνθρωπος at the beginning of parables with an appositional noun'. The case for a redactional origin of 'king' is persuasive.

Schlatter, p. 559, cites Josephus, *Ant.* 6.142 (ἀνθρώπῳ βασιλεῖ) and the rabbinic expression, 'king of flesh and blood', and suggests that in Mt 18.23 ἀνθρώπῳ βασιλεῖ means 'earthly king' (as opposed to the heavenly king, God). This is doubtful. ἄνθρωπος stands in apposition to a noun in other places in Matthew where it is simply a substitute for τις (1, p. 81). Moreover, why would the introduction to the parable wish to stress the earthly connexions of a figure who is a transparent symbol for God?[42]

ὃς ἠθέλησεν συνᾶραι λόγον μετὰ τῶν δούλων αὐτοῦ. συναίρω[43] + λόγον, a combination found in the papyri (BAGD, s.v., συναίρω) but not the LXX, means 'settle accounts' (cf. Latin *rationes conferre*). For other parables in which the kingdom is related to the settling of accounts see 24.45–51; 25.14–30 (cf. Lk 16.1–9). If one accepts the sum of 10,000 talents as an original part of the parable, δοῦλος must mean not 'slave' but, in accordance with oriental usage, 'minister' or 'official' (so BAGD, s.v., citing 1 Βασ 29.3; 4 Βασ 5.6; Josephus, *Ant.* 2.70). The parable would then be about a king and one of his governors or satraps. But a lesser sum—the solution we prefer—would permit one to think of a master and servant (and also permit one to give the σύνδουλοι of v. 31 its natural meaning: 'fellow servants').

24. ἀρξαμένου δὲ αὐτοῦ συναίρειν. The RSV rightly translates; 'when he began his reckoning'. The pattern of introductory participle followed by aorist indicative (so frequent in the parable of the prodigal son, Lk 15.11–32) is repeated in vv. 25, 27, 28, 30, 31 (*bis*), 34, and all but two sentences in our parable open with participles (vv. 23 and 30 are the exceptions).

---

[41] So De Boer (v). Jeremias, *Parables*, p. 28, n. 17, is undecided.
[42] We assume that the king, as so often in the parables, stands for God.
[43] NT: 3, all in Matthew: 18.23, 24; 25.19.

προσηνέχθη αὐτῷ εἷς ὀφειλέτης μυρίων ταλάντων.⁴⁴ For εἷς= τις (a Semitism) see 1, p. 82, and for the unclassical repetition of the subject after a genitive absolute BDF § 423.1 (cf. 1.20; 9.18). ὀφειλέτης (cf. 6.12) means 'debtor'. The word helps point the reader to religious realities, for the equation of sin with debt was well known (see 1, p. 612, to which add 1 En. 6.3). μυρίων⁴⁵ ταλάντων records the amount of debt: 10,000 talents. The τά λαντον⁴⁶ (usually in the LXX for *kikka(ā)r*) was a unit of coinage with relatively high value, equal in the first century to about 6,000 drachmas. According to Jeremias, *Parables*, p. 210, the sum of 10,000 talents 'exceeds any actual situation; it can only be explained if we realize that both μύρια and τάλαντα are the highest magnitudes in use (10,000 is the highest number used in reckoning,⁴⁷ and the talent is the largest currency unit in the whole of the Near East).' Josephus, *Ant.* 17.320, says that the total Judean tax for one year totalled only 600 talents, and when one compares the OT sums associated with the building of Solomon's great temple (see 1 Chron 29.4–7), the sum of 10,000 talents does appear incredible.⁴⁸ We suggested above, however, that Matthew may have greatly inflated the figure in order to magnify God's munificence.

Although προσηνέχθη probably implies that the debtor was brought forcibly, that is, against his will, the word does not necessarily imply that the man has just been brought from jail.⁴⁹

25. μὴ ἔχοντος δὲ αὐτοῦ ἀποδοῦναι. ἀποδίδωμι* is one of the key words of this parable, appearing in vv. 25 (*bis*), 26, 28, 29, 30, 34. For ἔχω= 'be able' (classical) see Lk 7.42; 14.14; Acts 4.14.

ἐκέλευσεν αὐτὸν ὁ κύριος πραθῆναι καὶ τὴν γυναῖκα καὶ τὰ τέκνα καὶ πάντα ὅσα εἶχεν⁵⁰, καὶ ἀποδοθῆναι. πραθῆναι

---

⁴⁴ c replaces μυριων with εκατον, no doubt because of the difficulties discussed on p. 795.

⁴⁵ μύριοι: NT: 1. Cf. 1 Clem. 34.6, quoting Dan 7.10.

⁴⁶ NT: 15, all in Matthew, all but one (18.24) in the parable in 25.14–30.

⁴⁷ He cites here Lk 12.1; 1 Cor 1.15; 14.19.

⁴⁸ Derrett 'Law' (v), calls attention to Josephus, *Ant.* 12.175–6, where a tax farmer offers to collect for Ptolemy taxes up to 16,000 talents. But the note to this by Ralph Marcus in the Loeb ed. (vol. 7, pp. 92–3) reads: 'This is obviously too large a sum in the light of other estimates of revenues which have come down to us. . . . Jerome gives the revenue from Egypt itself (*de Aegypto*) in the time of Ptolemy Philadelphus as 14,800 talents; Herodotus, iii.91, gives 350 talents as the tribute taken by Darius from Phoenicia, Palestine and Cyprus: Cicero estimates the total revenue of Ptolemy Auletes as 12,500 talents. Cf. also 2 Macc. iv. 8ff.'

⁴⁹ This against Jeremias, *Parables*, p. 211. See Linnemann (v), p. 176, n. 11.

⁵⁰ So HG, following ℵ D L W *f*¹³ Maj. NA²⁶ prints εχει (so B Θ *f*¹ *pc* Or; cf. 13.44).

is the aorist passive infinitive of πιπράσκω (= 'sell'), a word which occurs also in 13.46 and 26.9.

Diogenes Laertius, *Vit.* 4.46–58, tells the story of a tax farmer who, because he could not pay what he owed, was, with his family, sold into slavery. The practice of enslaving individuals on account of unpaid debts was not uncommon in the Graeco-Roman world (cf. Deissmann, *Light*, p. 270). There are also Jewish examples (cf. 1 Sam 22.2, Isa 50.1; Amos 2.6). In Exod 22.2 (MT 21.37) a man who cannot make restitution after he has stolen an ox or sheep 'shall be sold for his theft'. This legislation is referred to by Josephus (*Ant.* 16.3) as well as by the Mishnah and Tosepta, where it is stated that a woman cannot be so treated (*m. Soṭa* 3.8, *t.Soṭa* 2.9). Further, the OT contains stories in which children become enslaved to creditors when their parents' debt goes unpaid (2 Kgs 4.1; Neh 5.1–13), and wives and children were widely reckoned as property.

Given the average value of slaves in the ancient world, the selling of a family would not begin to pay back the debt owed (10,000 talents). So Jeremias (v), p. 211, writes: 'the king's order in v. 25 must be understood in the main as an expression of his wrath.' Linnemann (v), p. 109, on the contrary, thinks the action is an expression of justice. But as the huge sum of money is probably due to Matthew's hand, at one time the amount was probably small enough to be covered by the sale of family members.

26. πεσὼν οὖν ὁ δοῦλος προσεκύνει αὐτῷ λέγων.[51] If the imperfect προσεκύνει[52] does not here mean 'besought'[53] but bears the sense it does elsewhere in the Gospel ('worship', 'pay reverence to'), perhaps one should think the figure to be acting like a Gentile in that he is making prostration before a human king (cf. 1, pp. 236–7, 248). Or does the verb rather hint at the fact that the master or king represents God?

μακροθύμησον ἐπ' ἐμοί.[54] These exact words appear also in v. 29. μακροθυμέω followed by ἐπί + dative[55] here means 'show patience, be forbearing towards someone'. In the LXX the verb (cf. *'ārak*) and its cognates sometimes refer to God's longsuffering or patience (e.g. Wisd 15.1).

καὶ πάντα ἀποδώσω σοι. According to Derrett (v), this is in

[51] εκεινος follows δουλος (cf. vv. 27, 28) in ℵ² D L Δ Θ 33 892 *al* lat sy mae bo.

[52] Has it here replaced an original παρεκάλει (cf. vv. 29, 32)? So De Broer (v), citing 8.2; 9.18; 15.25.

[53] Both McNeile, p. 269, and Thompson, p. 215, n. 62, draw a distinction between προσκυνέω in the imperfect (= beseech) and the aorist (= worship). Cf. BDF § 328.

[54] κυριε is added at the beginning in ℵ L W 058 *f*[1.13] Maj it sy[p.h] co.

[55] Cf. LXX Eccles 8.12 v. 1.; Ecclus 18.11; 29.8; 35.19; Lk 18.7; Jas 5.7.

effect a request for a loan. That is, the unmerciful servant wants his current debt to be added to the amount due next year. Whether one can read so much into the words seems doubtful.

27. σπλαγχνισθεὶς δὲ ὁ κύριος τοῦ δούλου ἐκείνου ἀπέλυσεν αὐτόν. For σπλαγχνίζομαι see on 9.36. According to BDF § 176.1, the verb (which everywhere else in Matthew is used for Jesus) 'probably only appears to take the gen. of the person pitied . . . since ὁ κύριος τοῦ δούλου ἐκείνου . . . is to be taken together' (i.e.: 'the master of that servant').

καὶ τὸ δάνειον ἀφῆκεν αὐτῷ. The verb, which harks back to the previous paragraph and v. 21, appears again in vv. 32 and 35. For its use in connexion with cancellation of a debt see 1 Macc 10.29.

τὸ δάνειον (only here in the NT) is problematic. It means 'loan'. This has led Derrett (v) to urge that the master has made a loan and given the man another year in which to pay it. But is a loan of 10,000 talents credible?[56] Jeremias (v), p. 211, takes another course: 'The Syriac versions (sy^sin cur pal pesh) render τὸ δάνειον by ḥwbt' = "the debt". We may suppose that this word was used in the Aramic form of our parable and then too narrowly translated by τὸ δάνειον.' One suspects however that the Syriac rendering is just an attempt to obviate the very difficulty under discussion. We prefer to give the Greek its necessary meaning and conjecture that the story at one time had to do with a lord's loan (much less than 10,000 talents) to his servant.

28. What follows mirrors vv. 24–7, except that the response of the unmerciful servant is not the response of the master. The striking similarities function to show up the differences.

ἐξελθὼν δὲ ὁ δοῦλος ἐκεῖνος εὗρεν ἕνα τῶν συνδούλων αὐτοῦ. σύνδουλος* should be given its natural sense: 'fellow servant' (cf. 24.49).

ὃς ὤφειλεν αὐτῷ ἑκατὸν δηνάρια. The δηνάριον (= Lat. *denarius*; cf. 20.2, 9, 10, 13; 22.19), a Roman silver coin, had approximately the same value as the Greek δραχμή. According to Mt 20.1–16, it was the standard day's wage for a labourer. A hundred denarii is a trifle compared to what the unmerciful servant owed his lord.

καὶ κρατήσας αὐτὸν ἔπνιγεν λέγων. For πνίγω see on 13.7 and note *m. B. Bat.* 10.8: 'If a man seized a debtor by the throat on the street . . .' (cf. *b. 'Abod. Zar.* 4a).

---

[56] In addition, De Boer (v), p. 216, writes: Derrett takes δάνειον 'to mean "loan", but must then interpret the release of the servant by the master in v. 27a (*apelysen auton*) to include the conversion of the debt to a loan, a loan which the master then immediately forgives in v. 27b (*to daneion apheken auto*)! This explanation seems forced.'

ἀπόδος εἴ τι ὀφείλεις.⁵⁷ εἴ τι(ς) is probably the equivalent of ὅ τι: 'pay what(ever) you owe' (cf. BDF § 376 and recall the Aramaic *mâ dê*). But one could also render the words: 'Pay up— if you owe anything'.

29. **πεσὼν οὖν ὁ σύνδουλος αὐτοῦ παρεκάλει αὐτὸν λέγων.**⁵⁸ So v. 26, without αὐτοῦ and with προσεκύνει αὐτῷ. As already observed, the two lines may have been even closer in the pre-Matthean tradition (see on v. 26). But as they stand, the use of παρεκάλει instead of προσεκύνει underscores the social equality of the two characters.

μακροθύμησον ἐπ' ἐμοί, καὶ ἀποδώσω σοι. So also v. 26, with πάντα after καί. This request, unlike that in v. 26, is reasonable. The debt is sufficiently small that it could be paid back in time.

30. The plea for patience is ignored. The debtor is thrown in prison. The action is as surprising as the master's forgiveness of the unforgiving servant, not because it is unlawful or unjust but because it trumpets hypocrisy. The wicked servant asked for and benefited from mercy yet refuses to bestow it. He has broken the 'golden rule' of 7.12 and treated another as he would not wish to be treated.

ὁ δὲ οὐκ ἤθελεν. The meaning is: 'he refused' (with iterative force).

ἀλλὰ ἀπελθὼν ἔβαλεν αὐτὸν εἰς φυλακὴν ἕως ἀποδῷ τὸ ὀφειλό- μενον.⁵⁹ For βάλλω + εἰς φυλακήν (= 'throw in prison'), a common idiom, see 5.25; Lk 12.58; Jn 3.24; Acts 16.23–4; Rev 2.10. The requisite legal proceedings have been passed over as irrelevant to the story line.

31. All that has taken place is now related to the master by fellow servants, who recognize the terrible hypocrisy of a man who receives kindness but does not give it.⁶⁰

ἰδόντες οὖν οἱ σύνδουλοι αὐτοῦ τὰ γενόμενα ἐλυπήθησαν σφόδρα καὶ ἐλθόντες διεσάφησαν τῷ κυρίῳ ἑαυτῶν πάντα τὰ γενόμενα. λυπέω* + σφόδρα* (cf. 17.23; 26.22—the combination is redactional) appears in LXX Neh 5.6 and Jon 4.4, 9 for *hārâ* (= 'burn with anger').⁶¹ Does the expression here mean more

---

⁵⁷ C K Γ Δ *f*¹³ 28 892ᶜ 1010 1241 1424 Maj e f sy boᵐˢ add μοι before ει.
⁵⁸ C² W *f*¹³ Maj f q syᵖˑʰ mae add εις του ποδας αυτου.
⁵⁹ So NA²⁶. HG prints ου (so D W Θ *f*¹ˑ¹³ Maj) after εως. Is this original (cf. the variants for 5.26)?
⁶⁰ Weder, pp. 211–12, claims that v. 31 is editorial. The word statistics do not prove this. Only λυπεῖν* + σφόδρα* is clearly redactional (cf. 17.23 and 26.22; see on 2.10 and 14.9). We also doubt that Weder is right to see in v. 31 reflection of a communal situation, as though the indignation of the fellow servants is supposed to mirror the indignation of Christians over the sin of fellow believers (cf. Beare, p. 382).
⁶¹ Cf. also Tob 3.10; Dan 6.15; 1 Macc 10.68; 14.16.

than 'be exceedingly grieved, pained' and include feelings of anger? Manson, *Sayings*, p. 214, describes the fellow servants as 'indignant'.

32f. τότε προσκαλεσάμενος αὐτὸν ὁ κύριος αὐτοῦ λέγει αὐτῷ. Note the historical present. τότε* is often redactional, but προσκαλέομαι is almost always from the tradition.[62] δοῦλε πονηρέ. Compare 25.26 (reverse word order); Josephus, *Ant.* 2.55; 16.296. SB 1, p. 800, compares the Aramaic *'abdā' bîšā'*.

πᾶσαν τὴν ὀφειλὴν ἐκείνην ἀφῆκά σοι. This refers the reader back to v. 27. For ὀφειλή (LXX: 0) see also Rom 13.7; 1 Cor 7.3; Did 8.2.

ἐπεὶ παρεκάλεσάς με. ἐπεί is causal, not temporal. The master forgave the unmerciful servant his debt out of pure generosity. The one forgiven should have acted in kind. The one act of mercy should have begotten another.

οὐκ ἔδει καὶ σὲ ἐλεῆσαι τὸν σύνδουλόν σου, ὡς κἀγὼ σὲ ἠλέησα; Compare the δέω of 23.23 (certain commandments *must be* kept). Beneath this remark is the idea that God, the king of all, must be imitated in his goodness (see on 5.48). Compare Lk 6.36: 'Be merciful, even as your Father is merciful'. We have here the obverse of the fifth beatitude: if the merciful receive mercy, the unmerciful do not. We recall Browning: the sole death is 'lack of love from love made manifest'. Linnemann, *Parables*, p. 111, has appropriately written: 'Clearly mercy is essentially not something which we can accept with a feeling of relief at having got away with it once more, only to let things go on again just as we used to. It appears to have the character of an ordinance, just as justice is an ordinance'. The gospel is demand as well as gift.

34. We do not now read that the wicked servant asked for mercy (contrast vv. 26 and 29). He knows he stands condemned. There is no protest when the angry master hands the evil servant over to torturers and the last punishment becomes worse than the first.

καὶ ὀργισθεὶς ὁ κύριος αὐτοῦ παρέδωκεν αὐτὸν τοῖς βασανισταῖς. The use of the NT *hapax legomenon* βασανιστής (= 'torturers', not 'jailers'; cf. *T. Abr.* A 12.13) accents the severity of the punishment and may point to a non-Jewish environment (although Herod the Great did employ torture; cf. Josephus, *Bell.* 1.548). From the next line (ἕως οὗ ἀποδῷ) it follows that the defaulter is being punished in order to motivate him and

---

[62] Mt 10.1 (from Mark); 15.10 (from Mark), 32 (from Mark); 18.2 (redactional); 20.25 (from Mark).

those who care for him to raise the necessary funding (cf. Lev 25.47–52).

ἕως οὗ ἀποδῷ πᾶν τὸ ὀφειλόμενον.[63] Compare v. 30. ἕως οὗ is redactional in 14.22; 17.9; and 26.36. In this line we have the principle that like is punished by like. The unmerciful servant put another in prison for a debt unpaid (v. 30). This is now his own punishment. He too is put in prison, and for the same cause. As the parable now stands, with the debt amounting to 10,000 talents, the punishment must be perpetual, for a debt so immense could never be repaid. Thus the situation is a transparent symbol of eschatological judgement.

35. The parable ends with a redactional[64] warning which makes the moral of the parable impossible to miss. Compare 6.15: 'if you do not forgive men their trespasses, neither will your Father forgive you your trespasses'; also Jas 2.13: 'judgement is without mercy to him that shows no mercy' (cf. Hermas, *Sim.* 9.23).

οὕτως καὶ ὁ πατήρ μου ὁ οὐράνιος ποιήσει ὑμῖν, ἐὰν μὴ ἀφῆτε ἕκαστος τῷ ἀδελφῷ αὐτοῦ ἀπὸ τῶν καρδιῶν ὑμῶν.[65] Compare T. Gad. 6.7 ('And if he is shameless and persists in his wrong-doing, even so forgive him from the heart (ἄφες αὐτῷ ἀπὸ καρδίας), and leave to God the avenging'). 'From the heart' (= *milleb*) expresses sincerity and 'excludes all casuistry and legalism' (France, *Matthew*, p. 278). For the meaning of 'heart' see on 5.8 and 6.21. 'Forgiveness from the heart' is the antithesis of 'hatred from the heart' (cf. Lev 19.17; Prov 26.24). For οὕτως καὶ introducing the application of a parable see also 24.33 = Mk 13.29; Lk 17.10 (cf. Apoc. Jas. 8.23). ποιήσει is an eschatological future: the final judgement is in view. For the plural pronoun followed by a singular (ἕκαστος) see BDF § 305. οὕτως* introduces a threat: if one acts as the wicked servant did, one will be punished as he was punished. On fear as a motivation for action in the First Gospel see 1, pp. 728f.

(iv) *Concluding Observations*

(1) 'Let him be to you as a Gentile and toll-collector'. These

---

[63] αυτω is added at the end in ℵ*.2 C L W *f*¹ Maj sy^{p.h}. The reading is accepted by HG, not NA²⁶.

[64] So most recent commentators, including De Boer (v), pp. 219–22; Weder, p. 210. οὕτως*, πατήρ μου*, οὐράνιος*, ἀφίημι*, ἀδελφός*, and ἀπό* (instrumental) are all characteristic.

[65] C*^{vid} W Θ *f*^{(1).13} Maj have επουρανιος (on this word see Horsley 4, p. 149).

words, decidedly harsh and unpleasant, are nonetheless embedded in a section filled with kindness. The sinner is to be offered at least three opportunities to repent (vv. 15–17). And the one offended is to have forgiven the offender, no matter what—for Jesus demands forgiveness without measure (vv. 21–2). The motivation for such unbounded generosity is imitation of the Father in heaven (cf. 5.48). As he has forgiven undeserving Christians, so must they likewise forgive others (vv. 23–35). 'Freely you have received, freely give' (10.8). The appropriate attitude towards a wayward brother is like that of a shepherd seeking a stray sheep. The shepherd does not want to punish the stray but bring it back to the fold (cf. vv. 12–14). All this reveals two things. First, for Matthew, excommunication, when it comes, will in truth be self-imposed exile. The Christian community, if it is to be true to itself, if it is forbearing, anxious about the welfare of all its members, and animated by a spirit of forgiveness, will give sinners more than a fair chance. If, despite everything, excommunication follows, that can only be because the one excommunicated has finally refused to follow the commandments of Christ and therefore just does not belong in the Christian church.[66] Secondly, it is clear that chapter 18, including 18.15–35, has been shaped by Matthew's pastoral concern. The main teaching is in vv. 15–20, on excommunication. Vv. 21–2 and the long parable in vv. 23–35 are subsidiary. They function as a kind of commentary or 'gemara'. In a way reminiscent of 6.25–34; 7.7–11; and 10.26–31, the harsh demands in vv. 15–20 are tempered by the radical teaching on forgiveness in vv. 21–35. Those who involve themselves in deciding whether a brother is to be expelled must live and breath a spirit of forgiveness. The process of expulsion is too serious a matter to be left in the hands of any but the meek and merciful, who know that they themselves are the unworthy recipients of God's constant mercy and forgiveness.

(2) One might urge that 18.15–20 should be considered in relation to what the Germans call *Frühkatholizismus*, 'early catholicism'.[67] There is no denying that Matthew's text represents a development. Between Lk 17.3–4 and Mt 18.15–22 one can see the emerging institution of the church. But caution is very much in order. The very concept of *Frühkatholizismus* is controversial. It is defined differently by different scholars, and, speaking for ourselves, we are doubtful about its utility. If, however, one follows those who think it was characterized by ecclesiastical hierarchy

---

[66] Mt 18.15–20 is misinterpreted if it is taken as a mandate for a pure or sinless church. See Calvin's comments in his *Brieve instruction . . . Anabaptistes* 2.

[67] For lit. see the bibliography in J. D. G. Dunn, *Unity and Diversity in the New Testament*, Philadelphia and London, 1977, pp. 435–7.

and the fading of an imminent eschatological expectation, our Gospel satisfies on neither score. Not only do we detect little slackening of eschatological fervour in Matthew, but the First Gospel says nothing about ecclesiastical offices—so little, in fact, that E. Schweizer can even infer that Matthew's church had no place for elders or bishops or deacons. Whether he is right we do not know (his is an uncertain inference from silence). But the main point remains unassailable: Matthew has nothing explicit to say about any hierarchy. Furthermore, it would be a mistake to imagine that the legislation in Mt 18.15–22 could not go back to the early days of the church, that it could only have been formulated after the delay of the *parousia*. Bultmann, *Theology* 1, p. 48, affirms that rules such as those in Mt 18.15–22 became 'necessary in the course of time'. But how much time? Paul already in the 50's had to deal with matters of discipline in Corinth. Surely he was not the first. It is simply in the nature of things that close-knit groups will have rules or codes of behaviour and that there will always be some who bend or break the rules (cf. the Dead Sea Scrolls). Instructions on what to do in that case are inevitable.

If the key to Mt 18.15–22 is not 'early catholicism', should one rather look to the Dead Sea Scrolls? It has been suggested that the passage, along with other indications, points to an Essene influx into the early church (discussion in Davies, *SSM*, pp. 208–56, suggesting that in Mt 18 there is a conjunction of sectarian and rabbinic terminology). This is a real possibility (cf. Gnilka, *Matthäusevangelium* 2, p. 139). Indeed, the evidence for *some* Essene influence on the first-century church seems to us persuasive. But whether 18.15–22 in particular should be traced to Qumran is uncertain. It is always difficult to weigh parallels, and in the present instance the legislation on fraternal correction and excommunication has, as we have seen, parallels not only in the Scrolls but also in the Jewish wisdom tradition, the Testaments of the Twelve Patriarchs, and in rabbinic texts. What we suspect, although cannot prove, is this. Mt 18.15–22 was created, under the force of circumstances, by someone creatively combining a saying of Jesus with a common Jewish tradition about correcting a wayward brother. Which is to say: Mt 18.15–22 and the relevant Qumran texts are similar not because the latter begot the former but because both emerged from ancient Judaism.

(v) *Bibliography*

In addition to what follows see section (v) on pp. 788–90.

G. Barth, 'Auseinandersetzung um die Kirchenzucht im Umkreis des Matthäusevangeliums', *ZNW* 69 (1978), pp. 158–77.

Beasley-Murray, pp. 115–17.

F. H. Breukelmann, 'Eine Erklärung des Gleichnisses vom Schalksknecht (Matth. 18.23–35)', in *Parrhesia: Karl Barth zum achtzigsten Geburtstag*, ed. E. Busch et al., Zurich, 1966, pp. 261–87.

I. Broer, 'Die Parabel vom Verzicht auf das Prinzip von Leistung und Gegenleistung', in *À cause de l'Évangile*, LD 123, Paris, pp. 145–64.

Brooks, pp. 99–107.

D. R. Catchpole, 'Reproof and Reconciliation in the Q Community. A Study of the Tradition-History of Mt 18.15–17, 21–2/Lk 17.3–4', *SNTU* 8 (1983), pp. 79–90.

P. Christian, 'Was heisst für Matthäus "In meinen Namen versammelt" (Mt 18.20)', in *Dienst der Vermittlung*, ed. W. Ernst, Leipzig, 1977, pp. 97–105.

M. C. De Boer, 'Ten Thousand Talents? Matthew's Interpretation and Redaction of the Parable of the Unforgiving Servant (Matt. 18.23–35)', *CBQ* 50 (1988), pp. 214–32.

T. Deidun, 'The Parable of the Unmerciful Servant (Mt 18.23–35)', *BTB* 6 (1976), pp. 203–24.

Derrett, *Law*, pp. 32–47.

idem, '"Where two or three are convened in my name . . .": a sad misunderstanding', *ExpT* 91 (1979), pp. 83–6.

C. Dietzfelbinger, 'Das Gleichnis von der erlassenen Schuld', *EvTh* 32 (1972), pp. 437–51.

B. Englezakis, '*Thomas*, Logion 30', *NTS* 25 (1979), pp. 262–72.

Fiedler, pp. 195–204.

G. Forkman, *The Limits of Religious Community*, CB/NT 5, Lund, 1972.

E. Fuchs, 'The Parable of the Unmerciful Servant', in *Studia Evangelica*, vol. 1, ed. F. L. Cross, Berlin, 1959, pp. 487–94.

J. Galot, 'Qu'il soit pour toi comme le paien et le publicain', *NRTh* 96 (1974), pp. 1009–30.

J. Gnilka, 'Die Kirche des Matthäus und die Gemeinde von Qumran', *BZ* 7 (1963), pp. 43–63.

C. J. A. Hickling, 'Conflicting Motives in the Redaction of Matthew: Some Considerations on the Sermon on the Mount and Matthew 18.15–20', in *Studia Evangelica*, vol. 7, TU 126, ed. E. A. Livingstone, Berlin, 1982, pp. 247–60.

Jeremias, *Parables*, pp. 210–13.

Jülicher 2, pp. 302–14.

Linnemann, *Parables*, pp. 105–13.

P. K. Matthew, 'Authority and Discipline: Matt. 16.17–19 and 18.15–18 and the Exercise of Authority and Discipline in the Matthean Community', *CV* 28 (1985), pp. 119–25.

D. E. Oakman, 'Jesus and Agrarian Palestine: The Factor of Debt', in *Society of Biblical Literature 1985 Seminar Papers*, ed. K. H. Richards, Atlanta, 1985, pp. 57–73.

R. Pesch, '"Wo zwei oder drei versammelt sind auf meinen Namen hin . . ." (Mt 18.20)', in Schenke, *Studien*, pp. 227–43.

W. Pesch, passim.

V. C. Pfitzner, 'Purified Community—Purified Sinner. Expulsion from the Community according to Matthew 18.15–18 and 1 Corinthians 5.1–5', *AusBibRev* 30 (1982), pp. 34–55.

B. B. Scott, 'The King's Accounting: Matthew 18.23–34', *JBL* 104 (1985), pp. 429–42.

J. Sievers, '"Where Two or Three . . .": The Rabbinic Concept of Shekinah and Matthew 18.20', in *Standing Before God*, ed. A. Finkel and L. Frizzell, New York, 1981, pp. 171–82.

C. Spicq, *Dieu et l'homme selon le Nouveau Testament*, LD 29, Paris, 1961, pp. 54–61.

W. G. Thompson, passim.
D. O. Via, *The Parables*, Philadelphia, 1967, pp. 137–44.
Weder, pp. 210–18.
Weiser, pp. 75–104.
H. Zimmermann, 'Die innere Struktur der Kirche und das Petrusamt nach Mt 18.15–35', in *Petrus und Papst*, ed. A. Brandenburg and H. J. Urban, Munster, 1977, pp. 4–19.
Zumstein, pp. 386–96, 405–16.